The Garland Encyclopedia of World Music
Volume 2

South America, Mexico, Central America, and the Caribbean

Garland Reference Library of the Humanities, Volume 1193

Volume 1
AFRICA
edited by Ruth M. Stone

Volume 2
**SOUTH AMERICA, MEXICO,
CENTRAL AMERICA, AND THE CARIBBEAN**
edited by Dale A. Olsen and Daniel E. Sheehy

Volume 3
THE UNITED STATES AND CANADA
edited by Ellen Koskoff

Volume 4
SOUTHEAST ASIA
edited by Terry E. Miller and Sean Williams

Volume 5
SOUTH ASIA: THE INDIAN SUBCONTINENT
edited by Alison Arnold

Volume 6
THE MIDDLE EAST
edited by Virginia Danielson, Scott Marcus, and Dwight Reynolds

Volume 7
EAST ASIA: CHINA, JAPAN, AND KOREA
edited by Robert C. Provine, Yosihiko Tokumaru, and J. Lawrence Witzleben

Volume 8
EUROPE
edited by Timothy Rice, James Porter, and Christopher Goertzen

Volume 9
AUSTRALIA AND THE PACIFIC ISLANDS
edited by Adrienne L. Kaeppler and J. Wainwright Love

Volume 10
THE WORLD'S MUSIC: GENERAL PERSPECTIVES AND REFERENCE TOOLS

Advisory Editors
Bruno Nettl and Ruth M. Stone

Founding Editors
James Porter and Timothy Rice

The Garland Encyclopedia of World Music
Volume 2

South America, Mexico, Central America, and the Caribbean

Dale A. Olsen and Daniel E. Sheehy
Editors

GARLAND PUBLISHING, INC.
A member of the Taylor and Francis Group
New York and London
1998

The initial planning of The Garland Encyclopedia of World Music was assisted by a grant from the National Endowment for the Humanities.

Library of Congress Cataloging-in-Publication Data

The Garland encyclopedia of world music / [advisory editors, Bruno Nettl and Ruth M. Stone ; founding editors, James Porter and Timothy Rice].
        p.   cm.
    Includes bibliographical references, discographies, and indexes.
    Contents: v. 2. South America, Mexico, Central America, and the Caribbean / Dale A. Olsen and Daniel E. Sheehy, editors
    ISBN 0-8240-6040-7 (alk. paper)
    1. Music—Encyclopedias.   2. Folk music—Encyclopedias.
3. Popular music—Encyclopedias.   I. Nettl, Bruno, 1930–   .
II. Stone, Ruth M.   III. Porter, James, 1937–   . IV. Rice, Timothy, 1945–   .
ML100.G16   1998
780′.9—dc21   97-9671
                                                         CIP
                                                         MN

For Garland Publishing:

Vice-President: Leo Balk
Managing Editor: Richard Wallis
Director of Production: Anne Vinnicombe
Project Editor: Barbara Curialle Gerr
Copy Editor: J. Wainwright Love
Desktop publishing: Betty and Don Probert (Special Projects Group)
Glossary and index: Marilyn Bliss
Music typesetting: Hyunjung Choi
Maps: Indiana University Graphic Services
Cover design: Lawrence Wolfson Design, New York

Cover illustration: Musician from the village of Capagmarca, Peru (© Ken Laffal)

Contents

Audio Examples

The following examples are included on the accompanying audio compact disc packaged with this volume. Track numbers are also indicated on the pages listed below for easy reference to text discussions. Complete notes on each example can be found on pages 1023–1028.

About *The Garland Encyclopedia of World Music*

Scholars have created many kinds of encyclopedias devoted to preserving and transmitting knowledge about the world. The study of music has itself been the subject of numerous encyclopedias in many languages. Yet until now the term *music encyclopedia* has been synonymous with surveys of the history, theory, and performance practice of European-based traditions.

In July 1988, the editors of *The Garland Encyclopedia of World Music* gathered for a meeting to determine the nature and scope of a massive new undertaking. For this, the first encyclopedia devoted to the music of all the world's peoples, the editors decided against the traditional alphabetic approach to compartmentalizing knowledge from A to Z. Instead, they chose a geographic approach, with each volume devoted to a single region and coverage assigned to the world's experts on specific music cultures.

For several decades, ethnomusicologists (following the practice of previous generations of comparative musicologists) have been documenting the music of the world through fieldwork, recording, and analysis. Now, for the first time, they have created an encyclopedia that summarizes in one place the major findings that have resulted from the explosion in such documentation since the 1960s. The volumes in this series comprise contributions from all those specialists who have from the start defined the field of ethnomusicology: anthropologists, linguists, dance ethnologists, cultural historians, folklorists, literary scholars, and—of course—musicologists, composers, and performers. This multidisciplinary approach continues to enrich the field, and future generations of students and scholars will find *The Garland Encyclopedia of World Music* to be an invaluable resource that contributes to knowledge in all its varieties.

Each volume has a similar design and organization: three large sections that cover the major topics of a region from broad general issues to specific music practices. Each section consists of articles written by leading researchers, and extensive glossaries and indexes give the reader easy access to terms, names, and places of interest.

Part 1: an introduction to the region, its culture, and its music as well as a survey of previous music scholarship and research

Part 2: major issues and processes that link the musics of the region

Part 3: detailed accounts of individual music cultures

The editors of each volume have determined how this three-part structure is to be constructed and applied depending on the nature of their regions of interest. The concepts covered in Part 2 will therefore differ from volume to volume; likewise, the articles in Part 3 might be about the music of nations, ethnic groups, islands, or subregions. The picture of music presented in each volume is thus comprehensive yet remains focused on critical ideas and issues.

Complementing the texts of the encyclopedia's articles are numerous illustrations: photographs, drawings, maps, charts, song texts, and music examples. At the end of each volume is a useful set of study and research tools, including a glossary of terms, lists of audio and visual resources, and an extensive bibliography. An audio compact disc will be found inside the back cover of each volume, with sound examples that are linked (with a ☺ⁿ in the margin) to discussions in the text.

The Garland Encyclopedia of World Music represents the work of hundreds of specialists guided by a team of distinguished editors. With a sense of pride, Garland Publishing offers this new series to readers everywhere.

Preface

What we know about the music of South America, Mexico, Central America, and the Caribbean could fill many volumes. Even tiny islands of the West Indies have books written about their musical practices. Compiling a single reference volume on the music of this vast region has been a daunting task, but we are pleased to present the results of more than ten years of work by dozens of scholars and musicians. Here are gathered the writings of over forty contributors, each a specialist. Approximately one-third of the contributors are from the cultures about which they write; the others are researchers with vast knowledge, most of whom have direct fieldwork experience collecting, studying, and performing music in the region.

HOW THIS VOLUME IS ORGANIZED

This book, like its companion volumes in *The Garland Encyclopedia of World Music,* has a three-part structure that proceeds from the general to the specific. Part 1 provides an overview of the entire region, with two articles surveying the major background topics in geography, linguistics, history, performing arts, and research pertaining to the peoples south of the Río Grande.

Issues and Processes

The first article of Part 2 (THE DISTRIBUTION, SYMBOLISM, AND USE OF MUSICAL INSTRUMENTS) and the following three articles (MUSICAL GENRES AND CONTEXTS; SOCIAL STRUCTURE, MUSICIANS, AND BEHAVIOR; and MUSICAL DYNAMICS) are intended to be used as a user-friendly introduction to the musical arts of the region. They will help the reader understand how music is made, performed, used, received, appreciated, and changed by its practitioners and its audiences. The following seven articles document genres of music that cross national and cultural borders: the musics of Native American populations and of immigrant groups, popular music, and art music.

Nations and Musical Traditions

We have chosen to emphasize the information in Part 3 as the main body of this volume, and every country in South America, Central America, and the Caribbean is included. Relevant sections contain articles about the music cultures of numerous native American groups from South America and Central America (including Mexico). They are surveyed first because native Americans were the first to inhabit the regions and in order to stress the individualities of native Americans as people and developers of nations. Furthermore, recognizing that native American groups are justifiably nations in their own right (often having their own internal governments, religions, and moral codes), we have tried to include articles that represent a variety of indigenous cultures. Researchers on the native American traditions of these regions, however, are rare, and the number of cultures represented here is limited to twenty-seven, contained within twenty-five individual essays. Additional native

American cultures are included within certain country essays as well and, in some instances, are discussed by several authors. For example, the music of the Mapuche is discussed in its own article as well as in the "Mapuche" sections of the articles on Argentina and Chile. This provides the reader with a variety of information and approaches to scholarship.

Part 3 continues with essays about South America, Central America, and the Caribbean islands. The countries within these geographic regions are presented alphabetically by region.

Orthography

Hundreds of languages other than English, French, Spanish, and Portuguese are spoken in the Americas, but there is no consistent way to represent them in writing. Often, terms will be spelled with a modified phonetic alphabet, as in the use of *k* instead of *qu, w* rather than *gu, gü,* or *hu,* and so forth; the latter forms are derived from Spanish. Nevertheless, certain terms are so fixed in the minds of English readers that we have given spellings in the Spanish style: for example, *Inca* rather than *Inka, huayno* rather than *wayno,* and *quena* rather than *kena.* We have decided to retain the orthography preferred by the authors of particular entries. The large-scale rendering of native American languages, however, is consistent with recent linguistic scholarship. Thus, we have *Kechua* rather than *Quechua,* and *Warao* rather than *Guarao.* Regional varieties will nevertheless occur, as among the Quichua of Ecuador, who speak a dialect of Kechua; the Carib of Venezuela, who speak Karib; and the Guaraní of Paraguay, who speak Tupi-Waraní.

Some authors have chosen to use diacritics to indicate vowel or consonant sounds of particular native American terms, but none has chosen to use the International Phonetic Alphabet (IPA). Readers can consult a standard English dictionary to learn how to pronounce vowels that contain diacritic markings. Otherwise, vowel sounds are comparable to Spanish usage. Certain native American languages, however, require additional diacritic markings to represent their sounds properly. Kechua is one of these because of aspirated and explosive consonants. The Kechua-speaking Q'ero, for example, pronounce their name for themselves with an explosive "k" sound. Additionally, some languages have nasal sounds, rendered by the tilde (as in Portuguese): *Waiãpi,* for example, is pronounced with a nasalized sound on the second *a.*

ACKNOWLEDGMENTS

This volume in the *Garland Encyclopedia of World Music* has taken over a decade to complete. During that time we have steadfastly worked together to edit, re-edit, and polish the more than eighty essays as if we were two ethnomusicological Michelangelos chipping away stone in an attempt to free "The Captives" from their marble encasements. Michelangelo, it is said, never finished his masterpieces, but we have finished ours. However, it might be argued that an encyclopedia devoted to cultural practices can never be completed.

We wish to thank all the contributing authors whose patience has probably been tried many times but who never gave up. Without their expertise and wonderful work, we could never have undertaken the compilation of this volume. We are saddened by the death of our colleague Dr. Ronald R. Smith (PANAMA), and we hope this volume will stand as a memorial to him and to his love of Panama and Central America.

Furthermore, we wish to thank the many individuals who have been official and unofficial readers. Jacob Love, the volume's copy editor, deserves our highest praise—he is a true scholar with a breadth of knowledge and love of improvisation that are unsurpassed. Special thanks go to Martha Ellen Davis, T. M. Scruggs, and Anthony Seeger for their many comments and ideas about essays from particular geographic areas. We appreciate the critical comments on specific country articles supplied by Michael Alleyne, Michael Bakan, Gerard Béhague, Jennifer Duerden, Jane L. Florine, Carolyn J. Fulton, Katherine J. Hagedorn, and Diane Olsen.

Karl Barton and Michael O'Connor, respectively, assisted with organizing the glossary and checking reference materials. For translations we thank Carmen Arencíbia, Jane L. Florine, Rosemary McBride, and Timothy Watkins. We have greatly benefited from the photographic contributions of Cathy Collinge Herrera, Carolyn J. Fulton, Elena Constatinidou, and the many others who are credited in figure captions. On the audio compact disc, additional examples were submitted by Walter Coppens, Charles Sigmund, and Welson Tremura, while John Banks offered considerable assistance in producing the compact disc. And for its help with many aspects of production, we thank the School of Music of The Florida State University.

Finally, we are grateful to our wives, Diane and Laura, for their patience, understanding, and encouragement in helping us see this project through to its conclusion.

—Dale A. Olsen and Daniel E. Sheehy

List of Contributors

Olivia Ahyoung
Florida State Government Administrator
Tallahassee, Florida, U. S. A.

Olavo Alén Rodríguez
Center for Research and Development of Cuban Music (CIDMUC)
Havana, Cuba

Lawrence J. App
The Florida State University
Tallahassee, Florida, U. S. A.

Gage Averill
New York University
New York, New York, U. S. A.

Jean-Michel Beaudet
Meudon, France

Gerard Béhague
University of Texas
Austin, Texas, U. S. A.

Max H. Brandt
University of Pittsburgh
Pittsburgh, Pennsylvania, U. S. A.

Arturo Chamorro
Universidad de Guadalajara
Guadalajara, México

John Cohen
Putnam Valley, New York, U. S. A.

Larry Crook
University of Florida
Gainesville, Florida, U. S. A.

Martha Ellen Davis
University of Florida
Gainesville, Florida, U. S. A.

Monique Desroches
Université de Montréal
Montréal, Québec, Canada

Carlos A. Fernández
Indiana University
Bloomington, Indiana, U. S. A.

Jane L. Florine
Chicago State University
Chicago, Illinois, U. S. A.

Victor Fuks
Rio de Janeiro, Brazil

Juan Pablo González
Universidad de Chile
Santiago, Chile

William J. Gradante
Fort Worth Schools
Fort Worth, Texas, U. S. A.

Oliver Greene
Morris-Brown College
Atlanta, Georgia, U. S. A.

James S. Griffith
University of Arizona
Tucson, Arizona, U. S. A.

Jocelyne Guilbault
University of California
Berkeley, California, U. S. A.

J. Richard Haefer
Arizona State University
Tempe, Arizona

Olive Lewin
Office of the Prime Minister
Kingston, Jamaica

Salvador Marroquín
San Salvador, El Salvador

Lorna McDaniel
University of Michigan
Ann Arbor, Michigan, U. S. A.

John Messenger
The Ohio State University
Columbus, Ohio, U. S. A.

Janice Millington
Barbados Schools
Worthing Christ Church, Barbados

Ercilia Moreno Chá
Instituto Nacional de Antropología
Buenos Aires, Argentina

E. Fernando Nava L.
Universidad Nacional Autónoma de México
México, D.F., México

Linda O'Brien-Rothe
San Pedro School System
San Pedro, California, U. S. A.

Dale A. Olsen
The Florida State University
Tallahassee, Florida, U. S. A.

Deborah Pacini Hernández
Brown University
Providence, Rhode Island, U. S. A.

Charles A. Perrone
University of Florida
Gainesville, Florida, U. S. A.

Suzel Ana Reily
The Queen's University of Belfast
Belfast, Northern Ireland

Carol E. Robertson
University of Maryland
College Park, Maryland, U. S. A.

Raúl R. Romero
Pontífica Universidad Católica del Perú
Lima, Perú

John M. Schechter
University of California
Santa Cruz, California, U. S. A.

T. M. Scruggs
University of Iowa
Iowa City, Iowa, U. S. A.

Anthony Seeger
Smithsonian Institution
Washington, D. C., U. S. A.

Daniel E. Sheehy
National Endowment for the Arts
Washington, D. C., U. S. A.

Ronald R. Smith (deceased)
Indiana University
Bloomington, Indiana, U. S. A.

Sandra Smith
Forest Knolls, California, U. S. A.

Henry Stobart
Cambridge University
Cambridge, England

William David Tompkins
University of Calgary
Calgary, Alberta, Canada

Thomas Turino
University of Illinois
Urbana, Illinois, U. S. A.

Héctor Vega Drouet
University of Puerto Rico
San Juan, Puerto Rico

Timothy D. Watkins
The Florida State University
Tallahassee, Florida, U. S. A.

Lois Wilcken
Hunter College
New York, New York, U. S. A.

Vivian Nina Michelle Wood
Plantation, Florida, U. S. A.

Part 1
Introduction to the Music Cultures
of the Region

Cumbia, salsa, tango; carnival, fiesta, shamanic curing; mariachi, samba school, steelband; Victor Jara, Tom Jobim, Astor Piazzolla—these genres, contexts, bands, and musicians conjure up sinuous rhythms, lyrical melodies, pensive moods, ideological power, and above all, unforgettable musical art. Music, dance, and music-related behavior are of great importance to the people of the countries south of the Río Grande (the river that separates the United States from Mexico), the island countries south and east of Florida, and many native American cultures that thrive within those politically determined regions.

Señor Antonio Sulca, a blind Quechua Indian musician of Peru, wears a European-designed suit as he plays a Spanish-derived harp. His music tells of his people from Ayacucho, and his harp is adorned with a lute-playing siren, a possibly indigenous protective and amorous figure. Photo by Dale A. Olsen, 1979.

A Profile of the Lands and People of South America, Mexico, Central America, and the Caribbean
Dale A. Olsen

Geography
Demography
Cultural Settings

The articles in this volume cover the music of people from a vast region of the Western Hemisphere. Here you will find descriptions of the music of all the nations south of the Rio Grande (the river that separates the United States from Mexico); of many native American cultures that continue to thrive as autochthonous and somewhat homogeneous entities within these nations; and of all island states south and just east of Florida.

GEOGRAPHY

opposite: South America, Mexico, Central America, and the Caribbean

Because of political and cultural history, it can be difficult to make easy geographic classifications in this region. In fact, several problems of classification arise. First is the area known as the Falkland Islands (a British term) or Islas Malvinas (the Argentine term for the same place). These islands are problematic because of their political affiliation (should they be discussed as British or Argentine?) and because no scholarly musical research has been conducted there. Second is the phenomenon of Maroon culture, such as the several societies established by runaway African slaves in the interiors of French Guiana, Guyana, Surinam, and Jamaica, and formerly in Brazil. Like many native American groups, Maroon cultures may not be politically determined by non-Maroon people; like many native American groups, they have their own political systems. Maroon cultures have been studied, however, and much is known about their musics. A third problem concerns Isla de Pascua (Chilean term), Easter Island (English term), or Rapa Nui (Polynesian term), an island several thousand kilometers west of Chile. It is administered by Chile, though its aboriginal people were Polynesians. This region has also been studied; however, when the island is seen as a Polynesian culture, does the implied musical understanding have a Polynesian, non-Chilean tinge? and when studied from a Chilean's point of view, is the opposite true?

Central and South America include topographies of extreme contrast. In South America are the world's largest tropical forest (Amazon) and one of its driest deserts (Atacama). There are many lowland basins (Orinoco, La Plata, Amazon) and frigid highlands and glacial peaks (the Andes, including Aconcagua, the highest mountain in the Western Hemisphere). The country of Chile itself is, in reverse, a compressed

UNITED STATES OF AMERICA

MEXICO

THE BAHAMAS

CUBA

Puerto Rico (U.S.)

VIRGIN ISLANDS (U.S. and U.K.)

JAMAICA

HAITI

BELIZE

DOMINICAN REPUBLIC

HONDURAS

GUATEMALA

Guadeloupe (Fr.)

DOMINICA

Martinique (Fr.)

ST. LUCIA

BARBADOS

EL SALVADOR

NICARAGUA

GRENADA

ST. VINCENT AND THE GRENADINES

TRINIDAD AND TOBAGO

COSTA RICA

GUYANA

VENEZUELA

SURINAM

PANAMA

FRENCH GUIANA

COLOMBIA

Galápagos Islands (Ec.)

ECUADOR

PERU

BRAZIL

BOLIVIA

PARAGUAY

CHILE

URUGUAY

ARGENTINA

Falkland Islands (U.K.) (Islas Malvinas)

When music is made by a group of people or for a group of people, rarely does the musical event exist without dancing and the participation of members of the family. Music is an affair, an experience, an event to be shared.

version of the span from coastal Alaska to Baja California: its land goes from a northern dry desert, fertile central valleys, and lush southern pine forests, to extreme southern, rugged, canyonlike estuaries studded with glaciers, terminating in frigid mountains and waters of the area of the world that is the closest to Antarctica. Within the small country of Ecuador are tropical forests and perpetually snow-capped mountains—both at zero degrees latitude, the equator. Because of such topographies, most of the urban centers of South America are on or near the coasts of the Atlantic, Caribbean, or Pacific. All of these considerations have affected the music of Central and South America.

DEMOGRAPHY

Demography, the description of human populations, is more than a statistical science. When joined with cultural studies, demography becomes more complex than mere calculation of numbers and migration of people. There is probably no place on earth as racially and culturally diverse and complex as the Americas, especially the Americas covered in this volume.

As a way of explaining the complexity of a particular area, George List (1983) has tried to fit certain regions of South America within the framework of a tricultural heritage—native American, African, and Spanish. But within each of these areas there could be dozens of subareas of influence: which native American culture? which African culture? and even which Spanish culture? These are questions that must be asked (Bermúdez 1994).

Likewise, terms such as *mestizaje* 'miscegenation' (a mixing of race and culture, usually assumed between native American and Spanish or Portuguese) and *criolismo* 'creolism' (usually a mixing of African and European, or referring to European descendants born in the New World; usage depends on the country; in Haiti, Creole refers to the language) have been used to categorize people and cultures in Mexico, Central America, and the Caribbean. The terms *mestizo* and *creole* (*criollo*) are used throughout these areas by the people themselves; however, they are perhaps less useful today, with the amounts of urban migration taking place, the increasing possibilities of upward mobility, and the great influx of immigrants and their descendants from China, England, Germany, India, Indonesia, Italy, Japan, Korea, and elsewhere. Each country has its own ways of using the terms *mestizo* and *criollo* or uses other terms to accommodate its unique demographic mixture.

CULTURAL SETTINGS

Ethnomusicology is the study of music made by people for themselves, their gods, and/or other people. The people of South America, Mexico, Central America, and the Caribbean are diverse and the countries pluralistic, and their musical styles and other cultural attributes are equally so. When a person is making music for himself or herself, rarely is he or she completely alone: someone—a family member, a friend, a community—is listening, enjoying, crying, singing along. When music is made for God or the gods, rarely is it done in isolation: people are listening, learning the songs, perhaps praying or thinking spiritual thoughts. When music is made by a group of people or for a group of people, rarely does the musical event exist without dancing and the participation of members of the family. Music is an affair, an experience, an event to be shared.

REFERENCES

Bermúdez, Egberto. 1994. "Syncretism, Identity, and Creativity in Afro-Colombian Musical Traditions." In *Music and Black Ethnicity: The Caribbean and South America,* ed. Gerard H. Béhague, 225–238. Miami: North-South Center, University of Miami.

List, George. 1983. *Music and Poetry in a Colombian Village: A Tri-Cultural Heritage.* Bloomington: Indiana University Press.

Loukotka, Cestmír. 1968. *Classification of South American Indian Languages.* Los Angeles: Latin American Center, University of California.

Handbook of Middle American Indians. 1971. Edited by Robert Wauchope. Austin: University of Texas Press.

Approaches to Musical Scholarship
Dale A. Olsen

The Archaeological Record
The Iconographic Record
The Mythological Record
The Historiographic Record
Ethnology and Practice

Almost everything known about music and musical performance in the Americas comes from archaeology, iconology, mythology, history, ethnology, or current practice. Since antiquity, culture bearers, conquerors, missionaries, Peace Corps volunteers, politicians, grave robbers, scholars, students, travelers, visitors, and many others have contributed to musical knowledge in the Western Hemisphere.

THE ARCHAEOLOGICAL RECORD

Probably all ancient cultures in South America, Mexico, Central America, and the Caribbean—as, indeed, throughout the world—have used music for religious and social reasons. Many have used musical instruments for rhythmic or melodic purposes, or as some type of reinforcement of vocal sounds or dancing. Through archaeology it is possible to see (and even hear) some of the musical instruments of ancient people, because many extant musical instruments have been unearthed. Many of these, found in tombs, temples, and other ruins, are available for study in private and public collections. It is possible to see how musical instruments may have been held, which ones may have been played together, and what activities—such as dancing, sacrificing, healing, parading, hunting, and so on—they may have been used for. When musical instruments and performances are depicted in pottery, wood, and any other medium, their study is called music iconology. When such artifacts have been recovered from tombs, temples, and other sites lost in time, music iconology is a branch of archaeomusicology.

Nearly everything said about ancient musical instruments and events has to be qualified with the words *possibly,* and *may have,* and other modifiers indicating speculation; people living today can never be certain about artifacts from prehistoric times. The materials of ancient musical instruments can usually be ascertained, and the age of the instruments can be roughly determined—by carbon-14 dating for wood and bone, thermoluminescence (TL) for pottery, and other methods of dating. Instruments can be measured and physically described. Beyond these limits, however, archaeomusicologists must speculate.

The primary drawbacks in the study of ancient musics are the absence of emic points of view (what the bearers of the culture might say about it), observable cultural contexts, and actual sounds. Even if sounds are obtained from ancient musical instruments, it is still the researcher, rather than the bearers of the extinct culture, who causes the sounds to be made. For economic and other reasons, counterfeit artifacts—fakes!—are constructed and circulated, and determining the validity of supposed artifacts can be problematic. Furthermore, carbon-14 dating is not always possible because the procedure destroys part of the artifact, and it may not always be reliable because a buried instrument may receive contamination from seepage, garbage, vegetable matter, the chemical composition of the soil, and other sources, becoming nearly impossible to date by that method. TL dating is rare because few laboratories can do it, and its margin of accuracy is often too wide for it to be useful.

Sometimes, researchers designate as musical instruments ancient objects that may actually have been constructed and used for other purposes: a ceramic water vessel or beaker may be called a drum with its skin missing, a pipe for smoking may be said to be a flute, and so on. At other times, what may be termed an artifact may actually be an ecofact, as when a so-called bone flute is just a bone, or a geofact, as when a so-called polished stone is a naturally polished stone, rather than a human-crafted lithophone or stone chime.

Archaeomusicology is the study of music through archaeology, and music archaeology is the study of archaeology through musical instruments. Scholars who study the former are usually trained musicians, while those who study the latter are trained archaeologists (Hickmann 1983–1984). Because no etic conclusions (by an outsider) can be made with certainty, since no emic evaluations (by the ancient musician or maker of the instrument) are possible, both fields of study raise more questions than the answers they provide. Musical artifacts can be measured and described, but archaeomusicologists may never know beyond what they can speculate about the use and function of ancient musical instruments, and though the term *scientific speculation* seems like an oxymoron (a self-contradiction), some speculation can be undergirded by the methods of scientific inquiry. New World archaeomusicologists often consult the writings of Spanish chroniclers from the early years of the Encounter, though these writings may not always be accurate and reliable, may contain prejudiced or biased views, and may even transmit misinformation from their native American respondents who may have had some familiarity with their music-making ancestors. There may be difficulties translating the flowery language of early chroniclers—writers who themselves may not have clearly understood what they were describing. Additional scientific speculation can be based on the technique called ethnographic analogy (commonly used in ethnoarchaeology), whereby interpretations of the use and function of ancient culture are made by comparisons with modern cultures. This method can be particularly valuable when the cultures being compared are from the same geographic region, and especially when the living culture claims to be a descendant of the ancient one.

Within the Caribbean, few archaeomusicological studies have been conducted; most come from the Dominican Republic. Within Mexico, Central America, and South America, however, many studies exist; the cultures receiving the most frequent archaeomusicological investigation come from Mexico and Guatemala, including the Aztec, Maya, Nayarít, Olmec, and Toltec; the Central American countries of Costa Rica, Nicaragua, and Panama, including the Chorotega and Nicarao; northwestern Colombia, including the Sinú and the Tairona; the northern Andean countries of Colombia and Ecuador, including the Bahía, Chibcha, Guangala, Jama-Coaque, Manteño, Nariño, Piartal, Tuza, and Valdivia; the central Andean countries of Peru and northern Bolivia, including the Chancay, Chimu, Inca, Moche, Nasca, and Tiawanaku; and the southern Andean countries of Bolivia and Chile, including the Diaguita and San Pedro. Hundreds of ancient cultures thrived in these areas, each with musical activities that were possibly similar, judging by music iconography. This essay describes some extant musical instruments, and suggests ideas about ancient musical performance as determined from ancient pottery.

The Caribbean

Archaeological investigations in the Dominican Republic, Cuba, and Puerto Rico have revealed the existence of ancient bone flutes and ceramic vessel flutes with two or three holes for fingering (Boyrie Moya 1971:14–17; Moldes 1975:6–7; Veloz Maggiolo 1972:49). Specific details of their cultural derivations and contexts are unknown, and their use may have been ceremonial, for personal protection, or for diversion. A musical instrument used by the ancient Taino is the conch trumpet, which may have had a signaling function, as it does today in the Caribbean. It may also have had a ceremonial function, because the protuberances on it resemble those on a Taino idol (*zemi*), and they may symbolize a volcano or a sacred mountain (Fred Olsen 1974:96).

Mexico and Central America

Between 200 B.C. and A.D. 500 along the rugged coast of west-central Mexico, in the present states of Colima, Jalisco, and Nayarít, there lived some of the earliest Mexican cultures to produce musical instruments and depictions of musical performance, both done mostly in fired clay. These artifacts, buried in shaft tombs cut into the volcanic rocks of the highlands, were probably the belongings of a religious elite of shamans and rulers. The instruments include many idiophones (scraped, struck, and rattled); bodies of membranophones; and aerophones, such as ceramic duct globular flutes, duct tubular flutes, panpipes, and conch trumpets. In central Mexico are similar musical instruments, plus more elaborate tubular flutes with flared or disk-shaped distal ends that represent flowers or perhaps the sun (figure 1).

Ancient multiple duct flutes have been discovered in other parts of Mexico and as far south as Guatemala. Their existence suggests that multipart musical textures were used in Mexican and Central American antiquity, though a theory of polyphony is debatable, since no ancient flutists survive to prove or disprove it, and multitubed duct flutes are no longer used in the area.

Other types of duct tubular and globular edge aerophones, however, are common in Mexico today, and all have prototypes in ancient times (Crossley-Holland 1980). Robert M. Stevenson (1968) published the most comprehensive study of the ancient instruments and many others. Basing his findings on historical and archaeological records, he showed how native American—mostly Aztec (Nahuatl-speakers) and Maya—musical instruments and performing continued during Mexican colonial times, albeit with changes affected by or as a result of Spanish authority. These changes were structural (instruments made from cane rather than clay, six to seven holes for fingering rather than four, unornamented tubular rather than affixed with a disk at the distal end, a pipe-and-tabor rather than panpipe-and-rattle "solo" ensemble) and contextual (instruments no longer used for sacrificial rituals, but for Christian-related ceremonies).

Aztec and Maya influence stretched as far southward as Costa Rica and even Panama, and Chibchan and other South American influences are found in ancient Panama and northward into Costa Rica (Andrews V. 1972; Boggs 1974; Hammond 1972a, 1972b; Rivera y Rivera 1977). Among the former, northern influence is the use of log idiophones similar to Aztec and Maya examples. The latter, southern influence includes ceramic ocarinas (similar to those of Colombia) in the realistic shapes of animals, birds, fish, humans, and reptiles.

In the southern lowlands of the Nicaraguan Pacific Coast, archaeologists have found small tubular and globular duct flutes and evidence for the existence of a log

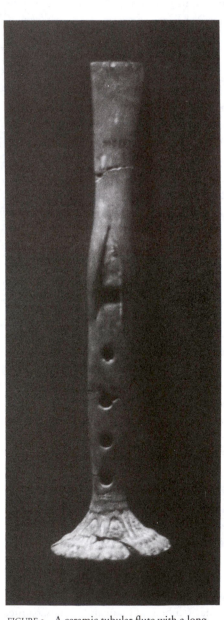

FIGURE 1   A ceramic tubular flute with a long duct mouthpiece, four fingerholes, and an elaborate flared or disk-shaped distal end that perhaps represents flowers or the sun. Perhaps Mexica (Aztec) culture, central Mexico, about A.D. 1300–1500. Photo by Dale A. Olsen, 1970.

idiophone (called *teponaztli* by Nahuatl-speaking people further north, whence early Nicaraguans probably came). It is believed that the Chorotega and Nicarao of Costa Rica also migrated from Mexico, and the ancient people from the Diquís region of Costa Rica show possible influences from South America, probably through and as an extension of the Chiriquí of ancient Panama (Acevedo Vargas 1987; Ferrero 1977). Many archaeological sites appear in Panama, though none of them were large ceremonial centers or cities. As found farther north into Mexico and farther south into Colombia, many of the musical instruments excavated by archaeologists in Panama are tubular and globular flutes made from clay.

South America

Hundreds of prehistoric sites are found throughout the northern extension of the Andes and the northern Caribbean littoral of present Colombia. The Spanish conquistadors regarded this region of South America as most probably the land of the fabled El Dorado (The Golden Man), and they made great efforts to locate his supplies and depositories of precious metal. As a consequence, indigenous nations were quickly destroyed. In the north, the great cities of the Sinú and villages of the Tairona were sacked and the people were killed, enslaved, or forced into the interior. Musically, the Sinú and Tairona are the most important cultures in the region now known as Colombia because of the numbers of their globular and tubular flutes that have been unearthed (Dale A. Olsen 1986, 1987, 1989, 1990). Colombia, however, is a grave robber's dream (an archaeologist's nightmare), and few excavated artifacts have been properly documented. Many sit today in museums in Bogotá, in private collections, and in stores that specialize in selling antiquities alongside numerous fakes.

The Sinú lived in large cities with elaborate ceremonial centers, situated in the lowlands of northwestern Colombia, along the Sinú River in the present department of Córdoba. Most of their musical instruments are elongated duct flutes made of fired clay. Rather than being tubular, they resemble two cones joined lengthwise at their widest points. Each instrument has four holes for fingering and is in the shape of a fish, or on the proximal cone has the adornment of a long-nosed reptile (figure 2). What these instruments were used for, and what the designs meant, are unknown. There are no living Sinú descendants who can interpret them. It is possible, judging from historical and current cultural attitudes about fish and reptiles, that the instru-

FIGURE 2   A ceramic double-cone-shaped tubular flute with a duct mouthpiece, four fingerholes, and an adornment of a long-nosed reptile on the proximal cone. Sinú culture, Colombia, about A.D. 1300–1500. Photo by Dale A. Olsen, 1974.

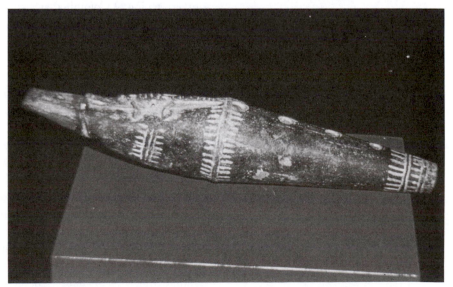

distal The portion of a musical instrument farthest from the mouthpiece

proximal The portion of a musical instrument closest to the mouthpiece

ments had magical power, possibly for protection against supernatural powers (Dale A. Olsen 1989).

More is known about the Tairona, who lived in villages in the rugged coastal foothills of the Sierra Nevada de Santa Marta in the present department of Magdalena [see KOGI]. Most Tairona musical instruments are vessel flutes in the shapes of animals, birds, reptiles, and humans, or anthropomorphic tubular flutes. Because Tairona terrain is higher and drier than the Sinú River basin, archaeologists have been able to excavate houses, ceremonial sites, and tombs, with yields of hundreds of ceramic and gold artifacts. Most ancient aerophones were unearthed in houses or tombs, but not in ceremonial centers, suggesting a personal rather than priestly use for them. To avoid slavery and death at the hands of the Spaniards, the Tairona escaped into the higher elevations of the Santa Marta mountains. Today, the Kogi claim to be their descendants. The Kogi do not play Tairona musical instruments, but they have interpretations for many Tairona artifacts, to which they attribute great power.

The Andean region of Colombia is archaeologically known more for its gold and statuary (as in the San Augustín area) than for its musical instruments. The myth of El Dorado probably began here among the ancient Chibcha, with the legend of the consecration of each new leader, who would have his body coated with gold dust. As an act of rebirth, he would dive from a raft into Lake Guatavita (near present-day Bogotá), to surface reborn as a pure being, free of his golden coating, and filled with the power of the spirit of the lake.

Little is known of the extant musical instruments of the Colombian Andes other than that they were primarily vessel flutes with little decoration. The Nariño (in the southern region of Colombia) and ancient cultures in northern Ecuador, however, had large numbers of decorative artifacts shaped like the shells of large land-living snails—artifacts that may possibly have been ductless vessel flutes (Nyberg 1974), though they may not have been flutes at all, but ritual vessels (figure 3).

Farther south, into present-day central Ecuador, the coastal lowlands have yielded numerous musical artifacts made from clay. Most of them are ductless vessel flutes in the shapes of animals and birds. The culture known as Bahía or Valdivia produced elaborate humanoid-shaped vessel flutes with two chambers and four holes for fingering. These instruments, capable of many multiple pitches, are elaborate in their exterior and interior design (Cubillos Ch. 1958; Hickmann 1990).

Possibly the richest area of the Americas for ancient musical artifacts is coastal Peru, from Lambayeque in the north to Nasca in the south (Bolaños 1981, 1988; Donnan 1982; Jiménez Borja 1951; Dale A. Olsen 1992; Stevenson 1968). One of the oldest known musical cultures in Peru, however, is Kotosh, high in the Andes in the department of Huánuco. There, what is thought to be a bone flute (with one hole exactly in the middle of its length) was discovered in the Tomb of the Crossed Hands, dating back to about 4500 B.C. (Bolaños 1988:11). Indeed, the precise uses

FIGURE 3 Two ceramic figurines (possibly cross-blown globular flutes) in the shape of a snail. Nariño culture, Colombia, about A.D. 1300–1500. Photo by Dale A. Olsen, 1974.

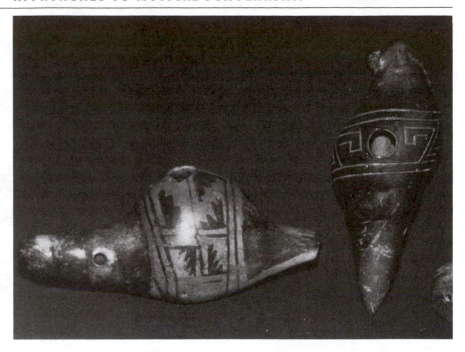

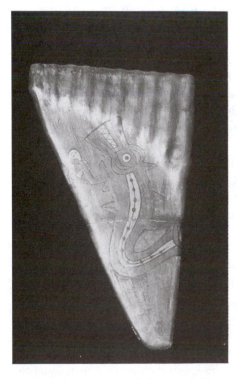

FIGURE 4 A ceramic ten-tubed panpipe with a painted fish deity. Nasca culture, Peru, about 100 B.C.–A.D. 600. Photo by Christopher Donnan, 1972.

of artifacts are not always clear, and what may seem to be a musical instrument may in fact be something else. In coastal Peru, some artifacts are undoubtedly tubular flutes because of their notched mouthpieces and holes, and numerous ceramic duct-less and duct globular flutes have been found (Dale A. Olsen 1992). It is curious, however, that though cross-blown tubular ceramic flutes existed in ancient Peru, tubular duct flutes did not—at least, none have been discovered.

Ceramic panpipes from the Nasca culture of southern coastal Peru have been unearthed and studied in detail (figure 4), and precise scientific measurements have been made of their pitches (Stevenson 1960, 1968; Haeberli 1979; Bolaños 1988); the measurements have dispelled the often-believed myth that Andean music had pentatonic roots. They have dispelled another belief: that Nasca panpipes were played in pairs using interlocking parts, as they are today in the southern Peruvian Andes. Scholars now believe that those panpipes were played in ensembles, because many instruments with nearly identical tunings have been discovered in common archaeological sites.

Trumpets, aerophones with cupped mouthpieces, were frequent among ancient coastal Peruvians. The Moche made instruments from the shells of conchs and ceramics shaped to resemble such shells. According to music iconography, these musical instruments were used by priests and shamans, or by the fanged deity in the afterlife. The Moche also played ceramic tubular straight and coiled trumpets, the latter depicting open-mouthed jaguars at their distal ends. The inland Recuay used trumpets that sometimes coiled around vases or beakers (figure 5). Farther south, on the southern Peruvian coast, straight trumpets were used by the Nasca and their neighbors in Paracas. These were often painted with motifs of feline, piscine, or solar deities (figure 6).

Numerous ceramic membranophones, some with skin intact, have been discovered at Moche, Nasca, and Paracas sites. Those from the Nasca and Paracas civilizations are the largest and most ornate. Some, reaching two meters high, are profusely painted with cat and snake deities (figure 7).

Farther south, in the area of present-day highland Bolivia, musical instruments have been archaeologically discovered from the Tiawanaku culture (1000 B.C.–A.D. 1000), an influential civilization. These artifacts include ceramic vessel flutes and

FIGURE 5 A ceramic coiled trumpet molded around a ceramic beaker. Recuay culture, Peru, about 200 B.C.–A.D. 550. Photo by Dale A. Olsen, 1974.

panpipes, bone tubular flutes, and wooden trumpets (figure 8). The Tiawanaku culture influenced the Diaguita and San Pedro cultures in the Atacama Desert region of northern Chile, where similar forms and designs among ceramic artifacts can been seen. María Ester Grebe (1974) has done a thorough study of the ancient musical instruments of Chile.

THE ICONOGRAPHIC RECORD

Music iconography is closely related to music archaeology because the source of information is artifactual. Iconography, however, studies the meanings attached, usually pictorially, to artifacts. *Music iconography* is the description (*music iconology,* the science) of music through its representation in sculpture, painting, and other plastic arts. Through it, researchers can gain an understanding of events, processes, and performances during the era in which the artifact was authentically used. It is a record of knowledge that is not fully reliable in itself, but when added to archaeological, historiographic, and ethnographic records, can tell much about a culture. Another aspect of music iconography is the study of the designs on musical instruments. One reason for iconography's unreliability is that so much is available only in secondary sources: the originals are difficult to locate because they are rare paintings or drawings or engravings from rare books or sometimes have disappeared altogether.

In South America, Mexico, and Central America, pre-Encounter musical iconography tells us about the uses of music among the Aztec, Maya, Moche, Nayarít, and other ancient civilizations. In the early post-Encounter period, paintings and drawings from codices and other compilations by chroniclers, missionaries, and others are valuable for their visual commentaries about music. After the Encounter, however, biases appear, and are often represented in art. Flutes, trumpets, and other instruments may be represented larger than life (or smaller), as more complex (or simpler), being played together in unlikely combinations, or in any number of incorrect ways. For this reason, music iconography must be joined with other types of documentation in a check-and-balance manner. As nationalism developed, painting and graphic arts became more detailed and representational. Artists were usually interested in more or less faithfully depicting life in their new countries, and this often included musical life, featuring such activities as playing instruments and dancing. Especially important are paintings of religious festivals, music during work, and music for pleasure. With the growth of tourism since the 1950s, music iconography

FIGURE 6   A ceramic straight trumpet. Nasca culture, Peru, about 100 B.C.–A.D. 600. Photo by Christopher Donnan, 1972.

FIGURE 7   A ceramic vase drum. Nasca culture, Peru. Photo by Dale A. Olsen, 1979.

in the form of items made for sale to tourists (carved gourds, figurines, statues, paintings) has proliferated. Once again, realism is not prevalent, and caricature is common.

The Caribbean

Drawings by chroniclers are somewhat informative about music in the Caribbean during historical times. The chronicler Gonzalo Fernández de Oviedo y Valdés included two drawings of a Taino idiophonic H-drum, a struck idiophone (which I call an H-drum because of the pattern formed by its two prongs cut into the top of a hollow wooden log) closed at both ends (1851, reproduced by Rouse 1963a:plate 90). These drawings are valuable because they suggest a possible connection with the Aztec *teponaztli* [see MEXICA] or the Maya *tunkul* [see MAYA] farther west on the mainland. The Taino idiophone is called *mayohuacán* by Moldes (1975:6), but Loven (1935:495) writes its name as *maguay,* the term for the century plant (*magüey*), from which it is made. The Taino H-drum was a large instrument according to René Currasco (former director of a noteworthy folkloric ballet in Santo Domingo, Dominican Republic), who built a reproduction inspired by the historical drawings, and played it while sitting on the floor as his ensemble performed a reconstructed Taino dance; his instrument stood about 1.2 meters high and measured about one meter in circumference. Loven explains that the Taino idiophonic H-drum was played by the chief (*cacique*) to accompany the festive song (*areito*) rather than a dance, though this song was possibly danced to. No mention is made of any melodic or linguistic communication on this particular instrument, though it could produce at least two tones. Ferrero (1977:133) reproduced an engraving by Benzoni from 1542, showing a similar instrument of the Gran Nicoya of Costa Rica, having three tongues and played with two sticks.

Rouse (1963b:plate 95) prints a picture by Picard (Fewkes 1907) showing container rattles being used in a Carib war-related dance. The instrument is apparently a large calabash rattle with a long stick handle, on the top of which are numerous vertically extending feathers, in the fashion of each player's headdress. The picture gives evidence of the importance attached to this seemingly sacred rattle, as it is shown being played by priests or shamans—three men of apparently high status, judging from their headdresses and costumes. Each man plays one rattle, while sixteen other men, without headdresses or costumes, dance in a circle around them.

According to music iconography, membranophones (skin drums) may have been used in the ancient Caribbean. A picture (Fewkes 1907, reproduced in Rouse 1963a:plate 92) depicts an Arawak dance to the goddess of the earth, in which two membranophones are played, each with two sticks in the European military-drum fashion. Lewin (1968:53) refers to skin drums among the Arawak during ceremonies of worship, explaining they are "made from the hollow stem of the trumpet tree with manatee skins stretched tightly across." If these portrayals of Arawak ceremonies are accurate, then perhaps European-style membranophones replaced the H-drum idiophones.

Mexico and Central America

The figurines of musicians unearthed in west Mexico (Nayarít, Colima) provide many details of instrumental performance, such as what instruments existed, who played them, and which instruments have been continuously used to the present. Some people depicted are musical soloists; others are members of musical ensembles. These were probably ceremonial musical performers, maybe shamans. Container rattles, rasps (figure 9), and tortoise-shell struck idiophones (figure 10) are commonly depicted on figurines as being played by men who often are shown speaking or

Music iconography can show how particular musicians were attired, and from that evidence, scholars can speculate about the performers' social status.

FIGURE 9   A ceramic figurine of a man playing a rasp. Nayarít culture, Mexico, about 200 B.C.–A.D. 300. Photo by Dale A. Olsen, 1989.

FIGURE 10   A ceramic figurine of a man playing a tortoise shell as a scraper or percussion instrument. Colima culture, Mexico, about 200 B.C.–A.D. 300. Photo by Dale A. Olsen, 1971.

FIGURE 8   A wooden straight trumpet. Tiawanaku culture, Bolivia, about A.D. 900–1200. Photo by Christopher Donnan, 1972.

singing. Single-headed drums and struck conch shells are shown being played in west Mexican iconography (figure 11). Players of aerophones are commonly depicted, giving us valuable information about performance that no longer occurs. Foremost are the player of a three-tubed flute (in figure 12, the way the flutist's fingers overlap the holes suggests that multiple sounds were used) and a panpipe-and-rattle "solo" ensemble (figure 13).

Though some musician-depicting artifacts are molded together in clay (figure 14), museums often display individual musician-depicting artifacts together as if to indicate ensemble playing (see figure 11). Grouping such artifacts together is purely speculative. Curators are often influenced by how musical instruments are played in combination today. This technique, called ethnographic analogy (Dale A. Olsen 1990:170), is usually the only way to determine the collectivity of musical instruments unless they are all arranged together in an archaeological site, but even that

FIGURE 11   Ceramic figurines: a man plays a single-headed drum with a mallet and a hand (?); another a man plays a rattle or strikes a conch. Colima culture, Mexico, about 200 B.C. –A.D. 300. Photo by Miguel Angel Sotelo.

FIGURE 12   A ceramic figurine of a man playing a three-tubed vertical flute. Colima culture, Mexico, about 200 B.C.–A.D. 300. Photo by Dale A. Olsen, 1989.

FIGURE 13   A ceramic figurine of a man playing a four-tubed panpipe with one hand and a rattle with another. West Mexico, about 200 B.C.–A.D. 300. Photo by Dale A. Olsen, 1989.

would not establish the orchestration of specific ensembles or explain how each instrument was used in relation to the others.

Music iconography can reveal information about musical contexts, but it cannot tell us many details about techniques of playing. It can suggest the big picture but not the little picture, the focus of musical detail. For example, the player of the single-headed drum pictured in figure 11 is probably playing with a mallet, but we cannot tell how he hits the drumhead (in the middle? on the rim of the skin? with his fingers? also with his palm?). Similarly, the player of the three-tubed flute in figure 12 is obviously playing with his fingers, but we cannot tell which parts of the fingers (tips or middle joints), nor can we tell which holes he covers with which fingers (this would be important information to know for the purposes of determining whether or not ancient Mexicans played multipart music on their multi-tubed flutes).

More important, music iconography can show how particular musicians were attired, and from that evidence, scholars can speculate about the performers' social status. For example, the drummer in figure 11 may have been a priest, judging from the elaborate headdress and fancy necklace, and the flutist in figure 12 may have been a commoner, judging from the simple hat and lack of fancy clothing. This is speculation, but scholars have nothing more on which to base their conclusions about musical contexts and musicians' status. Music iconography, at best, offers suggestions about how musical instruments might have been played and what sort of people the players might have been.

Stevenson explains that "at least forty codices record material of interest to the ethnomusicologist. Even late picture books such as the Codex Azcatitlan (painted *ca.* 1550 in the northern part of the Valley of Mexico) can yield extremely useful documentation on precontact Aztec music" (1968:10). The Bekker Codex (Martí 1968:83–86) pictures Mixtec musicians playing a variety of instruments in great detail. The Florentine Codex of Bernardino Sahagún shows how Aztec flutists smashed their flutes on the steps of the temple before being sacrificed (figure 15).

Another important source for ancient musical iconography of Mexico and Central America is Maya murals, originally painted in temples and tombs. The most famous is from Bonampak, Chiapas, Mexico. It shows numerous Mayan musicians performing together (Martí 1968:facing page 68). Such tomb art is found as far south as Honduras [see MAYA].

FIGURE 14   A ceramic figurine of a man and a woman singing together or yelling at each other. West Mexico, about 200 B.C.–A.D. 300. Photo by Dale A. Olsen, 1989.

In Panama and Costa Rica, several excavated gold artifacts are interpreted as depicting musicians. One of the most famous is from the Coclé culture (about A.D. 1300–1500) in Panama. It is often called the little man flutist (figure 16). The Society for Ethnomusicology (SEM) uses this figure as its logo (a choice made in 1955 by David P. McAllester), and today its form graces the journal *Ethnomusicology* and other SEM-published items. What is not known is whether the little man is actually playing a flute or a trumpet, smoking a cigar, or chewing sugarcane. Other figurines are clearer. These include a gold biped from the Panamian Veraguas culture (about A.D. 800–1540), who seemingly plays a flute with one hand and a rattle with the other (figure 17). This is a fine example of evidence of the one-man-band personage, who often plays a pipe and tabor in present Mexico and Central and South America (Boilès 1966). In this ancient artifact, however, the musician is playing a pipe-and-rattle combination. From Palmar Sur, an ancient Costa Rican site, Luis Ferrero (1977:plate 38) reproduces a photograph of a gold figurine of a double-headed flutist: each head plays what may be a flute that resembles the instrument in the Veraguas exemplar; this double-headed flutist is unique in the musical archaeology of the Americas.

South America

Perhaps nowhere in the Americas is music iconography so rich as among the prehistoric Moche of the north Peruvian coast [see PERU], who depicted musical instruments, singing, whistling, instrumental playing, dancing, and costumes on ceramic pots, often in exquisite detail. Some artifacts are difficult to interpret, such as deathlike figures who are playing panpipes (figure 18) (Benson 1975). Others are quite clear, such as scenes of panpipers where the instruments of two players are connected by a cord, suggesting that panpipes were played by paired musicians—perhaps in an interlocking fashion, as is commonly done today in southern Peru and Bolivia, though this is not known and can never be proven.

In colonial and more recent historic times throughout South America, many paintings, drawings, etchings, and other examples of the plastic arts have depicted musical instruments, singing, instrumental playing, and dancing. These are valuable for learning about colonial music. In colonial paintings of life in Rio de Janeiro, people of African descent are seen playing *mbira*-type plucked idiophones, instruments that have disappeared in modern Brazil.

THE MYTHOLOGICAL RECORD

People in all cultures tell stories. In English, stories passed on orally are called by a variety of names: folklore, folktales, mythology, myths, narratives, oral history, oral literature. Misunderstanding often arises when these terms enter into colloquial speech, because people usually think of a folktale, a myth, a story, and so on, as something that is not true. Actually, mythology is not concerned with proving or disproving truth. It is simply the study of a particular form of discourse. It may be true, or it may be false. Usually it is a little bit true and a little bit false.

Although such communications are often perceived as something other than fact, it is not for persons of one culture to determine whether or not the mythology of another culture is fact or fiction. The mythological record can be an important repository of information from which we can learn something about the meaning and contextualization of another culture's music. Much of what is learned may not exist in current practice (or perhaps it never existed, or exists only for the supernatural), but it may provide a framework on which cultural understanding can be built. This cultural understanding takes place, not usually with details that can be physically measured or scientifically studied, but with emotions, ideas, morals, and beliefs.

FIGURE 15   A picture from the Florentine Codex of Bernardino Sahagún (sixteenth century), showing how Aztec flutists smashed their flutes on the steps of the temple before being sacrificed.

FIGURE 16   A gold figurine of a man playing what may be a vertical flute. Coclé culture, Panama, about A.D. 1300–1500. Photo by Dale A. Olsen, 1989.

FIGURE 17   A gold figurine of a man playing what may be a vertical flute and rattle at the same time. Veraguas culture, Panama, about A.D. 800–1540. Photo by Dale A. Olsen, 1989.

A myth is an artifact. Unlike an archaeological artifact, it cannot be dated. Nevertheless, it can often provide data that researchers can use comparatively to help reconstruct cultural history. As a repository of historical fact, a myth is usually unreliable, though ideas about great tragedies (massacres, famines, plagues), large-scale migrations, wars, and other memorable events and situations may be related in narratives or songs. More often, myths may relate ideas about the creation of the universe, taboos on human conduct, and the daily lives of gods, cultural heroes, and ogres. Myths contextualize many musical instruments, and these native (albeit mythological) contexts can be compared with historical or contemporary uses of the same musical instruments. Likewise, myths may contextualize singing and dancing in ways that provide information about cultural continuity, acculturation, and cultural extinction.

Most of what we know from the mythological record of South America, Mexico, Central America, and the Caribbean comes from the twentieth century, the age of ethnographic investigation. Myths, usually transmitted orally, have been collected and written down by historians, travelers, missionaries, anthropologists, ethnomusicologists, and others. Written collections are important for study, but also important are the original rules of preservation (some myths are guarded by shamans, priests, elders, women, and so on) and dissemination, because those processes are essential in maintaining cultural cohesion and continuity. Therefore, mythology has tremendous internal importance for cultures. Scholars can learn much about a culture by study-

The king's drummer began to play on the great
drum. The elephants began to dance. The ground
shook with their stamping. The dancing went on
and on, all night.

—Haitian folktale

ing such internal dynamics (how, when, and why myths are preserved, transmitted, and remembered), and studying the myths themselves (what they mean, inside and outside the culture).

The Caribbean

Much of the folklore of the Caribbean region is Afro-Caribbean in origin. Telling stories, reciting proverbs, and singing songs—possibly African retentions passed on from generation to generation—are commonplace in areas where African slaves and their children lived in great numbers. Many Afro-Caribbean narratives refer to musical performance, musical instruments, dancing, and so forth. The following tale, entitled "Mérisier, Stronger than the Elephants" comes from Haiti, and portions of it tell us important information about local music (Courlander 1976:64–66):

> There was an old man with three sons. One day he fell ill, and he sent a message to his sons, asking them to come to his house. When they arrived, he said to them, "I am an old man, I am sick. If I should die, how will you bury me?"
>
> One son answered, "Father, may you grow strong again. But if you should die, I would have you buried in a mahogany coffin."
>
> Another son answered, "Father, may you live long. But if you should die, I would make you a coffin of brass."
>
> And the third son, named Brisé, replied, "Father, I would bury you in the great drum of the king of the elephants."
>
> "The great drum of the king of the elephants! Who before now has ever been buried so magnificently!" the old man said. "Yes, that is the way it should be." And he asked the son who had suggested it to bring him the drum of the king of the elephants.
>
> Brisé went home. He told his wife: "I said I would do this thing for my father, but it is impossible. Why didn't I say I would make him a coffin of silver? Even that would have been more possible. How shall I ever be able to do what I have promised?"

Thereupon Brisé sets off on a journey, looking for elephants so he can acquire the elephants' great drum. He travels far and visits many people, until he meets Mérisier, a Vodou priest. The story continues:

> Then Brisé understood that the old man was a houngan, a Vodoun priest with magical powers. The old man took out his bead-covered rattle. He shook it and went into a trance and talked with the gods. At last he put the rattle away and said: "Go that way, to the north, across the grassland. There is a great mapou tree, called Mapou Plus Grand Passe Tout. Wait there. The elephants come there with the drum. They dance until they are tired, then they fall asleep. When they sleep,

FIGURE 18   A stirrup-spout ceramic bottle depicts a male deathlike figure playing a pan-pipe. Moche culture, Peru, about 100 B.C.–A.D. 700. Photo by Dale A. Olsen, 1979.

take the drum. Travel fast. Here are four wari nuts for protection. If you are pursued, throw a wari nut behind you and say, 'Mérisier is stronger than the elephants.'"

When day came, Brisé went north across the grasslands. He came to the tree called Mapou Plus Grand Passe Tout. He climbed into the tree and waited. As the sun was going down, he saw a herd of elephants coming, led by their king. They gathered around the mapou tree. The king's drummer began to play on the great drum. The elephants began to dance. The ground shook with their stamping. The dancing went on and on, all night. They danced until the first cocks began to crow. Then they stopped, lay down on the ground, and slept.

Brisé came down from the tree. He was in the middle of a large circle of elephants. He took the great drum and placed it on his head. He climbed first over one sleeping elephant, then another, until he was outside the circle. He traveled as fast as he could with his heavy load.

The story continues to explain how the elephants come after Brisé, and how Brisé stops them each time by throwing a *wari* nut. The first nut produces a huge forest of pines as a barrier to the elephants, the second a large freshwater lake (which they drink to cross), the third a large saltwater lake (which they drink to cross, but all except the elephant king die). The story continues:

Brisé came out of the grassland. He followed the trails. He went to his father's house with the drum. When he arrived, his father was not dead; he was not sick; he was working with his hoe in the fields.

"Put the drum away," the father said. "I don't need it yet. I am feeling fine."

Brisé took the drum to his own house. He ate and slept. When he awoke, he heard a loud noise in the courtyard. He saw the king of elephants coming. The elephant ran straight toward the great drum and seized hold of it.

Brisé took the last wari nut that the Vodoun priest had given him and threw it on the ground, saying, "Mérisier is stronger than the elephants!"

Instantly the great drum broke into small pieces, and each piece became a small drum. The king of elephants broke into many pieces, and each piece became a drummer. The drummers went everywhere, each one taking a drum with him.

Thus it is that there are drums everywhere in the country. Thus it is that people have a proverb which says: "Every drum has a drummer."

This tale explains—though with tongue in cheek, of course—why Haiti has so many drums and drummers, but it also explains why Haiti has no elephants. It says the Vodou priest (*houngan*) plays a bead-covered rattle (similar to today's West African and Afro-Cuban instruments), which contrasts with container rattles often found in Haitian Vodou.

Mexico and Central America

Much of the mythology of Mexico and Central America is native American in origin. Probably all Amerindians have tales that can teach us something about their music. Especially noteworthy are narratives of the Aztec (Nahua), the Huichol, the Maya, and the Kuna. Some are creation myths. Others are everyday stories about animals, life in the forests, and so on. Musical performance, especially singing, is often a part of them.

Peter Furst and Barbara Myerhoff have shown (1966) how an elaborate cycle of myths, which they call an epic prose-poem, provides information about the birth, life, and death of a master sorcerer known as the Tree of the Wind. Also known as the

Datura Person, he was responsible for introducing the powerfully dangerous hallu-cinogen *datura* to the Huichol of northern Mexico. The cycle provides information about the power of singing and playing the violin by the Huichol, who consider the violin "among their most ancient instruments" (personal conversation, Ramón Medina Silva, a Huichol shaman, 1971). Similarly, Julio Estrada has shown how an Aztec (Nahua) myth explains the creation of the world through the power of the sacred conch trumpet of Quetzalcoatl, the Aztec cultural hero (Estrada 1992:341):

> But his shell horn had no holes: [Quetzalcoatl] then summoned forth the worms, which made the holes; thereupon the male and female bees flew into the shell and it sounded.

Estrada interprets this myth as explaining the "cultivation of the earth. When the shell is played, the wind god and the bees together spread the seed of a new culture" (1992:341). Many cultures (Aztec, Inca, Maya, Moche, and others) venerated conchs and used them as trumpets for sacred purposes; but for native Americans, conch trumpets have power especially when they are sounded, and myths help us under-stand why.

The sound of the trumpet, significant in prehistoric America, remains an impor-tant symbol. A week before carnival in Chamulá, Mexico, in 1969, the master of cer-emonies gave the following oral proclamation to the village (after Bricker 1973:85–86):

> Chamulas!
> Crazy February!
> Today is the ninth of February, 1969.
> The first soldier came to Mexico.
> He came to Guatemala;
> He came to Tuxtla;
> He came to Chiapa;
> He came to San Cristóbal.
> He came with flags;
> He came with drums;
> He came with trumpets.
> Viva! Viva!
>
> The last cavalier came to Mexico.
> He came to Guatemala;
> He came to Tuxtla;
> He came to Chiapa;
> He came to San Cristóbal.
> He came with fireworks;
> He came with cannons;
> He came with fifes;
> He came with bugles;
> He came with flags;
> He came with trumpets.
> Mariano Ortega and Juan Gutiérrez came with their young lady, Nana María
>   Cocorina.
> They go together into the wood to make love.
> They return eating toffee, eating candied squash, eating blood sausage.
> Viva Mariano Ortega!

Here we see trumpets, bugles, and other wind instruments as symbols of power, not only of victory in war (the Spanish conquests of Mexico, Guatemala, and Chiapas), but also of spreading the seed—because Nana María Cocorina becomes pregnant (Bricker 1973:118).

South America

The mythology of South American native people is rich. Telling stories is a way of life, and often the distinction between speaking and singing stories is slight. Among South American Amerindians, music is often a part of most myths, and numerous examples portray musical situations that differ from musical situations of the 1990s. Women do not usually play flutes; in myths, however, they are as likely to play flutes as men. An excerpt from a Warao narrative reveals how a woman plays a bamboo flute and sings for magical protection against a jaguar, who is actually a transformed man (Wilbert 1970:164–165):

> He had collected a lot of bamboo and threw it down, "Kerplum." When it became dark he lapped up some water with his tongue, "Beh, beh." After having built up the fire, the boys began to dance. She herself played the flute made of bamboo, "Tea, tea, tea, tail of a jaguar," she said.
>
> The jaguar rushed towards the woman, but she grabbed a piece of firewood and stuck him in the eye. The jaguar stopped. Again, in the dance place, she took the bamboo flute and played, "Tea, tea, tea, tail of a jaguar. Tea, tea, tea, tail of a jaguar." Again the jaguar rushed toward the seated woman. Again, she stuck a piece of firewood into his eye. . . .
>
> By dawn, he could take no more. He sat with his back to them. The woman's little brother arrived with arrows and spear. "Sister, you all survived the night?"

In anthropology, this is known as a reversal of social order (as when a musical instrument at one time was the domain of one sex, but then switches at some point in history), and often, mythology is the only record of such musical behavior. Furthermore, mythology often elaborates on the processes that produce such cultural changes.

Another trait seen in the above myth, and common in most narratives, is onomatopoeia, as when the jaguar throws the bamboo down and goes "Kerplum." Often such sounds symbolize musical instruments and the noises of everyday life, including the sounds of humans, animals, and spirits. Among the Kalapalo of Brazil, and possibly among most native South American people, spirits have a specially musical language: "Powerful beings are . . . capable of inventing musical forms, whereas humans are capable only of copying those forms in their performances" (Basso 1985:70). This is one of the main reasons that music has so much power among Amerindians, as shamans and nonshamans alike sing for protection, for curing, and for other types of theurgy (Dale A. Olsen 1996).

THE HISTORIOGRAPHIC RECORD

Musical historiography is essentially musical information written by chroniclers of a culture contemporary with their own. These writings are either emic (insider), such as the Maya writing about the Maya or the descendants of the Inca writing about the Inca (problematic because the notion that descendants have an emic claim on their ancestors can be controversial), Jesuits writing about music at their missions, and so forth, or etic (outsider), such as Spanish chroniclers (*cronistas*) writing about the music of ancient American civilizations, in which case the information may be biased. Another type of historiographic information is philology, which includes

During the colonial period, religious scholars produced many sources about Amerindian music because they believed that knowing about native music would help missionaries convert the Indians to Christianity. In essence, they provided some of the first ethnographies of native cultures.

descriptive treatises about musical instruments, musical practices, and language. (Early dictionaries are important sources about music.) Another area is oral history, though oral historians, folklorists, and anthropologists often disagree about whether oral history is history, folklore, or ethnography. Basically, historiographic information consists of ethnographies or travelogs from the past. Such sources can be quite different: some are objective, some are subjective, and some, because of bias or carelessness, may contain misinformation. Sources must always be carefully analyzed and compared with other types of information.

The Caribbean

Early chroniclers (cited in Boyrie Moya 1971:13–14; Loven 1935:492–497; Moldes 1975:6–7) described several musical instruments of the Taino, even though those Arawak-speakers were nearly extinct. These instruments included what the writers called a skinless drum made from a hollowed-out tree, with an H-shaped incision on the top forming two tongues that players struck; a small gourd or calabash container rattle used during a harvest festival; a large, double-handled gourd or calabash container rattle used by shamans for curing illnesses; snail-shell rattles strung around dancers' legs, arms, and hips; small, metal, castanet-type instruments held between a dancer's fingers; flutes; and conch trumpets. Most of these instruments were used to accompany the singing of religious songs (*areito*).

J. M. Coopersmith (1949:7–8), describing the Taino log idiophone, quotes the chronicler Oviedo y Valdés:

> They accompany their songs with a drum, which is made from a hollowed trunk of a tree, often as large as a man and sounding like the drums made by the Negroes. There is no parchment on the drum but, rather, holes or slits are made, from which the sound emanates. . . . The drum . . . (is cylindrical) in form and made from the trunk of a tree, as large as desired. . . . It is played with a stick like the tympanum (atabal). One sound-hole in the form of an "H" is cut in the middle of one side of the trunk. The two tongues formed by the "H" are beaten with a stick. On the opposite side of the trunk-section, near the base of the cylinder, a rectangular hole is cut. The drum must be held on the ground, for it does not sound if held elsewhere. . . . On the mainland, these drums are sometimes lined with the skin of a deer or some other animal. Both types of drum are used on the mainland.

This description is better than those of many other chroniclers, but it is typical because of what is *not* said. It was apparently uncommon to write about the cultural significance of musical instruments, their origins, or anything else about their seemingly extramusical functions. The obvious question, whether or not the Taino H-drum was borrowed from the Mexican mainland, was apparently never asked. Few other Taino instruments are mentioned, and musical occasions are not described at all.

The ancient Carib, by contrast, had more musical instruments, which the chroniclers (unknown writers cited in Petitjean-Roget 1961:51, 67–68 and Rouse 1963b:561; Rochefort 1666, cited by Stevenson 1975:52) described in fuller detail. Among them were container rattles made from gourds; a single-headed drum (membranophone) made from a hollowed tree; bamboo flutes and bone flutes; panpipes; conch trumpets; and even a single-stringed instrument made from a gourd. The chroniclers mentioned that mothers used rattles to soothe their children; men played flutes in the morning while women prepared breakfast and people bathed; panpipes accompanied dancing; and conch trumpets were blown to signal wars and hunting or fishing expeditions.

Mexico and Central America

Historical accounts of Amerindian music from Mexico and Central America—the area known as the Viceroyalty of New Spain, including the Caribbean islands—date from the early 1500s and were written mainly by Spanish chroniclers. Foremost among them was Bernal Díaz del Castillo, who lived between about 1492 and 1581 (Stevenson 1968:12–14). His accounts vividly describe ritual music for human sacrifices, music for battles, and festival music of the Aztecs.

During the colonial period, religious scholars produced many sources about Amerindian music because they believed that knowing about native music would help missionaries convert the Indians to Christianity. The Franciscan order was dominant in Mexico, where Pedro de Gante was the leading missionary who described Amerindian music during the early years of the conversion process. He wrote in letters to King Charles V of Spain about the Indians' musicality: "I can affirm that there are now trained singers among them who if they were to sing in Your Majesty's Chapel would at this moment do so well that perhaps you would have to see them actually singing in order to believe it possible" (Stevenson 1968:157). The printing of music appeared in Mexico as early as 1556, forty-five years before it appeared in Peru, and elaborate polyphonic scores attest to Amerindian choristers' musical skills.

South America

Spanish and Portuguese conquerors, explorers, religious zealots, and others wrote extensively about the new lands of South America—known as the Viceroyalties of New Granada, Peru, La Plata, and Brazil, the latter under Portuguese rule. One of the most important writers about sixteenth-century Peruvian music was Felipe Guamán Poma de Ayala (1936 [1612–1615/16]), who described Inca music and musical instruments in detail; Guamán Poma's source provides many drawings of Inca musical performance. Another sixteenth-century author, Garcilaso de la Vega (1966 [1609]), the son of a Spanish nobleman and an Incan princess, also wrote extensively about music among the Inca and other Amerindians.

The major religious orders in Spanish South America were the Augustinians, the Dominicans, the Franciscans, and the Jesuits; the last were musically active in Peru and Paraguay until their expulsion in 1767. Their goal was basically the same as that of missionaries in New Spain: spiritual conversion. Like those missionaries, they trained many musicians, chronicled many events involving music, described many musical instruments, and in essence provided some of the first ethnographies of native cultures.

Writings in the historiographic process often become ethnographies when they deal extensively with the behavior of a culture. Likewise, ethnographies become historiographic sources. Indeed, the difference between histories and ethnographies is often slight. Studies about the music of South America that are now important historiographic sources are numerous. Many of them are listed within the particular article references and in the general bibliography of this volume. They include such famous monographs from the first half of the twentieth century as *An Introductory Study of the Arts, Crafts, and Customs of the Guiana Indians* by Walter E. Roth (1924), *La musique des Incas et ses survivances* by Raoul and Marguerite d'Harcourt (1990 [1925]), and *Suriname Folk-Lore* by Melville and Frances Herskovits (1936).

ETHNOLOGY AND PRACTICE

Studies that go beyond the mere description of a culture and include analysis, interpretation, and synthesis based on participant observation, participation, and interaction have moved out of ethnography into ethnology, the science of culture. These include studies in anthropology, ethnobotany, ethnolinguistics, ethnomusicology, folklore, poetics, religion, and so forth, and they number in the thousands of volumes that add to our musical understanding of South America, Mexico, Central America, and the Caribbean.

In the realm of specific musical study, participation in and writing about the music of a culture by its bearers themselves (the emic, or "insider" approach) or by non-culturebearers (the etic, or "outsider" approach) has often resulted in the cultivation of knowledge acquired through practice. Two studies that help describe this approach are *Capoeira—A Brazilian Art Form: History, Philosophy, and Practice,* by Bira Almeida, known professionally as Mestre Acordeon (1986), and *Ring of Liberation,* by J. Lowell Lewis (1992). Both treat the same musical phenomenon, *capoeira,* a form of Afro-Brazilian music, dance, and martial art, from Salvador de Bahia, Brazil. Because these books differ widely in their approach to this topic, reading them both side by side will provide a better understanding of *capoeira* than reading only one of them. A thorough understanding of a particular musical topic requires the exploration of all the forms of musical scholarship available.

REFERENCES

Acevedo Vargas, Jorge. 1987. *La Música en las Reservas Indígenas de Costa Rica.* San José: Editorial de la Universidad de Costa Rica.

Almeida, Bira (Mestre Acordeon). 1986. *Capoeira—A Brazilian Art Form: History, Philosophy, and Practice.* Berkeley: North Atlantic Books.

Andrews V., E. Wyllys. 1972. *Flautas precolombinas procedentes de Quelepa, El Salvador.* San Salvador: Ministerio de Educación, Dirección de Cultura, Dirección de Publicaciones.

Basso, Ellen B. 1985. *A Musical View of the Universe.* Philadelphia: University of Pennsylvania Press.

Benson, Elizabeth P. 1975. "Death-Associated Figures on Mochica Pottery." In *Death and the Afterlife in Pre-Columbian America,* ed. Elizabeth P. Benson, 105–144. Washington, D.C.: Dumbarton Oaks Research Library and Collections.

Boilès, Charles L. 1966. "The Pipe and Tabor in Mesoamerica." *Yearbook for Inter-American Musical Research* 2:43–74.

Bolaños, César. 1981. *Música y Danza en el Antiguo Perú.* Lima: Museo Nacional de Antropología y Arqueología, Instituto Nacional de Cultura.

———. 1988. "La Música en el Antiguo Perú." In *La Música en el Perú,* 1–64. Lima: Patronato Popular y Porvenir Pro Música Clásica.

Boggs, Stanley H. 1974. "Notes on Pre-Columbian Wind Instruments from El Salvador." *Baessler-Archiv, Beiträge zur Völkerkunde* (Berlin) 22:23–71.

Boyrie Moya, Emile de. 1971. "Tres flautas-ocarinas de manufactura alfarera de los indígenas de la isla de Santo Domingo." *Revista dominicana de arqueología y antropología* 1(1):13–17.

Bricker, Victoria Reifler. 1973. *Ritual Humor in Highland Chiapas.* Austin: University of Texas Press.

Coopersmith, J. M. 1949. *Music and Musicians of the Dominican Republic.* Washington, D.C.: Pan American Union.

Courlander, Harold. 1976. *A Treasury of Afro-American Folklore.* New York: Crown Publishers.

Crossley-Holland, Peter. 1980. *Musical Artifacts of Pre-Hispanic West Mexico: Towards an Interdisciplinary Approach.* Los Angeles: Program in Ethnomusicology, Department of Music, University of California at Los Angeles.

Cubillos Ch., Julio César. 1958. "Apuntes Sobre Instrumentos Musicales Aborígines Hallados en Colombia." In *Homenaje al Profesor Paul Rivet,* 169–189. Bogotá: Editorial A B C.

Donnan, Christopher B. 1982. "Dance in Moche Art." *Nawpa Pacha* 20:97–120.

Estrada, Julio. 1992. "The Emergence of Myth as Explanation." In *Musical Repercussions of 1492: Encounters in Text and Performance,* ed. Carol E. Robertson, 337–350. Washington D.C.: Smithsonian Institution Press.

Ferrero, Luis. 1977. *Costa Rica Precolombina: Arqueología, Etnología, Tecnología, Arte.* San José: Editorial Costa Rica.

Fewkes, Jesse. 1907. "The Aborigines of Porto Rico and Neighboring Islands." *Twenty-Fifth Report of the Bureau of American Ethnology.* Washington, D.C.: U.S. Government Printing Office.

Furst, Peter, and Barbara Myerhoff. 1966. "Myth as History: The Jimson Weed Cycle of the Huichols of Mexico." *Antropológica* 17:3–39.

Garcilaso de la Vega, El Inca. 1966 [1609]. *The Incas: The Royal Commentaries of the Inca.* 2nd ed. Edited by Alain Gheerbrant. Translated by Maria Jolas. New York: Avon Books, Orion Press.

Grebe, María Ester. 1974. "Instrumentos musicales precolombinos de Chile." *Revista Musical Chilena* 128:5–55.

Guamán Poma de Ayala, Felipe. 1936 [1612–1615/16]. *Nueva Crónica y Buen Gobierno.* Paris: Institut d'Ethnologie.

Haeberli, Joerg. 1979. "Twelve Nasca Panpipes: A Study." *Ethnomusicology* 23(1):57–74.

Hammond, Norman. 1972a. "Classic Maya Music. Part I: Maya Drums." *Archaeology* 25(2):125–131.

———. 1972b. "Classic Maya Music. Part II: Rattles, Shakers, Raspers, Wind and String Instruments." *Archaeology* 25(3):222–228.

d'Harcourt, Raoul, and Marguerite d'Harcourt. 1990 [1925]. *La musique des Incas et ses survivances.* Paris: Librairie Orientaliste Paul Geuthner.

Herskovits, Melville J., and Frances S. Herskovits. 1936. *Suriname Folk-Lore.* New York: Columbia University Press.

Hickmann, Ellen. 1983–1984. "Terminology, Problems, Goals of Archaeomusicology." *Progress Reports in Ethnomusicology* 1(3):1–9.

———. 1990. *Musik aus dem Altertum der Neuen Welt: Archäologische Dokumente des Musizierens in präkolumbischen Kulturen Perus, Ekuadors und Kolumbiens.* Frankfurt am Main: Peter Lang.

Jiménez Borja, Arturo. 1951. *Instrumentos musicales del Peru.* Lima: Museo de la Cultura.

Lewin, Olive. 1968. "Jamaican Folk Music." *Caribbean Quarterly* 14(1–2):49–56.

Lewis, J. Lowell. 1992. *Ring of Liberation.* Chicago: University of Chicago Press.

Loven, Sven. 1935. *Origins of the Tainan Culture, West Indies.* Göteborg, Sweden: Elanders Boktryckeri Akfiebolag.

Martí, Samuel. 1968. *Instrumentos Musicales Precortesianos.* México, D.F.: Instituto Nacional de Antropología.

Moldes, Rhyna. 1975. *Música folklórica cubana.* Miami: Ediciones Universal.

Nyberg, John L. 1974. "An Examination of Vessel Flutes from Pre-Hispanic Cultures of Ecuador." Ph.D. dissertation, University of Minnesota.

Olsen, Dale A. 1986. "The Flutes of El Dorado: An Archaeomusicological Investigation of the Tairona Civilization of Colombia." *Journal of the American Musical Instrument Society* 12:107–136.

———. 1987. "The Flutes of El Dorado: Musical Guardian Spirit Effigies of the Tairona." *Imago Musicae: The International Yearbook of Musical Iconography* 3 (1986):79–102.

———. 1989. "The Magic Flutes of El Dorado: A Model for Research in Archaeomusicology as Applied to the Sinú of Ancient Colombia." In *Early Music Cultures, Selected Papers from the Third International Meeting of the ICTM Study Group on Music Archaeology,* ed. Ellen Hickmann and David Hughes, 305–328. Bonn: Verlag für Systematische Musikwissenschaft.

———. 1990. "The Ethnomusicology of Archaeology: A Model for Research in Ethnoarchaeomusicology." *Selected Reports in Ethnomusicology* 8:175–197. Issues in Organology.

———. 1992. "Music of the Ancient Americas: Music Technologies and Intellectual Implications in the Andes." In *Musical Repercussions of 1492: Exploration, Encounter, and Identities,* ed. Carol Robertson, 65–88. Washington, D.C.: Smithsonian Institution Press.

———. 1996. *Music of the Warao of Venezuela: Song People of the Rain Forest.* Gainesville: University Press of Florida.

Olsen, Fred. 1974. *On the Trail of the Ancient Arawaks.* Norman: University of Oklahoma Press.

Petitjean-Roget, Jacques. 1961. "The Caribs as seen through the Dictionary of the Rev. Father Breton." *Proceedings of the First International Convention for the Study of Pre-Columbian Culture in the Lesser Antilles (July 3–7, 1961).* Fort-de-France: Société d'Histoire de la Martinique.

Rivera y Rivera, Roberto. 1977. *Los instrumentos musicales de los Mayas.* México, D.F.: Instituto Nacional de Antropología e Historia.

Roth, Walter E. 1924. "An Introductory Study of the Arts, Crafts, and Customs of the Guiana Indians." *Thirty-Eighth Annual Report of the Bureau of American Ethnology to the Secretary of the Smithsonian Institution 1916–1917.* Washington, D.C.: U.S. Government Printing Office.

Rouse, Irving. 1963a. "The Arawak." *Handbook of South American Indians,* vol. 4, ed. Julian H. Steward, 507–546. New York: Cooper Square Publishers.

———. 1963b. "The Carib." *Handbook of South American Indians,* vol. 4, ed. Julian H. Steward, 547–566. New York: Cooper Square Publishers.

Stevenson, Robert M. 1960. *The Music of Peru: Aboriginal and Viceroyal Epochs.* Washington, D.C.: Organization of American States.

———. 1968. *Music in Aztec and Inca Territory.* Berkeley and Los Angeles: University of California Press.

———. 1975. *A Guide to Caribbean Music History.* Lima: Ediciones CULTURA.

Veloz Maggiolo, Marcio. 1972. *Arqueología prehistórica de Santo Domingo.* Singapore: McGraw-Hill Far Eastern Publishers.

Wilbert, Johannes. 1970. *Folk Literature of the Warao Indians.* Los Angeles: Center for Latin American Studies, UCLA.

Part 2
Issues and Processes in the Music of South America, Mexico, Central America, and the Caribbean

Music does not exist without a social context. Even music being recorded "out of context," as in a studio, is within a studio context. Likewise, all music is involved with some kind of social, religious, or economic issue, and a process is always at work. These are often complex phenomena, requiring extensive analysis to be understood.

Musical instruments, for example, do not function by themselves, but are entwined with cultural behavior. It is important to understand not only where musical instruments are found and why certain cultures have the instruments they do, but also what instruments physically and sonically symbolize and what roles they play. Musical genres too have typical contexts, entwined with social structure and human behavior.

The Americas are diverse for many reasons, especially because they are largely populated by immigrants, and music often negotiates ethnic and cultural identity among immigrant societies (most commonly in the Caribbean and South America). Music also changes because of inside influences and outside contacts, and new ideas come from the recent or "pop" musics of South America, Mexico, Central America, and the Caribbean.

Dance is a ritual behavior practiced by young and old. This little boy is a *chino* ('humble servant') dancer during the patronal festival of the Virgen de Guadalupe in Ayquina, Chile, 8 September 1968. Photo by Dale A. Olsen.

The Distribution, Symbolism, and Use of Musical Instruments

Dale A. Olsen

The Classification of Musical Instruments
The Distribution of Musical Instruments
Symbolic Interpretations of Musical Instruments
The Influence of Electronics

People make music by playing instruments, singing, or both, often at the same time. Musical instruments tell us much about cultures, not so much as items in themselves, but as tokens of meaning—what they signify to their cultures and how they came to mean what they mean. Musical instruments are artifacts and "ethnofacts"—the former because they are objects created by humans, and the latter because they have meaning, often of a symbolic kind.

The musical instruments found in South America, Mexico, Central America, and the Caribbean are diverse, and their number is large. From the Encounter in 1492 until the present, about two thousand languages have been spoken by native Americans, not including those of North America. If an average of three musical instruments per language group existed, that means that the names of probably six thousand instruments were once being used. The Spanish, Portuguese, Africans, and all the other foreigners who came after the Encounter and up to the present probably introduced another thousand names for musical instruments. Because of the disappearance of native American cultures, assimilation, modernization, and other forces of culture change, a much smaller quantity exists today. Nevertheless, we are still dealing with a vast number, and diversity is still a hallmark of these instruments. A systematic taxonomy of musical instrument classification, therefore, is necessary in order to understand the distribution, symbolism, and use of musical instruments in the area.

THE CLASSIFICATION OF MUSICAL INSTRUMENTS

This volume classifies musical instruments in two ways. First, whenever possible, they are classified according to the system designed by their culture itself. When an indigenous taxonomy is not known or does not exist, however, they are classified according to an extended set of terms derived from the work of Erich M. von Hornbostel and Curt Sachs: idiophone, membranophone, chordophone, aerophone (Jairazbhoy 1990), electrophone (Bakan et. al. 1990), and corpophone (Olsen 1986).

Sounds are transmitted via waves that travel from their sources through air (or water), strike the receiver's eardrum, and register in the receiver's brain. The shape of the wave determines whether what is received is music (and what kind of music),

FIGURE 1   A ceramic dog-shaped ocarina or globular flute with a cross-blown mouthpiece on its stomach (it was photographed upside down to show the mouthpiece) and two fingerholes. Ancient Moche culture, Peru. Photo by Dale A. Olsen, 1996.

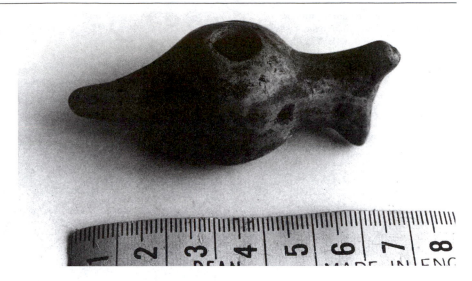

speech, noise, or whatever a culture calls it. The sources that produce what we may call music are what we shall call musical instruments. (These points are important because what we call music or musical instruments may not always be considered music or musical instruments by the people of the cultures themselves.) Given the diversity, large numbers, and complexity (or simplicity) of the sources of sound in the world, an objective system of classification must be employed; this is why the extended Hornbostel-Sachs taxonomy is often used.

An *idiophone* is defined as a 'self-sounder'; the entire instrument itself vibrates, sending off waves of sound. This is a huge category because of the cultural diversity of the geographic areas. Because of forced and unforced immigration, idiophones essentially include instruments from Africa, Europe, and Asia, in addition to those of native Americans. Examples of idiophones, using some common and general terms, range from dancers' ankle-tied bells to maracas (*maráka,* from the Tupí language), rhythm sticks, triangles, steel drums, marimbas, gongs, scrapers, and many more.

A *membranophone* is defined as a 'skin-sounder' in which a skin (or skins) stretched tightly over a rigid support vibrates, sending off waves of sound. Skin instruments are often called drums, a term otherwise used for the body or chamber. Confusion arises when *drum* is used for items without a skin, such as oil drums or steel drums—the former not a musical instrument, the latter an idiophone.

An *aerophone* is defined as an 'air-sounder', a wind instrument in which air within a column vibrates, or in which air acting on the instrument causes it to vibrate, sending off waves of sound. The aerophone category comprises the largest and most complex group of instruments in the Americas, and numerous subgroups can be included within it. Because of diversity, it would perhaps be prudent to refrain from employing terms derived from the classification of Western European orchestral instruments. For example, such terms as *edge aerophone* for *flute, lip-concussion aerophone* for *trumpet, single-reed-concussion aerophone* for *clarinet,* and *double-reed-concussion aerophone* for *oboe* or *shawm* (a European Renaissance kind of oboe) would be organologically clear. Common sense, however, suggests that for most readers, terms like *flute, trumpet, clarinet,* and *oboe* are easier to understand. In all cases, when the common European terms are used in this volume, they will never mean the European form of the instrument unless carefully stated so. Other terms such as *ocarina* for *globular flute* (figure 1) and *panpipe* for a multi-tubed flute without holes may be used. In addition, the terms *duct* (like the mouthpiece of a recorder) and *ductless* (like the mouthpiece of a Western flute, a single tube of a panpipe, or the Andean notched

FIGURE 2   Three bone flutes with notched mouthpieces and four fingerholes: *left and right,* the ancient Nasca culture; *middle,* the Chancay culture, Peru. Photo by Dale A. Olsen, 1973.

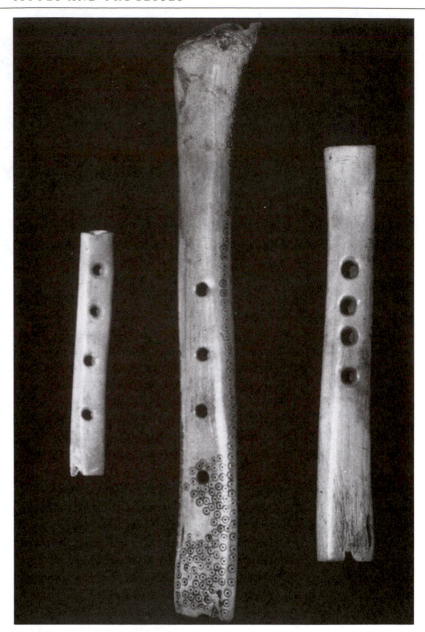

flute, figure 2) here serve to clarify the subcategory of flute-type instrument. Indeed, the literature on the subject of aerophones can be confusing because styles of writing are often unclear, and descriptions are often incomplete.

A *chordophone* is defined as a 'string-sounder' in which a string (or strings) stretched tightly over a rigid support vibrates, sending off waves of sound. Most musical instruments in this category derive from Iberian prototypes, and their names are most often given in their English forms, rather than Spanish or Portuguese (*guitar* for *guitarra,* *harp* for *arpa,* *mandolin* for *mandolina,* and *violin* for *violín,* for example). Sometimes *guitar type* or *small guitar* are used in scholarship, but that usage tends to confuse rather than clarify. Exceptions are the *tres* (figure 3) and the *cuatro,* whose names are determined by numbers of strings or string courses (except for the Puerto Rican *cuatro,* which has ten strings).

An *electrophone* is defined as an 'electronic sounder' in which a vibration or action is produced by electronic means, sending off waves of sound. This category serves for several instruments used in contemporary or pop music and includes the

FIGURE 3   The *tres,* a guitar-type instrument with six strings strung into three courses, common in Cuba and Dominican Republic. This man plays with a Dominican merengue quartet. Photo by Dale A. Olsen, 1977.

synthesizer and computer-generated devices. An electric guitar, however, may be a chordophone with an electronic attachment, a pickup, connected to an amplifier.

A *corpophone* is defined as a 'body sounder' in which a vibration or action is produced by a body part (or parts), sending off sound waves. This category includes handclaps, slaps of the buttocks, snaps of the fingers, and so forth, but does not include vocalizations. Musical vocal sounds are songs; the word *chant* is not used unless it is specifically defined within particular entries.

Karl Gustav Izikowitz attempted to list and analyze all the musical instruments of native South America (Izikowitz 1970 [1935]). Other scholars have made similar attempts for particular countries, including Argentina (Vega 1946), Bolivia (Diaz Gainza 1962), Colombia (Bermúdez 1985), Ecuador (Coba Andrade 1981), Guyana

edge aerophone A flute-type wind instrument

lip-concussion aerophone A trumpet-type wind instrument

single-reed-concussion aerophone A clarinet-type wind instrument

double-reed-concussion aerophone An oboe-type wind instrument (shawm)

(Roth 1924), Peru (Bolaños et al. 1978), and Venezuela (Aretz 1967). Izikowitz's book is a bibliographic study based on the descriptions of musical instruments published by anthropologists and other researchers; the other publications are primarily based on fieldwork by the authors. The above-listed country studies include more instruments than those of native peoples.

THE DISTRIBUTION OF MUSICAL INSTRUMENTS

A topic of scholars' concern is the distribution of musical instruments. At a general level, this distribution in the southern Americas is determined by one or more of these factors: the locations of the cultures that use them at present, the locations of the cultures that used them at one time, and the locations of their use in popular music.

The first factor is a logical truism, something to be expected. General examples are the distribution of African-derived membranophones around the coast of South America from Rio de Janeiro, Brazil, northward to the Caribbean coast of Colombia, northward from Colombia through Belize, southward from Colombia to coastal Ecuador, and into the cultures of the Caribbean basin—areas where the largest numbers of African slaves were concentrated. Particular examples are the use of *rum* membranophones in the Candomblé rituals of Bahia, Brazil, and *batá* drums in the Santería rituals of Cuba. Another example is the use of guitars or guitar-type instruments wherever Spanish or Portuguese heritage is strong.

The second factor relates to the use of instruments by people who were not the original users, but because the original users lived in the area in times past, they influenced the present users. An example of this is the use of *marimba* xylophones by Maya people in Guatemala, who learned the instruments from African former slaves or runaway slaves whose descendants no longer inhabit the area.

The third factor is determined by the importation of certain instruments because of popular music. An example is the use of the *charango* in Santiago, Chile, by performers of *nueva canción* in the 1960s and 1970s, such as Inti Illimani and Quilapayún, and its continued use in certain Chilean rock groups of the 1990s, such as Los Jaivas.

SYMBOLIC INTERPRETATIONS OF MUSICAL INSTRUMENTS

The distribution of musical instruments can be affected by culturally determined factors, most of them imbued with interpretations of symbolism or iconicity: concepts of ideal qualities of sound, concepts of physical duality, ideas about extramusical power, the need for giving signals, and the introduction of instruments by agents of foreign powers (such as Jesuit missionaries in 1700s and military bands in the 1800s).

Concepts of ideal qualities of sound

During pre-Columbian times, the predominant melodic musical instrument type was probably the edge aerophone, or flute. This conclusion is based on archaeology and is therefore verified only in areas where archaeological studies have been possible, namely the western third of South America and nearly all of Mexico and Central America. Because of humidity, tropical-forest terrain does not preserve items of material culture made from cane, clay, and bone, whereas dry climates do. The study of living tropical-forest cultures, however, reveals a high use of edge aerophones that are not related to European or African types (bone or cane tubular flutes played vertically, for example), suggesting that the tradition has probably continued from ancient times (see Okada 1995:video examples 26 and 27). Other edge aerophones, however, are found in archaeology but have not survived in living cultures. Globular flutes, for example, were common in ancient Mexico, Colombia, Peru, and elsewhere, but have disappeared from common use. Likewise, multiple tubular flutes with holes for fingering were prevalent among the Maya and Aztec but have since disappeared. In some regions of the Andes, such as the Mantaro Valley of Peru, many edge aerophones have been replaced by European clarinets and saxophones. Nevertheless, the ancient exemplars and the current usage (including the substitutions) suggest an edge-aerophone distribution wherever native Americans and their descendants (mestizos, or people of mixed race and/or culture) are located today. The distribution is, in fact, so prevalent that native Central America and western South America can be considered edge-aerophone (flute) cultures.

Evidence suggests that lip-concussion aerophones, or trumpets, have continued since antiquity in the Andes, though the materials have often changed from ceramic and wood to cow horn and sheet metal, while the shells of conchs remain fairly constant in certain areas, including Central America and Peru. Although evidence does not exist for single-reed-concussion aerophones in the ancient Americas, idioglot and heteroglot clarinets are common today in tropical-forest cultures (Waiãpi, Warao, Yekuana, for example) and elsewhere (Aymara, Guajiro). They may have existed in pre-Columbian times, and perhaps only their reeds disappeared; for example, tubes interpreted as bone, ceramic, or wooden "flutes" or "trumpets" in Mexican, Guatemalan, and Peruvian musical archaeology may have been single- or double-reed-concussion aerophones whose vegetable-matter reeds perished. Today's use of shawms (*chirisuya* and *chirimía*) in Peru and Guatemala, possibly introduced by Spanish missionaries, may actually suggest continuity rather than cultural borrowing, a sort of new wine in old bottles. The prevalence of lip- and reed-concussion aerophones among native Americans suggests a pairing or dualistic usage with the use of edge aerophones. Though the "flutes" are whistle-tone instruments, the "trumpets," "clarinets," and shawms are buzz-tone instruments.

Such dualism can be seen as a relationship of opposites, a common phenomenon with regard to the physical use of instruments, such as male and female pairs of instruments, especially in the *siku* 'panpipe' traditions of Bolivia and Peru. Dualism of sounds or tones exists in the Amazon tropical forest among the Tukano of Colombia, who attach sexual symbolism to the sounds of their instruments (Reichel-Dolmatoff 1971:115–116). The whistling tone of edge aerophones, for example, symbolizes sexual invitation, while the buzz of lip- and/or single-reed-concussion aerophones symbolizes male aggressiveness. These opposites are joined, and their union is supported by percussion sounds of membranophones and idiophones, which symbolize "a synthesis of opposites . . . an act of creation in which male and female energy have united" (Reichel-Dolmatoff 1971:116). This native tripartite theory of music explains the Tukano use of musical instruments and can possibly explain similar usage throughout native South America, especially in parts of the tropical forest, the Andes, and the circum-Caribbean area, where whistle-tone, buzz-tone, and staccato-tone sounds are common.

Throughout most of the central Andes of South America, the area at one time dominated by the Inca, there exists a preference for high-pitched sounds as exemplified by the whistle tones of flutes. This high-pitched aesthetic, favored by the Quechua (also Kechua) and the Aymara, is also found in their choice of the tightly strung *charango*, a small, guitar-type chordophone, as an accompanying instrument, and their style of singing, most often performed by women. The distribution of flutes throughout this region, from panpipes to duct and ductless edge aerophones, is related to the preference for high-pitched tones.

Concepts of physical duality

We have already seen how dualism is expressed in the sounds musical instruments make; the concepts of the whistle tone and buzz tone combine to create power, according to the Tukano. Many other native American cultures employ the concept of duality, but in a physical way: two instruments, or two halves of one instrument, symbolic of male and female, unite to create a whole. The distribution of symbolically male and female musical instruments coincides with cultures that interpret power as the union of opposites. Nowhere is this belief stronger than in the Andes of South America.

The *siku* panpipe set of the Peruvian and Bolivian Aymara requires two people to play each half of the instrument in an interlocking fashion. Called *ira* and *arca*, the halves are respectively male (the leader) and female (the follower). To play a melody together by joining individual notes in alternation is called in Aymara *jjaktasina irampi arcampi* 'to be in agreement between the *ira* and the *arca*' (Valencia-Chacón 1989:34, English version). This technique is related to the dualistic symbolism common among Andean native people, for whom the sun and the moon are dichotomous creator beings, associated respectively with male and female. But not all dualistic symbolism is mythological or cosmological; it can be sociological when each half of a panpipe ensemble known as *chiriwano* represents a particular community. Two metaphorical neighboring communities—each half of the panpipe ensemble— "play their particular melodies simultaneously in a type of counterpoint," like a musical duel, "in which each community unit tries to play its melody at a louder volume than the other, in order to dominate." This musical and physical dualism is a metaphor of the Andean society, in which two halves, the leaders of each community, "are structurally necessary to complete the whole" (Turino 1987:20, translated by Dale A. Olsen). This aspect of two parts working together to make a whole is related to the pre-Spanish concept called *mita* (*minga*), a communal work effort, in which the whistle tone of a *pinkullo* (*pingullo*) duct edge aerophone is coupled with the buzz tone of the bass snare drum as it produces its staccato synthesis of opposites to accompany work.

Panpipes of the Aymara and Chiriwano are not the only instruments played in a dualistic manner symbolizing male and female. Among the Yekuana of the southern Venezuelan tropical forest, *tekeya* single-reed-concussion aerophones are always played in pairs, one male and the other female. Their music is symbolic of "the movements and songs of a mythological animal pair" (Coppens 1975:1). Among the descendants of African slaves in the Pacific coast of Colombia (the Chocó region), two one-headed membranophones known as *cununo mayor* and *cununo menor* are designated as male and female, respectively (Whitten 1974:109).

Ideas about extramusical power

Many of the Andean *siku* traditions, though imbued with dualistic symbolism, are symbolic in other ways as expressed in particular musical occasions replete with elaborate costumes for the musician-dancers. One of the most symbolic is the Kechua *ayarachi* panpipe ensemble, "related to the cult of the condor, considered a totemic bird among Andean cultures. The garments of ayarachis and a ceremony alluding to this bird are indications of this character" (Valencia-Chacón 1989:69, English version).

The allusion to animals is an important use of symbol with regard to musical instruments. The animal for which an instrument has symbolic significance is usually a living animal. The Quechua *antara,* a monistic (having one part only) panpipe and an important instrument of the Inca, was often made from human bones. Human body parts imbued musical instruments with power, and *antara* panpipes made from human bones, "just like the drums from human skin, were not meant to be ordinary musical instruments. Instead, considering the joining of the parts: bones, skin, etc. for their essences, their voices should have been something alive" (Jiménez Borja 1951:39, translated by Dale A. Olsen). Indeed, life—its creation and continuation— is assured by fertility, by the joining of male and female, by the planting and harvesting of crops, by the abundance of rain.

In many regions of the Andes, the *pinkullo* duct aerophone (the term and the "flute" are used by the Aymara and the Kechua) is seasonal, played only during particular calendrical periods, such as the rainy season from October through March:

> This flute is played during the season when the great rains begin. . . . Before playing the instrument it is moistened in *chicha* [beer], alcohol, or water. The coincidence of . . . festivals with the arrival of the rains, the moistening of the wood before making the flutes, and the moistening of the instruments before playing them, is quite significant. (Jiménez Borja 1951:45, translated by Dale A. Olsen)

The *pinkullo* is associated with fertility, as the symbolism suggested above would indicate.

Flutes are obvious symbols of fertility because of their phallic shape, and they often have the role of a charm, endowed with power to entice a female lover to a male (they were played only by men in the Andes). So powerful was the sound of the *kena* ductless edge aerophone to the Inca in ancient Cuzco, Peru, that women could not resist it: "The flute . . . is calling me with such tenderness and passion that I can't resist it. . . . My love is calling me and I must answer him, that he may be my husband and I his wife" (Garcilaso de la Vega 1966 [1609]:87). One ancient technique was to play the *kena* within a clay pot—an obvious symbol of the sexual act, its musical imitation forbidden by the Roman Catholic Church. Nevertheless, the tradition persisted into the colonial period, and Borja describes such a jar found in Huamanga, department of Ayacucho, Peru. It has a small opening at the top for inserting the flute, two larger openings in the sides for the player's hands, and two eyelets on the sides so it can be suspended around the *kena* player's neck (Jiménez Borja 1951:37). He explains that to play the *kena* into such a specially designed clay vessel creates a magical voice that "defeats death and promotes life" (Jiménez Borja 1951:36). To further support the fertility symbolism of the Andean flute, especially as an instrument used during planting-related festivals, the term *pingullo* combines the Kechua *pinga* and *ullu,* words glossable as 'penis' (Carvalho-Neto 1964:342).

The need for giving signals
Musical iconicity (relationship between form and meaning) is another criterion for the use of musical instruments in Peru. The *clarín* is a long, side-blown, lip-concussion aerophone made from bamboo and cow horn, played outdoors by men during

The introduction of Western musical instruments by the Jesuits was new, but the idea of using musical instruments for religion and supernatural power was not. Since ancient times, musical instruments have been tools for supernatural communication and power.

Roman Catholic patronal festivals and *mingas,* traditional communal working parties. In the latter usage, the *clarinero* (player of the *clarín*) directs the work and sets the rhythms. Gisela Cánepa (cited in Romero 1987) delineates four sections in the *minga,* all determined by the music of the *clarinero* music: the *alabado,* or announcement; the *llamada,* which tells the workers to begin laboring; the *trabajo,* or working period; and the *despedida,* after the workers have returned home. During the *trabajo,* the musician plays melodies that announce and set the paces of the jobs to be accomplished; he even plays throughout the periods of rest.

The introduction of European musical instruments

Jesuit missionary influence of the 1700s

When the Spanish Jesuit missionaries came to South America in the mid-1500s to convert and teach the local inhabitants, they employed musical instruments that they thought would assist in the conversion because of their heavenliness. These instruments, also used to play bass, harmony, and melody in the absence of an organ, were the harp and the violin (figure 4), already introduced by musicians from the earliest days of the Encounter. The guitar, however, was considered too secular for converting the native Americans to the new religion. The introduction of Western musical instruments by the Jesuits was new, but the idea of using musical instruments for religion and supernatural power was not. Since ancient times, musical instruments have been tools for supernatural communication and power. This may be one of the major reasons that native Americans found the new musical tools acceptable.

After the expulsion of the Jesuits (in 1767), the harp and the violin continued to be played by native Americans until their religious use, and even their European derivation, were all but forgotten. José María Arguedas (1977:16) wrote: "Harp, violin, transverse flute, and chirimía are Indian instruments in the Peruvian mountains. . . . I remember with special . . . sentiment the expression of amazement of some of my friends, well known mistis or men of the village, upon finding that the harp, violin and flute are not Indian instruments, but European ones."

The shawm, known as *chirimía* in Colombia, Ecuador, Guatemala, and Mexico and *chirimía* and *chirisuya* in Peru, was brought, in its European form, by the Spanish colonists. It was used at Jesuit and other Roman Catholic missions as an outdoor instrument in processions, festivals, funerals, and other church-sponsored events. Additionally, it heralded the conquistadors' entrances into indigenous cities and was later played for social and political events of the Spanish aristocracy (Stevenson 1968:289). When many native peoples in the viceroyalties of New Spain, New Granada, and Peru learned how to play the *chirimía,* it took on indigenous characteristics (use of a split condor quill for a double reed, for example) and became considered one of their own.

The pipe and tabor—one person playing a vertical duct flute and drum at the

FIGURE 4   During the St. John the Baptist patronal festival in Acolla, Peru, a violinist and a harpist, members of an *orquesta típica del centro,* perform for a private party. Photo by Dale A. Olsen, 1979.

same time—was probably introduced by the Spanish, though there is evidence for one-person flute-and-drum or flute-and-rattle ensembles from ancient times in Mexico, Central America, and the Andes. In the Andes, the uniqueness of the ensemble is the use of the duct flute with drum, because duct vertical flutes were not known before the Spanish encounter (figure 5). Today in northern Peru, people not uncommonly make them from plastic tubing.

Military-band influences of the 1900s

Indigenous people, especially the Inca, had their own ensembles of military musical instruments, including the *kepu* (conch trumpet) and *wancar* (membranophone), as Garcilaso de la Vega wrote in 1609: "All night long, the two armies remained facing each other, on the alert. When day broke, the conch horns, timpani, and trumpets began to sound, and they marched toward each other, with loud shouting. Leading his troops, the Inca Viracocha struck the first blow and, in no time, there was a terrible struggle" (1966 [1609]:167). These musical instruments evoked fear in their ene-

FIGURE 5 Two pipe-and-tabor musicians (*cajeros*) perform at the Huanchaco patronal festival in Los Baños del Inca, Peru. Photo by Dale A. Olsen, 1979.

mies because the drums were often made from the skins of their families, killed in battle. Bernabé Cobo wrote in about 1650 that Tupac Inca Yupanqui, the tenth Inca king, "had the two main caciques [chiefs] skinned, and he ordered two drums to be made from their hides. With these drums and with the heads of the executed caciques placed on pikes, and with many prisoners to be sacrificed to the Sun, the Inca returned in triumph to his court, where he celebrated his victories with great sacrifices and fiestas" (1979:143). Therefore, the introduction by the Portuguese, Spanish, and *criollos* (Spanish-descended people) of "trumpets" and "drums" as military instruments into formerly Portuguese- and Spanish-held lands was modernization rather than innovation.

European-derived wind ensembles or bands (mainly German-influenced) were the result of the late-nineteenth- and early-twentieth-century introduction of the military-band concept into the recently independent countries of the Americas. The appearance of such instruments as trumpets, trombones, baritones, tubas, clarinets, saxophones, snare drums, and bass drums coincided with the development of modern armies. While the context was no longer to intimidate the enemy, bands played for processions and parades during religious festivals and military rituals, and provided music for dancing.

German immigrant influence of the 1900s

Besides the influence in the development of military bands, the German-manufactured accordion (*acordeón*) was introduced by German immigrants in the early 1900s. In Colombia, it replaced the locally fabricated *caña de millo,* a single-reed concussion aerophone used in popular ensembles to perform *vallenato,* a rural form of *cumbia* from the region of Vallenata. Today's *vallenato* groups use the button accordion (figure 6), several membranophones, a *guacharaca* (a scraper made from wood or bamboo), and an electric bass (Bermúdez 1985:74; see Marre 1983). In the cities of Colombia, Peru, and elsewhere, accordions are often used in *tunas* or *estudi-*

FIGURE 6   In a Colombian *vallenato* ensemble in Miami, Florida, a musician plays a button accordion. Photo by Dale A. Olsen, 1988.

Many countries, such as Brazil, Jamaica, and Mexico, have thriving music industries based on the electronic production of recordings. Since the 1980s, many urban centers have competed with the United States in producing *música latina*.

antinas, ensembles usually of student musicians who play Spanish-derived and other folkloric music on guitars, mandolins, violins, and other European instruments.

Related to the accordion because it has multiple single reeds is the harmonica (*rondín*) from Ecuador, Peru, and Colombia, where it is called *armónica, dulzaina,* and *sinfonía.* It was introduced by German immigrants in the late 1800s and early 1900s; today it is still manufactured in Germany by the Höhner company and imported to the Americas.

THE INFLUENCE OF ELECTRONICS

Electronics has been one of the most important influences in the producing and receiving, the preservation and learning, and the dissemination and commodification of music in South America, Mexico, Central America, and the Caribbean. Amplifiers for *charangos,* guitars, harps, flutes, panpipes, and other acoustic instruments are common in urban areas, but so are electrophones such as synthesizers. Equally important as musical instruments are the numerous devices for musical—and audio-visual, as in video cameras—recording and playback, such as boom boxes, radios, television sets, phonographs, and tape recorders. Also important are electronic-enhancement devices such as microphones, soundboards, speakers, and other elements of public-address systems and amplifiers. These, like the aerophones, chordophones, idiophones, and membranophones that they amplify, often require skilled technicians who function as performers in their own right.

Electronic production and reception of music

Just as brass bands have replaced weaker-volume panpipe ensembles in some regions of the Andes, so have electronically enhanced guitars and keyboards replaced weaker-volume samba bands in some regions of urban Brazil, and electronically enhanced horns and keyboards have replaced steel drums for some musical events in Trinidad. Stages in Córdoba, Argentina, are packed with speakers and electronic equipment during performances of *cuarteto* music; stages in Santiago and Viña del Mar, Chile, are likewise filled with sound-enhancement devices during rock concerts and performances by groups such as Los Jaivas and Inti Illimani.

Many countries, such as Brazil, Jamaica, and Mexico, have thriving music industries based on the electronic production of recordings. Since the 1980s, many urban centers have competed with the United States in producing *música latina.* The 45-rpm recording was the important medium of the 1970s, but the 1980s and 1990s are the decades of the cassette tape. By the mid-1990s, compact discs had become popular in large urban areas, and many musical stars were rereleasing on CDs and cassettes their recordings previously released on vinyl.

The reception of music, too, has become dependent on electronic devices. Probably every home in urban areas has a cassette recorder on which tapes of recent and nostalgic music can be played. Likewise, radios and television sets are important musical receivers found in most urban homes, delivering the latest songs by crooners and sexy stars such as Caetano Veloso and Xuxa.

Electronic preservation and learning of music

It is not unusual in the 1990s to see native Americans, mestizos, or even tourists recording music on boomboxes during patronal and other religious festivals in the Amazon of Brazil, the Andes of Peru and Bolivia, or other locations that normally do not have electricity. The effects of battery-operated recording devices are overwhelming, and often musical preservation on tape and dance preservation on video is a vital technique for the process of learning.

Musicians from many countries in the Caribbean, Central America, Mexico, and South America have interest in preserving music and dance for the purpose of learning and passing on traditions. In Brazil, the phenomenon known as *parafolclore* is based on the staging of folkloric events, and the learning process is often derived from the electronic preservation of traditional *folclore* events that have been recorded by amateurs with their boomboxes. In more sophisticated circles, recordings are made with Nagra and other professionally designed tape recorders, or on videotape, for preservation in institutes and other academic archives.

Electronic dissemination and commodification of music

Electronic dissemination of music is usually done for purposes of commodification. Money is usually the bottom line, though cultural patrimony and ethnic identity may be reasons for the popularity of karaoke among people of Asian descent in South America during the 1980s and 1990s. In São Paulo, Buenos Aires, and other cities where people of Chinese and Japanese descent live, karaoke bars feature the latest musical hits from Japan and the most recent audio, video, and laser-disc technologies. Karaoke in Spanish and Portuguese, featuring regional popular songs, is common in urban bars, where commodification—sales of food and liquor—is more important than the ideals of patrimony and ethnicity.

Sales of cassettes and CDs, however, are the most important means for making money by producers, whereas live concerts are probably the most lucrative means for the performers themselves [see CUARTETO, POP MUSIC OF ARGENTINA]. Both depend on musical dissemination via electronic sound-producing devices, the latest musical-instrument technologies.

REFERENCES

Arguedas, José María. 1977. *Nuestra Música Pópular y sus Intérpretes*. Lima: Mosca Azul & Horizonte.

Aretz, Isabel. 1967. *Instrumentos Musicales de Venezuela*. Caracas: Universidad de Oriente.

Bakan, Michael, Wanda Bryant, Guangming Li, David Martinelli, and Kathryn Vaughn. 1990. "Demystifying and Classifying Electronic Music Instruments." *Selected Reports in Ethnomusicology* 8:37–65.

Bermúdez, Egberto. 1985. *Los Instrumentos Musicales en Colombia*. Bogota: Universidad Nacional de Colombia.

Bolaños, César, Fernando García, Josafat Roel Pineda, and Alida Salazar. 1978. *Mapa de los Instrumentos Musicales de Uso Popular en el Perú*. Lima: Oficina de Música y Danza.

Carvalho-Neto, Paulo de. 1964. *Diccionario del Folklore Ecuatoriano*. Quito: Editorial Casa de la Cultura Ecuatoriana.

Coba Andrade, Carlos Alberto G. 1981. *Instrumentos Musicales Populares Registrados en el Ecuador*. Otavalo: Instituto Otavaleño de Antropología.

Cobo, Father Bernabé. 1979. *History of the Inca Empire*. Edited and translated by Roland Hamilton. Austin: University of Texas Press.

Coppens, Walter. 1975. *Music of the Venezuelan Yekuana Indians*. Liner notes. Folkways Records FE 4104. LP disk.

Diaz Gainza, José. 1962. *Historia Musical de Bolivia*. Potosí: Universidad Tomás Frias.

Garcilaso de la Vega, El Inca. 1966 [1609]. *The Incas: The Royal Commentaries of the Inca*. 2nd ed.

Edited by Alain Gheerbrant. Translated by Maria Jolas. New York: Avon Books, Orion Press.

Izikowitz, Karl Gustav. 1970 [1935]. *Musical Instruments of the South American Indians.* East Ardsley, Wakefield, Yorkshire: S. R. Publishers.

Jairazbhoy, Nazir Ali. 1990. "An Explication of the Sachs-Hornbostel Instrument Classification System." *Selected Reports in Ethnomusicology* 8:81–104.

Jiménez Borja, Arturo. 1951. *Instrumentos Musicales del Perú.* Lima: Museo de la Cultura.

Marre, Jeremy. 1983. *Shotguns and Accordions: Music of the Marijuana Growing Regions of Colombia.* Beats of the Heart series. Harcourt Films. Video.

Okada, Yuki. 1995. *Central and South America.* The JVC / Smithsonian Folkways Video Anthology of Music and Dance of the Americas, 6. Multicultural Media VTMV 230. Video.

Olsen, Dale A. 1986. "It Is Time for Another -Phone." *SEM Newsletter* 20(September):4.

Reichel-Domatoff, Gerardo. 1974. *Amazonian Cosmos: The Sexual and Religious Symbolism of the Tukano Indians.* Chicago: University of Chicago Press.

Romero, Raúl. 1987. *Música Andina del Perú.* Liner notes. Lima: Archivo de Música Tradicional, Pontificia Universidad Católica del Perú, Instituto Riva Agüero. LP disk.

Roth, Walter E. 1924. *An Introductory Study of the Arts, Crafts, and Customs of the Guiana Indians.* Annual Report 38, 1916–1917. Washington, D.C.: Bureau of American Ethnology.

Stevenson, Robert. 1968. *Music in Aztec and Inca Territory.* Berkeley: University of California Press.

Turino, Thomas. 1987. "Los Chiriguanos." In *Música Andina del Perú.* Liner notes. Lima: Archivo de Música Tradicional, Pontificia Universidad Católica del Perú, Instituto Riva Agüero. LP disk.

Valencia Chacón, Américo. 1989. *El Siku o Zampoña. The Altipano Bipolar Siku: Study and Projection of Peruvian Panpipe Orchestras.* Lima: Artex Editores.

Vega, Carlos. 1946. *Los Instrumentos Musicales Aborígenes y Criollos de la Argentina.* Buenos Aires: Ediciones Centurión.

Whitten, Norman E., Jr. 1974. *Black Frontiersmen. Afro-Hispanic Culture of Ecuador and Colombia.* Prospect Heights, Ill.: Waveland Press.

Musical Genres and Contexts
Anthony Seeger

Dance, Sounds, and Movements
Religious Music
Secular Music
Tourism
The Music Industry

Music is being played or listened to almost everywhere and most of the time in Mexico, Central America, South America, and the Caribbean. Ranging from the sound of a single flute played by a lonely shepherd in a high mountain valley, to privately performed curing ceremonies witnessed only by the curers and the ill, to radios playing in thousands of homes, to massive celebrations mobilizing hundreds of thousands of participants packed into the broad avenues and civic squares of densely populated cities, the richness and diversity of the musical traditions seem almost to defy description.

Yet this musical diversity has underlying patterns that enable observers to speak about the music of the entire region. This article presents some of the significant general features of the musical genres performed and the contexts in which music is played, drawing on the material from the entries on specific societies and nations, where these processes are described with more attention to local histories and the specifics of social processes, cultures, and styles.

The principal contexts of which music is a part in the Americas include religious activities, life-cycle celebrations, leisure, tourism, and to a lesser degree work. Some of these categories are general throughout the lands covered by this volume, but in other cases (such as tourism), music is more heavily involved in some areas than in others.

Many are the contexts for musical performance in the Americas. Although some new contexts replace older ones, what appears to happen more often is that new contexts are added to older ones, which after a generation they may eventually replace. The music changes, but the contexts often remain, and music itself goes on: work, life-cycle rituals, religious events, urban entertainment, tourism, and mass media all include musical performances of significance to their participants.

DANCE, SOUNDS, AND MOVEMENTS

Music and movement are closely intertwined in South America, Mexico, Central America, and the Caribbean. Some native South American communities use the same word for both, arguing that appropriate movements are as much a part of a performance as the sounds themselves. Stylized movements are often an important part

It is important to remember that rhythms for dancing usually involve distinctive body movements, and that the challenge, pleasure, exhilaration, and meaning of moving the body are an important part of musical events almost everywhere.

FIGURE 1   Two of the most outstanding tango dancers—Milena Plebs and Miguel Angel Zotto—in their show *Perfume do Tango* at the Sadler's Wells Theatre, London, 1993. Photo courtesy of Ercilia Moreno Chá.

of musicians' performances; dancing has been an important part of secular music for centuries, and the name of a rhythm or a dance may define a genre—such as the waltz, the tango (figure 1), and the samba. Also found throughout the region are dance-dramas, in which music, speech, and movement combine to depict a story (such as a battle between Moors and Christians or the crucifixion of Jesus), often performed in association with the religious calendar, and occasionally with civic and national holidays. Body movements, like the sounds with which they may be associated, are endowed with meaning and convey attitudes, values, and individual and shared emotions.

Ritualized movements throughout the region include children's games; musicians' movements while performing; processions; and solo, couple, and group dances. Though some common features can be discerned, dances of Amerindian, African, and European origins have distinctive features, often combined today in popular traditions. Traditional Amerindian dances tend to involve stamping or moving the legs and arms to a fairly regular rhythm, with the rest of the trunk and head fairly straight and rigid. Dances in circles and lines are common, usually with the genders separated; dancing in couples was extremely rare, if found at all. In European dance traditions, the trunk and head are fairly motionless, the legs usually move to a simple rhythm, and dancing in couples (and combinations of couples) is often a defining feature. Dances that originated in Africa frequently involve moving different parts of the body to different rhythms—resembling the polyrhythmic patterns of the music itself. Formations by individuals and in lines and circles are more common than dances in couples.

During the past five hundred years, whatever distinctness the dances of different ethnic groups once had has been blurred by adaptations of existing styles and creations of new ones. This situation is especially true of twentieth-century popular dances, which have often drawn heavily on African-descended traditions. Amerindian and African religious traditions reveal their origins with greater clarity than secular dances. European religions have had an ambivalent attitude toward music and dance altogether—often banning the performance of secular music and dance and discouraging dancing in religious services. Whereas music and dance open communication with spirits in many Amerindian and African-based religions, silent prayer is considered the most effective communication with the deity in many Christian churches.

Dance halls, nightclubs, and life-cycle celebrations of which dancing in couples is a part (birthday parties and weddings, for example) are important performance locations that provide the livelihood for many musicians. The importance of these locations may have influenced the development of musical technology (in favor of louder instruments that can be played for many hours), and technology has influenced the development of these venues. Many articles in this volume touch on the importance of secular social dancing in the musical environments of the different areas and describe specific dances that were, and are, popular. It is important to remember that rhythms for dancing usually involve distinctive body movements, and that the challenge, pleasure, exhilaration, and meaning of moving the body are an important part of musical events almost everywhere.

RELIGIOUS MUSIC

Amerindian belief systems

Before the colonization of the Americas by Europe beginning in 1492, it is quite likely that most musical events were in some form or another part of religious or state-sponsored events. Where states were based on religion, it is difficult to separate the concepts of religion and politics. The elaborate ceremonies described by the Maya and the Inca for their Spanish conquerors included musical performances by specialists. The religious rituals of the coastal Tupi-Guaraní in Brazil and the island-dwelling Arawak and Carib communities in the Caribbean featured unison singing, shouts, dancing, and the sound of flutes and rattles. The archaeological record is replete with examples of clay wind instruments; in the humid areas, little else has survived.

Intensive investigation of Amerindian music in the twentieth century has necessarily been restricted to areas where such groups survive and continue to practice what appear to be traditional religions and musical forms. They are often found living in "refuge areas"—remote locations, away from non-Indian settlements, in areas of relatively little economic importance to the national society, and where missionization is recent, tolerant, or ineffective. With small populations and facing the effects of new diseases and economic changes, these groups cannot serve for generalizing about the musical situation in the pre-Columbian empires. Their music, however, reveals striking similarities to descriptions written in the 1500s and 1600s of performances in the nonstate societies. In these refuge areas, music continues to be closely related to religious events, and to direct communications with spirits and interactions with spirits of animals (such as jaguars, deer, and vultures) or ancestors. In some cases, musical sounds are themselves the voices of spirits; the performers may or may not be hybrid humans or spirits, and the instruments themselves spirits. Dale Olsen, in his discussion of communication with spirits among the Warao, describes a feature that reappears throughout South America [see WARAO].

Shamanism and music

Shamanism is a widespread form of communication with spirits. It was found from the extreme southern tip of Argentina and Chile through northern Mexico and right up into the arctic. At one level, shamanism is communication with spirits for the purpose of healing or sickening an individual or a community. At another level, shamanism is a practice that demonstrates to onlookers the continued presence and power of spirits. It makes the sacred visible and experienced directly by the population. Shamans may use tobacco and other narcotics and hallucinogens in conjunction with singing, or they may rely on singing alone. In a few cases, they do not employ music at all. When music is part of shamanism, it can simultaneously structure the shaman's experiences and communicate them to the community as it teaches children how to be shamans and what the supernatural world is like. Like many aspects of community life, it is at once a religious, social, and instructional event.

Shamanism is often a domestic or community practice, but many communities perform larger ceremonies to which they invite neighboring communities. These may involve feasting, drinking homemade beer or ingesting narcotics or hallucinogens, and making music and dancing (as in the upper Rio Negro). Metamorphosis, a transformation into an animal or spirit, is characteristic of a great deal of native South

American religion. Shamans transform themselves into animals for their journeys. Through music, dance, and ritual structures, groups of performers are transformed into groups of animals and spirits. Amerindian religious experience is frequently achieved through altering perception by means that include deprivation, narcotics, hallucinogens, and long periods of activity, such as singing and dancing. Altered states are interpreted as the transformation of humans into more powerful beings. The transformation is achieved, in many cases, through music itself. The music is thought to originate in the natural or ancestral world and is taught to the performers by religious or musical specialists. Humans sing songs of the natural world and become themselves somewhat like the originators—ancestors, animals, or spirits. Rituals often involve some kind of terminating event in which the transformed beings are turned back into humans again.

The music in such events often appears repetitive and is frequently "interrupted" by "nonmusical" sounds, such as animal cries and shouts. Repetition is part of the efficacy of the music—it can provide the underlying structures on which the events develop. The development or drama may not be in melody and timbre, but in the texts and experiences recounted. Often, the music continues for the duration of the event—which may last hours, or even days and weeks. Where animal spirits are powerful and sometimes sacred, it should be no wonder that animal cries appear in the performances. They should not be considered extramusical, however, since their absence may result in a performance considered unsatisfactory or without effect. They may be nonmelodic, but they are not extramusical.

Syncretism and music

In Amerindian communities where missionaries have been active and there is a long history of contact with the colonizers, musical traditions developed that in many places combine aspects of native and colonizer religious events and similarly combine their musical forms and performances. The merging of styles and events through a colonial encounter is much more common than isolation in Mexico and Central and South America. Saint's-day celebrations in the Andes and the highlands of Mexico and Guatemala often combine public inebriation, shouts and cries rarely heard in European performances, and traditional Amerindian instruments with Roman Catholic holidays. In Andean communities in some areas of Peru, Christian holidays are the most important "traditional" musical events that survive.

In some Amerindian communities, especially those influenced by Protestant missionaries, the singing of hymns has replaced all traditional musical forms. In some places, this change has led to unusual new musical events, such as hymn-writing competitions and writing hymns in indigenous languages. In others, the singing of hymns and national and international popular music are the only genres performed today.

European-introduced Christianity

Most countries in Mexico, Central America, South America, and the Caribbean are nominally Christian, and most of their people are Roman Catholic. This situation is the result of extensive colonization by Spain and Portugal. Amerindians and enslaved African populations were converted to Christianity, and under colonial rule, the Roman Catholic Church influenced their beliefs and social institutions tremendously. The mass itself was seldom elaborated musically, and then for special occasions only, and the singing of hymns has only recently been introduced, but Roman Catholic missionaries were quite concerned with the musical development of the Amerindians they encountered. They set up music schools in several countries, and introduced their own music in part to replace the "diabolical" traditions they encountered. Some enslaved Africans were similarly taught to play European instruments and participated in many kinds of musical events.

The church supported the establishment of social groups called brotherhoods (Portuguese *irmandades,* Spanish *cofradías*), which had been organized in Europe but in the New World came to be one of the few organizations available to enslaved Africans and their descendants. These institutions had social and religious features and often included the performance of music and dancing on religious occasions. Voluntary religious organizations, continued by the descendants of these brotherhoods, survive in many parts of Mexico, Central America, South America, and the Caribbean, where they perform on saints' days and around Christmas.

For many communities of Amerindian, African, and European descent alike, the Christian religious calendar has structured the most important public musical events of the year. The birth of Jesus is celebrated in the end of December, at Christmas. Local community celebrations frequently extend to 6 January, with pageantlike wanderings of kings bearing gifts. Jesus' crucifixion and resurrection, celebrated during Holy Week (culminating in Easter), are preceded by a penitential period called Lent, which itself is preceded by enthusiastic celebrations of carnival during the final days before Ash Wednesday and the beginning of Lent. Carnival celebrations, not always welcomed by the church, are considered to be a kind of last chance for fleshly excesses before Lent, and music often plays an important role in the events. The most famous of these may be in the Caribbean, in Rio de Janeiro, and in New Orleans, but carnival celebrations and restrictions on musical performances during Lent are found in many communities throughout the area.

In addition to these religious events, the days of many different saints are celebrated in different areas. In some cases, a country may celebrate a saint (as Mexico does the Virgin of Guadalupe); in others, a certain saint may celebrated as the patron of a particular city, a particular trade, or a particular ethnic group. Often saints' days are occasions for competitions in music and dance. Communities with populations of African and Amerindian descent have often combined elements of previous beliefs with Roman Catholic ones—which has led to a multiplicity of traditions throughout the region.

In the twentieth century, evangelical Protestant groups have made considerable inroads into Roman Catholicism and African spirit-based religions. Hymns, sung in Spanish, Portuguese, English, and Amerindian languages, are a common musical form. Among the Protestant sects are Hallelujah groups, in which possession by spirits is common, often to the accompaniment of some form of participatory music. In some communities, considerable conflict occurs between religious groups, expressed in musical events, theology, and church rituals.

African-introduced religions

Africans were enslaved and brought to the Americas from widely variant societies and regions. They therefore had no unifying language, religion, or musical tradition. Many, however, shared general musical traits that transcended particular African communities—among them collective participation in making music, call-and-response singing, and dense and often interlocking rhythms played on drums.

Slaves of African descent turned to, and were in some cases encouraged to turn to, Christian churches for worship. They brought to these churches a musical tradition that persisted despite systematic efforts to suppress some of its African elements, such as the playing of drums (repeatedly outlawed in different countries). Important, too, were brotherhoods where slaves and free people of African descent could meet to socialize and to prepare ritual events. These have continued in such places as St. Lucia, Brazil, and Panama (figure 2), where their members perform on certain reli-

FIGURE 2   Cristo Negro (Black Christ); Christ's crucifixion celebrated by a *cofradía* (brotherhood in Portobelo, Panama. Photo by Ronald R. Smith.

A great deal of music is performed around events in human lives. These range from Amerindian initiations to European-influenced birthdays, weddings, anniversaries, and funerals. Many of these events include social dancing, drinking, and eating, and some are highly elaborate.

gious occasions. Important among the performances are *congos,* dramatic presentations of stories, combining special forms of speech, music, and highly coordinated dancing.

Among the later waves of peoples brought to the New World were Yoruba-speaking populations from West Africa, whose religion included the worship of spirits that would possess adepts and speak through them. These religions have persisted throughout the Caribbean and along Brazil's east coast right into Argentina, under various names and using various musical forms. Called Santería in Cuba, Vodou in Haiti, Candomblé in northeastern Brazil, and other names in other countries, they usually employ a set of three sacred drums and other instruments whose rhythms are specific to specific gods. Called by the rhythms, the gods descend and "ride" the bodies of specific worshipers. Though formerly persecuted in some countries, these religions are expanding to new audiences.

Other religious communities

Significant populations of peoples of Indian (from India) and Indonesian descent live in the Caribbean and the Guianas (Guyana, Surinam, French Guiana), and their celebrations are often related to ritual observances of their own. Some European immigrant groups have brought with them their own religious organizations, and these influence different countries to different degrees. Since 1898, Japanese immigrants have introduced their religions into South America [see MUSIC OF IMMIGRANTS].

SECULAR MUSIC

A great deal of musical performance may be characterized as nonreligious, or secular. There is no attempt in such music to address divinities or to call spirits to inhabit a space or a body. Some apparently secular events, such as saints' days, are intimately tied to the sacred calendar; some are tied to an agricultural calendar; some are related to life-cycle events; some are tied to national holidays and music festivals.

Music for work

A few kinds of music were developed to accompany collective labor. Before steam and electricity came to the aid of human muscles, coordinated labor was the most effective way to move heavy loads and raise heavy sails. In some situations, a fixed rhythm allowed laborers to work at a steady, slow pace, and served to while away the hours.

With the predominance of steam, gasoline, and electric energy, work-related songs are rarely performed. In many parts of the world, however, music continues to be part of the workplace. In Peru, certain collective agricultural work is accompanied by music played on flutes and drums or on other instruments. In many parts of the region, agricultural workers take a battery-operated radio to listen to popular music as they labor in the sun. The productivity of workers in offices may be carefully manipulated by local forms of Muzak in air-conditioned office buildings in the capital cities, and shoppers may be guided by music played in malls.

More frequently than actually creating the pace at which people work, music marks the beginning and ending of seasons: to begin the planting, to celebrate the harvest, to commemorate a particularly good manufacturing year. Agricultural rituals occur in most countries with large Amerindian populations and in Amerindian communities, but they also occur in communities of European immigrants and populations of African descent.

Life-cycle celebrations

A great deal of music is performed around events in human lives. These range from Amerindian initiations to European-influenced birthdays, weddings, anniversaries, and funerals. Many of these events include social dancing, drinking, and eating, and some are highly elaborate. In many countries, weddings are festive events, and performing at them is an important source of income for musicians. Fifteenth-birthday celebrations are major social occasions for young women and their families in much of Mexico and Central and South America. Courting, making new acquaintances, and renewing acquaintances are often part of life-cycle celebrations. They typically include a group of invited celebrants of both sexes and various ages and professional or semiprofessional musicians. Recorded music, occasionally with a disc jockey, may animate the events. Although birth and christening ceremonies are important in some communities, in others death is ritually elaborated. Funerals are usually occasions for sadness, but this does not detract from their musical elaboration. A good example is the wake for a child in Ecuador. These celebrations typically include a group of invited celebrants and a professional or semiprofessional group of musicians. The parties often begin in the afternoon and extend into the evening, or where rural roads and a large distance between neighbors make travel difficult, into the next day.

Nightclubs, bars, brothels, dance halls, clubs, streets

The urban-music scene includes a number of institutions where musicians are employed, music is performed, and people watch, listen, and dance. The audiences are mostly fairly young, attendees are not related to one another, and the musicians are professional and paid or receive contributions.

Bars and brothels are the legendary birthplaces of new forms of popular music, and are one of the reasons many musicians have often been associated with immorality and sexuality. For most of the twentieth century, bars and brothels have been important employers of musicians, and many genres of popular music have evolved from the urban Bohemia: the Cuban habanera, the Argentinean tango, the Brazilian *choro,* Dixieland jazz, and other forms have been associated with these urban institutions.

Nightclubs are a somewhat different institution. They run the gamut from bars with shows to tourist-oriented theaters where specially produced shows are presented to largely foreign audiences. In some cases, touristic nightclubs build on the foundations of earlier, less high-class institutions—as in the tango nightclubs of Buenos Aires; the jazz clubs of New Orleans; folkloric *peñas* in Santiago, La Paz, and Lima; steakhouses in Asunción; and others.

Dance halls are places where, for a small fee, singles or couples can enter to dance, mingle with others, buy drinks and food, and dance. Many of these businesses specialize in a certain kind of music, frequently a genre of popular music or the music of a group of immigrants who have moved to the city. Immigrant clubs are legion in Peru, in Brazil, and in some other countries. Dance halls specializing in disco music

FIGURE 3 The Port-au-Prince street musicians Jean and Narat Nicola, who call themselves the Beggar's Band. The two sing and play a variety of domestic utensils recycled as percussion instruments. Photo by Steve Winter, 1989.

(in the 1970s) and more recently hip-hop, house music, and other contemporary genres are outgrowths of these institutions. These are mostly frequented by young adults, though some clubs cater to an older clientele and usually play older forms of popular music.

Athletic competitions, political rallies, and other large, voluntary, public events often have musical components in Mexico, Central America, South America, and the Caribbean. Brazilian soccer games are noteworthy for the percussion bands that encourage the players with throbbing rhythms. Political rallies may be animated by protest songs, or by bands playing anthems. Civic holidays are often marked with parades and bands. When large groups of people meet, organizers may arrange for music that represents the event itself, or the participants may bring their own. The kind of music performed, and the interpretation of that music, is a significant part of the events.

The street is an open-air stage for arranged or spontaneous performances. Some musicians are the musical equivalents of hawkers and vendors. Others are beggars or simply entertainers. Often street musicians play homemade instruments (figure 3).

TOURISM

Tourism is an important feature of the economies of Mexico and many Central and South American and Caribbean nations. Drawing visitors from the United States, Canada, Europe, and Asia through their natural attractions (beaches, climates) and cultural attractions (festivals, carnivals, nightclubs) is essential to the economic health of most Caribbean nations, and it is important to most of the rest (figure 4). Artistically, the tourist industry is a double-edged sword: it supports local musicians but imposes changes on their art in the interest of pleasing a foreign audience that is largely ignorant of local traditions.

In large countries such as Brazil and Argentina, internal tourism is a significant feature of the economy. States in the northeast of Brazil are visited by wealthy residents of the south in much the same way that some Caribbean islands are visited by people from other countries. These visitors are looking for a rural life-style and often want to have the opportunity to see local traditions.

The traditional arts in many countries are supported to a greater or lesser degree

FIGURE 4   A masquerade being performed for tourists from a cruise ship on the beach in Soufrière, St. Lucia. The instruments are a bamboo flute, a bass drum, and a snare drum. The masquerader reaches out his left hand as he asks for money. Photo by Dale A. Olsen, 1977.

by tourism. In some cases, the tourist office pays for the performers' costumes and expenses; in other cases, it organizes events and controls who performs and who attends. Tourists, however, do not usually understand the traditions, and as they are on a holiday schedule, events are often shortened for their convenience. In the end, tourism may create venues and performances that differ distinctly from those of the community, and in some cases these can destroy the older, community-oriented traditions altogether.

THE MUSIC INDUSTRY

Mass media—radio, television, cassettes, CDs, videotapes—have transformed the musical environment at an ever-increasing rate during the twentieth century. The entertainment industry creates an important venue for performance and an influential conduit for new styles. Musical performance is no longer a face-to-face event, and new genres, new styles, and new audiences have been created through this transformation.

Technology has at times influenced musical performances in concrete ways. The standard three-minute length for recorded songs was determined in part by the playing time of a wax cylinder, and later by that of a ten-inch 78-rpm record. The difficulty of controlling radio emissions across national boundaries has led to exchange of musical ideas despite local laws and import restrictions. The possibility of creating certain sounds in a studio affects the way live performances are evaluated. The impact of these media is so widespread that it is difficult to imagine musical life without them.

Live performances often include topical songs and local references, but broadcast restrictions in many countries have limited which kinds of ideas can be expressed in music or image.

Radio and television

Satellite dishes are popular over much of the region. Music Television (MTV, VH1, and so on) has had a tremendous impact on musical performance in areas where its channels are received. So have local soap operas and other shows. The arrival of electricity, and with it radio and television, appears to result in a quick decline of domestic musical genres: the time that people used to spend singing to each another they now spend listening to or watching others perform.

A result of the impact of mass media on large populations has been the systematic attempts of national governments to control what is transmitted and to place various kinds of censorship on the media. Many countries have imposed some kind of control on radio networks and require a certain percentage of the transmissions to be music from their own country or region. The rest of the time, stations mostly feature popular music from several sources, especially North America. Television programs, being more expensive to produce, are often purchased directly from other countries.

Live performances often include topical songs and local references, but broadcast restrictions in many countries have limited which kinds of ideas can be expressed in music or image. This control has operated with varying degrees of success and has often been opposed by artists—many of whom have been imprisoned or even killed under military regimes as in Argentina, Brazil, and Chile. When music becomes associated with a lower-class or marginal life-style, its practitioners are likely to suffer various kinds of police and political repression.

Audio and video recordings

Many countries have a small recording industry that focuses on inexpensive media, such as audiocassettes, that feature local artists. A locally clandestine industry often produces pirated versions of international hits. Larger countries have subsidiaries of the large multinational recording companies, which publish local music and international popular music. Often local musical styles were adapted, recorded, and popularized by musicians in North America. In some cases, however, local styles became international ones: one need only think of calypso, reggae, samba, and tango. In most cases, the more popular singers were signed by transnational recording companies.

Recordings involve more than a performer and a machine that records sounds: producers, record-company executives, recording engineers, marketing specialists, and many others play important roles in determining the sound of a performance and its diffusion through mass media. Some artists feel they are losing control over their art; others welcome advice from those who know how to make them fit into a pattern that brings success. The relationship among artists, their record companies, and their music is quite complex and varies from genre to genre and place to place.

Widely separated communities within the same country, or communities whose members span several different countries, often create informal networks of audio and videotape exchanges. The Indian and Javanese communities in Trinidad and

Surinam exchange recordings with relatives in the home countries. Small shops in Miami, New York, and other North American cities feature local recordings from Mexico, Central America, and the Caribbean. Some record stores in the United States specialize in importing music from one area or another.

Social Structure, Musicians, and Behavior
Anthony Seeger

Music is firmly embedded in social life and contributes to the ways in which people in most societies work, play, worship, and reproduce themselves, socially and biologically. Music is part of social life because musicians and their audiences are part of larger groups and processes. Composers, performers, and audience members have families, participate in social life, have some attitude toward religious beliefs, and have been brought up under unique historical conditions. Musicians and their audiences use music as a resource for a variety of religious and social purposes. Small Amerindian villages and large nation-states may be seen as comprising social groups, each with its own kind of music, performing together or apart. As they perform, they express, create, or recreate the social fabric of the communities themselves in a constant musical process of reformulation and renewal.

In Mexico, Central America, South America, and the Caribbean, people have performed to attract lovers and to make fun of them, to support governments and to criticize them, to march to war and to oppose it, to worship gods and to be possessed by them. Some music has been taught in schools, supported by government funds, or sold through commerce. Other music has been prohibited or censored—by parents, slaveholders, governments, and religious leaders. Musical performances are among the ways people express personal, political, and religious beliefs. In so doing, they create and express attitudes about people, social groups, and various experiences.

It is easy to see that music is part of social life; it is more difficult to determine how. Simply looking at an event and asking straightforward, journalistic questions about it is a good start. Performances usually involve certain types of individuals and groups, to the exclusion of others. Different audiences express allegiances to different genres, attend at different times of day or night, and associate music with different goals.

The social contexts of many particular genres may be discovered in the individual entries of this volume, in which musical differences by gender, age, social class, ethnocultural group, and religion frequently appear. What needs to be stressed as a general principle is that most social identities—an individual's membership in a particular group—are partly constructed through music. Gender and age are relatively fixed, but an individual's membership in many ethnocultural and social-class groups

FIGURE 1   A young girl of Japanese descent (*sansei*, third generation) is spellbound at seeing and hearing a trombone being played in a *caipira* band during the 1981 *festa junina* (June Festival) in São Paulo, Brazil. Photo by Dale A. Olsen.

depends on demonstrating certain cultural preferences and styles, often including performance of or admiration for particular types of music, dress, bodily ornamentation, and cuisine. Different identities can be expressed with different musical forms: we can sing a national anthem as members of a nation and a regional song as a member of a region, or we can perform music that identifies us as an ethnic minority. People may activate different identities through the music they choose to perform or listen to. Or they may consciously introduce certain styles into their music to indicate specific cultural relationships, as when Peruvians or Brazilians of African descent introduce musical features learned in contemporary Africa to indicate the relationship of a genre to the African diaspora, or when a Paraguayan community of German descent adopts new German genres and styles.

Music is part of social life because musicians and their audiences are part of a larger society. In moments of ethnic or political crisis, music is a form of cultural expression that becomes an area of attention and conflict. Groups that earlier played various styles may begin to define themselves by a single genre; rallies of different political parties may feature different kinds of music, and arguments over what kind of music to play at a dance may express fundamental political and cultural differences. Music, and the performing arts more generally, can become the focus of intense interest (and violent repression), because art can be used to express complex social and political ideas.

Partly because societies are such large, complex subjects, the entries in this volume describe extremely different kinds of relationships between music and society. Taken as a whole, however, they reveal some regularities. One way to define the social features of musical performances is to look for answers to a few simple questions about a performance or genre: who is performing? for whom are they performing? what are they performing? where are they performing? when is it performed? why are people performing that music in that way? The first two questions direct our attention to the people involved; the fourth and fifth, to the specifics of the event itself; the third is about the music itself; and the sixth raises the issue of motivation. The answers to these questions are an introduction to the social contexts of musical performance.

DEFINING SOCIAL FEATURES OF MUSICAL PERFORMANCE

Who is performing?

The answer is usually simple: a group of children, a military band, an all-male chorus of retired truckers, an all-female unaccompanied group, a foreign rock band. The performers may be identified with an ethnocultural group (Amerindian, African or European descent, or more specifically German, Prussian, and so on). Yet the implications of who is performing begin to indicate the significance of the music. Individuals affiliate themselves with groups, and every group has relationships with other groups—relationships that usually change over time. Thus age, gender, occupation, and nationality can all be significant aspects of musical performance, especially since conflict often occurs between different ages, genders, occupations, and nationalities.

For whom are they performing?

For an analysis of the relationship of music to social behavior, the audience is just as important as the performers. Ethnomusicologists are not the only ones curious about who listens to a certain genre of music: record-company executives, radio stations, and professional musicians—all want to know about their audiences. The musicians may be performing for children (figure 1) or adults, for politicians or their critics, for members of their own ethnocultural group or of another one. Each context usually holds different meanings for the participants.

What are they performing?

Musical sounds are quite variable: they all have tone (pitch), timbre (quality), and amplitude (loudness), and are usually arranged into pulsing series (rhythms) that unfold in larger overall structures (strophic, binary, variational, and so on). At any given time, certain sounds are associated with certain groups (age, gender, occupation, ethnicity, cultural roots) and certain situations. These features may change over time; they are not fixed. The performance of a certain musical style, or attendance at the performance, often indicates some kind of statement about allegiance with a group or its goals. The exclusion of a musical genre or style may indicate opposition to the group with which it is identified. What kinds of music are *not* performed can be as important as what kinds of music *are* performed.

Where are they performing?

Music takes some of its meaning from the place in which it is performed. A song performed in a military parade in the civic center, surrounded by the president's palace, the ministry of justice, and large bank buildings, has different implications from the same song performed on a protest march, in a bar or a brothel, or in a church. Musical repertoire may move from context to context, but it often changes meaning as it does. It may bring some of its earlier meaning to its new context, permitting people to use music ironically, angrily, adoringly, and in many other ways. This ability is partly created by the contexts it is performed in, and by the way it is performed.

When is the music performed?

Different times can have different meanings. The dawn has tremendous significance for many Amerindian groups, and a great deal of music is performed at dawn. Many performances coincide with the agricultural cycle of planting, irrigating, and harvesting crops. Others are part of the Christian calendar of Christ's life (Christmas, Easter, saints' days), or Jewish, Hindu, or other religious calendars. Music associated with leisure, however, will be performed when people are not required to work: on weekends, in the evenings, on holidays and festivals. Some forms, such as Muzak, are designed to be played during working hours; but no one would confuse a quiet Muzak performance of a rock song in an air-conditioned office building with a late-night concert of the "same" song in a soccer stadium where thousands of people are dancing to deafening sounds from huge speakers. Like space, the time of a performance can indicate something about its significance.

Why are people performing that music in that way?

The question *why* has many answers that can come from many different positions. The musicians may say, "We perform to eat." The audience may say, "We listen because we like them." But that is only part of the answer. Why perform a given piece for a certain audience in a certain place at a certain time? The more specific the question, the more significant the answer may be. It might be: "We performed Mozart because the audience is so uneducated they wouldn't appreciate John Cage," or "We sang the national anthem as our protest march passed the police station so they wouldn't come out and beat us up," or "We had to play something loud to get the audience dancing," or "We thought it would be funny to play the brass-band piece on these instruments." All musicians have to eat, and most audiences have the option of being somewhere else, military and civic events excepted. But those alone do not explain an event. Instead, the specifics of each situation and the decisions made in it can be far more revealing than the generalities.

SOCIAL GROUPS AND MUSICAL PERFORMANCE

Small Amerindian communities and nation-states alike reveal musical distinctions based on gender, age, and other social groups.

Gender

Gender identity is distinct from sexual identity. A person has a sexual identity based on physiological traits; a person's gender identity is a social construction. Male humans are physiologically the same, and distinct from female humans. Different societies, however, define gender identities differently. This distinction is important because gender identity can change during an individual's lifetime, while biological identity does not (without surgical intervention). In some communities and some contexts, the musical roles of men and women may be rigidly separated when they are young, and then become more alike after a women's menopause. In other communities and other contexts, men and women may exchange roles, sing in one another's styles, and use gender definition (and ambiguity) as part of their musical performance.

Music is one of the ways gender and its meaning are established and perpetuated. The relationship of gender to musical performances is complex, varies considerably among different groups and at different times, and is changing rapidly as the relative positions of men and women change throughout Mexico, Central America, South America, and the Caribbean. The ambiguity of gay, lesbian, and bisexual gender roles receives musical and ritual expression in certain secular and religious music, among them transvestite performances in nightclubs (secular) and Brazilian Candomblé (religious). In most Amerindian communities, men play a greater number of musical instruments and are more deeply involved in public rituals than women. Women traditionally sang, but rarely played wind instruments, drums, or rattles. Sometimes women were prohibited from even seeing sacred instruments. But distinctions of gender are not restricted to Amerindian communities: worldwide, few orchestra conductors are women, and the Roman Catholic Church bars women from the priesthood; virtually all practitioners of the Brazilian martial art or dance called *capoeira* are male; most members of salsa or mariachi ensembles are men.

Amerindian women sometimes have entirely separate ceremonies in which they are full participants, ceremonies like *iamuricuma,* a ceremony in the Xingú region of Brazil, and *machitún,* a shamanistic role among the Mapuche of Argentina and Chile. In Amerindian and rural communities, where women's life-styles may remain more traditional than those of their husbands and sons, women often preserve traditions that once were performed by men: the last singers of the Selk'nam men's chants in Tierra del Fuego were women, as are most remaining singers of Spanish and Portuguese ballads (*romances*). With changes in gender roles can come changes in musical participation.

Age

Age may or may not be a significant factor in different musical performances, and it is hard to generalize across the region. Different societies define age somewhat differently: in some, age or status is determined, not by years alone, but also by a person's perceived stage in life—whether he or she is dependent on parents, married with children, a grandparent, and so on. Nevertheless, in almost every society, people of different ages perform or listen to different genres of music in groups to some degree differentiated by age. In some cases, they may perform the same genre in different ways. Children are sometimes included in musical events (figure 2), and at other times they are excluded; yet children often have their own musical genres, passed on intact from older child to younger child, quite outside the formal adult-to-child

FIGURE 2   A boy playing a *güiro* in a *conjunto típico* (typical ensemble) in Panama. A button accordion is to his right. Photo by Ronald R. Smith.

In urban communities, people seem to be attracted to new forms of popular music during their adolescence, and then to continue to be fans of that music for the ensuing decades, while new generations of youth find new types of music to identify with.

instructional hierarchy. This situation is true of many children's games and dances. Children learn a great deal about adult genres just by listening—things they may perform only many years later. Unmarried men and women are active participants in many social dances and music-related courting activities. Married adults have been the most frequent public performers, but many popular musicians are young adults. The elderly may participate less in public rituals, or they may be revered as a source of wisdom and knowledge, and be deeply involved in teaching younger generations. A few societies of the region have genres restricted to grandparents.

The most common form of age-related musical preference is the way different generations view different forms of popular music, often admiring most the forms that were popular when they were adolescents. In urban communities, people seem to be attracted to new forms of popular music during their adolescence, and then to continue to be fans of that music for the ensuing decades, while new generations of youth find new types of music to identify with. Dance-oriented clubs in such cities as Rio de Janeiro seem to have an almost age-grade quality to them. In popular music, musical preference is one of the classic conflicts between parents and children, and between schoolteachers and schoolchildren. The older generation almost always laments the passing of some form, the middle generation is letting it pass, and the younger generation has new interests. This succession, however, is not automatic: the younger generation sometimes becomes more interested in traditional forms as it ages, and eventually they become elders who lament the disappearance of the same traditions their parents and grandparents lamented—and yet the tradition survives.

Kinship

Kinship roles may be important in certain genres. Birthday parties, with their English, Spanish, or Portuguese versions of "The Birthday Song" ("Happy birthday to you") are typically attended by people of various ages and both sexes, many of whom are related by kinship or age to the celebrant. Many local bands include family members. Sometimes the significant groups are not the immediate family, but other kinship-based groups. Among the Gê-speaking Indians of Brazil, various social groups are identified by a musical genre, a style of performance, or even a musical text.

Occupation

Occupations often have traditions of their own, and some of these may be musical. Clearly the occupation of "musician" has musical features, but shamans and ritual specialists in tribal societies know more about musical performances than most other adults. Other occupations may have their own musical forms: seamen coordinated their labor through chanties; itinerant traders, with their packs filled with merchandise, carried musical traditions and stories to isolated settlements. In some places, different occupations have their own social clubs, with their own performances at leisure

FIGURE 3   A *caipira* band performs during the 1981 *festa junina* (June Festival) in São Paulo, Brazil. From left are a bass drum, an alto saxophone, and a snare drum. Photo by Dale A. Olsen.

times or holiday festivals. Today, travelers often bring cassettes and videos with them when they visit friends or relatives in distant places. Airline pilots are sometimes couriers in networks that bring recently released recordings of popular music directly to clubs and dance halls in Mexico, Central and South America, and the Caribbean. Taxi drivers may double as distributors of records.

Social class

Social class is often a factor in the performance in or attendance at musical events: just as people of different ages express their solidarity through participating in different musical traditions, so may people of different social classes choose to identify themselves with different genres or styles of performance. Social class is defined in a number of ways and can be quite complex in Mexico, Central and South America, and the Caribbean. Clearest of all are contrasts between urban elite and rural poor. The culture of the elites has traditionally been oriented toward Europe and the United States, including classical, popular, and avant-garde musical styles of performance. Urban workers often identify with a national form of popular music, whereas rural workers and recent immigrants to the large cities often prefer a rural-based country music such as the Brazilian *música caipira* (figure 3) or Amerindian-based popular music such as the Peruvian *huayno* (*wayno*).

How important these distinctions are will vary over time and by circumstance. Special cases contradict easy generalities, such as communities of Italian laborers who are enthusiastic fans of nineteenth-century Italian opera, a genre otherwise appreciated largely by an urban elite. When class conflicts are strong, the identification of a group with a particular type of music often has political implications. Then men and women of different social classes may identify themselves with the music of one of the classes as an expression of ethnic, cultural, or political unity, and governments may institute censorship or harassment.

Religion

Religions influence musical performances and audience participation. Many religions employ distinctive musical forms, and some forbid other kinds of musical performances or condemn music and dance. Amerindians under missionary influence sometimes saw their sacred instruments exposed and burned, and at other times were dissuaded from performing traditional genres by threats and coercion. Overall, European religious music has been a powerful influence on musical performances throughout the entire region. Sometimes religious genres appear in secular situations, and sometimes religions limit musical performances. Islam and some Christian Protestant fundamentalists prohibit drinking and mixed-sex dancing, and frown on participation in musical events in bars, brothels, and nightclubs. Different religious groups may have their own genres and their own professional musicians, as with Christian rock and Christian country (musical styles that may be spreading in the United States), with which members of the religious group identify.

Politics

Politics and music have a long history of association throughout the region—military bands, national anthems, warm-up groups at political rallies, composers of topical songs performing on street corners and in nightclubs. Music must be considered a potent political tool. Over the centuries, governments have harassed, censored, banned, exiled, jailed, tortured, and killed composers and performers from widely different social classes. In addition to the religious repression of musical styles, political persecutions have occurred repeatedly. In different countries, descendants of African slaves were forbidden to play drums and were pressured to abandon certain musical genres. In the 1940s, Brazilian country musicians were censored and jailed for their topical verses. In the 1960s and 1970s, many performers of new song (*nueva canción*), a genre that began in Chile and transformed topical singing over a wide region, were severely punished. The Chilean composer and performer Victor Jara was tortured and killed in reprisals against his songs. Sometimes just performing a certain genre of music is understood by all parties to be a protest. Not all music is political all of the time; but when other aspects of public life become intensely politicized, music tends to become so too.

Ethnicity

Throughout the twentieth century, ethnicity has been one of the most important mechanisms through mass movements have been created on the basis of perceived and created differences in ethnicity. The musical implications appear in movements based on identification with ancestors brought to the Americas from Africa. Musical styles clearly descended from musical traditions brought to the Americas and the Caribbean by enslaved Africans have been perpetuated and widely used by people of African descent as a means of affirming a collective identity, from which elements traceable to other ethnic groups have been removed. Frequently, musicians emulate contemporary African styles as they perpetuate older local styles. Certain Amerindian genres, and the practice of performing in unison ornamented with paint and feathers, or playing the flute, are means through which local groups affirm a native identity in many locations. Especially in places where Amerindian identity can confer a legal or social advantage, earlier traditions were revived or recreated. European identity is often more fragmented: German dance bands, Italian arias, Portuguese *fados* and *romances,* and Spanish lullabies survive in ethnic communities. Conflicts sometimes arise when the members of one ethnic group prohibit members of others from participating in their performances.

An ethnocultural group may formally identify itself with a particular musical genre, but its members may practice other genres, sometimes bringing to the other genres some of the musical styles of the formally adopted one. Muslim and Jewish communities do not celebrate Christmas or Easter but often participate in national civic rituals and music festivals. Japanese immigrants in Brazil perform and appreciate a number of Japanese musical genres, but a large part of the local Japanese population enjoys Brazilian popular music. The descendants of Italian immigrants may listen to more opera than other members of their social class, because of their pride in the genre itself.

Sometimes a reevaluation of an ethnocultural group will involve creating a new meaning for its music. This is the case of music performed by Brazilians of African descent in the late twentieth century: the musical relationships of their music to the musical traditions of Africa are not only recognized, but encouraged, through visits to Africa and a reevaluation of the history of the music of the Brazilian northeast.

Music is a social resource that can communicate statements of identity and attitudes. Musical performance has been shown to be a resource for expressing identity of and differences of gender, age, kinship, social class, ethnicity, religion, political persuasion, and nationality. The examination of almost any performance reveals how the practitioners and audiences are using these criteria to create meaningful events.

MUSICAL PERFORMANCE AND MUSICAL EVENTS

Music is not simply a sound in the air. Musical performance includes the intention of making sounds; the preparation for making them; the making of them; the sounds themselves; their reception, interpretation, and evaluation by an audience; and their perpetuation through new performances. An ethnomusicologist approaches musical performance by looking at many of those features: the goals, the rehearsals, the construction of the instruments and their use, the public performance, and its evaluation. An examination of these can assist in the understanding of the sounds themselves.

The structure of musical events varies considerably in Mexico, Central and South America, and the Caribbean. Some musical events are domestic and informal, and do not require special organization or written rules. Others are national events—wars, athletic competitions, and national holidays—where different types of music are often rigidly prescribed. Forms that require the cooperation of a group of musicians usually entail defined obligations. Most groups must meet on a regular basis to practice, to learn a new repertoire, and to socialize. The organizations through which this may be done can be occupational (in one Peruvian town, truck owners founded one dance group, truck drivers another), religious (as in the brotherhoods already described), regional (as in the neighborhood organization of the early samba schools in Rio de Janeiro), or based on age or kinship. Rehearsals, if any occur, are usually private and have rarely been studied. Yet many decisions central to the public performances of music are made in them. In some rural areas, practice sessions may often have formal and informal components, with dancing and parties lasting late into the night and many participants returning home only the next day. As the date set for the performance approaches, practices intensify and often become more frequent. In some cases, as in the samba schools (*escolas de samba*) of Rio de Janeiro, rehearsals become public events, with large numbers of tourists participating in the prepara-

Many national, civic, and sometimes even religious
events are staged in the form of competitions among
bands, for awards that may be monetary or purely
symbolic.

FIGURE 4   During the procession of the faithful
who carry the statue of the Virgin in the
patronal festival of the Virgen del Carmen in
Alto Otuzco, Cajamarca, Peru, music is performed by female singers, a pipe-and-tabor player, and a *clarinero* who plays a twelve-foot-long
clarín trumpet. Photo 1979 by Dale A. Olsen.

tions for carnival. The final, public performances vary widely. Processional forms are
common, as in parades during carnival in Rio, or in saint's-day processions in the
Andes and elsewhere, when an image of a saint is paraded around a community (figure 4). So, too, are social dances common, where large numbers of people gather in a
confined space—to eat, drink, and dance.

Another typical event in Mexico, Central and South America, and the
Caribbean is less familiar in other parts of the world: the competition. Many national, civic, and sometimes even religious events are staged in the form of competitions
among bands, for awards that may be monetary or purely symbolic. Brass bands, steel
bands, troupes of dancers, songwriters, and many other musical performers are
judged, and winners are announced. The rules are elaborately laid out, and what
seems like a spontaneous performance may well be defined as much by the rules of
the competition as by the performers' creativity. Judged-performance formats reap-
pear throughout the individual articles of this volume, but Rio de Janeiro's carnival is
one of the best examples. The neighborhood-based samba schools compete on several
fixed criteria for prestige, civic funds, and participation in three different levels of
competition. Each year, the two lowest-ranked groups in the top group go down to a
lower level, whereas the two highest-ranked ones in the lower level move up. Rio de
Janeiro's carnival is extremely structured: only percussion and friction instruments
can be used, no motorized floats are allowed, and a rigid timetable must be followed.
Elsewhere, competitions are more informal, as in patronal festivals in the Andes,

FIGURE 5   In Capachica, Department of Puno, Peru, a band consisting of brass instruments, clarinets, cymbals, and drums plays in celebration and informal competition with other bands during the patronal festival of San Salvador. Photo by Dale A. Olsen, 1979.

where one band tries to outdo the other, but there are no judges other than the participants, the dancers, and the crowd (figure 5).

Every performance has its own spatial organization—the way it uses or moves through space. Processions have their own spatial organization, which has been likened to that of the form of a comet: a small group in front, the center core of the procession in the middle, including the bands, and then a long tail of participants who follow along through the streets but are less involved in the performance. Some national parades are strings of such structures, with band after band moving down the avenues. In other cases, the movement from field or forest to the community, and the movement from the plaza to the edges of a settlement, are significant parts of the structure of the event.

MEDIATED MUSIC

When performers and audiences are separated by time and space, they may be called mediated. Performances are preserved and transmitted over media, preserved on wax cylinders, tapes, compact discs, or videotapes, and transmitted by radio, commercial recordings, television, videotape, or the Internet.

Mediated performances differ from the events described above because there is much more variety in the use of the performances. A person can listen to a recording of religious music anytime, not only in church. A television can transmit the sounds of deceased artists, whose contributions have long been adopted by different groups. And the commercial nature of the popular music recording and concert industry influences the social organization of its production and reproduction.

Live performances of large popular-music bands often involve managers, roadies, and promoters. Performance venues need to employ booking agents and all the employees of the location: ushers, ticket collectors, bartenders, security, stage crews, lighting-and-sound technicians, and so forth. Both sides may employ lawyers, insurance companies, and the services of innumerable specialists, though the specifics may vary from group to group and genre to genre. The tour of a large group is as much like a military campaign as anything else: it requires that a large number of people and heavy equipment arrive in a location that is prepared for them at a fixed time, and move out quickly afterward. Expectations vary considerably, however, and attitudes toward late arrivals and no-shows vary from genre to genre, from site to site. As the scope of the event increases, the amount of money that must be collected and paid out increases, and the number of positions and requirements increases proportionally.

The recording industry adds new roles to musical performance. Regardless of the type of group (whether it be a small community band with a homemade cassette recording, or a large popular group recording for a multinational recording company), some new roles are involved in the structure, the timbre, and the performance of the sounds. The industry itself applies some restrictions: the music on a CD cannot be more than seventy-five minutes long; a single song often will not receive airplay if it is more than four or five minutes long—a holdover from when 78-rpm records could hold no more than about five minutes of music.

Producers of records are a specialized group: their job is to help the band create a sound in the studio that will meet their needs, usually the need to sell as many copies as possible. Producers may have tremendous artistic control: they may insist that an electric bass be added to a genre where there has never been one before, or they may recommend that a full orchestra be added to a folk song. Depending on the power the group has with the record company itself, the producer may have final authority. Record companies themselves can be extremely bureaucratic. They tend to be uninterested in groups that will not quickly recoup the financial investment made in them. Record companies, too, have marketing departments, people who specialize in getting music played on radio, and sales forces that go to record stores. Record stores have their rents, their employees, their losses to theft, and payments to make on their stock.

Touring groups of musicians who make recordings attract a fairly large industry of specialists who are not themselves performers, but make their living from music. In large countries such as Brazil, Peru, and Argentina, the industry is quite complex and developed. In some smaller countries, more of the recorded music is imported, and there is a far less developed social organization of distribution, mass-media performance, and airplay.

OWNERSHIP AND RIGHTS

Another feature of musical performance that has grown alongside commercialization and a popular-music industry that emphasizes novelty is the industry of intellectual property. In many Amerindian and rural traditions, the actual ownership of a musical idea is considered unimportant, especially after the live performance at which it is introduced. European-modeled copyright laws, however, emphasize individual creativity and allow an author to copyright, or to keep other people from performing, a song or a musical idea unless they pay a royalty to the composer. A famous example is "The Birthday Song," composed in the 1920s. Anyone who records it on a cassette or a compact disc is expected to pay a royalty to the songwriter for each unit sold—anywhere in the world. Anyone who performs it in a film, on a stage, or on television is similarly expected to pay a music-publishing company for the use of the song.

The objective of copyright is to enable writers (including composers and songwriters) to earn income by giving them, or their music-publishing company, the exclusive right to record their composition. Anyone else who does so must request a license and pay a fee. For this reason, under international law, all "traditional" folk songs, and all Amerindian traditions without a single author and more than seventy-five years old, cannot be copyrighted. The law, therefore, rewards novelty and discourages tradition. It does more: a composer can base a composition on a traditional song and then copyright the new version in his or her name. This practice can lead to a kind of intellectual colonial exploitation: the musical ideas of a community that can be deemed "traditional" can be effectively taken and individualized and profited from. There are cases, especially in the Caribbean (whence have come elements of some popular North American genres), where fortunes have been made through musical copyright of previously traditional materials.

In many subtle ways, copyright laws influence the music performed and the music an audience hears. First, performers are encouraged to create their own material to make money from the royalties; second, record companies try to obtain the music-publishing rights on those songs to profit from them; third, certain performance locations, in an effort to avoid paying copyright fees, ask that groups restrict themselves to their own compositions or songs in the public domain (not under copyright); fourth, it can be less expensive for radio stations to play music by long-dead composers of classical music—safely beyond copyright concerns—than contemporary music.

To combat perceived inequities in the copyright law, some South American countries have taken steps to protect traditional music. Bolivia enacted a public-domain law that requires royalties to be paid to the state on all traditional songs. Brazil has proposed a law that would give Brazilian indigenous communities perpetual rights to their intellectual property (with the objective of protecting their shamans' pharmaceutical knowledge, and incidentally their music, dance, and other collective creations). The Brazilian law gives indigenous communities far more protection than it gives non-Indians, but it is consistent with a tendency toward longer-lasting terms and a broader extension of laws concerning intellectual property into all areas of life, among them music.

The way musicians and their audiences define themselves and their music are part of the social processes of the communities in which they claim membership. How they use age, gender, social class, ethnocultural affiliation, space, and time are important for understanding the musical performances themselves and the societies in general. The ethnomusicological approach to music is to examine the sounds of musical performances within the context of the social processes of which they are a part. As is repeatedly demonstrated in the articles of this volume, the relationships of the sounds of music to the social features of their performance is an intimate one.

Musical Dynamics
Anthony Seeger

Musical Enculturation or Socialization
Acculturation and Stylistic Change
Transnational and Transcultural Musical Influences

Most musical traditions are always changing, if at varying rates, through innovation by creators and performers, influences from other traditions, revivals of almost forgotten styles, changes in other features of social and cultural life, and many other causes. Yet outside of studies of popular music, we have little idea of how these changes occur. When a ceramic pot breaks and is discarded, its pieces are eventually covered by earth and preserved virtually unchanged for centuries. When a community is abandoned, the structures of its houses, the location of its hearths, trash from its residents, pollen from its gardens, and some remnants of its food often endure and give mute testimony to details of the life those residents led. But the operative word is *mute:* there is no sound.

Music could be preserved only in the minds of living practitioners until 1877, when Thomas Edison invented the phonograph using a tin-foil cylinder and an amplifying horn. Before then, people had no way to capture musical sounds. Various methods of musical notation had been developed, but these typically focused on only a few features of musical performances. The rest were transmitted through oral traditions (through teaching) and aural traditions (through hearing), and usually changed, in often unconscious ways, over time. Edison's invention of the phonograph spurred the emergence of ethnomusicology as a discipline, because at last it was possible to record sounds in distant places and to listen to them repeatedly for analysis. Researchers eventually took advantage of the phonograph for capturing the sounds of speech and music, and research centers soon appeared. In 1899, the first audio archive was founded in Vienna; in 1901, one was founded in Berlin. Later, archives were founded in the United States. The music industry grew up around audio recording and playback using three-minute wax cylinders or flat discs, and for many traditions, the relationship of tradition and change can be documented from then on.

In the late twentieth century, when audio- and video-recording devices are easy to use and virtually ubiquitous (they are even found in isolated Amazonian communities), it is hard to imagine musical traditions without any recording, playback, or radio. Until the twentieth century, however, the worldwide musical record is based on written descriptions, transcriptions, and manuscripts. For the Americas, the record is even poorer: Amerindians did not transcribe the details of their musical sounds, and the documents produced after Columbus's voyage, though better than nothing, are far less detailed than the manuscript materials available in Europe and parts of Asia.

Despite the sparseness of the records, we know that two associated waves of music were carried from Europe to the rest of the world, often transforming musical traditions and sometimes providing the basis for the creation of new local traditions. These were *religious hymns and other church music,* carried by missionaries, and *brass bands,* carried by soldiers, as the European powers explored and conquered. These became the first worldwide influences, eventually to be followed by certain dances and twentieth-century popular music. Mexico, Central and South America, and the Caribbean are filled with examples of religious and band-produced music—examples that have received local forms and are used in ways quite different from their original intentions. Musical changes, though somewhat difficult to document for earlier periods but dramatically represented today by satellite transmissions of popular music, are hundreds of years old in the Western Hemisphere.

Musical change has traditionally been discussed using concepts developed by anthropologists in the 1930s to describe the continuity and change of cultures. These concepts include music *enculturation* (the acquisition of musical knowledge, or music learning), *acculturation* (the changes that occur when members of different cultures come into continuous contact), and *transculturation* (what happens when distant cultural groups influence one another). Musical *deculturation* (the loss of culture without the implication of the replacement of it by another) is also described for some communities.

The trouble with these concepts is that they are inherited from a cultural anthropology that described cultures as unitary. In that view, a group has a single culture; two groups have two cultures, and when they are face to face, they interact and something happens. Today, researchers are likelier to view communities as comprising various groups with different sets of values that are often in conflict in specific social processes. Musical performance is one of the domains through which ideas and values are expressed, in which they may be contested, or in which they may be repressed and their participants eliminated. Similarly, individual members of communities may be masters of more than a single musical tradition—they may be bimusical or trimusical, able to shift from style to style with changes in contexts. The decision of which style to learn, which to perform on a given occasion, and which to pass on to one's children or disciples is shaped by many considerations that may have to do with ethnocultural affiliation, social class, political conjunctures, or economic or spiritual rewards. Unfortunately, ethnomusicologists lack a coherent analytic terminology with which to discuss these relationships.

Thus, though the words are used in this volume, *enculturation* and *acculturation* and the other such terms must be understood to represent complex interrelationships of groups of people, individual choices, and complex musical contexts. Unlike milk, culture is not something with which a person is filled like a jug, or with which various flavors can be mixed to create flavored milkshakes. Enculturation, or musical socialization, is in many communities a complex and many-layered process. Acculturation, or the combination of traits from two or more musical traditions, is often a representation of relationships of political and symbolic power whose musical expression is a conscious commentary on those relationships. Behind the words lies the complex situations described in the entries to this volume, filled with conflict, choice, and creativity.

MUSICAL ENCULTURATION OR SOCIALIZATION

Enculturation literally means 'giving culture' or 'endowing with culture'. In music, it usually refers to the ways members of a community become practitioners of their community's music. Music education is one form of musical enculturation; growing up in a family band is another.

Different musical traditions use sounds in different ways. Rhythms, pitches, timbres, and texts may all be employed differently within a certain community and among different groups. Children, born with the potential for all languages and all musical systems, are socialized into only a few of them—sometimes one, sometimes several. In most communities, every member is expected to be able at least to sing a few songs; in some, to perform on instruments and dance. Musical socialization also includes attitudes toward certain sounds and aural structures, and toward those who produce or enjoy them.

If all members of a community learn a few skills, attitudes, and values, a small number of community members usually learns how to innovate, often within fairly fixed, but constantly changing, limitations. These skills may be acquired through informal exposure, formal training, or years of apprenticeship. Musical knowledge may be voluntarily acquired or forced, but in most communities in Mexico, Central and South America, and the Caribbean, musical expertise is learned voluntarily by a self-selected group of individuals. It may be acquired from relatives, from friends and peers, in institutions such as schools and churches, from specialized teachers, from books, and more recently from audio and video recordings. Family and peers appear to be important everywhere; institutions, specialized teachers, and recordings are found in widely different relationships and interact in complex ways to influence a community's musical traditions.

Musical enculturation probably begins before birth, with patterns of sounds transmitted to the fetus with the sound of the pregnant woman's heartbeat. So far, we know little about what, if any, information a child retains from its prenatal musical experiences. After birth, throughout much of the region, infants are carried almost everywhere by their mothers or another female relative during the initial months, and they hear whatever music is being performed around them. It could be argued that children learn to sing before they learn to talk, in that systematic patterns of pitch, rhythm, and timbre appear in their vocalizations before referential language. Yet again, we have little information about cross-cultural parallels, or relationships of infant babbling to musical traditions, at that age.

By the time children are about three and begin to play together, a whole system of musical sounds and structures has probably been learned; and during later childhood, it is increasingly fixed. In some communities, adults sing special songs to children—often containing simplified melodies, rhythms, and words. In other communities (particularly Amerindian communities), there may be no lullabies and no special children's songs: the children fall asleep or stay awake to the sounds of adult music.

A child's first music teacher is often another child. Children in most communities learn to perform songs and games by playing with other children. These may be passed on for generations from one child to another, without involving adults. Collections of children's genres have been made in African-American and European-American communities; we know much less about children's music in Amerindian communities. The examples we have show that children often perform shortened and simple versions of adult genres.

Religious institutions and practices are important in musical education throughout South America, Mexico, Central America, and the Caribbean. Religious events (saints' days, Christmas, Easter, and so forth), most shamanism, and African-derived possession religions—all include music. Children and young adults of the region probably learn more music by participating in religious events than they do in schools. In areas where there are no schools at all, children may still be exposed to religious music. In the 1500s, the Jesuits taught Amerindians how to play European instruments and how to compose music in the European style of the period. Today, various choral settings of the Mass are available, as are musical performances around saints' days. Protestant services are punctuated by hymns, and many churches have children's choirs and adult choruses. The African-derived religions that invoke direct contact with saints and spirits—Santería in Cuba, Vodou in Haiti, Candomblé in Brazil—teach children other musical skills: multiple rhythms, forms of vocal interrelationships, postures, movements, and styles of performance. Before missionary repression, a great deal of Amerindian music was religious, and music and contact with powerful beings were closely related. In all these cases, children observe performances, and are exposed to musical styles that influence them throughout their lives.

Though religious institutions are found in almost every part of Mexico, Central and South America, and the Caribbean, formal education in schools and conservatories varies widely from place to place. Formal education is usually available only to part of the population, often differentiated from the rest by social class and geographic area, financial status, degree of urbanization, and other factors. In many rural areas, there is little formal education, and children acquire musical training by listening to their families, to other adults, to neighborhood performances, radio and recordings, and eventually performing themselves.

The availability of elementary and secondary schools does not mean that children learn much music there. Music is not usually a high-priority pedagogical subject. The music usually taught in most schools bears little resemblance to the music of the child's community or the genres favored by the child's peers. Musical curricula have usually been designed by educators and musicians of a different social class, ethnic group, part of the country, or (in colonial periods) by specialists completely removed from the local culture. The distance between the curriculum and the local community culture is being reduced in some countries in the region, but in others continues to grow, as forms of popular music continue to be ignored in schools in favor of exclusively European-influenced forms. Schoolchildren often learn choral singing; in urban areas, orchestras and bands are found occasionally. Children learn something in music lessons at school, but its relationship to the traditions into which they were born and that they may perform in the future is quite variable.

For children who are particularly interested in music, or whose families want to encourage them to be musicians, the methods through which they acquire advanced training vary according to some of the same factors that determine opportunities for formal education. Motivated children in most areas attach themselves formally or informally to local performers, and they learn through watching, performing, and eventually becoming part of the performing group. In large urban areas, an extracurricular network of music teachers may provide lessons in various instruments for a fee. Members of the elites of most Mexican, Central and South American, and Caribbean countries pay for music lessons in classical-music instruments, such as piano, violin, and classical guitar. Children perceived as being more talented or gifted or devoted to the subject may take further lessons with specialists of increasing ability, eventually entering music conservatories, in their own countries or abroad. The process is rather similar in every case: a child is motivated by outside encouragement, and this motivation is reinforced if he or she can master the required musical skills. Most music conservatories in the region specialize in advanced training in the performance, composition, and instruction of European classical music, though there are exceptions.

In addition to face-to-face means of learning skills, a large amount of music is learned today from recorded music, radio, and television. In most communities, chil-

The mechanisms through which songs have been learned vary: sometimes they were learned from captured enemies, sometimes from peaceful trading partners, sometimes through marriage exchanges, and now through radio and recordings.

dren are exposed to recorded music from the womb on. In addition to passive listening, many children pay careful attention to recordings or broadcasts, and they actively learn styles of songs, music, and dance that they practice and teach to one another. Children also learn attitudes toward different musical styles and performance practices from media sources. Since media can reach far from the source of performance, children can be influenced by forms entirely foreign to their area, by performers and styles they may never see in person. The increasingly extensive reach of media is having greater and greater impact on musical traditions throughout the Americas.

Parents, religious groups, and nations have all, at some time in the past few decades, tried to restrict the kinds of music to which children are exposed through the media. (Before electronic media had any important influence, people in the same roles regulated face-to-face musical performances.) Parents may forbid certain kinds of music in the home; churches may restrict their members' music or dance; and nations, to control the international, capital-intensive, market-oriented musical performances that predominate on public media, have offered incentives for certain kinds of music and censored others. These restrictions have met with varied success, pitting children against parents, religious leaders against nonbelievers, and nations against one other in such a way that some kinds of music are divisive rather than unifying. Forms of expression become domains for moral and political contention.

In general, repression seems to have only intermittent success. More successful are the encouragement of individuals and institutions to foster children's active participation in alternative musical events, and efforts to endow those events with positive value and status.

ACCULTURATION AND STYLISTIC CHANGE

The term *acculturation* was defined by Robert Redfield, Ralph Linton, and Melville Herskovits in an important paper: "Acculturation comprehends those phenomena which result when groups of individuals having different cultures come into continuous first-hand contact, with subsequent changes in the original cultural patterns of either or both groups" (1936:149). The term is often used to describe a process whereby individuals adopt the values, performance styles, and repertoire of another community. The advantage of the term is its vagueness; the problem is that it gives no indication of the relationship between the influencing and influenced culture(s). In music, the term was used extensively by Melville Herskovits and others, and continues in use precisely because its generality allows for further definition through examples.

In South America, Mexico, Central America, and the Caribbean, a great deal of observed acculturation has involved relationships of cultural, economic, and political dominance of one group over another. Music becomes one of the domains that expresses the relation of the groups to one another. This is not true everywhere. Scholars are still trying to discover a suitable language to express the processes through which communities produce cultural forms that combine features of different communities into new forms. Until such a language is developed, it is best to pay close attention to the details of the interaction of groups, and not simply to the musical results obtained by their members.

Amerindian communities in the Amazon have been learning one another's songs for hundreds of years. The mechanisms through which songs have been learned vary: sometimes they were learned from captured enemies, sometimes from peaceful trading partners, sometimes through marriage exchanges, and now through radio and recordings; but the result has been that part of the community's music has come from outside that culture. Amerindian communities often perform songs in a language they do not understand. They usually adopt other Amerindian styles selectively and continue to practice many of their own music and dance forms. Learning another community's musical style is not always, in these cases, a sign of cultural or political exploitation.

Members of different European communities also learned one another's styles. Examples are legion in classical concert music, where composers of one country were hired by patrons of another country to introduce prestigious forms to their courts. The combination of forms is obvious in communal dances in South America, where polkas (originally from Poland) are played between dances associated with other countries: a Viennese waltz (Austria), a schottische (Scotland), a fandango (Spain), a tango (Argentina), or a samba (Brazil). Here, too, the band's decision to play a given dance may be less a reflection of cultural dominance than of the dancers' interests in variety.

Most relationships between European colonists and Amerindians, and between European colonists and the Africans they used for labor, were dominating and exploitative. Amerindians were usually discouraged or prohibited from performing some or all of their traditional music, and new forms were imposed on them. Similarly, enslaved Africans were often prohibited from performing most genres, and in some cases European church music was offered as an exclusive replacement for their earlier traditions. Though the region reveals a complex variety of restrictions and alternatives, the relationships among communities from Europe, Africa, and the Americas differed from most of those among Amerindian groups.

An important thing to remember about South America, Mexico, Central America, and the Caribbean is that the large ethnocultural groups are not monolithic blocks. There are many different Amerindian societies, each with its own set of values, its own specific experience with other societies, and its own specific use of music in determining its future. There are many different groups of Europeans, each with its own musical traditions, some of which have tenaciously been preserved in the Americas long after they have disappeared in their homelands. Members of many different African communities were enslaved. Except for a few, such as the Yoruba, a large amount of the individual cultures has not survived. But in their place a general African-derived culture developed—in workplaces and the Maroon communities that coalesced in many countries. Significant populations of South Asians, Indonesians, and Japanese live in some countries. Important local differences occur in the cultural attributes found and community members' values and intentions, and it is unproductive to generalize without reviewing the data found in this volume.

Members of communities that are largely dominated by another community react in different ways to the forceful suppression of earlier traditions and the imposition of new ones. In some cases, they will actively embrace the new form and become creative within the new genre. The Waiwai of Brazil and the Guianas today sing little besides hymns, but they have adapted Protestant hymns to their intercommunal relationships; their villages engage in hymn-writing competitions, and the composition of hymns has become a culturally accepted creative activity. In other cases, stylistic features from some genres carry over into new musical forms. Some older traditions may be maintained as a form of protest, a means of transmitting knowledge and perpetuating other aspects of social and cultural life. African traditions have influenced a great deal of the music in the Caribbean, northeastern Brazil, and some areas on the Pacific coast, especially celebrations of carnival and popular music.

In some cases we can trace a trend called *deculturation*. This happens when the members of a community cease to practice their earlier culture but do not replace it with anything else. Deculturation may simply be a phase in the longer process by which some traditions are replaced by others, but it is often distressing to community elders and ethnomusicologists when a community abandons a long-established musical tradition and does not become proficient at another one. An Amerindian community, for example, might cease to perform its own traditions and simply stop making music, merely listening to recorded music on radio and cassettes.

More frequent, probably, are communities in which a few genres and some aspects of the former musical traditions are maintained somewhat unchanged, while others are adapted to new musical forms and contexts dictated by the dominating culture. European Christian music has been transformed by the musical contribution of African-American performers and composers. The celebration of saints' days in the Andes has been transformed by the use of Amerindian instruments and styles of performance. When used in these situations, *acculturation* usually means the combination, or fusion, of two or more styles. Another word often used for this is *creolization*. Once again, the terms are shifting in the 1990s, as scholars try to fit their concepts better to the complexity of the processes they see occurring.

Creolization takes its definition from linguistics, which describes a creole language as a complete language based on one or more other languages but distinct from any of them. Thus, in Haiti and elsewhere, French creole languages are unlike French and English and have proved relatively stable through time. Similarly, one could point to some musical styles that are neither European nor African in form but represent a fairly stable combination of traits. The important thing to remember here, though, is that musical fusion does not take place in a vacuum and is not free of values. It is a factor in the social situation of which it is a part.

When the word *creolization* is applied to music, it is a vague term, as it is more difficult to tell when a musical tradition is "independent" of its parent traditions. At one time, a group will point to certain fusion traditions with pride and say, "That's our music." At another time, they may denounce the same tradition with disdain and complain, "That's a terrible mixture of our beautiful tradition with their ugly one." Traditions that are seen as mixed are often the subject of considerable conflict. Over time, however, one can often trace how these adaptations of parts of other community's styles begin as criticized hybrids and become an integral part of a community's music. In other cases, one can trace how a shared musical tradition is eventually "purified," and becomes the symbolic property of only one of the contributing communities. Different countries reveal different dynamics, as the entries in this volume demonstrate.

The creative mixing of aspects of musical traditions is achieved in many ways: through instrumentation; musical texture, structure, and performance style; musical appropriation; and the creation of genres for new audiences. These features appear frequently throughout the entries.

Instrumentation

Musical instruments are at once sound-producing objects and highly significant representations of a community's history. Thus, a nationalist composer or regional folk-

FIGURE 1   In Santo Domingo, Dominican Republic, three musicians in a small merengue group play in front of a restaurant. *Left to right*: a *tambora*, a *güiro* or metal scraper, and a button accordion. Photo by Martha Ellen Davis, 1991.

rock group might use traditional Amerindian instruments to give their otherwise European compositions a national flavor; or, moving in the other direction, an Amerindian group might adopt an electric bass or rhythm section to make its music louder, more "modern," or commercially successful. The introduction of new musical instruments into a tradition does not, by itself, indicate whether the resulting change is considered to be highly significant. For example, the timbres of certain instruments have replaced others for practical or economic reasons. In the 1800s, the German accordion, with its loudness and versatility, replaced other instruments in dance-oriented bands throughout the region (figure 1). Many musical genres, however, continued to be performed on the new instrument. Musical instruments are sometimes identified with the communities in which they originated: rattles and flutes with Amerindians; percussion instruments, musical bows, and *xekeres* (*shekeres*) with Africans; and stringed and brass instruments with Europeans. New instruments, such as the electronic keyboard, have often been adapted to older forms. Sometimes old instruments are revived in new forms. South America has seen a great deal of creative use of musical instruments in traditions quite unlike those in which they originated.

Musical texture, structure, and performance

Chordal texture (harmony) was one of the defining features of sixteenth-century European music, and it continues to define much of the music of the region. The multipart, chordal approach to music was distinct from that of the Amerindians, whose polyphony did not work like harmony in the Western sense. Some African traditions employed multipart harmony; others did not. Amerindian communities and descendants of African slaves learned to perform harmonic structures, often in churches, and many of them carried this form into secular genres. The use of harmonies and the harmonic structures of pieces can be quite variable and are often defining features of genres.

Most Amerindian music featured a single, fairly steady, rhythmic pulse, with melodic syncopation in the vocal parts. A great deal of African music had complex, interlocking rhythms, played on membranophones or idiophones, or by slapping the body. European rhythms could be complex, but most dances were arranged in simple 2/4, 3/4, 4/4, or 6/8 time, and lacked the complexity of West African drumming. The rhythmic structures of African music have been greatly admired by people from

Most copyright laws exclude traditional music from their purview and give little protection to rural and less wealthy composers and performers. Popularizers have often shown little interest in crediting their sources, to say nothing of paying them a share of royalties.

many communities, and they have been widely adapted in some modified form to create new musical genres.

Call-and-response forms, improvisation, and broad community participation in making music have all been identified as having African origins. Certainly these performance processes appear in traditions bearing other obvious African influences. But not all examples of these features should be unquestionably traced to African influences, as they also appear in European and Amerindian traditions.

Musical appropriation

In Mexico, Central and South America, and the Caribbean, different groups have often adapted one another's styles, consciously or unconsciously, with the variety of results described in the individual entries. Powerful communities, often European and Christian, have sometimes forced their musical traditions on Amerindians and communities of African descent. Simultaneously, the same wealthy, European-influenced populations in many countries have admired and appropriated, often for their material benefit, the music of the poor and often African or Amerindian peoples in their countries. It has been argued that the poorer parts of the societies throughout Mexico, Central and South America, and the Caribbean have produced many of the musical styles that have subsequently become national styles or popular forms of music. There are different ways to interpret this phenomenon. It may be seen as cultural exploitation or as a musical parallel to classic colonialism (one group provides the raw materials; the other group packages it and sells it back) or simply an uncomplicated case of admiration and borrowing. In many cases, the evidence apparently supports the first two interpretations more than the last.

The patterns of cultural appropriation found in Central and South America and the Caribbean raise important issues of intellectual property and ethics. Most copyright laws exclude traditional music from their purview and give little protection to rural and less wealthy composers and performers. Popularizers have often shown little interest in crediting their sources, to say nothing of paying them a share of royalties (Wallis and Malm 1984). Although these attitudes are changing in a few countries, abuses have made many local musicians suspicious of outsiders carrying tape recorders or video cameras and may impede even legitimate and ethically aware investigations of musical performances in some communities and some countries. Some efforts are underway in various countries to modify the cultural and class biases of existing copyright laws, but most actual modifications apparently perpetuate and accentuate the rights of literate professional musicians with legal assistance over those of nonliterate but highly creative musicians whose work grows out of a strong vernacular tradition.

The creation of genres for new audiences

The most important face-to-face musical genre developed for specialized audiences, and one that often combines unusual mixtures of the above features, is music for tourists. Tourism is a major influence on the creation of musical styles considered appropriate to new audiences, especially those from outside the community (Lewin 1988). Throughout Mexico, Central and South America, and the Caribbean, tourism is an important part of national economies, and many aspects of culture have adapted to the new audiences tourism provides.

Touristic audiences are not neutral, however. They bring with them expectations of diversion, a short attention span, a lack of understanding of local languages and traditions, and often an ignorance of religious matters. Most performers voluntarily, often at organizers' request, adjust their performances to present them within times and in locations set by tourists' schedules. As surely as other economic systems have created or discouraged certain kinds of musical performance, so does tourism.

TRANSNATIONAL AND TRANSCULTURAL MUSICAL INFLUENCES

Since before Columbus, musical, economic, and other cultural influences have flowed back and forth between the highlands and the lowlands, between North and South America, and around the Caribbean. The arrival of Europeans and Africans stepped up the pace of interaction. Music probably followed the trade routes, with seaports and riverine ports becoming centers of creativity and patronage for the arts, and the trade routes carrying the new creations to other cities and other patrons. In the Atlantic, New Orleans, Havana, Rio de Janeiro, Buenos Aires and other ports were the originators of distinctive styles of music whose popularity spread far beyond the country's borders. In the Pacific, similar processes certainly occurred among the former Spanish colonies.

Few records of this transnational musical cross-fertilization existed until the era of sheet music, when popular music in its current form emerges in historical documents. The utilization of early recording devices at the start of the twentieth century escalated the trend, and a transnational popular-music industry began to flourish. At first, most recordings were produced in North America, but by the 1920s several countries had flourishing music industries, often owned or licensed by multinational corporations. The popular musical forms of Mexico, Central and South America, and the Caribbean have had a tremendous impact on the popular music of Europe, Africa, and other parts of the world.

Tango has had a tremendous impact on France and other parts of Europe, Japan, and the United States. Today, there are hundreds of tango clubs in Finland, where tango has become almost a national dance. As the tango retreats into the realm of tourist art in Argentina, it flourishes as a creative form in northern Europe.

Since the popular recording of "*El Cóndor Pasa*" in the 1960s by Simon and Garfunkel; since the residence of Andean musical ensembles such as Inti Illimani and Quilapayún in Europe following the 1973 military coup in Chile; since Bolivian, Chilean, Ecuadorian, and Peruvian street musicians have been performing in Europe; and since the formation of Andean music ensembles in American universities— Andean (or "pan-Andean") folkloric music has been popular outside of its homelands. Groups that perform at American universities (figure 2) or on the streets of European cities (figure 3) are commonplace.

Popular music from the Caribbean probably had a large influence on African highlife and other African genres of popular music that later swept back across the Atlantic to the Americas, and returned some of the influences with new features. Subsequently, merengue, reggae, salsa, soca, and other Caribbean musical genres have had a tremendous impact on the Americas and far beyond. The traditions from this region are influencing the development of musical traditions around the world.

What is the source of the impact of Caribbean music on the rest of the world?

FIGURE 2 The San Francisco–based Andean music ensemble Sukay performs on the campus of the University of Florida. *Left to right:* a guitar, a panpipe set, and a *charango.* Photo by Dale A. Olsen, 1986.

Part of it can be traced to the widespread adoption of a context common in many countries: the dance hall. Most widespread genres have been danceable genres. If any of them had religious aspects, such as reggae's relationship with Rastafarian beliefs, these aspects are largely shed by the time the form enters the hall. For some genres, socially and politically conscious vocals are attractive to audiences far from the political events in which the song originated. Not to be discounted either is the combination of musical familiarity with musical difference that the various mixtures of styles have brought about in the Americas. Record companies, tourism bureaus, music television, and the other parts of the music business also support the spread of music around the world. And new composer-musicians, hearing the music, will take it and create new forms, which will themselves come resounding back to the Americas from

FIGURE 3 A South American Andean music group plays on the streets of Helsinki, Finland. *Left to right:* a *bombo* (with *kena* and *siku* around the musician's neck), a *kena* (with *siku* around the musician's neck), and a *charango.* Photo by Arnold Perris, 1985.

places such as Bombay, Hong Kong, Jakarta, Kinshasa, Paris, and Tokyo. This process shows every sign of speeding up, as the Internet eases the sending of large and digitized music files, and home studios become more widespread.

Some of the music of Mexico, Central and South America, and the Caribbean continues to be heard only within its community. Others of its musical traditions have become part of the world's repertoire. The relationship between local and transnational musics is a theme that reappears again and again in these entries. It remains a challenge for all traditions in the coming century, when current trends will probably continue at an increasing rate.

Though the means by which musical traditions are learned, preserved, transformed, and even performed are constantly changing, the overall use of music in social life is probably increasing. The ways individuals and groups use music, the ways it is taught, the genres deemed significant, the genres that are transformed, the genres that spread across the globe, and the relationships among groups of people given expression through music will continue to be a significant part of musical performances in this hemisphere.

REFERENCES

Lewin, Olive. 1986. "Banana Boat Song Forever?" In *Come Mek Me Hol' Yu Han': The Impact of Tourism on Traditional Music*, ed. Adrienne L. Kaeppler, 1–5. Kingston: Jamaica Memory Bank.

Redfield, Robert, Ralph Linton, and Melville Herskovits. 1936. "Memorandum for the Study of Acculturation." *American Anthropologist* 38:149–152.

Wallis, Roger, and Krister Malm. 1984. *Big Sounds from Small Peoples: The Music Industry in Small Countries*. London: Constable; New York: Pendragon Press.

Native American Musical Cultures
Dale A. Olsen

Language Classifications
The Earliest Migrations
The Legacy of Native Americans

opposite: Native peoples of South America

On 12 October 1492, the Lucaya, a native people of the Caribbean, discovered Columbus. When he and his crew made landfall, on Samana Cay (San Salvador, present Bahamas), they thought they were in the East Indies; therefore they called these people Indians—a term that has caused confusion ever since, especially considering that hundreds of thousands of immigrants from India also live in the Caribbean today. (This volume uses the terms *native American, Amerindian,* and *Indian* interchangeably, reflecting particular authors' choices.) In 1492, the islands of the Caribbean and adjacent Atlantic were inhabited by native American peoples, including the peaceful Island Arawak or Taino (including the Lucaya subgroup) and the warlike Carib. And before them were other groups, including the Yamaye (Jamaica), the Borinquen (Puerto Rico), the Caliponau and Calinago (Lesser Antilles), the Siboney (Dominican Republic), and others (Loukotka 1968).

Columbus had no idea that the islands he encountered were but tiny specks compared to the huge landmasses in the Western Hemisphere, and that millions of people were dwelling in cities larger than many of those in Europe, were living and farming in lands higher in altitude than the Italian Alps, and were hunting and foraging in tropical forests unimaginable to him.

LANGUAGE CLASSIFICATIONS

At the time of the Encounter (a term preferred to *the Conquest,* because most native Americans were never conquered), it is believed that about 15 million people were living in the South American continent; about 26 million or more were living in Middle America (including present Mexico and Central America) and the Caribbean; and about 5 million were living in North America. These inhabitants of what was to become known as the Americas spoke more than two thousand languages, 1,492 of them in South America alone (Loukotka 1968:17). The South American aboriginal languages can be classified into seven large phyla: Macro-Ge, Macro-Panoan, Macro-Carib, Equatorial, Macro-Tucanoan, Andean, and Chibchan-Paezan; those in Middle America (Central America and Mexico) include three families within the collective group Central Amerind (Kiowa-Tanoan, Uto-Aztecan, and Oto-Mangue), plus Chibchan, Hokan, and Penutian, and Equatorial in the

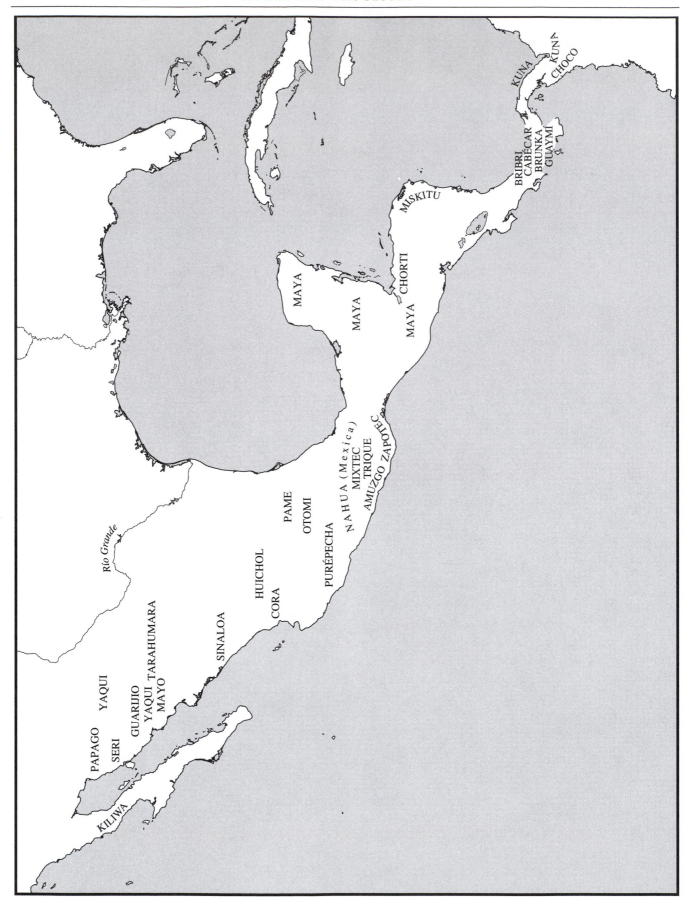

Caribbean basin (Greenberg 1987:63, 388–389). Scholars are not in complete agreement with this classification (mostly based on published works), and other systems can be devised. Nevertheless, for the sake of consistency, this system will be followed in this volume.

The native American cultures included in this section of the volume belong to many of those language areas. The map on page 79 shows the approximate locations of the South American native people discussed in this volume. The map on page 80 shows the approximate locations of those from Mexico and Central America. Many of these native American cultures are studied in individual essays organized alphabetically by region (for South American regions, see Steward 1949:5:674). Each is identified according to linguistic affiliation and cultural area, and described according to criteria presented in Parts 1 and 2, enabling the reader to make comparisons, observe trends, and so forth.

THE EARLIEST MIGRATIONS

The "Indians" are the native Americans. But even they are descendants of earlier peoples, who came from the Old World as discoverers, explorers, invaders, and conquerors. It is widely accepted that tens of thousands of years ago, hunters followed game across the land bridge between present Siberia and Alaska. During two ice ages, the first one about fifty thousand to thirty thousand years ago and the second one twenty-five thousand to twelve thousand years ago, the oceans receded to create a continuous stretch of tundra between Asia and North America, enabling animals to migrate in search of food, followed by nomadic hunting-gathering cultures (Layrisse and Wilbert 1966:17–18).

opposite: Native peoples of Mexico and Central America

For millennia, these early Americans migrated south and southeast, constantly in pursuit of game, being forced farther south by stronger groups of people, some building elaborate cities and ceremonial centers (Chichén Itzá, Mitla, Monte Albán, Tenochtitlán, Teotihuacán, and Tula in Mexico; Iximché, Kaminaljuyú, and Utatlán in Guatemala; Chan Chan and Cuzco in Peru; Tiawanaku in Bolivia; and others), some developing agricultural societies, others retaining hunting-gathering activities. Elaborate priest-god religions developed, while other systems of belief were based on shamanism, whereby a single entranced religious leader communes with the supernatural. In all cases, these peoples developed nations in their own right.

THE LEGACY OF NATIVE AMERICANS

The achievements of many American cultures and nations were distinguished and remarkable. Unfortunately, most of them did not survive the intruders' guns and swords, the enslavement inflicted on them for labor, the diseases unwittingly brought by the Europeans, and the dozens of other wrongs inflicted by one people on others. Hundreds of cultures have survived, however, some still maintaining life-styles and beliefs perhaps similar to those of ancient times, others existing in varying degrees of assimilation. We know little about the present music and musical performance of the native Americans in South America, Mexico, Central America, and the Caribbean, and much study remains to be done.

What remains may be but a mere echo of the past; nevertheless, many musical aspects of today's native Americans still resound and are vital to an understanding of the essence of Mexico, Central America, and South America. Many native American musical forms are being revived, others are being performed with renewed vigor, and still others are disappearing. Those that do continue are often important components of revolutionary movements by native Americans (as in Mexico and Guatemala) and non-Indians (as in *nueva canción chilena* 'Chilean new song' and the new-song movement throughout Central and South America). In many regions of Mexico and Central America (Bolivia, Brazil, Peru, and elsewhere), native people themselves make audio and video recordings of their indigenous events for learning and passing on the traditions and/or bringing attention to their way of life, its plights, and its beauties.

REFERENCES

Greenberg, Joseph H. 1987. *Language in the Americas.* Stanford: Stanford University Press.

Layrisse, Miguel, and Johannes Wilbert. 1966. *Indian Societies of Venezuela: Their Blood Group Types.* Caracas: Editorial Sucre.

Loukotka, Cestmír. 1968. *Classification of South American Indian Languages.* Los Angeles: University of California Press.

Steward, Julian H., ed. 1949. *Handbook of South American Indians.* 5 volumes. Washington, D.C.: U.S. Government Printing Office.

Music of Immigrant Groups
Dale A. Olsen

China

India

Japan

Germany

Italy

Spain

Chile

Out-Migration

By *immigrants* we mean people, other than individuals of the colonial powers of particular countries in the Americas, who entered the Americas of their own free will after about 1810, the beginning of the era of independence for most Central and South American countries. Therefore, native Americans and African slaves are not considered immigrants, even though their ancestral homes were not in the Americas (the original native Americans came from Asia). Likewise, people belonging to New World colonial powers who actually immigrated are not included because their cultural achievements were part of the national development of the countries to which they pertained; their musical achievements are discussed in Part 3 of this volume. Immigrants, then, in the context of this overview, are people who left their homelands to go to a new country in the Americas that had not been colonized by their ancestors, or to go to a new or another country after its independence. Thus, English people moving to Brazil are considered immigrants, whereas those going to Trinidad are not, until after its independence; French people moving to Chile are immigrants, whereas those going to French Guiana, which remains a department of France, are not; Spaniards going to Argentina before independence were not immigrants, but those going after were; Chileans going to Mexico were immigrants; and so on. Although these constraints seem arbitrary, they limit and help organize this survey.

Immigration basically began after 1850. It flourished until World War II and continues to a lesser degree. Its primary cause was the need for cheap labor in agricultural areas of South America, Central America, Mexico, and the Caribbean. The importation of African slaves provided inexpensive labor after the enslavement of native Americans was discontinued, but it, too, ended after the abolition of slavery in the mid-1800s. Even before emancipation, many countries had begun to import persons from several parts of Asia as indentured workers, drawing many from their colonies on the opposite side of the globe. The British in Trinidad and Guyana (then British Guiana) sought out workers from India; the Dutch in Surinam (then Dutch Guiana, sometimes spelled *Suriname*) brought laborers from Indonesia. Policies of immigration were contracted with governments of other Asian countries, resulting in the importation of workers from China and Japan (including Okinawa). Later, huge numbers of immigrants, including many Jews, came from Europe, especially Croatia,

When people immigrate in large numbers, they usually do at least three things to preserve their cultural identity: organize schools for their children, organize religious organizations, and organize cultural associations that sponsor sports, music, dancing, eating, handicrafts, and other socializing activities.

Germany, Greece, Italy, Lithuania, Poland, Russia, Serbia, and Spain; and sizable numbers came from West Asia, mostly from Lebanon, Syria, and Turkey. The incentive for these people to emigrate was also economic. Most of them came from the lower classes of their societies, and they wanted to elevate their status by making quick money and returning home. Others chose to emigrate because their own countries were overcrowded—another trait that affected personal economic welfare. These latter immigrants tended to stay in the new lands of opportunity. Many of the former stayed because their dreams had not always been based on reality—money was scant, disease caused problems that made returning impossible, marriage to locals created new family obligations, ships were rare, and fares were expensive.

In addition to the immigrants from across the Atlantic and Pacific Oceans, much internal immigration within the Western Hemisphere has occurred because of political turmoil or economic hardship. Many Chileans have immigrated to Mexico and Venezuela, Bolivians to Chile, Argentines to Brazil, Cubans to Panama—and of course multitudes to the United States of America.

Thus, ethnic groups and individuals of diverse national origins in the Caribbean, Central America, Mexico, and especially South America, are many. Overall, they have retained many cultural ways, including music, which often serves as a tool for retaining or teaching cultural identity. When people immigrate in large numbers, they usually do at least three things to preserve their cultural identity: organize schools for their children, with qualified teachers to continue instruction of their native languages (children's songs often serve for teaching language and culture); organize religious organizations and build houses of worship (music is part of traditional worship in most religions); and organize cultural associations that sponsor sports, music, dancing, eating, handicrafts, and other socializing activities.

Below, several of these immigrant groups are discussed by national (rather than ethnic or religious) origin, in the order in which they first arrived in noteworthy numbers. Many cultures are not included only because ethnomusicological research on them is lacking.

CHINA

The importation of indentured workers from China began as early as 1849 in Peru and 1853 in Surinam. By 1872, thousands of Chinese had entered Peru as laborers (Gardiner 1975:6), and about twenty-five hundred Chinese had come to the Dutch colony of present Surinam to work (de Waal Malefijt 1963:22). Roughly 150,000 Chinese, mostly from Canton, immigrated to the Spanish colony of Cuba. After Peru won its independence, Chinese came to the islands off the Peruvian coast to mine their deposits of guano (accumulated droppings from birds, used for fertilizer); they also came to work on the sugar plantations in coastal river oases, and in nitrate mines on the south coast. After 1930, thousands of Chinese workers immigrated to Argentina and Brazil, many from Peru.

After fulfilling their contracts as agricultural laborers, most Chinese moved to urban areas, where they opened laundries, restaurants, and grocery stores. Living near each other and relying on one another to survive persecutions resulting from the "yellow peril" (negative attitudes and oppression of Asians by non-Asians), they created Chinatowns. These became the locales of musical activities, mostly including theatrical presentations of Chinese operas and other forms of entertainment. The main purpose of such musical activities was socialization.

In the 1990s, Chinese musical activities in such urban areas as Buenos Aires, Lima, and São Paulo consist mostly of talent shows and karaoke contests. In number and variety, musical activities have never equaled those of the Chinese living in San Francisco or New York, most probably because of ethnic assimilation and the smaller numbers of Chinese in South America. Both factors resulted from the fact that Chinese immigration to South America and the Caribbean peaked early, leading to assimilation, and never reached the tidal-wave proportions that it did in the United States. Similarly, musical syncretism with European and African forms never materialized for the same reasons. Nevertheless, important musicians—notable not because they are Chinese, but because they are talented—have been of Chinese heritage. In Trinidad, for example, Kim Loy was a famous panman (steel drummer), and Selwyn Ahyoung, whose grandfather was Chinese and grandmother African, had a great future as an ethnomusicologist until his untimely death in 1987.

INDIA

The second immigrant culture to arrive in the New World as agricultural workers came from Calcutta to Surinam in 1873. Urban people, these Indians went straight to plantations to do labor at which they had no experience. Soon, rural people were brought over, and by 1916 more than thirty-four thousand lower-caste Indians had immigrated to Surinam (de Waal Malefijt 1963:23). Similarly, the British sent Hindu indentured servants for work in Trinidad and Guyana. In 1987, roughly 41 percent of the population of Trinidad was of East Indian descent.

Asian influence in the musics of Guyana, Surinam, and Trinidad has been extensive. These immigrants introduced two religions, Hinduism and Islam, and freedom of worship and musical expression has always been possible in the new lands. Singing is the most important medium of Asian Indian musical expression, including songs for festivals, ritual songs for childbirth, marriage, and death, work-related songs, and Hindu *bhajan,* devotional songs (Arya 1968:19–31; Manuel 1995:212).

Musical instruments used by the people of Asian Indian descent include numerous idiophones, membranophones, two chordophones, and an aerophone with a keyboard. The main instruments in the first category are two metal rods (*dantal*), two brass cymbals (*jhānjh*), and two brass cups (*majira*); each set of instruments is concussed (clashed together) to provide rhythmic accompaniment to membranophones. The most common membranophones include two single-headed and closed drums (in the shape of a kettle), one double-headed drum (in the shape of a barrel), and a tambourine. These are the *tassa* and the *nagara* (the kettle-shaped drums), and the *dholak* (the barrel-shaped drum). The *tassa,* played for Islamic festivals, is struck with a stick by men for the Muharram festival, and by women for the Matkor procession (Arya 1968:8). The *nagara* is played with two sticks for weddings and other festivities. The *dholak* is played during weddings. The chordophones include a bowed lute (*sarangi*) and a plucked lute (*tanpura*); as in India, the former is a melodic instrument for classical music, and the latter provides a drone. The most common melodic instrument is the harmonium, a reed organ or multiple single-reed aerophone with keyboard. This is the universal instrument for accompanying *bhajan* songs.

The singing of *bhajan,* Hindu religious songs of praise to God in any of his manifestations or incarnations, is quite common among people of Asian Indian heritage in Guyana, Surinam, and Trinidad. Performances, to the accompaniment of a harmonium, are often social in context.

Muharram or Hosay, a Muslim festival, is celebrated by Hindus in Guyana, Surinam, and Trinidad. It commemorates the martyrdom of the brothers Hasan and Husain, in A.D. 680. Matkor, a festival celebrated in Surinam, celebrates the mother-goddess's embodiment as the earth and other forms (Arya 1968:13).

Classical singing (*tan*) is performed by Asian Indians in Trinidad during their celebrations after wedding rituals, especially the dinner, when hired musicians with beaters (*dantal*), a *dholak,* and a harmonium accompany the singing of *tan* (Manuel 1995:215). This singing is followed by song duels (*picong*-style) and so-called chutney songs, which are danceable and easy to sing.

Asian Indians in the 1990s often maintain cultural contact with India by traveling to the motherland, reading India-oriented books and magazines, watching Indian films, and listening to Indian cassette tapes. At weekend public dances in Trinidad, they first listen to Indian film music, and then begin performing chutney dances, marked by special movements of the pelvis and gestures of the hands and accompanied by beer drinking. In the 1980s, chutney combined with soca (soul calypso) to become chutney-soca, a mixture of Trinidadian modern calypso, sung in Hindi with Indian vocal ornamentations and *dholak* accompaniment. Noted singers of this tradition are Anand Yankaran of Trinidad and Kries Ramkhelawan of Surinam. Rikki Jai and Drupatee Ramgoonai, Trinidadian Indian calypsonians, write popular calypsos with racial and cultural-unity themes. Also in Trinidad, the leader of the famous band known as Amoco Renegades is the Indian-Trinidadian Jit Samaroo (Manuel 1995:219–220). Even before the rise of these musical leaders of Indian heritage, the playing of *tassa* was an important influence in the development of steelband and soca.

JAPAN

Japanese indentured workers first reached Peru in 1899. Many came from Okinawa via Hawaii, where they had gone about thirty years before. The first Japanese workers to enter Peru (including people from Okinawa, politically but not ethnically Japanese) were 790 men who came to work in coastal sugarcane plantations (Morimoto 1979:13–14). Japanese immigration next included Brazil, beginning in June 1908, when 781 people (324 from Okinawa), including 158 families, arrived at the port of Santos to work in the coffee plantations (Ando 1976:138; Fujii and Smith 1959:3). By 1940, people of Japanese ancestry in Peru totaled 17,638, and in Brazil there were about 188,500 Japanese; more than 75 percent of those in rural areas were landowners (Cowles 1971:87). In the 1990s, the largest population of people of Japanese ancestry outside Japan is in Brazil; the second-largest is in the United States (including Hawaii), the third in Peru, the fourth in Canada, and the fifth in Argentina (Gardiner 1975:133). Sizable numbers of Japanese live in Bolivia, Colombia, Ecuador, Mexico, Paraguay, and other countries of the Americas.

The Japanese, like the Chinese, Indians, and Indonesians before them, chose to emigrate from their homelands to become wealthy—a promise usually made by immigration officials. However, wages were low, working conditions difficult, living conditions crowded, diseases rampant, persecution common, and loneliness almost unbearable. An added difficulty in Peru for the Japanese male workers was the initial lack of Japanese women; married men later had their families sent over, and single men married female immigrants, who were often "picture brides" (arranged marriages were based on photos).

In contrast, most Japanese in Brazil were admitted in family groups as colonists and drew strength from family socializing as a means of easing the pressures of being in a new country. Making music and drinking rice wine were two of these social activities. Their music consisted of singing popular songs or folk songs of the day, usually unaccompanied because musical instruments from Japan were rare (Handa 1971:220). The Japanese New Year's festival (O-Bon) and the Japanese emperor's birthday were two celebrations that always included music and dance.

After 1930, Japanese immigration included Argentina and Paraguay (in addition to Brazil and Peru), where colonists introduced new methods of horticulture—growing flowers and citrus. Most immigrants were peasant farmers, many from Okinawa, whose only musical performances had included singing folk and popular songs; by then, however, shamisen (Japanese orthography) and *sanshin* (Okinawan orthography) were available. These were lutes, often made locally from South American wood and local dogskin or imported snakeskin.

In all South American countries, Japanese immigration stopped during World War II. After the war, it remained closed in Peru, but resumed in Brazil in 1951. Additionally, in a program initiated by the U.S. Army, Okinawan immigrants came to Bolivia to establish farms in the Chaco region, east of the Andes; larger numbers came to Argentina and Paraguay. From 1951 to 1970, more than fifty-six thousand Japanese immigrated to Brazil, including many white-collar workers, intellectuals, and trained musicians who had lost their homes to the fires and bombs of the war. These new waves of Japanese immigration led to the performing and teaching of music in urban regions of Brazil and Argentina, most notably in São Paulo, Curitiba, and Londrina in Brazil, and Buenos Aires in Argentina. Japanese musical activity has not developed so strongly in Bolivia, Paraguay, and Peru (Olsen 1980), though acculturated forms such as *karaoke* 'empty orchestra'—recordings of pop and folk songs minus the singer, a type of sing-along to cassette tapes and videos—is extremely popular there, as it is in Argentina and Brazil.

Today, most people of Japanese descent live in urban areas of South America, where musical performance is often a means of socializing and maintaining ethnic identity (Olsen 1983). Many Japanese folk song (*minyō*) clubs have sprung up in the Japanese quarter of São Paulo (Liberdade), in Curitiba, and in Londrina in Brazil; and in Lima, Peru. Clubs dedicated to Okinawan *minyō* and *koten* (classical music) flourish in Buenos Aires, Lima (figure 1), and São Paulo. These organizations hold

FIGURE 1   In the Japanese-Peruvian Cultural Center in Lima, Okinawan-Peruvian women play zithers (*kutu*) and men play lutes (*sanshin*). Photo by Dale A. Olsen, 1979.

In the late 1990s, karaoke singing is the most important medium for maintaining a Japanese identity among the South American people of Japanese ancestry.

rehearsals weekly (when their members gather to drink tea or beer and eat cookies), present concerts, and often compete with each other in contests. Such activities are so well organized in São Paulo that each year's winner receives a trip to Japan and the opportunity to perform in Tokyo and make a recording with a famous Japanese singer. The singing of Japanese folk songs is usually promoted by Japanese cultural centers (São Paulo has two centers, one for Okinawan-Japanese and another for Naichi-Japanese, or ethnic Japanese), where yearly talent shows feature traditional musical, dance, and cultural genres.

The koto (Japanese orthography) and *kutu* (Okinawan orthography, a thirteen-stringed zither), the shamisen and *sanshin* (three-stringed plucked lutes), and the shakuhachi (a notched vertical bamboo flute) are the most popular Japanese classical musical instruments in São Paulo, Brazil, the capital of Japanese musical performance in all of South America, Mexico, Central America, and the Caribbean. These instruments are usually imported from Japan, since classically trained Japanese-Brazilian musicians desire the finest available instruments.

Brazil has several Japanese court-music orchestras (*gagaku* 'elegant music'), all associated with the Tenrikyō religious centers in São Paulo and Baurú, Brazil, where they serve ritual purposes. Tenrikyō, a Japanese religion that developed in the late 1800s, features dance as part of its daily ritual, usually to the accompaniment of koto and bowed shamisen (*kokyū*). Both instruments were manufactured in Brazil in the 1980s (Olsen 1982), but in the 1990s they are imported from Japan. The koto was made from Brazilian woods (especially cedar), and the *kokyū* was constructed from lard cans. Tenrikyō centers in Asunción and Piriapó, Paraguay, have kotos and shamisens donated by the main church in Tenri, Japan.

In São Paulo, Brazil, in the 1990s, classical Japanese music includes *nagauta, katarimono,* and *jiuta* (shamisen or *sangen* traditions); *sōkyoku* (koto tradition); *shakuhachi honkyoku*; *gagaku*; and *nō*. The Ikuta-*ryū* and Yamada-*ryū* styles of playing the koto are represented by teachers who are *nisei,* second-generation residents born overseas to Japanese-born parents. Likewise, both shakuhachi schools, Tozan-*ryū* and Kinko-*ryū*, are taught and performed in São Paulo by *issei*, first-generation residents born in Japan. Students of koto and shakuhachi often include non-Japanese people and adult Japanese of all generations who desire to learn more about their Japanese heritage. Tsuna Iwami (born 21 March 1923 in Tokyo; immigrated to Brazil in 1956) is the most important leader of classical Japanese chamber music in the southern hemisphere of the Americas. He is a master (*iemoto*) in the Kinko-school shakuhachi tradition, with the professional name of Baikyoku V, awarded to him by *iemoto* Araki Kodō IV in 1941 (Olsen 1986). In addition, Tsuna Iwami studied composition in Japan with Kishio Hirao, graduated from the University of Kyōto in chemical engineering and industrial administration, and retired in the early 1990s to continue composing music and making pottery. He has composed in a European postimpressionist idiom, and in the 1990s he has modernized his style, usually fusing shakuhachi and contemporary sounds. He performs widely in Brazil, where he is sought out as a teacher and lecturer.

Most young people of Japanese ancestry in South America have little knowledge of Japanese traditional music, but they are interested in learning about the heritage of their ancestors, especially the language, baseball (*béisbol,* which they claim the Japanese invented, and which they regard as a warrior attribute, *bushido*), and karaoke. The last is popular and is used to teach and maintain Japanese philosophy, morals, and culture. Youths who cannot speak Japanese learn to read and sing in the language by becoming temporary pop singers in the company of their friends. In the late 1990s, karaoke singing is the most important medium for maintaining a Japanese identity among the South American people of Japanese ancestry.

GERMANY

German communities arose especially in Argentina, Brazil, Chile, and Paraguay. Germans immigrated to the first three countries as colonists during open-immigration periods of the late 1800s and early 1900s; in Paraguay, many Germans are Mennonite farmers who received homesteading rights in the Chaco region; and in the 1930s, many German Jews emigrated to escape Nazi-sponsored persecution, and many *Volksdeutsche* (German-speaking Protestants living in Russia) immigrated into Argentina.

The obvious musical-instrument legacy of the immigrant German people is the accordion, of which two forms are found in the southern Americas: the button accordion (*acordeón de butones*) and the piano accordion (*acordeón de teclas*). In Argentina, a variant of the first type is known as *bandoneón*, invented in 1854 by Heinrich Band, after whom it is named. Most of today's accordions are German instruments made by Höhner, a company that manufactures musical instruments in Germany. Sometimes folkloric ensembles use both types, as seen among the German-derived groups on the island of Chiloé, in southern Chile (Yévenez 1980:57). The accordion has found its place in folk and popular music from the *tonada* in Chile to the tango in Argentina.

Additionally, German immigrants introduced dances, including the polka, the schottische, and the waltz. These dances have fused with national types to become the *gato polceado* in Argentina, the *polca* in Paraguay, and the *vals criollo* in Peru.

Germans first immigrated to Chile in the 1840s, when land was granted to them. Today in the southern lake district of Chile, several towns and cities (Valdivia, Osorno, Puerto Varas, and others) have large German-speaking populations. German architecture, breweries, and Lutheran churches abound in this area. Throughout central and southern Chile, the Chilean folklorist and singer Violeta Parra collected many German-influenced songs, especially waltzes.

In the German community of Alto Sampaio in southern Brazil, a singing society (*sociedad de canto*) was the most important cultural organization of the immigrants, "because the German loves to sing, and by singing he or she thematically reproduces German culture" (Flores 1983:256, translated by Dale A. Olsen).

ITALY

Italians constitute the largest immigrant culture in Argentina and make up large numbers of the immigrant population in southern and central Brazil and southern Chile. Although most Italian immigrants to the United States were from southern Italy and Sicily, most Italians who moved to Argentina were from northern Italy, including the border regions between Italy and Austria. For that reason, "the accordion . . . has challenged the guitar as the Argentine's favorite instrument" (Solberg

1966:19), signifying that Germany alone cannot take credit for the introduction of the accordion into Argentina.

Perhaps the most important Italian trait brought to South America is the singing of, and love for, Italian opera and art songs. The popularity of Italian opera in Buenos Aires was influential in the opening of the famous Teatro Colón in 1857. Bellini's *Norma* was first performed in Rio de Janeiro in 1844 (thirteen years after its premiere), and for the next twelve years, that city was the focal point of the Italian "prima donna personality cult" in Brazil (Béhague 1979:112). The popularity of opera among the rubber barons of the Brazilian Amazon led to the construction of an opera house in the city of Manaus; it was completed in 1910, at the end of the rubber boom [see ART MUSIC].

SPAIN

After the Italians, Spaniards (mostly from Galicia) were the second-largest immigrant group in Argentina. Because the national origin of most Argentines is Spanish, the Spanish immigrants had only slight adjustments to make, and upward mobility came quite easily. Many began as common laborers in Buenos Aires (garbage collectors, dock workers, street sweepers), but soon became retailers (Solberg 1966:20). The Spanish have retained their cultural identity, especially in Buenos Aires, where one of the main streets, the Avenida de Mayo, features Spanish *cantinas* (combination bars and coffeehouses) frequented by people who think of themselves as Spanish rather than Argentine.

The music of Argentina owes much to Spanish culture, but in this most European of the South American countries, this debt stems as much from the Spanish of the colonial period as it does from Spanish immigrants. It is not possible, for example, to slice the tango—the national music and dance of Argentina, especially Buenos Aires—into parts and claim that a certain percentage of it is musically a result of Spanish (or Italian) immigration. Perhaps it is wiser to view the tango as a musical product of common Spanish laborers who worked the docks of Buenos Aires. In any event, the concept of cultural identity through music, where the immigrants are of the same heritage as the colonists, is not so easily defined as that of persons who look and speak differently from those of the dominant culture.

CHILE

During the early years of the Chilean coup d'état (from September 1973), when President Allende was murdered and General Pinochet became the military dictator, many supporters of the deposed government—including musicians and artists—fled, fearing persecution and death. Because panpipes (*siku*), notch flutes (*quena*), and small guitars (*charango*) were featured in the protest movement called *nueva canción* 'new song', Pinochet made their playing unlawful. Other acts of oppression followed. The folksinger-guitarist-composer-poet Victor Jara was tortured and murdered. Jorge Peña, conductor of the children's orchestra in La Serena, was murdered because he had taken his orchestra on a tour to Cuba. In response, many Chilean musicians left for Brazil, Mexico, Venezuela, and elsewhere, especially Europe and the United States. Symphonic musicians left Santiago and joined orchestras in other cities outside Chile, such as Mexico City and San José, Costa Rica. Musicians such as Ángel and Isabel Parra fled to Mexico, where they continued to perform, compose, and record their music. The musical impact of Chilean immigrants since 1973 has been felt as far away as Paris, Rome, San Francisco, and Tokyo.

OUT-MIGRATION

The migration of people out of their homelands to other areas is emigration, or out-migration. It is caused by overt political oppression, as experienced in Chile in the

1970s, or by covert political oppression (when people are not recognized as political refugees), as experienced by thousands of Mayan people who fled political and economic oppression and death in Guatemala during the 1980s and 1990s, and have established new communities in Indiantown, Florida, and parts of southern California. In Indiantown, the Maya have continued their religious beliefs and lifestyles, replete with marimba music and song, in country settings reminiscent of their rural habitats in Guatemala. Although these out-migrations are recent, others happened shortly after independence and the abolition of slavery in the Americas and included Afro-Brazilians returning to Angola and African-Americans returning to Liberia. The out-migration of Cubans to Miami, New York, and elsewhere in the United States is another example of politically motivated movement, whereas the out-migration of Puerto Ricans to New York and Hawaii, and of Haitians to Miami and New York are examples of economically motivated movement. The out-migration of people from Mexico and every country in South America, Central America, and the Caribbean has deeply affected the music of the United States, and to a lesser degree other wealthy countries of the world where policies on immigration have been open.

REFERENCES

Ando, Zenpati. 1976. *Estudos Socio-Históricos da Imigração Japonesa.* São Paulo: Centro de Estudos Nipo-Brasileiros.

Arya, Usharbudh. 1968. *Ritual Songs and Folksongs of the Hindus of Surinam.* Leiden: E. J. Brill.

Béhague, Gerard. 1979. *Music in Latin America, an Introduction.* Englewood Cliffs, N. J.: Prentice-Hall.

de Waal Malefijt, Annemarie. 1963. *The Javanese of Surinam: Segment of a Plural Society.* Amsterdam: Royal Van Gorcum.

Flores, Hilda Agnes Hübner. 1983. *Canção dos Imigrantes.* Porto Alegre, Brazil: Escola Superior de Teologia São Lourenço de Brindes / Universidade de Caxias do Sul.

Fujii, Yukio, and T. Lynn Smith. 1959. *The Acculturation of the Japanese Immigrants in Brazil.* Gainesville: University of Florida Press.

Handa, Tomoo. 1971. "Senso Estético na Vida dos Imigrantes Japoneses." In *O Japonês em São Paulo e no Brasil,* 220–236. São Paulo: Centro de Estudos Nipo-Brasileiros.

———. 1980. *Memorias de un Imigrante Japonês no Brasil.* São Paulo: Centro de Estudos Nipo-Brasileiros.

Manuel, Peter. 1995. *Caribbean Currents.* Philadelphia: Temple University Press.

Olsen, Dale A. 1980. "Japanese Music in Peru." *Asian Music* 11(2):41–51.

———. 1982. "Japanese Music in Brazil." *Asian Music* 14(1):111–131.

———. 1983. "The Social Determinants of Japanese Musical Life in Peru and Brazil." *Ethnomusicology* 27(1):49–70.

———. 1986. "A Japanese Master Musician in a Brazilian Context." *Hôgaku* 2(2):19–30.

Solberg, Carl Edward. 1966. "The Response to Immigration in Argentina and Chile, 1890–1914." Ph.D. dissertation, Stanford University.

Yévenez S., Enrique. 1980. *Chile—Proyección Folklorica.* Santiago: Edward W. Leonard.

Popular Music: An Introduction
Gage Averill

Issues in Popular Music
Popular Musics Abroad

During the twentieth century, the world was blanketed by mass media and electronic communications while populations all over the globe experienced intense social and cultural changes, variously labeled Westernization, modernization, urbanization, secularization, industrialization, commercialization, and commodification. Mutually reinforcing, these processes overlapped in ways that made them potent constitutive forces of life.

New musics evolved in response to particular constellations of these processes. They arose from, and were marketed to, a mass audience of consumers (Manuel 1988). Most of them blended local and traditional forms with imported, usually Western, norms. Their classification under the rubric *popular* (or just *pop*) emphasizes their mass appeal and mass mediation, and distinguishes them from preexisting conceptual categories: folk (the orally transmitted musics of peasants) and art (the written musics of churches, courts, and elites). Musics dubbed popular typically function as entertainment in a variety of urban contexts: bars, bordellos, dance halls, hotels, clubs, restaurants, and streets. Most of them serve to accompany social dancing; hence, much of their persuasive power ties in with the pleasurable involvement of the body in motion. As broadcast media and personal sound systems have invaded homes and workplaces, popular musics have become pervasive in leisure and work. In day-to-day living, much of their impact is in the reassuring sonic presence of a familiar background noise.

Labels such as *folk, art,* and *popular* represent clusters of characteristics and do not define a rigid and universal scheme of classification. Popular styles typically share several traits. They are usually urban, mass-mediated, commodified (reproduced and commercially marketed), syncretic, rapidly obsolescent (though hits may be nostalgically preserved as markers of certain periods), and accessible (not overly demanding of listeners).

ISSUES IN POPULAR MUSIC

In Mexico, Central and South America, and the Caribbean, important developments in popular musics occurred during periods of rapid social change, such as emancipation and national independence. In particular, independence correlated with consolidations of popular genres, which national governments exploited to symbolize their nations-in-formation. At the New York World's Fair of 1964–1965, a newly independent Jamaica highlighted in its pavilion one such emergent genre, ska. In the 1960s, Trinidad and Tobago, also newly independent, installed steelbands in the country's schools. Popular movements, not political authorities, have sometimes connected popular music to national or ethnic identity: thus, in Martinique and Guadeloupe, where local identity often conflicts uneasily with French departmental status, *zouk* emerged as a symbol of residual locality (Guilbault 1993).

Popular music has served many political causes and movements in Mexico, Central and South America, and the Caribbean. Organizations and individuals have used pieces and styles to symbolize political affiliation, as in the Dominican Republic in the 1930s and 1940s, when Rafael Trujillo used merengues for campaign music and as symbols of his presidency (Austerlitz 1996). Governments have censored commercial artists, as in Brazil under the military dictatorship of the 1970s, and patronized sympathetic ones, as in Cuba since 1959. Opposition movements have used topical and critical popular musics as organizing tools and rallying cries, as in Chile in the late 1960s and early 1970s. Oppressed social classes have used popular music as part of the cultural fabric of resistance, as in Jamaica in the 1960s and 1970s. Dictators have offered dance music to the masses as a palliative in lieu of fundamental social change, as in Haiti in the 1960s. However, popular music achieves the desired political goals only if it functions effectively as entertainment.

Though some lay writers, including Barrow (1993), Gerard and Sheller (1989), and McGowan and Pessanha (1991), describe the general history and style of popular musics of the region, most scholarly works engage with more specific sets of issues, even if merely to assert that popular musics and their texts serve as windows into local culture, worldview, and ethos, especially with otherwise "silent" or disadvantaged social groups. The identification of African retentions, an early concern in popular-music research, is still an abiding issue (Liverpool 1993; Roberts 1974), though perhaps not to the same degree as in studies of the traditional music of the region. Perhaps the most fruitful line of investigation since the 1980s is concerned with how popular musics express social identity and stratification, and how they articulate differences in class, race, religion, gender, age, ethnicity, and geography (Austerlitz 1996; Averill 1989; Béhague 1994; Crook 1993; Hebdige 1987; Pacini Hernández 1995; Stuempfle 1995). The relationship of popular music to the political realm, including electoral politics, nation-state control, hegemony, and popular resistance, has inspired an increasing number of works (Averill 1997; Manuel 1991; Waters 1985). Biographical studies explain the influence of charismatic superstars such as Bob Marley, Carlos Gardel, the Mighty Sparrow, and how they have helped define and coalesce style, ethos, ideology, and identity (Collier 1990; White 1989). How new technologies, commercial-music industries, and the global flows of popular musics have affected local musical sounds and structures is of primary importance to Guilbault (1993), Hill (1993), and Wallis and Malm (1984), but the same questions crop up widely in the literature.

POPULAR MUSICS ABROAD

Popular musics of South America and the Caribbean—calypso, mambo, reggae, salsa, samba, steelband, tango, and many other genres—have competed in markets around the world, where they have influenced local trajectories of musical development (Roberts 1985 [1979]). For example, in the 1940s, Cuban music contributed to Congolese dance music, later called *soukous*. Numerous crazes for Latin American and Caribbean musics have affected European-American pop markets and figure prominently in the popularity of international musics currently marketed as world-beat.

Popular genres have helped attract and entertain tourists. As patrons of popular music, tourist bureaus and hotels have sponsored festivals, such as Reggae Sunsplash in Jamaica, and the Cartegena Festival in Colombia. In Brazil, Trinidad, Haiti, Cuba, and other countries, carnival serves a dual role as popular expression and tourist spectacle. In tailoring popular musics to foreign markets and tourists' expectations, promoters and industries have marketed tropical fantasies in exotic music, exemplified by the lambada craze of the late 1980s, but also visible in the early-twentieth-century fads for tango and maxixe.

Responding to the needs of audiences, strategies for marketing, and the world-views of populations, musicians have continued to interject enough meaningful content into music to make popular styles an integral part of emerging national identities in Mexico, Central and South America, and the Caribbean.

REFERENCES

Austerlitz, Paul. 1996. *Merengue: Dominican Music and Dominican Identity*. Philadelphia: Temple University Press.

Averill, Gage. 1989. "Haitian Dance Bands, 1915–1970: Class, Race, and Authenticity." *Latin American Music Review* 10(2):203–235.

———. 1997. *A Day for the Hunter, a Day for the Prey: Popular Music and Power in Haiti*. Chicago: University of Chicago Press.

Barrow, Steve. 1993. *Tougher than Tough: The Story of Jamaican Music*. Mango Records (Island Records), 400 Lafayette St., New York NY 10003. 4 compact discs and book.

Béhague, Gerard H., ed. 1994. *Music and Black Ethnicity: The Caribbean and South America*. Miami: North-South Center, University of Miami.

Collier, Simon. 1990. *The Life, Music, and Times of Carlos Gardel*. Pittsburgh: University of Pittsburgh Press.

Crook, Larry. 1993. "Black Consciousness, *Samba Reggae,* and the Re-Africanization of Bahian Carnival Music in Brazil." *The World of Music* 35(2):90–108.

Gerard, Charlie, and Marty Sheller. 1989. *Salsa: The Rhythm of Latin Music*. Crown Point, Ind.: White Cliffs Media.

Glasser, Ruth. 1995. *My Music Is My Flag: Puerto Rican Musicians and Their New York Communities, 1917–1940*. Berkeley: University of California Press.

Guilbault, Jocelyne, with Gage Averill et al. 1993. *Zouk: World Music in the West Indies*. Chicago and London: University of Chicago Press.

Hebdige, Dick. 1987. *Cut 'n' Mix: Culture, Identity, and Caribbean Music*. London: Methuen.

Hill, Donald R. 1993. *Calypso Calaloo: Early Carnival Music in Trinidad*. Gainesville: University Press of Florida.

Liverpool, Hollis Urban. 1993. "Rituals of Power and Rebellion: The Carnival Tradition in Trinidad and Tobago." Ph.D. dissertation, University of Michigan.

Manuel, Peter. 1988. *Popular Musics of the Non-Western World: An Introductory Survey*. New York: Oxford University Press.

———, ed. 1991. *Essays on Cuban Music: North American and Cuban Perspectives*. Lanham, New York, London: University Press of America.

McGowan, Chris, and Ricardo Pessanha. 1991. *The Brazilian Sound: Samba, Bossa Nova, and the Popular Music of Brazil*. New York: Billboard Books.

Pacini Hernández, Deborah. 1995. *Bachata: A Social History as a Dominican Popular Music*. Philadelphia: Temple University Press.

Roberts, John Storm. 1974. *Black Music of Two Worlds*. New York: Morrow.

———. 1985 [1979]. *The Latin Tinge: The Impact of Latin American Music on the United States*. Tivoli, N. Y.: Original Music.

Stuempfle, Stephen. 1995. *The Steelband Movement: The Forging of a National Art in Trinidad and Tobago*. Philadelphia: University of Pennsylvania Press.

Wallis, Roger, and Krister Malm. 1984. *Big Sounds from Small Peoples: The Music Industry in Small Countries*. New York: Pendragon Press.

Waters, Anita M. 1985. *Race Class and Political Symbols: Rastafari and Reggae in Jamaican Politics*. New Brunswick, N. J. and London: Transaction Publishers.

White, Timothy. 1989. *Catch a Fire: The Life of Bob Marley*. New York: Henry Holt.

Popular Music in the English-, French-, and Creole-Speaking Caribbean
Gage Averill

Anglophone Areas
Francophone Areas

One can speak of the English- and French- (Creole-) speaking islands together partly because of what they are not: they are not, in general, part of the sphere of Iberian cultural influence that includes Latin America, Central America, Cuba, and the Dominican Republic. The French and British colonies had a much higher ratio of African slaves and free blacks to European colonists than did most of their Spanish counterparts, and consequently, neo-African culture and European-African syncretisms are more evident.

The popular musics of the English-speaking and the Creole-speaking West Indies (Jamaica, Haiti, Trinidad and Tobago, the Bahamas, the Lesser Antilles) share some notable traits. They are highly syncretic forms with African and European secular antecedents, and they were developed by and for a largely lower-class Afro-Caribbean population. Because many of the English-speaking Lesser Antilles changed hands often during the colonial period, the islands reveal cultural influences from Great Britain and France, and much cross-fertilization occurred among the popular musics of these islands in the twentieth century.

As studies (Abrahams 1983; Guilbault 1985; McDaniel 1986) have shown, the Lesser Antilles retain vibrant traditional cultures, and some have produced dynamic popular forms. Nevertheless, the larger islands (Trinidad, Jamaica, Haiti, the French Antilles) have dominated the region culturally, especially since the arrival of commercial recordings and broadcast technologies. Genres originating on these islands—Trinidadian calypso, steelband, and soca; Jamaican ska, reggae, and dance hall; Haitian merengue, *konpa*, and roots music (*mizik rasin*), French Antillean beguine and *zouk*—have colonized other islands and foreign markets.

ANGLOPHONE AREAS

Trinidad and Tobago

In Trinidad, carnival was the main occasion for the performance and development of popular musics. Calypso, a topical genre called *cariso* in some nineteenth-century accounts, was sung by *chantwells,* a widespread term for singers in the Creole Caribbean (Cowley 1996). The transition from Creole to English song texts took

Steelbands have roots in the road march of carnival in Trinidad. Steelbands are now based in countries all over the globe, and pans are increasingly found in ensembles other than steelbands, such as jazz combos.

place in the decades at the start of the 1900s; at about the same time, the English term *calypsonian* replaced *chantwell*. The first commercial venues for calypso were tents, where calypsonians engaged in extemporized verbal duels (*picong*), and performed topical songs to the accompaniment of Venezuelan-style string bands. Early calypsoes used scales based on modes (locally called minor keys). Each took its name from the starting solfège note of the mode: *mi* minor, *re* minor, and *la* minor were most common. Later, especially after 1930, most calypsoes were composed in major tonality. Old calypsoes preserved vestiges of Creole, especially the formulaic cadential phrase *sandimanité,* from the French *sans humanité* 'without pity'.

Recordings of calypsonians were first made in 1914 by the Victor Gramophone Company (Warner 1985:22). Sporadic interest in calypso by multinational record companies has resulted in international releases by calypsonians such as Lord Invader, Lord Executor, Atilla the Hun, Roaring Lion, Mighty Sparrow, Mighty Chalkdust, and others (for a discussion of recorded calypsoes, see Hill 1993). Calypso's limited success in foreign markets may reflect partly the specificity of its lyrics to local political and social realities (including wordplay and allusion), and in part its near-total immersion in carnival.

In the 1970s, the rise of soca, a style of party-dance calypso influenced by American funk and soul, loosened musicians' reliance on carnival, and shifted the primary venue of musical performance to recording studios, often in the Trinidadian diaspora, especially Brooklyn, New York. Soca singers from other islands, such as Arrow (Montserrat) and Swallow (Antigua), achieved market success, though nationalistic restrictions prevented them from singing in Trinidadian carnival. Soca bands feature wind sections (saxophones, trumpets, trombones), synthesizers, electric guitars, electric bass, and trap drums, with strong bass-drum accents on downbeats, and lyrics that typically eschew topical themes in favor of a party ambience. The involvement of East Indians in Trinidadian popular musics has led to a variety of hybrid styles, such as chutney-soca, and youth-culture fusions with Jamaican dance hall and American rap (ragga and other genres) are common.

Steelbands

Steelbands have roots in the road march of carnival in Trinidad. Starting in the 1800s as neo-African percussion ensembles, road-march bands were restructured after the 1884 Peace Preservation Ordinance, as part of a long-standing campaign against lower-class and African cultural influence in carnival (Liverpool 1993), banned drumming, stick fighting (*kalenda*), and the brandishing of burning cane (*kanboulay*). Tamboo-bamboo bands, which resulted, featured percussive and concussive lengths of bamboo, progressively augmented by metallic devices (dust bins, pots, brake drums). In 1937, the vogue for metal sounds reached a peak with the appearance of an all-steel band (Alexander's Ragtime Band). In the 1940s, a series of innovations led to the development of tuned, sunken, multipitched oil drums (pans), which tuners elaborated into discrete pitch sets: twelve-basses, six-basses, tenor-basses, cellos, guitars, quads, double seconds, double tenors, and tenors or leads form the basic contemporary ensemble. In each band, a percussion section (the "engine room") featured trap drums, brake drums, and miscellaneous instruments.

At first, the social organization of the bands involved gangs of lower-class boys, "bad johns," the violence of whose confrontations triggered repressive measures from the authorities. In 1949, the government addressed the problem in a study, and in 1950 organized the Steel Band Association. In 1951, the tour of TASPO (Trinidad All-Steel Percussion Orchestra) to Britain raised the status of steelband as an indigenous orchestra. In the 1960s, the integration of pan into the school curriculum and the inception of prestigious competitions (Steelband Music Festival, Panorama) domesticated the bands' rivalries (Stuempfle 1995).

Steelbands spread quickly through the English-speaking eastern Caribbean. Recordings from the late 1950s and the 1960s featured bands from Antigua, Anguilla, St. Kitts, Barbados, and Nevis, where bands entertained tourists and accompanied limbo dances. Steelbands are now based in countries all over the globe, and pans are increasingly found in ensembles other than steelbands, such as jazz combos.

Jamaica

Jamaican popular music was influenced in its earliest phase by Trinidadian calypso, which bore a familial resemblance to mento, a Jamaican genre. In addition to "social bands," which performed mento and calypso, the popularity of American swing led to Jamaican big bands, the road bands. Sound-system operators (playing in the 1950s for "blue dances") specialized in imported rhythm-and-blues dance tunes on 45-rpm records—a style of music also heard on Radio Jamaica and Rediffusion (RJR), and on WINZ in Miami. These operators, such as Clement Dodd ("Sir Coxsone") and Duke Reid, competed on the strength of their systems and on the size and currency of their collections. Among the first to record local musicians, they formed the backbone of a local recording industry (Johnson and Pines 1982).

Locally, rhythm and blues developed an exaggerated backbeat and a quick tempo. This offshoot, ska, emerged in the years surrounding independence (1962); the classic studio-ska band, the Skatalites, was born in 1963. In the latter half of the 1960s, vocal ska recordings lionized ghetto street culture, known as "rudeness." Popular music became slower, and the bass and the drums rose to prominence. The newer sound, rock steady, was the immediate precursor of reggae. The influence of Rastafarianism on the lower class, especially among musicians, showed clearly, not only in aural texture (identified as "dread sound") but also in a preoccupation with biblical imagery and millenarian prophecy. Even non-Rastafarian performers widely copied Rastafarian beliefs, life-styles, and patterns of speaking (for a discussion of rastas, reggae, and politics in Jamaica, see Waters 1985).

"Catch a Fire" and "Burning," releases by Bob Marley and the Wailers, exported reggae to the world. Marley's synthesis of revolutionary ideology and Rastafarian spirituality appealed to disenfranchised peoples, especially those in the English-speaking Caribbean (White 1989). Among Caribbean youths from Trinidad to the Virgin Islands, reggae promoted "dread talk," the colloquial Rastafarian version of Jamaican patois. Jamaicans living in London exposed English youths to ska and reggae, and in London pubs there developed a parallel ska-reggae scene that appealed strongly to British punks (Hebdige 1987), inspiring two-tone, an antiracist movement and music, uniting black and white musicians.

Reggae's success in the United States and the United Kingdom—which included reggae-style hits for the Rolling Stones, Eric Clapton, the Beatles, Debby Harry, and others—inaugurated a new category of music for radio formats, record-store bins, and *Billboard* charts. At first called reggae, this category was later expanded to world-beat. The latter category testifies to the role of reggae in opening up European-American markets.

Jamaican artists on the island and abroad have made substantial contributions to the technology of popular music worldwide through their pioneering efforts to develop dub tracks and versions (with some original tracks deleted and new tracks superimposed) and their extensive use of sampling. Jamaican styles of chanted poetry to musical accompaniment—which include toasting, dub poetry, dance hall, and ragga—have influenced North American rap and hip-hop vocals and have found a substantial niche in world markets.

FRANCOPHONE AREAS

The Haitian *méringue* (Creole *mereng*) and its cousin, the St. Lucian and Martinican beguine (*béguine*) are syncretic couple dances descended from French courtly dances (contredanse and quadrille) and Kongo social dances, such as the *kalenda* and the *chica* (Fouchard 1988:19, Rosemain 1986:798). On both islands, elites patronized parlor and (in the twentieth century) jazz-band versions of their national dances. The parlor *méringue* is also called the *méringue lant* 'slow *méringue*'.

In the 1940s and 1950s, the major development in *méringue* was the fusion with Vodou rhythms in the hands of *négritude*-influenced composers, to produce the genre Vodou-jazz, popularized by the band Jazz des Jeunes (Averill 1989, 1997). But the most commercially significant development in Haitian dance music in the 1950s was the creation of *konpa-dirèk,* a new kind of *méringue,* patterned on the merengue of the Dominican Republic. The Ensemble Nemours Jean-Baptiste and the Ensemble Wébert Sicot made this dance the first commercially successful Creole popular music. In the 1960s, it was adapted for *mini-djaz,* rock-style ensembles (such as Shleu Shleu, Les Fantaisistes du Carrefour, Tabou Combo, and Les Difficiles de Pétion-Ville). These groups performed in Haiti and the Haitian diaspora (chiefly New York).

In the 1970s, musicians in Martinique, Guadeloupe, and Dominica adapted the *konpa* to produce the Antillean *kadans.* The late 1970s and early 1980s was a period in which *konpa,* calypso, and *kadans* influenced each other, drawing liberally from American funk and soul. In Dominica, the group Exile One created a hybrid, *kadans-lypso.* In France in the early 1980s, musicians from Martinique and Guadeloupe put together a dance music based on *kadans,* but with a high-tech sound (from multiple synthesizers) and Antillean rhythms. They called their band Kassav'; and their music, *zouk* (a Creole word for "party"). Within a few years, *zouk* became the dominant style of dancing in Martinique and Guadeloupe, and was among a handful of popular African and Caribbean dance musics in Paris. It even developed subgenres: *zouk*-love (light pieces, on romantic themes) and *zouk*-hard (upbeat tunes, on various themes) (Guilbault with Averill et al. 1993).

In Paris, French Antillean musicians absorb influences from an international community, utilize French technology to modernize their music, and reach an affluent "ethnic" market. In their respective diasporas, Caribbean musicians find potential crossover audiences for their music and a base for penetrating multinational markets.

REFERENCES

Abrahams, Roger D. 1983. *The Man-of-Words in the West Indies: Performance and the Emergence of Creole Culture.* Baltimore: Johns Hopkins University Press.

Averill, Gage. 1989. "Haitian Dance Bands, 1915–1970: Class, Race, and Authenticity." *Latin American Music Review* 10(2):203–235.

———. 1997. *A Day for the Hunter, a Day for the Prey: Popular Music and Power in Haiti.* Chicago: University of Chicago Press.

Cowley, John. 1996. *Carnival, Canboulay and Calypso: Traditions in the Making.* Cambridge: Cambridge University Press.

Fouchard, Jean. 1988. La Méringue, Danse Nationale d'Haïti. Port-au-Prince: Editions Henri Deschamps.

Guilbault, Jocelyne. 1985. "St. Lucian Kwadril Evening." *Latin American Music Review* 6(1):31–57.

Guilbault, Jocelyne, with Gage Averill et al. 1993. *Zouk: World Music in the West Indies.* Chicago: University of Chicago Press.

Hebdige, Dick. 1987. *Cut 'n' Mix: Culture, Identity and Caribbean Music.* London: Methuen.

Johnson, Howard, and Jim Pines. 1982. *Reggae: Deep Roots Music.* London: Proteus.

Hill, Donald. 1993. *Calypso Calaloo: Early Carnival Music in Trinidad.* Gainesville: University Press of Florida.

Liverpool, Hollis Urban. 1993. "Rituals of Power and Rebellion: The Carnival Tradition in Trinidad and Tobago." Ph.D. dissertation, University of Michigan.

McDaniel, Lorna. 1986. "Praisesongs for Rememory: The Big Drum of Carriacou and Rituals of the Caribbean." Ph.D. dissertation, University of Michigan.

Rosemain, Jacqueline. 1986. *La Musique dans la Société Antillaise, 1635–1902: Martinique Guadeloupe.* Paris: Editions L'Harmattan.

Stuempfle, Stephen. 1995. *The Steelband Movement: The Forging of a National Art in Trinidad and Tobago.* Philadelphia: University of Pennsylvania Press.

Wallis, Roger, and Krister Malm. 1984. *Big Sounds from Small Peoples: The Music Industry in Small Countries.* New York: Pendragon Press.

Warner, Keith Q. 1985. *Kaiso! The Trinidad Calypso: A Study of the Calypso as Oral Literature.* Washington: Three Continents Press.

Waters, Anita M. 1985. *Race Class and Political Symbols: Rastafari and Reggae in Jamaican Politics.* New Brunswick, N.J., and London: Transaction Publishers.

White, Timothy. 1989. *Catch a Fire: The Life of Bob Marley.* New York: Henry Holt.

Popular Music of the Spanish-Speaking Regions

Deborah Pacini Hernández

Transnational Influences
The Genres of Spanish-American Pop
Musicians' Social Backgrounds
Views from Outside the Region

Spanish-American popular musics are hybrids resulting from blending processes known as creolization, *mestizaje*, and syncretism, which developed in response to the encounter of European, Amerindian, and African cultures. Borrowing and blending have continued to enrich Spanish-American popular musics, most of which draw simultaneously from antecedent folkloric genres (themselves products of cultural blends) and contemporaneous popular musics.

Since the nature and extent of these musical changes typically reflect concurrent processes of social change, Spanish-American popular musics are valuable windows into the realities of the regions from which they have emerged. Useful as these musics may be for such analyses, however, their primary function is, and has always been recreational, whether for dancing, courtship, storytelling, or displaying artistic skill.

The historical trajectories of Spanish-American popular musics have been bound up with regional-cultural demographics and socioeconomic-political conditions, the processes of migration and urbanization, and the development of recording and broadcast technologies. In the early twentieth century, especially in urban areas, where people of European descent (who controlled musical production and dissemination) resided in greater proportions, the musical practices and aesthetics of popular music closely imitated prevailing European styles. Some European-derived musical traditions—contredanse, mazurka, polka, waltz—survive, though they have been creolized, like the local variations of the polka and the waltz that continue to flourish from Mexico to Paraguay.

In contrast, in rural areas (more heavily populated by people of African and/or Amerindian descent), musics were able to persist or develop according to traditional patterns, with little metropolitan interference. In public discourse, musics more informed by European aesthetics (like the Puerto Rican *danza* and the Cuban *contradanza*) were valued more highly than those with conspicuous Amerindian or African roots. However, in situations where nationalistic or indigenistic ideologies called for the rejection of anything associated with colonial powers, the latter musics (such as the African-Cuban rumba and the Chilean *cueca*) were celebrated as indigenous cultural expressions.

Urban migrations, which accelerated throughout the twentieth century, have increased the racial, ethnic, and cultural mix in cities, where various rural and urban forms came into closer contact, eventually resulting in the transformation of both. The direction of influence has always been two-way: migrants have inserted rural forms into urban areas, while returning migrants and the mass media have disseminated urban forms to provincial towns and cities. Early in the twentieth century, two originally urban genres—the Peruvian *vals criollo* and its close relative, the Ecuadorian *pasillo*—persisted as the popular music of choice in rural areas long after having been displaced by newer forms in these countries' capitals.

TRANSNATIONAL INFLUENCES

Many contemporary popular genres remain identified with the country whose root genre provided its framework (like the merengue of the Dominican Republic, the *cumbia* of Colombia, the *son* of Cuba), but most have been influenced by musics from beyond national borders. The extent of outside influences relates to the degree of linguistic and cultural commonalities shared by lenders and borrowers, but recording, broadcasting, and film have played important roles in expanding the pool of resources from which musicians have drawn; in particular, Cuba and Mexico have been important exporters of popular music styles to the rest of Latin America.

International migration has played a significant role in musical change by bringing musicians and audiences into direct contact with musical sources. In these cases, transformations have occurred far from the region where a music originated, as salsa has emerged in New York and the tango has become legitimate in Paris (Roberts 1985 [1979]).

Borrowing and blending have been more pronounced where similarities between old and new styles or instrumentation have facilitated transitions. For example, the single-reed sound of the European clarinet nicely replaced the indigenous single-reed *gaita* in the 1930s, when Colombian *cumbia* was modernized.

Sometimes outside influences have been limited and have not significantly changed the overall sound of a musical style; for example, the electric bass has been added to many otherwise still traditional ensembles. In other cases, borrowing has been extensive and sometimes less predictable; for example, in the 1970s, second-generation Andean migrants to Lima, Peru, creolized the Colombian *cumbia* by combining *cumbia* rhythms with highland *huayno* melodies, producing *chicha*, a distinctly Peruvian variant of *cumbia* (Turino 1990).

The evolution of Spanish-American popular musics has been characterized by incrementation and substitution; new forms have not always replaced preceding ones. Traditional and modern forms of a given genre, and a range of intermediate ones, can coexist with equal vigor, albeit with varying levels of commercial success (Manuel 1988): the Cuban *son* is still played by traditional guitar trios, by contemporary brass and percussion-based ensembles (*conjuntos*), and by jazz ensembles. Though distance from cities may partially explain the persistence of older rural forms, these musics, like their more modern and commercially lucrative counterparts, are recorded and disseminated through the mass media.

THE GENRES OF SPANISH-AMERICAN POP

The mixture of tradition and innovation characterizes Hispanic America's popular-music landscape, ranging from only slightly modernized but often mass-mediated versions of such regionally based genres as Mexico's *corridos* and *rancheras,* to a country-specific commercial music such as the Dominican Republic's merengue (Austerlitz 1996), Argentina's tango, and Peru's *huayno* (Turino 1993), to thoroughly transnational contemporary music styles such as salsa, *balada, rock en español, nueva canción,* and *cumbia.*

On the basis of record sales alone, popular musics with international projections (such as *balada*) would be considered most significant. National and locally based genres, however, have played far more consequential roles not only as sources for cross-fertilization but also as key symbols of national, regional, class, racial, gender, or political identities. As these musics are treated in other entries, the focus here is on transnational genres that might be omitted as foreign (such as rock or *balada*); or their connections with similar music in other Spanish American countries might not be articulated (such as salsa, *cumbia*, or *nueva canción*).

Salsa

Rooted in Cuban *son*, salsa has become so internationalized that it can no longer be associated with any one country (Boggs 1992; Manuel 1995, Rondón 1980). Beginning in the 1960s, Puerto Ricans and other Hispanic Caribbeans living in New York City modernized and transformed the *son* by paring down ensembles, combining elements of jazz, and using urban-oriented lyrics.

The term *salsa* distinguished it commercially from its Cuban predecessor, though musicians and audiences have always acknowledged its connections with *son*. New York has served as salsa's commercial center, but several Spanish-American countries have competed with New York: ensembles such as Oscar D'Leon of Venezuela and Grupo Niche of Colombia have the attention of an international salsa-loving public.

Music that elsewhere might be called salsa is still produced in Cuba, though locals reject the term as a U.S.-derived commercial name. In many parts of Spanish-speaking America, salsa often falls under the rubric *música tropical*, which includes other African-Caribbean dance musics, particularly *cumbia* and merengue.

Cumbia

In the 1800s, the traditional *cumbia* emerged among mixed African and Amerindian populations along the Caribbean coasts of Colombia. In the 1940s, coastal *cumbias* with strongly African-derived rhythms were adapted to large urban bands (*orquestas*), and recordings by performers like Pacho Galán and Lucho Bermúdez received international attention.

Today, *cumbia* is immensely popular throughout Latin America's Pacific-rim regions from Chile to Central America and Mexico, especially among consumers of Amerindian descent. In Mexico, it is so widespread it is considered Mexican rather than Colombian music; in Peru, *cumbia Andina* has become a distinct variant known as *chicha*.

In Colombia itself, most *cumbias* produced after 1970 were targeted at Central American audiences rather than coastal Colombian ones. These *cumbias* have lost their African flavor and are rejected by coastal Colombians as *cumbias del interior* (highland *cumbias*). However, a new generation of Colombian musicians (including Joe Arroyo) are producing *cumbias* with more pronounced African-derived rhythms and vocal styling (Pacini Hernández 1992).

Balada

The *balada*, commercially called Latin pop, can be considered the continuation of a long-standing pan-Hispanic tradition of guitar-based romantic song (including the *canción* and the *bolero*). In the 1960s, slickly produced romantic music by the Spanish singer Rafael emphasized sophisticated production and lush, densely textured arrangements, setting a new standard for romantic song. The frank eroticism of the texts challenged the sexual repression imposed by General Francisco Franco (Spanish head of state, 1936–1975).

Spanish-American romantic singers who adopted the sound of *baladas* in the 1970s found that upwardly aspiring urban middle-class audiences throughout the hemisphere increasingly preferred *balada*'s interpretations of modern romance to those expressed in older romantic musics. Male singers and points of view predominate; yet *baladas* suggest the more sensitive, emotional side of men, clearly appealing to women, *balada*'s most important consumers.

Since the 1980s, *balada* has become the most widely consumed and commercially successful music in Spanish America. The most famous *balada* superstars are the Spaniard Julio Iglesias and the Brazilian Roberto Carlos, but almost every Spanish-American country has an internationally known *balada* star, including Venezuela's José Luís Rodríguez (El Puma), Mexico's José José, and Argentina's Sandro. Since the mid-1980s, more and more singers formerly associated with *nueva canción* (such as Venezuela's Soledad Bravo and Puerto Rico's Danny Rivera) have been recording in the style of *baladas,* though they reject songs expressing coarse machismo and female subservience, which sometimes characterize *balada*.

Nueva canción

The neofolk-protest music known as *nueva canción* 'new song' is pan-Hispanic American. The term *nueva canción* originally referred specifically to Chilean folk-protest music, which emerged in the late 1960s and flourished in the political climate of the Allende years (1970–1973) [see CHILE]. It was inspired locally by singer-songwriter Violeta Parra's pioneer reinterpretations of Chilean folk music, and by her Argentine contemporary Atahualpa Yupanqui's similar work with his country's folk music.

Cuban musicians such as Sylvio Rodríguez and Pablo Milanés, whose less folk-rooted music (originally known as *canción protesta* and later as *nueva trova*) expressed the ideals of the Cuban revolution, were used as models. After September 1973, when the Pinochet dictatorship crushed *nueva canción,* its successor, clandestine or heavily veiled, became known as *canto nuevo* (also 'new song').

In the 1970s, politically conscious musicians from Mexico to Argentina began employing their own folkloric traditions as vehicles for commentary on local conditions, though they often continued to imitate the sound of their Chilean and Cuban models, as did Venezuela's Los Guaraguaos and Nicaragua's Carlos Mejía Godoy (Broughton et al. 1994).

These groups identify their music as *nueva canción* to establish solidarity with other Spanish-American ensembles similarly using music to raise political consciousness. Musicians and listeners insist that because *nueva canción* is noncommercial and has a serious social mission, it should be distinguished from recreational popular musics. Nevertheless, it must be considered popular music because its musical influences, social contexts, lyrical concerns, and mass-mediated forms of reproduction are unequivocally modern and urban based.

Rock

Rock was introduced to Latin America in the 1960s through television and radio and by the aggressive promotional campaigns of multinational record companies. Since then, it has become an appreciable part of the Latin American musical landscape.

Initially, most rock songs produced in Latin America were covers of U.S. or U.K. originals or highly derivative, prompting nationalists to denounce these efforts as an undesirable consequence of so-called Yankee cultural imperialism. By the late 1970s, bands in many countries were producing original rock, with Spanish lyrics referring directly to local conditions. In general, rock has been more important in Mexico and

In the 1940s, Cuba's all-female *orquesta* Anacaona broke new ground, but it was not until the 1970s that similar all-female ensembles or female-led ensembles began emerging elsewhere.

the southern cone (Argentina, Chile, Uruguay) than in the Caribbean region, where most people still prefer dance musics of traditional derivation.

During military dictatorships in Chile, Argentina, and Uruguay (1970s and early 1980s), when rock concerts were often the only large public gatherings allowed, they became an important forum for solidarity, albeit veiled and unfocused. Subsequently, *rock en español* (Spanish-American rock) lost its association with foreign imperialism and began to symbolize nationalism and resistance to political repression.

Spanish-American rock is not monolithic. Like its northern counterpart, it has a range of substyles—from what could be considered folk rock (combining modern and indigenous styles and instruments, as with Chile's Los Jaivas), to art rock (as with Argentina's Luis Alberto Spinetta), to punk (as with Chile's Los Prisioneros) and heavy metal and grunge (as with Mexico's Maná). In the late 1980s, reggae rhythms were increasingly incorporated into rock repertoires (as by Mexico's Los Caifanes).

Some rockers active since the 1960s (such as Argentina's Charly García) have produced innovative work in several of these subgenres. *Rock en español* is being produced in Cuba (by Carlos Varela) despite official preference for more autochthonous popular musics.

MUSICIANS' SOCIAL BACKGROUNDS

Through the broadcast media, most Spanish Americans have access to a wide range of popular musics, from local traditional genres, to nationally based commercial dance musics, to pan-Hispanic American genres, to imported pop, mostly from the United States. Latin American musical preferences tend to reflect self-perceived national, regional, class, racial, gender, or political affiliations as much as aesthetic decisions.

Attitudes toward tradition and modernity, toward rural and urban cultures, toward and between racial and ethnic groups, are often in conflict, symbolically or explicitly expressed in the competition between and valorization of available music forms. Designating a particular genre as being the national music of a given country is more often a response to political or racial ideologies than to actual widespread distribution of the music.

In this manner, nationalist Chilean musicians in the 1960s deliberately tried to transform what they perceived as a cultural identity oriented overly toward the North Atlantic into a more indigenous one by promoting as representative of the country's authentic national identity a variety of Andean music typical only of a small, remote area in northern Chile. Similarly, the racist ideology fostered by the Dominican Republic's dictator Rafael Trujillo in the 1930s precluded the designation of African-derived music played on long drums (*palos*) as a symbol of that country's national identity. Instead, with Trujillo's encouragement, a variety of merengue typical only of

Cibao Province, demographically more European than the rest of the country, was elevated to the status of representative of the national identity.

With the occasional exception of genres that have become symbols of a country's national identity, urban Spanish-Americans tend to reject musics closely associated with rural and poor segments of the population as backward and vulgar, preferring instead the transnational genres such as salsa, rock, and *balada*, or fully modernized, nationally based musics such as merengue and *cumbia*.

Alternatively, people who identify with rural ways prefer musics clearly grounded in more traditional styles. In the last decades of the twentieth century, as recently migrated urban poor have swelled the cities, new forms of music—the Dominican *bachata,* the Peruvian *chicha,* the Colombian *carrilera*—emerged to express the experience of transition between a rural past and an urban present (Pacini Hernández 1995). In Córdoba, Argentina, *cuarteto* has a somewhat similar background [see CUARTETO, POP MUSIC OF ARGENTINA]. Essentially urban, these musics are often publicly denigrated and denied equal access to media and distribution because of their association with the poor. In response, informal alternative production and distribution networks have arisen; low-quality recordings are sold by sidewalk or market vendors rather than by record stores; these networks serve as conduits for pirated recordings of mainstream commercial musics.

Among the noteworthy changes in contemporary popular music is the number of all-woman ensembles. Popular music has usually been dominated by men; women have always participated as vocalists, and to a lesser extent as composers, but seldom as instrumentalists.

In the 1940s, Cuba's all-female *orquesta* Anacaona broke new ground, but it was not until the 1970s that similar all-female ensembles (such as the Dominican Republic's merengue band Las Chicas del Can and Colombia's *vallenato* band Las Musas) or female-led ensembles (such as that of the Dominican Republic's accordionist Fefita la Grande) began emerging elsewhere.

VIEWS FROM OUTSIDE THE REGION

Although Spanish-Americans have usually maintained a keen interest in international musical developments, a corresponding interest in Spanish-American music from other world areas has been less noticeable. Often, Spanish-American music has been disseminated indirectly through others' interpretations rather than through original versions by Latin American musicians. Musical pieces are often transformed to conform to fit stereotypes of Latin American people and cultures. Dance musics such as the tango, the mambo, and the cha-cha received most of their international attention via watered-down versions in Hollywood films.

Since the 1950s, Latin American elements have appeared fairly regularly in Latino-flavored rock songs by U.S. musicians such as the Coasters ("Tequila") or the Drifters ("Rose in Spanish Harlem") (Roberts 1985 [1979]). Hispanic-American musicians such as Richie Valens, Carlos Santana, and members of Los Lobos have successfully fused Latino elements with rock (Loza 1993), but Spanish American popular music in its original versions had until the late 1980s achieved neither adequate exposure nor commercial success outside the region; even megahits, such as Calixto Ochoa's "*El Africano*" (1985), interpreted locally all over Latin America, is virtually unknown to most non-Hispanics. In contrast, since the 1950s, African-Cuban music in original versions exerted important influence on Central and West African popular music, particularly that of Senegal and Zaïre (Roberts 1974).

This situation has changed since the late 1980s, when a growing interest in world music (worldbeat) reflects and explains the growth of production and distribution companies (such as Arhoolie, Shanachie, Original Music, and GlobeStyle) that release or rerelease original recordings of Spanish and other third-world music to a new market of aficionados of music (Pacini Hernández 1993). Concurrently, scholarly interest in Spanish American popular musics, long considered too commercial to merit serious attention, has increased in quantity and quality.

REFERENCES

Austerlitz, Paul. 1996. *Merengue: Dominican Music and Dominican Identity.* Philadelphia: Temple University Press.

Broughton, Simon, Mark Ellingham, and David Muddyman. 1994. *World Music: The Rough Guide.* London: Rough Guides.

Boggs, Vernon. 1992. *Salsiology: Afro-Cuban Music and the Evolution of Salsa in New York City.* New York: Excelsior Music.

Loza, Steven. 1993. *Barrio Rhythm: Mexican American Music in Los Angeles.* Urbana and Chicago: University of Illinois Press.

Manuel, Peter. 1988. *Popular Musics of the Non-Western World.* New York: Oxford University Press.

Manuel, Peter, with Kenneth Bilby and Michael Largey. 1995. *Caribbean Currents: Caribbean Music from Rumba to Reggae.* Philadelphia: Temple University Press.

Pacini Hernández, Deborah. 1992. Review-essay on coastal Colombian music and recordings. *Ethnomusicology* 36(2):288–296.

———. 1993. "A View from the South: Spanish Caribbean Perspectives on World Beat." *The World of Music* 35(2):40–69.

———. 1995. *Bachata: A Social History of a Dominican Popular Music.* Philadelphia: Temple University Press.

Roberts, John Storm. 1974. *Black Music of Two Worlds.* New York: Morrow.

———. 1985 [1979]. *The Latin Tinge: The Impact of Latin American Music on the United States.* Tivoli, N. Y.: Original Music.

Rondón, César Miguel. 1980. *El Libro de la Salsa: Crónica de la Música del Caribe Urbano.* Caracas: Editorial Arte.

Turino, Thomas. 1990. "*Somos el Perú* (We Are Peru): *Cumbia Andina* and the Children of Andean Migrants in Lima." *Studies in Latin American Popular Culture* 9:15–32.

———. 1993. *Moving Away from Silence: Music of the Peruvian Altiplano and the Experience of Urban Migration.* Chicago: University of Chicago Press.

Popular Music of Brazil

Charles A. Perrone

Origins, Background, Foundations
Bossa Nova
MPB: Style and Label
Diversification and Variance

Popular music in Brazil is one of the world's most diverse musical phenomena. Besides the internationally known urban samba and bossa nova, Brazil has strong regional expressions, plus pop styles ranging from roots-oriented original composition to contemporary rock and hiphop. Significant centers of production and consumption exist in Bahia, Minas Gerais, and other states, but the major activity occurs in Rio de Janeiro, the nation's traditional cultural capital.

Brazil's recording industry is well developed. Worldwide, its market ranks among the top seven. The big five multinational corporations—EMI, BMG, Polygram, Sony, WEA—dominate the field, but the music branch of Globo, the world's fourth-largest private television network, plays a major role through nationwide broadcasting of soap operas with soundtracks, variety shows, musical specials, and advertising.

Radio is an enormous business; it favors cosmopolitan middle-class fashions but also attends to local, working-class, and rural tastes. Since the advent of recording in Brazil, national musics have competed with imports. In the 1980s, with the rise of Brazilian rock and new dance musics (especially lambada and samba-reggae), the commercial ratio of national production increased markedly.

A dialectic of national or foreign input and influence has been a constant in the formation and study of Brazilian popular music. Other key issues of scholarly inquiry have been migration, identity (class, ethnic, regional, national) via popular music, and the discourse of song, whether for social attitudes, political dissent, artistry, or musical history itself.

ORIGINS, BACKGROUND, FOUNDATIONS

The sources of Brazilian popular music are mainly Portuguese and African; indigenous Amerindian elements are negligible. In the late 1700s and 1800s, African-Brazilian *lundu* was a form of national expression. A historically important tradition of sentimental song was established with the *modinha,* cultivated extensively in different configurations at all social ranks. Other forms of song and dance music emerged from the imitation and adaptation of European models, including the polka, the schottische, and the waltz. Interaction between black and white musicians, which increased after the abolition of slavery (1888), fostered the definition of new styles.

In the Western Hemisphere, bossa nova had its greatest impact on jazz. In the early 1960s, before the Beatles craze, the style was widely imitated in the United States.

In the second decade of the twentieth century, urban samba emerged in Rio de Janeiro. Fueled by the recording and radio industries and by the growth of carnival, samba evolved musically, ascended from a station of social unacceptableness, and became the mainstay of modern popular music, especially for the (largely black) lower-class masses.

In the 1930s, a confluence of commercial, musical, intellectual, and political interests contributed to the establishment of samba as a symbol and vehicle of national identity (Vianna 1995). From its roots to the most recent mass-mediated manifestations, it has diversified in complex ways and gone through numerous phases [see BRAZIL: AFRO-BRAZILIAN TRADITIONS and BRAZIL: CENTRAL AND SOUTHERN REGIONS].

BOSSA NOVA

Bossa nova, a major development in popular music worldwide, began to take shape around 1958. It radically altered the traditional samba, offering the educated middle class a sophisticated alternative. The heavy binary beat gave way to lighter syncopation on a drum set; jazz-influenced (altered) chord progressions replaced standard harmonies; the melodic simplicity of romantic *samba-canção* 'song-samba' became elaborate vocal and instrumental lead lines, which could be sparse and chromatic or involved and dissonant; and melodramatic emphasis of tragic texts was left behind in favor of reserved vocal delivery of lyrics reflecting petit-bourgeois values. Bossa nova dynamically integrated restrained musical elements (Béhague 1973).

Vocal music was the mainstream of bossa nova, but instrumental ensembles (like Zimbo Trio) and solo guitarists (like Baden Powell) became a notable branch within the movement. Such 1960s groups, following the tradition of *choro,* laid the foundation for the expansion of improvisational music in the 1970s and 1980s in the work of such major exponents as Hermeto Pascoal and Egberto Gismonti, who also draw on regional sources, especially those of the Northeast.

In the Western Hemisphere, bossa nova had its greatest impact on jazz. In the early 1960s, before the Beatles craze, the style was widely imitated in the United States. After an ephemeral presence in the pop sphere, bossa nova became a permanent part of the jazz repertoire, in which more than ten of Antônio Carlos Jobim's compositions have achieved the status of contemporary standards.

Evolution of bossa nova

The second generation of bossa nova was stylistically and attitudinally heterogeneous in contrast to the first. The new style, having arisen in the sociopolitical context of developmentalism, changed in the populist climate of the early sixties, as musical activity in middle-class circles reflected the nationalism and political activism of the period. The disengaged sentimental discourse of mainstream bossa nova dissatisfied younger songwriters concerned with underdevelopment and living conditions. Although such themes as poverty and exploitation are constants in traditional and popular song cycles, social content took on new importance in the sixties. Employment of the terms *linha conteudística* 'content line' and *linha formalística* 'formalistic line' demonstrates the opposition of protest and topical songs to the original bossa-nova style and its prime concern with melody and harmony.

New songwriters tried to relate to urban and rural problems alike, applying non-standard diction and incorporating *samba de morro* or regional features into bossa-nova frames. In stylizations of rural genres, sometimes only the characteristic instrumentation or syncopation of bossa nova remained. In keeping with preferred themes, musicians took more forceful approaches. Use or imitation of folkloric melodies, rhythms, or instruments (such as the *viola*) often implied cultural nationalism or political commitment. A military coup d'état (1964) further heightened social awareness, leading to greater use of song as a vehicle of protest. The concurrent expansion of the music and television industries favored the growth of contestatory song until late 1968, when civil liberties were suspended and harsh control of the media began.

The success of the local rendition of early Beatles-like music provoked a nationalist reaction. Imitations of rock since the days of Elvis Presley had not constituted significant trends in Brazil; however, mid-sixties teen rock, called *iê-iê-iê* (yeah-yeah-yeah), attracted consumers who followed British-American pop and reached a mass TV audience. This movement, called Jovem Guarda (Young Guard), benefited from well-conceived promotional schemes. The music was denounced as alienated by those favoring what they called authenticity in popular music. The original leader of *iê-iê-iê* was Roberto Carlos, who went on to become Brazil's and Latin America's best-selling romantic singer in the widely cultivated genre known in Spanish America as *balada*.

MPB: STYLE AND LABEL

Nationally televised songwriters' competitions began in Brazil in 1965; at first, rock-type music was not accepted. During these festivals, the acronym MPB (Brazilian Popular Music) came into use to denote popular music of a national orientation (bossa nova, derivative forms, stylized regionalist composition). Though not a designation of a discrete style, MPB remained an indicator of the varied musics of the sixties generation, including such artists as Chico Buarque, Gilberto Gil, Edu Lobo, Milton Nascimento, and Caetano Veloso (Perrone 1989).

The original distinctions suggested by MPB would blur somewhat in the 1970s as rock styles were absorbed into the repertoires of artists who had been prominent in the late sixties, but the fundamental contrast between MPB and rock has never dissolved. In the 1980s, the initials MPB distinguished post-bossa hybrids from burgeoning national rock. The term MPB is used, less rigorously, to denote Brazilian popular music in general, including music from before the 1960s.

Several singer-songwriters of the MPB generation have established national (and to some extent international) reputations as exceptional performers, poet-composers, voices of political dissent, or vanguardists. Of these, Milton Nascimento achieved recognition as a unique vocal phenomenon and redefined possibilities of regional identity in pop. Chico Buarque challenged boundaries between the erudite and the popular and devised ingenious musico-poetic strategies of affective expressivity and resistance to the military regime (1964–1985).

The most controversial occurrence in Brazilian popular culture of the late sixties was *tropicalismo,* the vanguard movement led by Caetano Veloso and Gilberto Gil, who drew from a wide spectrum of sources—rock, pop, protest, sentimental ballad, folklore, experimental literature—to question schematic divisions of popular music into alienated-committed or national-foreign. Veloso, Gil, and their colleagues forged a music of diachronic and synchronic self-examination and satire.

Tropicalismo was an anomalous intellectualization of popular music, with its avant-garde posturing, juxtapositions of rural simplicity and urban sophistication, and metamusical commentary. Among its lessons were the inevitability of mass-media penetration of international cultural products and the advantages of critical assimilation of such information, as opposed to unthinking imitation. More than any other manifestation in Brazil, *tropicalismo* demonstrated that modern popular music, in addition to its traditional recreational uses, can fulfill political and aesthetic functions.

DIVERSIFICATION AND VARIANCE

Hybridization and eclecticism, by some measures attributable to the openings created by *tropicalismo,* characterized MPB in the 1970s and 1980s. There was ever-increasing adaptation of regional and foreign trends—rock, blues, soul, funk, disco, reggae, other Caribbean styles, and some African music. Popular musics of the Northeast region—which had come to Rio as early as the 1920s and had been a notable presence in the late 1940s and 1950s—illustrate the flexibility of the folk-traditional-popular-pop continuum and of more recent processes of syncretism involving bardic heritage and varied dance music genres [see BRAZIL: NORTHEAST REGION].

In the 1970s, national rock remained a minority countercultural activity, but in the early 1980s, a generation of home-bred rock bands proliferated and assumed prominence in major urban areas, eclipsing MPB and imports in middle-class preference. This new rock—composed, performed, and recorded in Brazil—used its own idioms and created its own idols, complicating the topic of cultural estrangement via music and stimulating more nuanced debate about alienation and authenticity (Perrone 1990). The Rock-in-Rio festivals (1985, 1991), two weeks long, were the largest ever staged anywhere in the world. In North America, samba, bossa nova, MPB, and Brazilian jazz were all part of the Brazilian wave, a renewal of interest in Brazilian popular music (McGowan and Pessanha 1991). Unlike those kinds of production, however, Brazilian rock has not developed an appreciable international following.

Rock and international romantic music have affected south-central Brazilian country music as *música sertaneja,* a massive, commercially active genre centered in São Paulo State. Related broadcast and performance circuits attend to tastes of agrarian and urban migrant workers. Scholars and the media have begun to pay attention to this music (Carvalho 1993; Reily 1992).

One of the most notable late-century developments came within the context of a renaissance of African-Bahian culture in Salvador. From the mid-1970s, black-focused musics for carnival and general consumption have flourished. One central fact is the spread of *bloco afro,* festive fraternal orders with novel approaches to samba (via Caribbean musics) and consciousness-raising programs. From local urban and carnival-specific contexts, African-Bahian material moved into local and national circuits of popular music for consumption via shows, recordings, radio, and TV. An industry term (*axé music*) was coined to refer to these phenomena. Commercialization has provoked criticism about the diluting of negritude and the potential superficiality of back-to-Africa ideologies. Despite unavoidable limitations, these practices involve the consolidation of fresh aesthetics and new processes of social identification for the black population, plus geographical and ethnic conceptualizations of musical practice and participation [see BRAZIL: AFRO-BRAZILIAN TRADITIONS].

The late twentieth century has witnessed the articulation of Brazilian versions of hip-hop. Rap has been most significant in working-class sectors of São Paulo. In Rio, large-scale funk dances, which have featured recorded black U.S. dance music since soul of the late 1970s, are an important nontraditional vehicle of identity for subaltern groups and have encouraged local renditions of dance-oriented funk and text-focused rap. These cases of appropriation express current dilemmas of disenfranchised black youth, confounding the consensus culture centered on samba (Yúdice 1994). As numerous originally marginalized forms, funk phenomena are now migrating to mainstream media.

REFERENCES

Béhague, Gerard. 1973. "Bossa and Bossas: Recent Changes in Brazilian Popular Music." *Ethnomusicology* 17(2):209–233.

Carvalho, Martha de Ulhôa. 1993. "Musical Style, Migration, and Urbanization: Some Considerations on Brazilian *Música Sertaneja.*" *Studies in Latin American Popular Culture* 12:75–93.

McGowan, Chris, and Ricardo Pessanha. 1991. *The Brazilian Sound: Samba, Bossa Nova and the Popular Music of Brazil.* New York: Billboard Press.

Perrone, Charles A. 1989. *Masters of Contemporary Brazilian Song: MPB 1965–1985.* Austin: University of Texas Press.

————. 1990. "Changing of the Guard: Questions and Contrasts of Brazilian Rock Phenomena." *Studies in Latin American Popular Culture* 9:65–83.

Reily, Suzel Ana. 1992. "*Música Sertaneja* and Migrant Identity: The Stylistic Development of a Brazilian Genre." *Popular Music* 11(3):337–358.

Vianna, Hermanno. 1995. *O mistério do samba.* Rio de Janeiro: Jorge Zahar / UFRJ.

Yúdice, George. 1994. "The Funkification of Rio." In *Microphone Fiends: Youth Music and Youth Culture,* ed. Tricia Rose and Andrew Ross, 193–217. New York: Routledge.

Art Music
Dale A. Olsen
Daniel E. Sheehy

The Concept of Art Music
Understanding Compositional Processes
Understanding Contextual Issues
Further Study

The creation of music requires a process—composition. It also involves an issue usually relating to social function or contextual use, such as shamanistic curing, ballroom dancing, lullaby singing, concert listening, and many others. What is often termed art music includes processes and issues and is therefore as much the domain of ethnomusicological study as it is the domain of historical musicology, music theory, and criticism. How ethnomusicologists study art music, however, is what makes their approach unique: ethnomusicologists emphasize processes and issues as aspects of human behavior.

THE CONCEPT OF ART MUSIC

By *art music* we mean the formally taught, notation-reliant European or European-derived tradition of music that is associated most closely with an educated elite. Art music includes the rich store of music created or performed for liturgical devotion and other Christian church events, and secular compositions intended for concert performance. Though art music is not the central focus of this encyclopedia, it has been, to varying degrees in different periods and among certain populations, a significant thread of musical culture in South America, Mexico, Central America, and the Caribbean. Several articles in this volume treat art music in national contexts.

The colonial era

The concept of art music did not exist in the pre-Columbian New World, so its history begins with its importation from Europe. The colonial era, spanning in most nations the early 1500s to around the 1820s, was marked by the widespread implantation of European musical style as well as genres and extraordinary accomplishments in the performance of religious art music. Missionaries, particularly Franciscans and Jesuits, used Gregorian chant and other church music to educate and persuade the Indian population to embrace Roman Catholicism. Many Indian populations, for whom music was an important element of pre-Christian worship, proved fertile ground for the transplanted music and became extremely proficient at singing and playing European music and making European musical instruments. In sixteenth-

century Mexico, some choirs were likened to their superlative counterparts in Spain,
though authorities criticized the abundance of "indecorous and improper instruments" employed in religious services as excessive (Stevenson 1952:63). In larger
cities of Hispanic America, cathedrals were prestigious centers of religious and public
life. They employed highly trained chapel masters to create music, train musicians,
organize ensembles, and perform for a wide range of events linked to church life.
"Cathedral musicians frequently supplied the musical needs of the viceroyal palaces
as well, and thus they were often responsible for a city's first attempts at secular
music" (Béhague 1979:5). Though the chapel masters and their New World disciples
concerned themselves with the creation of original works, they closely conformed to
European stylistic convention. Exceptions included the occasional use of Amerindian
language or Afro-mestizo dialect in texts. As largesse from the mother countries
declined during the final century of colonial times, the primacy of church music
waned—further evidence that art music in the New World was little more than an
extension of its European base.

Colonial secular music is known to have existed, but the documentation that
remains, such as guitar-tablature reinterpretations of secular genres of dancing, is
scarce. More prevalent are records of *villancicos,* secular songs with refrains, which
served as secular models for the chapel masters' creative production of devotional
music in polyphonic style. Many *villancicos,* such as those based on the well-known
late seventeenth-century texts by Sor Juana Inés de la Cruz in Puebla, Mexico, were
widely admired for their artistry. Tomás de Torrejón y Velasco's *La Púrpura de la Rosa,*
premiered in Lima, Peru in 1701, was the first opera created and produced in the
New World. It is the only extant score of colonial New World opera but was by no
means the only theatrical music produced. Operas and Spanish zarzuelas were performed in many theaters in the New World throughout the 1700s and 1800s. A popular theater for rubber barons was the Teatro Amazonas in Manaus, Brazil (figure 1).

Nineteenth-century changes

Beginning in the first decades of the nineteenth century, a wave of nationalism
brought sociopolitical independence for Latin American countries. The old church-

music models that had been controlled by the sociopolitical elite lost favor, and secular music moved to the fore. Definable national musical styles would not emerge until the final decades of the century. In the meantime, Italian opera, light theater music, songs, and piano music—all closely conforming to European models—ruled (Béhague 1979:96–97).

In the several decades after independence, foreign instrumentalists and singers, Italians in particular, toured and often resettled in the Americas. In larger cities, European operas and zarzuelas were frequently performed, and many opera singers had large followings. Opera was principally available through watered-down piano arrangements. With the lowering of previously strict class barriers and the growth of the upward-aspiring middle class came a demand for piano and other salon music (parlor music) as a means of personal improvement and achieving social status. Military bands performed arrangements of folk melodies and social dances, such as the waltz and schottische, plus Italian opera overtures and other light theater music.

The lack of widespread institutionalized music education was an impediment to supporting the performance and appreciation of purely instrumental orchestral music. By the end of the century, however, several music conservatories had been founded in Rio de Janeiro (1847), Santiago de Chile (1849), Mexico City (1866 and 1877), Quito (1870), and Buenos Aires (1893) (Béhague 1971).

UNDERSTANDING COMPOSITIONAL PROCESSES

The compositional processes of art music in nineteenth- and twentieth-century South America, Mexico, Central America, and the Caribbean probably do not differ from compositional processes elsewhere in the world where Western civilization is paramount or influential. The processes first involve searching for sources of inspiration, whether they are abstract ideas in a composer's mind, characteristic sounds of the tropical forest or Andes mountains, tonal possibilities of pre-Columbian musical instruments (or what composers thought they were), musical calculations based on mathematical formulas, impressions of people or places, and so forth. They involve notating such ideas on music paper, playing them on piano or guitar and writing them down on music paper, or creating them in a laboratory and writing down instructions for performance on music, graph, or plain paper. Ethnomusicologists study these processes as human behavior rather than just history or theory.

One of the most fruitful ways to study the composition of art music as a process is to examine composers' sources of inspiration. Throughout the Caribbean, Middle America, and South America, many composers have been influenced by the folk musics or Amerindian musics of their own country, paralleling nineteenth-century European romanticism, the movement exemplified in the works of such composers as Antonín Dvořák (Bohemia), Manuel de Falla (Spain), Edvard Grieg (Norway), Modest Mussorgsky (Russia), Jean Sibelius (Finland), and Bedřich Smetana (Bohemia), and the twentieth-century North American nationalistic movement, which informed works by composers as different as Aaron Copland, George Gershwin, and Roy Harris.

As nationalist sentiment permeated art-music sensibilities, Latin American composers began following the European model of incorporating nationalist vernacular elements into their music. Premiered in 1871, the opera *Guamotzín,* by the Mexican composer Aniceto Ortega (1823–1875), was based on a romanticized Aztec theme, appealing to nationalist sentiments. The previous year, the Brazilian António Carlos Gomes, the "most successful opera composer of the Americas in the nineteenth century," had achieved international fame through his work *Il Guarany,* complete with Indian heroes and idealized indigenous dance and music, set in an Italian style of the time (Béhague 1979:98, 113). The voluminous music written for piano during the final decades of the 1800s often reinterpreted national folk-music melodies, rhythms, and other elements. A pioneer in this trend was the U.S.-born Louis Moreau Gottschalk (1829–1869), famous for composing and performing piano pieces that developed African-American and Caribbean rhythms, viewed as "tropical" by North American and European audiences. Born in Louisiana, he studied in Paris, concertized all over, lived and taught in Cuba, and died in Rio de Janeiro.

Other influential nationalistic and folklore-inspired composers in Latin America include Carlos Chávez (1899–1978) and Silvestre Revueltas (1899–1940) in Mexico; Andrés Sas (1900–1967) and Teodoro Valcárcel (1902–1942) in Peru; Carlos Isamitt (1885–1974) and Carlos Lavín (1883–1962) in Chile; Alberto Ginastera (b. 1916) and Alberto Williams (1862–1952) in Argentina; and Carlos Gomes (1836–1896), Camargo Guarnieri (b. 1907), and Heitor Villa-Lobos (1887–1959) in Brazil. Some composers produced works inspired by Amerindian music or musical life: Villa-Lobos's *Amazonas* (1917), inspired by Brazil's native Amazonian cultures; Lavín's *Fiesta Araucana* (1926), inspired by Mapuche music from Chile; Valcárcel's *Suite Incaica* (1929); Chávez's *Sinfonía India* ("Indian Symphony," ca. 1940), based on Cora, Yaqui, and other Mexican Indian melodies; Aretz's *Yekuaná* (ca. 1974), based on material from the Yekuana Indians of Venezuela; and Ginastera's *La Pampa y la Puna,* which used a European flute to imitate the Andean *kena.* Works inspired by African-American music or folklore include *Sensemayá* (1938) by Revueltas, based on African-Cuban rhythms from the Abakuá society [see Cuba]; and *Três Poemas Afro-Brasileiros* (1955) by Guarnieri. Works inspired by rural mestizo or European-derived cowboys and the harshness of cowboy life include Williams's *El Rancho Abandonado* ("The Abandoned Ranch") (1890) and Ginastera's *Estancia* (1941), a ballet with a musical portrait of an Argentine ranch.

Twentieth-century changes

The twentieth century was marked first by a strong trend toward musical nationalism and subsequently by a swing toward universalism, two guiding philosophies that often coexisted to form a dialectic that defined much art music of the time. Many modern nationalist composers tried not so much to incorporate folkloric elements into their European-style compositions (in the fashion of their predecessors) as to create a distinctive nationalist style that abstracted from, synthesized, and transcended European and national antecedents. Universalism—the avoidance or outright rejection of nationalist tendencies in favor of a more personal vision and/or international sphere of influence and endeavor—won the hearts and minds of some composers, but sociopolitical loyalties or constraints compelled others not to alienate themselves from local musical traditions (Béhague 1979:125). Although the late twentieth century saw much musical experimentation in keeping with international trends, an abiding obstacle to the understanding and acceptance of experimental music—indeed, art music in general—was the limited degree of formal musical education available throughout the region.

UNDERSTANDING CONTEXTUAL ISSUES

These are just a few of the sources of inspiration, trends, and philosophies of some Latin American composers and some of their works. One way to study these and other compositions as reflections of a process is to compare them with their sources of inspiration. Several ways to study them as an issue would be to contextualize them by investigating letters and diaries to learn about the composers' reasons for crafting them; examining the reactions of audiences toward their performances and public

Art music is the musical voice of certain classes of people, just as folk music speaks for other classes and ritual music for still others.

opinion about them through reviews and newspaper articles; interviewing people who interacted with composers and knew their compositions and compositional techniques well; and so forth.

Important issues associated with art music in South America, Mexico, Central America, and the Caribbean generally involve contexts: participating in rituals, listening to concerts, watching ballets, and performing for oneself or one's group. Ethnomusicologists are interested in the broad concept of issue because it tells us something about the persons, peoples, and cultures for which the issue has meaning and importance. Ethnomusicologists ask what caused the art music to be composed, performed, recorded, listened to, or no longer listened to; who listens to it, when, where, and why; and who performs it, how, when, where, and why.

Art music is the musical voice of certain classes of people, just as folk music speaks for other classes and ritual music for still others. All music is made by humans for humans or their gods. Throughout this volume, many authors have written about art music as an aspect of culture.

FURTHER STUDY

The most valuable overview of the art music of South America, Mexico, Central America, and the Caribbean is by Gerard Béhague (1979). For each chapter, it includes annotated bibliographical notes that are useful for additional study. In addition, a portion of Béhague's doctoral dissertation (1971) presents details about musical nationalism in Brazil. More recently, David P. Appleby (1983) has written an overview about the art music of Brazil, offering cultural-historical data about many composers. Opera is an important medium for presenting nationalistic themes, and Malena Kuss (1992) has explored that topic for Argentina, Brazil, and Mexico. The most comprehensive source for the study of Latin American art music is the journal *Latin American Music Review*, edited by Gerard Béhague. The American father of Latin American art-music scholarship, however, is Robert M. Stevenson, whose many publications have inspired students and scholars alike for decades.

An ethnomusicological study of the art music of South America, Mexico, Central America, and the Caribbean (the entirety of so-called Latin America), however, has not been attempted. Although to many students and scholars of the Americas such an approach may not seem possible, it is certainly just as logical to examine the why, when, and how of musical occasions as the music itself.

REFERENCES

Appleby, David P. 1983. *The Music of Brazil.* Austin: University of Texas Press.

Béhague, Gerard. 1971. *The Beginnings of Musical Nationalism in Brazil.* Detroit Monographs in Musicology, 1. Detroit: Information Coordinators.

————. 1979. *Music in Latin America: An Introduction.* Englewood Cliffs, N.J.: Prentice-Hall.

Kuss, Malena. 1992. "Identity and Change: Nativism in Operas from Argentina, Brazil, and Mexico." In *Musical Repercussions of 1492: Encounters in Text and Performance,* ed. Carol E. Robertson, 299–335. Washington and London: Smithsonian Institution Press.

Stevenson, Robert M. 1952. *Music in Mexico: A Historical Survey.* New York: Thomas Y. Crowell.

Part 3
Nations and Musical Traditions

Excluding native cultures, the politically determined nations in South America, Mexico, Central America, and the Caribbean number less than fifty, but the names for their musical traditions—including dances, festivals, genres, musical instruments, and songs—number into the thousands. The people and their musical traditions are of native American, African, European, Asian, and other derivations. Most are a mixture of many heritages.

None of the nations, countries, or subcultures in South America, Mexico, Central America, and the Caribbean has developed or exists in isolation, and each has experienced musical and cultural growth. This photograph of a procession in northern Peru reveals one of the most important aspects of a culture: musical syncretism, possibly better described as cultural layering, because native American and Spanish elements often exist side by side.

A procession with the statue of the Virgen del Carmen during a patronal festival in Los Baños del Inca, Cajamarca, Peru, 16 July 1979. A *clarín* trumpeter precedes the religious statue while singers and dancers follow. Photograph by Dale A. Olsen.

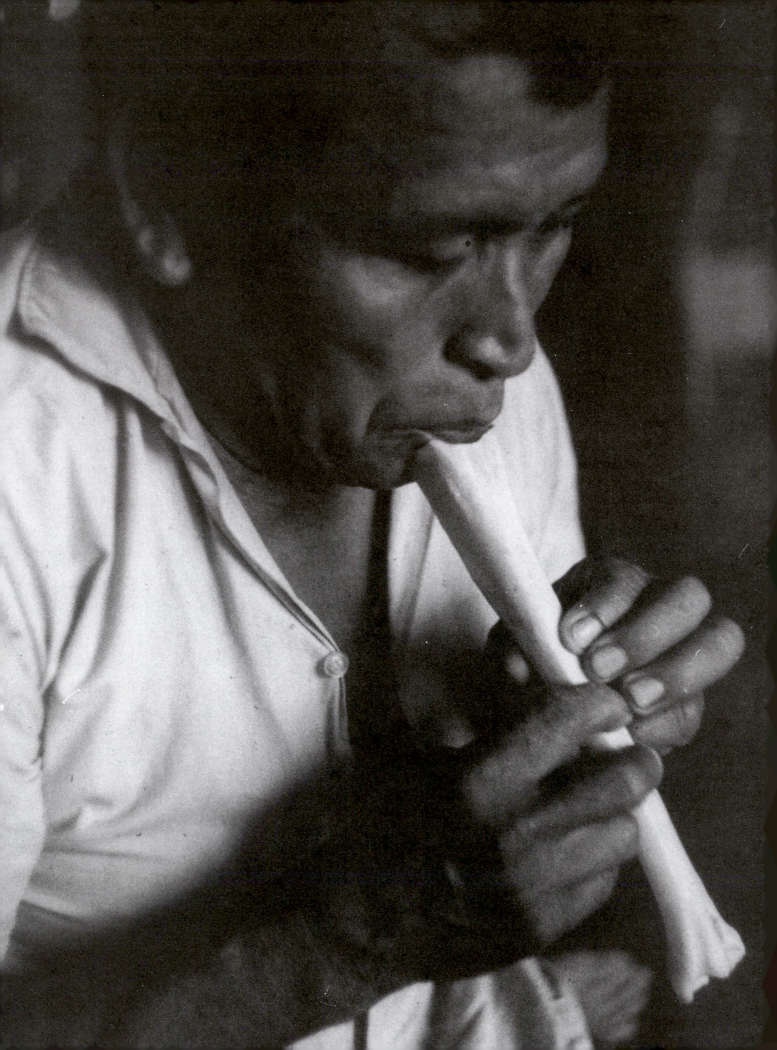

Section 1
Boundaries and Musics of Native South Americans

Since the Encounter of 1492, hundreds of native cultures in South America have become absorbed by the dominant cultures of Spanish, Portuguese, British, Dutch, and French heritage. Nevertheless, many indigenous "nations" remain. Neither acculturated nor traditional native people of South America are completely constrained by the political boundaries of countries, but inhabit broader geographic areas. Therefore, a reasonable plan for grouping the native people of South America is based on geographic areas: Amazon Basin, Circum-Caribbean, Chaco, and Andes (map 4). This grouping eases comparison and is helpful for quickly locating cultures. Another grouping could focus on ecosystems, including tropical forest, desert, mountain, and perhaps others. Of these, the tropical forest is so vast that many regions in the geography-based plan belong to it. The tropical forest is home to most of South America's native peoples. Within it live numerous game animals, many of which provide materials for musical instruments, such as this deer-bone flute, constructed by a Warao man in the Venezuelan jungle.

In the Orinoco Delta of Venezuela, a Warao man tests his newly crafted deer-bone flute. Photo by Dale A. Olsen, 1972.

The Tropical-Forest Region
Anthony Seeger

Musical Sounds and Processes
Social Hierarchies and Musical Performance
Musical Creativity and Innovation
Immigrant Musical Forms, 1500–1900
Immigration after the 1930s
Cultural Interactions

opposite: Geographic areas for grouping native peoples of South America

The tropical-forest region of South America includes much of Brazil and parts of at least eight other countries: Bolivia, Colombia, Ecuador, French Guiana, Guyana, Peru, Surinam, and Venezuela. It encompasses the Amazon and Orinoco river basins and much of the Guyana shield, extends to the coast of the Guyanas, Surinam, and eastern Venezuela, and reaches into the foothills of the Andes Mountains and toward the savannas of central and southern Brazil. It is huge, with a complex history of indigenous settlement and later, of colonization and economic transformation.

The music of the region is one of the least known in the world. We do not have enough musical information and analysis to define musical areas on a securely comparative basis and are lucky if we have one or two studies from a given family of languages. A great deal of research remains to be done.

There are several reasons for our lack of information: the physical and cultural disappearances of many Amerindian communities throughout the region, the difficulty of reaching the areas and conducting research, the tendency of ethnomusicologists to focus on surviving Amerindian traditions to the exclusion of others, and a concentration on other priorities by most other researchers. A few surveys have been prepared, however, including those by Isabel Aretz on South America (1984) and Venezuela (1991), and by Helza Cameu on Brazil (1977).

Though outsiders think of Indians as the primary residents of the tropical forest, other communities live there, and some have done so for centuries. Even before Columbus, Andean peoples probably influenced and were influenced by tropical-forest peoples. Later arrivals who have settled in the region and remained there included missionaries, gold miners, rubber tappers, farmers, and ranchers. More recent immigrants include factory workers, oil drillers, prospectors, members of new religious organizations, civil servants, and immigrants from rural areas in other areas or countries.

The Indian and non-Indian communities in the tropical forest have interacted over the past few centuries, with profound effects on the music of the former. External influence increased in the last few decades of the twentieth century, with the capital-intensive development of the region and the diffusion of shortwave radios, cameras, tape recorders, and television. In the 1990s, musical influences move in sev-

The tropical forest once was a complex mosaic of native communities, interacting with one another in a variety of ways. We do not know exactly what musical life was like before Columbus, because no one was asking questions then; but we can learn something of what it has been like since.

eral directions, as the Brazilian Indian leader Rauni tours with the British rock singer Sting, Milton Nascimento includes Brazilian Indian music on his album *Txai!* (1990), and Marlui Miranda (1995) arranges, composes, and performs new Indian music.

As with music almost everywhere, two simultaneous musical movements have affected this region. While some musicians looked backward to earlier forms, preserving or reinventing them, other musicians reached out to new forms, incorporating them into their styles to create new traditions. These musical choices are part of specific historical contexts, frequently those of political oppression, economic exploitation, and intentional cultural destruction. In this way, music reflects regional and transnational processes and local communities' reactions to them.

This article begins with a description of tropical-forest Indian musical sounds and a discussion of some pertinent musical processes. Later, it addresses the music of the early immigrants to the region. It concludes with a discussion of how these musical forms have interacted and are evolving.

MUSICAL SOUNDS AND PROCESSES

What does tropical-forest Indian music sound like? If you could hover over the region and listen to the music emanating from the hundreds of Indian communities during a twenty-four-hour period, you might hear a dramatic crescendo with the rise of the morning star, well before dawn, that would reach a peak in the dawn light before sunrise. The sounds would diminish as the day grew hotter then would pick up again in the late afternoon, dying down again around 8:00 P.M., but continuing in some form throughout the night into the predawn crescendo. You would hear flutes of all sizes, played for their overtones; you would hear reed instruments, some played in hocket; you would hear unison men's choruses accompanied by rattles and stamping feet, and unison women's choruses. Shouts, animal cries, whistles, and other sounds would sometimes obscure the text and tune. During the day, you would hear playing children imitate their elder's ceremonies, solo singers, shamans chanting, and lone fishermen and hunters humming to themselves in preparation for the evening's performance.

If your gaze could penetrate the forest and thatched roofs of the villages, you would often see people dancing almost everywhere you heard music. You might see elaborate bodily ornamentation of paint and feathers, and ceremonial dress made from palm fronds that would swish with the dancers' movements. Rattles might be hanging from their bodies; wind instruments might appear in various sizes. Men and women would usually be dancing in separate lines, not together, and sometimes the women would be hiding in the houses while the men alone performed. Somewhere you would see a lone shaman, singing over the sick, searching for the cause and cure of the illness. Nowhere would you see a conductor; indeed, the performers would not often be able to see one another while they perform.

In the early morning, when the sounds died down, you would see men heading for rivers and forests to fish and hunt, and women hurrying to gardens to gather crops to prepare food and, in some cases, fermented drink. Their labor must produce the sustenance that makes the performances memorable: "When we sing, we eat," say some; "when we perform, we drink," say others.

Somewhere you would see a person listening intently—to sounds coming from an unseen source within, or to a radio or a tape recorder, or to a person from a different community. After a time, the listener will be introducing to excited colleagues a new song, a new ceremony, a new aesthetic. Then the cacophony will crescendo again.

Ethnohistory

The tropical forest once was a complex mosaic of native communities, interacting with one another in a variety of ways. These groups nearly always lived in small, dispersed settlements. For thousands of years, they traded, intermarried, fought, and learned each others' music. Theirs were mostly traditions of straw and wood, using various kinds of grass, fronds, and vegetal material to construct residences, musical instruments, and symbolically important ritual regalia. As a result, we have little archaeological evidence from the region. Surviving materials include cook pots, charred wood, pollen from gardens, shells, and a few earthworks and other signs of social structure in isolated parts of the region.

Disease, violence, enslavement, missionization, and economic development have dramatically changed tropical-forest Indian settlements. Though some communities survived these ravages, the survivors often live in small, isolated settlements, surrounded by immigrant settlers. These communities are discouraged or actually forbidden to perform their traditional music, and are often deprived of the lands and resources once essential to their livelihood. Even ethnomusicologists who have gone to the most isolated regions and worked with recently contacted groups are studying a situation greatly altered by the colonization of South America. We do not know exactly what musical life was like before Columbus, because no one was asking those questions then; but we can learn something of what it has been like since.

Researchers discussing tropical-forest Indians usually talk about language families or cultural areas. The concept of "tribe" is sometimes helpful, but a tribal name is often a historical accident or a bureaucratic convenience. Peoples often have different names for themselves and often distinguish among communities that have been identified as a single people by a tribal name. As names have been used in the scholarly literature, a tribal name (for example *Suyá*) identifies a settlement or cluster of settlements with a distinct language or dialect. These linguistic units are themselves then classified as members of language families. Among the largest of these are the Arawak, the Chibcha, the Gê, the Karib, the Pano, and the Tupi (Nimuendaju 1980). Cultural, cosmological, and musical traditions are usually more similar among the members of a language family than between them, but not always. In some regions, communities of several language families share a single social organization, ceremonial life, and musical style: the Upper Xingu (the Xingu National Park, an Indian reserve, was established in 1967) and Northwest Amazon regions are good examples of this.

Regional traits

Despite the variety, some generalizations hold for most of the region: within a given culture, music and dance are often defined by the same word and are inextricably related; music is transmitted entirely in the oral-aural tradition; throughout the region, certain families of instruments are more common than others; societies with

FIGURE 1   Xavante (Shavante, Gê language group) men play side-blown bamboo trumpets (*upawã*) before singing and dancing *daño're.* Amazonas, Brazil. Photo by Laura Graham, 1986.

strong singing traditions usually have several types of oratory that are distinctly "musical" in the use of rhythm and pitch; much of the music is part of religious and social rituals rather than "entertainment"; music is often associated with transformation (as when a human spiritually becomes an animal) or travel (as when a shaman makes a spiritual journey); and music may be an important means for establishing a communal identity and making distinctions among peoples.

Lexical identity of music and dance

Among the Suyá Indians of Mato Grosso, music and dance are defined in a single word, *ngere,* and this practice seems widespread among land-based cultures. Most peoples seem to comprehend performed sounds and movements as a single, unified event. Often, a set of fairly stable sound structures and fairly consistent movements are identified as a named genre, as among the Xavante (Shavante) of Brazil (figures 1 and 2). This practice is distinct from that of societies in which dancers improvise to different musical performances.

In early accounts (1500–1900), observers provided better descriptions of the movements than of the sounds. After the introduction of audio field recorders (twentieth century), better information about the sounds became available. Only in the 1980s, when video recorders became viable field tools in the region, did we begin to get extensive recordings of the two aesthetic systems together.

Participants' costumes and bodily ornamentation and performers' choreography are often important clues to the musical process. When the Waiãpi are dancing the bumblebee ceremony, their instruments are supposed to sound like bumblebees, and they move like them (Fuks 1989); a similar association of dance and sounds is evident in Thomas Gregor's film on the Mehinaku (1973).

The oral-aural tradition

All musical traditions are learned and transmitted through the oral-aural tradition. There are no indigenous systems of notation, and if a tradition is not constantly performed, it is forgotten and cannot be revived.

In a purely oral culture, the lack of interest or performance during a single generation can mean the disappearance of the tradition. Musical traditions are as fragile as the tropical-forest ecosystems—once destroyed, they are virtually impossible to

FIGURE 2   After a log relay race, Xavante men sing and dance *daño're*. Photo by Laura Graham, 1986.

reconstruct. Audio and videotape recorders have changed this situation somewhat, and many communities are interested in preserving their traditions and teaching them through these means.

Preferred instruments

Idiophones (mostly rattles) and aerophones (a wide variety of flutes, trumpets [see figure 1], single-reed instruments, panpipes, nose-blown flutes, ocarinas, and so on) are widely distributed. Membranophones, mostly double headed, have played only a small role in the music in this region, though there are some. Chordophones are rare. Musical bows occur among the Shuar in Ecuador and the Yukpa in Colombia. Lute-type stringed instruments are found only in areas where they have been learned from immigrants. The best study on musical instruments of the region remains that of Karl G. Izikowitz (1970 [1935]).

Uses of instruments appear to correlate with language families. Members of the Gê family mostly use rattles to accompany singing; their aerophones are usually whistles, played to accompany song, rather than melodic instruments in their own right. In contrast, some Tupi peoples have many wind instruments, classified in considerable detail (Bastos 1978, 1986). Meanwhile, some Chibchan-speakers, such as the Warao, have dozens of musical instruments, but others, such as the Yanomamö, have none (Olsen 1981, 1996).

Everyone a musician

The societies of the region support no full-time native musical specialists or musicologists. Virtually all members of a certain age and gender engage in similar economic tasks and social processes. People make music in addition to all the other things they do in their lives and as part of those other things, rather than distinct from them. This fact distinguishes the tropical forest from some other parts of the world (most court-based societies, for example) and carries with it important implications for studies of tropical-forest music.

Since there are no full-time music specialists, practice is often part of performances. Since there are no full-time scholars of music, discourse about music tends to be phrased in diction borrowed from other domains. This diction appears to be

According to a widespread myth about the origin of sacred flutes, women once played flutes, and men were forbidden to touch them. By deceit, men overcame women and took the flutes, which they have kept to this day.

"metaphoric." In fact, most researchers in the region have had difficulty eliciting any "words about music" at all.

The functionality of music

Most tropical-forest music is associated with religious rituals, rites of passage, inter-communal visiting, annual-cycle rituals, or curing. Except for some lullabies and individual songs, most peoples do not set an "entertainment music" apart from these other forms. This tendency means that the contexts for musical performances are quite carefully defined.

In many cases, songs are known by the name of the ceremony to which they belong. Anthropological literature on these peoples frequently includes extensive analysis of rituals but virtually no discussion of music. This is frustrating for ethnomusicologists, but reflects a general tendency in anthropology to avoid discussions of sounds (and scents and feelings).

Song and oratory

Strong singing traditions often coexist with elaborate forms of speaking (Basso 1985; Sherzer and Urban 1986). Virtually all South American Indian groups distinguish between everyday speech and one or more forms of "oratory" or heightened speech. Elevated forms of speech may serve for formal encounters between humans, to recount myths, or to make political speeches.

Song itself may be considered an extreme of oratory—the extreme employment of fixed tonal relationships and rhythmic forms—and be systematically related to it, as I have suggested for the Suyá and as Olsen (1996) has suggested for the Warao. Instrumental music does not appear to be used to imitate the patterns of speech, even in communities with tonal languages, but to follow compositional rules that differ from those of speech.

Music and reality

Music is associated with cosmological transformations or travel. During ceremonies in many communities, singer-dancers are transformed into a kind of dual being, part-human, part-animal, or part-human, part-spirit. Some of the mystery and the efficacy of performances lies in these transformations. Among the Suyá, in the course of the mouse ceremony, the dancers become mice (Seeger 1987); among the Waiãpi, in the course of the bumblebee ceremony, they become bumblebees (Fuks 1989); among the Mehinaku, flutists become spirits.

Shamans are often transformed and travel, and their songs report their travels among the Arawete (Viveiros de Castro 1986), the Tenetehara (Wagley and Galvão 1949), the Kashinaua (Kensinger 1973), and the Shuar (Crawford 1976; Harner 1972, 1973).

What is this all about? Musical performance in the tropical forest appears to be a way to create a bridge between different types of reality. Musical performances bring together humans and animals, humans and spirits, the past and the present (Seeger 1987; Vidal 1977). These conjunctions are often reflected in sung texts, which may contain referential ambiguities: is the "I" in the text a human? a dead relative? an animal? a spirit?

Music may structure the hallucinogenic experience, acting like a "jungle-gym of consciousness" (Dobkin de Rios 1975). The role of music in these powerful conjunctions of everyday life with spirit-animal-otherworld through music is one of the reasons music plays such a central part in tropical-forest cosmology.

Music and identity

Communities use music to identify themselves in many ways. They may define themselves as against other Indian communities by the songs they perform (songs that make them uniquely human), or they may define themselves as "Indians" with respect to the national society around them (singing songs that make them uniquely political).

The use of music in forging and proclaiming an ethnic identity is widespread. In the tropical-forest region, the employment of music to this end varies according to the specific sociopolitical situation of the people. The same song may at one time have an internal meaning with little connection to ethnic identity, and only a short time later be performed primarily as a marker of that identity.

SOCIAL HIERARCHIES AND MUSICAL PERFORMANCE

Though in the tropical forest there are no social classes in the Marxist sense (of groups with distinct means of production), notions of hierarchy occur in most Indian peoples of the region. Hierarchy is established by gender, by age, by knowledge, by occupation (Hugh-Jones 1979), and by other means. It seems to become more pronounced toward the Andes.

In virtually all tropical-forest Indian communities, most public rituals are controlled by adult males. They make most important musical decisions. They select ceremonies, organize performances, and exclude women and children from some of the events. In some societies, men prohibit certain aerophones to women (Gregor 1977, 1985). In others, they let women sing but not play rattles; or women may accompany dancers with rattles but may not sing.

According to a widespread myth about the origin of sacred flutes, women once played flutes, and men were forbidden to touch them. Women at that time are often described as doing other men's tasks, such as hunting and warring. By deceit, men overcame women and took the flutes, which they have kept to this day. When these flutes are played, women are supposed to withdraw into houses and, under pain of severe sanctions, not even to look at them (Hill 1993).

The male dominance in performances is counterbalanced in many cases by ceremonies or musical genres controlled and performed exclusively by women. In the Upper Xingu, women have their own ceremony, Iamuricumã; the Gê have rituals of reversal and rituals in which women play central roles; in the Northwest Amazon, women have their own song genres (Harner 1972, 1973); and in other areas, the lament is an important women's genre, often also performed by men (Graham 1986:87).

Though women frequently know and are capable of teaching or performing certain musical genres, they do not often perform in the absence of a knowledgeable man. It is always important to distinguish between performance and knowledge. Female researchers have often had better access to women's knowledge than male researchers. The dominance of males over public ceremonies does not mean these societies are dominated by adult men; the reality is far more complex.

Age is also an important means of creating hierarchy. Older men tend to direct the activities of younger men and children (and of women), and older women often exercise authority over younger ones. Knowledge often confers status, and older men and women acquire status and authority over younger ones, partly through their knowledge of music, speech, and stories. Their authority lies in their knowledge and their culturally prescribed license to use it.

Other forms of social organization than age and gender may be important in musical performance. In Gê-speaking communities, musical performance of certain rituals may be under the control of name-based social groups. Among the Suyá, each social group has its own songs and sometimes its own way of singing: one moiety is supposed to sing more slowly than the other; young men are supposed to sing certain songs at a higher pitch than older men; and so on. In other areas, a certain community may control the ritual knowledge and musical performance of all the subareas.

MUSICAL CREATIVITY AND INNOVATION

Where does music come from? Contrary to some stereotypes, tropical-forest Indians do not sing the same thing all the time, but innovate frequently. New music enters their repertoires in a variety of ways. Among some groups, it comes during dreams, through earplugs, or from necklaces (Aytai 1985; Graham 1986; Olsen 1996). In other groups, songs are brought back from shamanic experiences or illnesses, in which individuals have learned songs from spirits.

Many communities are musically multicultural: they perform the music and often entire rituals of neighboring groups. The Suyá are the best documented in this respect: they sing songs from at least ten other societies, including two extinct groups, their former enemies, whose only cultural survivals live on in their music (Seeger 1987). As with all issues of music and identity, under certain circumstances all the music a group sings is "its own" music; under other circumstances, the same group will carefully distinguish the origins of each form.

What makes one performance better than another? Musical aesthetics are often difficult to investigate among tropical-forest communities because music is inextricably bound up with other social events and is rarely discussed dissociated from them. Among the Waiãpi, for example, the success of musical events is judged partly by the quality and quantity of manioc beer served during the performance.

Persistence often yields some forms of evaluation, but it may be worded in a manner that appears to be metaphoric. For example, Suyá descriptions of sound tend to focus on the throat: people with highly appreciated voices are said to have "beautiful throats," people with loud voices "strong throats," and people whose voices are neither strong nor beautiful "bad throats" or "ugly throats."

Children learn music by witnessing or participating in musical performances with their elders. There is rarely any special training, except in the case of shamans, who often undergo long and intensive training and initiations. But shamans' training is more directed toward interaction with spirits than toward musical performance in itself.

Children and young men and women often participate intensively in musical performances, thus gaining musical knowledge and understanding. As there are no full-time music specialists, there are no specialized music schools or other musical-training programs. Children and certain other relatives of particularly knowledgeable musicians often become musicians themselves, having heard a great deal of music during their youth.

IMMIGRANT MUSICAL FORMS, 1500–1900

The tropical forest was not heavily settled by non-Indians until the twentieth century. The local economies in the region were based on extractive industries, such as medicinal-plant collecting, lumbering, mining, rubber tapping, subsistence agriculture, hunting, and fishing. These required neither extensive clearing nor large settlements. In parts of the region, the rubber boom of the 1800s and the hunt for minerals profoundly affected the health and well-being of the Indian populations.

An important and distinct group of long-term immigrants who created communities that remained isolated from their national cultures were slaves who escaped into the tropical forest and founded free black communities. Settlements of this sort were located in parts of French Guiana, Surinam, Guyana, Venezuela, Colombia, and Brazil. Some of these communities, known as Maroons, continued a fairly separate existence even after slavery was abolished in their countries. Some spoke a creole language and developed their own culture from a combination of European, African, and locally indigenous traditions. In regions with large Maroon communities, these people may have had an influence on local Indian traditions [see SURINAM].

Missionaries and their musical baggage

Important beyond their numbers because of the influence they exercised over other groups, missionaries brought new musical forms to the tropical forest, based on harmony and sacred texts. In the interior of the region, large Roman Catholic missions became important institutions with considerable power and authority. They were often run by international orders and staffed by foreigners. Their effect on the Indian communities was often harsh: they forbade traditional music and ceremonies and restricted musical activities.

Later, missionaries of certain Protestant sects intensified the process, some with such success that hymns are the only music performed in certain tropical-forest Indian communities. Singing hymns may take unusual directions, however, as among the Waiwai, where communities compete in composing hymns.

With a few exceptions, the music of the church and the music of the Indians have apparently not mixed: the tunes for Christian services are hymns, and the Indian melodies continue without harmony where they are sung at all. In unusual cases, Indian communities employ some form of harmony that may have its origins in Christian music, as among the Kayabi (strict parallel fifths) and the Javae of Brazil, and the Moxo of Bolivia (Olsen 1976). In Guyana, among the Akawaio, the Makushi, and the Patamona, unusual music developed for the syncretic religion known as Hallelujah (Butt Colson 1971).

Handling the baggage

Why did Indian communities let the missionaries make them abandon their traditions? Part of the answer certainly lies with the missionaries' economic power. But part of it may have come from the missionaries' ability to win support among the less enfranchised parts of the Indian population—women, children, and young men. The missionaries often started schools for children and for extended periods of time took children away from their parents. They often tried to create new leadership of young men. Since adult men dominated the ritual and public life of the village, part of the missionaries' success may have been the willingness of women and young men to challenge the power of traditional leadership.

The tropical forest was not an area of florescence for Christian music; it did not produce the original Baroque compositions found in other parts of the Americas, and

cuatro 'Four', four-stringed small guitar from Venezuela and diffused to regions close to Venezuela

viola Brazilian plucked and strummed chordophone (from viola de mão, 'of the hand') with five double courses of ten or twelve metal strings

gaucho In Argentina, Uruguay, and southern Brazil, a rural dweller or cowboy of the pampa

música caipira Brazilian "country music"

huayno (also, *wayno*) Native American–derived (Quechua) Peruvian and other central Andean fast duple-metered song and dance form featuring long-short-short rhythmical pattern

Waiwai hymns have so far not had an impact on Protestant hymnals outside the region. Tropical-forest Indians' influence was quite large, however.

Other early immigrants to the tropical forest came from rural areas in the different countries and moved to the region to participate in its extractive economy. They brought with them rural musical traditions and annual celebrations. They played a variety of national styles on guitar, *cuatro,* viola, violin, and other stringed instruments, which they often made themselves. Aside from the music performed in churches, they made music at dance parties, in bars, at birthday parties, and during certain calendrical rituals such as saints' days and Christmas. In some communities, residents formed troupes to perform dance-dramas found in their own country and other Latin American countries, and larger settlements often had brass bands and some instruction in music. In some cases, rural forms survive in the tropical-forest settlements but have disappeared in the places from which they came.

Some itinerant poets and musicians probably made their living from their performances, but many more people now play part-time for their own communities. All music was live, face to face, and of course without amplification. The small settlements of Europeans and their descendants often developed distinct regional cultures, incorporating Indian material culture and in some cases a basic vocabulary. These communities usually remained economically and culturally tied to the commercial centers of each country, however, if only through an occasional boat that would exchange supplies for natural products. They remained linked to the national culture of which they were a regional part.

IMMIGRATION AFTER THE 1930s

Immigration increased in the twentieth century, and technological changes such as outboard motors, electric generators, recorded sound, radio, and extensive networks of roads in some areas have transformed the economy and the cultures of the entire tropical-forest region. There is now not a single part that lies beyond the reach of a radio transmitter; and with battery-operated portable radios, phonographs, and tape players, even the residents of the smallest settlements can play the latest music.

Pouring into the region on newly constructed roads or flying into newly enlarged airports, immigrants are rapidly altering the face of the tropical forest, physically and culturally. Quechua- and Aymara-speakers from the highlands have opened new communities in the lowlands; large numbers of gauchos from the southern states of Brazil have moved into Mato Grosso, Rondonia, and Acre; Protestant missionaries are making inroads among Roman Catholic worshipers; regional cities have swelled and created industries, established large governmental bureaucracies, and founded universities that bring wealthier and more highly educated people to the region. Each of these groups brings new music to the tropical forest and introduces some new traditions to it.

If you were to hover over the tropical-forest region today, in the haze of the smoke of burning clearings, and listen to the sound of the music, the cacophony would be even greater than before. From tens of thousands of terrible loudspeakers distorting the music from hundreds of sources, you could hear country and rock, industrial products of the world at large; from bars and nightclubs in towns and cities of all sizes, you would hear forms of regional rock, and professional musicians playing styles specific to their region; from Indian villages, a thousand tape recorders would be playing national music and even music from other places in the world. The predawn crescendo will have diminished, to be replaced by an evening one as leisure is fitted and fixed into set working hours. The oratorical styles are now often those of sports announcers and politicians, the national anthems of various countries sound out from thousands of rural schools, and religions have made certain days and hours specific to hymns and other religious genres.

If you could see through the smoke, you would see the separation of music and dance, a general secularization of performances, and a continued fascination with bodily ornamentation and swishing adornments, often now in the form of earrings, wristwatches, makeup, and cologne on the one hand, and machine-made clothing on the other.

The centers of the music industry are not to be found in the tropical-forest region, but a great deal of their product sells there. Whether by radio, by prerecorded cassettes, by magazine articles and photographs, or by television, the sounds and images of urban centers bombard the region. Exporting raw materials and importing finished products, the more remote parts of the region have more than a little colonial flavor. Ownership and patronage also come from the urban centers, and many professional musicians in the region eventually leave to pursue their careers elsewhere.

Probably the largest components of the music industry throughout the tropical forest are the country traditions (in Brazil, *música caipira*; in Peru, *huayno*; and in Venezuela, salsa), which have developed with the spread of recording and playback technology.

Most countries in the tropical-forest region have developed national country or rural-popular genres. Like U.S. country music, most of this music is instrumental dance music or verse-form singing in close parallel harmony by soloists, duets, trios, or quartets accompanying themselves primarily on stringed instruments. It draws heavily from folk music and has had a tremendous influence on it. Widespread and popular but little appreciated by urban sophisticates, this music (and the musical roots from which it draws) is a central part of the repertoire of many immigrants to the tropical forest. Because it does not appeal to middle-class urban sophisticates, we have few good studies of it.

The tropical-forest region continues to preserve some distinctiveness, for it is usually distant from the national capitals and the largest centers of population. The rhythms and songs of carnival, which dominate the popular music of the coastal cities of Brazil from November to February, are hardly heard in Acre. Hip-hop was not the craze in Roraima that it became in Rio de Janeiro. This pattern probably matches that of other national musical forms elsewhere in the region.

With increased communication and increased research, the music of the tropical forest has become an object of study in itself. In virtually every national capital, specialists are working to document and preserve tropical-forest musical traditions. They publish the books and recordings that are the best source most of us have for this kind of music. In each country too, bureaucrats are engaged in trying to turn the traditions into possible tourist attractions. In many small cities, the mayor's office works with the local board of tourism and local groups to ensure the continued distinctiveness of their part of the region. Ecotourism, adventure tourism, and the constant search for the exotic have brought new types of visitors to certain areas.

CULTURAL INTERACTIONS

In the intense interaction that typifies the cultures and communities of much of the tropical-forest region, music plays an important part in forging and demonstrating community or ethnic identity and sociopolitical positions. The transnational entertainment industry and the more commercial regional traditions have heavily influenced local populations through recordings, radio, and television. The processes are complex and ongoing. We do not know where they will lead.

For centuries, Indians have learned each other's songs, including hymns and other immigrant musical forms. This process continues. Upper Xingu Indians are great fans of Brazilian rock; elsewhere, country is the rage. Some Indian communities have consciously tried to reach accommodations with regional culture. For a while, some Eastern Timbira groups in Brazil were alternating their traditional ceremonies with dances in which regional musicians performed and couples danced together. How enduring such accommodations will be depends on whether new generations of "traditional" singers will emerge.

Indian music has become part of the creation and expression of an ethnic identity. Some groups are reviving older forms. To demonstrate authentic Indianness, by which to assert communal rights to land, health care, and other benefits denied to non-Indians, some peoples—whose oral tradition was so interrupted that there is nothing left to revive—are re-Indianizing themselves by learning traditions from other Indians. Music has become part of a complex set of interethnic relations, in which not only Indians but also ethnomusicologists and other researchers are often actual participants.

Indian music may be important in forging a certain kind of national identity, and Indian music from the tropical forest is of sufficient interest to the larger national society to support the production of documentary recordings on small independent labels. In an effort to affirm a distinct national identity, nationalist composers in several countries in the Americas have composed operas and other pieces that tried to combine European and Indian musical traditions. In *Nozanina*, for example, the Brazilian composer Heitor Villa-Lobos (1887–1959), with a Brazilian anthropologist, created a piece that combines European compositional styles with a text that is probably in Tupinambá. A similar association of musical forms and ethnic identity is important in certain Afro-Latin American communities, in which fairly isolated cultural forms of the Maroon and other largely black communities of the interior are becoming a source of pride and identity.

Concern with the future of the tropical forest and the appetite of the transnational popular-music industry for novelty have led to manifold results, but not to a great deal of tropical-forest influence on popular music. Some promoters of tropical-forest Indian music support the music to defend the tropical-forest ecosystem; others promote the music to broaden their fans' listening habits. Indian communities that have been given the chance are recording their traditions to defend their livelihood and culture. Some tropical-forest Indians, active in the defense of their ecosystems, fight against thoughtless industrialization. Through intensive political efforts, they make trips to the United States and to Geneva to talk with international organizations about how to invest in the regions in which they live. The Kayapo Indian leader Rauni toured with Sting in the 1980s, speaking out against the environmental destruction being inflicted on the region.

By the late 1990s, however, this activity had not led to a popular musical fusion the way the encounter with South African popular music, Afro-Brazilian music, or

Andean music had led to dramatic new styles of popular music in the Americas. Few non-Indian musicians dealt with the *sounds* of Brazilian Indian music in any serious musical way. When they used Indian sounds, they tended to opt for direct quotation, rather than for paraphrase or fusion.

Brazilian popular musicians have taken melodies from the tropical forest: in Brazil, Caetano Veloso uses a Juruna flute melody on one recording, and Milton Nascimento includes segments of Brazilian Indian songs in his recording *Txai!* (1990). Often laboring under a romantic vision of the noble primitive, many artists have gone to the tropical forest in search of something pure and missing in their own music. Sometimes their encounters have been completely perplexing; sometimes they have been enlightening for both parties; sometimes they have been more useful for one than the other.

CONCLUSION

Why have so few attempts been made to adapt the indigenous music of the tropical forest? I think it is a combination of social and musical features. Most Indian music is associated with ritual; it has little harmony or polyphony, and what polyphony it has is unfamiliar to unaccustomed ears. Drums and strings are not common in the Indian traditions but are absolutely central to popular music. The long, apparently repetitive performances are foreign to the popular music genre, in which three minutes, rather than all night, is the norm for recorded sound.

In many of these respects, tropical-forest Indian music differs from most African traditions and the Afro-*latino* traditions of the Americas. The indigenous South American form that has had international success is Andean popular music, whose several types are themselves the result of musical fusion in their home countries. Perhaps tropical-forest fusion will someday develop; perhaps it will not. One of the most enlightened and enlightening musical styles of native and pop fusion in the late 1990s, however, is the music of Marlui Miranda (1996), a Brazilian Indian.

The reasons for adopting or not adopting a certain musical form are only partly related to the sounds of the music. That is why the development of musical styles can be interesting. It is only slightly predictable. The past is obscured by a lack of archaeological record, the devastation of Indian populations before the arrival of the first researchers and the rapid destruction of communities by the advancing frontier, highly capitalized investment, and large-scale immigration. The present is obscured by its evanescence, and the future has yet to emerge.

The tropical-forest region of South America is huge. Its music is little researched and documented. Yet to the people who live there, music is often an indispensable part of life. Through it, they try to accomplish many different things. As with much music throughout the world, we hear and know about only a small fraction of what is performed.

REFERENCES

Aretz, Isabel. 1984. *Síntesis de la Etnomúsica en América Latina.* Biblioteca INIDEF, 6. Caracas: Monte Avila Editores.

———. 1991. *Música de Los Aborígenes de Venezuela.* Caracas: Fundación de Etnomusicología y Folklore.

Aytai, Desiderio. 1985. *O Mundo Sonoro Xavante.* Coleção Museu Paulista, Ethnologia, 5. São Paulo: Universidade de São Paulo.

Basso, Ellen B. 1985. *A Musical View of the Universe.* Philadelphia: University of Pennsylvania Press.

Bastos, Rafael Jose de Menezes. 1978. *A Musicológica Kamayurá.* Brasilia: Fundação Nacional do Indio.

———. 1986. "Música, Cultura e Sociedade no Alto-Xingu: A Teoria Musical dos Indios Kamayurá." *Latin American Music Review* 7:51–80.

Butt Colson, Audrey. 1971. "Hallelujah among

the Patamona Indians." *Antropológica* 28:25–58.

Cameu, Helza. 1977. *Introdução ao Estudo da Música Indígena Brasileira*. Rio de Janeiro: Conselho Federal de Cultura.

Crawford, Neelon. 1979. *Soul Vine Shaman*. Notes by Norman Whitten. Sacha Runa Research Foundation Occasional Paper 5. LP disk.

Dobkin de Rios, Marlene, and Fred Katz. 1975. "Some Relationships between Music and Hallucinogenic Ritual: The Jungle-Gym of Consciousness." *Ethos* 3:64–76.

Fuks, Victor. 1989. "Demonstration of Multiple Relationships between Music and Culture of the Waiãpi Indians of Brazil." Ph.D. dissertation, Indiana University.

Graham, Laura. 1986. "Three Modes of Shavante Vocal Expression: Wailing, Collective Singing, and Political Oratory." In *Native South American Discourse*, ed. Greg Urban and Joel Sherzer, 82–118. Berlin: Mouton de Gruyter.

———. 1990. "The Always Living: Discourse and the Male Lifecycle of the Xavante Indians of Central Brazil." Ph.D. dissertation, University of Texas at Austin.

Gregor, Thomas, ed. 1973. *Mehinaku*. 16-mm film.

———. 1977. *Mehinaku: The Drama of Everyday Life in a Brazilian Indian Village*. Chicago: University of Chicago Press.

———. 1985. *Anxious Pleasures: The Sexual Lives of an Amazonian People*. Chicago: University of Chicago Press.

Harner, Michael J. 1972. *Jivaro: People of the Sacred Waterfalls*. New York: Doubleday.

———. 1973. *Music of the Jívaro of Ecuador*. Folkways Records FE 4386. LP disk.

Hill, Jonathan D. 1993. *Keepers of the Sacred Chants—The Poetics of Ritual Power in an Amazonian Society*. Tucson: University of Arizona Press.

Hugh-Jones, Stephen. 1979. *The Palm and the Pleiades: Initiation and Cosmology in the Northwest Amazon*. Cambridge: Cambridge University Press.

Izikowitz, Karl G. 1970 [1935]. *Musical and Other Sound Instruments of the South American Indians*. East Ardsley, Wakefield, Yorkshire: S. R. Publishers.

Kensinger, Kenneth M. 1973. "*Banisteriopsis* Usage among the Peruvian Cashinahua." In *Hallucinogens and Shamanism*, ed. Michael J. Harner, 9–14. Oxford: Oxford University Press.

Miranda, Marlui. 1995. *Ihu, Todos os Sons*. Manaus, Brazil: Pau Brasil PB 001. Compact disc.

Nascimento, Milton. 1990. *Txai!* Brazil: Discos C.B.S. 177.228 / 1–464138. LP disk.

Nimuendaju, Curt. 1980. *Mapa Etno-Histórico de Curt Nimuendaju*. Rio de Janeiro: Fundação Instituto Brasileiro de Geografia e Estatística and Fundação Nacional Pró-Memória.

Olsen, Dale. 1976. "Música vesperal Mojo en San Miguel de Isiboro, Bolivia." *Revista Musical Chilena* 30(133):28–46.

———. 1981. "Symbol and Function in South American Indian Music." In *Musics of Many Cultures: An Introduction*, ed. Elizabeth May, 363–385. Berkeley: University of California Press.

———. 1996. *Music of the Warao of Venezuela: Song People of the Rain Forest*. Gainesville: University Press of Florida.

Seeger, Anthony. 1987. *Why Suyá Sing: A Musical Anthropology of an Amazonian People*. Cambridge: Cambridge University Press.

Sherzer, Joel, and Greg Urban, ed. 1986. *Native South American Discourse*. Berlin: Mouton de Gruyter.

Vidal, Lux. 1977. *Morte e Vida de uma Sociedade Indígena Brasileira*. São Paulo: Hucitec and EDUSP.

Viveiros de Castro, Eduardo B. 1986. *Arawete: Uma Visão da Cosmologia e da Pessoa Tukpi-Guarani*. Rio de Janeiro: Editora Zahar.

Wagley, Charles, and Eduardo Galvão. 1949. *The Tenetehara Indians of Brazil*. New York: Columbia University Press.

Moxo
Dale A. Olsen

Music at Jesuit Missions
Music of the Trinitarios of San Miguel de Isiboro
Further Study

The Amerindian people known as Moxo (Mojo in Spanish orthography) inhabit the Moxo Plains (*llanos de Mojos*), a large lowland area of grassland and scrub forest in northeastern Bolivia. This area of about 181,000 square kilometers extends from the eastern slopes of the Cordillera Oriental (Eastern Range) of the Andes to the Guaporé River, the present boundary with Brazil, largely within the Bolivian department of Beni. The capital of Beni, Trinidad (named for the Holy Trinity), is its largest city. Other towns include Concepción (named for the Immaculate Conception of the Blessed Virgin Mary), Magdalena (named for Mary Magdalene), and others with Christian names. These were three of twenty-one missions founded by the Jesuits, who controlled the area from the 1680s until their expulsion in 1767 (Claro 1969:9). According to a 1715 census, about thirty years after their first encounter with the Spanish, the Moxo numbered about eighteen thousand people (Steward and Faron 1959:254).

The Moxo, with their neighbors the Bauré, speak a language of the Macro-Arawakan linguistic phylum and Maipuran family (Greenberg 1987:384). The Jesuits imposed the Moxo language as the standard throughout the area, replacing others. After 1767, however, many villages returned to using their original languages. One, a Moxo dialect, is today called Trinitario by its speakers, whom others call Trinitarios. They, like most Moxo, have adopted European beliefs and practices, and their most frequent musical expressions occur as part of their Christian religious beliefs. In numbers and cultural development, the Moxo once dominated northeastern Bolivia.

MUSIC AT JESUIT MISSIONS

Jesuit missionaries taught Spanish Christian music to the Moxo, who like the Guaraní in Paraguay became excellent singers (as soloists and choristers), instrumentalists, builders of musical instruments, musical scribes, and even choir directors. The musical instruments built by the Moxo included European-style drums, organs, and violins. The Moxo fabricated a bass instrument by joining up to eleven of their traditional conical bark trumpets into enormous panpipes, which they sounded by buzzing the lips, not by blowing as flutes (Steward 1949:420, plate 39). These they

As an ancient dance, the *machetero* was associated with a shamanistic ritual held inside a special house where men sang, danced, and offered corn beer (*chicha*) to their jaguar god. The dance continues that tradition by replacing the jaguar deity with Saint Michael.

called big basses (*bajones*), which Samuel Claro erroneously called *fagót* 'bassoon', implying a double-reed instrument. *Bajones* probably provided the *basso continuo* part in sacred and secular musical performances. Even a century after the expulsion of the Jesuits, *bajones* joined flutes, violins, and drums to perform polkas and quadrilles (Claro 1969:12–13).

The Jesuits allowed the Moxo to perform traditional dances as acts of faith in Christian religious processions during the festivals of Corpus Christi, the Blessed Trinity, and the patron saint of each mission. One of these dances, the *machetero* 'swordsman dance', is still performed. Part of the remainder of this essay, based on research by the anthropologist Dori Reeks while she was a Peace Corps volunteer in the late 1960s, describes this dance and other religious musical expressions of the Trinitarios in the village of San Miguel de Isiboro (St. Michael of the Isiboro River) (Olsen 1974).

MUSIC OF THE TRINITARIOS OF SAN MIGUEL DE ISIBORO

Living in the Chaparé area of Bolivia, in the southern part of Beni, the Trinitarios form one of the last unassimilated communities of the Moxo. The Trinitario village of San Miguel on the Isiboro River, located about three days' travel by canoe from the nearest settlements, was founded in 1955 as a result of the Trinitarios' search for *tierra santa,* the land of peace and happiness. According to their belief, *tierra santa* will be a village guarded by jaguars and snakes who admit only the pure. There, living in harmony with an abundance of everything good, chosen Moxo people will be in the presence of God, manifested as Saint Michael (figure 1).

Vespers service for the patronal festival of Saint Michael

A deep religious conviction is basic to the culture of the Trinitarios of San Miguel de Isiboro, for whom religion is a mixture of traditional Moxo expressions and Roman Catholic Christianity, though the two systems of belief are invoked at different times during a religious event. This dichotomy is especially seen in the vespers service for the patronal festival of Saint Michael, which lasts from 5:00 P.M. on 28 September until 4:00 A.M. on 29 September. The indigenous portion of the evening is the *machetero*, which until 10:00 P.M. alternates with the more standard Christian musical worship. The remainder of the event includes praying and singing.

Machetero *music and dance*

A *machetero* is a swordsman who, brandishing a machete, symbolically fights off evil forces. Franz Keller-Leuzinger (1874:160) described the dance:

FIGURE 1 Altar and statue of San Miguel (Saint Michael), patron saint of the village of San Miguel de Isiboro, Beni, Bolivia, in the Roman Catholic Church. Photo by Dori Reeks, 1969.

A dozen of the sword-dancers (macheteiros), on the day of the consecration of a church, went singing and dancing and brandishing their broad knives and wooden swords, from cross to cross, headed by their chieftain, who carried a heavy silver

FIGURE 2 *Machetero* dancers, a bass drummer, and other participants during the vespers of the festival of Saint Michael in San Miguel de Isiboro, Beni, Bolivia. Photo by Dori Reeks, 1969.

cross, and followed by the whole tribe. They wore dazzling white camisetas, rattling stag's claws on their knuckles, and a fanciful head-gear composed of the long tail-feathers of the araras and of yellow and red toucan's breasts.

This description fits the *machetero* of 1969 as photographed in San Miguel de Isiboro (figure 2). The dancers, fewer than in 1864, still wear on their ankles—not their "knuckles" as Keller-Leuzinger writes—strung rattles, traditionally made from the shells of fruits or the hooves of deer (Steward 1959:420), and they are accompanied by a two-headed drum and a bird-bone flute (figure 3).

The exact significance of the *machetero* dance is unknown. Claro (1969:14) suggests that it symbolizes a warrior fighting against his enemies or against nature. Dori Reeks (personal communication, 1972) claims that the dancer represents the surrender of human beings to the infinite or to all the powers of nature. She learned from the Trinitarios that as an ancient dance, it was associated with a shamanistic ritual held inside a special house where men sang, danced, and offered corn beer (*chicha*) to their jaguar god. The dance continues that tradition by replacing the jaguar deity with Saint Michael. Keller-Leuzinger (1874:160) wrote, however, that the dance is "evidently representing the submission of the Indians and their conversion to Christianity." In Keller-Leuzinger's time, the dancer performed inside the church in front of the altar, but today he always performs outside the church.

FIGURE 3 *Machetero* dancers and a bird-bone flutist during the vespers of the festival of Saint Michael in San Miguel de Isiboro, Beni, Bolivia. Photo by Dori Reeks, 1969.

FIGURE 4   A young boy *machetero* dancer during the vespers of the festival of Saint Michael in San Miguel de Isiboro, Beni, Bolivia. Photo by Dori Reeks, 1969.

The instrumentation used for the music of today's *machetero* consists of a six-holed bird-bone flute with a fipple mouthpiece. The flutist is accompanied by a large bass drum played with one stick, and occasionally by a snare drum played with two sticks. Added to this are rhythms created by the dancer's anklet-strung rattles, which today are often metal jingle bells, especially used by children when they dance (figure 4). A portion of the music played by the flutist (figure 5) consists of a main melody (A) repeated several times, followed by a secondary melody (B) played once, and continuing with several repetitions of that pattern. Throughout the performance, the flutist ornaments the melody, as shown in the transcription.

Roman Catholic music for vespers

During the vespers, two musical events contrast strongly with the dance of the *macheteros:* the processional and the singing of the faithful followers as they approach the church. The processional musicians (figure 6) include several violinists and players of a cane transverse flute, a bass drum, and a snare drum. Their music is march-like, in duple meter. They alternate with a lead male singer (*taita*) and several female singers, accompanied by a violin in a slow style, reminiscent of plainchant.

The invocation or versicle sung by the *taita* is answered by the female chorus an octave higher, while the violin plays in mid-range parallel fifths with the *taita,* who sings in parallel fourths with the women (figure 7). To avoid the tritone, the violinist plays a D♮. This music seems to resound from Jesuit times, and the contrast with *machetero* music could not be greater. Both ritual expressions, however, celebrate the same patron saint, at least openly.

FURTHER STUDY

The sketchbook of Franz Keller-Leuzinger (1874) is important for understanding the *machetero* dance in historical times. His book has one of the best depictions of the *bajones* as they were played in church. Claro's article (1969) is the most important study of Moxo music during the Jesuit occupation. A recent book by Becerra Casanovas (1990) describes a number of Moxo dances, songs, and musical instruments.

FIGURE 5 Music performed on a bird-bone flute and a bass drum for the *machetero* dancer during the 1969 vespers of the festival of Saint Michael in San Miguel de Isiboro, Beni, Bolivia. Transcription by Dale A. Olsen, from a tape recorded by Dori Reeks.

continues

FIGURE 6 A flutist, two violinists, kneeling women, and standing *machetero* dancers during the 1969 vespers of the festival of Saint Michael in San Miguel de Isiboro, Beni, Bolivia. Photo by Dori Reeks, 1969.

FIGURE 7 Music performed on a violin and sung by a male leader and female responders during the 1969 vespers of the festival of Saint Michael in San Miguel de Isiboro, Beni, Bolivia. Transcription by Dale A. Olsen from a tape recorded by Dori Reeks.

REFERENCES

Becerra Casanovas, Rogers. 1990. *Reliquias de Moxos.* La Paz, Bolivia: Empresa Editora "Proinsa."

Claro, Samuel. 1969. "La Música en las Misiones Jesuitas de Moxos." *Revista Musical Chilena* 22 (108):7–31.

Greenberg, Joseph H. 1987. *Language in the Americas.* Stanford: Stanford University Press.

Keller-Leuzinger, Franz. 1874. *The Amazon and Madeira Rivers: Sketches and Descriptions from the Note-Book of an Explorer.* London: Chapman and Hall.

Olsen, Dale A. 1974. "Música vesperal Mojo en San Miguel de Isiboro, Bolivia." *Revista Musical Chilena* 30(133):28–46.

Steward, Julian H., ed. 1949. *Handbook of South American Indians.* Vol. 3, *Tropical Forest Tribes.* Washington, D.C.: U. S. Government Printing Office.

Steward, Julian H., and Louis C. Faron. 1959. *Native Peoples of South America.* New York: McGraw-Hill.

Suyá
Anthony Seeger

History
Musical Material Culture
Musical Contexts, Genres, and Structures
Social Structure, Musicians and Behavior, Musical Systems, and Performance Practices
Musical Enculturation
Musical Dynamics

Today the Suyá Indians live in a single village of about two hundred inhabitants on the banks of the Suiá-Miçu River, an affluent of the Xingu River at about 11 degrees south latitude (the Xingu flows north into the Amazon River). Horticulture, hunting, fishing, and gathering supply their basic needs, and trade or conflict with frontier settlements and ranches supplies them with salt, ammunition, trade goods, and some medical supplies and services. They speak a language belonging the northern branch of the Gê language family. Missionaries are not allowed to practice in the Xingu reserve, and the Suyá have little experience with Christian ideas and practices. Since shamanism is not highly elaborated, Western medical practices employed by Brazilian officials have not undermined the authority of traditional culture. The Suyá continue to perform many of their traditional ceremonies. They made peace with Brazilians in 1959.

Though language identity does not define cultural attributes, the Gê-speaking communities of Brazil share musical traits found among the Suyá: genres of speech and song are highly elaborated; most music is sung; unison singing marks important social groups; idiophones are common; aereophones are mostly played for emphasis and only rarely for melodies; songs originate from outside the community (from ancestors, animals, monsters, and other Indian communities); hallucinogens, alcohol, and tobacco are rarely central to musical performances; and most music is associated with rites of passage. Specific features of Suyá music that have not been documented among other Gê groups include an isomorphism of musical structures and cosmological structures, and the metamorphosis of performers into hybrid animal or human beings during ceremonies.

HISTORY

The historical record for the Suyá is shallow, with neither archaeological nor important ethnographic records extending back before 1884, when Karl von den Steinen (1942) visited the Suyá at the mouth of the Suiá-Miçu. Little cultural material can be preserved in the humid tropics, and most materials used by the Suyá were organic. Ethnographic evidence supports the Suyá claim that they made a long exodus from territory more than 1,100 kilometers to the northeast, fleeing and fighting enemies

Although their symbolism is not highly elaborated, hoof rattles are not to be attached to dancers' legs because there is always a danger of the dancer's changing into an animal.

throughout the 1700s and 1800s. Most Northern and Central Gê moved inland away from the advancing Brazilian frontier. What may be different about the Suyá is that they sing the songs of many groups they encountered during their travels. Suyá oral history (myths) recounts that, although Suyá society always existed, in the beginning the people had no fire, no names, no garden crops, no lip-disc ornaments, and few songs. They acquired fire from the jaguar, garden crops from the mouse, lip discs from enemy Indians, names from a cannibal people living under the ground, and songs from all of those. Suyá history is thus the recounting of a steady acquisition of desirable things (musical forms among them) from powerful outsiders. These acquisitions determined the shape and definition of Suyá society and music today: food must be cooked, body ornaments are significant markers of age and status, names are central to the definition of who a person is and the groups to which he or she belongs, and songs have their origins in beings outside everyday Suyá society.

MUSICAL MATERIAL CULTURE

Music performed by the Suyá is supremely vocal. Musical instruments play a small role in their performances; the most frequently used are idiophones that accompany singing and dancing. The principal rattle, *hwin krã,* is made of individual *piqui* pits strung with hand-spun cotton or occasionally burity-palm fiber to a central string. This can be held in the hand or tied to the knees so that the rattle sounds with each step. In addition to *piqui* pits, these rattles can be made from deer, tapir, or wild-pig hoofs. These rattles can be held in the hand, wrapped around the knees, or occasionally hung down the back. Although their symbolism is not highly elaborated, hoof rattles are not to be attached to dancers' legs because there is always a danger of the dancer's changing into an animal. In at least two myths the rattles turn into hooves on the singer, who irrevocably becomes an animal, unable to return to human form. Large gourds are sometimes suspended on a string down the back, knocking against the knee rattles.

A gourd rattle is played in certain ceremonies. It is made from a gourd partly filled with seeds with a wooden shaft going through the middle of it, decorated with a band of macaw down (young feathers) around the middle and a few parrot-wing feathers hanging from a string attached to the tip of the staff. In one ceremony, certain social groups carry red gourd rattles, other groups carry black rattles, and a third social group concludes the ceremony by chasing the singer-dancers and breaking their rattles.

Though the Suyá were aware of and even knew how to manufacture a variety of Upper Xingu woodwind instruments, they did not seriously make and play them, though they did seriously perform Upper Xingu sung ceremonies. Nor were any Brazilian musical instruments observed in the village between 1971 and 1998.

The Suyá are fairly well provided with electronic instruments. Their enjoyment of radio and cassette recorders is limited by the difficulty of obtaining batteries and the lack of generators or electric power near the village. In 1971, there were four shortwave radios in the village; by 1982, cassette recorders had made a tremendous impact. The Suyá recorded all their own ceremonies and exchanged tapes with other Indians. For non-literate Suyá, keeping a lot of identical-looking tapes straight was a problem. The man with the largest collection in 1981 had obtained a collection of pin-up wallet calendars, which he inserted in his cassette boxes. He would identify his tapes by the color of the J-card spine and the type of girl represented on the calendar ("the green box with the big-eyed girl on it"). In the late 1980s, the Suyá were operating two-way radios in contact with the Indian post and other villages. By 1994, they had become interested in video technology; through me had obtained a camera, solar panels, and rechargeable batteries; and had begun documenting their own ceremonies and other events. In recordings they made for themselves, they paid scrupulous attention to visual and sonic detail, and they often recorded aspects of events that outsiders might not have thought to record. By 1994 too, there was a Suyá-run bilingual school in the village, but it offered no outside musical influences; the school calendar featured Suyá ceremonies to mark the months. Many adults today can speak Portuguese, and a few can read and write.

MUSICAL CONTEXTS, GENRES, AND STRUCTURES IN 1995

The Suyá named their songs in two fashions. One was by performance style: *ngere* refers to unison songs, *akia* to individual shout songs, *iaren* to recitative-like speech, and *sangere* to invocations. The other was by ceremony: *amto ngere* 'mouse ceremony', *angroti ngere* 'wild-pig ceremony', *agachi ngere* 'day song (in rainy season)', and *kahran kaság ngere* 'big turtle song (for dry season)', and so on. Most Suyá rituals were related to the human life cycle, especially that part of it occurring from preadolescence through the birth of several children. The male life cycle was particularly marked by ceremonies involving musical performance. These ceremonies usually corresponded with certain agricultural or collecting seasons. Thus, the mouse ceremony was performed when the maize was ripe, and corn products figured prominently in the ritual foods prepared during it. Other ceremonies were performed in the dry season, when agricultural products and fish were plentiful.

The word *ngere* was the generic name for music and dance. The Suyá considered the sounds and their associated movements to be essentially part of the same performance. They sometimes hummed a tune without moving, but a real performance always involved specific bodily movements. Most Suyá dance was fairly simple walking or stamping in rhythm, moving clockwise or counterclockwise according to moiety membership, and holding or moving the hands in certain ways. But certain song-dances had more elaborate body movements, difficult enough for the less experienced young men or women to be embarrassed by trying to do them. Older people, supposedly less ashamed or shy, moved their bodies more freely as they sang.

Except for some rather generic songs that could be sung during a fairly long period of the year, most songs were restricted to the appropriate ceremonial period. A ceremonial period could last from a couple of days to an entire season, during which songs associated with the ceremony would be considered appropriate. After the opening evening, larger ceremonies would work their way slowly to a grand finale of all-night singing with full body ornamentation, multiple musical roles, collective euphoria, and some kind of spiritual metamorphosis. But there might be long periods without much activity beyond the seasonal songs in morning and evening.

Suyá shamanism was little developed. Most adults knew some invocations (*sangere*) they could use to influence the body, but these are quite distinct from the shamanistic efforts to recover souls found widely throughout South America. The fifty Suyá invocations that I collected were used as preventive care and first aid and included those to ease childbirth, to make a child grow tall, to heal a wound, to still a child with fever convulsions, and to heal snakebites and scorpion bites. The following example was performed to cure fevers that caused trembling and convulsions. It sought to blow into the patient the stillness and coolness of a particular animal—the cold-blooded white cayman, which can lie completely still in the water without causing a ripple. This would normally be recited by the singer quietly and rapidly under the breath, while blowing on the patient. The vocal tone would be musical rather than spoken. Glissandi marked the end of some phrases (indicated with multiple vowels).

> Master of the still waters [five times]
> Rough-skinned white cayman, his hand is spread out [without trembling], how cooooome?
> Animal, animal that lies there still
> Master of the still waters, with his rough skin, lying there in the stream
> Master of the still waters [five times]
> Master of our still waters
> White cayman, master of still waters
> His hand is spread out, his neck skin is spread out, his hand is spread out, he trembles not. How cooooome?
> Animal, animal, lying there
> Master of the still waters [three times]

The performer blew before the first and last lines.

Most invocations called on traits of things in the natural world to affect the human body. A slippery fish would be named to cause a fast and easy childbirth (the baby will slip out of the womb the way the fish escapes the hand); the strong-tusked wild pig would be invoked for a toothache; and so forth. The Suyá would give presents to people who performed invocations over a sick relative. In 1994, the first shaman in decades began to give cures using invocations and tobacco blowing and sucking similar to that found in neighboring Tupi-speaking societies such as the Kaiabi.

The most significant song-genre division was between unison and individual songs. Unison songs were called *ngere.* Most were strongly marked by rattles and stamping, in a steady 2/2 meter. Every Suyá social group had certain songs it sang in close unison. The melodies usually comprised between two and four musical phrases, repeated over and over with slowly changing texts. Unison songs were characterized by a steady upward drift in pitch of as much as a fourth—possibly a trait of musical development. When adult men were singing these, they would send children away because children could not sing as low as the adults. If women sang with the men, they would usually enter later and sing an octave above them. Some ceremonies were performed only by women, and men would watch silently.

In contrast to the unison songs were the shout songs (*akia*). These varied according to the age of the performer, had two to four phrases and an overall descending contour, and were often sung simultaneously to produce polyphony. These, too, were usually sung to the accompaniment of rattles and stamping in a regular 2/2 meter. Singers would often sing a variety of *akia* in a single night's performance.

Virtually all Suyá songs were constructed of a set of named nesting dual structures. Like the invocations, virtually every song named at least one animal. Each two- to eight-phrase strophe had a section sung with referential (directly meaningful) words and a part with only song syllables. In the Suyá language, almost every song was described as having two halves that named a different action and different animal but would be sung to the same melody. The different sections of each half were defined by the progressive unfolding of the text. Each half began with song syllables but no referential meaning, in a part called empty or without referential meaning. This would be followed by a section called approaching the name, which would name an action, but not the animal doing it. This would be followed in turn by telling the name, which would give the full text of the verse, sung several times until a coda would end the half. Here is an example from the mouse ceremony, which names two species of mouse. It is in two parts: the first half (*kradi*) and the second half (*sindaw*).

> First strophe (empty): Te-te-te-te-.... [twice]
> Third strophe [approaching the naming] : I paint my mask, I paint my mask and leap and sing, te-te-te-te-te... [five times]
> Later strophe [telling the name]: red mouse, I paint my mask and leap and sing, te-te-te-te-te. . . . [repeated many times]
> Final coda [*kure*]: only the second of the two melody phrases, the one without referential meaning: te-te-te-te-te-. . . . (once)
>
> First strophe (empty): Te-te-te-te-. . . . [twice]
> Third strophe (approaching the naming): I cut my mask, I cut my mask and leap and sing, te-te-te-te. . . . [five times]
> Later strophe (telling the name): big mouse, I paint my mask and leap and sing, te-te-te-te. . . . [many times]
> Final coda (*kure*), only the second of the melodic phrases, without referential meaning: te-te-te-te-te. . . . [once]

Over the course of a ceremony, the performances were often made more complex by the addition of simultaneous sounds: a unison song would be sung with a shout song, with keening, animal calls, and other sounds added to create a dense sonic environment much more complex than can be conveyed in the transcription of a single melodic line. This "development" often increased over the course of weeks, beginning with single performances and concluding with a rich overlay of contrasting sounds. These overlapping sounds were one of the ways a musical performance would be judged beautiful. The simultaneous sonic involvement of large parts of the community created the happiness or euphoria required for a successful event.

Virtually all Suyá music was apparently related to rituals and ceremonies. The link between music and ritual is widespread in South America, but seemed to be more extreme among the Suyá than in other reports. There were no work songs, no lullabies, no protest songs. Instead, ceremonial songs might be sung by a man under his breath during a long trip; children were soothed with a gentle shh-shh-shh-shh, but without melody; and protest and anger were indicated through refusing to sing. Silence was an indicator of anger, and refusing to sing was an aggressive act.

Because no missionaries had spent much time among the Suyá, they had no Christian songs, no patron-saint festivities. Unless ceremonies as a whole are considered as theater, there was no theater music as such. Some pantomimes were performed by an old man of the "clown" age grade in the center of the village plaza. They were hilarious but significantly silent; music is part of ritual. Some music may be shown to outsiders, and sometimes guests from other tribes were invited to watch (as were visiting Brazilian doctors, post administrators, and anthropologists), but there was no use of music for touristic purposes. Guests were fed and given gifts, not requested to give gifts. By 1995, the Suyá expected to receive royalties from publica-

The aesthetics of musical performances were couched in terms of the throat. Good singers were described as having strong or beautiful throats, whereas poor singers had weak or bad throats.

tions of their music and considered advance payment at the time of recording to be appropriate.

SOCIAL STRUCTURE, MUSICIANS AND BEHAVIOR, MUSICAL SYSTEMS, AND PERFORMANCE PRACTICES IN 1995

In Suyá society, people sang not what they wanted but who they were. And as they sang they (re-)constructed their society in a particular way. Each gender, and within the genders each age group, sang different songs or sang the same songs differently. To a certain extent, ceremonies and musical occasions created a village organized on principles different from those of the domestic and kinship relationships. The entire village would be divided up into two groups based on their names (received from uncles and aunts, not parents). The roles they played, the songs they sang, and the way they sang was a function of which group they belonged to and how old they were. Each ceremonial group had a certain repertoire and a way of singing. Each name group might have a particular right or obligation in a certain ceremony, such as being the last to stop singing, or the first in the line of dancers. Nor did the groups remain the same: name membership in the two large groups (ceremonial moieties) changed from dry season to rainy season; who a person sang with conferred and reaffirmed social identity, as did what and how a person sang. Women did not participate in many Suyá ceremonies as singers. Instead, they had other ritual roles and their own ceremonies, in which they took the lead parts while the men were silent, and participated in some ceremonies learned from other tribes. As with many other parts of Suyá life, women claimed no knowledge of domains in which they were knowledgeable and capable of performing. In a sense, Suyá society could be characterized as an orchestra in which each gender, age grade, and ceremonial group had its particular part.

Suyá songs were structured in the same way as their social groups (dual) and their cosmology (dualist). There is thus an isomorphism among Suyá society, cosmology, and song. This is apparently a rather unusual musical situation, yet it is fundamental to understanding Suyá music and Suyá social organization. This appears clearly in recordings and fuller analyses (Seeger 1982, 1987).

In addition to the social correlation between song structure and social structure, there is a cosmological component to most songs. The naming of animals invokes a kind of power that becomes particularly strong during the long finale of major rituals, when singers are considered to be transformed through their singing, dancing, and ornamentation into human or animal beings. At the end of the ceremony, they are transformed back into humans, but altered through the experience. The bringing together of the natural and social worlds in invocations and songs is a deliberate and symbolically rich part of musical performance.

According to the Suyá, music had been learned in "mythical times" from animals, learned in "historical times" from enemy Indians, and introduced by living members of the community who had particular powers that enabled them to hear the songs being sung by natural species and teach them to their fellow Suyá. The process through which a man or woman became an introducer of new songs was complex, but essentially these individuals had their souls (*megaron*) taken to the animals' communities, where the souls learned the animals' languages and songs. The individual could then learn the songs directly from the bees, the fish, the trees, or the animals, and teach it to those Suyá who did not have that capacity. Musical innovation was always brought from outside the village. Music was always brought from outside and was somewhat transformative. It was fairly easy for the rest of the Suyá to learn new songs because a general overall structure and a systematic development of text in each half of a song was carried over from one song to another.

Aesthetic concepts

It was difficult to discover Suyá aesthetic concepts, since the evaluation of a singer depended on the evaluator's kinship relation to him or her. The aesthetics of musical performances were couched in terms of the throat. Good singers were described as having strong or beautiful throats, whereas poor singers had weak or bad throats. Certain unison songs were beautiful because the singers had big throats (sang low pitches), whereas other genres required a high-pitched, small-throated performance. A singer who could learn quickly (had a good ear) and perform well (had a beautiful throat) would be highly praised. The Suyá say that when they sing they are happy (*kin*) or euphoric. When people were euphoric, the ceremony was a success.

MUSICAL ENCULTURATION

Children learned music by following the adults' example. Children sometimes accompanied adults' dancing and singing. They sometimes put on their own ceremonies, in which they recreated all the major parts of adults' ceremonies—usually after the adults had completed them. Boys were given short individual songs, more easily learned than those of adults. Certain ceremonies set up small camp sites in which the youths were instructed in singing. In late adolescence, the boys were expected to sing a lot. Women's singing followed the same pattern. Girls would sing with their mothers and learn the songs. There were no more formal forms of musical enculturation such as clubs, schools, and other organizations.

MUSICAL DYNAMICS

Suyá music has always been changing. The Suyá liked to learn new songs and continued to create music. Between 1971 and 1995, they sang the songs of more than ten different tribes or ethnic groups. They probably sang songs of groups with whom they interacted more frequently and had economic and other social relations. Though they listened to the radio and sometimes danced to recorded Brazilian music, they rarely performed Brazilian songs. Similarly, their music has had little influence on the rest of the world.

REFERENCES

Seeger, Anthony. 1981. *Nature and Society in Central Brazil: The Suyá Indians of Mato Grosso.* Cambridge, Mass.: Harvard University Press.

———, ed. 1982. *Musica Indigena: A Arte Vocal dos Suyá.* São João del Rei: Tacape 007 1982. LP disk.

———. 1987. *Why Suyá Sing: A Musical Anthropology of an Amazonian People.* Cambridge: Cambridge University Press. With accompanying audio cassette.

———. 1991. "When Music Makes History." In *Ethnomusicology and Modern Music History,* ed. Stephen Blum, Philip V. Bohlman, and Daniel M. Neuman, 23–35. Urbana and Chicago: University of Illinois Press.

Steinen, Karl von den. 1942 [1884]. *O Brasil Central.* São Paulo: Brasiliana.

Tukano
Dale A. Olsen

Musical Instruments
Genres and Contexts of Music and Dance
Further Study

Deep within the Amazon tropical forest of southeastern Colombia live the Tukano (Tucano), who belong to the Equatorial-Tucanoan linguistic phylum of the Macro-Tucanoan stock and the Tucano family of languages (Greenberg 1987:383–384). The Tucano family includes numerous subfamilies, such as the Cubeo, the Desana, the Makuna (Makú), the Tukano, and others. The names *Tukano* and *Tucano* are pronounced exactly the same, but the former spelling here denotes all the Tucano-speaking people in general; when specific information is known, however, particular names are used.

Altogether, the Tukano number perhaps no more than ten thousand people who maintain some traditional lifeways (Bermúdez 1990:110). Their location is on and between the Vaupés (Uaupes) and Caquetá rivers in southeastern Colombia and northwestern Brazil. Contact with rubber-tree tappers, missionaries, and other outsiders has brought disease and change to many Tukano. The lack of roads and the rapids on the rivers make travel difficult.

MUSICAL INSTRUMENTS

Traditional Tukano musical instruments include idiophones and aerophones and exclude membranophones and chordophones. The Desana, an eastern Tukano group, have about twenty musical instruments, each "associated with a certain ritual, a certain time of day, a certain age-group, and a certain animal" (Reichel-Dolmatoff 1981:91). Each has a particular sound that relates to a particular color, odor, temperature, and message. This kind of sound-classification taxonomy may be unique to the Tukano.

Idiophones

Tukano idiophones include internal container rattles and external anklet and staff rattles, tube stampers, coca-pounding pestle and mortar, struck log idiophones, and rubbed tortoiseshells. These are important collective ritual instruments, but the gourd container rattle is the most powerful. Called *nyahsánu* 'to shake' by the Desana, it is the sacred instrument of the shaman (*payé*), who employs it for curing illnesses. Within its body are quartz crystals, which, when the shaman is in a malevolent role, are supernaturally placed within the victim, bringing illness—and even death (Reichel-Dolmatoff (1971:49–50, 114). Like most Amerindian shamanistic rattles [see WARAO], the *nyahsánu* has symbolic properties that relate to power; the most obvious are the red handle, representing the penis and the earth, and the gourd, representing the uterus and the cosmos. At the point where the handle pierces the container are yellow feathers, which represent the sun's fertility. The body of the gourd is incised and painted with diamonds and stripes—geometric designs that "represent the skin of the mythical snake that brought the first men," the Snake-Canoe (Reichel-Dolmatoff 1971:119).

Tukano dance-music uses the gourd rattle (*nyahsánu*), with external strung rattles such as the *uaitúge* (from the word for 'bell', though the rattlers are dried seeds) worn on the dancers' ankles and/or upper arms; a staff rattle consisting of a *uaitúge* placed on a pole; a long and thin staff rattle with a slot containing seeds; and a tube stamper (*borépudearíyuhkë* 'white stick that strikes the ground') (Reichel-Dolmatoff 1971:119). The stampers are painted with the Snake-Canoe decoration, giving them female sexual imagery, but their phallic shape makes them male. To the Desana, this paradox symbolizes strength: the joining of female and male symbols in one instrument represents power.

The mortar and pestle is an implement of work, especially among the Tucano-speaking Cubeo, who use it to beat coca leaves into a narcotic powder. Performers often use several implements of different sizes at the same time, creating multipart rhythmic sounds, sometimes accompanied by panpipes (Tayler 1972:45).

The Tukano no longer use hollowed-out log idiophones. Figure 1 shows a large example housed in a museum in Rio de Janeiro, Brazil. Log idiophones—called *toá-toré* (from *toá,* the sound it makes, and *toré* 'cavity')—were hewn from the same type of trees used for canoes, and they were just as wide and deep. To play them for communication, the Tukano suspended them from four poles just outside the communal house (*maloca*); for storage or indoor music, they kept them indoors. As outdoor instruments, log idiophones announced festivals and other events; its sound was said to carry 30 kilometers. When these instruments were played indoors, the entire house reverberated as a resonator (Tayler 1972:47). Because of the cavity, the *toá-toré* symbolized a uterus; the slit symbolized a vagina, and the drumstick symbolized a penis, the "penis of the sun" (Reichel-Dolmatoff 1971:113–114).

A large tortoiseshell (Tatuya *goo,* Desana *peyú vári* 'turtle to scratch') is covered with beeswax and rubbed with the musician's hand, producing a low-pitched hum. Tortoiseshells are often played in pairs, producing multipart music. Sometimes the player of a *goo* accompanies himself by playing a panpipe, held in his free hand (Tayler 1972:45). Among the Desana, the instrument "symbolizes the vagina and clitoris of the Daughter of the Sun, clearly indicating its threatening character" (Reichel-Dolmatoff 1971:113).

Aerophones

Tukano wind instruments include a large number of multiple single-tubed cane ductless instruments or panpipes, cane and bone deflector duct flutes (some multiple tubed) without and with holes for fingering, and trumpets. Panpipes, called *veó-páme* (*veó* 'cane', *páme* 'parallel objects') by the Desana, have a varying number of tubes, depending on the musician's age: boys aged five through nine play panpipes of three tubes; at puberty, they play four or five tubes; and men play panpipes having eight or nine tubes. This arrangement is determined by the development of the musician's testicles: the more developed, the more tubes. Played in pairs called male and female, Tukano panpipes establish the fertility of humans and game animals. Among the Makuna, two or more musicians play "counter to one another in a type of antiphonal

FIGURE 1 A Tukano log idiophone (*toá-toré*) on display in the Indian Museum (Museo del Indio), Rio de Janeiro. Darin Olsen holds a rubber-tipped mallet, traditionally used to strike the instrument. Photo by Dale A. Olsen, 1981.

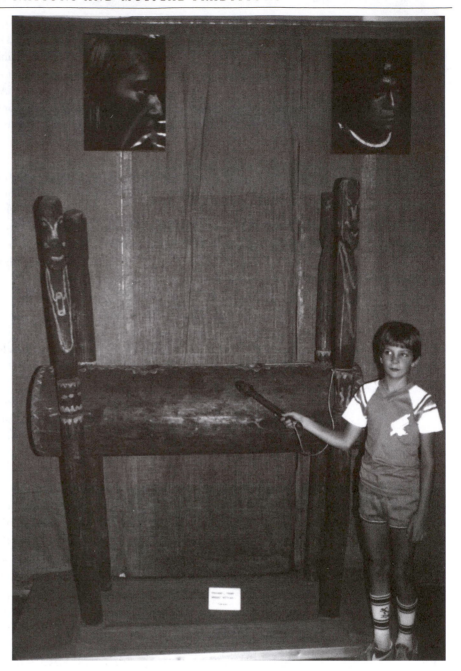

or orchestral manner, with upwards of thirty or more accompanying the dancers" (Tayler 1972:45). It is during these communal dances that many communal idiophones are used.

The Desana have a panpipe that is ducted with deflectors, making a double fipple mouthpiece. Karl Gustav Izikowitz (1970 [1935]:335) called it a double *mataco* whistle. Other small fipple flutes are three-holed, single-tubed, deer-bone instruments, played only by men. These instruments are all-powerful, and Reichel-Dolmatoff (1981:91) gives an example of how the Desana understand this power:

A small whistle is blown by adolescent boys early in the morning when they bathe in the river before dawn. The odor of the tune is said to be male, the color is red, and the temperature is hot; the tune evokes youthful happiness and the taste of a fleshy fruit of a certain tree. The vibrations carry an erotic message to a particular girl.

Such sexual metaphors relate to the use of the flute among Andean cultures and others around the world.

The most powerful Tukano aerophones are huge duct flutes, widely called *yurupari,* after a ceremony of the same name. The flutes come in pairs, male (*poré*) and female (*ponenó*); the Tukano believe that the "male flute produces a sustained sound that excites, while the sound produced by the female flute is interpreted as a threatening vibration" (Reichel-Dolmatoff 1971:112). This is a fitting symbolism because the *yurupari* ceremony is a fertility ritual for initiated men, and women are forbidden to see or hear the large flutes.

An irony is that according to Cubeo mythology, women were the original players of these instruments. A reversal of the social order occurred because the women played the flutes continually and did not work; therefore, a god took the flutes away from the women and gave them to the men; the god warned the men never to let a woman play or even see the flutes again (Tayler 1972:35). According to a Desana myth, however, men were the first players of the flutes. One day, when the men were away, the women found the flutes and handled them; but when they touched their own naked bodies, "suddenly hair grew on their pubis and under their armpits, places that previously had no hair" (Reichel-Dolmatoff 1971:169–170). Variations of the *yurupari* myth about flutes stretch across the Amazon basin (Hill 1993:58; Murphy and Murphy 1974:88–89).

Another aerophone used in the *yurupari* ceremony is a bark trumpet, made by wrapping long pieces of bark into a conical tube; the mouthpiece is made from wood. As a buzzing instrument, this is essential to the fertility ritual because it symbolizes male aggression.

One of the buzziest aerophones is a free-swinging aerophone, the whirled plaque (Desana *nurá-mëe* 'horsefly'). The people perceive that the sound of this instrument imitates the buzz of the horsefly and that its appearance—whirling around the player's head in a threatening fashion—imitates that insect's flight. The horsefly, a masculine symbol, is associated with fertility, but like a horsefly, whose sting is indiscriminate, the symbolism of penetration means 'lewd person' and even incest, which is taboo among the Desana. The swung plaque, though rare in the 1990s, functions as a reminder, a warning from the creator (the instrument's voice is "the voice of the power of the sun") to practice exogamy—marriage outside a particular group, rather than among siblings.

GENRES AND CONTEXTS OF MUSIC AND DANCE

Almost all music among the Tukano is for rituals or ceremonies. The available literature makes no mention of lullabies or of songs of leisure or work, except for panpipe music to accompany the mortar-and-pestle rhythms of the preparations of coca leaves. The ritual and ceremonial music can be divided into songs for shamanism (individual performances by the *payé*) and those of communal performance, including dance performance by the *kumú* for the community—festivals, Yurupari, mourning ritual, and courtship ritual.

Shamanism

The *payé* is the powerful Tukano shaman who cures illnesses, functions as the communicator between Tukano hunters and the supernatural masters of the animals, and presides over life-cycle ceremonies such as puberty, initiation, and burial (Reichel-Dolmatoff 1971:15). In his role as intermediary between the Tukano world and the spiritual realm, he uses hallucinogenic drugs—the drink *yajé* (*Banisteriopsis caapi*) or the snuff *vihó* (*Piptadenia* sp.), the latter inhaled through the nose. During rituals of

Yuruparí is a ceremonial complex in several parts, including the ritual of the sacred flutes and trumpets, along with the distribution of food. For several days, residents of neighboring villages unite to celebrate with music and dance, to eat, and to drink.

transformation, when he communicates with the supernatural, he sings and recites spells. His cosmological activities are closely interrelated: the ritual ceremony of ingesting *yajé,* for example, can be a part of curing; likewise, the communication with Vaí-mahsë, the Keeper of the Game, is related to curing. The most common cause of sickness is Vaí-mahsë's wrath, and curing must take place during daylight hours so as not to provoke Vaí-mahsë further (Reichel-Dolmatoff 1971:175–178). The Tukano interpret illness as a supernatural, patient-enveloping wrapping, which the process of healing removes by invoking various animals who destroy it and carry away the sickness, depositing it in the Milky Way. Each animal has a particular function, and the shaman, through his songs and spells, must invoke the correct one. After the cure has been effected, additional songs soothe and strengthen the patient.

Another religious practitioner is the *kumú,* who cures illnesses caused by the supernatural intrusion of pathogenic agents—stones, splinters, thorns—into the patient's body. He cures by blowing and sucking, rather than by singing and reciting spells. Nevertheless, he is an important singer in his other role, as spiritual leader of certain festivals, especially the ceremonial exchange of food.

Communal events

Dabucurí

The ceremonial exchange of food (*dabucurí*) is a three-day ritual of alliance between Tukano villages. During this event, the religious leader, *kumú,* sings songs of god (*go'a mëë bayári*), invoking the sun (Reichel-Dolmatoff 1971:136–137). This leader can be interpreted as a priest, and his role in Tukano culture is much higher than that of the *payé*; he is, in fact, the most important Tukano religious functionary.

Yuruparí

Held once a year, Yuruparí is a ceremonial complex in several parts, including the ritual of the sacred flutes and trumpets, along with the distribution of food. It is seen as a fertility festival, an initiation ceremony, and even as "a warning not to commit incest and to marry only the women from another group" (Reichel-Dolmatoff 1971:171). For several days, residents of neighboring villages unite to celebrate with music and dance, to eat, and to drink. Versions of this ceremonial complex occur throughout the Amazon basin.

Mourning ritual

On the death of a ceremonial leader or elder, the Cubeo hold an elaborate ceremony called *oyne* 'weeping', during which singing, playing musical instruments, and dancing occur over a long period. Beginning with wails, spells, and songs, the first part of the ceremony is followed by burial. A year later, the Cubeo stage a ritual that includes the playing of bark trumpets and other musical instruments, dances with masks, and songs. This is when spiritual animals, birds, fish, insects, demons, and all the ancestors return to mourn the deceased. The ancestors are represented by the low tones of two bark trumpets (*xudjiko, xudjiku*), 4.5 meters long (Tayler 1972:38).

Cachirí

A party featuring beer (*chicha*), the *cachirí* is a large social gathering that involves many people from neighboring villages. Often *cachirí* are held "to celebrate a special occasion, such as the completion of a new maloca, or a boy's naming ceremony, the end of a girl's isolation after puberty, or to honour the visit of some traveller, missionary, or ethnographer. But more often they may be held for no particular reason at all" (Tayler 1972:41). They include much making of music with panpipes, bone flutes, gourd rattles, strung rattles, dancing staffs, and almost any other musical instrument but sacred long flutes and trumpets. Men and women, with painted bodies, wear elaborate headdresses of egret, harpy eagle, and macaw feathers, and necklaces of many animal parts. Dancing and drinking last sixteen hours (Tayler 1972:42). This is the festival most travelers have commented about because of its lavishness and gaiety.

FURTHER STUDY

In 1938, Francisco de Igualada, a Spanish Roman Catholic missionary of the Capuchin order, published the article "Musicología Indígena de la Amazonia Colombiana," freely translated as "The Musicology of the Indians of the Colombian Amazon." Though based on European concepts, it was one of the first outside attempts to understand the music of the Indians of the Colombian Amazonian tropical forest, which included some Tukano villages; the title, however, is the best part of the article. A much more objective study was made between 1960 and 1961, when Brian Moser and Donald Tayler recorded and analyzed the music of the northwest Amazon and of other native people of Colombia. Tayler's publication (1972) resulted in well-documented LP recordings with an eighty-eight-page booklet, a map, and forty-four photographs. In 1966, Ettore Biocca published a multivolume study of Amerindian cultures from the upper Rio Negro and Orinoco, a study that includes recordings of Tukano music. The most prolific scholar of the Tukano, however, was Gerardo Reichel-Dolmatoff, who wrote many studies (1971, 1975, 1976, 1978, 1981, 1986) about the ethnography, folklore, mythology, and religion of the Desana; these studies include much contextualized information about Tukano music. This essay draws most of its information from the publications by Tayler and Reichel-Dolmatoff.

REFERENCES

Bermúdez, Egberto. 1990. Review of *Music of the Tukano and Cuna Peoples of Colombia* (Rogue Records FMS/NSA 002). *Latin American Music Review* 11(1):110–113.

Biocca, Ettore. 1966. *Viaggi tra gli indi: Alto Rio Negro-Alto Orinoco: Appunti de un Biologo.* 4 vols. Rome: Consiglio Nazionale delle Ricerche.

Greenberg, Joseph H. 1987. *Language in the Americas.* Stanford: Stanford University Press.

Hill, Jonathan D. 1993. *Keepers of the Sacred Chants: The Poetics of Ritual Power in an Amazonian Society.* Tucson: University of Arizona Press.

Igualada, Francisco de. 1938. "Musicología Indígena de la Amazonia Colombiana." *Boletín Latino Americano de Música* 4(4):675–708.

Izikowitz, Karl Gustav. 1970 [1935]. *Musical Instruments of the South American Indians.* East Ardsley, Wakefield, Yorkshire: S. R. Publishers.

Murphy, Yolanda, and Robert F. Murphy. 1974. *Women of the Forest.* New York: Columbia University Press.

Reichel-Dolmatoff, Gerardo. 1971. *Amazonian Cosmos: The Sexual and Religious Symbolism of the Tukano Indians.* Chicago: University of Chicago Press.

———. 1975. *The Shaman and the Jaguar: A Study of Narcotic Drugs among the Indians of Colombia.* Philadelphia: Temple University Press.

———. 1976. "Desana Curing Spells: An Analysis of Some Shamanistic Metaphors." *Journal of Latin American Lore* 2(2):157–220.

———. 1978. *Beyond the Milky Way: Hallucinatory Imagery of the Tukano Indians.* Los Angeles: UCLA Latin American Center, University of California.

———. 1981. "Brain and Mind in Desana Shamanism." *Journal of Latin American Lore* 7(1):73–98.

———. 1986. "A Hunter's Tale from the Colombian Northwest Amazon." *Journal of Latin American Lore* 12(1):65–74.

Tayler, Donald. 1972. *The Music of Some Indian Tribes of Colombia.* Book and three LP disks. London: British Institute of Recorded Sound.

Waiãpi

Victor Fuks

The Waiãpi (Wayãpi), whose language is included in the Tupi-Guaraní family, inhabit villages scattered throughout the northern territory of Brazil and the southern part of French Guiana [see FRENCH GUIANA]. Their area is part of the Guiana region of South America. About three hundred Waiãpi live in the Amapari area of Brazil, and an additional 650 live along the Oyapock River in French Guiana.

Though the Waiãpi constitute a single ethnic group, there are important differences between the Waiãpi of Brazil and the Waiãpi of French Guiana. The former initiated formal relations with sectors of Brazilian society only in 1973, but the Waiãpi of French Guiana have had contacts with French society since the 1700s. Other differences between the subgroups concern patterns of residence, language, music, and other forms of artistic expression. The French Waiãpi live along a major river, the Oyapock, and the forest-dwelling Brazilian Waiãpi inhabit inland villages close to small rivers, such as the Amapari. Thus, access to resources, mobility, and contacts with other societies vary. A friction idiophone (*pupu*) made out of a turtle shell is hardly used by the Brazilian Waiãpi but is regularly employed by their counterparts in French Guiana (Beaudet 1980:6). Likewise, the *kuripeawa*, a side-blown flute played by both groups, is a nasal flute among the French Guiana Waiãpi but a mouth-blown flute among the Brazilian Waiãpi.

A review of current knowledge of the Brazilian and French Waiãpi groups broadens understanding of the role of music in Waiãpi society as a whole. (Evidence of a yet uncontacted group of Waiãpi has surfaced, but details are limited.) Over time, identified Waiãpi groups have declined in number; some have merged with other Waiãpi groups and even with the Carib-speaking Wayana and Aparai Indians (Gallois 1983:110–112).

THE PEOPLE IN HISTORY

Most historical accounts of the Waiãpi, as of other Tupi-Guaraní-speaking groups, note the importance of music in these societies (Baldus 1970:1; Métraux 1927:30–37). Only recently have studies focused on the role of music in Waiãpi and

Cannibalistic themes still regularly occur in Waiãpi
musical performances, which are marked by the
consumption of large amounts of beer.

other Tupi-Guaraní-speaking societies (Menezes Bastos 1978; Beaudet 1980, 1983; Fuks 1989).

Historical descriptions of the Waiãpi are available in accounts written by missionaries, governmental officials, and travelers. At best, they reveal only general aspects of Waiãpi music and culture. The first written records can be traced back to the 1600s, when the Waiãpi (or Guaiapi) are believed to have inhabited the land along the Xingú, a major tributary of the Amazon (Bettendorf 1909:115–116; Gallois 1986:78). Pressure by colonizers in central Brazil probably led them to leave that area. Like other Tupi-Guaraní Indians, the Waiãpi had mythological reasons that led to extensive migrations to a "land without evil" (Métraux 1927:131–136). As a result, they migrated northward until arriving in the Guiana area in the early 1700s (Rivière 1963:185–186).

This new pattern of settling in the Guiana area was also marked by contacts with other ethnic groups, such as Portuguese and French colonizers, and with other indigenous groups, including the Wayana. In addition, the Waiãpi had commercial relations with the Boni (Maroons), who acted as middlemen between Indians and colonizers. From the Boni, the Waiãpi acquired such industrialized items as knives, metal pots, and glass beads, even before they had face-to-face ties with Westerners.

Newly arrived in the Guianas, the Waiãpi then had conflicts and major wars with the Wayana and other Carib-speaking groups, whom they fought for land and resources. These relations are described in the accounts of some travelers, who also alluded to Waiãpi music (Sausse 1951:73). Frédéric Thébault, Adam de Bauve, and Father Ferré were the first to attest that the Waiãpi were incorporating Wayana traits in their music and rituals (Thébault 1857:22); Bauve and Ferré cited Waiãpi songs that alluded to cannibalistic practices (1833:277).

These themes are included in Henri Anatole Coudreau's accounts of Waiãpi music, which note the use of manioc beer (caxiri) in Waiãpi musical performances (1886–1887, 1895:317). Cannibalistic themes still regularly occur in Waiãpi musical performances, which are marked by the consumption of large amounts of beer. Coudreau mentions the importance of bodily painting using the dyes genipapo, uru-cu, and tsipã during certain musical activities (1895:453). These are still important for the Waiãpi. At the end of the 1800s, several authors referred to the continuing decline in population primarily caused by the "bacteriological war" unwittingly waged by colonizers (Coudreau 1895:572; Crevaux 1883:217). Despite a devastating loss of population (Campbell 1982:4), the Waiãpi held firmly to their traditions. In the mid-1990s, a major musical revitalization has paralleled significant increases in the population.

Despite missionaries' negative attitude and the policies of the Brazilian Indian Agency (FUNAI), I witnessed in the mid-1980s almost daily collective musical performances, including the use of more than sixty-five different musical instruments. During my fieldwork, which lasted more than eight months between 1984 and

1987, the frequency of musical performances was remarkable. In addition to collective performances, some individuals often sing or play their flutes or other musical instruments while hunting, trekking, or simply lying in a hammock.

MUSICAL INSTRUMENTS

A large number of Waiãpi musical instruments are played in different contexts. Most Waiãpi musical instruments are aerophones, including flutes, clarinets, and trumpets (Fuks 1988, 1989:194). The only exceptions are the friction idiophone *pupu*, the rattles *maraka* or *marari* played only by shamans, and a shaker (*awai*) tied to the ankle of the leader (*jara*) of collective musical performances.

Waiãpi musical instruments are also classified in different families in which the same instruments, but of different sizes, are played by different people. The differences are based on knowledge, general repertoire, and each performer's physical limitations. Some flutes, such as the *erebo* panpipes, can be made in smaller sizes to suit children.

Waiãpi flutes (usually known as *nhimia*) vary in size, material, and performance context. The main distinction, however, relates to whether the instrument is played solo or in ensemble. Flutes and reeds of the class *ra'anga* can be played only in ensemble, and flutes such as the *so'o kangwera* are used by only a single player.

In classifying Waiãpi musical instruments we are faced with an incompatibility of Waiãpi and Western categories; for example, the Waiãpi term for flutes, *nhima*, may include the trumpet *nhimia poku*; and the class of *ra'anga* includes flutes, trumpets, and reeds. For that reason, I will outline some Waiãpi musical instruments and explain Waiãpi endogenous notions and translate them into musicological terms (Fuks 1989:195–209).

Flutes

The smallest Waiãpi notched flute, *so'o kangwera*, is made of deer bone; it is played by the person who killed the deer and made it. Its high pitches are believed to penetrate the forest as a request for the "owner of animal species" to release game for the Waiãpi to hunt. Like the bones, *so'o kangwera* are cross-sectionally triangular with rounded edges, have three holes, and like other Waiãpi musical instruments, generate a range of pleasurable emotions.

Another important Waiãpi flute, the *erebo*, is a panpipe, which can be played solo or collectively (figure 1). *Erebo* symbolically refers to animals, birds, and a mythical passage. The last is the case in Warikena, a festival reenacting the mythical origins of this flute. The number of pipes, their lengths, and their diameters vary from flutist to flutist; some adults make small, two-pipe *erebo* for their children. As with other Waiãpi musical instruments, performers commonly sing while blowing. At the end of every tune, each player quickly moves the pipes around his lips and produces a long yell (*opowe*). For other flutes, performers make a similar cue by moving the fingers quickly over the holes and yelling the *opowe*. Similarly, in vocal music, a cry serves as an endpoint.

The most common Waiãpi flute is the end-blown *pipimemyra*. It has five holes in front; in back, an additional hole always remains open. The term *pipimemyra* means 'aunt's daughter'— a potential wife, according to Waiãpi rules of cross-cousin marriage. *Pipimemyra* music thus symbolizes the love and happiness associated with marriage, birth, and hunters' good luck.

The side-blown flutes (*kuripeawa*) are played nasally by the French Waiãpi and with the mouth by the Brazilian Waiãpi (Beaudet 1980:10–11). Made of bamboo, these flutes have three holes for fingering and a large hole for the embouchure. Some have two attached parts, similar to the Western flute. The *kuripeawa* is often associat-

FIGURE 1   Waiãpi men play two *nhimia poku* trumpets, two *erebo* panpipes, and a *maraka* rattle (being recorded by a cassette tape recorder at lower left) during the *aisilili* bird dance, Upper Oyapock River, French Guiana. Photo by Jean-Michel Beaudet, 1981.

ed with the sounds of birds, especially certain parrots (the *kuri kuri* and the *kurei*); its name onomatopoetically represents these birds. Furthermore, the performer names these parrots while playing this flute, thus determining the attacks and timbres of each sound. This flute may only be played solo.

Nhimia miti and *nhimia mytare* are also for solo performances. Like the *kena* (used throughout the central Andes), they are ductless notched flutes. The distinction between *nhimia miti* (a small flute) and *nhimia mytare* relates to their sizes. Both may have three or four holes for fingering. *Nhimia mytare* follows a certain standard; it is usually longer, thus harder for children to play. These flutes are often associated with animals such as a certain monkey (*kwata*) and the *kuri kuri*. Like other Waiãpi flutes, they are used in times of happiness and are associated with such emotions.

Ra'anga: Edge flutes and reeds

The general class known as *ra'anga* includes more than sixty different musical instruments, including a variety of edge flutes and reeds. These instruments are "imitations" of some specific animal, fish, or insect, which each Waiãpi collective musical performance honors.

Some of the most common Waiãpi *ra'anga* are *pira ra'anga*, flutes specifically built for fish festivals. All *ra'anga* are used exclusively in such events, and at the end of the performance are disposed of. To emphasize the "likeness" with fish, *ra'anga* have carved wooden shapes of fish attached to their ends. These shapes and the names of each *pira ra'anga* vary according to the species of fish represented in performance. They include the *surubi*, the *paku wassu*, the *tucunaré*, and other species, with their specific *surubi ra'anga*, *paku wassu ra'anga*, and *tucunare ra'anga*.

Other *ra'anga* include the *cancan ra'anga*, a whistle associated with the *cancan*, a bird; the *mangangan ra'anga* of the bumblebee (*mangangan*); and the *tarutaru ra'anga* of the *tarutaru*, another bird (Fuks 1989:207–208, 231, 274).

Jawarun ra'anga are important musical instruments used in collective musical performances for jaguar. These instruments consist of two, three, or four reeds inserted into a larger, shallow pipe; they produce sounds considered similar to those of the jaguar.

The Waiãpi use other reed instruments, of which the most important are *turé*, called *tulé* by the Waiãpi of French Guiana. These instruments often accompany part of a major dance (Beaudet 1983:2). They are played in ensembles of at least three members. The leader plays alternatively two different *turé,* the *tay miti* and the *tay poku.* Two other instrumentalists play the other *turé* (*myte'i* and *myte'ru*), in hocket or interlocking style.

Trumpet

The Waiãpi trumpet known as *nhimia poku* 'long aerophone' can be used in a number of contexts. It is often played only solo, with the purpose of announcing special events or indicating structural points in the collective musical performances. In the latter case, only the "owner of the beer" (*caxiri jara*) is permitted to play. As "owner of the beer," he is not permitted to drink; and as a sober Waiãpi, he can control the performance sequence by cueing changes in it. The trumpets are played in pairs during the bird dance (*aisilili*), with panpipes and a rattle (see figure 1).

MUSICAL GENRES AND CONTEXTS

Music plays a major role in several Waiãpi activities. These include shamanistic rituals in which the shaman (*pajé*) evokes spirits by singing and playing his *maraka* (*marari*). Shamanistic music is performed in different contexts to cure the sick, scare away evil spirits, weaken enemies, and increase hunters' luck. The intensity of shamanistic song, and its accompaniment by the *maraka,* is believed to evoke the spirits of Waiãpi ancestors—and occasionally the spirits of the forest (*anhan*).

The Waiãpi make major distinctions according to the purpose of musical performances and whether they are solo or group performances. Vocal and instrumental musics performed in ensembles are usually marked by the consumption of manioc beer. Some Waiãpi say they can make music collectively only with beer.

One of the reasons performers drink beer derives from the fact that group performances often relate to another species of animal, a fish, or an insect; some mythical characters are the theme of collective musical performances. In the course of these events, the Waiãpi are transformed into jaguars, bumblebees, or fish. This transformation is emphasized by a change of behavior: the performers emphasize the attributes of the species they represent. In addition, the expressive sensations are modified, with the participants making the "music of this other non-Waiãpi." Nowhere, other than the use of the *ra'anga* and the change of text in these performances, does the transformation become so obvious.

The words used in the songs of these events are gradually modified as the participants dance, sing, and drink beer. At the start of each performance and before the transformation occurs, the participants name and call "the other." When "the other" entities arrive, the words of songs say "we are the jaguars" or name other species relevant for the performance. The literal translation of *ra'anga* denotes imitation. Thus, the sounds of the *ra'anga* are "like those of the 'other'." Playing these musical instruments shows that the Waiãpi are "becoming" the protagonist species of the performance. Though there are many Waiãpi musical performances, there is only one species per performance. Thus, in the fish festival, all participants become transformed into the honored fish.

Waiãpi men also sing or play solo music. Examples include a good hunter's songs, emphasizing his pleasure in hunting and eating game, and the playing of the *pipimemyra,* indicating the performer's upcoming marriage. Solo instrumental music is also performed while relaxing in a hammock and playing a Waiãpi flute. The announcements of special events are introduced by the trumpets *nhimia poku* and sometimes by vocal music.

Each Waiãpi is expected to have and to employ some form of musical ability. Every Waiãpi is a potential musician. Making music, especially singing, is considered as necessary as eating, sleeping, and socializing.

SOCIAL STRUCTURE AND MUSICAL PERFORMANCE

The Waiãpi distinguish music on the basis of performance context, whether it is solo or collective, and whether it is vocal or instrumental. Variation occurs according to the age of the performer or performers. Adults rarely perform children's songs unless they are used as musical satires of children's songs; these performances provoke laughter and highlight the importance of imitation in Waiãpi music.

The Waiãpi use several levels of imitation: vocal imitation of instrumental music and vice versa; imitation of the "music" of animals, insects, and fish; and imitation of music of people of other ages and the opposite sex. The sounds of nonhuman species inspire musical performances. Vocal music may similarly provide patterns for instrumental renditions. Instrumental tunes and timbres serve as models for vocal imitation and improvisation. The modification and reinterpretation of these models is the basis of Waiãpi musical improvisation.

Adults perform music in different contexts and unisex groups. Only men may play musical instruments. Thus, women's music is strictly vocal. In most cases, women sing their own repertoire, but during collective musical performances they sing the same songs male participants perform. Usually women's songs are associated with butterflies and garden products, such as manioc. The most important Waiãpi food, manioc requires long and arduous processing—a task undertaken only by women. From manioc, they make the basic staple and beer, plus items such as tapioca and *tucupi,* a sauce (Fuks 1987). Women's songs often describe the preparation of these items. Men usually sing about animals, fish, or insects.

Prescriptions for musical performance point to the importance the Waiãpi place on defining labor and expressive modes on the basis of sex. Despite the differences, the Waiãpi emphasize the complementarity of the sexes: men hunt game, which people eat with the women's manioc. Musically, the complementarity of male and female songs enrich the effect of collective musical performances. Despite these differences, each Waiãpi—man, woman, or child—is expected to have and to employ some form of musical ability. Every Waiãpi is a potential musician. Making music, especially singing, is considered as necessary as eating, sleeping, and socializing.

MUSICAL ACCULTURATION

In the late twentieth century, the Waiãpi began to be exposed to Western musical styles of Brazil. In addition, they have heard and seen Western musical instruments such as metal and plastic trumpets and flutes, and they use cassette tape recorders (see figure 1). The Waiãpi say these are "loud" instruments, unsuitable for the performance of their own music, but they recognize the different aesthetics involved and the ease of making a flute out of a plastic or metal pipe. The introduction of new materials for making musical instruments has had only a minor impact on Waiãpi instrumental music.

The Waiãpi are interested in the vocal music of other societies, and they have incorporated traits from neighboring communities of Wayana Indians and Boni (Maroons) from Surinam. The element of imitation, intrinsic in Waiãpi music, creates conditions necessary for different levels of incorporation of traits of non-Waiãpi music. With increased contact with missionaries and other sectors of Brazilian society, the Waiãpi will probably become more musically acculturated, combining their traditional music with elements of other musical styles, genres, and aesthetics.

REFERENCES

Baldus, Herbert. 1970. *Tapirapé: Tribo Tupi no Brasil Central.* São Paulo: Companhia Editora Nacional / EDUSP.

Bauve, Adam de, and P. Ferré. 1833. "Voyage dans l'intérieur de la Guyane." *Bulletin de la Société de Geographie* 20:265–298.

Beaudet, Jean-Michel, ed. 1980. *Wayãpi Guyane.* Paris: Musée de L'Homme ORSTOM-SELAF. LP disk.

———. 1983. "Les Orchestres de Clarinettes Tule des Wayãpi du Haut Oyapock." Ph.D. dissertation, Université de Paris X.

Bettendorf, João Felipe. 1910. "Chronica da Missão dos Padres da Companhia de Jesus no Estado do Maranhão." *Revista do Instituto Histórico e Geográfico Brazileiro (RHGB).*

Campbell, Alan. 1982. "Themes for Translating: An Account of the Wayãpí Indians of Amapá, Northern Brazil." Ph.D dissertation, Oxford University.

Coudreau, Henri Anatole. 1886–1887. *La France Équinoxiale (1881–1885).* 2 vols. with atlas. Paris: Challamel, Libraire Coloniale.

———. 1895. *Chez nos Indiens: Quatre années dans la Guyane Française (1887–1891).* Paris: Hachette.

Crevaux, Jules Nicolas. 1883. *Voyages dans l'Amérique du Sud.* 2 vols. Paris: Hachette.

Fuks, Victor. 1987. *Caxiri or Manioc Beer.* Indiana University Audio/Visual Center. Video.

———. 1988. *Waiãpi Instrumental Music.* Indiana University Audio/Visual Center. Video.

———. 1989. "Demonstration of Multiple Relationships between Music and Culture of the Waiãpi Indians of Brazil." Ph.D. dissertation, Indiana University.

Gallois, Dominique. 1983. "Wayãpi." In *Povos Indígenas do Brasil*, vol. 3, 99–137. São Paulo: CEDI.

———. 1986. *Migração, Guerra e Comércio: Os Waiãpi na Guiana.* São Paulo: FFLCH-USP.

Menezes Bastos, Rafael José de. 1978. *A Musicológica Kamayura: Para Uma Antropologia da Comunicação No Alto Xingu.* Brasília: FUNAI.

Métraux, Alfred. 1927. "Les Migrations Historiques des Tupi-Guaraní." *Journal de la Société des Americanistes* 19.

Rivière, Peter. 1963. "An Ethnographic Survey of the Indians on the Divide of the Guianese and Amazonian River Systems." B.Litt. thesis, Oxford University.

Sausse, André. 1951. *Populations primitives du Maroni (Guyane Française).* Paris: Institut Géographique National.

Thébault de la Monderie, Frédéric. 1857. *Voyages faits dans l'intérieur de l'Oyapock en 1819, 1822, 1836, 1842, 1843, 1844, 1845, 1846 et 1847.* Nantes: Bibliothèque Nationale.

Wayana
Victor Fuks

Musical History
Musical Instruments
Social Contexts and Musical Genres
The Indigenous Classification of Music
Outside Influences on Wayana Music

The Wayana inhabit a region bordering Brazil, French Guiana, and Surinam [see FRENCH GUIANA]. They speak a language that belongs to the Carib linguistic family. Carib-speaking communities, including the Panare, the Wayana, the Aparai, the Waiwai, and the Tyrio, constitute the linguistic majority in the Guiana region (Rivière 1984:1–12).

Carib culture has influenced that of other native American communities, including the Waiãpi [see WAIÃPI], Emerillon, and Palikur. The process of acculturation varies according to communally endogenous traits and to external influences of societies across the borders of Brazil, French Guiana, and Surinam. The Caribs' cultural impact has led some authors to study the "caribization" of the Guiana region (Gallois 1986:145). Carib communities have established forms of exchange with other Indian groups and with the descendants of Maroons (runaway slaves) known as Boni in French Guiana and as Mekoro by the Wayana.

Different Carib-speaking groups have occasionally fused to form a single local and cultural unity, as have the Wayana-Aparai of the eastern Paru River in Brazil (Velthem 1983:139). In 1985, the Wayana population was about 950 persons, of whom 250 lived in Brazil (some with the Aparai), 550 in French Guiana, and 150 in Surinam. They cluster in several villages. Individuals frequently cross the borders, especially during major celebrations marked by intense musical performances.

MUSICAL HISTORY

Only scattered records of Wayana music exist. They are mainly superficial descriptions written by travelers, governmental officials, or health specialists. In 1856, Thébault described Wayana music and its association with dance, rituals, and drinking beer (1857:22). Coudreau (1895:127, 158) also described musical performances, including the musical exchanges established between rival Wayana and Waiãpi settlements. One such exchange is exemplified by the use of the *tulé* (*turé, turè*), a single-reed musical instrument (Coudreau 1895:174).

The Wayana formerly warred with neighboring tribes, including the Galibis, the Pianoi (a Tyrio group), and the Waiãpi, a Tupi-Guaraní-speaking group (Velthem 1983:147). Though some travelers mention bellicose music and Waiãpi cannibalistic rituals, their evidence is inconclusive (Bauve and Ferré 1833:277). The Wayana no longer fight other tribes, and the war-music genre has become obsolete. Wayana bellicosity has gradually been transformed into a form of entrepreneurship, involving trade goods and songs. Musical exchanges mark the diplomatic phase of interethnic relations in the Guiana region. Major social and political changes have transformed the Wayana, who no longer need a highly centralized leadership or a military organization.

After peaceful exchanges with other cultures, the Wayana made an important cultural mark, including music, and they too incorporated some features from their former enemies, now their partners in trade (Beaudet 1983:20–26; Crevaux 1883:234; Grenand 1982:234; Schoepf 1972:92). Jules-Nicolas Crevaux (1883:217) alluded to the importance of shamanistic music performed in different contexts, such as curing, keeping away evil spirits, and increasing a hunter's luck.

The texts of songs, myths, and other narrative forms regularly performed by the Wayana are important sources of information about Wayana history. They provide an explanation of Wayana recent history (such as wars), reinforce a sense of ethnic identity, emphasize principles of social organization, and refer to belief systems, including shamanism. Shamanistic practices feature vocal musical performances for the purpose of scaring evil spirits, curing the sick, or weakening enemies. The shaman evokes spirits by singing appropriate songs and dancing. In addition, he wears special paraphernalia and ornamentation, symbolizing supernatural powers. Shamanistic songs are accompanied by the sounds of healers' rattles (*kuwai*) and whistles.

MUSICAL INSTRUMENTS

Asked about Wayana musical instruments, the Wayana say they simply play *lué*. The term includes all aerophones, especially flutes (*lué*) and trumpets (*titiru* or *tiroro*). The latter are low-pitched instruments that produce only one sound each, except for harmonics, occasionally produced by overblowing but considered to be in bad taste.

The flutes are wooden, with duct mouthpieces. They are played in pairs: two people alternate their single notes in interlocking fashion. Attached to the distal end, an armadillo's shell serves as a resonating box. Melodies played on paired flutes are improvisations based on vocal tunes; they are called *roriro*, an onomatopoeic representation of their sounds.

The term *lué* includes the end-blown *lué kôriró*, made of various types of bamboo, small trees, and bones of animals. To make these and other musical instruments in the late twentieth century, the Wayana have used plastic and metal pipes. Instrumental music is restricted to adolescent and adult males. Flutes can be played only by initiates.

In addition to aerophones, the Wayana use shakers when accompanying dances and collective musical performances. Attached to both legs or ankles of each participant, the shakers sound when the dancer stamps his feet. For collective ceremonies, shakers are attached to long sticks, which men strike on the ground while singing.

SOCIAL CONTEXTS AND MUSICAL GENRES

Wayana ceremonies are marked by different sections, each with specific music and dance. At a ceremony in 1985, the hosts (inhabiting the village of Twanke) sang a song of love while the guests sang and danced a song about the pleasures of drinking beer. Women brought food to the center of a plaza while the men and the initiates danced around it, wishing they could eat the food and drink more beer. They formed different circles of initiates, adults, and old persons. These circles occasionally merged: the initiates danced clockwise, while the others danced counterclockwise; previously initiated men sang tunes different from those of the new initiates.

Wayana musical events include a series of rituals marked by multisensory experiences. One of these, *okoma,* is a ceremonial part of the *marake,* the ritual for initiating boys. Other events requiring musical performances are the *karau* and the *irak.*

The *marake*

The entire *marake* may take several months, during which participants drink large quantities of beer, decorate their bodies, and wear long and elaborate clothes embroidered with glass beads. These events are formally opened after guests from different villages have arrived and have rested for a few days. Large amounts of manioc beer (*caxiri,* or *sakura* 'boiled *caxiri*'), kept in large wooden or aluminum pots, are served to the participants.

The *okoma* starts with the combined music and dance of hosts and guests. The hosts are represented by tapirs (*maipuli*), in opposition to the guests, represented by canoes (*kanaue*). The dance starts with the burning of pepper (*achi*), causing people to cry, cough, and move around. Young boys hold trays with the burning pepper, but most male children do not participate in the music and dance. Women remain on the dancers' right. They occasionally join their husbands in the singing and dancing, but never play musical instruments.

For several days, the protagonists (*maipuli* and *kanaue*) perform different music and remain separated. They unite only at the grand finale, the close of the ceremony, which marks the incorporation of boys into adulthood, allowing them to start playing flutes and trumpets and to engage in other men's activities and attributes. The end of the *marake* is marked by the unification of the protagonists in loud and multicolored action, achieved as the participants sing and play their musical instruments at full volume. Excitement is enhanced by the colorfulness of the participants' costumes and bodily ornamentation. Having drunk beer for several days, the dancers enter outboard-motorized canoes filled up with family members, fruits, pets, and other items. They navigate in circles on the river while singing, shouting, playing flutes and trumpets, and even shooting guns. The result is an ecstatic event, highlighted by loud sounds.

THE INDIGENOUS CLASSIFICATION OF MUSIC

The Wayana subdivide vocal music according to gender and age. Adult male songs often allude to animals, such as deer and tapirs. Men may sing *mareicāe* 'women's songs for Wayana males', songs to attract women. They have a large repertoire of *melanda,* songs that invoke the beauty of their wives and demonstrate affection. They have solo songs that serve to announce the performer's presence in the village and wake up friends; men who hear these songs invite the singer to go hunting with them.

Women's songs often refer to women's past experiences, especially to the times when they were children, and allude to food and insects. In addition, women have a large repertoire of lullabies and songs of love. Women's songs employ melodic and rhythmic structures similar to those of men's songs, but have a nostalgic feeling of their own.

Children sing versions of adult songs, male and female, such as the songs of the ceremonial protagonists described above. Some of their songs refer to games, sweets, and the virtues of their family members. Because of missionaries' impact, children have added hymns to their repertoire, emphasizing religious refrains, such as *alleluia.* Children also like songs from the Maroons, such as the song "*Sawaere,*" performed in Saranantogo, the Maroons' language. Wayana children do not seem to understand the meanings of the words of these songs.

OUTSIDE INFLUENCES ON WAYANA MUSIC

As a result of multiple influences, the Wayana have incorporated traits of different musical traditions. These aspects of acculturation include music and musical instruments from other indigenous groups and from the major colonizing countries (Brazil, French Guiana, Surinam). In addition, Maroons have affected Wayana society, though not much in musical traditions.

Perhaps the most important influence on Wayana musical performances is that of Protestant Christian missionaries, who not only teach hymns and modify traditional beliefs but also discourage participation in festivals featuring the consumption of beer and the performance of Wayana music. Traditional Wayana instruments are being replaced by Western musical instruments, such as harmonicas and guitars. The resulting impact is felt mostly among the young and adolescent. On several occasions, I witnessed children singing hymns and adolescents playing U.S. tunes on harmonicas.

Other Western influences vary according to the location of each village. In Surinam, the government has built cement houses for paramount chiefs it has appointed and has built airstrips and brought electricity to some villages. Some houses have stereos, radios, and even television sets, which play various kinds of non-Wayana music. Dutch and U.S. Roman Catholic and Protestant missionaries also encourage Wayana participation in Christian rituals to counterbalance their neglect of traditional Wayana music. In French Guiana, missionaries are not permitted to enter Wayana villages. Western impact is seen in the solar cells placed on the roofs of most houses; these generate electricity for lights, refrigerators, radios, and tape recorders. In Brazil, the source of outside influence, though not so apparent, is present through direct contact with the regional population and governmental officials. The Wayana also participate in parties organized by the local population, governmental agencies, and the church.

In all Wayana villages of Brazil, French Guiana, and Surinam, there is even a mixture of Brazilian, North American, Dutch, and French musical traditions. On several occasions, I heard calypso tunes, sambas, and American and European pop. The flow of French, Brazilian, and Dutch music, and of other modes of artistic expression, is fairly uninhibited. In turn, these musical exchanges combine with traditional Wayana music in complex musical expressions.

Though most Wayana participate in traditional musical performances, several individuals refuse to attend musical events—or when they do attend, participate passively, neither drinking beer nor playing musical instruments. They hide their traditional tattoos under Western clothes. In some cases, body-ornamentation motifs, such as snakes and birds, are replaced by tattoos of crosses and Christian names. However, most Wayana proudly execute different forms of traditional ornamentation at all times and especially during musical performances, which stress the importance of this ornamentation.

The Wayana consider some traditional performers musical specialists, as was the case of Anataka, son of the paramount chief of Kowen Hakon Village. A good singer, he knew many songs, which he could sing in high tessituras at full volume. Likewise, a good instrumentalist has a large repertoire and performs as loudly as possible, demonstrating traditional virtuosity associated with the rapid production of intense musical attacks.

REFERENCES

Bauve, Adam de, and P. Ferré. 1833. "Voyage dans l'intérieur de la Guyane." *Bulletin de la Société de Geographie* 20:265–298.

Beaudet, Jean-Michel. 1983. "Les Orchestres de Clarinettes Tule des Wayãpi du Haut Oyapock." Ph.D. dissertation, University of Paris.

Coudreau, Henri Anatole. 1895. *Chez nos Indiens: Quatre années dans la Guyane Française. (1887–1891).* Paris: Hachette.

Crevaux, Jules Nicolas. 1883. *Voyages dans l'Amérique du Sud.* 2 vols. Paris: Hachette.

Gallois, Dominique. 1986. *Migração, Guerra e Comércio: Os Waiãpi na Guiana.* São Paulo: FFLCH-USP.

Grenand, Pierre. 1982. *Ainsi parlaient nos ancêtres: Essai d'ethnohistorie Waiapi.* Paris: Travaux et Documents de l'ORSTOM, 148.

Hurault, Jean. 1961. "Les Indiens Oayana de la Guyane Française." *Journal de la Société des Americanistes de Paris* N.S. 3:135–183.

Rivière, Peter. 1984. *Individual and Society in Guiana.* Cambridge Studies in Social Anthropology, 51. Cambridge: Cambridge University Press.

Schoepf, Daniel. 1972. "Historique et situation actuelle des Indiens Wayana–Aparai du Brésil." *Bulletin Anuel du Musée d'Ethnographie* 15:33–64.

Thébault de la Monderie, Frédéric. 1857. *Voyages faits dans l'intérieur de l'Oyapock en 1819, 1822, 1836, 1842, 1843, 1844, 1845, 1846 et 1847.* Nantes: Bibliothèque Nationale.

Velthem, Lucia van. 1983. "Wayana-Aparai." *Povos Indígenas do Brasil,* 3:139–181.

Yanomamö (Yanomam and Sanima Subtribes)

Dale A. Olsen

Musical Contexts and Genres
Musical Aesthetics

The Yanomamö (also written *Yanomama, Yanoama,* and *Yanomami*) are hunter-gatherers who inhabit the tropical forests of the upper Orinoco highlands of southern Venezuela and northern Brazil. Their area covers about 260,000 square kilometers (Miagliazza 1980:101), and their total population has been estimated (Smole 1976:3) at fifteen thousand individuals, of whom in 1985, according to the national census of Indians, 9,717 lived in Venezuela.

Included within this culture are numerous subgroups whose names have often been designated by outsiders. *Sheriand, Sherishaná,* and *Guaharinbo,* for example, are terms applied to them by neighboring Carib-speaking Yekuana—terms that otherwise mean 'howler monkey'. *Waika* (*Guaika*) is a distasteful Yanomamö word meaning "to kill an animal (or man) that is already dying from a wound" (Chagnon 1968:38)—a term that one Yanomamö subtribe would apply, not to itself, but to other subtribes. Samatari, Pubmatari, Nabudub, and Casapare are other Yanomamö designations, often village names. Because of the inadequacy of some of these words, though they were chosen as subtribal designations by the scholars whose recordings and ethnographies are available (Layrisse and Wilbert 1966:182–208; Wilbert 1966:175–235, 1972a:13–64), only the following designations, because they are Yanomamö self-desgnations, should be employed: *Yanam, Yanomam, Yanomami* (*Yanomamö*), and *Sanima* (*Sanema*).

With dialects often as diverse as the names for the subtribes, the Yanomamö language, like Waraoan, was considered independent until Joseph Greenberg (1987:106) included it within the Macro-Chibchan language phylum. The discussion of Yanomamö language classification continues, and additional comparative linguistic research is needed.

Cultural similarities between the Yanomamö and the Warao occur, though these cultures are separated by about 1,300 kilometers. Numerous Carib-speaking cultures inhabit the grasslands and forests between them, but the Yanomamö and the Warao speak languages belonging to the same phylum, have similar views of the world, and share genetic similarities (Layrisse and Wilbert 1966:201–205). Despite these resemblances, however, a big difference between the Warao and the Yanomamö is that the latter traditionally have no musical instruments, whereas the Warao have many [see

The more the drug takes effect, the louder the
shaman sings. During the actual curing, the shaman
massages the patient's afflicted part to remove the
evil spirit causing the pain.

WARAO]. Only in the 1970s were several secular instruments introduced—via neighboring Yekuana villages (a bone flute) and non-Indian mission settlements (the
Venezuelan cuatro). Some of the most important cultural similarities between the
Yanomamö and the Warao occur within the realm of shamanism, the most frequent
context for Yanomamö men's musical performances.

MUSICAL CONTEXTS AND GENRES

Shamanism

The Yanomamö traditionally recognize three types of religious practitioners: the
häwiawan priest-shaman (similar to the Warao *wisiratu*); the *kailalá* doctor-shaman
(similar to the Warao *bahanarotu*); and the *shabori* or *sablí* shaman (similar to the
Warao *hoarotu*). Within today's subtribes, however, contact with Carib and Western
cultures has led to the development of variations on this pattern. Some groups, such
as the Yanomam, no longer have the priest-shaman (Layrisse and Wilbert 1966:186),
while among the Sanima that office has "degenerated" into a kind of wizard
(Barandiarán 1965:14).

The most musical of these religious practitioners is the *shabori* (Yanomam) or
sablí (Sanima), also known as *sapuli*, *saboli*, *shapori*, or *shaboliwa*, depending on the
subtribe. His is a favored office, and each Yanomam village "has as many *shabori* as
there are men who wish to enter this status: probably half of the men in each village
are shamans" (Chagnon 1968:52).

The most important function for which the *shabori* or *sablí* uses music is the
curing of illnesses. All illnesses among the Yanomamö, as indeed among most native
South Americans, are believed to be caused by supernatural forces. The intrusion of a
foreign *hekura* (Yanomam) or *híkola* (Sanima) into the patient's body is a common
cause of illness, one that is somewhat analogous to Warao concepts of pathogens. The
hekura is a spirit that "exists or lives above, in the top of the heavens or in the mountains," emanating from the "three kingdoms of nature: mineral, vegetable, and animal, and from giant prototypes of all the vegetable and animal species" (Barandiarán
1965:5, translated by Dale A. Olsen). Napoleon A. Chagnon (1992:139) explains
that according to Yanomamö belief, there may be thousands of *hekura*.

The Yanomamö have an additional cause of illness: soul loss. It is unlike Warao
concepts but resembles those of the Yekuana. "Transformed into *hekura*, the shamans
travel through cosmic space to recover a soul from a demon or from enemies. . . .
They transport themselves instantaneously to distant places, traveling horizontally
from one point of the compass to another, and vertically to reach the celestial disk or
to penetrate into the underworld" (Lizot 1986:124–126). Singing occurs during the
shaman's flight of ecstasy to recapture the lost soul, often in imitation of distant spirits the shaman meets.

TRACK 1   During the curing of intrusion-caused illnesses, singing is used by the *shabori* or the *sablí,* who must contact his *hekura* or *híkola* 'spiritual helpers', from within his chest or from afar, to help remove the illness-causing spirits from the patient's body. A specific spirit exists for each type of illness, and the shaman's responsibility is to contact the correct one. *Hekura* or *híkola* exist in every part of the real and cosmic world, "even from minerals and the natural elements" (Wilbert 1972:57), and if the shaman fails to contact the right one, he has not had sufficient power.

Besides singing, the principal catalyst used in contacting the spirits is a hallucinogenic snuff, Yanomamö *epena* or *ebena,* Spanish *yopo* (*Virala theidora* is the main ingredient). During the actual contacting, the drugged shaman dances in front of his own or his patient's section of the communal roundhouse (*shabono*) while singing and growling with a sound corresponding to whatever spirit he is contacting. The more the drug takes effect, the louder the shaman sings. During the actual curing, the shaman massages the patient's afflicted part to remove the evil spirit causing the pain. Then, by sucking or pulling, he extracts it from its victim and sends it off into the wind.

Musical style

The predominant melodic terminating patterns (cadences) of Yanomamö shamanistic songs are based on the interval of a third, manifested in many ways but especially as an approximate minor third. Also found in Yanomam musical grammar, however, are neutral thirds, major thirds, and even augmented thirds. (This intervallic pattern resembles that of Warao curing songs.) Some curing examples of the *shabori* and *sablí* begin with an approximate minor third, which after a few seconds expands into a neutral third or a major third. At other times, a minor third is instantly expanded by a glissando. These intervals should be conceived as manifestations of a basic third-ness, fluctuating with the various degrees of the shaman's altered state of consciousness.

Most Yanomam shamanistic music spans a range of only two or three tones (such as tonic, minor third, and fourth). Higher tones are rare, but lower tones are sometimes used in a secondary, grace-note fashion, often with fluctuating definite and indefinite pitches. Figure 1 demonstrates the use of a lower displaced tone and the common interval of the minor third. In keeping with its heavily rhythmic quality, pulsation is used on the sustained pitches.

Yanomamö shamanistic music is fast, often with seemingly metrical traits. The music accompanies often frenzied dancing by the shaman under the influence of *epena.* Grunts, yells, and other extramusical sounds may be employed (figure 2).

Another extramusical sound peculiar to Yanomamö shamanistic songs is buzzing of the lips, used in alternation with texted singing. During the portions of the shaman's ritual when he is communicating with his spirits, his buzzing functions as an imitation of the particular spirit being called, or more correctly, is said to be the spirit itself: "When the shaman begins to sing his special call, the distinct *hikolas* begin to come. The vegetable and animal *hikolas* come . . . with their whispers and hums or buzzes, and others, on the contrary, with thundering loud noises"

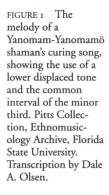

FIGURE 1 The melody of a Yanomam-Yanomamö shaman's curing song, showing the use of a lower displaced tone and the common interval of the minor third. Pitts Collection, Ethnomusicology Archive, Florida State University. Transcription by Dale A. Olsen.

continues

FIGURE 2   The melody of a Yanomam-Yanomamö shaman's curing song, employing extramusical sounds. The change in the "key signature" indicates a microtonal rise in pitch. Pitts Collection, Ethnomusicology Archive, Florida State University. Transcription by Dale A. Olsen.

(Barandiarán 1965:19, translated by Dale A. Olsen). Lizot describes the use of this buzzing and how it is produced: when the spirit of a jaguar, the Milky Way, or some other equally important essence arrives and speaks, the shaman must answer by buzzing his lips: "This is the way of the shamans when they communicate at night with the supernatural world. . . . He can hear their song—*arererere*—this is the sound the shamans make with their tongues at the time of the first call" (1986:101).

During shamanistic curing rituals, the Sanima make use of distinct musical sections, some based on a tiny range and others consistently larger; some involving only a buzzing of the lips and others using words; some fast and others slow. Of the songs of *sablí*, several are important:

(1) The song of the *okamo-haldiké* is a night song for exorcising all the adverse spirits and all the possible intrusion of adverse forces or of wandering spirits in the form of jaguars from within the dwelling area of the people. It contains some "*bbrrrrrrrbbbrrrrr bbbrrrrs..!!!*" that are noisy and grating, and tremendous yells like those used for chasing off enemies or obstacles. . . . (2) The song of the *haa-sulú-basú* is the song of the feeding preparation for receiving the *hikolas*. (3) The song of *kalidé* or song of the question "what happens?" is the great shamanistic song in which he explains all the phenomena of humanity, reverts to delimiting and naming the genre of the patient's infliction, and at the same time he calls the *hikolas*, beginning the job of creating the microcosmos within his soul and chest. (4) The supreme shamanistic song is the *huudumúsilibé* or "melody of the heaven." It is a humming or whispering song, excessively sweet and melodious, in which the shaman, after drugging himself with *yopo* and taking certain narcotic plants besides *yopo,* makes his celestial trip to the court of the Supreme Being Omao, asking him the final recourse of his own divine *híkola*.

These four principal shamanistic songs have the common name of *heekulamó,* forming part of the unity of performance that is properly shamanistic, with the eruption of the world of the *hekoras* or *hikilas.* (Barandiarán 1965:17, translated by Dale A. Olsen)

A large number of short and fast songs are sung by Sanima shamans. One shaman sang thirty-five different songs during a ritual, each sung as many as three times in succession, and almost all of them lasting only as long as a singer's breath. The singer cuts off abruptly, as if suddenly running out of air (figure 3). In this way, the Sanima shamanistic songs are similar to those of the Kogi of Colombia, another Macro-Chibchan culture [see KOGI]. After a short pause with muffled talking, the Sanima shaman usually repeats his song or may sing a different one. Cultural borrowing among upper Orinoco cultures is not uncommon, and since the 1940s the Sanima, experiencing close contact with Carib-speaking groups, have adopted some of their neighbors' material culture, with "elements of a typically Neo-Indian food economy" (Layrisse and Wilbert 1966:194).

FIGURE 3 The melody of a Sanima-Yanomamö shaman's curing song, showing its rapid and short character. Coppens Collection, Ethnomusicology Archive, Florida State University. Transcription by Dale A. Olsen.

Festivals

A feast (*reaho*), often to celebrate the dead, is a celebratory event, filled with wailing, singing, mock fighting, and a cannibalistic ritual during which the villagers ingest the ashes of the cremated deceased, mixed into a soup made with crushed bananas and water. Only in this way can the dead person's soul "be preserved as part of the energy reservoir of the community" (Wilbert 1972:61).

The ritual singing of the *reaho* is nocturnal, communal, and responsorial. A woman leads, followed by a chorus of women, or a shaman leads, followed by a chorus of men (Biocca 1966:252–253). Chagnon (1992:203–205) writes eloquently about his observation of this kind of singing, which occurred in 1965 when two war parties (visitors and hosts) met for a feast, singing, dancing, and chest-pounding duels in the Yanomamö village where he was doing research:

> Shortly after dark, the marathon chanting (*waiyamou*) began, and it continued until dawn. A man would chant softly, bidding for a man from the other group to come forth and chant with him. A second man would join in, also softly, responding melodically to the first one's chanted phrases. The first man would move slowly toward the second, gradually coming face to face with him, and then he would go into his routine, a highly ritualized, partially memorized monologue that sometimes crescendos into loud staccato screams. The second man, unable to predict what the first is going to say, must respond to each utterance with some twist or nuance of it. It might be a rhyming line or a clever counterpoint, or perhaps a scrambled version, with the words reversed or the order of the syllables changed. It is something like a fast game of Ping-Pong, with the melodic, staccato phrases as the ball. After some fifteen or twenty minutes, the man who has been leading the chant stops, and his partner takes the lead as they continue in the same fashion. When the first pair of chanters has finished, the last one to chant starts bidding for a new partner from the other group, and so it continues.

These exchanges exemplify the blurred boundaries of speech and song (see Okada 1995: example 25), and for that reason Chagnon uses the term *chant*, rather than *song*. It is during these melodic recitations that the men from the two villages conduct trade deals, using a highly metaphorical language; when wanting a dog, for example, a man asks for jaguar toenails (Chagnon 1992:205).

Individual and collective social and power songs

Men sing mostly during shamanistic and ritual events, but women sing for social reasons and during the feast. Social songs include lullabies, work-related songs, and songs about Yanomamö life. The last, especially, are important tools of enculturation. Wilbert (1972:40–41) recorded the following individual woman's song, which explains how hunters depend on the food gathered by women:

A shaman acquires the ability to sing during his initiation when, during a trance and under the effect of *epena*, he will supernaturally have "his tongue pulled out to be replaced with one capable of singing the beautiful shamanic chants."

The spider, *waikushihemu*,
Stood at the door of his house.
Along came the jaguar,
Who caught and devoured
Poor *waikushihemu*.

The Yanomamö explained the song this way: "Why did the mighty jaguar, the great hunter of the forest, bother to catch and eat a tiny spider? Because he was hungry and had nothing else to eat, that's why." To assist hunters, women sing and dance collectively, so their men will hunt successfully.

Individual songs of power are also sung by women. Kenneth Good, an American anthropologist who married a Yanomamö woman, explains (1991:319–320) how his wife sings to a rock-formation spirit, which, if the spirit hears her song, will bring rain, make the river rise, and enable boatmen to pass the rapids safely. Group songs and dances of power are performed by young men and women during evening rituals called *amoamo* to ensure the success of the men who are off in the forest on a ritual hunt (*heniyomou*) in preparation for the feast (Chagnon 1992:197).

MUSICAL AESTHETICS

A shaman acquires the ability to sing during his initiation, when, during a trance and under the effect of *epena,* he will supernaturally have "his flesh stripped from his bones and replaced with that of the bat, have his throat and chest opened and cleaned of blood, and his tongue pulled out to be replaced with one capable of singing the beautiful shamanic chants" (Wilbert 1972:59). These songs are the property of the male shamans only, and women must never sing them; if they did so, the women would become blind and deaf.

Except for the ritual songs of the *reaho* and *amoamo,* women sing their songs among themselves, except when asked by the men to sing for the community. Helena Valero, kidnapped by the Brazilian Yanomamö in 1937 and forced to live as the wife of a Yanomamö for twenty years, explains the following: "The women sing women's songs and the men sing men's songs. Every tribe has its favourite songs, and the men are never too shy to sing; but the women are often too shy." She explains how men and boys often ridicule the women: "Many were too shy and would not sing, because often, the next day, the youths who had listened while lying in their hammocks, jeered at them saying: 'You had a little voice, a wretched voice. How ugly your song was!' For this reason some of the young girls used afterwards to cry" (Biocca 1971:179, 181).

Yanomamö men are aware of the noisiness of their singing when they are under the influence of *ebena,* and how they are not alert to enemy attacks when they are singing: "In the evening, they performed their dances. Before they began their songs, the [headman] said 'Let no man take *epená*. At night, while we are singing, it is possible that the enemy may listen and come near. Nobody notices while singing" (Biocca 1971:179). The Yanomamö within a particular *shabono* realize that if enemy warriors hear their collective male singing while taking *epena,* they are vunerable to attack. This is especially important in the 1990s, when most male affiliates of a roundhouse collectively partake of the hallucenogenic snuff. At present, however, the enemy is often an outsider, searching for new lands to capture and exploit.

REFERENCES

Barandiarán, Daniel de. 1965. "Mundo Espiritual y Shamanismo Sanemá." *Antropológica* 15:1–28.

Biocca, Ettore. 1966. *Viaggi Tra Gli Indi.* Roma: Consiglio Nazionale delle Ricerche.

———. 1971. *Yanoáma: The Narrative of a White Girl Kidnapped by Amazonian Indians.* New York: Dutton.

Chagnon, Napoleon A. 1968. *Yanomamö, the Fierce People.* New York: Holt, Rinehart and Winston.

———. 1992. *Yanomamö. The Last Days of Eden.* San Diego, New York, London: Harcourt Brace & Company.

Greenberg, Joseph H. 1987. *Language in the Americas.* Stanford: Stanford University Press.

Good, Kenneth. 1991. *Into the Heart.* New York: Simon & Schuster.

Layrisse, Miguel, and Johannes Wilbert. 1966. *Indian Societies of Venezuela, Their Blood Types.* Monograph 13. Caracas: Instituto Caribe de Antropología y Sociología. Fundación La Salle de Ciencias Naturales.

Lizot, Jacques. 1986. *Tales of the Yanomami: Daily Life in the Venezuelan Forest.* Cambridge and Paris: Cambridge University Press and Éditions de la Maison des Sciences de l'Homme.

Okada, Yuki. 1995. *Central and South America.* The JVC / Smithsonian Folkways Video Anthology of Music and Dance of the Americas, 6. Multicultural Media VTMV 230. Video.

Smole, William J. 1976. *The Yanoama Indians: A Cultural Geography.* Austin: University of Texas Press.

Wilbert, Johannes. 1966. *Indios de la Region Orinoco-Ventuari.* Monograph 8. Caracas: Instituto Caribe de Antropología y Sociología. Fundación La Salle de Ciencias Naturales.

———. 1972. *Survivers of Eldorado.* New York: Praeger.

Yekuana
Dale A. Olsen

Musical Instruments
Musical Contexts and Genres
Musical Ideologies and Aesthetics

About three thousand tropical-forest people known as the Yekuana (Ye'kuana, Yecuana) inhabit portions of the Amazon Territory of southern Venezuela. These portions include the regions of the headwaters of the Ventuari, Cuntinamo, Padamo, and Cunucunuma rivers and the state of Bolívar, around the Caura, Erebato, and Paraguya rivers and their tributaries.

Residing in thirty-one villages (one is within Brazil), the Yekuana are Carib-speakers who for decades have erroneously been called by the Arawak term *Makiritare* 'Water People, River People'. This name was introduced by missionaries, and though it was once used by outsiders as a generic name (Layrisse and Wilbert 1966:72), it is no longer accepted. Among themselves, the people are known as *Yekuana* 'canoe people, person' (Guss 1989:7–8).

Of the Carib-speaking native Americans in Venezuela, only the Yekuana have managed to continue their traditional ways, which include shamanic rituals, elaborate group ceremonials, and individual music making at leisure. They have inhabited their present locale for several hundred years. They were first met in 1744 by the Jesuit priest Román, but musical documentation did not occur until 1911–1913, when the German explorer-ethnographer Theodor Koch-Grünberg made recordings, took photographs, and collected examples of Yekuana music and musical instruments. His recordings provide magnificent examples of what Yekuana music was like before the major acculturative influences of the second half of the twentieth century.

Surprisingly, much of the music associated with shamanism is virtually unchanged from the time of Koch-Grünberg's recordings; this is proof of the Yekuana people's cultural self-preservation. Outside pressures do exist, especially from American Protestant missionaries, who forbid old customs, drinks, myths, music, and lifeways. As with all other cultures, change is continuous; only the speed at which it occurs is variable.

MUSICAL INSTRUMENTS

Because artifacts made from vegetable matter deteriorate quickly in the tropical forest, no Yekuana musical instruments appear in the archaeological record. An array of

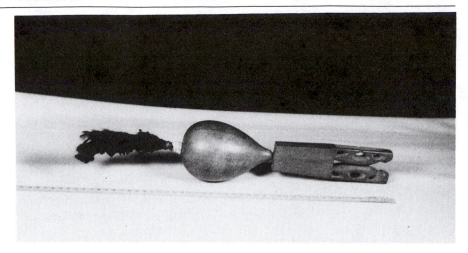

musical instruments, some sacred and some secular, are employed only by Yekuana men.

Idiophones

The most sacred Yekuana musical instrument is the shaman's rattle (*madaka*), a container idiophone. With singing, it is the shaman's most important tool. It is made from a single calabash, pierced with an intricately carved heartwood handle, depicting two shamans seated back to back in states of deep concentration or trance (Coppens 1975:2). A typical example is about 45 centimeters long (figure 1).

The extension of the handle, which pierces the upper end of the rattle, often includes an attachment of the black, velvety feathers of the crimson-crested woodpecker (*Campephilus melanoleucus*); the Yekuana believe this bird is the double of Wanadi, their cultural hero. The presence of these feathers therefore gives the rattle power. Additional power is provided by *wiriki* (also spelled *widiki*) or quartz pebbles, plus the roots of the *aiuku* and *kaahi* plants, the shaman's drugs—all of which, being contained within the rattle, give the instrument a distinctive sound when the shaman shakes it (Guss 1989:243).

Another sacred idiophone used by the Yekuana is the *wasaha,* a pole rattle or staff rattle. The rattles that are attached to the top of a pole by a vine consist of seed pods, which strike together when the pole is shaken or tapped on the ground. The musician executing the *wasaha* is the lead dancer, who keeps time for the chorus, which performs circular movements around the central pole of the circular communal house (Coppens 1975:2). Included within the ensemble of musician-dancers are bamboo clarinets and a drum; the lead clarinetist may manipulate the *wasaha* with one hand while playing his clarinet with the other.

The Yekuana make a rubbed or friction idiophone (*kodedo*) from the shell of a tortoise. This instrument is rarely used. The natural openings of the shell are filled with beeswax, and the musician rubs the shell with his hand. It often accompanies another musician playing a panpipe.

Membranophone

The Yekuana struck membranophone drum (*samhúda*) is constructed from a cylindrical section of hollowed-out tree trunk, covered at both ends with skins of jaguar, howler monkey, deer, or peccary. The skins are folded over a thick vine hoop, laced together with smaller vines. The *samhúda* is played with one stick in ensemble with bamboo clarinets and drum or by a singer accompanying himself.

Aerophones

The Yekuana use several edge aerophones, including a panpipe (*suduchu*), constructed from five small bamboo tubes. It is often accompanied by the friction idiophone. More common are the ductless bone flute (*kawadi dejë*) and the cane flute (*hito, wichu, fhidyu*), always played in recreational contexts.

Flutes

A small, end-blown flute is made from a deer's tibia. In exterior size and construction, it resembles the Warao *muhusemoi,* which has three fingerholes and a wide notched mouthpiece. In its interior, however, a small beeswax diaphragm is placed between the upper and middle holes. This diaphragm considerably changes the acoustical properties of the Yekuana flute: when a hole is covered, certain pitches ascend, rather than descend. The resulting music sounds like calls of birds.

The *hito* is a long-tubed end-blown flute with a duct mouthpiece, five holes for fingers, and one hole for a thumb. Unlike most other plug flutes throughout the world, the Yekuana instrument is closed at the distal end. Koch-Grünberg described this flute, noting the following traits: "the back hole is in the same place as the top front hole, which along with the others are covered with the fingers. The back hole stays open, because if it were not so, the sound would suddenly drop nearly an octave, given that the cane is closed in the distal end by a node, carrying somewhat of a sculpted tab, a particularity that distinguishes it from similar flutes" (quoted in Aretz 1967:219, translated by Dale A. Olsen). He added that the instrument was often played in pairs, and that the two instruments (each of a different size) were often attached by a string. In the 1990s, however, the *hito* is the favorite instrument of men's leisure, played alone, often in one's hammock.

Clarinet

The bamboo clarinet (*tekeyë, tekeya, wanna*) is a ritually important Yekuana instrument. It is an idioglottal single-reed aerophone of the *toré*-clarinet type (Izikowitz 1970:259), and it is always played in pairs, with one instrument considered male and the other female. The instruments measure from 1 to 1.5 meters long. Koch-Grünberg observed these clarinets as they were played during a new-house ritual, and his colleague Erich M. von Hornbostel added the following description of their construction:

> The tubes (*wana*) are 119 and 117 centimeters long. Each is divided by a partition of resin at 28 centimeters from its proximal end. In the middle of each partition is made a hole into which the sounding device (*suruidey*) is introduced (if necessary, a wool thread is wrapped around it to to make it fit snugly). This sounding device consists of a short green cane tube closed at its top by a natural node and open at its bottom. The middle portion of the cane is lightly filed, and in its wall a tongue is cut. A thread is attached around the tongue (in the manner of the tuning device for the tubes in our organs) which can be positioned so as to modify the freely vibrating portion of the tongue and thereby raise or lower the pitch of each instrument. (Aretz 1967:264–65, translated by Dale A. Olsen)

Each musician blows into the proximal end of the large tube, causing the single reed to vibrate freely without being touched by the player's lips. Because the single free-reed system cannot be seen while the instrument is being played, many observers erroneously call the *tekeyë* a bamboo trumpet.

According to Coppens (1975:3), "the music played on these clarinets symbolizes the movements and songs of a mythological animal pair." Paired instruments perform a musical dialogue: the male instrument plays the melody and the female instrument responds or answers: "The male imitates the squawks of a little starving parrot; the female reproduces the parent's answer" (Coppens 1975:4). Each musician modifies the pitch of his instrument by increasing or decreasing the pressure of the air. During an ensemble performance, the player of the longer instrument may play the *wasaha* with his free hand.

Trumpets

One of the most important musical instruments of the Yekuana is a bark trumpet (*siwo*) "made by rolling the inside part of the bark into tight, spiral funnels . . . decorated with flowers and fresh shoots, emblems of the new life soon to come" (Guss 1989:34). These trumpets are played by men for the female-fertility rituals of the garden, known as *adaha ademi hidi* 'garden-song festival'. The term *siwo* comes from the Yekuana word for the lower windpipe or thorax: "Wanato, the first human, discovered this music when he overheard a group of fish singing in the Orinoco headwaters" (Guss 1989:227).

The final musical instrument of the Yekuana is a conch trumpet (*hanawkwa*), which, because the Yekuana live a great distance from the ocean, they acquire through intertribal trade. They turn the shell into an end-blown trumpet by boring a hole into its apex. They blow the conch "to announce important events such as the departure for or the return from a long trading expedition or, in former times, the return of a warring party" (Coppens 1975:4).

MUSICAL CONTEXTS AND GENRES

Unlike Yanomamö society (in which as many as half the men are shamans) and Warao society (where *bahanarotu* shamanism is becoming increasingly popular among young men), the Yekuana have few shamans. A reason for this is that many Yekuana medicinal cures and religious festivities do not require the use of a shaman. Those illnesses that are supernaturally caused, however, can only be supernaturally cured by a shaman (*huuwai*), whose principal function is the curing of illnesses.

Yekuana shamanistic curing rituals take place in the forest, away from villagers' ears (Cesáreo de Armellada, personal communication, 1974), or at the foot of the central pole of the ceremonial roundhouse (*atta*), especially in the sacred space known as *annaka*, representing the innermost circle of heaven, reserved for men (Guss 1989:22).

Curing

The Yekuana categorize three types of illnesses by their causes. The first is an intrusive illness, caused by the bodily intrusion of a harmful essence, a pathogen that can be introduced in a variety of ways: by a malevolent *huuwai*; by the direct action of certain demons (such as Kanaima and Odo'sha); by the wandering of a dead person's soul, reluctant to leave its old home (Barandiarán 1962:84); by an animal spirit set loose because the beast was killed by a man who has a sick child; or by "the overwhelming charge of vital energy experienced by the invalid's progenitor in moments of danger" (Wilbert 1972:158). The second form of illness is caused by a violation or rupture of the strict hierarchy of the patient's vital energies, or by "a transgression of the moral or ethical code of the tribe" (Wilbert 1972:159). The third type of illness is caused by the loss or theft of the soul, a common ailment because the Yekuana believe that each person has six souls.

The intrusive illnesses are musically the most important. To help in the cure, the shaman usually uses song, his sacred rattle (which he shakes almost continuously), and tobacco smoke. Just as there are diverse causes for intrusive illness, so there is a

Individual songs of power are short and private, performed daily to name the spirits associated with each object with which a person comes in contact. Everything has to be made safe for human use through song.

diversity of cures, each with its ritual. When a malevolent shaman has inflicted spirit-intrusion damage, the curing often requires assistance from the community, which may include musical performance by a chorus of virgin girls or a solo adult male; these helpers are expected to repeat the curing shaman's verses. If the intrusion has been caused by a dead man's vagrant soul, the patient is placed in a secret place deep in the forest, apart from the community.

Possibly as a result of this diversity and the low number of shamans in a given community, recorded examples of Yekuana songs of curing are rare. Examples available include six songs recorded in 1971 and two others from one of the first expeditions among the Yekuana by Koch-Grünberg (Coppins 1975). Another example from the Koch-Grünberg collection exists in a notation made by von Hornbostel (1955–1956). These examples, recorded sixty years apart, reveal nearly identical melodies, showing the consistency of shamanic music for curing.

Figures 2 and 3 are melodic transcriptions of two Yekuana shamanistic curing songs. The first is from the Coppens Collection, recorded in 1971 by Walter Coppens. The second was recorded in 1912 by Koch-Grünberg. A comparison of them reveals important similarities, such as a sustained first pitch (with perhaps a microtonal rise in the second example), a descending melodic line based on the final interval of a major second (in cipher notation, figure 2 features the tones 4 3 2 1, while figure 2 features the tones 3 2 1), and a quarter-note pulse between 128 and 138 beats per minute). These traits stand in stark contrast with other shamanistic songs of curing from other Venezuelan cultures, especially with regard to the intervals. Indeed, throughout the tropical forest of South America, native American cultures choose particular intervals to construct certain melodic units employed for all particular functions (Olsen 1981: 366).

FIGURE 2   The melody of a Yekuana shaman's curing song. Walter Coppens Collection, Ethnomusicology Archive, Florida State University. Transcription by Dale A. Olsen.

FIGURE 3   The melody of a Yekuana shaman's curing song. Koch Grünberg Collection 1, 20, no. 37–1. Transcription by Erich M. von Hornbostel (1955–1956:439).

Other songs of power

Shamanism is a male domain, but the Yekuana have many other songs of power for everyday use among women and men, individually and collectively. Most items brought into use among the Yekuana must be purified with a solo song (*yechumadi*) or a collective song (*ademi*). Solo songs suffice for small items, such as the purification of healing herbs, body paints, food, artifacts, and so forth; collective songs, however, are employed for large things, such as the inauguration of a new communal roundhouse dwelling, the annual garden-song festival, or the welcoming of travelers (Guss 1989:65). Naturally, the collective songs take much longer than the individual songs—even several days, as each part of the large event or item must be musically named. The *atta ademi hidi* sung over a new house "must carefully focus on every detail, from the largest crossbeam to the smallest piece of thatch" (Guss 1989:66).

Other individual songs of power called *ademi* are short and private, performed daily to name the spirits associated with each object with which a person comes in contact, such as a particle of food, a musical instrument, a utensil for eating or drinking, a tool, a bow, an arrow, a hammock, and so on. Everything has to be made safe for human use through song: "It is through these chants, with the help of paints and herbs when appropriate, that the invisible dangers inherent in each object are neutralized. . . . No object, no matter what its origin, is ever integrated into the Yekuana world without first being purified by the corresponding chant" (Guss 1989:146). So important is this concept that death can result if a song is not properly performed. The power comes from the special words and the singer's breath; the proper union of words and breath (the singer's spiritual essence) provides the individual with power to communicate with the spiritual essence of the object and cleanse it, making it safe and suitable for use.

The garden-song festival

The largest communal musical event is the *adaha ademi hidi* 'garden-song festival' (literally, 'to sing garden'), which marks the transference of the gardens from men's concerns to women's. It converts the center of each garden into a centerpost linking the earth to heaven, serving as a conduit for the supernatural powers of growth.

During this festival, which may last several days, the women sing softly in a high register (always falsetto), and the men blow bark trumpets. The women's singing, led by a female songmaster, is a lengthy narrative (the "Garden Song") serving several functions: it recalls the origin of the plants and the first garden, explains the genesis of important entities in the physical world (celestial bodies, lightning, honey, various animals, cultural heroes), cleanses the men (infested by spirits in the forest), and protects the women (Guss 1989:36). It becomes a competition of music and dance. The ritual spaces shift from the communal male roundhouse to the communal female garden, endowing each with collective male-female power to exorcise and purify.

MUSICAL IDEOLOGIES AND AESTHETICS

Possibly because the Yekuana are an agricultural society, they make music and dance together as a way of strengthening their ideology. Living in a communal roundhouse, clearing and planting a communal garden, and undertaking other communal efforts habituate them to adopt cooperative approaches to many kinds of ritual endeavors.

Music and dance, when joined, create a pulsation describable as singing "in a syncopated responsive style" (Guss 1989:35). This contrasts with the quieter aesthetic of nondanced female singing, when women interpret their collective songs. Likewise, male shamanistic singing is quiet. When individual-to-spirit or group-to-spirit communication is involved and purification or curing is hoped for, the singer's words are often secretive and the delivery guarded. Although this behavior is perhaps not performed for aesthetic reasons, it is the only way the Yekuana want to do it, for to do otherwise may mean the failure of crops, the onset of illness, or the catastrophe of death.

REFERENCES

Aretz, Isabel. 1967. *Instrumentos Musicales de Venezuela.* Caracas: Universidad de Oriente.

Barandiarán, Daniel de. 1962. "Shamanismo Yekuana o Makiritare." *Antropológica* 11:61–90.

Coppens, Walter. 1975. *Music of the Venezuelan Yekuana Indians.* Folkways Records 4104. LP disk.

Guss, David M. 1989. *To Weave and Sing: Art, Symbol, and Narrative in the South American Rain Forest.* Berkeley: University of California Press.

Hornbostel, Erich M. von. 1955–1956. "La Música de los Makushí, Taulipang y Yekuaná." Translated from German by Federica de Ritter. *Archivos Venezolanos de Folklore* 4–5:3(1):137–158.

Layrisse, Miguel, and Johannes Wilbert. 1966. *Indian Societies of Venezuela: Their Blood Group Types.* Monograph 13. Caracas: Instituto Caribe de Antropología y Sociología. Fundación La Salle de Ciencias Naturales.

Olsen, Dale A. 1980. "Symbol and Function in South American Indian Music." In *Musics of Many Cultures: An Introduction,* ed. Elizabeth May, 363–385. Berkeley, Los Angeles: University of California Press.

Wilbert, Johannes. 1972. *Survivors of Eldorado.* New York: Praeger.

Kogi
Dale A. Olsen

Musical Instruments
Musical Contexts and Learning
Performance and the Aesthetics of Music and Dance

The Kogi (Cogui, Kogui; also called Kagaba and Cágaba), about six thousand native Americans, inhabit the northern foothills and slopes of the Sierra Nevada de Santa Marta in northeastern Colombia. Speaking a Macro-Chibchan-derived language, they are related to the Sáha (Sanká) on the eastern slopes of the sierra and to the Ika (Ijca, Bintukua, Arhuaco) in the southern region (Tayler 1972:13). Of these groups, the Ika are the most acculturated, and the Kogi are the least.

The Kogi life-style and system of beliefs reflect their isolation and religiosity. Scholars hypothesize, and the Kogi believe, that they are descendants of the ancient Tairona, a civilization that once inhabited the vicinity of the northern and western slopes of the Sierra Nevada. The conquistadors enslaved many Tairona men, women, and children, killed their chiefs and priests, and caused the remaining people (ancestors of the Kogi) to withdraw into rugged terrain, the forests of the sierra.

Archaeological investigation has revealed that the Tairona lived in numerous federations of large villages (Reichel-Dolmatoff 1965). Each village consisted of hundreds of circular dwellings built on stone foundations, much like Kogi settlements. Stone sepulchers, stone systems of irrigation, stone-walled terraces, and stone-paved roads led from one village to another. The Tairona founded ceremonial centers in mountain retreats, to which they made pilgrimages. In addition to working in stone, they were adept at ceramics and metallurgy.

Thousands of excavated ceramic objects detail many aspects of Tairona life and beliefs. Hundreds more are musical instruments (flutes and ocarinas), made in lifelike shapes of humans and animals and in highly stylized versions of both. Small, ceramic, some side-blown but most with fipple (duct) mouthpieces, these instruments were probably musical-effigy figurines, regarded as powerful tools for supernatural use. In addition to these items, early Spanish chroniclers mentioned several musical instruments of the Tairona and other Native Americans of the sierra. In 1514, Gonzalo Fernández de Oviedo y Valdés described log idiophones suspended from rafters inside Tairona temples: they "make large drums from about six or seven palms in length, made from the hollow trunk of large trees" (quoted in Reichel-Dolmatoff 1951:93). Other chroniclers describe "cornetas" and conch trumpets, instruments of loud sounds and possible priest-congregation ceremonial use. However, that these

Many Kogi individual and collective ceremonies that include music and dance address the anxiety Kogi men have about their mortality. Death preoccupies them.

accounts do not mention the excavated flutes suggests they served for private magical use rather than for public ceremonies. The Spanish may neither have known about their existence nor understood the cultural framework within which people played them.

MUSICAL INSTRUMENTS

Because the Kogi claim to be descendants of the Tairona, because of their proximity to the homeland of Tairona civilization, and because they often refer to the Tairona (and even use ancient artifacts for religious purposes), Kogi ideas about religious beliefs, the life-death cycle, magical protection, and other ideologies help explain the uses and functions of the Tairona musical-effigy figurines. Contemporary usage with regard to musical instruments, however, reveals little Tairona continuity (Bermúdez 1985; List n.d., 1983; Reichel-Dolmatoff 1949–1950, 1953).

Aerophones

Around their necks, Kogi dancers wear ceramic whistles (*huíbiju*), which they blow intermittently while dancing. The whistles may once have symbolized totemic animals (bats, foxes, jaguars, owls), though today, having lost their totemic power, they serve only as musical instruments. The continuity of their use, however, suggests a musical connection between the Tairona and the Kogi. By ethnographic analogy, one can hypothesize about the function of the ceramic musical-effigy figurines among the Tairona. By the 1950s, clay ocarinas that represent birds and other animals were serving in ceremonies whose function is to ward off illnesses.

The major Kogi aerophone is a duct flute, the *kuísi* (*kuizi*), a vertically held instrument, which mestizos colloquially call a hatchet flute. Its shape is unique: its mouthpiece—a quill, set into a flattened mass of beeswax mixed with charcoal—resembles the blade of an ax. The beeswax secures a thin quill (eagle, seagull, turkey), which serves as a tube to transmit the player's breath. The body of the flute, made from cane (*carrizo*), is up to 60 centimeters long and resembles the handle of an ax. With a smoldering splinter, the flutist himself (never a woman) burns in the holes for fingering, and he uses a hardened splinter to round them. He calculates the distances between the holes as the width of two fingers and half the width of his thumb; he calculates the length of the flute as three times the span of his extended thumb and little finger, plus the span of his extended thumb and index finger.

The Kogi play *kuísi* only in pairs, the *kuísi sigi* 'male flute' and the *kuísi bunzi* 'female flute'—or more commonly, *kuísi macho* and *kuísi hembra*, respectively. The male instrument has one hole for fingering, and the female has five (Reichel-Dolmatoff 1949–50:71 reverses the flutes and the number of holes). The player of the male flute shakes a rattle in one hand while playing his flute with the other. In the mestizo-Kogi village of Atánquez, the player of the female flute often fills one of the holes with wax—which "alters the series of fundamentals and overtones that can be produced" (List n.d.). There, the ensemble of flutes (*conjunto de carrizos*) often accompanies the *chicote,* an indigenous dance performed in a circle jointly by men and women. Since to the traditional Kogi the joint dancing of males and females is obscene, mixed dancing reveals outside influence.

The Kogi employ a large trumpet, the *nung-subaldá.* Each trumpet produces but one tone. Made from *totuma,* the fruit of the calabash tree (*Crescentia Cujete*), it can be fairly long and somewhat curved. Its mouthpiece is an opening in the calabash.

Other instruments

The *tani,* a container rattle, is about 20 centimeters long. It is an ovoid calabash into which small stones or dried seeds are placed. A short, cylindrical, wooden handle fits tightly into its bottom, fastened with cotton or hemp thread and packed with beeswax. The exterior of the calabash is sometimes decorated with dotted lines or is punctured many times with little holes. The instrument is played only by the man who plays the male flute. In acculturated situations, one man may play two rattles—one in each hand—as an accompaniment to flutes.

The Kogi make an idiophone from the shell of an armadillo and another from the shell of a tortoise. They scrape the former like a rasp and rub the latter. The shell (*morrocoyo*), covered with a resin and rubbed with a wet hand, produces a sound whose pitch depends on the size of the shell.

The Kogi employ several drums. One has a long, cylindrical body with a single oxskin head, fastened and tuned by rope and wedges. Placed on its end, it is struck with one stick and the fingers of one hand. The Kogi use it to make rain. Another membranophone, also played by a male, has two skins and is played with two sticks; its use is secular. Yet another, smaller drum has a single head; it is played by a woman, who holds it under her arm and strikes it with two sticks.

MUSICAL CONTEXTS AND LEARNING

The Kogi are unwilling to sing songs outside their proper contexts, especially for strangers; therefore, recorded examples are rare. As late as 1974, the Colombian Institute of Anthropology, in Bogotá, had in its archives only one recording of Kogi shamanistic music, including a song for making rain (figure 1). The recording, made that year, came from Pueblo Viejo (San Antonio) in the department of Guajira, on the northwestern slopes of the Sierra Nevada. The song's scale is similar to that of supernatural songs of other Macro-Chibchan-speakers, such as the Warao of Venezuela. It has the typical Macro-Chibchan interval of an approximate minor third. Short, it is vocalized without text (see also Olsen 1980:372).

The central person in Kogi musical performance is the priest (*mama*), who musically presides over religious ceremonies that probably derive from ancient Tairona rituals. Central to the Tairona religion, according to the Kogi, was a jaguar god, Kashindúcua; but in the mid-1900s, the Kogi sacred being was a mother-deity, Guateovan or Nebulwe, creator of the sun. Her sons and daughters are the founders of the ancient clans, Túxe and Dáke, representing male and female descent groups distinguished by colors and designs on cloaks, the plans of houses, words, songs, and dances (Tayler 1972:13).

Many Kogi individual and collective ceremonies that include music and dance address the anxiety Kogi men have about their mortality. Death preoccupies them,

FIGURE 1 Kogi rain-making song, sung without text by a shaman (*mama*) in one breath. Transcription by Dale A. Olsen.

and in daily conversation they often mention it (Reichel-Dolmatoff 1984:83). Ceremonial preoccupations are

> the prevention of illness, and masked dances are performed on these occasions with singing of chants and songs concerning the closing of gates and roads to illness. During these ceremonies, besides the masks, ceremonial staffs are used and clay whistles shaped like birds and felines are blown on. The ceremonies include the blowing of long-necked gourd trumpets, the playing of single and double membrane ceremonial drums, maracas and paired flutes (Tayler 1972:14).

Kogi culture teaches male children to follow strictly the culturally determined behavioral path, lest they be exposed to danger. Through mythology, transmitted in song or ceremonial speech, boys learn about the supernatural dangers of natural and atmospheric phenomena (echoes, lightning, rainbows, stones, thunder, trees) believed to be entities in whose presence one must carefully tread: most "myths, tribal traditions, descriptions of the ceremony, and other themes are sung, and the people learn by way of these songs" (Reichel-Dolmatoff 1949–1950:73).

Musical knowledge is a Kogi measure of status. Selected boys learn ceremonial songs and dances beginning at ages five or six. Seated, the *mama* puts his hands on the hips of a standing boy, who wears a heavy wooden mask. Humming, reciting, or shaking a rattle, he rhythmically molds the child's body. After two years of this education, he begins teaching the boys to sing. He guides them through songs, spells, and myths, covering the main cosmological figures and events. Some items are in an ancient ceremonial language that only he fully understands. The boys memorize related texts, melodies, and motions. The Kogi say children learn to dance before they learn to walk (Reichel-Dolmatoff 1976:279).

Giving importance to animals for protection against disease and misfortune, the Kogi consider them ancestors. Therefore, the Kogi practice a form of totemism in which a particular animal offers magical protection. One method for obtaining supernatural power from the animals is through dances and songs that imitate these animals: "animal imitation dances and songs, and those that are performed as a means of asking the animals for help, are the strict 'property' of those individuals who descended from a particular ancestral animal" (Reichel-Dolmatoff 1949–50:188). Thus, the preoccupation with death among Kogi males of all ages, priests and non-priests alike, has caused them to acquire methods for facing danger and ultimately for preventing death through the use of dance and music. The concern for prolonged life probably derives from the pre-Columbian past, since the intangible elements of belief, such as concern for the life-death cycle, are the most resistant to change.

PERFORMANCE AND THE AESTHETICS OF MUSIC AND DANCE

Kogi men's style of singing is unusual: a singer inhales audibly,

> contracts his abdominal muscles, and lets the air escape very slowly from his half open mouth, sustaining the singing tone until completely using up the air contained in his lungs. Violently and noisily he inhales again and then lets out the air again, all with great physical force and muscular tension. For the Kogi, the art of singing consists of retaining the air for the longest time possible while sustaining a tone or certain modulations of tones without breathing. Extreme volume contrasts are employed. Sometimes, for example, the beginning of the song is almost inaudible, then it slowly increases in volume and then diminishes, according to the rhythm of the song or the movement of the singer's body. Generally the songs

are nasalized and sung in a high falsetto, which is characteristic not only of the songs, but also for all the ceremonial conversation. From this falsetto he then descends one octave to his lowest tone which he sustains until he either rises again in pitch or sings the melody once more. This manner of singing requires considerable physical force, and the singer often finishes completely spent and covered in sweat. (Reichel-Dolmatoff 1949–1950:72; translated by Dale A. Olsen)

This description pertains to men's singing only, as the women rarely sing ceremonial songs. During ceremonies, the *mama* and other men employ ritual singing and ritual conversation, both of which are similarly intense in delivery.

Ritual songs often use vocables, lexically meaningless syllables, fixed from performance to performance. The song in figure 1 was explained as being textless (Benevides n.d.). An attempt to sing the transcription at the indicated speed can give a feel for the singers' respiratory capacity.

Singers of ceremonial songs sometimes accompany themselves by dancing. The performance has three sections. First, after starting to sing, the dancer

puts his weight from one foot to the other, slowing down little by little, while his arms dangle the length of his body, one hand holding the small calabash container filled with lime for his coca [a stimulant every Kogi male enjoys]. Slowly the rhythm again intensifies, and the dancer lifts one foot and stomps it on the floor, then the other, accompanying these gestures with rapid movements from his shoulders or head, resembling painful convulsions. (Reichel-Dolmatoff 1949–1950:72–73; translated by Dale A. Olsen).

In the second section, the dancer takes quick or short steps, or walks on his knees, moving in a straight line. He turns toward the spot where he began singing and dancing; again he makes convulsive gestures. In the third section, he circuitously returns to where he started. Sometimes he makes figure-eights, turns and moves in the opposite direction, or "jumps on one foot, rapidly crossing the other in front of or behind him after each jump" (Ibid.). In addition to these dances, the Kogi dance collectively for the fertility of crops. Such dances imitate "the movements of planting, harvest, or coitus. . . . Various individuals dance, forming lines, walking one behind the other. Only rarely do they dance in a circle and when they do the dancers hold hands" (Ibid.). Women do not dance during religious ceremonies. They dance only during the curing of illnesses, when their participation can drive away evil spirits and other dangers. Traditionally, Kogi men and women never danced together.

REFERENCES

Benevides, Manuel. n.d. *Música Indígena y Folklórica de Colombia.* Bogotá: Instituto Colombiano de Antropología. Liner notes to LP disk.

Bermúdez, Egberto. 1985. *Los Instrumentos Musicales en Colombia.* Bogotá: Universidad Nacional de Colombia.

List, George. n.d. "Two Flutes and a Rattel [sic]: The Evolution of an Ensemble." Unpublished paper.

———. 1983. *Music and Poetry in a Colombian Village: A Tri-Cultural Heritage.* Bloomington: Indiana University Press.

Olsen, Dale A. 1980. "Symbol and Function in South American Indian Music." In *Musics of Many Cultures: An Introduction,* ed. Elizabeth May, 363–385. Berkeley, Los Angeles: University of California Press.

Reichel-Dolmatoff, Gerardo. 1949–1950. "Los Kogi: Una Tribu de la Sierra Nevada de Santa Marta.—Colombia." *Revista del Instituto Etnológico Nacional* 4(1–2):71–297.

———. 1951. *Datos históricos-culturales sobre las tribus de la antigua gobernación de Santa Marta.* Bogotá: Instituto Etnológico de Magdalena.

———. 1953. "Contactos y Cambios Culturales en la Sierra Nevada de Santa Marta." *Revista Colombiana de Antropología* 1(1):15–122.

———. 1965. *Colombia.* Ancient Peoples and Places, 44. New York: Praeger.

———. 1976. "Training for the Priesthood among the Kogi of Colombia." In *Enculturation in Latin America: An Anthology,* ed. Johannes Wilbert, 265–288. Los Angeles: UCLA, Latin American Center Publications.

———. 1984. "Some Kogi Models of the Beyond." *Journal of Latin American Lore* 10(1):63–85.

Tayler, Donald. 1972. *The Music of Some Indian Tribes of Colombia.* London: British Institute of Recorded Sound. Booklet and 2 LP disks.

Warao
Dale A. Olsen

Musical Instruments
Musical Contexts and Genres
Performers and Performances
Further Study

Tropical-forest spirits singing with beautiful voices, fruit scattering on the forest floor, a scissors-tailed kite circling high above the forest canopy—it's time to sing a magical protection *hoa* song, or you will die! So believe the Warao of eastern Venezuela, deep within the tropical forest of the Orinoco River Delta. "And so many Warao die because they do not know the songs," says Jaime, a Warao elder and religious leader. The Warao speak and sing in a language believed to belong to the Chibchan-Paezan phylum, making them related to the Yanomamö, Kogi, Kuna, and other native Americans in northwestern South America (Greenberg 1987:382).

The designation *Warao* is their name for themselves; they are the canoe people (*wa* 'canoe', *arao* 'owners of'), and their traditional world is the swamp of the Orinoco River Delta, known politically as the Delta Amacuro Federal Territory. They are also the song people (*wara* 'ritual song communication', *arao* 'owners of'), and magical singing is as essential to them as canoeing (Olsen 1996).

Most Warao (also spelled Warrau, Guarao, Guarauno) live in houses built on pilings over water. Each extended family shares a cluster of houses. Because the delta is a web of rivers and streams, constituting about 26,500 square kilometers, the Warao are a riverine fishing people, though they were not always so. In ancient times, they lived in the jungle, siting their villages next to groves of *moriche* palms. This palm, then as today, has provided the Warao with essentials of life, including mortal food for themselves and spiritual food for their patron being, Kanobo (Our Grandfather). Also during ancient times, the Warao were primarily gatherers and occasionally hunters; today, they have added horticulture to their food-quest activities. They have always needed to travel through swampy jungles, by land as well as by water, in search of food or cosmological sustenance.

Until about the 1950s, isolation kept the Warao relatively free from contact with European- and African-derived cultures. For this reason, they are many in number and rich in traditional culture. Extensive missionization of the Warao began in 1925, when Spanish Capuchin missionaries founded mission schools in the delta. Even in the late 1990s, these missionaries control the area, and Protestant missionization, common in other parts of the South American tropical forest, has not been possible.

Other locally acculturative forces of the late twentieth century are creole-owned sawmills, with their attraction of outside traders, adventurers, and frontiersmen; exploration for oil; the building of roads and dikes; and research by anthropologists and other scientists. The Warao number over twenty-five thousand individuals, settled in about 250 villages (Girard 1997:332). An additional but much smaller number of Warao, the "Spanish Warao," inhabit the swampy coasts of Guyana between the Orinoco Delta and the Pomeroon River; they have mixed with the Spanish and are an acculturated group.

The Warao live closer to the Caribbean Islands than the people of any other native South American culture. Trinidad is a short distance by sea, north of the delta. Some musical traits of extant Warao culture resemble those noted in historical accounts of indigenous Caribbeans, especially the Taino or Island Arawak; the most important of these traits involve musical instruments, festivals, and shamanic tools common to the Warao and the Taino. These peoples share some religious and musical similarities with the Yanomamö, a thousand kilometers to the southwest.

MUSICAL INSTRUMENTS

The Warao use ten traditional musical and noisemaking instruments in shamanistic rituals, nonshamanistic ceremonies, and signaling. They play two borrowed instruments for entertainment. They retain knowledge of three other instruments, but these belong to an extinct part of the culture and are no longer used.

The ten surviving traditional instruments are four idiophones, *sewei* (strung rattle), *habi sanuka* (small container rattle), *hebu mataro* (large container rattle), and a small woven wicker container rattle; one membranophone, the *ehuru* (double-headed drum); and five aerophones, *muhusemoi* (deer-bone notched vertical flute), *hekunukabe* (cane vertical flute), *isimoi* (clarinet), *heresemoi* (conch trumpet), and *bakohi* (bamboo or cow-horn trumpet). The recently borrowed instruments are two chordophones: *sekeseke* (violin) and *wandora* (Venezuelan *cuatro*).

The following classification, based on the production of sounds, serves for an objective study. The Warao themselves suit their instruments to certain cultural contexts: religious ritual and dance, shamanism, traveling in the jungle or on water in search of food, entertainment, and tourism. Some of these contexts cause the overlapping use of certain instruments.

Idiophones

Strung rattles

The religious dances known as *habi sanuka* (for fertility) and *nahanamu* (for harvest) are occasions for attaching strung rattles (*sewei*) to male dancers' right ankles. Consisting of numerous small hoofs, seeds, nuts, fruits, or beetle wings threaded on a string, these rattles are sacred instruments, whose sounds enhance the rhythms of the dancing. Women never use strung rattles. As gifts from the Kanobo, they have great value; only village chiefs or shamans own them.

Container rattles

The *habi sanuka,* a small container rattle, is used by Warao men and women, led by a *bahanarotu* shaman during the fertility festival of the same name (see below). It is made from the fruit of the calabash tree *(Crescentia cujete)*, known as *mataro* or *totuma* in the delta. The fruit is filled with small stones, pieces of shells, or black seeds, and is pierced by a wooden handle. The total length of this rattle is 23 centimeters.

The *hebu mataro* is a huge calabash container rattle about 70 centimeters long. It serves for the festival of *nahanamu* and in *wisiratu* shamanism (see below). No instrument among the Warao is more important than this rattle, whose size, sound, sym-

FIGURE 1   A Warao *wisiratu* shaman's *hebu mataro* rattle in a *torotoro* basket. Photo by Dale A. Olsen, 1972.

bolism, and supernatural power are unsurpassable. When not used, it is stored in a *torotoro* basket (figure 1).

The Warao believe the *hebu mataro* capable of profound spiritual help as a "head-spirit" (Wilbert 1993:133). The handle (the leg), which pierces the calabash (the head), is made from a stick of wood, and the stones (the voice) are small quartz pebbles, which are not found in the central delta but must be brought from Tucupita, the territorial capital. When the *hebu mataro* belongs to a powerful *wisiratu* priest-

FIGURE 2   Bernardo Jiménez Tovar, a *wisiratu* shaman, uses his *hebu mataro* rattle in an attempt to cure a girl. Photo by Dale A. Olsen, 1972.

shaman (as opposed to a less powerful *wisiratu* shaman, one who has not yet inherited the position of priest), the instrument is adorned with feathers (the hair) where the handle protrudes from the top of the calabash. Selected red and yellow tail feathers from a live *cotorra* parrot are sewn into a long sash wound around the tip of the shaft. Two vertical and two horizontal slits (the mouth) always appear in the sides of the container, and geometric designs (the teeth) often adorn the slits. The shaft symbolizes fertility, an obvious symbol for the festival of *nahanamu* and logical for curing rituals, in which male and female power unite to restore a patient's health.

The *hebu mataro* is usually gripped and shaken with both hands while the player dances during the festival of *nahanamu* and while he cures illnesses. In the latter context, a *wisiratu* shaman will usually begin his work of curing by sitting on a bench, singing, and shaking his *hebu mataro* (figure 2). He will later stand to lean over his patient and shake it with all his might. At this time, the *hebu mataro* often produces a fiery glow, seen only by the shaman and the patient during a nighttime curing séance. When the *wisiratu* shaman vigorously shakes his rattle during the transitional part of the séance, the quartz pebbles repeatedly strike against the wooden handle, producing a fine dust. This dust, which has a low flashpoint, is in turn ignited by the heat produced by the concussion of pieces of quartz. Seeing a glow through the slits of the rattle has a psychological effect on the patient, reinforcing his or her belief in the shaman's curative powers.

Tourism accounts for the existence of one Warao musical instrument—a small, finely woven, wicker rattle, about the same size as the *habi sanuka*. It is simply a toy, most often made for sale to tourists in the Venezuelan towns of Tucupita and Barrancas.

Membranophone

A double-headed skin drum known as *ehuru* (or *eruru*) is used by the Warao while traveling through the jungle in quest of food and to the *morichal* (grove of *moriche* palms) to prepare for the *nahanamu*. In those contexts, it often accompanies singing; it has the secondary function of letting those behind the drummer and those ahead at the destination know where they are. Additionally, the Warao use the *ehuru* to frighten off jaguars and evil spirits that lurk in the jungle when the Warao go off to gather the starch for *nahanamu* (Turrado Moreno 1945:227).

Through an ecstatic technique, culturally induced with the aid of music and tobacco smoke, shamans transform themselves into powerful entities able to sustain contact with the spiritual world.

A hollowed log cut into the shape of an hourglass, the *ehuru* has heads usually made from the skins of howler monkeys. The player strikes one end with a single stick; the other end has a snare made of twisted *moriche*-fiber string and toothpick-sized thorns.

Chordophones

Solely for entertainment, the Warao use two stringed instruments: a violin and a *wandora*, a small, four-stringed guitar, like the Venezuelan *cuatro*.

Violin

The *sekeseke* is an often crude copy of a European violin, especially of the Renaissance prototype of the modern violin. A bow, slightly arched at each end, is made from a branch with several dozen loose strands of cotton fibers attached. Warao bowing especially resembles European Renaissance bowed-lute technique.

According to Warao lore, the *sekeseke* was first fabricated and transported to the Warao in a ship captained by Nakurao, a man-monkey from a far-off land. This creature, who had the upper torso of a man and the lower torso of a monkey, learned how to make the violin in a dream.

Aerophones

The music for the Warao *nahanamu* includes two wind instruments, the *muhusemoi* and the *isimoi*.

Flutes

The *muhusemoi* (*muhu* 'bone', *semoi* 'wind instrument') is a bone flute made from the tibia of a deer (figure 3). Its mouthpiece consists of a wide, obliquely cut notch, against which the flutist focuses his stream of air; its body has three holes for fingering. The Warao flutist has a unique way of fingering his *muhusemoi*: he opens only one hole at a time, producing a musical scale quite unlike any Western example. No two *muhusemoi* are alike, because no two deer's tibias are exactly the same size—and more important, each maker uses his own fingers as rulers for placing the holes.

During the *nahanamu*, several *muhusemoi* are played in ensemble with two *isimoi* clarinets, several strung rattles, and *hebu mataro*. Men may play several bone flutes with the *ehuru* drum while traveling by foot in the jungle. If a man does not own a *muhusemoi*, he may fabricate a *hekunakabe*, a disposable plant-stalk flute with the same proportions as the bone flute. After the travelers have reached their destination, the men play their instruments again while women collect and prepare *moriche*-palm starch (*yuruma*) for Kanobo—a process undertaken in preparation for the *nahanamu*.

FIGURE 3   Juan Bustillo Calderón plays a *muhusemoi* deerbone flute. Photo by Dale A. Olsen, 1972.

Clarinet

The most sacred wind instrument played during the festival is a heteroglot clarinet without holes, the *isimoi,* made and played by the musical leader of the festival, the "owner of the *isimoi.*" The Warao believe that, according to the ancients, the *isimoi* has a spirit that is the same as Kanobo.

The owner of an *isimoi* plays his instrument in duet with another *isimoi* played by an apprentice; the former has a lower pitch. Though the *isimoi* does not have holes, by increasing and decreasing the air pressure a skillful player can produce two distinct notes at the interval of a minor third, plus limited microtonal glissandi. Like the first interval produced by most *muhusemoi* flutes, and like the basic interval of Warao shamanistic music for curing, an approximate minor third is the interval that fundamentally identifies most Warao music.

Trumpet

The end-blown conch trumpet, *heresemoi,* is an important instrument in Warao culture, though it is associated primarily with canoeing during the crabbing season. Basically a signaling instrument used for giving directions to canoes at night, and to signal the departure and arrival of the crabbing canoes, it can be blown to announce the death of a tribal member, to signal the annual trek to the *morichal* in preparation for *nahanamu,* to announce the completion of a newly made canoe (Furst 1965:27), and "to herald each new phase in the process of felling and trimming the tree and scooping out . . . the trunk" of the tree from which a canoe is built (Wilbert 1993:55).

Electronic sound devices

Generally, modern Venezuelan material culture has had little effect on Warao music. A transistor radio may occasionally appear in a village, but the lack of receivable broadcasts and the expense of batteries work against its use and survival. In Warao villages adjacent to Roman Catholic missions, small phonographs can be found, and children can occasionally be seen dancing to Venezuelan creole music from scratchy 45-rpm records.

MUSICAL CONTEXTS AND GENRES

By far the most important Warao context for making music is theurgy (supernatural communication), and the most common kind is healing. Sickness and accidents abound, and though their causes are always attributed to the supernatural, some require the help of a shaman. Song, however, is always the most powerful medium for curing.

Music and the work of shamans

The Warao view of the world specifies three types of cosmological practitioners loosely classifiable as shamans: *wisiratu,* who oversee the apex of the Warao celestial dome and communicate with ancestral spirits; *bahanarotu,* who communicate with the eastern part of the cosmos where the sun rises, a good place; and *hoarotu,* who appease the spirits of the dead in the west where the sun sets, a bad place.

One of the most important duties of these specialists is curing illnesses caused by the intrusions of foreign essences. Through an ecstatic technique, culturally induced with the aid of music and tobacco smoke, shamans transform themselves into powerful entities able to sustain contact with the spiritual world to determine the illness-causing essences and how they got into their patients. Each type of shaman has a melodically and textually distinct set of songs for curing.

In all cases, the curer must name the illness-causing spiritual essence. When

FIGURE 4   A naming section of a *wisiratu* shamanistic curing-song cycle. Transcription by Dale A. Olsen.

properly named with the correct descending melody, this essence is removed, and the patient recovers. While curing, *hoarotu* shamans sing alone, or in twos or threes (as do, to a lesser degree, *wisiratu* shamans). Singing together, prescribed when the patient is an important person, results in a complex, multipart texture like a free round.

The wisiratu shaman

Only the *wisiratu* regularly rattles a large *hebu mataro* while curing illnesses. With this tool and its powerful properties, he is the most commonly consulted Warao doctor, primarily in charge of curing everyday respiratory and febrile diseases. Furthermore, as the mediator between man and ancestors, he can communicate with the major Warao supreme beings, known as Kanobotuma (Our Grandfathers). In addition to his curing role, therefore, he often functions as a priest in charge of Kanoboism, a Warao temple-idol religion in which the patron, Kanobo, is represented by a stone; and as a person in direct communication with the ancestors, he is greatly admired by all Warao.

The *wisiratu* shaman has three melodically and textually differentiated sections to his curing-song cycle. These respectively function to release and communicate with the helping spirits that reside within his chest, to name the illness-causing essence, and to communicate with the spirit essence after it has been removed and before it is blown off into the cosmos. The first of these, characterized by masking of the voice, has the narrowest melodic range, consisting of two or three notes based on the terminating interval (cadence) of a minor third (such as fourth, minor third, tonic). This section of his curing song is accompanied throughout by the *hebu mataro,* which is at times vigorously shaken as a means to punish the illness-causing *hebu.*

The second section is the naming section, in which the shaman seeks out the illness-causing spirit within the patient. It does not include masking of the voice, and in it the rattle is only minimally played. Guided by the patient's symptoms, the *wisiratu* names animate and inanimate objects from the Warao physical, vegetable, or cosmic world—objects that he suspects are causing the illness. This section is characterized by the widest melodic range, again based on the terminating interval of a minor third (such as fifth, fourth, minor third, tonic). In the naming excerpt transcribed in figure 4, the shaman begins by establishing rapport with his patient as he sings, "My friend, my friend, my friend, my friend, you are sad; my friend, you are sad."

The third section of the *wisiratu* curing-song cycle, when the shaman communicates with the illness-causing spirit, is an unmasked, high-pitched, one-note recitation.

The bahanarotu *shaman*

The *bahanarotu* shaman cures gastrointestinal and gynecological illnesses caused by the intrusion of essences of material objects (believed to be the material objects themselves) that living or ancestral malevolent *bahanarotu* shamans have placed into a victim via magical arrows. He is the ritual specialist pertaining to *hokonemu*, the misty, easternmost part of the Warao cosmos and the tobacco-smoke home of Mawari, the supreme *bahana* bird.

Like the *wisiratu,* the *bahanarotu* sings musical sections that differ melodically and functionally. The first, in which the shaman communicates and releases his helping spirits from his chest, is characterized by masking of the voice, and has a narrow range that emphasizes major-second and minor-third terminating intervals in about equal proportion. This is followed by a second section, similar to the first except that the voice is not masked, and the function includes dialogues with helping and malevolent spirits.

When the *bahanarotu* finishes the second part of his ritual, he begins to suck on the patient's body where the illness is believed to be located, removing the illness-causing material object. Accompanied by noisy slurps and gagging sounds, the shaman produces a saliva-covered object from his mouth, such as a thorn, a nail, or a piece of rope. This, he says, was causing the illness.

If the *bahanarotu* shaman does not detect and remove an object, or if the removal causes no relief, he will continue singing a third section, in which he names what he believes to be the illness-causing object itself and its supernatural cause. This third part, the naming section, which has the widest melodic range of his curing ritual and melodically resembles the naming section of *wisiratu* curing, is used only when an object has been placed within the patient via the magical arrows of the supernatural *bahana* wizards living in *hokonemu.* The curing wizard names as many objects as he can, until the patient's body begins to vibrate, when he once again applies suction to extract the pathogen.

The hoarotu *shaman*

The third type of Warao shaman, the *hoarotu,* attempts to cure deadly diarrheal or hemorrhagic illnesses, believed to be caused by the supreme deity of the western part of the Warao cosmos. This cosmic place where the sun dies is the abode of Hoebo (symbolically represented by a scarlet macaw) and his accomplices, the living-dead *hoarotu* shamans of eternity. Hoebo and his court, who feast on human flesh and drink human blood from human bones, must be fed by living *hoarotu* shamans. Through dreams, a living *hoarotu* receives a message to provide food for his supernatural leaders, which he accomplishes through inflicting songs ("sung" mentally) for killing other Warao (Olsen 1996), especially children. (Warao cite this practice in explanation of high infant mortality among them.) This inflicting genre employs an ascending two-note melody based on a major second (sung aloud only when being taught to an apprentice) in which the shaman names the essences that he will place into his victim.

Living *hoarao* (plural form) are called upon by the families of the patients to cure what are believed to be *hoa* illnesses. Through performing a curing ritual characterized by singing a descending naming melody similar to those employed by the *wisiratu* and *bahanarotu* shamans, but with different words and spiritual intent, a *hoarotu* tries to effect a cure; masking the voice does not occur. Inspired by the symptoms of

Lullabies are sung by men and women, and often have texts that teach older children about Warao life and beliefs, including the dangers of ogres and animals. The educative aspect of the lullabies is an important form of Warao enculturation.

the patient, a curing *hoarotu* names anything he can think of, from any aspect of the Warao tangible or intangible, mortal or immortal world. Many Warao die, it is said, because of the nearly impossible task of naming the correct intruding spiritual essence that is causing the *hoa* illness.

Other uses of music in healing, inflicting, and protecting

A fourth kind of affliction among the Warao requires musical healing, though the curer need not be a shaman. This is a physical and often external ailment of the body, such as a wound from a knife or a hatchet, the sting of a bee or a scorpion, the bite of a snake, a bruise, an internal problem during childbirth, an abscessed tooth, and others. These ailments are believed to be caused by supernatural powers possessing the objects or animals and causing them to harm the Warao. A cure is effected by knowing the proper prayerful song (*hoa*), sung directly to the body or the object or animal that inflicted the condition, and by blowing tobacco smoke over the patient.

The power of music can be used malevolently. Only the *hoarotu* shaman, however, inflicts illness—and even death—through song. This genre employs an ascending two-note melody, in which the shaman names the essences he will place into his victim.

Another kind of *hoa* serves for magical protection against supernaturally altered animals and ogres (Olsen 1996). These songs rely on the power of naming the danger, and on the melodic aspect of the song itself. The following musical text is for protection from a transformed *mera* 'lizard' about which the singer said: "The *mera* comes transformed to eat us. This isn't from here, but is in the jungle. It comes to hunt us and to kill us. This *hoa* is good for saving oneself, when he leaves for the jungle":

> You are arriving.
> You were born in the earth.
> This is your movement; this is your name.
> You were born in the earth.
> You are a small lizard of the earth, a little lizard of the jungle.
> This is your movement, and this is your name.
> Go away from me.
> Make your path, because the world is large.
> This is your movement, small lizard of the jungle, little lizard of the earth.

Like other Warao songs for controlling the supernatural, these have their own individual melodic patterns.

A supernatural charm, the *mare-hoa,* is employed for enticing a woman to love a man: the man names all the parts of a woman's body, causing her to find him irresistible. Another kind of *hoa* is sung during the ritual for felling a large tree from

FIGURE 5   A *dakoho* song about a stingray (*hue*). Transcription by Lawrence J. App.

which men make a canoe: a shaman's song in which the man has supernatural intercourse with the tree, the mythical mother of the forest.

Utility

Another common Warao context for music is utility, including lullabies and songs for working and traveling in the jungle, often with drum accompaniment.

Lullabies

Lullabies are sung by men and women, and often have texts that teach older children about Warao life and beliefs, including the dangers of ogres and animals. "Go to sleep, little child, or the jaguar-ogre which has no bones will think you are a deer and eat you" is a common theme. The educative aspect of the lullabies is an important form of Warao enculturation.

Work-related songs

Work-related songs once had an entertainment context. Known as *dakoho*, they are dance songs whose dance context is obsolete. They are more commonly sung to ease the work of men and women, to accompany the paddling of canoes, to augment drinking, or just for relaxing around the house. The excerpt transcribed as figure 5 is of an old *dakoho* about the stingray (*húe*), which can be seen in rivers during high tide. Most of its text contains vocables, such as the words *yanera, lanera, kwanera*, and *da-na-na-na-na*. It is a happy song, originally meant for dancing.

Unlike theurgical songs and the other songs of utility, most work-related songs have Western melodic traits. Many of them can effectively be accompanied with standard tonic, dominant, and subdominant harmonies, though the most common practice is to sing them unaccompanied. They are occasionally played on the *sekeseke*, or less often accompanied on the *wandora*. When and how this aspect of acculturation occurred is unknown. *Dakoho* from the 1930s and 1940s notated by the Spanish missionary Basilio María de Barral (1964:253–574) display more traditional traits than those I collected in the 1970s.

Songs for traveling in the jungle

When the Warao walk through the forest to get to the *morichal* to find large *cachicamo* trees (which they cut down for building canoes), to visit neighboring villages not easily accessible by canoe, or to gather food, they sing songs. Led by a male player of the *ehuru* drum, the songs keep the group together and help maintain the walking pace.

PERFORMERS AND PERFORMANCES

Most Warao makers of music are adults, though children, because of the constancy and closeness of family and village contact, learn all kinds of songs informally from adults. Occasionally children will sing *hoa* prayers to themselves to ease their pain from cuts, stings, or bruises. Likewise, dance songs and popular Venezuelan songs are a part of some children's musical repertoire, especially those who attend Roman Catholic mission schools in the delta.

Though women have been shamans, most singers of theurgical songs are men. The older the male adult, the more likely he knows the important theurgical songs, whether he is a shaman or some other leader of his village. Because Warao male elders are highly respected as leaders of families, knowledge of the songs increases the opportunity to sing them.

All Warao men must have a role within their society. Without a social position—as shaman, maker of baskets or canoes, keeper of the *isimoi,* and so forth—men would have no place to go with their wives after death except to the western part of the cosmos, the place of eternal death. And nearly all Warao roles, from shaman to artisan, include songs of power.

The underlying structure of Warao theurgical music is not an aesthetic one. It is based on the proper knowledge of the melodic formulas determined by context, and on the ability to choose words that will effectively communicate with the proper supernatural entities for accomplishing the appropriate tasks. This lack of aesthetic concern is typical of lullabies and other secular songs. The Warao sometimes, however, comment that someone is a good singer of *dakoho*—a reference to knowledge and ability. Other than the knowledge of *dakoho* or Venezuelan popular songs, there is no musical creolization or mestization between the Warao and African- or Spanish-derived Venezuelans—a factor caused by the Warao's physical isolation.

FURTHER STUDY

Recent books about the Warao are by Dale A. Olsen (1996), which explores the role of Warao music as power and pleasure, and by Johannes Wilbert (1993, 1996), which studies Warao cosmology, including some uses of music. Additionally, Charles L. Briggs (1993, 1996) has studied several areas of Warao music, including ritual wailing and healing.

REFERENCES

Barral, P. Basilio María de. 1964. *Los Indios Guaraúnos y su Cancionero.* Madrid: Consejo Superior de Investigaciones Científicas, Departamento de Misionología Española.

Briggs, Charles L. 1993. "Personal Sentiments and Polyphonic Voices in Warao Women's Ritual Wailing: Music and Poetics in a Critical and Collective Discourse." *American Anthropologist* 95(4):929–957.

———. 1996. "The Meaning of Nonsense, the Poetics of Embodiment, and the Production of Power in Warao Healing." In *The Performance of Healing,* ed. Carol Laderman and Marina Roseman, 185–232. New York: Routledge.

Furst, Peter T. 1965. "West Mexico, the Caribbean and Northern South America." *Antropológica* 14:1–37.

Girard, Sharon. 1997. Review of *Music of the Warao of Venezuela: Song People of the Rain Forest,* by Dale A. Olsen. *Latin American Music Review* 18(2):331–337.

Greenberg, Joseph H. 1987. *Language in the Americas.* Stanford: Stanford University Press.

Olsen, Dale A. 1996. *Music of the Warao of Venezuela. The Song People of the Rain Forest.* Gainesville: University Press of Florida. Book and compact disc.

Turrado Moreno, A. 1945. *Etnografía de los Indios Guaraúnos.* Interamerican Conference on Agriculture III. Cuadernos Verdes 15. Caracas: Lithografía y Tipografía Vargas.

Wilbert, Johannes. 1993. *Mystic Endowment: Religious Ethnography of the Warao Indians.* Cambridge, Mass.: Harvard University Press.

———. 1996. *Mindful of Famine: Religious Climatology of the Warao Indians.* Cambridge, Mass.: Harvard University Press.

Guaraní
Timothy D. Watkins

Musical Instruments
Musical Contexts and Genres
Further Study

The area the present-day Guaraní inhabit is much smaller than the area they inhabited in the 1500s, when they first encountered Europeans. Because of the activities of Jesuits, who gathered Guaraní people from various localities and put them in the same mission towns (*reducciónes* 'reductions'), and the genetic mixing of the Guaraní with Europeans, subtribes mentioned by Spanish conquistadors and missionaries have disappeared.

Since the 1700s, the Guaraní who resisted Jesuit missionary activities and did not become integrated into the greater mestizo Paraguayan culture have been known collectively as Cainguá or Ca'aguá ('inhabitants of the forest'). The names that designate individual Guaraní groups appear to have originated in the 1700s.

The Eastern Paraguayan Cainguá can be divided into three groups: the Mbyá (also known as Mbwiha, Ava-mbihá, Caayguá, Apyteré, and Baticola), the Chiripá (also known as Ava-Guaraní and Ava-katú-eté), and the Paí-tavyterá (also known as Pañ). The Mbyá live mostly in the departments of Alto Paraná and Itapúa. Some live in the region around Corpus in the Argentine province of Misiones, and others are widely scattered throughout the Brazilian states of Mato Grosso, Paraná, and Rio Grande do Sul. The Chiripá live south of the Jejuá-guazú River and along both banks of the upper Paraná River, along the Yuytorocaí River, and north of the Iguassú River. The Paí-tavyterá live north of the Jejui-Guazu River. Of these groups, the Mbyá remain the least acculturated, and the Chiripá are the most acculturated. In addition to these three groups, the Chiriguano (Chiriwano) are a Guaraní group in the Chaco area west of the Paraguay River, extending into Argentina and Bolivia. Several groups of Guaraní (including the Apapocuva and the Tañyguá) found in Brazil regard themselves as distinct from the Cainguá of Paraguay, though they are closely related.

The archaeological record of pre-Columbian Guaraní musical culture is scant; it contains only a few end-blown bone flutes. Among the reasons for the scarcity of archaeological musical artifacts is that the Guaraní led a seminomadic way of life, partly reflecting the belief that the souls of the dead continued to inhabit the structures that had been their homes during life. The climate and the soil have contributed to the nonsurvival of wooden instruments.

The most informative historical accounts of Guaraní music come from Jesuit

quena (also *kena, qina*) Spanish orthography of an Aymara name for a notched, end-blown edge aerophone of the central Andes

berimbau A struck musical bow with a calabash resonator common to Bahia, Brazil, and derived from Angola

records, the *Cartas anuas* (Leonhardt 1927 and 1929), annual reports made by each Jesuit province to the Jesuit general in Rome. On the expulsion of the Jesuits (in 1767), some of the Guaraní intermingled with mestizos and criollos; others returned to the forest, where they joined the Cainguá.

MUSICAL INSTRUMENTS

The anthropological literature does not specify a Guaraní taxonomy for musical instruments, though some instruments are used exclusively by men and others exclusively by women. Therefore, the common system used in ethnomusicology is followed.

Idiophones

One of the most important idiophones in use among all the Guaraní is the *mbaraká*, a spiked calabash rattle with small stones or seeds inside and a wooden handle, usually adorned with feathers. The *mbaraká* is a shamanistic instrument, played only by men. Its origin is attributed by the Chiripá to Hy'apú Guazú (the primordial father), and it is associated with thunder (Gómez-Perasso n.d.:114). They see it not as a receptacle for spirits but as an instrument for invoking them by its sound. During religious rituals, each man of the tribe uses his own *mbaraká*, but these are not regarded as being as potent as the shaman's instrument (Bartolomé 1977:98).

Another instrument used exclusively by men is a pair of wooden concussion sticks (*popygua'i*) about 30 centimeters long. According to Sequera (1987:70), who described their use among the Mbyá, the sticks are a shamanic instrument that accompanies *tangará*, a ritual dance performed within the ceremonial house (*opy*), and are played outside that house before ceremonial occasions for chasing away evil spirits. Each initiate (*yvyra'ijá*) makes his own sticks.

Women play a bamboo tube stamper (*takuapú*) whose length varies. The Mbyá instrument is between 70 and 90 centimeters long and about 10 centimeters wide. The Chiripá associate it with Ñande Sy Eté, the primordial mother, who plays it as she begins the search for Hy'apú Guazú (Gómez-Perasso n.d.:114). Strings of rattles may be attached to it and worn around the ankles, waists, or wrists; they are traditionally made from deer hooves, turtle shells, or other materials and may even consist of bottle caps strung together (Boettner n.d.:20).

Membranophones

Two-headed membranophones (*angu'á*) are distributed among the Guaraní groups. They are made of several materials (wood, clay, or even tin), and the material used for the membranes may be animal skin or cotton cloth. These drums may be played with sticks or with the hands and are of various sizes. Despite variations in details of construction, all are used only by men.

The *mba'e pu ovava'é* is a Mbyá cylindrical drum. The shaman usually plays it to accompany prayer-songs (*ñembo'e pöra*), but after a successful hunt, a hunter must use it to accompany propitiatory songs to the animals he has killed (Sequera 1987:70–71).

Aerophones

Guaraní flutes (*mimby*) may be vertical or transverse. Adjectives describe flutes, as in *mimby guazú* 'large flute'. The old-style flute (*mimby kué*) is a wooden, notched, vertical flute of the *quena* type, with five holes for fingers and one hole for a thumb. The *temimby ie piasá,* a Chiriguano transverse flute, is made from hollow cane and has six holes for fingers. The Mbyá long flute (*mimby pukú*) is a vertical duct flute with five holes for fingers and two for thumbs; its duct is formed by wax. Mbyá and Chiripá men use their flutes to attract potential spouses; they may play flutes with a two-headed drum (*angu'á pú*) to announce hunters' return to the village (Gómez-Perasso n.d.:115).

The Guaraní play raft panpipes. Chiriguano examples may be of Andean origin (Boettner n.d.:26). Mbyá panpipes (*mimby pú* 'sounding flute'), primarily women's instruments, are sometimes played by men (Sequera 1987:72–73).

Among the more uncommon aerophones is a bundle panpipe, played by Caingua women. It consists of five bamboo tubes, not bound together but held in a bunch with both hands. The Chiriguanos have a double flute.

The onomatopoeic word *turú* is the generic Guaraní name for trumpets. As with flutes, compound names are descriptive of size and material. The instruments are usually made of cane or bamboo, though cow horn sometimes serves. Of special note is the *uatapú*, a trumpet used to attract fish.

Chordophones

The Guaraní use several types of musical bows. The *guyrambau* (or simply *lambau*), a large Mbyá example, consists of a bow, the end of which is placed in the player's mouth while the string is plucked with the fingers or a small stick. It is played by men for recreation (Sequera 1987:71). A musical bow similar to the Brazilian *berimbau* is called *gualambau* in Guaraní. It has a gourd resonator close to one end. Harmonics are obtained by light placement of the fingers on the string, struck with a small stick. The *gualambau* seems to be falling into disuse (Boettner n.d.:31).

The *guyrapa-í* is a double musical bow in use among various Guaraní groups. It consists of a smaller bow (*embirekó* 'wife'), which rubs a larger bow (*imena* 'husband') whose end is placed in the player's mouth for resonance. Before playing, the string of the *imena* must be moistened with the lips. The player produces different notes by stopping the string of the male bow with the four fingers of the left hand. The instrument is associated with the *guyrapa-í yaretá* spirit and has obvious sexual symbolism. It is not played by women because they believe it would make them overly amorous (Boettner n.d.:31).

A chordophone that illustrates musical acculturation resulting from Jesuit missions is the Mbyá three-stringed fiddle (*ravé*). Apparently derived from the violin, it is considered by the Mbyá a sacred instrument. It is made of cedar, also considered sacred. Its strings were traditionally made from plant fibers, but nylon strings are now widely used. These strings are played by a small bow, made of wood and horsehair. The *ravé* measures from 45 to 52 centimeters long. Only men may play it, and it accompanies a ritual dance (*tangará*). Though all initiated men are expected to play it, the most proficient player receives the title *rave jára* 'master *ravé*-player' (Sequera 1987:71–72).

A five-stringed guitar (*kuminjaré*) is another example of musical acculturation. It is sometimes called *mbaraká*, the name given to the sacred rattle, distinguished from the guitar by the term *mirí* 'small'. The number of strings of the *kuminjaré* seems to point to its adoption by the Mbyá during the time of the Jesuit missions, when the European guitar had five courses. Like the *mbaraká mirí*, the *kuminjaré* is considered a shamanic instrument and is used within the *opy*. Unlike the *ravé*, it is not a melodic instrument; its strumming provides a rhythmic accompaniment for the *tangará* and ritual songs known as *ñembo'eí* (Sequera 1987:72).

MUSICAL CONTEXTS AND GENRES

Music is of great importance to Guaraní shamans, who use the sound of the *mbaraká* and songs to communicate with supernatural figures. Central to the recognition of an individual as a shaman is his supernatural inspiration with chants. Any Chiripá man or woman may have a personal sacred song (*guaú*), revealed to him or her by a dead relative. The recipient of the *guaú* may then teach it to the rest of the community. Its possession is believed to confer a certain immunity against accidents and has curative power. It is differentiated from *koti-hú*, songs with no religious significance and may be a true sacred song (*guaú eté*) or a lesser sacred song (*guaú aí*). The difference between the two genres seems to be that the *guaú eté* consists mainly of vocables (not understood even by the singers), whereas the *guaú aí* makes frequent use of archaic words and phrases; however, in importance, the texts seem to be secondary to the melodies (Bartolomé 1977:110).

A type of shaman, Ñandé Rú (Our Father), also known as Paí—derived from Mbaí 'the solitary one' because he lives figuratively between the upper world and the lower—is any man whose singing is unusually potent because of his spiritual force (Bartolomé 1977:110–112). According to local mythology Ñanderú Guazú (Our Great Father) created the earth (*yvy*). One day he encountered Ñanderú Mba'é Kua'á (Our Father Who Knows All). The two decided to create a woman, so Ñanderú Guazú fashioned a clay pot, which he instructed Ñanderú Mba'é Kua'á to break. From the broken pot emerged Ñaandesý (Our Great Mother). She had sex with both, and as a result bore twins. The older twin, the son of Ñanderú Guazú, received the responsibility of caring for the earth during the day; he is known as Ñaanderykeý (Our Older Brother) and became Sun (Kuarahý). The son of Ñanderú Mba'é Kua'á, having received the care of the earth at night, became Moon (Jacý); he is known as Ñandetyvý (Our Younger Brother). Ñanderú Guazú now resides in The Land of No Evil (Yvymaraeý), where he continues to communicate with shamans. He tells them that unless the Guaraní continue to pray, he will destroy the earth. If all the Guaraní obey his wishes, he will instruct the shamans to take their communities on a trek where they will be shown the way to Yvymaraeý, the place where good people go when they die.

The prayer dance

The most important ritual in the Guaraní religious complex is the prayer dance. It and its variations may be performed for a variety of reasons, but a good example is the prayer of the forest (*ñembo'é kaagüy*), a fertility-related dance traditionally celebrated once a year by the Chiripá. It takes place in the big house (*oga guazú*) in the center of the village. Typically, this house is a 3-meter by 6-meter area, covered with a low thatched roof. It may or may not have walls, though at least the side facing east (the direction of Yvymaraeý) is open. Along the eastern side is a candle holder (*tatáendey* 'fire holder'), which consists of three 1.5-meter-long poles (spaced a meter apart) and a crossbar on which candles and other sacred objects are placed. On the other side of the candle holder is a cedar-log trough filled with a fermented ceremonial drink made from the juice of maize, honey, or sugarcane. The canoelike shape of the trough may be linked to a mythical flood (Bartolomé 1977:123).

The *ñembo'é kaagüy* lasts for nine nights, from sundown to dawn. The celebration divides into two parts: the first eight nights are the sacred part, when only *guaú* are sung. The final night is secular: after a shaman sings a song indicating that the deity present for the *guaú* has departed, *koti-hú* may be sung. The dance and the songs it accompanies begin with all the men in a line, graduated from oldest to youngest, shaking their *mbaraká*. The shamans, shaking their own *mbaraká*, go into trance and begin to sing. At this point, some married women stand along the western wall of the big house and begin marking time with their *takuapú*. Single women begin to dance from side to side in the center of the house. The shamans may remain at the *tatáendey*, or they may lead the rest of the men on a simulated trek around the women and around the big house. The dance continues for ten to twenty minutes, until the shamans return to where they started, in front of the candle holder. After a minute or two of rest, dancing begins anew.

Other occasions besides the *ñembo'é kaagüy* that make use of variations of the prayer dance include the female puberty ritual, the initiatory dance for males, a name-giving dance, a dance for the dead, and a trek-related dance. This variety of occasions ensures that the prayer dance is celebrated quite frequently. In fact, shamans may call for its celebration for almost any reason. Its objectives are threefold: (1) to maintain a day-to-day contact with Our Great Father and Our Older brother, who provide guidance; (2) to please Our Great Father, who has instructed the shamans to keep dancing so they may ensure the earth's safety; and (3) to receive the final instructions that will guide them to Yvymaraeý (Albiol 1981:47).

In addition to the *guaú* and the *koti-hú*, a song-dance genre known as *mborahéi pukú* 'long song' is frequently found in the prayer dance and its variations. Its text consists of a responsorial retelling of the principal stories of Guaraní mythology. The singing is led by a *mborahéi jára*, a shaman renowned for his singing, who sings every verse twice. After hearing the verse and its repetition, the other singers repeat it twice more, after which the *mborahéi jára* goes to the next verse, and the same procedure is followed (Meliá, Grünberg, and Grünberg 1976:242).

Soul dances

A different kind of dance is linked to the Guaraní conception of life after death. The Guaraní believe that every person has two souls. The first soul, a spiritual one (Apapocuva *ayvucué*, Paí-tavyterá *ñe'e* 'word'), resides in the throat. Identified with a peaceful disposition, this soul enters the body during gestation or immediately after birth. A person's temperament is conditioned by an animal soul (*acyiguá*). In some traditions, these souls are aspects of the same soul, which after death separate. The spiritual soul tries to go to Yvymaraeý, but may linger for a while near its former home. The animal soul may turn into a ghost, showing itself sometimes as an actual animal. To drive the spiritual soul away, the shamans organize a dance in which two groups of dancers run past each other repeatedly, to confuse the soul and make it become lost. A shaman can then deliver it to the deity Tupã, who takes it to the land of the dead. The animal soul must be attacked with weapons (Nimuendajú 1914:305).

The search for Yvymaraeý has associations with dance. A legend says ancient Guaraní shamans gradually subjugated their animal soul through constant dancing, until their spiritual soul could fly to Yvymaraeý. The trek enacted in the prayer dance has occasionally been undertaken literally in migratory movements by villages and

A legend says ancient Guaraní shamans gradually subjugated their animal soul through constant dancing, until their spiritual soul could fly to Yvymaraeý.

groups of villages, which, believing the end of the world was near and that Yvymaraeý was beyond the Atlantic Ocean, were led eastward by their shamans. Bartolomé identifies the Apapocuva as one such migratory band of the Chiripá.

FURTHER STUDY

Moisés Bertoni's study *La civilización guaraní* (1922, 1956) is a good introduction to Guaraní culture. The pioneering work of Kurt Nimuendajú Unkel (1914) and León Cadogan (1949) are invaluable contributions to the study of Guaraní religion by anthropologists who actually underwent initiation as shamans. Branislava Susnik's *El rol de los indígenas en la formación y en la vivencia del Paraguay* (1982, 1983) deals with historical cultural change among the Guaraní through the 1800s. An excellent source for Guaraní oral literature is *Literatura guaraní del Paraguay* (Saguier 1980), which contains transcriptions of materials collected by anthropologists among the Mbyá, the Paí-Tavyterá, the Chiripá, and the Apapocuva. Georg and Friedl Grünberg's *Los Chiriguanos* (1975) is a good introduction to the culture of that sub-tribe.

REFERENCES

Albiol, Robert M. 1981. "The Ava-Guaraní: Their Development and Well-Being." M.A. thesis, University of Florida.

Bartolomé, Miguel Alberto. 1977. *Orekuera royhendú (Lo que escuchamos en sueños): Shamanismo y religión entre los Ava-katu-eté del Paraguay.* Mexico City: Instituto Indigenista Interamericano. Serie Antropología Social, 17.

Bertoni, Moisés L. 1922. *Etnología.* La civilización guaraní, 1. Puerto Bertoni: n.p.

———. 1956. *Religión y moral.* La civilización guaraní, 2. Buenos Aires: Editorial Indo-Americana.

Boettner, Juan Max. N.d. *Música y músicos del Paraguay.* Asunción: Autores Paraguayos Asociados.

Cadogan, León. 1948. "Los indios Jeguaká Tenondé (Mbyá) del Guairá." *América Indígena* 8(2):131–139.

Gómez-Perasso, José Antonio. N.d. *Ava guyrá kambí: Notas sobre la etnografía de los ava-kué-chiripá del Paraguay oriental.* Asunción: Centro Paraguayo de Estudios Sociológicos.

Grünberg, Georg, and Friedl Grünberg. 1975. *Los Chiriguanos.* Asunción: Centro de Estudios Antropológicos, Universidad Católica "Nuestra Señora de la Asunción."

Leonhardt, Carlos, ed. 1927, 1929. *Cartas anuas de la provincia del Paraguay, Chile y Tucumán, de la Compañía de Jesús.* 2 vols. Buenos Aires: Instituto de Investigaciónes Históricas.

Meliá, Bartolomeu, Georg Grünberg, and Friedl Grünberg. 1976. *Los Patavyterã: etnografía guaraní del Paraguay contemporáneo.* Asunción: Centro de Estudios Antropológicos, Universidad Católica "Nuestra Señora de la Asunción."

Nimuendajú Unkel, Curt. 1914. "Die Sagen von der Erschaffung und Vernichtung der Welt als Grundlagen der Religion der Apapokúva-Guaraní." *Zeitschrift für Ethnologie* 46:284–403. Translated into Spanish as "Los mitos de creación y de destrucción del mundo como fundamentos de la religión de los apapokuva-guaraní." Lima: Centro Amazónico de Antropología y Aplicación Práctica.

Saguier, Ruben Bareiro, ed. 1980. *Literatura guaraní del Paraguay.* Caracas: Biblioteca Ayacucho.

Sequera, Guillermo. 1987. "Cosmofonía de los indígenas Mbyá del Paraguay." *Caravelle* 49:65–75.

Susnik, Branislava. 1982, 1983. *El rol de los indígenas en la formación y en la vivencia del Paraguay.* 2 vols. Asunción: Instituto Paraguayo de Estudios Nacionales.

Quechua and Aymara
Thomas Turino

Musical Instruments
Song Traditions
Aesthetics and General Stylistic Traits
Musical Contexts
Pan-Andean Generalizations

Quechua (Kechua) was the official language of the Inca (Inka) empire, which stretched from northern Ecuador to central Chile. Most of the indigenous peoples of highland Ecuador speak it, as do the peoples of most of the Peruvian sierra and highland migrants in coastal cities. Aymara, the second most prominent native Andean language, is spoken in Peru, mostly in these areas within Puno Department: Huancané Province, on the northwest side of Lake Titicaca; Chucuito Province, on the south side of Lake Titicaca; and between Huancané and Chucuito, where Quechua- and Aymara-speaking peoples live. In Bolivia, Aymara-speaking communities cluster south and east of Lake Titicaca in the province of La Paz. The Bolivian linguistic situation is complex: Quechua and Aymara are spoken in areas juxtaposed throughout its highlands. To a much lesser extent, Aymara-speaking communities occur in northern Argentina and Chile (Tarapacá Province).

Population figures for speakers of Quechua and Aymara vary and are difficult to substantiate. In rural native Andean communities, Spanish bilingualism is common among middle-aged and young people, especially men.

The use of the linguistic terms *Quechua* and *Aymara* as ethnic, cultural rubrics is a late-twentieth-century development that remains restricted to certain contexts. For convenience, scholars and state institutions use these terms as cultural categories. Indigenous groups involved in political struggles have sometimes strategically used them as the basis of ethnic-bloc formation, especially in Ecuador and Bolivia. Notions of a Quechua or Aymara culture or nation, however, are alien to the discourse of villagers, who more frequently define their identities in terms of specific communities and regions (Montoya 1986).

Cultural and musical practices vary importantly by microregion and macroregion in the Andes but do not necessarily correspond with the language spoken. Quechua-speaking communities only 50 kilometers apart may differ fundamentally in their inventory of musical instruments, genres, and fiestas, whereas neighboring Aymara- and Quechua-speaking communities may share many similar traditions.

The only generalizable difference between making music in Quechua- and Aymara-speaking communities is the prevalence of vocal music among the former and its relative lack of importance among the latter. Beyond this, Quechua- and

antara (also, *andara*) Quechua for single-unit panpipe in Peru, played by one person

siku (also, *sico*) A double-unit panpipe consisting of six to eight (or more) closed cane tubes per half, requiring two people to play one instrument by interlocking the music

zampoña A Spanish term principally used in Chile for panpipe, especially the double-unit panpipe or *siku*

rondador Single-unit panpipe from Ecuador with up to thirty tubes

ira 'Leader' in Aymara, one of the halves (male) of the *siku* double-unit panpipe in the central Andes

arca (also, *arka*) 'Follower' in Aymara, one of the halves (female) of the *siku* double-unit panpipe in the central Andes

Aymara-speaking musicians can be considered together under the rubric *native Andean music*. This concept presents difficulties, however, since the boundaries between indigenous and mestizo identities and practices are fluid; yet certain aesthetic and musical features help distinguish a distinct native Andean musical sensibility.

To describe this sensibility and native Andean musical practice at a general level, I return continually to the themes of regionalism and ethnic and class divisions between people identified locally as criollos (whites, Spanish-Americans), mestizos (fusing Iberian and indigenous cultural heritages), and *indios* (Indians, self-defined as Quechua *runakuna* and Aymara *hak'enaka* 'people'). These divisions must be understood against the backdrop of a long history of harsh repression—by states (first colonial, later republican), by local elites, and at different times by the Roman Catholic church. Ethnic and class categories are social constructions, constantly negotiated within processes of social mobility, political confrontation, and urban migration; once established, however, these categories have real effects on peoples' lives.

Notwithstanding the intensity of ethnic and regional cultural diversity, general features of native Andean music can best be described in relation to two macromusical regions, located roughly to the north and to the south of the Lake Titicaca area of Peru and Bolivia, with the lake area belonging to the southern region. The southern region favors large-ensemble performance of indigenous wind instruments and drums. In the northern region, smaller ensembles and solo performance on indigenous winds and drums and on strings are more common, and stringed instruments in a greater variety have a more prominent role.

MUSICAL INSTRUMENTS

The prototypes for the idiophones, membranophones, and aerophones played in Andean villages arose in pre-Columbian societies; chordophones were not used before the 1530s.

Throughout the Andes, instrumental performance is a male domain. Exceptions are small, hand-held drums (like the *tinya*), and for dancing, rattles, leggings, and bells. Before the 1500s, women played different-sized drums, some of them resembling the late-twentieth-century *tinya*. Women accompany their singing with *tinya* in the central-southern Peruvian highlands (Junín, Huancavelica, Ayacucho, Apurimac, Cusco, Arequipa). Women in northern Potosí, Bolivia, play a similar drum, the *jochana*.

Idiophones and membranophones

Idiophones and membranophones are played as part of many Andean traditions involving instrumental ensembles, dancing, and singing. In native Andean music, the primary idiophones are leggings and shakers made of goats' hooves or metal attached to cloth, leather, string, or ribbons. In isolated localities, some peoples use other idiophones, such as the large metal triangle (*ch'iñisku*) that is a hallmark of the double-row-panpipe tradition of Charazani, Bolivia, and the separated scissor blades used in *dansaq* in Ayacucho, Huancavelica, and Apurimac, Peru. Most double-row-panpipe ensembles (two panpipe halves, played by two people) include drumming from any of several kinds of membranophones: large, deep, double-headed drums (*bombo, wankara*); large, thinner double-headed indigenous snare drums (*cajas*); and occasionally, Western snare and bass drums.

Aerophones

As suggested by the archaeological record on the Peruvian coast, panpipes, end-blown notched flutes, trumpets, whistles, and ocarinas were the major pre-Hispanic wind instruments. A transverse flute with two holes for fingering existed in Moche culture (Stevenson 1968:252–257, Olsen 1992:78–79), but side-blown flutes were probably much rarer than end-blown types. No good evidence for end-blown duct flutes has been found in the Andean area, though the presence of whistles and ocarinas indicates that the technology for duct flutes was available before the Spanish encounter.

Panpipes

Archaeological panpipes have received the greatest attention from scholars (Bolaños 1985, 1988; Haeberli 1979; Rossel 1977; Stevenson 1968; Valencia 1982), but they agree on little beyond three observations: single-row panpipes were used, they were sometimes played in consorts of two sizes tuned in octaves, and high-pitched tunings were favored.

Iconography on a pre-Columbian Moche pot from the north Peruvian coast shows two players' panpipes, connected by a cord. This illustration has often been cited as evidence that double-unit panpipes (with the series of pitches alternating between the halves) were played by paired musicians in interlocking, or hocket, fashion during the pre-Columbian period, as is commonly done in southern Peru and Bolivia. César Bolaños (1988:25, 105–106), however, argues that nothing in the archaeological record corroborates this; but he may have identified several consorts of single-unit Nasca panpipes with different-sized instruments tuned in octaves, plus panpipes with corresponding tubes tuned roughly a quarter-tone apart. The range of his measurements of variations in pitch between the instruments' corresponding tubes closely resembles the range of variations in pitch in contemporary panpipe consorts in southern Peru.

Our knowledge of pre-Columbian and early colonial panpipes in the Andean highlands derives largely from historical sources and iconography of the 1500s, such as Guamán Poma de Ayala. For the early colonial period, the chronicler Inca Garcilaso de la Vega (1966 [1609]:127) says "*los indios Collas*" (Qollas, Aymara-speakers from around the Lake Titicaca region) played double-unit panpipes in interlocking fashion. His reference to different vocal parts (*tiple,* tenor, contralto, *contrabajo*) in Colla panpipe performance may suggest that different-sized panpipes created polyphony (as they do today). Garcilaso, associated with the Inca elite of Cusco through his mother, apparently did not know the name of the instrument, which he says was a foreign instrument belonging to the Collas in the south. Bolaños uses this and other evidence to suggest that the Incas may not have used panpipes, but that peoples they subjugated did.

In accounts of highland societies from the early colonial period, panpipes were called *antara* (Guamán Poma 1980). *Siku* (or *sico*), a term for double-unit panpipes, appears in Ludovico Bertonio's Aymara dictionary of 1612 (1956). These terms, plus the Spanish word *zampoña,* are still used in the highlands.

FIGURE 1   A double-unit panpipe (*sikuri*) ensemble performs in the streets of Puno, Peru. Photo by Thomas Turino, 1984.

Types and distributions

Single-unit (a rafted set of pipes constituting one instrument) and double-unit (two rafted sets of pipes constituting one instrument) panpipes are played from northern Ecuador to northern Chile. Specific traditions are localized, and areas where the panpipe is played are not contiguous. In Ecuador and northern Peru, single-unit traditions, such as the *rondador* and the smaller, seven-tubed *antara*, are played solo, sometimes with drum by a single musician, and in groups with drum accompaniment.

The *antara* from the northern Peruvian department of Cajamarca is played solo for informal, personal performance while resting or herding animals (Romero and Cánepa 1988:4). Ecuadorian *rondadores* range from small panpipes with eight tubes (pentatonic) to larger hexatonic instruments with twenty, thirty, or more tubes (Moreno 1949:33); people of the central Ecuadorian provinces play the larger, single panpipes in fiestas throughout the year.

In the Peruvian departments from Ancash to Cusco, indigenous panpipe traditions are rare [see Q'ERO]. Double-unit panpipes are commonly played in the broad region surrounding Lake Titicaca in Peru (Puno and parts of Tacna and Moquegua departments), throughout Bolivia, and in northern Chile. A few localized single-unit traditions also occur in this area (Turino 1987:107–108) (figure 1) [see PERU: figures 1 and 2].

Many types of double-unit panpipes exist, with their names, construction (some have matching resonating tubes), tunings, and repertoire varying from one locale to another and from one occasion to another in the same locale. Many have a heptatonic series of pitches that alternates between the halves, played in interlocking fashion by a pair of musicians (*ira* 'leader', *arca* 'follower'). Unlike the single-unit instruments found in the north, most of the double-unit traditions involve large communal

FIGURE 2 A fiesta orchestra from Paucartambo, Cusco, Peru: two metal flutes (*kena*), a diatonic harp played upside-down, and a violin. Photo by Thomas Turino, 1982.

ensembles (often fourteen to thirty players); musicians often play drums at the same time. Consorts often include three or four different-size panpipes, each with its regional name, played in parallel octaves (as in *puneño ayarachi, chiriguano, siku,* and *sikuri* traditions); or between six and nine voices tuned in parallel fourths, fifths, and octaves (as in the *kantus* tradition in Charazani, Bolivia, and regional *siku* traditions in Huancané, Peru); or more rarely parallel thirds (as in regional *siku* traditions in Huancané, Peru).

Except for variable life-cycle fiestas, contractual performances at mestizo Roman Catholic fiestas, and state-sponsored folkloric festivals, double-unit panpipes in the southern Andean region are traditionally played mainly in the dry season, April through October.

End-blown flutes

The word *pinkullu* (also *pincollo* and *pingollo*; Aymara *pinkillu*), a pre-Columbian term, seems to have referred generically to end-blown flutes. Since there is no evidence of pre-Hispanic end-blown duct flutes in the Andes, we can assume that the term denoted end-blown notched flutes, which, with five or six holes for fingers and one for a thumb, are played from the central Peruvian department of Junín south through Bolivia; they are not traditionally used in northern Peru and Ecuador (Moreno 1949:36).

Notched flutes are known by the generic term *kena* (Spanish *quena*) and various local names, sometimes corresponding to dances, such as *pulipuli* in neighboring Huancané, Peru (Aymara), and Charazani, Bolivia (Quechua); *chokela* in the departments of Puno, Peru, and La Paz, Bolivia; and *lichiwayu* (or *lechewayo*) in Cochabamba and northern Potosí departments, Bolivia.

The smaller end-notched *kena* (35 to 38 centimeters) has become a prime solo instrument in urban folk-revivalist groups in Andean cities. In southern Peru, they sometimes combine with harps, violins, and other instruments in bands that typically play for dancing during mestizo fiestas (figure 2); within peasant communities, however, they remain a casual instrument, often played solo for personal enjoyment.

In the area around Lake Titicaca and to the east and south, longer end-notched flutes (about 55 centimeters or more) are played in large communal ensembles, often with drum accompaniment, for public ritual and festival occasions. In Bolivia, they are played in consorts of different sizes. Like panpipes, they tend to be strongly asso-

pinkullu Central Andean end-blown duct flute of Quechua origin with three to eight finger holes

pífano In Ecuador, a duct flute with six finger holes, and elsewhere in South America, a cane, plastic, or metal transverse flute with six finger holes

tarka In Bolivia, Chile, and Peru, a square- or slightly hexagonal-shaped (in its cross-section) wooden duct flute with a hoarse sound

pitu 'Pipe', Central Andean cane, metal, or plastic end-blown duct flute of Spanish or Quechua origin with three or four finger holes

ciated with dry-season festivals in the Lake Titicaca region and farther south; however, in various Quechua-speaking areas of the department of Cusco, Peru, they are used in ensembles with two to six flutists accompanied by snare and bass drums for agricultural ceremonies and for carnival during the rainy season.

In the twentieth century, the Quechua term *pinkullu* (in Ecuador, *pingullo*; Aymara *pinkillu*) most often denotes an end-blown duct flute, one of the most common instruments of the Andean area. In southern Cusco and Puno, Peru, and in Bolivia, these appear in sizes ranging from cane instruments 20 centimeters long to wooden instruments more than 100 centimeters long.

Combinations of flutes and drums

In Ecuador and central to northern Peru, cane or plastic duct flutes with two holes for fingers and one for a thumb, such as the *roncadora* of Ancash, Peru, are played in pipe-and-tabor fashion for religious festivals and work-related occasions. In various regions of Ecuador, three-holed *pingullo*-and-drum combinations accompany festival dances throughout the year; this music may be played by a single musician or an ensemble—eight persons playing three-holed *pingullo*-and-drum combinations in unison in Cotopaxi Province, Ecuador (Moreno 1949:111).

To drum accompaniment, people in Imbabura Province, Ecuador, play a six-hole duct flute, *pífano.* For the Fiesta del Coraza in Otavalo, Ecuador, villagers have a mixed ensemble including small eight-tubed panpipes (*rondadorcillos*), *pingullo,* and drums (Coba Andrade 1985:187). In Imbabura Province, Ecuador, villagers have a similar mixed ensemble (Aretz 1980:830), as they do for *el yumbo,* a dance. Three-holed duct flutes, played solo or in small groups in pipe-and-tabor style, are a central tradition in northern and central Peru. In the departments of Ancash and Junín, small, five- and six-hole cane duct flutes are combined in ensemble with other melody instruments, such as violins (Otter 1985, plate 48); as in Ecuador, people play duct flutes at different times of the year.

In Puno, Peru, and in Bolivia, large communal ensembles of five- or six-hole *pinkullus* play basically in unison, usually accompanied by indigenous snare drums (*cajas*) or Western snare and bass drums. In some regions in Bolivia and southern Peru, consorts of duct flutes comprise different-size instruments played in parallel fourths, fifths, and octaves, or in interlocking fashion. In northern Potosí, Bolivia, a consort of four different-size *pinkillos* occurs, each with its own name: *machu,* about 110 centimeters long; *k'ewa,* 70 centimeters; *tara,* 56 centimeters; and *juch'uy k'ewa,* 36 centimeters (Sánchez 1988:7). Neighboring southern Cochabamba has a similar consort (*charkas*), with flutes tuned in fifths but often played in parallel octaves (Baumann 1982:27). In the Titicaca region and throughout Bolivia, duct flutes are associated with rainy-season festivals beginning with All Saints Day and carrying on through March; *pinkullus* (*pinkillus*) and wooden flutes (*tarkas*) [see BOLIVIA] are strongly associated with carnival in this region.

FIGURE 3   A side-blown flute (*pitu*) band from Conima, Puno, Peru: two *pitus* and a Western-style bass drum (unplayed *bombo* in foreground). Photo by Thomas Turino, 1985.

Side-blown flutes

Cane or wooden side-blown flutes with six holes for fingers are played throughout the Andes. In the department of Puno, Peru, consorts of such flutes (*pitus, falawatus, falawitas*) include three sizes played in parallel fourths, fifths, and octaves, accompanied by Western snare and bass drums. Side-blown flutes are also played in large communal ensembles in the department of La Paz, Bolivia. From the departments of Ayacucho and Cusco, Peru, north to Ecuador, ensembles including one or two side-blown flutes, played in unison with snare and bass drums, accompany costumed dancing (figure 3). In the department of Cusco, these ensembles consist of indigenous peasant musicians, though they are often contracted for mestizo patronal fiestas.

Trumpets

Before the 1500s, coastal peoples used curved and straight ceramic and metal trumpets, and conch trumpets were important in the highlands. In the late 1990s, conch trumpets are still played by village headmen in the department of Cusco, Peru. Circular valveless trumpets (*wak'rapuku, cacho*), made of connected sections of bull horn, are played in the central-southern Peruvian highlands. In Junín, for Santiago (St. James) and other rituals connected with animal fertility, they are sometimes performed with violin, a drum (*tinya*), and singing; in the departments of Ayacucho and Apurimac, for bullfights, they combine with side-blown flutes and drums.

Trumpets such as the *pututu* and the *erke,* made from a single cow or bull horn, are played in Peru and as far south as Potosí, Bolivia. In Puno, Peru, and in Potosí, Bolivia, small, valveless, bull horn or metal trumpets (usually called *pututu*) are sometimes used like nonharmonic drones with *pinkullu* ensembles, and metal *pututus* are played in groups as noisemakers during carnival in Huancané, Peru. A single droning horn plays in the panpipe ensembles of Italaque, Bolivia.

Long (1.5 to 3 meters or more) valveless, side-blown, wooden or cane trumpets (*clarín, llungur*) have been documented in the northern Peruvian departments of Cajamarca and Ancash, and in the central-southern region of Junín and Huancavelica. As on all the trumpets mentioned here, pitches are produced on the *clarín* and *llungur* by overblowing. The *clarín* is blown during religious festivals (see p. 118) and communal agricultural labor in Cajamarca (CD track 21); the *llungur* is associated with agricultural occasions in central Peru; and musicians have been observed playing *clarín* during carnival in Ancash, Peru (Otter 1985:94). Similar long trumpets, known as *cañas,* are played in central Bolivia, associated with the dry season, according to the Bolivian ethnomusicologist Luz María Calvo.

Brass bands

Brass bands are the most ubiquitous type of ensemble in the Andean area. They point up the complexity of ethnic or class associations with instrument and ensemble types. Associated with mestizo fiestas in towns, they are popular at rural village festivals and weddings. The participating musicians in bands might be of mestizo or indigenous heritage; musicians often learn the band instruments and music literacy while in the military.

Typically, bands work on a contractual basis and are therefore often too expensive for indigenous village events—hence the more common association with mestizo occasions. Nonetheless, given the makeup of personnel and the bands' popularity across ethnic or class lines, it is currently difficult to ascribe a single ethnic identity or emblematic meaning to these ensembles, though identity and meaning vary locally.

In the Aymara-speaking district of Conima (Puno Department, Peru), two small, local, brass bands were associated with indigenous communities. They would occasionally play for weddings in the indigenous villages and on contract for mestizo fiestas in the district capital; local indigenous wind traditions (*siku,* five- and six-hole *pinkillu, tarka, pitu*), however, remained at the center of village musical life, with brass bands at the margins. By contrast, in the nearby Peruvian Aymara-speaking area to the south of Lake Titicaca (Puno and Chucuito provinces), brass bands rival the local panpipes and flutes in popularity; and in the region around Copacabana, Bolivia, on the south shore of the lake, they have effectively replaced the local winds.

Chordophones

To help convert Andean peoples to Christianity, missionaries of the 1500s and 1600s taught European music. Stringed instruments, especially the diatonic harp and violin, were diffused to many Andean regions in this way. From the departments of Cusco, Apurimac, and Ayacucho, Peru, to the northern province of Imbabura, Ecuador, these instruments are extremely important to indigenous and mestizo musicians.

In the Peruvian departments of Ayacucho, Huancavelica, and Apurimac, harp-violin duos accompany *dansaq* 'scissor dances', and in this area (Junín, Cusco, Ancash, and further north), the harp and violin play together and separately in various instrumental combinations. Dance-oriented bands in Cusco (associated with mestizo events but often involving native Andean musicians) include harp, two violins, two *kenas,* accordion, and bass drum. In Junín alone, standard ensembles include harp-violin duos; cow-horn trumpet, violin, and *tinya*; two violins and drums; violins, small duct flutes, and drums.

In Ecuador, the diatonic harp is important among Quichua-speaking peasants in some regions; solo harp with *golpeador* (person who beats the body of the harp) is played at children's wakes and at weddings in Imbabura Province, and harpists are contracted to play at private masses there (Schechter 1992:102). In some Ecuadorian areas, the violin is a central instrument.

Indigenous communities of the central-southern Bolivian sierra use violins, though traditions of playing violins, and especially playing harps, are relatively unimportant in the southern Andean area. Strings are of marginal importance and are often absent in Peruvian Aymara- and Bolivian-Quechua-speaking communities on the shore of Lake Titicaca.

For people in the Andean region, musical instruments and style indicate ethnic or class identity. The sixteen- to twenty-stringed *bandurria* (shaped somewhat like a mandolin) has become the main instrument among Quechua-speakers in the province of Canchis, department of Cusco, Peru. Mandolins have been more widely adopted by indigenous peasants in Peru, though mandolins, like guitars, often carry mestizo ethnic or class associations.

Charangos *and other guitar variants*

South and east of Lake Titicaca, the *charango* is the primary stringed instrument of indigenous peasants. Its traditional area of diffusion, for indigenous and mestizo performers, is the departments of Huancavelica and Cusco in Peru to northern Argentina, though it has been diffused more widely by urban folk revivalists.

Of central Andean origin, extant by the early 1700s, the *charango* is usually a small, guitar-shaped chordophone with a flat wooden back or a round back made of carved wood or armadillo shell; some *charangos* have round, rectangular, or teardrop-shaped boxes. The body is about 15 to 20 centimeters at the widest points. *Charangos* played by indigenous peasants usually have between eight and fifteen thin, metal strings, arranged in five courses. For a dense, driving sound, indigenous players typically strum a single-line melody or ostinato, using one or two courses with the other strings open.

Especially in the Huancavelica Valley, Laras and Canas provinces in Cusco, and Puno and Chucuito provinces in Puno (all in Peru), the *charango* is played primarily by indigenous young men as a part of courting activities. They may play a single genre (such as *kashua* in Canas and *kh'ajhelo* in Puno) or even a single melody associated with lovemaking and thus they aptly communicate their intentions (Turino 1983). Also in Cusco Department, the *charango* sometimes has its resonating body crafted into (or contains inlays depicting) a mermaid (*sirena* 'siren'), a symbol associated with magical powers for courtship (Turino 1983) (figure 4). In Canas, the *charango* is performed for dancing during the *papa tarpuy,* the communal potato-planting ceremony.

In northern Potosí, Bolivian *charangos* are associated with the dry season, and their performance is juxtaposed with a larger guitar variant known as *guitarrilla,* used during the rainy season (Luz María Calvo, personal communication). In southeast Cochabamba, Bolivia, a larger *tabla* (flat-backed) *charango* is used during the rainy season, and a smaller, round-backed *k'ullu charango* is associated with dry-season festivals. For northern Potosí, Walter Sánchez mentions the use of a round-backed *charango* during the dry season and a similar flat-backed *charango*-like instrument (known locally as *jitarrón*) during the rainy season. Both are played solo or in small groups of the same instrument, and the tunings vary according to the fiesta. As in Peru, the *charango* and the *jitarrón* are here associated with young men and lovemaking (Sánchez 1988:3–4, 13–14; 1989:2).

Among the Chipayas in the southeast of the department of Oruro, Bolivia, the *guitarrilla* is the only stringed instrument. The *guitarrilla,* about halfway between the size of a *charango* and a guitar, has five double courses of strings and a slightly rounded back. To accompany singing and dancing for marking animals, the Chipaya play it

Indigenous players criticize deeper-sounding mestizo *charangos* with nylon strings because they do not ring, or "cry out like a cat," as they believe *charangos* should.

FIGURE 4   Juan Tapara holds a *charango* whose body has the tail of a mermaid (*sirena*), Cusco, Peru. Photo by Thomas Turino, 1982.

in large *guitarrilla* ensembles (Baumann 1981:192–195). As in indigenous *charango* performance, they strum the *guitarrilla,* though the instrument's size and gut strings give it a decidedly lower-pitched, more muffled sound than that produced by metal-stringed *charangos.*

Like the inclusion of the *charango* in an agricultural ceremony in Canas, Cusco, the strong seasonal associations of *charangos* and *guitarrillas* in Cochabamba and Potosí suggest that this chordophone has been redefined as an indigenous instrument and is being conceptualized and used according to local musical principles.

SONG TRADITIONS

In Quechua-speaking communities throughout the Andes, songs are sung on most musical occasions, and even pieces performed instrumentally frequently have known texts. As with instrumental genres, indigenous genres of song are frequently labeled and defined according to context. People identify a song as a *matrimonio* 'wedding', a *carnaval,* or a *San Juan.*

Rodrigo, Edwin, and Luís Montoya (1987) published a major study and collection of Quechua song texts from twelve Peruvian departments. Themes they listed and contexts of performance that I have observed include agricultural, herding, and other work-related songs; songs for various life-cycle stages (including weddings, roof-raising activities, and death); songs of love and courtship; joking songs; political songs; songs associated with departure and migration; songs performed at Roman Catholic festivals and indigenous rituals; and others.

During carnival and other occasions associated with courting, a lively tradition of song duels between the sexes occurs in many Andean areas. The singing of Quechua hymns at Roman Catholic festivals is widespread. Quechua songs, performed solo or by groups, are accompanied by a wide range of instruments; they may be performed without accompaniment, as are agricultural songs (*harawis*), sung in the fields.

In contrast, songs are unimportant among Aymara-speakers (Tschopik 1946:555 for the south side of Titicaca; Turino 1989 and 1993 for Huancané, on the north side in Puno, Peru; Buechler 1980:97 for Bolivia). The members of Aymara-speaking communities may know local songs (and songs from the radio), but they rarely perform them in communal festivals. Over the course of a year and a half, I heard songs sung in fiestas in Conima on two of about fifteen occasions (Candlemas and Easter). In casual contexts, I did not encounter singing, though women may have sung in private. On the south shore of Lake Titicaca, Aymara-speaking women sometimes sing vocables with the men's *pinkillus* during carnival, and young men sing *kh'ajhelos* 'songs of courtship', accompanied by *charangos* (Paniagua 1982).

AESTHETICS AND GENERAL STYLISTIC TRAITS

Because of regional variation and fluid distinctions between indigenous and mestizo identities, useful generalizations about native Andean musical sound, practices, and aesthetics are few. Aural features that reflect general Andean aesthetic preferences include high pitch, dense sound, intensive and extensive repetition, and the use of subtle contrasts.

Tessitura and timbre

Indigenous *charango* players' use of high-pitched tunings and a strumming technique with numerous thin, metal strings ringing open fits with the preference for dense, high-pitched sound. Indigenous players criticize deeper-sounding mestizo *charangos* with nylon strings because they do not ring, or "cry out like a cat," as they believe *charangos* should. The creation of the *charango*, with its shorter length of string, may have involved the preference for higher tunings.

Though women do not usually play musical instruments, they are the preferred singers in indigenous Andean communities—especially young women, because of the preference for high-pitched music. Women often sing at the top of their range, using falsetto. They also use nasal head- and throat-singing techniques, which create a dense vocal sound; collective singing is often slightly heterophonic, as vocal overlapping adds to the aural density.

Flute ensembles mirror these traits. With the exception of panpipes, Andean flutes are usually played in their overblown ranges, and their potential for producing lower pitches is not utilized. Because of a greater abundance of overtones, overblowing contributes to the density of the sound and the height of the pitch. As with collective singing, a slightly heterophonic approach to wind-ensemble performance is common.

Adding to the density of ensembles of end-blown flutes, side-blown flutes, and panpipes, the preferred spectrum of tuning for "unisons" within a consort may be more than a quarter tone, resulting in abundant combination tones. The wide intonational spectrum that typifies most Andean wind ensembles is deliberately produced in the construction of the consort or, if the instruments are tuned in close unison, by some musicians blowing slightly sharp or flat off the median pitch. Bolaños's measurements of pre-Columbian Nasca panpipe tunings suggests that this preference is an old one. Studies of pre-Encounter panpipes also indicate an early predilection for high pitch. Many other examples point to a general native Andean preference for dense, high-pitched sounds. There are, however, a few exceptions, like the large *chiriguano* panpipes of Huancané, Peru, and the extremely dense but low-pitched long trumpets.

Andean ensembles of flutes and panpipes usually include low-pitched, resonant drums, which sonically balance high-pitched winds. In the wind consorts of southern Peru and Bolivia that have different-size instruments played in parallel octaves or polyphony, there is often an attempt to balance in volume the high and low sounds. In Conima, Puno, Peru, *sikus, pitus,* and *tarkas* are played (but never together) in three linear ranges; people state as an ideal that high and low sounds should be balanced in volume around the louder, main, melody-carrying center group. In the nearby *kantus* panpipe tradition of Charazani (Saavedra Province, department of La Paz, Bolivia), ensembles use three levels, tuned in fourths, fifths, and octaves, and players seek a balance in the volume of the more prominent high and low groups.

Repetition and contrast

Native Andean music generally has a great deal of repetition of small motives within and across phrases and sections of a piece, and of the same piece in performance. Forms such as AABB, AABBCC, and ABAB, consisting of short sections or phrases, are common. There is a strong tendency toward the use of subtle levels of contrast, or conversely, what appears to be almost an avoidance of stark contrasts. Hence, two sections or phrases of a piece may differ only by one or two short motives or by a different juxtaposition of previously used motives. In the context of extended repetition of a piece, there is a common tendency to perform subtle rhythmic and melodic variations on the basic melody in solo and ensemble performance throughout the Andes (such as substituting rhythm A for that of rhythm B in figure 5). In most performances, vocal or instrumental, the addition of melodic variations results in a heterophonic texture of shifting intensity. The construction of Quechua musical texts, usually strophic, often exhibits similar characteristics. The repetition of the same line within a strophe, the use of couplets or lines from one strophe to the next that differ only by one word and the ending of all lines of a song with the same word are common poetic devices.

Ensembles in the southern Andean area typically consist of one type of melodic instrument with or without percussive accompaniment. Timbral contrasts are not featured, as they are in many mestizo and urban folk-revivalist ensembles and native Andean ensembles further north. When trumpets are played with *pinkillu* ensembles (in Puno, Peru, and in Bolivia) or panpipe ensembles (in Italaque, Bolivia), the horns add to the sonic density but function more like nonharmonic, percussive drones than like melodic instruments. Similarly, native Andean performers do not typically utilize dynamic contrasts such as those created between strummed and plucked sections in mestizo *charango* performance.

In underlying rhythmic feel, native Andean music often follows a consistent, repetitive groove that facilitates collective dancing, singing, and working. Drums play repetitive patterns shaped in accord with specific melodies, or rolling, often driving ostinatos. The strummed patterns on the *charango* are those of the melody or of an ostinato accompanying a song or a dance. In Ecuadorian harp performance, a second person beats a driving, repetitive pattern on the body of the harp.

Tempo

Although repetition and constancy in most musical parameters within a piece are the rule, changes of tempo sometimes create contrast. In some faster genres of dance, such as *pinkillu* carnival music in the Lake Titicaca area, the last few repetitions of the piece will be played at a faster tempo (such as a quarter-note metronome marking of

a   *b*

FIGURE 5   Two rhythms commonly used in Andean music.

100 versus 88). The concluding section, sometimes known as *fuga,* is meant to animate the dancers.

More generally, native Andean musicians and listeners often seem to be acutely aware of tempo as a parameter. In Conima, Peru, community-ensemble styles were considered quite different, largely because the groups played the same genres at slightly different tempos. In the same region, two important *siku* genres are differentiated and labeled according to tempo ("slow ones" and "fast ones"). A similarly acute attention to issues of tempo occurs in Bolivia.

Sound and cultural associations

Native Andean music has been characterized as predominantly pentatonic (Harcourt and Harcourt 1990 [1925]). Though pentatonic melodies are common in mestizo and indigenous music, other scales occur in native Andean music, and they may vary from one instrumental genre to another within the same community (Olsen 1980:408–410). Scales with an initial minor third above the tonal center are in the majority, and people foreign to Andean villages have romantically interpreted the use of "minor modes" as signs of sorrows, hard lives, or melancholy. These scales, however, do not have the same emotional associations for mestizo or native Andeans as they do in European and Euroamerican musical conventions—native Andean composers might well cast joyful or joking songs in those scales.

Other musical parameters—timbre, tessitura, tempo—seem to correlate more commonly with locally defined associational meanings. The seasonal associations with certain instruments have community-specific meanings involving timbre. For Aymara-speakers in Compi, on the Bolivian side of Lake Titicaca:

> Between the end of the dry and the beginning of the wet seasons, a period during which rain falls irregularly, the tarka, a hoarse-sounding wooden flute, was strictly prohibited, for its sound could harm the freshly sown crops. . . .
>
> In the neighboring Chua, panpipe dances . . . were expected to assure a good harvest and were played between carnival and Rosario (first Sunday in October). An elderly informant assured me that when the brass bands replaced the panpipes, production decreased, only to regain its original level when the pipes were recently reintroduced. (Buechler 1980:41)

In another community south of La Paz, the hoarseness of the *tarka* was thought to attract dry spells, whereas the clarity of the pinkillu was thought to attract rain.

In Conima, Peru, the peasants do not seem to associate instrumental sounds with climatic conditions or agricultural phases per se. They explain their strong associations of duct flutes with the rainy season and panpipes with the dry season simply as a matter of custom. Of many questioned on instrument associations, only one Conimeño associated *siku* specifically with the harvest. The use of five-hole *pinkillus* for All Saints and carnival was simply explained in terms of the instrument's happy, lively sound being appropriate for these festivals (during All Saints to cheer the family of a person recently deceased). Conimeños considered the sound of the smaller, higher five-hole *pinkillus* happier, in contrast to the lower, more serious six-hole *pinkillu*—indicating that there may be emotional associations with different ranges of pitches. In Conima, genres with slower tempos tended to be considered more serious, profound, or emotionally moving, whereas faster tempos were associated with happier, upbeat occasions.

MUSICAL CONTEXTS

In the rural highlands, native Andean musicians perform in three basic types of situations that greatly influence the social and musical dynamics. The first type of context

A group's success in intercommunal competition is influenced by the popularity of its pieces. Ensembles are also judged on their volume, on the tuning and blending of the group, and on the length of time they spend performing in the plaza for public enjoyment.

includes agricultural and religious festivals, life-cycle ceremonies, and work projects within the musicians' indigenous community (*ayllu*). The second type comprises larger fiestas, as in a district capital, where various ensembles, representing different indigenous communities, interact. The third type of context involves performing for mestizos as the target audience. In any of these situations, the musicians may require payment, or they may play for free.

In-community festivals

Smaller in-community festivals, life-cycle celebrations, and work-related musical occasions in the Lake Titicaca region and further south usually involve a single communal ensemble. Any man from the village can voluntarily join with his communal group, whose musicians perform on a collaborative (nonprofessional) basis for the sponsor of the occasion and for the rest of the community. In such events, the musicians (and dancers, if a costumed troupe is required) are treated as honored guests, and from the sponsor and other community members they receive prestige, thanks, and offerings of food, drink, and coca. In this region, collaborative arrangements (or a contract with only minimal payment) might occasionally be made between musicians and someone in another indigenous community on the basis of friendship or ties of coparentage (*compadrazgo*), especially for weddings.

In the Cusco-Apurimac-Ayacucho region of Peru and further north, these types of in-community collaborative arrangements are found for the nonspecialized and specialized instrumental traditions, but musical specialists sometimes require contractual arrangements with cash payment. Solo harp performance at children's wakes, weddings, and private masses in Imbabura Province, Ecuador, seem to involve payment even within the community. Solo performance of three-holed *pincullu* and *tinya* for communal-work projects in Junín, Peru, has become a specialists' tradition, often with only one man in a community knowing the repertoire. Communities without such a specialist sometimes hire a musician from another community, and private landowners may do so for collective labor projects.

Intercommunal festivals

The second type of performance situation, intercommunal festivals, is distinguished from in-community events by size, and especially by the dynamics of musical competition. Because of the importance of music as an emblem and an activity constituting group identity, in intercommunity fiestas, musical and dance ensembles representing their communities, moieties, or barrios typically enter into direct competition with other ensembles for the honor and prestige of their group. Even when ensembles of specialists—such as *dansaq* 'scissor dance' groups in Huancavelica and Ayacucho, Peru—are hired by the sponsor of a fiesta, they still typically compete with the ensembles hired by other sponsors for the prestige of their employer and his social group. In these instances, success in competition is important for the ensembles' professional future.

Large intercommunal festivals usually occur in and around the central plaza of a district or provincial capital town or, on occasion, in a neutral place in the countryside. Each communal ensemble usually keeps to itself, celebrating separately alongside the other communities. The main form of intercommunal interaction is nonformal competition between the ensembles. Success in the competition is partially marked by the number of spectators and unaffiliated dancers a given ensemble attracts during the festival. Each ensemble may assert that they were the best or the most popular at a given festival, but people not directly involved in performing usually reach a loose consensus afterward.

In many areas of the Andes, in mestizo and native Andean contexts, musical competition constantly underlies the drive for musical innovation and quality. Among Aymara-speaking communities in Huancané, Peru, and Quechua musicians in the Charazani valley, Bolivia, composing new pieces for each major fiesta is an important component of the indigenous wind traditions. In Huancané, the quality and uniqueness of new compositions indexes an ensemble's competence and originality, and a group's success in intercommunal competition is influenced by the popularity of its pieces. In this region, *siku, pinkillu,* and *tarka* ensembles are also judged on their volume, on the tuning and blending of the group, and on the length of time they spend performing in the plaza for public enjoyment.

During intra- and intercommunity fiestas, native Andean musicians perform for the members of their own or other indigenous communities. In these situations, their performances are judged and appreciated according to shared aesthetic values and social expectations. Musicians are usually treated with respect, and they gain prestige when they perform well according to communal expectations.

Mestizo-sponsored events

An extremely different type of situation involves events organized by mestizos in which mestizos and criollos are the target audience. In many parts of the Andes, for patronal fiestas and weddings, mestizo sponsors may contract indigenous musicians and dancers to perform. In these instances, the hierarchical nature of relations between native Andeans and mestizos is often clearly articulated. In contrast to the favorable status and artistic freedom indigenous musicians enjoy in their home villages, even when contracted, they are frequently treated like lower-class servants by mestizo sponsors and their guests. The sponsor and his entourage typically dictate what and when the musicians will play and may sharply criticize musicians who perform below expectations.

In rural district and provincial capitals, and in highland cities, mestizo or criollo townspeople or state cultural institutions may organize folkloric festivals and contests involving native Andeans in staged performances for a nonparticipatory audience. This practice results in a variety of alterations in the spirit and manner of performance. In formal contests, usually with mestizo judges, the musicians and dancers may stylize their traditions according to their perception of what the judges and the audience will favor, and this stylization in turn is often based on the model of mestizo music and dance. Whether the performances are voluntary (as in contests) or are contracted, these situations are an important venue where mestizos, criollos, and the state exert influence on indigenous aesthetics and arts.

Native Andean musical occasions

Native Andean musical occasions are extremely varied. Each region has unique traditions regarding the number and kinds of festivals it celebrates within the annual

FIGURE 6   Aymara villagers in Conima, Puno, Peru, perform a *wifala* dance at an in-community ripening festival, 2 February 1985. Photo by Thomas Turino.

cycle. In some areas, the festival for the patron saint of a town or area is the most important celebration of the year. These events typically involve a regional market, a Mass, and a procession for the saint, with music-dance ensembles performing in the streets.

Dance-dramas are typical of patronal and other Roman Catholic festivals. In this type of tradition, a dance group represents a certain historical or mythical character, and the performance often embodies or is part of a larger narrative. Certain characters and motifs are found throughout the Andean region. Threatening outsiders—devils, jungle Indians, Spaniards, lawyers, government officials, and foreign soldiers—are frequently parodied. Blacks, old men, occupational groups, and local spiritual forces (such as mountain divinities) are other common characters represented in masked dance. Dance-dramas and many of these specific motifs are found throughout Latin America. They are partially rooted in Iberian traditions, especially colonial religious plays used for conversion, and dancing at carnival.

In some regions, indigenous communities may hold their own patronal fiestas, or they may participate voluntarily in the fiesta of a district or provincial capital as they would in any intercommunal event. In many places, however, patronal and other religious fiestas (such as Christmas, Holy Week, Easter, Corpus Christi) celebrated in large towns are controlled by mestizos, and native Andeans take part only on a contractual basis, or as passive observers.

It is typical for indigenous communities to celebrate festivals with Roman Catholic or European names but to invest them with local meaning and practices. Carnival (in February or March) and All Saints (*todos los santos*, 2 November), two major indigenous festivals in southern Peru and Bolivia, are prime examples. Carnival and other rainy-season fiestas (including Candelaria, 2 February) are typically redefined as agricultural, ripening, or earth-fertility festivals and occasions for dancing, courting and lovemaking. The *wifala* is a courting dance performed on such occasions (figure 6). Aymara-speaking communities celebrate All Saints in a special manner for three years after a person's death, feeding the spirit with coca and food to aid the journey from the underworld through this world to the upper world. Families in Junín, Peru, celebrate the feast of St. James (Santiago) by conducting animal-fertility rituals, which may involve special rites for the local mountain divinity. Given the harshness of Roman Catholic efforts to superimpose orthodox celebrations on indigenous ones (involving punishments and often the destruction of indigenous religious sites, musical instruments, and costumes), such combinations and juxtapositions of religious meaning and practice are hardly surprising.

In addition to native Andean agricultural and animal fertility rituals (with or without Roman Catholic names), music is often performed as part of communal work projects. Within communities, communally owned land and reciprocal labor exchange are the basis of collaborative agricultural labor. Often musicians lead the workers to and from the fields and perform during breaks. Other communal work projects involving music include the cleaning of irrigation canals and the building and roofing of houses. These types of events, like carnival and All Saints in southern Peru and Bolivia, typically involve noncostumed social dancing.

Life-cycle fiestas are the other major type of musical occasion in the Andes. Weddings typically involve music and social dancing. In the area of Lake Titicaca, Aymara weddings last three days, and to ensure widespread participation are often scheduled just before or after other communal festivals. In Ecuador, children's wakes are a primary event for harp performance. In some regions, families may elect to have music at first-haircutting ceremonies, which welcome babies into the community—a pre-Columbian Andean tradition.

PAN-ANDEAN GENERALIZATIONS

A few features have been suggested as characteristic of native Andean music. They include a predilection for high pitch; dense timbres and ensemble textures; intense repetition of motive, piece, and rhythmic movement; and minimalist contrasts, including constant subtle variations in the melody, resulting in varying degrees of heterophony in ensemble performance. In contrast to the tempered scale, wider tuning variances are favored. As a result, much native Andean music, particularly when played by larger ensembles, has a hard, driving, slightly dissonant quality that contrasts fundamentally with the sweeter, more consonant sound of the urban-revivalist Andean style, well known internationally as played by bands with solo *kena, zampoña, charango,* guitar, and drum. Pentatonic melodies are common but are not the hallmark of native Andean music, as formerly assumed: four-tone melodies are most common for traditional music in Canas, Cusco; three-tone scales are abundant in central Peruvian ritual music; and scales with six and seven tones are the mainstay in panpipe and *pinkillu* music in Huancané, Puno, Peru.

In the Andes generally, with the exception of small hand-held drums, rattles, and bells, instrumental performance is a male domain; women are often the preferred singers, and are active in dancing with men. In many genres, dance and music are conceptualized as an integrated unit, and musical genres are often defined (labeled) by context. In addition to noncostumed social dances, dance-drama traditions involving dramatic characters and narratives are performed at festivals throughout the Andean region. Generalizable musical contexts include Roman Catholic festivals and certain life-cycle ceremonies, especially weddings. Carnival tends to be one of the most important and popular festivals throughout the Andes; in southern Peru and Bolivia, at least, it often meshes with agricultural rituals for the earth. In contrast to the case with many native American groups, music does not seem to be an important adjunct of healing practices in the Andean region.

North-south distinctions

Though we must allow for further variations within, it seems possible to discuss the highland Andean area below 15 degrees latitude south of the equator as musically distinct from the Andean area to the north. The southern area has a greater prevalence of large wind ensembles (ten to fifty performers) accompanied by drums, and music-dance performance is more consistently a nonspecialist, large-group, or com-

marinera Peruvian dance and song genre, given its name in honor of seamen who died in the War of the Pacific (1879–1883)

cueca Chilean folk-urban criollo song and couple-dance genre that is considered a national symbol (also found in Bolivia), with song texts that sometimes reveal nationalistic, historical, or social commentary

yaraví From Quechua *hawari*, in Peru a slow, lyrical, and often emotional song section

dansaq Scissors dance from Ayacucho, Peru

munity affair. In such contexts, dancing tends to be a collective activity, involving circular choreography. Usually melodic instruments are not mixed in ensembles. Indigenous musicians of the southern region do not use stringed instruments with the exception of *charangos* and *guitarrillas*. Like wind instruments, *charangos* and *guitarrillas* are often played in larger ensembles, which do not mix instruments of different types.

People of the southern region make strong wet-dry seasonal associations with specific wind instruments, though the meanings of those associations vary locally. In Cochabamba and Potosí, Bolivia, different types of *charangos* (or the *charango* and the *guitarrilla*) are similarly contrasted. Like musical instruments, generic categories (and stylistic features that differentiate them) are usually identified by specific musical occasions, instruments, or dances, such as *matrimonio*, carnival, *todos los santos*, *pinkillada*, *chiriguano*, and *pulipuli*. Context-free generic categories (such as *wayno*, *marinera*, *cueca*, *yaraví*) are more typical of mestizo musical culture in the region.

In the Titicaca region and south, musical ensembles play for community-member life-cycle celebrations and communitywide festivals on a collaborative basis, though the fiesta sponsor and other community members often give musicians gifts of instruments, food, drink, and coca. Christian festivals are common in this area, but festivals and rituals for the earth, local mountain divinities, and ancestors take on a greater importance than in the northern region. In southern Peru and Bolivia, fiestas with Christian names are typically reinterpreted according to the local indigenous religion and agricultural cycle, whereas a more orthodox Roman Catholicism seems to become more important farther to the north. Musical traditions associated with communal agricultural labor and other work remain important in southern Peru and Bolivia, though they were once important but now are disappearing in the Peruvian department of Junín and to the north. Scholars make little mention of work-related music in Ecuador.

North of Lake Titicaca, the people of indigenous communities like to mix melodic instruments: harp and violin in Ayacucho, Peru; violins and *wakrapuku* in Junín, Peru; panpipes and duct flutes in Imbabura province, Ecuador. They favor strings—especially harp, violin, guitar, mandolin. Their ensembles are smaller. Even their large public events feature duets or solos. These traits imply musical specialization and professionalism: in central-southern Peru, hired harp-violin duos enliven indigenous *dansaq*; in Ancash, Peru, and in northern Ecuador, hired harpists and violinists grace indigenous weddings and children's wakes.

In the southern area, community wind traditions and *charango* traditions are typically learned by watching and imitating during rehearsals and performances. Young boys may receive guidance from their fathers or other men in private, but such instruction tends to be incidental.

The musical traditions of the northern area seem to involve pedagogical processes of greater formality. Evidence of more formal teaching exists in the north. Teacher-student relationships among harpists in Ancash, Peru, and in Imbabura, Ecuador, have been mentioned (Otter 1985:196–197; Schechter 1992:93), and Raúl Romero (1990:14) mentions teacher-disciple relationships for the solo *pincullo-tinya* agricultural musical tradition in Junín, Peru. Private practice on these instruments is also implied, whereas I found private practice to be quite rare for the wind traditions of the Titicaca area.

Aymara-Quechua distinctions

The only general Aymara-Quechua musical distinction I am aware of involves the centrality of songs among Quechua-speakers and the relative lack of importance of vocal music in Aymara-speaking communities. In pre-Columbian days, the southern Andean area was known as Collasuyo. Before the Inca period, independent Aymara-speaking states existed in what are now the Peruvian departments of Arequipa, Puno, and southern Cusco, and the Bolivian department of La Paz. Harry Tschopik (1946:503–504) noted that

> there is little doubt that in pre-Inca times, and probably until well into the Colonial Period, Aymara was more widely spoken than at present, but it is difficult to be certain of its former boundaries from the vague and scattered references to be gleaned from early Colonial documents.

The musical traits described here as belonging to the southern area are possibly the heritage of Aymara-speaking peoples, and the relative musical homogeneity of the southern area may be due to strong Aymara influence. Garcilaso's identification of double-unit panpipe performance with the Collas during the early colonial period is a hint in this direction. Yet this conclusion is speculative and requires further research. Until more locally specific information comes to light, it seems safe to say that most musical practices do not line up neatly with Andean linguistic groupings in the contemporary period, and therefore linguistic categories do not serve well as cultural categories. Indigenous peasants typically use community and region as the basis of social identity, and region provides a better basis for understanding Andean musical practices and styles than language does.

REFERENCES

Aretz, Isabel. 1980. "Ecuador II: Folk Music." *The New Grove Dictionary of Music and Musicians*, ed. Stanley Sadie. London: Macmillan.

Baumann, Max Peter. 1981. "Music, Dance and Song of the Chipayas (Bolivia)." *Latin American Music Review* 2(2):171–222.

———. 1982. *Musik im Andenhochland*. Museum Collection 14. Berlin: Museum für Volkerkunde. LP disk.

Bertonio, Ludovico. 1956. *Vocabulario de la lengua aymara*. La Paz: Editorial del Ministerio de Asuntos Campesinos.

Bolaños, César. 1985. "La música en el antiguo Perú." In *La Música en el Perú*, 1–64. Lima: Patronato Popular y Porvenir Pro Música Clásica.

———. 1988. *Las Antaras Nasca: Historia y Análisis*. Lima: Programa de Arqueomusicología del Instituto Andino de Estudios Arqueológicos (INDEA).

Buechler, Hans C. 1980. *The Masked Media: Aymara Fiestas and Social Interaction in the Bolivian Highlands*. The Hague: Mouton.

Coba Andrade, Carlos Alberto. 1985. "Danzas y bailes en el Ecuador." *Latin American Music Review* 6(2):166–200.

Garcilaso de la Vega, El Inca. 1966 [1609]. *The Incas: The Royal Commentaries of the Inca*. 2nd ed. Edited by Alain Gheerbrant. Translated by Maria Jolas. New York: Avon Books, Orion Press.

Guamán Poma de Ayala, Felipe. 1980. *El primer nueva crónica y buen gobierno*. México: Siglo Veíntiuno.

Haeberli, Joerg. 1979. "Twelve Nasca Panpipes: A Study." *Ethnomusicology* 23(1):57–73.

d'Harcourt, Raoul, and Marguerite d'Harcourt. 1990 [1925]. *La musique des Incas et ses survivances*. Paris: Librairie Orientaliste Paul Geuthner. Reprinted in Spanish, 1990, as *La música de los Incas y sus supervivencias.* Translated by Roberto Miro Quesada. Lima: Occidental Petroleum Corporation of Peru, Luis Alberto Sánchez, and Ismael Pinto.

Montoya, Rodrigo. 1986. "Identidad étnica y luchas agrarias en los andes peruanos." In *Identidades andinas y lógicas del campesinado,* 247–275. Lima: Mosca Azul.

Montoya, Rodrigo, Edwin Montoya, and Luís Montoya. 1987. *La Sangre de los Cerros: Antología de la poesía quechua que se canta en el Perú.* Lima: CEPES, Mosca Azul Editores y UNMSM.

Moreno, Segundo Luis. 1949. *Música y danzas autóctonas del Ecuador.* Quito: Editorial Fray Jacobo Ricke.

Olsen, Dale A. 1980. "Folk Music of South America—A Musical Mosaic." In *Musics of Many Cultures: An Introduction,* ed. Elizabeth May, 386–425. Berkeley: University of California Press.

———. 1992. "Implications of Music Technologies in the Pre-Columbian Andes." In *Musical Repercussions of 1492: Encounters in Text and Performance,* ed. Carol E. Robertson, 65–88. Washington, D.C.: Smithsonian Institution Press.

Otter, Elisabeth den. 1985. *Music and Dance of Indians and Mestizos in an Andean Valley of Peru.* Delft: Eburon.

Paniagua, Felix. 1982. "El kh'ajhelo." *Tarea* 6:65–69.

Romero, Raúl. 1990. "Musical Change and Cultural Resistance in the Central Andes of Peru." *Latin American Music Review* 11(1):1–35.

———, and Gisela Cánepa K. 1988. *Música Tradicional de Cajamarca.* Lima:Pontífica Universidad Católica del Perú, Instituto Riva-Agüero. LP disk.

Rossel, Alberto. 1977. *Arqueología sur del Perú.* Lima: Editorial Universo.

Sánchez, Walter. 1988. *Música Autóctona del Norte de Potosí.* Bulletin 6. Cochabamba: Centro de Documentación de Música Boliviana, Centro Pedagógico y Cultural de Portales.

———. 1989. *Circuitos Musicales: Recreación de la Música.* Bulletin 11. Cochabamba: Centro de Documentación de Música Boliviana, Centro Pedagógico y Cultural de Portales.

Schechter, John. 1992. *The Indispensable Harp: Historical Development, Modern Roles, Configurations, and Performance Practices in Ecuador and Latin America.* Kent, Ohio: Kent State University Press.

Stevenson, Robert M. 1968. *Music in Aztec and Inca Territory.* Berkeley: University of California Press.

Tschopik, Harry, Jr. 1946. "The Aymara." In *Handbook of South American Indians,* vol.2, *The Andean Civilizations,* ed. Julian H. Steward, 501–574. Washington, D.C.: U.S. Government Printing Office.

Turino, Thomas. 1983. "The Charango and the *Sirena:* Music, Magic, and the Power of Love." *Latin American Music Review* 4(1):81–119.

———. 1987. "Power Relations, Identity, and Musical Choice: Music in a Peruvian Altiplano Village and among its Migrants in the Metropolis." Ph.D. dissertation, University of Texas at Austin.

———. 1989. "The Coherence of Social Style and Musical Creation among the Aymara in Southern Peru." *Ethnomusicology* 33(1):1–30.

———. 1993. *Moving Away from Silence: Music of the Peruvian Altiplano and the Experience of Urban Migration.* Chicago: University of Chicago Press.

Valencia, Américo. 1982. "El siku bipolar en el antiguo Perú." *Boletín de Lima* 4(23):29–48.

Q'ero
John Cohen

Musical Instruments
Musical Genres and Contexts
Social Structure, Ideology, Aesthetics
Musical Acculturation
Further Study

The Q'ero are a Quechua-speaking people living high in the Andes east of Cusco, Peru. Their cultural traits include distinctive survivals. Though it is tempting to see the Q'ero as an Inka (Inca) survival, their unique musical practices probably reflect an even earlier Andean diversity with an Inka overlay.

Q'ero ceremonial music is heard throughout seasonal cycles, and the Q'ero exploit every local ecological zone from the mountaintops to the jungle. Centered on flocks of llamas and alpacas, music is an integral part of Q'ero rituals. The Q'ero share many social, economic, and cultural ties with their Andean neighbors, but they have been sufficiently isolated to have preserved their own cultural and musical traits in coexistence with contemporary elements.

Living at an elevation of 4.25 kilometers, the Q'ero are essentially herders, but they raise potatoes in the lower altitudes and grow corn, melons, and peppers in the jungle farther below. Each family has temporary wood shelters in the jungle, large stone houses in the ceremonial center at an elevation of 3.65 kilometers, and small stone houses located in isolated clusters in the high valleys. The total population is about four hundred people distributed in five hamlets (*ayllu,* a Quechua word for community, family, or other social grouping).

The Q'ero share certain musical traditions with the entire region of Cusco, but they have distinctly emblematic songs and music, heard only in their highland homeland. Their major festivals coincide with Spanish calendrical festivals, but with no European or colonial elements. Each of their festivals has songs and instruments specifically associated with it. For this reason, their music cannot be characterized by a single style, musical scale, or musical function. This diversity within the music of a single community is inherent in Andean cultural life.

MUSICAL INSTRUMENTS

Q'ero music is not influenced by European elements: it uses neither instruments introduced by the Spanish, nor any of the stringed instruments (like the *charango* and the *bandurria*) or the brass instruments that evolved in the Andes in the colonial era (see Cohen 1984). Though the Q'ero have had transistor radios since 1980 and can hear Andean radio programs of *huayno* (*wayno*) music broadcast from Cusco, they

> The *pinculu,* an end-blown notched flute capable of four notes, produces the music most uniquely associated with the Q'ero. This instrument is played at two fertility rituals: those for llamas and those for alpacas.

still use only musical instruments extant at the time of the Inkas: end-blown and side-blown flutes, panpipes, conch trumpets, and drums. Much Q'ero musical material culture consists of distinct musical instruments found only in Q'ero territory.

Panpipes

Canchis sipas are single-unit raft panpipes, two bound rows of seven reed tubes each [see QUECHUA-AYMARA]. One row is never played. The name means "seven young (unmarried) girls." These instruments and their related songs have their own scale. On the Nativity of Saint John the Baptist (24 June), Q'ero women address the songs associated with the *canchis sipas* to female alpacas, llamas, and sheep. One song says:

> Because you eat, we eat.
> Because you drink, we drink.
> Because you are, we are.

Another says:

> Mother, my mother [the female animal],
> Open me up [to luck], and speak inside of me.

In the department of Cusco, panpipes are rare, but they are common in the altiplano around Lake Titicaca. The presence of these panpipes (and the Q'ero use of four-stake looms) therefore suggests an earlier cultural connection to the Titicaca basin (Cohen 1980).

Flutes

The *pinculu,* an end-blown notched flute capable of four notes, produces the music most uniquely associated with the Q'ero. This instrument is played at two fertility rituals: those for llamas (Quechua *Ahata Uhuchichis,* Spanish *Santiago* 'Saint James') and those for alpacas (Quechua *Palchasqa* or *Palcha,* Spanish *Carnaval* 'carnival'). These flutes accompany the special four-note songs—including *"Bandarra," "Kius," "Palcha," "Serena," "Turpa,"* and *"Wallata"*— sung only for these festivals.

Wallata are the wild geese that fly in pairs over the mountains in Q'ero territory. The text includes these words:

> *Wallata,* black and white, with eyes of pearls;
> *Wallata,* black and white, with scalloped wings:
> The running waters which you drink in the highlands.

Turpa is an herb that grows on the mountain; the translation of the Q'ero words to this melody is: "Panti Turpa, why have you come to these desolate ravines?" *Palcha* is a gentian that grows at an elevation of 4.5 kilometers and blooms in February and March. *Serena* are waterfalls.

Always in connection with animals, shepherds play the *pinculu* in pastures while herding. Usually, several such flutes can be heard playing independently of each other across the high pastures (*puna*). The music directs and comforts the animals by locating their shepherd in space.

Pinculu are made from hollow reeds (*Arondo donax,* obtained in the jungle), ranging from 15 to 71 centimeters long. Four rectangular holes for fingering are evenly spaced toward the distal end of each tube to be made into a flute. Four-hole flutes of this description have not been found in other parts of the Andes; they are seen neither in Harcourt and Harcourt's collections (1990 [1925]) nor— except for some from Paracas culture—in ancient graves.

A person plays the *pinculu* by uncovering the four holes in sets of two fingers rather than one finger for each tone (see Okada 1995: example 12). Sometimes only the outline of the melody is heard with segments conceived under the breath without being audibly played (the musician plays mentally, silently). In addition, coloration is sometimes given to the music when the flutist overblows on the notch, producing short and high overtones or octaves. A technique frequently used in transitions from one note to another is to rapidly touch down two fingers, covering and uncovering two holes, producing a sound akin to a trill. In the lower register, intermediate notes are accessible by breathing with reduced force; these notes occur in passing, not as melodic terminal points. A particular Q'ero melody may have more notes in the sung version than when played on the flute. The flute gives the impression of an outline of the gist of a melody. Finally, *pinculu* are not tuned to each other and are not played together in unison. Three men playing in the same room will play the same tune together, though not at the same pitches, and not with shared points of starting or stopping (Cohen 1984).

Other musical instruments

The Q'ero use musical instruments found in other Andean communities. Of these instruments, the *pututu* is a conch trumpet, played by communal authorities as a sign of their position. The conch produces a blast of sound to announce the beginning of an event or a ceremony. *Pututu* are old: because the shells come originally from the sea, hundreds of kilometers away, they must be traded for and carried to the mountaintops.

Another outside musical instrument employed by the Q'ero is the *caña* (Spanish) 'cane, reed', an end-blown six-note ductless flute, made of reed or plastic pipe. Played by shepherds, *cañas* are used for melodies heard throughout the mountains.

A side-blown six-note flute, *pitu,* is used only for melodies of the *chunchu* (jungle Indian culture)—music played with drums during the fiesta of Corpus Christi and at the pilgrimage to Collariti. The *chunchu* melody is far richer than that performed on the *pinculu,* and it always ends with a sequence of notes unrelated to the tonal center of the melody. No texted songs are associated with this music. Dancers representing the *chunchu* dress in brightly colored feather headdresses, carrying long pieces of jungle wood (from a bow), festooned with short feathers. The *chunchu* as a visual motif is also seen in Q'ero weaving (Cohen 1957).

MUSICAL GENRES AND CONTEXTS

The Q'ero celebrate their annual festivals in their hamlets or at a lower elevation at the ceremonial center, where the entire community gathers several times a year for major feasts. In addition, they make a pilgrimage to Collariti during Corpus Christi and once a year join the neighboring communities in the *tinquy,* a dance on the passes at the geographic border between them. In sequence, the major festivals are Chayampuy, Palchasqa, Carnaval (and Tinquy), Paskwa, Corpus, San Juan, and Ahata Uhuchichis (Santiago).

The most unusual and emblematic Q'ero festivals, Palchasqa and Ahata Uhuchichis, occur roughly six months apart. Both focus on alpacas and llamas. The vocal and flute melodies associated with these festivals are sung and played throughout the year. During the festivals, however, they are performed with greater intensity.

At Palchasqa (February or March, based on the Christian calendar), individual Q'ero families hold rituals in their houses. The woman of the house sings, and the man plays a *pinculu*. They pour corn beer (*chicha*) onto grass from the pasture, and onto little statues of the animals. Then several families join together outside and throw flowers (*palcha*) at the alpacas while singing and playing *pinculu*. Five or more women sing at the same time, interspersing ritual phrases with complaints about their daily lives. Each tells her own story in song. At times, the musical texture consists of different people singing personalized songs simultaneously. Only occasionally do they meet on ritual phrases or on final notes.

The following translation from one woman's singing of a floral song is adapted from Cohen n.d.; the performance can be seen in Cohen 1984.

> Scatter the flower, Huaman [a mountain spirit].
> What suffering you leave me, my brother [refers to alpaca],
> Huaman, my brother sun [a mountain spirit].
> Don't leave me, mother [refers to the lineage of alpacas].
> The red flower that I gather,
> The earth hill that I climb [site of the ritual],
> You will make blossom.
> Come here, my mother [lineage of alpacas],
> Where I sleep with my lover.
> Leave those ancient things [old, male, infertile alpacas]:
> Black alpaca with red feet,
> You eat by the side of another,
> Or with the alpacas of Santo Domingo [a nearby mountain spirit].
> You drank to the earth.
> You gave me flowers, Huaman.
> Suffering takes away the happiness of my valley.
> Alpaca who leads the way,
> Flower that I have to give,
> Wouldn't you nurture me?
> Together you are sleeping.
> Don't look at me, mother [for you are sacred].
> Scatter the *panti* [flower], Huaman.

The ritual is repeated late in the day, with the animals in their corrals.

The following day, many elements come together. For carnival, the entire community descends from the isolated mountain hamlets, gathering at the central village, Hautun Q'ero, which serves as the ceremonial center. Each Q'ero family has a large house here, used only for community rituals. The male authorities are greeted with exchanges of conch trumpets, while other men play flutes and do a stomping dance (*kius*). The *ayllu* groups sing and play all night in the large houses. Twenty people may be packed together inside, drinking, singing heterophonically, with conch trumpets blasting. Sometimes, late in the night, the individual qualities become less apparent as people find accord between them, reaching a degree of musical consensus. At this point, the sustained final note of a phrase provides a drone beneath the individual voices. Occasional multipart texture occurs, and the whole event takes on a choral sound.

On the day of carnival, everyone gathers at the plaza (outside the church) overlooking the jungle. While the men dance, sing, and play *pinculu,* the women sing separately or in unison as *ayllu* groups. In this way, five sets of women representing the different *ayllus* sing the same song in overlapping disregard for each other. The women are arranged in a single line that arcs around the men, who dance, sing, and heterophonically play *pincullu.* There is a rich and pulsating texture to the event, perhaps more obvious to the outside listener than to the participants. This kind of heterophony does not occur elsewhere in the Andes, but it resembles celebrations in the Amazon basin. The structure of this Q'ero music may therefore suggest a cultural connection between the Andes and the Amazon.

The prevalent song at carnival is chosen or composed by the president of the Q'ero community (elected during Chayampuy, several weeks earlier) when he goes to Paucartambo, where the government registers his authority. During his trip, he reads the landscape for signs and composes a new song to be sung at carnival and throughout the year (Webster 1972).

Similar celebrations with music are held at the hamlets in the high valleys. From late July through August, individual families thank the gods for the strength and fertility of their llamas. In the corrals, they mark the male animals by putting tassels in their ears, and force them to drink corn beer. This festival is known as Ahata Uhuchichis (Let's Drink Corn Beer). Each family's ritual differs slightly from that of its neighbors. Though families celebrate on separate days, they all employ similar ritual items. A special cloth, the *uncunu,* is set on the ground as an altar (Spanish *mesa* 'table') on which ritual objects are placed. These are special ritual versions of items used in daily life: ropes, bells, and offerings of corn beer and coca leaves.

The ritual moves from the corral into the house. As it progresses through the night, the men increasingly mimic the animals, shaking llama bells and ropes, hitting each other with whips as if they themselves were llamas, and whistling as they do when they drive the animals along. Some men sing in a low, forced growl, in imitation of the llamas' humming. Often the women sing intensely, and some men play *pinculu.*

The music goes on continuously, but individuals start and stop as they please, sometimes not completing a phrase. After the ritual items are put away, the celebration becomes an expression of human fertility as couples go off to bed. This musical style allows for a maximum expression of the individual while retaining a distinctive communal identity.

Dances organized around specific symbols are associated with the ritual festivals. *Kius,* for example, is a legendary bird of the gods. It is danced during carnival with unmetered stamping and slight leaps. At the festival in Collariti, *ukuku* represents a bear with a shaggy costume, and *chunchu* represents the jungle Indian.

SOCIAL STRUCTURE, IDEOLOGY, AESTHETICS

Because Q'ero music functions as an integral part of ritual, considering music a separate entity may be a mistaken notion. The Q'ero explain music this way: "It's always like this, we sing this song of the Inkas. We compose the song from all things. Every song comes on its appropriate date. If there is no song, there is no fiesta; and without the fiesta, there is no song."

Q'ero songs reflect a complex cosmology that moves freely between mountain spirits (*auki* and *apu*) and personal events from daily life. The texts speak of parallels

At rituals for the fertility of the animals, gender differences in styles of singing are defined in terms of the animals: men imitate the sound of male alpacas; women imitate the sound of female alpacas.

between the lineage of animals and humans; they include metaphorical references to flowers as symbols of love and representatives of the gods. Wild birds and animals are seen as representatives of mountain spirits, whereas domesticated animals (llamas and alpacas) are associated with human counterparts. Songs that celebrate the fertility of the animals are mixtures of courtship, floral symbols, and giving thanks to the gods. The songs may contain calendrical and landscape references.

Though men and women know and sing the songs, women are the primary singers; only men play the accompanying *pinculu* or *canchis sipas.* (Consistent with indigenous Andean tradition, Q'ero women do not play instruments.) At rituals for the fertility of the animals, gender differences in styles of singing are defined in terms of the animals: men imitate the sound of male alpacas; women imitate the sound of female alpacas.

Often the flute serves as a prod to initiate women's participation, and the flutist will delineate a melody in anticipation of the singing. The woman's singing is more involving and intense than the flute. At communal gatherings, the maximal female vocal qualities find fullest expression. Their singing becomes emotional and intense rather than formal or dutiful. Men's singing can become an expression of a constrained explosion, a forceful assertion of local conceptions of maleness, complete with growls and explosive yelps.

The general Q'ero musical aesthetic allows different pitches, texts, and rhythms to sound at the same time. Though the Q'ero sometimes sing in perfect unison, their songs are structured to be sung individually. There is no sense of choral singing or harmony. A family, *ayllu,* or community may be singing and playing the same song at the same time, but each singer sets her or his own pace, pattern of breathing, and point of starting and stopping. Yet the melodies sung at communal occasions have a sustained note at the end of a phrase, permitting the other singers to catch up and share this prolonged duration, which serves as a drone. When the new verse starts, the heterophony begins anew.

MUSICAL ACCULTURATION

Although Q'ero practices may appear archaic and isolated, some Q'ero nonetheless deal with bank loans and interest rates to function economically. The value of their alpaca wool is affected by international market prices. When the Q'ero meet the world outside their boundaries, they disguise themselves. At Tinquy, they abandon their distinctive music, and conform to the music and costumes of their neighbors, dancing to popular *huaynos* and *carnavales* played on portable phonographs. This social dance, performed by couples in lines and often holding hands, in form resembles descriptions of an Inka dance known as *cashua taki.* About this dance, the Q'ero call themselves *Inka* and their neighbors *Qeshwa* 'People of the Valley'. When the Q'ero visit the commercial center at Ocongate, 30 kilometers away, they hide their traditional ponchos under neutral coverings. In the processes of presenting another face to the outside world, they protect their identities.

FURTHER STUDY

The material presented here is based on my visits to the Q'ero over a thirty-five-year period, when I attended most of their major festivals. My recordings of Q'ero music (1964, 1991) have provided ethnomusicologists with ways to construct a model for Inka-Andean tradition and to augment or refute Harcourt and Harcourt's pentatonic theories. Alan Lomax (1968) used a Q'ero example from this recording to characterize the Andes in his global musical map for cantometrics; Rodolpho Holzmann (1980, 1986) used this music to establish a tritonic basis for Inka music; Dale A. Olsen (1980) transcribed an excerpt to explain the use of tetratonic scales and to demonstrate the use of microtones; and Bruce Mannheim (1984) used a Q'ero example from the same source in his studies of subliminal verbal patterning in southern Quechua folk song. In Peru, Oscar Núñez del Prado has made recordings of Q'ero music (unissued). A published Peruvian mention of Q'ero music (Ochoa and Fries n.d.) derives from his writing or the sources above.

REFERENCES

Cohen, John. 1957. "An Investigation of Contemporary Weaving of the Peruvian Indians." M.F.A. thesis, Yale University.

————. 1979. *Q'eros, the Shape of Survival.* New York: Cinema Guild. Film, video.

————. 1980. *Peruvian Weaving, A Continuous Warp.* 1980. New York: Cinema Guild. Film, video

————. 1984. *Mountain Music of Peru.* New York: Cinema Guild. Film, video.

————. 1988. *Your Struggle Is Your Glory.* Music from films by John Cohen. Arhoolie Records.

————. 1990. *Carnival in Qeros.* Berkeley: University of California Extension Media Center. Film, video.

————. 1991 [1964]. *Mountain Music of Peru.* Smithsonian / Folkways CD SF 40020. 2 compact discs, reissued with additional material.

————. In press. "The Singular Music of Qeros." In *Making Culture and History in the Andes,* ed. Billie Jean Isbel. Ithaca, N.Y.: Cornell University Press.

d'Harcourt, Raoul, and Marguerite d'Harcourt. 1990 [1925]. *La musique des Incas et ses survivances.* Paris: Librairie Orientaliste Paul Geuthner.

Holzmann, Rodolfo. 1980. "Cuatro Ejemplos de Música Q'ero (Cuzco, Perú)." *Latin American Music Review* 1(1):74–91.

————. 1986. *Q'ero, pueblo y música.* Lima: Patronata Popular y Porvenir, Pro Música Clásica.

Lomax, Alan. 1968. *Folk Song Style and Culture.* Washington, D.C.: American Association for the Advancement of Science. Publication 88.

Mannheim, Bruce. 1984. "Subliminal Verbal Patterning in a Southern Quechua Folksong." In *Symposium of Latin American Indian Literatures.*

Okada, Yuki. 1995. *Central and South America.* The JVC / Smithsonian Folkways Video Anthology of Music and Dance of the Americas, 6. Montpelier, Vt.: Multicultural Media. VTMV-230. Video.

Olsen, Dale A. 1980. "Symbol and Function in South American Indian Music." In *Musics of Many Cultures: An Introduction,* ed. Elizabeth May, 363–385. Berkeley, Los Angeles: University of California Press.

Ochoa, Jorge Flores, and Ana María Fries. n.d. *Puna, Qeshwa, Yunga—El Hombre y su Medio en Q'ero.* Lima: Banco Central de Reserva.

Webster, Steven. 1972. "The Social Organization of a Native Andean Community." Ph.D. dissertation, University of Washington.

Mapuche
Carol E. Robertson

Musical Instruments
Musical Contexts and Genres
Acculturation
Further Study

The Mapuche (People of the Land) inhabit the lands between the Bío-Bío River and Chiloé Island in Chile and western Argentina. Anthropologists and government officials often use the name *Araucano* to designate these people, who share a common language (Araucanian, according to Joseph Greenberg 1989:383), though many continue to identify themselves as Pehuenche, Puelche, Tehuelche, Ranquel, Huarpe, and Pampa-Boroga. The politics of naming and specifying cultural identities in this area of Chile and Argentina is a puzzle that can be solved only through a discussion of archaeological records, musical forms, and ritual practices. The history of the southern Andes unites traditions of warriors, prophets, shamans, and nomadic pastoralists under a linguistic umbrella, *mapudungun* 'words of the land'.

Archaeological records and oral histories trace several migrations across the Andes Mountains. For millennia, peoples of the eastern pampas traded with their western neighbors and utilized the natural resources of the Atlantic and Pacific oceans. Ancient Moluche warriors and hunters from the pampas conquered the agriculturalists between the Bío-Bío and Toltén rivers more than a thousand years ago (Berdichewsky 1971). Between the 1400s and 1700s, the Chilean Mapuche reversed the direction of this influence by extending their military and trade empire all the way to what is now Buenos Aires (San Martín ca. 1919; Schoo Lastra 1928).

Clay vessels and stone panpipes suggest that trade routes extended from Patagonia to the southern borders of the Nasca, the Wari, and (much later) the Inca empires of Peru. In the late 1400s, the Inca incorporated the Kolla Suyu (Southern Kingdom) into their extensive domain and established military outposts south of the Maule River to protect their claims (Aldunate del Solar 1992). Thus, by the time of the Spanish invasions in the 1500s, the people we know as Mapuche had become a heterogeneous mixture of autonomous communities, formed into military confederations to resist incursions from Inca and Spanish forces.

Several centuries of contact between peoples on both sides of the Andes produced an intricate cosmology and a body of ceremonial lore loosely shared by peoples with differing systems of social organization (Faron 1956, 1961, 1964; Robertson 1979; Robertson-DeCarbo 1976).

Until about 1900, Mapuche military success was reinforced by a system of elaborate rituals, in which animal sacrifice and agricultural offerings to ancestors played a central part. For horses, women wove intricate wool blankets and belts, covered with protective signs and invocations of each warrior's personal power. To deepen the spiritual and physical fortitude of absent husbands and sons, wives and mothers performed lineage songs daily. To ensure the prosperity of those in battle and those at home, shamanic practitioners were consulted throughout the year.

Present-day Mapuche oral historians assert that formerly there were no permanent chiefs among Mapuche peoples; rather, in wartime, prominent citizens (often male diviners or heads of lineages) would be installed as military chiefs, expected to step back into the ranks once peace had been secured. Prominent women were consulted on matters of military strategy. Authority was negotiated through a system of lineage exchanges. The social and ritual power of each lineage was embodied in characteristic songs and dances.

The persistence of warfare over five centuries radically changed Mapuche social organization. Once the Argentine and Chilean armies usurped control of Mapuche lands, they established land-distribution patterns (Chile) and a system of reservations (Argentina) that altered access to the people's water, trade routes, animal herding, and authority structures. With men at war for long periods, social authority, ritual life, food gathering, and animal herding had fallen increasingly into the hands of women.

The Argentine and Chilean national governments were slow to recognize the rights of Mapuche women and restricted their claims to land and herds. The power arrangements that had prevailed in peacetime were replaced with permanent, hereditary chieftainships. Despite the conqueror's misogyny, several Mapuche women inherited the title of community chief (*lonko*) in Chile and Argentina. Each chief now answered to the white (*huinca*) military or provincial authorities of each territory (Martínez Sarasola 1992).

The ritual power of the shaman (*machi*) was undermined by missionization, public education, and governments, which feared shamans' power to energize the will of a subjugated people. Decreased access to fertile land and to the new economic system diminished a community's ability to provide feasts, horses, silver ornaments, and personnel requisite for important rituals, including seasonal rites of increase and female rites of passage (*katán kawil*).

MUSICAL INSTRUMENTS

The Mapuche have always challenged scholarly reduction, for while engaging in many musical practices common to other South American peoples, they have fashioned their dialogue with the sacred through unique uses of vocal and instrumental techniques.

The archaeological record offers extensive examples of *pitucahue,* stone panpipes of up to eight tubes, linking the Mapuche to panpipe traditions reaching as far north as Panama (Pérez de Arce 1986, 1987). Some Chilean *pitucahue* were carved as early as the tenth century. Stone, an unyielding medium, was eventually replaced by wood and cane.

Though stone panpipes were used to make melodies, their cane and wood counterparts (*pifülka*) were used as markers of rhythm. Most *pifülka* are double-tubed flutes open only on one end, yielding a fundamental and an overblown fourth, fifth, or octave. Wooden varieties became scarce in the 1900s and have been replaced by ensembles of single canes of varying lengths. Rather than playing cane flutes in melodic groups (as in the northern Andean traditions), Mapuche musicians play each tube separately: to create rhythmic patterns, each player coordinates the pitch of his tube with his fellows' pitches. When large numbers of *pifülka* players gather to dance around the altar (*rewe*) during the annual rites of increase (*ŋillipún*, also *nguillatún* and *kamarrikún*), the exact pitch of each cane is not important; instead of focusing on melody, the ensemble creates rhythmic patterns for movement.

Many other kinds of flutes have been found in archaeological sites, as have straight trumpets with oblique or transverse mouthpieces. Among the latter, the *trutruka* (with oblique mouthpiece) continues to be an important sonic element in the annual rites of increase [see ARGENTINA: figure 2]. This kind of trumpet, found in the Andes all the way to the Bolivian border, usually consists of a thick cane two to five meters long, wrapped in horse intestine (earlier, guanaco intestine), capped with a cow horn. Many *trutruka* players, having learned to play the trumpet in the army, often insert European military signals into the patterns traditionally associated with the annual rites of increase (Robertson 1975). Because the *trutruka* can be heard at a distance, it is still used for signaling in remote areas of the Andes.

Another instrument that has pre-Columbian antecedents is the *kultrún,* a single-headed drum central to Mapuche healing and ceremony. It consists of a wooden bowl (*mamül ralí*), covered with hide of guanaco, dog, or (in recent times) cow or horse, fastened with human hair or sinew. Drums are painted with symbols that denote the four directions, the four lines of ancestors, the sun, the moon, spirals, planets, and other forces of nature (Aldunate del Solar 1992; Grebe 1979–1980). They often appear in ancient rock drawings in scenes depicting important social changes, hunts, or spiritual revelations.

Many other instruments within the archaeological record have fallen out of use: shell rattles (*chunan*), calabash rattles (*huada*), shell rasps (*cadacada*), musical bows (*quinquerche* or *quinquercahue*), diverse flutes made of bone and cane, and a sucked trumpet (*lolkiñ* or *nolkín*). Of all the instruments mentioned, the *kultrún* is by far the most important, for it offers a point of entry into Mapuche cosmology.

MUSICAL CONTEXTS AND GENRES

In Mapuche ideology, each individual has two souls. The first, *alwé* or *almén,* is distinctly personal: it is born with each individual and yet survives the physical limitations of that individual. It is the source of each individual's creative energy. When a person dies, this soul wanders across the earth until it reaches the end of the western horizon, through which it enters the realm of gods and ancestors.

The second soul, *kimpeñ,* is an inherited soul embodying the life force of a lineage. It originates in the sacred ancestral past, but it is transmitted across the boundaries of time to the contemporary descendants of a lineage. This soul is individualized only in that it enters a person at birth. Its nature is cumulative, compounded through time, and contributed to by all deceased and living members of each lineage. Lines of kinship are traced through an individual's four grandparents. Though this soul can be traced to an individual's father's father, each person may invoke up to four sets of ancestors, according to circumstance and need.

The power of each *kimpeñ* is coded in its song, known as *tayil.* Each *tayil* is a signature—a shorthand statement of the natural powers and physical properties associated with a particular lineage, its guiding spirits, its animal totems, its spiritual history. As Andrés Epullán, a Mapuche elder of Andean Argentina, put it in 1978, "*Tayil* is a way of feeling. When the women pull out *tayil,* they do it with great emotion. In that moment, they are feeling everything that has ever flowed through the veins of those who hold that chant. They feel it through their wombs."

This genre can be performed only by women, for it is a form of giving birth to spirit. The verb used for vocalizing a *tayil* is the same verb used for the process of going through labor and giving birth. Many variations of *tayil* melodies exist, but

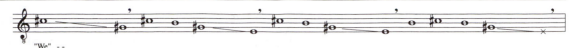

women say they know they are "tracking" the song correctly when they feel a certain tension in their wombs.

Specific melodic contours and coded syllables are combined to signal the character of a lineage (figure 1). For example, the word for sheep is *ufisha,* but the specific sung syllable identifying the sheep lineage is *we.* Likewise, the water lineage (*kó*) is coded into song as *yo-le-le.* When combined with the right song path or melodic contour, these syllables become the signature that identifies a specific family in the presence of ancestors and supernaturals.

The goal of performing *tayil* is to bridge the present and the past. Each performance consists of four phrases, and each phrase articulates the lineage soul in a different sphere of time and space. When a woman performs her husband's *tayil* (figure 2), phrase one departs the body of the singer and enters the body of the person whose lineage soul is being sung. Phrase two pulls this soul out of the husband's body and into the ritual space of the performance. Phrase three sends the performance into the realm of supernaturals. Phrase four brings it back into the body of the individual whose *à tayilfàf* is being performed (Robertson 1979).

Tayil are critical to the Mapuche process of ritual and healing. In Mapuche belief, most disease is caused by the wandering of the personal soul (*alwé*). This detachable aspect of self can become entangled in the spirit world or can be captured by another human being. An individual whose soul has been tampered with may suffer illnesses, exhibiting physical and spiritual symptoms. Treatment may be approached through several methods. In Chile, the most common is the *machitún,* wherein the *machi* uses her voice and her *kultrún* to journey for her patient and take the diseased soul through a cathartic process that will bring a release into wellness (Grebe 1979–1980; Grebe, Pacheco, and Segura 1972).

Persecution, intimidation, and missionization have made Argentine Mapuche wary of acknowledging the presence of shamanic practitioners in their midst (Robertson 1991). As in Chile, healers on the eastern slopes of the Andes are usually women. Men in this profession have always dressed and behaved socially as women, developing an artificial womb through which to channel healing.

In Argentina, ceremonial leaders are known as *witakultruntufe* 'women carrying the drum'. Like the Chilean *machi,* the *witakultruntufe* combines chant and drumming with herbal medicine and ritual action to create a healing gestalt in which the spiritual and social patterns and behavior of the patient may be modified. If illness is the result of a personal soul's wandering, the patient may be strengthened when the healer "pulls" the *tayil,* fusing past and present, creating a union of the mundane and sacred worlds. The healer may resonate sounds in parts of her body that correspond to affected parts of the patient's body. To treat respiratory diseases, she may sound

FIGURE 2   *Ufisha tayil* as performed by Tomasa Epulef, Zaina Yegua, Nenguén. Transcription by Carol Robertson.

Drummed rhythms accompany the emergence of the rhea from the egg, its wobbly attempts to walk, its strut as a mature bird, and its death and ascent.

tones in her chest and project the sound from her body into the patient's lungs. These techniques, developed over centuries of empirical experimentation, are based on a world view that perceives sound as central to the movement and balance of the universe, the community, and the individual.

Vocal genres

Several traditional vocal genres persist among the Mapuche. A precomposed style of ceremonial song (*öl*) accompanies dances at the annual rites of increase. Improvised songs (*kantún*) are often denoted by a Spanish term, *romanceo*. Spontaneous creations, these usually describe recent events and may cleverly juxtapose Spanish and Mapuche texts to cultivate the metaphors and puns of Mapuche humor. The melodies and rhythms of many *kantún* have been influenced by the Chilean *cueca*, and by *chamamé, chotis, milonga*, polka, and vals, styles introduced by frontier soldiers and gauchos. Late-twentieth-century examples may show traces of melodies by Mexican mariachis and even the Beatles.

Kantún may be composed and sung by men and women, unaccompanied or with guitar and accordion. The *öl* are often sung by women simultaneously with the hocketed melodies of *pifülka* ensembles; but *tayil* are the exclusive domain of women's voices.

Because Mapuche homes are often at great distances from one another, whole communities do not gather frequently. Men who work on road-construction sites or on cattle farms owned by non-Mapuche settlers may gather at makeshift *pulperías*, where alcohol lubricates the throat and loosens *cuecas* and *romanceos*. Since the 1960s, women have begun to join their men at *ramadas*, song-and-dance feasts held in criollo towns, in which participants may dance until they collapse from exhaustion.

The Mapuche are famous for their endurance in song and dance. Some boast that they have been well honed for *ramadas* by years of participation in the annual rites of increase, held at the end of each harvest season, and involving three or four days and nights of perpetual dancing and ceremony. The goal of the ceremony is to draw the ancestors' and deities' attention to the needs of their earthbound children. Sheep and horses are sacrificed and offered on an altar (*rewe*); women sing *tayil* and *öl* to fortify ritual actions that link the community to sacred time.

The dances of these rites vary from one community to another, depending on the mix of Andean and pampa groups that has resulted over centuries of migration and intermarriage. Among the most widely known dances are *puel purrún* and *lonkomeo*, performed in areas of Chile and Argentina. Their rhythms are signaled by the *kultrún* and are sometimes accompanied by young male dancers playing *pifülka* and *trutruka*.

Puel purrún means 'dance to the east', whence come light and life. The *puel*

FIGURE 3   *Ufisha tayil* as it might be performed by two kinswomen in the same ritual space. A composite transcription by Carol Robertson.

purrún involves the whole community. Women dance in one direction around the altar, and men dance in a circle in the opposite direction, or men and women face each other in parallel lines, dancing first to the right, and then to the left.

The *lonkomeo* 'moving the head' differs from *puel purrún* in that it is a virtuosic display of individual skill. The choreography of this dance depicts five stages in the life of the *choike,* a rhea, whose size and power impede its flight but which at death soars heavenward to meet the ancestors. Drummed rhythms accompany the emergence of the rhea from the egg, its wobbly attempts to walk, its strut as a mature bird, and its death and ascent. Old and young men alike are selected to form groups of four or five dancers representing the major lineages in a community. Kinswomen pull forth the lineage soul of each dancer so the dance, a ritual metaphor for life on earth, will evoke compassion in the beings of the spirit world.

Mapuche performance spaces often accommodate more than one event at a time, so instrumental and vocal genres often occur simultaneously without the need for synchrony. Thus, though dances, chants, and instrumental passages may accompany the same ritual action, they may do so as separate artistic statements. This is especially evident in group performances of *tayil,* in which each woman may begin her rendition on any pitch and perform at her own speed, for each woman is pulling her lineage soul forth as a separate, personal effort (figure 3).

This approach to performance often carries over into some of the musical genres learned from Argentine gauchos and performed at annual *señaladas,* when animals are branded, separated, and prepared for journeys to higher pastures where they will spend the summer. These events are capped in the late afternoon by house parties at which hosts provide meat, wine, and song. Guitars, accordions, and Western band instruments seldom seen in colder months may be brought down from the rafters for renditions of a late-nineteenth-century *vals* or *chotis,* and an occasional polka. Many of these styles were learned by grandfathers of the present generation while in captivity in frontier forts. Sometimes, an accordion, a guitar, and a trumpet may play in different keys and at different tempi, for although they are part of the same event, each performer asserts a degree of independence.

ACCULTURATION

Though many Mapuche children have been estranged from traditional world views by schools, missionization, and a world that hawks "modern" values and rejects old ways, they continue to participate in the agricultural and ritual cycles of their communities. Since the 1970s or earlier, Salesian missionaries have stressed traditional weaving and leatherworking as part of the curriculum, and Mapuche artisans have been receiving recognition for their textiles, pottery, silversmithing, and dance regalia. In turn, Mapuche communities continue to absorb influences from the outside, especially those transmitted by radio and village dance festivals. New generations are mediating the impact of military defeat through agricultural and animal-husbandry programs, and the Mapuche language is still spoken in many areas of the southern Andes.

In 1981, Gregorio Cayulef, a Mapuche elder from the Argentine-Chilean border, said:

> Chile and Argentina may declare war on each other forever. But we know that though our grandfathers came from many places, we are now one Mapuche people. We find seashells in the mountains and know these Andes were not always there. Change will come; but as for us, we must keep two things: our language and our chants.

FURTHER STUDY

The Chilean composer and scholar Carlos Isamitt was one of the first to study and write about the music and dance of the Mapuche, whom he called *los araucanos* (1937, 1938, 1941). Another Chilean composer interested in musical nationalism, Carlos Lavín, also published about the music of the Mapuche (1967). The Chilean composer, musicologist, and Indiana University professor Juan Orrego-Salas drew on the findings and publications of these Chilean scholars, those of Pedro Humberto Allende, and also his own laboratory research, resulting in an article in *Ethnomusicology* (1966) entitled "Araucanian Indian Instruments." This was one of the first studies in English on Mapuche music. With the expansion of the foremost Chilean scholarly journal, *Revista Musical Chilena*, into more ethnomusicological topics and themes, numerous articles on Mapuche music appeared in the 1970s and 1980s. Most important are those by María Ester Grebe (1973, 1974), Ernesto González (1986), Luis Merino (1974), and Carlos Munizaga (1974).

An early but important anthropological study of Chilean Mapuche music is by Titiev (1949), entitled *Social Singing among the Mapuche*. His studies (also 1951) and those by Louis Faron (1964, 1968) are important ethnographic works for contextualizing Mapuche music.

Two commercial recordings that include Mapuche music are by Dannemann and Wenzel (1975) and Clair-Vasiliadis, et al. (1975). Dannemann and Wenzel include several excerpts of *trutruka* music and a lengthy example of a *machi* shaman accompanied by a *kultrún*. Clair-Vasiliadis's recording includes numerous social songs, love songs, marriage songs, and other vocal examples, plus a short excerpt of a *trutruka* solo.

REFERENCES

Aldunate del Solar, Carlos. 1992. *Mapuche: Seeds of the Chilean Soil*. Philadelphia: Port of History Museum and Museo Chileno de Arte Precolombino.

Berdichewsky, Bernardo. 1971. "Fases culturales en la prehistoria de los araucanos de Chile." *Revista Chilena de Historia y Geografía* 139:105–112.

Clair-Vasiliadis, Christos, et al. 1975. *Amerindian*

Music of Chile: Aymara, Qaqashqar, Mapuche. Ethnic Folkways Records FE 4054. LP disk.

Dannemann, Manuel, and Jochen Wenzel. 1975. *Amerindian Ceremonial Music from Chile*. Unesco Collection. Musical Sources, Pre-Columbian America XI-1. Philips 6586 026. LP disk.

Faron, Louis C. 1956. "Araucanian Patri-Organization and the Omaha System." *American Anthropologist* 63:435–456.

————. 1961. *Mapuche Social Structure.* Urbana: University of Illinois Press.

————. 1964. *Hawks of the Sun: Mapuche Morality and Its Ritual Attributes.* Pittsburgh: University of Pittsburgh Press.

————. 1968. *The Mapuche Indians of Chile.* New York: Holt, Rinehart and Winston.

González, Ernesto. 1986. "Vigencias de Instrumentos Musicales Mapuches." *Revista Musical Chilena* 40(166):4–52.

Grebe, María Ester. 1973. "El kultrún mapuche: Un microcosmo simbólico." *Revista Musical Chilena* 27(123–124):3–42.

————. 1974. "Presencia del dualismo en la cultura y música mapuche." *Revista Musical Chilena* 28(126–127):47–79.

————. 1979–1980. "Relaciones entre música y cultura: El kultrún y su simbolismo." *Revista INIDEF* 4:7–25.

Grebe, María Ester, Sergio Pacheco, and José Segura. 1972. "Cosmovisión Mapuche." *Cuadernos de la Realidad Nacional* 14. Santiago: Universidad Católica de Chile.

Isamitt, Carlos. 1937. "Cuatro instrumentos musicales araucanos." *Boletín Latino Americano de Música* 3(3):55–66.

————. 1938. "Los instrumentos araucanos." *Boletín Latino Americano de Música* 4(4):307–312.

————. 1941. "La danza entre los araucanos." *Boletín Latino Americano de Música* 4(5):601–605.

Lavín, Carlos. 1967. "La música de los araucanos." *Revista Musical Chilena* 21(99):57–60.

Martínez Sarasola, Carlos. 1992. *Nuestros paisanos los indios: Vida, historia y destino de las comunidades indígenas en la Argentina.* Buenos Aires: Emecé.

Merino, Luis. 1974. "Instrumentos musicales, cultura mapuche y el Cautiverio feliz del Mestre de Campo Francisco Núñez de Pineda y Bascuñán." *Revista Musical Chilena* 28(128):56–95.

Munizaga, Carlos. 1974. "Atacameños, araucanos, alacalufes: Breve reseña de tres grupos étnicos chilenos." *Revista Musical Chilena* 28(126–127):7–20.

Orrego-Salas, Juan A. 1966. "Araucanian Indian Instruments." *Ethnomusicology* 10(1):48–57.

Pérez de Arce, José. 1986. "Cronología de los instrumentos sonoros del Area Extremo Sur Andina." *Revista Musical Chilena* 166:68–123.

————. 1987. "Flautas arqueológicas del extremo Sur Andino." *Boletín del Museo Chileno de Arte Precolombino* 2:55–87.

Robertson, Carol E. 1979. "'Pulling the Ancestors': Performance Practice and Praxis in Mapuche Ordering." *Ethnomusicology* 23(3):395–416.

————. 1991. "The Ethnomusicologist as Midwife." In *Music in the Dialogue of Cultures: Traditional Music and Cultural Policy,* ed. Max Peter Baumann, 347–364. Wilhelmshaven: Florian Noetzel Verlag.

Robertson-DeCarbo, Carol E. 1975. "Tayil: Musical Communication and Social Organization among the Mapuche of Argentina." Ph. D. dissertation, Indiana University.

————. 1976. "Tayil as Category and Communication among the Argentine Mapuche: A Methodological Suggestion." *Yearbook of the International Council for Traditional Music* 8:35–52.

San Martín, Félix. ca. 1919. *Neuquén.* Buenos Aires: Rodríguez Giles.

Schoo Lastra, Dionisio. 1928. *El indio del desierto.* Buenos Aires: Jacobo Peuser.

Titiev, Mischa. 1949. *Social Singing among the Mapuche.* Anthropological Papers of the Museum of Anthropology, 2. Ann Arbor: University of Michigan Press.

————. 1951. *Araucanian Culture in Transition.* Ann Arbor: University of Michigan Press.

Section 2
Countries and Peoples of South America and Their Music

What is the essence of South American music? Many will think of the guitar and its dozens of relatives. Others may think of skin-covered drums or hand-held rattles such as maracas. They are also right. South American music includes these instruments and many others, as it is a region of many heritages and great musical diversity. We think immediately of Spanish and Portuguese, African, and native American backgrounds. But we must also think of other Europeans, the great diversity of Africans forcibly brought to the New World, and the multitude of other immigrants whose musics have become part of the cultural mosaic of South America.

Señora Berta Indo, a rural guitarist, is from Curacaví, Santiago Province, central Chile, an area of South America that favors old musical traits, such as the use of metal rather than nylon strings. She holds her instrument in a manner deriving from Renaissance Spain, or even relating to performance by Spanish gypsies. Photo by Daniel E. Sheehy, 1973.

The Music of South America
Dale A. Olsen

Linguistic Diversity
History

South America is a continent of twelve politically independent countries and one department of France (maps pp. 243, 244, 246, 247). Five official or national languages are spoken—-Dutch, English, French, Spanish, and Portuguese—as are hundreds of native American tongues, dozens of imported languages [see MUSIC OF IMMIGRANT GROUPS], and several localized ones, such as Creole, Taki-taki, and Papiamento. Most of the continent's three hundred million people, however, speak Spanish or Portuguese.

LINGUISTIC DIVERSITY

opposite: Colombia, Venezuela, Guyana, Surinam, and French Guiana

Apart from the speakers of indigenous languages, the linguistic diversity of the South American continent originated from its colonial background. In the Treaty of Tordesillas (1494), Pope Alexander VI set a demarcation line that divided the New World between Spain and Portugal. It awarded Spain all lands 370 leagues west of the Cape Verde Islands and Portugal everything east of the line (Goodman 1992). This treaty led to the development of Brazil as an officially Portuguese-speaking country, whereas the other colonies in South America (except the Guianas) officially spoke Spanish. England, France, and the Netherlands, however, eventually established colonial outposts on the northern Atlantic coast of the continent, where their languages prevailed; this area, a sort of coastal buffer between Spain and Portugal, was known as the Guianas—British Guiana (Guyana), Dutch Guiana (Surinam), and French Guiana.

HISTORY

For the purpose of government, Spain divided its lands into four large domains, or viceroyalties (subkingdoms): New Spain (much of Central America north into the western half of the present United States), New Granada (present Colombia, Ecuador, and Venezuela), Peru (present Chile and Peru), and La Plata (present Argentina, Bolivia, Paraguay, and Uruguay). Portugal's domain became the viceroyalty of Brazil, which grew much larger than the land originally determined by the Treaty of Tordesillas. For almost three centuries, viceroys ruled these areas, representing the crowns of Spain and Portugal. Unique in South America, Brazil became the

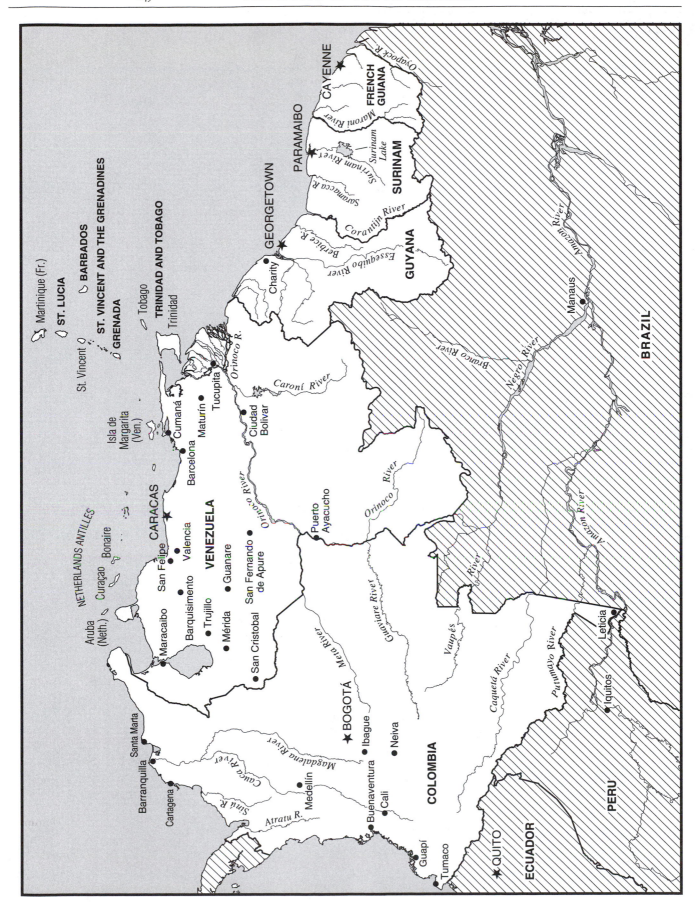

Ecuador, Peru, and Bolivia

FIGURE 1   During a floor show at the Brizas de Titicaca, a Puno club in Lima's downtown, young migrant musicians from Puno, Peru (or second-generation Puneños), wear ceremonial dress, dance, and play *siku* panpipes and drums while performing for fellow immigrants from Puno, other Peruvians, and tourists. Photo by Dale A. Olsen, 1996.

FIGURE 2   Accompanied by a solo guitarist, an Argentine couple dances the tango on a Sunday afternoon in a Buenos Aires street during the weekly San Elmio street fair. To the musician's left is a photo of the famous tango singer Carlos Gardel. To his right is a Gardel imitator, dressed like his idol. Photo by Dale A. Olsen, 1993.

home of a reigning European king, the king of Portugal himself; Dom João and his royal court escaped the Napoleonic takeover by sailing to Brazil in 1808, and in 1815 he proclaimed himself King of Brazil (Pendle 1963:120–124).

Independence movements started in the 1800s. Simón Bolívar and José de San Martín are considered the liberators of Spanish-speaking South America. Brazil, however, was given to Dom Pedro by his father, Dom João who returned to Portugal. Dom Pedro proclaimed Brazil's independence from Portugal in 1822 and had himself crowned emperor of Brazil. The remaining European colonies on the north coast (the Guianas) did not become independent until the 1900s, and French Guiana remains French territory. Since the 1800s, most South American nations have experienced dictatorships, elitist or military rule, and many changes of governments; only since the 1980s have some of them become democratic.

South America is a continent of great geographic contrasts. It contains one of the driest deserts on earth (the Atacama Desert in northern Chile), the highest mountain in the Western Hemisphere (Aconcagua, on the border between Argentina and Chile), one of the world's longest rivers (Río Marañón-Amazon, Amazon), the world's largest tropical forest (the Amazon), the world's highest waterfall (Angel Falls in Venezuela), and many other unique physical features.

In historical times, wars have been fought over some of these regions. From 1879 to 1883, Bolivia, Chile, and Peru fought the War of the Pacific over the discovery of nitrates (Chile won). From melted-down cannons, Argentina and Chile built a large statue of Jesus Christ (Cristo Redemptor, "Christ of the Andes") on their border between Mendoza and Santiago; its inscription translates: "Sooner shall these mountains crumble to dust than Argentines and Chileans break the peace sworn to at the feet of Christ the Redeemer" (Herring 1968:736). Border and internal skirmishes, and even wars, have been waged in the South American rain forests and foothills, mainly because of the desire for slaves, the discovery of minerals and hardwoods, or the possibility of finding deposits of oil. The Brazil-Paraguay war (1864–1870) was one of the bloodiest conflicts in all of South America, and the Chaco War, between Paraguay and Bolivia, was one of the longest (1928–1954) (Herring 1968:815–818). What can be termed genocidal wars against native Americans have continued in South America even into the late 1990s.

Native South Americans have been affected by the processing of rubber, narcotics, and gold and by intrusions into their lands by missionaries and nonmissionaries. In tropical forests, the Andes, the Caribbean coasts, and elsewhere, indigenous cultures and species of flora and fauna are in constant danger of extinction—mostly because of greed. Nevertheless, native South Americans have survived, though not without changes to most of their societies. Many musical occasions reveal these changes, as seen in musical instrument usage, ceremonial dress, dance styles, language, and musical genres—or the disappearance of any of the above (figure 1).

But just as the native South American music cultures have evolved, so have the Spanish, Portuguese, and many African music cultures. Most music of South America is a cultural mix, a musical mosaic (Olsen 1980). South America claims some of the world's most populous cities, greatest architectural achievements, and largest slums. It also claims some of the world's most exciting music and elaborate folkloric events. Much of this is because of the amalgamation of cultures—the fusion of dozens of heritages in a multitude of ways.

South Americans have great feelings of musical and cultural nationalism; art-music composers have borrowed on traditional themes, and popular-music composers have created national expressions. Throughout the centuries, many countries within South America have experienced musical censorship; however, some traditions, such as the tango in Argentina, never die (figure 2). Some military leaders pre-

PERU

BOLIVIA

BRAZIL

Arica

Iquique

PARAGUAY

Filadelfia

Yaví
Punta Corral

CHILE

Antofagasta

Jujuy
Salta

ASUNCÍON

Ciudad
del Este

Pilcomayo River

Paraguay River

Villarrica
Encarnación

San Miguel
de Tucumán

Copiapó

Posadas

Paraná River

Uruguay River

Iguaçú River

La Rioja

La Serena
Coquimbo

Cosquín

Santa Fe

Riviera

San Juan

Córdoba

Tacuarembo

Mendoza

URUGUAY

Valparaíso

San Luis

Rosario

Durazno
Florida

SANTIAGO

Colonia

Minas

ARGENTINA

BUENOS
AIRES

Punta del Este

La Plata

MONTEVIDEO

Maule R.

Santa Rosa

Río de la Plata

Concepción

Bío Bío R.

Colorado River

Bahía Blanca

Pinamar

Mar del Plata

Temuco

Neuquén

Negro River

Valdivia

Osorno

Bariloche

Viedma

Puerto Mont

Chiloé
Island

Chubut River

Rawson

Puerto
Aisen

GULF OF
SAN JORGE

Chile, Argentina, Paraguay, and Uruguay

Punta
Arenas

Río Gallegos

Falkland Islands (U.K.)
(Islas Malvinas)

Strait of Magellan

Tierra del
Fuego

Ushuaía

Beagle Channel

Brazil

fer German military marches to homegrown *cuecas*. Most South American countries have ministries of culture that concern themselves with music, and many have institutes of folklore that collect, preserve, and disseminate traditional music and dance. These vignettes suggest that music is highly important to the people of South America: it is one of their essential elements of life.

REFERENCES

Herring, Hubert. 1968. *A History of Latin America from the Beginnings to the Present.* New York: Knopf.

Goodman, Edward J. 1992. *The Explorers of South America.* Norman: University of Oklahoma Press.

Olsen, Dale A. 1980. "Folk Music of South America—A Musical Mosaic." In *Musics of Many Cultures: An Introduction,* ed. Elizabeth May, 386–425. Berkeley: University of California Press.

Pendle, George. 1963. *A History of Latin America.* Baltimore: Penguin.

Argentina
Ercilia Moreno Chá

Aboriginal Inhabitants
Musical Instruments
Religious Musical Contexts and Genres
Secular Musical Contexts and Genres
Enculturation and Learning
Musical Change

Located in the southern "cone" of South America, the Republic of Argentina is the southeast extreme of the Americas and covers about 2.77 million square kilometers of continental land. It extends westward to the Andes and Chile, eastward to the Atlantic Ocean, Uruguay, and Brazil, northward to the borders with Bolivia and Paraguay, and southward to Chile and the Atlantic Ocean. Its territory has a varied topography in which several cultural areas can be distinguished: Patagonia (Chubut, Neuquén, Río Negro, Santa Cruz, and Tierra del Fuego provinces), the area of the pampa (Buenos Aires, La Pampa, Santa Fe, the south of Córdoba), the area of Cuyo (Mendoza, San Juan, San Luis), the northwestern area (Catamarca, Jujuy, La Rioja, Salta, Tucumán), the central area (Santiago del Estero, the center and north of Córdoba), the area of Chaco (Chaco, Formosa, the east of Salta), and the littoral area (Corrientes, Entre Ríos, Misiones).

Argentina's population is about 34 million persons, of whom about 85 percent are of European descent. Natives and mestizos have been pushed aside or absorbed. A famous character, immortalized in literature, is a kind of mestizo called gaucho, a human stereotype synonymous with the country. The most representative music of Argentina, known all over the world, is tango, a popular dance for couples, with sensual and complex choreography.

ABORIGINAL INHABITANTS

The archaeological record for native Argentine music comes almost totally from the northwest; the historical record covers more of the country. Archaeological studies begun in the 1880s have centered in the northwestern Andean province of Jujuy, where numerous idiophones and aerophones have been found.

Ancient idiophones included rattles made of gourds and fruits, jingles (*cascabeles*) made of fruits, small metal and wooden bells (with and without clappers), and a gourd sistrum (Vignati 1982).

Aerophones included widely various flutes, whistles, and trumpets made from stone, ceramic, bone, and wood. Their forms were mostly abstract, though a few were zoomorphic. Excavations have revealed mostly ductless oval and pear-shaped globular flutes (ocarinas) made from stone or ceramic. One was made from an armadillo cranium, with an avian humerus for a duct (Vignati 1982:93). Bone end-blown flutes were found, with and without holes for fingering, with and without the rectangular notch of the *quena* (or *kena*). Raft panpipes of three or four closed tubes, made from stone, ceramic, and wood, were also found. Excavations have revealed trumpets, usually made from bone. The panpipes and trumpets have most commonly been found in Jujuy.

Historical records

Historical sources for the study of Argentine music began in 1520. They include the chronicles of explorers, travelers, colonizers, and missionaries. Most of these sources superficially describe the indigenous musics of Tierra del Fuego, Patagonia, Río de la Plata, and the Chaco.

Little has been published about the aboriginal music of Tierra del Fuego, except that music was related to birth, childhood, curing, and death (Vignati 1982). The Yámana and the Ona had collective songs and solo shamanistic songs, based on few pitches with small intervals (Gallardo 1910; Lothrop 1928; Segers 1891). There is no agreement about Yámana and Ona musical instruments, because the chroniclers could not competently determine whether or not an object was a musical instrument; only an aerophone and a women's rhythm stick have been mentioned (Furlong 1909; Gallardo 1910; Lothrop 1928).

Rattles made of gourd, bark, or leather (d'Orbigny 1835–1847; Hernández 1910 [1836]), rhythm sticks with and without rattles (Faulkner 1935 [1774]; Pigafetta 1800 [1534]; Transilvano 1837 [1829]), little bells (Hernández 1910 [1836]), a sistrum (Morris 1750), and drums (d'Orbigny 1835–1847; Sánchez Labrador 1936 [1772]) have been documented in Patagonia. In the 1800s, aerophones such as flutes, conch or cane trumpets, and whistles made of bone, wood, ceramics, and stone have been mentioned (d'Orbigny 1835–1847; Moreno 1890–1891; Vaulx 1898). Several mouth-resonated bows were reported during the last decades of 1800s, but the first mention was made by d'Orbigny, who saw such a bow among the Auca in 1829. Dances and songs were mentioned in association with birth, puberty, healing, death, marriage, religion, hunting, sadness, and thanksgiving.

The earliest sources dealing with the southern part of Argentina are by Pigafetta and Transilvano, chroniclers from Magellan's expedition (in 1520), followed by the chronicles of Fray García Jofré de Loaisa (in 1526), Simón de Alcazaba (in 1535), Sarmiento de Gamboa (in 1584), Francis Drake (in 1578), and Francis Fletcher (in 1578). None of the seventeenth-century Argentine sources mention music, and only about 1750 does music begin to be documented in quantity. Among the most important contributions are those of Joseph Sánchez Labrador (1936 [1772]), Alcides d'Orbigny (1835–1847), Estanislao Zeballos (1881), and a magnificent description by Hunt (in Despard 1854), a companion of the missionary George Pakenham Despard (1854). Hunt describes a melody sung by the Patagones in 1845, giving the texts and the rhythm on a musical staff.

Meager information from Río de la Plata mentions flutes, duct flutes (*pingollos*), drums, cornets, and trumpets associated with war. The main sources include the chronicle by Ruy Díaz de Guzmán (1969–1972 [1612]), who traveled between 1536 and 1538; the chronicle by Martín del Barco Centenera, who traveled between 1572 and 1581; and the monumental history written by Pedro Lozano (1874–1875) about the Jesuit missionaries' activities.

On the Chaco, few documentary sources before the 1700s are available, and only Martín del Barco Centenera and Pierre F. J. Charlevoix, the Jesuit historian, mentioned music, always in conjunction with dance (Vignati 1982). In the 1700s,

Jesuit works were produced by Florian Baucke (1942–1944), who traveled between 1749 and 1767, and Martin Dobrizhoffer (1784). Mentioned frequently are *clarines* (possibly a type of trumpet), flutes, cornets, trumpets, clarinets, duct flutes, and the ritual use of a rattle and a water drum in many villages. Music served various ceremonial functions having to do with health, death, war, evil spells, and the preparation of drinks.

Also important for the study of extinct Argentine cultures are recordings made by European and American scholars: fifty-one Tehuelche melodies were recorded by Robert Lehmann-Nitsche in 1905; more than forty recordings of the Yámana and the Selk'nam were made between 1907 and 1908 by Colonel Charles Wellington Furlong; and work in Tierra del Fuego was continued by Father Gusinde in 1923–1924 (all these recordings went to the Phonogramm-Archiv Berlin). Much later, Anne Chapman completed the last recordings of the Fueguian Selk'nam (1972, 1978). Beginning in 1931, documentary recordings of the music of living indigenous and creole cultures were made by Carlos Vega, Isabel Aretz, and other scholars; these recordings are preserved in the archives of the Instituto Nacional de Musicología "Carlos Vega."

MUSICAL INSTRUMENTS

Instruments associated with Argentine traditional music can be classified by type and organized into the categories indigenous and criollo. Ten of them are idiophones, of which six are in the indigenous category: rhythm sticks; rattles made of animals' toenails, metal bells, or calabashes; stick rattles; and Jew's harps (*birimbao*). Four idiophones are in the criollo category: triangle, sistrum, *matraca* (cog rattle), and *birimbao*. Nine are membranophones: five indigenous drums (four double-headed and one kettledrum) and four criollo tubular and frame drums. There are twenty-three aerophones, including eleven indigenous instruments (seven types of flute, two types of whistle, two types of trumpet) and twelve criollo types (six types of flute, harmonica, button accordion, keyed accordion, *bandoneón*, clarinet, trumpet). There are eleven chordophones: five in indigenous use (musical bow, rebec, guitar, two types of violin) and six used by criollos (*charango*, mandolin, guitar, *requinto*, violin, harp).

Various indigenous musical instruments, many of which are flutes, occur among the Mapuche, the Mbyá, the Chiriguano-Chané, the Chorote, the Chulupí, the Toba, the Pilagá, and the Mocoví. Except for the Mapuche (who live in Patagonia), the native groups are from Chaco and Misiones in the north and northeast, respectively.

The most complete collection of traditional Argentine musical instruments is in the Instituto Nacional de Musicología "Carlos Vega" in Buenos Aires, which has obsolete and currently used instruments from Argentine indigenous and criollo cultures. The collection is related to the institute's scientific archive, which includes related photographic and aural materials.

Among the indigenous idiophones, the jingle rattle is used only by the Mapuche and the Mataco, and the rhythm tube is used only by the Mbyá, a Guaraní group in the forest of Misiones. All the other idiophones are found among groups of the Mataco-Mataguayo and Mbyá-Guaycurú linguistic families of the Chaco. There, the gourd rattle is symbolic and is used by all the extant indigenous cultures for different types of shamanistic rituals: female initiation, fermentation of drinks, weather phenomena, birth-related rites, curing, and so forth. Particularly among the Mataco, the gourd rattle has an enormous power conferred by Tokwaj, a mythic hero who instituted therapeutic shamanic practices in which song and the gourd rattle are elements of power and communication.

bombo European-derived cylindrical double-headed bass drum membranophone, played with sticks

caja 'Box', small drum in many Spanish-speaking countries

charango In the Andes of northern Argentina, Bolivia, and southern Peru, a small guitar made with wood or an armadillo shell

erquencho Argentine single-reed-concussion aerophone without finger holes

tiple 'Treble', three-stringed chordophone

rabel European-derived stringed instrument originating in the Renaissance period, played with a bow like a violin, usually with three strings

The Mataco and to a lesser extent the Chorote each have a class of shaman who makes and uses a gourd rattle, never associated with dance as it is with other indigenous groups in the area. The Chiriguano-Chané gourd rattle is also a shamanic instrument with similar functions; however, this shaman accompanies his ritual with dance. Chiriguano-Chané shamans are solicited by the chief of a community to counteract an unfavorable meteorological effect; the assembled shamans smoke in the center of the village while conversing and divining the causes of the problem, then go to the fields where they dance (Pérez Bugallo 1982:225).

Of the indigenous membranophones, the *kultrún,* a single-headed kettledrum played with one stick, is used only by the Mapuche, who believe it has existed since the beginning of the world and that the gods of music (*tayiltufe*) teach the shaman (*machi*, always female today) how to paint the symbolic designs on its drumhead and how to play it. The *kultrún* has a complex symbolic content. As a shamanic tool, it represents the shaman along with her transcendent roles. It has value as a symbolic microcosm, representing the shaman and the Mapuche universe, conceived as a "complex network of relationships among diverse elements related through a good-evil polarity: colors, cosmic supernatural and natural areas, the cardinal directions, the stars, and earthly regions" (Grebe 1979–1980:12).

The supernatural world is reflected on the drumhead, always painted with abstract motifs, usually by the shaman herself. The natural world is represented by the body of the drum, constructed from the wood of a sacred tree, to which is attributed the power to help the shaman during her trance. In the cavity are placed various symbolic elements, such as rocks, feathers, medicinal herbs, and the hair of animals, which will confer efficacy to the shamanic endeavor (Pérez Bugallo 1993:42). The *kultrún* is always the leader of the instrumental ensemble in which it is played, carrying out the function of ritual communication in relation to sickness, death, initiation, and fertility.

Criollos commonly use several membranophones: one *bombo* is a large double-skinned cylindrical drum, beaten with two sticks and played with guitar (or, in the northwest, criollos commonly use guitar and accordion) to accompany several dances; another *bombo* is a double-skinned frame drum, beaten with one stick and used in religious ceremonies, in panpipe bands, and in some popular urban sports; a *caja* is a double-skinned frame drum, beaten with a stick and used to accompany songs (figure 1).

Two indigenous aerophones—*pifülka* and *trutruka*—are found among the Mapuche, and several others are found among groups in the northwest and northeast; most are symbolic. The *pifülka,* a wooden whistle whose sound recalls the whistle of a mythic vampire who musically announces his disgrace, is constructed so its shape suggests the mythic creature's wings (Pérez Bugallo 1993:92). The evolution of this instrument, first traced from archaeological sources and then through chroniclers and travelers to the present, shows it has accompanied the various historical situa-

FIGURE 1   A criollo from Yavi (Jujuy) with his *caja.* Photo by Ercilia Moreno Chá, 1968.

FIGURE 2   A Mapuche artisan tries a recently finished *trutruka*. Junín de los Andes, Río Negro. Photo by Cristina Argota, 1983.

FIGURE 2   A Mapuche artisan tries a recently finished *trutruka*. Junín de los Andes, Río Negro. Photo by Cristina Argota, 1983.

tions of the Mapuche in their struggle against Europeans. Originally used in shamanic curing, fertility rites, human sacrifices, battle, petitions, exorcisms, and funeral rites, it is currently used with the *trutruka* in the ŋillipún (*ngillatún*), the most important supplicatory ceremony of the Mapuche. The *trutruka* is a long (up to 3 meters), end-blown natural trumpet made from a hollowed bamboo pole covered with horse gut and adorned with a cow's horn at its distal end (figure 2). It resembles the *erke* (*erque*), used in the northwest by criollos, a side-blown trumpet whose length can be up to 7 meters.

The widespread belief that associates some flutes with male-female sexual attraction is present among the Chiriguano-Chané with respect to the end-blown flute called the *temïmbi-púku*. For this reason, men play the instrument in solitude to express feelings about their selection of a woman with whom to mate. Different melodies exist for courting, thanks, happiness over having found a woman, and sadness over wooing a married woman (Pérez Bugallo 1982:244). In numerous stories, animals and supernatural beings employ the flute as a vehicle of sexual attraction. Although the Andean *quena* once had similar symbolic significance in the Argentine altiplano, it is used more as a criollo instrument, alone or with a *charango,* or with a guitar and a *bombo.* Likewise, the Aymara *siku* are rarely used except in folkloric ensembles.

The aerophones the criollos use occur solely in the northwest, except for those with reeds, which are found mostly in the central and northeastern areas. Aerophones used in criollo music are numerous, and their distribution is well defined. Flutes, for example, are found in the northwest and have an old repertoire, but reed-concussion aerophones (single-reed and double-reed types), with a recent and mainly danceable repertoire, are found in the central and northeastern areas. Most notable among the vibrating reed instruments is the *erkencho* (*erquencho*), a single-reed clarinet made from cane and a cow's horn, found in the northwest. A multiple single-reed concussion aerophone is the accordion, introduced from Europe about 1850 (in some places, it has begun to be replaced by the guitar and violin). A similar instrument, the *bandoneón* (a concertina, whose popularity was spread by the tango) has become popular since 1950.

The native use of chordophones in Argentina occurs in the west, north, and northeast. The Mapuche may anciently have used a musical bow (*cunculcahue*), but the indigenous use of violin in the Chaco and Misiones is borrowed from European colonists. A traditional indigenous function of musical courtship includes the musical bow, the violin, the Jew's harp, and some types of flutes, especially in the Chaco.

Criollo chordophones are the mandolin, the *tiple* (rarely used), and the guitar, the most widely dispersed instrument in the country, except in the high Andes. The *charango,* a small plucked lute often made from an armadillo shell, is the only double-course chordophone of Argentina; usually having five courses, it is played in the Andean northwest. Bowed lutes such as the *rabel* and the violin are distributed in various parts of the west-central area and throughout the north and the northwest.

RELIGIOUS MUSICAL CONTEXTS AND GENRES

Mapuche

A strong female shamanic (*machi*) tradition is found among the Mapuche of the Patagonian Andes [see MAPUCHE]. The shaman's function is that of healer, ceremonial officiant, repository of mythology, poet, musician, dancer, and prophetess (Grebe 1979–1980:23). She leads the ceremonies in which the *kultrún* is used, and by singing sets up transcendent ritual communication with ancestors, spirits, and deities. She does this through the *tayil,* a paternally inherited song.

Each lineage has specific musical elements (pattern of vocalization, totem-related text, melodic contour) that unite its dead members with its living ones (Robertson 1979:236). At death, the shaman is transformed into a mythic being who goes to the place in the supernatural world that the spirits of the other deceased shamans, other ancestors, and gods inhabit. The *kultrún* is buried with her or is destroyed by her since, because of its ritual use, no other person may play it.

For the Mapuche, the most important seasonal ceremony is the *ŋillipún,* especially in the mountains of Neuquén and Chubut. Primarily a supplicatory ceremony, it takes place after harvest, but it can be performed during unfavorable meteorological conditions or in times of calamity. It lasts four days and follows a complex ritual. Throughout, music is important. Variations depend on where it is performed, but it invariantly consists of a reception (*alwünde*); the climbing of a nearby hill, on which men give ritual yells (*ipa*), imploring help for the supplications of the women; an ostrich (rhea) dance (*loncomeo*); and a women's suppliant song (*purrum*). The reception is performed on horseback, with a standard-bearer leading the participants; at its end, they gallop around the altar or sacred space.

The *lonkomeo* (*loncomeo*) dance is done by young Mapuche boys, who imitate the ostrich from its gestation in the egg through its birth and adult development (figure 3). In the *ŋillipún,* music plays an important role. Shamans serving as directors mark the stages of the ritual with different patterns on the *kultrún,* followed by performances by an ensemble including *trutruka, pifülka,* metal bells (usually played by the shaman with the same hand that holds the drumstick), and sometimes a bugle.

Mbyá

Every January, the Mbyá (Mbïá) of Misiones celebrate the *ñemongaraí,* a ceremony related to the ripening of fruits (Ruiz 1984). It has two principal objectives: the offering to the gods in thanksgiving for blessings received and supplication for the people's health and prosperity, and the naming of children beginning to walk.

The importance of naming consists in the belief that a child's soul is sent by one of the four deities, and the group's religious leader (*pa'í*) must ascertain which of the deities is responsible; only then can it be known what name the child will carry. On

FIGURE 3   Four Mapuche boys dance the *lonkomeo* during a *ŋillipún* celebrated in Anecón Grande, Neuquén. Photo by Cristina Argota, 1990.

the morning of the ceremonial day, women prepare an offering of bread, men search the forest for the sacred *gwembé* (fruit of a local philodendron), and the *pa'i* waits within the ceremonial enclosure.

After noon, adults enter the ceremonial enclosure—first the men, led by the ceremonial assistant and musicians (playing a *rabel* and a guitar), followed by the women, led by the wife of the *pa'i*. After placing the offerings, they leave, to return soon after sundown. The second stage also takes place in the ritual enclosure, which adults enter after dancing to the music of *rabel* and guitar. Once they are inside, the communication of the children's names takes place, followed by sacred songs to the accompaniment of guitar and rhythm sticks.

Daily at sundown, Mbyá men, women, and children dance to honor their deities. Accompanied by *rabel* and guitar, they perform in an open space in front of the ritual enclosure. After an hour or more, they enter the enclosure, where the *pa'i* leads the religious ceremony with more dancing and singing, accompanied by guitar and rhythm sticks.

Andes, Chaco, and the pampas

Harvest celebrations (often known as the *minga* in the Andes) are common in several countries of the Americas. They take on local traits in the northern and northeastern provinces of Argentina, however, and include the spontaneous and free collaboration of rural people for the labor of harvest and related tasks. The workers include employees, friends, and neighbors, who by day gather in a given field for the necessary amount of time and at night participate in traditional dances and other diversions.

In the northern area, people collectively gather the fruit of the *algarrobo,* from which *chicha,* one of the most popular local drinks, is made. At the end of spring (October–November), when the *algarrobo* pods are ripe, entire families go into the woods for several days of gathering, followed by parties and nightly dancing.

Among the indigenous groups in the Chaco, dancing—almost invariably in conjunction with singing—formerly occurred during such occasions as celebrations of victory in battle, preparation of beverages, the conjuring of evil spells and natural phenomena, courtship, and marriages. No current studies of the subject exist.

In the four northern Argentine provinces, where Brazilian and Paraguayan influence is felt, the celebration of the feast of Saint John the Baptist features bonfires, games with fire, and barefoot walks on burning coals. The nighttime celebration features music, often played on button accordion and guitar.

The ritual marking of animals is another musical context that takes on different local traits. It is usually celebrated in the fall (March–April) in the pampa, or at the beginning of winter (June) in the northern provinces. In the north, it is called *señalada,* because the marking takes the form of a shaped cut (*señal* 'signal') on the ear of each goat or sheep born the previous year. The *señalada* is followed by a fertility ritual in which two persons take two animals, position them as if they are mating, and then feed Pachamama (Mother Earth) in supplication of the production of manure. The entire celebration is accompanied by the music of a single-reed concussion aerophone (*erkencho*) and a snare drum and by the singing of *bagualas* with or without allusive texts. In the pampa, marking (there called *yerra*) implies certain outdoor skills, but not ritual ones. Music signals the end of the process of marking and the end of every workday, creating the ideal occasion for *milongas* and dances including the *chamamé,* the polka, the *ranchera,* and the the *vals.*

Roman Catholicism

Roman Catholic Christianity was introduced by the Spanish, who used it as a tool for cultural penetration and domination. Most festive Christian celebrations that utilize traditional music are found in the northern provinces and to a lesser degree in the rest of the country.

There are several types of Roman Catholic musical manifestations, some using an ecclesiastical repertoire that has fallen out of official use but appears in processions and masses. Others have local traits and texts obviously conceived for occasions such as patronal feasts, whereas still others include only instrumental performances that accompany the moving of saints' images.

Another Roman Catholic repertoire, though not overtly religious, accompanies feast-day celebrations of the saints at night, in places equipped for dancing, eating, and drinking. These celebrations have some or all of the following events: pilgrimage to the shrine, mass, vigil, novena, procession, and a fair where local artifacts, food, and drink are sold. This procession can be carried out with publicly venerated saints or family ones, and is usually accompanied by instrumental music performed on the *bombo* and violin.

A procession that attracts the largest number of faithful is that of the Virgin of Punta Corral in the province of Jujuy, where the religious statue is carried every year from Punta Corral to the village of Tilcara, where there is a church (Cortázar 1959). This procession, which takes a ten-hour march over steep mountains, is the occasion for the most splendid gathering of panpipe bands in Argentina. Playing *waynos* (*huaynos*) and marches, they make themselves heard during four stops made for the purpose of prayer and rest. Panpipe bands are made up of pairs of *siku* of three or four different sizes, military drums of three kinds, and a rattle.

According to Silvia P. García (1978), the summer solstice, celebrated in pre-

FIGURE 4   Men play a button accordion and a guitar, a common duet for dancing *chamamé, ranchera,* polka, and *vals.* Victorica, La Pampa. Photo by Ercilia Moreno Chá, 1975.

Christian antiquity, was changed by the Roman Catholic Church to the feast of the Nativity of Saint John the Baptist, celebrated throughout Latin America on 24 June. As with all festivals at the end of spring and the beginning of winter, rites of fertility and purification had great importance. Saint John the Baptist became associated with rites of water and fire. In the four northern Argentine provinces, where Brazilian and Paraguayan influence is felt, this celebration is more vigorous, and features bonfires, games with fire, and barefoot walks on burning coals. The nighttime celebration features music, often played on button accordion and guitar (figure 4), and traditional dances, especially the *chamamé,* the polka, and the *rasgueado doble.* It is interrupted periodically by four men dressed as women, pretending to fight a bull of wood and rags carried by two youths. The bull's head is actually a bull's skull, but in place of horns are lighted torches.

Patronal festivals in Argentina have acquired various features ranging from the official form, emanating from its use in Rome and predominating in urban centers, to forms typified by localized traits. In patronal celebrations, situations when the church is more influential, only the ecclesiastically approved form can be observed. In rural areas of the northwest, however, a different kind of festival is found. Examples are the fiestas of Saint James (Santiago) and Saint John the Baptist (San Juan); the latter, as the patron saint of sheep, inspires devotion among shepherds.

Both celebrations occur in front of family shrines with neighbors and friends in attendance, or at the churches, to which some of the saints' statues are carried. In some towns of Jujuy, both celebrations use a dance known as *cuarteada,* so named because the dancing couples carry the hindquarter of a sacrificed sheep or goat, advancing or retreating with it in front of the saint's statue, placed on a table in an open space. This dance shares some of the traits of the country dance, and is usually accompanied by the sounds of a long cane trumpet (*erke* [*erque*]). Displaying traits of a fertility ritual, it culminates with an attempt to rip the meat; whoever pulls at it with the most force keeps it, unless it tears in two.

In the town of Yavi, bordering Bolivia in Jujuy, an example of what the celebration of Holy Week was formerly like can be seen in small groups called *doctrinas,* originally formed to teach Christian doctrine to those preparing to take first Communion. These classes, commonly seen in the villages of the Andean altiplano until about 1900, can still be found in Yavi (Moreno Chá 1971). The entire ceremony on Good Friday night includes unaccompanied songs learned by the groups from their teachers through oral tradition. Many of the texts refer to Christ's passion and Mary's pain and are sung to pentatonic scales. They include *gozos* 'praises', *alabanzas, glorias, salves,* and other named genres. The study of Roman Catholic doctrine is no longer the purpose for the gatherings, now composed mainly of women and adolescents; instead, the occasion simply affords a chance for people to sing together.

Another type of religious celebration with a peculiar repertoire is the celebration of the Child-Mayor (*Niño-Alcalde*) in the province of La Rioja. A local veneration of the baby Jesus, this celebration goes back more than three hundred years. It relates to events in which, some people believe, the mediation of the baby Jesus made local native Americans submit to Spanish rule. In the ceremony, celebrated for three days starting on 31 December, the principal images are those of the Child-Mayor and Saint Nicholas, each having its own devotees who form its court in a hierarchical organization similar to those of European religious brotherhoods across Latin America (Aretz 1954).

Music is performed during the processions and the novena, which is said before both images. During the novena, *alabanzas* and *gozos* are sung. During the procession to the church and the novena, a special song for the occasion ("*Año Nuevo Pacari* 'Pacari New Year'," using the Quechua word *pacari* 'origin, beginning') is sung in Quechua to the accompaniment of a snare drum played by the Inca, a character who, representing indigenous vassals, belongs to the court of the Child-Mayor. The entire musical repertoire is European derived, syllabic, and in a major key.

Other European dances occur on 26 December in the province of San Juan during the celebration of the Virgin of Rosario de Andacollo; the major source of inspiration for this celebration is probably the fiesta of the same name occurring in the north-central Chilean town of Andacollo. The celebration usually consists of a novena prayed to the Virgin, followed by a procession and the climax of the fiesta, the presentation of the *chinos* (Quechua 'humble servant'), persons who honor the Virgin by dancing in fulfillment of vows (Olsen 1980:410). Many prayers and songs derived from the Chilean *chinos* interrupt this dance. Accordion, guitar, and triangle accompany the dances and marches of the procession.

Numerous indigenous life-cycle rituals have disappeared in Argentina; among the criollo populations of certain northwestern provinces, a few remain. The *rutichico* is a barely surviving Inca ceremony in Catamarca, Jujuy, Salta, and Santiago del Estero. In it, a boy's first haircut serves as a transition between his first and second childhoods. The haircut is initiated by the boy's godfather and is continued by the guests, who give the child gifts. Frequently, the freshly cut hair is offered to the Virgin Mary—an example of an old European practice superimposed on an indigenous one. The ceremony always ends with dancing.

At funeral rituals in the province of Santiago del Estero, women are hired to pray and sing Roman Catholic songs such as *salves* and *alabanzas* in the presence of the deceased. Wakes for children, formerly common, now occur only in remote areas. Argentinian Roman Catholics, who believe that children's souls go directly to heaven, do not see a child's death as a sorrowful loss. For this reason, manifestations of happiness, such as songs with couplets (*coplas*), are sung to the child and its parents, accompanied by a snare drum or a guitar. The Passion of Christ, similar to a wake, is dramatized in remote locales of this area. Calvary is simulated, and an effigy of Jesus is taken down from its cross, placed in a crystal coffin, veiled, and nocturnally paraded around villages.

The most vigorous dramatizations occur during carnival, when the women's ceremony known as *topamiento de comadres* occurs (a similar ceremony for men is now extinct). Women parody the baptism of an infant, thus sealing their relationship as godmothers (*comadres*). The *topamiento de comadres* includes the exchange of fruits, seeds, or homemade cheese. In some places, cheese in the shape of a baby is placed on the table, and a man in the role of a priest mimics the sprinkling of baptismal water on it.

After the ceremony, which includes singing with drummed accompaniment, the godmothers and their invited guests dance. After the carnival, a symbolic burial is enacted. Carnival can be represented by a human being, a rag or wooden doll, or the statue of the devil. Its death is symbolized by its burial or destruction by fire. This process is observed by all the revelers, and a mother of the personification (Quechua *pujllay,* in many places *carnaval*) accompanies this death with tears of farewell. In towns and cities, carnival has no dramatizations among the masqueraders (*murgas*).

Protestantism

Protestant Christianity was introduced in 1838, when Anglican missionaries began working in the south of the country among the indigenous people of Tierra del Fuego. In 1914, Protestants began proselytizing to the Mataco of the Chaco in the north. Protestantism spread quickly in the north and has competed since the 1940s with Pentecostalism, which has gained more adherents.

The first organized indigenous Pentecostal religious congregation, recognized officially in 1958, was the Iglesia Evangélica Unida (United Evangelical Church), which prospered most among the Toba living in their native Chaco and in the outskirts of larger cities. In addition to its religious function, it provides a feeling of identity and protection from global society.

Dance and music are extremely important in Toba Pentecostal worship. In only one of the five parts of the service are these genres absent. Different types of songs can be distinguished. Some have texts and music composed by the Toba; others have texts (in Toba or Spanish) taken from North American hymnals, though the original music (when it is available) is ignored. Most of the service is sung in unison by the congregation; sections are sung by small ensembles in two or three parts and by soloists. Until the 1970s, Toba Pentecostal singing was unaccompanied, but since then the guitar, the *bombo,* and the tambourine, and in the 1990s the *charango,* the *kena* (*quena*), and the accordion have been introduced. Influence of folk-derived music and lore can be seen in the incorporation and treatment of criollo instruments and in the use of *chamamé* and *zamba.*

Pentecostalism has been understood in indigenous terms (Roig 1990). The healing effected by the shaman as mediator is not replaced but is superimposed on the healing effected in worship by the pastor and the faithful. Originally the communication between the shaman and the supernatural was verified by song and rattle; now, power is realized through the song and dance of the pastor and the faithful, accompanied by criollo instruments. The gift of song to the shaman now comes from the Holy Spirit and often the learning of an instrument requires isolation, as it did for the shaman. In certain conventions or important meetings of the Toba Pentecostal church, dedications of musical ensembles of young people are reminiscent of forgotten initiation ceremonies, in which youths, in addition to marking their passage to adult life, entered the world of music.

Africanisms

The presence of African-derived beliefs in Argentina includes two variants of African-Brazilian religions: Umbanda and Batuque. The official opening of the first African-Brazilian temple was in 1966, and by the mid-1990s there were some three hundred churches, most in the Buenos Aires metropolitan area. Most of the adherents of Umbanda and Batuque are of the lower middle class (Frigerio 1991:23).

murga Urban carnival song genre in
Argentina

estilo 'Style', Argentine traditional musical
form from the pampa region

milonga Argentine song genre

chamamé Argentine polka-derived social
dance form

gato 'Cat', Argentine social dance genre

In most of the temples, both religions are practiced, but Batuque is sometimes replaced by other cults of the same origin, such as Candomblé. According to Alejandro Frigerio (personal interview, 1990), music and dance are of minimal importance in the Argentine versions, probably because the musical transplantation is abrupt and the repertoire has little in common with traditional or popular Argentine culture.

The repertoire of songs is learned through repeated listening to Brazilian recordings; the texts are in Portuguese and Yoruba, languages incomprehensible to most followers. The instrumental music is played on drums (and sometimes bells), often different from those used in Brazil. For Umbanda, however, the drums are Brazilian; for Batuque, they are locally available commercial instruments. A drummer's training is brief.

There is a relative homogeneity among these African-Brazilian cults from Belem do Pará (Brazil) to Asunción (Paraguay), and from Montevideo (Uruguay) to the Brazilian Northeast (Gallardo 1986:46). In the northeastern province of Corrientes, a syncretic celebration honors the black Saint Balthasar, not canonized by the Roman Catholic Church but popularly accepted as a saint to whom masses are offered. According to Roman Catholic traditions, Balthasar was one of the Magi, the three kings who journeyed to salute the baby Jesus in his crib on 6 January, the Epiphany. Though Argentina does not have a traditional black population, it once had a considerable one, which disappeared rapidly under mestization after the national abolition of slavery in 1853. In the present celebration of Saint Balthasar, African traits of social organization and music are superimposed on the structural base of the Roman Catholic saint's celebration (Kereilhac de Kussrow 1980). In certain localities in Corrientes, where the festival is celebrated, *candombe* (known locally as *charanda* or *ramba*) is still danced. It was found in Buenos Aires until about 1800 and is still found in Montevideo, Uruguay. Today, this dance appears with no racial connotations but with social ones, because it is danced by members of marginal social classes with remote native American or African ancestors.

In *candombe,* the coronation of African kings is represented and homage is given to them. Some traditional characters in *candombe,* such as the king and the *escobillero,* an acrobatic dancer (who dances with a small broom), were replaced by others of local significance and with Guaraní names such as *cambá-caraí* and *camba-ra-angá.* The music consists of simple melodies sung in Spanish and Guaraní in a major key and in binary rhythm, accompanied by *bombo* and triangle. Unlike the *bombo* of Andean music, for *candombe* the *bombo* is a double-headed conical membranophone with two heads attached to rings fastened by cords; it is played with the hands or with small sticks by two players seated astride it. The type of drum, its position on the ground, and its being played with the hands are unique features in traditional Argentine music. They suggest an African origin.

This ritual is now a votive dance found in the context of a Roman Catholic festival, which has assimilated it as the fulfillment of a vow to a saint. The dancers gather in pairs (of the same sex or opposite sexes), forming parallel lines. Formerly a dance of black brotherhoods during the carnivals of Montevideo and Buenos Aires, the *candombe* has become a votive dance.

SECULAR MUSICAL CONTEXTS AND GENRES

Music as entertainment is particularly important among Argentine criollos, who with music and dance often celebrate family events such as weddings or birthdays. They celebrate patriotic celebrations in much the same way, but on a local level. Since the 1960s, music has gained importance at sporting events and political rallies, where, as an expression of support, ridicule, or happiness, it occurs as multivoiced songs, usually improvised as quatrains or pairs of lines, or as multivoiced songs, transmitted orally by ensembles.

A large, double-headed bass drum has occupied a privileged place in this type of musical performance and is used with a European trumpet and a wooden noisemaker. The melodies have a strong beat. They are simple, catchy, and always in a major key, similar to the melodies used in *murgas*.

Apart from these musical traditions for public events, several large traditions stand out for having local, national, and international importance. These are folk-derived music, tango, tropical music, and rock. Some of them reflect social and cultural events that occurred in Argentina during the twentieth century.

Heavy European immigration—mainly from France, Germany, Italy, Poland, Russia, and Spain—began after 1870 and continued until the end of the 1940s. After the 1940s, the pace of immigration increased, with new waves arriving from the bordering countries and some arriving from Asia. This situation mainly oriented Argentinian society toward European cultural life. The relation between immigration and the origin of tango is strong, because tango permitted the immigrants to blend with other sectors of society.

Another migration took place within the country. From the late 1940s, a lot of people from rural areas moved to the urban centers, attracted by the increasing industry. This is related to the appearance of folkloric music in the cities.

Folkloric music

Since the 1960s, spectacles known as *jineteada* or *jineteada y doma* have appeared in rural and semiurban areas mostly in the central part of the country, organized by traditionalist societies, local municipal authorities, or special brokers. These spectacles include daylong displays of outdoor skills with ropes, horses, and colts. They are always accompanied by traditional pampa musical forms such as *cifras, estilos, milongas,* and *rancheras,* invariably used to set the mood while people display their skills. Some famous musicians often provide entertainment with their guitars for these events. At night, dancing marks the end of the celebration. Recordings are usually used, but instrumental ensembles occasionally accompany dances such as *chacarera, chamamé, gato, ranchera,* and *vals.*

Folkloric festivals (*festivales de folklore*) have occurred in Argentina since the late 1950s. The most important one, begun in 1960, takes place every year in Cosquín in the province of Córdoba. Similar festivals have appeared in neighboring countries. These festivals are competitions of singing, dancing, or both, usually celebrated annually in a consistent location under the auspices of local authorities. In addition to singing and dancing, the Cosquín competition features parallel events such as conferences, seminars, and craft-oriented fairs.

The music heard throughout a week by an enthusiastic crowd of about twenty-five thousand is not traditional, however, but revivalistic, composed in traditional styles by famous musicians who sometimes perform it themselves. A good performance in a competition like the Festival de Folklore de Cosquín can launch a performer's career at the national or international level, especially when followed by recordings and live appearances. The singer Mercedes Sosa started her career in this manner.

Though revivalist in intent, some folkloric repertoires reflect ideologies. A search for cultural and national identity marks the repertoires of the immigrant and of the nativist or traditionalist gaucho societies. These were formed in the late 1800s in defense of a nationality seen as endangered by the great European and Asian immigrations. They are still active preservers of the gaucho tradition, seen as the archetype of everything Argentine. Other ideologies are of a protest nature and can be seen in protest songs (*canciones de protesta*), which, partly as a consequence of the Cuban revolution of 1959, expanded throughout Latin America. Rock too became a vehicle for protest.

Public performances of traditional and popular musics can involve various scenarios. In rural areas, venues are set up for particular occasions, with buildings constructed from straw, canvas, or wood. As temporary structures, they provide spaces for nights of music and dancing after days of fairs. The structures where music and dance occur on a permanent basis acquire different names in different areas: *almacén, carpa, chichería,* and *ramada.* The music for these events may be recorded or live.

In urban areas, folk-derived music is performed in *peñas*—places where people of the same area meet, typical dances are performed, and local foods are consumed; they may be in the headquarters of traditionalist societies or in social or sports clubs. Some concerts by musicians of established fame take place in concert halls in large cities. Folk music reached its peak of popularity in the 1960s and has gradually lost its audience to national and international rock, which the middle and upper-middle class enjoy.

The so-called *música de proyección folklórica*, or simply 'folklore', is nothing more than the result of the process of urbanization of traditional rural repertoires that has occurred since the late 1800s. This was provoked by several internal and some external reasons. Internal reasons were the collection and documentation of traditional elements, the important activity of theater, circus, and *payadores* (singers of challenges and poets who sing with guitar), the emergence of musical nationalism, and the development of *peñas*. External reasons were the different streams of migration from Europe and Asia—streams that generated a local tendency to defend ethnic identity through music (Moreno Chá 1987). Since the 1920s, this process has been assisted by various official measures for the study, appreciation, and transmission of musical folklore and by internal migrations in which many rural inhabitants moved to the Buenos Aires metropolitan area in search of work. Aided by nationalistic fervor and governmental support, traditional music and culture have reached new geographical areas and social groups previously unfamiliar with them. Numerous ensembles (*conjuntos*) and instrumental groups of different kinds appeared, with repertoires not strictly traditional but based on traditional music. Different geographic areas were somewhat unequally represented by these groups, and there was a marked influence of the central and northwestern parts of the country.

Concurrently, between 1960 and 1965 a professionalization of composers and poets occurred, with an explosion of a movement known as the folklore boom. Famous singers, instrumentalists, and poets appeared widely on radio, television, and records. Theatrical events featuring music and dance were produced, the Festival de Folklore de Cosquín was founded, and several magazines covering the movement began to be published. The most famous magazine, *Folklore,* achieved a circulation of a hundred thousand in 1961. The most lasting and most internationally renowned works of the folklore revival were produced during this period. Perhaps the most representative work is the *Misa Criolla,* a musical setting of the mass composed by Ariel Ramírez and recorded with orchestra, chorus, and soloists on different occasions; one of the most outstanding performances was by the Spanish tenor José Carreras in 1990.

In the 1990s, the folklore revival experienced a soft revitalization, due in part to support by the national government through two radio stations—Radio Nacional and Radio Municipal. Folkloric music received a good amount of airplay on other radio stations (though little was on television) and was still performed in some of the more traditional festivals. It no longer had the widespread popularity that it did during the 1960s but is alive in the *peñas* and at family reunions of people with provincial roots. To a great extent, the repertoire is that of prior decades, performed by old and new musicians.

The most widely known folkloristic performers on the international stage who rose from this process—Eduardo Falú, Ariel Ramírez, Mercedes Sosa, Jaime Torres, and Atahualpa Yupanqui—remain influential through their recordings. Many of them attract audiences of a size that characterized this type of concert in its most glorious years.

Tango

Tango is music of nostalgia and melancholy, centered on one city—Buenos Aires. Its popularity peaked in the 1940s then declined, but in the 1980s began to rise again, nationally and internationally. It is a form of music and dance that in the late 1800s began to make its way through cafés, academies, halls for dancing, sites for dancing at carnival, theaters, variety shows, cabarets, and early recordings (Ferrer 1977). Today's tango continues to be danced in halls and clubs and is heard in *tanguerías,* a recent name for tango clubs given by its fans.

In its first stage of development, the tango did not reach the central locales of Buenos Aires but remained marginalized among lower-middle-class people and seedy characters. Beginning in 1912, political and social changes brought together various social classes in Buenos Aires. With the opening of cabarets downtown, the tango encountered more demanding venues, where it won not only new audiences but also new musicians who, being better trained, could make a living by playing it.

The early instrumentation of tangos included one *bandoneón* and two guitars; or a *bandoneón,* a violin, a flute, and a guitar; or a clarinet, a violin, and a piano; or a violin, a piano, and a *bandoneón*; or a similar trio or quartet. The 1920s saw the appearance of solo performers and the formation of the typical ensemble (*orquesta típica*): two violins, two *bandoneones,* a piano, and a string bass.

During the heyday of tango, different genres and expressions developed within the idiom. These included sung tangos (*tango canción* and *tango característico*), instrumental tangos (*tango romanza, milonga,* and others, performed by virtuosic ensembles), important lyrics, the appearance of prolific writers (such as Pascual Contursi and Celedonio Flores), and male and female singers who acquired tremendous popularity, of whom the most important was Carlos Gardel.

The most prominent musicians of this time were Julio De Caro, an icon in the development of the composition, arrangement, and performance of instrumental tangos, and Osvaldo Fresedo, who singlehandedly did away with the tango's chamber-music character (in which solo instruments were important) by consolidating the orchestra so groups of instruments were treated as single voices.

Since the 1980s, tango has been going through another phase of splendor and has occupied prominent places in such countries as Japan, Germany, and Finland.

The tango in the 1930s and later

The beginning of the 1930s was a difficult time for the tango and its musicians. Since most tango performances accompanied silent films, the arrival of movies with sound took away much of the market. From 1935 to 1950, however, the tango recovered its popularity and gained a new audience, particularly through the media of film and radio. Cabarets attracted a new audience, the middle class, which adopted the tango as its favorite dance because it acquired a stronger rhythm and became easier to dance. Instrumental parts continued to be treated homophonically (like voices in a chorus), and solos decreased.

The great orchestras of the 1930s and 1940s were those of Miguel Caló, Carlos Di Sarli, Enrique Mario Francini, Osmar Maderna, and Osvaldo Pugliese; major figures were Aníbal Troilo, Alfredo Gobbi, and Horacio Salgán. Singers acquired a new importance as soloists, because they began to sing all the lyrics rather than just the refrains. The vocalists Edmundo Rivero and Roberto Goyenche became highly popular.

The 1950s marked the end of tango's greatest creativity and popularity. It became associated with closed intellectual circles, which did not dance to it but listened to and studied it as a relic of earlier times. Beginning in 1955, however, a new stage of tango avant-garde began. It was headed by Astor Piazzolla and his octet: two *bandoneones*, two violins, piano, and electric guitar. New venues where the tango could be heard opened. These included Gotán 676, La Noche, and other clubs, frequented mainly by upper-middle-class *porteños* (people of the port, Buenos Aires) and international tourists.

The 1960s marked the appearance of Editorial Freeland, dedicated to the publication of the lyrics from the "golden age" of tango. Studies of dictionaries on the subject appeared, and the Academia Porteña del Lunfardo opened. It was a center for the study of the dialect (*lunfardo*) used by the social classes among which the tango originated and which is still used in some lyrics.

During the 1970s and especially in the 1980s, the tango had a resurgence, not so much in terms of new compositions but in the appearance of new singers and small instrumental ensembles (trios, quartets, sextets). The principal reason for this resurgence was tango's recovery as a dance. Since Piazzolla, beginning in 1955, the tango became just a music to listen to because of its rhythm. The success of tango shows abroad, especially *Tango Argentino* (Paris, 1983; Paris and Venice, 1984; Broadway, 1985), brought a renaissance of the dance in middle and high classes, especially in big Argentinian cities; however, much of the tango's popularity in Europe resulted from the international activity of Astor Piazzolla, Osvaldo Pugliese, Horacio Salgán, the Sexteto Mayor, and the singer Susana Rinaldi.

In 1990, the Academia Nacional del Tango (National Academy of Tango) was founded. Several scholars develop research on, preserve, and diffuse the tango through conferences, publications, courses, and concerts. Other factors were impor-

FIGURE 5   Two of the most outstanding tango dancers—Milena Plebs and Miguel Angel Zotto—in their show "Perfume de Tango" as performed at Sadler's Wells Theatre, London, 1993.

tant for tango's renewed popularity: the establishment in 1990 of FM Tango, a radio station dedicated exclusively to the genre, and the creation in 1991 of the University of the Tango of Buenos Aires, dedicated exclusively to the study of the tango from literary, historical, sociological, choreographic, and musical perspectives. Sólo Tango (Just Tango), the first TV channel devoted only to tango, was created in 1995.

Since the 1970s, tango as a dance has attracted the attention of important choreographers, including Maurice Béjart (Belgium), Dimitri Vassiliev (Russia), and Pina Bausch (Germany), and outstanding dancers, including Mikhail Baryshnikov (United States), Julio Bocca (Argentina), Milena Plebs, and Miguel Angel Zotto (figure 5).

Since the 1980s, tango has been going through another phase of splendor and has occupied prominent places in such countries as Japan, Germany, and Finland. In Argentina, it has been preserved by some sectors of Buenos Aires that never abandoned it and transmitted it by tradition. Tango began to obtain more visibility through films, literature, and research, and by embracing new audiences. These came from abroad and from the Argentinian middle and upper class, especially young people, anxious to learn from professional dancers called maestros (Moreno Chá 1995).

Tropical music

Caribbean music has been represented in Argentina since the 1960s by the *cumbia,* a Colombian dance, which became enormously popular. Ensembles such as Wawancó, Cuarteto Imperial, and Charanga del Caribe experienced such great success that their music, consisting mostly of *cumbias,* was widely recorded. Moreover, Caribbean music has been represented since the 1980s by genres like salsa, *son, guajira,* and reggae.

Caribbean-style music in Argentina is known generally as tropical music (*música tropical*). It gained popularity during the 1980s, and is heard in dance halls (*bailantas* or *bailables,* from *bailar* 'to dance') and in sport clubs and stadiums. In addition, the success of tropical music has revived an earlier genre, *música de cuarteto* or *música cuartetera,* which originated in the province of Córdoba and has become widely known because of the activities of the Cuarteto Leo [see CUARTETO, POP MUSIC OF ARGENTINA]. In the interior of the country, some ensembles do not hesitate to play a traditional melody to the rhythm of the *cumbia.*

Caribbean percussion is important as a defining element of tropical music. The genre may incorporate different mixtures of keyboards, accordion, electric bass, trumpets, trombones, saxophones, and other European-derived instruments. The lyrics are short, simple, and repetitive, and straightforwardly deal with dancing and love.

In Buenos Aires and its suburbs, a hundred thousand people visit no less than eighty tropical music venues every weekend, contributing to the proliferation of tropical music. The people who frequent these locales are of the middle and lower-middle classes, and the success of tropical music in the resorts of Mar del Plata and Pinamar and in the Uruguayan Punta del Este since the summer of 1990–1991 showed that the higher classes also enjoy this music.

The success of recordings has accompanied the popularity of this music. Each LP disk by popular singers such as Ricky Maravilla and Alcides surpasses two hundred thousand in sales. Two recording companies, Magenta and Leader Music, are dedicated to tropical music, and they produce vinyl discs at a cost one-third that of multinational record companies. Although the composers are unknown to the general public, they often share the credit with the performer who records the music for the first time.

The tropical music of the dance halls has enjoyed a boom that goes beyond the music to reach its typical locales, its own record labels, its specialized magazines, and its FM radio stations (Radio Fantástica and Radio Tropical) dedicated exclusively to the genre. It is a massive phenomenon based primarily on the desire for amusement through dancing, in couples or large groups, to sounds and lyrics that denote simple and contagious joy, often shared by entire families. It has variants defined by the origin of its principal performers and its fusion with traditional local genres. Some refrains of popular songs are sung, with adapted lyrics, at soccer matches.

Rock

Other popular musics, national and international, are danced to nightly in locales known as discos, *disquerías,* or boîtes, in social and sports clubs, and are heard in open-air or enclosed stadiums. These styles, known in Spanish by the English word "rock," have become most widespread in the mass media.

Argentine rock began about 1965 under the name *música progresiva nacional* 'progressive national music', in an attempt to differentiate it from the commercial music of the time and from British and American rock. Like those forms, it began as a young people's musical expression, challenging adult culture. The first stage in its development saw tension between an international rock-blues style and protest music based on urban concerns directed at a working-class audience (Vila 1989). It included a fusion of tango, jazz, and Argentine folklore dealing with lyric, personal themes. This stage reached its peak with the development of an ideology that sought to identify with the working class and resist the military dictatorship then in power. This ideology made rock a movement in which young people sought to construct their identity during the fifteen years when military dictatorships blocked or diverted their channels of expression.

Argentine rock thus attracted another audience, now not only from the working class but from the middle class also, and between 1975 and 1977 it typically incorporated Brazilian music, tango, Argentine–Latin American musical folklore, jazz, English rock, traditional rock, and ballads. This peculiar combination, which included a search for identity, different musical genres, and protest ideology, gave the movement great originality; however, it lost its meaning when the political stage again changed.

In 1981, university student organizations began to function once more, and young people were again able to participate in political parties. At that point, some national bands began to deal with the traditional themes of international rock for the first time, with lyrics centered on the body and leisure. This created a crisis in the movement, aggravated by the intervention of the recording industry and its broadcasting capabilities.

Then in 1982, the war over the Malvinas (Falkland Islands), claimed by both Argentina and the United Kingdom, provoked the prohibition of any music sung in English. From then on, *rock nacional* began to gain the airplay that for years had eluded it: television and recording studios at last opened their doors to it without reservation. Finally, the arrival of democracy in 1983 saw a flowering of new musical styles, and the movement lost the need to keep its branches united.

Since the 1970s, *rock nacional* has received the support of the written press through magazines such as *Pelo, Expreso Imaginario, Mordisco,* and *Estornudo*; but whereas radio programs have been dedicated to the genre since 1972, the support of radio stations was generally lacking. This changed in 1985, with the magazine *Rock & Pop,* followed by the appearance of additional magazines and inserts in the most widely distributed newspapers in Buenos Aires.

Other factors that played an important role in the development and popularity of *rock nacional* are related to technological advances. The amplification and electrification of musical instruments from the United States, Japan, and England; the development of recording studios with new resources; and festivals that incorporated high-tech sound-and-lighting effects attracted ever more enthusiastic followers.

Rock nacional has always incorporated different styles, such as pop, heavy metal, blues, folk, symphonic rock, tango rock, jazz rock, new wave, folklore rock, techno, reggae, and rap. Many of these styles were influenced by styles current in England and America and by the concerts of its famous performers in the large cities. Others had more local roots.

Rock nacional is no longer a locally Argentine phenomenon. Since about 1990, it has been the third most exported national variety of rock—after those of the United States and the United Kingdom (Vila 1989:1). It has had success in other Latin American countries. The existence of about six hundred bands and soloists and the production of more than five hundred recordings attest to the development of this genre.

In Argentina, *rock nacional* competes with British and American rock, which attracts a high-economic-level audience that can understand English. This music benefits from a great amount of airplay and record distribution, and the important support of music videos, broadcast nationally on Argentine television and internationally on cable television—including MTV, Music 21, and Much Music.

The displacement of *rock nacional* by imported music has been notable since 1988. In 1989, 9.23 percent of the music broadcast on the ten privately owned radio stations in Buenos Aires was sung in Spanish, Portuguese, or other languages, whereas 90.77 percent was sung in English. In the 1990s, this situation continued, improving the presence of U.S. rock groups and U.S. alternative music like that of Pearl Jam.

National and international rock (represented by famous performers from the United States and England) are featured in numerous festivals and concerts, and Argentine and foreign musicians often share the same stage. The festivals that take place every year in Buenos Aires, Córdoba, and elsewhere are special occasions that

Through censorship, the military governments impeded the activities of some folk musicians because of the musicians' sympathies with leftist ideologies.

occur in theaters and stadiums.

Argentina's audience for rock tries to identify itself with artists through appearance, dress, haircuts, and other details. Fans are young and strongly enthusiastic, often participating in concerts by singing along, clapping, swaying to the rhythm, showing approval by whistling, and lighting cigarette lighters. Some of these manifestations have become common in folk-music concerts, when musicians incite enthusiasm with their rhythms and lyrics.

The music-video industry began in Argentina in 1985 with local stars such as Soda Stereo, Virus, and Charly García. Though its product has seen success in Europe and the United States, the industry has not yet reached maturity. In the opinion of producers of videos, the reason for such underdevelopment in this part of the music business is the lack of economic support, despite the existence of numerous television programs dedicated to the genre. There are ten recording studios in Buenos Aires, but many of them cannot carry out the entire process of production.

ENCULTURATION AND LEARNING

The people of indigenous cultures teach and learn music informally and orally; voluntary repetition and the example of more experienced musicians are the most widespread methods of learning.

Indigenous cultures have another method, that of shamans, who believe in the gift of song from supernatural beings or ancestors. One of the most rigorous processes of learning is that of the Mapuche shaman. Among Protestant and African-Brazilian religious groups, learning is also informal, voluntary, and aural.

Among performers of popular music, learning for commercial distribution is unique. It usually occurs in formal settings. The level of expectation is greatest in the genres of rock and tango, and much less in tropical music, in which many musicians play by ear and barely read music.

The 1990s saw the rise of institutions that provided training in popular music. The Taller Latinoamericano de Música Popular (Latin American Popular Music Workshop), with headquarters in Rosario, has as its purpose the development of popular musicians and the awakening of critical and creative attitudes in composers, performers, teachers, journalists, and listeners. To train musicians of jazz, tango, and folk in a four-year program, the Escuela para Instrumentistas de Música Popular de América Latina (School for Instrumentalists in Popular Music of Latin America) was created in 1985 in Avellaneda, a suburb of Buenos Aires. In reality, however, pop musicians get their musical training almost exclusively from private teachers, sometimes the most famous musicians in the field, who own and operate workshops or labs for that purpose.

Another kind of institution eases the study of folk music: the secondary school with an artistic focus. In addition to studies leading to the *bachillerato* (high-school diploma), these schools offer specialization in different artistic fields, including folk-derived dance. Something similar takes place at the National Schools of Dance, where the same specialty is offered. All the schools of music have some course about traditional music of Argentina, and one of the most important ones, the Conservatorio Municipal, offers a career in ethnomusicology. In addition to a systemized pedagogical approach, some social and sports clubs and traditionalist societies offer training in the same areas.

Courses in musicology are offered at the university level. The Universidad Católica Argentina offers a major in musicology, in which students study music of oral traditions and others. Similar subjects are taught in the fields of arts or humanities at other universities. In general, however, the faculties of Argentine universities treat these subjects from highly theoretical and Western viewpoints.

MUSICAL CHANGE

During the twentieth century, traditional music in rural areas has been touched in varying degrees by three great events: the arrival of Protestantism, the European and Asian migrations, and the appearance of radio and television. European immigrant communities living in rural Argentina since about 1900—Germans, Greeks, Italians, Jews, Lithuanians, Spaniards, and others—have gained influence by introducing particular musical instruments, most notably the accordion, and styles of dancing. However, Chinese and Japanese immigrants (who came in the 1930s) have maintained the music and dances of their respective home countries as means of cultural identification. Rarely have their expressions reached wider audiences.

Because of newly introduced musical genres, mass communication has been the most profound agent of change in rural Argentina. Typical rural instrumental ensembles began to disappear, replaced by records and cassettes of folk and fashionable international musics.

These factors of change had consequences that differed from one place to another. In the northwest Andean area, the native tritonic scale disappeared, native pentatonic and criollo heptatonic major-minor scales yielded to European major and minor scales, and singing in parallel thirds gradually disappeared. In the central and northeastern area, European salon dances (such as the polka, the mazurka, and the waltz) were introduced in the early 1800s and become extremely popular. These changes initiated a process of creolization, resulting in genres with truly local traits. One of them, the polka, gave birth to other genres, such as the *chamamé* and the *rasgueado doble*. Since the 1970s, the *chamamé* has been the only traditional Argentinian music and dance form that is expanding, is spreading more and more (figures 6 and 7). It has even reached southern Chile.

Some Argentine governments have ignored the political aspect of music, but others have paid attention to it. Among the latter have been those of strong nationalistic and populist character, such as the Peron regime, which mandated the broadcasting of a certain percentage of music of national origin over all radio stations and in all places of entertainment. In 1949, a minimum of 50 percent of Argentine music was required to be aired; in 1969, that mandate was reiterated. In 1971, the proportion was increased to 70 percent, with the specification that this amount was to be divided equally between urban, folk, and "modern" musics. After 1983, with the return of democracy, all these requirements were abrogated.

Because rock was associated with subversive ideas, additional governmental actions included the suppression of rock concerts. Through censorship, the military governments impeded the activities of some folk musicians because of the musicians' sympathies with leftist ideologies. In contrast, the creation of a tango orchestra in the

FIGURE 6   Ivoti, one of the best-known bands dedicated to *chamamé*. Corrientes, 1995.

Subsecretariat for Culture dates from 1938, and in 1980 the first musicological study of tango (*Antología del Tango Rioplatense*) was published—by a state agency, the Instituto Nacional de Musicología "Carlos Vega."

Since the early 1990s, music of all types has been broadcast on about 2,100 radio stations and 330 television channels in Argentina. Especially important is the Servicio Oficial de Radiodifusión (SOR), made up of LRA Radio Nacional and its forty affiliates, and the Argentina Televisora Color (ATC) television channel. About another 470 closed-circuit channels and several cable broadcasts come from Europe and the rest of America.

—TRANSLATED BY TIMOTHY D. WATKINS

FIGURE 7   Wearing clothes typical of rural areas of Corrientes, a couple dances the *chamamé*. Photo by Jorge Prelorán, 1964.

REFERENCES

Aretz, Isabel. 1954. *Costumbres tradicionales argentinas.* Buenos Aires: Huemul.

Barco Centenera, Martín del. 1836. "La Argentina o la conquista del Río de la Plata." In *Colección de Obras y Documentos Relativos a la Historia Antigua y Moderna de la Provincias del Rio de la Plata,* ed. Pedro de Angelis, 2:183–332. Buenos Aires: Plus Ultra.

Baucke, Florian. 1942–1944. *Hacia allá y para acá: Una estada entre los indios Mocobíes, 1749–1767.* 4 vols. Tucumán and Buenos Aires: Universidad Nacional de Tucumán.

Chapman, Anne, ed. 1972. *Selk'nam Chants of Tierra del Fuego, Argentina.* Ethnic Folkways FE 4176. 2 LP disks.

———. 1978. *Selk'nam Chants of Tierra del Fuego, Argentina.* Ethnic Folkways Records FE 4179. 2 LP disks.

Cortázar, Augusto Raúl. 1959. "Usos y costumbres." *Folklore Argentino,* ed. José Imbelloni et al., 158–196. Buenos Aires: Nova.

Despard, George Pakenham, ed. 1854. *Hope Deferred, Not Lost: A Narrative of Missionary Effort in South America, in Connection with the Patagonian Missionary Society.* 2nd ed. London: J. Nisbet.

Díaz de Guzmán, Ruy. 1969–1972 [1612]. "Historia argentina del descubrimiento, población y conquista de las Provincias del Río de la Plata." In *Colección de Obras y Documentos Relativos a la Historia Antigua y Moderna de la Provincias del Rio de la Plata,* ed. Pedro de Angelis, 1:11-111. Buenos Aires: Plus Ultra.

Dobrizhoffer, Martin. 1784. *Historia de Aiponibus Equestri: Bellicosaque Paraguariae Natione.* 3 vols. Vienna: Kurzbek.

Faulkner, Thomas. 1935 [1774]. *A Description of Patagonia and the Adjoining Parts of South America.* Chicago: Armann and Armann.

Ferrer, Horacio. 1977. *El libro del tango.* 2 vols. Buenos Aires: Galerna.

Frigerio, Alejandro. 1991. "Umbanda o Africanismo en Buenos Aires: Duas etapas de un mesmo caminho religioso." *Comunicações do ISER* 35:52–63.

Furlong, Charles Wellington. 1909. "The Southernmost People of the World." *Harper's Monthly Magazine* 119(June).

Gallardo, Carlos R. 1910. *Tierra del Fuego: Los Onas.* Buenos Aires: Cabaut y Cía.

Gallardo, Jorge Emilio. 1986. *Presencia africana en la Cultura de América Latina: Vigencia de los cultos afroamericanos.* Buenos Aires: Fernando García Cambeiro.

García, Silvia. 1978. "La fiesta de San Juan en la Provincia de Formosa." *Cuadernos del Instituto Nacional de Antropología* 8:125–148.

Grebe, María Ester. 1979–1980. "Relaciones entre música y cultura: El kultrún y su simbolismo." *Revista INIDEF* 4:7–25.

Hernández, Juán Antonio. 1910 [1836]. "Diario que el capitán . . . ha hecho de la expedición contra los indios teguelches." In *Colección de Obras y Documentos Relativos a la Historia Antigua y Moderna de la Provincias del Rio de la Plata,* ed. Pedro de Angelis, 4:547–563. Buenos Aires: Librería Nacional.

Kereilhac de Kussrow, Alicia. 1980. *La fiesta de San Baltasar.* Buenos Aires: Ediciones Culturales Argentinas.

Lothrop, Samuel Kirkland. 1928. *The Indians of Tierra del Fuego.* New York: Museum of the American Indian, Heye Foundation.

Lozano, Pedro. 1874–1875. *Historia de la conquista del Paraguay, Río de la Plata y Tucumán.* 5 vols. Buenos Aires: Imprenta Popular.

Moreno, S. J. 1890–1891. "Exploración arqueológica de la provincia de Catamarca." *Revista del Museo de La Plata,* vol. 1.

Moreno Chá, Ercilia. 1971. "Semana Santa en Yavi." *Cuadernos del Instituto Nacional de Antropología* 7:1971.

———. 1987. "Alternativas del Proceso de Cambio de un Repertorio Tradicional Argentino." *Latin American Music Review* 8(1):94–111.

———, ed. 1995. *Tango tuyo, mío y nuestro.* Buenos Aires: Instituto Nacional de Antropología y Pensamiento Latinoamericano.

Morris, Isaac. 1750. *A Narrative of the Dangers and Distresses Which Befell Isaac Morris, and Seven More of the Crew. . . .* London: S. Birt.

Olsen, Dale A. 1980. "Folk Music of South America: A Musical Mosaic." In *Musics of Many Cultures: An Introduction,* ed. Elizabeth May (Berkeley: University of California Press), 386–425.

d'Orbigny, Alcide Dessalines. 1835–1847. *Voyage dans l'Amérique méridionale.* 7 vols. Paris: Pitois-Levrault.

Pérez Bugallo, Rubén. 1982. "Estudio etnomusicológico de los chiriguano-chané de la Argentina: Primera parte: Organología." *Cuadernos del Instituto Nacional de Antropología* 9:221–268.

———. 1993. *Pillantún: Estudios de etnoorganología patagónica y pampeana.* Buenos Aires: Búsqueda de Ayllu.

Pigafetta, Antonio. 1800 [1534]. *Primo viaggio intorno al globo terracqueo.* Milan and Paris: Amoretti.

Robertson, Carol E. 1979. "Pulling the Ancestors: Performance Practice and Praxis in Mapuche Ordering." *Ethnomusicology* 23(3):395–416.

Roig, Elizabeth. 1990. "La música toba en el contexto de la Iglesia Evangélica Unida." Paper presented at the "Séptimas Jornadas Argentinas de Musicología" of the Instituto Nacional de Musicología "Carlos Vega," Buenos Aires.

Ruiz, Irma. 1984. "La ceremonia *ñemongaraí* de los Mbïá de la Provincia de Misiones." *Temas de Etnomusicología* 1:45–102.

Sánchez Labrador, Joseph. 1936 [1772]. *Paraguay cathólico: Los Indios Pampas—Puelches—Patagones.* Buenos Aires: Viau y Zona.

Segers, Polidoro A. 1891. "Tierra del Fuego: Hábitos y costumbres de los indios onas." *Boletín del Museo de Historia Natural* 19(5–6).

Transilvano, Maximiliano. 1837 [1829]. "Relación escrita por . . . de cómo y por quién y en qué tiempo fueron descubiertas y halladas las islas Molucas." In *Colección de los viajes y descubrimientos que hicieron por mar los españoles desde fines del siglo XV.* Madrid: Imprenta Nacional.

Vaulx, Comte Henri de la. 1898. "À travers la Patagonie du Río Negro au détroit de Magellan." *Journal de la Société des Américanistes* 6:71–99.

Vignati, María Emilia. 1982. "La música aborigen." *Historia General del Arte en la Argentina,* 1:58–102. Buenos Aires: Academic Nacional de Bellas Artes.

Vila, Pablo. 1989. "Argentina's *Rock Nacional*: The Struggle for Meaning." *Latin American Music Review* 10(1):1–28.

Zeballos, Estanislao S. 1881. *Descripción amena de la República Argentina: Viaje al país de los araucanos.* 3 vols. Buenos Aires: Peuser.

Cuarteto: Pop Music of Argentina
Jane L. Florine

History of *Cuarteto*
***Cuarteto* in the 1990s**
Musicians' Social Class and Behavior
The Recording Industry
Musical Aesthetics

Cuarteto, also called *música cuartetera* 'quartet music', is a pop or dance music from Córdoba, Argentina. Long considered to be low-class music by many Argentines, it is a mass, working-class phenomenon; almost twenty thousand people dance to it every weekend in the city of Córdoba alone, and thousands more dance to it in the province of Córdoba and in neighboring provinces. Upper-class elitists, who look down on it, often hypocritically use it to liven up their own private parties. Weekend dances in the city of Córdoba are most commonly held at large athletic clubs, with an average of fifteen hundred to three thousand people in attendance per evening, whereas dances held on weeknights take place in smaller locales, which hold about eight hundred people. Other common sites, especially outside Córdoba, are gymnasiums, schools, outdoor athletic fields, and renovated movie theaters. Dances, which last four hours, normally run from 12:30 A.M. to 4:30 A.M. on weekends.

Besides the regular weekend dances, *música cuartetera* is performed and danced to on various occasions: patron saints' or seasonal festivals, carnival, gypsy celebrations for the Blessed Virgin Mary, Mother's Day, birthdays, wedding receptions, antidrug campaigns, and political rallies. It is basically a pop music to which people dance to forget their worries and have fun. Its lyrics usually refer to love (at times with erotic overtones and double meanings), the joy of dancing, and daily life. It is not normally heard in a concert.

HISTORY OF *CUARTETO*

Cuarteto was "invented" in 1943, when Leonor Marzano of the Cuarteto Leo (the first *cuarteto* group) developed an accompanimental pattern, the characteristic and identifying feature of all *cuarteto* music, called the *tunga-tunga* (Hepp 1988:59–60, 67–68). This pattern is played by the piano and the string bass (figure 1). Since the original Cuarteto Leo consisted of four instruments (violin, accordion, string bass, and piano) plus a singer, the genre was named *cuarteto*. This ensemble was in fact a pared-down version of larger musical groups called *orquestas características* 'characteristic orchestras' that traveled about the countryside playing European-derived genres, such as fox-trots, *pasodobles, rancheras, tarantelas,* and *valses,* for Spanish and Italian immigrant communities. *Orquestas características* differed from *orquestas típicas* 'typi-

Cuarteto music is a lucrative, highly competitive business in Córdoba. Groups earn most of their money at dances, perhaps netting 30,000 pesos in a single weekend. Additional income comes from record sales and royalties.

FIGURE 1   Four possibilities for the *tunga-tunga*, the underlying accompanimental pattern of *cuarteto* music. The right hand of the piano plays the top line (the off-beats); the left hand of the piano and the bass play the bottom line. Examples *a* and *b* show the most typical way to play the accompaniment, with a downward perfect fourth in the bass; examples *c* and *d* show another pattern in which the bass leaps up a fourth or a fifth. Transcription by Jane L. Florine.

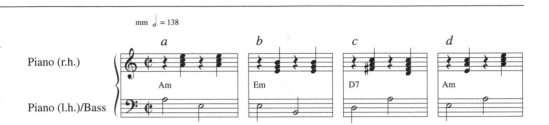

cal orchestras' (large ensembles that also traveled about the countryside), which mainly performed *milongas* and tangos. In the late 1950s, *orquestas características* began performing on the outskirts of Córdoba; later, in the 1970s, they penetrated the city itself.

Despite its apolitical nature, *cuarteto* music has occasionally suffered setbacks at the hands of government leaders. It was banned for a time after the 1976 military coup (Barei 1993:46), and recordings of it were removed from record stores in Córdoba during the World Cup of 1978 so tourists would not be exposed to it (Mero 1988:54–60).

CUARTETO IN THE 1990S

Though at times hundreds of *cuarteto* ensembles have been able to make a living simultaneously, only about forty remain active in Córdoba, where, in the late 1990s, three groups reign supreme: Chébere, Tru-la-lá, and Carlos "La Mona" (The Monkey) Jiménez. Over the years, *cuarteto* groups have evolved in instrumentation, style, and number of members. Though they are still called *cuartetos*, groups are now bands or orchestras usually having from eight to thirteen performers. Two of these performers are normally singers: one does *tropical* 'Caribbean-influenced' tunes, and the other sings *moderno* 'modern' genres (rock, jazz, and ballad-influenced selections). At times, as in the case of Carlos Jiménez, one singer covers all four hours of dances. Another of the performers is an announcer (*locutor*), who reads greetings and messages passed to him by members of the audience; this gives the dances a feeling of intimacy.

Instruments currently used by *cuarteto* groups are a combination of electronic keyboards or synthesizers, electric piano, electric guitar, electric bass guitar, Latin percussion, drum set, brass, and accordion. Only traditional-minded groups, such as that of Carlos Jiménez, maintain the use of the accordion; the style associated with this type of instrumentation is called *cuarteto-cuarteto*, which means "authentically *cuarteto*-style *cuarteto* music." Chébere, the group considered as having the most evolved style (so evolved that it may not be *cuarteto* music, say some people), has two trumpets and two trombones. Use of the other available instruments depends on each group's repertoire and style.

FIGURE 2   Recordings of *cuarteto* music, including *El Marginal* by Carlos Jiménez, displayed in the main window of the MJ Musical record store on San Martín Street in downtown Córdoba. Photo by Jane L. Florine, 1995.

On the road: traveling musicians

Cuarteto music is a lucrative, highly competitive business in Córdoba. Groups earn most of their money at dances (box-office receipts after taxes), perhaps netting 30,000 pesos (one peso equals one U.S. dollar) in a single weekend; additional income comes from record sales and royalties (figure 2). Publicity for dances, in the form of commercials on special radio programs and video clips on television, can cost from four to five thousand pesos per week. Though the financial rewards are high, groups must follow grueling schedules to prosper. Many bands travel to perform at sites outside Córdoba every weekend; only the three most important groups are successful in obtaining steady engagements in the city. Members travel in one or two buses (one is for sound or lighting personnel and handlers); they often meet at a central location downtown, get picked up, drive to a site hours away, have dinner together, play a dance, and return to Córdoba, all in the same evening. If dances are close by, they go in their own cars to save time. Though groups often follow this schedule from Friday through Sunday (the groups play in a different city or location each night and return to Córdoba after each performance), they play dances as many as six nights a week during the summer months. When bands go on tour, they sometimes stay in hotels. Some groups travel to Buenos Aires to perform in dance halls called *bailantas*; this has happened since 1988, when Carlos Jiménez and *cuarteto* music became known nationally after a huge crowd of fans got out of control during a Jiménez performance at the National Folklore Festival in Cosquín, Córdoba. (Since many people do not classify *cuarteto* as folk music, the genre was first heard at this annual festival only in 1987; because of the Jiménez episode, it has not been allowed there since 1988.) In Buenos Aires, *cuarteto* groups do not play in one locale for four hours, as they do in Córdoba; they normally play in as many as six or seven locales per evening for about forty-five minutes to an hour at each one.

Cuarteto fans are extremely loyal and normally follow only one group; some wear special hats and headbands with the names of their favorite group on them, and one official fan club exists—for the singer Gary and his band. The fans' social class depends on the band that they follow. For example, Chébere is noted for attracting university students whereas Jiménez crowds are from more disadvantaged populations. Many fans dance with their chosen group three or four nights a week, often

FIGURE 3   Carlos Jiménez strikes a typical pose as he sings at a *cuarteto* dance. Photo by Jane L. Florine, 1995.

FIGURE 4   A boy whose parents hope will someday be a *cuarteto* singer performs on stage with the band Tru-la-lá. He holds a tambourine in his right hand, sings into a plastic microphone, and wears an outfit made in the style of the bandsmen's uniforms. Photo by Jane L. Florine, 1995.

traveling to nearby cities to do so. Groups of friends, often girls, go together; it is the number of girls at a dance that makes or breaks it. In Córdoba, most dancers, except at special clubs for older people, are under thirty; more families attend dances outside of town than in Córdoba. Girls may dance with other girls, and old people with young people. People dance in small circles, in couples, or in the big "wheel" (*la rueda*) that rotates counterclockwise, like a solid disc of humanity, out on the dance floor. Fans buy recordings released by their favorite group(s), learn the lyrics, and sing along at dances. Especially before dances, they listen to special fan-oriented programs on FM stations. They normally buy recordings on San Martín Street, particularly at the record store MJ Musical (see figure 2). Older recordings are available for bargain prices at many stores on San Martín Street.

Dances normally feature four sets of music, which alternate between *moderno* and *tropical* styles (singers thus take turns) of about forty-five minutes each (Jiménez sings only the *cuarteto-cuarteto* style, however); at the end of the second *moderno* section, a lyric piece without the *tunga-tunga* might be performed. Recordings of *cuarteto* music are put on by a disc jockey during breaks, when fans buy alcoholic beverages, eat *choripan* (sausage sandwiches), and chat with the musicians. During breaks, bandsmen go to the bar and socialize with the public. Girls are often waiting to talk with them, especially when the dances are over. Those present at dances commonly have sexual encounters at nearby locations or hotels afterward.

Cuarteto personnel

Many different types of people are involved in the functioning of a *cuarteto* group. Musically speaking, members of the *cuarteto* world commonly label band personnel (those seen up on stage) in the following categories: owners (*dueños*), arrangers, singers, musicians, and announcers. Each person's level of musical influence usually falls into the same order; however, since there are cases in which some people fulfill multiple roles, the importance of individual members varies from group to group. For example, an owner who serves only as the announcer for his group will not have as much musical power as an owner who is the arranger, solo singer, and keyboard player of his own group. Behind the scenes, *cuarteto* groups employ orchestra managers, administrative personnel in charge of promotion and publicity, box-office personnel, drivers, lighting and sound-equipment men, and handlers (*plomos*, who carry, set up, and take down the equipment).

Women are seldom seen in *cuarteto* groups. Except for the singer Noelia, who has had some success, and two female choral singers in Gary's group, the *cuarteto* world is a male one. Since many owners believe musicians must look good and perform well (to attract female dancers), most men on stage are between the age of twenty and thirty, are physically attractive, and often have long hair (figure 3). Some veteran groups are made up of older performers, however, and one features children. Two unpaid boys often sing on stage with Tru-la-lá. The boys' parents, who want them to become famous *cuarteto* singers, bring them to dances to sing and play percussive instruments (such as tambourines) so they will learn the trade. These parents set up plastic microphones for their sons to sing into and have outfits in the style of bandsmen's uniforms made for them (figure 4). Though musicianship, by recommendation or audition, is always a criterion for hiring, a prospective musician-singer must be a *buena persona* 'good person'. In addition, since bandsmen spend much more time with their groups than they do with their own families, prospective members must be willing to adapt to a group's policies, personality, and musical style. They must come to all rehearsals and dances (or send a substitute if there is an emergency), be on time, not smoke on stage, and not drink to excess.

Owners are by far the most powerful and hard-working individuals in the *cuarteto* world. Since they have often had to invest or borrow as much as three hundred thousand pesos to start a group, they have a lot at stake; they keep most of the profits and pay other group members by the dance (group members do not get paid for canceled or rained-out dances). Some owners are singers who have broken away from other groups to try to make it as soloists. If not, they are normally performers in their own groups, and they arrange and compose. Owners often run their own offices and perform numerous administrative duties. They pick all personnel and establish group policy. Since *cuarteto* groups are incorporated companies and most group members are employees, owners must deal with issues such as taxes, salaries, benefits, retirement pay, and vacation time. Besides hiring personnel and establishing group policies, they must arrange everything that pertains to promotion, scheduling, travel, buses, equipment (sound and lighting), publicity (radio and television, in Córdoba and in other locations), uniforms (each group has several, often matching jackets and pants or shirts and pants), rehearsals, repertoire, recording, distribution, record companies, and record stores. They must keep up on new developments and trends in the music business, local and international.

Arrangers may or may not perform with the groups with whom they work. Besides composing, making musical arrangements, and copying parts by hand, they often conduct rehearsals. Since arrangers establish the musical sound of their groups, their own musical backgrounds influence group styles. Some groups, such as that of Carlos Jiménez, use no group arranger at all. Arrangers can suggest tunes for their groups to perform or record, but often the owners tell them what to arrange. In some instances, arrangers have great power in the recording studio, especially when they make demos (sequences are used to prepare most of the instrumental voices of the tunes) that subsequently serve as the basis of their groups' commercial recordings. In these cases, only the singers and a few musicians record live over what the arranger has prepared. By not having all group members record live, owners save in studio costs and time.

Though they often have little or no musical training, singers are normally more important in *cuarteto* groups than sidemen (accompanying musicians) or announcers, even if they are not soloists or owners. A successful singer is usually paid more than a sideman because it is his charisma that brings girls to the dances; since he is harder to replace, he is worth more. Though musicians' turnover in *cuarteto* groups is fairly high, especially as new groups are born and others die, singers often leave groups because entrepreneurs lure them away. Solo singers who own their own groups often dress as they please rather than in group uniforms, and only their faces appear on record covers (as opposed to shots of the entire group); they are free to make their own rules. For example, Carlos Jiménez (figure 3) dresses in the style of Elvis Presley in tight outfits with sequins, embroidery, and bright colors, and moves all over the stage. But Gary (whose real name is Edgardo Fuentes), despite having a *tropical* singer in his group (also called Gary), does all his recordings by himself. Singers, whether soloists or not, and musicians often compose tunes for their groups.

Announcers normally have small musical roles in *cuarteto* groups. Like singers, they may play percussion instruments when they are on stage. They may choose the selections to be performed during the evening, depending on the climate of the dance. If they are also owners or musicians, they can be influential in repertoire selection and composition of new tunes for the group.

MUSICIANS' SOCIAL CLASS AND BEHAVIOR

Most *cuarteto* owners, arrangers, singers, musicians, and announcers are from the city

Musicians who belong to groups that always play by ear feel they can be highly creative. Many say that they could not work in a group in which they were told to play what was on a written page.

of Córdoba. Though the remainder are mostly from the province of Córdoba, there are in the groups a few foreigners—from Brazil, Peru, Ecuador, and the Dominican Republic. Contrary to what many inhabitants of Córdoba believe, *cuarteto* group members are neither men who were born in the slums nor frustrated individuals who have gone into *cuarteto* music because they could not make it as soccer players. The social class, educational level, and musical training of members vary from group to group, but general observations can be made about the backgrounds of *cuarteto* personnel. Most of the men are not from musical families. Some attended dances when they were small, but many did so only because they were already performing at them, even at the age of ten. Many *cuarteto* members attended their first dance only when they began playing with their present groups. Though some older members have finished only primary school (they dropped out to work), most have finished high school. Many have begun, but not finished, university programs. Despite their heavy schedules, a few are still university or conservatory students and/or have second jobs. Several have degrees in music, but the musical training of most includes a combination of private lessons, music school or conservatory lessons, and participation in youth military bands (as brass players)—most of them read music to some degree. Most say they like what they do, but given a choice, most would rather play music other than *cuarteto* to make their living. Among their choices would be jazz, rock (most *cuarteto* guitarists have rock backgrounds), salsa, boleros, Argentine folk music, and Latin ballads. They listen to all styles of music in their free time and try to use these influences in their playing and composing. Since playing *cuarteto* music is almost the only way musicians can make a living in Córdoba (rock, folk, and jazz have not caught on), men who start in the *cuarteto* business normally remain with it for a long time; jobs in other lines of work do not pay so well.

Cuarteto musicians do not normally work their way up the ranks to positions of greater musical power. Though percussionists have learned how to play keyboards and/or other instruments by ear, most orchestra managers, handlers, and sound or lighting personnel are those who sometimes get "promoted" by being turned into musicians (players of congas or timbales, for example) or announcers.

On days they are not working with their groups (usually Mondays, Tuesdays, and Wednesdays), bandsmen must take care of their personal business and family affairs. Some can often be seen in downtown Córdoba in the *cuarteto* district, an area of a few blocks, especially in the Bon Que Bon bar, where bandsmen go to talk and exchange gossip. In better economic times, when many more *cuarteto* bands were performing in Córdoba and often needed substitute performers, people could hear about work opportunities at the Bon Que Bon. Owners are frequently seen downtown on their days off, since they must pay nearby radio stations and arrange for publicity. They may be seen at Rango TV, where their television commercials are usually made. It is common to see many people waiting in *cuarteto* offices on Tuesdays and Wednesdays—the only sure way to talk with owners.

Making Musical Decisions

The musical contribution that any one group member can make is largely determined by the group owner's (or owners') personality or style of management; a group member can make a contribution only if he is allowed to. Whether or not a group plays by ear affects an individual's musical influence. The impact of these factors can be seen in choice of repertoire, rehearsals, compositional style, performances, recording sessions, and aesthetics.

A group's repertoire is generally chosen by its owners, but other group members often suggest covers (of local, Latin American, and international hits) that can be adapted to the *tunga-tunga*. If the original lyrics are in English, they are translated into Spanish. Some groups introduce new cover tunes weekly at their dances so as always to have something new to offer their fans. Some groups, however, perform almost no covers; they prefer to do original material. When the time to cut records comes, the groups that mix covers and new material in their dances more often than not record both kinds of songs. Since musical royalties are lucrative, these might be tunes composed largely by an owner or a local composer. In many groups, however, owners encourage bandsmen to contribute their own compositions; by allowing their employees to earn money in royalties and contribute musically, they boost morale and lower the level of frustration. Owners who encourage contributions from their group members feel that it is wise to choose the best material—what will sell—instead of worrying about how much they will make in royalties. Many believe that eleven or twelve persons working together can come up with better ideas than can one person.

When new pieces are offered to owners, even by group members, they are normally presented in the form of demos. Nowadays, few tunes are presented sung only to piano or guitar accompaniment. Once the tunes for the next recording have been chosen, the group arranger and owner often switch around the lyrics and some arrangements; if this happens, they are listed on the recording as being partial composers of the song. In rehearsals, group members sometimes have a chance to modify newly chosen repertoire; at times, they give ideas for solos, breaks, introductions, and the like. The musicians of Carlos Jiménez are even expected to contribute ideas so as to enhance the repertoire; in this case, the compositional process is a collective one (the original composer's arrangement or demo is respected as much as possible, however).

Some groups try to rehearse once a week to add one or two new covers to their repertoire; in periods of extensive work, rehearsals are suspended. Other bands, for lack of time, rehearse only when they are getting ready to prepare a new recording; they often rehearse for ten to twelve hours a day for a few solid weeks to prepare and perfect the selections to be recorded. In the case of one ensemble, the final versions of tunes are invented live in the recording studio; when it performs at dances, the group then imitates what it has recorded. In groups that play with music, members try to be creative in rehearsals by working on ensemble playing, creating dance steps, and adding swing and stylistic knowledge to what is being performed. Musicians who belong to groups that always play by ear feel they can be highly creative; many say that they could not work in a group in which they were told to play what was on a written page, and even what timbre to add.

Even in groups that play with written-out parts, some individuals always perform by ear. The parts for piano, guitar, and bass often consist of no more than chord symbols (see figure 1); since the piano and the bass usually play the *tunga-tunga* accompaniment pattern and know what rhythms they must use, they do not need completely written-out parts. These musicians are allowed a certain amount of flexibility, with ostinato (*tumbao*) patterns in particular, so they can be more creative than group members who have every single note written out for them; however, after selections have been put together, no *cuarteto* music is improvised when it is performed. Before rehearsals, especially of covers, all the musicians listen to a tape of the selection(s) to be rehearsed. In some bands, these musicians are all expected to get their own parts off this recording by ear. It is common practice to ask percussionists and guitarists to imitate what they hear on recordings; percussionists are rarely given written-out parts. Singers are normally asked to get their lyrics off a tape they have listened to before rehearsals; they are not given written-out parts either.

THE RECORDING INDUSTRY

Groups that perform every weekend in Córdoba usually launch two recordings a year, on compact discs and cassettes; groups that play mostly outside the city usually release only one new recording a year. These discs are presented at special ceremonies, often complete with sets on stage, new uniforms, and other effects. A launching, with new material, is a type of rebirth, a shot in the arm for the public that constantly follows the groups. Recordings are often made in Buenos Aires, but are sometimes made in Córdoba. Chébere recorded a disc in Hollywood, California, however, and Gary is about to do the same. Some groups record live, one track at a time, and group members critique each other's performances. In other cases, however, demos of the new tunes are taken to the recording studio, and only the singers and a couple of musicians dub in their parts. Guest musicians, such as female singers or symphony musicians, may participate in these sessions. Mixing is normally done in Buenos Aires, usually by the owner-arrangers, but has been done in the United States. In the case of Carlos Jiménez, however, most of the musicians are consulted. The *cuarteto* recording industry is controlled by multinational companies, including BMG, Sony, and WEA, which handle local and international distribution, mostly to countries bordering Argentina. Chébere, which in 1995 signed a contract to have its discs distributed in the United States, reached the goal of all *cuarteto* artists: to conquer the international Latin music market, especially in the United States and Mexico (*Chébere* 1994).

MUSICAL AESTHETICS

Since the main aesthetic concern of *cuarteto* dancers is that the *tunga-tunga* be present in all *cuarteto* music, some owners feel limited in what they can do musically. At the same time, owners have another problem: their fans are constantly expecting them to come up with something new. (In fact, group members and fans get bored hearing the same repertoire for six months at a time, and they all want a change.) The constant need to have new material or ideas has created fierce competition among groups, and bands must keep up with the competition to retain their followers. To polish up *cuarteto* music, refine fans' musical tastes, and introduce changes, some owners have gone too far in their experimentation; they have lost their followers and have had to return to the generic *cuarteto* style to try to win them back. For this reason, owners are cautious with the novelties that they introduce; after all, *cuarteto* is a business venture. In 1994, one of the trends in *cuarteto* music was a risky one: Carlos Jiménez added Afro-Caribbean rhythms and percussion, mixing *cuarteto* with genres such as rap, conga, and *merengue* (Carlos Jiménez 1994). Then, in 1995, the band returned to the traditional *cuarteto* style (Carlos Jiménez 1995). Since Carlos Jiménez, despite the temporary use of African rhythms, is the last follower of the traditional *cuarteto* style, there is much speculation regarding the future of *música cuartetera* when Carlos retires. Indeed, change, competition, and commodification are the driving forces of pop music in Argentina, Latin America, and throughout the industrialized world.

REFERENCES

Barei, Silvia N. 1993. *El sentido de la fiesta en la cultura popular: los cuartetos de Córdoba*. Córdoba, Argentina: Alción Editora.

Carlos Jiménez. 1994. *Raza Negra*. BMG 74321–23116–2. Compact disc.

———. 1995. *El Marginal*. BMG 74321–30538–2. Compact disc.

Chebere. 1994. *Chébere*: A. C. E. '94. Clave Records CD 51413. Comapct disc.

Hepp, Osvaldo. 1988. *La soledad de los cuartetos*. Córdoba, Argentina: Editorial Letra.

Mero, Roberto. 1988. *La Mona, va! Carlos Jiménez y el fenómeno social del cuarteto*. Buenos Aires: Editorial Contrapunto.

Tru-la-lá. 1995. *Trulalazo*. BMG 74321-29135-2, Compact disc.

Bolivia
Henry Stobart

More than 75 percent of Bolivia's population of some 6.5 million lives in the highlands, an area dominated by the cold, high central plain (Spanish *altiplano* 'high plain'). At an altitude of 4 kilometers, the *altiplano* is bordered by two steep mountain ranges. The western cordillera follows the border with Chile, and the eastern cordillera drops through intermontane valleys toward the Amazon basin. The hot, eastern lowlands, which make up more than 60 percent of the country's area, are much less densely populated and comprise plains and tropical forest.

The official national languages are Spanish (spoken by 87 percent of the population), Quechua (34 percent), and Aymara (23 percent) (van Lindert and Verkoren 1994:72–73). In the lowlands, some forty Amerindian languages (including Guaraní, Moxo, and Yurakaré) are spoken, but mainly by small, dispersed groups [see MOXO]. With Peru, Bolivia is notable among South American countries for the strongly native American aspects of its culture and population [see QUECHUA AND AYMARA].

EARLY MUSICAL ACTIVITY

The archaeological record

Archaeological evidence of musical activity in the Andean highlands of Bolivia is poorly preserved in comparison with the wealth from early Peruvian coastal cultures. The earliest finds, said to date from 900 B.C. to A.D. 300, include clay panpipes, vessel flutes, and three-holed bone notch flutes. These are on deposit in the university museum at Cochabamba.

Tiwanaku (Tiahuanacu, Tiawanaku), at its height around A.D. 1000, was one of the most important early highland cultures, centered a few kilometers south of Lake Titicaca. The *zampoñero,* a large stone statue found there (kept in the Gold Museum, La Paz), is believed to represent a man holding a panpipe to his lips. Other finds include three bronze figurines depicting musicians holding end-blown flutes, a drum, and a four-tubed panpipe (Díaz Gainza 1988), and what appears to be a workshop for constructing panpipes.

The mythological record

A creation myth recorded by the seventeenth-century Spanish priest and chronicler

Bernabé Cobo (1990 [1653]) tells how humans were fashioned from mud at Tiwanaku, each endowed with language to sing their multiplicity of songs. Song and dance are often featured in accounts describing early mythological ages, when humans freely transformed themselves into animals. Even today, rural Andean music is especially linked with metamorphosing beings that may be said to take the form of humans or mermaids or to transform themselves into animals, and musical instruments are commonly said to have arrived with *Inkarrí,* the Inka (Inca) king.

Music and musical practices in Bolivia are often associated with enchantment and myth. These range from the consequences of breaking musical taboos to pacts with the devil to gain special musical powers and enchant members of the opposite sex. A Bolivian version of the almost universal story of the singing bones tells of a priest from Potosí who dug up his lover's body and fashioned a flute from her tibia. A more rural version of the same story (told as far north as Ecuador) tells of a young man who fashioned a flute from the bone of his lover (a partridge), which his parents had killed and eaten.

In many highland peasant communities of Bolivia, the image of three maidens connected with music is common. The Callawaya call these maidens Tusuy, the goddess of dance, compared to a spinning distaff; Wancay, the singer, who has the mouth of a toad; and Munakuy, love, the beautiful, who wears her heart outside her chest (Oblitas Poblete 1978). In other areas, three maidens with enchanting voices are said to have been invited to a wedding, but partway through the ceremony they turned into toads (Torrico 1988).

The historical record

The expansion of the Inka empire from Cuzco, Peru, around 1450 included all of today's highland Bolivia. Before this, the region was divided into kingdoms and ethnic groups, principally speaking Aymara, Pukina, and Uruqilla. The constant wars and shifting alliances among these kingdoms were exploited by the Quechua-speaking Inka, who introduced elements of their own culture, including music.

The Inka achieved uniformity and stability through implanting groups of loyal Quechua-speakers into troublesome parts of the empire, such as the valleys of Cochabamba, southern Potosí, Chuquisaca, and Tarija—areas now predominantly Quechua-speaking. The continued use of Aymara was accepted by the Inka, and Aymara remains the dominant indigenous language of the high plains of La Paz and Oruro departments.

In a late-sixteenth-century account of the musics of the Inka Empire, Guamán Poma de Ayala (1980 [1600?]) depicts altiplano women playing a large drum suspended from a frame, accompanying men who each blow across a two-tone pipe. The *jantarka*, a similar instrument, is still played by women during carnival in the village of Calcha, Potosí Department (Stobart 1987).

The Spanish invasion of the southern Andes in the 1530s followed less than a century of Inka rule. It brought from Europe new instruments that profoundly influenced indigenous music. In contrast, the invaders often viewed native American instruments with suspicion. They associated panpipes with those played back home in Spain by lowly castrators of pigs and grinders of knives. Spanish efforts to evangelize often repressed indigenous musical instruments, but the native Americans were immediately attracted to European instruments, and musical instruction was among the methods of Roman Catholic indoctrination. Lessons were given in plainsong and polyphony, and instruments such as shawms *(chirimías)* and recorders *(flautas)* were taught to provide processional or liturgical music.

Jesuit missions not only encouraged the use of instruments such as violins and transverse flutes, but also, unlike other Roman Catholic sects, sometimes adapted indigenous instruments to play European-style music. In the lowlands, these include the huge *bajón,* a multiple-tubed trumpet (resembling panpipes), and the *pífano,* a bird-bone flute. In secular music, the introduction of the *vihuela* and guitars resulted in imitations and hybrid instruments, such as the *charango.* Many European forms, styles, and rhythms were adopted; and even musical concepts, such as that of the siren (Spanish *sirena*) were blended into what appear to be pre-Hispanic musical practices.

In the 1570s, with the adoption of compulsory labor (*mit'a,* Spanish *mita*) to work the silver mines of Potosí, native Americans were drafted from communities all over the highlands, walking sometimes up to 1,600 kilometers from southern Peru. This glittering city was a melting pot of indigenous and foreign cultures. Descriptions of its legendary feasts by the chroniclers Arzans de Orsúa and Vela (1965) mention native American instruments such as cane flutes, trumpets (of conch, cane, or gourd), and a kind of marimba. These were played alongside instruments from every level of Spanish society, including bugles, guitars, harps, hornpipes, pipe and tabors, trumpets, *vihuelas,* and rebecs (Baptista Gumucio 1988).

Potosí and nearby La Plata (today Sucre) boasted theaters dating from the early 1600s, for which much music was composed. Several accounts mention the importance of persons of African descent as entertainers, and in 1568 a black and a mulatto were contracted in La Plata to open a school of music and dance (Stevenson 1968). Few manuscripts from that period survive, but a large collection of sacred pieces, dating mainly from the 1700s and 1800s, is held in the national archives in Sucre, mostly scored for voices, sometimes with violins and basso continuo, specifically harp and organ.

A school of military music was founded in La Paz in 1904, as were the National Conservatory in 1908 and the National Symphony Orchestra in 1944. Twentieth-century Bolivian composers adopted a nationalistic style, often through incorporating traditional elements or forms into their music. This was most successful, for example, in the stylized traditional dances (*cuecas*) for piano by Simeón Roncal (1870–1953). In the late twentieth century, composers tried to incorporate traditional instruments in a classical format, as in the Orquesta Experimental de Instrumentos Nativos (Experimental Orchestra of Native Instruments) of La Paz.

The introduction of the brass band, most especially in mining towns such as Oruro, had a huge impact on Bolivian popular music in the twentieth century. Similarly, accordions, saxophones, electric guitars, and keyboards (synthesizers) are widespread and exert increasing influence over popular styles of urban music.

MUSICAL INSTRUMENTS AMONG NATIVE AMERICANS

Bolivia is remarkable for the diversity of its musical instruments, which vary according to cultural group, area, time of year, and ritual function. In many highland zones, cane is the most common material, because of the proximity of the tropical valleys of the Yungas and Cochabamba; to the south and west, wood and bamboo are frequently used.

The names of many instruments are interchangeable, and a single generic term may refer to a variety of instruments of different construction. Confusions often arise in orthographic conventions between Spanish and indigenous languages; for example, the Spanish *quena* or *kena* is written as *qina* in standardized Quechua. Alterations and inconsistencies in spelling and pronunciation often make a word almost unrecognizable, as with the Spanish word for "flute," spelled variously *flauta, flawta, flawata, lawuta,* and *lawatu.* This article uses standardized spellings for indigenous languages and common Spanish spellings.

FIGURE 1   *Julajula* players kneel to perform a *kulwa* outside a church. Charka Province, northern Potosí, Bolivia. Photo by Henry Stobart, 1986.

Idiophones

Highland percussive instruments include triangles, bronze llama bells (*sinsiru, cencerro*), cog rattles (*matraca*), and heavy metal spurs attached to wooden sandals (*suila jut'as*). Among the lowland percussive instruments are seed-pod rattles (*paichochi*), worn on many dancers' ankles, drums and various idiophones, such as the gourd and beeswax *toá* of the Moré, a friction idiophone (Leigue Castedo 1957), and pestles and mortars played by paired women among the Chacobo (Prost 1970).

Membranophones

Double-headed drums are used throughout the highlands to accompany wind ensembles. Among the larger types are long cylinder drums (*phutu wankara*), commonly played with panpipes, as are shallower, military-style bass drums (*pumpu, bombo*). Military-style side drums (*tambora*) are particularly common in the altiplano, while vertically held drums (*wankara, caja*), often with a single beater and a snare of string, and sometimes porcupine quills, are universal there. Women sometimes play these types (*quchana, chinki*) in special rituals.

Aerophones

Panpipes

Panpipes are common throughout the highlands and are found in several parts of the lowlands. Among the lowland Chacobo, four tubes are simply grasped in the player's right hand; but in other regions, the tubes, ranging from two to seventeen, are usually tied together.

Highland panpipes are usually played in consort, on instruments of graduated sizes (tube lengths of 2.5 to 109 centimeters for the *julajula* of northern Potosí), typically tuned to play in parallel octaves or fifths (figure 1). For many types (double-unit panpipes), the tones of the scale are apportioned between two half instruments—a distribution of resources that requires two players to perform a melody in hocket or interlocking parts. With the pentatonic *julajula*, one person plays a four-tubed half (tuned to D–G–B–e), while the other plays a three-tubed half (tuned E–A–d). Thus, with a single half it is impossible to perform a complete melody (figure 2)—a performance aspect that has considerable social and symbolic significance.

Other double-unit panpipes played without drums range from the simple three-tubed (male) and two-tubed (female) bamboo pipes of the Chipayas (Baumann 1981) to three- and four-tubed varieties, such as the *julajula* (northern Potosí), the *chiriwanu* (La Paz and Cochabamba departments), and the *julujulu* (La Paz Department). These are respectively associated with ritual fighting, dances imitating combat, and hunting dances (Baumann 1982a).

Double-unit panpipes played with drums usually have more tubes (for example,

FIGURE 2   *Suna,* a processional dance played on paired *julajula,* often precedes ritual battles. About fifty musicians play their instruments in parallel octaves. Upper stems represent the four-tubed *qia* (the leader of the pair); lower stems, the three-tubed *arka* (the follower). Charka Province, Northern Potosí, Bolivia. Transcription by Henry Stobart.

The end-blown notched flute, commonly made of cane, is widespread in the highlands. In urban and mestizo contexts, it is popular and has become a highly expressive and virtuoso solo instrument.

pairs of eight and seven tubes) and are often constructed in double rows of pipes per unit of which only the row held nearer the player's lips is sounded (figure 3). Through sympathetic vibration, the outer, unstopped row (whose tubes are of similar lengths) enriches the harmonics of the stopped tubes. Such types of panpipe are commonly known as *siku*, *lakita*, or (Spanish) *zampoña*. They are played throughout the highlands and are often tuned approximately to a seven-note diatonic scale. In contrast, the seventeen-tube *siku* panpipes are played in parallel fifths, tuned so the tubes are arranged as a series of four five-note scalar units, each with a flatted third.

Flutes

The end-blown notched flute (*qina*, *qina-qina*, *lichiwayu*, *chuqila*, *mullu*, and others), commonly made of cane, is widespread in the highlands (figure 4). These are primarily played in consorts with drums and are tuned in unison or parallel fifths. Most have five or six holes, but the *mukululu* (La Paz Department) has only four, of which the lowest is never stopped—a practice common among many Bolivian flutes. In urban and mestizo contexts, the notched flute (*quena*, *kena*) is popular and has become a highly expressive and virtuoso solo instrument.

The six-holed cane side-blown flute (*flauta*, *pífano*) is common among lowland groups, especially those influenced by the Jesuits. In the highlands, it is played in consort to accompany certain dances, such as the *ch'unchu*, which caricatures lowland native Americans.

Several types of duct or fipple flutes (*pinkillus*, *flawtas*) are played in consort with drums in most highland regions and some lowland ones. Most types have six holes for fingering, but techniques of construction vary widely. Some types, such as the *pinkillu* (*flawta*) of northern Potosí, are made from branches with a pithy core, burned away with red-hot irons to form a hollow tube. Exceptional among flutes, groups of *pinkillu* of northern Potosí are played in hocket and are not accompanied by drums. In southern Potosí, among the Chipayas and in parts of La Paz Department, another form of *pinkillu* is made from curved branches that are split lengthways, hollowed out, and tied back together with tendons from an ox or a llama. Such instruments as the *saripalka* (figure 5) the *lawatu*, the *rollano*, and the *ch'utu*, like the northern Potosí *pinkillu*, are often wetted to swell the wood and fill any cracks before use.

FIGURE 3   During a Bolivian religious festival, a man plays a *siku* and a drum. Photo by Peter Smith, 1960s.

Most notable among the cane duct instruments of the plains of La Paz and Oruro departments are the *musiñu* (*mohoceño*) (figure 6). Within a consort, these range in size from the end-blown *sobre requinto* of 54 centimeters to the huge *liku* of 169 centimeters (5 centimeters in diameter), with the end-blown *irasu* in the middle. The *liku* and other larger sizes are played transversely with the aid of a narrow parallel extension-tube duct, enabling the player to reach the fingerholes. The intermediate instruments of the consort are organized in parallel fifths, octaves, and sometimes dissonant intervals.

FIGURE 4   During a Bolivian religious festival, men play notched flutes (*lichiwayu*). Photo by Peter Smith, 1960s.

FIGURE 5   At carnival, men play duct flutes (*saripalka*) and drums (*caja*). Calcha Province, Potosí Department, Bolivia. Photo by Henry Stobart, 1987.

FIGURE 6   A duct flute (*musiñu*) and drum ensemble of Villa Aroma, Aroma Province, Oruru Department, Bolivia. Photo by Henry Stobart, 1987.

Tarka (or *anata*) are duct flutes played throughout the highlands in parallel fifths and octaves (Mamani 1987). They are usually bored and cut from a solid block of wood (figure 7).

The three-holed pipe and tabor (*waka pinkillu* 'bull flute') is played in many highland areas. It is sometimes made from a condor's wing bone, when it is known as the *quri pinkillu* 'golden flute' (figure 8). Likewise, the wing bone of a local wading bird (*batu*) is used for the six-hole *pífano,* a duct flute that accompanies *macheteros,* dances of Trinidad, in lowland Beni Department (Olsen 1976) [see MOXO].

Trumpets

Highland natural trumpets include those made from conchs (now rare), animals' horns (*pututu, corneta, pulilitu*), and cane and gourd (*pululu*). Trumpets are often played nonmelodically in combination with wind ensembles or for signaling. However, certain types may be played melodically. These include the *caña,* a spectacular, 3-meter-long cane of Tarija, with a bell formed from the dried skin of a cow's tail (Calvo and Guzmán 1984), and the equally long *pututu* (or *tira-tira*) of northern Potosí, made of wood and the horns of oxen. Though resembling panpipes in shape, the huge *bajón* of the lowland Jesuit mission of San Ignacio de Moxos (Beni Department) is a multiple-tube trumpet (Becerra Casanovas 1977) that plays the bass in a European-style ensemble that usually includes violin and flute.

Single reed

A simple clarinet (*irki* or *erke*), consisting of a single idioglot reed inserted into the narrow end of an animal's horn, is played in many regions of the southern highlands, especially by the Jalq'as (near Sucre), where men and women play at distinctive pitches at carnival (Martínez n.d.). Such performance is especially notable in Tarija, where the *erke* is played as a solo instrument with drum (*caja chapaca*).

Chordophones

Musical bows are played by many lowland groups, such as the Moré in Beni Department, and others in Pando Department; they appear to be the only indige-

FIGURE 7   At carnival, men play duct flutes (*tarka*). Eucalyptus, Cercado Province, Oruro Department, Bolivia. Photo by Henry Stobart, 1987.

nous chordophones. In the highlands, chordophones are for the most part found among the Quechua-speakers of the central highlands and valleys. However, the *charango*, a small four- or five-course double-stringed (some have three strings) mandolin-like instrument, and the *guitarilla*, a deep-bodied five-course guitar, are particularly common among the Aymara-speakers of northern Potosí and the Chipayas of Oruro Department.

The peasant *charango*, often traditionally made using the carapace of an armadillo or half of a gourd, is especially associated with courtship (figure 9). Gut strings were originally used, but metal strings are used today, with a variety of tunings that in some regions alternate according to the time of year. Peasant *charangos* are strummed, and act primarily as a percussive and melodic, rather than harmonic, accompaniment to singing. In contrast, city and village styles tend to use full chords, fast strumming (*rasgueado*), and picking (*punteado*). Urban-style instruments are usually more finely constructed, are often carved from wood, use machine heads and nylon strings, and are commonly played in combination with the Spanish guitar, which is also popular as a solo instrument or as an accompaniment to songs (Cavour 1988).

The peasant guitar (*kitarra, guitarilla, qunquta, talachi, guitarrón*) is strummed to accompany singing. It uses sheep-gut (archaic), nylon, or metal strings, or a combination of nylon and metal. The depth of the sound box varies from 6 centimeters to more than 20. Many types are painted bright colors, depicting the growing crops of the rainy season, when these instruments are usually played.

Though widely used in churches and played in rural towns in the early 1900s, harps became rare by the end of the century. Violins, played in the valleys of Tarija, Chuquisaca, and Potosí to accompany dancing, are usually held below the shoulder, as was the practice in Europe before 1800. Locally constructed instruments may be made of a variety of materials, including cane of wide diameter.

Other Western instruments

Common in many larger towns, brass musical instruments from the West are becoming increasingly popular in the countryside. Most notable are the brass bands of Oruro and other mining centers, considered some of the finest in Latin America. These incorporate mostly imported trumpets, baritones (*bajos*), sousaphones, and, less commonly, trombones (often valve trombones).

The accordion sometimes replaces the *charango* and is commonly played in combination with saxophone or trumpet and percussion to supply music for dancing. Because Western instruments are costlier than local ones, they remain beyond the resources of most peasants.

The technology of music

Traditionally, many instruments, especially panpipes and flutes, were made in the communities where they were played. In valley regions with abundant wood, instrument-making traditions have tended to be stronger, and instruments are still commonly exchanged or bought by highland herders of llamas on their visits to the valleys in the dry winter months (June–August). However, certain highland communities specialize in manufacturing instruments, and some supply a variety of regions. These artisans have been influential in maintaining, revitalizing, and dispersing musical traditions.

Every large town has at least one radio station, and many stations broadcast in native American languages such as Quechua, Aymara, or Guaraní. Popular Latin American musical styles predominate, and outside the main cities most music broadcast on radio is local or national. Though peasant families living in remote regions often do not own a radio or are unable to afford batteries, radio–cassette recorders are

FIGURE 8   One man plays a "golden" flute (*quri pinkillus*) and a drum; the flute is made from a condor's wingbone. Chayanta Province, Northern Potosí Department, Bolivia Photo by Henry Stobart, 1991.

common in most other regions, where they are used to listen to radio networks and record local music. On the high plains of La Paz and Oruro departments, traditional music (such as a *musiñu* ensemble) may be recorded by as many as thirty to forty villagers using portable radio-cassette recorders.

Televisions are common in towns with electricity but rare in the countryside; the national average is one set per sixteen people (Myers 1992:470). The city of La Paz boasts more than seven channels, with a surprisingly large amount of time dedicated to music, mainly of the urban variety.

Neither musical notation nor other practical mnemonic devices are commonly used in peasant music; however, players in brass bands can often read Western notation and may use it when learning new melodies. In the 1990s, the famous *charango* player Ernesto Cavour developed forms of nonrhythmic notation for the *charango* and certain other instruments.

MUSICAL CONTEXTS AND GENRES

Maintaining a stable and creative relationship with the spiritual world is the central concern of most Andean and lowland ritual shamanic practices and curing. Traditional indigenous beliefs are highly complex, localized, and related to the surrounding environment, though most cosmogonies feature spirits of ancestors, the sun, the moon, lightning, and the earth, such as the Andean Pachamama (Mother Earth) and mountain deities. These beliefs are deeply syncretized with those of the Roman Catholic church, the official and dominant religion. In certain areas, the sun and moon are called *tata santísimu* 'holiest father' and *mama santísima* 'holiest mother' respectively, and thunder and lightning are called *gloria, Santa Barbara,* or *Santiago* 'St. James'.

Musical sound, often said to be the manifestation of spirit (*animu*), plays a central role in many rituals, especially at climactic moments. Most processions and many ceremonies are considered incomplete without the presence of appropriate music. In highland animal-fertility rituals such as *k'illpa,* special songs may refer directly to the animals, or *pinkillu* may be played. The sound of the flutes is said to engender the animals (causing them to multiply) and console the peaks (where the animals graze).

Seasonality and music

One of the most remarkable features of highland peasant music is the strong association of certain instruments, genres, and even tunings with specific times of year, the agricultural cycle, and other cyclical activities or celebrations. Over the course of a year, individual players from a single community may play as many as twelve instrumental types, each linked to a prescribed feast or season.

Musical instruments are often believed to influence agricultural production directly, and their sound is considered to affect the weather. Among the lowland Moré, for example, the *toá,* a friction idiophone, is considered to control rainfall. In highland northern Potosí, the high-pitched sound of the *charango* is said to attract the frost, necessary in the winter months for the preparation of *chuñu* (freeze-dried potatoes). In contrast, flute music is commonly said to bring rain and prevent frosts.

During periods of drought, people sometimes play *pinkillu* to call the rain, but the hoarse sound of the *tarka* is said to attract dry spells and is especially associated with carnival, when continued rain would spoil the ripening crops. In some regions during the growing season, *pinkillu* and *tarka* are alternated as required: the *pinkillu* bring rain, and the *tarka* attract dry spells (Buechler 1980). Some instruments (such as *kitarra* and *pinkillu*) are played continuously throughout a prescribed season, while others (such as *lichiwayu* and *julajula*) are confined to specific fiestas within a specific period.

FIGURE 9   On Easter, a young man in ritual-battle dress plays a *charango* with metal strings. Ayllu Macha, northern Potosí Department, Bolivia. Photo by Henry Stobart, 1991.

Huge crowds of people simultaneously playing different musics, widespread inebriation from alcohol, raised passions, fighting, and the spilling of blood—all are said to be essential to the success of a fiesta.

The rainy season (November to March) is especially associated with the souls of the dead, said to participate in agricultural production. According to Aymara legend, they "push the potatoes up from inside the earth" (Bastien 1978:81). At the feast of Todos Santos (1 and 2 November), the dead are invited back to the world of the living, and are ritually fed in family houses and the cemetery. In northern Potosí, *pinkillu* and *kitarra* begin to be played a few weeks before All Saints (1 November), when planting is begun or completed; their music continues until carnival, the ritual end of the growing season. On the final night of carnival, dancers imitating the spirits of the dead and devils dance out onto the mountainsides. At a climactic moment, the instruments of the rains are dramatically hushed and hidden away, and the people start singing the songs of the dry season to the strumming of the *charango* (Harris 1982a).

In contrast, the ritual start of the dry season is sometimes linked with the resurrection of Christ, following Lent and Holy Week, when music is often banned. During the vigil of Easter in Ingavi Province, La Paz Department, the musicians stand silent until the church bells ring *kalan kalan* (mnemonic, onomatopoeic vocables) to announce the resurrection. At this signal, musicians begin to play the *qina-qina*, which are not put away again until October. In many areas, the most intensive festal activity occurs between July and September, when a series of patronal festivals (saints' days) occurs. But in some areas (as Yura, Potosí Department), such activity is almost entirely confined to the growing and harvesting season, between the solstices of December and June (Rasnake 1989).

Strummed chordophones such as *charango* and *kitarra* commonly change tunings and performance techniques according to the time of year. As with the construction of instruments, many localized variations occur.

Fiestas and music

Most traditional musical performances occur at fiestas, events that serve a broad range of functions and mark a wide variety of celebrations and anniversaries. Carnival and All Saints are celebrated in most of the country, but the dates of other fiestas are subject to local variations. Besides acting as foci for ritual activity, celebration, recreation, and opportunities for courtship and social interaction, fiestas sometimes serve to provide contexts for public expressions of injustice or dispute.

In northern Potosí, full-scale battles may occur during fiestas, often within the context of ritual fighting (*tinku*). Some of the most intense moments of confrontation occur in the music itself, with aggressive stamping dances (*zapateo*) to the music of the *charango* and provocative performance on the *julajula*. This fighting expresses individual courage and communal solidarity, especially in territorial disputes.

Huge crowds of people simultaneously playing different musics, widespread inebriation from alcohol, raised passions, fighting, and the spilling of blood—all are said to be essential to the success of a fiesta. From this chaos and creativity emerges a new order. The fiesta marks a turning point, reflecting the Andean concept of *pachakuti* 'world turning', the end of an old period and the beginning of a new one. Time is specified in terms of the local cycle of fiestas rather than in months. The activities of these cycles are sometimes mirrored in the fiestas themselves, commonly accompanied by music. Participants may humorously mimic the mating of their domestic animals, making phallic allusions to their *pinkillu*; or, to the sound of *zampoña* and llama bells (*sinsiru*), they may carry sacks on their backs, imitating llamas journeying to the valleys to collect maize.

Some fiestas are centered on the sites of miracles or on villages with important patron saints and may involve pilgrimages of several days' walk carrying the community cross or standard, accompanied by almost continuous music *para alegrar el señor* 'to make the saint joyful'. On the participants' arrival, music is commonly performed in each corner of the village square, and then inside or facing the main door of the church in adoration or consolation of its patron. Social investment is another important aspect of fiestas, through sponsorship of fiesta-related activity and in the common experience of collective participation.

Many lowland peoples perform special dances at initiations and marriages. At the lip- and ear-piercing ceremony of ten- to twelve-year-old children, the Moré dance the *chiquít* to the sound of a gourd rattle of the same name. In the highlands, informal musical performance may follow baptisms and the ceremony of a child's first haircut, but it is almost always an important aspect of nuptial feasts, when special songs (*ipala*) are often sung by the bridegroom's sisters, or songs of insult (*takipayanaku*) are improvised between in-laws. Music may be provided for dancing by local wind instruments, brass bands, or *charangos,* for which a special tuning (*kasamintu*) is used in some areas.

For certain fiestas, married couples are expected to take part in hierarchical series of *cargos*, ritual-sponsorship obligations. In northern Potosí, for fiestas where *julajula* are played, the main sponsor (*alférez*) provides food and drink over the course of the festivities, while the minor sponsor (*mayura*) obtains the instruments, teaches the new melody, and carries a whip to discipline the dancing and control the ritual fighting (*tinku*). In other traditions, the sponsors (*pasantes* or *cabezas*) may contract local musicians who perform out of goodwill, or musicians from outside the community who for their services are paid with money or local produce. The sponsorship of fiestas in some regions alternates between sponsors (*alfereces*) and communal authorities (*kuraqkuna*) or *cabildos*. These positions of authority are rotated each year, and each married couple is obliged to take a turn.

Music is not usually played at funerals, but in La Paz Department, bamboo *alma pinkillus* are sometimes played for the Misa de Ocho Dias, a mass held on the eighth day after a death. Traditions vary widely for the feast of the dead at All Saints; in many areas, music is banned in favor of weeping in cemeteries, while in others the strains of *pinkillu* may replace prayers at the sites of graves. There is a special relationship between music and the ancestors or the recently dead.

Dance

In most Bolivian genres, music and dance are inseparable, and the physical action of dancing is often of great ritual significance. Dances in a circle are universal. Among the Tobas of the Gran Chaco, they were used in curing and life-cycle rituals. Encircling the patient would supposedly make the malignant spirits possessing the body depart with the dancer's perspiration (Karsten 1923). The courtship dance songs of the highlands often alternate sung verses with energetic stamping dances; the ring of dancers breaks periodically to rush energetically from one household or bar to another. Similarly, with much ritual wind music (played by flutes and panpipes), circles are formed at crossroads or the corners of village squares. At carnival, a band of musicians and dancers commonly accompanies the local authorities on a tour of territory and boundaries, and dances in a circle in the patio of each homestead.

In processional *julajula* dances of northern Potosí (linked with ritual battle), single files of sometimes up to a hundred players snake into village squares for major fiestas. For this dance, participants wear ox-hide fighting helmets, identical in shape to those of the Spanish conquistadors.

In the highlands of La Paz Department, many dances include a burlesque or pantomimic aspect (Harcourt and Harcourt 1959; Paredes Candia 1980), such as the *waka tokori,* which caricatures a bullfight; other dances represent mock combat or hunting, such as the *chuqila* (*chokela*), a ritual hunt for vicuñas (Baumann 1982b). Lowland dances are often connected with hunting or sometimes with the conversion of warlike tribes to Christianity. On Palm Sunday, *macheteros*—dancers with feather headdresses and large knives (machetes)—process through the streets of Trinidad (Beni Department) in a bowing dance of supplication before an image of Christ on a donkey (Rivero Parada 1989).

The most famous processional dances of Bolivia are the costumed and masked dances of Oruro carnival, which developed among urban miners and occur in other towns (Guerra Gutiérrez 1987). Two of its most spectacular dances are the choreographed *diablada* 'devil dance' and *morenada* 'black-slave dance', which feature huge, colorful, costly masks and are accompanied by brass bands. Among the many other urban dances of this type are those that caricature ethnic populations from other regions of Bolivia (such as Toba and Kallawaya) and even native North Americans. Partner dances or dance songs between men and women, such as the duple-time *huayño,* the compound-triple-meter *cueca* (a dance with handkerchiefs), and the *takirari* of the lowlands are popular in middle-class contexts but less common among traditional peasants.

The mimed dances, the extravagant costumes, and the dramatic aspect of many rituals are evidence of the popularity of theatrical presentation. A play based on the murder of the Inka Atahualpa by the Spanish is one of the few traditional dramas still performed. It appears as part of Oruro carnival, but early in the twentieth century it was staged in rural towns (Lara 1989). Music is an important aspect of the performance, especially in the laments of the Inka princesses.

MUSICAL PERFORMERS AND PERFORMANCES

The variety of musics and types of instruments is one of the salient markers of Bolivian cultural identity and differentiation, especially with the steady decline of traditional dress. People use music to express solidarity and competition at various levels. Some instruments and musical forms are closely associated with the immediate community and local agricultural production. Others are linked with the larger sociopolitical groups and may relate to the maintenance of territorial boundaries.

Competition often occurs between wind ensembles from different highland hamlets, communities, *ayllus,* or wards. Each attempts to dominate the other during a fiesta, in volume and assurance of melody, ideally causing their opponents to falter. But within the ensemble itself, there is a strong sense of solidarity, social leveling, and reciprocity, which reflect traditional forms of social organization and exchange.

Gender-based roles

With few exceptions, instrumental performance is the role of men. In the highlands, women are the main singers, and a song is said to be incomplete with only men's voices and without women's. Historically, women have often played drums to accompany singing and men's instruments, but the playing of drums by women is restricted to a few specific ritual contexts. Symbolically, men are commonly associated with the dynamic and engendering force of breath, while women are linked with the creative substance of water (Arnold Bush et al. 1991).

In the highlands and the lowlands, music is a central aspect of courtship. Many instruments—such as the *moró*, a ten-tube panpipe of the lowland Moré and the *pinkillu* and guitar-type instruments of the central highlands—are specifically associated with the young and unmarried. Songs of courtship are often laced with erotic metaphors, continually refer to marriage, and like the instruments themselves, are often linked with agricultural fertility.

North of Potosí, many couples meet only in the context of song and dance at fiestas and do not regularly spend time together until, after obtaining the permission of the woman's parents, the woman steals away to live with the man's family in concubinage. Following marriage (or concubinage), musical activity by women is sometimes frowned on because of its associations with courtship. In some regions, women are prohibited from singing and dancing. However, males of all ages, including boys, are expected to play in the massed panpipe bands that perform at certain highland festivals; in some places, older men are said to be better musicians because they have greater experience and know more tunes.

Class and ethnicity

Class structures are transitory and highly complex; they vary considerably according to region. Ethnicity, residence, wealth, education, occupation, and physical type may all contribute to the construction of class position. Distinctions of class as cultural identity are often clearly defined by the use of specific musical styles, techniques, rhythms, genres, and instruments. In many places, the choice of nylon or metal strings on a *charango* is not so much an issue of musical taste as one of class and ethnic identity. A peasant who uses nylon rather than metal strings may be understood to be rebelling against his ethnic origins and aspiring to a higher class.

The peasants (*campesinos, indios*) of the highlands are subsistence farmers or herders who principally speak Quechua or Aymara. In some regions, people retain traditional dress and strong ethnic identity. Their music is often closely linked to social considerations, cosmology, and agricultural production. Some dispersed indigenous groups remain in the lowlands, speaking a mosaic of languages, but few traditional musical practices survive among them.

The broad spectrum of middle classes ranges from those who speak indigenous languages and Spanish and retain localized music traditions, to educated monolingual Spanish-speakers with a strong sense of national cultural identity. The brass band developed among urban miners, but strong localized *charango*, guitar, and accordion styles developed among the more rural middle classes. A repertoire of nationally popular songs and dances, *música folklórica*, including many highland and lowland dances, is constantly played on the larger radio networks. Other Latin American styles and performers, such as the Colombian *cumbia* and the Peruvian *huayno* (*huayño* in Bolivia) are often heard, while younger generations sometimes favor rock and the fusion of these elements into the so-called commercial tropical style, known in Peru as *chicha* music.

The culture of the small, white, and wealthy mestizo population is more aligned with that of Europe and the United States, as is the growing migrant population of the lowlands, which includes many Okinawan Japanese [see MUSIC AND IMMIGRATION]. African Bolivians still perform *sayas* 'praise songs' in the streets of Cochabamba, and the *saya* is a popular musical form among pan-Andean folk groups such as Inti Illimani, Kjarkas, and Pacha.

In the tropical lowlands, music is often performed in a gentle, meditative manner. The Sirionó, for example, frequently sing while lying in hammocks. Such meditative and day-to-day performance is rare in highland peasant communities.

Composition

In rural communities of the highlands, the performance of new melodies each year and sometimes for individual fiestas (especially carnival) is commonly considered a ritual necessity. Old tunes are said to have no power and in Quechua are called *q'ayma* 'insipid'. In the high plains of La Paz and Oruro departments, new melodies are sometimes obtained through a process of collective composition. They may consist of no more than a few short motifs treated according to consistent formulae with, for example, rhythmic repetition at intervals of the fourth or fifth, or repetition of pitches with rhythmic variation.

It is often said that new melodies cannot be made up inside a house. Players describe how they are inspired when alone on a mountainside, beside a river, or sometimes when playing in an ensemble of *pinkillu*; often, a new tune appears under their fingers as if by magic, "played by the *sirínus*." Musical abilities and new melodies are commonly attributed to the *sirínus* 'sirens' or the *yawlus* 'devils' (Martínez 1990; Sánchez 1988) said to live beside streams and waterfalls or in caves or large rocks; these places are described as (Spanish) *lugares feos* 'ugly-evil places'. The *sirínus* supposedly take various forms, including that of humans, and can transform themselves into animals such as toads, doves, cats, dogs, and foxes.

Men sometimes visit *sirínus* late at night after buying a new instrument or shortly before fiestas, to endow their instruments with special magical powers. After making ritual offerings that may include the sacrifice of a red cockerel (made to crow before being killed), they leave the instruments beside a rock or a spring and retreat to a safe distance; they may leave the instruments for several nights. Traditions vary widely: in some places, people say if you hear the music of the *sirínus,* you will become mad; other people claim to listen to the music and copy it; in some parts, to frighten off the *sirínus* and collect the tuned instruments, people make a noise by throwing a tin can as soon as they hear the first tuning note. The tuned instruments are then said to have magical powers that attract girls with their enchanted music, as suggested in a text from Bustillos Province, Potosí Department:

Kay charanguytuyki	This *charango* of yours
Kasaru kustillu	Wants to get married
Sapa waqasqampi	Each time it weeps
Sirínu kustillu.	With the desire of the *sirínu.*

MUSICAL IDEOLOGIES AND AESTHETICS

In the tropical lowlands, music is often performed in a gentle, meditative manner; the Sirionó, for example, frequently sing while lying in hammocks (Key 1963; Riester 1978). Such meditative and day-to-day performance is rare in highland peasant communities, where most music is confined to fiestas, when women usually sing in a vigorous and often high-pitched style, sometimes reaching two octaves above

TRACK 10

middle C. This style is sometimes matched by shrill strumming from the *charango*, whose metal strings are often tensioned almost to the breaking point. Similarly, wind instruments are blown strongly in high registers, and gentle, mellow sounds are untypical and considered aesthetically unsatisfactory.

The dynamic aspect of musical performance emphasizes its ritual and socializing role in the reciprocal exchange of energies between paired performers (using interlocking technique) and between the worlds of humans and spirits. Such an exchange is analogous to the tradition of reciprocal labor in which work performed as aid to others is later returned with produce or a similar form of labor (Harris 1982b). In fiestas, dynamism and aesthetic saturation (food, drink, music, color) are considered ritually essential, contrasting vividly with the austerity of everyday life. Complaints about the quality of performance are rarely made, but if the music falters and stops, people are swift to criticize, even when the musicians are almost too drunk and exhausted to stand.

Many traditional wind instruments, especially of highland Oruro and La Paz departments, are played in consorts (*tropas*) of a single type of instrument made in graduated sizes and tuned in unison, parallel fifths, or octaves. Blending is essential, and people say the tonal color of the ensemble should be consistent, with each voice heard equally and no single voice standing out from the solidarity of the ensemble. In weaving, color is also often blended through chromatic graduations, *k'isas* 'sweetness' (Cereceda 1987); and what from a distance appears as a monochrome may be blended from, perhaps, fourteen shades and colors.

In contrast with the pure harmonics of the European flute, a broad tone, rich in harmonics (*tara*), is usually preferred in the highlands. *Tarka* or *taraka* probably derive their name from the Aymara word *tara*, which denotes a hoarse voice. When blown strongly, the sound of these flutes divides so the fundamental tone and the octave above are of near-equal intensity.

Rich, dense, and often dissonant tonal color is sometimes consciously added by an instrument that plays in parallel to the rest of the ensemble, but at a dissonant interval. For example, in the *tropa recto* (an ensemble of *musiñu*), all the instruments are tuned to play in parallel octaves or fifths; however, the single *sobre requinto,* tuned a fifth above the *irasu*-sized instruments, is pitched a tone above the four *requintos.* The resulting consistent parallel dissonance enlivens and enriches the timbre of the ensemble, *como órgano* 'like an organ'.

Fascination with sound is emphasized rather than developed instrumental technique, and little individual practice is necessary. Musical performance is essentially a socializing activity in which general participation and interaction are encouraged, reflecting traditional egalitarian social structures while discouraging excessive power or subordination. The notion of a soloist is contrary to many traditional highland musical practices. This presents a marked contrast to urban ensembles (*conjuntos*), which, following Western practices and tastes, combine a variety of instruments with contrasting timbres, use harmony and polyphony, and feature one person playing both panpipe halves to form a single instrument with the player periodically acting as a soloist.

Many types of double-unit panpipes and the *pinkillu* ensembles of northern Potosí divide the notes of the scale between paired instruments. The combination of paired instruments (that is, two halves), such as the three-tubed male panpipe and the two-tube female panpipe of the Chipayas, is usually stated to be "like older and younger brothers" but is sometimes compared with heterosexual intercourse. These concepts may be understood in terms of the organizing principle of duality or complementarity (Quechua *yanantin*) by which paired elements are said to belong together and to be incomplete or uncreative alone (Platt 1986).

Similarly, the hoarseness of *tara*, which refers to the timbre of some highland wind instruments, can be glossed 'double'. This vibrancy, rich in harmonics, is said to be in tune and creative like the balancing of male and female and the sexual union of a man and a woman. But when instruments produce a thin tone with few harmonics, do not sound well, or are out of tune with the rest of an ensemble, they may be called *q'iwa,* a concept said to imply singleness or aloneness, used to denote castrated animals, infertile plants, homosexuals, and misers with money or food. Associated with the inability to produce and with imbalance, *q'iwa* is understood in terms of agency and is of central importance to concepts of regeneration. In traditional communities, musical timbre is directly related to regeneration, productivity, and creation (Stobart 1992).

Poetry and music

The universality of dualistic principles in Bolivia may be attributed to certain musical forms and aesthetics, particularly in the poetry of Quechua songs. Each line is a union of two halves, and adjacent lines are commonly paired through common or opposing ideas or through vocabulary of similar sound, often as wordplay, as seen in a text from Ayllu Macha, Chayanta Province, Potosí Department:

Walli q'iririnqa,	Valley *q'iririnqa,*
Puna q'iririnqa:	Highland *q'iririnqa*:
Warmi wachakuqtin,	When the woman's giving birth,
Cholay q'ipirinqa.	My girl will be carrying.

This verse, sung by women, likens the *q'iririnqa* (a bird) to highland men who travel to the valleys with llama caravans each year to exchange salt for maize—a journey associated with amorous intrigue. The first and second lines suggestively contrast low and high (valleys or birth versus highlands or child on its mother's back). By semantic coupling, the single idea of "woman" is expressed in two contrasting words, *warmi* and *chola*; the words *q'iririnqa* and *q'ipirinqa* are almost identical in sound, though different in meaning.

The transmission of music

Traditionally, music is learned informally and socially through collective imitation and repetition. In the rural highlands, children and young men carry instruments while herding or on journeys; they learn alongside friends or while they are passing the time alone. New tunes on wind instruments are usually taught in collective contexts, through continual repetition of the complete melody.

Ensembles usually consist of members of existing social groups—a hamlet, a community, an *ayllu* (ethnic group), a ward, or even an urban migrant neighborhood or cultural center. But the brass bands and troupes of Oruro and several other towns are much institutionalized and autonomous, in themselves serving as a social focus.

The teaching of music in schools is mostly confined to singing local or national songs (especially the national anthem) and depends largely on the enthusiasm of individual teachers. Players in urban *conjuntos* sometimes take individual or collective lessons, and they may study Western classical music at the National Conservatory.

ACCULTURATION

Throughout history, highland Bolivian music has been subject to change, with the reinterpretation of new musical ideas, often brought from other cultures, within a cosmology centered on traditional economics, social structures, and agricultural production. But the latter half of the twentieth century, even more than the Spanish invasion hundreds of years before, saw an upheaval in the basis of Andean life. Music serves to reflect and motivate traditional values and structures, but as these concepts are abandoned or replaced by Western ideologies, music is no longer the necessity it was.

The introduction of radios and tape recorders and widespread migration to the cities have meant increased contact with urban mestizo and Western music in the countryside. The high prestige of such music, accompanied by increasing orientation toward Western values and aesthetics, means that traditional practices tend to be devalued and their significance forgotten. With increased ownership of tape recorders, tunes are becoming fixed, and taped music is beginning to replace live musicians, even in ritual contexts. Musical scales and melodic structures appear to be increasingly influenced by Western-based diatonic music; for example, a series of *lawatu* (flute) melodies recorded in southern Potosí in 1977 included a six-note scale, but *lawatu* tunes played in the same village ten years later commonly used a seven-note scale.

Among the middle classes, recorded music is heard in most buses, bars, and cafés. There are numerous radio networks, and sales of vinyl records and cassettes are high. Styles are diverse, but some of the most popular are the rhythmic lowland dance songs of such groups as Trío Oriental, who combine vocal harmonies with accordion, bass, and percussion. Besides incorporating forms such as the *taquirari* and the *saya* from Bolivia's own indigenous and black populations, this so-called tropical style is often influenced by African-Caribbean rhythms (such as the Columbian *cumbia* and the Peruvian *chicha*). Some highland bands have adopted similar forms and rhythms; for example, Maroyu's commercial style combines voice, electric guitars, organ, and percussion. Countless electric bands of this type, with considerable awareness of rock, are found in urban centers; typically, they supply music for dancing at weddings.

Since the agrarian reforms of 1953 and a policy of cultural unification, the state has encouraged folkloric festivals in certain regions. Many developmental agencies, radio stations, and political parties continue to organize competitions of peasant music, often with Westerners or mestizos as judges. These practices have served to transform essentially participatory music into a medium that differentiates musicians and audience. The radical reversal in ideology has often been accompanied by the abandonment of seasonal considerations, the encouragement of virtuoso instrumental techniques, and the development of new forms.

Nevertheless, traditional music is being rediscovered and valued again by many urban migrants. Far more than a hundred indigenous ensembles (*grupos autóctonos*) regularly perform in La Paz. Numerous urban ensembles (*conjuntos*) tour internationally on a regular basis. Andean music is often identified internationally with folkloric ensembles (*grupos folklóricos*), whose instruments typically include *charango,* guitar, *quena,* panpipes, and percussion, sometimes using highly developed instrumental techniques. Such ensembles are commonly seen on tour in international concert halls, or as migrants busking on sidewalks in Europe and the United States. Kjarkas, Rumillajta, and Savia Andina are among the most famous Bolivian ensembles of this type; their original songs and stylized versions of traditional dances are famous throughout the middle classes and are recognized as the popular national culture. Other groups, including Awatiñas, Los Masis, Norte de Potosí, and Los Yuras, often include examples of more traditional peasant styles in their programs. Many more localized mestizo *huayños* or other forms of dance and song are recorded and sold in large numbers, typically sung in a high, plaintive, full-voiced style, accompanied by *charango* and guitar or accordion.

The group Wara has combined more traditional folkloric instruments with elec-

nueva canción 'New song', generic name for pan-Latin American neofolk-protest music that began in Chile in the 1960s and spread throughout the Americas

peña In Andean cities where tourism is common, a private gathering place or touristic nightclub where folk musicians perform

tric guitars and a drum set, but the progressive exponents of a new style, *nueva canción* 'new song', often use traditional instruments alongside, for example, piano and flute. This intellectual movement represents an expression of broader Latin American identity and solidarity; such songs are popular in more educated circles. Famous artists include Emma Junaro, Jenny Cardenas, and Savia Nueva.

Formal concerts of classical music on Western instruments, and even new music especially composed for native instruments, take place in La Paz and other large towns. But public performances of more urban folk-derived music usually take place in the more informal setting of music clubs (*peñas*), where an array of professional and semiprofessional ensembles play styles likely to appeal to urbanites' and tourists' tastes; the most famous is Peña Naira in La Paz. One of the most famous groups to come out of the music clubs in La Paz is Los Jairas, featuring the virtuosic *charango* playing of Ernesto Cavour and the florid *quena* playing of the Swiss-born Gilberto "El Gringo" Favre.

Major competitions are held annually for folk-derived music in mestizo style, often resulting in prestigious coverage, recording contracts, and opportunities for the winners of prizes to travel abroad. Regional competitions are held for music from peasant communities and smaller towns, usually organized by radio stations or foreign-aid groups.

REFERENCES

Arnold Bush, Denise, Domingo Jiménez, and Juan de Diós Yapita. 1991. "Scattering the Seeds: Shared Thoughts on Some Songs to the Food Crops from an Andean Ayllu." *Amerindia* 16:106–178.

Baptista Gumucio, Mariano. 1988. *Potosí: Patrimonio cultural de la humanidad.* Santiago: Compañía Minerva del Sur.

Bastien, Joseph W. 1978. *Mountain of the Condor: Metaphor and Ritual in an Andean Ayllu.* St. Paul: West Publishing.

Baumann, Max Peter. 1981. "Music, Dance, and Song of the Chipayas (Bolivia)." *Latin American Music Review* 2(2):171–222.

———. 1982a. "Music of the Indios in Bolivia's Andean Highlands." *The World of Music* "Latin America" 25(2):80–98.

———. 1982b. *Musik im Andenhochland: Bolivien.* Berlin: Museum für Völkerkunde MC 14. 2 LP disks.

Becerra Casanovas, Rogers. 1977. *Reliquias de Moxos.* La Paz.

Buechler, Hans. 1980. *The Masked Media.* The Hague: Mouton.

Calvo, Luz María, and Roberto Guzmán. 1984. *Música tradicional de Bolivia. VI festival folklórico nacional "Luz Mila Patiño."* Cochabamba: Centro Portales y Lauro. LP disk.

Calvo, Luz María, and Walter Sánchez C. 1991. *Música autóctona del Norte de Potosí: VII Festival Folklorico "Luz Mila Patiño."* Cochabamba: Centro Portales y Lauro. LP disk and commentary.

Cavour, Ernesto. 1988. *El Charango.* La Paz: CIMA.

Cereceda, Verónica. 1987. "Aproximaciones a una estética andina: de la belleza al tinku." In *Tres Reflexiones sobre el pensamiento andino,* ed. T. Bouysse-Cassagne, Olivia Harris, T. Platt, and Verónica Cereceda, 133–231. La Paz: Hisbol.

Cobo, Bernabé. 1990 [1653]. *Inca Religion and Customs,* trans. and ed. Roland Hamilton. Austin: University of Texas Press.

Díaz Gainza, José. 1988. *Historia Musical de Bolivia.* La Paz: Puerta del Sol.

Guamán Poma de Ayala, Felipe. 1980 [c1600]. *Nueva crónica y buen gobierno,* ed. John V. Murra and Petena Adorno. México, D.F.: Siglo Veintiuno.

Guerra Gutiérrez, Alberto. 1987. *El carnaval de Oruro a su alcance.* Oruro, Bolivia: Editora Lilial.

d'Harcourt, Marguerite, and Raoul d'Harcourt. 1959. *La musique des Aymaras sur les hauts plateaux Boliviens d'après les enregistrements sonores de Louis Girault.* Paris: Société des Américanistes, Musée de l'Homme.

Harris, Olivia. 1982a. "The Dead and Devils amongst the Bolivian Laymis." In *Death and Regeneration of Life,* ed. Maurice Bloch and Jonathan Parry, 45–73. Cambridge: Cambridge University Press.

———. 1982b. "Labour and Produce in an Ethnic Economy, Northern Potosí, Bolivia." In *Ecology and Exchange in the Andes,* ed. David Lehmann, 70–96. Cambridge: Cambridge University Press.

Karsten, Rafael. 1923. *The Toba Indians of the Bolivian Gran Chaco.* Acta Humaniora 4, iv. Helsinki: Academiae Aboensis.

Key, Mary. 1963. "Music of the Sirionó (Guaranian)." *Ethnomusicology* 7(1):17–21.

Lara, Jesús. 1989. *Tragedía del fin de Atawallpa.* Cochabamba, Bolivia: Los Amigos del Libro.

Leigue Castedo, Luis D. 1957. *"El Itenez Salvaje": Influencia selvicola e indigenal sobre el Río Itenez.* La Paz: Ministerio de Educación y Bellas Artes.

Mamani P., Mauricio. 1987. *Los instumentos musicales en los Andes Bolivianos.* La Paz: Museo Nacional de Etnografía y Folklore.

Martínez, Rosalia. 1990. "Musique et démons: Carnival chez las Tarabuco (Bolivie)." *Journal de la Société des Américanistes* 76:155–76.

———. n.d. "Instrumentos de la zona Jalq'a." In *Guía de los instrumentos Bolivianos.* Cochabamba, Bolivia: Centro Portales.

Myers, Helen, ed. 1992. *Ethnomusicology: An Introduction.* London: Macmillan.

Oblitas Poblete, Enrique. 1978 [1960]. *Cultura Callawaya.* La Paz: Ediciones Populares Camarlinghi.

Olsen, Dale A. 1976. "Música Vesperal Mojo en San Miguel de Isiboro, Bolivia." *Revista Musical Chilena* 133:28–46.

Orsúa, Arzans de, and Bartolomé Vela. 1965. *Historia de la Villa Imperial de Potosí.* Providence: Brown University Press.

Paredes Candia, Antonio. 1980. *Folklore de Potosí.* La Paz: Ediciones ISLA.

———. 1984. *La danza folklórica en Bolivia.* La Paz: Ediciones ISLA.

Platt, Tristan. 1986. "Mirrors and Maize: The Concept of *Yanantin* among the Macha of Bolivia." In *Anthropological History of Andean Polities,* ed. John Murra, Nathan Wachtel, and Jacques Revel, 228–259. Cambridge: Cambridge University Press.

Prost, Marian D. 1970. *Costumbres, habilidades y cuadro de la vida humana entre los Chacobo.* Riberalta, Bolivia: Instituto Lingüístico de Verano, y el Ministerio de Educación y Cultura.

Rasnake, Roger. 1989. *Autoridad y poder en los Andes: Los Kuraqkuna de Yura.* La Paz: Hisbol.

Riester, Juergen 1978. *Canción y producción en la vida de un pueblo indígena.* La Paz and Cochabamba: Los Amigos del Libro.

Rivero Parada, Luis. 1989. "Principales Danzas y Danzarines de los nativos de San Ignacio de Mojos, Departamento del Beni—Bolivia." Santa Cruz, Bolivia: Casa de la Cultura "Raúl Otero Reiche."

Sánchez, C. Walter. 1988. *El proceso de creación musical (Música autóctona del norte de Potosí).* Cochabamba, Bolivia: Centro Pedagógico y Cultural de Portales, Centro de Documentación de música Boliviana. Bulletin 7.

Stevenson, Robert M. 1968. *Music in Aztec and Inca Territory.* Berkeley: University of California Press.

Stobart, Henry. 1987. *Primeros datos sobre la música campesina del norte de Potosí.* La Paz: Museo Nacional de Etnografia y Folklore.

———. 1992. "*Tara* and *Q'iwa*—Worlds of Sound and Meaning." In *Cosmología y música en los Andes.* Berlin: International Institute of Traditional Music.

Torrico, Cassandra. 1988. "Toads and Doves: The Symbolism of Storage Sacks' Design amongst Macha Herders."

van Lindert, Paul, and Otto Verkoren. 1994. *Bolivia in Focus.* London: Latin American Bureau.

Brazil: Central and Southern Areas
Suzel Ana Reily

Historical Overview
Musical Traits of Central and Southern Brazil
Musical Instruments
Music within Popular Roman Catholicism
Music in Urban Contexts
Music in Migrant Communities
Further Study

The music of central and southern Brazil is as diverse as the one hundred million people that populate the area. Gross topological contrasts occur throughout the rural areas of central and southern Brazil, which cover about 2,224,000 square kilometers, and an equally wide range of musical activities occur in such urban centers as Rio de Janeiro and São Paulo. These and other cities provide opportunities for hearing many kinds of Brazilian musics, including Brazilian popular music genres that have become known all over the world; traditional southeastern rural genres of medieval origin and their later developments; a wide variety of Afro-Brazilian traditions; northeastern traditional genres, brought by migrants searching for a better life in the south; and the musical traditions of the immigrant groups (Chinese, Germans, Italians, Japanese, Middle Easterners, Poles, Spaniards, and so on) that came to Brazil from the early 1800s on and particularly after 1888, when slavery was abolished in the country [see MUSIC OF IMMIGRANT GROUPS]. Concerts of Western art music are given regularly, and outlets of mass communication bombard the Brazilian public with the latest popular hits from abroad.

There are further distinctions between the musical preferences of different Brazilian social classes, ages, religious communities, professional categories, and even political parties. In effect, musical activities and preferences have become markers of identity for the social groups that make up Brazilian society.

HISTORICAL OVERVIEW

Little is known of the music of central and southern Brazil before the area's first encounter with Portuguese explorers on 22 April 1500. Information is also scant regarding the first three hundred years after that. During the colonial period, documents detail the musical activities of the major Roman Catholic cathedrals and the parlors of the upper classes, but data about musical life outside these domains are sparse. Some information is available in writings left by such travelers as Jean de Léry, who lived in Brazil from 1557 to 1558 and produced the first known transcriptions of native American music: two chants of the Tupinambá, near Rio de Janeiro (Léry 1980:150, 162). From his description of a "savage ritual," it is clear that, like other

Europeans, he was shocked by the rattles and flutes made from human skulls and bones. Other early documents on colonial musical life appear in the journals and graphic representations of such travelers as Theodor de Bry, Pero Vaz de Caminha, Gabriel Soares de Sousa, Hans Staden, and others.

The European settlement of Brazil was undertaken as a joint venture between Portugal and the Roman Catholic Church; with the sword came the cross. The Portuguese were allotted the landmass east of the demarcation set in the Treaty of Tordesillas in 1494, which included a large section of present-day Brazil. The colonization of the area combined economic, political, and religious objectives. Despite the Christianizing model of colonization, the Roman Catholic Church in Brazil was weak, and its weakness had important implications for colonial musical life: without ecclesiastical subsidies, musical performance—even for religious rituals—became almost exclusively the prerogative of lay people.

Since 1179, when the Portuguese crusade against the Moors began, the Portuguese crown had been on good terms with Rome, and a series of papal bulls had granted the king concessions over Portuguese religious institutions, rendering the church in Brazil subservient to the state. Though in the first years of colonization the goals of Portugal were seemingly congruent with those of the church, the crown's greater interest in gold than in souls had important consequences. About 250 years after the first encounter, Portugal had scarcely fulfilled its part of the bargain; there were but eight dioceses in the colony, and only a few thousand priests to serve a population of 1.4 million freemen and others. Most of the priests were employed on northeastern plantations to administer the sacraments to owners and their families.

Central and southern Brazil were especially affected by the crown's neglect. Unlike the northeast, where sugarcane had started generating profits almost immediately after the arrival of the Portuguese, the southern areas had little economic importance to the metropolis. The land was settled by Portuguese subsistence farmers, who moved farther and farther into the hinterland, displacing the indigenous population. They formed small, scattered communities (*bairros*) of around ten to fifteen households, which helped one another with tasks that a single family could not complete. These circumstances led to the emergence of a peasant ethos, marked by nomadism, community solidarity, and an emphasis on personalized social interaction.

In these communities, Christian festivities were the primary sociable contexts. In the absence of priests, colonists developed devotional forms based on rituals brought from Portugal, many rooted in late medieval musical traditions. Households alternated in promoting popular religious festivities. It was up to the host of the festival (*festeiro*) to invite musicians to lead the ritual proceedings at his house. The only leadership roles in these communities were those of popular Christian traditions. In rural areas, in such traditions as the baptism of Saint John the Baptist, the Saint Gonçalo dance, and the *folia de reis* (see below), the legacy of the household forms of popular Christianity can still be observed.

The communal work party (*mutirão*) was another important venue for making music and socializing in rural communities. At the end of the day, the host offered the workers a meal, followed by the *cateretê* (also *catira*), a widely practiced double line dance. In some areas, musical traditions developed to amuse the workers while they worked. In the Paraíba Valley, which lies between the cities of Rio de Janeiro and São Paulo, the *mutirão* is still accompanied by sung riddles (*brão*) sustained throughout the day (figure 1).

In southern Brazil, the church was far more active with the indigenous population than with the Portuguese. Jesuit missionaries, who arrived around 1550, were particularly fervent in their desire to convert the native Americans. By the late 1500s, more than five hundred Jesuits were in Brazil, baptizing and domesticating the

FIGURE 1 *Brão* singers rest for a moment to introduce new clues to help other singers solve the riddle. Photo by Suzel Ana Reily, 1985.

Tupinambá, the Guaraní, the Botocudos, and other indigenous groups, and the Jesuit order played an important role in the history of Brazilian music.

Music was often included in morality plays (*autos*) that priests enacted for the natives, and it is thought that even before the foundation of the Indian Theater of São Lourenço in Rio de Janeiro, there had been a native American theater in São Vicente. The first morality play believed to have been written in Brazil was the *Auto da Pregação Universal*, attributed to the missionaries José de Anchieta and Manoel da Nóbrega. It was first performed in Piratininga (now São Paulo) in 1567 before being taken to other coastal settlements.

The Jesuits were successful in acculturating native Americans through music and musical instruction, particularly within the missions (called reductions) they organized in the extreme southern parts of the country. By the mid-1600s, the Guaraní were not only playing European organs, harpsichords, woodwinds, and stringed instruments, but masterfully manufacturing instruments (Preiss 1988). Native orchestras accompanied religious songs sung in Latin, Portuguese, and native languages. Their ability to perform European music became a major argument in a scholastic debate as to whether or not native Americans had souls.

Although cultural interchange within the missions was essentially unilateral, some musicologists have claimed that the *cateretê* had a native origin (Andrade 1933:173). Anchieta (and later, other Jesuits) supposedly used it during religious festivals held among the Tupinambá, though evidence of this is weak. The acculturation of the native Brazilian population seems to have been so effective that at the level of the greater society, native American influence in almost all areas of life in Brazil is small. In the domain of musical expression, it may be limited to the preservation of a few indigenous terms, certain choreographic practices, and the occasional use of maraca-type rattles. In 1759, the Jesuits were expelled from Brazil, and the native Americans they had domesticated were enslaved. An important era of musical life in Brazil came to an end, and Rome lost its only strong ally in the colony.

Near the end of the 1600s, lay brotherhoods (*irmandades*) began to appear in urban centers throughout the colony. These voluntary associations became the main colonial institutions linking church and society. They built churches and maintained charitable institutions. Their main public activities involved the celebration of patronal festivals. Thus, they became particularly important in promoting the musical life of the colony.

The gold era

The significance of the lay brotherhoods becomes particularly evident with the rise of what has been called the *barroco mineiro* 'baroque of Minas Gerais'. This phase of artistic development occurred as a consequence of *bandeiras*, expeditions led by Portuguese colonizers from the São Vicente Captaincy into the interior of the country searching for gold. The rugged frontiersmen who left São Vicente and São Paulo on expeditions usually returned only with natives, whom they kept for themselves or sold as slaves to prosperous local aristocrats. Though these expeditions did not bring immediate prosperity to the colonizers of the São Vicente Captaincy, they paid off in the long term.

In 1698, prospectors found gold in the Serra do Espinhaço, and during the 1700s, the mines of Minas Gerais, Goiás, and Mato Grosso were producing 44 percent of the world's supply of gold. Gold attracted prospectors from all over the country, even from Europe. New communities grew up overnight, particularly around the major mining sites of Minas Gerais but also along the routes used for transporting the gold to the ports.

From about 1750 to about 1800, the concentration of wealth in gold-rush areas led to the development of an urban life-style in several of the important towns of Minas Gerais; unlike at any other moment in the colonial period, artistic activity in sculpture, painting, and music flourished. Though the music of the period, studied extensively by Francisco Curt Lange (1965, 1966), has been termed *barroco mineiro*, it is more closely associated with a preclassical homophonic style (like that of C. P. E. Bach and Franz Joseph Haydn), yet no single European musician stands out as the main influence on local composers. Many *mineiro* compositions involved a four-part mixed chorus with an orchestral accompaniment provided by two violins, a viola (or cellos), a bass, and two French horns, and occasionally oboes, flutes, and a harpsichord.

Between 1760 and 1800, nearly a thousand active musicians were associated with lay brotherhoods in Minas Gerais, primarily concentrated in Vila Rica (now Ouro Preto), Sabará, Mariana, Arraial de Tejuco (now Diamantina), São João del Rei, and São José del Rei (now Tiradentes). Many were free mulattoes, trained in family-based musical establishments, who studied Latin, voice, and instruments, and learned to read and copy music and to set liturgical texts to melodic lines.

The most outstanding local composer of the period was José Joaquim Emérico Lobo de Mesquita (ca. 1740–1805), who composed more than three hundred pieces, of which about forty have survived. Other important composers were Marcos Coelho Netto (d. 1823), Francisco Gomes da Rocha (d. 1808), and Ignacio Parreiras Neves (ca. 1730–1793). By 1820, the gold in the mines was becoming exhausted, and the golden era of Brazilian music was declining.

The coffee era

The gold-rush developments were followed by a boom in coffee, and the establishment of coffee plantations (*fazendas*) affected musical practices. In the early 1800s, coffee had become popular in Europe and the Americas. Coffee plants could be cultivated profitably in the soil of the Paraíba Valley, an area soon taken over by large landholdings, modeled on the northeastern plantation system. Around 1860, coffee moved westward to the areas around Campinas, and into Ribeirão Preto. By 1900, the state of São Paulo was producing nearly 75 percent of the world's supply. In the mid-1940s, northern Paraná became the locus of the new boom. Today, as coffee takes over the scrub lands of central Minas Gerais, fortunes are still being made.

As coffee made its westward march, rural communities were absorbed as sharecroppers into the plantation life-style. The coffee economy brought vast numbers of African slaves and their descendants, mostly of Bantu origin, plus European and other immigrant groups. The musical traditions of these social groups existed side by side, but in time they began to borrow from one another.

As in rural communities, sociability on plantations centered on Christian festivities. On special saints' days, landowners provided a hefty meal and entertainment for their workers. At these festivals, the landholding elites congregated in the parlor of the plantation house for European-style dancing in couples; sharecroppers participated in the *cateretê* in the front patio of the house; and slaves amused themselves in *batuques* near the slave quarters (*senzalas*). In the *batuque,* individual dancers entered a circle to perform acrobatic steps to other participants' singing, clapping, and percussive accompaniment. The soloist ended his or her performance with a belly bump (*umbigada*) against someone in the circle, transferring the role of soloist to that person.

As the population increased, patronal festivals became common in towns throughout the coffee-producing areas. The hosts (*festeiros*) of these festivals were mostly large landholders. To confront labor shortages, they competed with one another to produce ever grander festivals, demonstrating their benevolence toward

modinha   Brazilian sentimental song genre
    originating in late colonial period

lundu   Early Brazilian song type derived from
    Afro-Brazilian folk dance

batuque   Afro-Brazilian round dance of
    Angolese or Congolese origin

violão   (Portuguese, "guitar")   The common
    Iberian-six-stringed guitar

choro   Afro-Brazilian musical genre based on
    polka-*maxixe* rhythm

their workers. As the festivals became more and more elaborate new musical styles emerged to enhance them. Many communities founded brass bands, derived from the European military-band tradition, to lead their processions, and various Afro-Brazilian dramatic traditions of dance and music emerged, amalgamating Portuguese and African musical and ritual practices.

These ensembles still perform for patronal festivals throughout central and southern Brazil. In many rural communities, the patronal festival is the most important event of the calendar, bringing crowds of people to the streets, where they are bombarded with sounds, music, dancing, smells, and visual stimuli.

Musical life in Rio

Outside the mining areas, the only other colonial town of significant size in southern Brazil was Rio de Janeiro, where musical life centered on the monastery of São Bento and the cathedral of Saint Sebastian. In 1763, Rio became the capital of the colony, and throughout the 1800s it was Brazil's cultural center. The new musical trends and fashions that emerged in Rio radiated to other parts of the country. Thus, Rio set the tone for the country's art music and urban popular music.

Rio was the birthplace of Domingos Caldas Barbosa (1739–1800), the first known composer of *modinhas* and *lundus* whose texts are extant. His songs scandalized the Portuguese court because their manner of addressing women in the audience struck the court as being indecently direct (Tinhorão 1990:92–93). Gregório de Matos Guerra of Bahia (1623–1695) may already have written and sung *lundus* and *modinhas,* but none of his works has survived.

The *modinha* and the *lundu* developed in the early 1700s, competing for the distinction of being the first "truly Brazilian" musical form. The *lundu* made its way into upper-class parlors from the *batuque* circles, but the *modinha* evinces influences from Italian opera. The *lundu* is faster, and deals with comical and satirical themes. The *modinha* is more melodic, and incarnates the Brazilian romantic spirit, appropriate for serenades.

Even essentially art music composers such as José Maurício Nunes Garcia (1767–1830), Francisco Manuel da Silva (b. 1812), and Carlos Gomes made their contributions to the repertoire, exemplifying how fluid the dividing line between Brazilian popular music and art music has been.

In 1808, to escape the Napoleonic threat, the Portuguese court moved to Rio. Though the king, Dom João VI, remained in the colony only thirteen years, his presence gave new vitality to musical life in the capital. A patron of the arts, he stimulated musical activity, and Garcia, one of Brazil's most renowned priest-composers, soon found himself in the monarch's favor, much to the annoyance of the former court-based composer Marcos Portugal (1762–1830), who had also followed the king to the colony.

When Dom João returned to Portugal, he left the kingdom in the hands of his son, Dom Pedro I, who declared its independence in 1822. Though Dom Pedro was himself a composer (having received instruction from José Maurício, Marcos Portugal, and Sigmund Neukomm), he lacked his father's commitment to the arts, and cut state patronage to local musicians. In 1831 when he abdicated, the musical activities of the Brazilian imperial chapel had practically come to a standstill, with only twenty-seven musicians still under imperial patronage.

In 1840, his successor, Dom Pedro II, assumed the throne, and musical life in Rio was revitalized. This was due to the efforts of Francisco Manuel da Silva (1795–1865), the master composer of the imperial chapel, whose most famous work is the Brazilian national anthem. In Rio in 1847, Da Silva founded the Music Conservatory, which he directed until his death. In 1860, the National Lyric Opera was founded; its first production was *A Noite de São João* by Elias Alvares Lôbo (1834–1901), who based his libretto on poems by the Indianist writer José de Alencar. It was also through the National Lyric Opera that Brazilian audiences were introduced to Carlos Gomes (1836–1896), Brazil's most successful composer of operas. In his most celebrated pieces, *Il Guarany* and *Lo Schiavo*, he drew on the romantic image of the native Brazilian—which made him especially popular in Europe. Reminiscences of native Brazilian motifs and popular Brazilian urban genres were present in his music.

The arrival of the Portuguese court had other important implications for colonial musical activities. With the entourage came the first pianos, which families with sufficient means soon acquired. By 1834, pianos were being constructed in Brazil, and the piano remains an important status symbol for the upper classes. By 1834, Brazilian publishers were editing the music of the latest European dances (country dances, polkas, quadrilles, schottisches, waltzes, and others), which amateurs throughout the country played with enthusiasm. Popular composers, such as Chiquinha Gonzaga (1847–1935) and Ernesto Nazaré (1863–1933) Brazilianized these dances, providing the country's amateur pianists with a locally flavored repertoire. The influence of the *modinha* could be observed in the waltz, while the fusion of the polka with the *lundu* provided the matrix for the Brazilian tango and the *maxixe*, an early form of the samba.

While the upper classes gathered around their parlor pianos, Rio's bohemians were playing the same repertoire in the streets on *violões* (guitars) and *cavaquinhos* (small, four-stringed, guitarlike instruments similar to ukuleles, with metal strings). During the 1870s, a standardized ensemble evolved, consisting of an ebony flute (which played the melody), a *cavaquinho* (for the harmony), and a *violão* (guitar, which provided a bass). The musicians that played in this manner became known as *chorões*. Many early *chorões* were employed in military bands, which became important venues of musical instruction for those who could not afford private piano tuition. Near the end of the century, other band-derived wind instruments (such as the flute, the ophicleide, the clarinet, and the saxophone) would often play the melody. The repertoire became progressively faster and required greater virtuosity. It eventually evolved into a distinct musical genre, the *choro* (also *chorinho*).

Even in the late 1990s, the masterpieces of such popular composers as Pixinguinha, Zequinha de Abreu, Anacleto de Medeiros, and others were still being played and recorded, though *choros* were performed by larger ensembles, including tambourines and other percussion instruments. Small stringed instruments came to be used as melodic instruments.

Musical nationalism

By the late 1800s, musical nationalism had become a feature of Brazilian art music, particularly in the work of Joaquim Antônio da Silva Callado (1848–1880),

Alexandre Levy (1864–1892), and Alberto Nepomuceno (1864–1920). These nationalists drew primarily on Rio's urban musical traditions: the *lundu*, the *modinha*, and the *choro*.

Without doubt, Heitor Villa-Lobos (1887–1959), a native of Rio, was Brazil's most talented and prolific nationalist composer. He composed numerous orchestral pieces including twelve symphonies, thirteen tone poems, twelve suites, and more than twenty concertos. He also composed seven operas, numerous chamber and choral pieces, and a vast repertoire for solo instruments, especially piano and guitar. As a youth, he played with *chorões*, and later he traveled around the country, acquainting himself with the national soundscape, drawing on this material in his compositions. Among his most celebrated works are a series of *Choros*, composed between 1920 and 1929; the *Bachianas Brasileiras*, composed between 1930 and 1945; and his piano music, particularly the *Lenda do Caboclo*, composed in 1920; and suites based on children's songs, *A Prole do Bebê*, *No. 1* and *No. 2*, composed between 1918 and 1921.

Born in São Paulo, Mário de Andrade (1893–1945) was the intellectual leader of the nationalist movement. In a book about Brazilian music (1964 [1928]), he called on Brazilian composers to participate in the construction of a national serious music tradition through the use of Brazilian expressive elements. Though he was himself not a composer, he used his literary work to introduce his project to Brazilian music circles. Much of his work (especially 1975, 1982, 1983) was dedicated to the collection and analysis of the national repertoire, which provided composers with raw material for their compositions. His research inspired other artists and intellectuals to collect the musical folklore of the country. Among these are Oneyda Alvarenga (1946, 1982), Alceu Maynard de Araújo (1964), Augusto Meyer (1958), Baptista Siqueira (1979), and others.

Musical nationalism remained a hallmark of Brazilian art music well into the twentieth century, spearheaded by Camargo Guarnieri (1907–1993). The only composers who openly rejected it were those associated with Música Viva, a movement that congregated around Hans-Joachim Koellreutter (b. 1915), a German Jew who fled to Brazil to escape Nazi persecution, bringing with him the techniques of dodecaphonic composition. Some exponents of Música Viva did try to produce nationalist twelve-tone music, most notably Cláudio Santoro (1919–1989) and César Guerra-Peixe (1914–1993).

It was not until the 1960s that Brazilian composers began to break away from the nationalist mold. Through organizations such as the New Music Group in Santos and São Paulo, the Brazilian Society of Contemporary Music in Rio de Janeiro, and festivals of avant-garde music, Brazilian composers began to experiment with new compositional techniques—serialism, electronic music, aleatory procedures, atonality, and composition in mixed media. Major contemporary Brazilian composers active in central and southern Brazil include Gilberto Mendes (b. 1922), Willy Corrêa de Oliveira (b. 1938), Marlos Nobre (b. 1939), and Jorge Antunes (b. 1942).

MUSICAL TRAITS OF CENTRAL AND SOUTHERN BRAZIL

Contemporary musical traditions in central and southern Brazil resonate with the processes of interaction of the social groups in the area. Although Portuguese material has been substantially reinvented over the centuries, the strong sense of solidarity that had united peasant communities prior to the invasion of coffee culture has guaranteed the persistence of a marked Lusitanian-Hispanic legacy in the area. Iberian stylistic traits include arched melodies, conjunct melodic movement, parallel thirds and sixths, tonality, stanza-refrain alternation or strophic form, and the extensive use of stringed instruments.

FIGURE 2 Typical rhythmic sequence of a *cateretê*.

Many contemporary musical traditions associated with blacks and mulattos evince the influence of the *batuque*. These traditions often involve responsorial singing, syncopated rhythms (irregular accentuation and anticipation), and the extensive use of percussive accompaniment organized around an eight-pulse timeline.

In the process of acculturation or mestization, unique musical styles developed, reflecting the amalgamation of European and African musical practices. Many African traditions incorporated parallel thirds, functional harmony, and stringed instruments of European origin; likewise, the eight-pulse timeline became ubiquitous in the traditions of the Portuguese peasantry, as in the typical rhythmic sequence of the *cateretê* (figure 2).

Some forms (*embolada*, *moda-de-viola*, *xácara*, and others) have fixed texts, but many genres—particularly those involving musical duels, including the *cururu paulista* and the *porfia* of the extreme south, known as *cantoria* in the northeast [see BRAZIL, NORTHEAST REGION]—involve textual improvisation within the form of the Iberian quatrain. In these genres, two singers take turns improvising versified insults about each other until one is declared the winner. The texts of the *jongo*, the *brão*, and other riddle-based genres are also improvised, and the exposition of the enigmas and the quest for their answers involve song, as seen in the following example of a *jongo* improvisation. After a quatrain for the enigma, it has a quatrain for the answer.

Debaixo de papai velho,	Under old father,
Menino tá sepurtado.	Boy is buried.
Quero contar no meu ponto:	I want to tell you in my verse:
Menino foi interrado.	Boy was interred.
Meu irmão, sendo mais velho,	My brother, being older,
Licença peço pr'ocê:	I ask you to excuse me.
Vou desinterrar o menino	I'll now exhume the boy
Pra nós tudo aqui beber.	So all of us here can drink.

The "old father" is the *tambu*, the largest drum used in the *jongo*; the "boy" is a bottle of cane spirits. To protect the singer's knowledge from others' envy, he has hidden the drink under his instrument (Borges Ribeiro 1984:38).

In many popular Roman Catholic traditions of Brazil, competence in improvising verses is fundamental to ritual leadership. More than in other domains of performance competence, this ability is viewed as evidence of the leader's gift. Though age is a determining factor, criteria based on musical competence are important in constructing the internal hierarchies common to most popular Roman Catholic musical ensembles.

Some genres are sung solo (the *cururu paulista* and improvisations in the *carangueijo*) and others are sung collectively (processional prayers and refrains between improvisations in the *carangueijo*), but a common configuration throughout central and southern Brazil is that of the *dupla*, singing in parallel thirds or sixths. Its *modas* and *toadas* (tunes or melodic sequences) often encapsulate narrations related to rural social and religious life and traditional values.

One of the most typical features of rural traditional music is the consistent use of parallel thirds. The main voice is in the higher register, considered the more salient. Yet for the last chord of each verse, the first voice takes the mediant, while the second takes the tonic, rendering the first voice tonally subordinate to the second (figure 3).

The southern Brazilian states have received the musical legacy of waves of European immigrants, particularly Germans, who in isolated communities maintain their language and musical traditions.

FIGURE 3   *Toada paulista*, a rural traditional genre, showing a typical cadential pattern using parallel thirds. Transcription by Suzel Ana Reily.

The two voices are perceived as a unity; when one is not present, people feel something is missing. This kind of vocal construction can be viewed as a way of reconciling notions about the equality of the participants with the hierarchical aspects of vocal organization. Rendering the role of the first voice ambiguous causes its dominance to become structurally muted, and the two voices conjoin to form a complementary unit. Far from being merely an aesthetic preference, parallel thirds have probably been stable because they provide a sonic means of reconciling the asymmetry of social relations with notions of human equality—a fundamental issue of the Roman Catholic and socially oriented ethos of rural Brazil.

Only in the extreme south did the stereotype of the cowboy (*gaúcho*), androcentric and individualist, so influence the formation of the Lusitanian-Brazilian personality that parallel thirds and other polyphonic traits are less prevalent. There, male solos are far more common, and groups are more likely to sing in unison (Mendoza de Arce 1981). Distinctively, the southern Brazilian states have received the musical legacy of waves of European immigrants, particularly Germans, who in isolated communities maintain their language and musical traditions.

MUSICAL INSTRUMENTS

Numerous musical instruments are used during central and southern Brazilian social events; the rhythmic percussion instruments are used in ensembles, while the melodic instruments are played solo or in ensembles. The former include a great variety of idiophones and membranophones; the latter include aerophones, many influenced by use in military bands, and chordophones derived from colonial times. Only the most common musical instruments are included here.

Idiophones

The idiophones of central and southern Brazil are mostly small percussion instruments used to give timbral diversity to various ensembles. The *ganzá* (also *guaiá*, cylindrical shaker), *melê* (also *afoxé*, friction rattle), *rêco-rêco* (spring or bamboo scraper), and triangle are used in many different settings in urban and rural contexts. The double bell (*agogô*) is used exclusively in Afro-Brazilian urban traditions such as

Candomblé (an Afro-Brazilian possession cult) and the carnival associations known as samba schools (*escolas de samba*). Knee-tied bells (*paiás*) are unique to certain rural Afro-Brazilian dances, especially the *moçambique* of the Paraíba Valley. Large cymbals are an integral part of the percussion section of town bands.

Membranophones

Membranophones of various shapes and sizes are common throughout central and southern Brazil. Like idiophones, some are used in numerous traditions; others are only found in specific contexts. The tambourine (*pandeiro,* often known as *adufo* in some rural areas), and the *caixa* (a medium-sized double-headed drum, with or without snare) (figure 4) are the most versatile membranophones in the area, found in such diverse traditions as samba ensembles, *choros*, and popular Roman Catholic rural traditions of Portuguese or African influence.

Afro-Brazilian traditions, which use several drums of different sizes, often have distinct names for the different membranophones. In the popular traditions of Roman Catholic dramatic music and dance, the three most commonly found are a small drum (*repico*), a medium-size drum (*caixa*), and a large drum (*bumbo*). Two drums are used in the *jongo*: the *tambu*, the larger, and the *condonqueiro*, the smaller. A friction drum (*puíta*) is also used. *Baterias*, the percussion ensembles of samba schools, may have any number of small, single-headed frame drum (*tamborim*) (figure 5), *caixa*, *repique* (also *repinique*) (medium-size single-headed drum), *atabaque* (large narrow single-headed conical drum), *cuíca* (single-headed friction drum), and *surdo* (large double-headed bass drum). In these traditions, each drum type has its own basic rhythmic pattern, often in a polymetric relation to the other parts.

Aerophones

One of the most popular aerophones in Brazil is the accordion. Throughout the country, it is known as *sanfona,* but in the extreme south, it is called *gaita.* It was introduced into the country by German immigrants in the early 1800s but became popular with the population at large only after 1870. In southern Brazil, it is commonly associated with the fandango, a social dance; in southeastern and central Brazil, it often accompanies the *quadrilha,* danced during festivities in honor of Saint John the Baptist.

Military bands have left their legacy throughout central and southern Brazil, and many small towns maintain bands that perform for patronal and civic festivities. The wind instruments used in these ensembles often include flutes, clarinets, alto and tenor saxophones, cornets, trombones, saxhorns, tubas (*bombardinos*), and sousaphones (*baixos*). Their repertoire consists primarily of *dobrados* (marches in 2/4 time), appropriate for processions. Flutes, clarinets, and saxophones also serve as melodic instruments in *chorinhos.* In many percussive ensembles of African influence, the leader uses a whistle to cue stops and transitions.

Chordophones

The most common stringed instruments in the area include the *viola* (a guitar with five single or double courses of strings), the *violão* (the ordinary Portuguese term for guitar), the *cavaquinho* (a small, four-stringed guitarlike instrument similar to the ukulele, with metal or nylon strings), the *bandolim* (a small mandolinlike instrument with four double courses of strings), and the *rabeca* (folk-derived violin, the term reflecting the European word *rebec*).

The *viola,* the Brazilian descendant of the Spanish *vihuela,* is the most important instrument of central and southern Brazil, and it exists in a variety of types. A form of the instrument found in Mato Grosso do Sul is known as a *viola de cocho* 'trough

FIGURE 4   A man plays a *caixa* 'snare drum' for a *folia de reis* in Batatais, São Paulo. Photo by Suzel Ana Reily, 1988.

FIGURE 5   The *tamborim* 'frame-drum' section in a samba school in São Paulo. Photo by Suzel Ana Reily, 1982.

FIGURE 6 *Viola* tunings: *a, cebolão; b, rio abaixo.*

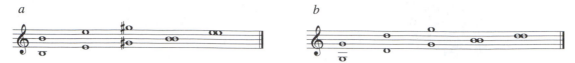

guitar'. The body of the instrument is dug out of a single trunk of soft wood and is covered with a thin layer of wood. Some instruments have a few small sound holes, but others have none. The *viola de cocho* has five single courses of strings, made of animal gut or fishing line. It produces a deep, hollow sound, more percussive than harmonic.

In southeastern Brazil, the most common *viola* is the *viola caipira* 'country guitar'. It is smaller than a guitar, and has five double courses of metal strings. In contrast with the *viola de cocho*, it has a full, metallic timbre. It can be tuned in many ways, the most common being the *cebolão* 'big onion' and the *rio abaixo* 'downriver' (figure 6). These tunings make the *viola* especially adequate for doubling the singers' parallel thirds. Quite often, other four-stringed instruments are tuned like the *viola* by eliminating the lowest string. Currently, the *viola dinâmica* (figure 7) is gaining popularity. Though larger than a *viola caipira*, it can be tuned in the same way, and it produces a louder sound.

A *violeiro* (*viola* player) must be competent to play in a tonality other than the one in which the instrument has been tuned. *Música sertaneja* (the Brazilian equivalent of North American country music) is accompanied by a *viola* and a *violão*, an instrumental configuration that has come to be known as *o casal* 'the couple'. Since the 1960s, however, the *violão* has been taking the place of the *viola*, since it is considered more modern and versatile.

Though the *viola* is the quintessential instrument of the Brazilian lower classes, the *violão* epitomizes the popular musical traditions of the upper and middle classes. It was celebrated in many pieces by Heitor Villa-Lobos, and it was the primary instrument of the bossa nova movement. Nonetheless, it is used in popular Roman Catholic traditions in rural areas, just as it is included in samba styles of the urban underprivileged. The *choro* musician (*chorão*) Horondino Silva created a seven-stringed guitar (*violão-sete-cordas*) to give him a wider range for his bass notes. The instrument continues to be used for *choros*.

FIGURE 7 A man plays a *viola dinâmica* in Monsenhor Paulo, Minas Gerais. Photo by Suzel Ana Reily, 1988.

The *cavaquinho* is primarily an urban instrument, used to accompany *choros* and samba. The *bandolim* is also used in the *choro* tradition, often as a melody instrument. The *rabeca*, however, is fundamentally a rural instrument, played primarily during popular Christian festivities.

MUSIC WITHIN POPULAR ROMAN CATHOLICISM

Musical activities in rural areas are associated with religious events, and many popular rituals still take place with little or no ecclesiastical intervention. Many saints who have become the objects of popular devotion in Brazil—the Virgin Mary, Saint John the Baptist, Saint Sebastian, and many others—are depicted with all-too-human traits, and quite frequently they are fun-loving musicians and dancers. Devotion to these saints typically involves making merry, eating heavily, performing music, and dancing.

The Saint Gonçalo dance

Saint Gonçalo of Amarante (flourished about 1250), patron of *violeiros*, is invariably depicted with a *viola*. It is said that every Saturday night he would take his instrument to the brothels of Amarante, Portugal, rounding up prostitutes, with whom he played and danced, tiring them so much that on Sunday they would not sin.

For this reason, the saint is honored through the Saint Gonçalo dance, a double line dance similar to the *cateretê*, involving rhythmic clapping and stamping. It is usually performed on a Saturday night in someone's yard to fulfill a promise made to the saint in return for a miracle, often a miraculous cure involving a person's legs. People with promises often dance holding the saint's image (figure 8). An entire social network assumes the responsibility of an individual's obligations toward the saint by attending the dance and participating in the activity. In this way, the institution of the promise and the actual event are as means of promoting social solidarity (Brandão 1981).

Folias de reis

🔊TRACK 11   The biblical Magi became musicians, according to stories told by people who participate in mummerlike ensembles known as *folias de reis* 'the kings' *folias*'. In Brazilian

FIGURE 8   Women of Atibaia, a suburb of São Paulo, dance with Saint Gonçalo. Photo by Suzel Ana Reily, 1983.

Most Brazilian musicologists concur that the word *samba* developed out of the Quimbundo term *semba*, which denotes the belly bump, one of the distinctive choreographic features of the *batuque*.

FIGURE 9   A *folia de reis* collects donations for the Festival of the Three Kings in Monsenhor Paulo, Minas Gerais. Photo by Suzel Ana Reily, 1988.

folklore, the wise men received their instruments—a *viola*, an *adufo*, a *caixa*—from the Virgin Mary; they returned to the east, singing from house to house to announce the birth of Jesus. Acting out this story, the *folia de reis* members go from house to house during the twelve days of Christmas, collecting donations to promote a festival on Epiphany (6 January), celebrated in Latin America as the day of the three kings (figure 9).

The tunes (*toadas*) used by *folias de reis* often involve an accumulation of voices (usually six), leading to a loud and prolonged major chord. The voices make successive entrances, each entrance tonally higher than the previous one; with each entrance, the texture becomes denser. Thus, the structure of the music reflects the ritual role of these ensembles: it is a sonic representation of the accumulation of donations, which, once collected, allows the community to stage its festival (Reily 1994b:13).

Ternos

In central and southern Brazil, ensembles of dramatic music and dance known as *caboclinhos, caiapós, congadas, moçambiques*, and others are collectively called *ternos*. They often perform in the streets during patronal festivals. They are usually dedicated to the Virgin Mary in her capacity as Our Lady of the Rosary and to Saint Benedict the Moor (d. 1589), but they may come out for festivals in honor of other saints.

Their typical choreography consists of a symbolic battle—between Christians and Moors, or Africans and slavers, or Indians and Portuguese—enacted through dialogues (*embaixadas*) and various uses of batons (figure 10). Symbolically, good (or the oppressed group) prevails over evil (or the oppressing group), thanks to the honored saint's intervention.

At large festivals, several *ternos*—some local, and others from neighboring municipalities—roam the streets. Each ensemble has unique uniforms and a unique combination of colors, and all the ensembles compete with one another, beating their instruments as loudly as possible.

In some areas, people distinguish between the music and the choreography of each type of *terno*. In the Paraíba Valley, *congadas* do not use batons and knee-tied bells, because these are associated with the poorer *moçambiques*. In other areas, *moçambiques* do not perform *embaixadas*, though both ensembles battle with batons.

Ternos are voluntary associations, but membership tends to be almost exclusively male; women may participate as bearers of banners (*porta-bandeiras*), leading the procession of musicians and dancers. The ensembles perform in two parallel lines, in which the leaders stay behind the instruments, in front of the dancers (*soldados* 'soldiers'). The dancers are organized in pairs according to their ages, with elders in front.

The musical performances of these ensembles begin with a slow *toada* sung in parallel thirds by the captain (*capitão*) and his helper (*ajudante*), immediately answered by the responder (*resposta*) and his helper (also *ajudante*). After this introduction, the first singers break into a faster *toada*, which, once presented, is repeated by the responder and his helper before the dancers behind them take it up (figure 11). Once the singing is under way, the captain blows his whistle, and the dancers begin to strike their batons in choreographed routines.

The parallel thirds and the harmonic accompaniment of the *toada* in figure 11 are signs of European input, but several of its features show African influence. Note the eight-pulse timeline underlying several parts, particularly the melody and those of the bass drum, the knee-tied bell, and the sticks. The other parts are in polyrhythmic relations to the timeline. Musical associations such as *congadas* and *moçambiques* may be Brazilian analogs to the tradition of secret societies brought to the New World by the slaves from the Kingdom of the Congo (Kazadi wa Mukuna 1979).

TRACK 12

MUSIC IN URBAN CONTEXTS

At the turn of the twentieth century, musical activities in the urban centers of central and southern Brazil were clearly defined along class lines: the elites congregated in enclosed spaces (parlors, concert halls, ballrooms) to participate in events involving European and national art music and dancing in couples; the middle classes were associated with *chorões*, which performed in the street, though in respectable places; and the lower classes, who were restricted to the hills overlooking Rio and poor peripheral neighborhoods, were recreating musical forms that had developed in *batuque* circles during the slave era. By the 1930s, however, samba had become a national phenomenon, cutting across these class-drawn barriers.

Samba

Samba is the best known of Brazil's musical expressive forms. Almost an international synonym for Brazilian music, it has become something of an umbrella term to designate a range of popular styles, including *samba carnavalesca* (carnival samba), *samba-enredo* (theme samba), *samba baiana* (Bahian samba), *samba-lenço* (handkerchief samba), *samba rural* (rural samba), *samba de morro* (hill samba), *samba da cidade* (city samba), *samba de terreiro* (yard samba), *samba de breque* (break samba), *samba de partido-alto* (specialist samba), *samba corrido* (verse samba), *samba-canção* (song samba), *samba-choro* (*choro* samba), and many others. All these genres have elements that at some level can be traced to African origins, particularly to Bantu traditions organized in eight- and sixteen-pulse timelines.

These timelines generate some rhythmic patterns (*batucadas*) played by several instruments in the percussion ensembles (*baterias*) of the urban carnival associations known as samba schools (*escolas de samba*) (figure 12). Note the eight-pulse cycle in the accents of the *caixa* and the *rêco-rêco,* and how the rhythmic patterns of the *agogô* and the *tamborim* are structured around a sixteen-pulse timeline. Other instruments such as the *surdo*, the *ganzá*, and the *cuíca,* are accented on offbeats creating a rich, polyrhythmic texture.

Brazilian musicologists argue about how and where the samba originated. Most concur that the word developed out of the Quimbundo (a Bantu language) term *semba*, which denotes the belly bump, one of the distinctive choreographic features of the *batuque*. According to Sílvio Romero (1954), the term was associated with a specific Bahian dance in the second half of the 1800s; Bahian ex-slaves then brought it to Rio de Janeiro, where it fused with such urban styles as the polka, the habanera, the *modinha*, and the *lundu*. Kazadi wa Mukuna (1979), however, argues that it may have developed on the coffee plantations of the Paraíba Valley before reaching the capital. Many rural forms of the samba are still danced throughout the coffee-pro-

FIGURE 10   *Moçambiques* dance at the Festival of the Divine Holy Spirit (Pentecost) in São Luís do Paraitinga, São Paulo. Photo by Suzel Ana Reily, 1982.

FIGURE 11   A *toada de moçambique* performed at the Festival of the Divine Holy Spirit (Pentecost) in São Luís do Paraitinga, São Paulo. Transcription by Suzel Ana Reily.

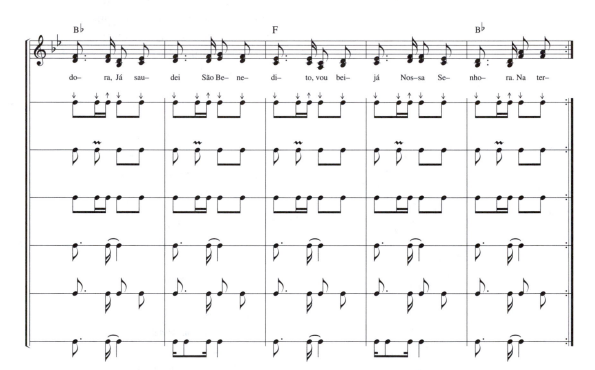

ducing areas, where they are known by various terms, such as *samba rural* and *samba-lenço*. In the contemporary forms of rural samba, the belly bump has been suppressed to make the dances more respectable. José Ramos Tinhorão (1986) argues that the samba was the product of a middle-class elaboration of Afro-Brazilian musical practices by professional musicians in Rio. It was then reappropriated in its more complex form by blacks and mulattos for their carnival parades.

Whatever the antecedents, samba first became associated with carnival (*carnaval*) in Rio de Janeiro. At carnival around 1900, mobile associations (*ranchos*, also *blocos*), made up of blacks, mulattoes, and unskilled white laborers danced down the streets to the rhythm of percussive instruments, singing responsorially to the

FIGURE 12   A rhythmic pattern played by a samba school's percussion ensemble. Transcription by Suzel Ana Reily.

short improvised verses of a leader. In Rio, this samba style became known as *samba baiana* or *samba carnavalesca*.

The new 2/4 rhythm proved particularly suitable for keeping unity in the movements of the mobile associations while allowing each dancer to move freely. By appearing to be more organized, these ensembles were less likely to attract official repression. Soon the samba became extremely popular among the lower-class inhabitants of Rio de Janeiro (*cariocas*), displacing practically all other musical genres. Samba and carnival would remain linked from then on, each lending its prestige to the other.

One afternoon in 1928, a group of samba musicians (*sambistas*) belonging to an association known as Deixa Falar (Let Them Speak) was rehearsing in a field in front of a teacher-training college. Inspired by this situation, they decided to call their own association a samba school (*escola de samba*). Thereafter, other carnival associations adopted the term, and samba schools began turning up in Rio neighborhoods.

Samba-enredo

During the 1930s, samba schools began presenting themes (*enredos*) in their parades, and these presentations soon led to the development of the *samba-enredo*, samba with a narrative text. Various uniformed dancers (*alas*) became clearly demarcated, each representing part of the story of the *samba-enredo*. Floats carrying *destaques* (people in special outfits placed on the floats) were added, also relating to the theme.

It did not take long for local politicians to perceive the political utility of the samba schools, for these were among the few associations capable of organizing the urban popular masses. In 1930, Getúlio Vargas came to power, and by 1937 he had instituted a nationalist regime, the new state (*estado novo*), modeled on Mussolini's Italy. The Vargas government was quick to coopt Rio's samba schools, incorporating them into its nationalist project.

The timid and quiet vocal style of bossa nova negated the stereotype of Brazilians as an overemotive, exuberant race, to portray them as contemplative, intimate, and sophisticated.

In 1934, carnival in Rio was made official, and only legally registered schools could receive public funds to help cover the costs of their exhibitions. By 1937, these groups had to develop themes that would stimulate nationalist feelings among the participants by glorifying patriotic symbols and national heroes. National glorification remained a dominant thematic trait of samba-school performances long after the Vargas era, which ended in 1954. In the mid-1960s, literary figures and Brazilian folklore became dominant themes.

With the onset of the 1980s, as the country faced redemocratization, many samba schools began to use the parades as a venue for addressing national issues, such as direct presidential elections, inflation, poverty, ecological devastation, discrimination against minorities, and other social and economic problems that afflict Brazil's people. One of the best examples of this change was "*O Luxo e o Lixo*" ('Luxury and Trash'), the 1989 theme developed by the producer (*carnavalesco*) Joãozinho 30 (whose surname is a number) for his samba school, Beija-Flor; it starkly depicted the inequalities of Brazilian society.

Hill samba and city samba

The distinction between hill samba and city samba emerged in the 1930s, when members of the ascending middle classes within urban contexts took to the new rhythm. Styles classed as sambas from the hills were those used by the lower classes that lived in shantytowns (*favelas*) overlooking the respectable neighborhoods. These included the various forms of carnival samba (*samba carnavalesco, samba baiana,* and *samba-enredo*), *samba de terreiro* (sambas played by samba school musicians outside the carnival period), *samba de partido-alto* (sambas in which prominent musicians improvised long verses between refrains), and *samba corrido* (a style of samba without refrains). City sambas catered to middle-class tastes; they emphasized melody and text, and their composers had better access to recording studios. Their dominant form was song samba (*samba-canção*), but break samba and *choro* samba were also included in this category.

The first recording of a samba, made in 1917, was of the composition "*Pelo Telefone*" ('By Telephone'). Only in the 1930s, when the radio was more widely diffused, did samba become a quasi-national phenomenon. With the popularization of the genre, the demand for it was no longer restricted to carnival, and composers of sambas responded by creating a new modality: *samba-canção,* samba for any time of the year. Performers and composers such as Ary Barroso, Noel Rosa, Araci Cortes, Carmen Miranda, Ataúlfo Alves, and many others could be heard year-round, all over the country.

As were the samba schools, the most popular musicians were quickly coopted by the Vargas government, which contracted with them to perform on National Radio, a state agency. During this period, Ary Barroso composed the internationally famous samba "*Aquarela do Brasil*" ('Watercolor of Brazil'). Grandiloquence became the trademark of the genre, as it exalted the country's greatness.

In the 1980s, a new form of samba, *samba de gafieira,* became popular in large urban centers. *Gafieiras* are large dance halls patronized by the urban working class, and *samba de gafieira* is the style of samba used in these establishments. In the early 1990s, the samba was fused with reggae to produce samba-reggae.

Bossa nova

After more than two decades of *samba-canção,* Brazilian audiences in the late 1950s welcomed the change brought by bossa nova. During the Vargas era, the country had undergone dramatic changes; as industry spearheaded the country's economic growth, rural bases of power had lost ground. Juscelino Kubitschek was elected president in 1955, espousing a platform encapsulated in the slogan Fifty Years in Five. He promised to lead the country in a developmental drive that in a single term of office would reduce its fifty-year lag in relation to the developed world. National pride was at a high, and the urban population was resolutely behind him.

In this era of national euphoria, the urban middle classes centered their preoccupations on making the most of the modern conveniences industrialization had brought them. By now, the lower and upper social classes of Rio had become spatially isolated from one another, and for the first time in Brazilian history, a new generation had grown up with only a superficial experience of interclass contact.

Youths who grew up within this context lived a carefree existence of sun, beaches, and romance, secure in their belief that Brazil was finally taking its place on the international scene. They were searching for a musical style that suited their self-image: it had to be simultaneously Brazilian and nonexotic; it had to be able to speak of traditional guitars and Rolliflex cameras.

Furthermore, nightlife for Rio's upper classes had moved out of the large big-band halls to the intimate dark setting of nightclubs, and such establishments were proliferating in the city's affluent neighborhoods. The nightclub context called for a mellow musical style, which could promote the romantic intimacy young dreamy-eyed couples were seeking.

Bossa nova answered all these requirements. While drawing on various traditions, the mellow sound of the guitar and the soft percussion highlighted their complex principles of rhythmic organization, rather than their visceral qualities; the timid and quiet vocal style of bossa nova negated the stereotype of Brazilians as an overemotive, exuberant race, to portray them as contemplative, intimate, and sophisticated.

The first recording of a bossa nova was made in 1958. The song was "*Chega de Saudade*" ('No More Longing'), which united the heavyweights of the movement, epitomizing their individual contributions. Antônio Carlos Jobim (1927–1994) wrote the music, which had a modal feeling set against altered and compact chords; the lyrics, by Vinícius de Morães (1913–1980), had a colloquial ethos, crafted to make full use of the timbre of each word, in a manner reminiscent of the symbolist poets of the late 1800s. João Gilberto's (b. 1931) nasal, speechlike vocal style, was ideally suited to bossa-nova aesthetics.

Gilberto's guitar technique attracted special attention: he slotted the chords between the syncopations of the melody, avoiding coincidences, a style that became known as the stuttering guitar. Gilberto derived the upper snaps of his beat from the rhythms of the *tamborim,* while the thumb reproduced the thump of the *surdo.* He produced chords with up to five tones by using the little finger of his right hand to pluck the highest string (Cabral n.d.:12).

Classics of the bossa nova repertoire, such as "*Desafinado*" ('Off Key', Antônio Carlos Jobim and Newton Mendonça), "*Samba de Uma Nota Só*" ('The One-Note Samba', Jobim and Mendonça), "*Garota de Ipanema*" ('The Girl from Ipanema', Jobim and Vinícius de Morães), "*Insensatez*" ('How Insensitive', Jobim and de Morães), "*Corcovado*" ('Quiet Night of Quiet Stars', Jobim), "*Wave*" (Jobim), and many others, became known internationally (Reily 1996).

Popular music after bossa nova

After bossa nova, Brazilian popular music (*música popular brasileira*, MPB) took many directions [see POPULAR MUSIC OF BRAZIL]. The 1960s saw the rise of a protest movement in which musicians such as Carlos Lyra, Geraldo Vandré, Chico Buarque, and others somewhat naively proposed to use their music for raising the consciousness of the underprivileged masses.

Various local styles were reformulated within the bossa-nova framework, and musical texts moved away from love, sun, and beaches to depict the harshness of life, especially for poor people. Though too distant from the reality of the lower classes to have any effect on them, these songs did help incite intellectualized sectors of the upper classes, who began to organize in opposition to the military dictatorship. But the 1960s was the decade of the young guard (*jovem guarda*), a romantic and alienated movement, which helped set the foundations for Brazilian rock (*roque brasileiro*). Trying to place Brazilian popular music back onto its "evolutionary track" (an expression used by Caetano Veloso in an interview with Augusto de Campos [1986a:63] in 1966), the *tropicália* movement of the late 1960s depicted Brazilian society as an amalgam of diverse and contradictory elements. In text and music, *tropicália* exposed the contradictions of this diversity. But the movement was cut short with a new law, Institutional Act No. 5 (1968), which led to the imprisonment of Veloso and Gilberto Gil and their subsequent exile in London.

The 1970s saw a series of revivalist and locally oriented movements. With the recognition that the national repertoire was made up of more than samba, Brazilian popular music in the 1980s became particularly heterogeneous; it was the decade of the independents. Alongside Brazilian rock, the *mineiros*, led by Milton Nascimento, were reinventing their local styles; the nativist (*nativista*) festivals of Rio Grande do Sul were reviving the cowboy-derived traditions; and various reformalized northeastern tendencies found niches in the southern commercial recording market.

In the early 1990s, traditional southeastern genres were being stylized, reviving for urban audiences the *viola caipira* and its repertoire. "*Pantanal*," a prime-time television soap opera (*novela*) set in an ecological reserve on the border between Brazil and Bolivia, provided a strong impulse in this direction by featuring Sérgio Reis, a leading figure of *música sertaneja*. Prime-time soaps are major setters of style in Brazil, influencing many domains of urban life-styles, including musical taste.

MUSIC IN MIGRANT COMMUNITIES

During the 1930s, Brazil began developing its industrial focus, and with that development the country moved from an essentially rural society to an urban one. From the 1950s, more and more migrants from the rural areas flooded into the large urban complexes, particularly those of the southeast, bringing with them their rural values and musical heritages. In the late 1990s, 75 percent of Brazil's population lived in cities or towns. Greater São Paulo and greater Rio de Janeiro together are home to nearly 20 percent of all Brazilians.

Unskilled on arrival, most migrants have been forced into marginal markets. They eke out a hand-to-mouth existence in the shantytowns surrounding the major industrial centers. Even so, they claim they are better off in the city than they were in the country, for in the urban centers they have access to cultural and technological benefits that are not rurally available. In effect, the experience of migration is marked by the development of strategies that can reconcile traditional values based on personalized social relations with projects of social ascent within a greater context based on impersonalized relations, and these contradictory aspirations can only be partially fulfilled.

In such contexts, participation in musical activities based on traditional rural genres has played an important role in providing the migrants with a means of processing their experience and of constructing mutual support groups in new contexts. Urban *folias*, *ternos*, and other devotional ensembles attract fellow townsmen (*conterrâneos*), providing the structure around which they can reconstitute their towns of origin in the big city. Northeasterners unite around their *repentistas* (performers of northeastern musical duels), and they congregate in establishments where they can dance the *forró* (a northeastern dance in couples). But it is in *música sertaneja* that the best example of a migrant musical creation appears. It is the most popular genre among the migrant populations of greater São Paulo, and the industry catering to this audience is booming.

Country in the city

Traditional southeastern genres of *dupla,* particularly the *moda-de-viola,* became *música sertaneja* when they started to be recorded commercially in the late 1920s. The musicians for these recordings were recruited from itinerant professional performers active in the circuses that have roamed the countryside throughout the year since 1900. Though the performances took place under circus tents, the attractions they offered were mostly melodramatic plays and comedies. *Duplas* were performed before the play, between acts, and after the play. Since the 1980s, many circus owners have dispensed with the play altogether, offering only performances of *dupla* in their tents. The term *música sertaneja* became current only in the late 1950s, replacing the more pejorative term *música caipira.* (*Caipira* might best be glossed 'hillbilly', though it officially refers to the inhabitants of the interior of the state of São Paulo.) The change in nomenclature coincides with the formation of the migration chains moving from the interior of the country toward the southeastern industrial centers.

No doubt "modern" *música sertaneja* is far removed from its rural origins, as it has taken the direction of technological sophistication and full-scale production. *Música sertaneja* proper, however, is typified by duos such as Tião Carreiro and Pardinho, and Pena Branca and Xavantinho, who have been able to derusticize traditional genres by using "correct" Portuguese and a more sophisticated vocabulary, while their sung narrations refer to themes related to the experience of migration.

Yet they have maintained some fundamental musical elements of the *caipira* aesthetic, such as continuous parallel thirds and the *viola* and *violão* accompaniment. Their performances pay attention to tuning, instrumental technique, and vocal simultaneity. The vocal timbre has lost some of its nasality without acquiring excessive vibrato. The music sounds like that of the *duplas caipiras,* but it has been cleaned up, so to speak. Furthermore, these duos are the ones most likely to be found performing in the circuses of the periphery, allowing the audience more personalized contact with them.

Through these elements, urban migrants have created a means of using music as a symbolic representation of those traits they feel they have acquired through migration and access to urban life. Just as the music has become more organized and "cleaner," so have those who participate in the performances; and inasmuch as the language in the verses has become more grammatical and sophisticated, it expresses

Through music, migrants have constructed a
symbolic universe, in which they have reconciled
contradictory experiences of urban and rural life,
creating a positive image of themselves.

the migrants' image of themselves as more cultured and better educated. The incorporation of these elements can thus be viewed as an attempt to create sound-based
structures that represent the process of social ascent they view themselves undergoing, or at least aspire to. By maintaining traditional elements associated with values
that focus on the family and on personalized social relations, they are making a parallel statement that they have not been contaminated by the negative side of the metropolitan experience, the excessive individualism that breeds greed, selfishness, arrogance, and other antisocial traits.

Migrant musical creations stand as symbols of the possibility of reconciling
urban economic mobility with a rural ethos of noncompetitive sociability. Through
music, migrants have constructed a symbolic universe, in which they have reconciled
contradictory experiences of urban and rural life, creating a positive image of themselves. In the long term, this process may give them dignity and confidence enough
to confront the society that marginalizes them.

FURTHER STUDY

Brazilian art music has received the attention of numerous scholars. General histories
of it include Renato Almeida (1942), David Appleby (1983), Gerard Béhague
(1979), Bruno Kiefer (1976), Vasco Mariz (1983a), and others. Other historical
musicologists have focused on specific periods or important figures in Brazilian art
music; these include José Maria Neves (1981), Vasco Mariz (1983b), and Bruno
Kiefer (1986). Studies of the social history of Brazilian art music are contained in Léa
Vinocur Freitag (1986), José Miguel Wisnik (1978, 1983), Enio Squeff (1983), and
others.

Documentation of the rural musical traditions of central and southeastern Brazil
abounds, but much of this research is purely descriptive. Since the early 1980s,
anthropologically oriented studies have emerged, though scholars have tended to
emphasize Amazonian and northeastern musical traditions. Studies of interest for
central and southern Brazil include Carlos Rodrigues Brandão (1981, 1985), Suzel
Ana Reily (1994a), Kilza Setti (1985) for central and southeastern Brazil, and Daniel
Mendoza de Arce (1981) and Richard Pinnell (1984) for the south of the country.

Special interest has been shown toward urban popular musics. Researchers in
this sphere include Edgar de Alencar (1965), Augusto de Campos (1986b), Chris
McGowan and Ricardo Pessanha (1991), Charles A. Perrone (1989), Claus Schreiner
(1993), José Ramos Tinhorão (1981, 1986), Ary Vasconcelos (1977), Hermano
Vianna (1995), and many others. More recently, scholars have been turning their
attention to the musical traditions of rural migrants in the urban context.
Northeastern musical traditions in São Paulo have been studied by Maria Ignez
Novais Ayala (1988); southeastern genres have been studied by Waldenyr Caldas
(1979), José de Souza Martins (1975), and Suzel Ana Reily (1992). Overviews of

musical research and annotated bibliographies can be found in Gerard Béhague (1985, 1991), Charles A. Perrone (1986), and Suzel Ana Reily (1994a).

REFERENCES

Alencar, Edigar de. 1965. *O Carnaval Carioca através da Música,* 2nd ed. 2 vols. Rio de Janeiro: Freitas Bastos.

Almeida, Renato. 1942. *História da Música Brasileira,* 2nd ed. Rio de Janeiro: F. Briguiet.

Alvarenga, Oneyda. 1946. *Melodias Registradas por Meios Não-Mecânicos.* São Paulo: Departamento de Cultura.

———. 1982. *Música Popular Brasileira,* 2nd ed. São Paulo: Duas Cidades.

Andrade, Mário de. 1933. *Compêndio de História da Música,* 2nd ed. São Paulo: Miranda.

———. 1963. *Música, Doce Música.* São Paulo: Martins.

———. 1964 [1928]. *Ensaio sobre a Música Brasileira,* 2nd ed. São Paulo: Martins.

———. 1975. *Aspectos da Música Brasileira,* 2nd ed. São Paulo: Martins.

———. 1982. *Danças Dramáticas do Brasil,* 2nd ed. São Paulo: Martins.

———. 1983. *Música de Feitiçaria no Brasil,* 2nd ed. São Paulo: Martins.

Appleby, David P. 1983. *The Music of Brazil.* Austin: University of Texas Press.

Araújo, Alceu Maynard. 1964. *Folclore Nacional.* 3 vols. São Paulo: Melhoramentos.

Ayala, Maria Ignez Novais. 1988. *No Arranco do Grito: Aspectos da Cantoria Nordestina.* São Paulo: Atica.

Béhague, Gerard. 1979. *Music in Latin America: An Introduction.* Englewood Cliffs, N.J.: Prentice-Hall.

———. 1985. "Popular Music." In *Handbook of Latin American Popular Culture,* ed. Harald Hinds, Jr. and Charles Tatum, 3–38. West Point, Conn.: Greenwood Press.

———. 1991. "Reflections on the Ideological History of Latin American Ethnomusicology." In *Comparative Musicology and Anthropology of Music,* ed. Bruno Nettl and Philip Bohlman, 56–68. Chicago: University of Chicago Press.

Borges Ribeiro, Maria de Lourdes. 1984. *O Jongo.* Rio de Janeiro: FUNARTE.

Brandão, Carlos Rodrigues. 1981. *Sacerdotes da Viola.* Petrópolis, Brazil: Vozes.

———. 1985. *A Festa do Santo Preto.* Rio de Janeiro: FUNARTE.

Caldas, Waldenyr. 1979. *Acorde na Aurora: Música Sertaneja e Indústria Cultural,* 2nd ed. São Paulo: Nacional.

Campos, Augusto de. 1986a. "Boa Palavra sobre a Músic Popular." In *Balanço da Bossa e Outras Bossas,* 4th edition, ed. Augusto de Campos, 59–65. São Paulo: Perspectiva.

———, ed. 1986b. *Balanço da Bossa e Outras Bossas,* 4th ed. São Paulo: Perspectiva.

Cabral, Sérgio. N.d. "Em Busca da Perfeição." In *Songbook: Bossa Nova,* ed. Almir Chediak, 10–17. Rio de Janeiro: Luminar.

Freitag, Léa Vinocur. 1986. *Momentos de Música Brasileira.* São Paulo: Nobel.

Kazadi wa Mukuna. 1979. *Contribuição Bantu na Música Popular Brasileira.* São Paulo: Globo.

Kiefer, Bruno. 1976. *História da Música Brasileira.* Porto Alegre, Brazil: Movimento.

———. 1986. *Villa-Lobos e o Modernismo na Música Brasileira.* Porto Alegre, Brazil: Movimento.

Lange, Francisco Curt. 1965. "Os Compositores na Capitania Geral das Minas Gerais." *Revista de Estudos Históricos* 3–4:33–111.

———. 1966. *A Organização Musical durante o Período Colonial.* Coimbra, Brazil: Separata do Volume IV das Actas do V Coloquio Internacional de Estudos Luso-Brasileiros.

Léry, Jean de. 1980. *Viagem à Terra do Brasil,* trans. Sérgio Milliet. São Paulo: Universidade de São Paulo.

Mariz, Vasco. 1983a. *História da Música no Brasil,* 2nd ed. Rio de Janeiro: Civilização Brasileira.

———. 1983b. *Três Musicólogos Brasileiros: Mário de Andrade, Renato Almeida, Luiz Heitor Correa de Azavedo.* Rio de Janeiro: Civilização Brasileira.

Martins, José de Souza. 1975. "Música Sertaneja: A Dissimulação na Linguagem dos Humilhados." In *Capitalismo e Tradicionalismo,* ed. J. S. Martins, 103–161. São Paulo: Pioneira.

McGowan, Chris, and Ricardo Pessanha. 1991. *The Billboard Book of Brazilian Music.* New York: Billboard Books.

Mendoza de Arce, Daniel. 1981. "A Structural Approach to the Rural Society and Music of the Río de la Plata and Southern Brazil." *Latin American Music Review* 2(1):66–90.

Meyer, Augusto. 1958. *Cancioneiro Gaúcho.* Porto Alegre, Brazil: Globo.

Neves, José Maria. 1981. *Música Contemporânea Brasileira.* São Paulo: Ricordi.

Perrone, Charles A. 1986. "An Annotated Interdisciplinary Bibliography and Discography of Brazilian Popular Music." *Latin American Music Review* 7(2):302–340.

———. 1989. *Masters of Contemporary Brazilian Song: MPB 1965–1985.* Austin: University of Texas Press.

Pinnell, Richard. 1984. "The Guitarist-Singer of Pre-1900 Gaucho Literature." *Latin American Music Review* 5(2):243–262.

Preiss, Jorge Hirt. 1988. *A Música nas Missões Jesuíticas nos Séculos XVII e XVIII.* Porto Alegre, Brazil: Martins Livreiro-Editor.

Reily, Suzel Ana. 1992. "*Música Sertaneja* and Migrant identity: The Stylistic Development of a Brazilian Genre." *Popular Music* 11(3):337–358.

———. 1994a. "Macunaíma's Music: National Identity and Ethnomusicological Research in Brazil." In *Ethnicity and Identity: the Musical Construction of Place,* ed. Martin Stokes, 71–96. Oxford: Oxford University Press.

———. 1994b. "Musical Performance at a Brazilian Festival." *British Journal of Ethnomusicology* 3:1–34.

———. 1996. "Tom Jobim and the Bossa Nova Era." *Popular Music* 15(1):1–16.

Romero, Sílvio. 1954. *Cantos Populares do Brasil.* Rio de Janeiro: José Olympio.

Schreiner, Claus. 1993. *Música Brasileira: A History of Popular Music and the People of Brazil.* New York: Marion Boyars.

Setti, Kilza. 1985. *Ubatuba nos Cantos das Praias: Estudo do Caiçara Paulista e de sua Produção Musical.* São Paulo: Atica.

Siqueira, Baptista. 1979. *Modinhas do Passado,* 2nd ed. Rio de Janeiro: Folha Carioca.

Squeff, Enio. 1983. "Refexões sobre um mesmo Tema." In *O Nacional e o Popular na Cultura Brasileira: Música,* ed. Enio Squeff and José Miguel Wisnik, 13–127. São Paulo: Brasiliense.

Tinhorão, José Ramos. 1981. *Música Popular—Do Gramofone ao Rádio e TV.* São Paulo: Atica.

———. 1986. *Pequena História da Música Popular: Da Modinha a Canção de Protesto,* 5th ed. Petrópolis, Brazil: Vozes.

———. 1990. *História Social da Música Popular Brasileira.* Lisbon: Caminho da Música.

Vasconcelos, Ary. 1977. *Raízes da Música Popular Brasileira.* São Paulo: Martins.

Vianna, Hermano. 1995. *O Mistério do Samba.* Rio de Janeiro: Jorge Zahar.

Wisnik, José Miguel. 1978. *O Coro dos Contrários: A Músic em Torno da Semana de 22.* São Paulo: Duas Cidades.

———. 1983. "Getúlio da Paixão Cearense (Villa-Lobos e o Estado Novo)." In *O Nacional o Popular na Cultura Brasileira: Música,* ed. Enio Squeff and José Miguel Wisnik, 129–191. São Paulo: Brasiliense.

Brazil: Northeast Area
Larry Crook

Musical Traditions of the Interior
Musical Traditions of the Coast

Northeast Brazil comprises all or parts of nine states—Alagoas, Bahia, Ceará, Maranhão, Paraíba, Pernambuco, Piauí, Rio Grande do Norte, Sergipe—with an area covering roughly 20 percent of Brazil. This region can be divided into the following three ecological-geographic zones: the *zona da mata,* a heavily populated, humid, coastal strip, running from Bahia through Rio Grande do Norte; the *agreste,* the zone mediating a wet coastal strip and a dry interior; and the *sertão,* a sparsely populated, drought-prone hinterland.

In size and population, the northeast is larger than most Latin American countries. It contains a mix of three principal ethnic groups: African, European, and Amerindian. Portuguese-descended people are found throughout the region; the *zona da mata* has the largest concentration of Brazilians of African descent, and the most pronounced degree of African cultural manifestations. Also in the *zona da mata* the mix of Portuguese and African populations is most evident. In the hinterlands, in the *agreste* and the *sertão,* live pockets of Amerindian groups, but the bulk of the population consists of *caboclos,* bronze-colored mestizos of Portuguese and Amerindian bloodlines, with a smaller degree of African heritage.

Common history, economic hardships, and the blending of cultural traditions have helped northeasterners develop a strong regional identity. Colonized by the Portuguese in the early 1500s, the region was intended to provide commodities (first brazilwood and then cocoa, coffee, cotton, and sugarcane) for European markets. The most prosperous center of early activity was in Pernambuco, but the original administrative center of Brazil was Salvador, in Bahia.

Slavery was institutionalized as first Amerindians and then Africans were exploited as workers. By the 1600s, a prosperous sugarcane colony in the *zona da mata* featured a feudalistic social and economic system. In the 1700s, the expanding livestock industry and the introduction of cotton pushed populations farther inland into the *agreste* and *sertão.* The decline of the economic and political importance of the northeast was foreshadowed by the move of the colonial capital from Salvador to Rio de Janeiro in 1763, accelerated in the 1800s with the discovery of precious stones and metals in south-central Brazil; it was completed by the growth of the cattle and coffee industries in the south. During the 1900s, the industrialization of the south widened

Racial and ethnic categories in the northeast are complex and cannot be defined by ancestry alone. Any division of musical traditions based solely on the racial descent of the producers or the consumers is riddled with problems and inconsistencies.

the gap with the northeast. To try to unify the country by drawing people away from the coast, in 1960 politicians inaugurated a new capital city, Brasília, in the central highlands.

Since the 1940s, swelling migrant *caboclo* populations in the cities, improved transportation, and a common diet of cultural stimuli via mass media have blurred distinctions between countryside and city. The northeast has an entrenched socioeconomic class system, with an extremely small, wealthy elite of landowners and businessmen, a small middle class, and a huge, disenfranchised underclass. Contrary to the myth of a Brazilian racial democracy, race does correlate with class: the underclass comprises primarily people of color, and the upper class continues to be almost exclusively white.

But racial and ethnic categories in the northeast (as in Brazil as a whole) are complex and cannot be defined by ancestry alone. Rather, they are constructed on a combination of physical attributes, socioeconomic standing, and cultural markers. Any division of musical traditions based solely on the racial descent of the producers or the consumers is riddled with problems and inconsistencies. Participation and identification with specific musical styles often correlates more with gender, class, region, and age than with race and ethnicity. Though specific instruments, genres, and stylistic features can sometimes be traced to a specific geographical origin (in Africa, Europe, or the Americas), most northeastern Brazilian musical traditions are the legacy of interaction among groups.

For the present discussion, the musical traditions of the northeast are divided into two categories: the music of the interior and the music of the coast. Traditions associated strongly with African heritage or African-Brazilian identity are discussed in AFRO-BRAZILIAN TRADITIONS.

MUSICAL TRADITIONS OF THE INTERIOR

The music that dominates rural areas, towns, and small cities of the *sertão* and the *agreste* (and migrant *caboclo* neighborhoods in coastal cities) is the result of ethnic diversity and the historical processes of colonialization and nation building. Closely identified with mestizo populations, *caboclo* music is viewed paternalistically as "folklore" by state-sponsored cultural institutions and the private culture industry. *Caboclo* musical traditions include *cantoria*, a repertoire of secular songs performed by singer-bards; religious songs, mainly those associated with Roman Catholicism; the music of instrumental ensembles, accompanying a variety of occasions; and social dance-music known generically as *forró*.

Brazilian scholars have noted that Amerindian inflections and intonations of speech, patterns of phrasing, and styles of dancing have influenced *caboclo* music, but they find it hard to pinpoint the precise Amerindian musical practices that persist. Certain instruments, such as cane flutes and gourd rattles, have strong Indian associations for *caboclos*; dramatic dances and carnival revelries frequently caricature native

FIGURE 1 Modes from northeastern Brazil: *a,* mode with flatted seventh; *b,* mode with sharped fourth and flatted seventh.

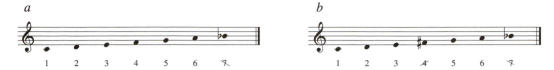

Brazilian Indians through stylized facial and body painting, the use of masks and costumes with feathers, and bows and arrows.

Iberian and African influences in *caboclo* music are more easily distinguished. The catechistic practices of Roman Catholic missionaries during Brazil's colonial period included medieval European modes, Gregorian chant, and Iberian musical elements. The ubiquity of modal structures led the noted Brazilian composer and musical scholar Guerra-Peixe to identify six northeastern modes with a variety of heptatonic scales (1985:95). Particularly distinctive are scales employing a flatted seventh (figure 1*a*) or a sharped fourth with a flatted seventh (figure 1*b*). The use of minor modes and the major diatonic scale is also common.

Intonation varies greatly from region to region and from musician to musician. In wind, string, and vocal performances, pitches frequently do not conform to the tempered system of tuning. Particularly noteworthy is intonational variance at the third, fourth, and seventh scale degrees. For instance, *caboclo* fifes (*pífanos*) are tuned to neutral thirds and sevenths (in relation to the tonic), which produce tonal frameworks that fall ambiguously between major and minor scales. Similar intonational characteristics exist in vocal styles. These practices distinguish traditional *caboclo* music from national and international popular styles (which conform to fixed tempered tuning) disseminated via broadcasts, recorded media, and live performances.

Harmonically, *caboclo* music emphasizes tonic and dominant relationships. Harmony is articulated chordally or by melodic outlining of chords, commonly by *violão* (guitar), *viola* (a medium-size guitar, with five double courses), or accordion. Singing and playing melodies in parallel diatonic thirds (typical of Iberian folk polyphony) and using harmonic or rhythmic drones are widespread practices.

Rhythmically, *caboclo* music demonstrates Iberian and African influences. Recitative-like singing, reminiscent of Gregorian chant, occurs in secular and religious repertoires of songs, and strict adherence to rules of text construction derived from Iberian poetic forms frequently results in irregular phrase lengths. In some genres such as the *aboios* (cattle-herding songs), certain tones are held for long and irregular durations, creating unpulsed and unmetered rhythms. In various dramatic dances, syncopated duple meter may alternate with unmetered recitative-like sections. Religious praise songs often feature tempo rubato effects at the beginnings and endings of phrases.

African-based rhythmic principles are particularly evident in *caboclo* dance music. Duple meter with syncopated accents, the interlocking of two or more cross rhythms, rhythmic-melodic ostinati (repeated patterns) of two to eight pulses in length, and subtle ambiguities between duple and triple subdivisions of the pulse suggest the influence of African rhythmic aesthetics. Most *caboclo* dance music features the interlocking of multiple rhythmic ostinati performed by ensembles of two to four percussion instruments. The repeats are typically subjected to continual variation and improvisation. *Caboclo* musicians value the ability to play "in the cracks" between duple- and triple-derived subdivisions of the beat.

Cantoria

Cantoria, the generic term for the sung poetry and singing contests of bards in the northeast, represents one of the richest forms of improvised poetry in Latin America. A singer-poet tradition related medieval Iberian minstrelsy, it dates to Brazilian colonial times, when bards served as primary sources of news for rural populations (Slater 1982:10). Today, *cantoria* is found throughout the northeast and in Brazilian cities where northeasterners have migrated, especially São Paulo, Brasília, and Rio de Janeiro. It is performed in homes; on street corners; at parks, fairs, and rodeos; in bars; on radio programs; in concert halls; at political rallies; and even on television. Most of its practitioners and audiences come from the lower class, but ranch owners, lawyers, and politicians also patronize it.

The subjects of the songs come from history, current affairs, myths and legends, political criticism, and especially the situation of the poor of the northeast: homelessness, poverty, misery, and the need for agrarian reform. The function of *cantoria* as political criticism is particularly evident during election season, when singers align with political candidates and perform at their public rallies, praising them and criticizing their opponents.

Songs of sociopolitical criticism have even been recorded by popular music luminaries. One example is Elba Ramalho's recording (1984) of "*Nordeste Independente*" ('Independent Northeast'), composed by Braúlio Tavares and Ivanildo Vila Nova. The jacket of this recording bears a warning: "Public broadcast of the song 'Nordeste Independente' is prohibited by the federal board of censorship." Local radio programs devoted to *cantoria* can be found throughout the northeast. Public and private sponsored competitions and concerts or festivals have become increasingly common since 1970 (Ayala 1988).

Cantoria singers are evaluated primarily for verbal, rather than musical, skills. *Cantoria* typically involves improvised song duels (*desafios*), performed by two singers accompanying themselves on a *viola* or percussion instruments such as a tambourine (*pandeiro*) or a metal cylindrical shaker (*ganzá*).

Prosodic forms of the poetry

Numerous prosodic forms are employed in *viola*-accompanied *cantoria* (*cantoria de viola*). The *desafio* involves two singers, who alternately improvise verses utilizing a series of fixed forms. *Desafios* begin with *sextilhas* (six-line heptasyllabic stanzas) featuring a rhyme scheme of *abcbdb*—in the past, four-line stanzas rhyming *abcb* were also common. Each singer (traditionally male) must begin his stanza with an obligatory rhyme (*deixa*) matching the last line of the preceding stanza. The following two *sextilhas* (from *A Arte da Cantoria* 1984), are linked by a *deixa* rhyming in -*ito*.

Neste momento sublime,	In this sublime moment,
Eu noto o tempo bonito	I note the beautiful time
Canta Otacílio Batista	Otacília Batista is singing
De São José do Egito,	From the town of São José do Egito,
Transporta versos da terra	Carrying the verses of the land
Para a casa do infinito.	To the house of the infinite.
Eu já sou doutro distrito.	I am from another district.
Declaro na minha loa	I declare in my praise song
Eu sou filho de Panelas,	I am a son of the town of Panelas,
Pernambuco, terra bõa;	Pernambuco, good land;
Que por impulso da arte	But because of the impetus of my art,
Moro hoje em João Pessoa.	I now live in João Pessoa.

The singing features many repeated notes, syllabic execution of the text, a steady stream of equal note values, and a high, tense tessitura with strong nasalization. As with *caboclo* music in general, modal structures with lowered sevenths are common. Melodies are constructed out of simple motives, sequences, and melodic cadences. The cadential rising or falling of a minor third is typical (figure 2*a*).

FIGURE 2 *Desafio* melody and *viola* accompaniment pattern: *a,* from a *sextilha* (transcribed by Larry Crook from Laurentino and da Silva 1978:A1); *b,* rhythmic pattern (*rojão*) played on the *viola.*

Sextilhas are usually sung in a quasi-duple meter, while some other poetic forms used in *cantoria de viola,* especially those based on the *décima,* tend to be unmetered.

During a *desafio, sextilhas* are followed by a variety of poetic forms, including *gemedeira,* a *sextilha* with the insertion of the call *ay-ay-ui-ui* between the fifth and sixth lines; *mourã o-de-sete-pés,* a dialogic seven-line stanza that one singer initiates and ends while the other singer provides lines three and four; *mourão-de-você-cai,* a dialogic twelve-line stanza with a fixed ninth line including the words *você cai* 'you will fall'; *oito-pés a quadrão,* eight-line stanzas with an *aaabbccb* rhyme scheme ending with the word *quadrão;* and *martelo,* primarily in ten-line stanzas featuring the rhyme scheme *abbaaccddc.*

Throughout a *desafio,* the *viola* supplies a harmonic-rhythmic drone (open fifths and octaves are typical), and fills in between stanzas with a syncopated ostinato known as a *rojão* or *baião de viola* (figure 2*b*). This interlude gives the next singer a moment to formulate his or her thoughts into the proper poetic-musical structure.

In addition to the *desafio, cantoria de viola* includes another poetic form inherited from the Iberian peninsula, the ballad (*romance*). Usually sung in quatrains with heptasyllabic lines, ballads cover the exploits of local folk heroes, historical events, the trials and tribulations of daily life, and other subjects. A large repertoire of ballads concerns Lampião, a twentieth-century bandit from the *sertão.* Another important form of *cantoria* is the ABC, so named because the beginning letter of the first word of each line must follow the sequence of the alphabet.

Contexts of performances

The several forms of *cantoria,* accompanied by tambourine or *ganzá* (or both together), are typically performed in outdoor public spaces such as street corners, parks, and fairs. For instance, *emboladores* (song duelers specializing in tongue twisters known as *emboladas*) accompanying themselves on *pandeiros* perform six days a week at a public square in the center of Recife. These performances include put-downs, appeals for money, and comical reference to the onlookers who encircle the singers. Most audiences belong to the working class (clerks, taxi drivers, maids, street vendors, night watchmen, and so forth) or are tourists. Nasalized, the style of singing is staccato and rapid fire, with many repeated notes within a small melodic range. The *pandeiro* parts that accompany these duels are based on additive patterns similar to the rhythm of the *rojão* (figure 3).

The *côco de embolada,* a special type of *embolada,* is associated with the African-Brazilian circular dance known as the *côco* but is also performed without the dance. It alternates between improvised stanzas and a fixed refrain, is usually satirical and comical in nature, and makes extensive use of double meanings and onomatopoeia.

Protestant proselytizing, which frequently occurs in parks and on street corners, involves the amplified singing of hymns accompanied by a small ensemble of electric guitar, electric bass guitar, drums, and other instruments.

FIGURE 3   Two common *pandeiro* patterns used for the *embolada*. Transcriptions by Larry Crook.

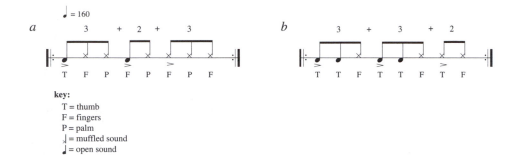

key:
T = thumb
F = fingers
P = palm
♩ = muffled sound
♩ = open sound

A purely unaccompanied form of *cantoria* is the *aboio,* which originated among cowboys (*vaqueiros*) of the northeast. It is freely improvised in unmetered rhythm with long-held notes, legato singing, and frequent glides between pitches. Mostly sung with nonlexical syllables, it utilizes stock endings, such as the phrase *ei boi.*

The rodeo song (*toada de vaqueajada*), a genre closely related to the *aboio,* is sung by professional and semiprofessional cowboy singers in competitions at rodeos. These strophic songs (typically set in heptasyllabic *sextilhas* with a rhyme scheme of *abcbdb*) are sung in parallel diatonic thirds by two singers. *Aboio*-style singing in a high falsetto, glides between tones, and imitations of cattle sounds and cowbells are typical of it.

Religious songs

The Roman Catholicism practiced by *caboclos* includes numerous acts of public and private devotion to saints and popular religious figures, such as making pilgrimages to holy sites, participating in religious processions, and hosting ritualized prayer sessions. In all these activities, devotional singing is ubiquitous. Women take active and dominant roles in religious life in general and in singing in particular. Loosely structured groups of female specialists (*turmas de mulheres* 'groups of women') that often lead praying and singing at domestic religious rituals have extensive repertoires of hymns, praise songs (*benditos*), funerary songs (*excelências*), and prayers (*rezas*). The whole month of May, women's groups organize nightly prayer sessions involving a sung rendition of the rosary with hymns and praise songs honoring the Virgin Mary. Female specialists also take leading roles in religious pilgrimages (*romarias*) to sacred locations such as Juazeiro do Norte in Ceará, where hundreds of thousands of devotees of Padre Cícero, a priest from Ceará (figure 4), travel each year to fulfill religious obligations. These pilgrimages involve hours of nonstop singing.

Songs praising God, the Virgin Mary, Padre Cícero, saints, and other important religious figures follow the modal traits of *caboclo* music (flatted sevenths, augmented fourths) but also make use of the major mode. Songs are strophic, and the text is usually set syllabically. The style of singing is smooth and legato in a flexible and fluid

FIGURE 4   Statue of Padre Cícero in a domestic shrine, displayed during a *novena*. Photo by Larry Crook, 1987.

tempo. Unison or parallel octaves are typical, as are improvised harmonies at the third and sixth. Occasional harmonies of fourths and fifths also occur.

One of the most popular praise songs, "*Ó que caminho tão longe*" ('Oh, What a Long Road'), is dedicated to Padre Cícero. Here are three stanzas from it.

Ó que caminho tão longe,	Oh, what a long road,
Cheio de pedra e areia!	Full of rock and sand!
Valei-me meu padrino Ciço,	I took refuge in my beloved Padre Cícero,
E a mãe de Deus das Candeias.	And in the mother of God of Candeias.
No céu só canta os anjos;	Only the angels sing in the sky;
No mar só canta as sereias.	Only the mermaids sing in the sea.
Valei-me meu padrinho Ciço,	I took refuge in my beloved Padre Cícero,
E a mãe de Deus das Candeias.	And in the mother of God of Candeias.
Ofereço este bendito	I offer this blessing
A luz que mais alumeia,	To the light that shines brightest,
Intenção do meu padrinho,	Intended for my beloved father,
E a mãe de Deus das Candeias.	And for the mother of God of Candeias.

The devotional quality of the song is typical of *benditos*. The first two lines of this song refer to the pilgrimage to Padre Cícero's burial site and to the hardships *caboclos* endure.

Caboclo wakes (Guerra-Peixe 1968) include a sung rendition of the rosary, prayers, and the singing of funerary and praise songs. Specific items are required at specific times: during the hour of clothing the deceased, in the morning, and at the time the casket is taken out of the house. The number of funerary songs conforms to the age of the deceased (for an adult twelve, for a baby seven). Songs with religious themes accompany various plays and dramatic dances, such as the *reisado,* depicting the story of the Nativity and the journey of the Wise Men, and the *pastoril,* recounting the shepherds' visit to the stable in Bethlehem.

The spread of Protestant religions in the northeast among *caboclos* has introduced Protestant hymn singing among born-again believers. Protestant proselytizing, which frequently occurs in parks and on street corners, involves the amplified singing of hymns accompanied by a small ensemble of electric guitar, electric bass guitar, drums, and other instruments.

Instrumental ensembles

Instrumental ensembles accompany secular and religious occasions in the northeast. The *Dança de São Gonçalo* (a dance performed by devotees of Saint Gonçalo, the patron saint of guitarists) is accompanied by string-and-percussion ensembles. In Sergipe, the ensemble includes *viola, violão, cavaquinho* (small guitar with four metal strings), folk violin (*rabeca*), small hand-held drum (*adufe*), tambourine (*pandeiro*), snare drum *(tarol)*, and bamboo scraper (*rêco-rêco*) (Dantas 1976). The choreography (in seven segments) involves two lines of dancers, led in front of an altar.

An important instrumental ensemble found throughout the northeast is the fife-and-drum band. Several such bands, performing for a wide range of social festivities and *caboclo* religious rituals, are known under a variety of names, including *banda cabaçal* (Ceará), *esquenta mulher* (Alagoas and Sergipe), and *terno de zabumba* (Paraíba); most, however, are generically called *zabumba* or *banda de pífanos* 'band of fifes' (figure 5). The ensembles typically comprise a core of four instruments: two transverse open-holed fifes (*pífanos*; in Sergipe and Alagoas, end-blown fipple flutes known as *gaitas* are used), a small snare drum, and a double-headed bass drum

FIGURE 5   During a St. Anthony's day celebration in Riacho das Almas, Pernambuco, Brazil, the *banda de pífanos* Dois Irmãos performs. Photo by Larry Crook, 1987.

TRACK 14

(*zabumba*). A medium-size tenor drum (*surdo*), a pair of hand-held cymbals (*pratos*), a triangle, and a metal shaker (*ganzá*) may be added.

The most important performance context of the fife-and-drum band is the *novena*, an all-night domestic prayer session honoring a saint or an important religious figure. In it, the ensemble accompanies the religious activities (such as the procession, reciting the rosary, singing devotions, and offering obligatory music) and animates a secular party that follows. Though largely identified with rural folkways, most fife-and-drum bands maintain a close relationship with life in towns and cities. Bands from rural areas frequently come to town on market days to play for tips and to participate in celebrations of patron saints' days and other festivities. Since the 1950s, many bands have relocated to urban areas in search of economic opportunities. There they continue to perform for traditional occasions such as the *novena* but have penetrated local and regional cultural industries and have developed a style they call folklore, which they identify with microphones, stages, showcase performances, colorful costumes, and tourism. A few groups have produced commercial records and tapes.

Fife-and-drum bands have two musical repertoires: devotional music appropriate for the veneration of saints, and secular music for dancing and partying. Conceived as an act of devotion, the performance of devotional songs is linked to the religious style of singing cultivated by the female specialists. This style features tempo rubato, fluid and legato connection of pitches, and a minimal ornamentation of the basic melody. As in most of the devotional repertoire, fifes play the melody legato, with glides and slurs between notes.

Fife-and-drum bands play marches and waltzes during processions at *novenas* and patronal celebrations. Most pieces have a simple binary form with symmetrical phrases, featuring parallel diatonic thirds, triadic outlining, and alternation of implied tonic and dominant harmonies (figure 6*a, b*). Percussion accompaniment for marches varies from group to group, but usually features the *zabumba,* alternating open and muffled strokes at the quarter-note level while the snare drum fills in a more active part combining ostinati, rolls, and single strokes at the eighth- and sixteenth-note level. Cymbals and tenor drum fill out the rhythmic texture.

Fife-and-drum bands share much of their repertoire of dances with accordion-based ensembles, which specialize in the highly syncopated *caboclo* dance-music known as *forró.* Figure 6*c* transcribes a *forró* using a two-measure ostinato played by a lower-pitched fife while a higher-pitched one improvises.

Music for social dancing and revelry (used to animate the secular portions of *novenas*, parties, stage presentations, and radio programs, and at commercial dance halls) features adaptations of European and Latin American social dances (bolero, mazurka, polka, quadrille, schottische, tango) and local genres (*abaianada, arrasta-pé, baiano, baião, forró*). In contrast to the legato style of the devotional repertoire, secular music features a distinctly articulated staccato style of playing and interlocking rhythmic patterns. The *abaianada,* a possible forerunner of the *baião* and *forró* (discussed below), is based on two interlocking parts performed on the heads of the *zabumba.* The drummer hits the top head with a soft mallet and the bottom head with an open hand (figure 7*b*).

Forró

TRACK 15
The most popular form of social dance music among *caboclos* is performed by accordion-based groups with a core instrumentation of accordion, triangle, and *zabumba,* to which other instruments—*agogô* (metal double bell), *ganzá,* bamboo scraper, *violão*—are freely added. Such groups are generically known as regional bands (*conjuntos regionais*), northeastern bands (*conjuntos nordestinos*), or northeastern trios (*trios*

FIGURE 6　*Pífano* parts: *a,* "Ó que caminho tão longe," an instrumental version of a *bendito* to Padre Cícero; *b,* "Marcha de novena" by the *banda de pífanos* Dois Irmãos; *c,* "Isso é bom," a *forró* by the Bandinha Cultural. Transcriptions by Larry Crook from recordings made in Pernambuco, Brazil, in 1988.

nordestinos). This tradition dates to the 1800s and has developed into the northeastern popular music known as *forró,* which has spread throughout Brazil.

The accordion was brought to southern Brazil by Italian immigrants in the mid-1800s (Almeida 1942:113) and was taken to the northeast in the 1860s by veterans returning from the war with Paraguay. During the same period, European social dances (mazurka, polka, quadrille, schottische, waltz) and Latin American dances (bolero, *ranchera,* tango) were spreading across the country. In the northeast, the accordion became a preferred instrument among *caboclos* to accompany their own versions of these dances, plus the *baião* and the *arrasta-pé.*

Accordion-based groups are particularly active during the month of June, when a series of winter festivals celebrate three Roman Catholic saints: Saint Anthony, Saint John, and Saint Joseph (figure 8). To hold dances, rural communities and working-class neighborhoods in towns and cities decorate their streets with paper flags, build large bonfires, and construct temporary huts (*palhoças*) with thatched roofs and dirt floors. Accordion-based groups provide accompaniment for a variety of activities, including satirical plays about the marriage of a country bumpkin (*casamento de matuto*), square dancing (*quadrilhas*), and social dancing for couples in the huts. The dancing and partying in the huts is collectively called *forró.*

During the 1970s and 1980s, experimentation with electric instruments (keyboards and electric guitar), drum set, and wind instruments evolved into a genre dubbed *forrock* (*forró* + rock).

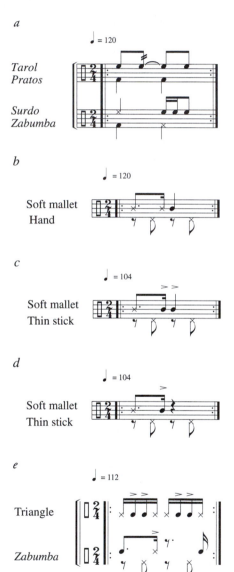

FIGURE 7   *Zabumba* percussion patterns: *a*, accompaniment to a processional march; *b*, the *abaianada*; *c*, the basic *baião* rhythm; *d*, a modern variant of the *baião* rhythm; *e*, the basic rhythmic accompaniment for the *forró*, played by triangle and *zabumba*. The symbol × designates a muffled stroke. Transcriptions by Larry Crook.

The main social dances of a *forró* include the *arrasta-pé* (a fast, foot-dragging dance), the *baião* (a syncopated dance), the *forró* (a syncopated modern hybrid of the *baião*), and the *xote* (a slow northeastern version of the schottische). Most of the music stresses a driving syncopated rhythm, exciting improvisation, and double-entendre (sometimes pornographic) lyrics. Though this music is seasonally associated with the June celebrations, it has been popularized throughout Brazil via broadcast media and commercial *forró* clubs that operate year-round. The history of the popularization of this music goes back to the 1940s or before.

Northeastern accordion music was first popularized nationally in the 1940s by Luiz Gonzaga, "King of the *Baião*," regarded as the creator of the genre. In an interview ("O eterno Rei do Baião" 1972), Gonzaga claims he took the rhythmic pattern (*baião de viola*) used by guitarists and mixed it with *zabumba* patterns common to fife-and-drum bands. The musical basis of the *baião* is thus a syncopated rhythmic pattern performed on the *zabumba* featuring two interlocking parts played on the top skin of the drum with a soft mallet and on the bottom skin with a thin stick (figure 7*c*; compare with the *zabumba* pattern for the *abaianada* in figure 7*b*).

Though the term *baião* already existed in popular usage in the northeast before Gonzaga popularized it—it even appeared on a recording in 1928 (Tinhorão 1986:221)—Gonzaga, with his partner Humberto Texeira, developed the *baião* into a genre of commercial popular music. Many credit Gonzaga with establishing the trio format: accordion, *zabumba*, triangle. His first big hit, in 1946, entitled "*Baião*," was coauthored with Texeira. During the 1940s and 1950s, Gonzaga released a string of hits based on the *baião* and other northeastern genres, such as *aboio*, *chamego* (dealing with themes of love), *toada* (melancholy romantic lyric song), *xaxado* (rhythmically resembling the *baião* but telling the history of northeastern banditry), and *xote*.

Between 1946 and 1956, northeastern music was a national fad, and the *baião* even made an international splash. By the mid-1950s, working-class *forró* dance halls featuring accordion trios emerged in Rio de Janeiro and São Paulo, catering to homesick migrant laborers from the northeast. Around the late 1950s or early 1960s, *zabumba* drummers began deleting the stroke that fell on beat two of the *baião*. This change produced a new, more syncopated *baião* (figure 7*d*).

Further experimentations with the *baião* yielded another variant, which came to be called *forró*. The rhythmic basis of the *forró* is a syncopated interlocking pattern performed with variously muffled and open strokes on the *zabumba*, featuring continual variations and improvisations (figure 7*e*).

During the 1960s, the national popularity of northeastern music waned. *Forró* groups began releasing records on so-called migrant labels, which catered primarily to working-class northeasterners in the south. Back in the northeast, *forró* groups continued to perform, especially during the June festivals. In Campina Grande in Paraíba, Caruaru in Pernambuco, and other cities, June celebrations became huge

FIGURE 8   A *forró* trio performs during the June festivities (*festa junina*) in Pernambuco. Photo by Larry Crook, 1984.

commercial affairs, rivaling carnival and drawing thousands of tourists. Large commercial *forró* clubs evolved in conjunction with these celebrations and now bring nationally and regionally famous *forró* musicians (*forroizeiros*) to perform as part of three weeks of activities. Caruaru, the so-called capital of *forró,* claims the largest *forró* club in Brazil, aptly named the Forrozão (Big Forró); it can accommodate more than four thousand people.

During the 1970s and 1980s, experimentation with electric instruments (keyboards and electric guitar), drum set, and wind instruments evolved into a genre dubbed *forrock* (*forró* + rock), infusing new commercial life into the music. Since the 1980s, northeastern musicians—Geraldo Azevedo, Alceu Valença, Fagner, Nando Cordel, Elba Ramalho, and others—have incorporated *forró* into mainstream Brazilian popular music. There is also a movement of roots-oriented musicians (Alcymar Monteiro and Jorge de Altinho, for instance) who, though incorporating wind and electronic instruments in their groups, stick close to an *arrasta-pé–forró–toada–xote* repertoire. All these musicians have now expanded *forró* beyond its seasonal association with June festivals to a year-round commercially successful music.

MUSICAL TRADITIONS OF THE COAST

Music of the northeastern coast is largely a mix of African and European traditions. The establishment of sugarcane plantations and the introduction of African slaves during colonial times left indelible marks on musical life. European erudite traditions were sustained by the Portuguese upper class (often by training slaves to play European music), while vernacular African and Iberian traditions were maintained and mixed by slaves and peasants.

Historical documentation shows that European-style erudite musical activities existed in the two major urban centers of Pernambuco (Recife) and Bahia (Salvador) from the 1500s (Béhague 1979). During the colonial period, art music was primarily related to activities sponsored by or relating to the Roman Catholic Church, as local chapel masters and organists composed and organized music for daily services and special rituals. Formalized music instruction was given to blacks and mulattoes as early as 1600, and some excelled as instrumentalists, singers, and composers. Private orchestras and choruses of slave musicians existed on large sugar plantations, and concert life and opera houses first appeared in the 1700s in Bahia and Pernambuco.

In addition to these activities, marching bands and concert bands have a long history in the cities and towns of the area and still serve for a variety of community functions including religious processions, ceremonies of state, and public concerts. In the 1800s, communal bands helped disseminate European social dances of the day. The abolition of slavery (1888) and the subsequent urbanization and proletarianization of former slaves had an important impact on the vernacular musical traditions of the area, and on the formation of urban popular musics that developed in the 1900s. The two most important coastal traditions are dramatic dances and carnival music.

Dramatic dances

The northeastern coast is the center of the danced folk plays that Mário de Andrade (1982) termed dramatic dances. These dances were mostly introduced by Jesuit priests during colonial times to instruct the non-Christian Indian and African populations in religious matters. They present stories of conversion or death and resurrection, divided into two parts: a procession and a sequence of choreographed scenes. Both parts are danced, involve stock characters and a cycle of songs, and are usually accompanied by a small instrumental ensemble. Though based loosely on religious themes, most dramatic dances include an abundance of secular action. Dramatic dances can be divided into three broad categories: the *baile pastoril,* a Christmas cycle; *cheganças,* recounting Portuguese maritime exploits and battles between Christians and infidels; and *reisados,* cyclic dances associated with Christmas and Epiphany.

Baile pastoril

In numerous forms, the *baile pastoril* occurs during the Christmas season, when it presents the story of the birth of Jesus. It is particularly popular in Alagoas, Pernambuco, Paraíba, and Rio Grande do Norte, where teenage girls dressed as shepherdesses form two lines (blue and red) and perform a series of danced segments (*jornadas*) that include songs and spoken dialogue accompanied by *pandeiros* and maracas (Alvarenga 1982:83). Small ensembles of string, wind, and brass instruments may accompany the singing. A secularized version, *pastoril de ponta-de-rua,* has been compared to a burlesque variety show. It includes sambas and *cançonetas* accompanied by accordion, triangle, and bombo (Mello 1990).

Chegança *and other dances*

The maritime exploits of the Portuguese are presented in *cheganças,* dances such as the *chegança de marujo* (of Alagoas), the *barca* (of Paraíba), the *nau catarineta* (of Paraíba), and the fandango (of Pernambuco, Paraíba, Rio Grande do Norte, and Maranhão). Epic stories of seafaring are told through a series of songs sung by men dressed as sailors, accompanying themselves on tambourines.

Other dances involving battle scenes between two opposing groups (commonly Christians against infidels, or blacks against Indians) also occur. The *quilombo* (from Alagoas), for instance, enacting a symbolic battle between blacks and Indians, is accompanied by a band of fifes that plays dance music specific to each group (Brandão 1978).

Reisado

The *reisado,* a cycle of dances associated with Christmastide, features a variety of human and animal figures presented in short scenes. The last dance in the cycle,

FIGURE 9   At the Festival de Jericos in Panelas, Pernambuco, the group Boi Tira Teima prepares to perform a *bumba-meu-boi*. Photo by Larry Crook, 1987.

bumba-meu-boi, has many regional variants in the northeast and throughout Brazil, such as *boi-surubi* (of Ceará), *boi-de-matraca, boi-de-zabumba,* and *boi de orquestra* (of Maranhão and Piauí).

Bumba-meu-boi

The *bumba-meu-boi* developed in the 1700s in Brazil among African slaves as a mechanism to criticize and ridicule the ruling class (Kazadi wa Mukuna 1994). Its principal figures include a bull (*boi*), a Portuguese master, a slave (Francisco) and his wife (Catarina), several cowboys, a priest, a Portuguese doctor, and an Indian shaman (figure 9). During the traditional nightlong presentation, the pregnant Catarina tells Francisco of a craving she has to eat the tongue of the master's favorite bull. Fearing for the health of the unborn child, Francisco shoots the animal and delivers the tongue to his wife, who cooks and eats it. Discovering his animal dead, the master orders Francisco to resurrect the bull or die. After several failed attempts by a Portuguese doctor, an Indian shaman succeeds in resurrecting the bull by placing a special leaf in his mouth. The bull then arises, and everyone dances.

Various instrumental ensembles accompany regional variants of the *bumba-meu boi.* A *cavaquinho,* an *onça* (a large friction drum), a tambourine, a folk violin, a bamboo scraper, a *violão,* a *zabumba,* and a variety of brasses and woodwinds may all be employed.

Carnival music

The northeast coast is renowned for the variety of its participatory traditions of carnival (*carnaval*). Though carnival is officially confined to the five days before Ash Wednesday, carnival season in the major cities involves six to eight weeks of intense activity. All cities and most towns sponsor carnival celebrations. The two major carnivals in the northeast occur in Pernambuco (Recife / Olinda) and Bahia (Salvador) and feature a variety of musical traditions unique to those cities.

Carnival season is a busy period for amateur and professional musicians, hired to play for a variety of activities. In addition to municipally sanctioned public parades, presentations, and competitions, masked balls in the private social clubs of the mid-

Salvador da Bahia has an elaborate carnival, with unique electrified music inspired by the *frevo* from Pernambuco. This form is the *trio elétrico.*

dle and upper class, employment by carnival associations, and presentations in restaurants and other commercial establishments keep musicians busy.

Frevo

TRACK 16

The most characteristic carnival music from Pernambuco is the *frevo,* a term likely derived from the Portuguese verb *ferver* 'boil over'. Three main types of *frevo* are recognized: *frevo de rua, frevo de bloco,* and *frevo-canção* (Oliveira 1971). *Frevo de rua* 'street *frevo*' originated in the late 1800s among the carnival clubs of urban laborers in Recife, which used military marching bands to accompany their parades. Competition among the clubs involved violent encounters between capoeira groups, which paraded in front of the clubs. From the bands' repertoires (especially the marches and polkas) and the choreographic movements of *capoeira* (game-dance) developed the aggressive dance and syncopated music that came to be known as *frevo.*

The early composers of *frevo* were mainly bandleaders and instrumentalists who did not know how to write music down. In contrast to the semi-erudite salon music cultivated by the more educated composers of the day, the *frevo de rua* was a loud street-band music, heavy on brasses, winds, and percussion. Typical instrumentation included four clarinets, five saxophones (combinations of alto, tenor, and baritone), four trumpets, four trombones, two tubas, a snare drum (*tarol*), a tambourine (*pandeiro*), and two tenor drums (*surdos*). The music of a *frevo de rua* is typically in a fast duple meter (figure 10).

A *frevo de rua* is typically organized into two repeated sections of sixteen measures each, separated by a short bridge or interlude. Highly syncopated melodies and countermelodies played by the brasses and woodwinds are accented and punctuated by the percussion. Individual compositions are strung together with drum cadences and rolloffs, allowing for nonstop music and dancing while the band is marching down the street with hundreds of dancers and revelers in tow. The instrumental *frevo de rua* continues to be an important part of *frevo* clubs (*clubes de frevo*) in Recife and Olinda, which hire bands to accompany their parades.

FIGURE 10   Percussion parts for the *frevo de rua.* Transcriptions by Larry Crook.

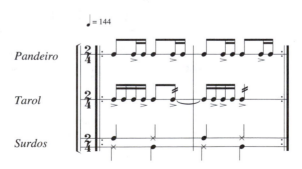

Because encounters between carnival clubs around 1900 often became violent and most of the revelers were from the lower strata of Recife society, the *frevo de rua* acquired an unfavorable reputation among the middle and upper classes. Around 1915, new carnival associations (called *blocos*) catering to middle-class tastes emerged in Recife. Among these groups developed the *frevo de bloco,* which featured songs sung by a female chorus accompanied by supposedly soft instruments—the flute, the clarinet, the *bandolín* (similar to a mandolin), the banjo, the *cavaquinho,* the violin, the *violão,* and a few percussion instruments. The *frevo de bloco* is distinguished from the *frevo de rua* by lighter instrumentation, the inclusion of a female chorus, slower tempo, frequent use of the minor mode, and lyrical sentimentality of the text.

To animate middle-class carnival balls held indoors in private clubs, the *frevo* song (*frevo-canção*) was first cultivated by popular composers in the 1930s in Recife. It is a solo song (with choral refrains) featuring an instrumental introduction (inspired by the *frevo de rua*), followed by a song. Two of the major composers of this genre are Capiba (Lourenço Barbosa) and Nelson Ferreira, who led popular jazz orchestras in Recife. In addition to writing for the three types of *frevo,* these composers experimented with a stylized version of the *maracatú* (an Afro-Brazilian carnival genre from Recife) and composed in other popular Brazilian and international genres.

The three main types of *frevo* are the primary moving forces behind the carnival in Recife and Olinda. Annual competitions for new *frevos* are sponsored by the city of Recife, and the top winners are recorded on commemorative albums. Popular *frevo* singers such as Claudionor Germano (specializing in *frevo-canção*), backed up by professional bands, release seasonal records each year in conjunction with carnival. Other popular musicians from Recife (Alceu Valença, for instance) include *frevos* in their repertoires.

Other traditions

Other major carnival traditions from Recife not specifically Afro-Brazilian in nature include the *caboclinhos* 'little *caboclos*' and the *maracatú rural* 'rural *maracatú*' (Real 1990). *Caboclinhos* typically comprise thirty to forty black and mestizo revelers from the rural regions of the *zona da mata* and neighborhoods surrounding Recife. They dress up as Brazilian Indians (with feathers, bows, and arrows) and perform a sequence of dances such as the *aldeia,* the *emboscada,* and the *toré,* accompanied by a *gaita* (end-blown flute with four holes for fingering), a snare drum, and a pair of metal maracas (*chocalhos*). The music is in a fast-paced duple meter, with highly ornamented melodic ostinati played on a *gaita.*

The *maracatú rural* is a *caboclo-* and African-inspired tradition that emerged in the outlying areas of Recife in the 1930s (Real 1990:72). Its most striking figures are the *caboclos de lança,* performers who imitate Indian warriors by carrying large lances and engaging in mock battles. Costuming is extremely creative and eclectic, combining brightly colored cellophane wigs, streamers, sneakers, and cowbells. Music for the *maracatú rural* combines semi-improvised narrative songs (related to *cantoria*) sung by the *mestre de toadas* (leader of the songs) and answered by a chorus. Accompaniment is provided by a small instrumental orchestra of snare drum, *ganzá,* large cowbell, and one or two brass instruments, commonly trumpet and trombone.

Salvador da Bahia has an elaborate carnival, with unique electrified music inspired by the *frevo* from Pernambuco (Góes 1982). This form is the *trio elétrico.* In the early 1950s, two Bahian musicians, Dodô and Osmar, began performing *frevos* on a trio of treble, tenor, and bass electric guitars, (respectively the *guitarra baiana, triolim,* and *pau-elétrico*), backed by a small percussion group of cymbals, snare drum, *zabumba,* and *surdo* from the back of a pickup truck, blasting their music into

FIGURE 11   During carnival in Salvador, Bahia, a 1960s-style sound truck makes *trío elétrico* presentations. Photo by Larry Crook, 1994.

the streets. During the 1970s and 1980s, these groups were associated with middle-class rockers in Salvador and provided inspiration for much of Bahia's popular music. *Trio elétrico* ensembles now perform atop multimillion-dollar sound trucks blasting out a fast-paced march music dubbed *frevo-baiano,* which incorporates a variety of styles including *frevo,* merengue, rock, and *ijexá* (figure 11).

Most of Bahia's stars of popular music perform atop sound trucks during carnival for the more than one million revelers who crowd the streets of Salvador. Some of the most dynamic and popular traditions—including *afoxés* (street manifestations of African-Brazilian religious cults) and *blocos-afros* (African blocs, which combine samba with Jamaican reggae)—are intimately associated with the renaissance of African-Bahian culture and contemporary black consciousness.

REFERENCES

A Arte da Cantoria. 1984. Vol. 2: *Regras da cantoria.* Fundação Nacional de Arte, Instituto do Folclore INF-1002. LP disk.

Almeida, Renato. 1942. *História da música brasileira.* 2nd ed. Rio de Janeiro: Briguiet.

Alvarenga, Oneyda. 1982. *Música popular brasileira.* São Paulo: Livraria Duas Cidades.

Andrade, Mário de. 1982. *Danças dramáticas do Brasil.* 2nd ed. 3 vols. Belo Horizonte, Brazil: Editorial Itatiaia.

Ayala, Maria Ignez Novais. 1988. "'Cantoria Nordestina': Its Spheres of Performance and its Relationship to the Cultural Industry." *Studies in Latin American Popular Culture* 7:183–197.

Béhague, Gerard. 1979. *Music in Latin America: An Introduction.* Englewood Cliffs, N.J.: Prentice-Hall.

Brandão, Théo. 1978. *Quilombo.* Cadernos de Folclore, 28. Rio de Janeiro: Fundação Nacional de Arte.

Dantas, Beatriz G. 1976. *Dança de São Gonçalo.*

Cadernos de Folclore, 9. Rio de Janeiro: Fundação Nacional de Arte.

Ferretti, Mundicarmo Maria Rocha. 1988. *Baião dos dois: a música de Zedantas e Luiz Gonzaga no seu contexto de produção e suya atualização de 70.* Recife, Brazil: Fundação Joaquim Nabuco, Editora Massangana.

Germano, Claudionor. 1980. *O bom do carnaval.* RCA / Cadmen 107.0317. LP disk.

Góes, Fred de. 1982. *O país do carnaval elétrico.* São Paulo: Editora Corrupio Comércio.

Gonzaga, Luiz. 1989. *O Melhor de Luiz Gonzaga.* RCA CDM 10032. LP disk.

Guerra-Peixe, César. 1968. "Rezas-de-defunto." *Revista brasileira de folclore* 8(22):235–268.

———. 1970. "Zabumba, orquesta nordestina." *Revista brasileira de folclore* 10(26):15–38.

———. 1985. "A influência africana na música do Brasil." In *Os afro-brasileiros,* ed. Roberto Mota, 89–104. Recife, Brazil: Fundação Joaquim Nabuco, Editora Massangana.

Kazadi wa Mukuna. 1994. "Sotaques: Style and Ethnicity in a Brazilian Folk Drama." In *Music and Black Ethnicity: The Caribbean and South America,* ed. Gerard Béhague, 207–224. Miami: North-South Center, University of Miami.

Laurentino, Moacir, and Sebastião da Silva. 1978. *Violas da minha terra.* Chantecler LP 2–04–405–075. LP disk.

McGowan, Chris, and Ricardo Pessanha. 1991. *The Brazilian Sound: Samba, Bossa Nova, and the Popular Music of Brazil.* New York: Billboard Books.

Mello, Luiz Gonzaga de. 1990. *O pastoril profano de Pernambuco.* Recife, Brazil: Fundação Joaquim Nabuco, Editora Massangana.

"O eterno Rei do Baião." 1972. *Veja e Leia* 184:80–82.

Oliveira, Valdemar de. 1971. *Frevo, capoeira, e "passo."* Recife, Brazil: Companhia Editora de Pernambuco.

Ramalho, Elba. 1984. *Do jeito que a gente gosta.* Barclay 823 030–1. LP disk.

Real, Katarina. 1990. *O folclore no carnaval do Recife.* 2d ed. Recife, Brazil: Fundação Joaquim Nabuco, Editora Massangana.

Rocha, José Maria Tenório. 1978. *Folguedos carnavalescos de Alagoas.* Maceió, Brazil: SENAC / AL.

Slater, Candace. 1982. *Stories on a String.* Berkeley: University of California Press.

Tinhorão, José Ramos. 1986. *Pequena história da música popular—da modinha ao tropicalismo.* 5th ed. São Paulo: Art Editora.

Afro-Brazilian Traditions
Gerard Béhague

Religious Musical Traditions
Secular Musical Traditions
Urban Popular Musical Traditions

Both nationally and around the world, the Afro-Brazilian traditions most clearly identify the musics of Brazil. Afro-Brazilian traditions shape the unique character of the musics of Brazil as recognized at the national and international levels. These traditions must be viewed, however, in their specific historical and regional contexts in order for their true meanings to be understood. A multiplicity of black identities emerges from the ambiguity of ethnic self-identities and the complexities of Brazilian social stratification.

Although historically Afro-Brazilians have remained at the lowest of the social strata and discrimination continues at certain levels, Brazil has seen deep racial integration throughout the twentieth century. Official segregation never became a reality in the post-slavery period. All of this facilitated the true nationalization of certain originally Afro-Brazilian popular musical expressions.

The history of African cultural transfers to Brazil is imprecise and often confused. The aftermath of the abolition of slavery brought such an overwhelming sense of national shame on the part of some governmental officials that in 1891 the minister of finances, Rui Barbosa, ordered the destruction of a large amount of archival documents relating to slavery in the naïve hope that such negative aspects of national history would be forgotten. Our sources of knowledge of early Afro-Brazilian musical traditions, therefore, are primarily oral, written, and iconographic sources dating mainly from the 1800s and throughout the twentieth century (Almeida 1942).

Traditional Afro-Brazilian musical manifestations are centered essentially in three parts of the country: the northeastern and northern states of Alagoas, Bahia, Maranhão, Pará, Paraíba, Pernambuco, and Sergipe; the southeastern regions of Espírito Santo, Minas Gerais, and Rio de Janeiro; and parts of São Paulo. As far south as Rio Grande do Sul, however, religious worship of African gods, as in the Batuque of Porto Alegre, survives. Moreover, significant aspects of Afro-Brazilian traditions are an integral part of some of the most significant genres of Brazilian popular music of the twentieth century.

Despite various racist policies at the beginning of the twentieth century (including advocacy of the cultural whitening of the black population), Brazil at the end of the twentieth century retains the position of being the second-largest black country in the world, after Nigeria. This, however, does not make it an African or neo-African culture, despite the establishment of trade and cultural contacts with West Africa following the abolition of slavery (1888) and an official opening to Africa since the 1970s.

After a period of sociopolitical vindication since the late 1970s, and especially after the centenary of the Brazilian abolition of slavery, the position of black musicians in the national market of the late 1990s remained ambivalent. In Bahia, these musicians have come of age in terms of their own involvement, freedom in, and control over their activities. In other areas, their future is uncertain. In general, however, at the end of the twentieth century, Afro-Brazilian musics command nationwide an unprecedented recognition and respect.

Brazilian racial democracy has remained a myth, yet the multicultural expressions of contemporary Afro-Brazilians are a reality. Indeed, Afro-Brazilian musical traditions cover a wide continuum—from traditional, Afro-related music integrated in religious systems inherited from Africa but developed independently, to obviously Iberian songs and dances also prevailing in nonblack Brazilian communities. This spectrum of musical expressions is not contradictory because it reflects the actual cultural experience and heritage of contemporary Afro-Brazilians (Tinhorão 1988). More than any other expressive means in numerous contexts, music in Brazil transcends social and ethnic boundaries. As some Afro-Brazilian musical traditions affect nonblack Brazilians, some Luso-Brazilian traditions are faithful expressions of Afro-Brazilians.

RELIGIOUS MUSICAL TRADITIONS

The stylistic continuity that can be observed in Afro-Brazilian religious music is most probably a case of cultural resistance during centuries of cultural confrontations—centuries that also involved cultural sharing. Afro-Brazilian religions present a complex configuration of dogmas and practices resulting from the local adaptation and transformation of systems of beliefs inherited from Africa and Europe, encapsulating the historical national experience.

The most nationally acknowledged popular religion, Umbanda, is found almost everywhere. Other religions, such as various types of Candomblé (Candomblé Gêge-Nagô, Congo-Angola, de Caboclo in Bahia and Sergipe, and Macumba in Rio de Janeiro), Xangô (Pernambuco) (Carvalho 1993), Tambor de Mina (Maranhão), Batuque (Pará), Pajelança (Amazonas), and others, are specific to certain regions. In varying degrees, they all recognize some aspects of the African Yoruba and Fon pantheon and the basic beliefs and practices of traditional African religions.

Animism, divination, initiation, ancestor worship, various kinds of offerings to the deities, ritual use of sacred plants, ritual music and dance, and specific social hierarchical organization prevail in all Afro-Brazilian religious communities. In Brazil, African religions underwent a great deal of transformation. On the one hand, Yoruba-Fon religions (of the *orixá / vodun* complex) exerted considerable influence on Bantu (Congo-Angola) religions; on the other hand, Roman Catholicism, imposed on slaves in Brazil, became integrated in varying degrees with African beliefs—which explains the so-called syncretism of Afro-Brazilian religions.

In the most traditional Candomblé religions of Brazil (Gêge-Nagô and Congo-Angola, in Bahia and Rio de Janeiro), syncretism is not so evident as it is in Candomblé de Caboclo, Macumba, Umbanda, and other religions, though African deities (*orixás* and *voduns*), usually have counterparts in Roman Catholic saints. Thus, the cult of *orixás* and *voduns* eventually became fused with that of *santos,* if only as a result of a historical accommodation, in which during the period of slavery, saints served to camouflage African deities.

Candomblé

In Candomblé, the center-leader, known as *babalorixá* or *pai de santo* (if a man) or *ialorixá* or *mãe de santo* (if a woman), assumes full responsibility in general liturgical matters and in the musical and choreographic training of the initiates and their subsequent position in the center. The ultimate authority in the knowledge of music and dance, he or she usually leads the performance of the proper sequence of songs. The religious leader also exercises power through the authority recognized and acknowledged by all. This power emanates primarily from ritual knowledge, including music and dance, in addition to the whole complex of esoteric knowledge of the precepts operating in the ceremonies. Among these, the most dramatic and richest is undoubtedly the cycle of initiation rites, representing the highest degree of participation in religious life. Initiates go through a severe education in ritual behavior, ritual language, music, and dance, all for serving their particular deity. In effect, this liturgical behavior results from a deep sociocultural conditioning, of which the performance of sacred songs and of specific dances represents an integral part. The relationship of music and spirit possession also results from this conditioning; that is, initiates are taught the meaning of certain songs within the mythology of their specific *orixá* and the corresponding expected behavorial response. It is therefore the association of such sacred ritual songs and corresponding accompanimental rhythms with their respective god that triggers the trance behavior, not necessarily fast and loud drumming as is usually believed. Initiation, the ultimate degree of participation in religion, consists in "placing the *orixá* in the candidate's head" (in local terminology, the *obrigação da cabeça*) so as to predict that deity's behavior when he or she takes possession of devotees. In actuality, spirit possession indicates the presence of the supernatural among humans (see Okada 1995: example 4). The possessed initiate is identified as the *orixá* himself or herself. Whether or not anyone should go through initiation is determined by the *ifá*, a divination game interpreted by the diviner (*babalaô*), frequently the same *pai* or *mãe de santo*.

The music of the Gêge-Nagô groups retains a strongly Yoruba style, both in the pentatonic and hexatonic melodic structures and in the rhythmic organization of the accompaniment. Overlapping responsorial singing prevails, the solo vocal lines performed in general by the cult leader, the master drummer, or less frequently by any of the official civil protectors of the group, known as *ogans*. The monophonic choral responses are provided by the initiates and any members of the congregation, male and female, who may wish to participate. The lyrics and most ritual speech of Gêge-Nagô groups are still in the Yoruba and Fon languages, though these languages are not spoken in Brazil as a rule, and few participants can give a word-for-word translation of the texts. This does not prevent them, however, from knowing the overall meaning and function of the songs. Portuguese dominates in Candomblé de Caboclo and Umbanda.

The extensive repertoires of song originate from the association of specific songs with each deity, with all private and public ceremonies, and within each ceremony with a rigorous sequence of ritual events. Each event or gesture has its corresponding songs. Thus, repertoires are classified according to their ritual functions: botanical songs, sacrificial songs, songs of offering, songs for calling the gods, songs for sending them away, and so on. The ritual power of musical sounds, combined with the liturgical significance of lyrics as components of myths, explains the length and complexity of Candomblé ritual songs.

The rhythmic structure of Candomblé music reveals a typically African sense of rhythm whereby regular motoric, unchangeable parts are contrasted with improvised parts. Ritual drumming occurs as an accompaniment to sung performances and in solos. Specific rhythmic patterns (figure 1) are associated with specific gods, such as *alujá* for Xangô (god of thunder and fire), *bravum* for Ogum (warrior deity and god of metal tools), *aguerê* for Oxossi (god of hunting), and *igbim* for Oxalá (god of creation). To each rhythm corresponds a given choreography associated with the specific god. The interlocking rhythmic organization common in traditional West African and Afro-Cuban religious music does not prevail in Brazil; however, the African type of hemiola is quite frequent. Cone-shaped, single-headed drums, known in Bahia as *atabaques*, are played in a battery of three sizes (figure 2). The largest drum, *rum*, is played with a stick and a bare hand by the master drummer, who, by improvising, controls the ritual dance. The middle-sized drum (the *rumpi*) and the smallest drum (the *lê*), played with sticks in Gêge-Nagô music, perform standard, unchanging patterns. The double bell (*agogô*), played with a metal stick, completes the accompanying ensemble. As drums constitute a significant symbol of communication with the *orixás,* they go through a sort of baptism before they can be used in ritual contexts (Béhague 1975, 1977, 1984, 1988, 1992b). The sacred role of drummers (*alabês*) is recognized by means of a ceremony of confirmation. The drummers' primary function is to call gods (figure 3), hence to bring about initiates' spirit possession (figure 4), but drummers themselves never fall into trance while drumming.

FIGURE 1
Schemes of some rhythmic patterns in Candomblé drumming (tempi, while constant, vary considerably among ensembles): *a, Aguerê de Iansã* for Oxossi; *b, Avaninha,* an entrance and exit pattern; *c, Bravum* for Ogum; *d, Ketu,* a generic drumming pattern without special attribute to any deity; *e, Opanijé,* generally for Omolu or Obaluaiê. Transcriptions by Gerard Béhague.

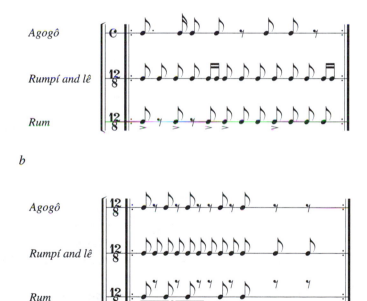

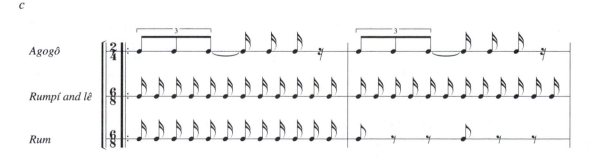

(*continued*)

Umbanda music caters to all segments of urban society, especially the lower middle class, by relying on a nationally omnipresent and familiar style, the folk-urban type of dance music most readily associated with the samba.

FIGURE 1 *(continued)* Schemes of some rhythmic patterns in Candomblé drumming (tempi, while constant, vary considerably among ensembles): *a, Aguerê de Iansã* for Oxossi; *b, Avaninha,* an entrance and exit pattern; *c, Bravum* for Ogum; *d, Ketu,* a generic drumming pattern without special attribute to any deity; *e, Opanijé,* generally for Omolu or Obaluaiê. Transcriptions by Gerard Béhague.

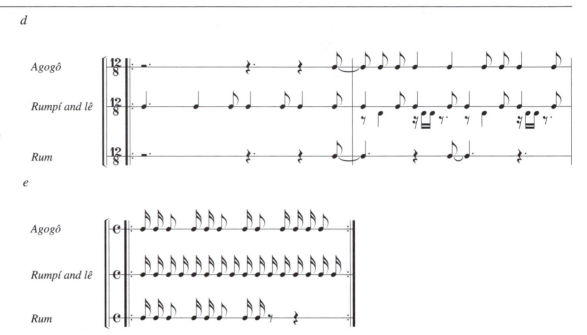

Umbanda

Since the 1950s, Brazilian religious music has gained a greater following as a result of the countrywide popularity of Umbanda, the religion that combines Candomblé beliefs, popular Roman Catholicism, spiritualism, and Kardecism (a Brazilian spiritualist movement, based on the writings of Allan Kardec). Umbanda music displays stylistic changes that illustrate how completely national values permeate strong regional and urban cultural settings. Indeed, Umbanda music caters to all segments of urban society, especially the lower middle class, by relying on a nationally omnipresent and familiar style, the folk-urban type of dance music most readily associated with the samba.

In contrast to traditional Candomblé religions, the repertoire of Umbanda music is in constant elaboration, albeit stylistically restricted. But this stylistic limitation appears the most effective in attracting worshippers from all social strata. In effect, Caboclo, Umbanda, and their expressive means (mostly music and dance) may be the most important factors contributing to the cultural, regional integration of Brazil in the last three decades of the twentieth century.

SECULAR MUSICAL TRADITIONS

The ancestry of secular traditions is not always easily established whenever the elements of a given musical genre and of specific sociocultural contexts of performance cannot be unequivocally related to an African derivation. Regardless of origin, one

FIGURE 2   *Atabaque* drums for Candomblé: *from left,* the *lê,* the *rumpi,* and the *rum.* They are painted to match the colors of the main god of the Candomblé house. Salvador, Bahia, Brazil. Photo by Gerard Béhague, 1978.

should consider traditions that are fully integrated in contemporary music making among self-defined Afro-Brazilian communities. Criteria of use, function, origin, and structure define the identification of traditions.

"Sacred" and "secular" are relative concepts, especially in Afro-Brazilian culture, in which songs and dances functioning outside a religious context frequently refer to sacred topics. As in Africa, religion sustains expressive culture in all its dimensions.

Capoeira

The game-dance known as *capoeira* is considered by some to have come from Angola, and by others to have been the creation of Brazilian blacks during slavery. Most probably, it is a local elaboration of some African model (Rego 1968). From a game fight believed to have been practiced by slaves during resting periods in the fields, it devel-

FIGURE 3   *A iconografia dos deuses africanos no candomblé da Bahia* 'The iconography of the African gods in Candomblé of Bahia'. Watercolor by Carybe (1980) of *alabês* (drummers and musicians) in Candomblé performance. Used by permission of the artist. Photo by Gerard Béhague, 1985.

FIGURE 4 A Candomblé initiate of Oxum in trance. Salvador, Bahia, Brazil. Photo by Gerard Béhague, 1973.

oped into a sort of martial art with subtle choreographic movements and rules—a well-defined musical repertoire of songs and accompanimental rhythms. It originated in Bahia but has extended to other major coastal cities, especially since the 1940s, and it became a main martial art taught in military schools. The traditional dance is known as *capoeira Angola*—a term that gives a linguistic justification to believers in the Angolese origin. The choreographic development involves a series of figures known as *golpes,* in which a swaying motion (*ginga*) is fundamental. Pairs of male dancer-fighters (*capoeiristas*) perform figures that include simulations of various motions of attack and defense (using the feet only), plus head-over-heels turns. The synchronization of movements between the attack of one dancer and the defense of the other (and vice versa) is remarkable (see Okada 1995: example 5; Fujii 1990: example 28-8).

Capoeira is accompanied by an ensemble (figure 5) of musical bow (*berimbau de barriga*), tambourine (*pandeiro*), double bell, and at least one drum (*atabaque*), and the singing is responsorial. The main instrument, the *berimbau* has a calabash resonator and is played by a wooden stick with a basket rattle (*caxixi*) (figure 6). By using a coin as a bridge, the player of the *berimbau* can produce two distinct pitches (usually a second apart), but the simultaneous performance of several bows of different sizes allows multipart and harmonic textures. Specific rhythmic patterns (*toques*) include the *São Bento grande,* the *São Bento pequeno,* the *Iúna,* the *Santa Maria,* the *Angola,* and the *cavalaria,* with specific functions and references to the dance. They differ mostly in tempo, rather than in rhythmic structure.

Capoeira songs—some 139 have been collected—constitute a rich source of Afro-Bahian expressive culture relating to slavery, the local lingo, and poetics. Except for the "hymn of the *capoeira*" and litanies (*ladainhas*), the repertoire of *capoeira* songs borrows a great deal from other repertoires, such as children's game songs of the *ciranda* genre. Other songs, such as "*Santa Maria, mãe de Deus*" ('St. Mary, mother of God'), invoke religious themes and figures.

Traditionally, *capoeira* has been taught and practiced in academies (*academias*) led by masters (*mestres*). Among historically known masters, none has enjoyed as much fame as Mestre Bimba, who developed a new form, *capoeira regional,* adding a number of dance figures resembling some of the strokes of other martial arts (Pinto 1991).

FIGURE 5 A *capoeira* group. Salvador, Bahia, Brazil. Photo by Max Brandt, 1996.

FIGURE 6   A *berimbau* player with *caxixi*. Salvador, Bahia, Brazil. Photo by Gerard Béhague, 1985.

Since the 1960s, the influence of tourism has resulted in the impoverishment of the *capoeira* tradition, in the performance of *golpes* and *toques* and the knowledge of songs. In addition, the popularity of *capoeira* abroad, primarily in Western Europe and the United States, has brought about fundamental changes in traditional performances.

Dramatic dances

Originating in missionaries' activities during the early colonization of the country, dramatic dances (*bailados*) have survived in contemporary Afro-Brazilian communities. These dances include processions and actual dramatic representation, with numerous characters, spoken dialogues, songs, and dances, accompanied by small instrumental ensembles. The major themes of such dramatic dances relate to the Iberian medieval catechistic theater, including conversion, resurrection, and battle scenes between Christians and infidels (Moors). Among significant dramatic dances enacted by Afro-Brazilians are the *bumba-meu-boi, congada, congo, marujada,* and *taieira,* all known by many different local names.

The bumba-meu-boi

The *bumba-meu-boi,* perhaps the most popular of all folk dramas, is known and practiced in various styles in several regions of the country, north and south. It has its origins in the triethnic heritage, but its Afro-Brazilian elements are especially evident in the northeastern and northern states. The main character is the bull (*boi*), representing for some an African totemic survival. The dramatic action enacts regional variants of a legend concerning characters of the colonial period—the Portuguese master, the black slave (variously named Mateus or Francisco), his wife Catarina, the captain (*cavalo marinho*), and others. Fantastic figures and animals participate in the representation, but only human characters actually sing. According to Mário de Andrade (1982), the dance includes fixed and variable elements, the former consisting of the main characters' entrances and dances, the latter also involving the secondary characters. Most of the songs exhibit characteristic elements of mestizo folk music, including the style of cattle-herding songs known as *aboios.*

Documentation of the dance in Maranhão (Kazadi wa Mukuna 1994) reveals the presence of three distinct styles, the *boi de zabumba* (*zabumba* is a double-headed bass drum), the *boi de matraca* (*matraca* is a type of wooden rattle), and the *boi de orquestra* (mostly brass-band instruments). Of these, the first is considered to represent a truly Afro-Brazilian tradition, not only through its instrumentation (including, besides the *zabumba,* the friction drum [*tambor onça*] and other percussion instruments), but also its musical and choreographic structures. The criticism of the dominating characters, hence of the ruling class, evidenced in the comic scenes of the bull's death and resurrection, is seen as an important clue that the drama originated in slaves' culture.

The marujada

The *marujada* (from *marujo* 'sailor') of the coastal area of the state of Bahia is performed entirely by black associations on specific feast days. It combines and celebrates Portuguese maritime feats and the confrontation of Christians and Moors. Performers representing Christians, dressed in Brazilian white navy uniforms, reenact episodes of exploration, including the hardship of life at sea, the battle with the Moors (dressed in red capes) and their imprisonment, the wounding and symbolic death of the leader of the Moors, and his eventual resurrection as a Christian, welcomed into his new community in a final scene. The performance includes choral numbers in a processional type of march by the sailors and several solo and duet

Mário de Andrade studied the *samba campineiro* of São Paulo (calling it Paulista rural samba) in 1937 and observed that samba was defined by its choreography rather than by its musical structure.

numbers in scenes by naval officers and Moors. Some scenes are spoken, and others are sung. Each community has developed a traditional oral script for the dramatic scenes. Responsorial singing between officers and sailors is common, with the sailors accompanying themselves on small hand-held drums. The melodic structures of the tunes belong almost entirely to the tradition of Luso-Brazilian folk songs. To a great extent, the *marujada* illustrates pertinently the biethnicity of Afro-Bahians' cultural heritage, for its participants are Candomblé worshipers, who obviously see no contradiction in their biculturalism.

Social dances

Dance music of a predominantly Afro-Brazilian tradition includes a variety of genres and instrumental ensembles. Quite frequently, collective singing forms an integral part of such genres, so singing combines with dancing. The performance of this music occurs on numerous social occasions, from spontaneous, informal performances in party gatherings to formal contexts associated with cyclical celebrations of life.

The substantial Afro-Brazilian contribution to and influence on Brazilian folk dances in general is reflected not only in the larger number of specific Afro-Brazilian dances, but also in the Brazilianization—that is, Afro-Brazilianization—of European dances, an important aspect of Brazilian urban popular music. The most common traits of folkloric choreographic structure are circular formation, frequently with solo dancers, and the presence of *umbigada* (from Portuguese *umbigo* 'navel'), the symbolic bumping of the couples' navels, signifying an invitation to the dance or challenge—and an indication that the dances originated in Africa.

Music and dance are inseparable—which explains why the name of a dance is applied to the music it accompanies. Among the dances of predominantly Brazilian blacks are the *batuque* and the samba, the *caxambu*, the *jongo*, the *côco*, the *baiano* (*baião*), and the former *lundu* and *sarambeque*, all with numerous regional names. Only a few can be considered here.

The batuque

A round dance given an Angolese or Congolese origin, the *batuque* is no longer performed as such, and the term has acquired the generic sense of black dance accompanied by singing and heavy percussion. However, in Rio Grande do Sul and Belém, Pará, *batuque* now designates Afro-Brazilian cults associated with different religious groups, and in São Paulo state, it is a specific dance of local Afro-Brazilian cults. The accompanying instruments of the latter include drums (*tambu, quinjengue*) and rattles (*matraca, guaiá*).

The samba

Many regional varieties of samba exist. As a folk dance, it was formerly important, but its importance has diminished in most regions of the country because of the popularity of some types of the urban samba. In the southern-central areas, the folk samba is known as *samba-lenço, samba de roda,* and *samba campineiro.* The choreographic arrangement of the *samba-lenço*—dancers with a kerchief (*lenço*) in their hand—resembles the old *batuque,* again in circular formation. With texts in the form of quatrains, the songs are performed in parallel thirds with snare drum and tambourine accompaniment. The songs are usually eight bars long, in duple meter with an anacrusis, and have a range of up to an octave, a descending motion with repeated notes, and isometric rhythm. The accompaniment exhibits typical Afro-Brazilian syncopation.

Mário de Andrade studied the *samba campineiro* of São Paulo (calling it Paulista rural samba) in 1937 and observed that samba was defined by its choreography rather than by its musical structure. The latter shows an arched melody in duple meter, syncopated rhythmic figuration, strophic and variable textual forms, and the relative importance of textual improvisation. The dance itself stresses collectivity—which explains the absence of the *umbigada.* Besides the instrumentalists (who also dance), the main participants are women. The *samba de roda* has lost its former importance in São Paulo, but in the northeast (especially in Bahia), it is still the most popular social dance. As a round dance involving soloists, it is usually performed responsorially, with frequent overlapping between the vocal soloist and the choral response.

The Bahian *samba de viola* is a type of *samba de roda* from a choreographic standpoint, but *violas* (various sizes of guitars, with five double-stringed courses as a rule) are the central instruments of the ensemble, completed by a *prato-e-faca* 'plate and knife', a *pandeiro,* a triangle, an occasional *atabaque,* and hand clapping. The lyrics (*chulas*) set this samba apart from others, in their extreme eclecticism in form and subject. In the 1980s and 1990s, the tradition of *samba de viola* lost its former importance and was known and performed by only a handful of older musicians (Waddey 1981).

The coconut

The coconut (*côco*) is a dance of poorer people in northern and northeastern Brazil. Its name derives from the fact that the dance is commonly accompanied by clapping with hands cupped to create a low-pitched sound, like that of a coconut shell being broken. Sometimes a drum or a rattle may be used, in which case the dance is named after the instrument: *côco-de-ganzá* (shaker), *côco-de-mugonguê* (drum), and so on. In the northern states, different names refer to the type of song associated with the coconut, such as *côco-de-décima, côco-de-embolada,* and *côco-desafio* (Alvarenga 1982). The choreographic structure dictates the alternation of stanza and refrain in the song: a solo dancer in the middle of the circle improvises a stanza and is answered by the other dancers. A frequent feature of coconut-song melodies (also present in *côco-de-embolada*) is the peculiar rhythm of short durations (usually sixteenth notes in 2/4 time) repeated continually, resulting in exciting ostinatos.

The maculelê

The Afro-Bahian *maculelê,* another martial dance, is believed to have originated in the city of Santo Amaro in the 1890s in celebration of the abolition of slavery. Strongly reminiscent of black African stick-fighting dances, the *maculelê* is performed with sticks used as mock weapons and percussive instruments. Responsorial singing with drum accompaniment praises two figures as having been responsible for the abolition of slavery: Our Lady of Conception is the main religious one, and Princess Isabel de Bragança (1846–1921) is the historical one. The songs are in Portuguese with numerous African words in the choral refrains. Some of the dance figures resemble those of *capoeira,* but in no way can it be said that *maculelê* functions as a preparation for *capoeira* practice, since it has its own autonomous repertoire and performance contexts.

URBAN POPULAR MUSICAL TRADITIONS

Brazilian popular music owes much of its character and creativity to Afro-Brazilians (Béhague 1985). In the 1700s, the Afro-Brazilian dance known as *lundu* had already been assimilated by upper-class composers as an expression of the tropical colony, and it had influenced the *modinha,* a sentimental genre (opposed to the Portuguese *moda*) in its characteristic syncopated rhythmic accompaniment (Araújo 1963; Béhague 1968). In the 1800s, the black flutist-composer Joaquim Antônio da Silva Callado, professor of flute at the Imperial Conservatory, Rio de Janeiro, began to nationalize European dances (including the polka, the schottische, and the waltz) by incorporating into his compositions in these genres melodic and rhythmic patterns associated with the popular scene of Rio de Janeiro. Reinforced by the introduction in Brazil in the mid-1800s of the habanera, with its typical dotted rhythm (dotted eighth, sixteenth, and two eighth notes), the Brazilian tango emerged. In effect, the systematic application of subtle variants of the habanera pattern, and the frequency of occurrence of a syncopation such as the sixteenth-eighth-sixteenth pattern in a duple meter, created the *maxixe,* at first the name only of a fast, syncopated style. The semipopular composer Ernesto Nazareth wrote for the piano many polkas and tangos that are true *maxixes* from a rhythmic point of view.

Chorões and the *choro*

In Rio between 1875 and 1900, popular instrumental ensembles of strolling street musician-serenaders known as weepers (*chorões*) appeared, performing dance music (*maxixes* and polkas) and arrangements of sentimental songs of the *modinha* type. This kind of ensemble, which came to be known as *choro,* typically included guitars (*violões,* sing. *violão*), a *cavaquinho* (small four-stringed guitar of Portuguese origin), a flute, a tambourine, and later a saxophone. While the ensemble's performance stressed improvisation and virtuosity, the musical genre *choro,* which developed after 1900, continued to use the same rhythmic foundation as *maxixes* and polkas. Many black popular musicians active during the period 1900–1930 became composers and performers of *choros.*

Urban sambas

The urban samba, which came to epitomize Brazilian popular music in general, has been strongly identified with Afro-Brazilian expressive urban culture. The first commercially recorded samba, "*Pelo Telefone*" (1917), was the work of the black composer Donga (Ernesto dos Santos). Sinhô, called the King of Samba in the 1920s (Alencar 1968), and Caninha, both black musicians, contributed greatly to the popularity of the genre; but it was Pixinguinha (Alfredo da Rocha Viana), another black composer, who had the greatest influence. With his bands Os Oito Batutas (1922), Orquestra Típica Pixinguinha-Donga (1928), and Grupo da Velha Guarda (1932), he popularized the urban samba among different social classes in the 1920s and 1930s (Alves 1968; Efegê 1978–1979).

In emphasizing a percussive ensemble and traditional responsorial singing, the so-called samba of the slums in the hills (*samba de morro*) maintained a closer identity with the folk samba. Out of this ensemble developed the *batucada* (percussion ensemble and percussive dance music) associated with the samba school (*escola de samba*), first organized as a carnival association in 1928. The music history of the samba school since then has been primarily associated with Afro-Brazilians as composers, arrangers, and performers (Alencar 1965). In addition to the *samba de morro,* other subgenres appeared from the 1920s to the 1940s, especially the *partido-alto* (a folklike dance of the primarily black connoisseurs) and the *samba de enredo* (samba with a story or plot), used by each group of samba schools.

In the 1970s and 1980s, the samba from Rio (*samba carioca*) regained vitality with the works of Martinho da Vila and others, especially the emergence of the *pagode,* as part of the complex world of Rio's slums (*favelas*). Some *pagode* pieces in the performance of Bezerra da Silva, such as "*O Preto e o Branco*" ('The Black and the White'), picture vividly the issues of racial relations and the deterioration of city life in the slums (Carvalho 1994).

Bahian genres

Urban popular music found its most notorious early cultivators in Rio de Janeiro, but the state of Bahia came second. As early as the mid-1930s, the Afro-Bahian Dorival Caymmi, through his fisherman or beach songs (*canções praieiras*) and his sambas (even before the advent of bossa nova), created an innovative style based on authentic, empathetic references to Afro-Bahian folklore and music. For several decades, his popularity throughout the country remained strong, perhaps because he was able to convey even to listeners alien to Bahia the essence of his cultural experience as a black Bahian worshiper of Candomblé and a cultivator of the most modern popular genres and styles. In addition, his lyrics, deeply rooted in the African linguistic and emotional tradition of his native state, represent a chief asset of his creativity (Risério 1993).

The innovations brought about in the samba tradition by bossa nova musicians beginning in the 1950s were the work of sophisticated musicians, primarily middle- and upper-class whites (Béhague 1973; Castro 1990). Some black performers, however, participated in the new trend, indicating their integration in the modern era of Brazilian popular music. In addition to Johnny Alf, Jair Rodrigues, Wilson Simonal, and especially the great guitarist of the 1960s, Baden Powell, bossa nova's second generation of black musicians included the internationally successful composers Gilberto Gil and Milton Nascimento, who each used a variety of styles and subjects to express and transcend their ethnic identity (Béhague 1980; Perrone 1989).

The city of Salvador, Bahia, the traditional bastion of Afro-Brazilian artistic expressions, has become a significant locus of popular-music developments since the 1960s. Besides the avant-garde movement of *tropicália,* whose members were mostly Bahians, a new carnival music appeared in the 1970s and 1980s. The Afro-Bahian phenomena of *afoxé, carnaval ijexá,* and *bloco afro* had significant sociopolitical and economic repercussions at that time. The traditional music and culture of Candomblé played an important role as a creative source and force in the concept of black ethnicity in the 1970s and 1980s. The emergence of an African consciousness among young people of African descent represents a social and human history of great significance, in which traditional music has had a fundamental function in the movement of ethnic and political vindication. Local black and mestizo young people have contributed to the re-Africanization of carnival (Risério 1981; repeated by Crook 1993). The process of a new black-consciousness movement, though it has much to do with the ideology of negritude, was never based on the cultural incorporation of contemporary African elements; rather, it originated in a new interpretation and rendition of the most traditional elements of Afro-Bahian culture. It would appear more accurate, therefore, to refer to a re-Afro-Brazilianization within a new concern of validation of the contemporary black culture and the necessity of expressing a new ethnicity.

The revitalization in the 1970s of the Afro-Bahian carnival associations called *afoxés* gave the new black movement a starting point. *Afoxés* whose members were

Bloco afro songs referred to a variety of Afro-Brazilian and other Afro-diaspora subjects, always expressing the black world, its history, and its problems.

devotees of Candomblé represented the first attempts in Bahia to transfer to the street, during carnival, the aura of the mythical world. The name of the oldest *afoxé,* Filhos de Gandhi (Sons of Gandhi), paid homage to the great statesman a few months after his assassination (1948) and revealed the ideological affinity of the group with Gandhi's anticolonialism, philosophy of nonviolence, and activism against European domination. Traditionally, the music performed in the carnival parades of *afoxés* was actually Candomblé music, specifically *ijexá* songs and rhythms. Filhos de Gandhi developed its own music but retained the main stylistic features of *ijexá* music.

By extension, the new carnival of the 1970s and 1980s became known as *carnaval ijexá,* primarily to establish a direct relationship with some of the most essential aspects of black culture. In a general sense, however, the word *ijexá* implied at that time Afro-Bahian culture associated with Candomblé, in which the term designates a specific drum rhythm resembling that of a slow samba. Actually, several lyrics composed for *afoxés* call *ijexá* a rhythm, a style, and a dance.

Beginning in the mid-1970s, new carnival organizations called *blocos afro* began to appear. The first one, founded in 1974, bore the linguistically and politically significant name Ilê Aiyê (from Yoruba *ilê* 'house, temple', and *aiyê* 'real world' in Yoruba cosmovision and mythology as opposed to Yoruba *orum* 'supernatural world'). At first, Ilê Aiyê barred white people's participation, and its compositions constantly mentioned the *aiyê* as the living, exciting, beautiful world of black people. The themes "black is beautiful" and "the living world is the black world" became part of the ideological manifesto of *blocos afro.* Reinforced by the appearance of the militant political group known as Movimento Negro Unificado (MNU), *blocos afro* took on the form of true activism in the 1980s. Their support of the MNU, however, was more a symbol of black identity and power than a direct political militancy. Their songs not only evoked the Afrocentricity of their origins, but also addressed the issues of racism and socioeconomic injustice. The creation of a new aesthetic involved the imitation and transformation of African and Afro-Caribbean models of music, dance, and dressing, known or imagined. The choice of instruments was limited to drums— several *surdos* (low pitched), *repiques* (high pitched), and snare drums—and other percussion, supporting a responsorial vocal structure (figure 7). At first, the basic rhythmic organization, known as the *toque afro-primitivo,* consisted of a slow-to-moderate-tempo samba in a rich and forceful percussive texture. *Bloco afro* songs referred to a variety of Afro-Brazilian and other Afro-diaspora subjects, always expressing the black world, its history, and its problems.

With the new *afoxés* and *blocos afro,* the direct relationship to Candomblé diminished considerably, since the young leaders were no longer Candomblé priests, the musicians not necessarily Candomblé drummers, and the songs no longer derived from liturgical repertoires. The members of the new groups, however, did not fail to recognize and adhere to some aspects of Candomblé traditions, as some members are

FIGURE 7   The *bloco afro* group Axé. Salvador, Bahia, Brazil. Photo by Max Brandt, 1996.

Candomblé worshippers. Before celebrating an important festivity (such as carnival), people sometimes perform rituals of offering to the *orixás* in the name of the groups. Some Candomblé rhythms have occasionally been incorporated into *bloco afro's* rhythmic section. In general, however, whether or not they are close to the Afro-Bahian religions, leaders of *blocos afro* are aware of and in tune with Candomblé's traditional function as a center of cultural resistance and of social and ethnic identity.

Among the Afro groups that emerged in the 1980s (including Araketu, Badauê, Ebony, Malê Debalê, and Muzenza) the most successful *bloco afro* undoubtedly has been Olodum, founded in 1979 by former members of Ilê Aiyê. Musically innovative, Olodum had by the mid-1980s introduced different patterns into their fundamental samba beat. These patterns were reminiscent of Afro-Caribbean rhythms (merengue, salsa), but the influence of Jamaican reggae was so strong that the new patterns of drumming, having acquired the interlocking structure of Afro-Caribbean rhythms, became known as samba-reggae (Béhague 1992a). Cuban *timbales* joined the percussive group of Olodum. Ideologically, the reference to Jamaica created a sense of affinity and solidarity with the Bahian-black movement. Through reggae and Rastafarianism, Jamaican black culture had been recognized the world over, and Bob Marley and Jimmy Cliff were idols of Afro-Bahian youths. Eventually Olodum created its own Banda Reggae, which toured extensively. The success of Olodum's sociopolitical program—schools, shelters and jobs for street children, a variety of community services—was due to the vision and determination of various leaders of the group, and to the inevitable selling out to the music industry. Though its first commercial success was local, its international popularity, translated into multimillion-dollar activity in a few years, has tarnished the ideological grounding of its beginnings, since Olodum is now viewed as another style of worldbeat.

In Bahia, samba-reggae was so successful that in the late 1980s several popular commercial bands, especially Banda Mel and Reflexu's, jumped at the opportunity to flood the pop market with synthesized renditions of the style. Among Afro-Bahian composers who specialized in the new genre has been Edson Gomes, one of the best representatives of resistance reggae (*reggae resistência*). Bahian mass-mediated popular music ended up establishing a trend called *axé* music (from Yoruba *axé,* denoting the vital spiritual force of Candomblé and everything and everyone associated with it)— an obvious misnomer, as this music has little or none of the Afro-Bahian religion's spirituality. The justification actually comes from the fact that this is music of Salvador, Bahia, often labeled the African city of Brazil, or the African Rome of the Americas, and, as such, its music needs to be qualified as African. *Axé* music, as in the works and interpretations of such figures as Margareth Menezes and Daniela Mercury, combines a variety of Afro-Bahian styles, *ijexá afoxé, bloco afro samba,* samba-reggae, and even occasionally lambada and *fricote,* all with heavily electrified accompaniment. As opposed to *bloco afro,* however, *axé* music has penetrated into the national pop market and, with the support of the multinational music industry, has resulted in a worldwide craze.

Another development that capitalized on *bloco afro*'s success was the early 1990s *timbalada,* so called because it involved an instrumentation in which the timbre of the *timbal* is the focus, provided with a plastic head and special tunings, in trying to approximate the percussive sound of *bloco afro.* Carlinhos Brown and others had a central role in popularizing *timbalada,* nationalizing a primarily regional style of popular music.

The Bahian pop star Luís Caldas, a light mulatto sometimes called the Brazilian Michael Jackson, won wide popularity in the 1980s with his lambadas, reggaes, and another genre of carnival dance music, *fricote.* His hit "*Fricote*" combines elements of *ijexá* and *bloco afro* rhythms, a lambada type of tune, and lyrics that have double meanings and overt sexual connotations. The lambada popularized in Bahia is actually an adaptation of the established popular dance from Pará known as *carimbó.* The market for international recordings fostered another short-lived craze for the lambada, of easy musical access and suggestive, acrobatic, sensual dancing. In Brazil, lambada continued in the 1990s only as a tourist attraction in the Bahian coastal resort of Porto Seguro.

Many Brazilian black pop musicians have been busy in adapting North American pop-music trends, such as funk and rap. Rock in Brazil has been associated predominantly with the white middle class. Funk and rap, introduced in Brazil in the 1980s, are heavily supported in big cities by people—especially teenagers—of the lower socioeconomic class, primarily blacks. Some musicians and singers of these styles "have associated themselves openly with the various black movements" (Carvalho 1994:30). In addition, funk musicians have frequently commented in their songs on the racial situation in Brazil and expressed black pride openly. In the late 1990s in Rio de Janeiro, articles in newspapers report that funk and rap are being used by the drug lords of the city.

Around 1990, in homage to the gangs, the "kings" of Rio rap, William Santos de Souza and Duda (Carlos Eduardo Cardoso Silva), who earned about $80,000 a month in 1995, recorded a famous rap, "*Rap do Borel*" ('Rap of Borel'), about a slum in the Tijuca neighborhood, where drug dealers operate. Raps exist for almost all the main *favelas* of Rio, and even as a challenge to drug enforcement, for the Division of the Repression against Drugs, as in the "*Rap da DRE*" ('Rap of the Divisão de Repressão a Entorpecentes'). Comando Vermelho (Red Command), the famous organized crime group, is known to have subsidized funk parties to recruit kids for dealing drugs. The more radical types of funk and rap, however, have served mostly for sociopolitical messages on local, regional, or national issues, as demonstrated by the rap groups Câmbio Negro (Black Exchange) and Chico Science. In opposition to hip-hop, Câmbio Negro adheres to consciousness rap (*rap consciência*). The noncompromising ideology of this group reflects militancy against racism and social injustice in deliberately shocking and foul language.

Charm, another form of urban popular music of the 1990s, attracts predominantly lower-to-middle-class blacks in Rio and São Paulo. A form of well-behaved, apolitical funk, it stresses bourgeois values.

REFERENCES

Alencar, Edigar de. 1965. *O carnaval carioca através da música.* 2 vols. Rio de Janeiro: Livraria Freitas Bastos.

———. 1968. *Nosso Sinhô do samba.* Rio de Janeiro: Civilização Brasileira Editora.

Almeida, Renato. 1942. *História da música brasileira.* 2nd ed. Rio de Janeiro: F. Briguiet.

Alvarenga, Oneyda. 1982. *Música popular brasileira.* São Paulo: Livraria Duas Cidades.

Alves, Henrique L. 1968. *Sua excelência o samba.* Palermo, Brazil: A. Palma.

Andrade, Mário de. 1982. *Danças dramáticas do Brasil.* 3 vols. Belo Horizonte, Brizil: Itatiaia.

Araújo, Mozart de. 1953. *A modinha e o lundu no século XVIII.* São Paulo: Ricordi Brasileira.

Béhague, Gerard. 1968. "Biblioteca da Ajuda (Lisbon) MSS 1595 / 1596: Two Eighteenth-Century Anonymous Collections of Modinhas." *Yearbook / Anuario* (Inter-American Institute for Musical Research, Tulane University) 4:44–81.

———. 1973. "Bossa & Bossas: Recent Changes in Brazilian Urban Popular Music." *Ethnomusicology* 17(2):209–233.

———. 1975. "Notes on Regional and National Trends in Afro-Brazilian Cult Music." In *Tradition and Renewal,* ed. Merlin H. Forster, 68–80. Urbana and London: University of Illinois Press.

———. 1977. "Some Liturgical Functions of Afro-Brazilian Religious Music in Salvador, Bahia." *The World of Music* 19(3–4):4–23.

———. 1980. "Brazilian Musical Values of the 1960s and 1970s: Popular Urban Music from Bossa Nova to Tropicalia." *Journal of Popular Culture* 14(3):437–452.

———. 1984. "Patterns of *Candomblé* Music Performance: An Afro-Brazilian Religious Setting." In *Performance Practice: Ethnomusicological Perspectives,* ed. Gerard Béhague, 222–254. Westport, Conn.: Greenwood Press.

———. 1985. "Popular Music." In *Handbook of Latin American Popular Culture,* ed. Charles Tatum and Harold Hinds, 3–38. Westport, Conn.: Greenwood Press.

———. 1988. "Fonctions Socio-Liturgiques de la Musique Religieuse Afro-Brésilienne, à Salvador, Bahia." In *Les Musiques Guadeloupéennes dans le Champs Culturel Afro-Américain, au Sein des Musiques du Monde,* ed. Michel Bangou, 195–208. Paris: Éditions Caribéennes.

———. 1992a. "La afinidad caribeña de la música popular de Bahia en la década de 1980." *Anales del Caribe* (Havana: Centro de Estudios del Caribe, Casa de las Américas) 12:183–191.

———. 1992b. "Regional and National Trends in Afro-Brazilian Religious Musics: A Case of Cultural Pluralism." In *Competing Gods: Religious Pluralism in Latin America,* Occasional Paper 11:10–25. Providence, R.I.: Thomas J. Watson Institute for International Studies, Brown University.

———, ed. 1994. *Music and Black Ethnicity: The Caribbean and South America.* Miami: North-South Center, University of Miami.

Carvalho, José Jorge de. 1993. "Aesthetics of Opacity and Transparence. Myth, Music, and Ritual in the Xangô Cult and in the Western Art Tradition." *Latin American Music Review* 14(2):202–231.

———. 1994. *The Multiplicity of Black Identities in Brazilian Popular Music.* Brasilia: Universidade de Brasilia.

Castro, Ruy. 1990. *Chega de saudades. A história e as histórias da bossa nova.* São Paulo: Companhia das Letras.

Crook, Larry N. 1993. "Black Consciousness, Samba Reggae, and the Re-Africanization of Bahian Carnival Music in Brazil." *The World of Music* 35(2):90–108.

Efegê, Jota. 1978–1979. *Figuras e coisas da música popular brasileira.* 2 vols. Rio de Janeiro: FUNARTE.

Fujii, Tomoaki, ed. 1990. *The Americas* II. Produced by Katsumori Ichikawa. JVC Video Anthology of World Music and Dance, 28. Video.

Kazadi wa Mukuna. 1994. "Sotaques: Style and Ethnicity in a Brazilian Folk Drama." In *Music and Black Ethnicity: The Caribbean and South America,* ed. Gerard Béhague, 207–224. Miami: North-South Center, University of Miami.

Okada, Yuki. 1995. *Central and South America.* JVC Smithsonian Folkways Video Anthology of Music and Dance of the Americas, 5. Montpelier, Vt.: Multicultural Media VTMV-229. Video.

Perrone, Charles. 1989. *Masters of Contemporary Brazilian Song: MPB 1965–1985.* Austin: University of Texas Press.

Pinto, Tiago de Oliveira. 1991. *Capoeira, Samba, Candomblé: Afro-brasilianische Musik im Recôncavo, Bahia.* Berlin: Staatliche Museen Preussischer Kulturbesitz.

Rego, Waldeloir. 1968. *Capoeira Angola: Ensaio sócio-etnográfico.* Salvador, Brazil: Itapuã.

Risério, Antonio. 1981. *Carnaval ijexá.* Salvador: Editora Corrupio.

———. 1993. *Caymmi: uma utopia de lugar.* São Paulo: Editora Perspectiva.

Tinhorão, José Ramos. 1988. *Os sons dos negros no Brasil.* São Paulo: Art Editora.

———. 1991. *História social da música popular brasileira.* São Paulo:

Waddey, Ralph C. 1981. "Viola de Samba and Samba de Viola." *Latin American Music Review* 2(1):196–212.

Chile
Juan Pablo González

The Republic of Chile, a long and narrow Spanish-speaking country, hugs south-western South America between the Pacific Ocean and the crest of the Andes Mountains. It is about 4,200 kilometers long and between 87 and 400 kilometers wide. Its terrain is extremely varied, from the driest desert in the world (Atacama Desert, in the Norte Grande) to glacier-filled estuaries and rugged peaks (Tierra del Fuego, south of the Magellan Strait). Because its location and terrain physically isolate it from the rest of South America, it is a rich repository of musical folklore.

NATIVE AMERICANS

A culture known archaeologically as San Pedro (named for the region of Atacama) originated about 500 B.C.; it was influenced by the Tiawanaku civilization (near Lake Titicaca in Bolivia) from A.D. 300 to 1000 and was dominated by the Incas from 1471 to 1533. Its descendants, named Atacameño by the Spanish after 1536, have retained certain agricultural techniques and folkways from ancient times.

The Atacameño, with the Aymara, the Mapuche, and the Fueguino, constitute the prevailing indigenous cultures of Chile; Rapa Nui (Easter Island, culturally Polynesian) can be considered an outside colonial addition [see OCEANIA VOLUME: EAST POLYNESIA: Rapa Nui]. These four broadly defined native Chilean cultures have been isolated from the concept of nation and nationality that was created and sustained by the dominant Chilean culture; thus, they have developed different levels of acculturation, resulting from a variety of contacts with the Western-derived Chilean world. The Fueguino are extinct.

The Atacameño live in oases of the Atacama Desert, Antofagasta Province. They call themselves Lican-antai and speak Kunza (their native language, now revived in their rituals) and Spanish. They developed a kind of urbanism by building villages, fortifications (*pukarás*), and irrigation systems, still used today. They practiced oasis agriculture, pasturing, and commerce among themselves and with the Inca and the Diaguita. Their social organization is based on small, autonomous kinship communities, and their indigenous religious system is linked to the earth, fertility, and water. They also practice Roman Catholicism (Munizaga 1974).

The Aymara live in Tarapacá Province, part of Bolivia before the War of the

Pacific (1879–1883). The fall of the Inca empire as a result of the Spanish invasion of Peru (1531–1533) transferred the Aymara and the other Indian nations to Spanish domination. The Aymara, conquered by the Inca in 1450, started their process of westernization by 1560 with the adoption of the Spanish language and Roman Catholicism. Today, they are bilingual and practice religious syncretism. The Aymara of the precordillera (foothills of the Andes) show a higher degree of acculturation than those of the highlands. Aymara youth immigrate to the coastal cities of Antofagasta, Arica, and Iquique, but for their festivals they return to the precordillera and the highlands. The culture of the Aymara region is the product of an acculturative process in which Aymara and Roman Catholic concepts blend. This mixture is expressed in the musical and choreographic features of the Aymara people.

The Mapuche are the main ethnic minority of Chile [see MAPUCHE]. About seven hundred thousand Mapuche live in the southern provinces of Arauco, Bío-Bío, Cautín, Llanquihue, Malleco, Osorno, and Valdivia, and in the cities of Santiago and Valparaíso. Their languages are Mapudungun and Spanish. They resisted the Inca and Spanish conquests but were defeated in 1884 by the Chilean army. A low degree of acculturation exists in their music and religious systems. Only the Pikunche (Mapuche of the north-central valley) and Williches (Mapuche of the south, Valdivia to Chiloé) were absorbed into Chilean mestizo culture.

The so-called Fueguino cultural group included four distinct nomadic nations that inhabited Tierra del Fuego. The Ona (or Selk'nam) and Patagones (or Tehuelches) were hunters, and the Yahgan (or Yamana) and Alacaluf (or Halakwalup) were fishermen. Little is known about the musical activities of these groups because of their remoteness, the secrecy of their rituals, and their meager population during recent history. The acculturation of the Alacaluf began in the 1930s. Since then, they have sought to integrate themselves into the Chilean economy, and since the 1960s they have identified themselves with Chilean culture rather than their traditional culture. Westernization produced a dramatic demographic reduction among them (only forty-nine Alacaluf remained alive in 1971), resulting in the extinction of their culture.

MUSICAL INSTRUMENTS

Chilean musical instruments can be classed as indigenous, Spanish, mestizo, or criollo, though the variety of mixtures makes classification somewhat unreliable. Many indigenous types can be described according to their native characteristics, uses, and functions.

Indigenous instruments

Atacameño

In the north of Chile, Atacameño musical instruments descending from pre-Hispanic times include two trumpets (*clarín*, *putu*) and a rattle (*chorimori*). The Atacameño adopted the snare drum (*caja chayera*) and the guitar from the Spanish. The *clarín* is a 2-meter transverse trumpet made of a cane bound with colored wool; the *putu* is a cow-horn trumpet decorated with wool; and the *chorimori* is a rattle of metal bells without clappers. The *clarín* and the *putu* are played together, respectively representing male and female principles during the native ritual of *talátur* 'praise to the water'. The *caja chayera*, a double-headed frame drum, is used in carnival with the guitar (Álvarez and Grebe 1974).

Aymara

Aymara musical instruments include the *kena* (*quena*, *lichiwayo*) and the *siku* (Spanish *zampoña*) [see QUECHUA-AYMARA; BOLIVIA]. The Chilean Aymara also

FIGURE 1   At the patronal festival of the Virgin of Guadalupe, 8 September 1968, a mestizo of Aymara descent plays a copper-tube *kena.* Aiquina, Antofagasta Province, Chile. Photo by Dale A. Olsen.

employ European instruments, including the guitar, the mandolin, the violin, the clarinet, the trumpet, and other brass instruments. Syncretic types include the *bandola,* the *tarka,* and the *pinquillo (pinkillo),* played by today's Aymara, alone and in orchestras and bands.

The *kena,* widely used in the Andean area from Ecuador to Chile, is a notched end-blown flute with five to eight fingerholes. Ancient *kena* made of cane, clay, and bone have been found in the Chilean Aymara region, and modern *kena* are made of cane, plastic, or copper, especially near the Chuquicamata copper mine, Antofagasta Province (figure 1). Today, the *kena* is played as a solo instrument (with accompaniment by *bandola* or guitar), or in ensemble (with two *kena,* a guitar, a mandolin, and a violin). The *lichiwayo (lichiguayo)* is a thick *kena* bound with llama tendons, played in ensembles of about six instruments.

The *siku* is a double-unit or paired, two-halved panpipe (a set of six to eight closed cane tubes per half), requiring two people to play one instrument. One half is called *ira* and the other *arca,* representing male and female principles and having respectively leading and following functions during performances. Each half of the instrument is a set of closed tubes, attached to a frame of open tubes. The *siku* was probably used in shamanistic practices during pre-Columbian times. Sets of *siku* are divided by register in the following categories: *sanha* (tenor), *contra* (alto), and *liku* (soprano).

The *tarka,* a wooden duct flute with a square-shaped outer surface, is played in ensembles known as *tarkeadas.* The *pinquillo,* a cane duct flute, is played alone or accompanied by a *bandola,* during carnival and while pasturing. The *bandola* is a guitar of four quadruple courses, derived from the Hispanic *bandurria.*

Mapuche

Among the Chilean Mapuche [see ARGENTINA; MAPUCHE]), the shaman (*machi*) plays three instruments: a *kultrún* (small kettledrum with internal rattle), a *wada* (gourd rattle), and a *kaskawilla* (bell rattle). The rest of the Mapuche community plays *kullkull* (cow-horn trumpet), *nolkín* (hollow-stem trumpet, played by inhaling), *trutruka* (2- to 6-meter-long cane trumpet, played by exhaling), *pifülka* (one- or two-tubed panpipe), *piloilo* (two- to five-tubed panpipe, made of stone, clay, cane, or wood), *pinkullwe* (cane transverse flute), and *makawa* (double-membrane drum).

FIGURE 2   A Mapuche man plays a *trutruka* in front of his house. Cautín Province, Chile. Photo by Juan Pablo González.

The *kultrún,* a symbolic microcosm of the Mapuche universe, is a leading Mapuche instrument. It signals the beginning and ending of musical performances, provides rhythmic patterns and tempos, and may induce the *machi*'s trance during rituals. It is made of sacred wood, filled with elements of animal, mineral, and plant origin, and painted with representations of the cosmos. It is played as a solo instrument, in a *kultrún* ensemble (with a *wada* or a *kaskawilla*), or with the other Mapuche sacred instruments (see Okada 1995: examples 11 and 12).

The *trutruka* is played as a solo or ensemble instrument by adult men during rituals, especially the *nguillatún*. Because of its length, its performance requires physical strength. It is constructed from a 2- to 6-meter-long hollowed-out section of *coligüe* cane, covered with a horse intestine; a cattle horn is usually attached at the distal end as a resonator (figure 2). The tubing is sometimes replaced by a straight or spiraled iron pipe, or is even replaced completely by a brass cornet (Grebe 1973, 1974).

Mapuche secular instrumental music is often played on the Jew's harp (*trompe*) adopted from the Spanish or other European settlers (especially Germans, who came to the Mapuche region during the mid-1800s). The Mapuche also adopted the accordion from the Germans.

Mestizo and creole musical culture

Spanish Roman Catholic and Arab-Andalucían traditions are the foundations of the traditional Chilean musical-poetic practice that can be called Chilean creole music (*música criolla chilena*) or mestizo music. This expressive art includes musical instruments, religious and secular music and dance, musical-poetic practices and forms, and performance styles that developed in central Chile, where the Spanish predominated.

Mestizo musical instruments in Chile (those of indigenous origin but played in Roman Catholic rituals) include the *flautones* or flutes of *chino* dancers, the oldest type of dance group in patronal festivals of central Chile (see Okada 1995: example 13). A *flautón* 'big flute' is a single-tubed panpipe, with extended sides in the shape of an elongated V added to a single cane tube (Olsen 1980). Sets of *flautones* play two-note melodies in hocket. The origin of the *chino* flutes is undoubtedly native American, and they may in fact derive from the Mapuche *pifülka*.

The *cauzúlor* shows the importance of water in oasis agriculture. To the Atacameños, water embodies music, and they learn the ritual melodies by listening to the flow of the water.

FIGURE 3   A zither (*charrango*) made by stringing four wires across a board (101 centimeters by 16 centimeters), supported by two beer bottles as bridges. Photo by Juan Pablo González, 1979.

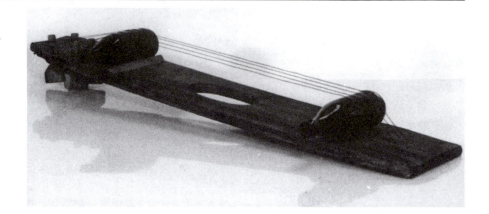

Chilean Spanish and criollo music is performed upon or accompanied by European or syncretic instruments. The European instruments include a three-stringed fiddle (*rabel*), a six-stringed guitar (*guitarra;* see photo, p. 240), a five-stringed guitar (*vihuela*), an accordion (*acordión*), a diatonic harp (*arpa*), the piano, the tambourine, and drums. Chilean creole instruments are the *guitarrón* 'big guitar', a five-course guitar with twenty-five strings, the *charrango* (board zither) (figure 3), the *tormento* (struck box with jingles), and the *quijada* (jawbone of an ass). In the creole tradition of Santiago and Valparaíso, the dances *cueca chilenera* and *cueca porteña* are performed by one or more singers and instrumental ensembles of two guitars, accordion, piano, harp, tambourine, and drums.

Patronal festivals in Chiloé include musical performances by an ensemble consisting of a guitar, an accordion, a double-skinned drum (*bombo*), a violin, and formerly a flute and a *rabel*. The last instrument is a Renaissance European transplant.

RELIGIOUS MUSICAL CONTEXTS AND GENRES

Indigenous

Atacameño

Two indigenous rituals (*cauzúlor* and *talátur*) and one mestizo ritual (*carnaval* 'carnival') provide the foundations for Atacameño musical practice. These rituals, devoted to fertility of the earth and abundance of water, are landmarks of the agrarian cycle. The people also perform rituals during patronal and livestock-marking festivals, as do the Aymara. Songs are sung in Kunza in native rituals; Kunza and Spanish are used in carnival. The Atacameño musical system is tritonic, based on notes that approximate the Western major triad; this acoustic foundation has ensured its survival and eased its mixture with Western tonality and instruments. Atacameño singing is syllabic and high-pitched; it is heterophonic and more improvisatory in the indigenous rituals, and solo or responsorial and more fixed during carnival.

In mid-August in Caspana, *cauzúlor* celebrates the end of the communal cleaning of the waterways, built in pre-Hispanic times. This ritual shows the importance of water in oasis agriculture. To the Atacameños, water embodies music, and they learn the ritual melodies by listening to the flow of the water. They express gratitude and pray for abundance, fertility, peace, and communal prosperity. While singing and dancing, they open the gate to the cleaned waterway and pour wine and throw corn into the water. Between August and October in Peine and Socaire, *talátur* praises the water, invoked to irrigate the earth. The songs for *talátur* are associated with singing to the water, according to the magical principle that the similar attracts the similar. The singing is collective, accompanied by a *clarín*, a *putu*, and a *chorimori*.

Carnival among the Atacameño is a harvest-celebrating rite, observed around Ash Wednesday in the regions of Atacama and Loa; it marks the end of the agrarian calendar, which culminates in the harvest of corn and wheat. The festivities performed in the Chilean Andean area coincide with Ash Wednesday, in preparation for the abstinence from eating meat during Lent. Under ecclesiastical benevolence, this coincidence allowed the pre-Columbian harvest rite to survive. In Chile, the Andean carnival is a rural phenomenon, practiced by the Aymara and Atacameño communities of the highlands and precordillera. Its syncretism is shown in Indian and Spanish musical features. The carnival couplet (*copla de carnaval*) is its main musical genre. Sung in Kunza or Spanish, these *coplas* are quatrains of eight-syllable lines rhyming *abcb*, linked by common themes. They include improvisational dialogues, usually competitions between men and women. The melodies are tritonic, with the accompaniment of *caja chayera* and guitar (Claro 1979; Grebe 1980).

Aymara

Aymara religious music is performed during seasonal rituals of carnival, sowing potatoes (*pachallampe*), and marking livestock (*enfloramiento*), and patronal and Marian festivals. The main genre of the Aymara carnival festival is the tone and round (*tono y rueda*), consisting of strophic melodies in major scales. Tones and rounds are played by *pinkillo* and *bandola* in the mountains and by guitar in the precordillera; they are danced in rounds by unmarried women in the highlands and by mixed people in the foothills. Two ensembles perform during carnival: a *tarqueada* plays *taquirari* songs, and an *orquesta* (ensemble with strings and winds) plays *cueca*, *cumbia*, *huayno*, *taquirari*, and *vals*.

To ask for agricultural fertility, the potato-sowing ritual is celebrated in October on the communal grounds of the church; during the celebration, tones and rounds are played. The rite for marking livestock (llama, alpaca, sheep, cattle) is celebrated within the corrals and animal-holding areas during February. Owners of livestock sing intimate songs to the animals to protect them and make them fertile. Accompanied by *bandola*, the songs are categorized according to the type and sex of the animal, and the function each animal performs.

The juxtaposition of Hispanic and native religious beliefs has developed since the 1500s in the Andean area, producing a blend of musical and choreographic features, which have their largest expression in the celebration of the religious festivals of the Roman Catholic calendar. A major patronal festival of the Chilean Aymara is celebrated in Isluga, a ritual town in the highlands, where the four *ayllu* (kinship divisions of the Aymara territory) are represented. There they celebrate two female patrons, St. Barbara (4 December) and the Immaculate Conception of the Blessed Virgin Mary (8 December), and two male patrons, St. Thomas, patron of Isluga (21 December), and Corpus Christi (Feast of the Blessed Sacrament). The festivals last three days each; during the first day, before vespers, non-Christian rites are performed; during the second day, at vespers, the Roman Catholic festivity is prepared; the third day, the day of the saint, culminates with processions and dances.

Several ensembles perform during Aymara patronal festivals: *lichiwayo*, *sikuri*, and brass bands. *Lichiwayo* lead the procession, playing heptatonic melodies in parallel fourths, in strophic and binary forms (AABB). The *sikuri* are ensembles of ten panpipe players, consisting of one *zanja*, two *contras*, and seven *liku*. Players of *contra* and *liku* also play a double membrane drum. Wearing hats with long rhea feathers (chucos), the musicians play *tonos de sikuri*, pentatonic tunes for procession. *Laquita* (*lakita*), ensembles of small panpipes, played by teenagers and other young people (trained by missionaries), play religious and dance music, especially *cueca*, *cumbia*, *huayno*, *taquirari*, and *vals*. Brass bands, derived from military bands, play the same repertoire as *laquita*.

Mapuche

The Mapuche divide their music into sacred (older, fixed, powerful) and secular (newer, freer, amusing). Mapuche sacred instrumental and vocal music is related to a fertility ritual (*nguillatún*), shamanic initiations (*machilwün* and *neikurrewén*), funeral rites (*elüwún*), and medical rituals (*pewutún* 'diagnostic', *datún* 'large therapy', *ülutún* and *lawentuchen* 'small therapies'). The shaman (*machi*), with her *kultrún*, is the leading performer in most Mapuche religious rituals. Mapuche music uses two basic scales: pentatonic and tritonic. Melodies are descending and include frequent portamentos and glissandos. Binary divisions prevail in metric and phrasal structures.

Christian Festivals of the Virgin Mary

The government of King Philip III of Spain (1578–1621) mandated devotion to the Virgin Mary in Hispanic America. The king ordered each town to have a manifestation of her as its patron. During the celebration of her day, guilds and fraternities danced and sang in front of her image. Today these troupes—as dance groups (*bailes*), confraternities (*confraternidades*), and brotherhoods (*hermandades*)— are formed by pilgrims who attend the festivals.

Each *baile* has an administrative director (*alférez* 'conductor'), who may personally finance the event, and an artistic director (*caporal* 'ringleader'), who instructs the pilgrims during the year and conducts the performances. The *bailes* dress emblematically and are categorized by choreography into step dances (*bailes de paso*) and jump dances (*bailes de salto*); the former are older.

In the Aymara region of Chile are found the following troupes: *chinos* (figure 4), miners who emigrated from central Chile to the saltpeter mines of the north in the late 1800s; *morenos*, mestizo people; and *cuyacas* and *llameras*, formed only by women. Most of the *bailes de salto* derive from *chunchos*, dressed as Amazon warriors transplanted by the Incas to the Andes. During the 1930s, members of the *bailes de chunchos* created new troupes, influenced by the North American Indians they saw in Hollywood movies. These new *bailes de salto* have been called redskins (*pieles rojas*), Apaches, Comanches, Cherokees, and Sioux. Other *bailes de salto* performed in the Aymara region are gypsies (*gitanos*), devils (*diabladas*, of Bolivian origin), and *sambas caporales* (of Brazilian-Bolivian influence). Differently costumed dancers (*figurines*), dressed like devils and bears, can join any troupe, making jokes and keeping the public separated from the dancers.

The structure of the festivity for the Virgin Mary derives from the relationship between the dancers and the image of the Virgin. Its arrival, entrance, and departure from the church, and the people's greeting, praise, and farewell to it at different times of the day are the high points of the ceremony. Most of the lyrics are sung or recited

FIGURE 4 *Chinos* from Petorca dance while playing *flautones* and drums. Photo by Juan Pablo González.

FIGURE 4 *Chinos* from Petorca dance while playing *flautones* and drums. Photo by Juan Pablo González.

in quatrains of eight-syllable lines. The melodies are strophic and in binary form (ABAB), in diatonic minor, major, or pentatonic modes, showing Spanish and Aymara-Quechua origins. These festivals include several hierarchical levels: official Roman Catholic rites (including masses) coexist with popular rituals (including physical penances and offerings) and native American and mestizo social practices (including the trading of goods during the festival). Official hymns coexist with Aymara and mestizo music and dance and with popular music.

The Virgin of the Pains

The festival of the Virgen de Las Peñas, celebrated 83 kilometers east of Arica on the first Sunday of October, is the oldest patronal festival of the Chilean Aymara. The earliest legend explaining the origin of this Virgin is carved in stone, dating from 1642. *Bailes* from Chile (*chunchos, morenos* 'browns', *gitanos* 'gypsies', and *cuyacas*), Peru (*lakitas* and *sikuri*), and Bolivia have attended this festival. They include bands consisting of two trumpets, two clarinets, a trombone, a snare drum, and a bass drum; or small flutes and snare drums; or two *kena* and a bass drum (for a similar musical event at the patronal festival of the Virgin of Guadalupe in Aiquina, see figure 1). The repertoire reveals various degrees of acculturation, from *huaynos* and *pasacalles* to military marches and hymns (Lavín 1948).

The Virgin of the Tyrant

The festival of the Virgin of Carmen, celebrated in La Tirana, 84 kilometers east of Iquique during the week of 16 July, is the biggest expression of religious syncretism in Chile (figure 5). According to legend, in about 1535 an Inca princess named Ñusta Huillac escaped from the Spaniards and established a stronghold in the Tamarugal pampa. She ruled the region with an iron fist until she fell in love with a Portuguese fugitive. She converted to Roman Catholicism and was murdered by her own warriors. A missionary found a cross in the place where she and her lover were sacrificed and built a sanctuary to the Virgin Mary there. Since 1883, Tamarugal has belonged to Chile; miners coming from the south began the present festival of La Tirana in 1886. Today, dozens of *bailes de paso* and *bailes de salto* perform an extensive itinerary

alférez　Administrative director, conductor, or main sponsor of a *baile* or *cofradía* dancing group in Chile

flautón　'Big flute', Chilean single-tubed *chino* dancer's ductless flute (like a single tube of a panpipe) played in sets

trote　'Trot', a term used in Chile for the Andean *huayno*

FIGURE 5　*Moreno* dancers and their accompanying brass band in front of the church during the patronal festival of the Virgin of Carmen, 16 July 1979. La Tirana, Tarapacá Province, Chile. Photo by Juan Pablo González.

of greetings and farewells in front of the cross and the image of the Virgin inside the church, plus honorific dances outside the church, usually to the accompaniment of brass bands or ensembles of *pitos* (side-blown fifes) and drums (Uribe Echevarría 1974).

The Virgin of the Candelaria

The festival of the Virgin of the Candelaria is celebrated for three days during the first weekend of February near the northern city of Copiapó. An ancient Christian festivity, it recalls the purification of the Virgin Mary after the birth of Jesus. The use of candles (from which the name *candelaria* derives) comes from a pagan Roman tradition, and other celebratory aspects reveal non-Christian origins. In Chile, the festivity started in 1780, with a muleteer's discovery of a stone icon of the Virgin. Originally, only regional *bailes* or confraternities known as *chinos* and *morenos* participated in the festival. Today, those traditional dance groups attend, as do newer ones, called devils (*diablos*), redskins (*pieles rojas*), sailors (*marinos*), and gypsies (*gitanos*), from other towns. The presence of these troupes gives the festival a carnivalesque character; strict regulations control the participants' discipline, moral behavior, honorableness, hierarchy, and duties.

During the first day, before vespers, the festival's sponsors (*mayordomos*) deposit a candle and an offering (*chuya*) of water, sweets, cinnamon, carnations, and coca leaves in front of images of the Virgin and Jesus Christ. During the night, ritual welcomes using coca leaves, alcohol, and tobacco are performed to honor the main sponsor and his family, his house, ancestral spirits, and Christian saints. At midnight, to remember the ancestral spirits, the sponsor sprinkles alcohol and coca leaves in front of the church; he then does the same in the four corners of the town square. Musical instruments (*flautones, tambores, zampoñas*) are sprinkled with alcohol and coca leaves; one note is played on each one to inaugurate the music.

On the second day, four rites are performed. In the first, at 3:00 A.M., the sponsor and the sacristan recite three Hail Marys in the church and remove the candles and the *chuyas* of the previous day. The sacristan sprinkles the cross, the church, and the bell tower with the *chuyas,* because the edifice and the tower, symbolizing female and male, protect and prosper the community. In the second rite, performed at dawn, people of the community gather in front of the church to ask forgiveness for their sins, and then walk to the opposite end of town and burn incense for Jesus (whom they think visible in the sunrise). In the third rite, performed during the afternoon in the house of the *alférez* and in the church, the images of the saints and the virgin are decorated, and candles and flowers are sprinkled with alcohol, coca leaves, and holy water. The fourth rite is performed in front of the church at night, when all the candles are lit. The community, the *alférez,* the sacristan, and the priest pray the rosary and sing religious songs, followed by dancing around the church by the *bailes.* When the sacristan closes the church, the dance groups retire to a house (*casa de baile*) to dance *cachimbos, cuecas, cumbias, huaynos,* and *trotes* all night.

The rituals of the third day, designated as the Virgin's day, start at noon with a mass, followed by a procession by the *bailes* and the populace. A new *alférez* is installed for the next year. The day ends with offerings to the authorities of the festival and more dancing in the dance house.

Our Lady of the Rosary

One of the oldest religious festivals in mestizo Spanish-speaking America has been celebrated every October and December since the late 1500s in the gold-mining town of Andacollo, in north-central Chile. According to folklore, the adoration and celebration of Our Lady of the Rosary (Nuestra Señora del Rosario) of Andacollo began when native Americans discovered an image of the Virgin Mary that Spaniards had hidden in the outskirts of La Serena. The festival has been attended by *bailes chinos* since 1584 (playing *flautones* and drums), *turbantes* since 1752 (playing guitar, mandolin, accordion, *flautas,* and triangle), *danzantes* since 1798 (playing guitar, *flautas,* and triangle), and *chunchos, diabladas,* and *indios* since 1958 (accompanied by brass bands). The *alférez* of each *baile* sings octosyllabic quatrains in front of the image, making promises and pledges, asking favors, and expressing gratitude to the Virgin—a practice that shows the preponderance of Hispanic influence.

Other Christian festivals

Spanish influences are prevalent in the one-day religious festivals of Cruz de Mayo (May Cross, 3 May), Corpus Christi, and Saints Peter and Paul (29 June), commonly celebrated in the provinces of Valparaíso and Aconcagua. These festivals are organized around *bailes* or *cofradías.* Each troupe consists of twenty to thirty members, a patron (called the owner), and an *alférez* (*abanderado* 'conductor'). The dances are of the *chino* type. Dancers perform in a reverent squat (see figure 4) while playing one- or two-tubed panpipes (*flautas, flautones,* or *pitos*) in hocket fashion, accompanied by double-skinned drums. The *alférez* sings octosyllabic quatrains of greeting and farewell to other *alféreces* and the priest, and *décimas* (ten-line strophes) to honor the festival's patron saint or the Virgin Mary (Plath 1979; Uribe Echevarría 1958;

Urrutia Blondel 1968). The verses, sung without accompaniment, are composed or improvised by the *alférez* himself or are already composed by other *alféreces* or popular poets. The *alféreces* of the visiting dance groups and the host *alférez* greet one another with dialogic singing of often improvised quatrains (*contrapuntos*), as seen in the following text (Uribe, 1958:41).

Cómo está, mi buen alférez?	How are you, my good director?
Cómo está? cómo le va?	How are you? how are you doing?
Me alegro de verlo bueno,	I'm glad to see you well,
Sin ninguna novedad.	Without any news.
Vengo bien, abanderado;	I'm fine, conductor;
Lo digo de corazón,	I say this from my heart.
El Baile de Campiche Afuera	The dance group of Campiche Afuera
Le hace saludación.	Gives you greeting.

The host sings the first stanza, and the visitor sings the second.

Chiloé Island festivals

The island known as Chiloé, situated in the northern part of the southern archipelago, was under the control of the Spanish until 1826. Therefore, Hispanic influence on the island is more evident than in other areas of Chile, which became independent in 1810. The Williche culture (the Mapuche of the south) was absorbed by Spanish influences, but descendants of the Williche maintain parts of their social organization. Beginning in the 1600s, Jesuits contributed to the process of change of Chiloé by developing a Baroque-influenced architecture and the teaching and practice of religious singing. Singing the rosary in novenas and at patronal festivals and wakes is a common practice in Chiloé. Rosary orations are sung as psalmody; sacred mysteries are sung in a Gregorian style; religious hymns precede the rosary, are interpolated, or conclude it. *Cantos de ángeles* 'songs of angels' are performed during wakes for infants. Chilotes (people from Chiloé) sing prayer songs for the dead, Christmas carols, and *salves* (songs with religious texts, promoted by missionaries since colonial times).

The patronal festivals celebrated in Chiloé are organized by local *cabildos* (male and female hierarchical organizations). After the religious festivals and communal-work efforts (*mingas*) are over, the Chilotes dance waltzes, *corridos, cuecas,* and *rancheras.* Dances once popular in Chiloé—the *cielito,* the *nave,* the *pavo,* the *pericona,* the *sajuriana,* the *trastrasera* (most of them derived from the Spanish *cuadrilla*)—are extinct. Children still play musical games and sing game songs (*rondas*) learned in school, and their parents sing lullabies, many from historical times (Dannemann 1978; Lavín 1952).

Starting in the late 1500s, the remoteness of Chiloé and the archipelago has led the Roman Catholic Church to instruct governmental leaders (*fiscales*) to replace the priest as conductor and controller of religious festivities. These leaders care for the church and teach and conduct religious singing.

SECULAR MUSICAL CONTEXTS AND GENRES

Indigenous

The Mapuche use a Jew's harp to play love songs, shepherds' songs, and lullabies. Mapuche secular vocal music is used to converse, argue, court, welcome, and express gratitude (Titiev 1949). Repetitions and variations of short melodic patterns of descending thirds are used in Mapuche secular songs (González 1986).

Spanish-derived and creole

Chilean Spanish-derived musical-poetic tradition originates from the genres, instruments, performance styles, and uses of music brought to Chile by Roman Catholic Spaniards (and Arab-Andalucíans) during the Encounter and the colonial period. The Spanish *romance, villancico, décima,* and quatrain and the Andalucían *nuba* (*nawba*) and *zejel* are among the ancestors of the musical-poetic tradition of the Chilean central valley. The narrative genres of Chilean creole music are the ballad (*romance, corrido*), the couplet (*copla*), the verse (*verso*), and the tune (*tonada*). All are based on genres of Spanish sung poetry brought to America during the colonial period by couplet singers (*copleros*), successors of European medieval minstrels.

The *romance* is formed by an indeterminate number of quatrains, recited or sung in one musical sentence (AB), in 6/8 or 3/4 meter, in the major mode, and with or without guitar accompaniment, usually with only tonic-dominant harmony. Its main textual themes have always been disaster, crime, love, and adventure. It survives only in the game song (*ronda*), the *canción,* the *corrido,* the *tonada,* and the *verso* (Barros 1970).

The *verso,* sung poetry accompanied by a guitar or a *guitarrón,* has the form of one octosyllabic quatrain plus five *décimas* (each rhyming *abbaaccddc*). The quatrain states the subject of the *verso,* which four *décimas* then gloss, each tenth line quoting one line of the quatrain; the fifth *décima* is a farewell. The *verso* has secular and religious themes (*fundamentos*), called *a lo humano* (to the human) and *a lo divino* (to the divine), respectively. Secular themes include modern and ancient history, astronomy, geography, nature, love, exaggerations, duels, and riddles; *versos a lo humano* are performed at weddings, baptisms, birthday parties, and recreational occasions, and after religious festivals. Religious themes derive from the Old and New Testaments and from Christian doctrine; *versos a lo divino* are performed at wakes, funerals, and novenas during the celebrations of the Cruz de Mayo and the festivals for the Virgin Mary. Both kinds of *verso* are maintained by oral and written traditions.

The melody of the *verso* is based on recitative-like patterns in major, minor, and Mixolydian modes, with half and full cadences (*requiebres* and *caídas*). The harmony is modal, tonal, or mixed, with or without bourdon (tonic pedal on open strings). The chords are often I, V^7 (with and without the third above the root), and flat VII (IV of IV). The accompaniment derives from the relationships between tuning and performing patterns (left-hand positions and right-hand strumming and plucking techniques).

The popular poets (*poetas populares*), the singer-composers of the *verso,* maintain a tradition of singing and improvising in rounds (*canto a lo pueta*)—a practice somewhat similar to that of the Andalucían *nuba.* During and after religious festivals, popular poets sing *versos a lo humano* and *versos a lo divino.* They participate in poetic duels by improvising quatrains of questions and answers in a dialogic style (*contrapunto*), developing a proposed theme given by the audience as an octosyllabic line (*paya*). The popular poets have great self-esteem; connoisseurs of the culture of the community and its ancestors, they have the capacity to express their knowledge in art.

Tonada

The genre known as *tonada,* widely performed in the central valley of Chile, may originate in part from the *zejel,* an Andalucían poetic form that alternates a refrain with stanzas. During the Chilean colonial period, the term *tonada* served to designate any intoned tune. Nowadays, the *tonada* is sung by one or two female or male singers (the duet style is in thirds) in a nasal style. It is accompanied by one or two guitars (with or without a harp), using normal or altered tunings (such as D–a–d–f♯–a–c♯)

romance   In Chile, an old-style narrative song with an indeterminate number of quatrains recited or sung in one musical sentence

villancico   'Rustic song', a popular Christmas song genre in Spanish-speaking countries, usually a *tonada* in Chile

tonada   'Tune', Chilean song performed by one or two singers in parallel thirds in nasal style

esquinazo   Chilean *tonada* performed as a serenade

parabién   'Best wishes', a Chilean genre similar to the *tonada*, performed as a marriage greeting and congratulatory song for a bride

playing I, IV, V of V, and V chords in the major mode. The *tonada* is commonly in moderate 6/8 and 3/4 meter, with strumming patterns that accentuate the shifting meter known as hemiola (*sesquiáltera*).

The octosyllabic quatrain is the common poetic meter of the *tonada,* though other poetic forms such as the *décima,* the *romance,* the *quintilla* (five-line stanza) and the ten- or eleven-syllabic line are used. The *tonada* may or may not have a refrain. Some quatrains start with the last line of the previous one (*de coleo*) or are the retrograde of each previous quatrain (*al revés*). A *cogollo,* a quatrain of farewell and homage to an important listener, is commonly added at the end. The *tonada,* which has a festive function, is played at rodeos, wheat harvests, and birthday parties. It is called *esquinazo, villancico,* and *parabién* when it is performed as a serenade, Christmas carol, and marriage greeting, respectively. It is also performed during wakes, when it is called *tonada de velorio* (Barros 1964; Pereira Salas 1941).

An urban form of the *tonada* developed in the 1920s, when rural peasants and plantation elites migrated to cities. This change gave impulse to the development of a popular music based on the *tonada,* evoking the relationship between the migrants and the countryside, nourished by a nostalgic attitude of paradise lost. Vocal quartets, accompanied by a harp, an accordion, and guitars, and wearing costumes of the Chilean cowboy (*huaso*), evoked the folklore of the central region of Chile. Though the cowboy does not usually sing (as a soloist or in a group), his costume is brilliantly impressive as a spectacle and reflection of authority from the countryside. It is also the attire used by landowners and other men of rank.

The first groups of singing cowboys were formed by university students who later divided their time between professional careers and artistic activities. The most distinguished quartets were Los Cuatro Huasos (founded 1927), Los Huasos Quincheros (1937), and Los Provincianos (1938) (figure 6). To capture the folklore of the Chilean countryside, these groups chose the *tonada* as their main musical expression because of its lyricism, its flexibility, the simplicity of its structure, and its roots in Chilean creole culture. Their polished arrangements and interpretations included virtuoso techniques on guitar and harp, with fancy introductions and interludes featuring parallel thirds and arpeggios in a Paraguayan style; they emphasized cultivated voices with articulate diction and precise intonation—appropriate traits, for the upper middle class greatly admired these types of quartets. To evoke the typical flavor (*sabor típico*) of this music, the singing cowboys included animated yells and farmers' speechways. This style of the *tonada,* often featured on recordings and during shows, was developed by Chilean folkloric composers, who also composed *cuecas* and other national musical forms.

Cueca

Most Chileans consider the *cueca* a national symbol, though not every Chilean appreciates it, and many Chilean musicians have not mastered it. Different cultural

FIGURE 6   The Chilean male vocal quartet Los Provincianos, dressed in decorative *huaso* costumes, 1939. Collection of Juan Pablo González.

FIGURE 6   The Chilean male vocal quartet Los Provincianos, dressed in decorative *huaso* costumes, 1939. Collection of Juan Pablo González.

origins have been postulated to explain its choreographic, musical, and poetic features. Afro-Peruvian and colonial (and now extinct) Afro-Chilean traits may survive in its polyrhythms and styles of dancing [see AFRO-PERUVIAN TRADITIONS]. Hispanic traits may survive in its harmonic and melodic structure and instrumentation. Arab-Andalucían traditions have been certified in its poetic structure, nasal vocal quality, and style of singing (Claro 1989; Garrido 1979).

The performance and theme of the *cueca* change with the setting. In the Andean mestizo areas of the north, it is performed by brass bands or panpipe ensembles; it has no lyrics and is danced before a *trote,* another name for *huayno* in parts of Chile. In traditional areas of the south, it is accompanied by guitar and accordion and sung in a chain of *seguidillas* (seven-line stanzas of five and seven syllables, ordered 5–7–5–7–7–5–7), with the fourth line repeated and lengthened with the syllable *si,* producing a longer variant. In the Chilean folk-urban tradition of Santiago and Valparaíso, two genres, *cueca chilenera* and *cueca porteña,* have been performed by singers and instrumental ensembles: two guitars, an accordion, a piano, a harp, a tambourine, and drums.

The *cueca* chronicles historic and social settings. The urban *cueca* has commented on historic events—Chilean independence from Spain (1810), the War of the Pacific (1879–1883), the Chilean revolution of 1891, and World War II. It has narrated catastrophes, accidents, and crimes. It has paid homage to Chilean men—the brave peasant (*roto* 'broken') and the he-man (*gallo* 'rooster'), sports stars, musicians, and poets. It has glorified and ridiculed love, and has exalted nature and wine.

The *cueca* is almost always performed in the major mode (principally with I and V chords), in a fast tempo in compound 6/8+3/4 time. Its structure is based on *coplas, seguidillas,* and *pareados* (two-line stanzas of seven- and five-syllable lines), sung with a ternary music sentence (ABB and ABA), as in the following text:

Tengo pena, tengo rabia,
tengo ganas de llorar,
Porque a la Corina Rojas la quieren ajusticiar.

> Dicen que la Corina,
> siendo una dama,
> Ha muerto a su marido,
> estando en la cama,
> estando en la cama, sí.
> No puede ser
> Que fusilen en Chile a una mujer.
>
> Le pasó a la Corina por asesina.

> I am sad, I am angry,
> I want to cry,
> Because they want to shoot Corina Rojas.

> They say Corina,
> being a lady,
> has killed her husband,
> being in bed,
> being in bed, yes.
> It can't be possible
> For them to shoot a woman in Chile.

> That happened to Corina for being a murderess.

The danced *cueca* is a choreographic account of a woman's conquest by a man, metaphorically represented as the conquest of a hen by a rooster. The stages of search, conquest, and victory correspond respectively to the *copla,* the *seguidilla,* and the *pareado.* Because the male dancer twirls a handkerchief, the *cueca* is often called a scarf dance (Claro 1982, 1989).

Folklorists and folkloric composers

Composers who cultivated Chilean folkloric music (*música típica chilena* 'typical Chilean music') such as the *tonada,* the *cueca,* and other genres include Nicanor Molinare (1896–1957), Victor Acosta (1905–1966), Violeta Parra (1917–1967), Luis Bahamonde (1920–1978), Clara Solovera (1909–1992), and Francisco Flores del Campo (1907–1993). Predominant themes in the songs of these composers are the idealization of the woman and the self-glorification of the man, with the man suffering love's deceit. The woman is presented in a dualistic fashion: on the one hand, she is virtuous, yet flirtatious; on the other, she is stubborn, yet reserved. The man appears with complementary traits: honesty and forcefulness, valor and patriotism.

Chilean folkloric music developed into a distinct style, as much because of its repertoire as because of its manner of interpretation. For the Chilean nation and the world, it forged Chile's sonic image and was the principal current of Chilean popular music until the early 1970s. Nevertheless, by providing knowledge of new genres, repertoires, and interpretive practices, folklorists such as Violeta Parra and Margot Loyola (b. 1918) contributed to the diversification of the notion of Chilean folklore prevalent in urban sectors of Chile until the 1960s.

Violeta Parra began transcribing folk songs in the early 1950s. She traveled throughout the country and became friends with popular poets and singers, from whom she learned the repertoire she preserved and disseminated while developing her own poetic and musical style (Parra 1979). A large portion of her songs are rhythmic, melodic, harmonic, and formal models of Chilean folk music, and are standards for the performance of such folk-musical genres as *cueca, parabién, pericona, rin, sirilla,* and *tonada.* Her lyrics, following poetic procedures appropriate to Chilean traditions, refer to traditional local customs and legends. Her songs often have archaic traits such as medieval European modality and Spanish poetry from the 1400s. She has faithfully maintained the original simplicity of Chilean folk music, intensifying it with a primitivism by which she has recreated an indigenous soundscape. This is clear especially with her use of tetraphonic melodies characteristic of the *trutruka,* repetitive rhythms of the *kultrún,* and harmonic drones.

Margot Loyola applied her academic musical training to the service of folk-musical collecting, transcribing, and preserving, especially by reconstructing and disseminating in traditional style a vast amount of her interpretations. She made recordings and gave concerts, developing an important pedagogy of folklore starting in 1949. From her efforts appeared Concumén (1955), a folk-musical ensemble dedicated to collecting and disseminating traditional songs, dances, and costumes from the central parts of Chile.

MUSICAL CHANGE

Since the 1800s, musical influences from Europe and Latin America have been incorporated into Chilean musical practices. During the twentieth century, many Latin American urban and rural folk-musical styles (especially Afro-Latin music) have been diffused via radio, film, and recordings and have been integrated into Chile's music (orally transmitted and composed) and dance. Especially between the 1930s and the 1960s, cultural expressions from Argentina, Mexico, and Cuba, including such genres as the tango, the *zamba,* the *corrido,* the *guaracha,* the *cha-cha-chá,* and the bolero became popular in Chile.

As early as the 1920s, the tango was danced in Santiago and Valparaíso, where it retained its traditional Argentine form. Repeated visits by Argentine musicians, along with Argentine films and recordings, ensured its presence in Chile. It was diffused through dance, musical performances, and composition contests; through the efforts of dance academies and professors; through the foundation of tango clubs; through the publication of special records, books, and magazines; and through the creative activities of Chilean composers, musicians, and dancers.

The Argentine *zamba* was diffused in Chile during the 1940s by the Argentine performers Antonio Tormo and Atahualpa Yupanqui and through records and broadcasts. During the later 1950s, the closeness of the *zamba* to peasant Chilean music, along with its harmonic and melodic richness, contributed to its popularity among Chilean youths, who sang Argentine songs and played Argentine guitars, enriching amateur musical performances and expanding interest in the guitar.

Throughout Latin America beginning in the 1930s, Mexican films began diffusing Mexican peasants' music. Chileans widely performed the Mexican *canción ranchera* and *corrido,* stripped of their narrativity and epic character. The Chilean people identified with the rurality of these genres; this identification led to the Chilean development of soloists and ensembles in mariachi styles, and of duets and trios in *norteño* styles [see MEXICO]. The Mexican-style singer Guadalupe del Carmen (1917–1987) and the quartets Los Veracruzanos, Los Queretanos, and Los Huastecos del Sur were active in Chile during the 1940s and 1950s. These ensembles, which formed part of the artistic programming of certain radio stations in Santiago, performed the most recent and fashionable *canciones rancheras* and *corridos* from Mexico. They also interpreted musical soundtracks from Mexican films shown in Chile.

The internationalization of Afro-Cuban music, helped by Mexican and U.S. music and films, brought to Chile between 1930 and 1950 the orchestral rumba of Xavier Cugat, the conga of Desi Arnaz, the mambo of Dámaso Pérez Prado, the

Nueva canción, which has common threads from a vast region of South America, symbolized the social and cultural unity of Latin America and reinvigorated the deprived and oppressed native people of the Andes.

FIGURE 7   An advertisement for a performance of Lucho Gatica in the Waldorf Theater (Santiago), 1953. Photo by Juan Pablo González, 1994.

guaracha, and the *cha-cha-chá.* These genres were interpreted, danced, composed, and recorded in Chile by local orchestras, including Cubanacán, Huambaly, Ritmo y Juventud, and Los Peniques. Burlesque of the *guaracha* gained popularity among Chilean peasants, whence it entered Chilean folklore. The same thing happened with the *cha-cha-chá* in the Andean region, as well as with the Colombian *cumbia,* which became a Chilean folkloric expression in the 1960s.

The bolero arrived in Chile in the mid-1930s via recordings and live performances by Mexican singers, including Juan Arvizu and Pedro Vargas. During the 1940s, the first Chilean bolero singers—Raúl Videla, Arturo Gatica, Mario Arancibia—appeared, followed in the 1950s by Lucho Gatica (figure 7), Arturo Prieto, and Sonia and Myriam. These performers sang boleros written by the Chilean composers Armando González Malbrán (1912–1950), Jaime Atria (1919–1984), and Francisco Flores del Campo (1907–1993), who cultivated an elegant and mundane orchestral style, appropriate for the regional dance salons, theaters, and auditoriums of Chile. The bolero was adopted during the 1950s as part of the *trío bolero,* brought to Latin America by the Mexican trio Los Panchos, who first performed in Santiago in 1951. This style was incorporated into a repertoire that included Peruvian waltzes, Chilean *tonadas,* and Paraguayan *guaranias* as duets and trios; this repertoire became popular in markets and restaurants throughout Chile. Chileans still appreciate the sentimentality of such ensembles.

POPULAR MUSIC

The incorporation of Andean music into popular urban Chilean music was a process that began in the 1950s with the countrywide diffusion of dances and songs tran-

FIGURE 8   The new-song ensemble Illapu in performance, with *bombo,* guitar, and singers (one is holding a *quena*). Photo by Juan Pablo González, 1978.

scribed in the north by Chilean folklorists. Performers and composers from Santiago became acquainted with the *cachimbo* and the *trote* (a 2/4 dance, similar to the *huayno*), composing with Andean sentiments songs that succeeded in penetrating the massive market of urban popular music.

Nueva canción

Beginning in the mid-1960s, the ensembles Inti Illimani and Quilapayún and the musicians Angel Parra, Isabel Parra, and Victor Jara were the founders of a movement that became known as new song (*nueva canción*). It incorporated Andean genres musical instruments (*siku* or *zampoña, kena, charango, bombo,* guitar) and native American sentiments from northern Chile, Bolivia, Peru, and Ecuador. Their music, which has common threads from a vast region of South America (even beyond the Andes), symbolized the social and cultural unity of Latin America and reinvigorated the deprived and oppressed native people of the Andes. It therefore was ideologically attached to the progressive spirit of the 1960s and the Allende years (until 1973). These musicians and the later ensemble Illapu (figure 8), polished the original native Andean sound, adapting it to the norms of popular music. At the same time, by associating Andean music with songs of social protest, they replaced the Andean people's nostalgia and pain with expressions of vigor and combativeness. The diffusion of Andean music by the musicians of the new-song movement enabled central and southern Chileans to accept this music as their own, identifying themselves with a sound that had until then been foreign to them.

Canto nuevo

After the military takeover of Chile (in 1973), new song was banned, its ensembles and musicians exiled (Inti Illimani lived in Italy until 1988, and Quilapayún has continued to live in France), or killed (Victor Jara, d. 1973). Chileans were not encouraged to play Andean instruments because those instruments were laced with the Marxist ideological overtones of the Allende years. Another movement followed, however. It inverted the term for new song, coining the term *canto nuevo,* also glossable as 'new song'. The ensemble Barroco Andino, using the same Andean instruments as had *nueva canción,* made recordings of music by Bach, Telemann, other classical composers, and the Beatles. Other ensembles were Ortiga, Aquelarre, and

Santiago del Nuevo Extremo, the last one closing the *canto nuevo* period in the early 1980s. Eventually, the ban on Andean musical sentiment was lifted, and the genre remained popular, mostly devoid, however, of overt social messages. Since 1994, when democracy was restored, Inti Illimani has composed and performed new pop music that fuses its earlier new-song sound with other world musics, especially Italian and Latin American.

Rock

After the 1960s, when an imitative rock movement known as new wave (*nueva ola*) developed in Chile, the fusion-rock band Los Jaivas electrified the Chilean pop scene in the early 1970s with the use of Andean *siku, kena,* electric guitars, keyboards, and other contemporary instruments. They released their thirteenth album, *Hijos de la tierra,* in 1995, recorded in Paris on the Sony label. The arrival of a new generation of Chileans by the early 1980s, more pragmatic and less idealistic than the previous ones, contributed to starting a pop-rock movement in Chile by the mid-1980s, with bands such as Los Prisioneros, Fulano, La Ley, and Los Tres. During the 1990s, some of them have reached popularity in Latin America and have been featured on MTV in the United States.

FURTHER STUDY

The investigation of Chile's musical cultures began in earnest with the creation of the Instituto de Investigaciones del Folklore Musical in 1943, integrated into the University of Chile in 1947. The institute sponsored musical fieldwork; managed teaching, recording, publication, and diffusion; and created an archive and library. Ethnomusicological research started in Chile during the 1960s with the publications by Manuel Dannemann (1978) and Raquel Barros (1958, 1964, 1970) on Chilean creole and mestizo music and by María Ester Grebe (1967, 1973, 1974, 1980) on Chilean creole and Indian music. Samuel Claro (1979, 1982, 1989), Luis Merino (1974), Ernesto González (1986), José Pérez de Arce, and Rodrigo Torres have also made ethnomusicological contributions in Chile.

REFERENCES

Álvarez, Cristina, and María Ester Grebe. 1974. "La trifonía atacameña y sus perspectivas interculturales." *Revista Musical Chilena* 28(126–127):21–46.

Barros, Raquel, and Manuel Dannemann. 1958. "La poesía folklórica de Melipilla." *Revista Musical Chilena* 12(60):48–70.

———. 1964. "Introducción al estudio de la tonada." *Revista Musical Chilena* 18(89):105–114.

———. 1970. "El romancero chileno." *Revista Musical Chilena* 24(111):12–119.

Claro, Samuel. 1979. *Oyendo a Chile.* Santiago: Editorial Andrés Bello.

———. 1982. "La cueca chilena, un nuevo enfoque." *Anuario Musical* 37:70–88.

———. 1989. "Herencia musical de las tres Españas en América." *Revista Musical Chilena* 43(171):7–41.

Dannemann, Manuel. 1978. "Plan multinacional de relevamiento etnomusicológico y folklórico." *Revista Musical Chilena* 32(141):17–41.

Garrido, Pablo. 1979. *Historial de la Cueca.* Valparaíso: Ediciones Universitarias de Valparaíso.

González, Ernesto. 1986. "Vigencias de instrumentos musicales mapuches." *Revista Musical Chilena* 40(166):4–52.

Grebe, María Ester. 1967. *The Chilean Verso: A Study in Musical Archaism.* Los Angeles: University of California Press.

———. 1973. "El kultrún mapuche: un microcosmo simbólico." *Revista Musical Chilena* 27(123–124):3–42.

———. 1974. "Presencia del dualismo en la cultura y música mapuche." *Revista Musical Chilena* 28(126–127):47–79.

———. 1980. "Chile: Folk music." *The New Grove Dictionary of Music and Musicians,* ed. Stanley Sadie. London: Macmillan.

Lavín, Carlos. 1948. "Nuestra Señora de las Peñas, 1ª parte." *Revista Musical Chilena* 4(31):9–20.

——. 1948. "Nuestra Señora de las Peñas, 2ª parte." *Revista Musical Chilena* 4(32):27–40.

——. 1952. "La Música Sacra de Chiloé." *Revista Musical Chilena* 8(43):76–82.

Merino, Luis. 1974. "Instrumentos musicales, cultura mapuche y el Cautiverio feliz del Mestre de Campo Francisco Núñez de Pineda y Bascuñán." *Revista Musical Chilena* 28(128):56–95.

Munizaga, Carlos. 1974. "Atacameños, araucanos, alacalufes: breve reseña de tres grupos étnicos chilenos." *Revista Musical Chilena* 28(126–127):7–20.

Okada, Yuki. 1995. *Central and South America.* JVC Smithsonian Folkways Video Anthology of Music and Dance of the Americas, 5. Montpelier, Vt.: Multicultural Media VTMV-229. Video.

Olsen, Dale A. 1980. "Folk Music of South America—A Musical Mosaic." In *Musics of Many Cultures: An Introduction,* ed. Elizabeth May, 386–425. Berkeley: University of California Press.

Parra, Violeta. 1979. *Cantos Folklóricos Chilenos.* Santiago: Editorial Nascimento.

Pereira-Salas, Eugenio. 1941. *Los orígenes del arte musical en Chile.* Santiago: Publicaciones de la Universidad de Chile.

Plath, Oreste. 1979. *Folklore Chileno.* Santiago: Editorial Nascimento.

Titiev, Mischa. 1949. *Social Singing among the Mapuche.* Anthropological Papers of the Museum of Anthropology, 2. Ann Arbor: University of Michigan Press.

Uribe Echevarría, Juan. 1958. *Contrapunto de Alféreces en la Provincia de Valparaíso.* Santiago: Anales de la Universidad de Chile.

——. 1962. *Cantos a lo divino y a lo humano en Aculeo.* Santiago: Editorial Universitaria.

——. 1974? *Fiesta de la Tirana de Tarapacá.* Valparaíso: Ediciones Universitarias de Valparaíso.

——. 1978. *Fiesta de la Virgen de la Candelaria de Copiapó: Las Candelarias del Sur.* Valparaíso: Ediciones Universitarias de Valparaíso.

Urrutia Blondel, Jorge. 1968. "Danzas rituales en la provincia de Santiago." *Revista Musical Chilena* 22(103):43–76.

Colombia
William J. Gradante

From Pacific mangrove swamps to the Amazon basin, from Caribbean beaches to Andean summits, Colombia is a land of contrasts. Because of the heterogeneity of its pre-Columbian peoples, the strength of its Iberian lineage, and the admixture of New World African culture, its musical heritage is extraordinarily rich and varied.

Colombia can be subdivided into five distinct regions, reflecting geographic features and cultural traits: the Pacific and Atlantic-Caribbean coasts, eastern plains (*llanos*), Andes, and Amazon basin. The focus of this essay is the musical culture of the Andean region, the homeland of most of the national population, especially those of primarily Hispanic descent.

MUSICAL INSTRUMENTS

Colombia has a tricultural heritage: Spanish, African, and native American. In the Andean region, however, the most important traditional music instruments are outright adoptions or creolized developments of archaic European originals. Instruments of indigenous or African origins have been incorporated into some regional ensembles; though these instruments remain among the less essential elements of a given ensemble, other evidence proves indigenous and African influence on Andean musical styles, instruments, and performance.

That some instruments occur almost everywhere in the world makes it difficult to determine whether they are indigenous to Colombia or are Old World imports. In popular culture, where these instruments are employed and enjoyed, such considerations are meaningless because all are cherished icons of Colombia's cultural history.

Idiophones

The *chucho,* a shaken tubular rattle, consists of a bamboo internode closed at both ends containing small rattling objects. In South America, such rattles may be divided into two historically distinct types: the first consists solely of a tube with internal rattling objects (probably pre-Columbian); the second features palm needles or wooden or metal nails, thrust through the tube walls into the interior resonating cavity, creating an enhanced percussive effect in acoustic duration and intensity. These are believed to represent either the outright adoption of rattles introduced by West African slaves during the colonial period or post-Columbian adaptations of indigenous rattles of the first type.

This idiophone has a variety of regional names: *chucho, chuchas,* or *alfandoque* in Boyacá, Cundinamarca, Huila, and Tolima; *guacho* (*guache*) in Antioquia; *carángano, guasá* (*guazá*) or *sonaja* in Cauca, Nariño, and Valle del Cauca. Among the more heavily African-influenced cultural groups inhabiting Colombia's Atlantic and Pacific coasts, tubular rattles tend to be played in pairs by one or two musicians; in the Andean region, more strongly influenced by traditional indigenous practices, it is a single instrument. In both regions, it is shaken, whether held horizontally by both hands or vertically in alternation, like a *maraca*. The *chucho* of southern Colombia is held horizontally in one hand, palm facing downward at waist level, the sound being produced through a deft dropping and catching of the instrument in alternating hands. Because of the absence of internally penetrating needles or nails, the sound produced is of short duration, precise, and crisp. When inserted into the context of a *dueto bambuquero,* the *chucho* may be held horizontally and played sitting, the player alternately tapping the ends on the thighs. The *chucho*'s relative of the eastern plains and the Atlantic Coast is the more familiar *maraca,* a gourd with a handle.

The *jalajala,* a strung or bunch rattle, is another shaken idiophone. The *jalajala* of the *rajaleña* ensemble consists of six 2-meter lengths of twine, strung with reed segments 15 to 20 centimeters long and a little more than a centimeter wide. Each of six pieces of twine is strung with a single reed before all six pieces are knotted together, ensuring that the reeds do not all slide toward one end of the twine. The second set of reeds is strung and knotted in place, and the process is repeated until all six segments, each made up of six strung reed rattles, have been completed. Finally, the ends of the twine are tied together, forming a large loop, which the musician wears over his head and across one shoulder. The player grasps the cords emerging from opposite ends of a single bunch of six loosely strung reeds and rattles them against each other. This motion produces a sympathetic rattling among the five remaining reed bunches, resulting in a delightful cacophony of percussion.

Indigenous populations throughout South America use similar rattles made of seashells and fruit shells, seeds, animal hooves, metal, bone, and reed. Among the mestizo populations of northeastern Colombia, where it is commonly played in the *conjunto guabinero,* this instrument is known as *quiribillo, quiriviño, piribique,* or *triviño.*

The jawbone (*quijada*) is a scraped, shaken, or struck idiophone [see AFRO-PERUVIAN TRADITIONS]. A player usually scrapes its teeth with a stick, but it is also a rattle, because the teeth chatter when the jawbone is shaken. The player may hit it with a fist. Its organological origins may have been among the indigenous peoples or the West African slaves who arrived in the colonial era. Across the savanna of Bogotá, burros' jaws are played by rural ensembles that call the instrument *cumbamba,* which means 'jawbone' in several indigenous languages. The jawbone is an integral part of the *guabinero* ensembles of northeastern Colombia (where it serves as a struck and a scraped idiophone), the *rajaleña* ensembles of southern and central Colombia, and the traditional *conjunto llanero* of Colombia's eastern plains region (where it is known as the *carraca*).

A notched gourd (*carrasca*), classifiable as a scraped idiophone, is known by many names. Some of these—*güiro, güira, güire*—derive directly from the Spanish name of the gourd from which it is typically constructed. After the gourd has been cleaned and dried, shallow transverse grooves are etched across its surface. To produce its rasping sound, a player scrapes a piece of stick or bone, sometimes coupled with several bits of stiff wire, across these grooves. The names of other instruments—*charrasca*, *carrasca*, and *carraca*, which tend to be made of wood, cane, reed, bone, or metal—reflect onomatopoeic influence. Known as the *guacharaca* or *raspa* in the *conjunto guabinero*, the instrument is simply a notched stick scraped with a bone or another stick.

Membranophones

The *tambora*, a double-headed cylindrical membranophone, is decidedly European in construction, though the manner in which it is played suggests African influence. Early accounts note that indigenous peoples regarded Spaniards' playing drums as a threat. With reed flutes and *fotutos* (gourd, shell, and ceramic trumpets), the drums of the native Americans performed a similar military function. The Spanish chroniclers reported encountering native drums they called *atambores*, *atabales*, *cajas*, and *bombos*, but none have survived archaeologically in Colombia. Such drums were described as being stood on the ground or held under one arm and played with bare hands or a single drumstick. Pebbles or other rattling objects were often enclosed in drums for an additional percussive effect. The hides used for membranes were fastened with wooden nails or loops of string, or a wet skin was stretched over the drum and allowed to dry in place. The tradition of slowly burning the centers out of tree trunks or stumps is still practiced in some regions. Documentation of the ancient indigenous custom of fashioning drums from inflated human skins also exists.

Drums similar to the *tambora* in construction, bracing, tuning, and performance are utilized throughout the Andean region of South America by indigenous, African-Hispanic, and mestizo ensembles. The modern Colombian *tambora* measures about 60 centimeters high and 35 centimeters wide. The heads are attached by means of indirect bracing, with the bracing cords running through equidistant holes in the outer hoops, laced in alternation from head to head. With the addition of supplementary ligatures, the simple tightening of two lateral cords running parallel to the outer hoops and perpendicular to the bracing cords (creating a netlike effect) is sufficient for tuning. Other traits assignable to European origins are the use of a counter-hoop shaped from a single piece of bent wood, and a small sound hole drilled in the upper side of the drum at a point equidistant from both heads, which in performance maintains air-pressure equilibrium inside the drum.

The player holds the *tambora* by slinging its strap over the right shoulder, across the back, and under the left arm. The drum hangs diagonally, almost horizontally across the front and left side of the player's body, resting on the left hip (figure 1). The manner in which the fundamental pattern of the *tambora* is traditionally executed suggests African influence and requires the right hand to strike the center of the (usually goatskin) drumhead with a large, heavy, padded stick, while the left hand strikes the (wooden) upper side of the drum with the side of a much thinner, headless stick. As part of improvised flourishes at the ends of phrases, the left head is occasionally struck with the smaller stick.

Friction drums are known throughout South America. In Colombia, a friction drum is called the *puerca* or *marrano* in the central and southern Andean *murga* ensemble, and the *zambomba* or *zambumbia* in the context of the *guabinero* ensemble. Although varying in size, friction drums consist of a wax-covered friction stick inserted and tied into a treated cow's bladder, which in turn is stretched over the open end of a dried gourd. Similar friction drums date at least to the Middle Ages, when they were known in Europe as *rommelpots*; correlates are known in Africa. Friction drums found in Brazil and Venezuela are called *cuíca* and *furruco*, respectively.

FIGURE 1   At the Fiesta de San Pedro, La Plata, Huila, Emidio Fajardo plays a *tambora*. Photo by William J. Gradante, 1976.

Aerophones

In various parts of Colombia, the Spanish term *flauta,* the generic denomination for 'flute', may denote panpipes, vertical flutes, or horizontal flutes. In most contemporary *murgas,* however, the term refers specifically to the transverse reed or cane edge aerophone. The transverse flute likely accompanied the fifteenth- and sixteenth-century conquistadors on their missions of conquest and colonization, probably with the military drum. Native Americans' affinity for the European flute, introduced to them by colonial-era missionaries, probably resulted from their previous experience with indigenous flutes. Whether these were of the horizontal or the vertical variety remains unknown.

Among contemporary native American groups in the central and southern Colombian Andes, the typical musical ensemble consists of two or more six-holed side-blown flutes, accompanied by drums closely resembling the *tambora* (figure 2). It is not clear whether the existence of such ensembles can be attributed to a process of adaptation of European musical instruments by native Americans, but it seems probable that the indigenous peoples were familiar with somewhat similar instruments in pre-Columbian times. It is known (Abadía Morales 1973:124 and personal observation) that transverse flutes are the preferred variety among numerous contemporary native American cultures of the Colombian Andes—Catío, Cholo, Guambiano, Ingano, Noanama, Páez, and others—though these cultures also use small panpipes. Similar findings have been reported among the Otavalo of northern Ecuador (Carvalho-Neto 1964:207–208 and personal observation).

The flute typical of southern Colombian ensembles is made of reed (cane), and is fashioned in pairs with reference to existing instruments (figure 3). The six nonequidistant finger holes are formed using a hot nail, spaced in accordance with a predetermined diatonic series of pitches. Whether the transverse flute is indigenous to the South American continent or was appropriated from the Europeans at some point during the past five centuries of conquest and colonization cannot be definitively determined, given the current state of archaeological research, at least in Colombia. Furthermore, the transverse flute was not unknown to Africans before slavery brought them to the Americas, and thus it may have been absorbed into

FIGURE 2   In Santa Rosa, Cauca, Páez Indians play side-blown flutes (*flautas*) and drums (*tamboras*). Photo by William J. Gradante, 1978.

FIGURE 3   At the Fiesta de San Pedro, La Plata, Huila, Carlos Ceballos (*left*) and Augusto Cuéllar play flutes. Photo by William J. Gradante, 1978.

The *tiple* has a big role in Colombian legends, where it is not only the lovesick troubadour's sympathetic companion but also the object of elves' and trolls' mischievous antics.

FIGURE 4   At the Fiesta de San Pedro, La Plata, Huila, Fernando Cuéllar plays a gourd "sousaphone" (*instrumento de calabazo*). Photo by William J. Gradante, 1978.

indigenous musical cultures through contact with African slaves brought to the country.

Perdomo Escobar (1963:17) reports the existence of the *fotuto,* a large, indigenous aerophone used by the Muisca in the 1500s. The *fotuto* was made from gourds, metal, wood, conch shells, clay, or animal horns, but present-day correlates are made almost exclusively from large gourds. In the department of Huila, such gourd instruments (*instrumentos de calabazo*) have acquired a central role in the celebration of carnivalesque June festivals, albeit with a humorous dimension. Gourds are wired together in the shape of orchestral instruments—tubas, contrabasses, violins, trombones, and saxophones—and played through carved gourd or manufactured metal mouthpieces (figure 4). Performance is usually limited to single foghorn-like notes, executed simply to help the array of percussion instruments mark time.

Chordophones

It is a subject of debate whether the pre-Columbian arsenal of musical instruments was devoid of stringed instruments of any kind (Izikowitz 1970:201–206), but the musical bows of the Yupka (Motilón), the Waru (Guajiro), and the Kogi of northeastern Colombia may be indigenous or an adoption from African-Colombian traditions extant on the Caribbean coast [See AFRO-COLOMBIAN TRADITIONS]. Musical ensembles of the Colombian Andes usually feature strummed and plucked chordophones of European origin.

The *carángano* is an idiochord tube zither used in mestizo ensembles of southern Colombia. Tube zithers are found primarily in Asia and West Africa, and Colombian specimens are probably the result of African influence. Instruments similar to the *carángano* of the mestizo *murgas* appear throughout Colombia and Venezuela, in predominantly African and relatively unacculturated indigenous cultural groups (Abadía Morales 1973:59; Aretz 1967:112–117; Davidson 1970:2:100–101; Liscano 1950:99–100; Perdomo Escobar 1963:328).

The bamboo used to make the *carángano* of southern Colombia measures from 2.5 to 3 meters long, and from 15 to 20 centimeters wide. A strip of the cortex a meter or two long is lifted from the middle of the tube, great care being taken neither to detach it at either end nor to puncture the hollow inner tube itself. After wooden bridges have been inserted at each extremity, raising the strip of cortex to a height of 6 or 8 centimeters, alternate segments of the main tube are punctured with rectangular sound holes.

In performance, the *carángano* is held at waist level by assistants at each end. The primary player alternately strikes the raised strip of cortex with two large sticks, causing it to vibrate noisily. Dried and inflated cow bladders partially filled with dried corn kernels (*vejigas*) are pressed against the vibrating strand of cortex by a second musician, making the *carángano* a chordophone and an idiophone simultaneously (figure 5). Whether stationary or in ambulatory contexts, the *carángano* serves as the centerpiece of the *murga* for its visual impact and its dominance in providing the timbre essential to the *rajaleña*.

The *tiple* is a medium-size, flat-backed chordophone related to the Spanish *vihuela* and is a descendant of the gittern of sixteenth-century Europe (figure 6). The earliest direct precursors of the modern *tiple* may have arrived in the New World as early as the first voyage of Columbus. Evidence points to the *tiple* as locally distinct from the guitar as early as the late 1600s, when the extant guitar featured four courses of strings, composed of a single chanterelle and three pairs of strings doubled at the octave, and the *tiple* might best be viewed as a development of it. The inhabitants of the Colombian Andes, however, perceive the *tiple* not as the conquistadors' legacy but as a revered product of the process of creolization.

The present-day *tiple* has twelve strings grouped in four courses and tuned as diagramed (figure 7*b*). It typically provides strummed *(rasgueado)* accompaniments for vocal, *bandola,* and guitar melodies. The *requinto* (or *tiple requinto*), its functional equivalent in *guabinero* ensembles of northeastern Colombia, is a slightly smaller version, and like the *tiple* is preferably made of pine, cedar, or walnut but with each course tuned in unison (see figure 7*c*). Some *requintos* have ten strings, with only the first and second, or first and fourth tripled, the others doubled. It may occasionally be plucked with a plectrum.

In the context of the performance of festive *rajaleñas* and *sanjuaneros,* the *tiple* renders a syncopated, percussive, chordal accompaniment. The combination of strumming the fingers and striking the palm or knuckles against the strings (*golpe apagado,* shown in figure 8 with x-shaped note heads), may be interpreted as a mestizo attempt to incorporate the percussive, rhythmic energy of the newly encountered African drumming styles into the otherwise predominantly Iberian musical tradition of early colonial Colombia.

The *tiple* has a big role in Colombian legends, where it is not only the lovesick troubadour's sympathetic companion but also the object of elves' and trolls' mischievous antics. The people and musicological scholars of the Andean region of Colombia romantically consider it the most Colombian of musical instruments, a product of the process of creolization, not unlike the mestizos themselves (Añez 1970 [1951]:31; Perdomo Escobar 1963:265, 388–392).

FIGURE 5   At the Fiesta de San Pedro, La Plata, Huila, Libardo Mejía (*left*) and Alfonso Sandoval play an inflated bladder (*vejiga*) and a struck idiochord zither (*carángano*). Photo by William J. Gradante, 1978.

FIGURE 6   At Santa Rosa, Cauca, a *dueto bambuquero* formed by Augusto Cuéllar (*left*) and Fernando Cuéllar plays a *tiple* and a guitar. Photo by William J. Gradante, 1978.

FIGURE 7   Chordophone tunings: *a, bandola; b, tiple; c, requinto; d, guitarra; e, cuatro.* These are the most common tunings in the Colombian Andes, according to folk musicians and instrument makers. Generally, however, respective strings are tuned using the intervals presented, rather than to precise pitches. The tuning for the *cuatro* may be the most variable (Aretz 1967:130–145).

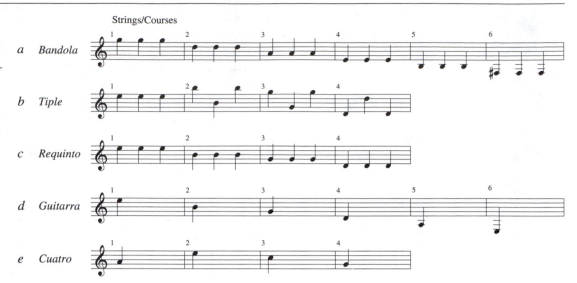

The *guitarra* (see figure 6) is the six-stringed classical guitar common throughout the Americas, though steel strings occasionally replace the usual nylon strings (see figure 7*d*). With the *tiple,* this guitar is an essential part of the *dueto bambuquero,* the *estudiantina,* and most other Colombian mestizo ensembles.

A relative of the mandolin and a direct descendant of the Spanish *bandurria,* the modern *bandola* or *lira* usually has a teardrop or circular shape, with a flat or slightly arched back (Añez 1970 [1951]:35). Its four courses of three steel strings and two pairs of copper-wound strings are tuned in descending fourths (see figure 7*a*) and played with a plectrum. They may be plucked in tremolo style when played in unison with or embellishing a vocal line, or in rapid-fire execution of *pasillo* and *bambuco* melodies to the rhythmic accompaniment of *tiples* and guitars. Twelve- and fourteen-string *bandolas* are extant, but a sixteen-string model is most common. *Bandolas* made of armadillo shells also occur, but they are quite unusual and may have been inspired by the *charango* of the central Andes.

A close relative of the guitar, the *cuatro,* has, as its name implies, four courses of single, usually nylon strings. Rhythmically complex, its strummed accompaniments are featured in the *conjunto llanero,* the harp-based ensemble typical of the eastern plains of Colombia, and in Venezuela, where alternative tunings occur (see figure 7*e*).

MUSICAL ENSEMBLES

Dueto bambuquero

In professional contexts, the musical genre known as *bambuco* is typically performed by the *dúo* or *dueto bambuquero,* consisting of two vocalists accompanying themselves on guitar and *tiple* (see figure 6). The *tiple* player strums chords while the guitarist provides an accompaniment combining full chords and bass motifs. Melodic instrumental introductions and interludes are usually performed on the guitar with *tiple* accompaniment, though these roles are occasionally reversed. Ensembles may double either instrument, adding one or more *bandolas* to perform instrumental interludes and vocal adornments. Originally a serenading song for the solo voice, the modern *bambuco* is sung as a duet in parallel thirds and sixths. It is not typically sung in unison or in more than two-part harmony, though brief responsorial or solo passages are not uncommon. Such music can be heard on Colombian radio stations specializing in folkloric music, but the airwaves have become increasingly filled with more commercially viable and danceable music such as *salsa* and *vallenato,* genres favored by the younger generation. The music of the *dueto bambuquero* is most often heard in nightly family gatherings, private parties, excursions to the countryside, or serenades. Although musicians tend to perform with preferred partners, membership is flexible, and in festive contexts duets easily become trios or quartets. Audience members' singing along is acceptable and often expected, as are improvisatory percussion accompaniment and, occasionally, dancing. The usual payment for providing music in a private party is food and alcohol.

When someone is organizing a serenade (*serenata*), the services of a *dueto bambuquero* may be obtained with the gift of bottled *aguardiente* (an alcoholic drink made from sugarcane) and a promise of more. Entire evenings may be spent locating musicians, rehearsing, and deciding which four or five musical selections will produce the desired effect on the recipient of the *serenata.* The actual performance takes place precisely at midnight, and lasts less than fifteen minutes. Approach and departure are executed in silence, and the recipient of the *serenata* makes no indication of her attendance other than, possibly, turning her light on. The identity of the male responsible for organizing the *serenata* is understood but remains unannounced.

Estudiantina

Bambucos are most commonly performed by the *dueto bambuquero,* but they provide a large percentage of the repertoire of the *estudiantina* ensemble. Also known as the *lira, rondalla,* or *tuna,* such ensembles specialize in instrumental music, sometimes of the classical variety, and in instrumental arrangements of *pasillos* and other genres of Colombian popular music.

The *estudiantina* is a large ensemble, adding any number of *bandolas* to a core group of *tiples* and guitars. Pedro Morales Pino formed La Lira Colombiana, Colombia's first *estudiantina,* in 1899 with three *bandolas,* two *tiples,* and a guitar. Morales Pino's second Lira Colombiana of 1912 featured five *bandolas,* four *tiples,* one guitar, and a cello. Reaching the zenith of their popularity on the professional level during the golden age of Colombian popular song (1890–1930), *estudiantinas* survive in schools, businesses, churches, and other social organizations where their size and flexibility of instrumentation allow for maximum participation among their members. Many *estudiantinas* work in association with choral groups, or like the Lira Colombiana, rely on their own instrumentalists to perform vocal parts. *Estudiantinas* may be observed in the context of a *serenata,* in an open-air recital on a bandstand in a park or a plaza, in schools or churches, or in the more formal setting of a concert hall.

Banda municipal

The municipal budget of most Colombian Andean towns provides for contracting a band director and paying for the services of such an ensemble as he can assemble. The only full-time professional musician, he recruits, teaches, rehearses, manages the budget for paying these instrumentalists, and maintains the equipment—several sets of uniforms and musical instruments typical of a small European or North American marching band. His responsibility is also to ensure satisfactory performances by his ensemble at their contracted occasions. Such contexts include welcoming visiting dignitaries, participating in parades on civic holidays, and providing a festive ambience during local festivals and fairs. The most common context is the regular public concert on the bandstand in the plaza in front of the church on Sunday afternoon and usually one other evening per week.

The parish priest and various local religious associations raise funds to hire the municipal band to provide appropriate music for public religious observances like

In the novel *María,* Jorge Isaacs referred to the *bambuco* extant in the department of Cauca in 1867 as a musical form brought to Colombia by slaves from an African kingdom known as Bambuk.

weddings, first communions, and even funerals, and for performance in processions associated with ecclesiastical holidays, the festival dedicated to the town's patron saint, and most important, Holy Week and Christmas. The band may be contracted privately for family celebrations, business openings, bullfights, and intermunicipality sporting events. Their musical repertoires consist of a mixture of hymns and dirges; popular television, radio, and movie themes; and brass-band arrangements of *bambucos, pasillos,* and currently popular Afro-Caribbean dances such as *cumbias, vallenatos,* and merengues.

Murga

The *murga* differs from each of the ensembles discussed above. Throughout the Hispanic world, the term *murga* commonly denotes an informal group of street musicians and merrymakers, and in Colombia it identifies typical ensembles performing at Andean Colombian festivals. The existence in the Colombian Andes of such ensembles, featuring *tiples,* clarinets, tambourines, *tamboras, quijadas,* and reed flutes, was documented as early as 1840 (Davidson 1970:3:123).

Unlike the musicians of an *estudiantina* or a *dueto bambuquero,* the members of a *murga* are frequently not only nonprofessionals, but also nonmusicians. Rather than concentrating on technique and execution, a *murga* tries for spontaneity and celebration. Contemporary *murgas* have neither rehearsals nor set personnel, and their instrumentation depends on their region. In the southern departments of Tolima and Huila, a typical *murga,* called a *cucamba* or a *rajaleña,* consists essentially of a pair of reed flutes, a *tiple,* and a *tambora* with a variety of percussion instruments: *carángano, carrasca, chucho, jalajala, puerca,* and *quijada.* In the northeastern departments of Santander and Boyacá, the typical *murga,* called *conjunto guabinero,* consists of a *tiple,* a *requinto,* a *quijada,* a *chucho,* a tambourine, and spoons; in the southwestern Andes, the typical *murga,* known as *chirimía,* may consist of *tiples,* reed flutes, guitars, and whatever other instruments happen to be available.

Improvisation is a theme that runs through virtually all aspects of a *murga.* Its membership is improvised; musicians may come and go during a performance. Instruments themselves are often improvised as individuals are drawn into the context. The predominant vehicle for textual expression by members of *murgas* is the *copla,* whether precomposed, traditional, or spontaneously improvised. Most performances feature *coplas* of all three varieties. Performances, often unscheduled, last for no set period of time.

The principal contexts for *murgas* are festivals for local patron saints, carnival, the extended Christmas and New Years' celebration, and the June festivals associated with the Nativity of St. John the Baptist (24 June, celebrated as *la fiesta de San Juan* in Tolima) and Saints Peter and Paul (29 June, celebrated as *la fiesta de San Pedro* in Huila). The principal function of a *murga* is to attract townspeople's attention and draw them into participating through dancing, singing, or even joining the *murga.*

Communal collection and consumption of alcoholic beverages is often central to the activities of the *murga*.

Conjunto llanero

The typical ensemble of the plains region of southern Venezuela and eastern Colombia is the *conjunto llanero*. In Colombia, it traditionally consisted of *cuatro, requinto,* and *carraca*. Abadía Morales (1973:75–76) and others, however, view the harp and maracas—which have long since replaced the *requinto* and the *carraca,* respectively— as tourism-inspired additions to the authentic *conjunto llanero,* though they may be considered traditional in Venezuela. Genres contributing to the repertoire of *conjuntos llaneros* are the *galerón,* the *corrido,* and, most prominently, the *joropo*.

MUSICAL CONTEXTS AND GENRES

Bambuco

In the novel *María,* Jorge Isaacs (1962 [1867]) referred to the *bambuco* extant in the department of Cauca as a musical form brought to Colombia by slaves from an African kingdom known as Bambuk. In the twentieth century, these remarks kindled controversy: as Colombian scholars began to research the history and origins of their beloved national dance, many were horrified to think that it might not be the product of the intermingling of Spanish and indigenous cultures.

Researchers (including Abadía Morales 1973:58–59 and Añez 1968 [1951]: 24–44) have put a great deal of effort into trying to determine the actual origin of the *bambuco*—or rather, to prove Isaacs wrong. Questions concerning whether or not, or the degree to which, African influences in the *bambuco*'s development should be acknowledged have been central to the resulting discussion. Less attention has been paid to the study of its actual musical traits and performances, or to the emergence of its contemporary varieties, the *bambuco de salón,* the *sanjuanero,* and the *rajaleña*. Researchers have disagreed about the most appropriate way to transcribe its rhythm and meter into staff notation. The controversy involves the employment of 3/4 or 6/8 time signatures (because of the juxtaposition of both, or *sesquiáltera*) and the proper placement of bar lines (figure 8*a*).

FIGURE 8   Characteristic strummed rhythms, *guitarra* on upper line and *tiple* on lower: *a, bambuco; b, pasillo lento; c, pasillo; d, vals; e, danza.*

a Bambuco

(continued)

FIGURE 8 *(continued)* Characteristic strummed rhythms, *guitarra* on upper line and *tiple* on lower: *b, pasillo lento; c, pasillo; d, vals; e, danza.*

b Pasillo lento

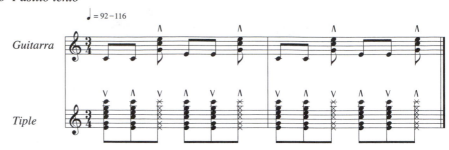

c Pasillo (Instrumental)

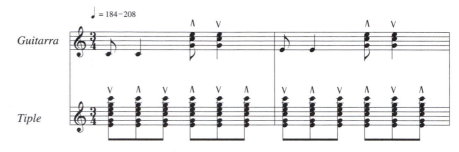

d Vals

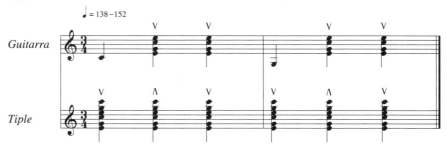

e Danza

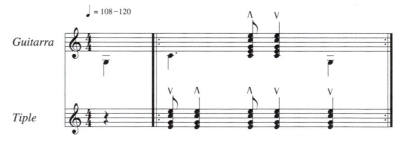

Examination of choreography, song texts, vocal styles, instrumentation, and musical functions associated with the *bambuco* show a high degree of inherent Hispanic influence. Little evidence of indigenous influence in the modern *bambuco* has come to light, and only when one analyzes the *bambuco*'s less-commercialized, unpolished, rustic cousins (such as the *rajaleña*) do African traits become obvious.

Early references to the *bambuco* identify it with the *bunde,* a scandalous genre. Documents mention *bundes* throughout the mid-1700s, often censuring individuals who had participated in them. Juan Crisóstomo Osorio y Ricaurte wrote in his *Diccionario de Música* (1867) that the *bambuco* was a brief sung and danced musical form in ternary meter, characterized by syncopation, appropriately performed by *tiple* and *bandola,* and always in a minor mode (Perdomo Escobar 1963:55–56). In a major mode, it loses its melancholy character, and is called *bunde.*

If this nexus can be established between *bambuco* and *bunde,* the former may be considered the oldest form extant in Colombian folk-musical traditions. The *bambuco* is believed to have been among the favorite dances of Simón Bolívar, the liberator of Colombia. In 1824, just after the battle of Ayacucho, Bolívar's troops celebrated to the sound of *bambucos* (Añez 1968 [1951]:38; Perdomo Escobar 1963:57), showing that the genre already had a widespread acceptance among the lower and middle classes.

By 1837, Colombian troubadours were delighting Guatemalan audiences already familiar with the *bambuco* and introduced the dancing of the *torbellino* (Añez 1968 [1951]:24). This date may demarcate the beginning of a second stage in the history of Colombian popular music, one that lasted until about 1890. During that stage, the composers Nicomedes Mata Guzmán, Rafael Padilla, Simón Ospina, and Pedro Morales Pino composed *bambucos, pasillos,* and other popular forms while leading Colombian popular music into its golden age. At the same time, Manuel María Párraga composed the first stylization of the *bambuco* in a piano work, *El Bambuco: Aires Nacionales Neo-Granadinos,* becoming the forerunner of a long line of composers of nationalistic art music.

Most modern Colombian folk musicians originally learned to play their instruments informally from friends and relatives, but learned Colombian traditional music from the radio. Nationally known *duetos bambuqueros* such as Garzón y Collazos, however, have established their own centers for formal instruction in *tiple,* guitar, and *bandola.* Such centers, located in Bogotá, tend to serve the upper echelons of Colombian society and deal primarily with the urban variety of the *bambuco* repertoire. This genre, also known as lyric *bambuco, bambuco de salón,* and *bambuco santafereño,* is the kind of *bambuco* most commonly heard on radio, on recordings, and in concert. Like most *sanjuaneros, bambucos* of this category have known authors, in some cases trained professional composers.

Performance of a given *bambuco* involves significant repetition of material, instrumental and textual. Nearly all begin with a melodic introduction performed by the guitar to chordal *tiple* accompaniment. The first stanza of text is then delivered, usually in a minor key, and after a second rendition of the instrumental interlude, it often repeats. Next, a new instrumental interlude is performed, or the same one is repeated, with a cadence in a new tonal center. The second stanza of text may now be sung and possibly repeated before the final dominant-tonic cadence. For *pasillos, guabinas, valses, danzas,* and *bambucos,* this hypothetical format is quite common, but the pattern of repetition is set by the performer, the audience, and the musical occasion. When texts include more than two stanzas, repetition may be limited accordingly.

The emotionality of *bambuco* texts is emphasized by modulations, usually from minor to parallel or relative major keys or to the subdominant; the associated vocal style involves the liberal use of dramatic pauses, rubato passages, and fermatas, all intended to enhance the emotional impact of the lyrics. Texts often consist of octosyllabic lines, but they may employ any form of traditional Spanish poetry. Concepts recurring in these texts include the extolling of a woman's beauty and desirability, the joys resulting from the idyllic love shared by a man and that woman, the anguish caused by the loss of that love, and pride in being Colombian or from a particular region.

Many *bambucos* are dedicated to the beloved *tiple,* as in the following example, an excerpt from *"Tiplecito Bambuquero"* ('Little *Tiple* the *Bambuco* Player'), by José Alejandro Morales:

And when my hands play upon
your enchanted fingerboard,
I feel that you and I are weeping
with a single heart.

—*Bambuco* text

Tiplecito, bambuquero,	Little *tiple,* you *bambuco* player,
tiplecito, embrujador,	little *tiple,* you enchanter,
eres tú mi compañero	you are my companion
en mi alegría y en mi dolor.	in my joy and in my sorrow.
Por eso es que yo te quiero	That is why I love you
como si fueras mi amor,	as if you were my lover,
tiplecito, bambuquero,	little *tiple, bambuco* player,
tiplecito, embrujador.	little *tiple,* enchanter.
Y cuando pulsan mis manos	And when my hands play upon
tu embrujado diapasón,	your enchanted fingerboard,
siento que tú y yo lloramos	I feel that you and I are weeping
en un solo corazón.	with a single heart.

Other lyrics comment on current events or make philosophical statements about everyday life, particularly the struggles of the peasant or proletarian classes. Since the late 1940s, the social changes that have convulsed Colombia have given rise to a class of *bambucos* which musicians have come to call *bambucos de protesta*. A sample of this subgenre is seen in the following example, an excerpt from "*'Ora Sí Entiendo Por Qué*" ('Now I Understand Why'), by Pedro J. Ramos:

Ayer que 'tuve en el pueblo,	Yesterday when I was in town,
compadrito Juan José,	dear old friend Juan José,
los estudiantes gritaban,	the students were shouting,
"¡Viva la rivolución!"	"Long live the revolution!"
y le decían al alcalde	and told the mayor
que se asomara a su balcón,	to come out onto his balcony,
Qu' es qu' "allí 'tán . . ."	"There they are . . ."
y qu' "esos son	and "Those are
los que venden . . ."	the ones selling . . ."
no sé qué. . . .	I'm not sure what. . . .
Qu' es qu' "allí 'tán . . ."	"There they are . . ."
ricuerdo ya—	I remember now—
"los que venden la nación."	"the ones selling out our country."

Written in the peasants' vernacular, the text uses *'tuve* for *estuve,* *'tán* for *están,* *rivolución* for *revolución,* and *ricuerdo* for *recuerdo.*

Bambuco choreography

Like most Latin American folkloric musical genres, the *bambuco* has a choreography that resembles its counterparts in that it is a pursuit dance: the partners rarely touch

FIGURE 9   At the Fiesta de San Pedro, La Plata, Huila, couples dance the *sanjuanero* (rustic *bambuco*). Photo by William J. Gradante, 1976.

each other, and they embrace only at its conclusion. It is essentially a courtship dance, in which the man plays the role of a gallant, respectful, but ardent pursuer of a timid but coquettish woman. Traditional attire, including the woman's full skirt and the man's neckerchief and palm-leaf hat, is essential to the execution of the traditional choreography.

Researchers (Jaramillo 1955:547–555; Koorn 1977:131–136; Perdomo Escobar 1963:271–272) agree that the proper performance of the *bambuco* involves eight basic steps: *invitación*, invitation to the dance; *ochos*, dancing in a figure-eight pattern; *codos*, dancing with elbows touching; *coqueteos*, flirtatious stepping, when the man tries unsuccessfully to steal a kiss; *perseguida*, the man pursuing the woman, dancing in a circle; *pañuelo*, neckerchief playing; *arrodillada*, the woman dancing in a circle around the kneeling man; *abrazo*, the man placing his right hand on the woman's waist, and dancing thus to her original position.

In southern Colombian June festivals, the *bambuco* is replaced by the *sanjuanero*, with more animated, athletic choreography, involving almost twice as many steps. When the *murga*'s drummers are inspired to perform an extended solo section, they can drive the dancers to joyous exhaustion. The *sanjuanero* features more extensive teasing and pursuit involving the traditional neckerchief and the sombrero, and several steps imply or require brief embraces (figure 9).

The festivity of the *sanjuanero*, also known as the *joropo huilense*, is evident in the following text, an excerpt from the festival theme song *"El Sanjuanero Huilense,"* by Anselmo Durán:

No hay guayabo que resista
este joropo caliente.
Por eso está con celos
su compadre, el aguardiente.

There's no hangover that can resist
this hot *joropo*.
That's why its partner,
cane-sugar liquor, is jealous.

Felices vienen y van,
sin pensar en el dinero,
trayendo tiples y guitarras
pa' cantar el sanjuanero.

Merrily they come and go,
never thinking of money,
bringing *tiples* and guitars
to sing the *sanjuanero*.

In festival contexts, where most spontaneous, unrehearsed *bambuco* dancing occurs, individual dancers interpret the national dance according to their own knowledge, preferences, and abilities: they may emphasize one step over another, or omit steps entirely. The order in which they perform steps is flexible.

Improvisation is permissible except in the context of a competition, the most prominent of which is the Festival Nacional del Bambuco, held in June in Neiva, the capital of the department of Huila. Such competitions may have saved the dance aspect of the genre from extinction, but they have frozen it: what was once a simple description of the characteristic steps has become a prescription that must be followed exactly. To earn maximal points from the judges, entrants must execute steps in the proper sequence and in the prescribed manner. They must wear folkloric costumes far costlier and more elegant than anything ever worn by any actual folk.

Copla

For the common people, the *copla* serves as the most eloquent mode of expression, especially when it has musical accompaniment. The term *copla* originally denoted the rhyming pairs of sixteen-syllable lines that made up the *romance* of Spanish balladry, dating from medieval times. In Colombia, the *copla* most commonly has four octosyllabic lines with the second and fourth rhyming assonantly (*abcb*). Improvisation emphasizes the text, which functions as a vehicle for the expression of humor and folk wisdom and as a forum for the public projection of local identity, class consciousness, and sociopolitical criticism. *Coplas* range from romantic poetry to blatant sexual joking.

Sung in Colombia since the 1500s, *coplas* continue to serve in established Colombian folkloric genres. The original corpus of *coplas,* inherited from Iberian tradition, has grown exponentially and exhibits considerable regional variety. The study of the informal musical performance of *coplas* may be the most exciting field of musicological research in Colombia, as the practice is still widespread among the populace and has not become commercialized by professional performers or inhibited by institutionalization. The genres of the *rajaleña* and the *guabina* appear to have the greatest potential for the further flowering of the art of singing *coplas,* at least until new forms emerge.

Rajaleña

The inherent style of *rajaleña* music, performed only in festival contexts—in which reversals and the reconciliation of opposites are dominant themes—virtually reverses the folkloric style employed during secular times of the year. Harmonically, rhythmically, melodically, and textually, and in instrumentation, ensemble, and vocal style, the *rajaleña* differs fundamentally from other local musical genres. The rhythm section's cross-rhythmic accompaniment, the vocal style, and the leader-chorus format are more typically African than Spanish. Melodic interest and vocal artistry are deemphasized, and the focus is the establishment of a context for the improvisation of *coplas.*

The term *rajaleña* refers literally to the chopping or splitting of wood, but the colloquial interpretation is 'insulting or criticizing without concern for consequences'. The behavioral license of *rajaleña* contexts permits and even encourages pornographic subject and language, and singers perform without the fear of resentment or retaliation. A few examples may be seen in the following lyrics:

Que nos gobiernen los godos	Let the conservatives govern,
o mande el liberalismo;	or give liberalism the game;
para tirarse a los pobres,	when it comes to screwing the poor,
todos resultan lo mismo.	they all turn out the same.
Todas las mujeres tienen	All women have
en la barriga el ombligo	a button in their tummy,
y más abajito tienen—	and a little bit lower, they have—
yo sí sé, pero no digo.	I know, but I'll play the dummy.
¿Cuándo será que estaremos	When will we be
como los pies del Señor?—	like the Lord's feet?—
uno encima del otro,	one on top of the other
y un clavito entre los dos.	and a nail to make us meet.

The social, psychological, and artistic aspects of the conceptualization and performance of *rajaleña* is the subject of Gradante's (1991) doctoral dissertation.

Guabina

Another vocal genre, the *guabina,* has unclear origins. Three different forms share the name. In central and southern Colombia, composed *guabinas*—humorous and lively as often as they are melancholy love songs or regional tributes—make up a big portion of the repertoires of *duetos bambuqueros.* Though popular among musicians and audiences alike, they do not hold nearly the status of the *bambuco* or even the *pasillo*. Literary evidence suggests the existence of another *guabina* extant in the province of Antioquia as late as 1900, but it has apparently disappeared, leaving only scattered couplets in collections of folklore (Gutiérrez 1955; Restrepo 1955).

The *guabina* of the departments of Santander and Boyacá has been described as a lyrical lament, *coplas* performed repetitively by laborers and travelers. Similar descriptions have been given of the *torbellino,* one species of which may be considered the instrumental counterpart of the *guabina*. The third and probably most vital *guabina* today is the *guabina veleña,* named for the municipality of Vélez, Santander, nationally known for its *guabina* competition in August. With the *rajaleña,* the *guabina veleña* is one of the least commercialized forms of popular music in Colombia. Performed by nonprofessionals and absent from radio (except during the annual festival), it is relatively unknown outside the region. It may owe its survival to the festival rules committee, which strictly prescribes how it must be composed and performed; however, such rules serve to freeze the genre in its present form, restricting its ability to evolve naturally, requiring purity at the cost of vitality.

Performances of the *guabina veleña* typically begin with an interlude plucked on one *tiple* while a second strums a chordal accompaniment. Percussion is provided ideally by a *carraca,* a *zambumbia,* a *quiribillo,* a *pandareta* (tambourine, usually without jingles), a *guacharaca,* and a *chucho* until the introduction is completed. *Coplas,* fixed or improvised, are then sung unaccompanied—a trait that makes the *guabina veleña* unique among Andean Colombian genres. After the first half of the *copla* has been rendered, the instrumental interlude is repeated, leading to the vocalist's completion of the *copla*. The melodic line is simple, almost modal—a trait that has led some observers to posit its origin in the plainsong taught to the region's inhabitants during the colonial era. As with the *rajaleña* of the southern Andean region, informal, noncompetitive performances may last from a few moments to a few hours, depending on the endurance and improvisatory skills of the *copleros.* The excerpts of *guabina* texts presented in the following example are typical (Koorn 1975:224, 226):

Tan alta que va la luna	How high is the moon
y un lucero la acompaña.	accompanied by a star.
Tan triste que queda un hombre	How sad is a man
cuando una mujer lo engaña.	when he is cheated by a woman.
Ayer pasé por tu casa,	Yesterday I went by your house,
te vide moliendo arepas;	and saw you grinding corn cakes;
La risa me reventaba	I broke up with laughter
de verte jondiar las tetas.	on seeing your tits jiggle.

The second of these *coplas* is commonly performed in the *rajaleña* of southern Colombia.

Pasillo

The *pasillo,* an adaptation of the Austrian waltz, was cultivated in Colombian bourgeois salons before Colombia became independent. It was known as the *valse del país* 'waltz of the country', the *valse redondo bogotano* 'the round waltz of Bogotá', the *valse apresurado* 'the hastened waltz', the *capuclinada,* the *estrós* 'Strauss', the *varsoviana* 'Warsaw thing'; and elsewhere in South America it had other names. A favorite among the elite classes, it was one of the few forms in which dancing couples embraced. Having gradually made its way into traditional culture, it exists in two forms, the romantic *pasillo lento* 'slow *pasillo*' and the *pasillo instrumental* 'instrumental *pasillo*', a faster version.

The *danza* enjoyed its greatest popularity beginning around the close of the 1800s in the salons of the privileged classes, but it never rivaled the status of its contemporary the *pasillo*.

The slow pasillo

The slow *pasillo* (*pasillo lento*), like the Ecuadorian version, is known for its nostalgic, effusively romantic texts and its melancholic melodies. Its origin among the aristocracy is evident in the choice of verse forms, which shun the *copla* in favor of the longer lines typical of Spanish lyric poetry. Individual lines go beyond the standard eight syllables of the *copla* and may have from ten to fourteen syllables. Slow *pasillos* tend to be romantic songs reflecting idyllic love or bitter rejection by the fickle object of a suffering man's attentions. The liberal use of fermatas and evocative pauses comes from the *bambuco,* as has the custom of alternating instrumental interludes and vocal sections and *sesquiáltera* (see figure 8*b*).

Probably the most famous *pasillo* of the Colombian tradition is *"Flores Negras"* ('Black Flowers'), composed in 1903 by Julio Flórez (1867–1923) and considered a masterpiece of the golden age of Colombian popular song. Two passages from this piece illustrate the textual style.

Oye: bajo las ruinas de mis pasiones
y en el fondo de esta alma que ya no alegras,
entre polvo de ensueños y de ilusiones
brotan entumecidas mis flores negras.

Guarda, pues, este triste, débil manojo
que te ofrezco de aquellas flores sombrías.
Guárdalo, nada temas, que es un despojo
del jardín de mis hondas melancolías.

Listen: beneath the ruins of my passions
and in the depths of this soul you no longer gladden,
amid the dust of my dreams and fantasies,
my black flowers bloom benumbed.

Keep, then, this sad, frail bouquet
of those gloomy flowers that I offer you.
Keep it, do not fear, for it's the spoils
of the garden of my deep melancholy.

The instrumental pasillo

Like its slower counterpart, the instrumental *pasillo* is sectional: it usually has three sections, each in a contrasting tonal area, typically a closely related key such as the subdominant or the relative or parallel major or minor. Syncopated and often sequentially related melodies and alternation of duple and triple meters in the *bandola* melodies and the guitarra and *tiple* accompaniment are typical (see figure 8*c*). The number and order of repetitions of given sections are at the performer's discretion. Pedro Morales Pino (1863–1926) and his student Fulgencio García (1880–1945) are known as the greatest *bandola* players in Colombian history, and as the composers of beloved instrumental *pasillos.*

Vals

A descendent of the waltz of the European tradition (see figure 8*d*), the *vals* or *valse* was cultivated by the Latin American colonial aristocracy as a formal dance (*baile de salón*). The *vals* of the nineteenth-century urban popular *salón* tradition was performed on piano. As a dance, it no longer enjoys the popularity it formerly commanded but remains a vital part of the repertoire of the *dueto bambuquero.* A perennial favorite is José Alejandro Morales' *"Pueblito Viejo"* ('Dear Little Old Village'), an excerpt of which is seen in the following example:

Pueblito de mis cuitas,	Hamlet of my heartaches,
de casas pequeñitas,	of tiny cottages,
por tus calles tranquilas	through your tranquil streets
corrió mi juventud.	ran my youth.
En ti aprendí a querer	With you I learned to love
por la primera vez,	for the first time,
y nunca me enseñaste	and you never taught me
lo que es la ingratitud.	the meaning of ingratitude.

Danza

In the early 1800s, the habanera, related to the independence era's *contradanza,* an adaptation of the English contredanse, spread across the Caribbean to Colombia, where it became known as the *danza.* The *danza* is the only Andean Colombian popular-music form set in duple meter (see figure 8*e*) and the only one to have been imported from a country other than Spain.

Structurally, the *danza* has two parts, the second frequently in the relative or parallel major of the (minor) key of the first. Like texts of *pasillos,* texts of *danzas* spring from the tradition of Spanish lyric poetry rather than that of the *copla.* The *danza* enjoyed its greatest popularity beginning around the close of the 1800s in the salons of the privileged classes, but it never rivaled the status of its contemporary the *pasillo.* Unlike the *pasillo,* it was never adopted by the common people but remained a symbol of the exclusivity of the colonial elite. Instrumental *danzas* are rare.

Luís Dueñas Perilla's composition *"Negrita,"* probably the most famous Colombian *danza,* remains a favorite serenade selection:

Negrita,	Dark-skinned girl,
Tú viniste en la noche	You came in the night
de mi amargo penar.	of my bitter suffering.
Tú llegaste a mi vida	You came into my life
y borraste la herida	and wiped away the wound
de mi pena letal.	of my grievous heartache.
La ilusión de mi vida	The revery of my life
es amarte, no más:	is to love you, nothing more:
implorarte el consuelo,	to beg of you the comfort,
el calor y el ensueño	the warmth, and the dreams
que jamás pude hallar.	that I've never found before.

As in this excerpt, the *danza* is suitable for serenading, in which the romance and sentimentality of its lyrics are especially appreciated.

Joropo

The *joropo* may be considered a close but more rhythmically complex relative of the *bambuco* or the *sanjuanero*. It is typical of the eastern plains and is only occasionally heard in the Andean highlands. Spanish influence in the musical aspect is strong and features frequent use of hemiolas and duple and ternary metric alternation. *Copla* form is prominent in the textual presentation of the *joropo* [for greater detail about the *joropo*, see VENEZUELA].

POPULAR MUSIC

What may be called folkloric music (*música folclórica,* also *música típica* 'typical music' and *música colombiana* 'Colombian music') began to evolve at the close of the 1800s in Bogotá. The setting was after hours in *piqueteaderos*—combination general stores and coffee houses, which became centers for informal congregation and the cultivation of a bohemian nightlife. Musicians there were young men, frequently with conservatory training, who spent their time teaching, performing religious music in churches, or singing in the chorus for visiting opera or zarzuela companies. They began to associate with the great poets Julio Flórez, Clímaco Soto Borda, Eduardo López, Carlos Villafañe, José Velásquez García ("Julio Vives Guerra"), Rafael Pombo, and others. Together, these artists—drinking, chatting, playing, singing, improvising—inspired and shared a new cultural milieu, which became known as the golden age of Colombian popular song. They collaborated in the creation of *bambucos, pasillos, valses, danzas,* and *guabinas,* which still serve as the foundation of traditional music performed in Colombia.

Pedro Morales Pino, the greatest *bandola* player in history, is remembered for the addition of a sixth course of strings to that instrument and for authoring method books for the guitar and the *bandola.* In 1890, he began transforming what had been an oral tradition into a written one, meticulously transcribing the melodies, rhythms, and texts of popular songs of his day. In 1898, he organized Colombia's first *estudiantina,* with which he toured the Andean region of Colombia, Central America, and the United States. Between 1901 and 1903, this ensemble performed in concert halls in New Orleans, St. Louis, Chicago, Buffalo, New York, Philadelphia, and Baltimore. Their repertoire featured not only Colombian popular music but also classical music, including pieces by Mozart, Beethoven, and Brahms, and pieces by Colombian composers. Reorganized and expanded, this *estudiantina* later toured the South American continent.

Morales Pino was an extraordinary arranger of classical music for *estudiantina* and is credited with more than a hundred compositions of his own, including orchestral works, in which he employed folkloric materials and nationalistic themes. His most famous popular songs include *"Cuatro Preguntas"* ('Four Questions'), a *bambuco,* words by Eduardo López; *"Trigueña"* ('Woman with Wheat-Colored Skin'), a *bambuco*; and *"Onda Fugaz"* ('Fleeting Ripple') and *"Divagación"* ('Melancholy Musings'), both *danzas* with words by Carlos Villafañe. Few educators can claim as impressive a group of students as those he nurtured at the Academia Nacional: Emilio Murillo, Alejandro Wills, Luís A. Calvo, Fulgencio García, and Carlos Escamilla.

Emilio Murillo (1880–1942), founder and director of the famous Estudiantina Murillo, was a prolific composer of popular songs, the most famous of which were *"El Trapiche"* ('The Sugar Mill'), a *bambuco,* words by Ismael Enrique Arciniegas; *"Fiebres"* ('Fevers'), a *canción,* words by Julio Flórez; and *"Hondos Pesares"* ('Deep Sorrows'), a *bambuco,* words by Julio Flórez. Searching for authentic Colombian musical lore, he engaged in extensive fieldwork, and in 1929, with Alejandro Wills,

Jerónimo Velasco, and Alberto Escobar, he traveled to Spain to represent Colombia in the Seville Exposition.

The golden age of Colombian popular song began with the emergence of vocal duets. Alejandro Wills (d. 1942) and Alberto Escobar (d. 1934) were the most popular musical duo in Colombian history. A guitarist and vocalist in Morales Pino's Lira Colombiana and the Estudiantina Murillo, Wills was an acclaimed composer and performer of popular music for some thirty years. Some of his best-loved works are "*Beso Robado*" ('Stolen Kiss'), a *bambuco*, 1930; "El Boga" ('The Oarsman'), a *bambuco*, words by Nicanor Velásquez Ortiz; and "*Los Arrayanes*" ('The Myrtles'), a *danza*, words by Julio Vives Guerra. In 1915 his two *danzas*, "*Ribereña*" ('The Woman Who Lives by the River'), words by Clímaco Soto Borda, and "*Sumercesita Linda*," words by Carlos Villafañe, achieved enormous success, and with "*Caramba*" (a *cuplé*, 1916), Wills became the leading Colombian popular-music composer of his day. Beginning in 1918, the duo Wills y Escobar toured Venezuela, Cuba, Mexico, and New York, where Wills created a sensation by performing on a carpenter's saw. While in New York, the duo made some of the earliest recordings of Colombian music—with the Victor Company.

Luís A. Calvo (1882–1945) was a prolific composer of religious music and orchestral pieces. Among his more successful popular music efforts are "*Serenata*," a *canción*; "Gitana," a *danza*; and "*El Republicano*" ('The Republican'), an instrumental *bambuco*. Fulgencio García (1880–1945), an extraordinary *bandola* player, composed several pieces of the *bandola* virtuoso repertoire, including the *pasillos* "*Coqueteos*" ('*Bandola* Riffs'), "*Vino Tinto*" ('Red Wine'), and "*La Gata Golosa*" ('The Sweet-Toothed [Greedy] Cat'), all composed in 1912. The last, originally named "*Soacha*," was renamed for Gaite Galoise (French Gaiety), a *piqueteadero* frequented by García. Patrons jokingly turned its name into Gata Golosa. The name stuck, not only to the establishment, but to this *pasillo*.

Carlos "El Ciego" ('The Blind') Escamilla is remembered as Colombia's greatest *tiple* player. A member of the first and second incarnations of the Lira Colombiana, he composed several still-popular pieces, among which figure the *pasillos* "*Nené*" ('Baby'), "*Colón*" (possibly named after the Teatro Colón in Bogotá, where the group played), "*13 de Marzo*" ('Thirteenth of March'), and "*Brisas del Amaime*."

Any survey of prominent composers of Colombian popular music must include Alberto Castilla (1883–1938), the founder of the Ibagué Conservatory and author of "*Bunde Tolimense*" ('*Bunde* of Tolima'), a *bunde*, words by Cesáreo Rocha Castilla; and "*Rondinela*" (named after a popular *piqueteadero*), a *pasillo*, 1916. Others worthy of inclusion are José A. Morales, author of "*Pescador, Lucero y Río*" ('Fisherman, Star, and River'), a *pasillo*; "*María Antonia*," a *bambuco*; and "*Yo También Tuve Veinte Años*" ('I, Too, Was Once Twenty Years Old'), a *bambuco*; and Carlos Vieco, composer of "*Hacia el Calvario*" ('Toward Calvary'), a *pasillo* comparing Christ's walk to Calvary with an orphan's suffering, words by Pablo Restrepo L.; "*Adiós Casita Blanca*" ('Goodbye, Little White House'), a *pasillo*, words by Padre Villarraga; and "*Campesina*" ('Peasant Girl'), a *bambuco*, words by Eladio Espinosa. Jorge Villamil Cordovez has had enormous success since the 1960s, supplying contemporary *duetos bambuqueros* with "*Espumas*" ('River Bubbles'), a *pasillo*; "*Oropel*" ('Fool's Gold'), a *vals*; "*Los Guaduales*" ('Bamboo Grove'), a *guabina*; "*Llamarada*" ('Flames'), a *vals*; and others, several of which have been recorded in various styles throughout Latin America. Ignacio "Papi" Tovar, Jorge Camargo, and Rodrigo Silva have also made their marks on contemporary Colombian popular-music history.

With the rise of the *dueto bambuquero*, Colombian traditional music first came to be performed by musicians with conservatory training. Performances moved from the countryside and the city's back streets into theaters and salons. Musicians discard-

By the mid-1800s, troupes of musicians primarily from Italy and Spain were doing their best to bring the Colombian privileged classes up to date with the latest European artistic trends.

ed the peasants' ponchos (*ruanas*) in favor of tuxedos and performed *música brillante,* an international menu of waltzes, gavottes, and minuets, alongside *danzas,* tangos, boleros, *bambucos,* and *pasillos.* To effect the right image, however, they later returned to performing in peasant-like costumes, and set off to tour the world.

Jorge Añez was a member of the second Lira Colombiana, the duet Briceño y Añez, and the Estudiantina Añez and composed popular songs, including the *bambucos* "*Los Cucaracheros,*" "*Agáchate el Sombrerito*" ('Put the Brim of Your Hat Down Lower'), and "*Ibaguereña*" ('Girl from Ibagé'), words by Eduardo López. Añez's quartet, the South American Troubadours, consisted of two Colombians, a Mexican, and a Panamanian opera singer and featured a pan-Hispanic repertoire. Whereas in the 1800s Europe had been the ideal destination for aspiring Colombian musicians, the recording studios of New York now began to claim their attention. In the 1910s, the first recordings of Colombian music were made in New York and Mexico City.

In his memoirs (1970 [1951]) Añez shares his insider's perspective on Colombian popular music during its golden age. He toured extensively in North and Central America and spent years in New York recording Colombian popular songs for Aeolian, Brunswick, Columbia, Victor, and other companies. In 1933, when he returned to Bogotá, he was bitterly disappointed to discover that the golden age was only a memory. The veteran musicians had died, and the *piqueteaderos* and bohemian atmosphere were gone.

ART MUSIC

The evangelization of the indigenous peoples of Colombia was helped by instruction in European music. Father José Dadey (1574–1660) founded musical education in Colombia. A Jesuit priest who came from Milan in 1604, he established the Colegio Seminario de San Bartolomé, which instructed indigenous people in religion and music, including reading, writing, singing, and organ playing. He ordered violins, harps, *chirimías* (single-reed aerophones), and flutes brought from Spain, and established the organ-building tradition in the Bogotá area.

The 1800s saw new beginnings in Colombia, then rebelling from Spain and struggling to create an identity of its own, politically and culturally. Two of the most important figures in this period were Juan Antonio de Velasco (d. 1859) and Nicolás Quevedo Rachadell (1803–1874), who introduced German and Italian music to Bogotá audiences. The first Spanish comic operas (*tonadillas*) had been presented in Bogotá in 1783. Their director, the composer Pedro Carricarte, established the first state-sponsored band in Colombia, La Banda de la Corona, in 1784.

By the mid-1800s, troupes of musicians primarily from Italy and Spain were doing their best to bring the Colombian privileged classes up to date with the latest European artistic trends. The first operatic selections in Colombia were presented in 1849. A twenty-eight-year-old tenor, Oreste Sindici, arrived in 1864 with an Italian opera company. Like others before him, he remained in Bogotá after his contract expired and became a prominent choral music educator, but is remembered today as the author of the Colombian national anthem.

Throughout the 1800s, the center of national musical activity remained in Bogotá. The piano became the instrument of choice for study, particularly by young ladies. By 1850, more than two thousand pianos were in the city—one for every fifteen people. Music-sponsoring organizations that focused the efforts of a growing nucleus of composers, performers, and consumers in the capital included the Sociedad Lírica (1848), founded by José Joaquín Guarín (1825–1854), pianist, composer and teacher; the Unión Musical (1858), founded by the composer Manuel María Párraga; and the Sociedad Filarmónica de Santa Cecilia (1868), founded by Pedro Vesoni. The English-born pianist and composer Enrique Price (1819–1863) founded the most important of these, the Sociedad Filarmónica de Bogotá, the basis on which all subsequent musical organizations in Colombia have been built. In 1847, he attached to it a professional school of music, the first in Colombia. With Rafael Pombo, his son Jorge W. Price (1853–1953) revived the Sociedad Filarmónica in 1875 and with state funding in 1882 opened the Academia Nacional de Música.

In 1888, the Colombian government contracted the Italian-born Manuel Conti to develop state bands, and by 1890 he had established the first musical-supply store in Colombia. It sold instruments, sheet music, and related items. The military bands he organized formed the basis for the Banda Nacional de Bogotá, which became the Orquesta Sinfónica Nacional (National Symphony Orchestra). In 1910, the Academia Nacional de Música was officially renamed Conservatorio Nacional de Música, under the directorship of Guillermo Uribe Holguín (1880–1971), who attached what is currently the Orquesta Sinfónica Nacional to it. The most influential composer of his generation, Uribe Holguín incorporated impressionistic, modernistic, and sometimes polytonal influences into his symphonic and piano works, many of which are clearly nationalistic, incorporating native rhythmic and melodic patterns, especially the *pasillo,* the *bambuco,* and less frequently the *joropo.* In 1936, Guillermo Espinosa (b. 1905) was appointed first director of the Orquesta Sinfónica Nacional. In his position as chief of the music division of the Pan American Union, he organized the Inter-American Music Festivals in Washington, D.C., promoting new works by Latin American composers.

Establishing nationwide musical training has been consistently difficult in Colombia because of a chronic lack of economic and political stability, further hampered by the failure of a sophisticated cultural ambience to materialize in the capital, where young students would be exposed to the highest caliber of international music production. All Colombian musicians of renown received their training at the national conservatory but continued their studies in Europe, many in Paris under the tutelage of Vincent d'Indy at the Schola Cantorum. Most returned to teach at the conservatory, in some cases assuming the directorship of the institution or founding similar centers in provincial capitals.

Another early nationalistic composer was José María Ponce de León (1846–1882), who composed zarzuelas, mazurkas, *bambucos, pasillos,* and *valses,* plus overtures and religious music. A forerunner of Colombian musical nationalism, he showed in his orchestral works the influence of Colombian folk dances. He composed the only two operas produced in Colombia in the 1800s: *Ester* (1874) and *Florinda* (1880), their librettos written by the poet Rafael Pombo.

Andrés Martínez Montoya (1869–1933), a composer and one of the great pianists and piano teachers of his time, was director of the Conservatorio Nacional de Música for many years and wrote a history of Colombian music. Santos Cifuentes (1870–1932), a composer, wrote texts on aesthetics and music theory that were adopted by the national conservatories of Colombia, Chile, and Mexico.

Antonio María Valencia (1902–1952) founded the Conservatory and School of Fine Arts at Cali in 1933, and introduced Colombia to modern European piano literature. In many compositions, he utilized impressionist techniques to incorporate nationalistic themes, including *bambucos, pasillos,* and *cumbias* [see AFRO-COLOMBIAN TRADITIONS]. In Colombian musicology, his former student and biographer, Andrés Pardo Tovar, is a key figure in his own right as the author of a series of articles entitled *Cultura Musical en Colombia* (1966) and for his other writings on music (1958).

Scholars in this field include composer Emirto de Lima (b. 1892), author of a treatise on Colombian folklore; Daniel G. Zamudio (1885–1952), noted composer, folklorist, and author of *El Folklore Musical de Colombia* (1950); and Guillermo Abadía Morales, the late director of the folklore and ethnomusicology program at the Universidad Nacional in Bogotá and author of many publications on Colombian music.

FURTHER STUDY

Scientifically researched, analytically oriented, and systematically presented ethnomusicological studies of any part of Andean Colombia are rare, in English or Spanish. Koorn's (1977) doctoral dissertation provides an analysis of Andean folk-musical culture, with particular attention to the northeastern highlands of the department of Santander. It includes description of musical instruments and a good, concise discussion of Spanish poetics in his treatment of the *copla.*

The literature on the folk-musical traditions of the Colombian Andes consists mostly of descriptive, outdated accounts of widely varying quality. Such studies are seldom analytical and rarely discuss associated human behaviors. Information concerning folk-musical instruments, associated masks, costumes, or dances tends to be included as briefly treated subtopics or genres within the context of larger compendia. Little emphasis has been placed on the study of folk music as a cultural expression or the projection of local identity within the context of folkloric performance.

Systematic analyses of the *copla,* the most important popular versifying in Andean Colombian folk-musical performance, are rare. Studies of *coplas* tend to take the form of collections, with little or no attention paid to the *copleros* and their roles as artistic creators and disseminators. Gradante's doctoral dissertation is a detailed analysis of the role of *coplas* and the musicians who create and perform them.

For insiders' accounts of the golden age of the Colombian popular song, the contributions by Añez (1970 [1951]) and Restrepo Duque (1971) are excellent. Davidson's three-volume collection is a treasury of resources for the study of Colombian musical folklore. Béhague's chapter on Colombia (1979) is a concise evaluation of the history of art music in Colombia. The folklorist Abadía's offering deals with Colombian mestizo, Afro-Colombian, and indigenous musical traditions in all regions of the country. Perdomo Escobar's work examines music in Colombian life from prehistoric times to the twentieth century and includes a glossary and an extensive bibliography. Piñeros Corpas (n.d.) is a good collection of recordings of African-Colombian and Andean Colombian music.

REFERENCES

Abadía Morales, Guillermo. 1973. *La Música Folklórica Colombiana.* Bogotá: Universidad Nacional de Colombia.

Añez, Jorge. 1968 [1951]. *Canciones y Recuerdos.* Bogotá: Ediciones Mundial.

Aretz, Isabel. 1967. *Instrumentos Musicales de Venezuela.* Cumaná, Venezuela: Editorial Universitaria de Oriente.

Béhague, Gerard. 1979. *Music in Latin America: An Introduction.* Englewood Cliffs, N.J.: Prentice-Hall.

Davidson, Harry C. 1970. *Diccionario Folklórico de Colombia: Música, Instrumentos y Danzas.* 3 vols. Bogotá: Banco de la República.

Gradante, William J. 1991. "*¡Viva el San Pedro en La Plata!*: Tradition, Creativity, and Folk Musical Performance in a Southern Colombian Festival." Ph.D. dissertation, University of Texas at Austin.

Gutiérrez, Benigno A. 1955. *El Folklore de Antioquia y Caldas.* Medellín: Editorial Bedout.

Isaacs, Jorge. 1962 [1867]. *María.* Buenos Aires: Editorial Kapelusa.

Izikowitz, Karl Gustav. 1970 [1935]. *Musical Instruments of the South American Indians.* East Ardsley, Wakefield, Yorkshire: S. R. Publishers.

Jaramillo J., Jacinto. 1955. "Coreografía del Bambuco." In *Folklore de Antioquia y Caldas,* ed. Benigno A. Gutiérrez, 547–555. (Medellín: Editorial Bedout)

Koorn, Dirk. 1977. "Folk Music of the Colombian Andes." Ph.D. dissertation, University of Washington.

Liscano Velutini, Juan. 1950. *Folklore y Cultura: Nuestra Tierra.* Caracas: Editorial Avila Gráfica.

Osorio y Ricaurte, Juan Crisóstomo. 1867. *Diccionario de Música, precedido de la teoría general del arte y especial del piano.* Bogotá: Imprenta de Gaitán.

Pardo Tovar, Andrés. 1958. *Antonio María Valencia: Artista Integral.* Cali: Biblioteca Vallecaucana, Extensión Cultural.

———. 1966. *La Cultural Musical en Colombia.* Bogotá: Ediciones Lerner.

Perdomo Escobar, José Ignacio. 1963. *Historia de la Música en Colombia,* 3rd ed.. Bogotá: Editorial ABC.

Piñeros Corpas, Joaquín. N.d. *Introducción al Cancionero Noble de Colombia.* Edición especial. Bogotá: Universidad de los Andes. 3 LP disks.

Restrepo, Antonio José. 1955. *El Cancionero de Antioquia.* Medellín: Editorial Bedout.

Restrepo Duque, Hernán. 1971. *Lo que Cuentan las Canciones: Cronicón Musical.* Bogotá: Ediciones Tercer Mundo.

Zamudio, Daniel G. 1950. "El Folklore Musical de Colombia." *Revista de las Indias,* suplemento 14.

Afro-Colombian Traditions
Lawrence J. App

Musical Instruments
Musical Contexts and Genres
Afro-Colombian Popular Music
Mediated and Live Performance
Further Study

During the past five centuries, African peoples and their descendants have contributed significantly to the development of music and culture in Colombia. From the beginning of Spanish colonization, they have blended their own music and musical practices with European and Amerindian influences, forming a rich and variegated musical tapestry. The specific ethnic origins of Colombian music are often blurred and complex because the process of *mestizaje* (the racial intermixing of European, Amerindian, and African peoples) began hybridizing cultural forms early on. As a result, few or no extant musical forms in Colombia are purely African; conversely, only a small portion of Colombian music has not been affected by African culture.

Africans were present from the beginning of Spanish exploration. They accompanied Pizarro on his expedition to the Pacific in 1526, and their numbers in Nueva Granada grew rapidly because of the demand for labor (Whitten 1968:1). An estimated one million enslaved Africans from as many as thirty-eight cultures passed through Cartagena, settling first in the Atlantic littoral—*la Costa*—then spreading to the Pacific coast as slaves were needed to work in the gold mines (List 1967:116). Though miscegenation created a triethnic population, *mestizaje* did not occur uniformly throughout Colombia, and the regional patterns of ethnic distribution established during the colonial period persist, with the highest concentration of Africans occurring on the two coasts and along the Cauca and Magdalena river valleys.

During the colonial period, Spanish influences were strongest in shaping the national character, including the arts. European musical forms including the *copla*, the *contradanza*, and the fandango and European musical instruments were brought to Colombia and blended with African and indigenous elements. Concurrently, as a result of social, economic, and religious factors, African culture developed in other regions with varying degrees of independence. For the slaves, Roman Catholic missionaries established *cabildos*, modeled after the *cofradías* in Spain but organized ostensibly by tribal origins, as places for religious conversion. In several areas, slaves rebelled and fled into the jungle, establishing independent communities. Havens for people of West African tribal origins, these communities often became microcosmic reconstructions of pan-African society and cultural practices.

Evolving economic and social patterns affected the distribution of blacks and the degree of *mestizaje*. The Pacific coast of Colombia has a long tradition of relatively unacculturated African societies, partially because of geographic isolation and environmental harshness. Most Colombian blacks are descendants of escaped slaves who intermarried with native Americans and formed independent communities as early as 1528 (Cáceres 1978:238). Though the Atlantic coast also had a large black population, the economy there was based on plantation agriculture and livestock, allowing greater movement and intermingling of ethnic groups. By the 1700s, large populations of blacks had settled in urban areas, where they formed distinct communities reflecting segregationist housing patterns. Though slavery was legally abolished in 1851, most blacks in Colombia had become free people during the 1700s, through manumission or escape.

The rising tide of nationalism that culminated in Colombia's independence (1819) sought ostensibly to break the influence of Spain on the national character; nevertheless, Colombian development continued to be guided by Western models of economic success. Though Colombia has one of the longest traditions of democratic rule in Latin America, partisan power struggles led to some of the bloodiest civil wars in the hemisphere. Behind the rhetoric of national unity, the white-mestizo political and social hegemony succeeded in maintaining class structures divided along racial lines. Many blacks chose to deny their African heritage in the collective search for upward mobility, which they associated with lighter shades of skin color. African-derived musics were ignored in Colombia's cultural mainstream; as a result, the most noticeably African-derived musical traditions persisted in marginalized communities. The vocal style of black Colombian music uses melodies and/or texts that originated in Europe, but African-derived traits predominate, including call-and-response singing, overlapping phrases, disjunct rhythmic cycles in phrasing, offbeat accents between text and melody, and the use of vocables and *gritos* (shouts of emotional expression). African influences are detectable on some music by the vocal tone quality. Especially noticeable, however, are African influences in musical instruments.

MUSICAL INSTRUMENTS

An organological overview of Afro-Colombian music shows that most instruments were developed from African sources, often blending with European or Amerindian influences.

Idiophones

Idiophones are the most numerous and diversified instruments in Afro-Colombian music. Tube rattles of native American origin, called *guasá* and *guacho* in the Pacific and Atlantic (Caribbean) areas, respectively, are constructed from sections of hollow bamboo, wood, or metal tubing and filled with seeds or pebbles. The main difference between the two is that the shell of the *guacho* is pierced with holes into which thorns or nails are thrust internally, altering the timbre. Though of Amerindian origin, *maracas* are used in many ensembles that perform African-derived music. The *guacharaca* is a scraper made of wooden tubing with notches cut into it and rubbed with a wire fork. *Palmetas* are wooden spatulas struck together to augment handclapping or substitute for it. The *marímbula,* a large member of the mbira family, consists of a wooden box and seven or more tuned metal keys, which are plucked. It is used in the Atlantic and Pacific coastal areas to provide bass accompaniment in some ensembles. It is believed to have been brought to Colombia from Africa via Cuba early in the twentieth century (List 1983:27).

Another tuned idiophone commonly used in Afro-Colombian traditional music is the marimba of the Pacific littoral. Black *libres* began constructing marimbas as early as the 1500s, based on principles brought from West Africa. The keys are cut from palm and laid across two strips of wood, with tuned bamboo resonators attached underneath. The number of keys may vary from eighteen to twenty-eight, but the construction and tuning are fairly consistent. The marimba is commonly played by two men; one *(bordonero)* plays a melodic ostinato on the lower keys, and the other *(tiplero, requintador)* improvises contrapuntal melodies and embellishments in the upper register. Usually, the marimba is suspended from the rafters of a specially built house (see figure 1)—an idea perhaps learned from native Americans, who suspended huge log idiophones from rafters.

Membranophones

Membranophones are the most prominent instruments used in Afro-Colombian music. In construction and performance, they bear a strong resemblance to their West African counterparts. The *tambor mayor* 'large drum' (also called *tambor macho* 'male drum') is a single-headed conical drum made from the trunk of a tree. The head, laced on and tuned with wooden wedges, is struck with the hands; the drum is sometimes lifted off the ground to change the tone. The *tambor menor* 'small drum' (*tambor hembra* 'female drum', *llamador* 'caller') is constructed and played in the same manner, though its musical role within an ensemble is different.

A third drum found in a typical coastal ensemble is the *bombo*, perhaps a hybrid of Spanish, Indian, and/or African influences. Barrel-shaped or cylindrical and double-headed, it is played with sticks on both heads and on the shell. In the Pacific coastal area, another conical drum called *cununo* is usually played in pairs (*cununo mayor* 'large' and *cununo menor* 'small'). Though the *cununo* and the *tambor* are similar in many respects, the primary difference between them is that the former is closed at the bottom except for a small hole.

Chordophone

The only chordophone of distinctly African origin in Colombia is the one-stringed musical bow, which may no longer be in use. Known as marimba in Palenque de San Basilio (a village near the Atlantic coast), it is played by striking the string with a thin stick and alternately stopping it with a piece of wood (List 1966). This produces two fundamental tones, amplified by the player's mouth, which serves as a resonator.

Aerophones

Two aerophones are commonly used in the African-derived genres of the Atlantic coast. The *caña de millo* (also called *pito*) is an idioglottal transverse clarinet used primarily in the *cumbia*. Possibly of Amerindian and African origin, it is made from cane or millet, and has four holes, played with the flats of the fingers, over a range of about a fifth.

A vertical duct flute (*gaita*) is probably of native American origin [see KOGI]. It is constructed from a hollowed-out section of cactus stalk, with a quill duct and a duct-encasing head made of beeswax and charcoal. *Gaitas* are usually played in pairs. The female instrument (*gaita hembra*) has five or six holes and is used for the melody, while the male instrument (*gaita macho*), having only one or two holes, plays accompaniment (see Bermúdez n.d.).

European instruments

European instruments have been incorporated into many black genres of music in Colombia. The button accordion, originally from Germany, has been used in different folkloric genres, but it primarily became identified as the signature instrument of *vallenato* (see below). The clarinet has been part of several brass-band traditions, including the *chirimía*; however, the clarinet's main use in Colombia has been in *cumbia* music, as this genre became syncretized. European brass instruments, especially the trumpet, the trombone, and the tuba, have become favorites of *chirimía,* contemporary *cumbia,* and Colombian *salsa* ensembles. By the mid-1950s, the use of cymbals *(platillos)* had become common in the *chirimía* bands of northwest Colombia. Modern electric instruments, especially the electric bass and synthesizer, have become popular in the more acculturated styles of African-derived music.

MUSICAL CONTEXTS AND GENRES

The settings in which African-derived music is performed in Colombia are almost as varied as the people themselves. Most musical contexts can be classified as religious, recreational, or related to labor, though some categories overlap. Colombians' localized and situationally determined perceptions of contexts and styles create a complex and somewhat ambiguous body of terms that may have multiple meanings. Furthermore, African influences in Colombia have become manifest in various ways. Blacks reconstructed or invented new forms and styles in response to whatever local conditions were present, often incorporating into their music European and Indian elements and new Africanisms brought by recent immigrants.

Religious contexts

Some of the oldest contexts with the longest traditions have evolved from religious practices. In many areas, Roman Catholicism became syncretized with West African religions, affecting the contexts and practices of black music in Colombia. In most of Colombia, festivals honoring Christian saints are organized locally on particular dates and are some of the prime musical occasions. These are religious festivals, but music, dance, celebration, and alcohol are frequently inseparable parts of them. Ritual sacrifices, spirit possession, symbolic choreography, initiatory rites, and group participation in religious observances are African-derived traits, whereas the use of the Bible, European melodies, the names of certain saints, and the burning of candles are Christian traits. By European standards, local distinctions between the sacred and the profane were obscured by the syncretism of African and European values, often bringing the disdain of priests and politicians.

In addition to the primary Christian holidays, most towns have a special festival in honor of the local patron saint. These festivals may last up to two weeks and are usually the largest community function of the year. While religious observances are occurring, the primary activities center on music, dance, and celebration; furthermore, these festivals may become vehicles for social and political commentary through lyrics, costumes, and dramatic scenes during parades. Music varies regionally, ranging from *arrullos,* a kind of religious praise song performed on the Pacific coast by a women's chorus in call-and-response manner, to brass bands playing *porros* and *cumbias* in the northeast. During the Advent and Christmas season, people perform special songs including *fugas* 'flights' and *alavados* 'hymns', incorporating European melodies and texts plus African-derived vocal and rhythmic techniques.

Wakes for the dead and funerals are another important religious context for African-derived music. Though practices vary among blacks in Colombia, the concern for the dead, use of funerary rites, and incorporation of music are generally derived from African ancestor-cult traditions. The wake for a small child *(velorio del angelito)* is a common practice on the Atlantic and Pacific coasts. Because people believe the child's soul goes directly to heaven, the music and the occasion are celebratory. In the Atlantic area, the *velorio* is usually held in the parents' home; relatives, friends, and people from the community attend. Music is provided by a specialized chorus of singers in leader-and-chorus refrain style, while the others sing and dance in a circle around the corpse. In the Pacific area, this wake also takes place in the fam-

In the *currulao* dance, a man asserts his freedom and a woman extols her ability to keep a man. The man advances while the woman retreats, rebuffing his invitations, but once the man symbolically gives up, the woman pursues him.

ily's home, but *chigualos* 'hymns for the dead' are sung by a chorus of well-known women singers accompanied by male kinfolk playing drums. The *arrullo* is another religious song sung in praise of a saint, for the death of a child, or as a hymn performed by a similarly percussion-accompanied vocal ensemble. Frequently, adaptations of Roman Catholic hymns, called *alavados* (*alabados*, *albaos*), are sung during the wake. *Alavados* are distinguished from *arrullos* by their more somber tone and textual origin—the former are European, but the latter are of local origin. These songs have a specialized function in that the social interaction is completely dependent on successful musical performance; conversely, the songs cannot be performed out of their context.

The use of music in wakes for adults varies throughout Colombia. In the Atlantic area, music for these occasions occurs only in Palenque de San Basilio, where traditional funerary music (*lumalú*) is performed by professional musicians—usually a chorus of female singers with two drummers playing a large drum and a small drum. A musical prelude signals the mourners to enter. The women sing, dance, clap their hands, and interject African vocables. In the Pacific area, the wake for an adult is a more solemn occasion: the attendance is more exclusive, there is no drumming, and everyone sings dirges. In both areas, the *novenaria* (*última novena*) is celebrated at the conclusion of the mourning period, usually nine days, to send the deceased's spirit to heaven. These rites were traditionally carried out in the community, but because authorities frowned on delayed interment, their practice has continued in secrecy. The *bunde*, once a generic term for African dancing, now denotes a kind of song primarily in funerary use. The rhythm is provided by *cununos*, *bombos*, and a *guasá*; the texts, usually praising a saint, are sung responsorially. The drums are believed to have magical powers to influence the spirits.

Recreational contexts

Another large category of musical contexts falls under the broad rubric of recreation. In many recreational functions, music and dance are closely associated, just as they are in religious functions. In the Pacific area, the *currulao* is danced at the local marimba house (*casa de la marimba,* where the instrument is kept). The *currulao* is believed to have originated in a seventeenth-century dance that may have been diffused from Cartagena, through the interior to the Pacific coast, by the migration of slaves (Wade 1993:275; Zapata 1967:94). The ensemble that performs the *currulao* (figure 1) consists of two *cununeros*, two *bomberos*, two *marimberos (tiplero and bordonero)*, a *guasá*, a male lead singer *(glosador)*, and a chorus of women *(respondadoras)*. The drums and marimba play highly syncopated, complex patterns, over which call-and-response singing is performed.

At least thirty distinct *currulao* melodies (*bordones*) can be combined with nine different rhythms, including the *bambuco*, the *agua larga*, the *fuga*, the *patacoré* (a rapid, complex rhythm), and others. The choreography and texts symbolize relation-

FIGURE 1 *Currulao* ensemble of the Pacific coast of Ecuador, which shares the marimba dance with the Colombian Pacific coast. Photo used with permission of Gráficas Feraud, Guayaquil, Ecuador.

ships between the sexes, in which a man asserts his freedom and a woman extols her ability to keep a man. The man advances while the woman retreats, rebuffing his invitations, but once the man symbolically gives up, the woman pursues him. Though husband and wife rarely attend together, the *currulao* may serve to preserve family social structure because new sexual liaisons are not formed. In contrast, new partnerships are formed in saloon contexts, where couples are allowed to touch each other when they dance (Whitten 1968:71). Traditionally, musical enculturation for children began with aural and tactile models of *currulaos,* provided through parental contact, followed by attendance at communal musical activities. Potential drummers and marimba players developed proficiency in an apprentice relationship with experienced musicians. During the 1960s and 1970s, as the traditional social structure in the Pacific area changed in response to urbanization, informal schools of folklore have helped preserve the *currulao,* both dance and music, by educating youngsters (Max Brandt, personal communication) (figure 2).

Festival contexts

Carnival is celebrated before Lent in Colombia as it is throughout Latin America. Though it is based on the Christian calendar, the church considers it secular or pagan, but in practice its celebration has many traits of Roman Catholic festivals. The *danza de negros congos* during carnival in Barranquilla, which features blacks parading in traditional African dress, probably originated from the *cabildos* in that area (Wade 1994:89). In Evitar, near Palenque de San Basilio, the *danza de negros* is performed by men who strip to the waist, paint themselves blue, and engage in a mock-battle with Indians, whom they defeat. The term *danza de negro* may also refer to a particular musical style, usually involving at least a male solo vocalist, a *tambor,* a *llamador,* and *palmetas.* Other styles played during the *danza de negro* include the *garabato,* created during the 1940s, and the *mapalé,* a distinctly African form. Accounts from the 1700s emphasized the fast rhythm and "frantic" drumming of the *mapalé* and the erotic nature of the choreography (Wade 1993: 89–90).

The *bullerengue* (also known as *tambor* or *chandé*) may have originated in African puberty rites (Zapata 1967:93). It has become a common musical form with many uses along the Caribbean (Atlantic) coast. It frequently occurs at the beginning

FIGURE 2 Children learn the *currulao* dance at an informal school of folklore in the home of Teófilo Potes, Buenaventura, 1973. Photo courtesy of Max Brandt.

of festivals and at *velorios* (wakes) and to accompany the *danza de negro*. It is performed by a group consisting of a *tambor*, a *llamador*, a *guaracha*, a male lead singer, and a female chorus, which adds clapping. The soloist sings texts on subjects such as relationships between the sexes, poverty, death, and the desire to leave his homeland, and the chorus responds with an unchanging refrain.

Nonfestival contexts

Music and dance occur on many informal, social occasions that do not necessarily mark a special festival or holiday. The *cumbia* is one of the most popular and widely diffused forms of African-derived music originating in *la Costa*. The name of the genre derives from the West African *cumbe* dance, and the genre itself may have appeared as early as the 1700s. Traditionally during the *cumbia*, dancers carried bundles of candles and circled around the musicians. The instrumentation of the *conjunto de cumbia* consists of three drums (*tambor, llamador, bombo*), shakers (*guachos*), and a *pito* or a *gaita*, which plays the melody (figure 3). Vocals may be added.

Complex polyrhythms and interplay between the drums, with a moderately fast tempo and melodic repetition, characterize the *cumbia*. In ensemble use, the *llamador* has the simplest part (marking time), the *bombo* plays a characteristic ostinato pattern, and the *tambor* improvises intricate counterrhythms. This trio forms the nucleus of the traditional *conjunto de cumbia*, but these drums are used in many other styles. The *porro*, a faster, more rhythmically regular style, may have developed from the *cumbia* (firgure 4). It is performed by local *conjuntos de cumbia* and adapted to *chirimía* bands. The *puya* is an even faster and more rhythmically complex style. Many variations on the conquest dance, a symbolically erotic dance of African origin that frequently includes the use of a handkerchief as a prop, may accompany all these styles.

The eclecticism of life in *la Costa* has produced music that, though associated with black culture, may come from diverse origins. The fandango is of Spanish origin, but the term has several meanings: it can denote a place where festivities occur, or a musical style used to accompany two kinds of dance (Zapata 1967:94). One is a dance in a circle, similar to the *cumbia*, and the other is a processional dance that commences nearly all carnivals. There is no set instrumentation: the *conjunto de pito*,

FIGURE 3   A *cumbia* ensemble. From top left: *guachos, pito, llamador, bombo, tambor mayor.* Photograph courtesy of George List.

conjunto de gaita, accordion, brass bands, or drums alone may perform the fandango. Even though it is a European genre, it has been appropriated by blacks in Colombia and adapted to African-derived performance, especially by the use of disjunct rhythms.

The *chirimía* band is believed to have originated in Chocó Province, northwest Colombia (Pacific coast). In its earlier forms, its instruments included *bombo, cununo,* brass instruments, and cymbals, playing European genres such as the *contradanza* and the fandango. The *chirimía* is an example of European instruments and genres being adapted to local, African-derived performance, evident in the rhythmic style of the drums. *Chirimía* groups have expanded and spread throughout Colombia. They usually perform outdoors at parades and festivals. Common genres adapted by them are the *jota,* the *bambuco,* and the *porro.*

Vallenato emerged early in the twentieth century in northeast Colombia, influenced by work-related songs (*zafras*) and the Spanish *romance.* The term *vallenato* referred to a trio—accordion, *caja* (small, single-headed drum), and stick rasp (*guacharaca*)—that performed merengues and *paseos* (figure 5). After a time, the term began to be used to describe a style and genre associated with the department of Valledupar. The music, though less polyrhythmic than the *cumbia,* had a rural, narra-

FIGURE 4   Percussion parts of a *porro,* performed by Los Gaiteros de San Jacinto (*gaitas* not shown). With sticks, a player strikes the *bombo* shell (downstems) and right head (upstems). The player strikes the single head of the *tambor mayor* on its edge (downstems) and in the center (upstems). Playing methods include: o = open; × = closed; > = slap; . = short; —= long. Transcription by Lawrence J. App from the video *Gaiteros: Music from the Northern Coast of Colombia* (Bermúdez n.d.).

jota A Spanish song and dance form from which the *cueca* and other Hispanic-American forms may have developed

bambuco Colombian "national" song and pursuit couple-dance genre performed most often on the *tiple* as the main instrument

vallenato A rural musical and dance genre of northern Colombia featuring accordion, drum, and scraper

copla 'Couplet', Spanish derived narrative musical genre of Chile, Colombia, and other Hispanic-American countries

zafra Colombian field song sung by farmers for their own entertainment

vaquería Colombian cattle song genre, sung by herders to quiet the animals and communicate among themselves

FIGURE 5 Melody and accompanying percussion parts of a *paseo* performed by a *conjunto de vallenato.* The single head of the *caja* is struck with sticks on the edge (downstems) and in the center (upstems). Transcription by Lawrence J. App from *The Noble Songbook of Colombia* (Piñeros Corpos n.d.).

tive style and a lively rhythm, which appealed to *costeños,* people from *la Costa.* In much of Colombia by the 1970s, *vallenato* groups had become popular as vehicles through which singers could romanticize rural life in the northeast coast and to extol their own virtues (see Marre 1983).

Another source of diversion through music is the performance of songs of praise or derision. Traditionally, *décimas* are a strictly vocal form of ten lines, whose melodies and verses derive from the European *copla.* The vocal style and lack of synchronization between accent and text indicate an African influence. Usually, two *decimeros* compete in a display of musical skill that includes adherence to strict musical formulas and ingenuity at incorporating texts that alternately praise themselves and deride their opponents. The audience helps determine the outcome of the competition and may even become the subject of the *coplas.*

Zafras appear to have been common among blacks in the Atlantic coastal area. They consist of *coplas* sung by a farmer for his or her own amusement, with texts usually based on humorous or philosophical topics. *Vaquerías* are songs used by cattle herders to quiet the animals and communicate among themselves. Children's game-playing songs and lullabies, called *arrullos* (not the same genre as on the Pacific coast), are mostly European derived, but the use of free rhythm and melodic overlap show some African influence. The continued use and dispersion of *zafras* and *vaquerías* is unlikely.

The music of the interior is generally more European in character, but traces of Africanisms have diffused into it from the coastal areas, earlier by migration of blacks and later through technological means. Throughout Colombia since the 1800s, the *bambuco* (not the same as with the *currulao*) has been a popular genre and a source of national pride [see COLOMBIA]. Though the melodies are distinctly European and the compound *sesquiáltera* pattern, combining 6/8 and 3/4, recalls "colonial rhythm" (Olsen 1980:392), the disjunct placement of rhythmic cycles and offbeat accents seem to be African traits.

AFRO-COLOMBIAN POPULAR MUSIC

Modern Colombia has been shaped by many of the processes affecting other developing nations, including urbanization, technological advancement, and political and social unrest. As blacks have migrated to the cities, African-derived forms have been diffused into mainstream culture or sometimes abandoned in favor of more modern forms. The availability of technology, especially radio and sound recordings, has hastened the processes of acculturation and diffusion. Some traditional black musics such as *cumbia* and *vallenato* have spread far beyond their local roots and have affected national and international styles. Conversely, black populations, even in some remote areas, are exposed to an increasing variety of outside music. They incorporate these influences in their own styles, often bringing in other African-derived music, including that from Cuba (*son*), Jamaica (*reggae*), and Nigeria (*jùjú*), and music from Europe and the United States.

In the late twentieth century, the violence traditionally associated with the instability of Colombia's political system was exacerbated by increased factionalism. Leftist guerrilla groups, exporters of illicit drugs, and right-wing paramilitary troops undermine hopes for democracy, as struggles for power often end in bloodshed. Efforts for black political solidarity and preservation of black cultural identity were reflected in the constitution of 1991, which provided for the protection of cultural identity of ethnic groups, but basic issues of human rights have taken precedence for most Colombians. Despite these problems, Afro-Colombian musics are being increasingly accepted into the Colombian mainstream, especially by younger people. As an avenue for defining social identity and expressing protest, music provides a safer outlet than political activism. An emerging sense of black identity is being negotiated and defined through the re-Africanization of Colombian pop music and cultural borrowing of other black musics.

Cumbia

Historically, *cumbia* and *vallenato* are the two most popular styles that have evolved out of the traditional music of Colombia. *Cumbia* began appearing in the coastal towns in the 1920s, and by the 1930s it had spread to the interior. As it attracted a more sophisticated (that is, mestizo) audience, it lost much of its polyrhythmic vigor, gradually developing a four-beat, loping rhythm. *Costeño* bands that played *cumbia*, such as *Los Corraleros de Majagual*, added brass, electric bass, and occasionally accordion, but the clarinet became the most popular melody instrument for the commercial style. By the 1960s, *cumbia* was the nonpareil music of Colombia; it was standard fare at any dance or fiesta, and it took on the air of a national music.

As *cumbia* gradually went out of style in Colombia during the 1970s, it gained popularity elsewhere, spreading through Central America to Mexico and into Tex-

Mex bands. *Cumbia* became part of the repertoire of many salsa groups, which frequently used electric instruments and slick brass arrangements to accommodate the tastes of new audiences. The term *cumbia* now refers to three different genres: the rural *cumbia* of the *conjunto de pito*; the style of *cumbia* popularized by *costeño* groups in the 1960s, and the salsa-influenced *cumbia*. The traditional form of *cumbia* is now mostly performed at festivals by folkloric groups such as Totó la Momposina y Sus Tambores (1993), whereas contemporary artists have revitalized the genre's popularity by reincorporating African polyrhythms into the modern style.

When salsa emerged as a style in the 1970s, it rapidly displaced *cumbia* as the most popular style in Colombia. Though it had originated in New York and Puerto Rico, many Colombians adopted it as their own music. Many Colombian artists had successful careers in the salsa market, at home and abroad. Over time, many recordings followed the proven formulas of the salsa industry, yet some Colombian artists, such as Jairo Varela y Grupo Niche (from Medellín), have used salsa as a vehicle for expressing their black musical and cultural identity. The black Colombian salsa star Joe Arroyo (1992, 1993a, 1993b) has gained popularity by incorporating African-derived musics into the salsa idiom. Considered one of the most innovative and exciting composer-performers in Colombia and abroad, he has fused *cumbia*, merengue, and salsa with music of the French and English Caribbean into vibrant new forms.

Vallenato

When *vallenato* spread from its rural context into the cities, its rhythms got simpler and other instruments—bass, guitar, conga, cowbell—joined the accordion-drum-scraper trio, modernizing the sound of the ensemble. By the 1980s, *vallenato* superseded salsa as the preferred music among blacks throughout much of Colombia. *Vallenato* groups developed a rhythmic intensity, exciting basses, and virtuosic displays on the accordion by artists such as Alejo Durán, but the main focus remained on lyrics, whose subjects ranged from sentimental ballads to political protest and praise of wealthy patrons. Sensationalism probably exaggerates the influence of Colombian drug money on promoting *vallenato*, since its popularity transcended many social sectors. It is now commercially exported to audiences outside Colombia in various forms—the more traditional style, versions that include salsa brass arrangements, and a new style called *charanga-vallenato*.

Outside influences

Along the Atlantic coast, particularly in Cartagena and Barranquilla, other African-derived music began to be imported, perhaps as early as the 1960s. By the 1970s, recordings of African-derived popular music were being appropriated and recontextualized by local DJs as symbols of an emerging black identity. Caribbean styles such as soca, merengue, reggae, and Haitian music have a strong appeal to black communities as do African *jùjú* and *soukous*. The Colombian middle class originally referred to this style by the pejorative term *música champeta* (meaning something crude), but gradually a broad range of younger audiences began calling African-derived musics therapy music (*música terapía*), a way to feel good (Pacini 1993a). Colombian artists have responded to this demand by creating local styles from various sources, such as *caribeños* (*zouk* and salsa), *cumbiamberos* (*cumbia* and *son*), and *reggaespañol* (hiphop or dance-hall reggae with Spanish lyrics). The revolutionary lyrics of Fela Anikulapo Kuti (of Nigeria) and Bob Marley (of Jamaica) have inspired a movement toward messages of black identity and resistance in popular Afro-Colombian lyrics. These contemporary styles became even more popular among blacks as older music was appropriated by the mainstream, mestizo population.

MEDIATED AND LIVE PERFORMANCE

Technology, particularly the media and recordings, has had the biggest impact on musical contexts in Colombia. Discos Fuentes was the first Colombian recording company to promote national artists abroad, but current European and American appetites for exotic music have encouraged an ever greater market for Colombian musicians, many of whom receive distribution through major international labels, including Sony, Virgin, and Mango records. At the other end of the spectrum, cassette piracy supplies many of Colombia's poorer peoples with cheap copies of local and international pop musics. Beginning in the 1950s, DJs with mobile sound systems (*picós*) began playing a variety of music catering to black *costeños* and by the 1970s had become an important factor in disseminating African-derived music. For local dances, DJs often featured unauthorized recordings of *soukous* and other Afro-Pop musics on powerful and elaborately decorated *picós*. In response to changing social conditions, the context for *picó* performances gradually changed from family parties in private homes to hired engagements for dances held in temporary structures called *casetas* 'cottages' (Pacini 1993b).

Music festivals sponsored by private companies or by the government have appeared throughout Colombia, providing exposure for artists and venues for a variety of styles. The popularity of *vallenato* spawned several festivals or competitions, some sponsored by record companies such as the one in San Pelayo, or state events such as the Valledupar Fiesta de Vallenato, held each spring. The winner of the competition is decided on the basis of musical talent and the singer's cleverness at devising musical texts. African-derived folkloric music of Colombia is being performed by groups such as La Negra Grande de Colombia at festivals, with lesser-known *gaitero* and *pitero* ensembles. The Festival de Música del Caribe, founded in Cartagena in 1983, has grown to include major Caribbean and African artists representing many different styles. The Green Moon Festival, another festival emphasizing musics of common African heritage, began in 1987 on the Colombian island of San Andrés.

Besides mass media, recordings, and festivals, several contexts have evolved to incorporate music and/or dance. Beginning in the 1960s, *bailaderos* were established in private homes; these operate primarily on weekends and holidays, serving food, alcohol, and music for dancing, usually from a stereo system. As a focal point for urban black culture, the *bailaderos* were defined largely by the music played there. In the 1980s, *vallenato* music was featured exclusively at the *bailaderos* as an emblem of black community at a time when it was not accepted by mestizo culture (Wade 1993). Salsa or *vallenato* bars cater to a mixed, though primarily black clientele, and feature music and alcohol—but no dancing because it interferes with liquor sales. A venue that includes music and dancing is the *discoteca*, modeled after discos in Europe and the United States. *Discotecas* are usually elaborately decorated with lights and sound systems. Though patronized mostly by mestizos, they play salsa, *vallenato*, and other Latin, Caribbean, and American styles.

FURTHER STUDY

The primary ethnomusicological studies of the Colombian coastal areas were conducted during the 1960s by Norman E. Whitten Jr. on the Pacific coast, which historically includes coastal Ecuador and Colombia as a contiguous culture area (n.d., 1965, 1967, 1968, 1974; Whitten and Contreras 1966), and George List on the Atlantic coast (1966, 1967, 1973, 1980, 1983). Important studies of contemporary Colombian coastal musical culture include works of Egberto Bermúdez (1985, 1994), Jeremy Marre and Hannah Charlton (1985), and Deborah Pacini Hernández (1992, 1993a, 1993b), the ethnographic work of Peter Wade (1993), and studies of political economy by Charles Bergquist et al. (1992). Films by Marre (1983) and

Bermúdez (n.d.) are particularly important for contextualizing the music of northern Colombia.

REFERENCES

Bergquist, Charles, Ricardo Peñaranda, and Gonzalo Sánchez, eds. 1992. *Violence in Colombia: The Contemporary Crisis in Historical Perspective.* Wilmington, Del.: Scholarly Resources.

Bermúdez, Egberto. 1985. *Los instrumentos musicales en Colombia.* Bogotá: Universidad Nacional de Colombia.

———. 1994. "Syncretism, Identity, and Creativity in Afro-Colombian Musical Traditions." In *Music and Black Ethnicity: The Caribbean and South America*, ed. Gerard Béhague, 225–238. Miami: North- South Center, University of Miami.

———. N.d. *Gaiteros: Music from the Northern Coast of Colombia.* Video.

Cáceres, Abraham. 1978. "Preliminary Comments on the Marimba in the Americas." In *Discourse in Ethnomusicology: Essays in Honor of George List,* ed. Caroline Card et al., 225–250. Bloomington: Archives of Traditional Music, Indiana University.

Cantos Costeños: Folksongs of the Atlantic Coastal Region of Colombia. 1973. Produced and recorded by George List with the assistance of Delia Zapata Olivella, Manuel Zapata Olivella, and Winston Caballero Salguedo. Ethnosound EST 8003. LP disk.

Joe Arroyo y La Verdad. 1992. *Rebellión.* World Circuit WCD 015. Compact disc.

———. 1993a. *Fuego.* Sony CDZ 81063. Compact disc.

———. 1993b. *Grandes éxitos.* Vol. 2. Vedisco 1017–2. Compact disc.

List, George. 1966. "The Musical Bow at Palenque." *Journal of the International Folk Music Council* 18:36–50.

———. 1967. "The Folk Music of the Atlantic Littoral of Colombia, An Introduction." In *Music in the Americas,* ed. George List and Juan Orrego-Salas, 115–122. The Hague: Indiana University Research Center in Anthropology, Folklore, and Linguistics.

———. 1980. "African Influences in the Rhythmic Organization of Colombian Costeño Music." *Latin American Music Review* 1(1):6–17.

———. 1983. *Music and Poetry in a Colombian Village.* Bloomington: Indiana University Press.

Marre, Jeremy. 1983. *Shotguns and Accordions.* Newton, N. J.: Shanachie Records. Video.

Marre, Jeremy, and Hannah Charlton. 1985. *Beats of the Heart: Popular Music of the World.* New York: Pantheon.

Olsen, Dale A. 1980. "Folk Music of South America—A Musical Mosaic." In *Musics of Many Cultures: An Introduction,* ed. Elizabeth May, 386–425. Berkeley: University of California Press.

Pacini Hernández, Deborah. 1992. Review of *Cumbia, Cumbia! Ethnomusicology* 36(2):288–296.

———. 1993a. "Spanish Caribbean Perspectives on World Beat." *The World of Music* 35(2):48–69.

———. 1993b. "The Picó Phenomenon at Cartagena, Colombia." *América Negra* 6:69–115.

Piñeros Corpos, Joaquín. N.d. *The Noble Songbook of Colombia.* Bogotá: Universidad de los Andes, LP 501–503. LP disk and liner notes.

Totó la Momposina y Sus Tambores. 1993. *La candela vida.* Carol / Real World CD 2337–2. Compact disc.

Wade, Peter. 1993. *Blackness and Race Mixture: The Dynamics of Racial Identity in Colombia.* Baltimore: Johns Hopkins University Press.

Whitten, Norman E., Jr. 1967. Liner notes to *Afro-Hispanic Music from Western Colombia and Ecuador.* Folkways Records FE 4376.

———. 1965. *Class, Kinship, and Power in an Ecuadorian Town: The Negroes of San Lorenzo.* Stanford: Stanford University Press.

———. 1968. "Personal Networks and Musical Contexts in the Pacific Lowlands of Colombia and Ecuador." *Man* 3:50–63.

———. 1974. *Black Frontiersman: A South American Case.* Cambridge, Mass.: Shenkman.

Whitten, Norman E., Jr., and Aurelio Fuentes Contreras. 1966. "¡Baile Marimba!" *Journal of the Folklore Institute* 3(2):170–183.

Zapata Olivella, Delia. 1967. "An Introduction to the Folk Dances of Colombia." *Ethnomusicology* 11(1):91–96.

Ecuador
John M. Schechter

Musical Instruments
Musical Contexts and Genres
Performers and Performances
Musical Ideologies and Aesthetics
Further Study

One of the smallest countries in South America, Ecuador is extremely varied—geographically, climatologically, and culturally. Its name means 'equator', from the fact that the equator goes right through it. Yet Ecuador has snow-capped mountains because it is an Andean country, and it has a dense tropical forest because east of the Andes is the Amazon basin. Between the Andes and the Amazon is the densely and tropically forested *montaña,* the rugged foothills of the Andes.

The native American populations of Ecuador include descendants of many pre-Inca people and those whom the Inca subjugated. Some, such as the Shuar (earlier called Jívaro) of the tropical forest, were feared as headhunters by colonists and explorers; others, such as the Otavaleños (Quichua, native Americans in the Otavalo Valley), have become wealthy textile artisans.

Ecuador is archaeologically rich. Prehistoric coastal cultures, especially, produced elaborate figurines and musical instruments. Likewise, the highlands were the sites of ancient cultures that used music in a variety of contexts, some of them partially explained by the iconography of ceramic vases. The archaeological ceramic musical instruments in the collection of the Museo Arqueológico of the Banco Central del Ecuador, Quito, reveal a lengthy development with considerable formal variety. The roughly 130 vessel flutes in this collection are ductless, and their resonating chambers are globular in shape. Of the four types of vessel flutes in this collection, the first is a miscellaneous group, having an unobstructed resonating chamber; the external shapes are most often those of animals or birds. These instruments represent the archaeological phases of Manteño, Bahía, Jama-Coaque, and Guangala of the coastal region. The second type of vessel flute has the northern sierra as provenance, representing the ceramic styles of Piartal and Tuza; these display a consistent design, all having four holes for fingers and one for the embouchure. The fundamental shape of these instruments is of a stylized conch shell whose construction mimics the interior spiral of the shell. Decoration includes geometric motives, monkeys, and birds. The third group is the largest, also with consistency of design—in this case a single finger hole and a large embouchure hole; once again, there is the imitation of a natural shell, and decorative motives are geometric and zoomorphic. These instruments belong to the ceramic styles of Piartal and Tuza. The fourth type is miscellaneous in shape; these vessels appear to be designed primarily as containers, though they can also create sounds. Pitch analysis reveals that the second group has the largest average gamut and the smallest average interval. The coastal instruments have generally greater variety in shape, whereas highland instruments are typically larger and evince a higher-quality ceramic technique (Nyberg 1974).

MUSICAL INSTRUMENTS

Currently housed in the Casa de la Cultura, Quito, the Pedro Pablo Traversari Collection of Musical Instruments is an important repository of European and South American archaeological and modern exemplars. Perhaps one-third of the instruments are on display; the remainder are in storage. Many stored instruments are broken and in disarray, lacking proper identification. A wonderfully diverse collection—including a harp with crocodile-shell sound box, a lyre-guitar, a rabel, a pre-Columbian *kena,* an eighteenth-century Italian oboe—it has been carefully catalogued by Richard Rephann (1978).

Idiophones

The variety in idiophones in Ecuador is greater than that for aerophones or membranophones. Struck idiophones include *tuntui* and marimbas [see AFRO-COLOMBIAN TRADITIONS]. The Shuar play the *tuntui* (or *tunduy*), a large hollow log idiophone. Taboo for women, it is used to send signals of war, death, or event. It has a penetrating sound that carries up to 5 kilometers away. Used by Cayapa Indians and Afro-Ecuadorians in Esmeraldas Province, marimbas are discussed below.

Shaken idiophones include fruit-capsule rattles, cowbell chains, gourd rattles, tubular rattles (including the *guasá*), and *maracas.* The Shuar play the *shakap, makich,* and *chilchil*—all types of fruit-capsule rattle. Women place the *shakap* on their waists and dance with it, whereas the *makich* is attached to the ankles for dancing. As described below, the Quichua of Imbabura and Pichincha provinces wear chains ("series") of typically twelve *cencerros,* or cowbells, tied to a leather cape; the bells sound as dancing men play side-blown flutes. *Cencerros,* likewise mounted on the back, may be seen today also at dancing during the Fiesta de los Diablos (2 February) in Spain. Afro-Ecuadorians of the Chota River Valley, Imbabura, and of neighboring Esmeraldas Province play gourd rattles (*maracas*) and tubular rattles (*alfandoques* and *guasás*). The usage of *alfandoques* dates back at least to the 1800s in the Chota River Valley (Carvalho-Neto 1964:80).

Scraped idiophones include an animal's jawbone whose teeth are scraped—or the jawbone is shaken (called *quijada* in some places of Ecuador, Colombia, Peru, and Mexico; in Colombia, the term *carraca llanera* is also found). The jawbone is used by Ibero-Ecuadorians and Afro-Ecuadorians in Imbabura and Esmeraldas. The notched gourd (*güiro*), scraped with a nail or comb, is found among the same two groups in the same regions; moreover, the *güiro* is being incorporated into Quichua ensembles in Imbabura (Coba Andrade 1979:71–73).

Membranophones

Single-headed and double-headed membranophones appear in Ecuador. Double-headed types probably predominate in the 1990s. Single-headed drums include the *cununo* and the *zambomba.* The *cununo,* found in cylindrical and conical shapes, is tuned by means of wooden wedges and is played with the hands. It resembles the *tambor mayor* of the Atlantic coastal region of Colombia. Two *cununos* form part of the ensemble for the *currulao,* a secular ritual of Afro-Ecuadorians of Esmeraldas Province in the Pacific littoral region of northwestern Ecuador. The *currulao* ensemble incorporates the double-headed *bombo* drum, a marimba suspended from the rafters of a special house and played by two men, and *guasás*, bamboo rattles played by women. The *zambomba,* a clay friction drum, utilizes a cane rod as a friction stick. It is played by mestizos of Pichincha Province. Organological cousins in Spain include the *eltzagor* (Basque region), *sanbomba, zambomba,* and *ximbomba* (Catalonia and the Balearic Islands).

Three important types of double-headed drum are the *caja,* the *bombo,* and the *bomba*. A frame drum, the *caja* is found among Afro-Americans of Imbabura and Esmeraldas provinces and Quichua of Tungurahua Province. In Tungurahua, the *caja* is played along with *bombo* and side-blown flutes during the festival of Corpus Christi. With these other instruments, it creates the *orquesta de toros,* which accompanies masked youths (*toros*) as they dart about the plaza. A larger frame drum than the *caja,* the *bombo* appears notably among highland Quichua. The *bombos* of the Salasaca Indians of Tungurahua Province are among the largest drums in the country. The Salasaca are known for the elaborate painted designs on their drumheads (for a contextual photo, see Schechter 1994a:61).

At Corpus Christi in central highland Tungurahua and Cotopaxi provinces, *bombos* are played alone (by a single musician), in consort with *cajas,* and in pipe-and-tabor fashion with *pingullo* (the painted-drumhead version). Salasaca painted drums may contain a snare. Elsewhere in the Ecuadorian highlands, the *bombo* appears in Licán, Chimborazo Province, and among Afro-Ecuadorians of the Chota River Valley, Imbabura and Carchi provinces.

Afro-Ecuadorians of certain villages in the Intag and Chota river valley region of Imbabura and in Río Limones, Esmeraldas, play *bombas* with their hands while seated, holding them between the knees (for a contextual photo, see Schechter 1994c:288). The *bomba* has been used by Afro-Ecuadorians for at least a hundred years in Chota (Carvalho-Neto 1964:99), where it provides accompaniment for ensembles that otherwise incorporate guitars, *guasás* (bamboo or metal rattles, filled with seeds or stones), and vocals. These ensembles perform the *bomba* (same name as drum), a lively dance in *sesquiáltera* meter (juxtaposed 6/8 and 3/4), and other genres.

Aerophones

Pipe and tabor and other flutes

The pipe-and-tabor technique, mentioned above in the discussion of *bombo,* joins a membranophone and an aerophone into a single instrument played by one person (figure 1). Evidence for pipe-and-tabor technique suggests traditions deeply rooted in Spain and in the Americas: the Iberian *txistu* with *tamboril* [*thun thun*] (Basque), *flaviol* with *tamboret* (Catalonia), *txirula* with *salteri,* the latter a box zither, not a drum (Basque), and *pito* with *tambor* (Salamanca, León) find Western Hemispheric counterparts in several different types of panpipe-with-drum combinations on the Peruvian-Bolivian altiplano—in the *erkencho* (clarinet, made of horn, with reed) with *caja* of northwest Argentina; and in the *pingullo*-with-*bombo* of the Ecuadorian central Andes (Tungurahua and Cotopaxi).

Known as *pingullo* in Ecuador (written variously *pincullo, pincollo, pinkayllo, pinkillo, pinkullo, pinquillo* for its different manifestations in Peru, Bolivia, and northwestern Argentina), the aerophone part of this instrument is an end-blown duct flute. Often made of bamboo, the *pingullo* typically has two anterior finger holes and one posterior, making it apt for pipe-and-tabor usage.

A duct flute with six anterior finger holes, the *pífano* is played by one person (often a Quichua musician), typically with a second musician playing the *tamboril,* a double-headed drum varying in size. On ritual, festive, or amatory occasions in the

FIGURE 1 A man plays a *pingullo* and a *bombo* in the street of a barrio in Quito, Ecuador. Photo by Charles Sigmund, 1975.

The use of harps dates back in Ecuador to the 1700s, when they played an important role in the evangelistic work of Jesuits in the Marañón River zone of the Peruvian-Ecuadorian Oriente.

Oriente region of Ecuador, Shuar musicians play the *pinkui*, a side-blown flute with one blowhole and two finger holes. The *kena*, an open notched flute, found traditionally in the southern and central Andes of Peru and Bolivia, respectively, and in northwestern Argentina and less often in Ecuador, is nevertheless played in ensembles by many younger Quichua in northern Ecuadorian Andean villages and towns.

Trumpets

In Ecuador, the *bocina*, a simple trumpet, encompasses a large family of aerophones. It may be long and straight like the *huarumu* (Carvalho-Neto 1964:228–229) or, as among the Salasaca in central highland Tungurahua Province, composed of several curved segments of cow horn joined with a *guadúa* bamboo bell (Coba 1979:79, 93). The Afro-Ecuadorians of the Chota Valley play different-size *puros,* gourd aerophones (such as the *chile frito* of Guerrero, Mexico) in the traditional *banda mocha* ensemble of this region: gourds, leaves, small combs, *bombo,* and cymbals, perhaps with a European trumpet (Coba 1979:87, 94).

The people of several Ecuadorian highland provinces use a conch-shell trumpet (*churu*). Since at least the 1800s, its sounding has called Quichua to congregate for festive occasions or for *minga,* a communal work gang. For the same purposes, the *churu,* also known as *quipa* (after the Peruvian Quechua *qquepa*), is used not only in Imbabura but also in Cotopaxi, Tungurahua, and Chimborazo provinces. Peruvian conch-shell trumpets date back to the Chavín era (900–200 B.C.) and were used through the Inca period and into the twentieth century.

Panpipes

The *rondador,* a single-unit Ecuadorian panpipe, comprises from eight to thirty-four or more tubes set not in staircase arrangement (as in the central Andes), but in zigzag fashion. Like the harp, it is frequently played by blind musicians on street corners and in marketplaces (figure 2). Performance on either of these instruments affords the (typically male) musician a means by which to earn an income when traditional agricultural pursuits might be impossible.

TRACK 19

In addition to the unique array of tubes, the tuning and performance of the *rondador* are also distinctive: adjacent tubes may be a major second apart, or a major or minor third, a perfect fourth or fifth, or a major or minor sixth; and adjacent tubes (especially thirds and perfect fourths) are typically played simultaneously, notably at the ends of phrases (Olsen et al. 1987). *Rondadores* are typically of cane, sometimes painted with the yellow, blue, and red of the Ecuadorian flag; smaller types may be made of condor or vulture quills.

Chordophones

Chordophones include *tumank (tsayantur), paruntsi, keer (kitiar), bandolín,* guitar (*guitarra*), harp (*arpa*), and numerous variations. The *tumank,* or *tsayantur,* and the

FIGURE 2   A beggar at the market in Cotacachi, Ecuador, plays a *rondador*. Photo by Charles Sigmund, 1975.

paruntsi are musical bows. With the mouth used as resonator, the *tumank* appears among the Shuar in the Oriente region; the *paruntsi* is found among the Quichua of Imbabura. The *keer*, or *kitiar*, is a bowed lute with which the Shuar accompany love songs and shamanic chanting (see Crawford 1979). The *bandolín* is a type of flat-backed mandolin with five courses of triple strings struck with a plectrum. It is played by Quichua and Iberian-Ecuadorians in the highlands; certain Imbabura villages, such as Ilumán, used to be famous for their proliferation of *bandolines*. In the region of Cotacachi, Imbabura, one finds the tuning g″–e♭″–c″–g″–e♭″.

Guitar and guitar variants

Quichua and Ibero-Ecuadorians in the highlands play the guitar, basic for the accompaniment of such folkloric genres (*música nacional*) as *albazo*, *pasacalle*, and *pasillo*. The Quichua regularly use it to accompany the *sanjuán*. Moreover, the Afro-Ecuadorians of Chota are guitarists. Certain Chota musicians, such as Germán Congo, have achieved notable virtuosity on the *requinto* (sometimes slightly smaller in size than the regional guitar), which leads ensembles.

The *charango*, a small guitar whose center of diffusion is Peru-Bolivia, is sold in quantities in music stores in Imbabura—frequented by large numbers of Western tourists; some ensembles of younger Quichua are now incorporating it, since they see it included by visiting Peruvian groups who come to play in the larger Ecuadorian cities.

Harps

The use of harps dates back in Ecuador to the 1700s, when they played an important role in the evangelistic work of Jesuits in the Marañón River zone of the Peruvian-Ecuadorian Oriente (Chantre y Herrera 1901:653–654, 661–662) and the Andean highlands, where harps are said to have been extremely widespread among indigenous peoples (Recio 1947 [1773]:426). In eighteenth-century highland Ecuador, Indians at missions played harps for the mass, baptism, and Via Crucis; in the Marañón region, the harp took its place alongside the violin to perform in Corpus Christi processions (Chantre y Herrera 1901:661–662).

Three principal kinds of Ecuadorian diatonic harps are in use in rural towns and

FIGURE 3   While a harpist and a beater (*gol-peador*) from Imbabura play, two women and a child listen, near Cotacachi, Ecuador. Photo by John Schechter, August 1990.

FIGURE 3   While a harpist and a beater (*gol-peador*) from Imbabura play, two women and a child listen, near Cotacachi, Ecuador. Photo by John Schechter, August 1990.

villages: the Imbabura harp (*arpa imbabureña*), the folk harp (*arpa folclórica*), and the Ecuadorian-Paraguayan harp (*arpa ecuatoriana-paraguaya*) (Schechter 1992a).

The Imbabura harp is of cedar, with wooden nails in the construction of the sound box; sound emanates from three holes in the sound box, the holes on either side of the short forepillar. The neck is uncarved. Quichua male musicians in Imbabura Province perform pieces from the *sanjuán*, *pareja*, and *vacación* genres on this instrument at children's wakes and at weddings; rhythmic accompaniment for the harpist is provided by a *golpeador*—a friend or family member who kneels by the harp and beats the sound box in rhythm. Quichua harpists are typically soloists, with *golpeador* (figure 3).

TRACK 20

The folkloric harp is considerably larger than the Imbabura harp; fine exemplars of the former are made in Ambato, Tungurahua Province, in furniture makers' workshops. This high-headed harp with a tall pillar is distinguished by an elaborately carved neck, the carving typically in leaf or floral patterns (Ambato is well known for its fruits and flowers); moreover, the finial, or top, of the pillar is also carved—commonly with rounded scrollwork or a human head (for photo, see Schechter 1992a: chapter 2).

The Ecuadorian-Paraguayan harp has a neck in the form of an exaggerated inverted arch, a shape that dates back in Ecuador to the early 1800s and characterizes Paraguayan harps of the 1990s. The design of soundholes in the Ecuadorian-Paraguayan harp—a painted S shape, terminating in small holes—dates back to harps of seventeenth-century Spain (Schechter 1992a). Iberian-Ecuadorian harpists play *música nacional* genres on the folk harp and the Ecuadorian-Paraguayan harp as soloists or with other stringed instruments. Noted practitioners are Elías Imbaquingo (of a community near Cotacachi) on the Imbabura harp and Don César Muquinche (of Izamba, near Ambato) on folk harp and Ecuadorian-Paraguayan harp (Schechter 1992b:415–420).

MUSICAL CONTEXTS AND GENRES

This section treats musical genres in six broad contexts: religious settings, life-cycle rites, seasonal rites, the San Juan patronal festival, dance and music, and music as entertainment. The discussion of religious settings encompasses shamanic practices and the Christian festivals of Holy Week and Corpus Christi. The section on life-cycle focuses on the festive child's wake and the wedding. Seasonal rituals discussed include harvest songs (*jawaykuna,* sing. *jaway*) and the New Year's celebration (*año viejo* 'old year'). Music as entertainment focuses on the *currulao,* the marimba dance of Esmeraldas Province.

Coverage here is selective; one can find an enormous variety of musical genres and contexts in Ecuador, where multiple native American, Afro-American, and Ibero-American cultural groups exploit multiple ecological-geographical niches.

Shamanic healing

Native American peoples of Ecuador, like those of Venezuela, Peru, Chile, and other nations of South America, practice shamanic healing. Through song, frequently self-accompanied by idiophone, Ecuadorian jungle Quichua and Shuar shamans travel in the therapeutic process between this world and a realm of spirits. Musical style comparisons may be made between the shamanic songs of these two lowland groups, inasmuch as they share similar underlying etiological beliefs and behavioral aspects.

Notations by Karsten (1935) and melodies transcribed by Moreno Andrade (1830) point to tritonicity (triadic or nontriadic) as the traditional Shuar tonal gamut, especially in social dance-songs (Harner 1973); in many whistling and sung segments of shamanic curing, the established Shuar features—extensive tonic repetition, tritonicity, and dotted figures—are present (Harner 1973; List 1965). Shamanic songs in the curing ceremonies of Shuar and lowland Quichua are syllabic (Crawford 1979), reflecting the need in both cultures for extensive commentary during the ritual.

Processions

Whereas the shamanic phenomenon reflects an indigenous view of the nature and power of spirits to affect health, prominent processions in highland Ecuador—notably those for Holy Week and Corpus Christi—betray strong links to an imported belief system, Roman Catholicism, the most significant influence in colonial Latin America. Arriving in the Americas in the 1500s, 1600s, and 1700s, missionaries—notably in South America, the Jesuits—brought their European musical forms, musical instruments (violin, harp), and religious philosophy and practices. Thus, we find celebrations associated with prominent saints, processions at major junctures of the Roman Catholic liturgical calendar, and the ritual of the child's wake.

Holy Week

In highland Ecuador, indigenous processions for Holy Week date from at least the 1800s (Hassaurek 1867:161). During *Semana Santa* (Holy Week), the week before Easter, the Quichua who live in small communities (*comunas*) outside Cotacachi, Imbabura Province, conduct processions organized by *comuna*, each with its own icon (*santo*) that is adorned and carried during all Holy Week processions. Many icons depict stations of the cross; others venerate the Virgin Mary. The processions begin on Palm Sunday and are repeated on Wednesday evening, Holy Thursday evening, Good Friday at midday, and that evening.

On Palm Sunday in 1980, two types of musical performance were in evidence—the same types that were heard in each of the other daylight and evening processions observed in Cotacachi during Holy Week that year: cane side-blown flute (six finger holes) duos and trios, and the responsorial song of Jesus' Passion in Quichua. In the midst of each of these processions, a male Quichua ritual specialist (*catequista*) led responsorial singing of one of the Passions. Musical settings of Jesus' sufferings and death as told by the evangelists, the Passions were sung a cappella, in this case in the

In medieval Europe and in twentieth-century Andean South America, theater occurred and occurs outdoors: Europe had its miracle and mystery plays, and modern Ecuador has its pantomime involving the simulation of planting.

Quichua language. None of the singers performed from written music: only the *catequista* carried the hand-printed text, and the choral respondents (usually all female) echoed the *catequista's* sung lines.

Performed in Quichua and sharing the pentatonic mode with much Imbabura-area Quichua secular dance music, this and all Holy Week processional renditions by both men and women were sung without vibrato, with the same rhythmic freedom of phrase with which Gregorian chant, an import from Europe, is performed in church or cloister. An example that illustrates these features (figure 4) adapts a biblical Passion text:

> Huañuna horas ñami chayashka,
> Nishpa Jesusca, Diospac churica,
> Oracionmanta anchurijushpa,
> Huirto punguman chayagrijucpi. . . .

> Now having arrived at the hours of his death,
> He called Jesus, son of God,
> Going away, on account of the sentence imposed on him,
> Having arrived at the door of the garden. . . .

Strongly traditional in Spain, Holy Week appears vital in this hemisphere among Ibero-Americans and native Americans. The emphasis observed on the contribution of each Quichua *comuna* in Cotacachi Holy Week finds an echo in Silvia, Colombia, where each neighborhood (*barrio*) contributes to and participates in the celebration (Gradante 1980:45).

Corpus Christi

A similarly long lineage appears for the festival of Corpus Christi, a movable feast held on the Thursday after the seventh Sunday after Easter. The Spanish form of the rite was first incorporated in 1280 in Toledo, then Seville in 1282 and Barcelona in 1319 (Carreras y Candi 1933:556).

The syncretism of Corpus Christi in Ecuador is perhaps more profound than that of Holy Week. In the central highlands (Cotopaxi and Tungurahua provinces), the festival of "Corpus," as it is known there, brilliantly displays features drawn from medieval Roman Catholic ritual and native American Andean ritual. The rite juxtaposes the European facets of elaborate processional, incorporating pipe-and-tabor performance with a native Andean harvest celebration at the June solstice, the approximate date of Corpus Christi. Moreover, in medieval Europe and in twentieth-century Andean South America, theater occurred and occurs outdoors: in Europe, miracle and mystery plays; in modern Ecuador, pantomime involving simulation of planting (which follows close after the harvest), pairs of actors (with one often taking

FIGURE 4 Responsorial singing in the streets of Cotacachi, Imbabura Province, Ecuador; Wednesday of Holy Week, 2 April 1990. The text adapts a biblical Passion text. The melody shares the pentatonic mode with much Imbabura-area Quichua secular dance music. Transcription by John Schechter.

an animal role), and portrayals of devils—an aspect of street theater that has analogs to the north (black-Satan portrayals in Trinidad and Cumaná, Venezuela) and the south (multitiered devil-personages of carnival in Oruro, Bolivia).

The rite of the Ecuadorian "Corpus" incorporates at least three elements that have a two-hundred-year heritage: *danzantes*, pipe-and-tabor musical accompaniment for the *danzantes*, costumed indigenous dancers; and the erection of *castillos*, fruit-bearing poles. On 5 June 1980, I recorded the processional music of two musicians, each playing *pingullo* and *bombo* in a small village outside Patate, Tungurahua; they were accompanying the dancing of two processional *danzantes* (for a contextual photo, see Schechter 1994a:61).

Much the same type of pipe-and-tabor accompaniment to performing *danzantes* is described by an eighteenth-century Jesuit writer recording a "Corpus" in the Marañón Español region along the Peruvian-Ecuadorian border (Chantre y Herrera 1901:661–662). In addition, this writer describes the building of *castillos* along the route of the procession; he saw live animals, fish, fruit, and other foods. The *castillos* I observed, on "Corpus" proper (5 June 1980) and on its octave, were telephone-pole-like structures, sustaining one or two large, wooden, inverted triangles to which networks of strings had been attached; these strings held potatoes, peppers, bananas, gourds, and other fruits of the harvest. After they had been erected (in June 1980), one, two, or three men climbed them and tossed the fruits of the harvest down to the community, gathered in the plaza below. Following this sharing out of the harvest, two of the young men who had earlier formed an informal group of mischievous bulls (with cow-horn masks over their faces) took their place in front of an actual plow and, now as oxen, pulled the plow around the plaza, followed by a bull ensemble (*orquesta de toros*): one side-blown flute, one *caja* (small double-headed drum), and one *bombo*. The plow was followed by a man tossing out flour to simulate sowing.

In June 1980, "Corpus" proper featured musical performances by several ensembles (a local brass band, stationed on the church patio in the plaza, played national folk music), but the octave had only the bull ensemble. Rather than a musical celebration, the octave was dedicated primarily to street theater, notably pantomime. Most of the acting was in pairs. At one point, a man in normal dress entered the plaza; behind him came the master, in a Caucasian mask (*blanco*) and wearing an old suit with a large hat. They dropped the log for the small *castillo*. Then the master pretended that his hobbyhorse was bucking; the servant came over, grabbed the reins, patted it on the head, and calmed it down. This mime pair continued the bucking-calming routine for a short time then left the plaza. One more pair of mimes then appeared: a ram with four horns on his head, tied by rope to his master; they ran along together, the master repeatedly calling his ram, "Pachito, Pachito!"

One may find multiple transcriptions of "Corpus" *pingullo* melodies (to accompany *danzantes*) emanating all the way from northern Carchi down to southern Cañar and Azuay provinces (Moreno Andrade 1972). Comparisons reveal significant uniformities of style among these melodies; many are heavily tetratonic, some extending the tonal gamut to upper 7, thus creating pentatony, and others using the arpeggio of the minor dominant (Schechter 1994a).

Children's wakes

In native American, Afro-American, and Ibero-American cultures throughout Roman Catholic Latin America, a festive wake is celebrated at the death of an infant or young child. One finds accounts of such occasions in nineteenth-century Mediterranean-coastal Spain; in the Western Hemisphere, the rite is described back as far as 1788 (in Puerto Rico). This celebration is called most broadly *velorio del angelito*, or *wawa velorio* (as it is known among northern Ecuadorian highland Quichua), or *wawallo* (as it is known among Afro-Ecuadorians of the Chota River Valley, northern Ecuador), or *baquiné* (as it is known among African-Antillans of Puerto Rico). In the nineteenth or twentieth centuries, children's wakes have appeared in Argentina, Brazil, Chile, Colombia, Cuba, the Dominican Republic, Ecuador, Mexico, Nicaragua, Panama, Paraguay, Peru, Puerto Rico, and Venezuela. With rates of infant mortality high in Ecuadorian rural areas, the ritual continues to be practiced, though many believe it is dying out.

In Roman Catholic belief, a vital regeneration in Christ occurs through the administration of baptism, a sacrament that unconditionally promises salvation to a child dying in infancy. In Roman Catholic Spain and Latin America, the deceased infant is believed to dwell among the angels. This is a cause for rejoicing. Wherever the ritual has been celebrated, the body of the child has always been conspicuous by its presence, typically in the same room in which family and friends dance to the favorite music of the region, either the Valencian *jota* in the 1870s in Alicante Province, Spain (Davillier 1874:409), the *gato* in rural Buenos Aires Province, Argentina, in the 1870s (d'Aurignac 1890), or the *sanjuán* in rural Imbabura, Ecuador, in 1980 and 1990 (Schechter 1983, 1992b, 1994b).

The ritual makes a profound impact on those who observe it, whether nationals or foreign visitors. In some works of art, such as the painting *Velorio de Indios* by Ecuador's Joaquín Pinto (1842–1906), the ritual is depicted in a fundamentally objective fashion, with little "commentary" by the artist. In other instances, such as the canvas *El Velorio* (1893) by Puerto Rico's Francisco Oller y Cestero, or the short story *El Angelito* by Baldomero Lillo (1867–1923) of Chile, artists portray the festivity of the wake with considerable cynicism—even thinly veiled revulsion (Schechter 1994b).

In Ecuador, the child's prominent display sometimes takes on traits that might relate to earlier Inca practices. As depicted by Felipe Guamán Poma de Ayala, during the month of November (*Aia Marcai Quilla* 'Carry the Dead Month'), the dead were taken from their stone crypts, dressed in fine clothes, given food and drink, put onto litters, and carried through the streets from house to house and through the plaza (1836 [1615]:256–257). The 1573 *Relación (Geográfica de Indias)*, "*La Cibdad* [*sic*] *de Sant Francisco de Quito,*" discussing the burial rites of Quito-area Indians, is similar: the deceased is carried on a seat placed on a litter that the bearers carry on their shoulders; the corpse is also buried thus seated ("*La Cibdad de Sant Francisco del Quito*" 1897 [1573]:3:60–104). In nineteenth-century Quito, this custom was employed explicitly in Indian child burials: "The Indians and other indigent people [in Quito] bury their children after a very curious fashion. They hire an angel's suit and other ornaments in a church or convent, trick up the dead body, place it on a chair in a sitting posture, and carry it about in procession before they take it to the grave-yard" (Hassaurek 1867:151). A nearly identical description occurs in Charles Wiener's (1880:94–96) account of an Afro-Peruvian child's wake observed in the 1870s in Trujillo. Wiener describes the child being placed into a chair, paper wings being attached to the back (sometimes themselves attached to an owl's wings), and a crown of flowers being placed on the head. The child is thus processionally borne to the homes of relatives and friends. Wherever the cadaver is set down, a fiesta takes place.

A vivid account of a similar indigenous child-cadaver procession and festivity appears in Bemelmans's (1941:97–98) description for Baños, Ecuador, in the twentieth century. As for the northern Ecuadorian Quichua, Elsie Clews Parsons (1945:78–80, 83) provides an extended description of a child's wake and procession in Peguche, a village near Otavalo. A violinist provided dance music for the wake and the funeral procession the following morning. Again, as with the indigenous celebration documented outside Baños perhaps ten years earlier, Collier and Buitrón's (1971:151) description of a child's wake in and around Otavalo includes mention of the deceased child's being seated on a table or a platform.

From my own observations of four children's wakes (three in 1979–1980, one in 1990) in Quichua *comunas* on the slopes of Mount Cotacachi, Imbabura, many of the preceding facets are found, as always tempered by those aspects that pinpoint the rite to a specific locale. Indeed, research has supported the hypothesis that wherever it occurs in time and space, the Latin American or Iberian child's wake serves as a kind of microcosm of local cultural preferences in types of music, instruments, and dances. Thus, we are not surprised to find the Cotacachi Quichua *wawa velorio* reflecting its own locality's preferences. Violinists had provided the music some fifty years ago at a Quichua child's wake in Peguche (only some thirty minutes' drive from the wakes I attended outside the town of Cotacachi), but the Cotacachi Quichua tradition specifies solo harp, not violin, for the ritual. Pinto's *Velorio de Indios* describes a solo harp providing the music one hundred years ago. Like Valencian *jota* and Argentinian *gato* in their own times and places, the Cotacachi *sanjuán* and *pareja*, musical genres of Imbabura, are performed at the child's wake.

The most prominent dance music type in the area, *sanjuán,* is in simple duple meter, consisting of the regular repetition of a single, primary motive, with a secondary motive occasionally inserted. As noted above, Cotacachi Quichua harp per-

sanjuán In Imbabura, Ecuador, dance music for a child's wake performed on harp with *golpeador*

pareja In Imbabura, Ecuador, dance music for a child's wake performed on harp with *golpeador*

vacación In Imbabura, Ecuador, harp music for a child's wake, meant to drive away the

demon from beneath the platform supporting the dead child

albazo Ecuadoran national folk music genre

bomba Ecuadoran circle dance (often performed around a cross) and its music

sanjuanito 'Little *sanjuán*', an expanded form of *sanjuán*

formance practice calls for the hitting of a one-handed, rhythmic *golpe* on the harp's sound box by a second musician, who also typically sings. Whenever performed, *sanjuán* is danced with a strong back-and-forth stomp that coincides with the accent of the *golpe*. Slightly faster than *sanjuán* and in simple or compound duple meter, *pareja* requires a two-handed *golpe*. This genre, performed usually without text, has associations with couples, dancing, newlyweds, and dawn.

Complementing *sanjuán* and *pareja* at *wawa velorio* was a musical form called *vacación*, performed by harpists. An unmetrical genre with no sung text, it is a steady, percussive music, comprising several consecutive cycles of a gradually descending melody. It was always the first music performed in the deceased's home at the evening vigil, prefaced only by the harpist's tuning. Cotacachi Quichua harpists (*maistrus*) explained that performance of *vacación* at the beginning of the ritual was to drive away the *demonio* from beneath the platform supporting the child. Whenever action centered on the child (as during the late-night adorning of the body or the mother's lament at dawn), *vacación* would be performed as a kind of musical child marker. Unlike *sanjuán* and *pareja*, it is not danced, nor is it accompanied by a *golpe*. In the Pacific coastal area of Ecuador-Colombia, where the ritual is termed *chigualo*, Afro-Ecuadorians commence the rite with a man beating a rapid rhythm on the *bombo;* Whitten (1974:138) notes that one function of this percussive music is "frightening the body- or soul-snatching Tunda apparition away."

At *wawa velorio* in Cotacachi, merrymaking is compulsory. Visiting family and friends are continuously barraged with food (stewed corn, maize gruel) and drink (*trago* 'cane alcohol'). They are entreated throughout the night to dance to the music, and they are involved in tricks (notably played on those who fall asleep), teasing, and horseplay. The degree of lightheartedness and sheer playfulness cannot be overstated. Even at about 10:30 P.M., when the child is removed from its platform, placed on the floor, and adorned with ribbons on its wrists and waist and with a wreath of flowers on its head, the laughter and teasing continue, coinciding with the mother and god-mother's lamenting.

Weddings

The importance of the harp, and the degree to which the solo harp with *golpeador* is embedded in Cotacachi Quichua culture, are underscored by that instrument's prominence in marriage (*matrimonio*), another life-cycle ritual of the Imbabura region. The Imbabura Quichua wedding typically lasts five days, often from Saturday to Wednesday. At the conclusion of the nuptial mass (held in a church), all go to a local tavern, where a meal is served. Thereafter, all retire to the groom's father's house, for another meal (*miza*). The evening is spent in expressing gratitude to the godparents for their assistance.

The next morning, people may dance to the music of a local band performing Quichua *sanjuanes* and perhaps mestizo *albazos,* often with amplifiers and speakers.

FIGURE 5 Around a cross, the principals and the most honored guests at a Quichua wedding perform a circular dance (*bomba*); sitting in the shade beneath the eaves, a harpist plays. A *comuna* of Cotacachi, Imbabura Province, Ecuador. Photo by John Schechter, 1990.

At some point that morning, however (at 11:00 A.M. at a Cotacachi *comuna* wedding celebration I attended in October 1990), the *ñavi maillai* takes place. This is a traditional ritual, with *pareja* and *sanjuán* dance music provided throughout by solo harp and *golpeador*. The bandsmen, in my experience, retire from their musical instruments, temporarily leaving the site or staying to observe the ritual (Moreno Andrade 1972:191–195; Parsons 1945:58; Rubio Orbe 1946:286–287).

Carefully organized and led by a male Quichua, the *ñaupador* 'he who goes ahead', *ñavi maillai* is a mutual washing of the face and feet. After a community elder has recited prayers, the series of mutual face and feet washings takes place. The *ñaupador* first washes the face of the bride's mother, who then washes his feet; then he washes her feet. Thereafter may follow the godfather's washing of the face and/or feet of the godmother, then the godmother's washing of the godfather. The bride and groom then wash each other's face and feet. Then the groom's parents—the hosts, for the moment—take their turn washing each other's face and feet. This concluded, the principals and the most honored guests (community leaders and close friends) form a *bomba*, a circle around a cross, and dance to the harpist's music (figure 5). They suddenly break the circle and take it once around the house, only to rejoin it again when they return. *Trago* and *chicha* (a drink made from fermented maize) are consumed at the celebration, which moves the next day to the home of the bride's parents, where *ñavi maillai* is repeated.

Harvest

The Inca performed responsorial harvest songs; similarly, responsorial harvest work songs using the word *jaway* date back to seventeenth-century Quito (Carvalho-Neto 1964:255). In central-highland Chimborazo Province, indigenous men and women perform harvest songs (*jaway*), which set the pace of the chore of harvesting grain. In this genre, a male lead singer (*paki*) reignites traditional village rivalries or comments on love affairs while a chorus responds "*Jaway, jaway*" (Harrison 1989:21–22). The term for these songs varies with the province: *jaway* (the generic term) in Chimborazo, Tungurahua, Cañar, and Azuay; *jauchihua* in Cotopaxi; *jaichima* in Pichincha; and *jailima* in Imbabura (Carvalho-Neto 1964:256).

New Year's Eve

In many regions of the Ecuadorian highlands and coast, New Year's Eve is termed *año viejo* 'old year'. In a practice that dates back to the 1800s in Guayaquil and that was still observed among Quichua on Cotacachi's slopes in 1979–1980, the Old Man (Viejo), a gigantic straw-filled male effigy in old clothes—effectively symbolizing the year now completed—is constructed, often by children. At the moment of the new year's arrival, it is torched, and the crowd tosses its burning pieces around.

At *año viejo* in the Cotacachi *comuna* of Topo Grande (still lacking electricity in 1979–1980), two *comuna* guitarists performed *sanjuanes* while the straw man's burning garments were tossed about in the darkness. In the Quito version of the ritual, black clothes and a black mask cover the effigy, the Widow (*Viuda*). This ritual has parallels in Uruguay, where similar effigies, bearing the name of Judas, are burned at Christmastime; in Mexico, giant bamboo Judases are constructed to be burned or exploded on Good Friday evening or Holy Saturday morning. In certain parts of Eastern Europe, an effigy of a hag is borne and burned by children in a spring rite: the old woman stands for winter and must die, allowing spring rains to arrive for the crops (Slobin 1992:167–168). In the Andes, New Year's Eve falls during the same season when rains are needed to nourish corn and beans planted in September and October.

Festival of St. John the Baptist

The festival of the Nativity of St. John the Baptist (San Juan) dates back at least to the 1860s in Imbabura and neighboring Pichincha provinces (Hassaurek 1867:266–267; see also Jiménez de la Espada 2:1884:21). The festival remains strong in Cotacachi, Imbabura, where, two weeks to one month before the onset of the fiesta, one hears on Cotacachi's slopes the sound of a conch trumpet (*churu*), which apprises the Cotacachi Quichua that San Juan is approaching. On the eve of San Juan, they dance throughout the night to the sound of transverse flutes and guitars. The next morning (24 June), Quichua from all the *comunas*, in costume, go down to the plaza in front of the principal Cotacachi cathedral, completely packing it. They dance in the park and elsewhere to the sound of flutes, guitars, and *churu*.

During San Juan, long-standing communal rivalries resurface. These recall the traditional, annual encounter ritual (Quechua *tinku*), which still takes place in certain communities of the Bolivian altiplano, such as Chayanta, in northern Potosí (Delgado P. 1980:1–2); in the plaza, Quichua from, or allied with, "opposing" Cotacachi-area communities engage in fistfights and throwing stones. Days later, on the eve of the feast of Saints Peter and Paul (29 June), the same dancing as on the eve of San Juan occurs, and Quichua once again gather in the plaza the following day, where dancing continues for up to five days (Andrade Albuja 1979).

Specific ritual phenomena at Imbabura San Juan include *culebrillando* and *aruchicos* (Carvalho-Neto 1964:88–89; Coba Andrade 1985:35–38). *Culebrillando* is single-file serpentine dancing that may simulate a snake's movement in the view of some or the path of a sun's ray in the view of others. Arriving at the predetermined site (a plaza, or a street corner), the "snake" forms into a circle and stomps its feet to the cries of *jalajajaja!* Each group is led by a foot-captain (*chaqui-capitán*) who wields a cattle whip. In certain towns of Imbabura and neighboring Pichincha, the *aruchicos* are featured. Their dress is unique: long sheepskin coat, poncho, cloth hat, dark glasses, and leather cape from which hang lines of bronze bells that sound with the forceful dancing to the sound of flute duos and perhaps *rondador*.

The principal genre of dance of Imbabura is the *sanjuán*. In some parts of the province, Quichua musicians call the genre *sanjuanito*, the term used by mestizo and Afro-Ecuadorian musicians to denote an expanded form of *sanjuán*. *Sanjuanes* in

Imbabura may be traditional, lacking a known composer. One example, "*Ruku kuskungu,*" has a text that dates back at least 120 years in Ecuador. The Ecuadorian folklorist Juan León Mera published much the same text in 1868 under the title "*Atahualpa Huañui*" ('The Death of Atahualpa'). Known as the Quito Inca, Atahualpa was the son of Wayna Capac, who campaigned in Ecuador; Atahualpa had dominion over the Quito area in the last days of the Inca Empire. Mera's (1868, 1892:345–347) verses refer to the Inca father (Atahualpa), but the "*Ruku kuskungu*" verses I collected outside Cotacachi in 1980 do not. One quatrain has been preserved in the Cotacachi Quichua *comuna* exactly as it was sung in the Ecuadorian highlands in the mid-1800s. In sum, what seems roughly 150 years ago—and likely earlier—to have been a lament on the Inca Atahualpa's death is still sung and danced, if without the specific references to the Inca and his demise.

A *sanjuanito* may be autobiographical (see below; the *sanjuanitos* of the Ilumán composer Segundo Galo Maigua), or it may enumerate the multitudinous features of a beloved animal such as the sheep (the word *llama* is used among northern highland Quichua to refer to sheep) in "*Ñuka llama di mi vida*" (Schechter 1982:2:410–411). It may speak of disaster, inebriation and its effects, and courting, as in "*Rusa María wasi rupajmi*" (Schechter 1992b). It may exploit semantic juxtaposition and syntactic paralleling to strong effect, as in "*Juyalla,*" where we hear: "As a girl I was fine, as an old woman I have deteriorated; / As a girl I was lovely, as an old woman I shall become ugly" (Schechter 1987).

Mestizos of the highlands dance to *pasacalles* and *albazos*, both of which commonly glorify a prized aspect of one's own region: its women (as in the *pasacalle* "*Cotacacheñita de mi corazón*"), one of its favored musical instruments (as in the *albazo* "*Arpita de mis canciones*"), or its beautiful flora and abundant fruits (as in the *pasacalle* "*Ambato, Tierra de Flores*").

Entertainment

Not tied to fixed season or ritual, music serves a vital function as entertainment, notably in the highland and coastal regions of Ecuador. In the highlands, groups of mestizo musicians—perhaps guitarists, an accordionist, a trumpeter, a *güiro*-player, and a drummer—will jump in the back of a pickup truck and travel throughout a community, giving serenades of perhaps three songs at each home. The purpose will often be fund raising: to buy gifts for the schoolchildren at Christmastime, or perhaps to purchase uniforms for the local soccer team. These musicians will play famous pieces from the repertoire of traditional music (*música nacional* 'national music'): *albazos, pasacalles, pasillos*. Established local ensembles, such as Cotacachi's "*Rumba Havana,*" will perform regularly at the large outdoor coliseums of cantonal capitals, drawing sizable crowds for their amplified music.

Among Afro-Ecuadorians in the tropical forest of coastal Esmeraldas, the marimba dance (*currulao*) is a kind of secular ritual. Performed on holidays, special occasions, or Saturday nights, a *currulao* takes place in a house built on piles, whose owner has made most of the instruments of the ensemble, including the marimba (Whitten and Fuentes 1966). This marimba, suspended by ropes from rafters, is a xylophone with bamboo resonators (*guadúa*) and a *chonta*-palm keyboard. Played by two men, the instrument has from twenty-one to twenty-six keys and forms part of an ensemble that includes a *glosador* (typically male vocal soloist); *respondedoras* (female chorus) who shake *guasás*; two *cununo* membranophones; and two *bombos*. The marimba part is played by two persons, a *bordonero* and a *tiplero*. The *bordonero* plays the lower part, the *bordón*, an ostinato repeated with slight variations; the *tiplero* plays the *tiple* (treble), or *requinta*, a contrapuntal and/or harmonic improvisation based on the ground bass part, the *bordón*. Whereas the marimba music of

In rural highland Ecuador, instrumentalists are
nearly always men. This contrasts with rural Chile,
where women are harpists—a heritage from
sixteenth-century Spain, when certain women
were virtuosos on the instrument.

Central America is fundamentally homophonic, that of the Ecuadorian-Colombian
coast is essentially contrapuntal, incorporating rhythmic cycles (additive rhythm)
that, when juxtaposed, create polyrhythmic complexes involving rhythmic organization and texture typical of West Africa (Cáceres 1978:239–241) [see AFRO-
COLOMBIAN TRADITIONS].

The marimba dance is a *baile de respeto*—a respectful and intense dance, which
usually does not involve touching. It is characterized by the interplay between the
glosador and the *solista* (the *respondedora* who answers the *glosador* and sings melody,
as opposed to harmony, for the other *respondedoras*); the two sing of their respective
sex roles and difficulties, and of life in the region. Of the nine different types of *currulao*, the *bambuco*, a pursuit dance, is the most commonly performed.

The increasing contact of coastal Afro-Ecuadorians with highland mestizos has
inflated economic aspirations, and *currulao* has been scorned by upwardly mobile
blacks. Higher per-capita income and the arrival of electricity have resulted in more
saloon dancing, featuring such popular forms as *cumbia* and *bolero*. Hence, marimba
dancing has become more and more a commercial activity, produced for the benefit
of fee-paying highland tourists. Traditional practices and motivations are disappearing, as the *costeños* modify their instrumentation to conform to tourists' image of
what their music should be (Cáceres 1978:233–234).

Afro-Ecuadorian musicians of the Chota River Valley, in highland Imbabura and
Carchi provinces, bordering on Esmeraldas, also perform for tourists; but they preserve a unique *sesquiáltera* genre, the *bomba*. One ensemble, Grupo Ecuador de Los
Hermanos Congo y Milton Tadeo (figure 6), is locally acknowledged to be the premier representative of the dance music of Chota (Schechter 1994c).

PERFORMERS AND PERFORMANCES

In rural highland Ecuador, instrumentalists are nearly always men, whether one
speaks of Quichua, Afro-Ecuadorian, or mestizo musicians. In particular, Quichua
harpists and their *golpeadores* are always men, as are most mestizo harpists.

This contrasts with rural Chile, where women are harpists—a heritage from sixteenth-century Spain, when certain women were virtuosos on the instrument
(Schechter 1992a). Quichua girls, though, as well as boys, will know and sing *sanjuanes* in Imbabura. Harpists (males), even those known to be masters on the instrument, will often suffer ill repute: at the occasions for which they perform, such as
wedding and child's wake, they are frequently entreated to drink *trago* nearly inces-
santly, despite their attempts at denial. Thus, the reputation of harpists as being
heavy drinkers is often reluctantly acquired (Schechter 1992b:415–420).

In the Otavalo Valley, teenagers and young men are actively engaged in musical
performance. The number of ensembles of Quichua musicians is high; one famous
group, Conjunto Ilumán, is shown in figure 7. Annual radio festivals are filled to
overflowing with ensembles' participation. Musical performance is a major form of

FIGURE 6   The musical ensemble Grupo Ecuador de Los Hermanos Congo y Milton Tadeo, near Ibarra, Ecuador. Photo by John Schechter, 1990.

socialization among Quichua youths who, having dropped out of school, find few community activities available to them—except for volleyball, pursued with a vengeance in the *comunas* of Imbabura. One hears Quichua teenagers rehearsing diligently on weekends at a member's home performing a few traditional *sanjuanes* and often experimenting with their own compositions.

MUSICAL IDEOLOGIES AND AESTHETICS

Among highland and lowland Quichua in Ecuador, women's songs are important avenues for expressing a variety of sentiments. In highland Chimborazo, Regina Harrison (1989:122–125) recorded a song in which a Quichua woman expresses a willingness to do myriad domestic tasks in her husband's absence; she speaks of the need for a husband and a wife to work together to sustain their family.

FIGURE 7   The musical ensemble Conjunto Ilumán. Their instruments, *left to right:* guitar, guitar, *bombo, raspa, requinto,* Imbabura, Ecuador. Photo by John Schechter, 1990.

In contrast, in Amazonian Ecuador, Harrison (1989:132–133) found Quichua women's songs that speak openly of physical abuse. A clear tone of self-assertiveness appears in women's songs from this region. One woman sings of her physical strength (working in the fields), the powers she has received from her family, and her sexual powers (Harrison 1989:139–140).

Also in the tropical forest, a woman may privately sing songs with which to enchant, often seeking out upper elevations (with strong winds), whence her sung words might be borne a great distance (Harrison 1989:145–147). These are known as *llakichina* 'to make sad'. Rich in jungle imagery, they are often sung to make the person to whom they are directed—husband or lover—return to the singer. Thus, they might stress love, loyalty, and/or the singer's desirability (Seitz 1981:228, 233). The recipient may perceive the song's message through the song of a bird or in a dream; the message is made to appear through the intermediary of the singer's spirit helper (Seitz 1981:243).

In the jungle region, Canelos Quichua women create highly artistic *mucahuas*, decorated pottery bowls for drinking *chicha*; in the course of their work, these women "think-sing" special songs, "owned" by the spirit or soul beings about whom they are singing. The women believe that, in the process of decorating, they are imparting various types of souls—such as the "*huarmi huasimanda ayatian,* household soul continuity," and the "*ahuashca huarmi aya,* woman's soul built into the clay by labor and knowledge of technique and design" (Whitten 1976:90).

Composition

Mention (above) of the Congo brothers and Milton Tadeo (Grupo Ecuador) brings us to the subject of their and other Ecuadorian musicians' creative processes. In the Chota Valley, traditional *bomba* (genre) texts, such as for "*Este pañuelito,*" dealt with themes such as love. In the 1980s and 1990s, Fabián Congo (the vocalist-guitarist of the ensemble) was composing songs with distinctly political content. Though his *bomba* "*Promesas políticas*" expresses a growing disillusionment of the people with their government's promises, his "*Deber y dolor*" and his brother Germán's (lead guitarist) "*El Ecuador y Colombia*" reflect the musician brothers' consciousness of the special geography of Chota—within highland Imbabura, Ecuador, and close to the Colombian border. In effect, the Congos' musical compositions are directed outward: they express regional pride and regional consciousness, yet with a strong admixture of commentary and topicality.

In contrast, the compositions of an Imbabura Quichua composer, Segundo Galo Maigua of Ilumán (see figure 7, far right), near Otavalo, reveal a different artistic point of departure. Working within the genre of *sanjuán* (or, as it is termed more often in Ilumán, *sanjuanito*), he produces songs prompted largely by autobiographical, not regional, forces. His "*Rusita Andranga*" speaks of a woman with whom he fell in love while traveling with friends through the Quichua *comunas* of Mount Cotacachi, across the valley. His famous *sanjuanito*, "*Ilumán Tiyu*" ('Man of Ilumán'), written when he thought he was near death, was meant as a final statement of his own musical identity. And his "*Antonio Mocho,*" widely popular in 1990, enacts musical vengeance on a fellow guitarist who attacked him in a jam session and was notorious as a wife-beater—a morbid trait highlighted in this *sanjuanito*. More than regional expressions, Galo Maigua's *sanjuanitos* are personal balladry, the emotional core of experiences from his own life. Thus, his creative process is inward looking.

Discussion of Galo Maigua's *sanjuanitos* brings us to formulaic expression, a fundamental compositional technique for *sanjuanito*. In multiple performances within the cycle of dispersion, an Imbabura *sanjuán* or *sanjuanito* will maintain its general melodic and rhythmic character. In relation to text, however, certain words, phrases, or lines appear widely in different *sanjuanes*, regularly interchanging with other elements of the same order.

The pattern is that of Milman Parry's concept of the formula, in which certain groups of words are typically used within identical metrical conditions to express certain fundamental ideas (Lord 1978 [1960]:4). The most stable formulas are those correlating with the most often used ideas. Verbs, in particular, often serve as formulas in and of themselves. Examining Cotacachi Quichua *sanjuán* texts, one can pinpoint this formulaic operation; one finds, in Parry's phrase, "systems," mostly but not exclusively of verbs, in *sanjuán* lines of from seven to twelve syllables. Prominent verbs in these systems are the Quichua verbs for 'to dance', 'to turn', 'to say', 'to get drunk', 'to be', 'to go this and that way', 'to come', and 'to walk.' The prominence of 'to dance' reflects the multiplicity of festive occasions in which *sanjuanes* are performed; thus, it often appears in imperative form; 'to turn' is used partly for the same reasons—to turn while dancing. 'To say' appears solely in a quotational function. 'To get drunk' is fixed to particular personages in certain popular *sanjuán* texts. 'To be' facilitates the elaboration of certain static conditions, such as the diverse sheep features in the *sanjuán* "*Ñuka llama de mi vida*" 'My Sheep of My Life'. The three verbs 'to go this and that way', 'to come', and 'to walk' are tied neither to particular festive occasions nor to famously fixed texts; instead, they are used metaphorically and freely to mean, roughly, "walking" or "going this and that way" on account of a loved one. Finally, *sanjuanes* frequently appear in textual couplets, the patterns for which (involving balance, antithesis, apposition, parallelisms) seem to be characteristic of the workings of the oral mind (Schechter 1987:39–42).

FURTHER STUDY

Primary and secondary sources for the study of historical and modern Ecuadorian musical instruments include Carvalho-Neto (1964), Coba Andrade (1979, 1981, 1992), Jijón (1971), Rephann (1978), Schechter (1992a), and Traversari Salazar (1961).

Though good beginnings have been made in organological studies for Ecuador, further studies are called for on the musics of Ecuadorian central and southern highland Quichua. Despite studies by Carrión (1975), Morlás Gutiérrez (1961), and Riedel (1986) on the Ecuadorian *pasillo,* and anthologies of text and music such as that of Godoy Aguirre (1980s), major scholarly work still remains in documentation and analysis of the stylistic character of other genres of national folkloric music.

Afro-Ecuadorian musics have been explored by Thomas White, Norman E. Whitten, Jr. (1967, 1974) and Whitten and Fuentes C. (1966) for coastal Esmeraldas, and by Carlos Alberto Coba Andrade (1980) and John Schechter (1994c) for the coastal and highland (Chota) regions. Work on lowland Quichua and Shuar and other Oriente musics has been sporadic; see Belzner (1981), List (1965), Muriel (1976), and Monteros (1942), and the important recordings of Coba Andrade (1990), Crawford (1979), and Harner (1973).

Finally, Ecuadorian ethnomusicology owes a debt to the pioneering works of Segundo Luis Moreno Andrade and subsequently of Carlos Alberto Coba Andrade—studies that are foundational for their breadth and depth. Since the late 1970s, after a slow start, the field of Ecuadorian music-cultural studies has begun to make substantial progress.

REFERENCES

Andrade Albuja, Enrique. 1979. "Cai San Juan Fiestamanta." *Quichua Monologue* (19 November). El Ejido, Cotacachi, Imbabura, Ecuador.

d'Aurignac, Romain. 1890. *Amérique du Sud: Trois ans chez les Argentins.* Paris: E. Plon, Nourrit.

Béhague, Gerard. 1979. *Music in Latin America: An Introduction.* Englewood Cliffs, N. J.: Prentice-Hall.

Belzner, William. 1981. "Music, Modernization, and Westernization among the Macuma Shuar." In *Cultural Transformations and Ethnicity in Modern Ecuador,* ed. Norman E. Whitten, Jr., 731–748. Urbana: University of Illinois Press.

Bemelmans, Ludwig. 1941. *The Donkey Inside.* New York: Viking Press.

Boilès, Charles L. 1966. "The Pipe and Tabor in Mesoamerica." *Inter-American Institute for Musical Research Yearbook* 2:43–74.

Cáceres, Abraham. 1978. "Preliminary Comments on the Marimba in the Americas." In *Discourse in Ethnomusicology: Essays in Honor of George List,* ed. Caroline Card, John Hasse, Roberta L. Singer, and Ruth M. Stone, 225–250. Bloomington, Ind.: Ethnomusicology Publications Group.

Carreras y Candi, F., ed. 1931–1933. *Folklore y Costumbres de España.* 3 vols. Barcelona: Casa Editorial Alberto Martín.

Carrión, Isabel V. 1975. *Antología del Pasillo Ecuatoriano.* Cuenca, Ecuador: publisher unknown.

Carvalho-Neto, Paulo de. 1964. *Diccionario del Folklore Ecuatoriano.* Tratado del Folklore Ecuatoriano, 1. Quito: Editorial Casa de la Cultura Ecuatoriana.

Chantre y Herrera, José. 1901. *Historia de la misión de los indios Mainas y de otras muchas naciones situadas en el Marañón español y en otros varios ríos que desembocan en él.* Madrid: A. Avrial.

"La Cibdad [sic] de Sant [sic] Francisco del Quito." 1897 [1573]. In *Perú,* pp. 60–104. Relaciones Geográficas de Indias, 3. Madrid: Hijos de M. G. Hernández.

Coba Andrade, Carlos Alberto. 1979. "Instrumentos Musicales Ecuatorianos." *Sarance* 7:70–95.

———. 1980. *Literatura popular afroecuatoriana.* Otavalo, Ecuador: Instituto Otavaleño de Antropología.

———. 1981. *Instrumentos musicales populares registrados en el Ecuador.* Vol. 1. Otavalo, Ecuador: Instituto Otavaleño de Antropología.

———. 1985. *Danzas y bailes en el Ecuador.* Quito: Ediciones Abya- yala.

———, ed. 1990. *Música etnográfica y folklórica del Ecuador: Culturas: Shuar, Chachi, Quichua, Afro, Mestizo.* Otavalo: Instituto Otavaleño de Antropología. 2 LP disks.

———. 1992. *Instrumentos musicales populares registrados en Ecuador.* Vol. 2. Quito: Banco Central del Ecuador.

———, general coordinator. 1990. *Música etnográfica y folklórica del Ecuador.* Otavalo: Instituto Otavaleño de Antropología, LP 5748, 5750. 2 LP disks.

Collier, John, Jr., and Aníbal Buitrón. 1971. *The Awakening Valley.* Quito: Talleres Gráficos del Instituto Geográfico Militar.

Crawford, Neelon, ed. 1979. *Soul Vine Shaman.* New York: Neelon Crawford. LP disk.

Davillier, Le Baron [Jean] Ch[arles]. 1874. *L'Espagne.* Illustrated by Gustave Doré. Paris: Librairie Hachette.

Delgado P., Guillermo. 1980. "Apología del Tinku de Chayanta." *Presencia,* sec. 2 (La Paz, Bolivia), 18 May, 1–2.

Godoy Aguirre, Mario. 1980s. *Florilegio de la música Ecuatoriana: Breve estudio.* Guayaquil: Editorial del Pacífico.

Gradante, William J. 1980. "'Somos Todos Silvianos': Semana Santa and Communitas in Silvia." In *Folklore Papers of the University Folklore Association,* no. 9, ed. K. F. Turner, 27–55. Austin: Center for Intercultural Studies in Folklore and Ethnomusicology, University of Texas at Austin.

Los Grandes de la Bomba: Con Fabián Congo y Milton Tadeo. 1989. Novedades 323102. LP disk.

Harner, Michael J. 1973. *Music of the Jívaro of Ecuador.* Ethnic Folkways FE 4386. LP disk.

Harrison, Regina. 1989. *Signs, Songs, and Memory in the Andes: Translating Quechua Language and Culture.* Austin: University of Texas Press.

Hassaurek, Friedrich. 1867. *Four Years among Spanish-Americans.* New York: Hurd and Houghton.

Jijón, Inés. 1971. *Museo de Instrumentos Musicales "Pedro Pablo Traversari."* Quito: Casa de la Cultura Ecuatoriana.

Jiménez de la Espada, D. Marcos. 1884. "Yaravíes Quiteños." In *Actas de la Cuarta Reunión, Congreso Internacional de Americanistas, Madrid, 1881,* 2:I–LXXXII. Madrid: Imprenta de Fortanet.

Karsten, Rafael. 1935. *The Head-Hunters of Western Amazonas: The Life and Culture of the Jíbaro Indians of Eastern Ecuador and Peru.* Societas Scientiarum Fennica, Commentationes Humanarum Litterarum VII.l. Helsingfors: Centraltryckeriet.

List, George. 1965. "Music in the Culture of the Jíbaro Indians of the Ecuadorian Montaña." In *Primera Conferencia Interamericana de Etnomusicología (1963): Trabajos Presentados,* 131–151. Washington, D.C.: Secretaría General de la OEA, Unión Panamericana.

Lord, Albert B. 1978 [1960]. *The Singer of Tales.* New York: Atheneum.

Mera, Juan León. 1868. *Ojeada Histórico-Crítica sobre la Poesía Ecuatoriana, desde su Época más Remota hasta Nuestros Días.* Quito: J. Pablo Sanz.

———. 1892. *Antología Ecuatoriana: Cantares del Pueblo Ecuatoriano.* Quito: Imprenta de la Universidad Central del Ecuador.

Monteros, Raimundo M. 1942. *Música autóctona del oriente ecuatoriano.* Quito: Ministerio de Gobierno.

Moreno Andrade, Segundo Luis. 1930. "La Música en el Ecuador." In *El Ecuador en cien años de independencia: 1830-1930,* 2:187–276. Quito: Imprenta de la Escuela de Artes y Oficios.

———. 1972. *Historia de la música en el ecuador—Volumen Primero: Prehistoria.* Quito: Editorial Casa de la Cultura Ecuatoriana.

Morlás, Gutiérrez, Alberto. 1961. *Florilegio del Pasillo Ecuatoriano.* Quito: Editorial Jodoco Ricke.

Muriel, Inés. 1976. "Contribución a la Cultura Musical de los Jívaros del Ecuador." *Folklore Americano* 21:141–157.

Nyberg, John Leroy. 1974. "An Examination of Vessel Flutes from Pre-Hispanic Cultures of Ecuador." Ph.D. dissertation, University of Minnesota.

Olsen, Dale A., Daniel E. Sheehy, and Charles A. Perrone. 1987. "Music of Latin America: Mexico, Ecuador, Brazil." In *Study Guide for Sounds of the World Series.* Reston, Va.: Music Educators National Conference.

Parsons, Elsie Clews. 1945. *Peguche, Canton of Otavalo, Province of Imbabura, Ecuador: A Study of Andean Indians.* Chicago: University of Chicago Press.

Recio, Bernardo. 1947 [1773]. *Compendiosa Relación de la Cristiandad (en el Reino-) de Quito.* Madrid: Consejo Superior de Investigaciones Científicas Instituto Santo Toribio de Mogrovejo.

Rephann, Richard. 1978. *A Catalogue of the Pedro Traversari Collection of Musical Instruments / Catálogo de la Colección de Instrumentos Musicales Pedro Traversari.* Organization of American States and Yale University Collection of Musical Instruments. Quito: Casa de la Cultura Ecuatoriana.

Riedel, Johannes. 1986. "The Ecuadorean *Pasillo:* 'Música Popular,' 'Música Nacional,' or 'Música Folklórica'?" *Latin American Music Review* 7(1):1–25.

Rubio Orbe, Gonzalo. 1946. *Nuestros Indios (Estudio Geográfico, Histórico y Social de los Indios Ecuatorianos, especialmente aplicado a la Provincia de Imbabura).* Quito: Imprenta de la Universidad.

Schechter, John M. 1982. "Music in a Northern Ecuadorian Highland Locus: Diatonic Harp, Genres, Harpists, and Their Ritual Junction in the Quechua Child's Wake." 3 vols. Ph.D. dissertation, University of Texas at Austin.

———. 1983. "*Corona y Baile*: Music in the Child's Wake of Ecuador and Hispanic South America, Past and Present." *Latin American Music Review* 4(1):1–80.

———. 1987. "Quechua *Sanjuán* in Northern Highland Ecuador: Harp Music as Structural Metaphor on *Purina.*" *Journal of Latin American Lore* 13(1):27–46.

———. 1992a. *The Indispensable Harp: Historical Development, Modern Roles, Configurations, and Performance Practices in Ecuador and Latin America.* Kent, Ohio, and London: Kent State University Press.

———. 1992b. "Latin America / Ecuador." In *Worlds of Music: An Introduction to the Music of the World's Peoples,* 2nd ed, ed. Jeff Todd Titon, 376–428. New York: Schirmer Books.

———. 1994a. "Corpus Christi and its Octave in Andean Ecuador: Procession and Music, 'Castles' and 'Bulls'." In *Music-Cultures in Contact: Convergences and Collisions,* ed. Margaret J. Kartomi and Stephen Blum, 59–72. Sydney, Australia, and Newark, New Jersey: Currency Press and Gordon & Breach.

———. 1994b. "Divergent Perspectives on the *velorio del angelito:* Ritual Imagery, Artistic Condemnation, and Ethnographic Valve." *Journal of Ritual Studies* 8(2):43–84.

———. 1994c. "*Los Hermanos Congo y Milton Tadeo* Ten Years Later: Evolution of an Afro-Ecuadorian Tradition of the *Valle del Chota,* Highland Ecuador." In *Music and Black Ethnicity: The Caribbean and South America,* ed. Gerard H. Béhague, 285–305. Miami: North-South Center, University of Miami.

Seitz, Barbara. 1981. "Quichua Songs to Sadden the Heart: Music in a Communication Event." *Latin American Music Review* 2(2):223–251.

Slobin, Mark. 1992. "Europe / Peasant Music-Cultures of Eastern Europe." In *Worlds of Music: An Introduction to the Music of the World's Peoples,* 2nd ed., ed. Jeff Todd Titon, 167–208. New York: Schirmer Books.

Stevenson, Robert M. 1959. "Ancient Peruvian Instruments." *Galpin Society Journal* 12:17–43.

———. 1963. "Music in Quito: Four Centuries." *Hispanic American Historical Review* 43:247–266.

Taylor, William B. 1908. Photograph on view at the American Museum of Natural History, New York, July 1995.

Traversari Salazar, Pedro Pablo, ed. 1961. *Catálogo General del Museo de Instrumentos Musicales,* ed. Pedro Pablo. Quito: Editorial Casa de la Cultura Ecuatoriana.

Whitten, Norman E., Jr., ed. 1967. *Afro-Hispanic Music from Western Colombia and Ecuador.* Ethnic Folkways FE 4376. LP disk.

———. 1974. "Ritual Enactment of Sex Roles in the Pacific Lowlands of Ecuador-Colombia." *Ethnology* 13(2):129–143.

———. 1976. *Sacha Runa: Ethnicity and Adaptation of Ecuadorian Jungle Quichua.* Urbana: University of Illinois Press.

Whitten, Norman E., Jr. and Aurelio Fuentes C. 1966. "Baile Marimba! Negro Folk Music in Northwest Ecuador." *Journal of the Folklore Institute* 3(2):168–191.

Wiener, Charles. 1880. *Pérou et Bolivie: Récit de Voyage.* Paris: Librairie Hachette.

French Guiana
Jean-Michel Beaudet

Amerindians
Creoles
Maroons
Interrelationships among Local Cultures

Bordered to the east by the Oyapock River and Brazil, and to the west by the Maroni River and Surinam, French Guiana has an area of 90,500 square kilometers. Situated just below the equator, it is crisscrossed by innumerable currents of water and is almost entirely covered by a tropical forest. Administratively linked to France, it is one of the last areas of South America that is not politically independent.

Colonization dating from the 1600s has directly formed the population, which totaled 114,800 persons in 1990. The first people to occupy the land were Amerindians, whose number has risen to 4,200 (about 4 percent of the total population), indicating a strong demographic dynamism after the epidemics that decimated the indigenous populations of the Americas in past centuries.

The most numerous people of French Guiana are creoles, descendants of slaves taken from Africa and freed in 1850. Creole culture resembles that of other peoples in the Guianas and the Antilles. Next to the creoles are Maroons, descendants of slaves who escaped from plantations in the 1600s and 1700s and reconstructed their original civilizations, imprinted with strong African components. French Guiana's ethnic mosaic is completed with French people and numerous families originally from Brazil, China, Haiti, Indonesia, Lebanon, and Vietnam. Since these populations are largely minorities, their musical practices do not represent the major traits of the country.

This demographic composition is comparable with that of Surinam, with, however, clearer cultural boundaries and a tendency to partition in French Guiana. Few cultural exchanges occur among the various cultures, which live alongside each other more than they mix. Thus, local musical life resembles a juxtaposition of traditions and practices.

AMERINDIANS

The Amerindian people of French Guiana live in two different native milieus and are distributed according to three cultural linguistic families. Six distinct languages are still spoken in the country: the Arawak and the Palikur (Parikwene) belong to the Arawak linguistic family and are established in the north, in the coastal zone; the

Emerillon and the Waiãpí [see WAIÃPI] are of Tupi culture and language, and live in the south of the country; finally, the Wayana [see WAYANA], who also live in the south just above the Maroni River, and the Kalina (Galibi), in the north at the mouth of this river, speak the same Carib language. The Kalina are the most numerous and the most active in the French Guianese Amerindian rights movement (Tiouka 1985).

The most salient differences and the likenesses among the musics of these peoples can be outlined first by these two geographic regions: the musical systems of the people in the south are comparable among themselves, whereas the three ethnic groups have different historical origins; we can assume there was an important network of communications among the groups of the south in previous centuries. These cultural exchanges are much less apparent for the people of the coast (the Arawak, the Kalina, and the Palikur), who have been in continued contact with colonizers for three centuries.

In repertoire, performance, and discussion, all Amerindian people of French Guiana distinguish between collective music, danced and accompanied by manioc beer, and individual music, played or sung solo, not characterized by public participation or drinking. This distinction is does not strictly make a ritual-profane opposition; in particular, shamans usually sing alone, addressing a group. Cetain repertoires or circumstances of performance have an intermediate significance between these poles. Individual music includes masculine repertoires (mainly flute airs) and feminine repertoires (love songs, lullabies, and lamentations). Performances of feminine pieces are becoming progressively rarer.

Among the Emerillon, the Wayana, and the Waiãpí, women sometimes accompany men in collective songs, but their place is clearly secondary. Of the three ethnicities in the south, men are responsible for music; at the time of festivals, women are primarily responsible for beer, served according to formal codes regarding the exchanges between music and drink (Beaudet 1992). On the coast, the situation differs. Palikur women have an original and voluminous repertoire of collective songs sung in unison, including *wawapna* 'song of the rattle', whose rhythm they mark three times with small rattles (*waw*) attached to long, pointed sticks; *mayapna* 'song of the Mayes', the people who formed the present Palikur nation; *wukikapna,* the song for haircuts after a disease; and *kuwapna* 'song of the butterflies'. Kalina women have a specific repertoire associated with the stages of the ceremonial cycle of the funeral procession; they sing the rhythm of these songs in unison to the slow, steady pulse of the large basket rattles (*ka:lawa:si*), which, for most stages of the ceremonial cycle, are set on long pointed sticks.

Musical instruments

Apart from the Palikur and Kalina rattles, all Amerindian instruments are reserved for men. This distribution of instruments by sex conforms to a general law among the Amerindian cultures of the Americas (Beaudet 1983). Structural analysis shows that this prohibition contributes to a polarization between, on the one side, women (who have reached menses and have borne children) and on the other side, men, aerophones, and political prestige.

Like most indigenous people of South America, those in French Guiana make flutes, trumpets, and clarinets (Beaudet 1989a), and these aerophones usually have significant social and religious functions. We find characteristic instruments in the center and north of the Amazon, such as the large *turè* (*turé*) clarinets (Beaudet 1980 and 1989b) (figure 1) and the instruments most often found on the circumference north and west of the Amazon: raft panpipes with three or four tubes, sometimes accompanied by a struck turtle shell.

FIGURE 1   For the *kausikman* dance in the village of Saint Georges de l'Oyapock, two Palikur men play *turè* clarinets. Photo by Jean-Michel Beaudet, 1979.

To add rhythm for dancing, the Amerindians in the south of French Guiana use cowbells with seeds of yellow oleander (*Thevetia peruviana*), a tree of the dogbane family. According to the Kalina, in their mourning rituals they give preponderant significance to the *sambula,* a large drum with two skins, probably of European origin. The first sequences of these rituals present two distinct musics: on one side, six to eight men sing with their drums in one powerful voice, and on the other side, women (their number increasing as the ceremony proceeds) shake their rattles and in a high-pitched and plaintive voice sing songs from a different repertoire (Kloos 1975). Collective vocal music is popular with all groups. There are always unison songs, except among the Waiãpí, or when the women sing with the men to produce heterophony, a high-pitched heterogeneous canon superimposed on the men's grave, low unison.

Repertoires and social organization

In each of these musical traditions, the repertoires could have several origins—the mythical world or neighboring groups. The musical form usually described is in effect a transmission from the spirits of the forest or the river through the mediation of shamans, whose musical inspiration is explicitly defined as coming from the spiritual powers of their environment and village.

Wayãpí musical practices are organized in correspondence with social organization: instruments and repertoire exist for each social level (individual, nuclear family, extended family, village, regional group). Little known, Emerillon music must be understood as a component that affirms a strong identity, a miraculous affirmation if we account for the demographic catastrophe of the past—after many epidemics, the Emerillon were but fifty-three in 1952.

The sociomusical organization of the Wayana seems oriented toward two poles: the shamanistic and the *marake,* adolescents' major rite of initiation (Hurault 1968). The repertoire and musical practices of the Palikur are evidence of the federated dynamics that for many centuries have shaped these people. As for other Arawak and the Kalina, this group is equally engaged in a strong folkloric movement associated with a cultural revival supported by current trends. Individual music, threatened for years by the increasing demands and pressures of tourism, everywhere disappears more quickly than collective music.

CREOLES

Within French Guianan creole culture, we could once distinguish between more rural life and more urban life—two constantly interrelated worlds. Today, rural life has almost completely disappeared, and creole culture is more unified. Creole musical practices have always divided into two large groups. The first, called folkloric music (*musique folklorique*) or local dances (*danses locales),* are the dances accompanied by singing, derived from drum ensembles with originally African rhythms. The second group, typical music (*musique typique*), is a dance music played by orchestras of different forms, depending on the season and social categories; these dances and their music have the most pronounced European origins, but they have been reappropriated and remodeled along forms common in the Antilles (Jolivet 1989).

The *danses locales,* which first appeared as slaves' dances, were divided into two subgroups according to whether they were considered more reserved or more "devilish." The first could be danced in front of masters and in parlors. The *grage* is a dance that is particularly presented in the Sinnamary region, driven by *tambourins,* frame drums of different sizes. The *lerol* is a form of quadrille accompanied by three drums and a rattle (*chacha-lerol*). The *kamouge* is a dance accompanied by two long, cylindroconical, single-headed drums resting on the ground. The first (*foule*), 3 meters long, is considered male and plays ostinato rhythms; the drummer hits the skin with his hands, while another musician beats on the barrel with two short sticks (*tibwa*). On another drum (*coupe* 'cut'), shorter and considered female, various formulas are executed.

The most "devilish" dances were executed among slaves; these are the *belya* and the *kaseko* (*casser le corps*). The *kaseko* is the only creole dance that remains alive in French Guiana; it is accompanied by *tibwa* and two single-headed cylindrical drums, made from small barrels and held between the knees. Among the dances born among the slaves, the *kaseko* is the most favored; it is sometimes danced at night in the courtyards of particular houses in the suburbs of Cayenne or in market towns, but like the other folkloric dances, it is particularly performed in shows associated with the revival movement or with tourism.

If *musiques folkloriques* are associated with a strong territorial feeling (people say the *grage* from the Approuage is different from the *grage* from Sinnamary), the creoles resent *musique typique* groups, which they believe unoriginal, "copied" from the other Antilles. Orchestral genres and styles have always been imported from the French Caribbean, English, and least often Spanish people. Sometimes, the musicians themselves originally come from Sainte Lucie (St. Lucia), or today, from Haiti.

The middle class of Cayenne, like all the creole middle class, has tried to imitate European classical music for piano and violin, but the real musical life was in ballroom orchestras. Changes in the instrumentation and repertoire of these orchestras has followed the musical transformations throughout the Antilles. In French Guiana, the most creative period was during the rush for gold at the end of the 1800s, which gave birth to many orchestras. For more than a century, banjos, clarinets, guitars,

During funerals, the body of the deceased is carried down the river, accompanied by drums and singers, one or the other equipped with loudspeakers. Electric bands go on the same barge, where old people pray and young girls dance.

trombones, accordions, saxophones, electric guitars, and finally synthesizers have served as the major orchestral instruments, performing waltzes, mazurkas, schottisches, biguines, merengues, *compas, kadens,* reggae, and finally *zouk.*

The most original aspect of these musics (*folklorique* and *typique*) always seems situated in the lyrics, where the particularities of local creole culture find expression. The poetry and infectiousness of French Guianese songs are presented in the danced and drummed repertoires (*gragé* and *kaséko* especially), and in the carnival parade music (*vidé*) and among songwriters, of whom the best known are Sabas, Lubin, the Volmar brothers, and Ruffinel in the first half of the twentieth century, and of whom Viviane Emigré could be considered a typical representative of the 1980s (Play 1989).

MAROONS

Less numerous than in Surinam, the Maroons of French Guiana live primarily along the Maroni River in four large, distinct groups: the Aluku (also called Boni), the Djuka, the Paramaka, and the Saramaka. The Aluku coalesced the most belatedly, at the end of the 1700s; most live in French Guiana. Though each of these people has a different history, they all share numerous common traits—in particular, a pronounced African heritage. They have synthesized with their original music some elements from Amerindian culture and creoles of the region. Creativity is another common trait found among these cultures, a trait manifested particularly in the arts (Price and Price 1980). In musical life, this creativity translates into valuation of improvisation and games, even during ceremonies. The barriers between speech and song, among the daily amusements and the formal ceremonials, are fuzzy and movable.

Aluku women and men like to create songs spontaneously to comment allusively on everyday life or to mark the rhythm of the heaviest chores. For several decades, men have sometimes accompanied their songs with a resonating pluriarc (*agwado*) whose playing can lead certain hiding games. The most important Aluku ceremonies are the funeral songs *booko deo* and the relief of mourning *puu baaka* (Bilby 1989), accompanied by an ensemble of three cylindroconical drums of different dimensions: the large drum (*gaan doon*), the small drum (*pikin doon*), and the *tun.* These drums have one skin, often ornamented with engravings (Hurault 1970) and are similar in shape to drums of West Africa. The cowbell (*kaway*) is another rhythmic instrument important in ceremonial music; its name and shape clearly indicate that it has been directly taken from the neighboring Wayana.

Aluku rites of mourning consist of a series of sequences—*mato, susa, songe, awawa, awasa*—that mix song, recitation, dance, virtuosic demonstrations, provocations, improvisations, women, men, and drummers. Besides these funeral ceremonies are many other occasions for performance. Certain circumstances are formal, such as other festivals (*pee*), of which the primary reason is to maintain an exchange with the gods, but the amusement dances of the young, called *aleke,* are also prized. All these performances are intense, sensual, dramatic, and emotional. This vivacity, this formal dynamism gives evidence of the conscious and successful synthesis between the affirmed African tradition, the valuing of creative play, the physical memory of their historical struggle for liberty, and the incorporation of foreign elements: on returning to the city, young people amuse themselves by recreating on their drums the rhythm of a cola-bottling machine (Price and Price 1980). The ritual demonstrations of agility during a song can be heard alternatively in the rhythms of village drums and in African popular music, easily purchased on cassette in cities. During funerals, the body of the deceased is carried down the river, accompanied by drums and singers, one or the other equipped with loudspeakers; microphones, amplifiers, loudspeakers, and electric bands go on the same barge, where old people pray and young girls dance.

INTERRELATIONSHIPS AMONG LOCAL CULTURES

The large cultural groups—Amerindians, Maroons, creoles—present three manners of acting on the relation between tradition and creation. The creoles of French Guiana are considered the main imitators of musical currents that travel from the Caribbean region. They produce few original compositions in popular music, whereas the ancient drum-accompanied dances are particularly the objects of revival.

As this population is influenced by the media, the creole music of the Antilles and the African popular music they listen to have become a sort of slang music (*musique véhiculaire*) among the younger generations of all the cultural groups in the image of Creole, the language that serves as *langue véhiculaire* of French Guiana. Amerindian musical behaviors divide into two clearly distinct domains from the viewpoint of practices and the viewpoint of discourses: one part of Amerindian musics, not being acclaimed, is continually weakening, in accordance with contact with colonial society; and the other part is an adhesion of the young to the popular music broadcast by creole ensembles. Finally, the Maroons affirm their creativity across the synthesis of cultures present in every level of their musical civilization.

—TRANSLATED BY ROSEMARY McBRIDE

REFERENCES

Beaudet, Jean-Michel. 1980. *Wayãpí-Guyane.* Société d'Études Linguistiques et Anthropologiques de France Orstom-Selaf CETO 792. LP disk.

———. 1983. "Les Orchestres de clarinettes *tule* des Wayãpí du haut Oyapock (Guyane française)." Ph.D. dissertation, Université de Paris X, Nanterre.

———. 1989a. "La Musique amérindienne, un art du souffle." In *Musiques en Guyane,* ed. Bureau du Patrimoine ethnologique, 25–39. Cayenne: Conseil Régional de la Guyane.

———. 1989b. "Les *turè*, des clarinettes amazoniennes." *Latin American Music Review* 10(1):92–115.

———. 1992. "Musique et alcool en Amazonie du Nord-Est." *Cahiers de Sociologie Economique et Culturelle* 18:79–88.

Bilby, Kenneth.1989. "La musique aluku, un héritage africain." In *Musiques en Guyane,* ed. Bureau du Patrimoine Ethnologique, 49–68. Cayenne: Conseil Régional de la Guyane.

Hurault, Jean-Marcel. 1968. *Musique Boni et Wayana de Guyane.* Paris: Vogue LVLX 290 (Musée de l'Homme). LP disk.

———. 1970. *Africains de Guyane.* La Haye and Paris: Mouton.

Jolivet, Marie-José. 1989. "Les formes de la tradition musicale en Guyane créole." In *Musiques en Guyane,* ed. Bureau du Patrimoine Ethnologique, 73–90. Cayenne: Conseil Régional de la Guyane.

Kloos, Peter. 1975. *Amerindian Songs from Surinam: The Maroni River Caribs.* Amsterdam: Royal Tropical Institute STEMRA, VR 20158. LP disk.

Play, Dany, ed. 1989. *Typiquement D.O.M. Compilation 89 Antilles-Guyane.* Cayenne: TDM production. LP disk.

Price, Richard, and Sally Price. 1980. *Afro-American Arts of the Surinam Rain Forest.* Los Angeles: Museum of Cultural History and University of California Press.

Tiouka, Félix. 1985. "Adresse au gouvernement et au peuple français." *Ethnies* 1(1–2):7–10.

Guyana
Olivia Ahyoung

The Cultural Traditions of Guyana
National Musical Contexts and Genres

The republic of Guyana is one of three former colonies originally known as the Guianas, which lie side by side on the northeastern coast of South America. The Arawak word *guaianá* 'land of many waters' (Tremblay 1988:58) was the name given the area, sighted by Columbus in 1498 and comprising today's Guyana, Surinam (formerly Dutch Guiana), French Guiana, and parts of Brazil and Venezuela. Guyana (bordered by Surinam to the east, Brazil to the south, Venezuela to the west, and the Atlantic Ocean to the north), is the only English speaking-country on the South American continent. The British divided Guyana into three counties: Essequibo, Demerara, and Berbice. In 1982, through a process called regionalism, the country was politically divided into ten regions. Most of its eight hundred thousand inhabitants live in the coastal regions, and most of its 215,000 square kilometers are covered by tropical forests.

Originally believed to be the mythical El Dorado (legendarily believed to be rich in gold and precious stones), it was first sought out by early Spanish explorers. Between the 1500s and 1800s it was invaded by the Dutch, French, Portuguese, and British. The first European settlers were the Dutch, whom in the late 1500s the indigenous inhabitants welcomed as trading partners. The area was partially settled in 1616, when the Dutch established a fort at Kyk-Ober-Al in the present county of Essequibo. In 1621, the colony was placed under the direction of the Dutch West Indian Company, which administered it for the next 170 years, interrupted briefly by periods of French and British rule.

During the Dutch occupation, British settlers began migrating to the region in large numbers, and by 1760 they were a majority of the population in Demerara. The Dutch held the three colonies until 1796, when they were captured by a British fleet. The territory was restored to the Dutch in 1802, but a year later the British retook it. In 1815, the Congress of Vienna assigned the three counties to Britain. In 1831, they merged to form British Guiana, which remained a British colony until 1966, when Britain granted it independence.

THE CULTURAL TRADITIONS OF GUYANA

Guyana's history resembles that of the former British West Indies, culturally linking

Immigrants from India to Guyana brought with them their religious and cultural patterns, which they have maintained (with slight variations), forming a thriving subculture.

the country more closely to those islands than to South America. Its cultural expression reflects its separate ethnic contributions.

The peoples who contributed to Guyana's cultural heritage and development include the aboriginal inhabitants; British, Dutch, and Portuguese colonists; African slaves; and East Indian and Chinese indentured laborers brought in to relieve the labor shortage created by the Emancipation Act (1833). The merging of these peoples' cultural traditions in a common sociocultural context over an extended period stimulated processes that shaped the evolution of Guyanese music.

Native Americans (Amerindians)

The continuing presence of native Americans distinguishes Guyana from much of the immediate English-speaking Caribbean. Unlike their counterparts in the West Indies, who became extinct, the Amerindians of Guyana escaped that fate by retreating into the forests and savannas. Among the population today are small groups of Arawak, Waiwái (Waiwai, Wai-Wai), Patamona, Wapishana, and Macushi, the last group being the most prominent of the savanna peoples. There are also mixed groups: Spanish Arawaks, such as the Arecuna of the Moruka River area, and Spanish Warao, living on and near the border with Venezuela. The savanna peoples, rarely seen in the populated coastal areas, subsist by farming, hunting, fishing, and to a lesser degree selling their crafts—polished stone implements, weaving, and beadwork.

Though historians have recorded sketches and pictures of aboriginal carvings, paintings, stonework, basketry, and beadwork, scant collections of Amerindian musical culture in the form of instruments, dance, and song exist. Since about 1975, the Guyanese government has tried to address the need for documentation. In 1985, the artist-historian Denis Williams founded the Amerindian Museum, which displays life-size replicas, artifacts, and literature of each of the indigenous cultures of Guyana. Some information on local Amerindians can also be found in the Georgetown Museum, whose founding curator, Sir Everard Im Thurn, wrote a pioneering work on the Amerindians in 1883. Sister Noel Menezes, a Carmelite nun and historian, has researched and written extensively about the culture of the Amerindians of Guyana. Other studies have been made by Walter Roth (1924), Niels Fock (1963), and Jens Yde (1965) for the Waiwái.

Local Amerindians had a song for every aspect of life. Vocal music making occurred around campfires, in fields while sowing or harvesting, or at the feasting after a successful hunt (*mashramani,* also the name for a carnival-like celebration in Guyana). Sometimes, dance would accompany vocal music, usually performed in a circle. In the Caribbean as a whole, with the early demise of the Arawak and Carib populations, indigenous religious expression was wiped out; however, the tribes remaining in Guyana give evidence of traditional rituals and feasts that have remained intact. Music in the form of divine incantations is utilized for the purpose of healing, and Hallelujah, a syncretic religion, includes ritual singing (Butt Colson 1971).

The most popular Amerindian instrumental types in Guyana are membranophonic drums and flutes. Skin drums vary in size according to their use (hunting, feasting, dancing, warfare). They are mostly made from the hollow trunks of trees, with the skins of animals to cover the ends. Rawhide thongs or bush ropes (made of vines) tighten and keep the skins in position. Bamboo flutes were often used, and as with the skin drum, different types were used depending upon the occasion. Flutes were made from long-jointed or short-jointed bamboo, the latter being favored for instrumental merrymaking.

The influence of other people's musics has not escaped these groups entirely, so today locally made instruments such as the guitar, the violin, the banjo, the maracas (*shak-shak*), the side-blown bamboo flute, and occasionally a tambourine are found.

People of East Indian heritage

Indians, most from North India, first came to Guyana in May 1838, and continued coming until 1917. The majority were of the Hindu religion, about 10 percent were Muslim, and some were Christian. By 1917, about forty-two thousand Muslim Indians were in Guyana; in the late 1990s, their numbers probably totaled about seventy-five thousand. They brought with them their religious and cultural patterns, which they have maintained (with slight variations), forming a thriving subculture in Guyana. They kept up their celebratory practices of Ramadan and other rituals, such as Phagwa (which honors the Hindu god Lord Krishna), Divali (a Hindu festival associated with lights and rejoicing, signifying the triumph of light over darkness), and Hosay (an Islamic festival). Other cultural ties were continued through folk music, storytelling, traditional weddings, and especially language, which they retained. By the end of the indentureship period (1917), Indians who had chosen not to return to their homeland began to participate actively in the society of their adopted country. In the 1990s, East Indians accounted for about 41 percent (328,000) of the Guyanese population.

Instrumental music, song, dance, and drama always played a significant role in the daily existence of these people. Since the Indian people of Guyana practiced their culture strictly among themselves, there has been a dearth of written information about local Indian musical instruments, their construction, and methods of performance. With the establishment of the National History and Arts Council (now the Department of Culture), local Indian musical ensembles flourished during the late 1970s and early 1980s. Membranophones were their major instruments, including the *dholak,* the *tabla,* the *taja,* and *tassa* drums [see MUSIC OF IMMIGRANT GROUPS]. The *dholak* and *tabla* were usually brought from India. Until the late 1970s, some were available for purchase in Indian merchants' stores.

The *dholak* is a double-headed barrel-shaped drum whose shell is hollowed out of a solid block of wood to a thickness of 25 millimeters. It is about 45 to 50 centimeters long, with a diameter of 30 centimeters on one end and 18 to 23 centimeters on the other; the size, however, can vary. Both heads are covered with stretched leather. Attached to the heads are thick cotton thongs that pass through circular rings of metal near the middle of the shell; these rings help tune the heads. The *dholak* is used for folk music and festivals.

The *tabla,* which consists of two drums, is the most widely used percussive instrument in Indian vocal and instrumental music in Guyana. The *bayan,* played with the left hand, is made of clay or copper; the *dayan* is usually hollowed out of a block of wood and played with the right hand. Both drums have single leather goatskin heads fastened to leather hooks and stretched over the drum bodies. The heads are made tight by leather laces that pass through the hooks and by cylindrical blocks of wood wedged between the laces and the shell. To raise or lower the pitch, the player pushes these wedges up or down. The drums are usually tuned an octave apart. A flour-and-water paste applied to the left drumhead lowers the pitch, giving a dull low sound. Since the paste is applied only once, it is mixed with iron filings for permanence. In Guyana, the *tabla* serves extensively as accompaniment to dancing and singing.

The *taja* was always popular in Guyana and was played by Indian immigrants during the 1800s. It is a double-headed membranophone made from an oak barrel covered with goatskin on both ends. The skins are held securely by thick cotton laces that pass through small metal rings; the tension of the laces regulates the pitch. The *taja* is not usually mentioned with other instruments of Indian origin, so it is believed that this drum may have been originally built by local Indians for entertainment rather than rituals.

The *tassa*, known as the wedding drum, is a popular membranophone among the Hindus in Guyana. It is usually played alongside another large drum, the *baydam,* during weddings, *mundan* (shaving of the head of a child), and other ceremonies. Kettle-shaped, the body of the drum is made of metal, 45 to 60 centimeters in diameter. Goatskin covers the single opening, held in place with goatskin straps. The *tassa* is played with two small bamboo sticks and is usually accompanied by a pair of small metallic cymbals (*jhāñjh*).

Since the early 1960s, European instruments have infiltrated the few East Indian popular film-music bands found in Guyana—a clear indication of the impact of European and North American culture. Most Indian musical ensembles are not complete without a harmonium, a portable reed organ with a keyboard ranging about three octaves and a bellows. The harmonium player sings as he accompanies himself, playing melodies with his right hand while operating the bellows with the left.

Because of their initial isolation on the sugar plantations in the rural areas of Guyana, the Indian community maintained and recreated many aspects of their traditional life, including worship, thus keeping their musical traditions somewhat intact. By modeling, older Guyanese Indians teach Hindi devotional songs (*bhajan*) to their children. The East Indians, however, still practice religious and secular festivals from India (with reinterpretations), and some of these, such as Divali, Phagwah, and Eid, are nationally observed. During these ceremonies, many East Indian musical traditions are expressed, including classical, secular, and religious Indian song and dance, some strongly influenced by the film industry of India.

With the wave of nationalism that spread throughout the country after independence, Guyanese East Indian cultural traditions began to develop a local flavor, becoming distinct from those of India. Early in the 1970s, the National School of Dance, through its choreographers, incorporated East Indian dance steps into its performances, accompanied by traditional Indian instruments such as the *tabla*. Some choreographers were Indians, but the majority were not.

People of African heritage

Thirty-seven percent of Guyana's population is of African heritage, descendants of slaves mainly from West Africa who brought with them their languages and a cultural heritage that included traditions of storytelling. In colonial British Guiana, people of African heritage experienced considerable prejudice and discrimination. Their cultural practices were deemed pagan and immoral and were seen to be potentially dangerous, having the capacity to incite the emotions. Drumming in particular was held in contempt and at one time was even outlawed. Yet enslaved Africans kept their music and religious traditions alive by secretly maintaining them. Over time, these traditions mixed with other influences from the colonists, giving rise to new forms. The African heritage is still rich in Guyana, where numerous examples of survivals and retentions exist.

Tapping vivid memories of home, African slaves in Guyana built African musical instruments in their new land; several have survived, especially skin drums. Today, there remains a strong tradition of drumming, singing, and dancing. Two surviving membranophones are a conga and a tam-tam (variant spelling of tom-tom, a large and slightly convex-shaped drum, played with the hands).

The conga is an elongated bass drum, about 40 centimeters in diameter, whose body is made of wood. It is about 1.2 meters high, covered at one end with skin and open at the other. Wooden stakes attached to loops affixed to the skin are hammered into the side of the drum body, making the skin tight and allowing the drum to be tuned. The tam-tam is similar in style except for its diameter, about half that of the conga; as a result, it produces a higher sound. These drums, held between the legs of seated musicians, are played with the hands. Drumming is heard only in specific social and religious contexts such as weddings and wakes (rituals lasting nine nights after a person's death), particularly in rural areas.

Another African retention is the *que-que,* a ceremonial song-and-dance sequence, performed mainly as a celebration honoring a couple intending to marry. In this context, singing and dancing accompany each other, with the dancers' bare feet simulating drum patterns. The dancers line up in two files, men on one side, women on the other, while spectators gather in a ring. A soloist improvises a line or a stanza (usually in quadruple time), and spectators and dancers answer, clapping their hands. The dancers move around in a circle, stamping on the ground in a one-two-three pattern, and kicking in the air on the fourth beat. The *que-que* usually lasts several hours, since it follows a sequential pattern of songs. During it, food and drink are served.

Enslaved Africans kept their religious traditions alive as they had done with their music and language. Dale Bisnauth describes a syncretic sect unique to Guyana; known as the Church of the Western Evangelical Millennium Pilgrims (WEMP) and founded by Nathaniel Jordan, it draws beliefs and practices from Christianity, Hinduism, and traditional religions of Africa (1993:42). Because of the attire prescribed by the church, members are commonly called the Jordanites or the White-Robed Army. They come mainly from the black working class. Derived practices include singing a cappella, the use of Protestant hymns and European harmonies, the technique of lining out, rhythmic hand clapping, and responsorial texture.

Calypso and steelbands

Another common musical form in Guyana is calypso, whose roots lie in African oral traditions. Because it originated in Trinidad, however, its musical influences include French and Spanish concepts from the colonial periods, East Indian drumming (*tassa* drumming), and African revivalist spirituals. In style, it also shows influences of rhythm and blues, swing, and bebop, brought to Trinidad by United States troops stationed there during World War II. Calypso can be described as witty, using satirical poetry in song. It serves as a vehicle for the town crier, village gossip, and rich entertainment.

The average Guyanese does not use calypso as an everyday means of expression; therefore the calypsonian is a specialist to whom many people can relate because he offers clever commentaries on current social ills. The Guyanese form of calypso is usually four stanzas long, with a chorus after each stanza. The tunes are catchy,

Work songs include those sung by gold diggers, locally known as pork-knockers, who paddle boats to and from the goldfields and diamond fields in the interior of Guyana.

singable, and easy to remember. Audience participation in the chorus serves as a measure of the popularity of a particular calypso.

The steelband, which came to Guyana from Trinidad in 1952, is in part a descendant and reinterpretation of the hollow log idiophones and xylophones of Africa. It includes steel idiophones (pans) made from 55-gallon oil drums. Pans range from full-size basses to the ping pong, cut to about 15 centimeters from the top of the barrel. Steelbands play any type of music on any occasion but play mostly during national festivals [see TRINIDAD AND TOBAGO].

Masquerade bands

In Guyana, the late-twentieth-century reawakening of masquerade bands, though not widespread, represents a revival of African elements. A tradition of music, dance, mask, and mime, the masquerade can be found in several islands of the Caribbean. Though its roots are strongly African, Al Creighton (1994) cites other influences, such as Morris dancing and medieval mumming plays. The name *masquerade* (used in Nigeria) may come from the Yoruba word *egungun* 'masquerader'.

In Guyana, the masquerade is performed mainly at Christmas, though it has no traditional links with the Christian nativity. It is made up of instrumentalists playing fife and two types of drums, flouncers (dancers who perform a series of intricate steps), and various masked and costumed characters (see Okada 1995: example 21). The last include stilt dancers (symbols of agility and strength recreating the steps of ancestral gods), the mad cow (which drives fear into onlookers and controls crowds), and Mother Sally (a towering, 2-meter image, dancing wildly with flailing hands).

Music and dance play equal roles in masquerades. The fife, with its size and piercing quality akin to those of the piccolo, plays a rhythmic melodic line above the drumbeats. Dictating the dancers' steps, the *bhoom* (bass drum) keeps the beat, while the *kittle* (a smaller drum) plays counter-rhythms to the bass. Both drums are played with sticks. Despite attempts in the 1990s to revive interest and elevate its status, masquerade is a dying art in Guyana.

British traditions

Guyanese formal music education was developed mainly by the British. Generations of young people were and still are being taught music theory, piano performance, and other instrumental playing in preparation for the examinations set by the British Royal Schools of Music. These examinations are an external equivalent to those held in England and are adjudicated by an examiner sent from England. High standards of instrumental performance were attained by some of these candidates, who were later to form the nucleus of a concertgoing public and patrons of the arts.

As part of their legacy, the British (with the help of musically trained Guyanese) established in 1952 the Music Festival, a biennial competition, which continued until 1973. As with the examinations, an adjudicator was sent from England to judge instrumental and vocal performances, verse, and choral speaking at varying age levels through adulthood. All the music chosen for competition was classical. Later, the scope of the festival expanded to include categories in folk song and composition. The latter category was included to encourage musical settings of poetry about the flora, fauna, and rivers of Guyana. It gave rise to two collections of Guyanese national songs, with titles such as "Buttercup," "My Guyana El Dorado," "Way Down Demerara" (the name of a river), "My Native Land," and "O Beautiful Guyana."

The outstanding vocal work by a Guyanese composer is a three-movement musical setting of A. J. Seymour's poem "The Legend of Kaieteur," referring to a Guyanese waterfall. Composed in 1944 by the late Philip Pilgrim, this work was intended for orchestra, solo piano, three soloists, and a choir of a hundred voices. The composer died before completing the orchestral score, but the work has been performed (in 1944, and again in 1970) with two pianos substituting for the orchestra. For the first Caribbean Festival of the Arts (CARIFESTA), held in Guyana in 1972, the composer's brother rescored the work for two pianos and steelband. As far as is known, this was the first time a steelband was used in an extended work of its kind. The event served to highlight a perceived need for the region's traditional instruments to be fully recognized and used in nontraditional ways.

The British also established military bands and chamber orchestras. In the initial stages, a military band known as the B. G. Militia Band was made up of British foreign nationals under the directorship of a British bandleader. One former director, Major S. W. Henwood, wrote compositions for the band and encouraged bandsmen to compose. A few compositions by former bandsmen are still performed. Gradually, in the early 1960s, the makeup of the band changed to include young local men (taught to play wind instruments) and a local bandmaster. During the 1970s and 1980s, the band, now known as the Guyana Police Force Band, began to include women among its members.

In the 1950s, British expatriates' establishment of the Theater Guild of Guyana allowed for the production of several British plays and operettas, particularly those of Gilbert and Sullivan. Dance bands that flourished during the 1930s and 1940s played the music of the swing era for ballroom dancing. During British rule, music and music education flourished in schools, churches, and concerts.

NATIONAL MUSICAL CONTEXTS AND GENRES

The great influence of dance and folk drama on the music of Guyana is reflected in festivals and dramatic presentations that have become part of everyday life. Singing has always been a major part of Caribbean culture, and in the vocal repertoire of Guyana, many forms of songs appear. Among these are the spirituals, chanties, work songs, classical European art songs, English folk songs, and religious songs. Examples of these genres are not always sung but are sometimes used instrumentally as part of dramatic presentations. Examples of this practice can be found during Mashramani (an Amerindian term for celebrations after a successful hunt or harvest). During these celebrations (formerly marked by national competitions called Mass Games, inspired by similar events held in other socialist countries, especially North Korea), music, movement, dance, choral speaking, and visual art combine to produce exciting dramas.

Guyanese work songs formed a considerable portion of the vocal literature in the pre- and early postindependence eras. Work songs can be described as songs that accompany and stimulate workers during periods of communal labor. In Guyana, many of these songs dealt with activities of the sea and shipbuilding. That Guyana borders the sea is reflected in the many boat songs and chanties in the musical repertoire. However, with the increase in movement from rural to urban areas, beginning in the early 1970s, many of these musical traditions are no longer practiced.

Among the work songs peculiar to Guyana are timber workers' songs. Others are used by builders who believe in the need to appease evil spirits, thus ensuring safe and proper construction. The foreman customarily leads these songs, and the other builders or loggers join in on the chorus. Also in the work-song category are those sung by gold diggers, locally known as pork-knockers, who paddle boats to and from the goldfields and diamond fields in the interior of Guyana. To save time, these workers often engage in the dangerous practice of riding the rapids; their songs offer them comfort and protection. One of the most famous of their songs is "Itanamee," referring to a Guyanese river; in its text, a frightened man pleads with the captain to be put ashore. Completing this group are boat-race songs and chanties, formerly sung at the annual regatta (Brathwaite 1962:6).

Starting in 1970, after the attainment of independence and on a change in the form of government to a republic, a wave of nationalism spread through the country, fostered and reflected in governmental cultural policies of the 1970s. A few jazz musicians experimented with various rhythms and motifs in an attempt to create a Guyanese beat. Two beats that enjoyed brief spells of popularity were the *bhoom* and the *lopi,* the first in the 1960s and the second in the 1970s.

Other evidence of the growth of musical nationalism was seen in the creation of the Guyana Festival of the Arts (GUYFESTA), which replaced the British-style Music Festival in 1973 with several folkloric arts. It allowed competitors, even those who had received no formal music training, the freedom to compose and perform their own works, mostly for voice with guitar accompaniment, on any theme—folk, national, political, social. It helped showcase a young breed of composers whose compositions were more rhythmic and syncopated than the earlier, hymn-style pieces (figure 1). In the 1990s, the Mass Games were discontinued, partly for lack of interest after the death of President Forbes Burnham in 1985. GUYFESTA was replaced with a revived version of the Music Festival, now with a regional adjudicator and higher standards.

Tourism, media, and musical outreach

Unlike most West Indian islands, Guyana does not boast blue waters and sandy beaches. As a result, tourism has never been a large part of the Guyanese economy. Foreign nationals staying in the country are mainly there at the request of the government, working on national projects through their embassies. Much Guyanese music is heard in the context of social events: Mass Games; Mashramani, a kind of carnival (figure 2); and classical and folk concerts.

There is no public television station in the country. Not until 1992 was a private station begun—CNS, devoted to East Indian culture (Manuel 1995:214). Radio, however, plays an important role. It devotes airtime to Indian programs of religious and secular music, but most of its fare is American popular music. Musical competitions continue during Mashramani, with calypso, steelband, and fife-and-drum competitions.

Some importance must be placed on the contributions made by visiting artists and foreign nationals living in Guyana, as on the roles played by the cultural arms of various embassies. Guyana has been fortunate in this respect, and the contributions made by the Indian Cultural Center, the USIS Information Services, and several other foreign embassies, have helped in no small measure to broaden the cultural outlook of the Guyanese people.

The social class structure, which arose even musically as a consequence of British traditions, no longer exists, and instruments and those who make and use them have

FIGURE 1 "Cooperate," a song (and publication layout) with social content composed by Olivia Ahyoung in 1985 for the unpublished children's book, "My Community, My Nation." Art by Barrington Braithwaite. Copyright Olivia Ahyoung, 1985.

Though Guyana boasts many formally trained
musicians, they have yet to make a musical impact
on the world scene, as performers in Jamaica and
Trinidad have.

FIGURE 2   "Mashramani," a song (and publica-
tion layout) with social content composed by
Olivia Ahyoung in 1985 for the unpublished
children's book, "My Community, My Nation."
Art by Barrington Braithwaite. Copyright Olivia
Ahyoung, 1985.

acquired new status. However, despite the shift in emphasis to local and regional culture, with an upsurge of performances of folk music, more school steelbands, and
with young people involved in masquerade bands, the general teenage population,
exposed to large doses of American popular music, feels a conflict of interest.

Though Guyana boasts many formally trained musicians, they have yet to make
a musical impact on the world scene, as performers in Jamaica and Trinidad have.
Such an achievement can be possible only through the combined efforts and cooperation of the Department of Culture and the Ministry of Education, the agencies
responsible for determining the direction of music and music education in Guyana,
and their subsequent export abroad.

REFERENCES

Bisnauth, Dale. 1993. "Roots: Religious Crossroads." In *The Caribbean: Culture of Resistance, Spirit of Hope,* ed. Oscar L. Bolioli, 36–45. New York: Friendship Press.

Brathwaite, P. A. 1962. *Musical Traditions, Aspects of Racial Elements with Influence on a Guianese Community.* Georgetown, Guyana: Georgetown Press.

Butt Colson, Audrey. 1971. "Hallelujah among the Patamona Indians." *Antropológica* 28:25–58.

Creighton, Al. 1994. "The Jester Dances On, but the Gods Are Gone." *Stabroek News* (Georgetown, Guyana, 25 December): 5A.

Fock, Niels. 1963. *Waiwai. Religion and Society of an Amazonian Tribe.* Nationalmuseets Skrifter, Etnografisk Roekke, 8. Copenhagen: National Museum.

Manuel, Peter. 1995. *Caribbean Currents.* Philadelphia: Temple University Press.

Okada, Yuki. 1995. *Central and South America.* JVC Smithsonian Folkways Video Anthology of Music and Dance of the Americas, 5. Montpelier, Vt.: Multicultural Media VTMV-229. Video.

Roth, Walters E. 1924. "An Introductory Study of the Arts, Crafts, and Customs of the Guiana Indians." In *Thirty-Eighth Annual Report of the Bureau of American Ethnology to the Secretary of the Smithsonian Institution 1916–1917.* Washington, D.C.: U. S. Government Printing Office.

Tremblay, Hélène. 1988. *Families of the World.* Vol. 1, *The Americas and the Caribbean.* New York: Farrar, Straus and Giroux.

Yde, Jens. 1965. *Material Culture of the Waiwái.* Nationalmuseets Skrifter, Etnografisk Roekke, 10. Copenhagen: National Museum.

Paraguay
Timothy D. Watkins

The Colonial Period
Musical Instruments
Musical Contexts and Genres
Social Structure and Musicians
Popular Music and Electronic Media
Further Study

Paraguay is often called by its citizens the heart of South America, because of its land-locked position in the center of South America and national pride in its cultural riches. About 95 percent of the population is of mixed Spanish and Guaraní Indian descent. Though little else of Guaraní culture has survived, the Guaraní language has left a strong mark, and its use is a focus of national pride. Most of the population is bilingual; 90 percent of the population speak Guaraní, and 75 percent speak Spanish. Widespread bilingualism has led to frequent mixing of the languages, creating a linguistic hybrid, Jopará. Racial and linguistic mixtures contribute to the ethnic, cultural, and social homogeneity of the population. This homogeneity, in turn, contributes to a strong sense of cultural identity, often expressed in music.

Though the landmass of Paraguay (406,750 square kilometers) is almost the size of California, most of the 4.5 million population has traditionally occupied an area within 160 kilometers of the capital, Asunción. Large-scale migrations to the east and south since the early 1970s have reduced this concentration, but most of the population still lives in the eastern half of the country. Though the western area accounts for 60 percent of the landmass, only about 4 percent of the people live west of the Paraguay River, in the area known as the Chaco.

The Paraguay River serves as a cultural divider among the country's Indians. The four groups in eastern Paraguay all speak varieties of Guaraní [see GUARANÍ] or Guayakí, a related language. Those in the Chaco represent five language families: the Ayoreo and Chamakoko belong to the Zamuko family; the Angaité, Guana, Lengua, and Sanapana belong to the Maskoy family; the Chorotí, Chulupí (Churupí), and Maká belong to the Matako family; and the Guaykurú family is represented by the Toba language. The only Guaraní group in the Chaco is the Chiriguano. The Guaraní language often serves as a lingua franca among the native populations.

The archaeological musical record of pre-Columbian Paraguay is scant; it contains only a few bone vertical end-blown ductless flutes (*mimby*) of Guaraní origin. Besides the climate and the soil, among the reasons for the paucity of archaeological musical artifacts is that the indigenous inhabitants led a seminomadic way of life, occasioned at least in part among Guaraní tribes by the belief that the souls of the dead continued to inhabit the structures that were their homes during life.

THE COLONIAL PERIOD

The historical musical record begins with the arrival of the Portuguese explorer Aleixo García in 1524. Among the chroniclers, Martín del Barco Centenera (1982 [1602]), who in 1572 accompanied the expedition of Juan Ortiz de Zárate, mentioned the *mbaraká* (large rattle), horns, and drums. Ruy Díaz de Guzmán (1945:187) wrote of trumpets (*cornetas*) and horns (*bocinas*), sounded by the Indians before an attack. Ulrich Schmiedel, a Bavarian soldier who accompanied Pedro de Mendoza in the exploration up the Paraná and Paraguay rivers, recounted that music was played while the chief of the Jerús—scholars have not identified this culture; it may have been the name of a village—ate his meals, and that at noon, if the chief so wished, the most attractive men and women danced before him (1942:60).

Some of the most informative accounts of natives' musical performance come from Jesuit records. The *Cartas anuas,* annual reports made by each Jesuit province to the Jesuit general in Rome (Leonhardt 1927–1929), tell us that some Guaraní surrounded the house of a certain Spaniard and for several nights played their horns and drums "in a warlike manner." The Jesuit historians praised Guaraní musical abilities, which they used for missionizing other Indians. Gonzal Carrasco recounted how the missionaries would travel into new areas by canoe, taking Indian converts. As they headed upriver, the missionaries, echoed by their recent converts, sang songs to attract the attention of other Guaraní, who came out of the forest to the riverbanks, and sometimes even swam after the canoes, at least in part because of their fascination with the music they heard (Charlevoix 1769 [1756]:60).

The Jesuit accounts focus on life in the thirty mission towns (*reducciones* 'reductions') established by the Jesuits among the Guaraní. These accounts have little to say regarding native musical practices among the Guaraní, but they do attest to the extent to which the missionaries instructed the Indians in European musical styles. As early as 1609, the year the first mission towns were founded, the Jesuit provincial (the highest-ranking Jesuit in the province), Diego de Torres, ordered that the Indian inhabitants should be taught "not only doctrine and singing, but to read and write music with ease." By 1620, Pedro de Oñate reported that in the mission town of San Ignacio the missionaries had taught the Indians to sing well in three voices, and there was a good trio of *chirimías* (shawms). By about 1700, all the mission towns had choirs and instrumentalists trained in European styles, whom observers frequently compared favorably with European performers. The Guaraní musicians performed music imported from Europe and written by Jesuit missionaries, including the Italian composer Domenico Zipoli (1688–1726).

In addition to the musical instruction available in each mission town, Guaraní youths who showed musical talent were sometimes sent to the music school established at Yapeyú, near the Uruguay River. The most important figure in the musical life of Yapeyú was Anton Sepp von Reinegg (1691–1733) from Tirol, whose accounts (1696, 1973 [1710]) of his life as a missionary shed important light on the development of music not only at Yapeyú but in all the mission towns. He is credited with the introduction of the harp, an instrument that has obtained musical primacy in Paraguayan folk music, and he built the first organ to have been constructed in the mission towns. This organ seems to have been moved from Itapúa, where it was built, to Yapeyú.

Guaraní from the mission towns sometimes visited Argentine cities, including Córdoba and Buenos Aires. In 1628, Francisco de Céspedes, governor of Río de la Plata, wrote about having seen in Buenos Aires a group of more than twenty Indians from San Ignacio. He described them as "great musicians" who played "the organ, violin, and other instruments," and performed the "dances of the Sacrament." He insisted they were as skilled as if they had been educated in Spain (Peña 1916:173).

MUSICAL INSTRUMENTS

Inventories made of the mission towns on the expulsion of the Jesuits from Spanish lands show the use of a remarkable number and variety of musical instruments. Among them were harps, guitars, *vihuelas, bandurrias,* violins, violas, harpsichords, spinets, horns, trumpets, trombones, *chirimías, bajones,* flutes, and organs. Some of these instruments had been imported from Europe, but many had been made by the Guaraní. The only instrument with precontact roots recorded in the inventories was a conch trumpet.

In addition to the written inventories, an iconographic record of some instruments found in the mission towns still exists. High on the walls of the church in the partially restored ruins of the town of Trinidad is a frieze depicting angels playing many of the instruments mentioned in the written accounts of musical life in the Jesuit mission towns (figure 1).

Numerous musical instruments are in use today among the indigenous, mestizo, and European-descended inhabitants of Paraguay, though there is no record that indigenous instruments were used in Jesuit mission towns.

Idiophones

One of the most important idiophones in use among the Guaraní is the *mbaraká,* a spiked calabash rattle with small stones or seeds inside, and a wooden handle usually adorned with feathers. It is regarded as a shamanistic instrument [see GUARANÍ].

The *takuapú,* a Guaraní word for an indigenous bamboo stamped tube, is played only by women among themselves and other groups. Among the Maká and other Chaco indigenous groups, the length may vary between 1.5 and 2 meters. The *takuapú* tubes in the Chaco may have strings of rattles attached and are used in women's dances to mark the beat. Strings of rattles, such as those attached to the *takuapú,* may be worn around dancers' ankle, waists, or wrists. They are traditionally made from deer hooves, tortoiseshells, or other materials or may even consist of bottle caps strung together (Boettner n.d.:20).

Membranophones

Indigenous groups use various types of drums. Water drums are used by the Toba, the Maká, the Guaykurú, and other groups living in the Chaco. The bodies of these

FIGURE 1 Section of a frieze in the ruins of the church of Trinidad, Itapúa, Paraguay. *Left to right:* violin, harp, and guitar. Photo by Timothy D. Watkins, 1992.

FIGURE 2   Two Aché-Guayakí women play *krywá* resonating tubes. Photo by Timothy D. Watkins, 1992.

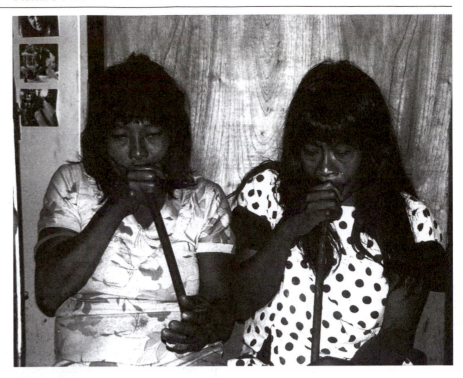

drums may be made of wood, ceramic, or tin, and are covered at their tops with deerskin or lizardskin. The heads are beaten with a single stick, a gourd, or the hand.

Aerophones

Flutes are the most frequent type of aerophone among all indigenous groups in Paraguay. The generic term for flutes among the Guaraní is *mimby*, but a wide variety exists. One of the most notable flutes among the non-Guaraní Paraguayan groups is a wooden globular flute found among the Chulupí.

The *krywá,* a resonating tube played exclusively by Aché-Guayakí women, consists of a simple cane tube, open on both ends but with no holes for fingering (figure 2). It is held so the player hums into one of her hands, which acts as a duct to the proximal end of the tube. The player's other hand alternately covers and uncovers the distal end of the tube, producing a rhythmic change of timbre. Individual players may use single or double tubes. In the latter case, the alternate covering and uncovering of the distal end occurs on only one of the two tubes. Though the *krywá* is used exclusively by women, there does not appear to be any taboo against its handling by men, and it is frequently played in mixed gatherings.

Chordophones

Traditional chordophones played by members of indigenous groups in Paraguay include several types of musical bows. The *cajuavé* is a small, mouth-resonated bow found in the Chaco. It is held between the front teeth and struck with a small stick; the musician's mouth serves as a resonator and a means of changing the amplitude of the overtones. The sound of the *cajuavé* is soft, and it is a personal instrument, played by men on occasions such as the death of, or separation from, their wives (Boettner n.d.:30).

The Aché-Guayakí hunting bow (*rapá*) serves as a musical instrument. Players place it over a resonating container, and strum it to produce a monotone ostinato. Traditionally, clay pots were the resonators of choice, but metal buckets are sometimes used. A possibly related chordophone used by the Aché-Guayakí is the

Traditionally, harpists made their own instruments—
a practice that can still be observed in the interior
of the country. However, a thriving harp-making
industry now exists in and around Asunción.

terokará, a board zither with five to seven strings. One end of it is placed inside (rather than over) a resonating container, which, like that used for the *rapá,* may be of pottery or metal.

A one-stringed violin is used by the Maká and the Lengua of the Chaco, probably as a result of contact with missionaries. The hairs of the bow are moistened by the player's mouth to produce sound when drawn across the string. The body of the violin is made from wood or a tin can.

The most ubiquitous instruments in the folk music of the population of Paraguay are the guitar (*guitarra*) and the harp (*arpa*). These are considered indispensable for folkloric ensembles (*conjuntos*). The guitar, called *mbaraká* in Guaraní, is of standard European design, with six nylon strings.

Harps and harpists

The diatonic Paraguayan harp (sometimes called *arpa india* 'Indian harp', though it is of European descent) is usually the featured instrument of a *conjunto,* and the harpist is often the director of the group. The Paraguayan harp produces a bright, powerful sound. The neck is made of two halves of laminated wood, through which the tuning pegs pass, and the strings (usually 36 to 40) come out of holes in the bottom side of the neck. This construction causes a centralization of pressure in the neck, which makes a high string tension that creates a bright sound. This construction allows for a lightweight instrument, usually between 3 and 5 kilograms. Tuning pegs were traditionally made of wood, though most harps now feature guitar-type mechanical pegs. The body of the Paraguayan harp is about 1.4 meters long and about 40 centimeters wide at its widest point. The sound resonates from the body through a single, large, round hole in the base of the sound box. Traditionally, harpists made their own instruments—a practice that can still be observed in the interior of the country. However, a thriving harp-making industry now exists in and around Asunción, providing harps for professional harpists in Paraguay and throughout the world. The popularity of the Paraguayan harp has spread widely since 1970, even as far as Japan (figure 3).

An important aspect of harp-performance technique in Paraguay is the lack of standardization. Harpists learn by experimentation and observation. This results in widely various techniques and special effects, which become part of the tradition. Techniques of muffling and glissando are especially important in harp pieces such as "*Pájaro Campana*" ('The Bellbird'), "*Cascada*" ('Waterfall'), and "*El Tren Lechero*" ('The Milk Train'), based largely on natural or human-made sounds.

The most influential Paraguayan harpist-composer was Felix Pérez Cardozo (1908–1952), composer of the onomatopoeic "*Llegada*" and "*El Tren Lechero,*" and arranger of the famous traditional melody "*Pájaro Campana.*" He was one of the first harpists to popularize the Paraguayan harp outside the country. Other famous harpists include Luís Bordón, who lived for many years in Brazil; Digno García, the

FIGURE 3 A young Japanese woman, "T-san," who immigrated to Asunción, Paraguay, specifically to study the Paraguayan harp, poses with her instrument. Photo by Dale A. Olsen, 1993.

original harpist with the internationally acclaimed Trío Los Paraguayos and the composer of "*Cascada*"; and Santiago Cortesi, who in addition to his fame as a performer has gained wide renown as a harp teacher.

When the harp is played at home or in concert as a solo instrument, the harpist is usually seated; in a *conjunto* performance, usually with two or three guitars, the harpist usually stands, sometimes placing the legs of the instrument on a small stool to obtain the correct height. In addition to the harp and standard guitars, a *requinto* (a smaller guitar) is sometimes used in folkloric ensembles.

MUSICAL CONTEXTS AND GENRES

Religious

Religious contexts form an important part of musical life in Paraguay. Music is an important part of shamanism among the Indian groups, where sickness is often believed to be caused by intrusion of substances into the patient. Healing results from naming and extracting the intrusion, which follows several hours of chanting by the shaman.

African-derived music

Though Paraguay never had as many African slaves as did regions along the Atlantic and Pacific coasts, there was in the 1800s a small number of Paraguayans of African ancestry. They have mostly been absorbed into the population at large, leaving little trace of their African heritage except the musical bow (*gualambau, guyrambau, lambau,* and other names) and possibly the *mbarimbau.* The one exception is the community of Laurelty, where the celebration of the feast of Saint Balthazar is observed by the descendants of the blacks who had followed the Uruguayan General Artigas into exile. This celebration retains certain Africanisms, especially the primacy of drums, played exclusively by men.

In the 1980s and 1990s, African-Brazilian cults including Umbanda and Candomblé made inroads into Paraguay, principally because of large numbers of Brazilian immigrants in the western part of the country. There has been little study of these cults in Paraguay, and even less of their music. Given the relative homogeneity among African-Brazilian cults from Belem and Bahia in the Brazilian northeast to Asunción, Montevideo, and Buenos Aires, it is to be assumed that the music of these cults in Paraguay is similar to that practiced by their adherents in Brazil. The most important *terreiros* (centers of African-Brazilian worship) in Paraguay are in Asunción, Caaguazú, Campo Nueve, Coronel Oviedo, Itá, and Itaguá (Gallardo 1986:43).

Roman Catholic festivals

About 95 percent of Paraguay's population is Roman Catholic. Most of the other 5 percent are Mennonites, Baptists, or Pentecostals, or belong to smaller Protestant denominations. Beginning with the Jesuit mission towns, Roman Catholicism has been a significant cultural force through Paraguay's history. Given the greater freedom that began after the second Vatican Council (1962–1965), liturgical music has been somewhat influenced by the *coritos* (short choruses) prominent in many of the Protestant churches. Much music associated with the Roman Catholic Church, especially in religious festivals, is greatly influenced by folkloric traditions. Traditional religious songs include *gozos* 'joys', *alabanzas* 'praises', and *villancicos* 'rustic songs'.

An important musical event that occurs during Holy Week is the activity of the *pasioneros* (relating to the Passion of Christ), also called *estacioneros* (relating to the

Stations of the Cross). These are associations of men who process to the church or to a replica of Calvary, the hill on which Jesus was crucified. Dressed in uniforms, they carry the banner of the association and a cross. The uniforms usually consist of black or navy pants, plain or with yellow stripes down the legs; or white pants with colored stripes; black belts; and white shirts with the association's own emblem or a cross enclosed in a triangle on the pocket. Sometimes a black or purple sash, crossing from the right shoulder to the left side of the waist, is worn. A short cape, which may be black, purple, blue, dark yellow, or gray, decorated with a cross, is also part of the uniform. Sometimes a white cap is worn. As these uniformed *pasioneros* process, they sing somber songs, known as cried song (*purahéi jahe'ó*) or mournful song (*purahéi asy*), on the subject of the Passion, stopping every few steps to kneel, as if observing the Stations of the Cross. The songs, which may be in Spanish, Guaraní, or a mixture of the two, are sung in unison or in thirds and have mostly conjunct melodies, simple harmonies (usually only tonic and dominant), and rather free rhythm. Musical instruments are not used.

Patronal festivals

Patronal festivals are especially important musical occasions, in which a complex of religious and secular ceremonies forms a unified whole, providing an occasion for celebration and strengthening communal bonds, often marked by the return of family members who have moved away from the community. The festivals are usually organized by a festivity commission (*comisión de festejos*), composed of prominent men and women in the community. The religious observance begins nine days before the feast of the patron saint. Masses are said for community members who have died in the past year, and for the sick. Weddings are an important part of the celebration.

Traditionally, the image of the patron saint is kept in the home of a caretaker, but this custom is no longer widely observed. From the caretaker's home, the image is taken in a large procession to the church for the beginning of the novena. In communities where the image is kept in a chapel, the procession from the chapel to the church takes place on the eve of the feast, accompanied by a joyful celebratory procession marked by fireworks, band music, flying flags, and people on foot and (in rural areas) on horseback. After the image of the saint arrives in the church, masses are celebrated.

The feast proper begins before dawn with a trumpet signal (*diana mbajá*), the pealing of bells, brass-band music, and fireworks. The national flag and the standard of the patron saint are raised in the central plazas. If the patron saint is female, young men may serenade her, accompanying themselves with guitars and harps.

The central ceremony of the patronal feast is a high mass (always sung), in which a *conjunto* often supplies the musical accompaniment. Frequently, especially in rural areas, the mass is in the Guaraní language. The church is highly decorated for the occasion. The entire town attends the mass, as do residents of neighboring localities and towns. Many pilgrims or *promeseros,* children and adults, come dressed as the patron saint or at least wear elements of clothing such as habits, cloak, belt, or tiara associated with the saint. They may carry the standard or insignia of the saint and as a sign of penance may carry stones on their heads. These *promeseros* may walk great distances; in the days immediately before 8 December, the feast of the Virgin of Caacupé, attended by pilgrims from all over the country, it is common to see *promeseros* walking for many miles up rugged hills on their knees in supplication or in recognition of answered prayers.

After mass, the image of the saint is carried in a solemn procession through the streets of the town, which have been adorned with bamboo arches, small flags, flowers, ticker tape, and aeolian noisemakers, which sound in the wind. The procession is led by a brass band, followed by the various religious confraternities, brotherhoods, and associations, each carrying its standards and flags and led by its own color guard. The patronal festivals of some isolated towns still feature bands composed entirely of men and boys who play *mimby* and drums resembling those used by the Guaraní. These include the Banda Para'í in the town of Tobatí and Peteke (also known as Angu'a Pararä) in the town of Guayaivity. *Peteke* and *Pararä* (*Parará*) are onomatopoeic words, recalling the sound of the drums (Gómez-Perasso and Szarán 1978).

More secular events also take place. In the plaza in front of the church or on a vacant lot, a temporary amusement park (*kermese*) is usually set up. Tents and booths provide cover for various activities, including raffles, darts, target shooting, cards, and other games. Typical foods and drinks, alcoholic and nonalcoholic, are sold as are local arts and crafts. A merry-go-round is an indispensable part of the festivities. Bullfights are frequent occurrences as is the *toro candil* 'lighted bull', in which one or two men inside a mock-bull play the part of a fighting bull. The bull's body is made of cowhide or canvas over a wooden frame; its head is fashioned of a cow skull, to the horns of which are tied flaming torches.

An important part of the celebration surrounding patronal festivals is the concerts provided by military bands (from the local army post) or by similar civilian bands (*banda koyguá*) and by *conjuntos* performing folk music, which may accompany folk dances like the *polca paraguaya,* the *galopa,* and the *golondriana.* Groups of musicians may go from house to house serenading ecclesiastical, civil, and military authorities and prominent families.

Social and athletic clubs hold their own festivities. These events frequently feature rock bands, and are characterized as *bailes.* Those who attend come to dance. Dances (*danzas*) are not so frequent in the celebrations at these clubs.

Other feasts

Alongside the feasts of local patron saints and of the Virgin of Caacupé, the most important patronal festivals are those of San Blas, patron saint of the nation (3 February), and Saint John the Baptist (24 June). The festivities of the night of 23 June are anticipated the entire year. Besides the typical revelry, musical performance, and dancing, a particular feature of this celebration is fire. Around dusk, a large bonfire (*fogata de San Juan,* or in Guaraní, *San Juan ratá*) is lighted. Around midnight, when the fire dies down, the white-hot coals are raked out into a uniform bed on the ground, about 1 meter wide by 4 or 5 meters long, over which the faithful walk barefoot after exclaiming "*Viva San Juan!*" This practice, which apparently does no harm to the practitioners' feet, is known as *tatá ari jehasá* 'to walk on fire'. Other important activities of this feast involving fire are the crowd's kicking around a fireball (*pelota tatá*), a ball of rags soaked in tar and kerosene and set afire, and the burning of Judas in effigy (*Juda kái*). The figure of Judas is often filled with fireworks, causing a great commotion. The *Juda kái* and *tatá ari jehasá* mark the highlight of the festivities and for that reason bring the music to a temporary halt.

Protestant music

The music of the Protestant churches formerly tended to resemble that of the denominations in the United States and Europe to which they were related. Many of the Protestant hymns were Spanish translations of European and North American hymns and gospel songs. Since the 1970s, however, short repetitive choruses (*coritos*), written originally in Spanish, have been gaining popularity. These may or may not be settings of Scripture. Their texts are much more subjective and emotionally charged than those of traditional hymns. Musically, they tend toward diatonic, conjunct

conjunto 'Ensemble', throughout the Spanish-speaking Americas, a musical ensemble that performs folk music

polca paraguaya 'Paraguayan polka', the pre-eminent national genre of Paraguay, vastly different from the European polka

galopa 'Gallop', Paraguayan outdoor fast dance consisting of two contrasting musical sections

Jopará The widespread language mixture of Guaraní and Spanish spoken in Paraguay

guaránia National song genre tradition of Paraguay, created in 1925 by José Asunción Flores

sesquiáltera A Spanish-derived dual meter consisting of superimposed 3/4 and 6/8, often with alternation or hemiola

---

melodies with uncomplicated harmonies easily accompanied by guitars, frequently even in churches that have a piano or an electronic keyboard.

Secular music and dance

Folkloric music, a primary vehicle for expressing Paraguayan ideology, is particularly linked with a sense of national identity. Much of this musical nationalism is related to the importance of the Guaraní language and mythology in mestizo culture. Many musical texts are in Guaraní or Jopará. Several songs of wide renown are based on Guaraní mythology. Much folkloric music is composed by individuals but is generally conceded folkloric status based on preconceived notions of genre. The executive branch of the government demonstrated the nationalistic importance of music in a 1959 decree, which ordered that 50 percent of the music played on the radio be by Paraguayan composers. The decree is still technically in effect, though unenforced.

The musical genre known as *guaránia,* created in 1925 by José Asunción Flores (1904–1972) and later adopted by other composers, is widely acknowledged as an important national tradition. Often in minor mode, the *guaránia* is slower than a *polca,* though it makes use of the same dual-meter (*sesquiáltera*) rhythmic device. It is defined primarily by the characteristic *rasgueado,* or guitar strum. The texts of many *guaránias* assume a nostalgic viewpoint, expressing a yearning to return to a particular locality as does the song "Asunción," or remembering a lost love as does "*Recuerdos de Ypacaraí,*" which became famous throughout the world. The following partial text of "*Recuerdo de Ypacaraí*" reveals the typical nationalistic and romantic flavor of the *guaránia,* including the Guaraní term for "girl" (*cuñataí*):

Donde estás ahora cuñataí,	Where are you now, *cuñataí,*
Que tu suave canto no llega a mí?	That your gentle song does not reach me?
Donde estás ahora?	Where are you now?
Mi ser te adora	My being adores you
Con frenesí.	With frenzy.
Todo te recuerda, mi dulce amor	Everything is reminiscent of you, my sweet love.
Junto al lago azul de Ypacaraí,	Near the blue lake Ypacaraí,
Todo te recuerda.	Everything is reminiscent of you.
Mi amor te llama, cuñataí.	My love calls you, *cuñataí.*

The *polca* (polka, though vastly different from the European and American dance by that name), in various forms, is a preeminent national genre. The texts of the sung *polca* and the related genre of song (*canción,* Guaraní *purahéi*), commonly known together as *polca canción,* are frequently about explicitly nationalistic, military, or political subjects. Accounts of important battles in the Triple Alliance War (1864–1870) against Argentina, Brazil, and Uruguay, and the Chaco War (1932–

1935) against Bolivia, are common topics. The use of music to declare ideological and organizational allegiances can be seen in the fact that all major political parties and even soccer teams have official *polcas*.

Dancing frequently accompanies folkloric music. Especially prominent are several varieties of *polca*. The dance music of the *polca paraguaya* is unlike that of the European and North American polka. Whereas its most prominent feature is the melody's duple rhythm, it uses a dual meter—a syncopated compound binary in the melody against simple triple meter in the bass.

Polcas are often qualified by terms that describe how they are danced: *polca syryrý* 'smooth, slippery', *polca popó* or *jeroky popó* 'jumping polca, jumping dance', *polca jekutú* 'stationary (in which the dancer does not cover much space)', *polca valseado* 'characterized by a smooth balance of the dancer's body as in the waltz'.

The gallop (*galopa*) consists of two musical sections: the first resembles a *polca*, but the second has notable syncopation, emphasized by percussion instruments. It is performed by an instrumental ensemble usually consisting of brass and woodwind instruments, bass drum, snare drum, and cymbals. The dancers (*galoperas*) are women who dance to fulfill religious vows. The *galopa* usually takes place outdoors, in a space prepared for the occasion, lit with torches and adorned with flowers and paper pennants. The *galoperas,* in traditional dress, improvise steps as they dance with pitchers of water or bottles of alcoholic *caña* balanced on their heads, from which they offer drinks to observers. Formerly, some *galoperas* would carry baskets of fruit on their heads rather than pitchers or bottles. The symbolism of water and fruit and sensuous motions of the dancers, most of whom are young, seem to identify this dance as a type of disguised fertility ritual.

Other important folkloric dances include the *chopí* (also known as the *Santa Fe*), the *palomita*, the *golondriana*, the *london karapé*, the *pericón,* the *solito,* and the *cazador.* All of these are couple dances, performed in traditional clothes.

Steakhouses and touristic performance

An important context for Paraguayan folkloric music and dance can be found in the steakhouses (*parrilladas*) of Asunción, especially those catering to tourists from Argentina, Brazil, the United States, Japan, and the rest of the world. These restaurants, featuring typical Paraguayan cuisine, frequently offer performances of *conjuntos* of singers accompanying themselves with harp and guitars, as well as performances of folk dances.

One of the most impressive dances, and a popular tourist attraction, is the bottle dance (*danza de las botellas*), usually accompanied by *polca* music (figure 4). Probably derived from the *galopera,* it can be danced by couples, a group of women, or by solo women. The steps are often improvised, and the distinguishing mark of the dance is the balancing of bottles on the heads of the female dancer(s). As the dance progresses, more and more bottles are added, one on top of the other (the top of one may fit into a groove in the bottom of another).

Sometimes feats such as picking up a handkerchief from the dance floor with the teeth emphasize the dancer's agility and balance. In particularly lavish productions, as many as fourteen or fifteen bottles may be placed one on top of the other on the dancer's head by a helper, who may need to ascend a ladder to stack them. The final bottle is usually decorated by the insertion of flowers or by the attachment of a tricolor ribbon.

Music and life-cycle events

Life-cycle rituals are frequently settings for musical performance in Paraguay. Especially notable is the *quinceañera,* a girl's fifteenth-birthday celebration. This

FIGURE 4   In a Paraguayan steakhouse, a woman performs the *danza de las botellas* 'bottle dance'. Photo by Timothy D. Watkins, 1992.

event marks her coming of age and is celebrated as lavishly her family can afford. Dances featuring rock bands are often held; if the family's resources do not permit a live band, recordings are played.

Serenades

The serenade (*serenata*) is a frequent occurrence at a *quinceañera,* often performed by a young woman's suitor, who may be accompanied by his male friends. The serenade may be a surprise to the recipient, or she may have had prior knowledge of the event, usually as the result of gossip. The music usually begins with a love song, frequently a *guaránia,* sung to the accompaniment of guitars, and is followed by two or three faster songs such as *polcas.* At the end of the serenade, the recipient and her family are expected to thank the musicians graciously, and if they had prior knowledge of the event, to invite them into the house for an *ambigú,* food and drink. Longer *serenatas* are sometimes called *musiqueadas.* Both are performed as a sign of respect for family members, important members of the community, and girlfriends.

Wakes

A wake, especially that of a young child, is an important musical event. According to popular belief, the spirit of a young dead child (less than about eight years of age) bypasses purgatory and goes directly to heaven, where he or she becomes an angel or even a star. For this reason, the wake of a young child is called a little angel's wake (*velorio de angelito*) and is the scene of festivities (Gonzalez Torres 1991:312–313). The child wears a white crown; the clothes are white or pink for a girl or light blue for a boy. A small crucifix or palm leaves are placed in the child's hands, folded on the chest. The body is placed in a white casket whose edges are decorated with white flowers and is displayed on a table covered with a white sheet. Candles are lighted at the head of the casket. Family members and friends who attend the wake place flowers and sometimes money on the body or on the table.

During the wake, a *conjunto* (an ensemble of harp, guitar, and flute, or at least two guitars) plays and sings. Alcoholic beverages, including *caña* (sugarcane alcohol) and beer, flow freely. Those attending the wake frequently dance all night, and fireworks are not uncommon. The mourning parents of the deceased child usually remain in a separate room, where friends and family console them.

A burial procession is headed by musicians. The casket may be carried by four children—friends, relatives, or schoolmates—or may be carried by the mother or godmother on her head. The lid of the casket is carried by other children. Once at the cemetery, the crucifix or palm leaves are taken out of the child's hands, and the casket is closed for burial. In some parts of the country (such as Alto Paraná and Itapúa), store owners commonly pay for the expenses of wakes and provide money to deceased children's parents. This service entitles store owners to sell food and drinks to the guests.

SOCIAL STRUCTURE AND MUSICIANS

Musical performance in Paraguayan culture is widespread within all ages and social classes. Singing among groups of friends is perceived to have great entertainment value and is a frequent pastime. Guitars are widely played, though mostly by ear; few players have any formal training in music. Men and women play guitars, but few women play harps. Some professional and semiprofessional *conjuntos* include women, who tend to be singers rather than harpists or guitarists.

The intentional role of music in the promotion of cultural identity can also be seen among various ethnic groups of foreign extraction, such as the communities of Japanese, Koreans, Germans, Russians, Ukrainians, and Arabs, some of whom maintain cultural centers that occasionally sponsor concerts to promote the traditional music of the group. Particularly notable are the Japanese, who operate cultural centers in Asunción, Ciudad del Este, Encarnación, and smaller towns [see MUSIC OF IMMIGRANT GROUPS].

Most musical education in Paraguay takes place informally, based on oral tradition. Basic study of music is part of the public school curriculum, but not many people learn to read music. The Ateneo Paraguayo, founded in 1883, is one of the oldest and most highly regarded musical institutions of the country. It offers lessons in applied music and music theory. The Escuela de Bellas Artes, part of the National University of Asunción, was established in 1957; it is made up of departments of music, voice, classical dance, and plastic arts. More or less advanced musical training is available at the Baptist and Mennonite seminaries, which also sponsor choirs. The offerings of these educational institutions are supplemented by the Orquesta Sinfónica de la Ciudad de Asunción, which, in addition to concert seasons of art music from the Western tradition, carries on educational activities for young people.

Individual teachers, primarily in Asunción, provide private music lessons. The most frequently studied instruments are harp, guitar, and piano. The study of classical guitar is particularly prestigious, and Paraguayans take pride in the two guitarists of world fame Paraguay has produced: Agustín Barrios Mangoré (1885–1944) and Cayo Sila Godoy (b. 1920).

POPULAR MUSIC AND ELECTRONIC MEDIA

Paraguayan folk music such as *polcas* and *guaránias* continues to exercise great appeal, but other styles are popular. Local rock bands are in constant demand for public dances (*bailes*). These bands perform music of their own composition, plus covers of songs that have obtained success through recordings or on the radio, including those by musicians from the United States, Europe, and the rest of Latin America. Rock bands are somewhat influenced by popular Caribbean styles. The influence of Argentine rock is especially apparent.

Electronic musical culture in Paraguay includes a widespread network of forty-two AM and forty-eight FM radio stations, covering the entire country. Eight television stations and a cable television system cover the main population centers, in the eastern half of the country. Television and radio signals from Brazil and Argentina can be received in the areas bordering those countries. Several small recording studios are located in Asunción; these produce mainly cassette recordings by Paraguayan folkloric and popular musicians.

FURTHER STUDY

The Jesuit accounts provide most of the historical records regarding music in Paraguay during the 1600s and 1700s. Most important are those by Pierre François Charlevoix (1769 [1756]), Anton Sepp von Reinegg (1973 [1710]), Martin Dobrizhoffer (1784), and Florian Paucke (1696).

One of the best sources on Paraguayan folklore is Mauricio Cardozo Ocampo's *Mundo folklórico paraguayo* (1989). The first volume, *Paraguay folklórico,* is devoted almost entirely to Paraguayan folkloric music and is notable for the number of musical texts included. Most of the music in the volume has been arranged for piano by the author.

The definitive work on Paraguayan dance is Celia Ruiz Rivas de Domínguez's *Danzas paraguayas, método de enseñanza: Reseña histórica de la danza en el Paraguay y nociones sobre el folklore* (1974b), an excellent overview of the history and choreography of Paraguayan folk dances. It is supplemented by the same author's *Album musi-*

Paraguayan folk music such as *polcas* and *guaránias* continues to exercise great appeal, but other styles are popular. Local rock bands are in constant demand for public dances, with the influence of Argentine rock especially apparent.

cal: Suplemento del libro de Celia Ruiz Rivas de Domínguez "Danzas tradicionales paraguayas" (1974a).

Brief biographies of Paraguayan musicians can be found in Miguel Angel Rodríguez's *Semblanzas biográficas de creadores e intérpretes populares paraguayos* (1992). More extensive works about individual musicians include Armando Almada Roche's *José Asunción Flores: Pájaro musical y lírico* (1984), and Richard Stover's *Six Silver Moonbeams: The Life and Times of Agustín Barrios Mangoré* (1992).

For further information on the Paraguayan harp, see Alfredo Rolando Ortíz's *Latin American Harp Music and Techniques for Pedal and Non-Pedal Harpists* (1984) and John M. Schechter's *The Indispensable Harp* (1992).

The section on Paraguay in Paulo de Carvalho-Neto's *Estudios afros: Brasil, Paraguay, Uruguay, Ecuador* (1971) is an invaluable overview of the sources on African descendants in Paraguay. Josefina Plá's *Hermano Negro: La esclavitud en el Paraguay* (1972), in addition to discussing the history and social context of slavery in Paraguay, dedicated a chapter to the cultural legacy of Paraguayans of African descent.

REFERENCES

Almada Roche, Armando. 1984. *José Asunción Flores: Pájaro musical y lírico.* Buenos Aires: Ediciones el pez del pez.

Barco Centenera, Martín del. 1982 [1602]. *Argentina y conquita del Río de la Plata.* Madrid: Institución Cultural "El Brocene" de la Excelentísima Diputación Provincial de Cáceres.

Bartolomé, Miguel Alberto. 1977. *Orekuera royhendú (Lo que escuchamos en sueños): Shamanismo y religion entre los Ava-katú-eté del Paraguay.* Serie Antropología Social 17. Mexico: Instituto Indigenista Interamericano.

Boettner, Juan Max. n.d. *Música y músicos del Paraguay.* Asunción: Autores Paraguayos Asociados.

Cardozo Ocampo, Mauricio. *Mundo folklórico paraguayo.* 3 vols. Asunción: Editorial Cuadernos Republicanos.

Carvalho-Neto, Paulo de. 1971. *Estudios afros: Brasil, Paraguay, Uruguay, Ecuador.* Serie de Folklore—Instituto de Antropología e Historia, Universidad Central de Venezuela. Caracas: Instituto de Antropología e Historia, Facultad de Humanidades y Educación, Universidad Central de Venezuela.

Centurión, Carlos R. 1961. *Historia de la cultura paraguaya.* Asunción: Biblioteca Ortiz Guerrero.

Charlevoix, Pierre François. 1769 [1756]. *Histoire du Paraguay.* Translated as *The History of Paraguay.* London: L. Davis.

Díaz de Guzmán, Ruy. 1945. *La Argentina.* Buenos Aires: Espasa-Calpe.

Dobrizhoffer, Martin. 1784. *Historia de Abipones.* Translated by Sarah Coleridge as *An Account of the Abipones: An Equestrian People of Paraguay.* 3 vols. London, 1822. Reprint, New York: Johnson Reprint Corporation, 1970.

Gallardo, Jorge Emilio. 1986. *Presencia africana en la cultura de américa latina: vigencia de los cultos afroamericanos.* Buenos Aires: Fernando García Cambeiro.

Gómez-Perasso, José Antonio. n.d. *Ava guyrá kambí: notas sobre la etnografía de los ava-kué-chiripá del Paraguay oriental.* Asunción: Centro Paraguayo de Estudios Sociológicos.

Gómez-Perasso, José Antonio, and Luís Szarán. 1978. *Angu'á pararä.* Estudios Folklóricos Paraguayos 1(1). Asunción: Editorial Arte Nuevo.

González Torres, Dionisio M. 1991. *Folklore del Paraguay.* Asunción: Editora Litocolor.

Leonhardt, Carlos, ed. 1927–1929. *Cartas anuas de la provincia del Paraguay, Chile y Tucumán, de la Compañía de Jesús*. 2 vols. Buenos Aires: Instituto de Investigaciones Históricas.

Ortiz, Alfredo Rolando. 1984. *Latin American Harp Music and Techniques for Pedal and Non-Pedal Harpists*. 2nd ed. Revised and enlarged. Corona, Calif.: author.

Paucke, Florian. 1696. *Florian Pauckes Reise in die Missionen nach Paraguay und Geschichte der Missionen S. Xavier und S. Peter Brixen*. Translated by Edmundo Wenicke as *Hacia allá y para acá*. Tucumán: Universidad Nacional de Tucumán (1942).

Peña, Enrique. 1916. *Don Francisco de Céspedes, noticias sobre su gobierno en el Río de la Plata* (1624–1632). Buenos Aires: Coni Hermanos.

Plá, Josefina. 1972. *Hermano Negro: La esclavitud en el Paraguay*. Madrid: Paraninfo.

Rodríguez, Miguel Angel. 1992. *Semblanzas biográficas de creadores e intérpretes populares paraguayos*. Asunción: Ediciones Compugraph.

Ruiz Rivas de Domínguez, Celia. 1974a. *Album musical: Suplemento del libro de Celia Ruiz Rivas de Domínguez "Danzas tradicionales paraguayas."* Asunción: Impresa Makrografic.

——. 1974b. *Danzas paraguayas, método de enseñanza: Reseña histórica de la danza en el Paraguay y nociones sobre el folklore*. Asunción: Impresa Makrografic.

Schechter, John M. 1992. *The Indispensable Harp: Historical Development, Modern Roles, Configurations, and Performance Practices in Ecuador and Latin America*. Kent, Ohio: Kent State University Press.

Schmiedel, Ulrich. 1942. *Viaje al Río de la Plata*. Buenos Aires.

Sepp von Reinegg, Anton. 1696. *Reissbeschreibung*. Translated by Werner Hoffman and Monica Wrang as *Relación de viaje a las misiones Jesuíticas*. Buenos Aires: Eudeba, 1971.

——. 1973 [1710]. *Continuation oder Fortsetzung der Beschreibung deren denkwuerdigeren paraguarischen Sachen*. Translated by Werner Hoffman as *Continuación de las labores apostólicas*. Buenos Aires: Editorial Universitaria de Buenos Aires.

Stover, Richard D. 1992. *Silver Moonbeams: The Life and Times of Agustín Barrios Mangoré*. Clovis, Calif.: Querico.

Peru
Raúl R. Romero

Peru is a country of diverse geographical regions, languages, races, and cultural traditions. It is the third-largest nation in South America, with more than 20 million inhabitants distributed within its coastal, Andean, and Amazonian regions. It borders Ecuador and Colombia to the north, Brazil and Bolivia to the east, Chile to the south, and the Pacific Ocean to the west. Spanish, Quechua (Kechua), and Aymara are the principal languages spoken in Peru, along with numerous languages of Amazonian peoples.

The pre-Hispanic cultural heritage of Peru can be traced back to about 1400 B.C., when the Chavín culture surged in the central Andes of Peru. Throughout the centuries after its decline, there emerged successive and prosperous regional cultures, all of which the Inca Empire subdued in the 1400s. The Spanish incursion of the 1500s put an abrupt end to the autonomous development of indigenous cultures in coastal and Andean Peru. The colonial system introduced an era of economic exploitation of the Peruvian Indians through such institutions as the *encomienda,* a system by which land and peasants were governed by Spanish landlords (*encomenderos*), the *mita* (coercive labor for the colonial administration), and the collection of forced tribute (Indian contributions in kind to the Spanish crown). With these tactics, ideological struggles against indigenous religious practices, such as the extirpation-of-idolatries campaign conducted by the Spanish clergy in the 1600s, were enforced. These actions and the diseases brought by Europeans caused a dramatic depopulation of indigenous peoples.

Distinctive social and ethnic groups began to emerge soon after the arrival of Europeans. A solid difference was made between the Spanish born on the Iberian Peninsula and those born in the colonies; the latter, labeled creole (*criollo*), were considered socially inferior to the former. Early miscegenation between Spanish men and Indian women created a mestizo racial group, which during most of the colonial period occupied an ambivalent social position between Spanish and Indian. The importation of African slaves added another ethnic dimension to the colonial social framework.

The modern nation of Peru resulted from the political and economic independence of the creoles from Spanish jurisdiction in 1821, after which a new sector of rich and influential plantation owners (*hacendados*) replaced the *encomenderos*. Thus, the political and economic structures of the new nation remained in the same hands, and the subordination of Peruvian Indians and mestizos persisted.

In pre-Hispanic Peru, indigenous cultures had occupied the coast and the mountains, but during the colonial domination, the Spaniards settled mostly in the coast, while the mostly Quechua Indian peasants (Aymara in the far south) inhabited primarily the Andean region [see QUECHUA-AYMARA]. Thus, coastal Peru became a bastion for white and creole culture (with the important presence of the black slaves, eventually liberated in 1854), whereas the Andes became a stronghold for Indian and mestizo communities. The geographical and cultural partition of the country began to blur with massive migrations to the capital, Lima, beginning in the 1950s and given the consequences of the revolutionary régime of 1968–1980, which implemented radical agrarian reforms and structural changes crucial to the Peruvian economy. The Peruvian Amazonian region, the third important geographical region in the country, continued to be occupied by more than fifty scattered and seminomadic ethnolinguistic groups, which for centuries remained isolated from the national scene.

ARCHAEOLOGICAL BACKGROUND

Among the earliest musical instruments are a sixth-century-B.C. panpipe (Kechua *antara,* also *andara*) and an end-notched flute (Aymara *kena,* also spelled *quena*) found in the Chilca region. One of the oldest samples of musical iconography is from the Chavín horizon, around 1400 B.C. It shows musicians playing conch trumpets (Bolaños 1985:11, 14).

The musical iconography of the pre-Incan Moche (Mochica) culture, around 100 B.C., is one of the richest in Peru. Moche ceramics depict musical instruments, costumes, and dances in detail. Among the most significant representations is that of two panpipers facing each other, their instruments attached with a string—evidence that these instruments were played in pairs in pre-Hispanic times. Musical iconography depicting panpipes exists in textiles from the Huari culture, around A.D. 600 (Rowe 1979).

Clay panpipes from the Nasca culture have been the most studied and debated pre-Hispanic musical instruments. The excellence of their condition (most are housed in the National Museum of Anthropology and Archaeology in Lima), enabled several investigators to measure their pitches and hypothesize about pre-Hispanic musical scales. Carlos Vega (1932) and Andrés Sas concluded that blowing the panpipe produces a series of semitones and quarter tones. Sas also concluded that the Nasca used diatonic and chromatic scales (1936:232). Later, Stevenson (1968), Haeberli (1979), and Bolaños (1988) restudied Nasca panpipes with new methodologies; they provided new data and arrived at similar conclusions about pre-Hispanic musical scales. These studies rejected the conclusion by Raoul and Marguerite d'Harcourt (1990 [1925]) that pentatonicism was the dominant scale in ancient times [see APPROACHES TO MUSICAL SCHOLARSHIP].

HISTORICAL BACKGROUND

Spanish chroniclers of the 1500s and 1600s first documented the musical practices of the Inca period. Guamán Poma de Ayala (1956 [1613]) committed many pages to describing musical expressions and activities. In his famous drawings of pre-Hispanic life, he depicted musical instruments and performance settings. Other chroniclers, such as Pedro Cieza de León (1967), Bernabé Cobo (1956), and Garcilaso de la Vega (1959), profusely described and commented on various pre-Hispanic musical manifestations. Colonial dictionaries of Quechua and Aymara by Diego Gonzales Holguín (1608) and Ludovico Bertonio (1612), respectively, contain important definitions about musical genres, musical instruments, and dances at the time of the Spanish Encounter.

Among the issues addressed by these chroniclers are the regional and ethnic diversity in music and dance. Guamán Poma de Ayala (1956:242) and Cobo (1956:270) agreed that each province or part of the Tawantinsuyu (the Inca empire) had unique songs and dances. The relationship between music and society was another concern of these writers, who claimed that certain kinds of music were performed only by elites during particular rituals and thus were not intended for popular use.

Regional and ethnic diversity in pre-Hispanic times was paralleled by a process of musical differentiation whose corollary was various songs and dances. In the post-Encounter period, it was frequent to observe "many and diverse" dances in massive fiestas and processions; on one occasion, forty different dances occurred in the Corpus Christi procession in the province of Collao (Cobo 1956:270–271). The chroniclers characterized songs and dances on the basis of texts rather than on musical traits. For these reasons, most of their references to musical genres are in the domain of literary pictures, and their information does not permit a clear understanding of the musical structure of actual pieces. In general, references to musical genres therefore tend to be merely nominative or defined in relation to the character of the sound. Guamán Poma (1956: 233–235), for instance, mentioned various musical genres, indicating their character and transcribing their lyrics, among them the *harawi* (*haravi,* a nostalgic love song), the *kashwa* (*cachua,* a cheerful song), the *wanka* (*uanca,* also a love song), and the *haylli* (a harvest song) as the most important ones. Early definitions of musical genres already included the *cachua,* described by Cobo as a dance of men and women joining hands in a circle, and Gonzales Holguin's portrayed *haylli* as joyful, victorious songs, sung during the sowing of the fields and *harawi* as songs dealing with unrequited love (Stevenson 1960:169).

Musical instruments are probably the most fully documented musical phenomena of pre-Hispanic times. The references about them are abundant, and note their uses in everyday life. Chroniclers confirm the presence of numerous idiophones, drums (*huancar*), flutes (*pincullu, quenaquena, antara*), and trumpets (*k'epa*) in the Inca empire, and the absence of stringed instruments. Although allusions to aspects of musical performances are scanty, they constitute the only extant references for the pre-Hispanic period. Garcilaso de la Vega's description of panpipe ensembles is one of the most prominent (1959:201). He narrated, briefly but concisely, the interlocking technique of performance by panpipe ensembles, and suggested that fifths were the foremost tonal intervals in these ensembles. He also noted the presence of larger intervals at the expense of smaller ones in musical scales. Carlos Vega (1932:350) thought that in this passage, Garcilaso was trying to describe a pentatonic scale. Guamán Poma de Ayala referred to the musical accompaniment of the *pingollo* and the *quenaquena* in several dances and songs, and highlighted two cases of antiphonal dances of men and women (1956:233). The first of these, the *uaricza araui,* was sung by the Inca and his women, the *cuyas* and the *ñustas.* The Inca's chant imitated the gentle moan of an animal, and was repeated over and over again until it resembled the high sound of a dying animal. His chant was answered by the women. The second case of an antiphonal chant was the *saynata,* in which a man responded to a women's chorus.

No chronicler provided a musical transcription, but later colonial sources do include notation. In the second half of the 1700s, Bishop Baltasar Martínez Compañón included the notations of seventeen traditional songs and three instrumental dances in the ninth volume of his encyclopedia of life and nature in Trujillo, the province to which he was assigned. In a five-hundred-page encyclopedia, the

Franciscan brother Gregorio de Zoula, who served in Cusco in the late 1600s, left seventeen musical transcriptions of anonymous songs. In contrast to the more regional flavor of Martínez Compañón's collection, Zoula's transcriptions revealed a marked Renaissance style. A *zapateo* (a creole popular form) and a hymn to the Virgin Mary were transcribed by Amédée François Frézier. Though not strictly a transcription but a composition based on an autochthonous theme, the four-part polyphonic piece "*Hanacpachap Cussicuinin,*" published in Quechua by the Franciscan Juan Pérez Bocanegra (1631), is related to the work of missions in Peru (facsimiles in Quezada Machiavello 1985:76 and Stevenson 1960:48–49).

MUSICAL INSTRUMENTS

The Andean area

Many pre-Hispanic musical instruments, including a drum (*tinya*), a flute (*quena*), and a panpipe (*antara*), are still used in the Peruvian Andes. Other instruments developed during the colonial domination as a consequence of the cultural encounter between European and indigenous models. These included a small guitar (*charango*) and a coiled cow-horn trumpet (*wak'rapuku*). Various European musical instruments, including the guitar, the accordion, the harp, and the violin, were introduced by the Spaniards. Among the European instruments that since the 1890s have been adopted by the Andean peasantry are the trumpet, the saxophone, the clarinet, and other band instruments.

Membranophones

Drums receive different names according to their sizes and localities. These names include *tinya, wankara,* and the Spanish terms *bombo, caja,* and *tambor.* There are drums of different sizes, ranging from a *tinya* of about 20 centimeters in diameter to a *caja* of 70 centimeters in diameter. Most, however, are double-headed cylindrical drums. Contrasting with aerophones (played only by men), small drums like the *tinya* are, as in pre-Hispanic times, mostly played by women, on several occasions, including music for marking animals in the central Andes. Bigger drums are played by men, mostly for accompaniment, in small or large ensembles.

Aerophones

Traditional panpipes such as the *ayarachi,* the *chiriguano,* and the *sikuri* in Puno are always played collectively (Valencia 1983). These panpipes are usually named after the ensemble of which they are part and are tuned to a diatonic scale. These are double-unit panpipes, designed to be played in pairs, each component having complementary pitches. One of them is designated *ira* 'leader'; the other, *arca* 'follower'. The playing technique of these groups is complex. *Sikuri* ensembles consist of different sizes of panpipe (*siku*, figure 1). Some are tuned in octaves, whereas others are tuned to the fifth (called *contras*). An ideal orchestration would include eight different groups of instruments, but not all ensembles always present all the possible combinations (Valencia 1989:46–53). Other panpipe traditions such as those of the *ayarachi* and *chiriguano,* are subdivided in three groups, each of which is tuned to the octave (Valencia 1989:65, 71). *Sikuri* and other panpipe ensembles perform intensively throughout the annual calendar of fiestas, in weddings, and other life-cycle events, such as a child's first haircut (*corte de pelo,* Turino 1993:46). In several traditions in the Puno area and in Lima among migrants from Puno, individual players of each panpipe half play a drum at the same time (figure 2). Elsewhere, a single-unit panpipe is played as a solo instrument, like the *andara* in Cajamarca (Instituto Nacional de Cultura 1978:209–210).

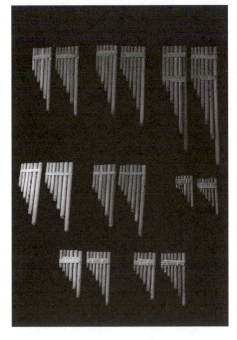

FIGURE 1 A set of *siku* panpipes of the Aymara, Quechua, and/or mestizo people of Puno, southern Peru, represents the *ira* 'leader' (male) and *arka* 'follower' (female) pairs in their assorted four sizes. Photo by Raúl R. Romero, 1985.

Pipe-and-tabor players perform widely in public festivals. They fulfill a central role in ceremonies associated with communal labor in the fields and in the construction of buildings.

FIGURE 2   In a street in La Victoria, a *barrio* in Lima, a panpipe group consisting of migrants from the department of Puno and their descendants performs for an event. The ethnomusicologist Thomas Turino is in the left background. Photo by Cathy Collinge Herrera, 1984.

Different kinds of vertical end-notched flutes (*quena*), vertical duct flutes (*pincullo, tarka*), and side-blown flutes (*pito*) are widely disseminated in the Andes. The *quena*, also known by local names, including *lawata, chaqallo,* and *quenacho,* is usually made from cane but also from wood and since the 1970s from plastic. It can have diverse lengths, but most are between 25 centimeters and 120 centimeters. It may have three to eight holes for fingering. One of the most ubiquitous types, measuring 30 to 40 centimeters long has six holes in the front and one in the back. The *quena* can be played as a solo instrument in private and contemplative situations, but in public performances it is usually played with other instruments in ensembles, such as the *conjunto* in Cusco, or with large ensembles of instruments of the same type as for *choquela* dances in Puno (Cuentas Ormachea 1982:59) and carnival dances in the Colca valley, Arequipa (Ráez 1993:286).

No archaeological evidence has been discovered for determining the origins of duct tubular flutes, though globular flutes with duct mouthpieces are found archaeologically in Peru [see APPROACHES TO MUSICAL SCHOLARSHIP]. It is therefore generally considered that they originated during the colonial period. The term *pingollo,* however, was usually employed by the early chroniclers to denote pre-Hispanic flutes. Today's duct flute is most frequently made of wood or cane, may be of different sizes (from 30 to 120 centimeters long), and may have a variable number of holes, stopped with the fingers of one or two hands. One of the most common names for duct flutes (played with two hands) in the Peruvian Andes is *pincullu* (also spelled *pincullo,*

FIGURE 3   During a communal work effort in the fields of Paccha, Jauja, Peru, a *pincullo* and *tinya* pipe-and-tabor musician performs. Photo by Raúl R. Romero, 1985.

pinkillo, pinkuyllo), called *flauta* in many areas and *chiska* and *rayán* in Ancash. One of the most disseminated types is the three-holed one-handed duct flute, played in a pipe-and-tabor mode. In northern Peru, pipe-and-tabor duct flutes are of two types, the *roncador* 'snorer', characterized by a rough sound (found in Ancash and Huánuco), and the *silbadora* 'whistler' (also *flauta*), with a more mellow timbre (found in Cajamarca and La Libertad). Pipe-and-tabor players perform widely in public festivals. They fulfill a central role in ceremonies associated with communal labor in the fields (figure 3) and in the construction of buildings in Junín (Romero 1990:14) and Ancash (den Otter 1985:112). In the Colca Valley, a six-hole *pinkuyllo* 120 centimeters long, played by one performer accompanied by a drum played by a woman, is used exclusively in fertility rituals (Ráez 1993:291). Duct flutes can be played in ensembles of instruments of the same type, including the five- and six-hole *pinkillo* in Conima, Puno; from eight to fifteen performers play them in unison, accompanied by drums (Turino 1993:48).

The *tarka,* another popular duct flute, occurs only in the southern department of Puno. The feature that distinguishes it from other duct flutes is its hexagonal cross-sectional shape [see BOLIVIA]. Usually with six holes for fingering, it is played in public festivals in large ensembles (*tarkeadas*), but it has been reported to be played as a solo instrument in private situations by shepherds in the mountains (Bellenger 1981:24).

In the Andes, the side-blown flute is known by diverse local names, including *flauta, pito, phalahuita,* and even *quena* (Instituto Nacional de Cultura 1978:221). In Puno, where it is called *pitu,* it is made of cane, has six holes in the upper side, and is played in large ensembles of multiple side-blown flutes in community festivals (Turino 1993:57). In Cusco, two six-holed *pitus* are accompanied by drums in the war bands (*bandas de guerra*), ensembles recurrent in public festivals throughout the region.

Different kinds of locally constructed trumpets are widely used. These include the *wak'rapuku* in the central Andes, the *clarín* in the northern Andes, and the *pampa corneta* in Huancavelica. The *wak'rapuku* (figure 4), made of cattle-horn pieces spirally joined together, is usually played in pairs called *primera* and *segunda,* tuned a third apart. It is played but once a year, during animal-marking fertility rituals. Its origins

TRACK 21

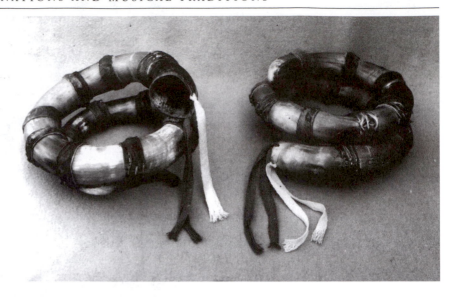

FIGURE 4   Two *wak'rapuku* coiled cow-horn trumpets: *cacho primero* 'first horn' on left, *cacho segundo* 'second horn' on right. Pitched a third apart, they are traditionally played in Junín, Peru, for the *herranza* 'marking of the animals' fertility ritual, often with a violin and *tinya* drum. Photo by Raúl R. Romero, 1985.

TRACK 22

are no doubt colonial, because cattle were introduced by Europeans. The *clarín*, popular in Cajamarca, is a cane side-blown trumpet 3 meters long, used in festivals (figure 5) and in agricultural music (Canepa-Koch 1993:150). The *pampa corneta* is a straight wooden trumpet, 3 to 4 meters long. Restricted to Ayacucho and Huancavelica, it is usually played only in the ritual of marking the animals. The *pututu* (conch trumpet) is still used in the southern Andes for signaling and opening special communal ceremonies. It is called *churu* in Amazonas and *quipa* in San Martín. In Cusco, it is used in communal labor (*faenas*) in Pisac and Paucartambo.

The Spanish introduced double-reed instruments such as the *chirimía* (a shawm made of wood), which during colonial times was frequently played for official ceremonies related to municipal affairs in urban centers. The *chirimía* is still played in the northern coastal and Andean areas in public festivals (Casas Roque 1993: 324–326) and in highland Lima, Huancavelica, and Ayacucho, where it is known as *chirisuya* (Jiménez Borja 1951:79).

FIGURE 5   During the patronal festival of the Virgin of Carmen in Alto Otuzco, Cajamarca, Peru (16 July), a man plays a *clarín*. Photo by Dale A. Olsen, 1979.

FIGURE 6 Nicanor Abarca Puma, a *charango* maker and player from Arequipa, Peru, plays a *charango de caja.* Resembling a small guitar, it has five triple courses of metal strings. Photo by Dale A. Olsen, 1979.

Chordophones

Since ancient Peruvians used no chordophones, it is reasonable to conclude that many chordophones currently in use were introduced by the Spaniards during the colonial period—the guitar, the mandolin, the *bandurria,* the harp, and the violin. The *charango,* in certain localities also called *quirquincho* 'armadillo' and *chillador* 'screamer', is a small guitar, made of wood (figure 6) or armadillo shell. Common to southern Peru, it is from 23 to 45 centimeters long (Bellenger 1981:42). It has diverse tunings and regionally variable numbers of strings; the most common tuning is the *Santo Domingo* for the five-stringed *charango* (E–A–E–C–G). The six-stringed variant usually duplicates the third string, one of which is tuned to the octave of the other. In Cusco, the *charango* is played by Andean peasants with a predominant strumming style while a single string carries the melody; mestizo performers play it in a plucked melodic mode, interspersed with strumming sections (Turino 1984:259).

The European guitar has not suffered any drastic morphological changes in its adaptation to Andean musical practices, though its tuning varies by region. Besides the standard system, other tunings depend on the locality, each of them with a specific name. In Ayacucho, the most common tuning, *comuncha* (E–B–G–D–B–G), predominates in rural areas. This tuning serves primarily for playing peasant *huaynos* (*waynos*) in E minor. Other tunings, such as harp tuning (*temple arpa,* E–B–F♯–D–A–F♯), used to play *huaynos* and *carnavales* in B minor, and devil tuning (*temple diablo,* E–C–G–D–B♭–G), used to play *yaravies* in G minor, are also widely used (Pinto 1987:84–86). In Jesús, Huánuco, Villareal Vara (1958:35) found six different tunings in carnival guitar music, one of which, called plain (*llano*), corresponds to the standard European tuning E–A–D–G–B–E.

Spanish missionaries propagated the European harp and the violin throughout all the Andean area. Today, both instruments are widely dispersed in the communities of the Peruvian Andes; they are usually played individually or together as part of larger ensembles. The harp, contrasting with the guitar and the violin, has experienced considerable morphological adaptation, ranging from the triangle-shaped *arpa indigena* (figure 7) to the smaller *domingacha* type with a pear-shaped sound box (Olsen 1986–87, 56:57). The Peruvian harp is diatonic, usually tuned to the C major

FIGURE 7 The late Fausto Dolorier Abregu, professional harpist and former professor of harp at the National School of Folkloric Arts, Lima. Photo by Dale A. Olsen, 1979.

tamborero In Peru, a person who beats on the box of the harp as on a percussion instrument while the harpist plucks the strings

estudiantina 'Student ensemble', an ensemble in Puno that includes guitars, *charangos*, mandolins, and an accordion

orquesta típica 'Typical orchestra', an ensemble in the central Peruvian highlands consisting of saxophones, clarinets, violins, and a harp

banda 'Band', usually a brass band or a large ensemble of mixed European-derived wind instruments

herranza Marking of animals in the Andes, a context for ritual music making

conjunto de cuerdas String orchestra of Ancash, Peru, consisting of several guitars, mandolin, violins, and often a harp

scale. It uses from twenty-six to thirty-six metal or nylon strings and has no pedals. It is so lightweight that it can be easily played upside down and over the shoulders during processions and festivals (see figures 9 and 10).

Harp performance styles vary by region. Olsen (1986–1987) has distinguished six principal regional styles in Peru: Callejón de Huaylas–Huánuco in the northern Andes, Mantaro in the central Andes, Ayacucho in the south-central Andes, Urubamba-Abancay in the southern Andes, Chancay in the central coastal region, and urbanized in Lima. The harp can be played solo and in ensemble, where it provides bass and harmonic functions. In some regions of the country, it is played as an accompanying percussion instrument by a *tamborero,* a person who beats his fingers on its body while someone else plucks the strings [see ECUADOR].

Ensembles

Andean music has adopted the accordion, widely used throughout the region but especially in *conjuntos* in Cusco, in string ensembles in the Callejón de Huaylas (den Otter 1985:91), and in the *estudiantina* group of stringed instruments in Puno. Wind instruments—clarinet, saxophone, trumpet, trombone, tuba—make up brass bands (figure 8). Saxophones (alto, tenor, baritone), clarinets, harps, and violins form the basis of the typical orchestra (*orquesta típica*), the most popular ensemble in the central Andes department of Junín and neighboring areas (figure 9).

TRACK 23

FIGURE 8   A military band performs in procession during a patronal festival in Los Baños del Inca, Cajamarca, Peru. The musicians are reading music affixed with clothespins to each other's backs. Photo by Dale A. Olsen, 1979.

FIGURE 9   The *orquesta típica* 'typical orchestra' Los Piratos del Centro (the Pirates from the Center [central Mantaro Valley]), from Huancayo, perform in Junín, Peru. *Left to right:* baritone saxophone, three tenor saxophones, four alto saxophones, a harp carried upside down, a clarinet, a violin, and another clarinet. Photo by Raúl R. Romero, 1985.

Regional instrumental ensembles play in various contexts. Throughout the Andes, ensembles combining a harp and violins are pervasive, as is the combination of flute and drum played by a single performer or by several, as in the *banda de guerra* of Cusco, which combines *quena* (*kena*) flutes, accordion, mandolin, harp, and a violin. The *banda típica* in northern Cajamarca mixes *quenas* and percussion instruments (snare drum and cymbals). Large ensembles of one instrumental type—for example, aerophones such as *pitu, pinkillu,* and *tarka*—are also common in the south. The *estudiantina* ensemble of Puno includes guitars, *charangos,* mandolins, and an accordion. The *herranza,* an ensemble that accompanies herding rituals in the central Andes, merges a violin, several *wak'rapuku,* and a *tinya.* The string ensemble (*conjunto de cuerdas*) of Ancash combines a violin, a mandolin, and sometimes a harp or a *quena* and an accordion.

The Coast

After the lute (*laúd*) and the *bandurria* had disappeared, the guitar became the most important instrument in creole music of the urbanized coast (Santa Cruz 1977:49). It serves as a solo instrument or for voice-accompanying duos and trios, especially in the *vals criollo.* After the 1950s, when creole music began to be disseminated primarily via commercial records and the mass media, the creole repertoire began to be performed by various musical instruments and ensembles. The guitar remained the most vital instrument in live performances, but percussion instruments—such as the *cajón* 'big box' and Iberian castanets (usually replaced by a pair of spoons in live performances)—were introduced. The *cajón* is a variably sized wooden box with a hole in its back, commonly used by Afro-Peruvians [see AFRO-PERUVIAN TRADITIONS]. The performer sits atop the instrument and strikes it with both hands.

In the rural areas of the Peruvian coast, other instruments can be found. Many of them—such as the *pinkullo* and the *caja* (played by a single performer, as in the highlands), the harp, the *chirimía,* and the instruments that form the brass band in Lambayeque—are also played in the Andes. For *marineras* (dance music in 6/8 meter), a *tamborero* beats on a harp's sound box while the harpist plucks the strings and sings. The banjo, introduced in some areas of the north Peruvian coast around 1900, is now used to play *valses* and *marineras* (Casas Roque 1993).

The guitar is the most important instrument in the Afro-Peruvian tradition. Peruvian blacks incorporated it and the harp in street fiestas as early as the 1700s, but this tradition has been forgotten (Estenssoro 1988:163). Still in use are the *quijada* (or *carachacha*), the jawbone of an ass, mule, or horse, whose teeth rattle when the jawbone is struck with a hand. After the 1950s, when a process of revitalization of Afro-Peruvian music took place, Caribbean instruments (including congas, cowbell, and bongos) were incorporated.

The Amazonian Region

An extensive assortment of musical instruments can be found among the nearly sixty ethnolinguistic groups that inhabit the Amazonian region (see Okada 1995: examples 9–11). Among numerous types of wooden and membranophonic drums are those used to send messages and signal the group or other parties (Pawlik 1951). Many classes of musical bows are employed as are diverse types of European-derived wooden zithers and violins. Cane and bamboo trumpets and vertical and side-blown flutes of different sizes and number of holes are also common. The panpipe is played as a solo instrument or in ensembles.

MUSICAL GENRES AND CONTEXTS

The Andean area

Current Andean musical expressions are re-creations of pre-Hispanic indigenous genres, local developments based on colonial European models, or recent configurations derived from the encounter with national and transnational urban musical forms. Among the pre-Hispanic genres of song cited by early chroniclers and still persisting among Andean peasantry is the *harawi,* a monophonic genre of song that consists of one musical phrase repeated several times with extensive melismatic passages and long glissandos. It is associated with specific ceremonies and rituals (including farewells and marriages) and agricultural labor (including sowing and harvesting) in the southern Andes. It is usually sung in a high-pitched, nasal voice by a group of elder women called *harawiq* (Cavero 1985:237). In Cusco, this genre, known as *wanka,* is associated with the same ritual contexts (Arguedas, cited in Pinilla 1980:390). The *kashwa,* a pre-Hispanic genre usually associated with nocturnal harvest rituals, is performed in a circle by young, unmarried men and women (Roel 1959). *Haylli* is a responsorial genre, performed during communal agricultural work in the fields.

Among other Andean musical genres associated with specific contexts is the *carnaval,* a song and dance for the homonymous festivity. This genre has several regional variants and designations, such as *wifala* and *puqllay* (in Ayacucho, Puno, and Cusco), *araskaska* and the recently introduced *pumpín* (Ayacucho), and the more disseminated *pasacalle* (in Ancash and the southern Andes). The *walina,* a genre linked with the ritual cleaning of the irrigation channels in the highlands of the department of Lima, is customarily sung by men, with a *chirimía* playing a countermelody.

Some genres have become dissociated from their original contexts. These include the *santiago* (originally a kind of song from the Central Andes, performed by a woman during the ritual marking of animals), the *huaylas* (once a ritual harvest song, also from the Central Andes), and the *carnaval* of the southern Andes. These genres became accepted beyond their villages, achieving regional significance in traditional fiestas. Later, they began to be distributed by the record industry, achieving national coverage and eventually emancipating themselves from their original ritual contexts.

The most widely disseminated and popular song-dance genre in the Andes is the *huayno* (*wayno*). In view of meager early colonial references to it as a musical form, Roel (1959) has postulated that its popularity grew during the colonial period, and that this acceptance was achieved to the detriment of the *kashwa*. He has further explained that the *kashwa* as a collective and rural manifestation could not survive within a colonial system that implied spatial and ideological limitations. In this sense, the *huayno* as a freely choreographed couple dance was better suited to urban, narrow spaces.

The *huayno* has many regional variants and adopts different names, including *chuscada* (Ancash), *pampeña* (Arequipa), *cachua* (Cajamarca), *chymaycha* (Amazonas and Huanuco), and *huaylacha* (Colca Valley). Usually in duple meter, it consists of a pair of musical phrases in periodic form (AABB). Like other Andean genres, it may have a closing section, called *fuga* or *qawachan,* which consists of a contrasting theme in a faster tempo. Today, it reflects the styles of the different social and ethnic groups that perform it. As an autonomous expression of contextual and ritual constraints, it can be performed at any time and in various settings (see Cohen 1984).

The *yaraví* is a slow, lyrical, mestizo genre in triple meter and binary form. Mostly sung in the southern Andes, it is usually associated with afflicted love affairs and nostalgic moods. Arguedas has suggested that in Cusco the mestizo *yaraví* evolved from the indigenous *harawi,* from which it took its main sentimental theme (Pinilla 1980:390). Its melody is built on a minor tonality, is usually sung in parallel thirds, and has a flexible tempo (Carpio Muñoz 1976; Pagaza Galdo 1961) (see Okada 1995: example 13). Having analogous musical characteristics is the *triste,* pervasive in northern Peru. In the central Andes, the *muliza,* though distinctive in style and form, is similar to the *yaraví* and serves the same evocative function. These genres are usually followed by a *fuga de huayno,* a *huayno*-like closing section.

Contrasting with fixed genres are nonfixed genres organically linked to specific ritual contexts, including fertility rituals, agricultural communal work, the cleaning of irrigation channels, the building of edifices, and life-cycle ceremonial phases (baptism, courting, marriage, funerals). In many cases, the accompanying music bears the name of the ritual involved, though in some cases a fixed musical form may be associated with the ritual.

In the Mantaro Valley in the department of Junín, the nocturnal harrowing of grain was until the 1950s accomplished by young unmarried men and women who sang unaccompanied or with guitar accompaniment and danced on top of a mound of grain, separating the seeds from the husks. In the same region, the music of a *pincullo* and a *tinya,* played by one performer in a pipe-and-tabor fashion, is reserved for times when the peasant community gathers to work in the fields in specific moments of the agricultural calendar, especially the first tilling of the soil and the harvest. Each musical repertoire pertains solely to its corresponding performance context, and although each tune is given a descriptive name, the whole repertoire lacks any concrete name other than the occasion for which it is intended. In Cajamarca in the northern Andes, the *clarín* is played during the *minka* (communal work in the fields), especially during the harvest of grain (Cánepa-Koch 1993:150; Jiménez Borja 1951:75).

The marking (*marcación*) of animals is one of the most ubiquitous fertility rituals in the central and southern Andes of Peru. Associated with the Andean mountain deities (the *wamani,* the *apu,* or the *achachila,* depending on the region), it is usually performed during specific seasons of the year [see Q'ERO]. In the highland areas of the Colca Valley, the music of a large *pincuyllo* and a *tinya* is played in the *tinka,* a ceremony during carnival when a llama is sacrificed and ritual offerings are buried for the deities. Music accompanies the steps of the ritual and is played during rest periods when, after the ritual, the participants dance and relax. An ensemble of eighteen

When an infant dies in Puno, a lively *huayno* is sung with *charango* accompaniment because it is believed that the dead baby goes to heaven in a state of grace. Thus, the death is an occasion to celebrate rather than grieve.

quenas or *chaqallos* accompanied by two *bombos* and a snare drum fulfills the same function during a similar ritual called *wylancha* in Puno (Canepa-Koch 1991). In the Mantaro River Valley, the musical ensemble of the marking of animals or *herranza* consists of one or two *wak'rapuku*, a violin, a singer, and a *tinya* (see Okada 1995: example 16) The repertoire of this ensemble is strictly linked with each step of the ritual and like the previously mentioned cases is exclusively reserved for this occasion.

The cleaning of irrigation channels (*michicoq, fiesta del agua* 'festival of the water') is a ceremonial task performed by all the members of the peasant community. It is an especially strong tradition in Puquio, Ayacucho, and San Pedro de Casta, Lima (see Okada 1995: example 15). Here, the *walina* is a fixed genre associated exclusively with this ritual. A large repertoire of *walina* is sung only by the men, who perform the ceremonial cleaning; it is accompanied by the *chirimía*, which plays a relatively independent countermelody to the lead singer's melody.

The communal construction of buildings (*pirkansa*) is an event in which communal labor fulfills an indispensable function and in which music is ceremonially vital. In the Mantaro Valley, the *pirkansa* occurs when the walls of an edifice are being built: during the ritual, a performer of *pincullo* and *tinya* music (as in agricultural music) participates. A similar instrumental combination is employed in Ancash (*flauta* and *caja*) in the same setting (den Otter 1985:113).

Ceremonial life-cycle phases (baptism, courting, marriage, funeral) are also contexts for major musical repertoires. The role of music in courting rituals is particularly solid in Cusco. In Canas, young unmarried men summon their chosen women by playing the *tuta kashwa* ('night dance', a particular melody) on their *charangos* during the fiestas of Saint Andrew (San Andrés) and the Holy Cross (Santa Cruz) (Turino 1983:85). Funeral music is usually sung by specialists at the wake or actual burial as in the festivity of the Día de los Muertos (Day of the Dead). In the Mantaro Valley, items in the repertoire of the funeral-song singers (*responseros*) have Quechua texts with strong musical-liturgical influence. In other areas, the relatives of the deceased themselves may weep and grieve, combining spoken passages with musical cadences. When an infant dies in Puno, a lively *huayno* is sung with *charango* accompaniment because it is believed that the dead baby goes to heaven in a state of grace; thus, the death is an occasion to celebrate rather than grieve.

The annual festival calendar is the natural context for the numerous dance-dramas that exist in the Peruvian Andes. The fiesta calendar, prolific throughout all the Andean region, is the result of the blending of the pre-Hispanic agricultural calendar with the Christian annual calendar. Different types of festivals are celebrated with greater or lesser intensity according to each region and locality. Some fiestas have achieved pan-Andean relevance. These include the Purification of Our Lady (Virgen de la Calendaria, 2 February), Fiesta de la Cruz (3 May), the Nativity of St. John the Baptist (San Juan, 24 June), Saints Peter and Paul (San Pedro y San Pablo, 29 June), Our Lady of Mount Carmel (16 July), St. James the Apostle (Santiago Apóstol, 25

FIGURE 10   On Sunday, the main day of the patronal festival of San Juan Bautista (Saint John the Baptist) in Acolla, Junín, Peru, dancers known as *tunantadas* and *chunginos,* representing Spanish nobility, perform to the accompaniment of an *orquesta típica* (only the upside-down harp is in view). Photo by Dale A. Olsen, 1979.

July), St. Rose of Lima (Santa Rosa de Lima, 30 August), the Nativity of the Blessed Virgin Mary (8 September), and Christian seasonal observances such as Christmas, the Epiphany, Holy Week (especially Palm Sunday), and Corpus Christi. Carnival is celebrated throughout the Andes, often closely linked with the Purification of Our Lady.

Frequently, the actual fiesta lasts from three to five days, depending on the type of festivity and the region. The main events usually occur during vespers the evening before the central day, on the central day itself, and on the closing day or the farewell. In the Colca Valley, fiestas usually consist of five parts, coinciding with the five days of the fiesta. First is the *antealba,* when the communal preparations are concluded and the musicians begin to rehearse. Second, the *alba* constitutes the evening of the principal day, when fireworks are set off. Third is the *principal,* the main day, when all the dance-dramas are performed and the customary bullfights or horse races are presented. Fourth is the *bendición,* when the fiesta continues and the organizers for the next year are chosen; during that night, a general farewell takes effect with music and dance, and continues until the following day, the fifth and closing day, known as *kacharpari* (Ráez 1993:278–279). In Ishua, Ayacucho, the fiestas have a similar temporal division, but different names: *anticipo, víspera, día, cabildo,* and *despacho* (Bradby 1987:200).

Music and dance are integral parts of the Andean fiesta (figure 10). The music for dance-dramas follows the structure of the dance-dramas themselves—a multisectional form of two to six parts, each with different tempos and styles. The dance-drama choreography is usually fixed and repeats itself year after year. In Cusco, most dances include formations in columns, zigzag movements, and circular patterns—figures that ultimately express local concepts of social space and hierarchy (Poole 1991:325). Similar choreographic patterns have been observed in the province of Cajamarca in the dances of the *chunchu* and the *palla* (Canepa-Koch 1993:170). Dance-drama music is unique, exclusively linked with the choreography of the dance from which it takes it name. Besides the dances in the fiestas, other festive music

FIGURE 11   During a festival in central Peru, a bass drum, snare drum, and two violins are played. Photo by Raúl R. Romero, 1985.

includes music for fireworks, bullfights, horse races, processions, special offerings, and orchestral salutes (welcomes and farewells).

Music for dance-dramas can be performed by a single musician, several performers (figure 11), or a large ensemble. The performers may be members of the community or hired musicians who play professionally in regional markets. In many regions, mestizo sponsors of fiestas hire Indian performers to be closer to the tradition. In this sense, performers of music for dance-dramas may have a less conspicuous profile than the dancers themselves. In some contexts, the latter usually dance because of a religious promise to the Virgin, whereas musicians are usually hired to play (Canepa-Koch 1994:270). Brass bands, including winds, drums, and cymbals, became widely popular in the Andes in the beginning of the twentieth century, largely because military service had become mandatory, and few young men could avoid it (Romero 1985:250). Brass bands remain one of the most popular vehicles for dance-dramas in the southern Peruvian Andes.

There are numerous dance groups and choreographic representations in the Andes, and their classification has seldom been agreed on. Using thematic criteria, Luis Valcarcel (1951:11–13) distinguished the following thematic types in Andean dances: religious, totemic, martial, associational (guilds), satirical, regional, pantomimes, entertainment, agricultural, and strolling dances. Mildred Merino de Zela (1977:70), preferring to use a chronological model, classified them as pre-Hispanic, conquest, colonial, independence, and republican dances. Poole (1990:101), however, has highlighted the fact that ethnic or historic representation, if in fact the most important external trait that these classification systems emphasize, is not necessarily the most important factor involved in Andean dance. The significance of local concepts of time, space, and hierarchy in representing "the other" go beyond the plain illustration of a personage.

Musical competition is pervasive in the Andes, where competitiveness is an essential trait intended to encourage social productivity and solidarity (Montoya 1987). In the Mantaro Valley, after a ceremonial labor day, the laborer who worked fastest and best was elected to inspire the other workers. During traditional festivals throughout the Andean region, contests in which a jury of selected personalities chooses the best music-and-dance group are pervasive. In other instances, a jury is not involved, but the participants themselves decide which group is best. Competition is indispensable in the scissors dance (*danza de tijeras, dansaq*), performed in the context of public fiestas in Ayacucho and adjacent areas. In this dance, two groups compete, each including a harp, a violin, and one or two dancers who play the scissors as an idiophone (see Cohen 1986). Competing dancers alternatively perform up to twenty-one choreographic segments of increasing difficulty (Núñez Rebaza 1990:18–21). Competition also involves singing, as in the carnival songs called *coplas* in Cajamarca. In a succession of challenges and responses among musicians, each singer sings a *copla* in open competition with the others (Canepa-Koch and Romero 1988). In these instances, the principal competition is immersed in Andean established values, but in new contexts (such as the *concurso* 'contest'), the focus shifts to external and formal elements. Dances and musical groups are taken out of context to compete in the urban theater or stadium, and competition is based on formal and ornamental criteria.

The Coast

The waltz (*vals criollo*), the most representative genre of the repertoire, is generally called creole music (*música criolla*), and many Peruvians consider it the foremost national music. A development of its European counterpart, it had achieved regional consolidation by the end of the 1800s. It developed from the Spanish *jota* and *mazurca* and from the Viennese waltz, popularized in Lima by the mid-1800s (Santa Cruz 1977). The Peruvian *vals* originated in the lower classes and neighborhoods of Lima. It was the genre the working classes in the *barrios* preferred, while the upper classes rejected it (Stein 1982).

The polka, now seldom performed, is also part of the creole repertoire. The *marinera*—until about 1900 known as *zamacueca, chilena, mozamala,* and *resbalosa*—is one of the most widely disseminated song-and-dance genres in the country. Originally from coastal Peru, it is widely performed in Andean regions. In compound duple and triple meter (6/8 and 3/4), it has three distinctive parts: the song itself (three stanzas), the *resbalosa* (one stanza), and a closing *fuga* ('flight', not a fugue in the European sense). The *tondero,* a related genre, followed a parallel evolution in the northern coastal departments of La Libertad, Lambayeque, and Píura. In music and choreography, the *tondero* resembles the *marinera,* but it exhibits a distinctive harmonic structure: the first section (*glosa*) begins in the major mode, the second is in the relative minor mode (*dulce*), and the piece returns to the major mode in the third (*fuga*). Both genres are usually accompanied by guitars and a *cajón.* In northern Peru, the latter is replaced by a harp and a banjo.

Creole musical contexts in Peru are limited to the city of Lima and adjacent coastal areas. In coastal Lambayeque, dance-dramas (including *pastoras, margaros,* and *diablicos*) are accompanied by a *pincullo* and a *caja* (played in pipe-and-tabor style), brass instruments, and a *chirimía* (Casas Roque 1993:304–318).

The practice and performance of African-derived music, dances, and rituals by black slaves in Peru since the early years of the conquest is well established in colonial and republican sources. The 1700s marked the beginning of creolization of the music of Peruvian blacks. With their integration into the dominant society, they began to accept and adopt creole cultural and musical expressions. During the 1800s, after the abolition of slavery, they intensified this process. By the 1950s, a small number of specialists remembered a few genres of song associated with them, the repertoire had contracted to a minimum, and the choreographies of most were lost.

This repertoire was the subject of a revival and reconstruction that labeled it Afro-Peruvian, as put forward by the brother and sister Nicomedes and Victoria Santa Cruz, who performed, produced, and promoted Afro-Peruvian music and

In the Peruvian tropical forest, music is customarily linked with ritual and festival cycles, which are strongly influenced by the Roman Catholic calendar. Ritual songs are most prominent in healing ceremonies.

dances (Romero 1994). The movement singled out black-associated genres that had previously been intermingled with the white creole repertoire. Genres such as the *festejo,* the *ingá,* the *socabón,* and the *panalivio* were commercially disseminated by the Santa Cruz family in the late 1950s. In the next decade, the *landó* (or the *zambalandó*), the *son de los diablos,* the habanera, the *zaña,* the *samba-malato,* the *agua de nieve,* the *alcatraz,* and other genres were favored [see AFRO-PERUVIAN TRADITIONS].

The Amazonian Region

Among the groups that inhabit the Amazonian region, the musical cultures of the Aguaruna (border with Ecuador), the Huitoto (frontier with Colombia), the Culina (frontier with Brazil) and the Campa, Cashibo, Shipibo, and Yagua (central Amazon) are better known than others. In the Peruvian tropical forest, music is customarily linked with ritual and festival cycles, which (as in the Yagua group) are strongly influenced by the Roman Catholic calendar. Ritual songs are most prominent in healing ceremonies such as the *ayahuasca* ritual (in which a hallucinogenic drink made from a vine is imbibed) and other shamanistic activities. Vocal music is more pervasive than instrumental music. The vocal imitation of animal and jungle sounds is especially emphasized by the Cashibo. Widely various scales have been reported, ranging from two to seven pitches. Among these, pentatonic scales are quite common in groups such as the Culina. Although heterophony is most commonly observed in musical renditions, two-voice polyphony in intervals of fourths and canonic singing have also been observed (Pinilla 1980:380–384).

SOCIAL STRUCTURE AND ETHNICITY

In assessing matters of social and performance styles in the Peruvian Andes, ethnic distinctions between Indian and mestizo musical cultures have played a fundamental role (Arguedas 1985). These terms no longer exclusively indicate racial types as in the colonial period, but normally refer to cultural and aesthetic orientations. The categories of "Indian" and "mestizo" have generally been understood as polar entities, the Indian usually contemplated in the context of a rural, closed, corporate community, and the mestizo as being an intermediary, equally fluent in a rural milieu and an urban setting. Along these lines, Indians have been assumed to be monolingual in Quechua, wear only Indian clothes, practice ancient customs, and live according to communal rules and principles. Mestizos, in contrast, have been described as bilingual, favoring European dress, and holding urban values (Adams 1959:92).

Nevertheless, the concepts of Indian and mestizo are in fact relational and refer to abstract social units. Therefore they should not be considered descriptive of individuals or social groupings, fixed in time and place. Mestizos of one locality may be considered Indians by the standards of another locality, and Indians and mestizos may assume the opposite condition in variable situations and contexts (de la Cadena

1995:331). By the same token, Indian music can at times be performed by mestizos (Arguedas 1989:14).

With these considerations in mind, we can distinguish Indian aesthetics from mestizo aesthetics in various ways. Most rural Indian music tends to look simpler in form, consisting frequently of a single phrase repeated several times, with extensive melodic variation in the repetitions. Mestizo forms usually consist of a two-phrase symmetrical structure in a periodic form, like the *huayno* (*wayno*). Monophony prevails in rural Indian musical genres such as the *harawi,* the *wanka,* and the *haylli,* whereas homophony and the presence of European harmony are pervasive and indispensable in mestizo forms, like the *huayno,* the *marinera,* and the *yaraví.* Indian music can also be antiphonal or responsorial, as in the *haylli* or liturgical hymns sung during pilgrimages. Indian singing generally features high-pitched, nasal, tense vocalizations, especially noticeable among women. In collective singing, unison is preferred, contrasting with the pervasive intervals of thirds in mestizo musical performances. (It is not uncommon, however, to find intervals of thirds in Indian music.) Parallel voicing at the fifth is featured in panpipe-ensemble traditions in southern Peru. Music for dance-dramas follows a suitelike plan, in which each section has its own style and form.

TRADITION AND MUSICAL CHANGE

Most Andean communities are concerned about safeguarding their traditions, which, for them, represent the past, though their origins are not necessarily thought archaic. Several musical expressions in the Andes are locally considered traditional, though their origins can be traced back only to the beginning of this century. In the cities of Puno, young people regard the panpipe group Qantati Ururi of Conima as the true keepers of the panpipe tradition, though this band uses intervals of thirds—a practice introduced as a result of urban influence in Conima during the first decades of the twentieth century (Turino 1993:130). In the Mantaro Valley, a variant of the typical orchestra—clarinets, violins, harp—is considered to represent authentic performance, though clarinets were introduced into the valley only in the 1920s. In Cusco, the dance *los majeños* 'the men of Majes [a town in Arequipa]', normally accompanied by a brass band, is considered traditional regional folklore, though it became popular only in the 1960s (Mendoza-Walker 1994:55).

Trends in musical change include the spread of brass bands throughout the Andean region at the cost of smaller traditional ensembles with less dazzling instrumentation. This change happened especially in the case of dance-dramas. In the Mantaro Valley (Romero 1985:21), in the Colca Valley (Ráez 1993:280), and in most of the Andean region, brass bands have displaced Indian and rural ensembles and have achieved intense popularity. One of the factors in their expansion is that they are more elastic in repertoire than are the regional ensembles. They can play any musical genre—*cumbia, marinera, pasodoble,* tropical music, and even the latest popular music hit—and this versatility adds to their popularity among younger people.

The *cumbia,* originally a genre from Colombia, is immensely popular in the Peruvian Andes. It is commonly performed by the ubiquitous brass band and is danced at special times in traditional fiestas. In regional ensembles, called jazz bands by the people of Cusco, its basic rhythmic pattern has influenced the rhythmic accompaniment of mestizo genres like the *huayno* and those of festival music. The similarity of this rhythmic pattern with that of the *huayno* is striking.

ANDEAN MIGRANT MUSIC IN THE CITIES

Andean music had been present in Lima since the 1930s in the festival of Amancaes every *día del indio* (24 June), and well before that through the works and performances of Peruvian academic composers who have borrowed Andean musical materials and themes (Núñez and Llorens 1981:54–55). Since the late 1940s, processes of massive migration and the presence of Andean peoples in the urban centers of the country, especially in Lima, has continued and expanded highland traditions (see figure 2) and generated new musical styles, which combined Andean musical traditions with the popular musical trends available in the cities. The appearance of the first commercial records of Andean music marked the birth of a new style of urban mestizo popular song. These records were distributed in Lima in 1949 because of an initiative by José María Arguedas (1975:125), who promoted the pilot edition of a series of 78-rpm records on the (now locally extinct) label Odeon. The success was overwhelming, so Odeon began to mass-produce them independently of Arguedas.

In the 1950s, the sale of Andean records grew considerably in urban sectors of Peru, mainly because of the increasing migration of Andean rural peoples into the capital. The appearance of the first folkloric programs (*programas folklóricos*) on commercial radio stations in Lima dedicated to the diffusion of Andean music and the promotion of folkloric festivals contributed to this success (Llorens 1991:180). In the 1960s, as a result of this outburst of production and consumption, Andean mestizo celebrities—songwriters, instrumentalists, performers—achieved popularity and recognition. Singers including the Pastorcita Huaracina, el Jilguero del Huascarán, and Picaflor de los Andes sold thousand of records and became celebrities. The effort was not limited to records but also included live performances in marginal spaces where migrant musicians could play and migrant consumers could attend, such as live radio shows, open theaters (*coliseos*), and regional associations.

Coliseos were the most influential musical settings for these musical styles. Beginning in the late 1940s, masses of Andean migrants congregated in them, usually on Sundays and holidays, to watch their favorite professional and amateur performers. Today, these venues have disappeared, replaced by public performances and musical festivals in provincial clubs and athletic stadiums. Many provincial associations celebrate their regional fiestas in Lima, recreating their own music and dances (Núñez and Llorens 1981:66–70).

Until the 1970s, commercial records were produced by major Peruvian record companies, including FTA, IEMPSA, Mag, Sono Radio, and Virrey. Only the first two survive and are now the biggest record producers in Peru. Both maintain an Andean music division, one of their most important production departments. It was not until the 1970s that small and independent record companies in open competition with IEMPSA and Virrey began to record nonprofessional peasant performers. Consequently, *huayno* songs were less emphasized by these companies, and widely various songs and dance genres (including ritual music) began to be recorded on commercial discs. These recordings are not distributed on a national scale, but prevail in local and regional markets (Romero 1992:198).

During the early 1960s, the popularity of the *cumbia* among Andean residents and migrants was boosted by the appearance of a new urban musical genre, called *chicha* or *cumbia andina,* which blended musical elements from the *huayno* with the *cumbia. Chicha* achieved great approval among the younger generations of Andean origins, and became especially important in its center of operations, Lima, though many of its principal performers came from the central Andes. *Chicha* style and the instrumental makeup of its musical groups reflect the influence that since the early 1960s international Latin American popular styles and American and British rock have had on young Andean migrants (Turino 1990:19). A typical group (figure 12) consists of two electric guitars, an electric organ (replaced in the 1990s by a synthesizer), an electric bass, Latin percussion (*timbales,* congas, bongos, cowbell), and a vocalist, who performs in a style recalling that of Andean mestizo songs.

FIGURE 12   On stage in Lima, Peru, the *chicha* (also known as *cumbia andina*) ensemble Alegría performs. *Left to right:* musicians play bongos, electric bass, *timbales,* keyboard, and electric guitar. Photo by Raúl R. Romero, 1985.

Chicha music became a nucleus around which young unmarried men and women from first- and second-generation cohorts in Lima congregated every Sunday and holidays. Several *chichódromos* (locales for *chicha* events) opened in downtown Lima and in the outskirts, and such groups as the Shapis, Alegría, and Chacalón y la Nueva Crema gained fame. Though most *chicha* lyrics deal with romantic love, other themes directly linked to the problems of the migrant in Lima also prevail. As a product of migrant Andean people, *chicha* was regarded by the upper classes and by the mass media as a low cultural product in bad taste, and its performances were considered dangerous and promiscuous. With time, however, *chicha* has opened new channels for migrant music on FM radio stations and during prime-time television. This reversal does not mean that upper and middle classes in Peru have changed their attitudes toward *chicha* music but that Andean migrants have achieved an influential position in Peruvian society. The role of *chicha* as the urban expression of a new Andean cultural identity transcending regional characters to achieve national significance has been emphasized by Peruvian social scientists since the 1980s (Hurtado Suárez 1995).

In rural areas, as in Paccha in Junín, *chicha* is usually played in public buildings at night in social dances (*bailes*) organized during the traditional fiestas. Without disturbing the normal development of the fiesta during daytime, the *bailes* in Paccha gather young unmarried men and women together. In this setting, they may interact freely and independently in ways that they cannot during traditional festivities. In the context of a social dance, *chicha* functions as a courting ritual, does not require heavy expenses, and may be enjoyed at any period of the year (Romero 1989:131).

THE MASS MEDIA AND POPULAR MUSICS

The mass media have been responsible for disseminating transnational musical genres and styles since the first decades of this century. Peruvians with access to the radio and movie theaters became familiar as early as the 1920s with the Argentine tango, the Mexican ranchera, and the North American fox-trot, one-step, and charleston (Basadre 1964). Local orchestras disseminated these genres in social and private dances and events. Jazz has been played in Lima since the first decades of the twentieth century, especially by orchestras influenced by the styles of New Orleans. In the late 1960s, Jaime Delgado Aparicio, a pianist, arranger, and musical director trained

The regular visits of renowned Cuban and Caribbean performers and bandleaders consolidated the popularity of these genres throughout the years. Today, salsa music is one of the most popular genres throughout Peru.

at Berklee College in Boston, returned to Peru and became a jazz advocate. He was the main disseminator of modern jazz until his death in the early 1980s. He recorded three jazz LPs and performed and conducted widely in public concerts in Lima. Despite his advocacy, however, jazz audiences in Lima remained limited to a narrow circle, drawn mainly from the middle and upper classes. In the late 1990s, live jazz performances in Lima are scarce, though recorded performances are broadcast on radio regularly alongside Brazilian popular music, which has been present in the Peruvian media since the 1960s.

In the 1960s, rock and roll became popular among the younger generations in urban centers, thanks to the massive influence of radio, the LP-recording industry, and national television. In that decade, local singers and groups sang rock in Spanish (*rock en español*), gaining for the genre a sudden, though short-lived, fame. In 1985, rock and roll in Spanish reemerged as Micky Gonzales, a performer and composer, sold thousands of copies of his first rock album and suggested the same path to subsequent rockers. In the 1990s, rock in Spanish, with lyrics based on nationally significant themes, regained popularity among young people of different social sectors. Other bands have been equally open to influences of pop, reggae, rap, and worldbeat, but the most consequential musical influence is Argentine *rock en español,* whose popularity in Peru preceded the development of Peruvian rock in the 1980s. Unlike Argentine rock bands, however, Peruvian bands have had only a limited international distribution. The most commercially successful band in writing lyrics portraying national reality with a satiric touch is No Sé Quien y No Sé Cuantos (I Don't Know Who and I Don't Know How Many), the best-selling Peruvian rock band of all time. Most Peruvian bands have begun producing CDs, cassettes, and videos, all of which the national media broadcast intensively.

In the early 1970s, the movement known as *nueva canción latinoamericana* 'new Latin American song' began to influence politically conscious university students. As a result, many performing groups emerged. The main influences that had achieved immense popularity among university students were groups performing *nueva canción chilena* 'new Chilean song' and *nueva trova* 'new song', a Cuban genre. In the early 1980s, the movement lost its vitality in Peru, and political-oriented Peruvian musical groups dissolved. Among them were ensembles formed within the Taller de la Canción Popular (Popular-Song Workshop), which the composer Celso Garrido Lecca had established at the National Conservatory of Music in the 1970s.

The *nueva canción* movement in Peru precipitated the rise of numerous neofolkloric groups that later achieved worldwide popularity. Mainly directed to the foreign-tourist market, these groups, which usually combine the *siku,* the *quena,* the *charango,* the guitar, and the Argentine *bombo,* play Andean musical genres, usually in faster tempos and altered in their rhythmic, harmonic, and instrumental aspects, furthering their commercial aims. In the 1990s, it is common to find these groups playing in *peñas folklóricas* (coffeehouses and/or restaurants featuring neofolkloric music) or as street musicians in Europe and the United States. Record production and sales of these groups in Peru is minimal, despite their national ubiquity.

In the 1950s, Cuban and Caribbean popular genres such as the *son,* the rumba, and the bolero began to gain wide acceptance in Peru, as did (later) the most commercial versions such as the *cha-cha-chá* and the mambo. The regular visits of renowned Cuban and Caribbean performers and bandleaders consolidated the popularity of these genres throughout the years. Today, salsa music is one of the most popular genres throughout Peru. Live performances of salsa are frequent in *salsódromos* (nightclubs for dancing to salsa) around the country, and numerous AM and FM radio stations exclusively broadcast salsa music at all hours. Most local salsa activity consists of the performance of covers of hits from New York and Puerto Rico. Peruvian composers and performers of salsa have not yet achieved international distribution, with the exception of the singer-composer Antonio Cartagena.

Latin pop dominates Peruvian markets and record sales. In the mass media, it is the most disseminated genre, closely followed by Top 40 international hits. Both are highly popularized by the media, and both styles fill the stacks at local record stores. A survey of the musical preferences of *limeños* (people of Lima) in the early 1990s revealed that more than 57 percent of *limeños* who listen to radio prefer Latin pop and salsa, 19 percent prefer Andean and creole music, and 17 percent prefer rock and roll. Jazz and classical music were the least-represented categories, with 3 percent total (Bolaños 1995:111). The remaining 4 percent is accounted for by other categories.

Today, the Peruvian recording industry is in a transitional stage. Recordings in the LP format ceased to be produced in the late 1980s, and since then the cassette industry has controlled the market. Though the bigger companies are slowly switching to the CD format, they are unable to compete with small and informal companies that market inexpensive cassettes. Illegal copying and cassette piracy are common throughout the country, as are ambulatory retailers who frequent the busiest streets and local markets.

Radio is a powerful medium in contemporary Peru. It reaches even distant rural communities. In 1992, there were 331 AM and 180 FM radio stations in the country. Of these, only forty-seven AM and thirty-nine FM stations were located in Lima. In the 1980s, television networks experienced a notable growth. Today, Peru has six private television stations and one state-supported channel, most with national coverage. Cable television, available only in the capital, airs TV programming from Europe, the United States, and other Latin American countries. Parabolic antennas, which pick up satellite waves, are widely dispersed in the rest of the country, providing television to rural communities that cannot receive signals from national television stations.

FURTHER STUDY

An excellent survey of traditional musical instruments in Peru is Jiménez Borja's seminal book on the subject (1951). A more recent and exhaustive organological inventory for all three geographical regions of Peru can be found in the *Mapa de los Intrumentos Musicales de Uso Popular en el Perú* (Instituto Nacional de Cultura 1978).

The first known wax-cylinder recordings made in Peru were made by the French couple Raoul and Marguerite d'Harcourt in the 1920s. The d'Harcourts recorded extensively throughout the Andean areas of Ecuador, Peru, and Bolivia, and used these recordings as the basis for a book (1990 [1925]). The current location of these recordings is unknown, and it is widely assumed that they are lost. Around 1900, Heinrich Brünning recorded wax cylinders in the north coast of Peru, documenting musical renditions and oral expressions in the Mochica language, now largely extinct. The location of Brünning's materials is unknown.

The first recordings of Andean Peruvian music known to be extant are those made in the 1940s by the South American ethnomusicologists Isabel Aretz and Luís Felipe Ramón y Rivera, who recorded extensively on reel-to-reel tape in the southern Andes of Peru. Their collection is deposited in the National Institute of Musicology in Buenos Aires, Argentina, and in the Fundación Interamericana de Etnomusicología y Folklore in Caracas, Venezuela. More recent recordings of Peruvian traditional music are deposited in the Library of Congress and the Archives of Traditional Music of Indiana University, Bloomington. The largest collection of unpublished audiovisual materials is housed in Lima, in the Archives of Andean Traditional Music of the Catholic University of Peru.

REFERENCES

Adams, Richard. 1959. *A Community in the Andes*. Seattle: University of Washington Press.

Archivo de Música Tradicional Andina. 1995. *Catálogo del Archivo de Música Tradicional Andina*. Lima: Pontífica Universidad Católica del Peru, Instituto Riva Agüero.

Arguedas, José María. 1975. *Formación de una Cultura Nacional Indoamericana*. México: Siglo XXI.

———. 1985. *Indios, Mestizos y Señores*. Lima: Horizonte.

———. 1989 [1938]. *Canto Kechua*. Lima: Horizonte.

Bellenger, Xavier. 1981. "Les Instruments de Musique dans les Pays Andins: Deuxième Partie." *Bulletin de L'Institut d'Études Andines* 10(1–2):23–50.

Basadre, Jorge. 1964. "Notas sobre la Música en el Perú." In *Historia de la República del Perú*, ed. Jorge Basadre, 10:4603–4619. Lima: Editorial Universitaria.

Bolaños, César. 1985. "La Música en el Antiguo Perú." In La Música en el Perú, 1–64. Lima: Patronato Popular y Porvenir Pro Música Clásica.

———. 1988. *Las Antaras Nasca*. Lima: Instituto Andino de Estudios Arqueológicos.

———. 1995. *La Música Nacional en los Medios de Comunicación Electrónicos de Lima Metropolitana*. Cuadernos CICOSUL. Lima: Universidad de Lima, Facultad de Ciencias de la Comunicación.

Bradby, Barbara. 1987. "Symmetry around a Centre: Music of an Andean Community." *Popular Music* 6(2):197–218.

Canepa-Koch, Gisela. 1991. *Wylancha*. 28 mins. Lima: Pontificia Universidad Católica del Perú, Archivo de Música Tradicional Andina. Video, VHS-NTSC.

———. 1993. "Los chu'nchu y las palla de Cajamarca en el ciclo de la representación de la muerte del Inca." In *Música, Danzas y Máscaras en los Andes*, ed. Raúl R. Romero, 139–178. Lima: Pontífica Universidad Católica del Perú.

———. 1994. "Danzas, Identidad y Modernidad en los Andes: Las Danzas en la Fiesta de la Virgen del Carmen en Paucartambo." *Anthropológica* 11:255–282.

Canepa-Koch, Gisela, and Raúl R. Romero. 1988. "Música Tradicional de Cajamarca." Lima: Pontífica Universidad Católica del Perú, Instituto Riva-Agüero. Notes to LP disk.

Carpio Muñoz, Juan. 1976. *El Yaraví Arequipeño*. Arequipa: La Colmena.

Casas Roque, Leonidas. 1993. "Fiestas, Danzas y Música de la Costa de Lambayeque." In *Música, Danzas y Máscaras en los Andes*, ed. Raúl R. Romero, 299–337. Lima: Pontífica Universidad Católica del Perú.

Cavero, Jesús A. 1985. "El Qarawi y su Función Social." *Allpanchis* 25:233–270.

Cieza de León, Pedro. 1967 [1553]. *El Señorío de los Incas*. Lima: Instituto de Estudios Peruanos.

Cobo, Bernabé. 1956 [1653]. *Historia del Nuevo Mundo*. Vol. 2. Madrid: Ediciones Atlas.

Cohen, John. 1984. *Mountain Music of Peru*. New York: Cinema Guild. Film, video.

Cuentas Ormachea, Enrique. 1982. "La Danza Choquela y su Contenido Mágico Religioso." *Boletín de Lima* 4(19):54–70.

de la Cadena, Marisol. 1995. "Women Are More Indian: Ethnicity and Gender in a Community near Cuzco." In *Ethnicity, Markets, and Migration in the Andes: At the Crossroads of History and Anthropology*, ed. Brooke Larson and Olivia Harris, 329–348. Durham, N.C.: Duke University Press.

den Otter, Elisabeth. 1985. *Music and Dance of Indians and Mestizos in an Andean Valley of Peru*. Delft: Eburon.

Estenssoro, Juán Carlos. 1988. "Música y Comportamiento Festivo de la Población Negra en Lima Colonial." *Cuadernos Hispanoamericanos* 451–452:161–166.

Garcilaso de la Vega, El Inca. 1959 [1603]. *Comentarios Reales de los Incas*. Vol. 1. Lima: Universidad Nacional de San Marcos.

Guamán Poma de Ayala, Felipe. 1956 [?1567–1615?]. *La Nueva Crónica y Buén Gobierno*. Lima: Ministerio de Educación.

Haeberli, Joerg. 1979. "Twelve Nasca Panpipes." *Ethnomusicology* 23(1):57–74.

d'Harcourt, Raoul, and Marguerite d'Harcourt. 1990 [1925]. *La Musique des Incas et ses Survivances.* Paris: Paul Geuthner. Reprinted in Spanish, 1990, as *La música de los Incas y sus supervivencias.* Translated by Roberto Miro Quesada. Lima: Occidental Petroleum Corporation of Peru, Luis Alberto Sánchez, and Ismael Pinto.

Hurtado Suárez, Wilfredo. 1995. *Chicha Peruana: Música de los Nuevos Migrantes.* Lima: Eco-Grupo de Investigaciones Económicas.

Instituto Nacional de Cultura. 1978. *Mapa de los Instrumentos Musicales de Uso Popular en el Perú.* Lima: Instituto Nacional de Cultura.

Jiménez Borja, Arturo. 1951. "Instrumentos musicales Peruanos." *Revista del Museo Nacional* 19–20:37–190.

Llorens, José Antonio. 1991. "Andean Voices on Lima Airwaves: Highland Migrants and Radio Broadcasting in Peru." *Studies in Latin American Popular Culture* 10:177–189.

Matos Mar, José, and Jorge A. Carbajal. 1974. *Erasmo: Yanacón del Valle de Chancay.* Lima: Instituto de Estudios Peruanos.

Mendoza-Walker, Zoila. 1994. "Contesting Identities through Dance: Mestizo Performance in the Southern Andes of Peru." *Repercussions* 3(2):50–80.

Merino de Zela, Mildred. 1977. "Folklore Coreográfico e Historia." *Folklore Americano* 24:67–94.

Montoya, Rodrigo. 1987. *La Cultura Quechua Hoy.* Lima: Mosca Azul.

Núñez Rebaza, Lucy. 1990. *Los Dansaq.* Lima: Instituto Nacional de Cultura, Museo Nacional de la Cultura Peruana.

Núñez Rebaza, Lucy, and José A. Llorens. 1981. "La música tradicional andina en Lima metropolitana." *América Indígena* 41(1):53–74.

Okada, Yuki. 1995. *Central and South America.* JVC Smithsonian Folkways Video Anthology of Music and Dance of the Americas, 6. Montpelier, Vt.: Multicultural Media VTMV-230. Video.

Olsen, Dale A. 1986–87. "The Peruvian Folk Harp Tradition: Determinants of Style." *Folk Harp Journal* 53:48–54, 54:41–48, 55:55–59, 56:57–60, 57:38–42, 58:47–48, 59:60–62.

Pagaza Galdo, Consuelo. 1961. "El Yaraví." *Folklore Americano* 8–9:75–141.

Pinilla, Enrique. 1980. "Informe sobre la Música en el Perú." In *Historia del Perú,* vol. 9, ed. Juan Mejia Baca, 363–677. Lima: Juan Mejia Baca.

Pinto, Arturo. 1987. "Afinaciones de la Guitarra en Ayacucho." *Boletín de Lima* 9(49):83–87.

Poole, Deborah A. 1990. "Accommodation and Resistance in Andean Ritual Dance." *The Drama Review* 34(2):98–126.

———. 1991. "Rituals of Movements, Rites of Transformation: Pilgrimage and Dance in the Highlands of Cuzco, Peru." In *Pilgrimage in Latin America,* ed. Ross Crumrine and Alan Morinis, 307–338. New York: Greenwood Press.

Quezada Macchiavello, José. 1985. "La Música en el Virreinato." In *La Música en el Perú,* 65–102. Lima: Patronato Popular y Porvenir Pro Música Clásica.

Ráez Retamozo, Manuel. 1993. "Los ciclos ceremoniales y la percepción del tiempo festivo en al valle del Colca." In *Música, Danzas y Máscaras en los Andes,* ed. Raúl R. Romero, 253–298. Lima: Pontífica Universidad Católica del Perú.

Roel Pineda, Josafát. 1959. "El Wayno del Cusco." *Folklore Americano* 6–7:129–245.

Romero, Raúl R. 1985. "La Música Tradicional y Popular." In *La Música en el Perú,* 215–283. Lima: Patronato Popular y Porvenir Pro Música Clásica.

———. 1989. "Música Urbana en un Contexto Rural: Tradición y Modernidad en Paccha, Junín." *Anthropológica* 7(7):121–133.

———. 1990. "Musical Change and Cultural Resistance in the Central Andes of Peru." *Latin American Music Review* 11(1):1–35.

———. 1992. "Preservation, the Mass Media and Dissemination of Traditional Music." In *World Music, Musics of the World: Aspects of Documentation, Mass Media and Acculturation,* ed. Max Peter Baumann, 191–210. Wilhelmshaven: Florian Noetzel.

———. 1993. *Música, Danzas y Máscaras en el Perú.* Lima: Pontífica Universidad Católica del Perú.

———. 1994. "Black Music and Identity in Peru: Reconstruction and Revival of Afro-Peruvian Musical Traditions." In *Music and Black Ethnicity: The Caribbean and South America,* ed. Gerard H. Béhague, 307–330. Miami: North-South Center, University of Miami.

Rowe, Ann Pollard. 1979. "Textile Evidence for Huari Music." *Textile Museum Journal* 18:5–18.

Santa Cruz, César. 1977. *El Waltz y el Vals Criollo.* Lima: Instituto Nacional de Cultura.

Sas, Andres. 1936. "Ensayo Sobre la Música Nazca." *Boletín Latinoamericano de Música* 4:221–233.

Stevenson, Robert M. 1960. *The Music of Peru.* Washington, D.C.: Organization of American States.

———. 1968. *Music in Aztec and Inca Territory.* Berkeley: University of California Press.

Stein, Stephen. 1982. "El vals criollo y los valores de la clase trabajadora en la Lima de comienzos del siglo XX." *Socialismo y Participación* 17:43–50.

Turino, Thomas. 1983. "The Charango and the *Sirena:* Music, Magic, and the Power of Love." *Latin American Music Review* 4(1):81–119.

———. 1984. "The Urban-Mestizo Charango Tradition in Southern Peru: A Statement of Shifting Identity." *Ethnomusicology* 28(2):253–270.

———. 1990. "Somos el Perú: 'Cumbia Andina'

and the Children of Andean Migrants in Lima." *Studies in Latin American Popular Culture* 9:15–37.

———. 1993. *Moving Away from Silence: Music of the Peruvian Altiplano and the Experience of Urban Migration.* Chicago: University of Chicago Press.

Valcarcel, Luís E. 1951. "Introducción." In *Fiestas y Danzas en el Cuzco y en los Andes,* ed. Pierre Verger. Buenos Aires: Editorial Sudamericana.

Valencia Chacón, Américo. 1983. *El Siku Bipolar Altiplánico.* Lima: Artex Editores.

———. 1989. *The Altiplano Bipolar Siku: Study and Projection of the Peruvian Panpipe Orchestra.* Lima: Artex Editores.

Vega, Carlos. 1932. "Escalas con Semitonos en la Música de los Antiguos Peruanos." *Actas y Trabajos Científicos del XXV Congreso Internacional de Americanistas* (La Plata) 1:349–381.

Villareal Vara, Felix. 1958. "Las Afinaciones de la Guitarra en Huánuco, Perú." *Revista Musical Chilena* 12(62):33–36.

Afro-Peruvian Traditions
William David Tompkins

The African Heritage
The Spanish Heritage
Traditional Afro-Peruvian Genres
Creole Musical Genres
Twentieth-Century Developments
Academic Folklorists and Further Study

The African presence in coastal Peru began with the Spanish encounter in the early 1500s and increased over the next three centuries. Afro-Peruvian musical development was a function of black exposure to the musical traditions of African, Spanish, and indigenous people. Though the link with Africa was reinforced with each new arrival of slaves, blacks in colonial Peru worked closely with the Spaniards, for receptivity to Spanish culture, language, and religion was the key to their social advancement. Interracial mixing and the eventual decline of the black population relative to others on the coast also promoted acculturation.

The strength of the African heritage varied in intensity, following social and cultural changes in Peru that affected black behavioral attitudes—particularly the growth of political and folkloric nationalism, and ultimately, in the late twentieth century, the worldwide movement of negritude. Despite Afro-Peruvian eclecticism, however, blacks in Peru not only retained much of the integrity of their musical style, but also profoundly influenced the development of national music in coastal Peru.

THE AFRICAN HERITAGE

One of the principal sources of cultural unity and community for Peruvian blacks from about the 1550s to the 1850s was the *cofradías,* religious brotherhoods or sodalities for black slaves, established by the Roman Catholic Church in the 1540s. Each *cofradía* was devoted to a particular saint and served the members' spiritual and physical well-being. Though much activity of the *cofradías* was supervised by the church, it apparently included African ritual elements.

The *cofradías* were a major factor in the preservation of African musical traditions, as evidenced by descriptions of them in colonial literature. Though most accounts of the music and dance of non-Hispanicized slaves (*bozales*) in the *cofradías* were biased and critical (Lee 1935:144), the municipal leaders of Lima still required the *cofradías* to take part in the city's state and religious processions. An ordinance called the *cofradías* to assemble according to their respective nations of origin with their typical dress and musical instruments, and to dance and sing their traditional music.

marimba African term for a xylophone

cajita 'Little box', coastal Afro-Peruvian idiophone made from a small wooden box with a hinged lid, played by shutting the lid in rhythm and striking the box with a stick

quijada African-derived scraped or struck idiophone made from the defleshed, dried jawbone of an ass, mule, or horse

son de los diablos Choreographed musical spectacle performed in the streets of Lima during carnival

festejo Afro-Peruvian form often interrupted at phrase endings by a sudden pause or a long-held pitch

cajón 'Big box', Afro-Peruvian and criollo idiophone made from a wooden box with a soundhole in the back

FIGURE 1   In Lima, Peru, a member of Perú Negro plays a *cajita*. Photo by William David Tompkins, 1974.

FIGURE 2   In Lima, Peru, a member of Perú Negro plays a *quijada*. Photo by William David Tompkins, 1974.

From the descriptions of musical instruments in the colonial literature, blacks showed a marked preference for percussion instruments. Their only aerophone was a nose-blown flute ("Rasgo . . . de los Negros Bozales" 1791), and their only chordophone was a musical bow, strung with catgut and struck with a small cane (W. B. Stevenson 1825:304). They had several membranophones, particularly those formed from hollow logs or large conical, ceramic vessels (*botijas de barro*). Both types are described in eighteenth- and nineteenth-century sources and are remembered by elderly consultants as being used in rural areas until the early 1900s.

Of now obsolete idiophones, the marimba was once among the most popular. It consisted of wooden tablets placed on an arch of wood over the mouths of gourd resonators. The tablets were struck with sticks by a player who squatted in front of them. The existence of the marimba in northern Peru in the 1780s is documented by Martínez Compañón (1978: plate 142), who ordered a watercolor made of it. The last known reference to it is in a travel account from the first decades of the nineteenth century (Rushenberge 1834:39).

Black slaves also employed other idiophones, including a notched stick, a bamboo rasp, and a long stamped pole hung with pieces of tin, ribbons, and tinsel, the base of which was struck on the ground.

Perhaps the most unusual musical instrument used by Afro-Peruvians until the first decades of the twentieth century was a *mesa de ruidos* 'table of noises', called *tamborete* in Lima and *tormento* in Chile. It consisted of a sheet of wood placed on four legs, with a possible box resonator underneath. On top of the sheet were (perhaps partially nailed) bottle tops with chips of wood on top of them. Agile fingers played rhythms on top of the sheet, causing the bottle tops and wood chips to vibrate.

Among the idiophones still extant are the *cajita* and the *quijada*. The *cajita* consists of a small wooden box with a hinged wooden lid. It is suspended in front of the player by a cord that passes around his neck or waist. He plays rhythms by striking the side of the box with a stick and opening and closing the lid (figure 1).

The *quijada,* also called *carraca* or *carachacha,* is the lower jawbone of an ass, mule, or horse, stripped of its flesh and with the teeth loosened so they can rattle in their sockets (figure 2). While the left hand holds the jawbone at the chin, the right scrapes a piece of sheep rib across the face of the jaw or the surface of the molars, or the clenched fist strikes the side of the jaw, buzzing the molars in their sockets.

A watercolor "by Pancho Fierro" from the mid-1800s illustrates the use of the *cajita* and the *quijada* to accompany the *son de los diablos,* a dance performed during carnival (figure 3). The *cajita* is still used primarily in stage renditions of the *son de los diablos,* and the *quijada* accompanies various Afro-Peruvian genres, most notably the *festejo* (described below).

In northern Peru, the idiophones *angara* and *checo* are also used. Each is fabricated from an empty calabash with one of its sides opened. The player puts it between

FIGURE 3 Watercolor by Pancho Fierro (1803–1879) showing a *cajita,* a harp, and a *quijada* accompanying a *son de los diablos,* performed during carnival. Municipality of Lima. Used with permission.

El son de los diablos.

FIGURE 4 A young man of Guayabo plays a *cajón.* Photo by William David Tompkins, 1974.

his thighs, the aperture facing down, and strikes its top with his hands. Ignacio Merino (1817–1876) painted the *angara* as it was played during the 1800s.

The Afro-Peruvian idiophone used most widely in the twentieth century is the *cajón,* a simple wooden box about 50 centimeters high, 30 wide, and 25 deep, with a sound hole about 10 centimeters in diameter in the back. The player normally sits on top of the *cajón,* rhythmically striking the front and sides of it with his hands (figure 4). During the late 1800s, the nails in the planks of the *cajón* were purposely loosened to add a kind of vibration when the *cajón* was struck (Fuentes 1925:112). The instrument probably developed during the 1800s and became popular shortly after 1850; before then, membranophones had more commonly been used. Today, the *cajón* provides rhythmic accompaniment to various forms of Afro-Peruvian and other coastal music.

Many of these instruments seem to be of African origin or inspiration. The African affinity for percussive instruments is evident, and the buzzing produced by numerous African instruments reappears in the Peruvian marimba, rasps, *quijada, cajón,* and *tamborete.* After the 1950s, as folkloric groups strove to reconstruct their African musical heritage, they rediscovered some of these instruments.

THE SPANISH HERITAGE

Colonial literature shows that blacks in Peru used two forms of musical expression. Music rooted in African traditions continued to be performed in the *cofradías* into the 1800s; however, blacks skilled in playing Spanish musical instruments had long performed military music, and soon Afro-Peruvian musicians became commonplace in all facets of social, religious, and musical life in Spanish Peru.

As early as the 1500s, but especially during the 1800s, many blacks developed proficiency in the graces of European salon music and dance. Some black dance masters attained considerable fame (Fuentes 1925:110–111; R. M. Stevenson 1968:304). Even the church exploited blacks' musical talents: in the 1600s, the College of San

Pablo had a fine band of black musicians who played trumpets (*clarines*), shawms (*chirimías*), drums, flutes, and various kinds of plucked lutes (Bowser 1974:246).

As black musicians encountered more European music, they adapted and reinterpreted elements into their own music. New Afro-Peruvian genres emerged. Some of them were indigenous to Peruvian blacks; others were black stylizations of Spanish musical forms. The pantomimic *moros y cristianos,* one such musical tradition, was eventually absorbed into black culture from Spanish folklore. Several chroniclers wrote about it during the 1800s, and Pancho Fierro portrayed it in a watercolor in 1830. This mime-drama has probably disappeared from coastal Peru, and already by the 1970s, only the oldest people in rural areas remembered having seen it.

Another Afro-Peruvian genre that originated in Spanish traditions is the *son de los diablos,* danced by several blacks dressed in devil costumes and masks (see figure 3). This dance seems to have its more remote origins in the short religious plays of Corpus Christi and the processions of Low Sunday (Quasimodo Sunday). After 1817, it passed to the secular context of carnival (Fuentes 1925:80). Various written accounts of it, and paintings of Pancho Fierro, show that the performing group normally consisted of a major devil (*diablo mayor*) and several minor devils, masked and dressed in pantaloons, accompanied by musicians playing the harp or a guitarlike plucked lute (possibly the *vihuela*), the *cajita,* and the *quijada.* The group formed a circle on street corners, and each devil would dance in turn. During the first few decades of the twentieth century, the *son de los diablos* gradually disappeared from Lima's carnivals. It was revived in the mid-1950s in the context of a staged Afro-Peruvian folk dance.

Celebrations of Christmas

Christmas in Peruvian homes takes place around often elaborate crèches (*nacimientos, belenes*). In some rural areas and small towns, late December also brings out the *hatajos de negritos* (see Okada 1995: example 22), boys dressed as Magi, who sing and dance in adoration of the Infant Jesus to the accompaniment of a solo violin in front of crèches. Mestizos and even indigenous peoples have dances *de negros* that imitate blacks. The songs and dances of the *hatajos* from the more densely black-populated areas of Ica, however, are rooted in their own history and heritage. In their performances, boys represent not only kings and shepherds, but also enslaved blacks.

The costumes of the *negritos* vary from group to group but generally consist of an ornate cap representing a crown, and a band of bright red or blue cloth, crossing diagonally over the upper body like a royal sash. The crown and the band bear a profusion of tinkle bells, bits of bright paper, bolts of cloth, and tiny mirrors—and paper currency, donated to the dancer. Each *negrito* holds a handbell (*campanilla*) and a decorated rope whip (*chicotillo*). At one time, small jingle bells (*cascabeles*) attached to the dancers' ankles would sound with each movement of their feet. The *negritos* dance repetitive choreographic figures in two lines, employing rhythmic stamping reminiscent of the *wayno* (*huayno*) but with more frequent use of *zapateado* (rhythmic striking of the heels and toes of the shoes against the floor or against each other) and *escobillada* (a brushing movement of the shoe or bare foot along the floor or ground).

TRACK 25

The songs and dances of the *hatajo de negritos* of the town of El Carmen, province of Chincha, represent a notable example of acculturation and assimilation of Spanish, African, and highland native musical elements. Like the nineteenth-century Spanish *villancico,* the songs of the *negritos* employ pastoral, amorous, or sacred Christmas themes set syllabically to a simple melody in a short strophic form. The dramatic element in the performances of the *negritos* probably owes much to the *vil-*

lancico's occasional association with the theater and the old Christmas plays (*autos*) introduced by the Spanish missionaries.

Some songs reveal native American influences in the texts and melodies, and occasionally even in the vocal style—particularly the broken, wailing voice at points where the melody suddenly descends. The *hatajo* of El Carmen, composed mainly of blacks, employs a more kinetic style than does that of mestizo groups. Residents of the area consider black dancers particularly skillful in *zapateado*. Many of the texts employ black dialect and make frequent references to life under slavery.

Spanish prosody

Afro-Peruvian traditions have absorbed several recited or competitively sung Spanish poetic forms, some of which may be recited or sung competitively. Among the most important of these is the *décima,* a poetic form consisting of ten octosyllabic lines, developed in Spain during the 1500s and popularized throughout Latin America. The *décima* deals with biblical subjects (*a lo divino*) or themes of philosophy, politics, satire, or love (*a lo humano*). It is usually recited but may be sung in a declamatory, syllabic style with guitar providing an unobtrusive chordal accompaniment (*socabón* or *socavón*).

Décimas can be presented *sueltas* 'individually' or *en pié forzado* 'forced foot'. The structure of the *décima en pié forzado* varies in different regions of Latin America. In Peru, it consists of four *décimas* preceded by an octosyllabic quatrain (*glosa*) that becomes the skeleton on which four ten-line strophes hang, thematically and structurally. Each line of the quatrain in turn becomes the final line of one of the corresponding *décimas.*

The *cumanana* and *amor fino,* less complicated coastal poetic forms, are sung in declamatory style. They are accompanied by the guitar and, like the *décima,* are often performed competitively by two or more poet-musicians. The *cumanana,* found in the northern Peruvian departments of Piura and Lambayeque, consists of four octosyllabic verses of text set to a melody, the style of which closely resembles that of the *triste* and the native *yaraví.* When it is performed in competition, the singers alternate *cumananas* but must retain the same melody throughout. Their texts present a dialogue in which each singer draws from his own repertoire or demonstrates his improvisatory skill in responding to the thoughts or questions presented by his opponent. An almost obsolete sister form of the *cumanana* is the *amor fino* (in the department of Lima), also based on a quatrain of essentially octosyllabic lines but with an optional two-line refrain (*estribillo*), making it somewhat similar to the Argentine *payada.*

The *décima,* the *cumanana,* and the *amor fino* have roots in the Spanish poetic tradition. Representative of all cultural groups in coastal Peru, they do not belong exclusively to any one group. Nevertheless, many African-derived cultures demonstrate an affinity for verbal dueling, and my oldest consultants in Peru remember many of the masters of these poetic forms as being of African descent.

TRADITIONAL AFRO-PERUVIAN GENRES

As blacks became integrated into the social and economic order of colonial Peru, they developed musical genres that reflected the realities of the New World. The *penalivio* or *panalivio* 'ease-pain', a satirical dance and song of lament dating from the 1700s, commented on the conditions of slavery. Afro-Peruvian work songs, street vendors' songs (*pregones*), and songs accompanying the watermelon-harvest festival (*maca-maca*) in Ica also reflect something of the nineteenth-century black life-style (Vizarreta 1941).

fuga 'Flight', Afro-Peruvian musical appendage used as a lively closing section

zapateo From *zapateado* 'foot stamping' a dance technique involving rhythmic striking of heels and toes against the floor or each other

alcatraz Afro-Peruvian novely couple dance

ingá Afro-Peruvian novelty circle dance

landó Afro-Peruvian song and dance form, said to have come from the Brazilian *lundú*

The *festejo*

Probably the most important Afro-Peruvian musical form is the *festejo* (see Okada 1995: examples 19 and 20), whose rhythms occur in several genres. A typical *festejo* melody consists of short phrases with a surging rhythm, frequently interrupted at phrase-endings by a sudden pause, or by a tone of longer duration. The question-answer character of the melodic line in consecutive phrases is exaggerated in the final section (*fuga*), composed of melodic fragments sung responsorially by soloist and chorus. Considerable metric variety and even simultaneous use of two different meters can be found, but the underlying meter is essentially 6/8 with a stilted iambic rhythm.

A typical example (figure 5) has balanced four-bar phrases (repeated), rhythmic contrasts, the use of *fugas,* accent displacement, and a responsorial nature:

A don Antonio Mina	They stabbed and killed
lo pican y lo mataron.	Sir Anthony Mina.
Arriba en la huaca grande	Up at the old ancient tomb
al don lo vido yo.	I saw the gentleman myself.
Atiralalá, atiralalá, atiralalá	Throw it, throw it, throw it
desde Lima a Lunahuana.	from Lima to Lunahuana.
Cachaplaca, chaplaca, chaplac.	Mark of the blade.
Un jarro de agua y un dulce.	A jar of water and a candy.
El turronero de yema.	The candy maker.

The texts often follow a set strophic form. They usually treat a festive theme, often in a historical setting reflecting the era of slavery. Texts and melodies are sometimes interchanged between *festejos,* and texts may even be borrowed from another musical genre and set to a *festejo* melody and rhythm. This swapping of melodies and texts is common in the Afro-Peruvian musical tradition as elsewhere in the world (Levine 1977:196–198). The guitar, the *cajón,* and clapping provide the basic instrumental accompaniment. The use of the *cajón* in the *festejo* is an innovation of the 1950s, replacing the ceramic vessel or hollow log membranophones that were used previously, and most modern performances include the *quijada.*

The *festejo* was probably danced in free style. In addition, several other genres of dance are based melodically and rhythmically on the *festejo*. These include the *son de los diablos* (described above), the *alcatraz,* the *ingá,* the *zapateo* (*zapateado*) *criollo,* and the *agua 'e nieve.*

Novelty dances based on the *festejo*

These include the *alcatraz* and the *ingá.* My oldest consultants remember them only as sources of entertainment. The *alcatraz* is performed in a circle. One male-female

FIGURE 5 Excerpt from "*Don Antonio Mina*," a typical *festejo*. Transcribed by William David Tompkins, from *El Festejo* (n.d.:B4).

couple at a time dances in the center. Either or both dancers carry a flaming stick or candle, with which he or she tries to light a paper streamer attached like a tail behind the partner, while the other makes such pelvic movements that the streamer flicks about, dodging the flame. To perform the *ingá* (onomatopoeic of a baby's cry), also called *ungá*, and *baile del muñeco* 'doll's dance', the dancers also form a circle. In its center, embracing a large doll, pillow, or anything that could be used to represent an infant, one performer dances alone. After several minutes of dancing, the soloist passes the doll to someone of the opposite sex within the circle. This person takes a turn, and the sequence proceeds in that manner until all have danced.

Competitive dances based on the *festejo*

Two dances utilizing *festejo* rhythms in a competitive demonstration of skill are the *zapateo* (*zapateado*) *criollo* (or the *pasada*) and the *agua 'e nieve* (or *agüenieve*). The *zapateo criollo* is danced by a solo male who demonstrates his skill by improvising intricate rhythmic patterns with his feet, supplemented by rhythmic slapping (see Okada 1995: example 21). An element of virtuosity and even acrobatics is often present. The dance is usually performed competitively by two or more individuals who take turns trying to impress onlookers or to score points with the person chosen to judge their contest. The *agua 'e nieve* is essentially the same, but based on *escobillada* technique.

The only rhythmic accompaniment used in these dances comes from the guitar, which provides a simple, unobtrusive musical framework on which the dancer improvises. When these dances are performed by the *hatajo de negritos,* however, rather than using the *festejo* rhythm, the violin plays an accompaniment resembling that used for *villancicos,* and boys combine *zapateado* and *escobillada* techniques.

The *landó*

Another Afro-Peruvian musical genre, rhythmically distinct and more complex than the *festejo,* is the *landó*. Colonial-period literature provides no information that reli-

FIGURE 6 Excerpts from a traditional *landó* from Guayabo, Chincha Province, Peru, arranged and performed by Perú Negro: *a,* instrumental introduction, showing polyrhythms on guitar and *quijada; b,* call-and-response pattern between a male soloist and a chorus of men and women. Transcribed by William David Tompkins, from *Perú Negro* (Byrne and Evelev 1995: track 13).

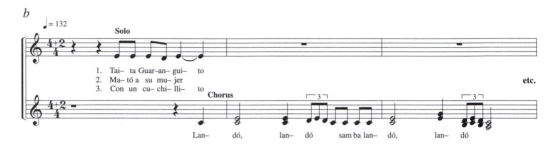

ably confirms the origin of this dance. Because the original choreography for the dance has essentially been lost, modern Afro-Peruvian troupes have created their own steps, utilizing accentuated movements of the hips. The original rhythm of the *landó,* which has also been lost, was replaced by a rhythm created by the guitarist Vicente Vásquez Díaz (Vásquez Rodríguez 1982:44).

Fragments of a few traditional *landós* have survived, and new ones are being composed. The *landó* exhibits richly syncopated rhythmic variety using six units per bar, conceivable as (4+2)/4 time. The primary accentuation is on the first and fifth quarter notes; a secondary accent occurs on the third. Contrasting meters, especially 6/4 time, often occur in instrumental and vocal parts, producing polyrhythms and cross-accents (figure 6*a*). Frequently in minor mode, the music of the *landó* is in a responsorial format: a soloist sings a one- or two-bar phrase, answered by a chorus singing a short refrain (figure 6*b*). As they alternate, the soloist repeats the same melodic fragment, using different verses in a kind of miniature strophic form, and the chorus repeats a refrain, such as "*Samba landó, landó/Samba malató landó.*" Some *landós* also employ a contrasting lyrical section (see Byrne and Evelev 1995: example 13).

CREOLE MUSICAL GENRES

The nineteenth century was a critical period in the development of Peruvian culture. Political and cultural alienation from Spain led to national independence (1821), the abolition of slavery (1865), and the War of the Pacific with Chile (1879–1883). In all these movements and events, blacks played important roles.

Concurrently, nationalism in folk music was evidenced by the emergence of new national genres of music. Thus, even as the mixture of races along the Peruvian coast produced a distinctive *mestizaje,* the blending of Hispano-European, native American, and African music traditions gradually synthesized a creole music (*música criolla*), truly representative of coastal Peruvian culture.

The *zamacueca* and its offshoots

Probably the most important new national musical genre of the nineteenth century was the *zamacueca* (or *zambacueca*), which appeared in coastal Peru not long after 1800. Its choreographic theme, shared with dances derived from it, was a courtship pantomime, performed by a man and a woman amid a crowd that accompanied them with rhythmic clapping and supportive shouting. As the dancers advanced and retreated from each other, they rhythmically and provocatively flipped a handkerchief about. The instrumentation varied, but frequently consisted of plucked stringed instruments and a percussive instrument such as the *cajón.*

Other coastal dances choreographically related to the *zamacueca* appeared during the 1800s. The most notable were the *tondero* and the *resbalosa.* These dances are distinctive in their musical form and style. The *tondero,* still found in northern coastal Peru, has a ternary structure: *glosa* (always in minor mode), *dulce* or *canto* (always in the relative major), and *fuga* (in the original minor mode). The *resbalosa,* found in the areas closer to Lima, is musically more syncopated, and its steps are based on *escobillada.*

The *zamacueca* became popular in many Latin American countries during the mid-1800s, and numerous regional and national variations developed. In the 1860s and 1870s, the *zamacueca chilena,* a Chilean version of it, was the most popular form in Peru. After the War of the Pacific, however, Peruvians, not wanting their national dance to carry their enemies' name, renamed it the *marinera,* honoring their seamen who had died in the war. Modern, commercial Afro-Peruvian renditions of the *zamacueca,* which began with Victoria Santa Cruz's popular "*Ven a mi encuentro,*" bear little resemblance to the historical version.

The *marinera* has a choreography similar to that of the *zamacueca,* with regional variations throughout Peru (see Okada 1995: example 24). Most important to a study of Afro-Peruvian music is the *marinera* of Lima (*marinera limeña*), which functions in one of two contexts: as a *jarana,* a competition (*contrapunto*) between or among singers; or as a noncompetitive performance of a simple *marinera* with singing and/or dancing. Unlike the *marineras* of other regions, the *marinera limeña* follows strict rules of performance in dancing and singing. The essential accompaniment consists of two guitars, the *cajón,* and clapping. The poetic structure of a *marinera limeña* is ternary, consisting of three strophes, each of which must adhere to set poetic and musical structures.

The *jarana* is performed by two or more singers who sing alternate strophes in a series of *marineras.* A singer may choose strophes from traditional Spanish poetry, or from verses composed before the competition, or may even improvise strophes. According to strict rules, the texts of the strophes of a given *marinera* must be adapted spontaneously to fit the melody, chosen or improvised by the performer who sings the first strophe (Hayre 1973).

A complete performance of a *jarana* consists of three to five *marineras,* each having three strophes followed by a *resbalosa* and *fugas.* The *resbalosa,* the complementary movement to the *marinera,* consists of two or more strophes sung in a somewhat livelier and more syncopated rhythm than that of the *marinera,* with fewer metrical and musical restrictions than its counterpart. The *fugas* are the climax of the piece and the competition. In them, the competitors test each other's knowledge by singing couplets or quatrains of verses back and forth to each other in rapid succession. If a singer makes an error during the *jarana,* or is unable to answer at all, his opponent wins. Many of the greatest interpreters of the *marinera* and performers of *jarana* have been Afro-Peruvian, including Bartola Sancho Dávila, Manuel Quintana, Elías and Augusto Ascuez, Augusto Gonzales, and Abelardo Vásquez. Only a few individuals who know how to sing *jaranas* are still alive. The only commercially available traditional performance is the LP disk *La Marinera Limeña es Así* (n. d.).

The creole waltz

The creole waltz (*vals criollo*) is the most popular national form of music among most races and social classes in coastal Peru. Though it has its roots in the Viennese waltz,

Beginning in the 1920s, semiprofessional musical ensembles of Afro-Peruvian musicians and singers attained renown in the performance of creole music, often entertaining on stage or at late-night parties.

it bears little resemblance to its aristocratic progenitor. Many of its national traits reflect black influences.

By the 1850s, the *vals* already differed considerably from the European waltz. It had, and still has, a free choreography consisting of short, slow steps with considerable rhythmic movement of the hips, arms, and shoulders. Its melody usually abounds in displaced accents, anticipated and retarded beats, and occasional use of rubato. In the early 1900s, the traditional instrumental accompaniment of two guitars was enriched by the addition of the *cajón*. Most composers of *valses* have been whites or mestizos, but Afro-Peruvians are among the carriers of the tradition, and their influence has helped make its character unique.

TWENTIETH-CENTURY DEVELOPMENTS

Folkloric nationalism (*criollismo*) continued to develop throughout the twentieth century in Peru, with the black population always playing an important role. Many musical genres identified principally with Afro-Peruvian culture, however, began to fall into disuse in the late 1800s and the early 1900s.

Only a few families of black musicians in Lima and rural areas remained familiar with the forms. Black composers, singers, and dancers showed little interest in traditional Afro-Peruvian music. Instead, they dedicated themselves to creole music in vogue, especially the *marinera,* the *resbalosa,* and the *vals,* plus imported popular music such as the tango (from Argentina), the boston and shimmy (from North America), and even the zarzuela.

Beginning in the 1920s, semiprofessional musical ensembles of Afro-Peruvian musicians and singers attained renown in the performance of creole music, often entertaining on stage or at late-night parties (also called *jaranas*). These groups, usually living in and identified with particular neighborhoods of Lima, developed repertoires of *valses,* polkas, *marineras, resbalosas*, and *tonderos.* One musician of Afro-Peruvian heritage, Samuel Márquez, formed the ensemble Ricardo Palma, which in addition to popular creole genres performed some old Afro-Peruvian songs. In 1936, he presented this repertoire in the theatrical performance *Del 96 al 36* 'From [18]96 to [19]36'. Much Afro-Peruvian music had already been lost by then, and often only portions of choruses survived; therefore, Márquez made arrangements based on surviving fragments. His presentation was a success, and for the next couple of decades, Ricardo Palma performed Afro-Peruvian folkloric music at many kinds of celebrations.

The first attempt to bring an entire program of Afro-Peruvian music to the stage was achieved through the efforts of José Durand, a white creole. Frequenting festivities where the foremost black singers and musicians performed, he collected information and songs from knowledgeable elderly blacks. The result was La Cuadrilla Morena de Pancho Fierro (The Brown Company of Pancho Fierro), which made its début in the Teatro Municipal of Lima in the summer of 1956. This engagement marked the beginning of organized commercial companies of Afro-Peruvian musicians and dancers.

Though Durand's ensemble eventually disintegrated, it inspired other commercial Afro-Peruvian groups. During the 1960s, Victoria and Nicomedes Santa Cruz formed Danzas Negros del Perú and Cumanana. Other groups initiated in the 1970s included Perú Negro (founded by Ronaldo Campos), Gente, Morena, Los Frejoles Negros, and the Afro-Peruvian ensembles of the Conjunto Nacional de Folklore (led by Victoria Santa Cruz). The next two decades saw the formation of many more commercial Afro-Peruvian groups in Lima and some smaller coastal towns. Several scholars' research has confirmed that most of the repertoire of these commercial groups since the 1950s has been stylized, newly invented, or Africanized "folklore," with few roots in Afro-Peruvian tradition (Vásquez Rodríguez 1982:44–51).

Festejos, landós, and other Afro-Peruvian music can now frequently be heard in nightclubs, *peñas criollas,* and *centros musicales.* Though *peñas* were originally where amateur performers of creole (and occasionally Andean) music met for jam sessions, the term is now loosely used by entrepreneurs to describe cover-charge dinner concerts of popular Peruvian music with professional performers or even dinner dances with Latin American music provided by a disk jockey. Numerous vinyl records, cassettes, and compact discs of commercialized Afro-Peruvian music have been issued.

In Cañete every August, the Festival Negroide promotes Afro-Peruvian musics. It gives awards for the best black dancers, vocalists, and composers. Governmental agencies promote creole and Afro-Peruvian music by requiring a certain portion of the programming of radio and television stations to include national music.

ACADEMIC FOLKLORISTS AND FURTHER STUDY

The twentieth century saw the beginning of scholarly research on Afro-Peruvian music. In the 1930s and 1940s, Fernando Romero began studying African influence on Peruvian coastal music. Other scholars—including Abraham and Felipe Arias Larreta, Fernando Assunçao (1969), José Mejía Baca (1938), José Durand (1961, 1971, 1973), Carlos Hayre (1973), Arturo Jiménez Borja, Robert M. Stevenson, Rosa Elena Vásquez Rodríguez (1982), and Carlos Vega (1936, 1953)—have researched diverse aspects of coastal creole and black culture.

Possibly the most popular Afro-Peruvian folklorist and prolific writer of the 1960s and 1970s was Nicomedes Santa Cruz. Most scholars have taken issue with his theories, especially those concerning the nature and origins of colonial Afro-Peruvian and creole musical instruments and genres, but no other folklorist during this period did more to make Peruvians aware of the richness of their Afro-Peruvian heritage.

Most elderly Afro-Peruvian consultants who remembered traditional black music as it was performed around 1900 have now died. They asserted that contemporary Afro-Peruvian "folklore" is an invention of modern black ensembles that wish to Africanize performances to make them more exotic. Afro-Peruvian music has entered into the commercial music industry. To succeed, it must be marketable and competitive with other youth-favored music, particularly Caribbean dance music. Only the Hatajo de Negritos has remained uncommercialized and totally within the realm of tradition.

Despite the arguments about "true" Afro-Peruvian traditions, however, one must avoid the misconception that the only authentic Afro-Peruvian music is that which has remained unchanged from former centuries. Culture is not static, and African-derived culture has been characterized by resilience throughout history as it interacted between the past and present, absorbing and reinterpreting elements from the musical traditions around it.

Similarly, modern Afro-Peruvian music reflects the ethos and group consciousness of the present-day black population. The social struggles of the 1800s (calling for greater cultural integration) had taken a turn by the late twentieth century, when blacks were beginning to take new pride in their African heritage, inspired by the worldwide development of negritude. Many Afro-Peruvians have embraced these new musical expressions as their own and consider them to be rooted in their history and traditions as they perceive them, expressive of their values and views.

REFERENCES

Assunçao, Fernando. 1969. "Aportaciones Para un Estudio Sobre Los Orígines de la Zamacueca." *Folklore Americano* 17(16).

Bowser, Frederick Park. 1974. *The African Slave in Colonial Peru 1524–1650*. Stanford, Calif.: Stanford University Press.

Byrne, David, and Yale Evelev. 1995. *Afro-Peruvian Classics: The Soul of Black Peru*. Warner Brothers Records CD-9-45878-2. Compact disc.

Durand, José. 1961. "Del Fandango a la Marinera." *Fanal* 16(59):10–15.

———. 1971. "De la Zamacueca a la Marinera." *Mensajes* 15:23–27.

———. 1973. "La Resbalosa Limeña." *Mensajes* 19:8–14.

El Festejo. N.d. Lima: Sono Radio LPL 9239. LP disk.

Fuentes, Manuel. 1925. *Lima: Apuntes Históricos, Descriptivos, Estadísticos y de Costumbres*. Lima: E. Moreno.

Hayre, Carlos. 1973. "Apuntes para el análisis de la marinera limeña." Mimeogram, 23 pp. Lima: author.

Lee, Bertram T., ed. 1935. *Libros de Cabildos de Lima*. Vol. 6, part 2, 16 de agosto, 1563. Lima: Consejo Provincial.

Levine, Lawrence W. 1977. *Black Culture and Black Consciousness*. New York: Oxford University Press.

La Marinera es Así. N.d. Lima: Odeon ELD-2215. LP disk.

Martínez Compañón, Baltasar Jaime. 1978. *La Obra del Obispo Martínez Compañón Sobre Trujillo del Perú en el Siglo XVII*. Madrid:

Ediciones Cultural Hispánica del Centro Iberoamericano de Cooperación.

Mejía Baca, José. 1938. *Algunas Noticias Sobre la Conga*. Lima.

Okada, Yuki. 1995. *Central and South America*. JVC Smithsonian Folkways Video Anthology of Music and Dance of the Americas, 6. Montpelier, Vt.: Multicultural Media VTMV-230. Video.

Perú Negro, Lima. 1974. Virrey Recording VIR 920. LP disk.

"Rasgo . . . de los Negros Bozales." 1791. *Mercurio Peruano*, 16 June.

Rushenberge, William. 1834. *Three Years in the Pacific*. 2 vols. Philadelphia: Carey, Lea & Blanchard.

Stevenson, Robert M. 1968. *Music in Aztec and Inca Territory*. Berkeley: University of California Press.

Stevenson, William Bennett. 1825. *A Historical and Descriptive Narrative of Twenty Years Residence in South America*. 3 vols. London: Hurst, Robinson.

Vásquez Rodríguez, Rosa Elena. 1982. *La Práctica Musical de la Población Negra en el Perú*. Havana: Casa de las Américas.

Vega, Carlos. 1936. "Eliminación del Factor Africano en la Formación del Cancionero Criollo." *Cursos y Conferencias* 10(7):765–779.

———. 1953. *La Zamacueca (Cueca, Zamba, Chilena, Marinera)*. Buenos Aires: Editorial Julio Korn.

Vizarreta, Juan Donaire. 1941. *Campiña Iqueña*. Lima: Imprenta La Moderna.

Surinam
Dale A. Olsen

Native Americans
African Influence
Indonesian Influence
Urban Creole Music

The small country known as Suriname (from *surinam,* an Arawak name) in its early colonial period, then as Dutch Guiana before its independence in 1975, and today as Surinam or Suriname, is unique because of its cultural extremes. It is home to native Arawak- and Carib-speaking inhabitants of its interior forests; it is the domain of the most African-derived subcultures in South America, the Maroons (formerly "Bush Negroes") in its interior forests and savannas; and it is the home of descendants of Portuguese Jews and indentured workers from China, India, and Indonesia. Added to this are an overlay of Dutch and English culture and a population speaking mostly Sranan, an English-based creole, along a partially urbanized and highly populated Atlantic seaboard (Manuel 1995:222).

A country of 163,265 square kilometers, Surinam lies in northeastern South America between French Guiana to its east and Guyana to its west. Of its population of about four hundred thousand people, about 95 percent live along the Atlantic coast, and about a third dwell in Paramaribo, its capital. The country was controlled by the British until 1667, when they traded it to the Dutch in exchange for Manhattan Island in New York.

NATIVE AMERICANS

As in other colonial settlements in the Western Hemisphere, many indigenous people of Surinam were enslaved by Europeans or migrated deep into its interior. Others have always inhabited the humid regions bordering Brazil to the south. Native Americans near the Atlantic coast were Arawak- and Carib-speakers about whom little is known. What is left of their cultures reveals high levels of acculturation. The major forest people include the Akumo (Ocomayana), the Tirió (Trio), and the Wayana (Oayana) [see WAYANA]. All three groups speak Carib-derived languages within the Gê-Pano-Carib phylum (Loukotka 1968). Their cultures are somewhat preserved, but missionization has led to acculturated and syncretic musical forms of expression. Wayana music can be heard on *Musique Boni et Wayana de Guyana* (1968).

The Tirió number about a thousand people; they have received evangelical indoctrination since the arrival of American missionaries in the 1970s. As a result,

"The missionaries taught us new songs," he replied
excitedly. "Here, listen to this." The tune he sang
sounded vaguely familiar, but it took me a minute
to recognize it: a Tirió version of "Jingle Bells."
—a Tirió shaman

traditional shamanism is on the wane, and Westernized medicine has replaced many
Tirió curing beliefs. Some elderly shamans cling to their traditional songs for curing,
but it is more common to hear American and European folk songs sung in the forest.
Mark J. Plotkin (1993:276) writes the following about the demise of traditional
songs and dances, the latter known for realistic depictions of "hunting scenes, jaguars
chasing a herd of peccaries, and cock-of-the-rock males displaying their feathers and
strutting about to attract the females of the species":

> I couldn't believe the Tiriós had been forced to give up such an essential part of
> their culture in exchange for an imported religion. "So what do you sing now?" I
> asked. "The missionaries taught us new songs," he replied excitedly. "Here, listen
> to this." The tune he sang sounded vaguely familiar, but it took me a minute to
> recognize it: a Tirió version of "Jingle Bells."

American missionaries have introduced portable radios into the forest, enabling the
Tirió and others to hear Brazilian popular music broadcast from Amazonian stations.
Nevertheless, Tirió shamanic lore is being passed on to apprentice shamans, ensuring
that curing songs and ethnobotanical agents will continue to be used for another generation (Plotkin 1993:285).

AFRICAN INFLUENCE

Slaves from Africa—from the region of West Africa formerly known as the Gold
Coast (principally Ashanti, Fon, and Yoruba cultures)—first arrived in about 1650,
and some three hundred thousand Africans entered Surinam until the end of slavery
in 1863. During several political-economic conflicts involving the Dutch, the
English, and the French beginning in 1663 and lasting for a hundred years, many
African slaves escaped from the European-owned sugarcane plantations into the interior, where they established communities fashioned on African models (Bastide
1971:52–53). Known as Maroons (meaning 'runaways'), they live in three main cultural groups, having a total population of about forty thousand: the Saramaca (the
largest, numbering about twenty thousand), the Auca (also known as Djuka or
Ndjuka), and the Boni (also known as Aluku). They collectively obtained official
governmental recognition (their own independence) in the 1770s, and today, in
terms of their cultural identity, they are among the most African of South American
people.

The Maroon "river cultures" of Surinam have retained many African beliefs.
Most notable is the belief in a supreme deity known by several names: Nyan Kompon
(a Fanti-Ashanti name) among the Saramaka; Nana (an Agni name) among the
Djuka; and Masu Gadu (a Fon name) among the Boni. Beneath the supreme deity
are many lesser gods or spirits. Many have particular foods, colors, taboos, songs,
drum rhythms, and dances (Bastide 1971:58–59). Village priests supervise the

Maroon rituals, which often include animal sacrifices, songs, dances, music of three ritual drums, and possession by spirits.

Musical instruments

The Maroons of Surinam use musical instruments of all four organological classes, but most prominent are struck idiophones and membranophones.

Idiophones

Small container rattles made from beautifully incised calabashes are important instruments for ritual use (Dark 1970). By themselves, their sounds can induce possession in believers. Saramaka and Djuka religious dancers use strung rattles made from seed pods and attached to their ankles. These the Maroons originally acquired from their indigenous neighbors, but today the Maroons themselves make them.

Struck idiophones that accompany drumming include two pieces of iron that are hit together, the *felu-ko-felu* 'iron-against-iron', a concussion idiophone that provides a steady pulse during ritual musical performances. Another instrument that provides a steady pulse is the *kwakwa,* a squat wooden bench or stool beaten with two sticks. Both instruments are played by men and women. In addition, women clap to accompany singing and dancing.

Surinam is the only country in the Americas where a plucked idiophone similar to the African mbira is used. This instrument can be heard on *Music from Saramaka* (Price and Price 1977). Known as the *benta,* it consists of a board that supports split bamboo reeds, plucked with the fingers. A versatile instrument, it is played only by young men—for entertainment, for imitating animals or birds, communicating via the Maroon language, and dancing (Price and Price 1991:211–212). Power to play the instrument was attributed to spirits of the forest, and it is said that "some players were able to walk on water across the river while playing" (Price and Price 1977).

Membranophones

Single-headed open-ended drums are the most powerful Maroon instruments in Surinam. They come in various shapes and have various names, depending on the subculture they pertain to and on the deity they communicate with. The three most important of these membranophones are the *agida,* the *apinti,* and the *tumao.* All have the power to summon gods and ancestral spirits, function as the voices of supernatural beings and articulate their messages in a specially drummed language, and send the gods and spirits back to their celestial or metaphysical homes at the conclusion of the ceremonies. All the drums are in the domain of male players, and "no woman may play drums, or even touch them. Belief has it that if a woman plays the drums, her breasts will grow until they reach the ground" (Herskovits and Herskovits 1969:523).

The *agida,* measuring up to nearly a meter long, is the lowest-pitched drum of the battery of ritual drums. Its head, tightened with pegs driven into the side of a log body, is played with a single drumstick, providing a steady pulse for evoking earth gods and snake gods. Meanwhile, the player's other hand plays intricate cross-rhythms on the same skin. Herskovits and Herskovits observed an *agida* that was more than 2.4 meters long, and "so powerful was its call, that only a few minutes after it began to sound the invocations to the Snake god, devotees from nearby villages, under possession, made their appearance" (1969:522). The ritual to the snake god is known as *vodu* or *papagadu,* the latter being the name of the deity that lives in anacondas and boa constrictors (a good example can be heard on Price and Price 1977).

The *apinti* derives from the *apentemma* of the Ashanti in Ghana. It is a pegged drum whose skin is attached to a goblet-shaped body hewn from a log. This body is often carved in low relief and adorned with brass tacks. Smaller than the *agida* and pitched as a tenor drum, it is played with the hands and is associated with *kromanti* 'warrior gods, ancestral spirits'. It is a talking drum (Price and Price 1980:180). The drummer can produce two tones (near the rim and in the middle of the head), enabling the drum to "speak." The two pitches are related to the tonal spoken language. In ritual contexts, the *apinti* provides the most intricate rhythms of the three drums. Its player is the musical equivalent of the Ghanaian master drummer.

The *tumao* is a medium-to-long cylindrical log drum (slightly larger at the top than the bottom, but not enough to be called a conically shaped instrument). Its skin is tensioned by wedges driven downward through a hoop attached to the head. It is larger than the *apinti* and smaller than the *agida,* has plain sides, and is played with the hands. In its ritual context, it is dedicated to bush spirits (Herskovits and Herskovits 1969:521).

Religious music

Many Maroon gods pertain to the fauna and flora of the forest and other natural things—animals (snakes, especially anacondas and boa constrictors), the bush (the fierce *kromanti*), rivers, and even the sea (far from their villages, but probably an African retention). Some gods are known throughout the subcultures, but others are regional and pertain to particular villages and clans. Many aspects of Maroon ritual life are related to African (especially Ghanaian) counterparts.

Secular music

One of the most important kinds of secular music among the Maroons is *sêkêti,* "often cryptic" songs and dances, "drawing on heavily poetic, metaphorical language, . . . composed by both men and women as expressions of love, despair, admiration or derision, and . . . a major form of social commentary" (Price and Price 1977:4). *Sêkêti* are usually performed responsorially, with leader and chorus dancing while singing, accompanied by clapping and drumming (listen to Gillis 1977a and Price and Price 1977). They can be performed in settings of solitude as when paddling alone in a canoe or sewing alone at home; they are often performed by women. Saramaka women say *sêkêti* are "songs of love (*lóbi*), cursing (*kósi*), or hardship (*fukâ*)" (S. Price 1984:167). An example of the last refers to the hardship of loneliness experienced by a woman when her husband leaves home to work away from the village (after S. Price 1984:178):

> M'á ó láfu môò-éé.
> Dí wómi dê a Lendema lío.
> M'á ó láfu môò.

> I won't laugh anymore.
> The man's at Lendema's River.
> I won't laugh anymore.

A reason for not laughing anymore was the flooding of the Surinam River (called Lendema's River in the song, after the man responsible for constructing a dam), creating a huge artificial lake (Lendema Wata) for hydroelectric power. This project destroyed several Saramaka villages upstream from the dam; the displaced families were relocated in government-built houses on the coast—a factor causing major cultural changes for many Maroons.

INDONESIAN INFLUENCE

In 1891, the Dutch in Surinam began to import Javanese indentured laborers from their Indonesian colony, the Dutch East Indies. By 1940, about thirty-three thousand Javanese had immigrated to the former Dutch Guiana (Waal Malefijt 1963:25–28). Some forty thousand people of Javanese descent still live in Javanese communities in Surinam, where performances of gamelan music and shadow-puppet plays occasionally occur.

As former members of the Javanese rural class or their descendants, those that have continued to work in agriculture follow beliefs that are something of a mixture of Islam and the worship of spirits. Rain and harvest rituals; traditional curing of illnesses; magic; rituals of birth, circumcision, marriage, and death; various *slametan* rituals, "a constant re-affirmation of the unity of the community, which makes everything right, and enables the people to live 'the good life'" (Waal Malefijt 1963:161); wayang; and the celebration of Ramadan—all these occasions incite singing and musical performance. Musical specialists include the *dukun* (a male or female shaman who performs love-controlling magic and curing), the *lèdèk* (a female religious dancer), and the *dalang* (leader of the wayang, a puppet theater that employs a gamelan, an orchestra consisting mostly of struck idiophones). The most musical of these specialists is the *dalang,* and the gamelan is the major musical expression of the Javanese in Surinam.

Instruments for the traditional Javanese gamelan were not brought over by the original laborers, who had to make the voyage without possessions. In the early 1900s, bronze instruments were imported, but without their wooden frames, which were built in Surinam from local woods. In Surinam, Annemarie de Waal Malefijt (1963:154) interviewed many elderly Javanese who commented on how beautifully carved the gamelan instruments were in Java, and how plain they were in Surinam. This situation is because the aristocratic court elite (*prijaji*) did not emigrate from Java, and therefore did not support the manufacture of gamelan instruments in Surinam. The instruments in a Surinam-Javanese gamelan include *gendèr*, metal-keyed marimbas with bamboo resonators; *saron* and *demung*, metal-keyed marimbas without resonators; suspended metal gongs, in several sizes; and *kendang*, double-headed membranophones (Gillis 1977).

Though Waal Malefijt (1963) photographed and described only Javanese-style gamelan instruments, I observed and photographed a Balinese *gamelan angklung* from Surinam that was on display in the Jaap Kunst Museum in Amsterdam. Several accompanying photographs documented its use in processions, as in Bali.

The Javanese gamelan provides musical accompaniment for wayang in Surinam. The *dalang* manipulates the puppets, singing and reciting the dialogue. Only the elderly Javanese-born in Surinam understand the dialogue of the *dalang*. Nevertheless, theatrical presentations still last from 8:00 P.M. to 6 A.M., and attention is demanded from young and old. At outdoor performances, children usually fall asleep by midnight.

The only other Javanese musical instrument employed by the mostly Islamic population in the rural settlements is the *bedug*. This is a ritual drum, sounded for the traditional and daily Islamic call to prayer (as it is in Java) and for announcing death by the Islamic religious leader (*ka'um*), who beats a rhythm that the community recognizes.

The annual, monthlong celebration of Ramadan (Pasa in Surinam and Java) requires fasting and other Islamic ritual acts. It ends with Bodo (also Lebaran), a holiday that government officials erroneously call the Javanese New Year, when Javanese music is played on the radio.

Beginning in the 1970s, the Indonesian government has furnished Surinam with

Kaseko merges many Caribbean and African styles, often blending Caribbean calypso, reggae, and *zouk* with West African *soukous* and Surinam Maroon Djuka drumming.

professional Javanese gamelan teachers and has provided scholarships for Surinam-Javanese to study traditional music and other aspects of culture in Java for one year, allowing them to return to Surinam and teach the people of Javanese descent more about their ethnic heritage. The Indonesian government has donated elaborate gamelans to the people of Surinam (Gillis 1977).

URBAN CREOLE MUSIC

Along the Atlantic seaboard is a thriving but largely unknown musical scene, which has produced three musical genres that reveal Maroon musical traits. These genres—*kawina, kaseko,* and *aleke*—have been researched by Peter Manuel (1995:221–231). His work, the only recent study of popular Surinamese music in English, provides the foundation for the following descriptions.

Kawina

This is the oldest creole musical form of Surinam, developed by the people of African descent who remained in the coastal region rather than escaping into the interior forest as did the Maroons. *Kawina* probably originated in the late 1800s as a mixture of musical traits from creoles, Maroons, and foreign migrant prospectors; these included Afro-Surinamese drums, European accordions and clarinets, and responsorial singing. The European instruments were discarded in favor of percussion instruments, and in the 1990s, *kawina* ensembles have included a small bench struck with sticks, hand-held container rattles, *timbal* membranophones (large single-headed drums, not to be confused with Caribbean *timbales*), and *koti kawina* and *hari kawina*, small double-headed drums, all as rhythmical accompanying instruments to responsorial singing laced with European harmonies.

Kawina can function as religious or secular music. The former (*winti kawina*) accompanies Afro-Surinamese ceremonials associated with the Winti religion, while the latter (*prisiri kawina* 'good-time *kawina*') accompanies social dancing and singing (the lyrics often make comments on current events and people). Since more than half of the world's Surinamese live in the Netherlands, many popular *kawina* bands reside and record overseas in Amsterdam (Manuel 1995:223).

Kaseko

More contemporary than *kawina* music, *kaseko* merges many Caribbean and African styles, often blending Caribbean calypso, reggae, and *zouk* with West African *soukous* and Surinam Maroon Djuka drumming (Manuel (1995:224–226). The result is a highly danceable music, popular in the Netherlands and Surinam. The Netherlands issues CDs, but Surinam relies mostly on its cassette-producing industry.

Like many other contemporary Caribbean and West African musics, *kaseko* features trumpets, saxophones, keyboards, electric guitar, electric bass, and percussion (including some Maroon drums); the melodic instruments play extended ostinatos and jazz-inspired solos, whereas the percussion features steady rhythms, interspersed with syncopated accents.

Aleke

As a more recent contrast to *kawina* and *kaseko, aleke* is heavily percussive, featuring Djuka drums in spirit and *aleke* drums (such as a combination *agida* and conga) in actuality. A battery of three *aleke* drums (the use of three drums also retains the Djuka concept) and a horizontally placed bass drum (*djas* 'jazz') and a high-hat cymbal are used. In addition, *aleke* is a vocal music with communication in mind; its lyrics often "deal with decidedly modern themes, from AIDS and poverty to the pros and cons of condoms" (Manuel 1995:230).

REFERENCES

Bastide, Roger. 1971. *African Civilisations in the New World.* Translated by Peter Green. New York: Harper & Row.

Dark, Philip. 1970. *Bush Negro Art.* London: Alec Tiranti.

Gillis, Verna. 1977a. *From Slavery to Freedom: Music of the Saramaka Maroons of Suriname.* Lyrichord LLST 7354. LP disk.

———. 1977b. *Javanese Music from Suriname.* Lyrichord LLST 7317. LP disk.

Herskovits, Melville J., and Frances S. Herskovits. 1969. *Suriname Folk-Lore.* New York: AMS Press. Columbia Contributions to Anthropology, 27, 3.

Loukotka, Cestmir. 1968. *Classification of South American Indian Languages.* Los Angeles: Latin American Center, UCLA.

Manuel, Peter. 1995. *Caribbean Currents.* Philadelphia: Temple University Press.

Musique Boni et Wayana de Guyana. 1968. Paris: Collection Musée de l'Homme. Vogue LVLX 290. LP disk.

Plotkin, Mark J. 1993. *Tales of a Shaman's Apprentice.* New York: Penguin Books.

Price, Richard, and Sally Price. 1977. *Music from Saramaka.* Ethnic Folkways Records FE 4225. LP disk.

———. 1980. *Afro-American Arts of the Suriname Rain Forest.* Los Angeles: Museum of Cultural History, University of California at Los Angeles.

———. 1991. *Two Evenings in Saramaka.* Chicago: University of Chicago Press.

Price, Sally. 1984. *Co-Wives and Calabashes.* Ann Arbor: University of Michigan Press.

Waal Malefijt, Annemarie de. 1963. *The Javanese of Surinam: Segment of a Plural Society.* Assen: Van Gorcum.

Uruguay

Ercilia Moreno Chá

Native American Inhabitats
Traditional Musical Instruments
Religious Musical Contexts and Genres
Secular Musical Contexts and Genres
Musical Behavior and Creativity
Learning Music
Musical Change

Uruguay, officially named the República Oriental del Uruguay, is one of the smallest countries of the Americas, with an area of 177,508 square kilometers. It extends northward to Brazil and the Atlantic Ocean, eastward to the Atlantic, and westward and southward to its border with Argentina across two rivers, the Uruguay and the Río de la Plata. The population, mostly descendants of Spanish and Italian settlers, was 3,168,000 in 1994. The native population is extinct, and vestiges of Africans who came as slaves remain in some cities, especially in the capital, Montevideo.

The political, cultural, and musical history of Uruguay is closely related to that of its larger neighbors; nevertheless, since colonial times, Uruguay has developed special musical genres related to carnival, to the tango (which it shares with Argentina), and to Uruguayan popular song (*canto popular uruguayo*), the most important Uruguayan musical movement of the second half of the twentieth century.

The writings of Spanish and Portuguese sailors, geographers, and conquistadors provide the principal historical sources for the study of Uruguayan traditional music, including references to native American religious and secular dances, songs, and instrumental music. No archaeological evidence for Uruguayan indigenous music exists. Governmental archives and private collections have held traditional Uruguayan music only since 1944.

NATIVE AMERICAN INHABITANTS

The ethnic group that predominantly inhabited this region at the time of the Spanish encounter was the Chaná-Charrúa. The first musical reference to these people was made in 1531 by the Portuguese Lopes de Souza (1927), who related that when his men landed on a beach in search of fresh water, the natives approached them singing (Ayestarán 1953:6).

The first reference to Chaná-Charrúa musical instruments was made by the Spaniard Martín del Barco Centenera (1602); in his poem "*Argentina y conquista del Río de la Plata*" ('Argentina and Conquest of the River of Silver'), recounting his travels along the river, he mentions trumpets (*trompas*), horns (*bocinas*), and drums, which the Charrúas used in battle (Ayestarán 1953:7). Later, a French observer described a musical bow brought to Montevideo by four presumably Charrúa

Indians, one of whom played it. In Paris, these natives were exhibited as the last remaining examples of a culture in the process of extinction. Their musical bow was probably a single-stringed mouth-resonated bow without resonator (Ayestarán 1953:17, 20). The Chaná-Charrúa declined in numbers, and nothing more is known about their music.

Another group that inhabited the territory of present Uruguay was the Tupí-Guaraní, among whom Franciscan and Jesuit missionaries proselytized. In 1680, some participated in a Spanish-led battle against the Portuguese. Cristóbal Altamirano admonished them to "take their *pingollos* or fifes, or flutes with which they encouraged themselves in battle" (Ayestarán 1953:15). Altamirano used the Quechua term *pingollo* perhaps because he was Spanish, and several Jesuits of this time had been working in Peru.

After 1767, when the pope expelled the Jesuits from the Americas, many Guaraní from Jesuit missions in the north wandered southward into the area now known as Uruguay. There are many references to their activities as instrumentalists and singers—skills that had been well developed during their time in the missions. Some of these musicians made up the fife-and-drum corps that performed during Uruguay's struggle for independence from Spain. The Tupí-Guaraní were absorbed into the new cultural system of the 1800s, which arose from Uruguay's independence.

Little else is known about Uruguayan Indian music. Lauro Ayestarán amassed a collection of about four thousand recordings from all over the country between 1944 and 1966; they are housed in an archive named after him, kept in the Museo Histórico Nacional. His research is important for understanding Uruguayan music and musical performance.

TRADITIONAL MUSICAL INSTRUMENTS

The major sources for the study of Uruguayan musical instruments are by Fornaro (1989) and Ayestarán (1953, 1967). Uruguay's traditional musical instruments derive mostly from Europe; some are of African-Brazilian derivation. In the former group are chordophones such as the guitar and the violin. Aerophones include the usual military-band instruments, plus the harmonica, the button-and-keyboard accordion, and the *bandoneón* (a square accordion, used just for tango). Membranophones and idiophones are mostly military-band instruments, such as bass drum, snare drum (*redoblante*), and cymbals; with *tamboriles,* they are strongly connected to *murgas,* groups of dancers and singers that appear at carnival.

Instruments of African-Brazilian derivation are membranophones such as *atabaques* (mostly single-headed cylindrical drums, struck with the hands), and idiophones such as the *agé* (a hollow gourd, covered with a net into which seeds, beads, or shells are woven) and the *adjá* (a small bronze bell).

RELIGIOUS MUSICAL CONTEXTS AND GENRES

Musical expressions related to Roman Catholicism are not so abundant in Uruguay as in other parts of Spanish-speaking Latin America, but there does exist a familiar tradition of unaccompanied songs among women and children, including religious and secular lyrics. Religious songs deal with the infant Jesus, saints' lives, and miracles. Secular songs can accompany some children's games and can be Christmas carols, lullabies, narrative songs (*romances*), songs of love, and other musical genres (Fornaro 1990b).

Two occasions of national celebration relate to the calendar of saints: the feast of the Virgin of Verdun, whose celebration is centered in Minas, in the department of

Lavalleja, and the feast of San Cono, celebrated in the city of Florida, in the department of Florida; these celebrations attract people from all over the country.

Other festivities take place in other locations. These include the feasts of Saint John and Saint Isidro Labrador, particularly popular in rural agricultural areas. Also popular are patron saints' festivals, which incorporate sacred and secular elements. In addition to the observation of appropriate Roman Catholic ritual behavior, the selling of food, drink, and other items, and participation in games and other activities are important (Fornaro 1990b:48–49). Traditional music, performed on guitars, accordions, concertinas, *bandoneones,* and harmonicas, and traditional dance occur spontaneously at these celebrations, enlivening, in addition to the processions, various contexts.

The feast of the Virgin of Verdun, for example, is one of the main venues for a *payada,* a poetic and musical duel between *payadores,* competitors in improvising to the same melody. A *payador* is a singer who improvises poetic texts to a given musical form (such as the *milonga*), accompanied by a guitar. The subject of a typical competition deals with country life and rural dwellers, among whom the gaucho has a symbolic role; historical and nationalistic themes are not so prevalent. *Payadas,* which occur most frequently during Holy Week, include performances by *payadores* from all over the country. Organized by criollo societies, this celebration includes other events stressing outdoorsmanship (activities of the gaucho). Usually the winning *payador* is determined by the spectators' applause, rewarding the competitor who shows the most wit, sagacity, and ability to improvise rhymes.

Figure 1 is an excerpt from a *payada* in which a jury has imposed on the singers the subject of marital infidelity. The first stanza is sung by *payador* A; the second, by *payador* B.

Se nos pide la opinión,	We are being asked for an opinion,
el concepto, el testimonio	a concept, a testimony
sobre el tema matrimonio,	on the theme of marriage,
convivencia y comprensión:	living together, and understanding:
y el jurado y la reunión,	and the jury and the audience,
sin ninguna terquedad,	without any obstinacy,
pero con mucha ansiedad	but with great anxiety
en sus discretos reclamos,	over their discreet allurements,
quiere saber que opinamos	want to know what we think
sobre la infidelidad.	about infidelity.
Pues bien, si la gente insiste,	Well, if people insist,
debemos con claridad	we must clearly
hablar de infidelidad	speak about infidelity
y explicar en qué consiste.	and explain what it includes:
La infidelidad es triste,	infidelity is sad,
destructora de la paz,	destroyer of peace,
obra cruel de Satanás,	cruel work of Satan,
hecho nefasto y nefando,	fateful and infamous fact,
lamentable siempre—y cuando	always lamentable—
lo cometan los demás.	when others commit it.

The contestants sing different melodies of *milonga,* the most common genre for this kind of contest.

Africanisms

The use of music in the context of African religious systems is totally different from that in celebrations derived from Roman Catholic culture. In African-derived events,

FIGURE 1 A *payada* in *milonga* rhythm as performed by Washington Montañés (*payador* A) and Héctor Umpiérrez (*payador* B). Transcription by Ercilia Moreno Chá, from *Contrapunto 3* n.d.:A1.

(continued)

music is not peripheral to the religious act but is essential to it. The 1950s and 1960s saw an increase in the penetration of Afro-Brazilian religions into areas bordering Brazil. Another focus of that penetration is Montevideo, whence Afro-Brazilian religions have spread into the southern departments of Uruguay. These cults are practiced mostly by descendants of European immigrants and a few Afro-Uruguayans.

These manifestations are characterized by their liturgies, the musical repertoire that accompanies their public acts (mostly performed in Portuguese), and records and cassettes of Brazilian origin. As in Brazil, these religions, known collectively as Umbanda and Macumba, are highly syncretic, combining Yoruba beliefs with Bantu,

Usually the winning *payador* is determined by the spectators' applause, rewarding the competitor who shows the most wit, sagacity, and ability to improvise rhymes.

FIGURE 1 *(continued)* A *payada* in *milonga* rhythm as performed by Washington Montañés (*payador* A) and Héctor Umpiérrez (*payador* B). Transcription by Ercilia Moreno Chá, from *Contrapunto 3* n.d.:A1.

Roman Catholic, Spiritist, and indigenous Brazilian beliefs (Fornaro 1990a:3). In addition to personal devotion, collective acts of worship take place in temples (*terreiros*). An estimated seven hundred temples are registered with the Uruguayan authorities, and about three hundred more are not (Pallavicino 1987:13).

Music and dance serve as means of communication with different deities. Songs may be performed by soloists or ensembles, accompanied or unaccompanied. Accompaniment consists of the following instruments: one to three differently sized *atabaques,* a hollow gourd, and a small bell (*adjá, sineta*). The most popular ceremony is devoted to Iemanjá, goddess of the waters. It takes place on 2 February on the beaches of Montevideo, and by riverbanks and streambeds throughout the country (figure 2).

Another African-derived dance is found in Montevideo's carnival. This dance was brought by Africans who entered the country as slaves after the mid-1700s. The carnival dance known as *candombe* (whose name in the 1800s denoted African-Uruguayan dances and locales for dancing) commemorates the coronation of Congo kings. It imitates certain non-African state organizations and reveals syncretism between Bantu fetishism and Roman Catholicism (Ayestarán 1953:103). Its nineteenth-century precursor was celebrated every year in Montevideo between the feasts of Christmas and Epiphany (6 January). It survives not only among the descendants of Uruguayan slaves but also among other persons, who dance it during the celebration of carnival in Montevideo and on sporadic occasions. An expansion of this dance occurs in the interior of the country, where some of its elements grace political, athletic, and cultural events outside of carnival contexts.

It is in carnival celebrations, however, that *candombe* takes its most typical form as presented by Black Lubolos, the carnival ensembles approved by the municipal carnival regulations of the city of Montevideo. Black Lubolo societies perform in various carnival parades on different dates, their appearance announced by drummed calls (*llamadas*) lasting from two to fifteen hours, played at different sites from the end of December until the beginning of Holy Week. The *candombe* itself is performed to the sound of at least twelve drums (a number set by a municipal regulation), but sometimes up to thirty drums. This kind of drum, called *tamboril afro-uruguayo,* is considered an emblematic instrument of Uruguay. It is an open, barrel-shaped drum, constructed from many slats of wood; the membrane for each instrument, previously tacked in a traditional manner, is now usually attached mechanically. The *tamboril afrouruguayo* was formerly played in sets of four, but in the 1980s the bass (*bajo*) was gradually eliminated, and in the 1990s most performances use only the three remaining types, each having a different register: *chico, repique,* and *piano* (Fornaro 1987). These drums are struck with a stick and a hand.

SECULAR MUSICAL CONTEXTS AND GENRES

Several secular dances of European origin are performed throughout Uruguay. These include the polka, the mazurka (known as the *ranchera*), and the waltz, the last two being the most widespread. All of them passed from urban to rural surroundings in the late 1800s and can be found in organized rural-dance festivals and in family settings. In addition, Brazilian folk dances such as the *chimarrita,* the *tirana,* and the *carangueijo* may be present along the border.

Music is used in *criollas,* societies whose principal objective is the preservation of traditional rural festivals. In certain localities, music affords a special occasion for entertainment through *retretas,* Sunday musical performances by bands supported by municipalities, police departments, or the armed forces. Folk-music festivals take place in the interior of the country, attracting rural and urban spectators. The most important ones occur in the cities of Tacuarembó and Durazno.

In schools and homes, children's music is found in songs and musical games. Lullabies continue to be widespread. Most of these genres derive from the children's repertoire of the European tradition, which has spread all over Latin America.

The musical stage

Since the 1940s in Montevideo, a kind of light theater known as *teatro de revistas* developed along the Río de la Plata. Related to the Spanish *tonadilla escénica* and the French *variété,* it alternates comic or satirical dialogue with music and dance, usually presented by luxuriously costumed players. It has a roguish and even impudent character, in which there is not usually a dramatic flow so much as a succession of independent scenes, including opportunities for performances of tangos. It enjoyed a brief renaissance in the 1980s (Fornaro 1990b:22).

Carnival

In Uruguay, carnival retains aspects of the medieval European one, in which popular sectors questioned the existing social order by parody, satire, or other resources. For five weeks before carnival, officially competing ensembles perform on street stages (*tablados*), in athletic clubs, in the Teatro de Verano in Montevideo, and at other locales throughout Uruguay. The official competition of carnival groups, the responsibility of the municipal government of Montevideo and the Uruguayan Associated Directors of Popular Carnival Shows, occurs every year (figure 3). Monetary prizes are given to the best ensembles in each category, which includes theater. To help determine the winners, governmental officials and organizations related to the celebration designate a committee of judges. The judges take into account the opinion of the "popular jury," the audience. The official regulations specify the criteria the entrants must meet and the mechanisms that will determine the winners.

The relationship of Montevideo's carnival to tourism is evidenced by the annual publication of the municipal carnival regulations (the 1991 version consisted of twenty pages) by the Tourism Division of the Municipality of Montevideo. Because carnival attracts national and international tourists, some celebrations are performed in Punta del Este, where some groups go in search of foreign audiences.

The murga

During Montevideo's carnival, theatrical presentations abound. Each year, the

FIGURE 3 Program of the official competition of carnival groups, presented during carnival 1994 at the Municipal Summer Theatre "Ramón Collazo" in Montevideo.

FIGURE 4   The *murga* Los Arlequines performs during the carnival parade in the streets of Montevideo in 1995. Photo from the archive of the newspaper *El País* (Montevideo).

municipal government of Montevideo publishes regulations governing the presentations. The regulations specify five categories of groups: *negros lubolos, revistas, parodistas, humoristas,* and *murgas.* All of them use musical accompaniment, but the *murga,* documented since 1909, is the one whose conventions most closely resemble those of Western theater (figure 4).

The *murga* is a popular art. In contrast with genres considered cultured, it relates to popular genres such as *teatro callejero,* zarzuela, and operetta and has developed its own stock characters (Diverso 1989:14). Its presentations satirize political and social events that have happened since the last carnival. Figure 5 transcribes a presentation of Araca la Cana, one of the most traditional *murgas* of Uruguay. The first stanza below is the chorus; soloist A sings the next stanza, and soloist B sings the last.

Yo quiero ver que esta noche	Tonight I want to see
la alegría te siga;	Happiness catching you;
quiero ver en tu cara	I want to see in your face
sonrisa de cariño.	A smile of love.
Quiero que esta noche ría	I want you to smile tonight,
que usted disfrute a mi lado.	And enjoy being with me.
Yo quiero hablar del presente;	I want to talk about the present;
no quiero hablar del pasado.	I don't want to talk about the past.
Quiero encontrar una calle	I want to find a street
que no esté llena de ahujeros,	That isn't full of potholes,
para decirle a Pacheco:	So I can ask Pacheco:
"¿Cómo le vá, compañero?"	"How's it goin', buddy?"

Pacheco was Jorge Pacheco Areco, president of Uruguay (1967–1971).

A show has four parts: the presentation (*presentación*), consisting of the director's speech and a choral song; the potpourri (*potpurrí*), performed by the chorus and soloists; the *cuplé,* performed by soloists and the chorus, appealing to social, moral, or political interests; and the leaving (*retirada*), containing the richest harmonies of the unaccompanied chorus. Only at the end do drums emphasize the high point of the action. The chorus begins in three, four, or five voices, and displays canonic imi-

The *murga* is a popular art. Its presentations satirize political and social events that have happened since the last carnival.

FIGURE 5   A performance by the *murga* Araca la Cana in Montevideo during carnival 1994. Transcription by Ercilia Moreno Chá.

tation and other complex techniques. The melodies sung each year are selected from the most popular songs, to which original texts are set. The instrumentation required by the regulations includes bass drum, cymbal, snare drum, and occasionally aerophones, including flute, trumpet, and saxophone. The music is of great importance, not only because of the songs, but because it serves as the basis for choreography.

Popular music

Tango

The tango, a ballroom dance in 4/4 time [see ARGENTINA], is the most characteristic urban dance along the Río de la Plata. It developed on both riverbanks, with its Uruguayan center in Montevideo and its Argentine center in Buenos Aires. Since its popular origins (after the 1860s), it has had a long development in duets and trios that combined violin, guitar, flute, accordion, *bandoneón,* clarinet, and harp, until the development of the typical ensembles of the mid-1900s.

In comparison with the Argentinian capital, the development of the tango in Uruguay was delayed because of the slow development of music publishing and recording (Legido 1994:36–37) and because the rise of talking movies in Buenos Aires at the end of the 1930s gave tango a relevant presence there. Several artists migrated to Buenos Aires and Europe to start international careers, thus becoming important names in the history of tango. This was the case with Alfredo Gobbi, a composer and musician who made recordings of tango in Paris in 1907 and was one of the first teachers of tango in France; and with Francisco Canaro (1897–1948) prolific composer and representative character of the traditional tango of his time. Similar cases include the singer Carlos Gardel (1890–1935), the world-famous singer of tangos, and Julio Sosa, his best successor, who did influential work in Buenos Aires between 1949 and 1964. Horacio Ferrer, the most important living poet of tango, has dedicated himself to diffusing, studying, and promoting tango in both capitals (Montevideo and Buenos Aires), in each of which he founded the National Academy of Tango.

The tango is now an internationally recognized dance, widely found in Europe and America, and played by various ensembles, at the core of which are the piano, the violin, and the *bandoneón.* It has a widespread popular appeal throughout Uruguay, especially among the generation born before the 1940s, who early in their lives experienced the genre at the height of its popularity.

Two institutions in Montevideo—Joventango since 1977 and Fundación Tango since 1987—have helped disseminate tango music and dancing. Tango festivals celebrated each year include Festival de Tango de Montevideo, Viva el Tango, and Buscando la Voz del Tango. Tango shows are becoming popular: in 1995, "*Todos somos Gardel*" ('We're All Gardel'), "*Mano a mano*" ('Hand to Hand'), and "*Tangueces*" attracted large audiences. El Tango Ha Vuelto a las Calles de Montevideo (The Tango Has Returned to the Streets of Montevideo) is a traveling production performed on spring weekends. The show ends with tango classes given by teachers in the streets of different neighborhoods of the capital.

Popular Uruguayan song

In popular music, the most typical expression from the 1970s to 1990s is the movement known as *canto popular uruguayo*—a name chosen to differentiate it from the rising movement of folkloric music occurring in Argentina at the same time. This movement began in the 1960s, and its essence was testimonial: its protest songs dealt with a great economical and political crisis. Thus, its texts expressed the desire for social and political change and a search for national and regional identity. This search was effected by including in the repertoire the performers' texts and music, by using Spanish (contrasted with English, used in rock), and by incorporating rhythms of Uruguayan and Latin American derivation (Martins 1986:23–24).

The music showed strong affinities with that of Uruguayan folklore, *candombe,* the tango, and the *murga.* The most common instrument was the guitar, but in the 1970s the *bandoneón* and sets of *tamboriles* joined the ensemble. The main promoters of this movement included Jaime Roos, Braulio López, Rubén Rada, and Eduardo Darnuchans. From Jaime Roos and Raúl Castro come the lyrics of the song "*Que el letrista no se olvide*" ('Hope the Poet Doesn't Forget'), devoted to the authors of lyrics for carnival *murgas*; here is a stanza:

No te olvides de cantarle a los *cracks* que no llegaron.
Dedícale alguna estrofa al borracho y su amistad,
y no vayas a olvidarte de dudar de tanto verso.
¿Cuántas veces el silencio es la voz de la verdad?

Don't forget to sing to the experts who haven't arrived.
Devote a stanza to the drunkard and his friendship,
and please don't forget to distrust such a verse.
How often is silence the voice of truth?

This song reminds listeners of subjects that must be in the lyrics.

International Music

Uruguayan disco is strongly associated with American and British recordings of international music, mainly from the United States, England, Germany, and the Netherlands. Uruguay's youth, more familiar with the English language than are their elders, are attracted to this music. They also enjoy tropical music (*música tropical*), an influx of Caribbean genres such as salsa, merengue, *cumbia, plena,* and others. This musical movement has brought typical Caribbean percussion instruments and styles to Uruguay, and has encouraged the formation of local bands dedicated to playing the new repertoires.

Events for rock and popular Uruguayan song (*canto popular uruguayo*) are usually held in large urban settings, such as athletic stadiums, clubs, and theaters. Rock concerts are usually performed by international figures apportioning their performances among Rio de Janeiro, Buenos Aires, and Montevideo. During summers, Punta del Este (an important international tourist destination) joins this circuit. Rock and other kinds of popular music are broadcast over eighty-six AM and sixty-six FM radio stations and twenty-four television channels in Uruguay. Numerous recording companies release national and international music, on records and cassettes.

MUSICAL BEHAVIOR AND CREATIVITY

Instrumental performance in Uruguay and the construction of musical instruments is almost exclusively the province of men, while women join them by dancing and singing. Different social groups are centered around various musical events; carnival and Afro-Brazilian rituals (such as Umbanda) attract the widest cultural and social diversity; they appear in urban and rural locales, reaching widely various ages and social groups. Events involving mostly traditional criollo music occur predominantly in rural areas, whether on beaches, arenas, streets, or soccer fields.

Audiences include people of all ages, who may participate by singing and dancing or, as with the *payada,* by simply observing. In urban areas, popular music is performed in the streets and large athletic stadiums, dance halls, social clubs, and *tanguerías,* locales in which live performances of tangos can be heard, sometimes accompanied by dance.

In the cities, the young people are more divided. The young people of the middle and upper-middle classes prefer rock, but members of the older generation cling to the repertoire of performers of tangos (*tangueros*), which includes *milongas*, waltzes, and tangos. In the 1990s, traditional dance halls of Montevideo, including Palacio Salvo and Sudamérica, are devoting themselves to tango and tropical music. Some cafés, including La Vieja Cumparsita, Tanguería del 40, and Café Sorocabana, have started to give room to the tango. Without regard to age, the lower classes prefer folk music. In the case of the *murga,* there is a class-based division between the actors (from the lower-middle class) and the spectators (from every level of the social spectrum).

Uruguayan musicians' creativity is situational, conditioned by the repertoire and its function. Musicians who perform rock and popular Uruguayan song enjoy a certain creative liberty, but carnival musician-composers employ established popular melodies, to which they add their own instrumentation and texts. The texts and the music of Afro-Brazilian ritual songs come mostly from Brazil, but drummers enjoy rhythmic latitude. For criollo instrumentalists who perform traditional music, creativity is shown especially in special tunings for the guitar and in strums, which sometimes acquire a virtuosic character.

The reaction of the public to the diversity of repertoires is also varied. It runs from the participation common in the Afro-Brazilian cults (in which parts of the audience sing while the initiates sing, dance, and enter into trance) to the nonparticipation (listening and applauding only) of audiences at theatrical performances of popular music (such as *teatros de revista, canto popular uruguayo,* and others). Between these extremes are the active participation of the audiences at rock concerts, which includes whistling, singing, clapping, and dancing, and the passive participation of *murga* audiences, represented in the texts sung by the chorus.

Ideologies underlie some musical expressions. Throughout the repertoires of *payadores* and personified by gaucho mentality is a nationalist sentiment, linked to traditionalist movements from the late 1800s; these movements tried to contrast national elements with the great wave of European immigration which the country was experiencing. Yoruba mythology is the obvious basis of the Afro-Brazilian cults, whereas a politically and socially questioning attitude dominates the movement of popular Uruguayan song. Social and political satire predominate in the texts of some carnival songs, especially the *murgas*. At sporting and political events, music increasingly serves as a rallying force; drummed rhythms, marches associated with athletic clubs or political parties, and improvisation of short texts over simple and catchy melodies are traditionally associated with these events.

LEARNING MUSIC

The learning of traditional criollo music is voluntary and unsystematic. It takes place through observation of other musicians, the same process that occurs among immigrant communities. In the music of the Afro-Brazilian religious rituals, the same process is in operation for the songs and the training of advanced instrumentalists. In the music of carnival, the director of the group takes the teacher's role, but learning still takes place mainly by ear. In popular commercial music, musicans sometimes have a basic knowledge of musical rudiments that permits them to read scores and learn instruments in conservatories or with private teachers; usually, however, commercial musicians play from memory or by ear.

Uruguay has several private or official conservatories. Most are oriented toward European academic music, but two in Montevideo teach folk and pop. These are the Centro de Cultura Popular, operated by the Ministry of Education and Culture (includes a traditional dance program), and the Taller Uruguayo de Música Popular (Uruguayan Popular-Music Workshop).

Yoruba mythology is the obvious basis of the Afro-Brazilian cults, whereas a politically and socially questioning attitude dominates the movement of popular Uruguayan song.

Entities such as criollo societies and athletic clubs often facilitate the learning of dances through courses that supplement the teaching of folk music at the high-school level. At a higher level, there is the Conservatorio Nacional de Música and the musicology program at the Universidad de la República, both oriented toward European music.

MUSICAL CHANGE

The Uruguayan ethnomusicologist Marita Fornaro (personal communication) gives three main reasons for change in traditional Uruguayan music: the depopulation of rural areas, which has led to the presence in Montevideo of more than half the national population; the increasing technology in agricultural areas, which has led to the disappearance of traditional festivals and their attendant musical events; and the influence of mass communication since the 1960s. Of these reasons, the last has been the most influential in several ways: radio has introduced new genres, especially Argentine folk music and Caribbean forms of music and dance; television has spread the popularity of Rio de Janeiro's carnival, with the consequent influence of its costumes, musical genres, and samba schools; and television has influenced traditional children's songs. The process of musical creolization began early in the colonial period, and certain extant dances reveal that the process was still occurring during the twentieth century, when the mazurka and the polka acquired local traits. Most mestization of the late 1990s relates to the extant Africanisms in certain religious contexts and the *candombe* of Montevideo's carnival.

—Translated by Timothy D. Watkins

REFERENCES

Ayestarán, Lauro. 1953. *La música en el Uruguay.* Montevideo: Servicio Oficial de Difusión Radioeléctrica.

———. 1967. *El folklore musical uruguayo.* Montevideo: Arca.

Barco Centenera, Martín del. 1602. *Argentina y conquista del Río de la Plata.* Lisbon: Pedro Crasbeeck.

Contrapunto 3. N.d. Sondor 84.291. Cassette.

Diverso, Gustavo. 1989. *Murgas: La representación del carnaval.* Montevideo: Coopren.

Fornaro, Marita. 1988. "El 'Cancionero Europeo Antiguo' presente en el Uruguay." In *Terceras Jornadas Argentinas de Musicología,* 65–74. Buenos

Aires: Instituto Nacional de Musicología "Carlos Vega."

———. 1989. "Organología tradicional uruguaya: Panorama general y caracterización." In *Cuartas Jornadas Argentinas de Musicología.* Buenos Aires: Instituto Nacional de Musicología "Carlos Vega."

———. 1990a. "La música en los cultos de origen afrobrasileño presentes en el Uruguay." Paper presented at the third annual conference of the Asociación de Musicología, Buenos Aires.

———. 1990b. "La música tradicional del Uruguay." Manuscript.

Fornaro, Marita, and Antonio Díaz. 1987. "La música afromontevideana y su contexto sociocultural en la década de los años 80." Paper present-

ed at the first annual conference of the Asociación Argentina de Musicología, Buenos Aires.

Legido, Juan Carlos. 1994. *La orilla oriental del tango: Historia del tango uruguayo.* Montevideo: Ediciones de la Plaza.

Lopes de Souza, Pedro. 1927. *Diario de Navegação.* Rio de Janeiro: Paulo Prado.

Martins, Carlos A. 1986. *Música popular uruguaya 1973–1982: Un fenómeno de comunicación alternativa.* Montevideo: Ediciones de la Banda Oriental.

Pallavicino, María L. 1987. *Umbanda: Religiosidad afro-brasileña en Montevideo.* Montevideo: Pettirossi.

Venezuela
Max H. Brandt

When Spanish explorers encountered the bay of Maracaibo, on South America's north coast, it reminded them of Venice; therefore, they called the land *Venezuela* 'little Venice'. Today, the country of Venezuela has a land area of 912,050 square kilometers (more than twice the size of California) and 2,800 kilometers of Caribbean coastline, and in 1992 had a population of 20,675,970. Its five major cities are Caracas (the capital, founded in 1567, with close to 25 percent of the national population), Maracaibo, Valencia, Maracay, and Barquisimeto. From the early colonial period through the first decades of the twentieth century, most of Venezuela's inhabitants lived in rural communities, but today, more than 90 percent of its population resides in urban centers.

Traditional Venezuelan music derives from the cultures that have influenced most Latin American and Caribbean countries: the indigenous (or aboriginal, Indian, Amerindian, native American), the European, and the African. Venezuela still manifests pockets of unacculturated indigenous music, but most of its traditional music is an assortment of genres and styles stemming from Spain and Africa. Two pioneering twentieth-century ethnomusicologists of Venezuela, Luís Felipe Ramón y Rivera and Isabel Aretz de Ramón y Rivera, have classified traditional Venezuelan music into three categories: indigenous, folk, and popular music—a classification often criticized for being too rigid and simplistic. In it, the indigenous category pertains to pre-Columbian music, remaining essentially unacculturated. Folk music encompasses the music of Spain and Africa—music that has been transformed in Venezuela and is not attributable to specific authors. According to Aretz and Ramón y Rivera, popular music is music composed by known authors using traditional forms, primarily European. Aretz and Ramón y Rivera recognize art music (academic music) and latter-day popular forms such as salsa, but do not view them as "traditional" music.

Though this overview follows the three categories of traditional music presented above, a more comprehensive study of traditional Venezuelan music might utilize classifications proposed by Rafael Salazar (1992a) or other Venezuelan musicologists. The question of what is indigenous, folk, or popular is widely debated in Latin America today. The term *traditional popular,* for example, is sometimes used in place of *folk.*

In 1498, when European explorers arrived on Columbus's third voyage to the New World, about fifty thousand native Americans were thought to be living along the central Caribbean coast of Venezuela, an area no longer populated by indigenous peoples. Indigenous music survives primarily in the Amazon region, the Orinoco Delta, and the Guajira Peninsula. European and African influences predominate along the coast of north-central Venezuela, the most densely populated part of the country. Perhaps more than two-thirds of the Spanish who arrived during the first century of colonization came from Andalucía, in southern Spain. With colonization came Moorish influences; thus, when the term *European* is employed here, it is used in its broadest sense, including influences from Arabic, Islamic, and West Asian sources that were part of Andalucía during the colonizing of the Americas.

In the Andes, Spanish influences predominate. Spanish-derived vocal forms and musical instruments form a plurality of Venezuela's existing folk music, and Isabel Aretz (personal communication) has identified twelve families of song (*cancioneros*) in Venezuela's folk music, eleven of which she calls Spanish in origin; the remaining one is African-Venezuelan. Likewise, though in any survey of musical instruments indigenous-inspired rattles and African-derived drums abound, the stringed instruments of Spanish origin are the most notable. The national instrument of Venezuela, a four-stringed lute (*cuatro*) closely resembling the ukulele, and Venezuela's next most prominent musical instrument, a harp (*arpa*), derive from Spain.

A Caribbean-island character is also apparent in much of Venezuela's music, linking this country musically to places such as Cuba, Curaçao, the Dominican Republic, Haiti, Puerto Rico, and Trinidad and Tobago. Much of this influence is African, and the influence of Africa on Venezuela as a whole is much greater than is often perceived. Venezuelans often emphasize their European and indigenous cultural roots, but the African impact on local culture, and music in particular, is undeniable. From the earliest colonial times, Africans were taken to Venezuela directly from the African continent, but the greatest number of Africans and their immediate descendants came indirectly to Venezuela—from Spain, Colombia, and Caribbean islands. These people represented cultures from widely dispersed areas of Africa. In particular, vestiges of West Africa and Central Africa survive in Venezuela today, although Central African influences appear to be more prevalent (García 1990).

No social groups or religious organizations in Venezuela can be traced directly to a specific African ethnic group (Pollak-Eltz 1972, 1994). In Venezuela, the importation of slaves from Africa ended early in the 1800s, while it continued in other countries of the Americas. By 1930, African-Venezuelans knew little about the African origin of their principal musical instruments and forms. Not until the research of Juan Pablo Sojo (1976 [1943]), Juan Liscano (1943), Luís Felipe Ramón y Rivera (1950), and others did interest in the African heritage of Venezuela arise.

INDIGENOUS MUSIC

The indigenous societies encountered by Europeans during the early 1500s in the area known today as Venezuela were neither so numerous nor so complex in social organization as those found in other territories in South America. Spanish chroniclers documented Venezuelan indigenous music from the 1500s through the 1700s (Quintana 1995). Many of these societies no longer exist. About thirty indigenous languages survive, spoken by some two hundred thousand people.

Supernatural and symbolic phenomena are associated with most Venezuelan Amerindian instruments. Some groups give human and/or spiritual significance to their musical instruments. Symbolism, as when the handle and the gourd of a rattle represent male and female spheres of influence, respectively, are common [see

YEKUANA]. Some groups that have few musical instruments rely solely on vocal music [see YANOMAMÖ].

The forms of vocal music—solo songs and collective songs, men's songs and women's songs, songs dealing with the supernatural world and songs dealing with mundane activities (such as working and walking in the forest)—vary widely from one indigenous group to another. Musical texts commonly deal with nature and the supernatural world, and songs are sometimes sung by shamans in secret or in bygone languages or even mentally, without sounds [see WARAO].

Musical structure among indigenous Venezuelans is much like that of other aboriginal groups of the Americas. Indigenous groups of Venezuela share no comprehensive system of tonal organization, and the number of tones used in performances varies greatly among individuals and ethnic groups. One song might be sung on a single tone, whereas other songs use five or more (Olsen 1980b:365). Multipart singing may be heterophonic or canonic, as in singing rounds. Rhythmic practices also vary. Free rhythm is common in solo singing, whereas collective singing is often clearly metered, especially when it accompanies dancing.

Among the indigenous peoples of Venezuela, shamans are the key individuals and usually the most important makers of music. Responsible for the mental and physical health of their people and for singing the myths and legends that tell the people's history, they are the vital link between society and the supernatural world. They combine spiritual leadership, divination, healing, and historical narration, and they use their voices (and often rattles) as the paramount implements in conducting their official duties.

Some indigenous groups have several kinds of shaman, each with a unique musical repertoire. The Piaroa (Wothuha) of the Amazon region have two: the *dzuwèwè ruwa,* who fights to protect his people from hostile and evil spirits, and the *mèñeruwa,* the master of the *mèñe,* sacred songs that men perform at nighttime rituals in communal houses (Agerkop 1983:13). *Mèñe* have four functions: combating the fatal illnesses caused by consuming the meat of certain animals; insuring the well-being of agricultural crops and pregnant women; curing acute afflictions, such as snakebites or wounds caused by wild animals; and accompanying the blowing of incense when someone dies or at the beginning of a special ceremony called *warime.*

Musical acculturation among native Venezuelans began in the 1500s with the coming of Europeans and Africans, and especially Christian missionaries. The adoption of Christian music often led to a repudiation of traditional music, which missionaries felt was too closely integrated with indigenous beliefs. Increasing contact with Venezuelan creole culture led indigenous people into new musical realms, affecting their music. Some indigenous groups have been in contact with nonindigenous cultures for decades, but still maintain most of the traditional music they had on first contact. Venezuelan indigenous music was some of the earliest to be recorded by modern technology (around 1900), so to study musical continuity and change, ethnomusicologists can compare early recordings with present-day performances.

FOLK MUSIC

Though elite and urbane individuals—from native American shamans and African princes to Spanish priests—have influenced traditional music in Venezuela, the main subjects in this development have been peasants. European and African traits predominate in most folk-musical forms; indigenous phenomena are less apparent. Some Venezuelan folk music blends European and African music, but most of it is European- or African-based. Some songs are obviously European in form. Others feature the leader-response form of African music. Certain ensembles feature Iberian

In parts of Latin America and the Caribbean, the term creole is used to identify cultural elements of purely European ancestry. In Venezuela, it usually refers to the cultural trinity of indigenous America, Europe, and Africa.

strings, but others feature African-style drums. Occasionally we find a juxtaposition of both, with European-derived lutes and African-derived drums in the same ensemble. Distinctions are sometimes obvious, sometimes subtle. Most of this folk music is associated with the many fiestas that take place in Venezuela throughout the year (Hernández 1993).

The music of Venezuelan peasants of mixed ancestry is often called creole music (*música criolla*). Ramón y Rivera (1969) uses the term *folk* in classifying and describing this music, but he and other Venezuelans often use the term *criolla* when discussing the music created in Venezuela since the arrival of the Europeans and Africans. In parts of Latin America and the Caribbean this term is used to identify those of purely European ancestry; in Venezuela, it usually refers to the cultural trinity of indigenous America, Europe, and Africa. Likewise, *creole* often designates the traditional music of Venezuela. Even music sometimes called African-Venezuelan music (Ramón y Rivera 1971) is occasionally designated as creole music by those who perform it.

As in other parts of the Americas, European musical influences are the easiest to trace through written sources. We have not only published accounts of music and musical instruments in Europe during colonial days (elements that may or may not have reached Venezuela), but also explorers', officials', and clerics' inventories of instruments and vocal music brought from Spain. Europeans reported extensively on indigenous music and instruments but hardly mentioned early musical imports from Africa. For those imports, we must rely more on comparisons of existing phenomena with recent ethnomusicological research in Africa.

Traditional Musical Instruments

The roots of creole music in Venezuela can be traced in part through the study of musical instruments. Two important organological contributions to creole music from indigenous sources are rattles and wind instruments. The major instruments from Spain are stringed instruments, and African-Venezuelans are locally known for their knowledge of drums and drumming.

Idiophones

Container rattles (maracas), usually in pairs, accompany just about every genre of creole music. Indigenous Venezuelans commonly use a single rattle to accompany singing, but creole ensembles commonly employ a pair. (An exception is the use of a single rattle in some African-Venezuelan ensembles of the central coast.) Paired maracas are not usually equal in size or sound. One, usually larger, with more seeds, emits a deep, raspy sound; the other, with fewer seeds, emits a clearer and brighter sound. Often, a gender designation is assigned to each: the lower-sounding instrument is male, the higher-pitched is female.

The most prominent idiophones of African derivation are the sides of wooden-

FIGURE 1 During the festival of Saint John the Baptist in Curiepe, Miranda (Barlovento area), Venezuela, two men beat sticks on the side of a drum. Photo by Dale A. Olsen, 1974.

bodied drums, struck with sticks commonly called *palos* and sometimes *laures* (figure 1). They embellish the rhythms of drums, and children often play them while listening to rhythms of drums.

Another African-derived instrument, from the area of Barlovento, is an ensemble of stamped bamboo tubes called *quitiplás* (figure 2), an onomatopoeic word representing the rhythm of the two smallest tubes. The player holds one tube in each hand, striking one to the ground, followed by the other, and then striking both against each other, producing the last syllable of the word (*plás*), in a cyclic or continuous rhythm. Two or three other players each hold a larger tube, which they strike on the ground with one hand while using the other hand to cup the top of the tube for special effects. *Quitiplás* sometimes accompany songs and dances of the *redondo*

FIGURE 2 On a street in Tacarigua, Miranda (Barlovento area), Venezuela, three men stamp bamboo tubes (*quitiplás*). Photo by Max H. Brandt, 1973.

ensemble, using the same basic rhythms performed on these membranophones. Children often play *quitiplás* as a way of learning the rhythms of the drums.

Also of African derivation is the *marímbola* [see DOMINICAN REPUBLIC: figure 1], a wooden box with metal strips or tongues, plucked by the musician as he sits on the instrument. The *marímbola* is played in various parts of Venezuela and in certain neighboring Caribbean countries. Other African and European-based idiophones commonly played in Venezuelan folk music are metal triangles, concussion sticks, bells, Jew's harps (*trompa* or *birimbao*), and ridged instruments scraped with a stick (most commonly called *charrascas*). Steel drums are played in some urban centers and in the town of Callao in Bolívar State, where people from Caribbean islands have been relocating for decades.

Membranophones

Though indigenous peoples of Venezuela used numerous kinds of drums, most drums used today are of African and European origin. From Europe came at least two double-headed drums, the bass drum (*bombo*) and the side drum (*redoblante*). The drum found most widely in the country, the *tambora*, may have been inspired by both traditions.

Africa is responsible for the greatest variety of drums. Barlovento (Windward), on the central coast in Miranda State, is famous for its African-Venezuelan drumming. It has produced three distinct sets of membranophones: *minas, redondos,* and *tamboras.* Its stamped bamboo tubes, musically related to *redondos* and sometimes called drums themselves, are part of its heritage. Though multiple sets of drums commonly occur among ethnic groups in Africa (as among the Yoruba of Nigeria, who have different families of drums), they rarely do in communities of the African diaspora in the Americas. Barlovento is an exception. Unlike in Africa, though, where a variety of composite rhythms or instrumental pieces can be played within the context of one family of drums, the drum sets of Barlovento each feature only one composite rhythm. The only exception to this rule is the *malembe* rhythm and song form, performed for processions rather than dancing, primarily by *redondo* ensembles, but also sometimes by *mina* ensembles.

Long, heavy log drums with a skin at one end—*burro, cumaco, mina, tambor grande*—are common in Venezuela. In performance, each is most often placed on the ground. The main drummer straddles the end near the skin, and one or more other musicians beat the side of the drum with *palos* or *laures*.

The Barlovento variant of this drum, the *mina,* is not placed on the ground. When played, it rests on crossed poles (see figure 1). The ensemble consists of two drums, one long (*mina*) and one short (*curbata*), made from the same log, always of strong, heavy wood such as that of the avocado tree. The largest piece, about 2 meters long, becomes the *mina* (*tambor grande*); it is propped up on two long poles tied together in an X, with the upper V of the X being much smaller than the lower. The *curbata,* less than half the length of the *mina,* stands upright on three or four V-shaped legs, cut at its bottom and open end. Each drummer uses two sticks, one in each hand, while one or more (usually two to four) musicians play rhythms on the lower end of the *mina* with sticks (*laures*), one in each hand (Olsen 1980a:403–407). The ensemble usually includes one maraca or a pair of them.

Two other drum types of the central coast, *redondos* and *tamboras,* have skins at both ends. The commonest are *tamboras,* the main instruments that accompany all-night observances for honoring a saint or the Holy Cross. In Barlovento, *tamboras* can be played alone, or in ensembles of up to four or five instruments, by performers who hold the drums between their knees while sitting. The physical traits of the *tamboras* and the rhythms played on them recall those of the *redondo* ensemble. The

FIGURE 3 During the festival of Saint John the Baptist in El Tigre, Miranda, Venezuela, three men play drums (*redondos*) with one stick and one hand, as a woman shakes maracas. Photo by Max H. Brandt, 1973.

tambora, like the *redondo* drum, is played with one stick, which sometimes (depending upon the particular drum) strikes the side of the drum and the skin.

Redondos, found in a smaller area south and east of Caracas, are longer than *tamboras,* and are held between standing drummers' legs (figure 3). The three drums of the set are made from the same trunk of a balsa tree (called *lano* in Barlovento), whose wood is soft and lightweight. Each drum, varying slightly in size, is hollowed to resemble an hourglass inside and is covered at each end with skins connected to each other with thin rope lacings forming W-shaped patterns. The drummer strikes the drum with a stick held in one hand and the fingers of the other hand. These drums have various individual names and are most commonly called *tamborcitos, tambores redondos,* or *culo 'e puya.* The only other musical instruments accompanying this ensemble are maracas.

Neither the *mina* nor the *redondo* tradition seems to have a direct link to a specific community in Africa; scholars have not found any drumming traditions in Africa that exactly match those of either ensemble; however, generic links are traceable to parts of Africa. The most direct links with central Africa, specifically the Republic of Congo (Brazzaville), have been made by the Venezuelan researcher Jesús García (1990), a native of Barlovento. Other links have been made to West Africa. The construction of the *mina,* with its skin held in place by ropes tied to pegs that protrude into the body of the drum, recalls construction techniques in West Africa. Furthermore, there may be some connection between the term *mina* and the name of Almina, an important port in Ghana from which many slaves embarked for the Americas. Aspects of this ensemble found in central Africa include sitting over the end of the drumhead while playing it and using the heel of the foot to alter the sound of the drum. Similarities exist between *redondos* and instruments in the Museum of the Belgian Congo in Tervuren, Belgium (Liscano 1960). In the film *Salto al Atlántico* (Esparragoza 1991), García presents evidence linking Venezuela and Africa.

Scholarly focus has been on Barlovento, but three neighboring areas, also called Barlovento by some people, have similarly African-Venezuelan genres and instruments. The Litoral (shore) and the Guarenas-Guatire Valley lie between Caracas and Barlovento proper, separated from each other by a chain of mountains running along

mina   Venezuelan set of two single-headed drums; also the longer drum of the *mina* pair

redondo   Venezuelan double-headed drum with internal hourglass shape

tambora   A long, tubular Afro-Venezuelan membranophone made from a log with two skin heads, played with one stick while held between the knees

laures   Venezuelan sticks (also *palos*) beaten on the side of the wooden-bodied *mina* drum

chimbangueles   A set of four to seven Afro-Venezuelan conical drums

furruco   A single-headed Venezuelan friction membranophone played by rubbing a long stick attached to and protruding from the top of the drum skin

the coast. The upper Tuy Valley is the third area, just south of the Guarenas-Guatire Valley and southwest of Barlovento proper, including the towns of Cúa, Ocumare del Tuy, Santa Lucía, and Santa Teresa.

The drumming traditions of the Litoral are closely related to those from Barlovento proper. The *cumaco*, also commonly called *tambor grande*, closely resembles the large *mina* but has a drumhead nailed to one end rather than being fastened by pegs and wedges. Unlike the *mina* (propped up on two poles), the *cumaco* is placed on the ground while the drummer sits on it, playing it with bare hands and sometimes controlling the sound with the heel of one foot. One, two, or three *cumacos* can be played at the same time. Other musicians play sticks on the trunk of the drum. Other names for *cumaco*-like drums in this area are *burro negro, campanita, mayor, piano, pujo, macizo, primero,* and *segundo*. Some communities also have a *curbata,* an instrument much like that of Barlovento with the same name. The town of Naiguata, in addition to having *cumacos,* has drums made of barrels called *pipas. Tamboras* or *tamboritas,* much like those of Barlovento, accompany *fulias* at *velorios*. There are no *redondo*-type drums in this area, but *redondo*-type rhythms are played on *cumacos* to accompany songs and dances, much as in the *redondo* tradition of Barlovento.

In the Tuy Valley, southwest of Barlovento, *redondos* rule. They are somewhat shorter than the *redondos* of Barlovento, and their rhythms and combinations are somewhat different from those of Barlovento.

In the Guarenas-Guatire Valley, two *tambora*-like drums (*prima, cruzao*), and a military-style side drum (*grande*) (Ramón y Rivera 1969:92) accompany *redondo*-like songs and dances during the festivals of the Nativity of Saint John the Baptist (24 June). The best-known fiesta of this area is the Parranda de San Pedro (Saint Peter's Procession), which takes place in the town of Guatire on 29 June. The procession and dancing of this fiesta are accompanied by *cuatros,* maracas, foot stamping, and singing. The characters in this reenactment of early colonial days, all of whom are men with faces blackened to represent their African ancestors, are María Ignacia (a man dressed as a woman), one who carries and dances with an image of Saint Peter, a flag bearer, two boys who dance next to María Ignacia, and two dancers with squares of thick, hard leather attached to their sandals, enhancing the sound of their stamping. Other men (often three) play *cuatros* and maracas. María Ignacia represents a legendary colonial woman who had promised to dance in honor of Saint Peter every year if the saint would help with a cure for her ill daughter. The daughter survived, but María Ignacia died soon after, so her husband, dressed in María Ignacia's clothes, danced every year in his wife's place. Today, the man portraying María Ignacia carries a black doll, representing the cured daughter.

Around Lake Maracaibo, San Benito (Saint Benedict the Moor, of San Fratello and Palermo) is honored during the Christmas and New Year's season by drumming on *chimbangueles*. The music is primarily African-Venezuelan. Documents about *chimbangueles* describe sets of four to seven drums. The communities of Bobures, Gibraltar, and El Batey, at the southern end of Lake Maracaibo, use seven drums, four designated male and three designated female (B. Salazar 1990). The male drums are *el tambor mayor, el respuesta, el cantante,* and *el segundo;* the female drums are *la primera requinta, la secunda requinta,* and *la media requinta.* The drums are conical. At the large end is a skin, held in place by cords attached to a hoop or a loop, also often made of cord, placed near the bottom or narrow end of the drum. This hoop or loop is held in place by wooden wedges placed between the hoop and the body of the drum. Supported by a strap over the drummer's shoulder, *chimbangueles* are played with a stick in one hand. The rhythms played on them have specific names, including *el chocho* 'the doting', *el ajé* 'the accompaniment', *el chimbanguelero vaya* 'the *chimbanguele* drummer goes', *el misericordia* 'the mercy', *cantica y San Gorongomez* 'invocation', and *saludo a los capitanes* 'salute to the captains'.

A single-headed friction drum known as *furruco* (*furro*) is used in *aguinaldo* ensembles (see figure 7) during the Christmas season. It is similar to the Spanish *zambomba* and African friction drums, whose sounds are produced by rubbing a stick attached to the skin.

Chordophones

The most important Spanish contribution to the instrumental music of Venezuela was the introduction of stringed instruments. Today, the four-stringed *cuatro,* found everywhere in Venezuela, even among indigenous groups, is considered the national instrument (figure 4). The diatonic or creole harp (*arpa*), though found in only two areas of Venezuela, is also recognized as an important symbol of Venezuelan music (see figure 4), as attested to by miniature models in the gift shops of Caracas and other tourist-frequented communities.

In large cities, the *cuatro* is played as much as, or more than, in the countryside. It is often called a guitar (*guitarra*), since it is the most commonly used instrument of the guitar family in Venezuela. It is also known by diminutives—*guitarra pequeña, guitarrita, guitarilla, guitarillo*—and by other names, such as *discante.* Primarily an accompanying instrument, it plays chords, mostly the tonic, dominant, and subdominant, but virtuosos such as Fredy Reyna (*Danzas y Canciones Para Los Niños* 1981) include exquisite melodic techniques in their performances.

Small guitars with nylon strings are used primarily as accompanying instruments. Most, like the *cuatro* 'four', are named for the number of their strings. They include the *cuatro y medio* 'four and a half', *cinco* 'five', *cinco y medio, seis* 'six' (but smaller than the standard six-stringed guitar), *cuatro con cinco cuerdas* 'cuatro with five strings', and *cinco de seis cuerdas* 'six-stringed *cinco*'. In the west of Venezuela, the *tiple* 'treble' is common [see COLOMBIA]. Used as a melodic or chordally accompanying instrument, the *tiple* most commonly has four double or triple sets of strings.

Plucked lutes (*bandolas* and *mandolinas*) serve as melodic instruments in Venezuela. The best-known *bandola,* from the plains, uses four gut or nylon strings. It has been publicized by the virtuoso Anselmo López from Barinas, the only plains state where the *bandola* is as popular as the harp—or perhaps even more popular. The *bandola* of the central coast has four courses of double strings, the higher-sounding ones from metal. The *bandola* of the eastern area (more commonly called *bandolín* or *mandolina*), also smaller than the plains *bandola,* has four double courses of nylon strings. The *bandola* of the Guayana area (surrounding Ciudad Guayana, where the Caroní River meets the Orinoco, in Bolívar State) borrows elements from the plains. The *bandola andina* (also known as a *bandurría*), found in the Andes area of western Venezuela, has five or six courses of double or triple strings.

FIGURE 4   Accompanied by a *cuatro*, the Venezuelan musician Jesús Rodríguez plays a plains harp (*arpa llanera*) in Miami, Florida. Photo by Dale A. Olsen, 1983.

Of the stringed instruments used to play melodies, the violin (*violín*) is the most widely used instrument in Venezuela. It is a European model, like that used throughout the world.

The diatonic harp, once popular in Spain, is an important creole instrument in many countries of Latin America [see COLOMBIA; ECUADOR; MEXICO; PARAGUAY; PERU]. The *arpa criolla* usually has between thirty and thirty-seven strings; thirty-three and thirty-four are the commonest numbers. Its main performance styles in Venezuela are that of the plains (*arpa llanera*) and that of Aragua (*arpa aragüeña*, from the state of Aragua). Because the latter style also occurs in the federal district, the state of Miranda, and states closer to the coast than the plains states, it can conveniently be called the style of the central-coast harp. More commonly, it is specified by adjectives derived from the names of places, including Aragua (*arpa aragüeña*), Miranda (*arpa mirandina*), and the Tuy River area (*arpa tuyera*).

The instruments differ slightly from one area to another. The plains harp has a narrower sound board than does the central-coast harp and now uses only nylon strings. The coastal harp sometimes has gut or nylon strings in its lower register, but metallic upper strings give it a more brilliant sound. Performance brings out an even more prominent difference between these harps (see below, in relation to the *joropo*).

The diatonic harp was taught to indigenous Venezuelans by Spanish priests during the early colonial period, and its music was fashionable in the salons of the urban upper class. The harp music heard today in Venezuela has roots in seventeenth- and eighteenth-century Spain, when the Renaissance modes had not yet been fully replaced by major and minor tonalities (Garfias 1979:13). Keyboard music was performed on diatonically tuned harps, then popular in Spain. The harp-playing styles of Venezuela closely resemble Spanish Baroque keyboard styles.

Aerophones

Wind instruments are notable in the music of marginalized creoles such as the people of Falcon State, who dance to the music of an ensemble featuring *turas,* end-blown flutes, one male and the other female. Other flutes of this ensemble are *cachos,* made from a deer's skull with antlers attached; these are played in pairs, one large and one small.

Another popular Venezuelan aerophone is the panpipe, locally called by several names, including *carrizo* 'cane' and *maremare* 'happy-happy', played by creoles in many parts of Venezuela. Especially well known are the panpipes of Cumanacoa, in Sucre State, and those of San José de Guaribe, in Guarico State. There are many other kinds of creole aerophones, including cane and wooden flutes (vertical and transverse types) and conch trumpets (*trompetas de caracol, guaruras*). The last instruments play in drum ensembles of the Barlovento area.

MUSICAL CONTEXTS AND GENRES

Folk Catholicism

Venezuelan folk-religious music is based primarily on Christian conventions. There are no clear links to specific African religions, nor do the traces of syncretism between Christianity and African beliefs in Venezuela reveal the same levels of importance found, for example, in musical performances of Cuban Santería or Brazilian Candomblé. The concept of Saint John the Baptist may have syncretic links to African deities and celebrations but no direct links to African prototypes are obvious.

Folk-religious music in Venezuela accompanies rituals that are apparently Christian, though many are not based on formal Roman Catholic teachings. Instead, this music has evolved with a creole version of Roman Catholicism developed from early colonial days to the present. The church was less influential in colonial Venezuela than in such places as Colombia and Mexico, and Spanish priests were not in abundance. Peasants (*campesinos*) observing native American, African, and Spanish beliefs and customs were at liberty to develop and conduct religious ceremonies, embellishing them with music, dance, costumes, and practices not always acceptable to visiting clerics. Even today, representatives of the official church frown on many ritual aspects of Venezuelan fiestas.

Not all this music can be considered entirely religious in design. Much of it is dedicated to Christian saints, but texts and meanings are often interspersed with secular ideas and words. Some aspects of a particular fiesta (such as *salves,* sung at the beginning of a *tamunangue* in Lara) are traditional and acceptable facets of the Roman tradition, yet the music and dance known as *la perrendenga,* performed in front of the image of San Antonio later in the fiesta, has little to do with Christianity. Therefore, although the fiestas described below are Christian in name, creole Roman Catholicism plays a dominant role as they unfold. Furthermore, alcoholic beverages are almost invariably associated with these quasi-religious celebrations; it would be most unusual for the members of a participating music ensemble, usually men, not to share a bottle of rum or some other kind of spirits.

The combination of music and dance as tribute to deities is locally important, as is the concept of *la promesa,* the promise to honor a saint through music and/or dance for certain favors. The interplay and coexistence of beliefs and performances has produced a wealth of religiously inspired creole music and dance.

Though *malembe* means 'softly, slowly, take it easy' in various Bantu languages, the people of Barlovento are not aware of its African roots and use it simply as the name of a kind of music.

Velorios

Velorios, nightlong celebrations or night watches to honor a saint or the Holy Cross (not to be confused with wakes for a deceased person, also *velorios*) are common in Venezuela. In the plains, the music of the *velorio* is primarily Spanish in origin, with stringed instruments predominating, whereas in the central coastal region the music is more African in origin, where the *tambora* drums accompany songs called *fulias*. Perhaps the *velorio* most widely celebrated in the Venezuelan plains is the wake of the Holy Cross (*velorio de cruz*) or May Cross (*cruz de mayo*). Table altars are decorated with flowers, and a chapel or a temporary roof is often constructed of fronds, papier mâché, flowers, or other materials to honor a cross, usually made of wood and decorated with the same materials. In the plains and surrounding areas, especially in the states of Apure, Carabobo, Cojedes, Guárico, Lara, Portuguesa, and Yaracuy, the Holy Cross is venerated by performances of three-part polyphonic pieces (*tonos*), usually sung by men, sometimes unaccompanied, but more often accompanied by one or more *cuatros*. The music and texts came from Spain during the early days of the colony. Most harmonic singing in Venezuela is in two parts (usually at intervals of a third), but plains wakes use more complex polyphony, unique in Latin America. The lead singer (*guía* 'guide') usually sings a solo phrase and is then joined by two other men improvising a harmonic response—a higher part (*falsa,* also *contrato* and other names), and a lower part (*tenor,* also *tenorete*). In *velorios* of the central coast (especially in the federal district, the state of Miranda, and parts of the state of Aragua), vocal harmony is less important than melody. Here, the *velorios* are centered on the singing of *fulias,* accompanied by at least one *tambora* (but usually three or four), the scraping of a metal plate with a fork, a spoon, or other utensils, and usually one maraca or a pair of maracas. The *tamboras* are held between seated musicians' knees. The most complex of the drum-accompanied vocal genres of Barlovento, the *fulia* is found in a more widely dispersed area of the central coast than are the songs associated with other drums. It has an alternating solo-chorus form of singing, like the other drum songs. The solo is sung by a man or a woman, and the choruses usually consist of male and female singers. The verses have fairly complex texts, but the choruses almost always include vocables or syllables, such as *o lo lo la lo lai na.*

Though the vigil continues until dawn, *fulias* and the accompanying *tamboras* do not play constantly. The music is broken up every twenty to forty minutes with the recitation of *décimas,* ten-line stanzas of poetry brought from Spain in the early days of the colony. Men and women (usually men) recite this poetry after an order is given to the musicians to stop playing, usually with the words *hasta ahí,* suggesting that the musicians take a pause. Some people, even those who cannot read and write, are recognized as specialists in *décimas.* Dancing is never part of celebrations that employ the singing of *fulias* and the playing of *tamboras.* The *fulia-tambora* tradition is not limited to Barlovento; it occurs in more or less the same form in neighboring areas of the central coast.

Mampulorios

Nightlong *velorios* for the deceased occur in Venezuela, but they are not usually associated with music. An exception to this were angel's wakes (*velorios de angelito*) for infants and young children. In the central coast, these *velorios*, called *mampulorios*, were festive occasions to celebrate the purity of sinless souls, which would ascend directly into heaven. Primarily religious in intent, they lasted all night, with the adorned body of the child present. Attendees ate food, drank alcoholic beverages, and played games. *Mampulorios* rarely occur now, and little is known about their music.

San Juan Bautista (Saint John the Baptist)

From the state of Yaracuy in the west to the state of Miranda, south and east of Caracas, the central Caribbean coast of Venezuela is home to many Venezuelans of African origin. Most of their communities lie along the coast; some are 50 kilometers or more inland. These people claim St. John the Baptist (or simply *San Juan*) as their patron saint. Juan Liscano (1973), the pioneer twentieth-century Venezuelan folklorist, noted the connection between the celebration of Saint John the Baptist (24 June) and summer-solstice celebrations elsewhere in the world. In central coastal Venezuela, Saint John the Baptist is honored with African-derived music and dancing beginning on 23 June and ending on 25 June, with ritual and musical observations varying from place to place.

Barlovento is known for the music of the feast of Saint John the Baptist. Especially important is one of its major towns, Curiepe, an important slave-trading center in the early 1700s. During the feast of Saint John the Baptist, a standard musical form is associated with drumming on *mina,* and a dance requires many people to participate at the same time, usually multiple pairs or three or more people dancing in a line or a circle, each with an arm or a hand on his or her neighbor's shoulder. The *redondos* accompany a standard song and dance performed by one male-female couple at a time, the person of each gender being alternately replaced by someone from the audience. A man and a woman dance provocatively in circular movements as spectators form a circular arena around them. The dancers' movements and the formation of the onlookers—not the shape of the drums—are said to give this drum and its music the name *redondo* 'round.'

A rhythm and song known as *malembe* accompanies the street processions with the image of Saint John the Baptist. *Minas* or *redondos* accompany the *malembes* and processions with a unison rhythm or its variants notated in figure 5. Though *malembe* means 'softly, slowly, take it easy' in various Bantu languages, the people of Barlovento are not aware of its African roots and use it simply as the name of a kind of music.

In some communities, a statue of Saint John the Baptist is kept in the local church or chapel; in others, it may be kept in the home of a devotee or leader of a San Juan society. For his fiesta, the saint is dressed in red vestments and is paraded through the streets. Some larger images of the saint, such as that in Curiepe, are placed on platforms and carried on the shoulders of four or more people, who are more likely to be dancing than walking. At times, because of the carriers' gyrations, it seems that the statue will surely fall off the platform. One or more of the images may be danced about in the hands of a devotee. Saint John the Baptist is said to love danc-

FIGURE 5   Typical rhythms performed on drums (*minas* or *redondos*) to accompany the *malembe,* sung during street processionals when the statue of St. John the Baptist is carried on the Sunday morning of the saint's feast. Transcription by Max H. Brandt.

ing, and at certain moments during the festival, libations of rum or cane alcohol are sprinkled over the icon, giving the saint the reputation of a true reveler and the name San Juan Borrachero (Saint John the Drunkard). He is sometimes called San Juan Congo, San Juan Congolé, and San Juan Guaricongo (Liscano 1973:54), revealing a connection to the Congo basin of central Africa.

Tamunangue

One of the most famous expressions of music and dance in Venezuela is the *tamunangue,* from the state of Lara in the northwest of the country. It is a suite of dances and music, usually performed in honor of San Antonio de Padua (Saint Anthony of Padua), the patron saint of Lara. It is regularly performed on 13 June, the saint's feast, but can occur during the weeks before or after.

The music for the *tamunangue* consists of singing accompanied by stringed instruments or maracas and a drum of African origin. The *tamunangue* usually begins with the singing of *salves* dedicated to the Virgin Mary in a church or a chapel outside which the dance of the *tamunangue* will be performed. The *salves* are usually accompanied only by stringed instruments—the *cuatro,* the *cinco,* the *quinto,* the *lira,* the *cuatro de cinco cuerdas,* and the *cinco de seis cuerdas.* A *tamunangue* ensemble could have a minimum of two such instruments (one *cuatro* and one *cinco*), but many ensembles, often composed of musicians from diverse communities, have seven to ten.

The principal drum of the *tamunangue* (usually called *tamunango* but also called *tambor grande* and *cumaco*) resembles the *tambor grande* and the *cumaco* from the central coast. With one head nailed in place, the drum normally measures slightly more than one meter long and sits on the ground during performance. In addition to the rhythms played by hand on the drumhead by a drummer who sits on the drum while playing it, sticks (*palos,* also *laures*) are played on its side by one, two, or three men (*paleros* 'palo players') who bend over one or both sides of the drum behind the seated drummer. On some occasions, and especially when the ensemble graces processions, the large double-headed drum known in most parts of the country as *tambora* is used.

The *tamunangue* begins with the piece "*La Batalla*" ('The Battle'), also called a game (*juego*). It is followed by distinctive dances and pieces of music that vary slightly from one community to another. Aretz (1970) analyzes the most commonly performed eight pieces of the suite, which she lists in order of performance as "*La Batalla,*" "*La Bella,*" "*El Chichivamos*" or "*Yeyevamos,*" "*La Juruminga,*" "*El Poco a Poco,*" "*La Perrendenga,*" "*El Galerón,*" and "*El Seis Figuriao.*" "*La Batalla*" is a graceful stick dance accompanied by music. The stick (*palo*) or staff (*vera*), the size of a walking stick, is usually decorated. The battle, always between two men (regularly replaced), is gracefully executed with stick hitting stick, never touching opponents' bodies. Four lines of verse are sung in 2/4 time.

San Benito el Moro (Saint Benedict the Moor)

Saint Benedict the Moor, also known as Saint Benedict of Palermo and of San Fratello, is the patron saint of people from Venezuela's northwest coast around Lake Maracaibo, especially those of African descent. The festivities for the saint take place after Christmas and into the new year, accompanied by three or four drums mentioned earlier, called *chimbangueles.* The saint is represented by images or statues of a black man. Like Saint John the Baptist in central Venezuela, he takes on the Venezuelan creole mix of traits from Spanish, African, and possibly native American sources, resulting in a zest for both the profound and the sacred. Saint Benedict is associated with the drinking of rum, and he is thought to have an eye for beautiful women.

FIGURE 6   During the feast of Corpus Christi in San Francisco de Yare, Miranda, Venezuela, the dancing devils of Yare (*los diablos danzantes de Yare*) perform. *Left to right*: an unmasked musician-dancer plays a single maraca, another plays a *redoblante* (military-style drum), and a masked man dances. Photo by Max H. Brandt, 1973.

Los diablos danzantes de Yare *'The dancing devils of Yare'*

Many central-coastal communities, including Cata, Chuao, Naiguata, Patanemo, and San Francisco de Yare, have organizations of masked devil dancers who perform during the feast of Corpus Christi (Ortiz 1982). The most famous of them is San Francisco de Yare, in the upper Tuy Valley (figure 6). Music is less important in this tradition than in other Venezuelan festivals. The dancing devils of Yare are accompanied by a military-style drum (*redoblante*), single maracas carried by many masked dancers, and jingle bells attached to their clothing.

Secular music

The lullabies and children's songs of creole Venezuelans are based on European models. A rich corpus of children's music exists among many African cultures, but this kind of music seems not to have come to the Americas with African slavery. Scholars who have studied children's songs around the world have noted that they are more likely to be passed on from one generation of children to another than from adults to children. (This is not true, of course, of lullabies and other kinds of children's music.) Since few children were brought to the Americas as slaves, this might be one reason that traditional African children's songs are not found among African-Venezuelans. European migrations to Venezuela, however, did include children—which may have had some impact on the children's songs sung in Venezuela today and on children's songs fostered by the formal education of the Spanish elite.

Most chores and tasks in the Venezuelan countryside have songs to ease the burden of the labor. The most common are grain-pounding songs and milking songs. A once common sight in the Venezuelan countryside was *el pilón* 'the mortar', often operated by two women, each with a pestle, to grind or pound grain to the rhythm of a song. These songs, though, are seldom heard today, but we can still hear the milking songs, sung to pass the time and put the cow at ease so the milk will come easily. They are especially popular in the plains states. Other kinds of work-related songs include coffee-picking songs, clothes-washing songs, and songs to encourage beasts of burden that turn the machines that press juice from sugarcane (Ramón y Rivera 1969:30–31).

To most Venezuelans, the epitome of folk dance is the *joropo,* a music and dance influenced by both Africa and Europe and known as the national dance of Venezuela. This is a couple dance, and each participant normally holds one or both hands of the partner, in the same dance position used by European couples to dance a waltz.

FIGURE 7　Around Christmas, an *aguinaldo* ensemble plays in a Maracaibo home. *Left to right*: singer, *cuatro,* two *tambor* drums (played with sticks, rather than hands), and a *furruco* friction drum. Photo by Elena Constatinidou, 1996.

Year-end music: aguinaldos *and* gaitas

Several types of music performed during December (Christmastime) are nonliturgical and bridge the religious and secular categories. *Aguinaldos* are Christmas carols. Their texts can be religious and secular. The word *aguinaldo* in Venezuela also means 'Christmas gift'. Itinerant musicians perform this music at Christmastime as they go from house to house, a tradition called the *parranda.* (In neighboring Trinidad this tradition is called *parang,* a word thought to be an anglicized rendition of the Spanish word *parranda.*) The *aguinaldo* musicians usually expect a gift, which could well be a shot of rum or an *hallaca,* a Venezuelan Christmas delicacy, wrapped in a banana leaf.

The most characteristic musical instrument of the *aguinaldo* ensemble is the friction drum (*furruco,* also *furro*) (figure 7). Other instruments include one or two double-headed *tamboras,* one or more lutes (like the *cuatro* and the guitar), maracas, and a *charrasca. Aguinaldos* with religious texts usually accompany a Christmas procession called Las Pastoras, but the house-to-house revel (*la parranda*) is more likely to exhibit secular *aguinaldos.*

The music of the plains seems to dominate the traditional music scene during much of the year, and *aguinaldos* can be heard throughout cities, towns, and villages at Christmastime, along with holiday favorites from abroad. It is the *gaita,* though, that reigns at the end of the year, not only in the Lake Maracaibo area (where it originates), but also in Caracas and other communities. The traditional *gaita* of the state of Zulia is accompanied by a friction drum (*furruco*) and drums called *tamboras,* which can be of the standard double-headed type or small barrel-type or bongolike drums. Quite evident is how these drums are played: the drummer performs with a stick in each hand, one of which beats the side of the drum. *Tamboras* can be played between the legs while the player is sitting or supported by a strap while the player is standing. Standard secondary instruments, such as maracas and *charrascas,* also accompany *gaitas.*

Many *gaitas* heard today use electronic keyboards and other modern instruments in addition to the standard percussion instruments. The rapid beats of the *tambora,* though, and the growling of the *furruco,* make this kind of music easy to distinguish from other genres.

Secular dance and music: the *joropo* and its variants

Some creole music is not associated with dance, but most is. Partly because of urbanization, contemporary Venezuelans are less skilled at folk dancing than were their ancestors, though Venezuelan folk dancing is taught in most grade schools; most recorded folk music heard today on public broadcasting systems and on private systems in homes and vehicles is played for listening rather than for dancing. Venezuelan young people are no longer brought up in surroundings where folk dancing is a natural aspect of daily life. Nevertheless, most Venezuelans are aware of the association of dance with most of their folk music. The pieces of the *tamunangue* suite, for example, are more often associated with the dances than with the music accompanying them. Perhaps the greatest joy of participating in the San Juan festival in Barlovento, unless one is a key musician, comes from joining the public dancing to the *mina* ensemble or propelling oneself into the dances of the *redondos,* in which only one couple, through interchanges of partners, is dancing at any one time.

To most Venezuelans, the epitome of folk dance is the *joropo,* a music and dance influenced by both Africa and Europe and known as the national dance of Venezuela. The term *joropo* refers to more than just dance. It also denotes a genre of music and the event in which the music and dance are performed. A person can attend a *joropo* (event), request the performance of a particular *joropo* (musical piece), and then execute a *joropo* (dance). Most often, the term names the dance. This is a couple dance, and each participant normally holds one or both hands of the partner, in the same dance position used by European couples to dance a waltz, for example. (Usually many couples dance at once.) The dance involves both basic and intricate footwork. It is similar in style throughout Venezuela, but the musical ensembles that accompany it vary locally.

The term *joropo* was first used to describe an event in a rural setting with dance, string music, and song, and its meaning as a genre of dancing probably came in common usage around 1850; before then, a dance of this style was probably called a *fandango* (Ramón y Rivera 1969:191). People in the countryside may speak of a particular *joropo* as an event that took place in the past or one planned for the future. It can be on a small scale, organized by a family or a segment of a community, and may take place in a house. An excuse to have a modest *joropo* might be a baptism, a birthday party, or a visit by a special friend. Alternatively, it might be a more public event, perhaps as part of a communitywide fiesta coinciding with a national holiday or a religious celebration, such as that for the local patron saint. Such a *joropo* would probably take place in an outdoor public area or a community hall. Like many fiestas in Venezuela, it would probably start early in the evening and last until sunrise. In the early 1920s, it was much more important than it is today. It included not only musical entertainment and dancing but also special food and drink, children's play, and courtship.

As a musical piece, a *joropo* can be rather complex. There are many names for the musical forms that accompany the dance (Ramón y Rivera 1953). The list includes *joropo,* but four other words are more appropriate for classification: *corrido, galerón, golpe,* and *pasaje.* Even these are not mutually used in the same context by all musicians. The term *joropo* is often used for pieces that some might call *golpes* and especially for pieces in three, four, or more parts, written by famous composers, such as Pedro Elías Gutiérrez, Francisco de Paula Aguirre, and Carlos Bonet. The *joropos* of urban composers are now often performed in rural areas of Venezuela, and traditional pieces that might once have been called *golpes* or other names forgotten by younger performers are now simply called *joropos* (Ramón y Rivera 1967:54, 1969:191). *Revuelta* is another commonly used term for *joropo* music. It is usually an extended version of a *pasaje,* though both names are often used for the same kind of piece. Yet another commonly used term, *hornada* (a batch or ovenful), denotes a medley of *revueltas* or *pasajes.* Other names usually refer to particular movements, literary texts, or specific pieces, such as the *corrido* called "El Pajarillo" and the *golpe* called "La Refalosa."

Joropo music is rhythmically sophisticated, commonly notated with a double-time signature of 3/4 and 6/8, producing polyrhythms and an always present polymetric sense of simultaneous duple and triple figures (hemiola or *sesquiáltera*), which provide creative possibilities for instrumentalists and dancers. The tempo is always brisk (a common pace is 208 quarter notes a minute), keeping dancers and musicians active. Some vocal lines conform strictly to the accompaniment, especially in *golpes,* but much of singing demonstrates the "melodic independence" that Ramón y Rivera has often written about. This is a free style of singing, in which, excepting the beginnings or endings of certain long phrases, much of the vocal line does not coincide rhythmically or metrically with the instrumental accompaniment.

Melodies are clearly Spanish in character, but they have roots in Andalucía. The texts, sung in Spanish, relate to Spanish genres of early colonial days (such as the *romance* and the *décima*). Most melodies have fixed texts, but some texts are improvised. All this music is distinguished by having one musical note for each syllable of text.

The *joropo* *and the plains harp ensemble*

For accompanying *joropos,* the plains harp ensemble is probably the most famous in Venezuela. This is almost always an all-male ensemble and can be purely instrumental or can have one vocalist, also usually male. It is often presented as the trademark of Venezuelan traditional music, in part because of the attractiveness of the instrumental combination and its repertoire. During the dictatorship of Pérez Jiménez (1950–1958), this music came to the fore as a national symbol, supported by that government.

The *arpa llanera* is the featured melody instrument of the ensemble, sharing the melody role with the vocalist, who does not usually play an instrument. The other two instrumentalists play a *cuatro* and maracas. Since the mid-1900s, a fifth musician, playing an acoustic or electric string bass, has been added to accentuate the bass, traditionally played by the lower strings of the harp.

The *bandola,* a four-stringed, pear-shaped lute that takes the place of the harp in many ensembles (and which may have preceded the *arpa* in some Venezuelan communities), remains the melodic instrument of choice in the states of Barinas and Portuguesa; it is also played in Apure and Cojedes. An eight-stringed version of it appears in Miranda, Sucre, and Anzoategui. The virtuosity possible on the *bandola* has been ably demonstrated by Anselmo López, master of this lute. The instrument is plucked with a pick, so the lower two strings provide an ostinato, much like that of the lower strings of the harp; the higher strings, on alternate beats, play the melody. Performances on the plains harp are usually dashing and impressionistic, but the plains ensemble is equally appealing to most listeners when the *bandola* is the leading instrument.

In the plains ensemble, the *cuatro* provides the basic harmonic framework, plus a rhythmic pulse through its strumming (*rasgueado*). One might expect the maracas to provide a basic rhythmic background, but a good player of maracas (*maraquero*) can steal the show with rapid rhythmic embellishments, a subtle shifting of accents from triple to duple meter, and a masterful visual display of arm and hand techniques.

Joropo *and the central-coastal harp ensemble*

The *joropo* of the central coast (especially in the states of Aragua, Miranda, and the federal district, and in parts of Anzoategui, Sucre, and Carabobo) is traditionally accompanied by two male musicians—one who plays the harp and one who sings and plays maracas. An eight-stringed *bandola* (four double courses and similar in shape to the plains *bandola*) sometimes takes the place of the harp. The harp also differs somewhat from that of the plains; the sound board is slightly wider at the bottom, and the upper strings are metal, not nylon, though the lower strings are usually nylon or gut.

Central-coastal *joropo* music is less flamboyant than plains *joropo* music, and in form it is quite different. The vocal and instrumental melodies of the plains ensembles are songs with European-based harmonies and fixed texts, but the coastal style features shorter and more repetitive phrases, with melodies and texts more likely to be improvised. The harp makes complex melodic patterns.

The African cultural presence is more concentrated on the coast than on the plains. Because Barlovento is at the heart of this area, one would expect to find more African influences in this music than in plains *joropo* music. Indeed, the vocalist's improvisation recalls African musical traditions, as does the repetitiveness of themes and phrases—an important musical trait not always appreciated by those who do not know African music.

The golpe *of Lara*

The *golpe* of Lara State, somewhat northwest of the plains, is a cousin of the plains *joropo* in music and dance (Fernaud 1984). Its standard instrumentation is one or two *cuatros*, a *cinco*, a *tambora*, and a pair of maracas. Occasionally, other instruments—a violin, the large drum used for the *tamunangue*, a standard guitar—substitute or join the ensemble. Other instruments (such as an *arpa*, a *bandola*, and a *bandolín*) were formerly used but seldom appear today.

Instrumental and vocal *golpes* are almost always performed by men; women, however, participate in the dancing. Unless a bowed chordophone is involved, the melodies are carried by vocalists, usually a duo singing in thirds. Musicians claim that *golpe* music and dance are distinct from the plains *joropo,* especially in tempo, said to be slower and more sedate.

Other joropo *ensembles*

Though the two harp ensembles mentioned above are conspicuous for performing *joropo* music, other notable *joropo* ensembles exist. Many Venezuelans argue that the vocal part is the most important musical component of the *joropo,* but some *joropos* are purely instrumental, especially in the plains. If only one instrument is used, it probably would be a *cuatro.* If another musician were to accompany the *cuatrista,* it would probably be a *maraquero* ('maracas player'). A *joropo* with maracas alone or with maracas and voice would be possible but rare.

Children are expected to clap and sing, and certain instruments (such as sticks struck on the wooden bodies of the large drums) provide access for young people to play minor parts, even at the height of important celebrations.

SOCIAL STRUCTURE AND PERFORMANCE

Presentations of Venezuelan folk music in urban settings, at home and abroad, have since the 1960s often been organized and performed by university students and middle-class devotees of these traditions—citizens of ethnic and social backgrounds somewhat different from those who claim this music as their own. With the decline of the petroleum market in the final two decades of the twentieth century, a change that has brought economic strife to Venezuela, the number of urban performances by young people with roots in rural areas has surged. The core of this music remains in the countryside, performed by agricultural workers who, though not always having the educational and financial resources of their urban cousins, do have access to the carriers and surroundings of traditional culture. It has been passed on to them orally by older relatives and neighbors, who in turn lend their musical skills from earlier generations of local contacts. Since the 1980s, a revival of interest in creole traditions has produced hundreds of community-based performance groups scattered throughout the *ranchos* (poorer neighborhoods of Caracas), where few existed in the 1960s and 1970s.

Most instrumentalists continue to be men. Women contribute in an equally important way to the vocal music and dancing. Drummers in Barlovento, harpists in Apure, and players of cane flutes in the states of Zulia and Falcón to Sucre are almost always men, reflecting similar practices in native American, Iberian, and African cultures. Often a woman will play a maraca or another supporting instrument, but seldom do women serve as lead instrumentalists. In addition to enhancing vocal music, they usually play a prominent part in organizing fiestas, without which performances would not occur.

Middle-age and older men and women usually take the most prominent musical roles, but young people—from babies to teenagers—are always present at fiestas, encouraged to participate in making music. Children are expected to clap and sing, and certain instruments, such as sticks struck on the wooden bodies of the large drums, provide access for young people to play minor parts, even at the height of important celebrations. During less festive occasions, as when instruments are being made or prepared for performances, children are encouraged to touch and play them. Formal courses of instruction in folk music are more likely to be found in the schools of cities and major towns than in rural settings.

Most music described here was once maintained solely by rural people, including people of European descent, whereas the upper classes in towns and cities, especially the elite descendants of Europeans, regarded this music as inferior. This situation has changed, and Venezuelans of all social classes and walks of life tend to be proud of their folk music. In the last decade of the twentieth century, sometime during their schooling most Caraqueños are encouraged to learn to play the *cuatro,* dance the *joropo,* and absorb other aspects of Venezuelan folklore.

Musical Acculturation

Venezuelan folk music began to undergo substantial change during the mid-1900s, when large migrations from rural areas to urban centers began. The African-Venezuelan area of Barlovento is a good example of musical change.

Though Barlovento is close to Caracas, it was until the 1940s isolated by mountains, the lack of modern roads, and a reputation for malaria and other tropical illnesses. Isolation had an impact on the cultivation of African music, leading to its present fame. Since the early 1950s, these traditions have undergone major transformations, primarily because Venezuela's major eastern highway now penetrates Barlovento, allowing wealthy Venezuelans from the capital to purchase and develop its land. Likewise, in a reverse migration, many African-Venezuelans who have called Barlovento home for generations have moved to Caracas for better jobs, education, and health care. These changes at first had a detrimental impact on traditional drumming, since these people usually did not bring the instruments and their music, but folk music from the countryside became much more acceptable during the last decade of the twentieth century.

POPULAR MUSIC

The cities of Venezuela, especially Caracas, have genres of popular music, influenced in varying degrees by the music of the Venezuelan countryside and of other countries in the Americas and Europe. Ensembles and individual performers who became popular in the 1960s for drawing on Venezuelan folk music in their compositions and performances include such famous recording artists as the *cuatro* player Fredy Reyna, the internationally known folk singer Soledad Bravo, and popular groups such as El Cuarteto, Gurrufío, Quinteto Contrapunto, and Serenata Guayanesa.

Perhaps the best-known group to perform and promote both folk and popular music in Venezuela during the last decade of the twentieth century is Un Solo Pueblo, which has produce many CDs. Another important group is Tambor Urbano, with a CD entitled La Rumba, especially popular in 1997 and 1998, which features African-Venezuelan music of the central coast and especially the region of Barlovento. In 1998 the group known as ODILA (Orquesta de Instrumentos LatinAmericanos), the performance component of the Fundación de Etnomusicología y Folklore (FUNDEF), celebrated its fifteenth anniversary promoting not only Venezuelan folk music, but also music from various other countries of Latin America and the Caribbean. The performances of ODILA are based primarily on recordings and research conducted since the 1950s under the auspices of the former Instituto Nacional de Folklore (INAF), the former Instituto Interamericano de Etnomusicología y Folklore (INIDEF), and their succeeding organizations, such as FUNDEF.

The music of Venezuela portrays an exquisite model of the Amerindian, European and African layers of culture that make up the identity of this important region of Latin America. Intertwined with rituals, fiestas, and dances, the music unique to this vibrant South American country continues to endure and embodies a fundamental ingredient of the national psyche. To experience Venezuelan music is to capture the essence of a positive national pride and beauty that is truly remarkable.

FURTHER STUDY

The most comprehensive study of indigenous Venezuelan music is by Aretz (1991), who presents a survey of twenty-three Venezuelan societies that exist in various states of acculturation. A brief synopsis of her work on this subject appears as an article in *The World of Music* (1982). Before making a detailed musical inventory of each ethnic group, Aretz discusses the consequences of musical contact with Europeans, gives an overview of studies, and presents the general traits of Venezuelan indigenous vocal and instrumental music. She cites publications that deal with the missionaries and explorers of early colonial days, the scientific expeditions of the eighteenth and early twentieth centuries that mention musical culture, and the more concentrated efforts of ethnomusicologists and other scholars interested in this subject. Photos, illustrations, and charts make this publication important, even for those who do not read Spanish. Other important studies (including recordings) of Venezuelan Amerindians include Agerkop (1983), Coppens (1975), Olsen (1996), and Ramón y Rivera (1992).

A publication on the music of Caracas (R. Salazar 1994) surveys the music of the Caracas valley from the time of the first known encounters between Amerindians and Europeans to the most famous popular groups of the late twentieth century. It covers scores of urban genres and performers—those with minimal ties to rural Venezuela and individuals and ensembles using Venezuelan rural sources in their works. A perspective on the music of the *joropo,* the first major work on this subject since Ramón y Rivera's classic work of 1953, is a book and compact disc by Rafael Salazar entitled *El Joropo y Sus Andanzas* (1992a). The *décima* has been studied in detail by Ramón y Rivera (1992). Other relevant works by Rafael Salazar are *Latinoamérica es Música* (1992b) and *Memorial del Canto* (n.d.).

Since music is an important part of most festivals (*fiestas*) in Venezuela, at least two books are important. One is *Fiestas Tradicionales de Venezuela* by Daria Hernández and Cecilia Fuentes (1993), with photographs by Nelson Garrido. The other is *Diablos Danzantes de Venezuela,* edited by Manuel Antonio Ortiz (1982).

A study of African-Venezuelan music by Max H. Brandt (1994) focuses on the aspect of music as identity among the people and musicians of Barlovento. It includes photos of African-Venezuelan drummers. In addition to written sources that address musical instruments (especially Aretz 1967), excellent recordings outline the distribution of creole instruments in Venezuela, such as *Folklore de Venezuela* (1971), *The Music of Venezuela* (1990), *Música Popular Tradicional de Venezuela* (1983), and those by Lares (1969, 1978a, 1978b).

REFERENCES

Agerkop, Terry. 1983. *Piaroa.* Caracas: Cajas Audiovisuales INIDEF.

Anuario FUNDEF, Año IV. 1993. Caracas: Fundación de Etnomusicología y Folklore.

Aretz, Isabel. 1967. *Instrumentos Musicales de Venezuela.* Cumaná: Universidad de Oriente.

———. 1970. *El Tamunangue.* Barquisimeto: Universidad Centro Occidental.

———. 1982. "Indigenous Music of Venezuela." *The World of Music* 25(2): 22–35.

———.1991. *Música de Los Aborígenes de Venezuela.* Caracas: Fundación de Etnomusicología y Folklore.

Brandt, Max H. 1994. "African Drumming from Rural Communities around Caracas and Its Impact on Venezuelan Music and Ethnic Identity." In *Music and Black Ethnicity: The Caribbean and South America,* ed. Gerard H. Béhague, 267–284. Miami: North-South Center, University of Miami.

Coppens, Walter. 1975. *Music of the Venezuelan Yekuana Indians.* Folkways Records FE 4101. LP disk.

Danzas y Canciones Para Los Niños. 1981. Caracas: Ediciones Fredy Reyna. LP disk.

Esparragoza, Maria Eugenia. 1991. *Salto en el Atlántico.* Research by Jesús García. 16mm film.

Fernaud, Alvaro. 1984. *El Golpe Larense.* Caracas: Fundación de Etnomusicología y Folklore.

Folklore de Venezuela. 1971. Caracas: Sonido Laffer. 8 LP disks.

García, Jesús. 1990. *Africa en Venezuela: Pieza de Indias.* Caracas: Cuadernos Lagoven.

Garfias, Robert. 1979. "The Venezuelan Harp." *Folk Harp Journal* 24:13–16.

Hernández, Daria, and Cecilia Fuentes. 1993. *Fiestas Tradicionales de Venezuela.* Caracas: Fundación Bigott.

Lares, Oswaldo. 1969. *Música de Venezuela: Indio Figueredo (Homenaje al Indio Figueredo).* Caracas: Oswaldo Lares. LP disk.

———. 1978a. *Danzas y Cantos Afrovenezolanos.* 1978. Caracas: Oswaldo Lares. LP disk.

———. 1978b. *Música de Venezuela: Cantos y*

Danzas e La Costa Central. Caracas: Oswaldo Lares. LP disk.

Liscano, Juan. 1943. "Baile de tambor." *Boletín de la Sociedad Venezolana de Ciencias Naturales* 8(5):245–252.

———. 1960. "Lugar de origen de los tambores redondos barloventeños." *Revista Shell* 8(35): June.

———. 1973. *La Fiesta de San Juan El Bautista.* Caracas: Monte Avila Editores.

The Music of Venezuela. 1990. Memphis: Memphis State University. High Water Recording Company, LP1013. LP disk.

Música Popular Tradicional de Venezuela. 1983. Caracas: Instituto Nacional del Folklore. LP disk.

Olsen, Dale A. 1980a. "Folk Music of South America—A Musical Mosaic." In *Musics of Many Cultures: An Introduction,* ed. Elizabeth May, 386–425. Berkeley: University of California Press.

———. 1980b. "Symbol and Function in South American Indian Music." In *Musics of Many Cultures: An Introduction,* ed. Elizabeth May, 363–385. Berkeley: University of California Press.

———. 1996. *Music of the Warao of Venezuela: Song People of the Rain Forest.* Gainesville: University Press of Florida. Compact disc with book.

Ortiz, Manuel Antonio. 1982. *Diablos Danzantes de Venezuela.* Caracas: Fundación La Salle de Ciencias Naturales.

Pollak-Eltz, Angelina. 1972. *Cultos Afroamericanos.* Caracas: Universidad Católica Andres Bello.

———. 1994. *Black Culture and Society in Venezuela.* Caracas: Lagoven.

Quintana M., Hugo J. 1995. "Música aborigen en los cronistas de Indias." *Revista Montalbán* 8:157–175.

Ramón y Rivera, Luís Felipe. 1950. "La percusión de los negros en la música americana." *Boletín de la Sociedad Venezolana de Ciencias Naturales* 8(5):245–252.

———. 1953. *El joropo, baile nacional de Venezuela.* Caracas: Ediciones del Ministerio de Educación.

———. 1967. *Música Indígena, Folklórica y Popular de Venezuela.* Buenos Aires: Ricordi Americana.

———. 1969. *La Música Folklórica de Venezuela.* Caracas: Monte Ávila Editores.

———. 1971. *La Música Afrovenezolana.* Caracas: Universidad Central de Venezuela.

———. 1992. *La Música de la Décima.* Caracas: Fundación de Etnomusicología y Folklore.

Salazar, Briseida. 1990. *San Benito: Canta y Baila Con Sus Chimbangueleros.* Caracas: Fundación Bigott.

Salazar, Rafael. N.d. *Memorial del Canto.* Caracas: Banco Industrial de Venezuela.

———. 1992a. *Del Joropo y Sus Andanzas.* Caracas: Disco Club Venezolano. Book and compact disc.

———. 1992b. *Latinoamérica es Música.* Caracas: Ediciones Disco Club Venezolano.

———. 1994. *Caracas: Espiga Musical del Ávila.* Caracas: Disco Club Venezolano. Book and compact disc.

Sojo, Juan Pablo. 1976 [1943]. *Nochebuena negra.* Los Teques: Biblioteca Popular Mirandina, Gobernación del Estado Miranda.

Section 3
Mexico: One Country, Many Musics

Mexico is often seen as a land with a varied topography and at least three cultural identities—native pre-Columbian, Spanish colonial, and modern mestizo—but in reality it is much more complex and varied. Contemporary native Mexican groups speak fifty-four languages, and the twentieth-century emergence of a national identity has embraced diverse strands of regional mestizo culture. Music has been a major signifier of these cultures. The large bass guitar shown opposite and known as the *guitarrón* is featured in mariachi groups that seem to typify Mexico by their presence in many Mexican restaurants in the United States. In reality, the instrument and mariachi itself are rooted in just one of Mexico's cultures—that of Jalisco and the surrounding states of western central Mexico—and especially in the city of Guadalajara.

Major population growth and serious unemployment brought massive migration that moved three-quarters of the Mexican people to urban areas and made Mexico City the most populous city in the world. An influential commercial media industry centered in Mexico City disseminates popular music from Mexico and abroad—particularly from the United States—and exports Mexican music to countries throughout the Americas.

Francisco Castro of Guadalajara, a *guitarrón* player in a strolling mariachi orchestra, poses in a café. Photo by Daniel E. Sheehy, 1984.

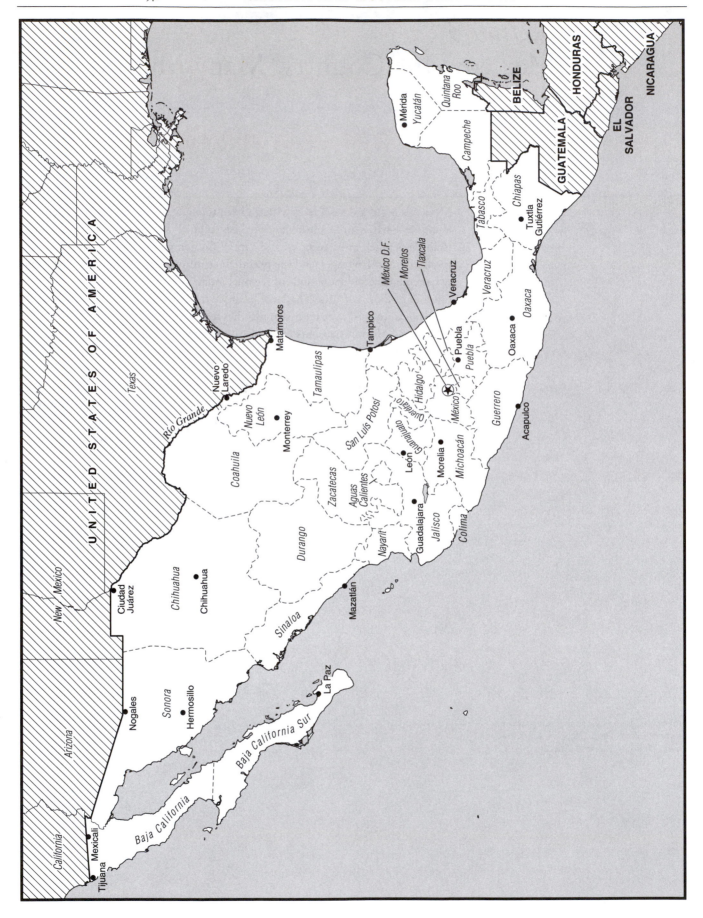

The Music of Mexico's Native People

Daniel E. Sheehy

Native Musical Traditions
Native Musical Instruments

opposite: Mexico

Mexican Amerindian culture is varied and complex, and there are many native American musical traditions in Mexican territory (see map 3). Fifty-four native languages are spoken in Mexico, perhaps half the number thought to have been extant at the time of the Encounter. Although a few native groups have lived in relative isolation since the early 1500s, most have experienced significant political and cultural oppression, evangelization, and acculturation. About 10 percent of Mexicans speak Amerindian languages; most of those also speak Spanish. Through isolation, as with the Lacandón Maya [see MAYA], or resistance, as with the Yaqui [see YAQUI AND MAYO], some groups have maintained a high degree of continuity in many of their cultural and musical practices. Many communities maintain a sense of native American identity while accepting Spanish religious beliefs and customs and adopting Spanish musical practices, instruments, and occasions for performance. It is often difficult to draw a line between native American and mestizo musics, given that the latter are by definition a blend of native American and other cultural elements.

NATIVE MUSICAL TRADITIONS

The variety of Mexican Amerindian musical traditions defies generalization, but a few traits are shared by nearly all: music is strongly linked to ceremonial or ritual occasions, though songs of love, lullabies, and humorous songs also exist; most music is intended to accompany dance and has a regular, marked, rhythmic pulse; instrumental performance predominates; singing is usually in a high range. The ritual occasion may be one of many possibilities: a Maya shamanic chant to encourage sufficient rain for the season's crops; the Totonac dance of the flying men (*danza de los voladores*), in which four men swing around a pole from a rope tied to their feet, to the accompaniment of a cane flute and drum in seasonal homage to Mother Earth; or a Mixtec *banda* performing on the village saint's day as a promise (*manda*) to God, a saint, the Virgin Mary, or some other religious figure. In keeping with its ties to social and religious function, music is generally not conceived of as "art for art's sake," a separate activity to be cultivated solely for aesthetic pleasure. Dancing can be communal, or it can be quite individualized as in the Yaqui dance of the deer (*danza del venado*), in which a single dancer evokes the spirit and movements of the deer.

huéhuetl Nahua large single-headed, cylindrical, hollowed-out log drum, also used by the Maya

teponaztli Nahua hollowed-out log slit drum or gong with an H-shaped incision on the top

ayotl Nahua name for a tortoiseshell idiophone struck with deer antlers

banda 'Band,' usually a brass band or large ensemble of European-derived wind instruments

Dance music most often takes the form of one or more *sones,* short melodies of one or two simple phrases. *Sones* are usually repeated at least several times each, and when they are strung together in continuous fashion, the changing of the *son* usually coincides with the changing of the choreography.

NATIVE MUSICAL INSTRUMENTS

There is a great diversity of musical instruments across the native American cultures of Mexico. Certain instruments—such as the Yaqui *baa wéhai,* an idiophone consisting of half a large gourd placed closed side up in a container of water and struck with a stick—are particular to a given group. Many musical instruments are distributed widely among multiple groups. The pipe-and-tabor combination of duct flute and double-headed drum played by a single person is found in virtually all areas of Mexico. The *huéhuetl* and *teponaztli* have survived from pre-Encounter times in the east-central and southern parts of the country. Small rattles strung around dancers' legs, gourd stick rattles, and a tortoiseshell idiophone (*ayotl*) are found in various places. Instruments of European origin are used widely by many groups: the harp, the violin, and the guitar took root early in the colonial period, and one or all of them are now central to the traditional music of the Tzotzil Maya, the Yaqui, the Purépecha (also Tarascan) [see PURÉPECHA], and many others. Typical of the conservatism of Amerindian music, another early colonial importation, the double-reed aerophone *chirimía,* is now played exclusively by native Americans, particularly the Purépecha of Michoacán and the Nahua of Puebla and Tlaxcala. Wind and percussion instruments associated with brass bands make up the instrumentation of small and large *bandas* in Amerindian towns and villages in central and southern Mexico.

Guarijio

J. Richard Haefer

Guarijio History and Ethnography
Ceremonial Music
Further Study

About two thousand Guarijio (Varojió, Warihio, Huaraijió) live in the foothills, low mesas, banks (*barrancas*), and mountain slopes along the upper Río Mayo, on the western side of the Sierra Madre Occidental in southern Sonora, Mexico. This area, northeast of Navajoa, Sonora, varies from lowland desert to steep mountainsides covered with trees and shrubs, predominantly oak at lower elevations and pine forests at higher ones. Possibly the least known of all the indigenous peoples of Mexico, the Guarijio are members of the Sonoran Tara-Cahitan branch of the Uto-Aztecan language family (Miller 1983). The majority live in the state of Sonora; those who live on the highest peaks dwell in the state of Chihuahua. This distribution is important, not for governmental demographic reasons, but because environmental considerations functionally divide the Guarijio into upland and lowland dialects. Ceremonially and musically, however, these groups celebrate the same rites with the same instruments and songs.

GUARIJIO HISTORY AND ETHNOGRAPHY

Little is known about Guarijio prehistory. Because of the geographic distance from central Mexico, all the Sonoran peoples showed little of late Mesoamerican origin in their customs at the time of the Encounter. Early missionaries said the Chínipas, Guasapan (Guazapares), and Témoris (most likely extinct Guarijio groups of dialects, or possibly peoples related to the Tarahumara) lived near the Guarijio, who may have separated from the Tarahumarans some five hundred years ago. Proselytized in the late 1600s, the Guarijio were uncooperative. Rather than remaining in mission life, they often revolted and returned to the sierras (Pérez de Ribas 1944 [1645]). Only one major mission church remains in the heart of Guarijio land.

Though Hispanic contact and its attendant missionization was made nearly four hundred years ago, Mexican ranchers now dominate the area by owning most of the land. The Guarijio were thought to be extinct but were rediscovered in the early 1930s, when about sixteen hundred Guarijio were living (Gentry 1963). The lowland peoples were "much acculturated" and the upland peoples "remain[ed] distinct" (Hinton 1983). Most lowland men are employed by local ranchers, though their socioeconomic position resembles late-eighteenth-century indenturement more than

Guarijio ceremonial texts, presented in a variant musical language, speak of things native to the locale, such as bees, beehives, birds, various animals and plants, and the natural process of reproduction.

modern wage-based employment. Lowland men speak enough Spanish to function as workers, but children and women were monolingual in the native language into the 1980s. Families continue living in small villages in the mountains, but men live at the hamlets (*rancherías*) where they work. Only a few families live in Mexican-Indian villages such as San Bernardo, near the southern edge of their homeland.

Most families reside in one- or two-room huts (*jacales*) made of wattle and daub, and occasionally of adobe or stone, with thatched roofs and an attached brush enclosure (*ramada*). Household possessions are centered in the *ramada,* which serves for cooking and sleeping, and consists of coiled and scraped pottery ollas and bowls, twilled baskets and sleeping mats, woven woolen blankets and sashes, and handmade wooden stools, benches, and tables. Modern appurtenances, including portable radios or boomboxes, are available only to those living in the Mexican-style villages. Musicians' rattles, violins, and harps are stored in one of the rooms when not in use.

The primary method of transportation is walking, usually following the river and streambeds. Once a month, if they walk to one of the local Mexican-Indian villages, Guarijio who get a government stipend receive transportation to a town where they can buy staples more cheaply than in the hamlets. In the early 1980s, a government school and clinic was opened at Mesa Colorado, providing the first formal schooling and first local medical treatment for the Guarijio. However, for most of them, the coming of education and medical treatment has brought few changes in their lifeways.

CEREMONIAL MUSIC

The major ceremony practiced by the Guarijio, the *túmari,* includes two distinct activities: the *tuburada* and the *pascola.* All known musical activities center on these rites, normally presented simultaneously in adjacent spaces; the former may be performed without benefit of the latter. A brief description of the events illustrates local musical material culture, music, and dances; enculturation and syncretisms in the events; and social relationships and musical interactions.

The *túmari* (*túguri, tuwúri,* cognate with Tarahumara *tutubúri*) is celebrated irregularly throughout the year for thanksgiving, benediction, propitiation, fertilization, and/or curing, possibly (but not always) related to the agricultural cycle. It functions as a social and religious celebration, and it may have been the basis for pre-Columbian communitywide interaction (Hinton 1983). Guarijio territory may be divided into four overlapping *túmari* areas on the basis of attendance patterns (Gentry 1963). Contemporary ceremonies appear to attract members of localized groups of hamlets, with minimal attendance from more distant villages and a few Mayo visitors. Local Mexican ranchers are asked to leave before the ceremony starts.

Túmari begins with the placement of a shrouded cross, a censer, and a rosary (made from local seeds) in the plaza. A chanter (*wikatáme turélo, seleme*) conducts a preliminary rite, which contains elements of Christianity such as making the sign of the cross (in the threefold Mexican manner) and perfuming the cross with incense, and traditional elements including offering ritual food or seeds (depending on the intent of the ritual and its relation to the agricultural cycle) and playing rattles. In the preliminary rite, men place their hats near the cross. The preliminary rite ends with an extensive extemporaneous sermon preached to all assembled around the *tuburada* area, women on the east, men on the west. This discourse, spoken in Guarijio, often invokes the aid of Roman Catholic saints, especially the Blessed Virgin Mary and San Isidro (Saint Isidore the Farmer, patron of agriculture), while informing the people about the reasons for the celebration and encouraging them to act responsibly by not consuming alcoholic beverages, though agave liquor (*tesgüino*) was consumed in the past (Gentry 1963).

The *tuburada,* which begins after the admonition and a triple blessing of the people, is the only documented autochthonous Guarijio ritual event, despite its aspects of Christianity. It is led by a chanter (*turélo*) and two assistants, who sit on a bench facing the plaza. The dance begins when several younger girls form a line shoulder to shoulder, facing the singers and moving forward and backward between the singers and the cross. To the beat of the song, they stamp their right feet loudly on the hard *caliche* surface of the ground. As the night progresses, they are joined by successively older women, at times in groups of two dozen or more. Each singer shakes a gourd rattle (*hali'*), the only traditional musical instrument used by the Guarijio; it is made from *buli,* a native gourd (*Lagenaria siceraria*).

The songs are brief and repetitive (two or three phrases with variations), but have a rising feature resembling that of songs of Yuman and Baja cultures to the north, including the typical change in the rattle-played pattern from a strong-beat sequence to a continuous roll at the rise. A second genre progresses at a faster tempo and lacks the rise. Guarijio ceremonial texts, presented in a variant musical language, speak of things native to the locale, such as bees, beehives, birds, various animals and plants, and the natural process of reproduction. The singing lasts all night (about twelve hours), with pauses from time to time.

A while after the *tuburada* is firmly established, the sound of violins and harp can be heard from the *pascola ramada,* about 50 to 75 meters away. Normally, two violinists (*yaweros*) play their violins (*yaweras*) with a single harpist. The *yaweras,* patterned after the Brescian-style violin of the late 1600s, are made entirely of local woods. The harp (*paracá*) usually has twenty-five strings, the highest nineteen made of monofilament, and the lowest six made of twisted goat gut. The Guarijio are known as the finest craftsmen of these instruments in the area, though similar instruments made by their Yaqui, Mayo, and Tarahumara neighbors are more widely known outside the area. The group performs throughout the night with the exception of a brief period in the middle when the violinists leave to eat, and the harpist will then perform solos.

The music is of two types—the *contradanza* and the *son principal*— distinguishable by variations in tempo, meter, and accompanimental rhythmic pattern; the forms are similar, and the opening and closing formulas are constant. The *contradanza* is in duple meter with a triple subdivision (6/8) at a tempo of about 120 beats per minute. The accompanying pattern in the bass of the harp consists of chords played on the beat, interrupted with the Mexican style *contratiempo* syncopation every four to twelve beats. The *sòn principal* is in duple meter with a duple subdivision and a faster tempo (about 144 beats per minute). It is usually played without syncopation, accompanied by a short–short–long rhythm in the harp. Formally, both genres consist of short stanzas lasting less than a minute and a half, repeating for up to twelve minutes, depending on the dancers' wishes. Each stanza has four phrases in an *aabc* or *abcd* pattern, the final phrase being as long as the first three. Melodic intensity is developed by repetition and variation. The second violin harmonizes in thirds with the first. Both genres begin with a stylized introductory formula consisting of eight to twelve beats sounding the tonic chord. The closing formula is a progression in a I–IV–V–I chordal pattern. Most scales have seven tones; a few have five. Though the harmony and instruments are of European derivation, the melodies appear to be traditional. Throughout the night, the tempi increase and the tuning of the instruments rises, as is typical of the Guarijio-Mayo-Yaqui *pascola* complex. The tunings are named for local animals (frog, owl, and so on).

The dancing of the *pascola* provides a comic relief to the solemnity of the *tuburada*. Three *pascola* are led to the *ramada* by their manager (*moro*), masks covering their heads. The opening rite, a speech (in mixed Spanish and Guarijio) mocking that of the chanter and exhorting the people to enjoy the fiesta, is followed by a risqué burlesque, in which the *pascola* mimic a sexual act by inserting the manager's stick into the sound holes of the harp to shouts of encouragement from the observers, mostly men, though a few women may watch this opening rite. After the opening dance, the *pascola* perform in turn (youngest to oldest), wearing their masks on the backs of their heads—a practice different from that of the Yaqui and the Mayo, who wear the mask on the side of their heads. Several noisemakers are part of the regalia. The most unusual are *chairígoas* (better known by the Yaqui term *teneboim*), rattles made from the cocoons of the giant silkmoth and wrapped around the dancers' legs from ankle to knee. Exacting footwork produces a swishing sound from them. A *coyole,* a belt with "hawk's bells" (small, claw-shaped metal bells), is worn around the dancer's waist. In the middle of the dancer's back, under the *coyole,* is stuck a sistrum (*senasum*), which the *pascola* shake with their hands only during the first and last dances.

Soon after daybreak, the *pascola* stop dancing, and the chanter concludes the ceremony with communal prayers to the supernatural and an oration to the community. The *pascola* then terminate the activities with one final dance, which all gather to watch. The *túmari* ends with a meal of goat stew (*wepasuni*).

FURTHER STUDY

The study by Gentry (1963), though dated, remains the most comprehensive survey of the Guarijio. So little has been written about Guarijio music, however, and so little recorded sound—only one cut on a commercial LP disk (*Indian Music of Northwestern Mexico* 1978)—is available that it is virtually impossible to make suggestions for further study that would not require fieldwork or access to tapes in private collections.

REFERENCES

Gentry, Howard S. 1963. *The Warihio Indians of Sonora-Chihuahua: An Ethnographic Survey.* Washiongton, D.C.: Bureau of American Ethnology. Bulletin 186.

Hinton, Thomas B. 1983. "Southern Periphery: West." In *Southwest,* ed. Alfonso Ortiz, 315–328. Handbook of North American Indians, 10. Washington, D.C.: Smithsonian Institution Press.

Indian Music of Northwestern Mexico. 1978. Canyon Records C8001. LP disk.

Miller, Wick. 1983. "Uto-Aztecan Languages." *Southwest,* ed. Alfonso Ortiz, 113–124. Handbook of North American Indians, 10. Washington, D.C.: Smithsonian Institution Press.

Pérez de Ribas, Andrés. 1944 [1645]. *Historia de los triumfos de nuestra Santa Fé entre gentes las más bárbaras y fieras del Nuevo Orbe.* México, D.F.: Editorial "Layac."

Mexica (Aztec or Nahua People)

Arturo Chamorro

Early Mexica Culture
Musical Instruments
Musical Contexts and Genres

The oldest known version of Náhuatl, a member of the Uto-Aztecan linguistic family (Greenberg 1987:381), was spoken by the Mexica people in pre-Columbian times. During the expansion of the Aztec Empire, it spread to other parts of Mesoamerica and served many native Americans as a lingua franca. Today, it has regional dialects. The Mexica were the bearers of a strong tradition of music and dance, particularly in the context of religious ceremonies, which they disseminated widely in many parts of what is now Mexico and Central America; like their language, these traits have regional variants in contemporary life.

EARLY MEXICA CULTURE

Archaeological discoveries of the twentieth century have revealed the former use of ceramic tubular duct flutes with holes (many with multiple tubes), globular flutes (some with multiple chambers) with and without holes, and other ductless aerophones. There is evidence pro and con for the existence of polyphony or multipart texture in ancient Mexico. Charles Boilès (1965:218) posited that a particular notion of harmony could be explored based on archaeological evidence from the Totonacapán region in Veracruz, where he found triple vertical flutes made of clay. Samuel Martí (1968: 210) came to the same conclusion, on the basis of the discovery of quadruple vertical flutes from Teotihuacán. José Raúl Hellmer (1960) noticed that quadruple vertical flutes produce not only chords but two or more melodic lines. Robert M. Stevenson (1968:84) agreed that pre-Columbian cultures had harmony; however, he insisted that the notion of multipart texture has to be understood within the concept of parallelism.

In pre-Columbian times, the notion of melody may have been subordinated to the prosody of native languages (Mendoza 1984:28). Ceramic flutes may not necessarily have been used for musical purposes because they were found only in burials for their symbolic content (Schöndoube 1986:99).

Archaeological and historical evidence, the latter including chronicles written by Franciscan and Augustinian missionaries shortly after the Spanish conquest, indicate that within the Aztec Empire during the early 1500s there was probably no Nahua concept equivalent to the Spanish notion of music. The latter was introduced primar-

"With the rattling sounds and with their mouths
they produced great noise, diverse body movements
that were disordered and out of beat, and every so
often they uttered some sounds, saying words that
probably nobody would understand."
—Sixteenth-century Spanish account
of Aztec music and dance

ily by Roman Catholic missionaries, who taught European religious songs and
hymns. Many terms in classic Náhuatl, however, reveal indigenous concepts related
to music, including singing (*cuica tlamatiliztli*), dancing (*netotiliztli*), sound or noise
(*caquiliztli*), and the sound of trumpets (*tlatlazcaliztli*) (Molina 1966). Although it
is not wise to explain Nahua music in terms of parallel musical concepts in European
cultures, Nahua notions about the organized production of sounds were often
expressed in terms of sound-producing actions and expressive movements of the
human body, such as blowing through certain aerophones, using different manners
of percussion, and creating sounds with the feet. From these facts, we may surmise
that there was a strong link between music and dance.

One typical written historical reference concerning this connection (Durán
1967:121) reveals that the Spaniards perceived Aztec instrumental sounds as being
senseless and disorganized, though demonstrating deep religiosity:

> As a guide for their dance, they had an Indian who was dressed in the same way as
> their idol was dressed, like a bird or a bat, with its wings, ornamented comb, and
> long feathers. On their feet and wrists the dancers wore rattles, according to cus-
> tom. With the rattling sounds and with their mouths they produced great noise,
> many expressions, diverse body movements that were disordered and out of beat
> with the others, and every so often they uttered some sounds, saying words that
> few people or probably nobody would understand.

This performance occurred during the celebration of the ancient Aztec calendrical
month Xocotl Huetzi (When the Fruits Fall), a festival among several dedicated to
Xiuhtecuhtli (Yellow Face), the god of fire, one of the main deities of the Mexica
pantheon (Sahagún 1956:1:2:188). Other festivals with dances and music honored
Xochiquetzali (Feathered Flower), goddess of the moon. But two specific gods for
music and dance were honored in the festival Xochilhuitl (Flower Festival). One of
them was Xochipilli (Flower Prince), the solar deity of dance, music, flowers, games,
love, pleasure, and poetry, whose counterpart was Macuilxóchitl (Five Flowers), the
patron of dance and games (Stevenson 1968:8).

Xochipilli had a close affiliation with Xochiquetzali (Fernández 1959:35;
Soustelle 1950:40,88). There was a difference, however: Xochipilli was a solar and
masculine deity, the patron of poetry, dance, music, and art; Xochiquetzali was a
lunar and feminine deity, the patron of painters and other artisans, and partner of
Tezcatlipoca (Smoked Mirror), one of the main gods of the Mexica pantheon.

MUSICAL INSTRUMENTS

Important musical instruments used for music and dance included struck idiophones
and membranophones, plus certain aerophones. Two of the former—the *teponaztle*
and the *huéhuetl*—were legendary in Mesoamerica. The *teponaztle* (also *teponaztli*)

FIGURE 1   Two pre-Columbian Nahua slit
drums (*teponaztle*), preserved in the National
Museum of Anthropology in Mexico City. The
upper instrument is wood engraved with an
image of Cuauhtli-Ocelotl (Eagle-Ocelot); the
lower instrument is ceramic, probably used for
votive offerings. Photo by Dale A. Olsen, 1970.

was a log idiophone made from a small, hollowed-out trunk of a tree, with an H-shaped slit cut into it, producing two tongues. This instrument was positioned horizontally and struck with mallets. Each tongue produced a distinct pitch. Some ancient *teponaztle* preserved in the National Museum of Anthropology in Mexico City (figure 1) are of woods that produce a loud sound and are intricately engraved with important images such as the deities Macuilxóchitl and Cuauhtli-Ocelotl (Eagle-Ocelot) and a serpent (*cóatl*). The *huéhuetl* was a single-headed cylindrical membranophone fashioned from a hollowed-out log (figure 2). Its size varied, but its dimensions reached a meter in length and 42 centimeters in diameter. Set in a vertical position with a head made from an animal skin, it was played with the hands.

Pictographs in early colonial codices, particularly the Florentine Codex (Sahagún 1956), offer important information about how the ancient Nahua played their percussion instruments in particular situations. The Codex Borbonicus (Paso y Troncoso 1979) describes the ancient calendars, rituals, cyclical celebrations, ceremonies commemorating the months of the Aztec year and other celebrations of the Aztec world. These codices offer ancient visual representations of Mexica culture and include many images of the dance associated with the sounds of the *teponaztle*, the *huéhuetl,* rattles, and conch trumpets. There are frequent allusions to the *teponaztle* and the *huéhuetl* in sixteenth-century chronicles by Durán, Sahagún, Diego de Landa (1959), Bernal Díaz del Castillo (1928), and Diego Muñoz Camargo (1947) and in precolonial native paintings such as those found in the Florentine Codex, the *Atlas Durán* (appended to Durán 1967), and other codices from the Mexica culture (Seler 1960).

A description by Diego Muñoz Camargo (1947:146) tells how the *huéhuetl* and *teponaztle* were often played to accompany dances:

> They had drums made with great beauty, tall ones, more than a half a man's height; and another instrument called *teponaxtle* [sic], made of a single log, rounded and hollowed out, whose sound carries more than half a league. Together with the drum they make strange and smooth sounds. With these drums, along with wooden trumpets and other instruments such as flutes, they produce a strange and admirable noise, and songs and dances so in rhythm that it is a sight to behold.

FIGURE 2   A pre-Columbian Nahua drum (*huéhuetl*) body fashioned from a hollowed-out log and preserved in the National Museum of Anthropology, Mexico City. Photo by Dale A. Olsen, 1970.

Modern uses of ancient instruments

Today, the *teponaztle* is still in use and has various functions. Among some Nahua people from middle and west Mexico, certain patterns of sound played on the instrument have a communicative function. In Tlaxcala, a few such patterns have been learned through syllabic formulas in the Nahua language, like the following:

Nahua:	nacatamal	kemaca	tleco kix	kemaca
Syllabic formulas:	na-ca-ta-mal	ke-ma-ca	tle-co kix	ke-ma-ca
English:	corn dumpling	yes there are	fire to get	yes there are

In San Bernardino Contla, Tlaxcala, Nahua drummers play this pattern on a tall vertical drum of the *huéhuetl* type to announce from afar a festival in honor of the patron saint. The sound of the drum is audible at a great distance. The Nahua of Pómaro, Michoacán, still play the *teponahuastle* (a version of the *teponaztle*) to announce the events of Christian ceremonies (figure 3).

In the valley of Puebla and Tlaxcala in central Mexico, the *huéhuetl* accompanies certain parts of Christian ceremonies, calls people to mass, and announces the beginning of patron saints' celebrations. In these settings, it forms part of the *conjunto azteca,* an ensemble that includes a *huéhuetl*-style drum, a snare drum, and a pair of *chirimías* (double-reed aerophones). This type of ensemble is heard during Christian festivities in most Nahua- and Otomí-speaking towns in the Puebla-Tlaxcala Valley.

FIGURE 3   A man from Pómaro, Michoacán, Mexico, holds a *matraca* rattle, with a slit drum (*teponahuastle*) on the table. Photo by Abraham Cáceres D., 1981.

In relation to dance, the *teponaztle* and *huéhuetl* have been preserved mainly among *conchero* groups in Mexico City and in several other central Mexican cities. The *conchero* dancers play armadillo-shell guitars while they dance in public displays tied to Christian traditions, especially the annual commemoration of the Virgin of Guadalupe (12 December). This is one of the main occasions for such performances, when groups from many central Mexican towns congregate and perform to the accompaniment of *teponaztle* and *huéhuetl*.

Notwithstanding the indisputably Mesoamerican character of the use of *teponaztle* and *huéhuetl*, contact and fusion of indigenous and Spanish musical traditions occurred during the conversion of the indigenous peoples to Christianity, beginning in the early 1500s. This change coincided with changes in the Nahua people's values and view of the world and has transformed the music significantly. New European instrumental sources were adapted for and accepted in emergent musical ensembles. The three instruments that significantly reflect the European musical tradition—violin, guitar, harp—have been those that most faithfully represent the preferred sound of indigenous peoples in contemporary times. It is difficult to conceive of a traditional Mexican indigenous musical tradition that would not include bowed, strummed, or plucked chordophones. Most currently active ensembles are not reconstructions of European ensembles but fusions with Mesoamerican instruments including rattles, usually played in ceremonially danced rituals. Most of these stringed instruments are manufactured by indigenous people and mainly take the form of the four-stringed European violin, a small guitar (*jarana,* a high-pitched variation, with five strings or courses of strings), and a diatonic harp with twelve or twenty-eight strings.

TRACK 28

jarana Nahua five-stringed, hourglass-shaped
   chordophone
son Nahua indigenous and mestizo dance-
   music tradition associated with regional
   musical styles

corpus Nahua dance performed in mid-
   March, accompanied by violin, guitar, and
   rattles

Important centers for the making of these instruments are Acayucan, Chicontepec, Mexcatla, and Pajapan, all in Veracruz in the eastern Gulf region, and Tecomán and Paracho in the western Mexican states of Colima and Michoacán, respectively. A mestizo community widely known as a center for the construction of *jaranas* and large, thirty-six-stringed harps is San Juan de los Plátanos, in Michoacán.

MUSICAL CONTEXTS AND GENRES

The native style of playing these instruments, formulating chordal progressions, and creating repertoires gave rise to *son,* a new musical genre. In the mestizo tradition, the word *son* is most often associated with regional musical styles performed on chordophones such as the violin, the *jarana,* and the harp. In indigenous music, however, especially Nahua music, the term *son* (pl. *sones,* diminutive *sonecito*) relates not to geographical locations but to the close relationship of the music with body movements and the symbolic representation of personages in ceremonial dances. In the Malinche dance (of Acayucan and Pajapan, Veracruz), a first group of musical pieces and a dance are formed by five *sones,* and a second group of musical pieces and a dance are formed by six *sones.* The Malinche dance begins with a musical piece and dance called *la cortesía* or *reverencia* (the act of demonstrating respect for the dance), performed as the first encounter with La Malinche. This is an allegory of the native woman, Malinche, Cortés's concubine, adviser, and interpreter.

In this first group of *sones,* minor details in the dance receive local names. The first is the *son de cinco pasos y vuelta* 'son of five steps and a turn', the second is the *son de tres pasos y golpe de talón* 'son of three steps and a heelstroke', the third is the *son de la vuelta entera* 'son of a whole turn', the fourth is the *son de cuatro pasos al frente* 'son of four steps ahead', and the fifth is the *son de cuatro pasos* 'son of four steps'. A second group of *sones* indicates a change in attitude to that of a warlike confrontation (an allegory of the conquest of Mexico by the Spanish); it includes a sixth *son* (the *corrida del monarca* 'the monarch's run'), a seventh *son* (the *son de la guerra* 'son of war') and an eighth *son,* with textual strophes about La Malinche (Anguiano and Munch 1979).

Another example is the *danza de cuauileros* (or *danza de cuauilones*), found in the towns of Aquila, Coire, Maruata, Ostula, and Pómaro, near the Pacific Ocean in Michoacán (Chamorro 1984). Also known as the *coloquio de la conquista de Hernán Cortés* 'colloquy of the conquest by Hernán Cortés', the dance represents the battle between the native Americans and the Spaniards. The performance is introduced with simulated combat using a wooden cudgel (*cuauitl*), Nahua warriors' favored weapon. The accompanying *sones* have different local Spanish names: the first one is *pata volando* 'flying foot'; the second, *cruzado* 'crosswise motion'; the third, *la cortesía* 'the paying of respect'; the fourth, *moviendo cadera* 'hip shaking'; the fifth, *primer paloteo* 'first attack with cudgels'; the sixth, *el brinquito* 'the little jump'; the seventh, *segundo paloteo* 'second attack with cudgels'; the eighth, *la cuchilla* 'the knife'; the ninth, *el engaño* 'the trick'; the tenth, *tercer paloteo* 'third attack with cudgels'; the eleventh, *pata ligera* 'agile foot'; and the twelfth (still with a Nahua name), *mochi nimochikahua* 'the leavetaking'. In addition to the cudgels, the dancers play rattles, coordinating their movements to the structures of the *sones*.

The titles of all these *sones* mainly indicate a display of skill in a simulation of battle. This display represents how the ancient Mexicans developed their military training. In addition, the attack with cudgels has to be precise and in accordance with the musical accents. The striking of the cudgels always occurs on the strong accents of every part of the musical piece; thus, there is no syncopation.

Some choreographies, such as those of the *cortesía* and *mochi nimochikahua,* are actually addressed to the saint. The body motions in certain parts of the dance stereotypically evoke religious attitudes; however, dancers' display of skill and competence earns high social status in Nahua society. Such dancers will gain prestige and will be recommended to other festival leaders.

The same towns in Michoacán have another dance known by the Nahua terms *xayácatl* or *xayacates* 'the disguised men' (Chamorro 1984), a parody of the famous Spanish dance *moros y cristianos* 'Moors and Christians', which reenacts the battles of the expulsion of the Moors from Spain. Disguised men perform stylized simulated scenes of combat in which the dancers appear as grotesque personages with rudimentary costumes made of coconut palms, leather masks, and tree branches. Accompanied by violin and guitar, the dance has two sections: *xayácatl de alastik* 'the disguised men of the flat disguise', and *xayácatl pasultik* 'the disguised men of the curled disguise'. In both parts of the dance, symbolism involves the domination of evil. Within the *xayácatl de alastik* occurs a representation of All Saints Day, performed two days later on the evening of 3 November with the following four types of *son*: *niños disfrazados* 'disguised boys', in which disguised children enter with small canes, cowbells, and jingle bells; *quebrado* 'broken or turned motion'; *mihkuhika* 'the first change'; and *mihtutilo* 'the later change'. At the end of this final choreographed *son,* a new set of dancers, clothed in branches, thick grass, and other vegetation, enters, dancing and clapping their hands to the *son de pasultik.* The Nahua people of the Mexican Pacific Coast frequently allude to this event not as a dance, but as a game to frighten people (*mauiltic* 'to frighten, to play').

TRACK ⊕-29   From the same Nahua region of Michoacán comes the dance of *corpus,* performed in mid-March to the accompaniment of violin, guitar, and rattles. The dancers are commanded by one male chief (*capitán*) and two female chiefs (*capitanas*). The dancers interweave long ribbons attached to a long rope stretched out horizontally. The role of each dancer is to hold one of the ribbons, interweaving it with others, and then after a pause to undo the weaving through contrary movements. During this process, various choreographed *sones* are performed, including *la reata* 'the rope', *de rodillas* 'on one's knees', *el zapateado* 'the foot stamping', *el machetazo* 'the hit with a machete', *la cortesía* 'the paying of respect', and *la procesión* 'the pilgrimage'.

The most important musical trait of *sones* for Nahua dances is an ostinato bass in the harp, supporting a tonality that normally alternates between tonic and dominant chords. The musical meter does not change, there is no prominent syncopation, and there is no emphasis on improvisation, in contrast to the mestizo music of the nearby Michoacán region known as hot land (*tierra caliente*), where improvisation, syncopation, and changes in metrical emphasis are characteristic. With the use of harp and *jarana,* the Nahua musical tradition shows a tendency toward isorhythm in its repetitive rhythms and short musical phrases. This is evidently the result of the link between the phrases of *sones* and the kinetic requirements of the dance.

The Nahua *sones* for dancing are included in most important nonliturgical ceremonies within the Roman Catholic tradition, particularly in the celebrations in honor of patron saints. They are part of syncretized Mexican Christianity, a religious form that began to take shape in the 1500s by a substitution of divinities and an indigenous reinterpretation of Christian imagery and the Christian calendar. Out of this process came a native Christian tradition involving Náhuatl-speaking people in a system of ceremonial responsibilities such as *mayordomías* (the institution of having principals and elected native chiefs who organize rituals) and *pagar mandas, promesas,* or *ofrendas* (fulfilling religious vows, promises, or offerings, usually made in return for divine intervention). Among the Nahua along the Gulf of Mexico coast, the Christian personages with the most *mayordomías* and traditions of offerings are the Virgin of Guadalupe (celebrated 12 December), Saint Isidore the Farmer (between 14 and 17 May), Saint Joseph (17 May), and Saint Mary Magdalen (16 May). All of these events include the performance of *sones* and the *danza de Malinche*. Among Nahua people of the Pacific Coast, the more festive events are those honoring Saint Anthony (13 June), celebrated with *cuauileros* and *corpus,* and the Virgin of Guadalupe (locally, 12 December and Good Friday), celebrated with *xayácatl.*

REFERENCES

Anguiano, Marina, and Guido Munch. 1979. *La Danza de Malinche.* México, D.F.: Culturas Populares, Secretaría de Educación Pública.

Boilès, Charles. 1965. "La flauta triple de Tenenexpan." In *La Palabra y el Hombre: Revista de la Universidad Veracruzana.* Xalapa: Universidad Veracruzana.

Díaz del Castillo, Bernal. 1928. *Historia Verdadera de la Conquista de la Nueva España.* México, D.F.: Ediciones Espasa-Calpe.

Dibble, Charles E., and Arthur J. O. Anderson. 1951. *Florentine Codex: General History of the Things of New Spain by Fray Bernardino de Sahagún, Book 2.* Santa Fé: School of American Research.

Durán, Diego. 1967. *Historia de las Indias de la Nueva España.* México, D.F.: Editorial Porrúa.

Fernández, Justino. 1959. "Una aproximación a Xochipilli." *Estudios de Cultura Náhuatl* 1:31–41. México, D.F.: Instituto de Historía, Universidad Nacional Autónoma de México.

Hellmer, José Raúl. 1960. "Mexican Indian Music Today." *Toluca Gazette* (1 June). Toluca: Gobierno del Estado de México.

Landa, Diego de. 1959. *Relación de las Cosas de Yucatán.* México, D.F.: Editorial Porrúa.

Martí, Samuel. 1968. *Instrumentos Musicales Precortesianos.* México, D.F.: Instituto Nacional de Antropología e Historia.

Mendoza T., Vicente. 1984. *Panorama de la Música Tradicional de México.* México, D.F.: Universidad Nacional Autónoma de México, Instituto de Investigaciones Estéticas.

Molina, Alonso de. 1966. *Vocabulario náhuatl-castellano y castellano-náhuatl.* México, D.F.: Ediciones Colofon.

Muñoz Camargo, Diego. 1947. *Historia de Tlaxcala.* México, D.F.: Lauro Rosell.

Paso y Troncoso, Francisco del. 1979. *Códice Borbónico: Manuscrito mexicano de la Biblioteca del Palais Bourbon.* México, D.F.: Siglo XXI Editores.

Sahagún, Bernardino de. 1956. *Historia General de la Cosas de Nueva España,* vol. 1. México, D.F.: Editorial Porrúa.

Seler, Eduard. 1960. *Gesammelte Abhandlungen zur Amerikanischen Sprach- und Alterthumskunde.* Berlin: A. Asher.

Schöndoube, Otto. 1986. "Instrumentos musicales del Occidente de México: las tumbas de tiro y otras evidencias." *Relaciones: Estudios de Historia y Sociedad* 7(28):85–110.

Soustelle, Jacques. 1950. *La Pensée Cosmologique des Anciens Mexicaines.* Paris: Hermann.

Stevenson, Robert M. 1968. *Music in Aztec and Inca Territory.* Berkeley: University of California Press.

Mixtec
E. Fernando Nava L.

Early Mixtec Culture
Present Mixtec Music Culture
National Policy
Further Study

The term *Mixtec* 'Cloud People' (Spanish *Mixtecano*) encompasses four indigenous groups of Mexico: Mixteco (476,000 people), Amuzgo (33,000), Trique (18,000), and Cuicatec (15,000). They are located in the Mixteca region of Mexico, divided into Mixteca Alta, Mixteca Baja, and Mixteca de la Costa—upper, lower, and coastal subregions, respectively. The region is a mostly mountainous area of about 30,000 square kilometers extending from northwestern Oaxaca State to the Atlantic coast, from eastern Guerrero State to the Atlantic coast, and in southeast Puebla. The Mixtec occupy practically the whole region, the Trique and Amuzgo reside within the region, and the Cuicatec are located on the northeastern side. Two non-Mixtecan groups, the Ixcatec and Chocho, also reside within the region. Outside neighboring groups of the Mixtecan people include the Mazatec, the Nahua, the Popoloca, the Tlapanec, and the Zapotec.

Except for the Nahua, all groups in the area speak Oto-Mangue languages within the Central Amerind phylum (Greenberg 1987:381). The Mixtec branch of Oto-Mangue has thirty varieties of the Mixteco language, two of the Amuzgo, two of the Trique, and one of the Cuicatec. These languages are tonal—which explains the name *Cuicatec* as 'Song People' (Náhuatl *cuica* 'song', *teco* 'people').

EARLY MIXTEC CULTURE

In pre-Columbian times, Mixtec culture was prominent, like that of the Zapotec and the Maya. At the time of the Spanish encounter, they were under the control of the Aztecs, to whom they paid taxes. There is much information about the music of the early Mixtec from pre-Hispanic documents, archaeological findings, and descriptions in chronicles by Europeans who arrived in the region during the 1500s. Such sources describe the following idiophones: *ke'e,* a log idiophone similar to the Nahua *teponaxtli* (*teponaztli*); *tiyoo,* a tortoiseshell struck by a deer's antler, similar to the Nahua *ayotl*; *tôndáxin,* a rattle; a scraper (made from bone, with a human skull as a resonator); and jingle bells, preferred as decoration of artifacts used in celebrations and applied as decoration on bracelets, necklaces, earrings, and breastplates. Gold jingle bells made for dancing were considered valuable jewels; some were preserved as a communal heritage rather than as private possessions. The membranophone most

The chronicles say that a chief's attire included anklet jingle bells, and when in battle the Mixtec warriors lost to the Nahua, the former played their conch trumpets as a sign of surrender.

cited is the *óuu,* a single-headed, deep-bodied wooden drum resembling the Nahua *huéhuetl.* A flute, a conch trumpet, and a calabash trumpet having a tubular mouthpiece with a mirliton (*zumbador,* a membrane placed over a hole in the central part of the calabash) were the most widely used aerophones.

Many Mixtec practices were documented in pre-Hispanic books (codices) depicting musical ensembles. Spanish chronicles mention war-related music and how the native people, in dances and songs, cried to their gods for victory in battle. The chronicles say that a chief's attire included anklet jingle bells, and when in battle the Mixtec warriors lost to the Nahua, the former played their conch trumpets as a sign of surrender. They add that during preparations for a new monarch's celebration, orchestras of cane flutes, conch trumpets, and tortoiseshell idiophones, with other percussive instruments, were organized.

Researchers have speculated that each ancient Mixtec town had at least one annual festival for its supreme god and that during this festival, dances were held. Every four years, the men cut their hair and held celebrations. With the healing of an ill governor, the clergy held dances. Women who were about to give birth prepared festivities of singing and dancing for the goddess of baths. There were celebrations twenty days after a child's birth and on the child's first birthday. Weddings were elaborate sequences of rituals that ended in dance. Other rituals included variations on the flier's dance (*baile del volador*), some executed by only one man, though among the Cuicatec by four. A similar Totonac dance, *los voladores de Papantla* 'the fliers of Papantla', is still performed in Veracruz. The Mixtec played another danced game that survives among the Totonac, who call it *huahua.*

Sources from the period of national independence (1810) until the beginning of the twentieth century are devoid of information about Mexican indigenous groups; they mainly concentrate on the growth of the mestizo population. Mixtec musical practices were influenced by this mestizo group—and remarkably by a growing black population in the Atlantic coastal region, where African influence is evident.

PRESENT MIXTEC MUSIC CULTURE

Today, even with mixtures of native American, mestizo, and African traits, traces of ancient Mixtec music remain. These include the rites of initiation practiced by initiate musicians in caves in Guerrero, just west of Mixtec territory. Elsewhere within caves, the Trique venerate their lightning god (*diós rayo*), syncretized with Saint Mark (San Marcos). They dance to a special melody played on a three-stringed violin, a small guitar (*jarana*), and a drum. Trique mythology includes *la nuera* 'the daughter-in-law', sung and danced for the wind god (*diós del viento*) and the forest god (*diós del monte*). This practice contrasts with later songs sung to Spaniards (*dioses sucios* 'dirty gods'). A survival east of the Mixtec region is acrobats (*maromeros*), who during celebrations walk a tightrope and do other stunts associated with the flier's dance.

FIGURE I   In Chichuaxtla, Oaxaca, Mexico, Triqui men (Mixtec-speakers) play guitar and violin for the festival of the dead. Photo by César Ramírez, 1987.

Musical instruments and ensembles

Present Mixtec idiophones include a container rattle used for dancing and African-influenced percussion instruments, including the *cajón de tapeo* (a wooden box struck with the hands, similar to the *cajón* of Peru) and a scraped *charrasca* (*quijada de burro* 'donkey's jawbone' or *quijada de caballo* 'horse's jawbone'). Membranophones most often correspond to the *tarola* (a snare drum from the European tradition) or the double-headed African-styled tubular drums that use a ring-rope system for tension. Additionally, the Mixtec make a friction idiophone (*oticonte,* a Nahua term, also called Spanish *bote del diablo* 'devil's can' and *arcuza*) from half a calabash by covering it with a skin into which they fasten a stick, which players rub. Surviving Mixtec aerophones are tubular cane duct flutes, now used to play Western melodies.

The most common ensembles are string groups (violin and guitar) (figure 1), joined along the Atlantic coast by a clay jug held between the knees of a seated performer who hits the mouth of the jug with a rag held in one hand and regulates the closure of the mouth with the other hand; the sound obtained is low in pitch. Sometimes a violin and/or a harmonica are grouped with the *oticonte* and the *charrasca*; these are exclusive to Afro-mestizo dances. Some dances are accompanied by flute and drum; others by violin and drum. Also on the coast is the *jarana,* the local version of a small, five-stringed guitar of Spanish origin. In a couple of northern towns, the psaltery is still played.

Bands (*bandas*), consisting of European-derived clarinets, trumpets (figure 2), saxophones, trombones, cymbals, bass drum (*tambora*), and snare drum (*tarola*), are found throughout the regions. All elections and other official governmental ceremonies, military and sports parades, and patriotic holidays are accompanied by marching bands, which, with other musical ensembles and dances, accompany processions on patronal saints' holidays and other important days in the liturgical calendar.

Except for a few band musicians, most performers cannot read music. Singers of praises, who cannot read music, occupy a place in the religious hierarchy. Only men lead religious musical practices and singing. Women participate by singing in several dances and the responsorial choruses of religious songs; children participate only in the latter.

FIGURE 2   During carnival near Oaxaca, Mixtec men and boys play trumpets in a band. Photo by César Ramírez, 1987.

Festivals

Sacred and secular festivities are the foundation on which music and dance are built. Festivals include dances with such topics as Moors and Christians (*moros y cristianos*) and *chareos* (related to Saint James), *doce pares de Francia* (twelve French couples), *la conquista* (a drama about the battle between the Aztecs and the Spanish), *tortuga* (turtle), and *tejón* (badger). In Mixteca de la Costa, there are organizations of dancers called *los tejorones* who perform for free and may engage in dances such as the tiger (*el tigre,* actually a jaguar).

Ten religious festivities have major importance. These include especially *la Virgen de Calendaria* (for blessing seeds) and carnival, which has comic dances, the he-mule (*macho mula*) and the he-rope (*macho riata*), representing herders' jolly activities, and graceful dances called little masks (*mascaritas*), imitating quadrilles of the 1800s. During these holidays in Mixteca Alta, masked people roam the streets, and in Mixteca de la Costa, the *tejorones* dance; both activities are accompanied by string music (often violin and *jarana*). The playing of bull horns announces the Trique carnival. Special musical pieces marking each stage of the ritual include the cloud-flower (*flor de nube*), a song with string accompaniment; the dance of the bull that jumps (*el toro que brinca*); and music danced by men in women's clothing. Other religious festivities are the third Friday of Lent, a great Trique fair; Holy Week, with several processions; a *petición de lluvia* asking for rain on St. Mark's day; the feast of the Holy Cross; the day the Cuicatec pray for a good harvest; All Saints; All Souls, celebrated by visits to cemeteries and the custom called the raising of the dead (*la levantada de muertos*), when people in disguise roam around the town accompanied by music; La Virgen de Guadalupe, important for all Mixtec; and the nativity cycle (*ciclo navideño*), celebrated in some places with shepherd's dances (*bailes de pastores*).

Life-cycle events

Among Mixtec life-cycle events, a celebration held by Trique women at the time of childbirth stands out. It consists of dancing accompanied by string music from the genre called flowers (*flores*), which refers to the ancient ritual of the bath (*rito del baño*).

Baptisms and weddings are also times of musical celebration. When a Trique wedding is arranged, parties occur simultaneously at the homes of the bride and the bridegroom. In many places, newlyweds go out on the town accompanied by music played by a band, while at the bride's house the guests perform mestizo dances, including the dove (*el palomo*). In Mixteca Baja, the turkey (*el guajolote*) is a nuptial dance in which the dancers carry a live turkey and other foods that will be served at the wedding banquet: tortillas, beer, and *mole*.

For death, aside from the communal observations, music is performed at private occasions. When an old civil servant dies among the Mixteco, the authorities take a band to the home of the deceased to pay homage. Among the Amuzgo, funerals are accompanied by songs of praise, sometimes sung in Latin. During the wake (*la velación*), which lasts all night, a band, a string group, or a singer participates. Music accompanies the body of the deceased to the cemetery and is played during the burial.

Specific Mixtec pieces are played for children and adults, establishing an important dichotomy between so-called happy genres (in a fast tempo) and sad ones (at a slow tempo). Music performed at a child's wake is happy (songs of love), but music at an adult's wake is sad (marches). The existence of many different dances possibly reflects the aesthetics of ancient Mixtec culture.

Secular music

A separate repertoire of musical pieces includes Afro-mestizo dances—the devils' dance (*danza de los diablos*); the *son* of the trough (*son de artesa*), to which people perform stamping (*zapateado*) atop a wooden platform (*tarima*); and the *chilena*, a famous couple dance with Afro-Hispanic rhythms and Spanish stanzas, related to the *marinera* (formerly *zamacueca*) and the *cueca* of the Pacific coast of Peru and Chile.

Euro-mestizo genres are the ones most widely performed. These include boleros, *chiflateras, corridos, cumbias, jarabes,* marches, *oaxacados,* and polkas, sung in Spanish. All over Mixtec territory are strong reminders of European influence, such as religious songs with Latin texts; polyphonic music performed by two brass bands during Holy Week; and overtures, mazurkas, and waltzes played by bands whose members can read music.

Other songs in the native language include a genre known as *katikubi,* whose structure is non-Western, with improvised texts and topics that describe everyday people and common situations, including marital conflicts, though some are especially dedicated to brides. The Amuzgo sing these songs unaccompanied, but the Mixteco sing with harmonica accompaniment. A genre of minor importance is the *tarántula,* sung to provoke and encourage movement in those who have been stung by a poisonous insect.

NATIONAL POLICY

Since the 1980s, Mexican governmental organizations have encouraged the performance of Mixtec music and dance by organizing and supporting fairs, festivals, and festivities. The Mixteca region has three cultural-indigenous radio stations (Radiodifusoras Culturales Indigenistas del Instituto Nacional Indigenista): La Voz de la Mixteca (The Voice of the Mixtec, serving the Mixteco and the Trique), La Voz de la Montaña (The Voice of the Mountain, serving the Mixtec, the Tlapanec, and the Nahua), and La Voz de la Costa Chica (The Voice of the Little Coast, serving the Mixteco and the Amuzgo). Aside from broadcasting in Spanish, the stations broadcast in the native languages, play folk music, and organize festivals.

For years, the economy of the region has caused large migrations, especially of the Mixtec. The two main destinations are California (both the U.S. state and Baja California, Mexico) and Mexico City. The former region has another indigenous radio station, La Voz del Valle (The Voice of the Valley), serving the Mixtec, the

Since the 1980s, Mexican governmental organizations have encouraged the performance of Mixtec music and dance by organizing and supporting fairs, festivals, and festivities.

Trique, and the Zapotec, in San Quintín, Ensenada. In Mexico City, children, young adults, and adults earn money by performing popular music in the streets, accompanied by accordion or a trio of a clarinet, a trumpet, and a bass drum.

FURTHER STUDY

For a Mixtec overview that includes contextual information about music and dance, books by María Luisa Acevedo (1992), Juan Julián Caballero (1994), Barbro Dahlgren de Jordan (1954), Kent V. Flannery and Joyce Marcus (1983), César Huerta Ríos (1994), and Robert S. Ravicz (1965) are of value. Thomas Stanford has written important studies about Mexican Amerindian musical and dance terms during the colonial period (1966) and contemporary Mixtec music and dances (1963, 1977). Recent articles and books about contemporary Mixtec music within festivals and funeral contexts are by Luciano Mendoza Cruz (1994), E. Fernando Nava L. (1984, 1987), and Françoise Neff (1995). A series of recordings by the Mexican Instituto Nacional Indigenista (National Institute for Indigenous Studies, 1994a, 1994b, 1994c, 1994d, 1994e, 1995) provide valuable documentation of Mixtec music. Thomas Stanford (1977) and Rosa María Garza Marcue (1995) have issued recordings of Mixtec traditional and popular music, respectively.

—Translated by Carmen Arencíbia

REFERENCES

Acevedo, María Luisa. 1994. *Mixtecos*. México, D.F.: Instituto Nacional Indigenista y Secretaría de Desarrollo Social. Colección Pueblos indígenas de México.

Caballero, Juan Julián. 1994. *Amuzgos de Oaxaca*. México, D.F.: Instituto Nacional Indigenista y Secretaría de Desarrollo Social. Colección Pueblos indígenas de México.

Dahlgren de Jordan, Barbro. 1954. *La Mixteca, su cultura e historia prehispánicas*. México, D.F.: Universidad Nacional Autónoma de México.

Flannery, Kent V., and Joyce Marcus, eds. 1983. *The Cloud People: Divergent Evolution of the Zapotec and Mixtec Civilizations*. New York: Academic Press.

Garza Marcue, Rosa María. 1995. *Música Popular Poblana. Homenaje a don Vicente T. Mendoza*. México, D.F.: Fonoteca del Instituto Nacional de Antropología e Historia. INAH 032. Cassette.

Huerta Ríos, César. 1994. *Triquis*. México, D.F.: Instituto Nacional Indigenista y Secretaría de

Desarrollo Social. Colección Pueblos indígenas de México.

Instituto Nacional Indigenista. 1994a. *La Voz de la Costa Chica*. México, D.F.: Subdirección de Radio del I.N.I. y Secretaría de Desarrollo Social. INI-RAD-I-3; XEJAM. Compact disc.

———. 1994b. *Mixtecos y triquis en la frontera norte*. México, D.F.: Subdirección de Radio del I.N.I. y Secretaría de Desarrollo Social. Series 5, "Sonidos del México Profundo," INI-RAD-II-5; XEQIN. Cassette.

———. 1994c. *La música en la Mixteca*. México, D.F.: Subdirección de Radio del I.N.I. y Secretaría de Desarrollo Social. Series 7, "Sonidos del México Profundo," INI-RAD-II-7; XETLA. Cassette.

———. 1994d. *La música en la Montaña de Guerrero*. México, D.F.: Subdirección de Radio del I.N.I. y Secretaría de Desarrollo Social. Series 10, "Sonidos del México Profundo," INI-RAD-II-10; XEZV. Compact disc.

———. 1994e. *V Festival de Música y Danza Indígena.* México, D.F.: Departamento de Etnomusicología del I.N.I. Series 8, "Archivo sonoro digital de la música indígena," INI-ETM-VIII-01. Compact disc.

———. 1995 *Sistema de Radiodifusoras Culturales Indigenistas. Testimonio musical del trabajo radiofónico.* México, D.F.: Subdirección de Radio del I.N.I. y Secretaría de Desarrollo Social. INI-RAD-I-5. Compact disc.

Mendoza Cruz, Luciano. 1994. *Festival Costeño de la Danza.* Oaxaca: Instituto Oaxaqueño de las Culturas.

Nava L., E. Fernando. 1984. "Las defunciones y su música en San Pedro Amuzgos, Oaxaca." *La música en México* (México, D.F.: monthly supplement of *El Día*), 148:3–4.

———. 1987. "Notas fúnebres: Música indígena para muertos." *México Indígena,* 2nd series, 3(19):57–59.

Neff, Françoise. 1995. *El rayo y el arcoiris: La fiesta indígena en la montaña de Guerrero y el oeste de Oaxaca.* México, D.F.: Instituto Nacional Indigenista.

Ravicz, Robert S. 1965. *Organización social de los Mixtecos.* México, D.F.: Instituto Nacional Indigenista.

Stanford, Thomas. 1963. "Datos sobre la música y danzas de Jamiltepec, Oaxaca." *Anales del Instituto Nacional de Antropología e Historia* (1962) 15:187.

———. 1966. "A Linguistic Analysis of Music and Dance Terms from Three Sixteenth-Century Dictionaries of Mexican Indian Languages." *Yearbook* 2:101–159. New Orleans: Tulane University, Inter-American Institute for Musical Research.

———. 1977. *Música de la Costa Chica de Guerrero y Oaxaca.* México, D.F.: Instituto Nacional de Antropología e Historia. INAH 21. LP disk.

Otopame (Chichimec, Otomí, and Pame)

E. Fernando Nava L.

Musical Instruments
Musical Contexts and Genres
Further Study

In the east-central part of Mexico are three indigenous groups known collectively as the Otopame: the Pame, Chichimec, and Otomí. Joseph Greenberg (1987:381) places their language in the Oto-Mangue family of languages of the Central Amerind phylum. The Pame (2,650 people), calling themselves Xi'úi, reside primarily in the state of San Luis Potosí. The Chichimec (1,500 people), calling themselves Ezar, live in one community within the state of Guanajuato. The Otomí, or Ñahñú (about 5,500 people), divide into several groups; most live in the eastern part of the state of Guanajuato and in the western part of the state of Querétaro; the rest are spread throughout Mexico.

Otopame groups are living exponents of the oldest culture of central Mexico. Their antiquity is supported by archaeological studies that have unearthed musical instruments from various parts of these territories. Clay aerophones have been found, but none of the indigenous groups preserves a musical tradition that uses them. During the colonial period, except for some dances whose aspects survive in contemporary indigenous practices, colonialists were more interested in describing warfare than art. Even in modern times, a predominantly mestizo culture's lack of interest in indigenous culture has led to few studies of Otopame culture. Still, all three groups show multiple levels of extant musical traditions.

MUSICAL INSTRUMENTS

Pame music has two flute traditions. Some musicians still play a pre-Hispanic flute they call *mitote* (a Nahua term), made of thin cane and measuring about 40 centimeters long. It has five holes—four for covering by the fingers, and one (near the proximal end) covered by a matted cobweb protected by an *elote* leaf, acting as a mirliton. A duct mouthpiece is made from a turkey quill held in place with wax. Traditionally this flute was always played in pairs; today, because of a shortage of musicians who carry on the tradition, it is usually played solo. It is used only to accompany the dance called *xancaa* and *mitote* (after the flute), also of pre-Hispanic origin.

The other Pame aerophone is an end-blown cane flute (*nipjiiht*), measuring more than 40 centimeters long by 3.5 centimeters wide. It is found in most of

Mexico. The Pame usually play it during religious rites and processions, accompanied by a drum played by a second performer.

The Otomí have end-blown duct flutes, played in three ways: a flutist accompanied by a drummer; a pipe-and-tabor soloist, who plays the flute while accompanying himself on a small drum, struck with a drumstick; and a pipe-and-tabor duet, with each performer playing a flute and a drum. The last are called *tunditos,* and their repertoire includes sacred and secular music. Currently, the Chichimec do not use these aerophones.

String music is played throughout the whole eastern-central region of Mexico. The Pame and the Chichimec share the most complex of chordophone musics: the *huapango arribeño* 'highland *huapango*', a variety of *son* [see MEXICO]. The Pame preserve the traditional ensemble: two violins and a *guitarra sexta* the standard six-stringed guitar. The Chichimec have a more recent and mestizo-influenced arrangement of instruments: *guitarra huapanguera* (resembling the *guitarra sexta,* but slightly larger, with a bigger resonator, a deeper sound, and five courses of three double and two single strings), two violins, and a Jalisco-style *vihuela* (a round-backed small guitar). These ensembles usually accompany Spanish literary genres (secular and sacred), such as poems in couplets (*coplas*) and ten-line stanzas (*décimas*), and songs and instrumental music for deceased infants and children (*angelitos* 'little angels'). Otopame ensembles of one or two violins and one guitar are common. Such ensembles alone perform almost half the highland repertoire. Groups known as *música de golpe* 'strike music'—a violin accompanied by double-headed membranophones (snare drum, bass drum)—are equally common among the Otomí and the Chichimec.

The Otopame, especially the Otomí and the Chichimec, have a strictly percussive dance music, played only by a double-headed bass drum and a snare drum, or by a single bass drum. These dances come from the period of the Encounter (early 1500s) and were traditionally performed by male dancers, though today women also dance them; the dancers' shell ankle-tied rattles emit a sound that adds to the timbral sonority of the music. On special occasions, such as Holy Week, the Pame use a pair of snare drums during their processions; these they play in alternation, much like a dialogue.

Of all the Otopame, only the Otomí have wind bands and percussion bands. The iconography of some small chapels shows that they formerly had larger ensembles. Friezes depict groups of aerophones, chordophones, and membranophones, though these ensembles are not used today.

MUSICAL CONTEXTS AND GENRES

All Otopame groups have religious songs (*alabanzas* 'praises') sung unaccompanied, mostly in Spanish, in two, three, or four voices. Only the Otomí sing songs in their native language. A subgenre of Pame religious songs is the linnet (*jilguero,* a kind of finch), a genre employed in a duel or challenge in which two singers or groups of singers compete and show off their memory skills.

Of secular songs, the *décima* is performed in two ways: as poetry (*poesía*), a series of five or six recited ten-line stanzas that alternate with a sung quatrain whose first line repeats the last line of the stanza; or as *valona,* a quatrain glossed by four stanzas, each of which ends with its respective line of the quatrain, and the whole is sung in recitative, like a *salmodia.* These genres are performed only by the Pame, but are enjoyed by all three groups. The character of these verses is historical and narrative. The verses relate to Otopame ritual practices documented during the colonial period. In them, singers often engage in dialogues that describe nocturnal reunions of

FIGURE 1   Three Pame *malinche* dancers with *xichat* rattles in Santa Catarina, San Luís Potosí, Mexico. Photo courtesy of the Ethnographic Audio-Visual Archive, Instituto Nacional Indigenista, Mexico, with permission.

ancient warriors, their rites, battles, conquests, and dances. *Décimas* are performed during dances called *topadas* ('buttings'), musical duels that last all night while listeners dance to the rhythms of the *jarabe,* the *poesía,* the *son,* and the *valona.*

Otopame songs in native languages are rare. The indigenous languages are tonal, but a lyrical tradition among them does not exist. The only group in the area that has some native lyrical manifestations is the Otomí. A recent wave of interest in the preservation of indigenous cultures has resulted in the compositions of some lyrical songs in the native languages of the groups.

Singing and dancing

All three groups preserve male dances that commemorate, from a European perspective, the Spanish conquest of Mexico. No version includes spoken dialogue, but with choreography and gestures (representing anger, threats, battles, and courtship fights) these dances narrate episodes of this historical period. The Pame have two similar versions accompanied by violin and guitar: *malinche* and *monarca.* The Chichimec call them by the general name *danza chichimeca* 'Chichimec dance', and accompany them with violin and snare drum or by drum only, while dancers play calabash rattles (*xichat*) (figure 1). The Otomí, who dedicate these dances to the conquerors' souls, accompany them with paired pipe-and-tabor players and call them *rayados contra franceses* or simply *rayados* 'striped ones' (people who paint stripes on themselves).

The Otomí also preserve the conquest dance of the *concheros* (players of armadillo-shell guitars), which originated in the Otopame region. Though these dances were extremely popular in the central part of the country, only the Chichimec performed them until the 1950s. The accompaniment consisted of mandolins (*mandolinas*) or small guitars (*conchas de armadillo,* each with an armadillo shell for a resonator) played by several dancers.

Other dramatic manifestations include the shepherds (*pastorelas*), derived from Christmas celebrations first organized locally during colonial times. The Pame of the north preserve some that last an entire night. Between extensive dialogues, a violinist and a guitarist perform songs and instrumental pieces. The main characters of another dance genre accompanied by a violin and a guitar are a leader, a bull, and cowboys. The Pame depiction of these characters is playful, bordering on mockery.

Several dances are exclusive to the Pame. In *la ropa del muerto y el arco* 'the deceased's clothing and the bow', men and women enact the passage from life to death. This dance is performed during festivals for All Saints Day (Todos los Santos), All Souls Day (Fieles Difuntos), and most days during November. Another Pame dance is the *mitote,* accompanied by the cobweb-mirliton flute of the same name. Men stand side by side, each with his arms on his neighbors' shoulders, moving backward and forward in rhythm. It is performed only in one Pame town on festive occasions and after a community project has been finished.

Other musical genres

The *minuete,* a purely instrumental genre, is practiced by the Chichimec and the Pame. All compositions in this genre are anonymous. Most are in ABCD structure, with melodies modulating to neighboring keys. Among the tonalities used, D, G, A, C, and F are the most frequent and are associated with specific rituals. Different tonalities have different functions, such as *minuetes* for ceremonies with religious statues and to escort the bodies of deceased infants to the cemetery. Despite the name, these pieces bear no resemblance to the European minuet. They resemble those of a genre played by the Cora of Nayarit—a music whose basic elements led to the mariachi genre.

Mestizo genres that are widely performed throughout the Otopame indigenous regions include the *jarabe,* the *canción,* the *corrido,* and the *polca.* Other genres considered local are the *huapango huasteco* and the *son arribeño.* The former is played by a string trio with a fast rhythm; the latter is the *son* music performed during the *huapango arribeño.*

All three groups observe the traditional holidays of Holy Week, the feast of the Holy Cross (Santa Cruz), Corpus Christi, and All Saints. The only group that celebrates carnival in a joyful manner is the Otomí. Each town's major celebration is its patronal festival. Some are special celebrations, like those in which the Otomí and the Chichimec visit each other's towns; or Saint Michael's Day (Día de San Miguel) among the Otomí of Tolimán in Querétaro, which starts two months early so they can perform all the daily dances and pilgrimages that they must complete for their celebrations.

Outside the festive calendar, the most important Otopame celebrations are weddings, for which modern groups with electronic equipment are usually hired. An important event for the Chichimec is the wake, for which they play sacred pieces (*piezas sagradas*). The Pame also perform these pieces for musicians' and dancers' wakes. Specific pieces are for adults, some are for children, and others are for important moments in the wake. These pieces differ primarily in tonality, which changes to suit the purpose.

Not much music remains associated with agricultural rituals. The Pame and Otomí are the only ones who still have ceremonies in which a singer leads a group in praise. The only other occasion when the Chichimec and Pame had a labor-related celebration was for the completion of a house, when the owners were responsible for hosting a party for the whole town. Pame and Otomí leadership roles are played by indigenous governors. Though they lead dances, it is the musician's job to lead the ceremonies of civil and religious events.

FURTHER STUDY

General works on the Otopame are by Doris Bartholomew (1994) and Jacques Soustelle (1993). Studies of specific cultures are by Carlo Bonfiglioli (1996), Raúl García Flores (1993), Gabriel Moedano (1972), and E. Fernando Nava L. (1994a) for the Chichimec; Heidi Chemín Bässler (1993) for the Otomí; and Dominique Chemín (1994), Chemín Bässler (1984), Nava (1994b), and Miguel Ángel Rubio

Outside the festive calendar, the most important Otopame celebrations are weddings, for which modern groups with electronic equipment are usually hired.

and Saúl Millán (1994) for the Pame. In addition, Nava (1987) has written about Otopame funeral music. Recent recordings include one cassette produced by María Isabel Flores Solano et al. (1995) and four published by the Instituto Nacional Indigenista of Mexico (1994, 1995a, 1995b, 1996).

—TRANSLATED BY CARMEN ARENCÍBIA

REFERENCES

Bartholomew, Doris. 1994. "Panorama of Studies in Otopamean Languages." In *Panorama de los estudios de las lenguas indígenas de México,* ed. Doris Bartholomew, Yolanda Lastra, and Leonardo Manrique, 335–377. Colección Biblioteca Abya-Yala, 16, 1. Quito: Ediciones Abya-Yala.

Bonfiglioli, Carlo. 1996. "Chichimecas contra Franceses: De los 'salvajes' y los 'conquistadores'." In *Las Danzas de Conquista en el México Contemporáneo,* 91–115. México, D.F.: Fondo de Cultura Económica.

Chemín Bässler, Heidi. 1979. "La fête des morts chez les pames septentrionaux de l'état de San Luis Potosí au Mexique." In *Les hommes et la mort: Rituels funéraires a travers le monde,* ed. Jean Guiart, 75–84. Objets et Mondes, La Revue du Musée de l'Homme, 19. Paris: Le Sycomore.

———. 1984. *Los Pames Septentrionales de San Luis Potosí.* México, D.F.: Instituto Nacional Indigenista.

———. 1993. *Las Capillas Oratorios Otomies de San Miguel Tolimán.* Colección "Documentos," 15. Querétaro: Consejo Estatal para la Cultura y las Artes.

Chemín, Dominique. 1994. *Imagen Pame Xi'oi.* San Luis Potosí: Editorial Ponciano Arriaga. Archivo Histórico del Estado de San Luis Potosí.

Flores Solano, María Isabel, et al. 1995. *La Sierra Gorda que canta: A lo Divino y a lo Humano.* Guanajuato: Instituto de la Cultura del Estado de Guanajuato, Dirección General de Culturas Populares y Discos Corason. Cassette.

García Flores, Raúl. 1993. *¡Puro mitote! La música, el canto y la danza entre los chichimecas del Noreste.* Monterrey, Nuevo León: Fondo Editorial Nuevo León.

Greenberg, Joseph H. 1987. *Language in the Americas.* Stanford, Calif.: Stanford University Press.

Instituto Nacional Indigenista. 1994. *La Voz de las Huastecas.* México, D.F.: Subdirección de Radio del I.N.I. y Secretaría de Desarrollo Social (INI–RAD–I–2; XEANT). Compact disc.

———. 1995a. *Flautas Indígenas de México.* México: Departamento de Etnomusicología del I.N.I.; series 7: Organología Indígena, vol.1 (INI–VII–01). Cassette.

———. 1995b. *Sistema de Radiodifusoras Culturales Indigenistas: Testimonio musical del trabajo radiofónico.* México, D.F.: Subdirección de Radio del I.N.I. y Secretaría de Desarrollo Social (INI–RAD–I–5). Compact disc.

———. 1996. *KUNDA ERER MA-IR RANTO NIUFF: Águilas que no se olvidan: Grupo indígena chichimeca de San Luis de la Paz, Guanajuato.* México: Departamento de Etnomusicología del I.N.I. (INI–VI–05). Cassette.

Moedano N., Gabriel. 1972. "Los hermanos de la Santa Cuenta: Un culto de crisis de origen chichimeca." In *Religión en Mesoamérica,* 599–609. México, D.F.: Sociedad Mexicana de Antropología.

Nava L., E. Fernando. 1987. "Notas fúnebres: Música indígena para muertos." *México Indígena,* second series 3(19):57–59.

———. 1994a. *Chichimecas Jonaz.* Colección Pueblos indígenas de México. México, D.F.: Instituto Nacional Indigenista y Secretaría de Desarrollo Social.

———. 1994b. *Pames de San Luis Potosí.* Colección Pueblos indígenas de México. México, D.F.: Instituto Nacional Indigenista y Secretaría de Desarrollo Social.

Rubio, Miguel Ángel, and Saúl Millán. 1994. *Pames de Querétaro.* Colección Pueblos Indígenas de México. México, D.F.: Instituto Nacional Indigenista y Secretaría de Desarrollo Social.

Soustelle, Jacques. 1993. *La Familia Otomí-pame del Centro de México.* Toluca: Instituto Mexiquense de Cultura.

Purépecha (Tarascan)

Arturo Chamorro

The Ceremonial Tarascan Cultural Universe
The Christian Purépecha Cultural Universe
The Secularized Purépecha Cultural Universe
Further Study

The Purépecha (P'urhépecha) or Tarascan are an Amerindian group in west Mexico. Their territory is delimited by an ecological system formed by four areas: the Tarascan Plateau (including the main portion of Paricutín Volcano), Lake Pátzcuaro, La Cañada (a stream near the Zamora Valley) and Zacapu (toward the north of Lake Pátzcuaro).

The Purépecha are descendants of an older ethnic group known as Wacúsecha (People of the Eagle Dynasty), who took up residence at Lake Pátzcuaro a few centuries before the Spanish conquest. The more recently used term Purépecha, an autodesignation meaning 'newly arrived' or 'arrived from somewhere else', has replaced another older term, Tarascan, meaning 'son-in-law'. Joseph Greenberg (1987:382) classifies the Tarascan language within the Chibchan family of the Chibchan-Paezan phylum.

To understand the development of Purépecha music, the existence of three etic universes in the history and culture of Purépecha has to be considered. In the first cultural universe is the music of the ancient Tarascans from the precolonial period, which can be identified as the Tarascan ceremonial universe of culture. The second one departs from the Spanish colonial period and is the Christian Purépecha universe of culture. The third is also from the influence of the Christian world; however, it must be understood as the secularized Purépecha universe of culture.

THE CEREMONIAL TARASCAN CULTURAL UNIVERSE

This cultural universe is archaeologically documented with ancient evidence from the Lake Pátzcuaro Basin. Ritual burial grounds have produced widely various clay, stone, bone, seashell, and copper artifacts, probably used for ceremonial purposes. Collars of seashell pieces and copper bells made with the lost-wax technique were common (figure 1). Carl Lumholtz (1960:403) found tortoiseshell-shaped copper bells in archaeological sites in Jilotlán, Naranja, and Pátzcuaro. Otto Shondoube (1986:93–95) found flutes, whistles, and other artifacts made from clay in a grave in Chupícuaro, dated between 1200 and 600 B.C. Besides these instruments, several written sources from the 1500s mention large trumpets and cylindrical drums that produced powerful sounds, audible for long distances and used for communication

The priests said, "Gentlemen, please stand up because the goddess Cuerauaperi has already opened the door." They started to play their trumpets and drums while burning incense, singing with her as they bathed and dressed her.

—Sixteenth-century chronicle

FIGURE 1   An ancient collar made from 165 pieces of seashell and nineteen copper bells, each with a rounded loose clapper inside. Regional Museum of Guadalajara. Photo by Miguel Angel Sotelo. Used with permission.

and perhaps war-related ceremonials. These were probably played during ceremonial occasions as tributes to local gods, as with Nahua music [see MEXICA].

Within the Tarascan pantheon, the main deity among terrestrial gods was Cuerauaperi, mother of all terrestrial gods and spirit of creation, to whom the main festivals with sounds, dances, and ceremonial libations were dedicated. Jerónimo de Alcalá (1980:11) described the predictions and dreams these people had before the Spaniards came to their province, where their main gods came from, the feast they celebrated, and the importance of the butterfly dance (*parakata uarakua*), in which the main priests, accompanied by drums and large trumpets, danced with a big butterfly in honor of Cuerauaperi, embodied as a beautiful maiden:

> The priests said, "Gentlemen, please stand up because the goddess Cuerauaperi has already opened the door." . . . All the priests were naked, covered with soot, and seated with trefoil garlands on their heads. . . . They started to play their trumpets and drums while burning incense . . . , singing with her as they bathed and dressed her. . . . They put very fine clothes on her, . . . a trefoil garland on her head, . . . bells on her ankles, . . . and they brought much wine, which they offered for drinking. . . . On the day after the feast, all the women from the village were taken to the kitchen fire, where they prepared toasted corn. . . . Thereafter, a few dancers came in and performed a dance called *Paracata Uaraqua* in the patio surrounded by a wooden fence or in the houses of the priests. And the priest of this goddess danced there, wearing a snake as a waistband and a paper butterfly.

Funerals in honor of a *cazonci,* a rank equivalent to a king or a main ruler, were accompanied by conch trumpets and diverse percussion instruments, such as tortoiseshell idiophones struck with bone mallets. In the *Crónica de Michoacán,* written by Pablo de Beaumont in the 1500s (1932:54–58), information about these ensembles as used for certain ceremonials was provided by elderly Tarascan informants; however, they were described through the author's own interpretation of the native discourse:

> Solemnity in burials . . . [was] memorable for Tarascan kings. . . . Upon the death of the king, his successor gave the news about it to the rest of the lords . . . [and] the first thing they did was to wash the entire body, dress it with a shirt and shoes, and put a few small golden bells on the dead king's ankles. . . . After all the pomp, and with musical accompaniment, they took out the corpse from the main palace at midnight . . . . A double sound was made with tortoiseshells percussed with crocodile bones, instead of the double sound by bells. . . . In the middle of many bonfires, conch and horn trumpets were sounded in alternation with songs in a doleful tone, which were created as praises for the dead king.

THE CHRISTIAN PURÉPECHA CULTURAL UNIVERSE

An ideological change took place from the Spanish encounter until the late 1500s. The ceremonial Tarascan dimension moved toward the Christianized Purépecha world by means of evangelization, using Christian vocal practices and other methods of religious conversion, as performed by Christian friars of the orders of Saint Francis and Saint Augustine. Visual resources were also useful in evangelization. Pablo de Beaumont (1932) relates how Christian missionaries handled diverse paintings and icons representing the mysteries of faith so they could be learned more easily by the natives; moreover, they assisted in an attempt to eradicate cult practices of the ancient Tarascan gods. Some evidences of painting and icons as tools of evangelization among the Purépecha can be seen from the images of angel musicians in some local Christian churches. Angel-musicians are shown magnificently dressed and playing musical instruments including a double-reed aerophone (*chirimía*), a krummhorn (*orlo*), an early bassoon (*bajón*), a bowed viola (*vihuela de arco*), a six-stringed sixteenth-century guitar (*vihuela de mano*), and a harp (*arpa*). These are wooden icons, carved into the wooden roofs of Christian churches in Cocucho, Naranján, Quinceo, Zacán, and other places. With this evidence, the arrival of European music in the Purépecha territory is clear.

These visual images can be compared with the written sources provided by the Augustinian friars. Diego Basalenque (1963:62, 63, 85) describes the chapels in Tacámbaro and Tiripetío, where the Spanish commissioner Cristóbal Oñate established centers for teaching European music, and Christian music in particular. Minor centers (*visitas* 'visits') were also established, the most important at Parangaricutiro. The Franciscan Isidro Félix de Espinosa (1945:148–151) mentions the remarkable work of Juan de San Miguel, a friar devoted to teaching organ and choral music, who organized a native American chorus (*semaneros* 'weekday workers') to sing hymns.

Chirimías were also played in the musical ensembles of the *visitas* in Purépecha territory, as explained by Diego Basalenque (1963:45) in his description of the sounds during an Easter celebration at Tiripetío:

> Easter and solemn days required that all the *visitas* should assist the priest, and those in the procession should bring their crosses and candlesticks with their trumpet music. These days were of great rejoicing to the people, especially the

Corpus Christi festival, which was established with particular devotion; thus it was instituted, and devotion still grows with the invention of services which they perform in the streets, such as dances and performances of trumpet and *chirimía* music at each altar—because each *visita* brings its own music.

The role of *chirimías* in Purépecha religious thought is important for understanding the Purépecha view of the world. *Chirimía* performance has been maintained as a permanent custom during Corpus Christi celebrations, even today. Jesús Hernández Tziandón, an elderly *chirimía* player from Cherán Atzícurin Village, explains that during Corpus Christi, the *chirimía* is played as a part of a religious responsibility in that the modern Christian Purépecha consider the instrument a symbol of the divine world.

Another cultural legacy from the Christian world still in use by the Purépecha consists of songs, prayers, and *alabanzas,* hymns in praise of the Eucharist, performed responsorially in Spanish or in Purépecha by an elderly male or female leader (*kéngi,* a native authority on celebrations) and a choir of native women and men.

THE SECULARIZED PURÉPECHA CULTURAL UNIVERSE

Within the Purépecha secular or social festival universe is the *chanántskua,* a carnival tradition of dances and games. Included is a symbolic element known as the little bull (*torito*), represented in three forms: as music, as a handcrafted cardboard costume for a dance-drama, and as a musical instrument shaped in wood. As music, little bulls are characterized by short and redundant melodies in 6/8 meter, played by local brass bands to accompany dances and games. In the village of Cherán, little-bull melodies are played during the holy-child-awakening ceremony (*levantamiento del Niño*) in February or March. As an artifact for dances and games, a cardboard bull is carried by one or two men as a body-enveloping mask for dancing and a device for charging and butting onlookers. As a musical instrument, especially in the village of Ahuiran, a little bull is an idiophone also known as *kiringua.* Manufactured from a small carved log and played with two sticks while carried by a man who dances while he plays, it resounds throughout the village.

Also within the Purépecha secularized universe are social events that include new native musical traditions born after the end of the Spanish colonial period. Since the 1800s, such new musical genres as *abajeño, son regional*, and *pirekua* have reshaped a Purépecha musical culture with some European influences.

Abajeño is a genre of instrumental music whose name comes from western Mexican Spanish, meaning 'from lower lands', referring to the lowland musical traditions of mestizos of Jalisco, Colima, and Michoacán. This music is characterized by the plucking of a thirty-six-stringed harp, the strumming of a guitar, and the bowing of a violin. Its structure includes rhythmic alternations in 6/8 and 3/4 meters, syncopated basses, and parts that are improvised—possible African influence. Eduardo Ruíz (1969) asserted that this mestizo tradition comes from the 1800s in Michoacán, according to written sources that mention popular dances called *zapateados* 'foot stampings', accompanied by a harp and performed during the War of French Intervention (1862–1867). Purépecha musicians rework *abajeños* in their own way by performing them with string orchestras and brass bands. String-orchestra *abajeños* are played by violins, a guitar, *vihuelas,* violoncellos (for rhythmic and harmonic accompaniment), and a string bass. Brass-band *abajeños* are mainly characterized by the sounds of tuba and trombone playing bass lines and percussion instruments playing rhythmic combinations. Also included are E♭ saxhorns (like medium-size euphoniums) called *armonías* 'harmonies' because of their harmonic-rhythmic function, and clarinets. Purépecha *abajeños* are structured by repeated melodies in fast tempo, with two or three melodic themes developed in turn. In many of them, the melodic themes are lyrically played by clarinets, and contrasted tutti sections are highly percussive with alternating 6/8 and 3/4 meters. As musical genres Purépecha and mestizo *abajeños* accompany *zapateados*. This use is especially common in the secularized contexts of popular festivals. *Zapateados* can be performed spontaneously by the audience during a popular festival or formally choreographed and performed as part of traditional Purépecha dances, including *viejitos* (with masks of old men), *negritos* (with masks of black men), *rancheros de pastorela* (songs of Christmas shepherds), and *kúrpites* (young men with Spaniard masks).

A clearly nineteenth-century European influence appears in the genres *son regional* (a mostly instrumental 'regional *son*' genre) and *pirekua* (a vocal genre); both are related to the waltz in rhythm and tempo. Henrietta Yurchenco (1983:255–256) asserted that the waltz characterizes the *son* and the *pirekua* in a special way because both genres are in a slow triple meter and are enriched by abundant diatonic melodies that are played and sung as duets with a rhythmic sequence of two to five notes against fixed patterns in the accompaniment. Two or three chords (usually I, IV, and V) provide harmonic motion in major or minor keys, with little use of modulation. *Sones* and *pirekuas* are intended only for listening—as serenades and for musical competitions during a feast.

Purépecha composers make use of a rhythmic feature known as *cuatrillo,* in which four grouped notes are played in the place of three in 3/8 time. This combination produces the effect of a syncopated rhythmic pattern in some of the instruments. A variant of *pirekua,* called *abajeño,* is sung and accompanied in fast tempo in a combination of 6/8 and 3/4 meter. Beyond these characteristics, *sones* and *pirekuas* are identified by their instrumentation and interpretation. *Sones* can be performed by a violin, a violoncello, a string bass, a clarinet, a saxophone, and a trombone (old orchestras added a flute) (figure 2), whereas *pirekuas* are performed by either two to three guitars, strings and winds, a small brass band, or unaccompanied. Yurchenco's recordings (1970) include a few examples of ensembles consisting of mandolins and guitars, but such groups are no longer used.

If vocally interpreted, *sones* are normally sung in Spanish, but *pirekuas* are usually sung in Tarascan. *Sones* textually express ideas about everyday events, feelings, people, and places, but *pirekuas* are poetic expressions that describe the Purépecha worldview.

FIGURE 2   In Zopoco, Michoacán, an ensemble of strings and winds performs *sones. From left:* violin, string bass, violin, trombone, metal clarinet, and string bass. Photo by María del Carmen Díaz, 1981. Used with permission.

> # The meanings derived from *pirekua* lyrics about flowers are basically references to femininity and passion, as in songs of love.

Pirekua lyrics refer to several aspects of daily life and people's emotions. From the diversity of lyrics in *pirekuas* emerges a frequent allusion to flowers related to native femininity, passions, recollection, death, nostalgia about old times, myths, and ecology, but other lyrics are critical of unsolved communal problems. Frances Toor (1930) interpreted flower symbolism in *pirekuas* sung for weddings during the distribution of ceremonial crowns or crowns of flowers (*canakuas*). The meanings derived from lyrics about flowers are basically references to femininity and passion, as in songs of love. An example of this (figure 3) is the following *pirekua,* entitled "Elbirita," composed by Agapito Secundino, a native of Lake Pátzcuaro:

FIGURE 3   "Elbirita," a *pirekua* composed by Agapito Secundino and performed in San Jerónimo Purenché-cuaro in 1981 (Chamorro 1981). Transcription by Arturo Chamorro.

Tsïtsïki sapichu,	Little flower,
shánkari sési jáshika!	How beautiful you are!
Nári arhíkuariski?	What is your name?
Nánina? pirini para p'ikukuarini?	How can I take her?
Nótaru modu jarasti.	There is no way.
Nirásinga kétsimani juchit amigu.	I am walking downtown with my friend.
Juchit amigu nirásinga kétsimani	My friend, I am walking downtown
Elbiritani eshéni.	to meet Elbirita.
K'uinchikua janónguasti.	The feast is already here.
Tsinari, tsinari, malesita.	Wake up, wake up, my dear girl.
K'uinchikua janónguasti.	The feast is already here.
Animacha andámutanisti k'oru.	It is close to the Animas feast.
Arí tsïtsïki sháni p'untsumika,	This flower has so much fragrance,
oktubri jimbó anapu.	from October precisely.
Elbirita sháni terékuarka k'oru.	Elbirita is smiling so much.

Other Purépecha *pirekuas* have gained prestige abroad for their composers, including "*La Josefinita*" by Uriel Bravo and Juan Méndez (from Zacán), "*Male Seberiana*" by Jesús Chávez (also from Zacán), and examples by Jacinto Rita (from Angaguán), Juan Crisóstomo (from Quinceo), Francisco Salmerón (from Quinceo), Salvador Próspero (from Tingambato), Cruz Jacobo (from Sevina), and Juan Victoriano (from San Lorenzo). The last is the composer to whom Henrietta Yurchenco (1970) devoted a great part of her local research between the 1940s and the 1960s.

FURTHER STUDY

The major study of Purépecha music is a recent book by Arturo Chamorro (1994). In Spanish, it provides a cultural and semiotic analysis of music and musical performance by focusing on the *son* and its variants. Sources in English are few but include a study of rural Mexican festivals by Brandes (1989) and Henrietta Yurchenco's liner notes to a recording (1970).

REFERENCES

Alcalá, Jerónimo de. 1980. *La Relación de Michoacán*. Morelia: Fimax Publicistas Editores.

Basalenque, Diego. 1963. *Historia de la Provincia de San Nicolás de Tolentino de Michoacán*. México, D.F.: Editorial Jus.

Beaumont, Pablo. 1932. *Crónica de Michoacán*. México, D.F.: Publicaciones del Archivo General de la Nación.

Brandes, Stanley H. 1989. *Power and Persuasion: Fiestas and Social Control in Rural Mexico*. Philadelphia: University of Pennsylvania Press.

Chamorro, Arturo. 1981. *Abajeños y Sones de la Fiesta P'urhépecha*. Instituto Nacional de Antropología e Historia INAH-SEP 24. LP disk.

———. 1994. *Sones de la Guerra: Rivalidad y emoción en la práctica de la música P'urhépecha*. Zamora: El Colegio de Michoacán.

Espinosa, Isidro Félix de. 1945. *Crónica de la Provincia Franciscana de los Apóstoles San Pedro y San Pablo de Michoacán*. México, D.F.: Editorial Santiago.

Greenberg, Joseph H. 1987. *Language in the Americas*. Stanford, Calif.: Stanford University Press.

Lumholtz, Carl. 1960. *El México Desconocido*. Vol. 2. México, D.F.: Editoria Nacional.

Ruíz, Eduardo. 1969. *Historia de la Guerra de Intervención en Michoacán*. Morelia: Balsal Editores.

Shondoube, Otto. 1986. "Instrumentos musicales del occidente de México: Las tumbas de tiro y otras evidencias." *Relaciones: Estudios de historia y sociedad* 7(28):85–110.

Toor, Frances. 1930. "Nota sobre las canacuas." *Mexican Folkways* 6(3):108–109.

Yurchenco, Henrietta. 1970. "Music of the Tarascan Indians of Mexico: Music of Michoacán and Nearby Mestizo Country." Folkways 4217. Notes to LP disk.

———. 1983. "Estilos de ejecución en la música indígena mexicana con énfasis particular en la pirekua tarasca." In *Sabiduría Popular*, 248–260. Zamora: El Colegio de Michoacán.

Tarahumara
J. Richard Haefer

Environment and Living Conditions
Musical Instruments
Musical Contexts and Genres
Further Study

The Tarahumara (Tarahumar, Rarámuri, or 'runners') of northwest Mexico occupy the meadows, canyons, valleys, and uplands of central and southern Chihuahua. Numbering some fifty thousand, they have lived in this area for more than two thousand years. They were contacted by Jesuits as early as 1610 (Pérez de Ribas 1944 [1645]). In 1767, at the time of the Jesuit expulsion, they supported nearly thirty missions and more than fifty *visitas,* small, nearby suburbs of a mission. The Franciscans replaced the Jesuits in northern Mexico, but mission activity declined among the Tarahumara, and many of them retreated into the mountains in the southwest corner of Chihuahua.

Despite the presence of missionaries, miners, and cattlemen, little acculturation occurred before the middle of the twentieth century, when the Mexican government opened facilities for the Indians. In the early 1960s, with the opening of the trans–Sierra Madre railroad (Ferrocarril de Chihuahua al Pacífico), outside influences expanded rapidly. Even so, the Tarahumara have selectively adopted outsiders' cultural traits. Few archaeological investigations have been conducted in their area.

ENVIRONMENT AND LIVING CONDITIONS

The climate of the Sierra Madre varies from tropical in the valleys to extreme cold in the highlands in winter. Lowland areas are desert, but the mountainous valleys are heavily wooded; in the uplands, heavy rainfalls provide adequate water for junipers, pines, and many other trees. Most Tarahumara live in hamlets (*rancherías*) of several families, each occupying a one- or two-room house. Until early in the 1900s, when outsiders opened local sawmills, houses were made of stone with earthen roofs; many Tarahumara still live in caves in the upper regions of the territory. Local leaders and ceremonial practitioners are elected, or more often appointed, as needed.

The Tarahumara practice hunting, gathering, and farming, mostly of corn, squash, and beans. Some, especially the lowlanders, work in a wage-based system. Corn is the staple, used for food and drink, especially the alcoholic *tesgüino.*

MUSICAL INSTRUMENTS

Indigenous musical instruments are limited to the gourd rattle, though a handheld drum may have been present in precontact days. Archaeological sites show the use of

the rattle and a musical bow during the precontact period (Zingg 1940:63–64).
Several instruments were adopted from the Europeans early in the time of contact.

The gourd rattle is normally made from a bottle gourd (*arisiki*), which grows in
the valleys. It grows in pear and globular shapes, and when cleaned out and partially
filled with seeds or pebbles serves for dances—the traditional *yúmari* and the adopted
matachín. With the coming of sawmills, some Tarahumara began making a distinctive four-sided rattle from thin *uré*-wood shavings glued to each other and held
together by two disks where the rattle handle passed through the container. These are
normally topped with a small cross and used by *matachines*. Rattles may also have
been made of hide, deer hooves, and ankle-tied cocoon versions.

Nonindigenous instruments

Instruments adopted from early Europeans are the guitar and the violin, and possibly
the pipe and tabor (there is evidence in pre-Columbian Mexico for the pipe and
tabor combination). Guitar and violin soundboards are made from local woods, usually pine or ash (*uré, cabarí, sawá, watosí*; for scientific names, see Pennington
1963:163), and fingerboards are made from *inóko,* a hardwood. The guitar is less
waisted than a modern instrument, but the bend is well above the center of the
sound box. Metal frets are inserted in the fingerboard, and commercial guitar strings
are purchased from local stores. Most guitars are undecorated, though occasionally
colored tin from a fruit can serves to hold the strings. The guitar is found much less
frequently than the violin; when used, it plays chords beneath the violin melody for
the *matachín* dancers.

The violin is somewhat larger than a modern European instrument, nearly the
size of a viola, sometimes with an extreme waist. It is made of the same woods as the
guitar, with *inóko* used for the fingerboard, pegs, and bow. The bridge may be made
of local woods, or sometimes of another material, such as plastic. Commercial violin
strings or guitar strings are used, and the tail piece is made of wood or tin from a can.
The head of the scroll box is often carved, usually in the shape of an animal's head
(horse heads often occur), and geometric patterns are frequently cut into the lower
part of the fingerboard. Horsetail hair is used for the bow, and a peg is sometimes
used to apply tension to it. Stringed instruments are normally unvarnished and
undecorated. Makers may use colored pencils to outline the eyes of the scroll animal
and the large f-holes.

Held in the old-fashioned way (against the bottom of the collarbone) violins are
played in large ensembles for *matachín* dancers, often with as many as eight to twelve
violinists; for small fiestas, a single violinist will do. The music consists of one to
three short phrases, repeated with variations lasting from five to thirty minutes,
depending on the dancers' patterns. Velasco Rivero (1983:170–77) outlines some of
the typical line-dance patterns as figure-eights, crisscrossing lines, and reverse loops.
Melodies may be played in unison or in parts, usually thirds, and infrequently with a
drone. Little is known about the songs of the *matachines*. The system is somewhat
complex, with different tunings used throughout a night's performance and possibly
different repertoires for different activities, such as playing for private fiestas at home
and dancing in front of or inside a church, or in procession (Griffith 1979). After
tuning, one performer begins playing, and others will join in as soon as they feel
comfortable with the composition.

The pipe and tabor consists of a duct flute and double-sided drum. The drum is
held with the little finger of the left hand, which plays the notes on the pipe, and
struck with a stick held in the right hand. Sometimes the drum may be rested against
the knee or the ground (figure 1). The drums are often as large as 60 centimeters or
more in diameter and about 10 centimeters deep; smaller ones are made and sold to

FIGURE 1   A Tarahumara pipe and tabor player with members of the soldiers' society seated beside him during Holy Week daytime ceremonies. Photo by J. Richard Haefer.

tourists, especially along the railroad. The pipe is a modified version of the European recorder, but with an external duct made by tying a short piece of larger-diameter cane atop the main body of the instrument. It may have as many as four holes for fingering, but three is the norm. During Lenten celebrations, pipes and tabors accompany the dancing of the *pariseos* (Spanish *fariseos* 'Pharisees', associated with Judas). Modern drums, made of wooden hoops, usually have several beads strung across one head as a snare. Older drums were fashioned from a hollowed-out section of a log and were deeper in shape. Drums may also be played without the pipe—a further indication of their antiquity within Tarahumaran culture. The drumhead, made of goatskin, may be decorated with red ochre paint, usually in geometric patterns, or left undecorated.

MUSICAL CONTEXTS AND GENRES

Tarahumara musical performances blend indigenous and European ideas, freely reinterpreted after the expulsion of the Jesuits from the area (Merrill 1983:296). In local cosmography, the universe consists of seven layers. One god—the father (*ononrúam*), the father god (*tata riósi*), the sun (*rayénari*, called *el padre* 'the father' by González Rodríguez 1982:78)—inhabits the uppermost level, and the god of the lower house—*terégor*, the devil—inhabits the lowest. The Tarahumara live in the middle levels. Other levels are occupied by mother, the moon, the Virgin Mary (*metsaka*, called *la madre* 'the mother' by González Rodríguez 1982:79), Mexicans, other non-Tarahumara (*cabóci* 'whiskered ones'), and others. The people "conceive of human beings as composed of a body 'sapá' and one or more [autonomous] souls" (Merrill 1988:87).

Tarahumara rituals perpetuate goodness and restore the well-being of particular individuals or the community, but most elements of either kind of celebration are the same. Rituals derived from Christian customs mark the feasts of the Virgin of Guadalupe (12 December), Christmas, the Feast of the Three Kings (Epiphany, 6 January), and Holy Week (especially Palm Sunday and Maundy Thursday through Holy Saturday). Less important or localized celebrations may take place for the Immaculate Conception of the Blessed Virgin Mary (8 December), Candlemas (2 February), Corpus Christi (in June), and various local saints. Fiestas normally begin on the eve of the holy day and continue for eight to twenty-four hours, ending with a dinner for all present. The sponsors (*pisteros,* Spanish *fiesteros*), assisted by their relatives, must provide for all aspects of the celebration including the dancers, musicians, and food.

Traditional ceremonies

González Rodríguez (1982:145) lists eight genres of dances: *tutuguri, yúmari, matachín* (not precontact), *pascola, warishíwami, kuwari, ayena,* and *yo'é,* indicating that the last four are rare indeed, if found at all. Among Tarahumara ceremonial practices, other sources list *bakánawi* as a curing ceremony, *korima* as a harvest ceremony, and *nawesari* as 'ritualized public sermons' that apparently occur within larger ceremonial contexts. Merrill (1988) and Velasco Rivero (1983) present analyses and examples of sermons, the primary method for presenting reproductions of knowledge through words as a means of restructuring Tarahumaran customs. Merrill discusses curing, including the processes of diagnosis and the prevention and alleviation of sickness, especially in relation to the concept of soul. Such cures are led by a curer (*owirúame*). Other sources describe curing only in relation to *tutuguri.*

Most sources state that *tutuguri* and *yúmari* are names for the same ceremony. It is suspected, however, that further research will show that *tutuguri* is the name for the entire ceremony complex, and *yúmari* may more specifically refer to the dance performed in a circle within the larger ceremony. Some sources indicate that the two names may be specific to particular geographical regions, though that concept seems less justifiable, or that *yúmari* is a generic Spanish term for native dances in this area. *Tutuguri,* a precontact ceremony, is often called a curing ceremony, but is actually practiced to maintain harmony—curing in the most general sense. Led by a chanter (*wikaráame, sawéame*) who presents the sermon and with two additional singers leads the singing, the *tutuguri* consists of a synthesis of indigenous and Roman Catholic elements, including a sacrifice of food—a white goat or chickens, plus food to be consumed in the fiesta following—to the sun god, line and circle dancing, and the use of a cross, incense, and a rosary (this resembles the Guarijio *túmari*) [see GUARIJIO]. *Tutuguri* is also celebrated at eclipses and the winter solstice, with a representation of the sun painted on large drums played during the night.

Tutuguri songs differ from most Middle and North American Indian songs in that they start low and ascend, though the overall structure has successive phrases beginning at lower tones. Songs are usually quite brief, as few as three phrases of only about four seconds each, repeated for up to five minutes or more. A rattle pattern is played with downward strokes throughout most of the song, alternating with rolls at the ascent (*Indian Music of Northwest Mexico* 1978). Nearly all sources report the musical texts as being unintelligible, but a seventeenth-century observer (Guadalaxara 1683) translated a musical text loosely into a Spanish sentence glossable as "she asks the moon to take care of her sheep so they can have much wool to card, comb, and knit for good blankets" (González Rodríguez 1982:110). *Tutuguri,* therefore, is sung and danced for curing, for propitiation, and for entreating the gods on behalf of all Tarahumara, or as they say, asking forgiveness (*wikálawi tánia*) for a long and healthy life, abundant crops, and many children.

Tutuguri ends with the offering of food in the early-morning hours, followed by a feast for all in attendance. A *tutuguri* performed during Lent may be accompanied by *fariseos* dancing to the pipe and tabor; the rest of the year, *matachines* may or may not be present.

Several sources, including the seventeenth-century authors Cajas Castro (1992:199–211) and Rodríguez (1982), mention the use of peyote (*jíkuri*) by the Tarahumara. Cajas Castro believes this practice to be older than that of *yúmari,* but

On their heads, the *matachín* dancers wear crowns made from a shell of wood covered with bright, meter-long streamers and mirrors or reflective pieces of metal.

few details are known. Peyote celebrations take place only in winter and may involve a *tutuguri* or a *matachín*. González Rodríguez (1982:117) mentions its function for the purification of the dead in a private ceremony led by a *sipáame*. Permission of the local village governor is required, and the ceremony includes the drinking of *tesgüino,* plus such Christian elements as a cross.

Acculturated ceremonies

European-derived ceremonies center on the Christian liturgical calendar. In remote locations, they follow an outmoded calendar, modified by time and the absence of priests. Being an oral-tradition culture, the Tarahumara are not attuned to changes in the dates for the celebration of various ceremonies as dictated by the ecumenical council known as Vatican II. Therefore, they continue to celebrate the ceremonies as they think they always have, using the dates of the former calendar.

Two main organizations are found: the *matachines* and the societies of Holy Week. *Matachines* dance throughout the year, except during Lent and Easter, especially for Our Lady of Guadalupe day, Christmas, and Epiphany, though they may appear at private fiestas and even dance at *tutuguri*. *Matachines,* introduced from Europe in the 1600s, were first noted in the village of Norogachi in September 1737 by the missionary Lorenzo Gero (González Rodríguez 1982:146), and again in January 1752 by Bartholomé Braun—the latter undoubtedly for an Epiphany celebration, the former probably for the Exaltation of the Holy Cross.

Dancing in front of the church or a private home, the *matachines* (called *awíeme* 'dancer') are led by one or two organizers (*monarkos,* rather like booking agents but physically present to lead the group) and a *chapeyó* (another kind of dancer, found principally at smaller, home ceremonies) wearing a deer's head. From four to twenty or more *matachines* move in intricate lines, changing directions at the organizers' shouts and occasionally performing elaborate circle-eight figurations (see Velasco Rivero 1983:170–177, for movement diagrams). On their heads, the *matachín* dancers wear crowns made from a shell of wood covered with bright, meter-long streamers and mirrors or reflective pieces of metal, distinctively different from those of their northern neighbors, the Yaqui and Mayos. Their lower face and shoulders are covered by scarves, as is the front of the waist; brightly colored shirts and jeans are worn beneath. In some regions, colorful bolts of cloth may be draped around the body. In their right hand they carry a gourd rattle and in the left a wand, sometimes shaped like a heart, covered with crepe paper. The dancers, all men, move to the music of violins, in a few places accompanied by one or two guitarists.

Holy Week celebrations are more elaborate and involve two sodalities: *pariseos* (Spanish *fariseos* 'Pharisees') and *sontárusi* (Spanish *soldados* 'soldiers'). Leaders appoint appropriate boys and men from the village to dance with each group. Between mass and other ritual devotions, different activities take place daily, including dancing inside and outside the church, and processions. A straw-stuffed effigy of

Judas is hidden by the *pariseos*, and when it is found by the soldiers, it is "killed," burned, or mutilated genitally, depending on local custom. On Holy Saturday, individuals from the two groups wrestle one another, and in some regions one or two *pascola*-like dancers appear. Griffith (1983:775) identifies the *pascola* as "a clown and dancer whose appearance enlivens certain fiestas," but who is not part of a separate cult, as in other Northern Mexican Indian cultures. *Pariseos* are identified by costuming that includes a bare chest and back with large white scarves or cloth tied over the lower body. Long scarves are tied around the head and hang down the back. The leaders wear turkey-feather headdresses. In some regions, a few dancers have large spots of white clay painted on their chests, backs, and legs, and are accordingly called *pintos*. Elsewhere additional dancers, such as *tenanches* 'outsiders' and *mulatos,* appear. Pharisees dance to the pipe and tabor or the drum alone.

The soldiers dance simultaneously with and against the *pariseos*, are dressed distinctively in long white cloths draped over their bodies, and wear long, red headbands. The leader carries a large red banner of office, and all carry long lances. Holy Week festivities are sponsored by one or two *pisteros* assisted by their relatives and friends, who may take a year or more to save enough money to pay for the occasion. As with all Tarahumara celebrations, the dancing ends with feasting for all and much drinking of *tesgüino,* often continuing in private homes for several days after Easter.

FURTHER STUDY

Detailed descriptions of the presentations of *matachines* (including more information about organizers and *chapeyos*) are given in Bennett and Zingg (1976 [1935]), Cajas Castro (1992:154–163), Fontana et al. (1977, 1979), González Rodríguez (1982), Merrill (1983), and Velasco Rivero (1983:152–188). Tarahumara Holy Week celebrations have been studied by González Rodríguez (1982), Velasco Rivero (1983:189–233), Cajas Castro (1992:164–187), and Merrill (1983).

REFERENCES

Bennett, Wendell Clark, and Robert M. Zingg. 1976 [1935]. *The Tarahumara, an Indian Tribe of Northern Mexico.* Glorieta, N. M.: Rio Grande Press.

Cajas Castro, Juan. 1992. *La sierra tarahumara o los desvelos de la modernidad en Mexico.* México, D.F.: Consejo Nacional para la Cultura y las Artes.

Fontana, Bernard, et al. 1977. *The Other Southwest, Indian Arts and Crafts of Northwestern Mexico.* Phoenix: Heard Museum.

———. 1979. *The Material World of the Tarahumara.* Tucson: Arizona State Museum.

Griffith, James S. 1979. *Tarahumara Matachin Music.* Phoenix: Canyon Records, C-8000. Notes to LP disk.

———. 1983. "Kachinas and Masking." In *Southwest,* ed. Alfonso Ortiz, 764–777. Handbook of North American Indians, 10. Washington, D.C.: Smithsonian Institution Press.

González Rodríguez, Luis. 1982. *Tarahumara, La sierra y el hombre.* México, D.F.: Fondo de Cultura Económica.

Guadalaxara, Tomás de. 1683. *Compendio del arte de la lengue de los tarahumares y guazapares.* Puebla: Imprenta Real.

Indian Music of Northwest Mexico. 1978. Canyon Records C-8001. LP disk.

Merrill, William L. 1983. "Tarahumara Social Organization, Political Organization, and Religion." In *Southwest,* ed. Alfonso Ortiz, 290–303. Handbook of North American Indians, 10. Washington, D.C.: Smithsonian Institution Press.

———. 1988. *Rarámuri Souls, Knowledge and Social Process in Northern Mexico.* Washington, D.C.: Smithsonian Institution Press.

Pennington, Campbell W. 1963. *The Tarahumar of Mexico, Their Environment and Material Culture.* Salt Lake City: University of Utah Press.

Velasco Rivero, Pedro de. 1983. *Danzar o morir, religión y resistencia a la dominación en la cultura tarahumara.* México, D.F.: Centro de Reflexión Teológica.

Zingg, Robert M. 1940. *The Tarahumara, an Indian Tribe of Northern Mexico.* Chicago: University of Chicago Press.

Yaqui and Mayo
James S. Griffith

The Yaqui and Their Music
The Mayo and Their Music
The Music of Neighboring Tribes
Further Study

The traditional homeland of the Yaqui and the Mayo is in northwest Mexico. Yaqui territory was, and is, along the lower Río Yaqui in central Sonora; the culturally related Mayo live along the banks of the Río Mayo in southern Sonora and the Río Fuerte and the Río Ocoroni in northern Sinaloa. The two groups are sometimes called Cáhitan-speaking peoples (Beals 1945:1003). They speak closely related languages belonging to the Uto-Aztecan stock (Greenberg 1987:381). The Yaqui call themselves Yoeme, and the Mayo call themselves Yoreme.

Both groups have an uncertain archaeological record, and they may have arrived in their homelands fairly late in the prehistoric period. Both groups experienced intensive contacts with Jesuit missionaries in the 1600s and 1700s and developed religious and ceremonial systems blending European and native elements. Yaqui and Mayo musics resemble each other in general form and in how they are used within their cultures. Inasmuch as the Yaqui have been much more thoroughly studied, written about, and recorded, they may serve as a baseline in describing the music of both groups.

THE YAQUI AND THEIR MUSIC

The earliest recorded contact between the Yaqui and Europeans was in 1533, when the Yaqui fought a Spanish slave-raiding expedition to a standstill. As the Spaniards expanded their missions and permanent settlements up the West coast of Mexico, this pattern continued, with Spanish attempts at entering Yaqui territory being repulsed. Finally, in the early 1600s, the Yaqui formally requested that missionaries be sent to them. This was done in 1617, when the Jesuits Tomás Basilio and Andrés Pérez de Ribas arrived on the Río Yaqui. They received an enthusiastic welcome, and thus began a Yaqui-Jesuit association that lasted until increasing Spanish pressure led to armed revolts on the part of the Yaqui.

These revolts started in 1740 and continued off and on until the early twentieth century. The earlier issues involved Yaqui autonomy; later on, the sacredness of Yaqui land became an issue, especially during the 1800s, when Mexican pressures to put that land to "civilized" uses increased. Facing a policy of genocide and deportation around 1900, many Yaqui fled across the border to the United States, where they found work, often on railroads, and formed squatters' communities that eventually developed into Yaqui villages.

Today in Arizona, there are several settlements of Yaqui in addition to the traditional villages on the Río Yaqui. Guadalupe near Tempe, Yoem Pueblo at Marana, and three communities in or near Tucson hold the bulk of the Yaqui population in the United States. All these but the Marana community hold the annual cycle of Yaqui Roman Catholic ceremonies. The Yaqui were federally recognized as a tribe in 1978, when the Pascua Yaqui Reservation was established southwest of Tucson.

Older forms of Yaqui music

The earliest mention of Yaqui music is in a 1645 account (cited in Beals 1945:31–32) that describes the Yaqui as having flageolets, probably the two-piece, three-hole flutes that are still in use; trumpets, possibly made from conchs; *atabales,* kettledrums, possibly flat single- or double-headed drums resembling contemporary drums; and *teponaztli,* a term used in central Mexico to describe cylindrical idiophones with an H-shaped slit creating two lamellas that were struck.

Other instruments found in contemporary Cáhitan-speaking culture may be of native American origin. Rasping sticks (*hirukiam*) of a hardwood (often brazilwood) are played while supported on gourd resonators (*bweham*). A waxed half gourd is floated in a basin of water and struck with a wrapped stick, making a hollow "thunk"; in Yaqui, the instrument, a struck idiophone, is called *ba kubahe* 'water drum'. Gourd and split cane rattles are also used, and may have existed before the Spaniards arrived. Other instruments of probable native origin are idiophones worn by ritual dancers, such as leg rattles (*teneboim*), made from cocoons of the giant silk moth (*Rothschildia jorulla*) that are dried, filled with seeds, and strung together. The deer dancer wears a belt of deer-hoof rattles (*rihhutiam*), which, like the dance itself, may also be of pre-Hispanic origin.

Traditional Yaqui music is closely tied to the Christian ceremonial cycle and Yaqui ceremonialism. Yaqui (and Mayo) religion is a syncretic blending of native concepts and practices with those introduced in the early 1600s by Jesuit missionaries. The annual ceremonial cycle involves a series of public and private religious fiestas. These may celebrate patronal saints' days and other important Christian feasts, including Palm Sunday and Easter.

Deer dance

The oldest level of Yaqui ceremonialism seems to be the deer dance (figure 1) and the songs accompanying it. Deer songs are sung by three or four men who sit on the ground and play their accompanying instruments. Two or three men play rasps on gourd resonators; another strikes a water drum. The singers follow the lead singer, resulting in a slightly echoic sound. Descending melodies are common in these songs, which represent an ancient level of Yaqui music and poetry. In a difficult, archaic form of the Yaqui language, they refer to happenings and conditions in *seyewailo,* the world of the enchanted wilderness, which for the Yaqui parallels the universal world of sensations (Evers and Molina 1987).

The deer dancer wears cocoon-husk leg rattles and a deer-hoof rattle belt and carries two gourd rattles (*ayam*) in his hands. During his dance, he becomes the deer, whose voice the singers provide. The rasp is said to be his breath, and the water drum his heartbeat. Many Yaqui believe the dance and the songs came from the time in Yaqui history when they relied heavily on hunting and performed the dance at an all-night feast before the hunt took place to "please the deer and ask his pardon for having to kill him" (Griffith and Molina 1980:34).

FIGURE 1   At a Yaqui deer dance just south of Tucson, Arizona, a dancer wears cocoon-husk strung rattles (*teneboim*) on his legs and a deer-hoof strung rattle (*rihhutiam*) as a belt; he holds two gourd rattles (*ayam*). Three singers are behind the dancer, and the instrumentalists, from the left, include a man striking a water drum (*ba kubahe*), two men playing rasping sticks (*hirukiam*) held on gourd resonators (*bweham*), and a pipe and tabor player (*tampaleo*). Photo by James S. Griffith, 1976.

Pascola *dance*

Appearing in the same context as the deer dancer is the *pascola* dancer. Any religious fiesta (*pahko*) must have at least one *pascola* present. *Pascolas* play many roles. They formally open and close the fiesta with speeches and dances. They act as ritual clowns, focusing people's attention on the unfolding *pahko*. They act as ritual hosts, dispensing water and cigarettes to spectators, and they dance to two kinds of music.

While the musicians are playing harp and violin (a small harp, supported on the player's lap, and one violin for the Yaqui; a larger harp and two violins for the Mayo), the dancer performs a complex, European-appearing dance (figure 2) by elaborating on the rhythm of the music with his feet, with head down and arms loosely at his sides. Idiophones—leg rattles (*teneboim*) about his lower legs, brass bells (*coyolim*) dangling from his belt—accentuate the rhythm. The melodies are called *sonim* in Yaqui and *sones* in Spanish. When the music changes to the vertical flute and double-headed frame drum played by the same man (pipe and tabor fashion), the *pascola*'s dance changes. He slips a small wooden mask over his face and takes up a rattle (*senasawim*) in his right hand. This rattle has a wooden handle and a slotted wooden body with metal discs strung on two nails crossing the slot like a sistrum. Peering with his masked face and pawing with his feet, the *pascola* engages in complex manipulations of the rattle against the palm of his left hand.

The violin and the harp are European instruments, probably introduced by Jesuit missionaries to provide suitable music for the mass and other ceremonial occasions. Though the vertical three-hole flute may be native American in origin, its simultaneous use by a drummer is distributed over much of Mexico and has strong parallels with European usage dating back to the 1200s.

FIGURE 2 Just south of Tucson, Arizona, Yaqui *pascola* dancers perform, accompanied by a harp and a violin. The senior dancer on the right is wearing *teneboim* on his legs and a belt with pendant metal bells. He is being watched by two younger *pascolas* awaiting their turns to dance. Photo by James S. Griffith, 1979.

Matachines (*contradances*)

Another body of Yaqui and Mayo music is played on violins and guitars for *matachines,* contradances done by men and boys as an act of devotion to the Virgin Mary. Some *matachín* melodies bear a haunting resemblance to Anglo-Celtic fiddle melodies, but it is hard to carry this comparison beyond the realm of generality (Spicer 1980:99–103).

Matachines are known over much of what was northern New Spain. Pueblo Indians in New Mexico and mestizos in many parts of northern Mexico and the United States Southwest perform them. Among the Yaqui (and to a lesser extent among the Mayo), they are intensely sacred and are never performed on secular occasions. This practice contrasts with performance of the deer dance and *pascola* dances, which can be part of purely secular celebrations.

Though the use of the violin and guitar shows European influence, the Yaqui and the Mayo play a perhaps more ancient mouth-resonated bow (*baka aapa* 'cane harp'), in its modern form a length of local cane with a tuning peg at one end and a single nylon string. Coastal Mayo and Yaqui frequently use fishing line for the string. This is strictly a solo instrument, played usually for the musician's enjoyment; he plays melodies (*sones*— each *son* has its own title) that include those from *pascola* and deer dances (Warman 1976).

A purely secular Yaqui song is the *corrido,* sung in Yaqui, often to the accompaniment of a guitar. *Corridos* are sung narrative poems that deal with persons or incidents of interest to the Yaqui community. They are frequently sung by groups of men in the same manner as deer songs (Nuss 1976).

matachines   Sacred dance in northern Mexico and adjacent areas of the southwestern United States

corrido   Yaqui narrative song genre

mariachi   The most nationally prominent folk-derived Mexican musical ensemble since the 1930s, usually with guitars, *vihuela, guitarrón,* violins, trumpets, and singers

trío romántico   Mexican-derived ensemble of three male musicians who sing sad, nostalgic, and romantic songs while accompanying themselves on guitars

Yaqui norteño *music*

The Yaqui have always been quick to take up new instruments and new kinds of music. Since the end of World War II, many Yaqui musicians have been performing in the *norteño* style, which has spread from Texas into the Arizona-Sonora border country. Several Yaqui combos (*conjuntos*) have been active around Tucson; in 1972, one of these, El Conjunto Murrietta, recorded two LP disks (*"Chicken Scratch": Popular Dance Music of the Indians of Southern Arizona* 1972). In 1993, Los Hermanos Cuatro, a Yaqui *norteño* quartet from Old Pascua Village in Tucson, performed at the Festival of American Folklife in Washington, D.C. This group has been extremely popular among working-class Yaqui and Mexicans on Tucson's southwest side. Yaqui *norteño* activity has been also strong in Sonora. The polka *"Flor de Capomo"* ('Water-Lily Flower'), with words in Spanish and Yaqui, was composed by a Yaqui named José Molina. It was popular during the mid-1990s in Arizona and Sonora. Arizona Yaqui also participate in mariachis and *tríos románticos.*

THE MAYO AND THEIR MUSIC

The Spanish contacted the Mayo shortly before they contacted the Yaqui, as the Spanish expedition was moving up the coast of Mexico. Differences between the two peoples that appeared at this first contact have persisted. The Mayo seemed to accept the incursions of outsiders (at least to some degree), but the Yaqui have always resisted foreign entry into their land unless it was on Yaqui terms. The Mayo participated in revolts against the Spanish and later the Mexican governments, but their resistance basically ended in the late 1800s, and they never experienced the genocidal programs directed by the Mexican government against the Yaqui (Crumrine 1977; Spicer 1962:46–85). The Mayo continue to live along the Mayo and Fuerte rivers, experiencing constantly greater disruption and incursions on the part of their Mexican neighbors.

Mayo music is extremely similar to Yaqui music, but small differences occur. Mayo *pascola* groups usually use two violins and a harp, but the harp is larger than the standard Yaqui lap-held harp. Mayo deer dancing tends to be heavier than that of the Yaqui. But these are differences of style within the same general pattern.

THE MUSIC OF NEIGHBORING TRIBES

Several other native groups in northwestern Mexico and southern Arizona have music that appears to have derived from Yaqui or Mayo sources. The Tarahumara of the Chihuahuan Sierra Madre have a *pascola* dancer who performs on sacred and secular occasions to the music of a solo violin [see TARAHUMARA]. The Tarahumara also have a strong *matachín* tradition in which the music is supplied by a violin (heard on *Tarahumara Matachin Music / Matachines Tarahumaras* 1979).

The Warihio [see GUARIJIO] of the Sonoran mountains play *pascola* music that closely resembles that of the nearby Mayo. The Tohono O'odham (formerly Papago)

in southern Arizona have *pascola* dancers who perform to the music of a violin and a guitar. Farther north, the Gila River Pima have at least one group of *matachines*. Members of both these Arizona cultures agree that their music derives from that of the Yaqui.

FURTHER STUDY

For an overview of Yaqui history, see Spicer 1962:46–85 and 1980. Leticia Varela (1986) takes a detailed look at Yaqui traditional music and musical instruments as they existed in the 1970s and early 1980s.

Recordings of Yaqui music have been made by anthropologists and others since the 1920s. The earliest known recordings were made in Guadalupe, Arizona, by Frances Densmore during Holy Week of 1922 (Densmore 1932); these cylinders, housed in the Library of Congress, contain deer songs and Yaqui *corridos*. In the early 1940s, Laura Boulton visited the Yaqui Regiment in Tlaxcala, south and east of Mexico City. During the 1930s, trying to neutralize the Yaqui as potential armed defenders of Yaqui land, the army recruited able-bodied Yaqui males into this regiment, gave them decent pay, and stationed them far from Yaqui country. Boulton's expedition, which occurred during Holy Week, resulted in a Folkways recording (Boulton 1957). In 1940, Edward Spicer of the University of Arizona arranged for John Green to bring portable recording equipment into Pascua Village near Tucson, Arizona, during Holy Week. Green recorded deer and *pascola* music, antiphonally sung hymns, and *matachín* music; this was released on the General label, and reissued on Canyon in 1980. Henrietta Yurchenco recorded in Vicam on the Río Yaqui in 1946, and some of her materials were released on Folkways (Yurchenco 1952). Samuel Charters, vacationing in Guaymas, Sonora, in 1956, happened on a Yaqui harpist playing *pascola* music on the streets while his son danced; another Folkways album resulted from that encounter (Charters 1957). Finally, the Canyon Record company arranged recording sessions in the Río Yaqui village of Potam (1972), in Old Pascua Village in Tucson (1976) and in a studio near Phoenix; these sessions resulted in three albums (1972, 1976, 1980) containing deer and *pascola* music, *matachín* melodies, and Yaqui *corridos*.

With few exceptions, Yaqui music has been recorded wherever there have been large concentrations of Yaqui in the twentieth century. The contexts of Yaqui recordings have included actual ceremonies, field-recording sessions using portable equipment, and studio sessions. For a videotaped presentation of part of a Yaqui deer and *pascola* performance see *Seyewailo, the Flower World: Yaqui Deer Songs* (1978).

Mayo music, like Mayo culture in general, is less recorded, less studied, and less available. The Instituto Nacional de Antropología e Historia of Mexico issued some Mayo music, including the elusive mouth-resonated bow (*baka aapa*), on an LP album with notes by Arturo Warman (1976). Canyon issued the album *Indian Music of Northwest Mexico* (1977), containing recordings of Mayo and related Warihio music. But as with anthropological studies and general attention from the outside world, the Yaqui have received much more notice than their Mayo cousins. Written transcripts of music collected in 1933 from Yaqui and Mayo appear in Domínguez (1962).

REFERENCES

Beals, Ralph L. 1945. "The Aboriginal Culture of the Cáhita Indians." *Ibero-Americana* 19:31–32, 67–70.

Boulton, Laura. 1957. *Indian Music of Mexico.* Folkways FW-8851. LP disk.

Charters, Samuel. 1957. *Yaqui Dances—the Pascola Music of the Yaqui Indians of Sonora, Mexico.* Folkways FW-957. LP disk.

"Chicken Scratch": Popular Dance Music of the Indians of Southern Arizona. 1972. Canyon C-6085 and C-6162. LP disk.

El Conjunto Murrietta Tocando Norteño. 1978. Canyon C-6162. LP disk.

Crumrine, N. Ross. 1977. *The Mayo Indians of Sonora: A People Who Refuse to Die.* Tucson: University of Arizona Press.

Densmore, Frances. 1932. *Yuman and Yaqui Music.* Washington: U.S. Government Printing Office. Smithsonian Institution Bureau of American Ethnology. Bulletin 110.

Domínguez, Francisco. 1962. "Informe Sobre la Investigacíon Folklórico-Musical Realizada en las Regiones de los Yaquis, Seris y Mayos, Estado de Sonora, en Abril y Mayo de 1933." In *Investigación Folklórica en México—Materiales,* vol. 1, ed. Baltasar Samper et al. México, D.F.: Secretaría de Educación Pública, Instituto Nacional de Bellas Artes.

Evers, Laurence J., and Felipe Molina. 1987. *Yaqui Deer Songs: Maso Bwikam: A Native American Poetry.* Tucson: University of Arizona Press.

Greenberg, Joseph H. 1987. *Language in the Americas.* Stanford: Stanford University Press.

Griffith, James S., and Felipe S. Molina. 1980. *Old Men of the Fiesta: An Introduction to the Pascola Arts.* Phoenix: The Heard Museum.

Indian Music of Northwest Mexico. 1977. Canyon C-8001. LP disk.

Nuss, Robert. 1976. *Yaqui Ritual and Festive Music.* Canyon C-6140. Notes to LP disk.

Seyewailo, the Flower World: Yaqui Deer Songs. 1978. Produced by Larry Evers. University of Arizona Radio-TV-Film Bureau. Video.

Spicer, Edward H. 1962. *Cycles of Conquest: The Impact of Spain, Mexico, and the United States on the Indians of the Southwest, 1533–1960.* Tucson: University of Arizona Press.

———. 1980. *The Yaquis: A Cultural History.* Tucson: University of Arizona Press.

Tarahumara Matachin Music / Matachines Tarahumaras. 1979. Canyon C-8000. LP disk.

Varela, Leticia. 1986. *La Música en la Vida de los Yaquis.* Hermosillo, Sonora, México, D.F.: El Gobierno del Estado de Sonora, Secretaría de Fomento Educativo y Cultura.

Warman, Arturo. 1976. *Música Indígena de México, Vol. 5—Música Indígena del Noroeste.* México, D.F.: Instituto Nacional de Antropología e Historia. Notes to LP disk.

Yaqui Festive and Ritual Music. 1972. Canyon C-6140. LP disk.

Yaqui Fiesta and Religious Music—Historic Recordings from Old Pascua Village. 1980. Recorded by Edward H. Spicer. Canyon CR-7999. LP disk.

Yaqui—Music of the Pascola and Deer Dance. 1976. Canyon C-6099. LP disk.

Yaqui Pascola Music of Arizona. 1980. Canyon CR-7998. LP disk.

Yurchenco, Henrietta. 1952. *Indian Music of Mexico.* Folkways FE- 4413. LP disk.

Yuma

E. Fernando Nava L.

Musical Contexts and Genres
Musical Instruments
Learning Music
Musical Change
Further Study

The Yuma are an Amerindian people residing in northern Mexico and the southwestern United States. They divide into several subgroups with common cultural traits. The Yuma who occupy Mexican territory include the Cucapá (136 persons), the Kumiai (96), the Pai-pai (360), and the Kiliwa (41); all four groups have been in existence for hundreds of years. That each group's language has words and names for the other groups shows that intergroup communication has occurred for generations. Joseph Greenberg (1987:381) places the Esselen-Yuman language in the Hokan family of the Northern Amerind phylum. Data from colonial chroniclers to present-day ethnographers confirms that the Yuma groups have maintained similar cultures. In the beginning, they were hunter-gatherers with a militaristic tradition that made their colonization difficult. Today, they are farmers, cattlemen, and laborers.

One of the first kinds of music described for the native Yuma was not indigenous. It was music taught by religious colonists, including friars Eusebio Francisco Kino and Juan María Salvatierra. No indigenous Yuma music has survived. Colonists outlawed shamanic songs and established religious holidays and celebrations, especially that of Saint Francis. Written accounts of native music and musical practice survive. To gain local trust, Salvatierra participated in a performance: "entering a circle of dancers, he danced with them for a long time a piece they call, in their language, *nimbé*" (Lemmon 1977:10[55]:16).

MUSICAL CONTEXTS AND GENRES

It was not until the 1800s that Yuma regional genres began to be transcribed. Among these pieces are dances and songs that the Yuma used to retain their cultural identity and to defend themselves from Spanish influences. These songs have an important function, characteristic of the Yuma macroculture and its present subgroups: they represent the convergence of communal, intertribal, interethnic, and regional identities. Their homogeneity, which includes mythological references, allows a discussion of Yuma musical tradition with minor internal differences.

Though the Yuma have repertoires sung exclusively by men, men and women participate in music. There are five genres of Yuma song: songs within the narrations

Some song-dance cycles mark specific times of day: the wildcat is a cycle that begins at sunset, but at midnight, with the coyote's howl, morning pieces begin to be played. When the owl hoots at dawn, the dancing ends.

of myths, lullabies (*arrullos*), personal songs (for good luck in fight or games), shamanistic songs, and social dance-songs with occasional mythological content. Only shamanistic and social dance-songs remain in the present repertoire, organized into cycles and single songs, the former being more important. The soul of their tradition is a sung dance accompanied by a rattle.

From a structural viewpoint, the songs usually follow the pattern AABA, with repetitions ad libitum. Each section has anywhere from one to four phrases of about the same length and a range of five to twelve tones. From a melodic perspective, section B (*levantada*) is unique among indigenous musical styles. It involves imitation, partial substitution, lengthening, or insertion of the main melodic principle several tones higher than the tonic while a rattle makes a sort of crescendo-tremolo. In some cases, the "transposed" fragment is sung on tones not used in the main melody. After it, the melody goes back to its former, quieter state, and in some cases it uses an altogether different range of pitches from that of the initial melody. The main melodic character is descending. The melodic range is restricted to anywhere from a perfect fifth to a major ninth. The range of most of a song's parts is limited to major seconds, minor thirds, and major thirds. The tonic is usually the lowest melodic tone, and the major third, perfect fourth, and perfect fifth above it are the most important tones. The scales are essentially pentatonic.

Literary forms such as prose and stanzas are sung and are repeated according to the duration of the melody. Often texts include vocables or words from Yuma languages. At times, the lyrics of the *levantada* differ from those of the main melody. Though this process might seem confusing, it actually helps the music by emphasizing the melodic line and making it an efficient system of communication. Most songs are shared by the Yuma subgroups, making them part of a long-standing intertribal tradition.

Each song begins with the shaking of a rattle (figure 1) and ends with a rhythmic sequence of the rattle and the vocables *ha-ha-ha*. Specific cries or yells end specific cycles. Except for brief breaks when the melody and the rattle stop, the rattle plays throughout the song. The rhythm usually follows that of the text. If the text is short, the rhythm follows a regular pattern; if the text is long, the words are distributed in asymmetrical patterns modifying the rhythm. In some cases the rhythm of the voice and the rhythm of the rattle coincide; in others they do not. Syncopation and triplets are common.

The practice of Yuma shamanistic singing has decreased but it is performed in curative practices and rituals. The Cucapá shaman alternates singing with movements of his hand, rocking of his body, and cries similar to those in the dance. These practices transcended Yuma territory. In previous times, the Cucapá and other groups sought Pima healers (related to the Uto-Aztec), who sang in a style resembling that of the Yuma. Some movements of rattles are specific to shamanic practice.

FIGURE 1   Señor don Trinidad Ochurte, a Yuma elder of the Kiliwa group, near Ensenada, Baja California, Mexico, sings and shakes his rattle. Photo by Lorenzo Armendariz, 1992.

Dancing

In social dancing, up to four rows of ten persons holding each other's shoulders move in advancing and retreating patterns. While they dance, a singer and backup singers (*ayudantes* 'helpers') standing in front of them sing in unison. The Kiliwa have another way of dancing: in a squatting position. The singers begin singing while seated, but stand up to join the dance after the first *levantada*. At times, the bodily movements and rhythms, with accompanying cries, do not follow the musical beat. Some song-dance cycles mark specific times of day: the wildcat (*gato salvaje*) is a cycle that begins at sunset, with songs about the first stars of the evening; but at midnight, with the coyote's howl, morning pieces begin to be played. When the owl (*tecolote*) hoots at dawn, the dancing ends.

Festivals and other celebrations

Yuma dances are performed during holidays, times when the Yuma visit other groups. These intertribal, interethnic visits may entail traveling across the border between Mexico and the United States. Such holidays demonstrate the groups' cooperation, particularly in dances that were sometimes the only way men and women met potential mates. Cycles of songs about birds, the *peón* (a guessing game with bets), cats, and the *kuri-kuri* (the Yuma cannot translate this word) are sung during holidays like the one held in September, which may fuse an agricultural festival and Mexico's independence day. Aside from holidays, the Yuma attend festivals organized by indigenous institutions on both sides of the border.

Though weddings and birthdays are also celebratory occasions, more emphasis is given to celebrations of funerals and holidays related to death and the dead, though ritual behavior has formally decreased. Until the 1950s, cremation-related ceremonies were common; these were all-night rituals with singing, dancing, and wailing. As in religious and harvest ceremonies, any cycle of songs could be performed, but the Yuma preferred the favorite songs of the deceased.

MUSICAL INSTRUMENTS

A rattle is the only instrument now used to accompany Yuma singing (see figure 1). It is made of a gourd that is prepared and cooked in salt and cleaned out with wire. It is then filled with *palmilla* seeds and sealed with an oak stick, inserted to serve as a handle. Sometimes, if the singer wishes, small holes are drilled into the gourd, raising its pitch slightly. The body of the rattle may have the decoration of painted stripes or a solid color. The importance of this rattle is underlined by its citations in myths, where it is sometimes not made of gourd, but, as in one tale, from the scrotum of a hero's divine father.

Two other idiophones formerly served in alternation with the rattle for the accompaniment of song: a rattle made of deer's hoofs strung together with strings (believed to have originated among the Kumiai, but used only by the Cucapá); and the tortoiseshell rattle (among the Kiliwa, the shell's designs were sketches of a future world). A flute and a drum, the only Yuma aerophone and membranophone, are seldom used.

LEARNING MUSIC

According to the Yuma, people learn melodies, accompanying rhythms, and ceremonies in which singing and dancing play a part, through dreams. Another method of learning is through listening and repeating the songs of festive celebrations. Arizona Yuma culture is considered the creative center for songs, and the Cucapá are credited as those who have contributed most to the diffusion of songs. The place of origin of some songs is known, especially of songs that have become diffused during the twentieth century. An example is that of the Pai-pai man who went to learn from the Mohave in Arizona and brought his knowledge to the Yuma, Cucapá, and others. Another is that of a Kumiai man who learned to sing in Yuma and taught a Pai-pai man. The Kiliwa consider themselves to be the least skilled in this art, but they attend the performances of their Pai-pai neighbors.

Some Yuma songs are so old that their origins are unknown. Not only do single songs travel; complete cycles of songs have spread throughout different regions. This diffusion of song is common not only among the Yuma, but also among the Uto-Aztec (Yutonahua) people and the Papago (Tohono O'odham), groups that share cycles, genres, and styles of singing. Yuma singers usually attend Uto-Aztec celebrations, and vice versa. Back-and-forth exchange of the Yuma repertoire makes it coherent.

MUSICAL CHANGE

The extensive repertoire of songs accompanied by a rattle suggests that the Yuma have preferred rattle-accompanied songs for generations. This theory is strengthened by the fact that unlike neighboring tribes, the Yuma do not use readily available artifacts, such as pottery and baskets, as percussion instruments.

In the 1970s, the Yuma adopted the six-stringed Spanish guitar (*guitarra sexta*), the button accordion, the violin, and the bass, with the genres these instruments usually perform in Mexico, such as the popular mestizo tunes heard through the media. Nevertheless, such ensembles rarely appear in the heart of the culture, and they never perform traditional repertoire. On the radio, all groups listen to genres such as *corridos* and other (near the U.S. border) *norteño-fronterizo* music played by accordion-driven ensembles.

Musicians, their songs, and holidays have played important social roles, especially during moments of cultural crisis, because they preserve the social continuity of each community. This is why each group tries to have at least one singer who can hand down his knowledge and art to local children.

FURTHER STUDY

Because some Yuma live in the United States, several excellent studies are in English. Two classics are by Frances Densmore (1932) on the Yuma and Yaqui and by George Herzog (1928) on the Yuma. More recently are studies of the Cocopa (Cucapá) by William Kelly (1977) and the Kiliwa by Mauricio Mixco (1983, 1985). Numerous investigations of the Yuma in Baja California include those by Gema Camacho Fajardo (1989); Thomas B. Hinton and Roger C. Owen (1957); Jorge Martínez Zepeda (1989); Roger C. Owen, Nancy E. Walstrom, and Ralph C. Michelsen (1969); and María Teresa Uriarte Castañeda (1974). This region has been important for Yuma research because of Jesuit influence in Baja California. Alfred E. Lemmon (1977) has written about the Jesuits and their music in that part of Mexico, and Miguel Del Barco (1973) has studied the colonial chroniclers' writings; both studies deal with early Yuma music.

—TRANSLATED BY CARMEN ARENCÍBIA

REFERENCES

Camacho Fajardo, Gema, and E. Fernando Nava L. 1989. "Estructura de los cantos tradicionales de los grupos indígenas de Baja California Norte." In *Música en la Frontera Norte: Memorias del Coloquio de Historia de la Música en la Frontera Norte,* ed. Comite Mexicana de Ciencias Históricas, 37–43. México, D.F.: Comité Mexicano de Ciencias Históricas.

Del Barco, Miguel. 1973. *Historia Natural y Crónica de la Antigua California,* ed. Miguel León-Portilla, 167–229. México, D.F.: Universidad Nacional Autónoma de México.

Densmore, Frances. 1932. *Yuman and Yaqui Music.* Bulletin 110. Washington: Bureau of American Ethnology.

Herzog, George. 1928. "The Yuman Musical Style." *Journal of American Folklore* 41(160):183–231.

Hinton, Thomas B., and Roger C. Owen. 1957. "Some Surviving Yuman Groups in Northern Baja California." *América Indígena* 17(1):87–102.

Kelly, William H. 1977. *Cocopa Ethnography.* Anthropological paper 29. Tucson: University of Arizona Press.

Lemmon, Alfred E. 1977. "Los Jesuitas y la música de la Baja California." *Heterofonía* 10(55):13–17, 10(56):4–17, 40–44.

Martínez Zepeda, Jorge. 1989. "Música indígena en Baja California Norte." In *Música en la Frontera Norte: Memorias del Coloquio de Historia de la Música en la Frontera Norte,* ed. Comite Mexicana de Ciencias Históricas, 57–64. México, D.F.: Comité Mexicano de Ciencias Históricas.

Mixco, Mauricio. 1983. *Kiliwa Texts: "When I Have Donned My Crest of Stars."* Anthropological paper 107. Salt Lake City: University of Utah Press.

———. 1985. *Kiliwa Dictionary.* Anthropological paper 109. Salt Lake City: University of Utah Press.

Owen, Roger C., Nancy E. Walstrom, and Ralph C. Michelsen. 1969. "Musical Culture and Ethnic Solidarity: A Baja California Case Study." *Journal of American Folklore* 82(324):99–111.

Uriarte Castañeda, María Teresa. 1974. *Las costumbres y los ritos funerarios de los indígenas de la Baja California.* México, D.F.: Universidad Nacional Autónoma de México.

Mexico
Daniel E. Sheehy

In 1843, when Frances Calderón de la Barca, the wife of the Spanish ambassador to Mexico, wrote that for Mexicans, "music is a sixth sense," she joined a long line of distinguished observers singing the praise of Mexican musical performance. Evidence of the musical achievements of Mexico's indigenous people is abundant. Archaeological remains bear witness to the complexity of musical instruments and performance in native American cultures more than a millennium before contact with Europeans. Sixteenth-century European chroniclers described the prestige and prominence of musical life among the indigenous peoples they encountered, and twentieth-century documentation has revealed that many distinctive native musical cultures survive nearly five centuries after the Spanish conquistador Hernán Cortés defeated the Aztec Emperor Moctezuma.

During the colonial period, Franciscan, Dominican, Augustinian, Jesuit, and other Roman Catholic missionaries found European sacred music a valuable means of teaching the indigenous population the tenets and customs of Christianity. Many pre-Conquest indigenous musical practices were easily transferred to Roman Catholic contexts, so church music prospered. As deadly diseases and Spanish oppression diminished the native American population and as Amerindians, Europeans, and Africans intermingled, a new, mestizo ("mixed") population gradually rose to prominence. African peoples, most brought to Mexico as slaves, had a profound influence on the shaping of mestizo culture and music—an impact not yet fully understood or appreciated.

In the century after 1810, when Mexico achieved independence from Spain, many observers published accounts of regionally distinct traditions of music among rural mestizos. After the revolution of 1910, many of these traditions were officially promoted as symbols of national identity, or were widely popularized through the power of Mexico's media. Also, from the adoring nineteenth-century accounts of visiting Italian-style opera singers and from the strong following of nationalist composers in the twentieth century, we know that European secular fine-art music did not escape the Mexican attraction to music.

Many musical threads of Mexico's past have continued to the end of the twentieth century. Rapid urbanization, the intensified commodification of music, an increasingly powerful and centralized media complex, and other twentieth-century trends, however, have worked to magnify and coopt certain musical styles, leaving others to languish in the shadow of neglect, and to introduce and promulgate new musical fashions from abroad, especially from the United States.

THE SCHOLARLY RECORD

Written sources on Mexican music history reflect four major periods: the pre-Encounter era (before 1521); the colonial period (1521–1810); the so-called Independence Period (1810–1910); and the twentieth century after 1910. Most musicological sources were written after 1930. Earlier writings were penned mainly by soldiers and missionaries in colonial times, foreign and urban travelers, journalists, and observers of traditional lifeways in the 1800s, and antiquarians around the turn of the twentieth century.

The pre-Conquest and post-Conquest eras are marked by events that began in 1519, when Spanish conquistador Hernán Cortés and his comrades arrived at what is now San Juan de Uloa, Veracruz. They made their way to Tenochtitlán, slew the Aztec emperor, Moctezuma (1520), and took his nephew Cuauhtémoc captive (1521), bringing an end to Aztec rule over a multitude of Mesoamerican tribes. Since 1325, when Tenochtitlán was founded, Aztec domination had extended over territory extending from north and east of what is now Mexico City south to Central America. A rich store of archaeological and written evidence has allowed scholars to surmise much concerning the importance and centrality of music to Aztec public and ritual life, but fewer archaeological remains of other native American civilizations and their greater chronological distance from European documentarians have greatly limited our knowledge of their music. Most notable among the latter civilizations are the Olmec along the Gulf Coast (circa 1200–400 B.C.), the Maya (flourishing circa A.D. 300–900), and pre-Aztec groups of west-central Mexico.

PRE-ENCOUNTER MUSIC

Extensive historical evidence supports the claims that during many periods and in numerous areas of what is now Mexico, music was complex and important. Tubular duct flutes with multiple tubes that were apparently played simultaneously, unearthed on the east and west coasts and perhaps going back more than two thousand years, point to the existence of polyphony. With the possible exception of the musical bow, chordophones are thought to have been absent before their importation by Europeans. Other musical instruments were abundant, and many were found widely throughout Aztec territory. Many tribes used the same instruments, though with names in the local tongue rather than in Náhuatl, the language of the Aztecs.

Important ancient Mexican musical instruments include the following, given in their Náhuatl names. Idiophones included an *ayacachtli,* a gourd or gourd-shaped rattle made from clay or gold; an *ayotl,* a tortoiseshell struck with deer's antlers; a *coyolli* made of clay, copper, dried fruit, gold, or nutshells (Stevenson 1968:40), often strung around a dancer's legs or waist; a rasp (*omichicahuaztli*) made from the bone of a deer or a deerlike animal; and a log idiophone (*teponaztli*). Membranophones included a single-headed drum (*huéhuetl*). Aerophones included a conch trumpet (*atecocoli*), a clay whistle (*huilacapiztli*), a wooden or metal trumpet (*tepuzquiquiztli*), and a *tlapitzalli,* an end-blown clay or bone tubular duct flute with four holes. Many similar instruments continue in use among native American peoples [see NAHUA].

The Aztec held the *huéhuetl* and the *teponaztli* in particularly high esteem. They considered these instruments sacred and often paired them and situated them at the center of important ritual dances and other events. The *huéhuetl* was typically fashioned from a hollowed log with three supporting legs carved at one end. Its head, of skin, was struck with the hands while the performer sat or stood. The *teponaztli* was most often made of a hollowed log with a slit in the shape of the letter "H" on one side, resulting in two tongues that were struck with sticks. It was placed horizontally on the ground, with a sound hole opening on the side opposite the slit pointing downward. The following account by Spanish chronicler Francisco López de Gómara (1511–1566) is one of many describing the *huéhuetl* and *teponaztli* (1554, quoted in Stevenson 1968:105–106):

> These two drums playing in unison with the voices stood out quite strikingly, and sounded not at all badly. The performers sang merry, joyful, and amusing melodies, or else some ballad in praise of past kings, recounting wars and such things. This was all in rhymed couplets and sounded well and pleasing. . . . When it was at last time to begin, eight or ten men would blow their whistles lustily. . . . Many times a thousand dancers would assemble for this dance and at the least four hundred. They were all leading men, nobles, and even lords. The higher the man's quality the closer was his position with respect to the drums.

Tubular duct flutes were also prominent in Aztec music (see p. 17). An account by Fray Bernardino Sahagún, in his *Historia general de las cosas de Nueva España* (Stevenson 1952:23–24), points to the social and ritual importance of such flutes:

> At the festival of the sixth month they sacrificed a handsome youth whose body was perfectly proportioned. . . . They selected for this purpose the best looking among their captives . . . and took great pains to choose the most intelligent . . . and one without the least physical defect. The youth chosen was carefully trained to play the flute well, and taught . . . how to walk about as do the nobles and people of the court. . . . The one chosen for the sacrifice . . . was greatly venerated by all those who met him. . . . He who was thus chosen to die at the next great feast went through the streets playing the flute and carrying flowers. . . . On his legs he wore golden bells which rang at every step he took. . . . Twenty days before the feast . . . they married him to four beautiful maidens. . . . Five days before the sacrifice they worshiped the young man as one of their gods. . . . [After four days of preparation, they at last] took him to a small and poorly decorated temple which stood near the highway outside the city. . . . Upon reaching the foot [of the temple] the young man mounted the steps by himself. As he mounted the first step he broke one of the flutes he had played during the past year of his prosperity; on the second step, another, and so on successively until he had broken them all, and had reached the summit. There he was awaited by the priests who were to kill him, and these now grabbed him and threw him on the stone-block. After seeing him pinned down on his back with feet, hands, and head securely held, the priest who had the stone knife buried it deep in the victim's breast. Then drawing the knife out, the priest thrust one hand into the opening and tore out the heart, which he at once offered to the sun.

In Aztec civilization, music was closely linked to spiritual and material life. Accounts by sixteenth-century Spanish chroniclers, including Toribio de Motolinía (1941 [1858]), Sahagún (1956 [1547]), and Diego Durán (1867–1880), describe many elaborate ceremonies and rituals with music at their center. Robert M. Stevenson has drawn from such accounts to reach numerous conclusions about music in Aztec life. These accounts point to musicians' prestige, the closeness of music's link to ritual and specific ceremonial occasions, the communality of music performance, belief in the divinity and origin of certain instruments, attention to accuracy of pitch and rhythm, and other traits. Music education included formal schools, called *cuicalli* (Martí 1955:112, 115). Unfortunately, there are no known transcriptions of native American melodies from that era (Stevenson 1968:89–91, 125).

THE HISTORICAL RECORD

Music in the colonial period (1521–1810)

New Spain, as Mexico was called when it was a Spanish colony, enjoyed an active musical life. Most documentation surviving from the 1500s and 1600s tells of the learning, creation, and performance of European fine-art music, particularly that associated with the Roman Catholic Church. Missionaries relied heavily on music as a means of enculturating the indigenous population in the principles and ways of the Spanish Catholic tradition. Native Americans responded by taking up European music in large numbers; many of them attained a high degree of musicianship in choral and instrumental performance. New Spain's church life was a rich vein of European musical production until its decline in the 1700s.

Vernacular European and mestizo music outside religious contexts seldom made their way into musical notation. Official documents suggest that musical performance was abundant. It often attracted the reprimand of religious authorities on moral grounds. A violist named Ortiz was among the followers of Hernán Cortés. Locally made Spanish musical instruments were abundant soon after the Encounter. In the 1600s and 1700s, blacks gave profane musical performances (*oratorios, escapularios*) during religious festivities, ridiculing the sacred event. Colonial documents show that blacks played harps and guitars, danced publicly, and played important roles in shaping the people's grass-roots music (Saldívar 1934:220–222).

In the late 1700s, as Spanish influence over the New World waned, the vernacular music of New Spain's criollos and mestizos took on a more local character, different from its Spanish roots. Spanish *seguidillas,* fandangos, sung verses called *coplas* and *letrillas,* and other folkloric genres were the models for the creation of new pieces called *sones,* first documented as such in 1766 in Spanish Inquisition records. Popular theater performed in the Coliseo in Mexico City around 1800 featured *tonadillas escénicas*—short, simple dramas replete with new *sones* and other local melodies. The *jarabe,* a *son* intended especially for dancing, also emerged around 1800.

Music in the Independence Period: 1810–1910

Independence from Spain and the decline of ecclesiastical influence brought Mexican secular music to greater prominence. *Sones, jarabes,* and other melodies associated with political insurgence were honored as symbols of national identity. Writers of that time described a Mexican culture alive with musical activity marked by regional traditions and interregional sharing (Calderón de la Barca 1843; Esteva 1844a, 1844b; Prieto 1906:347–351). Traditional Mexican melodies were arranged for piano and exalted in genteel society as national airs (*aires nacionales*) and little *sones* of the country (*sonecitos del país*). *Jarabes* flourished, especially in west and central Mexico, gradually evolving into potpourris of excerpts from *sones* and other popular melodies.

Independence led to the importation of music from Europe, especially Italy and France. Italian opera was imported, imitated, and emulated by Mexican musicians and composers. Outside the confines of the Roman Catholic Church, instrumental fine-art music was virtually unknown in Mexico until the first wave of foreign performers, after 1840 (Mayer-Serra 1941:30). The piano became a standard piece of furniture in the homes of an expanding middle class. European fashions in dancing were adopted unchanged. The waltz (*vals*), introduced by 1815, met frequent con-

Beginning in 1910, intellectuals elevated and idealized Mexico's Amerindian past, and music scholars combed through archives and archaeological relics, recovering pre-Encounter musical achievements.

demnation as a "licentious" French import and was quite popular throughout the period. One of the most internationally renowned Mexican compositions of the 1800s was "*Sobre las Olas*" ('Over the Waves'), a waltz written by the Otomí native American Juventino Rosas in 1891. "*La Paloma*," the most popular song during the time of the French occupation (1862–1867), had been written in the 1840s by the Spaniard Sebastián de Yradier in the style of a Cuban habanera—a form that left a deep mark on Mexican music of later years. A voluminous repertoire of mazurkas (*mazurcas*), polkas (*polcas*), schottisches (*chotices*), waltzes (*valses*), and other pieces for dancing were written in European styles by Mexicans in the late 1800s (Stevenson 1952:208). In bandstands (*quioscos*) set up in town plazas across the country, brass bands (*bandas del pueblo*) performed *marchas,* European dances, *sonecitos,* and *jarabes.*

The composition of fine-art music in the 1800s largely imitated European models. Some works, such as *Ecos de México* (1880) by Julio Ituarte (1845–1905), drew heavily from Mexican melodies but were entirely European in style. Mexican composers Melesio Morales (1838–1908), Gustavo Campa (1863–1934), and Julián Carrillo (1875–1965) emulated Italian, French, and German musical conventions, respectively (Stevenson 1952:227). Salon music consisted of popular operatic melodies, other diluted versions of elite music (Mayer-Serra 1941:70), and Romantic-style *romanzas, contradanzas, caprichos,* and so forth. A truly nationalist movement did not occur until the revolution of 1910 put an end to the thirty-five-year presidency of Porfirio Díaz and the hegemony of European cultural models it had encouraged.

Music in the postrevolutionary twentieth century

With the Mexican Revolution, beginning in 1910, came a nationalist movement in cultural thought and policy. Intellectuals elevated and idealized Mexico's Amerindian past, and music scholars combed through archives and archaeological relics, recovering pre-Encounter musical achievements. Native American and mestizo songs and dances were collected and published. Mexico's centralized educational system codified and disseminated a select repertoire of music and dance. José Vasconcelos, Secretary of Public Education from 1921 to 1924, directed his agency, through its Aesthetic Culture Department, to encourage traditional dance; on the hundredth anniversary of the founding of the republic (1921), thousands watched as thirty couples danced "*El Jarabe Tapatío*" in a Mexico City ceremony unveiling the version to be taught throughout the country (Saldívar 1937:9). Rural musicians representing locally distinctive mestizo styles migrated to Mexico City in search of professional musical opportunities.

Art-music composer Manuel M. Ponce (1882–1948) successfully blended traditional harmonic and melodic material into a Romantic musical style and was among the first generation of nationalist composers (Mayer-Serra 1941:147). Carlos Chávez led the next generation a step further as he incorporated native American instruments, rhythms, and melodic traits into many of his works to evoke impressions of an ancient Amerindian past. With the indigenous-inspired rhythms of his *Sinfonía India,* he broke all connection to the Mexican Romantic past. Silvestre Revueltas also wrote in a modern musical style, though he took his inspiration from modern Mexico (Mayer-Serra 1941:162–165). In the late 1960s, the avant-garde compositional techniques and aesthetics of Manuel Enríquez, Manuel de Elías, Eduardo Mata, Mario Lavista, Héctor Quintanar, and others signaled a move away from nationalist styles (Béhague 1979:292).

In the 1930s and 1940s, the nationwide expansion of the radio and recording industries created a demand for local musics that possessed the potential for broad appeal. In the same decades, the Mexican film industry, while it created star entertainers singing in pseudo-folk styles, contributed to public awareness of certain styles of traditional music. All these media were powerful vehicles for foreign music to infiltrate local culture. For intellectuals, music from the United States was a major source of concern—a fear that led the music historian Gabriel Saldívar (1937:21) to promote national music as "a barrier of pure nationalism to the avalanche . . . of shabby [*quinto patio* 'slum'] songs" that had invaded Mexico.

Postrevolutionary nationalism remains a potent frame of reference among intellectuals, in government cultural policies, and for the population at large, but other social forces have a major bearing on musical life. A high birthrate, bringing Mexico's population to near a hundred million at the end of the twentieth century, has made it the most populous Spanish-speaking country in the world, with a high proportion of young people. More than 20 million people reside in metropolitan Mexico City, the most populous city in the world. The country's population is three-fourths urban, though many people have rural roots. The media industry is one of the most influential in Latin America and is in turn greatly influenced by the fashions of the United States. There are more than four hundred radio stations nationwide, most of them commercial. Although the media are the central force in shaping musical tastes, the fabric of Mexico's musical life, like that of most twentieth-century large urban societies, is made up of hundreds of threads, commonly described in several ways: music of "ethnic groups," referring principally to Amerindians; regional musical culture (*música regional*); certain widespread genres of music, such as narrative ballads (*corridos*); folk-derived popular music; international pop-music fashions; and fine-art music.

MÚSICA REGIONAL: THE MESTIZO *SON*

As mestizo culture took shape, the particular cultural blend, the shared life experiences over time, and the isolation of local communities and regions led to considerable cultural diversity among mestizos. Musical life was more local and regional than it was national, and this tendency was reflected in the mestizo music that had evolved by the 1800s. During the time of self-discovery after national independence, writers such as José María Esteva (1844a:234–235) described many of these traditions in detail:

> The *sones* danced by the *jarochos* [of Veracruz] are composed by the *jarochos* themselves and by other Spaniards [sic], or are from the interior of the republic, and rearranged according to their own tastes; consequently, they dance [the local genres] *Canelo, Tusa, Guanábana,* etc., along with *Manola, Agualulco,* and *Tapatío* [genres from other areas]. Most *jarocho* women dance the same way, but with much grace, and sometimes in certain *sones* like the *Bamba,* one admires the agility with which they tap their heels and make a thousand movements, carrying a glass filled with water on their heads without spilling a single drop, or forming a

noose from a sash laid on the ground that they adjust with their feet and which they then untie without using their hands at all.

Jarocho musicians continue to perform most of these *sones*.

In the postrevolutionary era, a national road-building effort, other improvements in transportation, a powerful media industry (which bombarded even the most distant village with the latest musical fads), governmental efforts to educate the population about its national culture, and professional opportunities in urban areas for rural musicians altered these patterns profoundly. But even as local and regional musical distinctions were fading, several regional styles of music were increasingly heard, incorporated into a national canon of region-based national identity. This canon has reinforced regional musical identity at its roots, creating national and international markets for the performance of regional music by professional musicians. Regional musical identity persists, though in part solely as a musical style and as an emblem of an idealized rural, regional heritage. Regional musical distinctions are based on repertoire, typical instrumentation, style of performance, related regional traits such as style of speech and vocabulary, traditional dress, local topics alluded to in song texts, and other factors.

At the core of most regional musical styles that emerged with the formation of mestizo culture, particularly those of central Mexico, is the musical genre known as *son*. As the Spanish *seguidillas*, fandangos, *zapateados*, and secular forms widely known as *tonadillas* were accepted and reinterpreted by mestizos, new genres of music were created, based on their Spanish predecessors. In the early 1800s, the Gran Teatro Coliseo de la Metrópoli in Mexico City and other theaters in the provinces were clearinghouses for a variety of genres of song and dance. Short theatrical interludes featured Spanish and mestizo melodies and dances that circulated throughout New Spain. These pieces, often called *sones*, exemplified a variety of forms, including that of *jarabes*, pieces documented as early as the late 1700s. Writing in the 1950s, the folklorist Vicente Mendoza stated that the *son* was "one of the most genuinely Mexican of musical genres," and he estimated that 60 percent of Mexican traditional music, with the *son* as its nucleus, had origins in the *tonadillas* popular nearly 150 years before (1956:59, 66). Indeed, many extant *sones*, including "*La Bamba*," "*El Perico*," and "*El Palomo*," were documented in the early 1800s.

The mestizo *son* continues to be diverse in form, but a few generalizations are possible. It is oriented toward accompanying social dance, with vigorous, marked rhythm and fast tempo. It is performed most often by small ensembles in which string instruments predominate, with notable region-specific exceptions. Its formal structure is based on the alternation of instrumental sections and the singing of short poetic units called *coplas*. The mode is usually major, with harmonic vocabulary mostly limited to progressions drawing from I, IV, II^7, V, and V^7. In contrast to the Amerindian *son*, the mestizo *son* is fundamentally secular as is reflected in its textual amorousness and wit, its overall extraversion, and its performative settings.

When danced, the *son* is usually performed by couples, though some *sones* have special choreography that may call for other groupings. Triple meter (6/8, 3/4, or a combination of both) predominates, with many exceptions in duple meter. The performing ensembles include melodic instruments, such as violins and harps, and instruments that provide chordal and rhythmic accompaniment corresponding to specific regional styles, especially guitars. Singing is usually in a high vocal range, often in parallel thirds. Men predominate in the public performance of *sones*, though many women may learn and perform *sones*, particularly in family settings. *Sones* are often among the repertoire of music performed at important life-cycle events (especially baptisms, birthdays, and weddings), in public commemorations of the civic-religious calendar (independence day, patronal saints' days), and in entertainment-oriented venues, including bars, restaurants, and theaters. Many government- and private-sponsored public concerts feature *sones* and other forms of folkloric music and dance.

Coplas performed for *sones* are short poetic stanzas that stand alone as complete thoughts, as opposed to being linked together in a long narrative (as in some other Mexican genres). They usually consist of four to six octosyllabic lines. The even-numbered lines rhyme; the odd-numbered lines may end in consonance or assonance. Two typical *coplas* are the following:

Date gusto, vida mía,	Give yourself pleasure, my love,
que yo me daría otro tanto.	for I'd give myself some.
No vaya a hacer que algún día	Don't let it happen that someday
el gusto se vuelva llanto.	the pleasure changes to tears.
Buenas noches, señoritas;	Good evening, misses;
muy buenas noches señores.	a very good evening, sirs.
A todas las florecitas	To all the little flowers
de rostros cautivadores	with captivating faces
van las trovas más bonitas	go the prettiest verses
de estos pobres cantadores.	from these poor troubadours.

Two major exceptions to this form are textual patterns derived from the *seguidilla* and the *décima*. In the former, seven-syllable lines alternate with five-syllable lines:

Para bailar la bamba,	To dance the *bamba,*
se necesita	one needs
una poca de gracia	a little grace
y otra cosita.	and some other little thing.

Often, filler such as *cielito lindo* 'dear, sweetheart' will be added to the stanza, achieving greater congruence with the accompanying musical phrase:

Ese lunar que tienes,	That mole that you have,
cielito lindo, junto a la boca:	dear, next to your mouth:
no se lo des a nadie,	don't give it to anyone,
cielito lindo, que a mi me toca.	dear, for it belongs to me.

The décima is a ten-line stanza rhyming *abbaaccddc:*

Señora, está usted servida.	Madame, you are served
Sólo le encargo a usted:	I only ask this of you:
que las décimas no se dé,	that the *décimas* not be given away,
aunque el propio rey las pida.	even if the king himself requests them.
Si las tienes aprendida(s)	If you have them learned
y alguno las necesita,	and someone needs them,
no le dé, porque le quita	don't give them to him, because it takes away
la gracia y la decorrupta,	their grace and purity,
que a todo el mundo le gusta(n)	for everyone loves
las décimas bonitas.	pretty *décimas.*

Rhymes may reflect regional pronunciation (*aprendida* for *aprendidas*) or near-rhyme (*gusta* for *gustan*).

Décimas are present in certain *sones* of southern Veracruz, and in the *valonas,* a

Many regional styles of Mexican music are distinguished by their forms of *sones* and several other styles in which the *son* has been historically influential, but not currently central to their identity.

musical genre with several declaimed *décimas,* of the hotlands (*tierra caliente*), the western part of the state of Michoacán (see *Music of Mexico, Vol. 2*).

Regional *sones*

Although these and other unifying traits make a case for mestizo *son* "supergenre," many regional styles of *son* are easily recognizable by the distinctiveness of their instrumentation, instrumental techniques, treatment of the *copla,* vocal nuances, repertoire, associated dances, and other factors. Many regional styles of Mexican music are distinguished by their forms of *sones* and several other styles in which the *son* has been historically influential, but not currently central to their identity. Seven principal kinds of *son* that mark regional musical styles are *son huasteco* of the northwestern geocultural region known as the Huasteca; *son jarocho* of the southern coastal plain of the state of Veracruz; *son istmeño* or *son oaxaqueño* of the Isthmus of Tehuantepec, mainly in the southwest portion of Oaxaca, overlapping with Chiapas; *chilena* of the Costa Chica along the Pacific coast of Oaxaca and Guerrero; *son guerrerense* (*son calenteño*) of the Balsas River basin hotlands in Guerrero; *son michoacano* (*son calentano*) from the neighboring hotland region of Michoacán; and the *son jalisciense* of Jalisco. Many regional styles in which the *son* is influential but not central are those found in Yucatán and the northern border area.

Son huasteco

The Huasteca comprises portions of the states of Tamaulipas, Hidalgo, Veracruz, Querétaro, and Puebla. The *son huasteco,* also known as *huapango,* possibly developed from the Náhuatl *cuauh-panco* 'over the wood', a dance performed on a wooden platform. *Son huasteco* is typically performed by a trio of musicians playing a violin, a *huapanguera* (*guitarra quinta,* a deep-bodied guitar with eight strings in five single and double courses), and a *jarana* (small five-stringed guitar) (figure 1). The violinist plays melodies that are often complex and highly syncopated, requiring a high degree of skill and the ability to improvise. The two guitars play in strummed (*rasgueado*) fashion, with the *huapanguera* player occasionally adding single-string countermelodies. The vocal style includes brief, ornamental breaks into falsetto. *Quintillas* and *sextillas* (five- and six-line *coplas,* respectively) are favored. Singers often improvise texts befitting the particular performance situation. The singing of the *copla* typically involves certain patterns of repeating lines of the *copla* that allow fuller vocal treatment of the text and time for the singer to compose improvised *coplas.* Typical *sones huastecos* are "*Cielito Lindo,*" "*La Rosa,*" "*La Azucena,*" "*El Llorar,*" "*El Toro Sacamandú,*" "*El Gusto,*" and "*La Huasanga*" (see *Music of Mexico, Vol. 3*).

Son jarocho

The *son jarocho* takes its name from a term of uncertain origin (possibly from *jaras,* clubs said to have been wielded by colonial militia) denoting the people of the south-

FIGURE 1   A *trío huasteco* plays at a member's home in Mexico City. *Left to right:* Eduardo Bustos Valenzuela, violin; Domitilio Zubiria, *jarana huasteca;* and Mario Zubiria, *huapanguera* (*guitarra quinta*). Photo by Daniel Sheehy, 1992.

TRACK 30   ern coastal plain of Veracruz. The most widespread typical instrumentation (figure 2) centers on the thirty-two- to thirty-six-stringed diatonic harp (*arpa jarocha*), a *jarana* (shallow-bodied guitar with eight strings in five courses), and a *requinto* ("*guitarra de son,*" a four-stringed, narrow-bodied guitar, plucked with a 7.5-centimeter plectrum fashioned from cow horn or a plastic comb). The use of the *requinto* appears to be on the wane. In the southern area, near the border with Tabasco, the harp is rare, and smaller sizes of *jarana* are found. In the central town of Tlacotalpan, a *pandero* (octagonal frame drum, with jingles like a tambourine) joins the ensemble. The harpist plays melody and bass. The *jarana* player employs a variety of patterns (*maniqueos*) to strum a rhythmic-chordal accompaniment appropriate to the meter, tempo, and character of the particular *son*. The *requinto* player (*requintero*) supplies an additional, largely improvisatory, melodic line, often interacting with the harpist's

FIGURE 2   A *conjunto jarocho* in Boca del Río, Veracruz. *Left to right:* Daniel Valencia on *requinto jarocho*, Rufino Velásquez on *arpa jarocha,* and Inés Rivas on *jarana jarocha.* Photo by Daniel Sheehy, 1978.

melody. Six-line *coplas* are most common and are the preferred medium for most textual improvisation, of which a great deal occurs.

It is often supposed that the *son jarocho,* more than any other regional *son* tradition, is of African origin. Most *sones jarochos* are based on a short, cyclical rhythmic-chordal pattern (*compás*) that drives the music through continuous repetition in the fashion of the West African timeline usually played on a bell or the African-Cuban beat played on claves. Certain *sones*—"*El Coco*" and "*La Iguana*"—have a responsorial refrain. The style and degree of interaction between musicians, dancers, and audience also suggest a more African style. These factors, with the prominence of African and mulatto people in the region's ethnographic history, further support this notion.

Son istmeño *or* son oaxaqueño

Unlike most regional *son* styles, the *son istmeño* customarily is neither performed by string ensembles nor sung. Wind-and-percussion *bandas* follow the basic pattern of "sung" sections alternating with instrumental interludes, though sections sung in other areas are performed instrumentally in a cantabile style. The *bandas* follow the models of European brass bands of the 1800s. Most *bandas* are composed exclusively of native Americans, the *banda* being a central social institution of many Amerindian communities. The performances at civic and religious celebrations, however, are part of the musical life of mestizos and native Americans alike.

In the southernmost state of Chiapas and the southern edge of Oaxaca, the marimba (figure 3) is similar to the *banda* in its treatment of the *son*. Though the marimba was probably modeled on African xylophone prototypes during colonial times, it has been the domain of primarily mestizo musicians since at least the mid-1800s. It has become an important icon of Chiapan identity and is closely associated with the towns of Tehuantepec (Chiapas) and Juchitán (Oaxaca). The marimba may be *sencilla* (a single instrument) or *doble* (a combination of a smaller and a larger instrument) and may be played by two, three, or more players. It is often accompanied by percussion and other instruments. Although the marimba continues to consist of a set of rectangular wooden slats of graduated lengths suspended over resonator tubes (each with a small membrane that buzzes as its slat is struck), the wooden slatboard of the modern marimba has been transformed to resemble the piano keyboard, with the black keys located above and set into the white keys. Marimba ensembles typically perform a wide-ranging repertoire, from pieces often called *sones* to a special repertoire for Amerindian events to current melodies spread through the popular media. The pieces most closely resembling the *sones* of other regions follow two main models: waltz-rhythm melodies that are instrumental interpretations of songs; and fast-tempo *zapateados* cast in a 6/8 rhythmic mold with frequent shifts to 3/4.

Chilena

Though the cultural antecedents of the *chilena* from the Costa Chica differ from those of *sones* rooted in the colonial era, the overall character and musical traits of the genre argue for its inclusion in the *son* family. It is derived from the *cueca,* a musical genre and dance performed by Chilean and Peruvian adventurers who stopped in Acapulco on their voyage to California during the gold rush of the mid-1800s. Its Chilean origins are found in the structure of the text and in the choreography, with its dancers' use of handkerchiefs. Until its decline in the mid-twentieth century, an ensemble of harp, five-course *jarana,* and some form of percussion typically accompanied the *chilena*. Today, the guitar and six-stringed *requinto,* the latter similar to the guitar, but smaller and tuned a perfect fourth higher, most often fill that role.

FIGURE 3 Near several restaurants in downtown Veracruz, a quartet plays a marimba and accompanying instruments. *Left to right:* two musicians playing the marimba, a drummer, and a *güiro* player. Photo by Daniel Sheehy, 1978.

Son guerrerense *or* son calentano

From Guerrero, this *son,* also called *son calentano* (from *caliente* 'hot', referring to the hotlands of Guerrero and Michoacán) is associated with the ensemble consisting of one or two violins, six-stringed guitar (formerly a smaller *jarana*), a *tamborita* (small, double-headed drum, played on the head and rim with two drumsticks), and occasionally a bass (*guitarrón*), borrowed from contemporary mariachis. The tradition is found mainly in the area of the Balsas River basin of Guerrero. Most *sones* in this region are called by different names, reflecting differing characters. Those called *son* are usually fast-paced instrumental melodies intended for dancing, those called *gustos* are typically strophic songs in triple meter, and those called *chilenas* resemble those of the Costa Chica.

Son michoacano

In the neighboring hotlands of Michoacán, the *son michoacano* (*son calenteño*) is closely identified with a string ensemble consisting of a large diatonic harp (*arpa grande*), two violins, a *vihuela* (five-stringed guitar with a convex back), and a *jarana* (also known as *guitarra de golpe,* a deep-bodied guitar with five strings). Unlike the *sones* of Veracruz and the Huasteca, the *son michoacano* has fixed musical interludes that separate the sung sections. Occasionally during these instrumental interludes, a violinist or guitarist will kneel down and beat the lower face of the harp with his hands as a percussive accompaniment (figure 4)—a practice that was apparently more widespread in earlier times.

The *son* is central to the ensemble's repertoire, but two other traditional genres, the *jarabe* and the *valona,* are also distinctive of the region. The *jarabe* is similar in

The *son jalisciense* (*son* from around the state of Jalisco) is perhaps the most widely known of Mexican *sones* through its performance by mariachis throughout the country.

FIGURE 4   A *conjunto de arpa grande* from the hotlands of Michoacán. *Left to right:* Ricardo Gutiérrez Villa, violin; an onlooker; second violinist (name unknown) momentarily kneeling and beating the harp with his hands; Rubén Cuevas Maldonado, *arpa grande*; *vihuela* (name unknown); and Ovaldo Ríos Yáñez, *guitarra de golpe* (*jarana*). Photo by Daniel Sheehy, 1991.

form to its counterparts in other regions of west-central Mexico—a string of perhaps five to seven melodies performed instrumentally, each section corresponding to a particular pattern of movement. The *valona* (the word is thought to derive from "Walloon," perhaps introduced during the presence of Flemish troops in the 1700s), more widespread in the 1800s, is a local version of *décima*-based forms found in several parts of Latin America. Generally, a four-line *copla* precedes four *décimas,* the last line of each *décima* duplicating the first, second, third, and fourth lines of the introductory *copla,* in that order. A single basic melodic pattern functions as the introduction and as musical interludes between sections of text. The subjects are almost invariably witty or picaresque.

Son jalisciense

The *son jalisciense* (*son* from around the state of Jalisco) is perhaps the most widely known of Mexican *sones* through its performance by mariachis throughout the country. The *son jalisciense* is closely related to the *son michoacano* and to a lesser extent to other *sones* throughout territory stretching from southern Sinaloa to Guerrero. Previous to the introduction and standardization of trumpets in mariachis during the 1920s through 1940s, the accompaniment to this *son* was one or two violins, a *vihuela,* perhaps a *guitarra de golpe,* and a harp or a *guitarrón.* Most *sones jaliscienses* are strophic songs in which *coplas* alternate with melodically fixed instrumental interludes. Some *sones* are quite complex rhythmically, with ornate patterns of strumming the guitars and 3/4–6/8 metrical ambiguities.

Other regional forms

Two other musical regions influenced by the *son,* but not identified by a distinct kind of *son,* are Yucatán and the northern border area. Regional music of Yucatán is distinguished by the *jarana* and the *bambuco.* The *jarana* is a couple dance resembling the Spanish *jota* in its choreography and the meter of its music. The *jarana* is performed instrumentally, most often by a small orchestra of wind and percussion instruments, and has no text, excepting occasional brief breaks, when a dancer declaims a *copla.* The compositions usually consist of a series of short melodies, similar to those of a *jarabe.* Although the *jarana* may have been rooted partially in the *sonecitos* of the 1800s and earlier, its repertoire and overall style show few close similarities with those of regional *sones.* The *bambuco* is a slow, often melancholic genre of song, apparently brought to the region by Colombian musicians perhaps as late as the early 1900s. It is often sung in two or three-part harmony, accompanied by a guitar, a six-stringed *requinto,* and a percussion instrument or a bass.

El Norte (the north), the vast and arid region stretching from Tamaulipas to Sonora, took shape as a distinctive cultural region in the nineteenth and twentieth centuries. It was sparsely populated through colonial times. In the second half of the 1800s, the growth of ranching and, more important, mining attracted an enormous migration of workers from other regions of Mexico and of professionals and others from European countries such as Germany, Poland, and France. The lack of a strongly unified cultural base made the region fertile ground for the implantation of the European musical and dance vogues that held sway over most of urban nineteenth-century Mexico. Mazurkas, polkas, schottisches, waltzes, and other European dances attained a preeminence that endured throughout the twentieth century. No unique form of *son* emerged in the north. However, songs, *corridos* in particular, were set to the rhythms of the European dances, with the 2/4 polka meter being the most favored. The *son's* overall form of *coplas* alternating with instrumental melodies and its strong identification with the people (*el pueblo*) may have deeply influenced this music, which has long been considered distinctive of the north (Reuter 1985:185). This polka-rhythm song, accompanied by accordion as lead melodic instrument, a large twelve-stringed guitar (*bajo sexto*), an acoustic or electric bass, and perhaps a drumset or a *redova* (small, hollow woodblock played with two sticks), much like the mariachi, became widely known through its success in the commercial media (figure 5).

WIDESPREAD GENRES

Many regional musical customs, genres, and pieces are shared widely, especially by mestizos. Religious observances paying homage to the Virgin of Guadalupe or reenacting Mary and Joseph's journey to Bethlehem, songs sung by and for children, *corridos,* serenades (*serenatas*), the song "*Las Mañanitas,*" and a canon of "national" music and dance derived from regional traditions are some of the most pervasive.

Religious music

More than 90 percent of the Mexican population is nominally Roman Catholic. In addition to more universal liturgical music and sacramental events that include secular music (such as baptisms, weddings, and funerals), there are specifically Mexican religious occasions with their own musical repertoires. Key to the conversion of Mexican Amerindians to Roman Catholicism was the belief that in 1531 the Virgin Mary appeared to an Amerindian named Juan Diego on the hill Tepeyac, located in

what is now Mexico City. Ecclesiastical authorities confirmed the miraculous appearance, opening the door to the widespread adoration by native Americans and mestizos throughout Mexico and beyond of this figure, closely identified with their own cultural past. Among Mexican communities in Mexico and abroad, 12 December and the preceding weeks have become a time of ceremonial devotion to the Virgin of Guadalupe. Special hymns and other songs of praise to the Virgin of Guadalupe are sung during processions, celebrations of the Mass, and late-evening or early-morning serenades in front of statues of her.

Early December is one of the most important occasions for devotional performances by musical-choreographic groups often known as *concheros,* named for the guitar many of them play, fashioned from an armadillo shell. *Concheros,* whose performance also may be known as Aztec dance (*danza azteca*), are active in many parts of Mexico and the southwestern United States, but especially in the federal district (Mexico City) and in the neighboring states to its north and east. Consisting mainly of blue-collar and lower-middle-class mestizo and Amerindian people of both sexes and all ages, these groups take part in many saint's-day celebrations, singing, playing, and dancing while dressed in highly ornate costumes, evoking images of ancient Aztecs. Many carry out long-distance pilgrimages to the Basílica de Guadalupe at the foot of Tepeyac, where they perform tightly coordinated devotional choreographies.

With Christmastide comes *las posadas,* the musical reenactment of Mary and Joseph's journey to Bethlehem. Churches, social groups, and individuals organize these events so children and adults can dress up as characters in local interpretations of the story: Mary, Joseph, shepherds, Bedouins, Romans, devils, and others. The participants divide into pilgrims and innkeepers (*caseros*). The pilgrims ask for lodging (*versos para pedir posada*), and the innkeepers deny them a place to stay. In the following lyrics (after Reuter 1985:101–102), the pilgrims sing the first two stanzas, and the innkeepers sing the second two:

En nombre del cielo,	In the name of heaven,
os pido posada,	I ask of thee shelter,
pues no puede andar	for my beloved wife
mi esposa amada.	cannot go on walking.

No seas inhumano;	Don't be inhumane;
tennos caridad,	have charity with us,
que el Dios de los Cielos	for the God of the heavens
te lo premiará.	will reward you.
Aquí no es mesón;	This is not an inn;
sigan adelante.	continue on your way.
Yo no debo abrir;	I don't have to open;
no sea algún tunante.	don't be a pest.
Ya se pueden ir	Now you can go away,
y no molestar,	and don't bother,
porque si me enfado,	because if I get angry,
los voy a apalear.	I'm going to hit you.

In the end, a door is opened, and the pilgrims are invited in, to the following lyrics (after Reuter 1985:103):

Entren, santos peregrinos;	Enter, holy pilgrims;
reciban esta mansión,	receive this lodging,
que aunque es pobre la morada,	for though the abode is humble,
os la doy de corazón.	it is given to you from the heart.

To the joy of all present, a fiesta begins, at the center of which is a piñata. While children are bludgeoning the piñata, two melodies are often sung, to the following texts (after Reuter 1985:106–107):

Dale, dale, dale.	Hit it, hit it, hit it.
No pierdas el tino,	Don't lose your aim,
porque si lo pierdes,	for if you lose it,
pierdes el camino.	you lose your way.
No quiero oro;	I don't want gold;
no quiero plata:	I don't want silver:
yo lo que quiero	what I myself want
es romper la piñata.	is to break the piñata.

In southern Veracruz and neighboring areas, the Advent tradition known as *la rama* involves groups of adults and/or children going from home to home asking for an *aguinaldo,* a gift of coins, candy, food, or drink. They typically carry with them a decorated branch (*rama*) and sing verses to the melody "*La Rama*" ('The Branch'). There are local variations of "*La Rama*," but it is distinguished by verses sung by individuals alternating with the refrain beginning *Naranjas y limas, limas y limones, más linda es la Virgen, que todas las flores* 'Oranges and lemons, lemons and limes, the Virgin is prettier than all the flowers'. An example from Tlacotalpan, Veracruz is the following:

Licencia queremos,	We request permission,
familia decente,	good family,
y sin ofenderlos	and without offending you
dispense a esta gente.	forgive these people.
Naranjas y limas	Oranges and lemons,
limas y limones	lemons and limes,
más linda es la Virgen	the Virgin is prettier
que todas las flores.	than all the flowers.

Battles between police and smugglers (*contra-bandistas*), assassinations, horse races, and a wide range of tragic and comic stories provide fodder for the composers of *corridos*—on both sides of the Mexico–U.S. border.

Dispense a esta gente	Forgive these people
que venga a su casa,	who come to your house,
y si son gustosos,	and if you are pleasant,
verán lo que pasa.	you will see what happens.
Naranjas y limas, etc.	Oranges and lemons, etc.
Ya se va la rama	The *rama* is leaving
muy agradecida,	very thankful,
porque en esta casa	because in this house
fue bien recibida.	it was welcomed.
Naranjas y limas, etc.	Oranges and lemons, etc.

The texts may refer in some way to the birth of Jesus, or they may be entirely secular or picaresque in content.

The *corrido*

The *corrido* is distributed widely throughout Mexico but has been favored particularly by people in northern and western areas. In simple terms, its historical roots are thought to be in the Spanish *romance,* a long, often epic ballad, structured in a series of *coplas,* and the nineteenth-century printed *décimas* distributed in the fashion of English broadsides as a means of spreading accessible accounts of socially notable events. The revolution beginning in 1910, however, provided the intense popular interest that catapulted the *corrido* to prominence, as it conveyed the events and often heroic exploits of such revolutionary figures as Francisco Madero, Francisco Villa, Emiliano Zapata, and myriad others.

It was in the era of the Revolution (1910–1917) that the form and function of the *corrido* became relatively fixed. Structurally, the *corrido* most often consists of a simple melody the length of a *copla* cast in a I–V^7 harmonic framework and repeated for a variable number of *coplas* constituting the piece. The meter is usually 3/4, though 2/4 is common, particularly in renditions from later years when *música norteña* with its polka rhythm came into fashion. The emphasis is on the text, sung in a straightforward fashion unfettered by musical complexities. Usually, the first *copla* is a formal introduction, and the final *copla* is a formal farewell. An excerpt from the *corrido "Valentín de la Sierra"* illustrates this structure:

Voy a cantar un corrido	I'm going to sing a *corrido*
de un amigo de mi tierra.	about a friend from my land.
Llamábase Valentín	He was called Valentín,
y fue fusilado y colgado en la sierra.	and he was shot and hung in the sierra.

No me quisiera acordar:	I don't want to recall:
fue una tarde 'el invierno	it was a winter afternoon
cuando, por su mala suerte,	when, from bad luck,
cayó Valentín en manos del gobierno.	Valentín fell into the hands of the government forces.
Vuela, vuela, palomita.	Fly, fly, little dove.
Párate en ese fortín.	Go alight on that fortress.
Estas son las mañanitas	These are the *mañanitas*
de un hombre valiente que fue Valentín.	of a valiant man who was Valentín.

The last stanza (*despedida* 'farewell') makes a formal farewell by shifting its stance: after telling of Valentín's capture, interrogation, and execution, it wraps up, under the term *mañanitas* (see below), the information of the previous *coplas*.

The *corrido* continued in its function of memorializing current events, real or imaginary, long after the revolution subsided, in 1917. Battles between police and smugglers (*contrabandistas*), assassinations, horse races, and a wide range of tragic and comic stories provide fodder for the composers of *corridos*—on both sides of the Mexico–U.S. border.

Songs by and for children

Children's game-playing songs are "probably one of the most traditional and persistent" musical repertoires in Mexico (Mendoza 1956:55). This conservatism is undoubtedly tied to the group identities that the songs reflect and engender in the children who sing them. Most Mexican game-playing songs are clearly of Hispanic origin, though many variations on those Spanish prototypes have emerged over the centuries of practice in the New World. Circular games (*rondas*), the most prominent, include jump rope and clapping songs, in which the song guides the movements of the game. "*La pájara pinta*," "*Amo ató matarile rilerón*," "*Doña Blanca*," "*A la víbora de la mar*," "*Juan Pirulero*," and many others are heard on school playgrounds, parks, streets, and other places where children play. The variety of melodies and texts is great, but most involve constant repetition and the use of nonlexical syllables (Reuter 1985:118).

Lyric songs not associated with playing games

Mexican children have three other general kinds of children's song: lyric songs not associated with playing games, songs derived from adults' songs, and songs sung by adults to young children. Of the first variety, "*La Rana*" ('The Frog') exemplifies songs that tell cumulative stories (in the fashion of "Old MacDonald Had a Farm") (after Mendoza 1956: musical example 85):

Cuando la rana se sale a solear,	When the frog goes out to sun itself,
viene la mosca y la quiere picar:	the fly comes along and wants to bite it:
la mosca a la rana,	the fly to the frog,
la rana en el agua:	the frog in the water:
¡cua, cua, cua!	croak, croak, croak!

A new element is added to each successive repetition, resulting in a chain of entities, each trying to do in the one that follows. Death ends the series:

Cuando el herrero se sale a pasear,	When the blacksmith goes out for a walk,
viene la Muerte y lo quiere matar:	Death comes and wants to kill him:
la Muerte al herrero,	Death to the blacksmith,
el herrero al cuchillo,	the blacksmith to the knife,
y el cuchillo al buey,	and the knife to the ox,
y el buey al agua,	and the ox to the water,
y el agua a la lumbre,	and the water to the fire,
y la lumbre al pato,	and the fire to the duck,
y el pato al perro,	and the duck to the dog,
y el perro al gato,	and the dog to the cat,
y el gato al ratón,	and the cat to the mouse,
y el ratón a la rana,	and the mouse to the frog,
la rana a la mosca,	the frog to the fly,
la mosca a la rana,	the fly to the frog,
la rana en el agua:	the frog in the water:
¡cua, cua, cua!	croak, croak, croak!

Children's songs derived from adults' songs

Children's songs derived from adults' songs are of several kinds. Centuries-old Spanish romances, such as "*Delgadina,*" "*Mambrú se fue a la guerra,*" and "*El señor don gato,*" were appropriated and developed by children. Many songs created and recorded especially for children by composer-singers such as Francisco Gabilondo Soler (pseudonym *Cri-Cri, el Grillito Cantor* 'Cri-cri, the Little Cricket Minstrel') have made their way into oral tradition. And of course, the unrelenting presence of commercial advertising jingles and theme songs from soap operas and children's programs in the popular media has left its mark on the songs children sing, particularly in urban areas.

Songs sung by adults to children

Songs sung by adults to children consist mainly of lullabies (*arrullos*) and coddling songs (*cantos de nana*). *Arrullos* often involve repetition and nonlexical syllables, in keeping with the purpose of putting an infant to sleep. *Cantos de nana* often refer to the parts of the body and are combined with movements to develop the infant's physical coordination.

Serenatas

Other musical practices widespread in Mexico include *serenatas,* the related song "*Las Mañanitas,*" and songs and dances (usually associated with a particular cultural region) that have spread through the educational system or the popular media. *Serenatas* (apparently from *sereno* 'night watchman', referring to the early hours when their performances traditionally occur) are courting, congratulatory, or devotional serenades. A man may contract or organize a group of musicians and unexpectedly serenade his lover outside her home. The recipient of the serenade may otherwise be a person celebrating a birthday or other happy event—or even a statue of the Virgin of Guadalupe (particularly on 12 December).

The song "*Las Mañanitas*" is often the first song sung on these occasions. In earlier times, the term *mañanitas* 'early morning' was nearly synonymous with *serenata,* and included a range of songs that varied greatly according to local custom. Currently, it often refers to a specific song, an arrangement combining portions of two different *mañanitas*—"*Las Mañanitas Mexicanas*" and "*Las Mañanitas Tapatías.*"

MUSIC AND PUBLIC POLICY

In the postrevolutionary era, numerous governmental efforts have promoted a common canon of folklore throughout the country. Public-school curricula include a small repertoire of traditional songs and dances, and many universities have ongoing ensembles studying and performing folkloric music and dance from a variety of styles. The federal government's social security agency (Seguro Social) sponsors music-and-dance groups and presentations as part of its concern for the well-being of the population. Representations of folkloric traditions are a key element in public and privately funded efforts to promote tourism. Other sectors of government, the armed forces and police departments, for example, may subsidize the performance of such music and dance.

There is no greater archetype of this canon than "*El Jarabe Tapatío.*" *Jarabe* ('syrup' in Mexican Spanish) referred in Mexico to a dance piece as early as 1789, when "*El Jarabe Gatuno*" was condemned by Inquisition authorities on moral grounds. In the early 1800s, the *jarabe* was still a single, short dance, most likely included in what were called *sones.* Its identity as part of an oppressed mestizo culture catapulted it to prominence as the Mexican insurgents won independence from Spain. It thus became one of the earliest musical symbols of national identity. By 1900, it was a series of short *sones* linked together as one composition and was most prevalent in the west-central states of Colima, Durango, Jalisco, Michoacán, and Nayarit. Some of these *jarabes,* such as "*El Jarabe Tapatío,*" were arranged for piano and published, becoming established as standard versions. In performances of "*El Jarabe Tapatío*" in Mexico City in 1918, the Russian ballerina Anna Pavlova popularized choreographic innovations that further standardized the piece. By 1921, when, in Mexico City, performers premiered the version of "*El Jarabe Tapatío*" to be taught in the nation's public schools, its primacy and the title of "*El Jarabe Nacional*" were fixed, though at the expense of losing much of its dynamic quality as a social dance.

POPULAR MUSIC

Folk-derived popular music

Though the recording and broadcasting of regional musics had already been underway during the second and third decades of the twentieth century, the major explosion in Mexico's popular media history did not occur until the fourth decade. The powerful radio station XEW began broadcasting in 1930. It was followed by XEB and others, creating an enormous demand for live musical performances to fill the air time. Seeking opportunities, musicians representing regional musical traditions flocked to Mexico City. In 1935, the Victor Talking Machine Company opened Mexico's first major record-production facility, expanding the availability of recordings of homegrown music. The Mexican film industry prospered in the 1930s and 1940s, and many influential films, such as "*Allá en el Rancho Grande*" (1936), "*Cielito Lindo*" (1936), and "*Ay Jalisco no te rajes!*" (1941) portrayed regional musicians, often to evoke an idealized sense of rural life. Mariachi, *jarocho,* marimba, and other kinds of typical music (*música típica*) were heard and seen throughout Mexico and abroad.

The dramatic growth of the radio, recording, and film industries during this time had major and profound effects on Mexican musical life. Professional composers proliferated, many building on the Mexican tradition of the nineteenth-century romantic song (*canción romántica*). Pseudo-folk and urban derivative styles of music emerged from rural predecessors. The communal character of regional music was displaced by a star system promoted by the commercial media. Foreign folk-derived genres, such as the Cuban bolero and the *cumbia* [see PANAMA], took hold at

Since the 1930s, the mariachi has been the most nationally prominent folk-derived Mexican musical ensemble. Postrevolutionary nationalism and the rising radio and film industries contributed to its important role.

the cultural grass roots. American popular-music exports, from the foxtrot to rock and rap, held enormous sway over urban Mexicans' musical tastes.

Mexican song: the *canción romántica* and the *canción ranchera*

The gamut of Mexican genres, structures, styles of interpretation, and accompanying instrumentation is great. Its range and diversity reflect the musical currents influencing the creation and performance of song in Mexico, particularly since the mid-1800s. It was during this time—of European romanticism, Italian opera, and the rise of the middle class—that a strain of sentimental and nostalgic composition emerged in Mexico. The terms *canción romántica* and *canción sentimental* described this musical vein, which was much in vogue into the early twentieth century and still constitutes a major thread of contemporary Mexican musical life. With Yradier's "*La Paloma*" (see above), Veracruzan composer Narciso Serradell's "*La Golondrina*," cast similarly in an *habanera* meter, was an important prototype for songwriters between 1870 and 1900.

In the first decades of the twentieth century, Yucatecan composers, influenced by the Colombian *bambuco* and Cuban parlor music, contributed greatly to the shaping of *canciones románticas*. The prolific Yucatecan songwriter Augusto "Guty" Cárdenas Pinelo (1905–1932) wrote many songs, such as "*Rayito de Luna*," that became embedded in the growing national musical repertoire. María Grever (1884–1951), based in New York for most of her musical career, created songs such as "*Júrame*," "*Cuando Vuelva a Tu Lado*," and "*Muñequita Linda*," and movie music with wide appeal in the United States, Latin America, and abroad. Agustín Lara (1897?–1970) brought a new urban and more openly sensual sensibility to the *canción romántica* in more than five hundred compositions, such as "*Mujer.*" His early prominence on Mexican radio and in films in the 1930s had a broad impact on musical tastes and contributed to the popularity of his music.

Typically, the *canción romántica* was, and continues to be, performed by a soloist or a duo or trio of singers, often accompanying themselves on guitars, perhaps with a form of subtle percussion such as maracas or *güiro*. One such group, Trío Los Panchos, which became enormously popular in the late 1940s, contributed greatly to the subsequent prominence of the Cuban-derived, slow-tempo, romantic bolero. Its style of interpreting a variety of songs with suave, mellifluous voices singing in two- or three-part harmony forwarded the close association of such groups to *canciones románticas* and the status of the romantic trio as a major Mexican musical stereotype.

The *canción ranchera* came about with the mass migration of rural people to urban areas, Mexico City in particular. Near the end of the twentieth century, urban Mexicans preserved a strong identity with their rural roots. The emergence of the *canción ranchera* is closely linked to the rise of the popular media and to the popularity of folk-derived ensembles such as the modern mariachi. Beginning in the 1930s and continuing through the century, popular singer-actor stars of the screen such as

Pedro Infante and Jorge Negrete portrayed idealized ranchers, Mexican cowboys (*charros*), and other rural stereotypes, singing country songs (*canciones rancheras*) with straightforward messages of love, romantic betrayal, and adventurous exploits. These songs, finding a niche in the commercial-music market, attracted countless songwriters. The most prolific and influential composer of *canciones rancheras* was José Alfredo Jiménez (1926–1973), who composed and recorded more than four hundred popular compositions beginning in the late 1940s. *Canciones rancheras* are typically in a simple binary form, cast in a slow duple or triple or fast duple meter and sung by a soloist in a direct, extroverted, passionate style somewhat reminiscent of *bel canto*. The term is often extended to refer to any song sung in a *ranchero* style and particularly such songs accompanied by a mariachi. The *bolero ranchero,* for example, is a version of the romantic bolero, interpreted in a more open-voiced, solo fashion.

Mariachi

Since the 1930s, the mariachi (figure 6) has been the most nationally prominent folk-derived Mexican musical ensemble. Postrevolutionary nationalism, which elevated grass-roots cultural expression, and the rising radio and film industries, which disseminated it, contributed to its important role. The term *mariachi* was formerly thought to have derived from the French *mariage,* based on the fanciful notion that west Mexican folk string ensembles had played at weddings for the French imperialists who tried to rule the country from 1862 to 1867. Research, however, has unearthed two documents that gainsay this etymology. In one, dated 1852, the priest Cosme Santa Anna in Rosamorada, Jalisco, told his archbishop that the diversions called mariachis were disrupting holy days. In the other, a diary entry written in Guerrero in 1859, the priest Ignacio Aguilar referred to *Mariache* as a musical ensemble (Jáuregui 1990:15–18). That both these sources predate the French occupation nullifies unsubstantiated accounts of a French imperialist origin.

The old-time mariachi—one or two violins, a *guitarra de golpe* and/or a *vihuela,* and a harp or some form of string bass—still exists in some rural communities of Jalisco and Nayarít, where it plays a generations-old repertoire of *sones, jarabes,* and religious pieces called *minuetes.* Its presence has been eclipsed almost entirely, though,

FIGURE 6   A mariachi in Mexico City poses in front of the historic cabaret Salón Tenampa, located on Plaza Garibaldi, where mariachis gather and perform daily. *Left to right:* two trumpets, two violins, a *guitarrón,* and a *vihuela.* Photo by Daniel Sheehy, 1991.

by the modern mariachi, which evolved largely in response to the success of Mexico City's commercial-music industry in radio, film, recordings, and later, television. The instrumentation was expanded to include sections called *melodía* (two trumpets and three to six or more violins) and *armonía* (a *vihuela*, a guitar, a *guitarrón*, and occasionally a harp). Since the 1930s, the evolution of the mariachi was tied closely to that of *música ranchera* and its star system.

The preeminent and archetypal modern mariachi since the 1940s has been Mariachi Vargas de Tecalitlán. Under the guidance of the late Silvestre Vargas, Mariachi Vargas came to dominate commercial mariachi music. It appeared regularly in the major electronic media, accompanying the most prominent singers of *música ranchera,* and producing countless recordings. Its musical arrangements of traditional pieces and modern compositions set the standard for virtually all modern mariachis throughout Mexico and abroad. Since the 1950s, the group's close collaboration with the composer-arranger Rubén Fuentes, who joined Vargas as a musician in 1945, had a profound impact on mariachi music. His innovations brought the harmonic language of contemporary popular music and new instrumental techniques and rhythms into the canon of mariachi conventions.

Other folk-derived popular musics

The twentieth century saw the creation of many folk-derived musical expressions. In the early decades, the *orquesta típica,* an ensemble of musicians in folkloric garb, played regional melodies on a variety of (primarily stringed) instruments. Miguel Lerdo de Tejada was its leading exponent. The Veracruzan harpist Andrés Huesca, the *requinto* player Lino Chávez, and others brought standardized arrangements and compositions in a modified *son jarocho* style to audiences in the 1940s and later.

Other regional styles of music penetrated or were coopted by the mainstream Mexican commercial media. In the 1950s, the accordion-driven *música norteña* entered the commercial market through actor-singers such as the witty Lalo González "Piporro," and in the 1960s and 1970s through successful recording artists such as Cornelio Reyna. By the early 1990s, "new" pop groups called *bandas*, emulating the raucous, brass-woodwind-percussion sounds of two closely related ensembles, Sinaloa-style bands (*bandas sinaloenses*) and Zacatecas-style bands (*tamborazos zacatecanos*), dominated Mexican pop. The marimba ensemble, though never a major force in the popular media, was an indispensable musical icon, often used to represent the cultural milieu of Chiapas and southern Oaxaca. Although each of these styles reflected the fads of commercial popularity, through widespread recognition as a music representing part of Mexico's national cultural identity, they all filled a long-lasting niche in Mexican musical tastes.

International popular music in Mexico and Mexican music abroad

Although homegrown musical strains, *música ranchera* in particular, account for a major share of the commercially dominant popular music in Mexico, pop-music fashions from abroad hold sway among urban people. Interest in foreign musical models is not new. The Mexican middle class that emerged in the 1800s adored European salon music and opera. A passionate interest in the Cuban *danzón*, kindled in the 1920s and 1930s, waned but continued throughout the century. American dance orchestras of the 1940s and 1950s spawned countless Mexican imitators and internationally popular composer-bandleaders such as Luis Arcaraz. *Música tropical*—in its most general sense, referring to rhythmically lively urban dance music of Caribbean origin—gained a large following. Beginning in the late 1940s, the mambo, the *cha-cha-chá,* the *cumbia,* and, later, salsa penetrated Mexican markets and entered the repertoires of many kinds of musical ensembles throughout the country. North American, Brazilian, and other romantic ballad styles were incorporated into the *balada,* an extension of the *canción romántica.* Beginning in the 1950s, large numbers of young Mexicans flocked to American rock. Mexican bands did Spanish-language covers of popular melodies and composed new pieces, though they never managed to forge a long-lasting and distinctly Mexican style of rock.

Much Mexican popular music and, to a much lesser extent, grass-roots traditional music has found a following outside Mexico. With the rise of the commercial music complex in the early twentieth century, Mexican musicians recorded and performed abroad. The first mariachi recording is thought to have been made in Mexico City in 1908. Folkloric troupes of dancers and musicians presented theatrical renditions of regional music and dance on every continent, especially in Europe and the Americas. Trío Los Panchos, which formed in New York, toured widely in the United States before settling in Mexico. Commercially aspiring ensembles saw touring abroad, particularly to economically prosperous locations like New York and Los Angeles, as means of gaining greater recognition and profits. Powerful radio stations such as XEW broadcast Mexican music deep into Latin America. Many Mexican musicians resettled in other countries. At the first annual Encuento del Mariachi in Guadalajara in 1994, mariachis from the United States, Canada, Costa Rica, Aruba, Venezuela, Italy, Belgium, Japan, and other countries joined their Mexican counterparts. In the final decades of the twentieth century, many Mexican artists, from Mariachi Vargas de Tecalitlán, to singers such as Angeles Ochoa and the veteran Lola Beltrán (d. 1996), to composer-singers such as Armando Manzanero, Luis Miguel, and Juan Gabriel, had major followings abroad. The combination of long-proven Mexican musical productivity and a large and successful Mexican music industry exporting music around the world opened a broad swath in many parts of the world, especially among Spanish-speaking communities.

FURTHER STUDY

English-language sources on pre-Conquest, colonial, and nineteenth-century music in Mexico are few, but Robert M. Stevenson offered a cornucopia of insightful documentation, synthesis, and critical references of previous scholarship in *Music in Aztec and Inca Territory* (1968) and his earlier *Music in Mexico: A Historical Survey* (1952). Peter Crossley-Holland offered new analysis of pre-Aztec musical instruments of West Mexico and an appeal for greater scholarly collaboration among musicologists, archaeologists, anthropologists, physicists, and others in his *Musical Artifacts of Pre-Hispanic West Mexico* (1980). Among the milestone English-language articles on the topic are Charles Boilès' works on flutes and the musical bow (1965, 1966a, 1966b) and E. Thomas Stanford's analysis of music-and-dance terms in three sixteenth-century native-language dictionaries (1966).

Several Mexican scholars have published important works in Spanish on Mexican music history. Gabriel Saldívar broke much new ground through his examination of colonial documents and ancient instruments, resulting in his *Historia de la música en México (épocas precortesiana y colonial)* (1934). Samuel Martí's *Instrumentos musicales precortesianos* (1955; second edition, 1968) offers photographic illustrations of musical artifacts, and his *Canto, danza y música precortesianos* (1961) employs iconography, historical accounts, and ethnographic musical transcriptions in search of knowledge about Aztec song, dance, and music. Articles and book chapters by the folklorist Vicente T. Mendoza (1938, 1956), Daniel Castañeda (1933, 1942), and Carmen Sordo Sodi (1964) are among the many shorter publications treating preencounter music. Otto Mayer-Serra's *Panorama de la música mexicana desde la independencia hasta la actualidad* (1941) offered a critical treatment of fine-art music from 1810 to the 1930s.

Much Mexican popular music has found a following outside Mexico. The first mariachi recording is thought to have been made in Mexico City in 1908; powerful radio stations such as XEW broadcast Mexican music deep into Latin America.

Though scholarly research on tribal, folk, and popular music in the final decades of the twentieth century has built on and advanced the accomplishments of Saldívar, Mendoza, Stevenson, and others, many musical traditions still lack comprehensive, in-depth, authoritative documentation. Jas Reuter's *La música popular de México* (fourth edition, 1985) offers a brief, introductory overview of tribal and mestizo music. The *Serie de discos* edited by Irene Vázquez Valle (1967–1979) is the most comprehensive effort to document a panorama of native American and mestizo musical traditions through recordings and descriptive notes. Other important recordings of Mexican music are by Lieberman et al. (1985), Montes de Oca H. (1994), Strachwitz (1992, 1993, 1995), and Strachwitz and Sheehy (1994). In *Historia de la música popular mexicana* (1989), Yolanda Moreno Rivas synthesized much background and biographical detail on the origins, leading personalities, and major trends of popular musical styles. The music of Mexico's Amerindian peoples, particularly that of smaller, more marginal, groups, is acutely in need of further documentation.

REFERENCES

Béhague, Gerard. 1979. *Music in Latin America: An Introduction*. Englewood Cliffs, N.J.: Prentice-Hall.

Boilès, Charles Lafayette. 1965. "La Flauta Triple de Tenenexpan." *La Palabra y el Hombre (Revista de la Universidad Veracruzana)* 34 (April-June).

———. 1966a. "El Arco Musical, ¿Una Pervivencia?" *La Palabra y el Hombre (Revista de la Universidad Veracruzana)* 39 (July–Sept.).

———. 1966b. "The Pipe and Tabor in Mesoamerica." In *Yearbook 2* of the Inter-American Institute for Musical Research, 43–74. New Orleans: Tulane University.

Calderón de la Barca, Frances Erskine. 1843. *Life in Mexico during a Residence of Two Years in That Country*. London: Chapman and Hall.

Castañeda, Daniel. 1942. "Una flauta de la cultura tarasca." *Revista Musical Mexicana* (7 March).

Castañeda, Daniel, and Vicente T. Mendoza. 1933. *Los Teponaztlis, Los Percutores Precortesianos, Los Huehuetls*. Anales del Museo Nacional de Arqueología, Historia y Etnografía, 8. México, D.F.: Museo Nacional de Arqueología, Historia y Etnografía.

Crossley-Holland, Peter. 1980. *Musical Artifacts of Pre-Hispanic West Mexico: Towards an Interdisciplinary Approach*. Monograph Series in Ethnomusicology, 1. Los Angeles: Department of Ethnomusicology, University of California at Los Angeles.

Durán, Diego. 1867–1880. *Historia de las Indias de Nueva-España*. 2 vols. México, D.F.: J. M. Andrade and F. Escalante.

Esteva, José María. 1844a. "Costumbres y trages nacionales: La jarochita." *El museo mexicano*, 3:234–235.

———. 1844b. "Trages y costumbres nacionales: El jarocho." *El museo mexicano* 4:60–62.

Jáuregui, Jesús. 1990. *El mariachi: Símbolo musical de México*. México, D.F.: Banpaís.

Lieberman, Baruj, Eduardo Llerenas, and Enrique Ramírez de Arellano. 1985. *Antología del Son de México*. Discos Corason / Música Tradicional (México) MTCD 01–03. 3 compact discs.

Martí, Samuel. 1955. *Instrumentos musicales precortesianos*. México, D.F.: Instituto Nacional de Antropología.

———. 1961. *Canto, Danza y Música Precortesianos*. México, D.F.: Fondo de Cultura Económica.

———. 1968. *Instrumentos musicales precortesianos*, 2nd ed. México, D.F.: Instituto Nacional de Antropología e Historia.

Mayer-Serra, Otto. 1941. *Panorama de la música mexicana desde la independencia hasta la actualidad*. México, D.F.: El Colegio de México.

Mendoza, Vicente T. 1938. "Música Precolombina de América." *Boletín Latino-Americana de Música* 4(4):235–257.

———. 1939. *El romance español y el corrido mexicano: Estudio comparativo.* México, D.F.: Ediciones de la Universidad Nacional Autónoma de México.

———. 1956. *Panorama de la música tradicional de México.* México, D.F.: Imprenta Universitaria.

Montes de Oca H., Ignacio. 1994. *Music of Mexico, Vol. 2: Michoacán: Conjunto Alma de Apatzingán, "Arriba Tierra Caliente."* Arhoolie CD426. Compact disc.

Moreno Rivas, Yolanda. 1989. *Historia de la música popular mexicana,* 2nd ed. México, D.F.: Consejo Nacional para la Cultura y las Artes, Alianza Editorial Mexicana.

Motolinía, Toribio de. 1941 [1858]. *Historia de los Indios de Nueva España,* ed. Salvador Chávez Hayhoe. México, D.F.

Prieto, Guillermo. 1906. *Memorias de mis tiempos.* 2 vols. México, D.F.: Viuda de C. Bouret.

Reuter, Jas. 1985. *La música popular de México: Origen e historia de la música que canta y toca el pueblo mexicano.* México, D.F.: Panorama Editoria.

Sahagún, Bernardino. 1956 [1547]. *Historia general de las cosas de Nueva España.* New edition, with numeration, annotation, and appendices, ed. Angel M. Garibay K. México, D.F.: Editorial Porrúa.

Saldívar, Gabriel. 1934. *Historia de la música en México: Épocas precortesiana y colonial.* México, D.F.: Editorial "Cultura."

———. 1937. *El Jarabe, baile popular mexicano.* México, D.F.: Talleres Gráficos de la Nación.

Sordo Sodi, María del Carmen. 1964. "Los dioses de la música y de la danza en el Códice Borgia." *Revista del Conservatorio* (Mexico City), 7 (June).

Stanford, E. Thomas. 1966. "A Linguistic Analysis of Music and Dance Terms from Three Sixteenth-Century Dictionaries of Mexican Indian Languages." In *Yearbook 2* of the Inter-American Institute for Musical Research, 101–159. New Orleans: Tulane University.

Stevenson, Robert M. 1952. *Music in Mexico: A Historical Survey.* New York: Thomas Y. Crowell.

———. 1968. *Music in Aztec and Inca Territory.* Berkeley and Los Angeles: University of California Press.

Strachwitz, Chris. 1992. *Mexico's Pioneer Mariachis, Vol. 3: Mariachi Vargas de Tecalitlán: Their First Recordings 1937–1947.* Arhoolie-Folklyric CD7015. Compact disc.

———. 1993. *Mexico's Pioneer Mariachis, Vol. 1: Mariachi Coculense de Cirilo Marmolejo, Plus Several Sones by Cuarteto Coculense: The Very First Mariachi Recordings from 1908.* Arhoolie-Folklyric CD7011. Compact disc.

———. 1995. *Music of Mexico, Vol. 3: La Huasteca; Huapangos y Sones Huastecos; Los Caimanes (1995) y Los Caporales de Panuco (1978).* Arhoolie 431. Compact disc.

Strachwitz, Chris, and Dan Sheehy. 1994. *Music of Mexico, Vol.1: Veracruz: Conjunto Alma Jarocha, "Sones Jarochos."* Arhoolie CD354. Compact disc.

Vázquez Valle, Irene. 1967–1979. *Serie de discos.* México, D.F.: Instituto Nacional de Antropología. 24 LP disks with notes.

Section 4
Central America: Connecting North and South America

Central America connects Mexico and South America. In pre-Columbian times, the region was the center of one of the world's most celebrated and musically complex civilizations—the Maya. Three centuries of Spanish colonial rule and independent evolution since 1821 have wrought differing national complexions from varied cultural roots. For example, most Guatemalans are Amerindians, most Costa Ricans claim European heritage, and nearly half the Belizean population is African. Musical cultures of the region reflect these differences. European-derived musical instruments such as the harp, guitar, and violin are popular among native American and mestizo groups.

Showing Spanish influence in his violin and native American influence in his clothing, Panamanian Efraín Gutiérrez performs on stage with the group Panamá la Vieja. Photo by Ronald R. Smith.

The Music of Central America
Daniel E. Sheehy

Amerindian Cultures

Spanish, African, and Mestizo Heritages

Urban Migration

opposite: Central America

The term *Central America* denotes the region comprising seven nations: Guatemala, Belize, Honduras, El Salvador, Nicaragua, Costa Rica, and Panama (map 10). To their north is Mexico, with 92 million people living in 1,216,510 square kilometers. The seven countries of Central America, by contrast, have an aggregate population of 32 million, only one-third as large as that of Mexico, and with 325,142 square kilometers of territory, about one-fourth the size of Mexico.

With the exceptions of Belize and Panama, the Central American countries were briefly united after their declaration of independence from Spain (1821) as the United Provinces of Central America (1823–1826). A mild desire for greater unity remains, though it is consistently thwarted by nationalism and a long-standing tradition of local political control. Immediately after independence, Panama joined its southern neighbor, Colombia, but separated from Colombia in 1903 and came to be considered part of Central America. Belize was a British colony, British Honduras, until 1973, when it attained independence.

AMERINDIAN CULTURES

Prehistoric Central America was home to two of the world's most celebrated civilizations. The apogee of Mayan civilization, centered in Guatemala, Honduras, and Belize (A.D. 600 to 900), saw notable accomplishments in astronomy, mathematics, systems of writing, and expressive culture. The Aztec Empire, farther north, encountered in 1519 by the conquistador Hernán Cortés, impressed the Spanish adventurers with its pyramids, ceremonies, and music. Its influence extended from the northern areas of central Mexico southward to what is now the Pacific coast of Nicaragua. Native American culture in Central America is often simplistically expressed in terms of these civilizations, but hundreds of distinctive cultures and languages existed within and alongside them (see map 3).

SPANISH, AFRICAN, AND MESTIZO HERITAGES

The Amerindian population suffered a steep decline in the 1500s, as the Spanish invaders practiced abusive policies toward their New World subjects and unwittingly carried diseases against which native peoples had little resistance. Nevertheless,

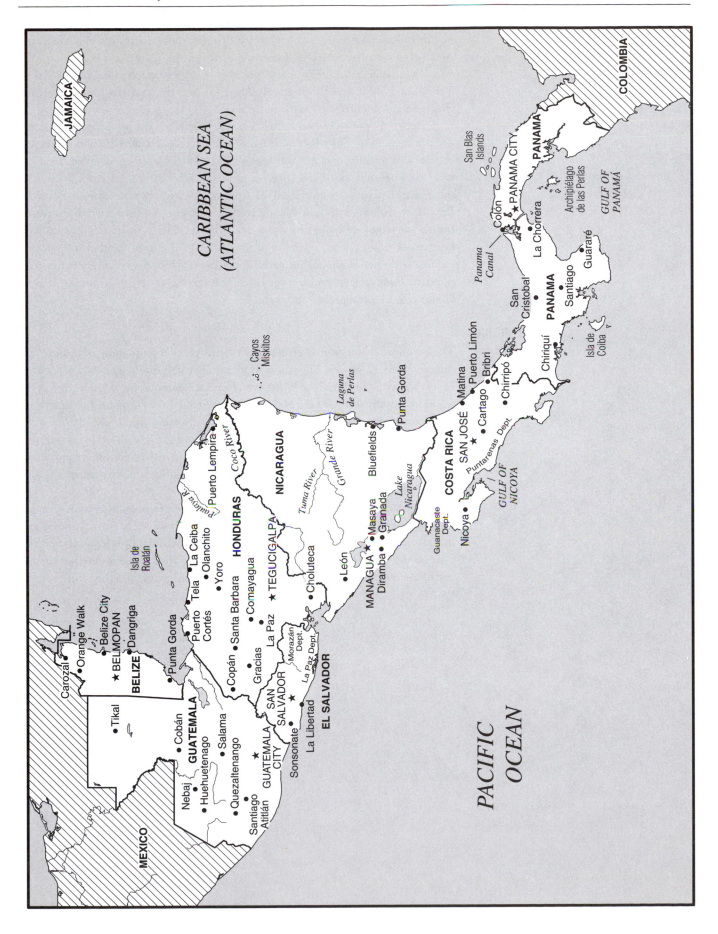

Amerindians formed the base for the modern-day populations that resulted from the mixing of Europeans, Africans, and Indians. Today, more than two-thirds of Central Americans are mestizos. The dominant contributors to mestizo culture are the Spanish language and lifeways and the Roman Catholic religion. African slaves, brought mainly in the 1500s and 1600s, and their descendants have had strong effects on mestizo life, particularly in music.

Localized practices vary the general pattern. Most Guatemalans are Amerindians, most Costa Ricans primarily claim European heritage, and nearly half the Belizean population is African. Spanish is the official language of six of the countries, but English is the official language of Belize and is the lingua franca in much of the sparsely populated east coast of Central America, where immigrants from English-speaking Caribbean islands settled. Numerous Maya-related and other Indian languages are spoken by about one-fifth of Central Americans, especially in Guatemala. More than 85 percent of the Central American population is at least nominally Roman Catholic, but native American religious beliefs and practices continue in some places, and evangelistic Protestant sects have gained ground in Guatemala, El Salvador, and elsewhere.

URBAN MIGRATION

The twentieth century saw sweeping societal changes that profoundly influenced culture and music. Massive migration to urban areas left about one-half of Central Americans living in cities. The birthrate in Central America, one of the highest in the world, drastically increased the population. Poverty and civil unrest led to significant migration northward to Mexico and beyond. The growth of electronic media and the music industry gave an advantage to popular musics of the more developed countries. On radio and television and in films, Mexican music had an enormous impact on Spanish-speaking Central Americans and was in turn influenced by popular music of the United States.

Central America is a region of striking cultural contrasts and hundreds of musical threads. The modern descendants of ancient Amerindian cultures, rural-rooted mestizo traditions, African-derived traits, and international urban popular musics exist side by side, giving rise to new musical hybrids. Musical life is filled with possibilities as an increasingly younger population charts its course into the future.

Bribri and Cabécar

Carlos A. Fernández

Musical Instruments
Musical Contexts and Genres
Further Study

The Bribri and the Cabécar live in six tropically forested reservations along the Atlantic and Pacific slopes of the Talamanca Mountains in southeastern Costa Rica. At the time of their first contacts with Spaniards (1502), these peoples appear to have inhabited the Matina Valley on the Caribbean coast (Stone 1977:165). Fleeing from Spanish settlers, they settled in Talamanca. In 1605, captain Diego de Sojo y Peñaranda succeeded in overpowering them and founding Santiago de Talamanca, which became the first Franciscan mission in the area (Fernández Guardia 1975:168).

Until the late 1800s, the Bribri and the Cabécar strongly resisted non-Indians' attempts to convert and settle the area, first by colonial powers and later by Costa Rican authorities. In 1909, the Costa Rican government and the Chiriquí Land Company, a subsidiary of United Fruit Company, signed an agreement by which the latter acquired rights to begin banana production in the Talamanca Valley (Borge and Villalobos 1994:35–45). Most Bribri and Cabécar were removed from the lower portions of the valley and established in the upper floodplain. After the 1930s, when the United Fruit Company abandoned the area, indigenous populations returned and resettled there.

Bribri and Cabécar clans are traditionally matrilineal. They distinguish themselves by mythical territorial origins defining their kin relationships, positions within political and religious hierarchies, and occupational specialties. Communities that resettled the lower floodplain of the Talamanca Valley have undergone acculturation since 1940, marked to a large extent by the establishment of schools for Indians and the pressure of agricultural, timber, oil, and other industries. In 1977, after intense lobbying by indigenous organizations, the Costa Rican congress created the Bribri and Cabécar reserves, now administered by local populations.

Because the languages, kin relationships, and political and religious organization are similar, the Bribri and the Cabécar are often considered a tribal unity (Bozzoli 1986:86). Both their languages fall within the Western or Archaic Group of the Macro-Chibchan Phylum. Most Bribri and Cabécar maintain their languages, with many of their traditional customs and beliefs. It is estimated that in the mid-1990s

Healing songs directed to patients or their illnesses are *siwa' kulè* 'shouted knowledge', whereas those done to communicate with Sibö's messengers are *siwa' kus* 'whispered knowledge', which is sometimes only thought.

their population was 11,800 Bribri (of whom roughly 80 percent are bilingual in Spanish and their native language) and 8,300 Cabécar.

MUSICAL INSTRUMENTS

A maraca (*tönö*), made of a gourd (*Crescentia cujete*) filled with platanillo seeds (*Heliconia* spp.), is used in traditional Bribri and Cabécar funerals and medicine. Through perforations drilled in one end of the gourd, a cord is passed to a bird-bone handle. The *blur cue,* a sun-dried armadillo shell, is played by rubbing its ribbed sides with a wooden stick or a large seed (Salazar 1992:36–37). It accompanies songs and dances, usually with the *sabak* (figure 1), a single-headed membranophone usually made of Spanish cedar (*Cedrela alliodora*), a wood that the Cabécar and Bribri believe Sibö, creator of the world, created for its resonance (Salazar 1992:77). The head, made of iguana skin, is attached to the rim of the drum by the animal's gelatin or blood, held in place with a cord for a few days while it sets, and finally fixed to the rim with India rubber. The instrument is tuned by rubbing the surface of the head with the palm of a hand. It is played by hitting the head with the fingertips of the right hand while holding it under the left arm, usually suspended from the left shoulder by a cord attached to either end of the drum. It accompanies songs and dances, ritual and secular.

The Bribri and Cabécar have three kinds of aerophones (Salazar 1992). The *talacabe* is an end-blown flute made of bird bone or carrizo (*Chusquea* spp.) with a

FIGURE 1   Cabécar men play *sabak* drums during the *muakuke* 'game of the drum' at Alto Chirripó Reservation, Province of Cartago, Costa Rica. Photo by Rodrigo Salazar Salvatierra, 1977.

beeswax embouchure. The instrument has six holes for fingering, all positioned close to the embouchure near the upper end of the instrument. Cabécar medical practitioners believe sounds produced on this instrument extricate spirits causing illness in their patients. The instrument also accompanies agricultural work and is used for entertainment. The *etka talacabe,* another end-blown flute made of carrizo, has no embouchure and no holes for fingering. One end of the instrument is closed, and different pitches are produced by overblowing. It is used in funerary ceremonies as a means of freeing the soul of the dead and accompanying it on its way to Sibö. The *yöcsoro* consists of an end-blown snail shell. Beeswax is fitted onto the shell's opening to enhance the angle at which air strikes the inner cavity. A hole for fingering is made toward the tip of the shell's spiral, usually four turns from the opening, to allow two tones to be produced. The instrument is played during recreational activities and as a signaling device.

MUSICAL CONTEXTS AND GENRES

According to Bribri respondents, singing is the preferred communicative medium of Sibö. An essential aspect of Bribri culture, it appears in traditional narratives, life-cycle rituals, and medicine. Until the early 1900s, the Bribri, like the Cabécar, were governed by a hierarchy of ritual specialists, official carriers of the oral traditions: a high priest (*úsêköl,* the last of whom died in 1910), a funerary singer (*stsököl*), a manipulator and burier of corpses (*ököm*), a master of ceremonies (*bikàkla*), and a doctor (*awá*). Ritual specialists retain an important role in the political and religious lives of indigenous populations. Members of certain clans continue to train to become practitioners of these ritual offices, of which singing is an important component.

Ritual songs

Sacred narratives (*siwa' páköl* 'histories') include sung dialogues between Sibö and other characters. Ritual specialists perform them at night for adults and children. These narratives, mythological in content, serve as a major means of preserving and shaping Bribri and Cabécar history, custom, and morals, and are an important form of entertainment.

According to one mythic narrative, the Bribri are descendants of maize seed that Sibö left in Alto Lari, about 400 meters above sea level along the Lari River in the Talamanca Valley. Some seeds sprouted and became animals, which formed clans and tribes. Other narratives tell of the creation of the world, the sea, the sky, and other salient aspects of the Talamanca landscape, flora, and fauna (Bozzoli 1977).

Birth, menarche, pregnancy, illness, and death call upon the *awá* to care for members of his community. The therapy he provides usually involves singing to the rhythm of his rattle, cleansing by blowing tobacco on the patient, and treating the patient with forest-collected plants. The Bribri traditionally believe that illness is caused by entities that can be set free by *olóbsó,* the guardian of "where the sun rises." The *awá* heals people or cleanses objects by sending these entities to the realm of *bukublu,* guardian of "where the sun sets" (Bozzoli 1983:126–127).

To become an *awá* (pl. *awápa*), an apprentice must memorize lengthy ritual songs and sacred narratives—a process called *se' sulétèke* 'our learning'. The songs, put under the category of *siwa'* 'knowledge', are classified according to particular textural traits and performance contexts. Healing songs directed to patients or their illnesses are *siwa' kulè* 'shouted knowledge', whereas those done to communicate with Sibö's messengers are *siwa' kus* 'whispered knowledge', which is sometimes only thought. The *awá* recognize two other styles of singing used in teaching an apprentice: *siwa' ajköbta* 'recited knowledge' and *siwa' ajköki* 'sung knowledge'.

Ritual songs performed by *awá* have a series of repeated melodic phrases in irregular rhythms with accents depending on textual requirements, plus a nasal quality (Jones 1974:429–433). The songs are sung in a linguistic register different from everyday speech, featuring repetition, vocables, and archaic vocabulary. They follow this sequence: those in which the *awá* presents himself and the patient to Sibö; those directed to the particular illness, describing its nature and history; and those asking Sibö to send the illness back to "where the sun sets." For serious illnesses, the last follows the drawing of images on a piece of barkwood (*Ochroma lagopus*) that represent Sibö, the illness, and the animals and plants that cure it (Bozzoli 1982:88).

Public schools, health-care clinics, and missionaries have discouraged traditional medicine, but *awápa* continue to be sought, usually in conjunction with non-Indian medicine, by older members of the community and sometimes by non-Indians from urban centers outside reservations. Many *awápa* are well known locally, and even internationally, and since the 1980s have created organizations working to maintain traditional knowledge and ways and to develop projects of benefit for their communities.

Bribri funerals have several main events: wrapping the cadaver and placing it in the forest (done shortly after an individual's death); packing the disjointed skeleton and storing it in a provisional shelter (done six to nine months after the death); *sulàr* 'music for our people', a ceremony; and a procession to the ossuary of the clan of the deceased, leading to burial of the bone-bearing package (Cervantes 1990:26–47). In the course of these funerary activities, members of the community narrate the life of the deceased on several occasions, each time in an increasingly elaborated fashion, and always in recitative.

Though all ritual specialists have some knowledge of the musical traditions, the *stsökölpa* (sing. *stsököl*) are assigned the role of specialists in funerary music. The songs for the *sulàr,* known as *sbláuk,* are sung by the *stsököl,* accompanying himself on a ceremonial gourd rattle (*tönö*), and by his assistants, the *stsököl sini'pa* (Cervantes 1990:42–43). The *stsököl* sings while his assistants and other men play *sabak* or armadillo shells, dancing in a circle. On such occasions, women do not play instruments, but they participate in a linear dance also carried on during the *sulàr,* though the funerary singer, his assistants, and other players stand outside the row.

Traditionally, funerary singers came only from certain clans. According to one mythical narrative, they originated from four tropical-forest birds: the macaw (*Ara macao*), the toucan (*Ramphasta swainsonii*), the parrot (*Amazona* sp.), and the quetzal (*Pharomachrus mocinno*). Each bird is said to have its own vocal style that characterizes funerary singers from different clans. These birds in turn had been born from *tá,* a plant whose seeds are used in ceremonial rattles (Bozzoli 1977:185–186). The institution of the *stsököl* has practically disappeared, and in most areas the *awá* has taken over his ritual functions.

Secular song and dance

Other Bribri songs fall under the general category of *jtsök* 'to sing'. Bribri men sing work-accompanying songs (also called *kulè*); women and girls sing *ajkòyönuk* 'extemporaneous song' as they wash clothes or grind foodstuffs. The latter term also denotes dialogues sung between women (Bozzoli 1982:66). To kinfolk on birthdays and other occasions, women often sing personalized songs, seen as amicable expressive gestures. Other Bribri songs, known as *ajköki* 'songs elaborated or prepared with a goal', tell of the birth or death of someone in the community, or mark first menstruations and weddings.

People commonly dance during the corn-beer fiesta and communal meetings. The *sörbö,* a dance done in a circle by men and women, young and old, commemorates the creation of the Bribri world. One of the most important public symbols of Bribri identity, it describes Sibö's creation of the earth and the sky and roles played by his assistants in that process.

When danced by a group, the *sörbö* is performed responsorially by a singer (*awá, óköm,* or *bikakla*) and dancers. The main singer sings a musical phrase that all other participants repeat. As the dancers repeat this phrase, the singer interjects more elaborate phrases. The *sörbö* and other song-dances are often accompanied by a *sabak,* which the Cabécar of Chirripó use to accompany other dances, including the *muakuke* 'game of the drums' and the *bulsique*. The latter resembles the *sörbö,* but the songs that accompany it, exhibiting greater variation in pitch, rhythm, and accent, are more complex than those sung by the *awá* (Jones 1974:430).

Singing and dancing add to youthful entertainment. Amateur musicians are often called to prepare ensembles for villagewide celebrations. Vocal and instrumental music performed by Bribri young people is markedly influenced by the popular music of Colombia, the Dominican Republic, Mexico, Panama, and even the United States, partly because of the impact of national and local broadcasts, and partly, later in the twentieth century, by the increasing availability of boomboxes.

FURTHER STUDY

The Bribri and the Cabécar have been the focus of numerous ethnographic studies, including those by Bozzoli (1982, 1986), Gabb (1875), Salazar (1980), Sapper (1978), Skinner (1920), and Stone (1962). These works provide historical depth to current understandings of Bribri and Cabécar ceremonial uses of song and music, particularly in funerals and medicine. Sapper (1978) transcribes several *yöcsoro* melodies collected in the Chirripó area; Stone (1962) includes the texts of more than fifteen songs and other information about music. Bozzoli (1986) provides the most detailed study of Bribri medicine to date.

Acevedo (1986) gives an introduction to Bribri and Cabécar musical culture. Jones (1974) and Salazar (1992) have studied musical systems and instruments in detail. Cervantes (1990) deals with local funerary rites and songs from an ethnography-of-communication perspective, and provides important analyses of linguistic, oral-poetic, and communicative features of these events. Further research is needed on native musical style and performance, oral composition, participant aesthetics, and indigenous systems of classifying genres and instruments. Linguistic and oral-poetic analyses of other genres such as *siwa'* and *jtsök* are lacking.

REFERENCES

Acevedo, Jorge L. 1986. *La Música en las reservas indígenas de Costa Rica.* San José: Universidad de Costa Rica.

Borge, Carlos, and Victoria Villalobos. 1994. *Talamanca en la encrucijada.* San José: Editorial Universidad Estatal a Distancia.

Bozzoli, María E. 1977. "Narraciones Bribris." *Vínculos* 2(2):166–199.

———. 1982. *Especialidades en la medicina aborigen bribri.* San José: Departamento de Antropología, Universidad de Costa Rica.

———. 1983. "De donde el sol nace a donde el sol se pone: Mitología talamanqueña del clima y de las enfermedades." *América Indígena* 43(1):125–145.

———. 1986. *El nacimiento y la muerte entre los Bribris.* San José: Editorial Universidad de Costa Rica.

Cervantes, Laura. 1990. "Sulàr: Playing for the Dead." M.A. thesis, State University of New York at Albany.

Fernández Guardia, Ricardo. 1975 [1913]. *El Descubrimiento y la Conquista.* 5th ed. San José: Editorial Costa Rica.

Gabb, William M. 1875. "On the Indian Tribes and Languages of Costa Rica." *Proceedings of the American Philosophical Society* 14:483–602.

Jones, Pedro K. 1974. "Una Breve Descripción de la Cultura Musical Chirripó." *América Indígena* 34(2):427–37.

Salazar, Rodrigo. 1980. *Los Cabécares (crónica de viaje).* San José: Centro Universitario del Atlántico, Universidad de Costa Rica.

———. 1992. *Los instrumentos de la música folclórica costarricense.* Cartago: Editorial Instituto Technológico de Costa Rica.

Sapper, Carl. 1978 [1924]. *Visita a varias partes de Costa Rica.* San José: Ministerio de Cultura, Juventud y Deportes.

Skinner, Alanson. 1920. "Notes on the Bribri of Costa Rica." In *Indian Notes and Monographs,* 6:3:41–106. New York: Heye Foundation, Museum of the American Indian.

Stone, Doris Z. 1962. *The Talamanca Tribes of Costa Rica.* Papers of the Peabody Museum of American Archaeology and Ethnology, 43, part 2. Cambridge, Mass.: Peabody Museum Press.

——. 1977. *Pre-Columbian Man in Costa Rica.* Cambridge, Mass.: Peabody Museum Press.

Kuna
Sandra Smith

Kuna compositions and choreographies unfold according to musical principles that predate European contact. The Kuna are famous for their ability to modernize their lives, reflecting the world around them in ways that preserve and maintain what is uniquely theirs. As a display of knowledge and artistic skill, they weave foreign elements into their traditional music. Men who have worked on foreign ships relay stories of their travels; these are woven into lullabies and historical chants. Kuna groups that have danced in festivals in Panama, Latin America, North America, and Europe bring back foreign styles of dancing that are imitated in Kuna choreographic sequences, as in "The Way Americans Dance," which depicts square-dance figures. The cultural cohesion and adaptability of the Kuna people are related to their historical dispersion over a wide geographical area.

CUSTOMS AND MUSICAL CULTURE

Numbering about thirty thousand, the Kuna (Cuna) live along several rivers in northern Colombia and eastern Panama, and along Panama's Caribbean coast and on the San Blas Islands. Kuna expressive culture displays the wealth and imagination afforded by leisure, strong communal organization, and an unbroken heritage of indigenous civilization. The Kuna are among the most extensively documented living nations of Latin America. They comprise several slightly different cultural groups sharing a common language and traditions, including music. These groups are distinguished by slight differences in vocabulary, style of speaking, interpretation of oral traditions, and music.

Kuna ancestors once lived in the northern Colombian highlands, where the development of their material and expressive culture reflected a riverine way of life. Some village groups spread along the rivers into the Colombian lowlands toward the Gulf of Uraba. Others spread northward through the mountains into eastern Panama, where they settled along rivers that flow into the Atlantic Ocean. These populations ranged across 300 kilometers and were separated from each other by dense jungle and, in some cases, by other native groups. Offshoots of the mountain and river populations in eastern Panama and northern Colombia formed coastal vil-

The instruments were animate beings that existed in social combinations, such as couples or groups of three or six. They each 'sang' their own language and danced their own dance, and they all arrived singing and dancing.

lages near the mouths of rivers at about the time of earliest European contact there. The people of most of these villages subsequently moved offshore to the San Blas Islands, which stretch from the Colombian border all along Panama's eastern coast. Though these islands have neither fresh water nor soil suitable for farming, they provide a healthier environment than the coastal areas. Island-dwelling Kuna make daily forays to the mainland to farm, hunt, and fetch water. They frequently travel upriver to visit their relatives in the mountains. They associate the variation in their styles of speaking and cultural traditions with each of their populations.

The island-dwelling Kuna, now far outnumbering the mountain- and river-dwelling Kuna, maintain their highland heritage. They travel up and down the coast in canoes, they use the metaphorical structure of rivers and pathways to describe their traditional arts, and they construct their musical instruments, mostly flutes and panpipes, of materials from the mountains. These instruments have a closer affinity with instruments used by Andean peoples of South America than with those used by neighboring lowland peoples of Central America. Each island village maintains social, cultural, and political ties with its mainland relatives, whose linguistic and musical styles are consequently reflected throughout the island population.

Because the Kuna are geographically scattered, interspersed with other native groups and with Latin American populations, they place a high premium on communication between the distant members of each of their cultural groups, and among their different groups as a whole. Much of this communication is carried out musically during periodic gatherings when the cultural leaders of different villages convene to perform tribal oral histories and discuss social and political issues.

Kuna music consists of vocal and instrumental genres. Most of the latter are associated with dance. Individuals of all ages and both genders participate in musical performances, though most musical genres are gender-specific. The following examination of Kuna music uses as a framework Kuna beliefs about the origin and development of their musical traditions and Kuna terminology for musical items and activities.

The Kuna believe that musical traditions, which encompass ways of singing, playing instrumental music, and dancing, exist almost in a Platonic sense in an otherworldly realm. This is the realm of the ancestors and the gods, from where the legendary hero, Ibeorgun, helped bring to the Kuna certain musical instruments, mostly end-blown flutes and panpipes, each with its particular music and dance. The instruments were animate beings that existed in social combinations, such as couples or groups of three or six; they each 'sang' their own language and danced their own dance, and they all arrived singing and dancing. The Kuna believe they have undergone legendary and historical periods of cultural decline and renewal, and when they have sought to relearn forgotten traditions, their cultural leaders, like Ibeorgun, have helped them hear the tradition-carrying ancestral voices. The Kuna believe that their musical traditions are continually modified in the slow march of culture, and that new ways of singing, playing instruments, and dancing emerge from ancestral voices to answer current needs.

The Kuna language does not employ terms that correspond directly to English concepts of "music," "chant," "song," and "dance." Most Kuna vocal genres are directly associated with the term *igar* (also *igala*) which can be glossed 'way' or 'path'. *Igar* is more broadly associated with formalized ways of speaking, which can include knowledge about communicating with the world of spirits. Each vocal musical genre with *igar* employs specific linguistic and musical conventions; musicality is part of the *igar* of these specialized ways of speaking. Each piece or text of one of these genres with *igar* has a name and a 'way' or manner of expression. It follows a specific 'path' that guides expression along a theme or spiritual journey and directs the expression toward an audience of common villagers or trained cultural leaders, Kuna-speakers or Spanish-speakers, nonhuman living things, or spirits or ancestors. Vocal genres with *igar* are learned in formal apprenticeships.

Vocal genres without *igar* use ordinary language. The texts of these genres are neither named nor formalized; they are freely improvised around common themes. Musically, these genres, like those with *igar*, follow certain conventions, but they have greater individual freedom of musical expression than those with *igar*.

Most instrumental genres are associated with musical instruments that have *igar*. Each genre employs a unique musical system, compositional structure, and style of dancing, and all are used in specific social contexts. The pieces within each genre are named, and they are learned in formal apprenticeships. Instruments without *igar* are used for free improvisation or for playing the musical pieces of the instruments having *igar*.

The term *namaked* denotes the performance of vocal genres with or without *igar;* normal speaking is called *soged*. *Namaked* denotes all kinds of human 'calling' and individual kinds of flute-produced music. A parallel term, *gormaked,* denotes all nonhuman calling and the sound of flutes in a generic sense ("the calling of the flutes"). Birdcalls are also *gormaked*. To indicate improvisation on flutes without *igar,* the Kuna say the name of the flute followed by the words *binsae* 'thinking up' and *namaked* 'calling'. They use the term *dodoed* to denote flute-produced music associated with dance, and the term *dodoged* to refer to the dancing itself. They also use the term *dodoged* to denote the playing of flutes in ensemble, whether or not the performance is choreographed.

I use the term *chanting* to denote vocal *namaked* with *igar,* and *singing* to denote vocal *namaked* without *igar*. This usage is consistent with the usage of Sherzer (1983), who has made the most extensive ethnography of Kuna speaking to date. I use *music* to denote human and flute *namaked* and flute *dodoed*. I use *dancing* to denote formally structured human movements.

Considering Kuna beliefs about Kuna musical traditions and the terminology the Kuna use to define musical instruments, compositions, and performances directs attention toward certain features. Broadly speaking, the Kuna do not have an all-encompassing musical system that can be defined tonally or compositionally; rather, musical systems are genre specific. Kuna musical instruments, compositions, and performances are primarily constructed and organized around the interactive roles characteristic of the specific kinds of social groupings represented by the instruments being used or by chanters' or singers' interactions with their audiences. As a vehicle for enhanced communication to certain audiences, music includes formalized patterns of interaction. Cultural leaders are responsible for learning and teaching musical traditions and providing and supporting the contexts that require musical expression.

Each Kuna musical instrument is described below, with emphasis placed on the kinds of groupings in which it is constructed and played. Following this is a discussion of musical contexts and genres, focusing first on vocal genres and second on instrumental genres. Finally, the social aspects of music, including musical enculturation and acculturation and the role that aesthetic evaluation plays in the homogeneity of Kuna musical traditions, are described.

MUSICAL INSTRUMENTS

Kuna instrumental music is represented only by idiophones and aerophones. Musical instruments are neither abundantly nor evenly distributed in Kuna territories, and outside knowledge about their use is limited. There is homogeneity in construction and repertoire among the communities that are in mutual contact. Although variation occurs between community groups that are not in frequent contact, Kuna music on a tribal level shows greater homogeneity than variation.

Of eight reported idiophones, seven are rattles, and one is a humming top. Only one rattle remains in use: the single calabash rattle (*nasis*), shaken by women when singing lullabies and by men when chanting during celebrations of female puberty.

The Kuna have seventeen aerophones, including shell trumpets, voice-modifying instruments made of animal skulls and bamboo, and flutes and panpipes made of wood, bone, and bamboo. Kuna aerophones fall into nine organological classes, distributed among twelve Kuna-defined genres. Most Kuna aerophones are designed to be played in sets of two, three, or six component instruments. Some paired instruments are made up of a complementary male-female couple; others are composed of a primary and secondary speaker. The three-part aerophone contains members arranged in a sequential hierarchy, with the members providing different numbers of pitches. The six-part aerophone contains members that are alike, each producing only one pitch. Each aerophone is associated with a different genre of dance. Some flutes, such as *suara,* are associated with a single dance or way of dancing, but others, such as *gammu burui,* have a large repertoire.

The Kuna do not construct their flutes and panpipes according to a single scale at a standardized pitch. Each kind of aerophone is made to produce a particular array of tones, but its size and range can vary. When matching sets of aerophones are used, as when dancers need three sets of the paired *gammu burui* panpipe, the sets are constructed exactly alike. Different kinds of aerophones are not played together in concert except to produce a cacophony used to drive away harmful spirits.

Flutes

The Kuna distinguish nine kinds of end-blown flutes. A single end-blown flute with external duct (*dolo*) is used for improvisation or for playing the repertoire of the other aerophones. It is constructed like the Kogi hatchet flute [see KOGI]. An external duct made from a pelican's quill is embedded in a large wad of pitch built up from the proximal end of the bamboo tube. There are four equidistant holes for fingers and sometimes one for a thumb.

A single end-blown vessel flute (*dede*) made of an armadillo skull is used to purify the space where musical performances occur. Medicinally, armadillo spirits open pathways or tunnels into Kuna spiritual dimensions.

Four kinds of end-blown internal duct flutes (*sulupgala, gorgigala, mulagala, uasgala*) made of wing bones of eagles, pelicans, and vultures were reported to have been used singly and in sets during celebrations of puberty. Several of these flutes are suspended on necklaces and worn by dancers to make a percussive sound while they dance; this use continues in the late 1990s during celebrations of puberty.

Paired end-blown flutes with external duct (*supe*) resemble the Kogi hatchet flute, but they are constructed in male-female pairs that Kuna musicians call primary

FIGURE 1   Two puberty rite chanters use single end-blown flutes (*gammu suid*) and rattles (*nasis*) in their performances. Around them, Digir Villagers dance in a line at the close of the ceremonies. Photo by Sandra Smith, 1979.

and secondary speakers. The male flute, with four equidistant holes for fingers and one for a thumb, is shorter than the female flute, which has one or two holes for fingers. Melodies with many notes, often imitating birds, are played on the male flute, and the female flute intersperses notes between male-flute passages.

Paired end-blown notched flutes (*suara*) are constructed like the Andean *kena* (*quena*) in male-female couples. The male flute has four equally spaced holes for fingers and sometimes one for a thumb; the female flute has no, one, or two holes. The pair is played in interlocking patterns indigenously described as *su-ar-aaa, su-ar-aaa,* with the male flute sounding *su-ar* and the female flute sounding *aaa*. Paired end-blown ductless and unmodified flutes (*gammu suid*) are also constructed as male and female. Both flutes have two holes for fingers and together produce four consecutive pitches, spanning a fourth. Two chanters use these flutes to chant through and to play overlapping melodic motifs during celebrations of puberty (figure 1).

The Kuna describe one side-blown flute (*galabigbili*). It is constructed of bone or wood and has four holes for fingers. Its use has not been reported in print.

An end-blown conch trumpet (*dutu*) is used to call performers from their homes. Two voice-modifying instruments, one made of a jaguar's skull (*achunono*) and the other of a deer's skull (*goenono*), are constructed with an unmodified open-ended bamboo tube attached to the nape of the skull. Each performer, making jaguarlike or deerlike sounds, directs his voice through the bamboo tube into the skull. Together, the performers pantomime a jaguar hunting a deer (figure 2).

Panpipes

The Kuna have two kinds of bamboo panpipes, bound and unbound, distinguished in three different groupings: paired panpipes; a panpipe made up of three different members; and a panpipe made up of six similar members. Each kind of panpipe is played in an ensemble of six players. The paired panpipe is played in three matching sets; the panpipe having three members is played in two matching sets; the six-part panpipe is played by six performers.

The paired panpipe (*gammu burui*) is made up of fourteen lengths of bamboo tubes in total, giving fourteen consecutive pitches of an equiheptatonic scale, spanning one note short of two octaves. The tubes are distributed alternately between a

Titles given to *gammu burui* compositions name birds and animals, human relationships, techniques of playing the instruments, and activities of the celebrations, with each piece following certain compositional principles.

FIGURE 2   In the dramatic dance performed in Digir Village with the *achunono* and *goenono* voice-modifying instruments, the jaguar triumphs over the deer. Photo by Sandra Smith, 1979.

FIGURE 3   A Kuna woman plays a single *gammu burui* panpipe set (two halves). Photo by Ronald R. Smith.

male and a female instrument, played in duet. The seven tubes of each instrument are again distributed alternately between two bound rafts. The adjacent tubes within each raft are a fifth apart. Each player holds a three-tube raft and a four-tube raft side by side, with the shortest tubes in the center (figure 3). The interval between the rafts (the two short tubes) is a neutral third. Each tube of the male instrument is one step longer and lower in pitch than the corresponding tube of the female instrument. Melodic statements are produced in an alternating and interlocking pattern between two players. Danced performances use three matching sets, so that six players, all men, dance with six women who each have a rattle (figure 4).

Some *gammu burui* pieces consist of the repetition and modification of two or more melodic statements, each usually closing with the figure presented in the introduction of the piece. The melodic themes are stated and repeated in their shortest forms in the first section; then they are each expanded by a few notes by internal segmental repetition or the insertion of new material. The expanded statements are in turn repeated several times; in the last portion of the piece, the melodic themes contract to their original forms. The total length of a piece is fifteen to twenty minutes.

In a *gammu burui* composition of this sort (figure 5) the last segment of the introduction appears at the end of each theme. Themes A and B are expanded to create A' and B'. The compositional structure is section 1, AABB (four times); section 2, A'A'B'B' (four times); section 3, AABB, A'A'B'B' (once); section 4, AAB'B' (once). In section 3, the entire piece to this point is contracted into a single statement of sections 1 and 2; finally, in section 4, section 3 is further contracted.

FIGURE 4   In Digir Village, the head couple of *gammu burui* dancers leads the other dancers through choreographic formations. The men play panpipes and the women shake rattles. Photo by Sandra Smith, 1979.

Titles given to *gammu burui* compositions name birds and animals, human relationships, techniques of playing the instruments, and activities of the celebrations, with each piece following certain compositional principles. Pieces about birds and animals imitate calls and behaviors in a theme and a series of variations; compositions about techniques of playing instruments feature specific interlocking patterns of movement.

The three-part panpipe (*goke*) is constructed of three bound tubes, two bound tubes, and a single tube. The set is duplicated so that six players perform together. The tubes are graduated in size and are arranged to produce six consecutive pitches. The lowest pitch, which I call pitch 1, is produced by the player of the single tube. Pitches 2 and 3 are produced by the player of the two-tube raft. Pitches 4, 5, and 6 are produced by the player of the three-tube raft. The pitches are equally spaced, with the intervals slightly smaller than a whole step; all together, from lowest to highest, the pitches span a sixth. The ensemble plays together, but their musical parts are arranged hierarchically. The music, called *gokedom,* is composed of three short melodic statements of equal length. Each statement can be notated as two eighths followed by a quarter. In each statement, the player of the single tube plays on the quarter, whereas the player of the two-tube raft plays pitches 2, 3, and 2 for each statement. The player of the three-tube raft plays a different sequence in each statement: first he uses only two tubes, playing pitches 4, 5, and 4; then he uses all three tubes, playing pitches 6, 5, and 4; finally, using only one tube, he plays the phrase on pitch 4 as 4, 4, and 4. The three statements are each repeated once, and the entire sequence is played over and over.

The last panpipe, *guli,* has six single unbound tubes producing six closely spaced consecutive pitches spanning a third to a fifth. Six men play single tubes in alternation, interlocking their notes to create a melodic line. *Guli* is an onomatopoeic name of the song of the golden-collared *manakin,* a bird whose sounds and movements are imitated in a dance associated with this panpipe.

FIGURE 5   "Buruiguad, Dummad" ('Little Ones, Big Ones'), a *gammu burui* panpipe piece from Nalunega. Interlocking of notes is shown by upward stems for one panpipe and downward stems for the other. Transcription by Sandra Smith.

MUSICAL CONTEXTS AND GENRES

An outline of Kuna musical genres closely parallels the Kuna division of specialized knowledge into eight named disciplines, all but one of which—the discipline of prophecy and prognosis—involve music. The disciplines of specialized knowledge that utilize music include traditional chanting for history, medicine, exorcism, puberty rites, and funeral rites; traditional *gammu burui* music and dance; and the discipline that includes all other forms of traditional instrumental music.

Chanting

The disciplines involving chanting are practiced by men who, though not shamans, are trained specialists in traditional medicine, history, exorcism, puberty rites, and funeral rites (Sherzer 1986.) Chanters neither transform themselves into spiritual entities nor perform extraordinary acts, but their practices are embedded in a framework that includes beliefs about spiritual matters. Medicinal and exorcistic specialists chant in fixed texts to a collection of wooden doll-like spiritual helpers, informing them how to carry out specific acts. The spiritual helpers then interact with other spiritual entities on behalf of a specialist and his patient.

Addressing the members of their village, historical specialists chant texts woven from fixed stories and accounts to describe mythical and historical events, report on their travels, and recount humorous parables. Christian and other religious groups have established missions, schools, and social projects in some Kuna villages, where the singing of hymns is taught. This music is not combined with indigenous chanting or other Kuna musical traditions, though Christian beliefs and personages are in some places woven into the stories and historical chants.

Funeral specialists perform chants that guide the soul of the deceased to the cemetery and protect the released soul as it begins its journey to the world of spirits. Specialists in puberty rites chant through *gammu suid,* addressing entities in the spiritual world. The word *gormaked* denotes the calling of the chants through, or by, the flutes. The long, fixed texts prescribe all the special preparations and activities of the puberty ceremony, but they are in a linguistic form that the Kuna do not understand. The calling of the *gammu suid* accompanies all the activities, linking the participants and their actions to the spiritual world.

Musically, the performance of all these kinds of chanting, except those used for puberty rites, share stylistic features (Sherzer and Wicks 1982): they are not accompanied by musical instruments; their statements consist of short parallel phrases beginning on a high pitch and ending on a low pitch while diminishing in volume and tempo; and the final phrase of each statement terminates with a long tone. The overall melodic shapes of the phrases suit each chant, but all of them contain strings of syllables on a single pitch: some descend in a steady pattern; others seesaw up and down; others cluster in repeating patterns corresponding to repeated linguistic phrases. As the chanter proceeds, the range of the chanting ascends and increases in volume, strength, and tempo.

Chants for puberty-related rites have a different musical style. The statements are chanted in short notes with a change of pitch on nearly every syllable. One or two musical tones are played on the flutes to introduce each chanted line. Standing side by side, the chanters shake rattles in a continuous, steady rhythm, slowly rotating their bodies as a pair while stepping in place (see figure 1).

Medicinal, exorcistic, and funeral chanters perform alone; historical chanters perform in pairs, the primary one chanting two or more phrases at a time, ending with a long final vowel; the secondary responder overlaps a short phrase of confirmation. The responder uses a single tone, near the midpoint of the range of tones used by the primary chanter. Before the responder finishes, the primary chanter overlaps the beginning of his next statement. In this way, the men create a continuous sound that may last several hours. These men are cultural leaders, and the chants take the form of a dialogue between them in an archaic language, understood only by other trained leaders or their initiates. Afterward, an initiate interprets the chant to the audience.

Chanters of puberty rites perform in pairs and are replaced by their students from time to time during the ceremonies, which last several days. During the celebrations, all villagers participate in four days of ritual and informal music and dance. Though only girls are celebrated in this way, men and women carry out official tasks, participating equally. Before the celebrations begin, many items—food, fermented drink, flutes, rattles, special hammock-supporting ropes, pictographic boards, medicinal materials—are prepared. Male and female specialists are appointed to direct each aspect of preparation; as part of the preparations, some men perform chants. Throughout, the specialists tend to the villagers and the girl or girls being celebrated by serving them food and drink in ritualized, dancelike ways and by performing specific kinds of flute-and-panpipe music and dance at appointed times. This kind of performance is limited because most villages no longer have the proper musical specialists. Outsiders' knowledge of this music is speculative, primarily based on observations in other contexts. Away from the ceremonial activities, men informally perform for each other as entertainment.

At the close of the celebrations, a villagewide dance spirals around the two chanters, first at a running pace in a large circle, and gradually at a slower pace, as the line of dancers closes in. Alternating along the line, men and women intertwine their arms, with their hands on the shoulders of dancers to either side.

Dancing

Only adults perform the chanting traditions and the instrumental music of puberty-related festivals, but people of all ages participate in *gammu burui* music and dance. In several villages, *gammu burui* dancers organize themselves into societies. They hold regular rehearsals and performances; their music is suitable for group learning and participation because once a lead pair of *gammu burui* players has learned a piece, other players can follow in unison. Dancers are led through formations by principal male and female dancers. Sometimes groups of dancers from several villages compete (figure 6).

The defining movement of *gammu burui* dances is a step and a hop in place, which becomes a skip when the dance speeds up. Men and women use the same step, though men perform it more vigorously than women. Choreographies consist of formations such as parallel lines, circles, and squares, with men and women dancing as a group, rather than as couples. In each dance, the tempo and intensity develop from a slow, calm, walking pace to a fast, vigorous, running pace.

Most danced pieces last twenty to thirty minutes; some contexts require shorter versions. Melodic themes and choreographies are sometimes slightly varied by each group; however, the repertoire shows a high degree of homogeneity, and most pieces are known by all the groups. A few troupes perform for tourists who visit the uppermost end of the archipelago. These performances consist of a few dances, each one abbreviated to about five minutes.

Improvised singing

Musical genres that are not named and are not considered to be special disciplines are the vocal genres without *igar:* lullabies sung by women to calm and quiet children, songs women sing to each other during puberty celebrations, and laments sung by women to their dying and deceased relatives. These genres are performed in private,

The Kuna have developed a form of notation to help them memorize their long chants. Colored pictographs, measuring one to two centimeters square, each correspond to an event, an episode, a character, or an entity.

FIGURE 6   At an annual dance festival in Digir Village, groups from different villages compete. Here, the host group performs with an unusually large *gammu burui* ensemble of twelve men playing panpipes and twelve women playing rattles. Photo by Sandra Smith, 1979.

within the household or in a female-only area of a community's festival hall. The texts are improvised in ordinary language, and they are not named.

The singing of lullabies occurs every day and throughout the day. Lullabies are performed within the privacy of the matrilocal household by female relatives of the child: an older sister, cousin, aunt, mother, or grandmother. They are improvised around common themes, but always address the circumstances of the child at hand. Musical phrases are short and rhythmically regular. Their melodic shapes are oscillating, each phrase ending on a low tone and the last ending with a long tone. The singer, sitting in a hammock with a child, shakes a rattle at a fast and steady pace close to the child's head. This sound, combined with the rapid swinging of the hammock, quickly puts the child to sleep.

When women sing beside a dying relative, they use a weeping style. Sometimes several individuals sing simultaneously, though each is singing about her own feelings and memories. This kind of singing has no rhythmic accompaniment, and it is not rhythmically regular. It continues after the relative dies and the body is taken to the burial site, where women may continue singing for a short while after the burial.

A third kind of improvised singing is performed by women in private but outside the home. This is when a village's adult women gather in the festival hall during the first few days of a puberty-related celebration. They are sequestered in a small space and served fermented drink by younger girls. Sitting as close to each other as possible in two facing rows with shoulders, hips, and knees touching, they sing for several hours, one woman at a time. The texts concern the women's mutual friendships. The musical style is like the singing of lullabies, but without rhythmic accompaniment. As the singers become tipsy, the melodies become freer and punctuated by laughter.

SOCIAL ASPECTS OF MUSIC

Kuna chanters, players of aerophones, and makers of instruments are men. For some genres of dancing, rattle-playing women join men. Improvised singing is the purview of women. No classes defined by kinship or economic level occur in Kuna society. Cultural leaders are men who have learned the chants associated with the disciplines of traditional knowledge in history, medicine, exorcism, and puberty and funeral rites. Through one-on-one apprenticeships, they train younger men according to their talents. An apprentice studies sequentially with several teachers, and each teacher may instruct several apprentices. Novices strive to obtain widespread training, often including periods of study at universities in Panama or abroad. Their courses of study might be in history, political science, law, anthropology, social science, or medicine. The Kuna expect that the period of training will last ten to twenty years.

Most Kuna are bilingual in Kuna and Spanish, and some are multilingual, speaking also English, French, or German. They use Panamanian newspapers, radio, and television to follow international, national, and tribal events. With these media, they have become familiar with foreign musics. Nevertheless, they keep their own music compartmentalized and private. They do not incorporate foreign musical instruments with their own in performances, and they do not play foreign music on their own instruments. They keep their music mostly inaccessible to foreigners.

The Kuna have developed a form of notation to help them memorize their long chants (figure 7). Teachers and apprentices use colored pictographs as educational tools. Each pictograph, measuring one to two centimeters square, corresponds to an event, an episode, a character, or an entity. A long tabulation of pictographs, running in boustrophedon, represents the path or way of the chant depicting spirits and spiritual helpers on their travels to spiritual abodes. No forms of traditional notation were developed for instrumental music.

Musical enculturation and acculturation

Beginning with lullabies in infancy, Kuna individuals learn traditional language, song, and customs. Lullabies describe the duties a child has toward other relatives, the village, and the tribe. The singing of lullabies is learned through exposure and imitation, as mothers sing to their children and girls sing to their younger siblings. In nightly or weekly gatherings, villagers listen to their leaders' historical chants. Topics of concern are embedded in the context of mythical and historical tribal lore. In annual puberty celebrations, all kinds of traditional music and dance are displayed. Through music and dance, all villagers participate in the ceremonial rebirth of the girl being celebrated.

Most Kuna musical settings are rural, occurring in indigenous villages. Festivals organized by the *gammu burui* dance societies take place in some villages (see figure 6) and in Panama's cities during folkloric presentations in which national dances are presented. Kuna urban centers for young people organize presentations by and for their members. Dance societies in some villages arrange performances for tourists. Sometimes, for personal use, the Kuna make cassette recordings at festivals.

Electronic media

Electronic media form a small part of the material culture of Kuna music. The Kuna use cassettes to transmit oral letters, and in this way they often send entire speeches

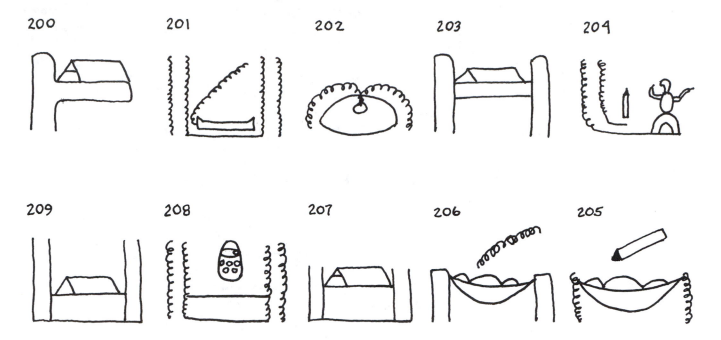

FIGURE 7 A pictograph, an indigenous form of Kuna chant notation. Each figure corresponds to a mental map of a chant, depicting spirits and spirit helpers on their travels to different spiritual abodes. Here, the final portion of the first section (called *Gamma* 'Flute') of the chant "*Sergan Igala*" ('Way of the Elders'), consisting of 564 pictographs, is shown. Each pictograph corresponds to one or two lines chanted from memory. The pictographs depict midnight (the house), when the cool winds (wiggly lines) from the flutes (shown in 201, 202, 204, 205) cool the feverish body (hammock), destroying the seeds of sickness. Drawing by Sandra Smith, after Holmer and Wassén 1963:32, 49.

and chants from one community to another. Battery-powered radios, phonographs, and televisions expose them to music from outside Kuna society.

Musical evaluation

Most Kuna consider aesthetic judgments inappropriate, and leave evaluations to musical specialists, men who judge the uniformity of dancing and playing, the enthusiasm and vigor of dancers and musicians, and the speed and tightness (or closeness) of interlocking musical parts and choreographic figures.

Kuna women look for similar features in evaluating their textiles, which include appliqué blouses and beaded bands worn on arms and legs. They judge uniformity of colors and designs used by groups of women (such as members of dance groups, the friends of a girl going through the celebrations of her puberty, and even all the women of a single village), brightness and contrast among the colors, intricacy, tightness, closeness, and evenness of interlocking visual patterns. In the images depicted in appliqué blouses, they evaluate humor and the play of multiple levels of meaning. The Kuna similarly value these features in historical chants and their colloquial interpretations and in some *gammu burui* pieces.

Kuna music and dance are meant for human and nonhuman receivers. Most traditional chanting is addressed to nonhuman entities. Human participants are merely witnesses with passive reactions. These relationships characterize the music and dance that occur in the ceremonial contexts of puberty-related festivals. Performances for public entertainment, however, are also addressed to human audiences. Reactions are mostly passive, but exceptionally good performances stimulate bursts of approval.

Some individuals and communities gain reputations for being more innovative than others. Creativity is expected and encouraged from these, while orthodoxy is expected from others. Chanters develop individual styles by combining styles learned from different teachers. In some traditions, they tailor their chanting to specific situations. In this sense, chants are always developing. Women's songs, however, are spontaneously created at each sitting. Each group slightly varies instrumental compositions and choreographies, but new compositions are few, introduced only by leaders of the group.

FURTHER STUDY

Musical texts have been published in translation and in the Kuna language, keyed to transcriptions of indigenous colored pictographs (Holmer and Wassén 1953, 1963; Nordenskiold 1928); an ethnographic study of curing (Chapin 1983) links the pictographs more closely with Kuna medicinal knowledge than with textual translations. A description of Kuna rites of passage (Prestán 1975) contains detailed accounts of the preparations and ceremonial activities for girls' puberty rites. The Kuna history-chanting tradition is documented in Howe's ethnography on political organization (1985), and general descriptions of the musical aspects of chanting and women's singing were made by Frances Densmore (1925, 1926) and Narciso Garay (1930). (For the Kuna, Densmore uses the name *Tule,* which means 'person' in the Kuna language.) Most recently, the singing of lullabies (McCosker 1974) and the performance of instrumental music (Smith 1984) have been studied.

Museums in Germany, Panama, Sweden, and the United States of America house collections of Kuna domestic equipment, textiles, and musical instruments. The Kuna construct and use all but a few of their instruments in pairs or sets, but most collections contain only partial or mismatched sets, or instruments in disrepair. Consequently, misinformed photographs, illustrations, and descriptions of construction and usage have persisted.

Few recordings of the musical instruments of the Kuna are commercially available. Moser and Taylor (1987) released excerpts from recordings made in Panama in 1960 for the British Institute of Recorded Sound. The complete recordings are available for study in the Archives of Traditional Music, Indiana University.

REFERENCES

Chapin, Norman A. 1983. "Curing among the San Blas Kuna of Panama." Ph.D. dissertation, University of Arizona.

Densmore, Frances. 1925. "A Study of Tule Indian Music." In *Exploration and Fieldwork,* 115–127. Washington, D.C.: Smithsonian Institution.

———. 1926. "Music of the Tule Indians of Panama." *Smithsonian Miscellaneous Collections* 77(11):1–39.

Garay, Narciso. 1930. *Tradiciones y Cantares de Panamá.* Panama: Ensayo Folklórico.

Holmer, Nils M., and S. H. Wassén. 1953. *The Complete Mu-Igala in Picture Writing.* Göteborgs Etnografiska Museum, Ethnologiska Studier, 21. Göteborg: Elanders Boktryckeri Aktiebolag.

———. 1963. *Dos Cantos Shamanísticos de los Indios Cunas.* Göteborgs Etnografiska Museum, Etnologiska Studier, 27. Göteborg: Elanders Boktryckeri Aktiebolag.

Howe, James. 1985. *The Kuna Gathering: Contemporary Village Politics in Panama.* Institute of Latin American Studies, Latin American Monograph 67. Austin: University of Texas Press.

———. 1990. "Mission Rivalry and Conflict in San Blas, Panama." In *Class Politics and Popular Religion in Mexico and Central America,* ed. Lynn Stephen and James Dow, 143–166. Washington, D.C.: American Anthropological Association.

McCosker, Sandra Smith. 1974. *The Lullabies of the San Blas Cuna Indians of Panama.* Göteborgs

Etnografiska Museum, Etnologiska Studier, 33. Göteborg: Elanders Boktryckeri Aktiebolag.

Moser, Brian, and Donald Taylor, eds. 1987. *Music of the Tukano and Cuna Peoples of Colombia.* Rogue Records FMS / NSA 002. LP disk.

Nordenskiöld, Erland. 1938. *An Historical and Ethnological Survey of the Cuna Indians.* Comparative Ethnographical Studies, 10. Göteborg: Göteborgs Museum.

Prestán, Arnulfo. 1975. *El Uso de la Chicha y la Sociedad Kuna.* Ediciones Especiales, 72. México, D.F.: Instituto Indigenista Interamericano.

Sherzer, Joel. 1983. *Kuna Ways of Speaking: An Ethnographic Perspective.* Austin: University of Texas Press.

———. 1986. "The Report of a Kuna Curing Specialist: The Poetics and Rhetoric of an Oral Performance." In *Native South American Discourse,* ed. Joel Sherzer and Greg Urban, 169–212. New York and Berlin: Walter de Gruyter.

Sherzer, Joel, and Sammie Ann Wicks. 1982. "The Intersection of Music and Language in Kuna Discourse." *Latin American Music Review* 3:147–164.

Smith, Sandra. 1984. "Panpipes for Power, Panpipes for Play: The Social Management of Cultural Expression in Kuna Society." Ph.D. dissertation, University of California at Berkeley.

Maya

Linda O'Brien-Rothe

The Highland Maya
The Lowland Maya
Further Study

Some 2.5 million Maya live in the southern Mexican states of Campeche, Chiapas, Quintana Roo, Tabasco, and Yucatán, and in Belize, Guatemala, and parts of El Salvador and Honduras. Most contemporary Maya live in towns and villages, practice subsistence cultivation of maize, follow traditional culture, wear distinctive dress, and speak one of twenty Mayan languages or dialects. Their worldview, myths, and religious customs include elements of Christianity, which the Maya have combined with their ancestors' religion.

Maya civilization developed and flourished roughly between 200 B.C. and A.D. 900 in the forested highlands and lowlands of southern Mexico and Central America. It reached its artistic and intellectual peak in the eighth century and then fell into abrupt decline. Pre-Columbian Maya musical life is known from Spanish records written in the early years after European contact and from Maya art and writings, which record history, genealogies, religious beliefs, and ritual practices. These records survive in murals, figurines, sculptures, and painted ceramic vessels. Three lowland-Maya books—the Dresden Codex, the Codex Paris, and the Codex Madrid (Tro-Cortesianus)—contain glyphic texts associated with pictures, some of which depict Maya instruments, ensembles, and musical occasions. The archaeological remains of musical instruments and the contexts in which they are found provide information about instruments made of ceramic and bone. Instruments of perishable materials—cane, wood, and other organic products—have not survived.

Shortly after the initial Spanish contact, musical texts were written down in indigenous languages in the Spanish alphabet. These include texts in *Los Cantares de Dzitbalché* (*The Songs of Dzitbalché*) a manuscript from Campeche, Mexico (Barrera Vásquez 1965), and in the *Popol Vuh* (*Book of Counsel*), a mythology and tribal history of the Quiché [see GUATEMALA]. These and similar sources contain texts of ritual and calendric songs, lyric songs, and laments. The descriptions of the Maya left by Spanish colonists of the 1500s and 1600s contain scattered references to music and instruments. No comprehensive, systematic study of the musical life of the ancient Maya exists, but some understanding can be gained from these sources.

The music of the ancient Maya was part of a unified cosmos in which all things had sacred significance and function. Certain gods—notably the sun god, for whose cult a log idiophone was played, and a monkey god, god of music and dance—were associated with music. Music and musical instruments played an essential role in communicating between people and spirits and were important in rituals and rites of passage. Scenes painted on ceramic vessels show musicians in attendance or playing in the presence of royalty and during rituals. A scene from the great murals at Bonampák in Chiapas shows an ensemble of musicians playing drums, trumpets, tortoise-carapace idiophones, and spiked vessel rattles at the ritual sacrifice of a captive or a slave (see reproduction in Martí 1968:68). The tomb furnishings of kings and priests, outfitted with items needed for the journey to the afterlife, often included musical instruments. At a cemetery for priests and dignitaries on Jaina, an island off the north coast of the Yucatán Peninsula, virtually every excavated figurine is a rattle, drum, or vessel (globular) flute, and many figurines depict musicians.

Survivals of musical instruments show that the Maya developed various aerophones, principally vessel flutes, of unique forms and acoustical properties. Double-duct or double-tube and triple-duct or triple-tube flutes evidence the use of paired and multiple tunings (Martí 1968:191–212). Bone mouthpieces were probably used with trumpets, whose flared bells were made of basketry impregnated with wax or of wood, as depicted on some painted vessels and murals.

Maya idiophones included rattles, strings of shells or seed pods (draped on dancers or sewn to their clothing), spiked vessel rattles, and the hollow feet of ceramic offering bowls, which contained clay pellets or pebbles. Bone or wood rasps and struck wood or carapace idiophones were common. Maya membranophones included a waist-high single-headed wooden drum and smaller ceramic hourglass-shaped single-headed drums, sometimes joined in pairs. Murals and painted vessels reveal that the Maya combined instruments of different kinds to form ensembles. Stringed instruments were absent from ancient Maya music.

Maya culture has a perceptible homogeneity, but natural environments and historical developments have differentiated Maya musical life into two streams: that of the highlands of Chiapas and Guatemala, and that of the lowlands of Belize, Guatemala, and southern Mexico. It is therefore convenient to discuss highland and lowland Maya musics separately.

THE HIGHLAND MAYA

The Maya who live in Chiapas and the Guatemalan highlands are among the least assimilated indigenous peoples in Mexico and Central America. Though surrounded by Ladinos (people of non-Maya culture whose first language is Spanish and who still function as semiautonomous groups in social, economic, political, and religious affairs), these Maya have resisted mestization. They share a common history as part of the Audiencia de Guatemala, a colonial administrative unit that tied Chiapas more closely to Guatemala than to the rest of colonial Mexico.

The Roman Catholic missionaries of the 1500s and 1600s were dedicated to the Spanish musical education of indigenous people, particularly in styles practiced in Seville. They trained singers for choirs that sang plainchant and polyphony, and developed ensembles of strings and winds to accompany them. Spanish secular music too was implanted in the Maya colonies (Harrison and Harrison 1968:2). In the 1800s, it became fashionable among the upper classes to collect Maya melodies and write them down in European musical notation, adjusting their details to conform to Western musical concepts.

In Mexico, the music of the Tzeltal, the Chol of Tojolabal, and the Tzotzil-speakers in the neighboring villages of San Lorenzo Zinacantán and San Juan Chamula are the most extensively documented. In Guatemala, the music of Quiché groups, especially the Tzutujil-Maya of Santiago Atitlán, is best documented

(O'Brien 1975). Local style and repertoire, details of the construction and tuning of instruments, and the components of ensembles differ from one language to another and even from one town to another.

Musical contexts and genres

The traditional music of the highland Maya reflects the profound influence of colonial Spanish music, of which it contains some striking survivals, such as the singing of the texts of Tenebrae services (psalms and prayers of the Divine Office for Holy Thursday, Good Friday, and Holy Saturday) and late-sixteenth- and seventeenth-century style "falsobordone" settings, in which a plainchant melody is transposed to a higher octave and harmonized below in three or four parallel parts—a texture still cultivated in Santiago Atitlán, Guatemala. Survivals of Spanish folkloric and secular styles appear in pieces whose style and form recall those of the chaconne and the sarabande, now played in Chiapas and Guatemala on instruments that conform to European models of the late Middle Ages and the early Renaissance. Examples are ritual songs frequently sung on a single melody (known as *bolonchón* in Zinacantán) and some ancestral songs of the Tzutujil-Maya in Guatemala. In highland Guatemala, the term *zarabanda* denotes certain forms of popular music.

Among the highland Maya, traditional music is closely connected to events of the ritual calendar, in which indigenous and Christian cycles are intertwined. Little survives that has no European influence, but the least acculturated genres are shamanic songs, addressed to the ancestral gods by the shaman (*curandero*), a native ritual healer or maker of prayers. These songs cure illnesses and injuries, heal women after childbirths, bless new houses and fields, and enhance calendric rituals. They are freely sung to nonmetrical or (less frequently) metrical texts that contain standard material, improvised in what are known as Maya couplets, paired lines of poetic text in parallel construction, in which the second line repeats and varies the first. These are sung or declaimed to formulas that govern melodic contour, mainly on a single tone, except for an occasional drop to a lower tone before the performer breathes or a rise at the end of a phrase, but they sometimes require more complex melodies.

Stemming from Spanish colonial origins, yet thoroughly revamped by Maya musical style, are guitar-accompanied songs (*bix rxin nawal* 'songs of the ancestors') of the Tzutujil-Maya [see GUATEMALA]. Among them is a melody identical to the *bolonchón* of Chamula, performed in Chiapas instrumentally or sung in unison without words.

The most frequent contexts for public musical performance in highland towns are fiestas, celebrations of feasts of patron saints of towns, according to the Christian calendar. For these celebrations, which may last from three to eight days, musicians from surrounding towns and villages join the throng and play in their local style, often simultaneously with other musicians, creating a characteristic combination of multiple kinds of music. Typical of such festivities in Chiapas is the celebration of the fiesta in Zinacantán. In the central plaza on 20 January, the feast of Saint Sebastian, a local trio of harp, guitar, and violin plays the piece most typical of Zinacantán, the "*Canto de San Sebastián*" ('Song of Saint Sebastian'), a piece strongly reminiscent of the chaconne, with a sarabande-style rhythmic accompaniment. A similar ensemble accompanies ritual officials on their way to the church. Other musicians stroll with guitars, visitors from Chamula play button accordions, and a wind band hired from out of town plays clarinets, saxhorns, and drums. Near the church, other ritual officials dance to the music of a three-holed flute and two large drums (*tambores*).

In Chiapas, a few melodies serve for many deities, so a single melody has many names. Similarly, the Tzutujil of Guatemala know a melody or a melodic formula by a broad title, such as "Song to Face-of-the-Earth," but may also call it "Rain Song" or

"Song to Control the Winds" or "Song to Our Father the Sun," depending on the occasion or motive for its use and on the text, which the singer improvises. All these songs come under the province of the god called Face-of-the-Earth (O'Brien 1975). Apart from laments (sung during funerals and at the graveside), lullabies to children, and the occasional playing of the *tun,* no musical performance by Maya women of the highlands is documented.

In Chiapas and Guatemala, commercialized and media-dispersed popular music is pervasive. It is predominantly the popular music of Mexico, but also that of Latin America as a whole, and, to a lesser extent, the Caribbean. Recorded popular music—*canciones rancheras, corridos, cumbias,* or whatever is currently broadcast on radio and television—is played on loudspeakers during the fiesta, sometimes drowning out the ritual music. Hymns of evangelical missionary churches, mostly from the repertoire used in the United States (in Spanish or Mayan translation), are broadcast daily over loudspeakers in virtually every rural village and town, influencing popular musical taste.

Musical instruments

The Tzutujil classify their musical instruments as male and female [see GUATEMALA]. Whether other Maya employ a similar taxonomy is unknown. Therefore, this overview follows the general system employed in this volume, rather than assuming all Maya have the same taxonomy.

Idiophones

An important Maya instrument is the log idiophone (*tun,* also *t'ent'en* and *c'unc'un;* Náhuatl *teponaztli*) [see GUATEMALA: figure 1]. It is a hollowed-out section of the trunk of a tree, into the side of which an H-shaped slit is cut, forming two tuned tongues, which players strike with sticks or dry corn cobs. Typical is the *t'ent'en* of Zinacantán, constructed of two lateral sections, one of Spanish cedar and another of black cherry. This instrument is 62 centimeters long and 15 centimeters in diameter, but much larger sizes exist. Holes allow it to be suspended on a bearer's back with a tumpline passing around his forehead, while the player walks behind, playing it and a cane flute. Personifying the instrument by name (Our Holy Father *T'ent'en*) demonstrates regard for it as powerful, living, and preeminently sacred. When not in use, it is housed in a special chapel with the tumpline, the drumsticks, and two small sets of bow and arrows carried by the bearer and the player; in the chapel, these objects receive a daily offering of incense and candles. Before being used for the festival of Saint Sebastian or for the yearly rainmaking ritual (its only public appearances in Zinacantán), it is washed with water containing sacred herbs, reglued, and decorated with ribbons. It is sometimes played with gourd rattles and frame rattles.

In Guatemala, where the log idiophone has the same names, it is treated with similar reverence. For rituals associated with rain and the sun, log idiophones are often played in pairs of a larger and a smaller instrument. In the town of Rabinal, Department of Baja Verapaz, Guatemala, the log idiophone forms part of the ensemble that plays for the dance-drama *Rabinal Achí,* called *baile del tun* 'dance of the drum'.

Similar to the log idiophone is the *tortuga,* made of the carapace of a tortoise struck on the ventral side with a stick or an antler. The *tortuga* is mainly associated with *posadas* processions, which occur during Advent.

Membranophones

A cylindrical, double-headed wooden drum has skins of deer or dog tensioned by cords laced through the hoop, to which the heads are fastened. The drum is known

The Chiapan harp has a curved neck with a carved design that usually represents angels or birds facing each other, perhaps suggesting the ability of winged creatures to fly to a world above the earth and the power of ritual music to contact the gods.

by many names: Tzotzil *tampor, tampol, cayobil*; Quiché *k'ojom*; Spanish *tambor, tamborón*. The diameter of the head and the height of the drum are of about the same size, from about 38 centimeters to 1 meter. The player sometimes performs seated, using one or two padded sticks while holding the drum between the knees; in procession, the drum is carried on a bearer's back; the player follows, often playing the flute with one hand and beating the drum with a stick held in the other, in alternating phrases of rhythm and melody. In ritual contexts, the drum maintains a steady rhythm while the flute plays rhythmically free phrases that typically end with an ascending slide or interval of a fourth or a fifth. Flute melodies come from the same repertoire as those of string trios, but the flute reproduces the melodic contour rather than the exact tones of the melody, and does so in a freer rhythm than a guitar or a harp.

A drum to which snares made of knotted leather cords have been added is smaller than the *tambor* and in Quiché languages is called *caj* (from Spanish *caja*). In some highland Chiapas towns (Magdalenas, Tenejapa, Venustiano Carranza), several drums combine with valveless trumpets and sometimes three- or seven-holed cane flutes. Their repertoire includes pieces in strict and rapid rhythms, plus melodies closely related to the European fife-and-drum tradition, imported from Spain during the early contact period.

Aerophones

A Maya end-blown cane fipple (duct) flute, with one hole for a thumb and two to six holes for fingering, is known by various names (Tzotzil *'ama, amael*; Quiché *xul, zu, zubac*; Spanish *pito*). It measures about 15 to 35 centimeters long, and 1.5 to 2 centimeters in diameter. A three-holed flute (*tzijolah*) produces various tones by overblowing. Because in this and other highland Maya styles exact pitch is less important than melodic contour, broad variations in flute-produced scales occur.

Chordophones

The Maya violin (*violín*) has a flat bridge, long f-holes, three pegs, and two or three strings. When played, it is held against the chest, not under the chin. The strings are stopped with the flats of the fingers. Each note is played with a full stroke of the bow, whose tension is adjusted with pressure from the player's thumb. Double-stopping is common. European prototypes of these violins are probably from the early 1600s.

The guitar (*ctar*) has several forms and sizes. The Chamula guitar has four courses, the first double and the rest triple, with one unstrung peg. The Zinacantán guitar has five courses, the first triple and the rest double, with one peg unstrung.

In Chiapas, a large, four-string bass guitar (*kin*) has strings widely splayed at the bridge, resembling its late-sixteenth or early-seventeenth-century European prototypes. The technique of playing predominantly involves chordal strumming (*rasgueado*), which makes all the strings sound with a single stroke of the nails. The number of instruments of each kind in a string trio may vary. Sometimes an accordion, drums, or maracas are added. Guitars provide chordal rhythm, a harp plays the bass and the melody, and a violin plays the melody. In unison falsetto, players may sing vocables, or texts in Maya couplets.

The Chiapan harp (*arpa*) is from 1.5 to 2 meters high, has a straight forepillar with incised decorations and a curved neck with a carved design. The design usually represents angels or birds facing each other, perhaps suggesting the ability of winged creatures to fly to a world above the earth and the power of ritual music to contact the gods. The back, made of five panels, is tapered, and the soundboard has three holes. The tuning pegs and feet are of wood, and the strings are of metal or nylon. It is leaned against the right shoulder with the right hand playing the upper register and the left the lower. Zinacantecos play with the fingernails of the right hand and fingertips of the left; Chamulas use fingernails only.

Ensembles

At highland Guatemalan fiestas, a mixture of musical genres and ensembles is common, though the marimba or the marimba band is practically universal, and string trios are rare. A principal difference in the musical practice of the areas is the importance and frequency of use of the marimba: it is much more commonly played by Ladinos than by the Maya in Chiapas, where it is regarded as a Ladino instrument; but in Guatemala, it is equally claimed by both cultures and is ubiquitous at festivities of all kinds. In Chiapas, marimbas usually have chromatic keyboards and wooden, boxlike resonators; they are built by Ladino makers in the major municipal centers, including Tuxtla Gutiérrez and Venustiano Carranza. In Guatemala, marimbas with gourd resonators, though rare, are still used, and diatonic and chromatic keyboards are common; there, marimbas are commonly built by Maya and Ladino makers. Marimba players in Chiapas tend to play mestizo-style music, but Guatemala has a sizable repertoire of traditional Maya marimba music, some of which has African roots or early colonial origins.

Most widespread among the highland Maya is the ensemble of cane flute and drum. In highland towns, it heralds a ritual action or the event that follows it, often in procession [see GUATEMALA: figure 5]. Thus, a flute and a drum lead participants into the center of town, musically telling of the nature of the ritual and of its commencement. This ensemble is reserved for sacred events. In general, each town has one such ensemble. The official position of flutist and drummer, often the same person, is passed through the male line and is usually a lifetime service.

Among the most common ensembles in Chiapas is the string trio, which combines one or more guitars, harps, and violins. This ensemble plays for religious rituals but may be hired to entertain at private parties. The instruments are locally made.

An important part of the musical spectrum at highland fiestas is the brass band, which may be hired from the Ladino community if no Maya ensemble is available. In Chiapas, where the marimba is identified with Ladinos, a marimba band is usually hired from outside for fiestas. Its main components are the *marimba grande,* a chromatic, six-octave instrument with boxlike resonators beneath the keys and played by two or three players; and the *marimba tenor,* with four or five octaves and two or three players. To these marimbas are added saxophones, trumpets, a string bass, drums, and claves, maracas, or güiros.

THE LOWLAND MAYA

The traditional indigenous music of the lowland Maya groups of Yucatán (including the Mexican states of Campeche, Quintana Roo, Tabasco, Yucatán, and parts of Chiapas; and the country Belize) is little documented. In lowland Chiapas, the

Lacandón—the smallest branch of the Maya family—are unique for having remained isolated from European culture after initial contact until the late 1800s, when the arrival of woodsmen, gatherers of chicle, and traveling merchants brought diseases that caused the degeneration of their society and the reduction of their numbers to less than five hundred in the mid-1990s. They live in small clans in the tropical forest of southern Chiapas.

Musical contexts and genres

Singing is the principal Lacandón musical expression. In rituals, men sing solo songs honoring local gods and spirits, petitioning them for health and protection, accompanying rites of passage, and appealing to the spirits of animals. Their texts usually describe the actions being performed, as in the "Song for Offering Ma'atz to the Gods" (*En Busca de la Música Maya: Canción de la Selva Lacandona* 1976:3:2):

> O god, please descend from heaven.
> We have prepared maize, please drink it.
> We will also eat it.

Some songs, such as lullabies or those to ward off animals, try to influence events (*En Busca de la Música Maya: Canción de la Selva Lacandona* 1976:5:13).

> Ya ha ha!
> Here is your mother.
> Sleep, sleep, it's your mother.

Among such songs are those for the yearly renewal rites of the sacred vessels, including the sacred drums (*k'ayum,* also the name of the god of music). Lacandón singing is syllabic, and syllables may be lengthened, elided, or slurred. Some songs are on a single pitch, and some are inflected by a loose melodic formula. Rhythm is governed by the rhythmic pattern of the text, or sometimes a rhythmic formula is repeated in each phrase. The male falsetto voice is often used, as is a wide vibrato.

In lowland Maya villages outside the Lacandón area, songs are sung for ritual occasions, extended hunting trips, curing, giving thanks for the harvest, and protecting crops, cattle, and similar objects and activities. Many towns have teacher-singers (*maestros cantores*), men who carry on an office established by Franciscan missionaries in colonial times. They formerly acted as lay assistants to priests, providing daily observances of Roman Catholic rituals. Today, after a long and widespread sacerdotal absence, they have come to be in charge of Christian and indigenous rituals. They sing hymns and songs that have been in oral tradition for many generations, and they play violins and single-headed drums (about 36 centimeters high) suspended at the player's side, and sometimes a cornet or trumpet. In the Guatemalan highlands, men who perform these functions are called sacristans (*sacristanes*).

The Yucatec Maya's most widely known ancient costumed dance is the ribbon dance (*xtoles*). It was formerly done in public during carnival in Mérida, Mexico. Recalling pre-Columbian lowland iconographic depictions, fourteen male dancers (seven dressed as women and seven as men) carried spiked vessel calabash rattles, which sounded with metal pellet bells sewn to their clothing. The accompaniment was provided by two musicians each playing an end-blown duct flute (*pito,* a long tin tube, pierced with holes for fingering) and a single-headed cylindrical tin drum, played with the hands. The *xtoles* song was sung in Maya during the dance. For public festivities a band played before and after the dancing, going from house to house.

Another dance, once widespread in Yucatán, probably as part of a fertility ritual, is the pig's head (*cabeza del cochino*) or dance of the head (*okot pol*). It is danced during a ceremony celebrating the slaughtering of a pig and the sharing of its flesh. A song of some twenty verses on agrarian themes accompanies this dance and its procession, in which the pig's head is carried.

The Maya of Yucatán have largely adopted the musical styles of local mestizos. The Spanish *jota* has left its influences of rapid triple meter and the percussive staccato of its castanet accompaniment, and the styles of nearby cultures—the Colombian *bambuco*, the Cuban *habanera*, the Mexican *jarana*—have submerged indigenous features.

Social structure, musicians, and behavior

In traditional Maya perspectives, the musician's role is one of communal service (*cargo*), in which an individual holds a civil-religious office for a year at a time (and if he chooses, in successive years), passing through various stages of a hierarchy and finally becoming an elder of his community. The *cargo* holders' function is to carry out ancestral customs to placate the gods and ensure the people's well-being. A musician's vocation is typically a lifetime service, reserved to males and often passed down in a family through the male line. To serve in calendric rituals, some musicians are appointed by ritual officials on a rotating yearly basis.

There is no formal instruction in traditional Maya music. Musicians report receiving inspiration and instruction from ancestors in dreams. Technique and style are absorbed through observation and imitation. Apprentice musicians will often be allowed to play percussion in an ensemble before being permitted to play strings or winds. Formal instruction in styles regarded as non-Maya, such as playing brass-band instruments or playing a six-stringed guitar for popular music, is available to some through public schools and private instructors.

Musical instruments

The Lacandón use a ceremonial vessel stick rattle (*soot*) fashioned from a gourd (*jícara*) pierced by a stick that traverses it to serve as a handle, held in place with wax or thongs of bark. The crown of the gourd is decorated with perforations that form a cross—perhaps the four cardinal directions—painted in red and white. Another kind of rattle is a tortoiseshell filled with pebbles and sealed; it is used in rituals by the maker of prayers, who shakes it while singing softly to communicate the people's desires to the gods (Villa Rojas 1967:51).

The *k'ayum* is a Lacandón drum made of a ceramic bowl around 50 centimeters in height and somewhat smaller in diameter, with a lip over which a skin is stretched. Its base rests on a hoop of braided reeds. On one side is an effigy of K'ayum, the singing god, the god of music. Prayers and incense are frequently offered to K'ayum, embodied in the drum. New drums are fashioned each year during the spring rites of renewal (of which chants form a significant part), when the old ones are destroyed.

The Lacandón have an external-duct cane flute (*sur*) about 36 centimeters long and 1 centimeter wide, with four to six holes for fingering close to the distal end. A small reed tube, held in place with beeswax, directs the player's breath against a sharp edge (Baer and Baer 1952:43). Another Lacandón aeropohone is a whistling jar of terra cotta, about 3.5 centimeters high by 3 centimeters wide. It emits a low sound, used for calling in the forest. The Lacandón use a conch trumpet to sound a single tone toward each point of the compass after food is offered to the gods, to call them down to partake of the offerings.

The other lowland Maya use a stringed instrument (*hichoch*) whose body is a tortoise carapace or an armadillo shell; a conch trumpet (*hub*), used to assemble people or make announcements; a cane or wooden flute (*h'chul*); a hollowed log idio-

The Lacandón use a conch trumpet to sound a single tone toward each point of the compass after food is offered to the gods, to call them down to partake of the offerings.

phone (Yucatec Maya *tunkul,* Quiché *tun*) with two vibrating tongues cut in the side, each producing a pitch when struck; and a struck mouth-resonated bow (*hool*) with a string-tensing stick between the bow and the string, used for *jaranas.*

FURTHER STUDY

The major study of pre-Columbian Maya musical instruments is by Martí (1968). He has compared many of the ancient instruments from Mexico with Mexican instruments in current use and has explored ancient Mexican musical contexts by studying pre-Columbian musical iconography and comparing it with how musical instruments have been used in Mexico during the twentieth century. Other, more scientific studies are by Flores and Flores (1981), Hammond (1972a, 1972b), and Rivera y Rivera (1980). Three important studies that include descriptions of musical performance by late-twentieth-century Maya are by Daniel Alfaro (1982), Gary H. Gossen (1974), and Raúl G. Guerrero (1949). Linda O'Brien's dissertation (1975) studies Maya music of Santiago Atitlán, Guatemala. Two recordings, *Modern Maya: The Indian Music of Chiapas, Mexico* (1975) and *Musiques des communautés indigènes du Mexique* (1969–1970), offer valuable recorded material.

REFERENCES

Alfaro, Daniel. 1982. "Folk Music of the Yucatán Peninsula." Ph.D. dissertation, University of Colorado.

Baer, Phillip, and Mary Baer. 1952. "Materials on the Lacandon Culture of the Petha Region." University of Chicago Library Manuscripts on Middle American Anthropology, 34.

Barrera Vásquez, Alfredo. 1965. *El Libro de los Cantares de Dzitbalché.* México, D.F.: Instituto Nacional de Antropología e Historia.

En Busca de la Música Maya: Canción de la Selva Lacandona. 1976. King Records GXH (k) 5001–5003. LP disk.

Flores Dorantes, Felipe, and Lorenza Flores García. 1981. *Organología aplicada a instrumentos musicales prehispánicos: SILBATOS MAYAS.* Colección Científica 102. México, D.F.: Museo Nacional de Antropología, Instituto Nacional de Antropología e Historia.

Gossen, Gary H. 1974. *Chamulas in the World of the Sun: Time and Space in a Maya Oral Tradition.* Cambridge, Mass.: Harvard University Press.

Guerrero, Raul G. 1949. "Música de Chiapas." *Revista de Estudios Musicales* 1(2):129–150.

Hammond, Norman. 1972. "Classic Maya Music. Part I: Maya Drums." *Archaeology* 25(2):124–131.

———. 1972b. "Classic Maya Music. Part I: Rattles, Shakers, Raspers, Wind and String Instruments." *Archaeology* 25(3):222–228.

Harrison, Frank, and Joan Harrison. 1968. "Spanish Elements in the Music of Two Maya Groups in Chiapas." *Selected Reports in Ethnomusicology* 1(2):1–44.

Martí, Samuel. 1968. *Instrumentos Musicales Precortesianos,* 2nd ed. México, D.F.: Instituto Nacional de Antropología e Historia.

Modern Maya: The Indian Music of Chiapas, Mexico. 1975. Folkways FE 4377. LP disk.

Musiques des communautés indigènes du Mexique. 1969–1970. Vogue LDM 30103. LP disk.

O'Brien, Linda. 1975. "Songs of the Face of the Earth: Ancestor Songs of the Tzutujil Maya of Santiago Atitlán." Ph.D. dissertation, University of California at Los Angeles.

Rivera y Rivera, Roberto. 1980. *Los Instrumentos Musicales de los Mayas.* México, D. F.: Instituto Nacional de Antropología e Historia.

Villa Rojas, Alfonso. 1967. "Los Lacandones: su origen, costumbres y problemas vitales." *América Indígena* 27(1):25–53.

Miskitu

T. M. Scruggs

Musical Instruments
Musical Contexts and Genres
Further Study

The Miskitu are an Amerindian people whose current population totals about 170,000, including 120,000 within the borders of Nicaragua (calculated from Hale and Gordon 1987:18), fifty thousand in Honduras (calculated from Ashby 1976:6 and Velásquez and Agerkop 1979:11), and a small number of families in Managua, Nicaragua, and along the coast in northeastern Costa Rica. With the neighboring Sumu [see NICARAGUA], the Miskitu speak a language belonging to the Macro-Chibcha linguistic phylum. Chibchan-speakers once occupied the greater part of the Caribbean coastal region known as the Atlantic Coast (Holm 1978:298; Stone 1966:210).

The Miskitu's first development of a distinct ethnic identity most likely dates to the 1600s, when the first references to Miskitu appear in documents (Holm 1978:306–309; for an earlier dating, see Nietschmann 1973:23). The name has no relation to the insect but probably came from the association of the group with muskets they had purchased from English buccaneers. Different spellings of the name are still common (for example, *Mosquito* in English and *Miskito* in Spanish), but the Miskitu language has no /o/ sound.

Contemporary Miskitu identify themselves, and are considered by outsiders, as essentially of native American descent, but in the last five centuries they have mixed genetically with Europeans and Africans. Their early openness to contact and trade with Europeans led to their military and economic dominance over the native American groups related to them that became collectively known as the Sumu and the Paya [see HONDURAS]. The Miskitu eventually expanded their control to encompass their current area of habitation, running along the Caribbean coast from Río Negro, Honduras, to Río Escondido, Nicaragua, and extending far upriver of most major tributaries, especially along the Río Coco, which forms the Honduran-Nicaraguan border. In the 1700s and 1800s, the Miskitu further intensified mutually beneficial relations with the English, who until the end of the 1800s promoted the concept of a Miskitu king and a kingdom of Mosquitia. From escaped slaves originally brought to the Atlantic Coast by the English, and possibly from survivors of shipwrecked slave ships, several Miskitu communities acquired a significant African genetic heritage (Bell 1989:3; Helms 1971:16).

To create an *ispara almuk*, a performer drives an old machete into a tree trunk. Standing up, he presses his abdomen against the handle and strikes the blade with a long nail to provide rhythmic accompaniment.

In the 1880s, the proselytizing efforts of German and German-American Moravians led to mass conversions to Moravian Christianity among the Miskitu. Over time, the Moravians successfully reduced the political power of traditional shamans (*sukia*), but the shamans' role in traditional healing and funerary rituals remains strong (Hale 1994:40, 50). Twentieth-century missionary efforts attacked some of these functions, and the viability of several traditional genres of music and dance may be precarious (Velásquez and Agerkop 1979:56). Except where otherwise noted, the following discussion is drawn from research conducted in the mid-1970s by Terry Agerkop (1977 [1992]) and Ronny Velásquez (1987, 1988) among Miskitu in Honduras, and research of Eduard Conzemius in Nicaragua in the 1920s.

MUSICAL INSTRUMENTS

Idiophones

The *insuba* (also *simbaika*) is a handleless rattle, made from a dry gourd filled with small stones or hard seeds. Shamans use a small size (about 8 centimeters in diameter) in curative practices. Women formerly utilized a larger size (about 15 centimeters in diameter) to accompany their songs during funerary rituals (*sikru*); it is now limited to the wakes (*kwal taya*).

The *kuswa taya* is a tortoiseshell that produces two tones when struck on the free ends of its ventral side with a deer's horn, wooden stick, or large nail. Formerly used in funerary rituals, it can currently be used in a variety of musical contexts.

To create an *ispara almuk,* a performer drives an old machete into a tree trunk. Standing up, he presses his abdomen against the handle and strikes the blade with a long nail. This instrument provides rhythmic accompaniment to the player's whistling and/or singing of songs related to laments (*inanka*) and in young people's musical repertoires. It is also played during children's wakes.

A deer's horn or large nail is used to rasp the loose teeth of the jawbone of a horse (*aras napat*) and to strike the base of the mandible. This instrument accompanies songs called *tiun* (see below). Another rasp is the *krita,* a food grater.

Membranophones

The *turu-turu* is a mirliton no longer than 3 centimeters, made by stretching a bat's wing between two small pieces of reed, held together by beeswax, which covers the entire instrument. The player positions the instrument entirely in his mouth, and the vibration of its membrane modifies his voice. The *turu-turu* was primarily used in funeral rituals, in which it was a medium for communicating with the ancestral spirit to whom the ritual was dedicated.

The *klisang,* another mirliton, is made from a piece of cane, 8 to 10 centimeters long. One end is stopped by the natural growth between segments, and a membrane (from a bat's wing, a cow's gut, or thin paper) is wrapped around the other end and tied with a thread or vegetable fiber. A hole is bored on a side of the tube near the membrane, over which the performer places his lips while singing. Restricted before around 1930 to the *sikru,* it serves today in other kinds of funerary rituals.

The *kungbi,* a large drum, is likely a result of contact with coastal populations of African descent. Measuring 40 to 50 centimeters in diameter and 1 to 1.5 meters long, it is made from the hollowed section of a mahogany (*yulo*) log. The skin used for the heads is rolled at the edges around a circular bent branch and fitted over one end of the barrel. To secure the skin, a second wooden hoop is fitted over the first. This assembly is held in place by cords wrapped around the second, outer hoop and tied to five pegs driven into the body of the drum. The drum is laid on the ground and the player sits atop it, beating with his hands to accompany the singer, who sits immediately behind him on the same drum. The *kungbi* has traditionally been used in funeral rituals. The influence of the Moravians, who have attacked it as demonic, has diminished its ritual presence and resulted in its being used supremely for secular entertainment.

Chordophones

The *kitar* (from English *guitar*) is a rustically manufactured plucked wooden lute. Its strings, once made from catgut, are nowadays purchased commercially. The peg-holding end of the fingerboard is designed for six strings, but the *kitar* used by youths to accompany their *tiun* customarily employ fewer. The standard six-stringed Spanish guitar is now also widely used.

The *tina* (from Spanish *tina* 'washtub') consists of a single string made from vegetable fiber and fixed between the protruding end of a meter-long wooden pole and the bottom of an upturned tin washtub. The string passes through a hole bored through the bottom of the tub and held with a stick on the other side. Players obtain different pitches and timbres by placing the pole along the edge of the tub, plucking it at different places, and varying the tension by moving the pole. The *tina* is principally used to accompany Christian hymns and, less often, young people's *tiun.*

The *lungku* is a musical bow made from a thin and flexible wooden branch about 50 to 80 centimeters long and a cord from the dried fiber of the *sani* (Spanish *majao*) plant. The player places the bow in his or her mouth to act as a resonator and plucks the string with the right hand. The left hand holds the bow, creating two fundamental tones by alternately letting the string vibrate freely and tightening the length of the string with the thumb and index finger (figure 1). From these fundamental tones the player can produce a series of harmonics. The *lungku* can barely be heard by anyone other than the performer and therefore serves mainly for individual introspection. Compositions tend to imitate the sounds of animals and are highly personal in nature. Though perhaps once the province only of women, it is currently played by men too.

Aerophones

The *bra-tara,* a vertical notched flute around 30 centimeters long, has four holes with a beeswax-molded mouthpiece. Both beeswax and the kind of cane used are difficult to find. At the present time, *bra-tara* are manufactured only in Mocorón Village, on the Ibantara River.

MUSICAL CONTEXTS AND GENRES

The only Miskitu calendrical festival is *Krismis,* a dance in a circle, named after the month in which it is performed, *Krismis* (from English *Christmas,* Miskitu for December). A soloist among the ring of dancers calls out improvised phrases in a strongly marked, regular rhythm that the rest of the participants repeat. Each perfor-

FIGURE 1   Castelo Pederik plays a Miskitu musical bow (*lungku*). Tikiwraya, La Mosquitia, Honduras. Photo by Ronny Velásquez, late 1970s.

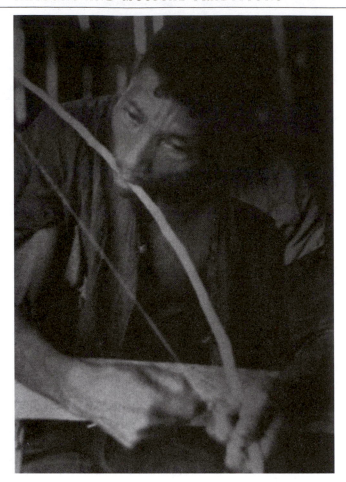

mance lasts until the dancers tire (from thirty to forty minutes), and several are usually performed at each occasion. *Krismis* dances are often interspersed with *inanka* (see below).

Several kinds of song are related to curative rituals. An *iumu,* the harmful spirit responsible for the person's ailment, can be removed from an afflicted person who drinks water that has been empowered through song by a specialist in the community. The specialist collects fresh water in a bottle. He sanctifies the water by singing and blowing through a hollow cane (*klisang*). Each illness requires a specific song; the specialist may need to try several songs and bottles before making a correct diagnosis. For a more serious illness, when the Miskitu believe a dead person's soul has invaded the patient, the shaman performs a daylong *isingni ulan* (from *isingni* 'soul' and *ulan* 'mounted'). This ritual revolves around the shaman's spoken incantations and solo singing, accompanied by a handleless rattle (*insuba*). During the ceremony, younger members of the community may perform *tiun* to distract the harmful soul and help the shaman capture it.

At the end of the 1600s, the English buccaneer and navigator William Dampier (1652–1715) witnessed a performance of the *sikru* and made the earliest extant written reference to Miskitu music (Dampier 1699:10). Long *bara* (flutes, larger cousins of the *bra-tara*) and *kungbi* were prominent and remained so, as described in the twentieth century in detail by Conzemius (1932:161–164). Pressure from Moravian missionaries forced many Miskitu to abandon the ceremony around the 1950s, and only fragments of the cycle of songs once used by the shaman survive.

Despite the atrophy of the *sikru,* funerary ceremonies remain important occasions for traditional musical performance. Laments (*inanka*), sung by women at wakes (*upla pruan bara*), refer to the life of the deceased, mourn their departure, and idealize the world in the afterlife (see examples in Grossmann 1988:65–66). The singers perform a mixture of laments and crying sounds while seated around the body of the deceased. The melodic contour of laments describes a descending pattern, with a repetition of the lowest note at the end of each phrase. Women's laments accompany the burial. A wake for a dead child can include a greater variety of instruments and music: people may play a musical bow and a machete (*ispara almuk*) and may sing *tiun* containing textual allusions to death.

Three days after a death, a shaman begins an extended *kwal taya,* or wake for the deceased (*isingni* 'soul'). To first capture the soul, he sings and accompanies himself with an *insuba* while hunting for the manifestation of the soul in a firefly (also called *isingni*). On a night set by the shaman, the main section of the wake takes place. Again, the principal musical expression are laments; however, the shaman dances and sings to the soul, manifested as a firefly trapped in his hands. The shaman's dance is accompanied by one or more *kitar,* food-grater rasps, handleless rattles, and the jawbone of a horse. Simultaneously, younger men perform their own *tiun,* accompanied by the same instrumentation. Contemporary ritual celebrations have incorporated portable radios and record players, combining popular music with the above-mentioned traditional music. As the sky lightens, the performers move to the grave, where the shaman buries the firefly with the body. After this ceremony, the eldest women of the family are required to sing laments about the deceased for a series of specific occasions, including at the beginning of each day; when strong rain and storms approach; when something negative, such as a major illness, befalls the community; and when something especially positive happens, such as a good harvest or an abundance of fish.

The principal secular form of Miskitu music is *kitarlawana* (from *kitar* and *lawana,* song) or *tiun,* which Agerkop suggests spelling "tune" to correspond to the English original of the word (1977:16). These are songs composed by men, and their lyrical content centers on a woman. Most often, their sentiments are of longing and desire, but they can express a range of emotions, including strong negative feelings (see examples from the late 1800s in Bell 1989 [1899]:89, 312). Their performances can be accompanied by one or more *kitar* and/or guitars, plus the percussion of scrapers (*kritas*) and horse's jawbones (*aras napats*). The impact of centuries of European contact and an intensive European missionary presence are evident in the melodic design and full use of functional harmony. *Tiun* are sung solo or harmonized in a roughly followed pattern of parallel thirds and sixths. Their vocal style can vary from a forceful production that borders on shouting to relaxed, often plaintive timbres, in which the singer cracks his voice at the end of phrases. The tonality is overwhelmingly in a major key. The meters can be in either 3/4 or 4/4 at a moderate-to-slow tempo. Dotted rhythmic accompaniment is pervasive, as shown in figure 2, an excerpt from one of the oldest and most popular *tiun.*

FURTHER STUDY

The first recordings of Miskitu music, *Nicaragua—música y canto* (1992 [1977]), were made by Salvador Cardenal Argüello in Managua in the early 1960s. Miskitu music was first exposed to the mestizo population of Nicaragua when these recordings and live performances by Miskitu visiting Cardenal Argüello's studios in Managua were broadcast over his radio station. In the 1980s, groups of young Miskitu presented nationally televised versions of traditional dances, and Pacific Coast mestizo folk-dancing troupes usually included a representation of Miskitu dance in their repertoire. Several cassettes of Miskitu musicians performing *tiun* were produced by the state recording label initiated by the Sandinistas (Grupo Lanlaya

To first capture the soul, a shaman sings and accompanies himself while hunting for the manifestation of the soul in a firefly. The shaman dances and sings to the soul, manifested as a firefly trapped in his hands.

FIGURE 2   Excerpt from "*Silpiki Mairin*," a *tiun*, performed by the group Saumuk Raya (New Seed), from the recording *Saumuk Raya—Semilla Nueva* 1986:A5. Transcription by T. M. Scruggs; lyrics translated from Miskitu to Spanish by Terry Agerkop and from Spanish by T. M. Scruggs.

1987; Saumuk Raya—Semilla Nueva [1986]). Other recordings, including *Music of the Miskito Indians of Honduras and Nicaragua* (1981), were made by non-Nicaraguan investigators. The change in government in 1990 and economic decline have prevented the release of more Miskitu recordings in Nicaragua. Miskitu music remains virtually unknown to non-Miskitu in Honduras.

REFERENCES

Agerkop, Terry. 1977. "Música de los Miskitos de Honduras." *Folklore Americano* (Instituto Panamericano de Geografía e Historia, Lima, Peru) 23:7–37.

Ashby, Maggie. 1976. *The Miskitia of Honduras.* CHR Volunteer Field Report. London.

Bell, C. Napier. 1989 [1899]. *Tangweera: Life and Adventures among Gentle Savages.* Austin: University of Texas Press.

Cardenal Argüello, Salvador. 1977. *Nicaragua: Música y canto.* Managua: Banco de América. Liner notes.

Conzemius, Eduard. 1932. *Ethnographical Survey of the Miskito and Sumu Indians of Honduras and Nicaragua.* Washington D.C.: Bureau of American Ethnology, Smithsonian Institution.

Dampier, William. 1699. *A New Voyage Round the World.* 4th ed. 2 vols. London.

Grossmann, Guido. 1988. *La Costa Atlántica de Nicaragua.* Managua: Editorial La Ocarina.

Grupo Lanlaya. 1987. *"Lanlaya"—Canciones de Amor Miskito.* ENIGRAC CE–021. Cassette.

Hale, Charles R. 1994. *Resistance and Contradiction: Miskitu Indians and the Nicaraguan State, 1894–1987.* Stanford, Calif.: Stanford University Press.

Hale, Charles R., and Edmund T. Gordon. 1987. "Costeño Demography: Historical and Contemporary Demography of Nicaragua's Atlantic Coast." In *Ethnic Groups and the Nation State: The Case of the Atlantic Coast in Nicaragua,* ed. Charles R. Hale and Edmund T. Gordon,

7–32. Stockholm: Department of Social Anthropology, University of Stockholm.

Helms, Mary W. 1971. *Asang: Adaptations to Culture Contact in a Miskito Community.* Gainesville: University of Florida Press.

Music of the Miskito Indians of Honduras and Nicaragua. 1981. Smithsonian Folkways 4237. Cassette.

Nicaragua—Música y canto. 1992 [1977]. Radio Güegüence. Seven compact discs.

Nietschmann, Bernard. 1973. *Between Land and Water—The Subsistence Ecology of the Miskitu Indians, Eastern Nicaragua.* New York: Seminar Press.

Saumuk Raya—Semilla Nueva. 1986. *Saumuk Raya—Semilla Nueva.* ENIGRAC 018. LP disk, cassette.

Velásquez, Ronny. 1987. *Chamanismo, Mito y Religión en Cuarto Naciones Étnicas de América Aborigen.* Caracas: Biblioteca de la Academia Nacional de la Historia.

———. 1988. "Instrumentos musicales pertenecientes a la cultura Miskita." In *Organología del Folklore Hondureño,* ed. Jesús Muñoz Tábora, 105–124. Tegucigalpa: Secretaría del Turismo y Cultura.

Velásquez, Ronny, and Terry Agerkop. 1979. *Miskitos—Honduras.* Cajas audiovisuales INIDEF 2. Caracas: Instituto Interamericano de Etnomusicología y Folklore. Cassette.

Belize
Oliver Greene

The Maya
The Garifuna
Creole Music
Further Study

Belize, formerly known as British Honduras, is the only English-speaking country in Central America. Located on the Yucatán Peninsula bordering Mexico to the north and northwest, Guatemala to the west and south, and the Caribbean Sea to the east, Belize has a land area of 22,965 square kilometers. Geographically, the country divides into six major districts: Belize, Cayo, Corozal, Orange Walk, Stann Creek, and Toledo.

Belize has a population of 189,392 (1991 census), composed mainly of the following cultural and ethnic groups, in descending order of population: mestizos (of European and Amerindian descent, 81,253 or 42.9 percent; creole (of African descent, with varying degrees of admixture from other ethnic groups), 55,364 or 29.2 percent; Maya (three Amerindian groups, including the K'ekchi, the Mopán, and the Yucatec), 20,438 or 10.8 percent; Garifuna (of African and Caribbean Amerindian descent), 12,335 or 6.5 percent; and East Indians, 6,457 or 3.4 percent. Other cultural or ethnic groups in Belize are Arabs, Chinese, Koreans, Mennonites, and Rastafarians. There is much debate over this census, which for the first time identified the mestizos, rather than the creoles, as the largest ethnic group.

Though English is the official language of the country, Creole (a synthesis of English, African languages, and Spanish) is the lingua franca, especially in Belize City. Other local languages include Garifuna, low German (as spoken by Mennonites), Hindi, Maya (K'ekchi, Mopán, and Yucatec), and Spanish. Recent arrivals include Haitians, Hondurans, Jamaicans, and Taiwanese. Musically, Belize reflects European, Amerindian, and African cultural practices and their synthesis.

Several historical events affected the development of Belize's cultural and ethnic fabric. In 1519, the Spanish conquistador Hernán Cortés landed in Yucatán. By 1650, the coast of Belize had become a haven for British pirates, who attacked Spanish vessels carrying gold and silver back to the Spain. In the 1720s, the British began importing African slaves to the region. The emancipation of slaves occurred in 1838, opening the way for people from India to be brought to Belize (and other British colonies in the Caribbean) as indentured servants between 1844 and 1917. During the Caste War in the Mexican Yucatán (1847–1850), thousands of Maya and mestizos fled the Spaniards and entered Belize as refugees. In 1862, Belize became

British Honduras, a British colony. From 1958 to 1962, descendants of Swiss Mennonites migrated from Mexico to Belize. Rastafarians from Jamaica are the most recent arrivals. In 1964, British Honduras began self-government and in 1973, anticipating independence, local residents changed the name of the colony back to Belize (the original name of the area). Belize was granted full independence from the United Kingdom in 1981.

THE MAYA

In pre-Columbian times, the Maya inhabited many Middle American areas that include portions of the present countries of Belize, El Salvador, Guatemala, Honduras, and Mexico [see MAYA]. In the Belizean area of the Yucatán Peninsula alone, more than thirty-five sites of ancient Maya centers have been discovered. The earliest indication of Maya existence in Belize has long been debated. Carbon-14 testing of wood from the settlement of Cuello suggests Maya occupation as early as 2600 B.C., but some archaeologists think the testing results are incorrect.

Knowledge about the music of the ancient Maya in Belize has been gained from archaeological remains of actual instruments, iconography, writings in Maya manuscripts, and sixteenth-century Spanish accounts of the Maya from the end of the Postclassic Period (1500s). Archaeological excavations in Belize, conducted at sites including Altun Ha, Barton Ramie, Benque Viejo, Lubaantun, Pacbitún, San José, and Santa Rita, have yielded valuable information on Maya music of the Late Classic (A.D. 600–900), Postclassic, and earlier periods.

Fragments of musical instruments and complete exemplars of eight ceramic globular flutes (ocarinas), five tubular flutes, two composite flute-rattles, and ceramic hand-held drums were found in 1986 in Late Classic tombs of two elite women in Pacbitún. Some globular flutes represent a fat god (associated with death) and a kneeling water-lily-holding woman (associated with the afterlife). Each of the tubular flutes has two holes for fingering, a circular mouthpiece (probably a ducted fipple mouthpiece, like other Maya flutes), and a globular resonating chamber in the middle. The distal ends of four of them are in the shape of ornate flowers. These flutes were capable of playing in several octaves. The most suggestive discovery in the Pacbitún tombs was two composite flute-rattles. Each instrument, about 16 centimeters long, is evenly divided between a flute handle and an incised rattle ball, containing fifteen to twenty ceramic pebbles. One instrument, painted red, has two holes for fingering; the other, with "a stubby, perpendicular projection" for a mouthpiece, was painted blue and has four holes (Healy 1988:28–30).

Contemporary Maya music

Little research has been conducted on the music of Maya Indians currently living in Belize. Contemporary Mayan music is a syncretization of indigenous and Spanish elements. The pre-Columbian combination of flute and drum (two musicians) can still be heard, but the marimba is commonly found in the Cayo District in central Belize, the home of many Mopán Maya. Spanish musical influences from neighboring Guatemala are also quite prevalent; the K'ekchi Maya of the Toledo District in southern Belize play melodies on harps, violins, and guitars. The romantic lyrics and extensive use of the guitar among the Yucatec Maya in the districts of Orange Walk and Corozal can be attributed to the influence of traditional Mexican music. The Maya festival of the feast of Saint Louis (San Luís) includes drumming to signal the beginning of the procession, playing marimbas and rattles, singing, ceremonial dancing of the tiger dance and the holy-deer dance, and more drumming to signal the culminating event of the festival, the raising of the greased pole (Mallán 1993:45–47).

String music of the K'ekchi

Music of the typical K'ekchi harp ensemble serves for entertainment, such as dancing in a circle involving male-female interaction, mostly through hoplike steps. The music is always instrumental, with guitar, a thirty-stringed diatonic harp, and a violin mostly doubling the main melody one octave lower than the harp. The K'ekchi harp is plucked with the thumb and the first three fingers of both hands. The resonator doubles as a percussion instrument when a second musician beats on it.

Legends in some Maya communities attest that K'ekchi harp music was created and named by the Maya gods. Others maintain that the pieces were named by the Spaniards as they converted the Maya to Christianity. The effects of indirect Spanish influence on Maya music are clear in the occasions when the harp is typically played: Easter, Christmas, and other major feasts, all of them Christian events. The performers are usually men who learn to play from childhood by being apprenticed with masters in villages. Florencio Mes (Palacio 1988), in his fifties in 1996, is one of the few bearers of this ancient tradition. As a typical Maya harpist, he not only plays but builds all his instruments, using traditional tools, local hardwoods, and nylon fishing line for strings. A highly respected elder in his community (San Miguel, in the Toledo district of Belize), he has represented his country at major Caribbean and European festivals (Scott 1996b).

THE GARIFUNA

The Garifuna of Belize and adjacent coasts [see GUATEMALA; HONDURAS; NICARAGUA] are products of the genetic mixture of former West Africans and Carib and Arawak (also Taino) who occupied the island of St. Vincent, in the Lesser Antilles. Sebastian Cayetano (1989:31–32), a Garifuna historian and linguist, states that the Garifuna ancestry can be traced back to the Yoruba, Ibo, and Ashanti cultures of West Africa, in the lands that today comprise Nigeria, Ghana, Sierra Leone, and Mali. The encounter between Africans and Amerindians began in 1635 (and perhaps centuries earlier; see Lawrence 1987), when two Spanish vessels carrying West African slaves en route to Barbados were assumed to be destroyed at sea during a storm; surviving Africans swam to St. Vincent Island and took refuge among the Amerindians there. Some sources suggest that the population of Garifuna on St. Vincent was augmented by runaway slaves from nearby islands: Maroons, also of West African origin, from groups including Ashanti-Fanti, Congo, Efik, Fon, and Yoruba (Coelho 1955:6–8).

The Amerindian origin of the Garifuna is intricate. Douglas Taylor (1951:32), a noted ethnographer of the Garifuna, stated that the Island Carib who had intermixed with the West Africans were the offspring of the Arawak people known as Igneri and the Carib people known as Kallina or Galibi. During raids on Arawak (Taino) villages, Carib warriors would kill the men and take Arawak women as wives. Therefore, the Island Carib women spoke an Arawak language, whereas the men spoke a Carib language. Though Carib prevailed as the dominant language of the Garifuna, numerous examples of men's and women's using different words for the same object survive. The term Garifuna may reflect the Africanizing of the pronunciation of the terms *karifuna* and *kalinago* as *Garifuna* and *Garinagu,* respectively (Foster 1982:9). The former are words the Island Carib used when referring to themselves; today, the word *Garifuna* refers to the people and the language. The word *Garinagu,* the plural form of Garifuna, is used primarily by the people when referring to themselves.

The Garifuna, also called the Black Carib by foreign observers, were defeated in battle by the British and exiled to Roatan Island, off the coast of Honduras, in 1797. The first Garifuna migrated to Belize from Honduras in 1802 (S. Cayetano

1990:43). To escape being massacred after the civil war in Honduras, another group left Honduras and settled in Dangriga on 19 November 1832, now recognized as National Garifuna Settlement Day. Currently, most Belizean Garifuna reside in six communities in the districts of Stann Creek and Toledo: Barranco, Dangriga, Georgetown, Hopkins, Punta Gorda Town, and Seine Bight.

Garifuna ritual music and musical instruments

The ritual music of the Garifuna displays elements of the music of West African worship of ancestors and Amerindian shamanism. Religious practices, conducted by a shaman (*buyei*), include shamanistic healing and spirit-possession ceremonies, of which *adügürühani* (feasting the dead, the last of the postmortem rituals), also known as *dügü,* is the most elaborate. Postmortem rituals that follow the funeral and precede *dügü* are *beluria,* nine nights of family prayers, often concluding with communitywide participation in singing, drumming, and dancing; a Garifuna mass, a translation of the Roman Catholic mass into the vernacular, with hymns sung to the accompaniment of a *garawoun primero* and a *segunda* (see below); *arairaguni,* an invocation to determine the cause of illness; *amuyadahani* 'refreshing the dead', a private ritual, in which family members make offerings to their ancestors; and *achuguhani* 'feeding the dead' (also called *chugú*), usually a single day's ancestral-spirit-placating ritual that may or may not include singing and drumming. The influence of West African drumming and Amerindian vocal music and modality is apparent in the music of *adügürühani.* The Garifuna of Nicaragua call this ritual *walagayo* (Wells 1980:5), a term whose use in Nicaragua may be attributed to its use in a popular *dügü* song referring to a crowing fowl (Garifuna *gayo*).

Feasting the dead (*dügü*)

The most extensive sacred music of the Garifuna occurs in *dügü,* for supplicating and placating ancestral spirits (*gubida*). The term *gubida* is most commonly used when referring to ancestral spirits that inflict illness; the term *ahari,* a deceased relative's spirit (E. Cayetano 1993:17), is frequently used in reference to ancestral spirits in general. When an individual of the Garifuna community becomes ill and cannot be cured by conventional medicine, a shaman is consulted to determine the cause of the illness. With the assistance of his or her spiritual helpers (*hiúruha*), the shaman conducts an invocation ceremony (*arairaguni*). With the shaman acting as a medium, the *gubida* reveals that it has caused the relative to become ill because it feels neglected. The *gubida* is always of consanguineal relation to the afflicted individual. The *gubida* may then request *achuguhani* or *dügü.* Good health is restored to the individual if the *gubida* and the officiating shaman consider the ceremony a success. The spirit may request that the patient's family build a new temple (*dabuyaba*) within which to hold the *dügü* and other religious rituals. Essential to all Garifuna communities, the temple symbolizes cultural and religious continuity (figure 1). *Dügü* are often the results of generations of neglecting the ancestors. Parents and grandparents, near the end of their lives, may request that a *dügü* be given in their honor or in honor of one or more ancestors, frequently a married couple. Generation after generation of offspring may fail to do the ritual until one relative becomes deathly ill, and the ritual must be done.

The primary function of music during the *dügü* is theurgy (communication with the realm of the spirits), in which songs and drums are the principal media. The Garifuna do not believe that ancestral spirits literally reside in the drums; they believe that the sound of the heart drum (*lanigi garawoun*), the central and largest instrument of the three *segundas,* has a calming effect on ritual participants, especially those who have become possessed by *gubida* (John Mariano, personal communication).

When first constructed, drums are anointed with *hiu,* a cassava wine, and blessed with the smoke of *buwe,* a sacred herb. These techniques and methods suggest a combination of native American traits and African ones.

FIGURE 1   A Garifuna temple (*dabuyaba*) in Dangriga, Belize. Photo by Oliver Greene, 1994.

The calming effect on participants in a state of great excitement may be attributed to the regularity and repetition of the drumming, a simple pattern in triple meter. Most instances of possession by ancestors occur during *dügü,* but instances of possession in other contexts have been reported. During ritual occasions, three drums are always used, though two are employed for secular dances and songs (Bilby 1993:5). The rhythm of the heart drum is thought to symbolize the heartbeat; with a shaman's rattle, it attracts the spirit from the mud floor of the temple (Foster 1986:8). During the rituals, the chief shaman (*sinebui*) plays a container rattle (*sísira, maraga*) whose design is Amerindian, though similar rattles are found in Africa. It also serves in secular contexts (see figure 4).

In design and construction, *garawoun* reveal African and Amerindian traits; however, unlike many drums used in African, African-derived, and native American religious practices, they are played only with the hands. They are constructed in the following manner (figure 2). First, a hardwood log, usually mahogany or mayflower, is hollowed out with fire and water; then, holes are drilled into the bottom of the drum to secure the drumhead, which will be attached later; the heads, made of animal skin (usually of deer, and sometimes of goat or peccary), are then sewn to a rim made from a beach-growing vine; the heads are then fitted against a second rim, and laced to this rim and the wooden frame with rope; eight to ten short sticks, 3 to 6 centimeters long, are then placed into the lacing and twisted to tighten the cords and raise the pitch of the drum; finally, drumheads are equipped with snares made by attaching nylon, cotton, or metal strings across the heads to create a buzzing sound. When first constructed, drums are anointed with *hiu,* a cassava wine, and blessed

FIGURE 2 Two Garifuna *garawoun* drums; *left to right, primero* and *segunda.* The tension sticks and snares are visible. Photo by Oliver Greene, 1994.

with the smoke of *buwe,* a sacred herb. These techniques and methods suggest a combination of native American traits (the lacing of the heads, the use of snares) and African ones (the use of goatskins, sticks for increasing skin tension).

Traditional Garifuna music features two kinds of *garawoun: primero* 'lead drum' and *segunda* 'supporting drum' (figure 3). The *primero,* a treble drum about 30 to 45 centimeters in diameter and 60 centimeters high, provides rhythmic variety with syncopations and improvisatory passages. The *segunda,* a bass drum, about 60 to 90 centimeters in diameter and 90 centimeters in height, maintains the steady pulse in duple or triple meter. The sizes of drums have not been standardized. The dimensions of *garawoun* depend solely on the diameter of the log from which they are cut. If the tree is quite large in diameter, up to five drums may be cut from a single section of wood. During a *dügü,* however, three *segunda* play a simple unison beat in triple meter (a battery of three drums is common to African-derived cultures). In sacred and secular settings, the ensemble of drummers is called *dangbu.*

FIGURE 3 Playing the *garawoun* drums; *left to right, primero, segunda,* and *primero,* in procession to the Roman Catholic church on National Garifuna Settlement Day in Dangriga, Belize, 19 November 1994. Photo by Oliver Greene.

Several song-and-dance genres are performed during the *dügü: abelagudahani, ámalihani,* and *ugulendu. Abelagudahani,* a "bringing-in" song, is performed at the beginning of the ritual to escort fishermen to the temple from the sea, where they gather ritual food at the outlying cays. *Ámalihani,* a complex dance, characterized by movement in a circular pattern and reversals of direction, is used to placate the spirit. Spiritual possession (*ónwehani*) frequently occurs as female participants dance, forming lines behind the shaman, who faces the drummers; maintaining this configuration, they move first in a clockwise direction, and then counterclockwise around the temple. Possession by ancestral spirits may occur during ordinary daily activities and has even occurred during Christian church services.

Possession has occurred in contexts without the influence of musical accompaniment. Performers shuffle while stopping at positions that mark the four cardinal directions. Standing in front of the drummers, the shaman lowers his container rattle to the ground and raises it again in the directions of the spirits—where they live, and whence power may be drawn. *Ugulendu,* the fundamental sacred dance of the *dügü,* thought to be of Carib origin, is a tightly bound shuffle (legs and feet held close together) performed in a circular pattern. *Awangulahani,* a circular dance of rejoicing for having fulfilled the spirit's request, is one of the final events of the ritual. Three themes associated with this dance are the drawing of elder participants into the circle, the calming effect of the dance and its ability to make participants happy, and the circle as a symbol of completeness (Wells 1980:5). Many songs for the *dügü* are composed in remembrance of a specific ancestor.

Sociological benefits attributed to the *dügü* in general are a psychological catharsis, the curing of illness, and the reassertion of solidarity as expressed by relatives and friends in the community (S. Cayetano 1989:15).

Gender roles

Gender roles in the musical performances of *dügü* (and in other kinds of ritual) are apparent. Drumming has traditionally been considered the men's domain, but in most collective vocal genres (in sacred and secular contexts) women predominate as singers (*gayusa*). However, when no women are present, men serve as lead and responsorial singers. At the *beluria* and similar events, men who play *garawoun* often serve as lead singers. Traditional vocal ensemble music is always performed in unison. Responsorial singing occurs most often when a vocalist introduces a new song to the ensemble. The introductory phrase, the solo vocalist's call, is quickly overpowered by a unison choral response—the preferred method of collective singing. Songs of the same genre are usually performed successively without interruption to the continuous accompaniment of *garawoun* drums and sometimes two *sisira.*

Texts of most *dügü* songs refer to ancestors as female (grandmother or great-grandmother, even if the *dügü* is being given in honor of a man), perhaps reflecting the matrilineality and matrifocality of Garifuna society. It may also be a reflection of gender-based empowerment, because older women predominate as organizers, ritual participants, and composers of ritual songs. Skilled composers, dancers, and drummers who know sacred and secular genres are highly respected in their villages and become known from one community to another.

Semisacred genres

Úyanu are unaccompanied, semisacred, usually mournful gesture-accompanying songs in irregular meter (Jenkins 1982a:2). They fall into two categories: *abeimahani* and *arumahani,* for ensembles of women's and men's voices, respectively. Only women compose the melody and the text for *abeimahani,* and only men compose the melody and text for *arumahani.* Two kinds of lyrics are associated with each genre:

songs that describe events personally experienced by the composer and songs of historical nature about the origin of the Garifuna people. John Mariano, the shaman of the temple in Dangriga, states that ancestors give the melody and text of songs of the latter kind to individuals in dreams (Foley 1995:49–50). *Uyanu* have an irregular meter or lack of strict metrical rhythm, which can be attributed to the syllabic setting of the text.

Abeimahani, once performed at events such as house parties and to comfort the sick, are performed during the liminal period of the *dügü,* between midnight and 3:00 A.M., when the *segunda* are silent. *Abeimahani* are performed by women who stand in a line with their fingers linked (the manner in which hands are linked may vary from one community to another) while gesturing to irregularly metered music. Gestures include unison swinging of the arms forward and backward, slightly bending the knees, and moving the upper torso forward in coordination with the backward swing of both arms. The number of singers of *abeimahani* may range from only a few women to several dozen. The genre is clearly of Amerindian origin (S. Cayetano 1989:77; Jenkins 1982b).

Arumahani, reported by many non-Garifuna scholars as all but extinct, are performed almost exclusively in the temple during *dügü.* Though *arumahani* are performed less frequently than *abeimahani,* the genre is not in danger of becoming extinct (John Mariano and Rolando Gómez, personal communication). Most of these songs are performed by the men present (usually only a few) and women who know the texts.

Garifuna shamanistic songs are said to be songs given to a shaman by his spiritual helpers during times of struggle and transformation. Some shamanistic songs call specific spiritual helpers by name. Shamanic songs are often unaccompanied, in free rhythm, have a range of about one octave and a descending melodic contour, and are based on repetitive melodic material characterized by descending leaps of thirds and fourths followed by short passages of whole tones and semitones. These traits show Amerindian influence.

Garifuna secular music and dance

Traditional Garifuna secular music and dance display a synthesis of West African, Amerindian, English, Spanish, and creole traits. The Garifuna use idiophones, membranophones, and chordophones to accompany many secular kinds of songs and dances. Drums are the most prevalent musical instruments of Garifuna traditional secular music, and rattles are often used with them to accompany some singing and dancing (figure 4). Occasionally hollowed-out turtle shells of varying sizes, struck with wooden sticks, and blown conch shells are added to the ensembles; these instruments provide additional timbres, pitches, and rhythmic variety. The European harmonica is sometimes played, but the Spanish guitar is the only European instrument that has found a lasting place in Garifuna music, usually as an accompaniment for singing. Some secular genres, however, are sung unaccompanied.

In secular Garifuna contexts, music is used for accompanying processions and mime-dances, wakes, and work, and as social commentary, lullabies, and entertainment. Specific rhythmic accompaniments and lyrics are associated with particular dances.

Processions and mime-dances

Processions performed during the Christmas holidays are frequently accompanied by a combination of membranophones and aerophones, perhaps influenced by the British fife-and-drum tradition. The Garifuna perform four specific processions and mime-dances: *charikanari, pia manadi, wanaragua,* and *wárini.* Traditionally per-

FIGURE 4 A Garifuna man plays *sísira* rattles during an evening of social song and dance before the National Garifuna Settlement Day celebration, Dangriga, Belize, 18 November 1994. Photo by Oliver Greene.

As an expression of sexual politics, the *punta* is a variation of the cock-and-hen mating dance common to many African-influenced cultures of the southern Americas and the Caribbean.

formed by men during Christmastime, they are frequently incorporated into the repertoire of folk-dance companies. These are short dramas performed by stock characters who travel from yard to yard, collecting money for their performances (Whipple 1976:1).

Charikanari is a mime-dance that depicts the meeting of a hunter, a cave man, and a cow that taunts children and spectators (S. Cayetano 1989:77). *Primeros, segundas,* and a harmonica provide accompaniment.

Pia manadi, a processional play, uniquely involves the death and resurrection of one of the characters and displays traits resembling those of English mumming plays. Pia, a Carib hero from the Guianas, was one of the twin children of the sun and a genius of the forest. He and Manadi, a man dressed as a woman, are characters in the comedy (Taylor 1951:7–8). This play is accompanied by a horizontal cross-blown cane flute, one *primero,* and one *segunda,* in a style reminiscent of the British fife-and-drum tradition. Few performances of this drama are seen today.

Little has been written about *wárini.* It is simply defined as a masked dance that is a prelude to *wanaragua* (E. Cayetano 1977:87). The costume for *warini* includes palm leaves attached with a cord or string and worn around the shoulders and waist, the latter extending to the knees. *Wanaragua,* commonly known as John Canoe, is an old song-and-dance genre, composed and performed solely by men. Formerly presented throughout Afro-Caribbean cultures at Christmas, it is perhaps derived from the *egungun* festival of the Yoruba, in which participants appeared in whiteface, which symbolized the death transformation of the ancestor spirits. In the 1990s in Belize, performers disguised as men and women use painted wire masks resembling Europeans as they travel from yard to yard, amusing the children. Each performer wears a headdress known as *wababa,* a term that may come from the Yoruba, meaning 'father' (Felix Miranda, personal communication). Performers also wear knee-tied rattles. Wárini are composed by men only and consist of a single call-and-response pattern, continuously repeated until a new song is introduced (Hadel 1973:91). Free duple patterns on the *primero* are superimposed on the three-against-two rhythm of the accompanying *segunda,* and the meter seems to shift from 2/4 to 6/8, or even 3/4 (Whipple 1971:91). Accompaniment for *wanaragua* and *wárini* is provided solely by *primeros* and *segundas.*

Wakes

The texts of numerous songs mournfully address death, the dead, ancestors' power, misfortunes, and other common Garifuna matters. Nonritual songs of death and mourning convey the importance of kinship, the influence of the dead, and the relationship of mutual dependency between the living and the dead as a source of power. Garifuna songs do not address imaginary events and feelings (E. Cayetano 1977:17).

In the *beluria,* the Garifuna sacred and secular worlds meet. An all-night event in commemoration of a recently deceased relative, the *beluria* is the culmination of nine nights of prayers and songs for the deceased and his or her family. Music plays an important part in its sequence of activities: prayers, hymns in Garifuna, and scriptural readings before an altar or shrine called a *cielo,* erected for the deceased; drumming and traditional secular songs and dances; the Garifuna mass; more drumming, singing, and dancing; and disassembling the *cielo* and taking portions to the grave.

Bérusu, a musical form for solo voice and guitar, is for general entertainment and is often played at wakes. In the *berusu* performed on the recording by Jenkins (1982c:3), the composer says he has seen God and dreamed of his own death. Some traits of this song include a simple harmonic structure based on alternations of tonic, dominant, and subdominant chords, a formal structure of ABAB, and the repetition of melodic material during interludes between verses.

Work

Leremuna wadaguman and *leremuna egí* are work-accompanying songs for men and women, respectively. *Leremuna wadaguman* is usually performed as men work cooperatively at strenuous tasks, such as chopping down large trees and hauling logs downriver and onto the beach to make boats; the title derives directly from the Garifuna word for work, *wadagimanu. Leremuna egí,* performed by women when grating manioc, is accompanied by rhythms produced when the manioc root is beaten against a wooden grater. The title derives from the Garifuna word *eremuha* 'to sing' (E. Cayetano 1993:42). Musical traits of the second grating song on the recording by Jenkins (1982c:3) are a small ensemble of female voices, responsorial form, a repetitive rhythmic motive (usually a quarter followed by a dotted eighth and a sixteenth) as the only accompanimental sound, the range of a minor tenth, and repetition of melodic material. Grating songs, incorporating exclamatory vocables and repetitions in a typically Amerindian style, are performed with a high nasal timbre.

Songs of social commentary

Paranda, a Garifuna genre resembling a serenade and serving as a vehicle of social criticism, is usually composed by men. It was influenced by Hispanic musical genres, and it has a particularly Hispanic sound because of the close relationship maintained between the people of Barranco, in southern Belize, and their nearby Guatemalan and Honduran neighbors. The *primero* plays variations of a basically duple meter—an eighth, two sixteenths, and a quarter—against the *segunda,* which emphasizes a strong accent on the second half of beat two, producing syncopation. As a song about love, a *paranda* incorporates the unison singing of one man and two women, repetition and alternation of verse and refrain, and a simple harmonic chordal structure, played on a guitar. When performed solely as a dance, it is a slow march accompanied by drums, guitar, and *sísira* or maracas (Ugundani Dance Company 1994).

Another social-commentary song-and-dance form, the most popular and best-liked Garifuna genre, is *punta.* In duple meter, dancers employ quick alternating movements of the hips and feet, keeping their upper torsos upright. As an expression of sexual politics, it is a variation of the cock-and-hen mating dance common to many African-influenced cultures of the southern Americas and the Caribbean. Also the favorite form of social commentary by women, it provides an arena for exposing unacceptable behavior in personal affairs. *Puntas* seem to be composed only by women and are performed responsorially (Hadel 1973:5); the call, usually half a sentence sung by the leader, is followed by the response and the completion of the sentence by the chorus. Andy Palacio, a celebrated performer of the contemporary genre punta-rock, suggests that the call-and-response form encourages community participation, and that drumming characterizes *puntas* (Pillich 1992:6). A transcription of the accompaniment for a *punta* (figure 5) shows the *primero* playing a repetitive

FIGURE 5 The *primero* and *segunda* accompanimental patterns for a *punta* narrated by Andy Palacio in *Gimme Punta-Rock . . . Belizean Music* (1995). The *primero* plays a repetitive rhythmic motive in compound duple meter; the *segunda* plays an ostinato rhythm in duple meter. Transcription by Oliver Greene.

rhythmic motive (on which later improvisatory passages are based) in compound duple meter against an ostinato rhythm in duple meter performed on the *segunda*.

Additional secular dances

Hüngühüngü, a popular Garifuna dance in triple meter with unison singing, is frequently performed for holidays, processionals, and other festive occasions. Lyrics may vary from relating historical events, such as the departure from St. Vincent, to describing a deceased loved one. It is a secular version of *ugulendu*. Its step is a sort of shuffle, similar to a slide, in which the upper torso is held upright at times and bent slightly forward at others (Whipple 1971:109).

The genre called "combination" is a dance with alternating sections of the rhythms of *punta* and *hüngühüngü*. As the accompanying *garawoun* drums shift from the duple meter of *punta* to the triple meter of *hüngühüngü* and back again (as cued by the *primero*), dancers also shift to proper movements for the corresponding accompaniment.

In *gunjéi,* a graceful dance staged in a circle, partners switch at the call of the word *sarse* (Jenkins 1982c:4). The identifying duple-meter ostinato rhythm is played on the *segunda* and consists of an eighth and two sixteenths followed by four sixteenths. The *primero* presents improvisatory passages based on the ostinato rhythm of the *segunda*.

Chumba is an old dance performed by a soloist in a highly individualized manner. Each dancer in turn moves to the center to perform gestures that portray aspects of everyday life. S. Cayetano describes *chumba* as highly accented and probably related to the *chumba* found in the Caribbean, such as that of Grenada and Carriacou. The identifying rhythmic pattern played on the *segunda* is in duple meter and consists of a dotted eighth and a sixteenth, followed by two sixteenths. Improvisatory patterns are performed on the *primero*.

In the *senbei,* each performer salutes the drum and jumps into the dancers' circle, displaying fancy footwork. The identifying rhythmic pattern is played on the *segunda* in lively compound duple meter. It consists of three eighths, beginning on the second principal beat of the measure, followed by an accented dotted quarter on the first principal beat. Recent attempts to revive this genre have been successful.

Preservation of traditional Garifuna cultural practices

As subjects of anthropological, sociological, and musicological studies since the 1950s and recipients of Western cultural influences, the Garifuna of Belize, like those of Honduras and elsewhere, have become aware of the importance of preserving their traditional cultural practices. The Belize National Folklore Company, founded in 1996 as a division of the Belize National Dance Company of the Belize Arts Council, is devoted to preserving the traditional and indigenous dance and music of Belize. The Ugundani Dance Company is devoted solely to the preservation of traditional Garifuna dance and music.

Garifuna popular music: punta-rock

The most popular of the contemporary genres of dance-music in Belize, punta-rock, features the synthesis of electric instruments (as used in rhythm and blues and reg-

FIGURE 6 Using two mallets, a Garifuna man plays four tortoiseshell idiophones suspended around his neck; each shell, unique in size, produces a particular pitch when struck. National Garifuna Settlement Day celebration, Dangriga, Belize, 19 November 1994. Photo by Chris Mawuenah.

gae), traditional drums (*primero* and *segunda*), and rhythmic patterns of the *punta* dance. The creation of punta-rock in the late 1970s is attributed to Pen Cayetano, a musician and painter from Dangriga. His band, Pen Cayetano and the Turtles, is recognized as being the first to add electric guitars and percussion instruments such as turtle shells, sticks, cowbells, *shaka* (*shakshak* or rattles), and tambourines to the original rhythms of *punta,* as played on traditional drums. He fused traditional Garifuna rhythms with Rastafarian ideologies, occasionally incorporating tortoiseshell idiophones (figure 6). By 1980, the popularity of his band had spread from Dangriga to Belmopan, the capital, and to Belize City (Scott 1996c). Highly celebrated performers of punta-rock in 1997 include Mohobob Flores, Andy Palacio, and Chico Ramos. Its performing venues include nightclubs, football games, and blocked-off streets. Punta-rock band members are of creole, mestizo, and Garifuna ethnicity and come from throughout the country. This genre has transcended its initial ethnic focus to become the most popular form of national music.

The trio that today makes up the second generation of the Original Turtle Shell Band are blood relatives of Cayetano, practitioners of Rastafarianism, and part-time farmers. In their most recent recording, *Serewe* (1996), they use the sound of a conch trumpet, maintain call-and-response forms, refer to Garifuna spiritual ideals and culinary arts, and borrow rhythmic material from indigenous genres, such as *punta, paranda,* and *hüngühüngü* (Scott 1996c).

CREOLE MUSIC

I greatly acknowledge Gina Scott, an authority on the creole music of Belize, for her input for the following section.

Some creole songs are based on national and international issues (including those of the Caribbean), but most are about historical and domestic incidents, often embarrassments, whose publicity subjects their participants to the rhymed and sung gossip of the onlooking community. The transformation of domestic event into song is a universal cultural phenomenon, not limited to the Caribbean area (Beck 1980b:17).

A major appeal of creole music is responsorial structure. The traditional performances of creole songs require a minimum of two voices. One, the call, sings the first, third, and subsequent alternating lines, each of which varies the basic line in melody and words. The other, the response, sings an unvarying, one-line refrain. Some performances involve a group of singers, with a solo voice presenting the call and an audience giving the unison response. Call and response overlap (Beck 1980a:10–11). Traits of creole songs include a simple harmonic structure, a refrain, structures that may include ABA and three-part rondo forms, and melodies frequently in common time based on diatonic movement, arpeggios, and sequential figures.

Brukdown

The term *brukdown* denotes a kind of dance and song reflecting usual and unusual events in the life of the common Belizean, or a specific rhythmic organization. The instrumentation may be as simple as one guitar providing the harmony, with an ostinato pattern played by a broomstick pounded on the floor for rhythmic stability. At the other extreme, a brukdown ensemble may include guitars, banjos, accordions, a double-sided *gumbeh* or boom drum, and various percussive devices, including a horse's jawbone rasped with a metal rod.

Brukdown reflects African slaves' journey into the mahogany camps of Belize and the resulting culture of survival—the Belizean creole culture. It uses syncopated rhythms and responsorial patterns firmly rooted in Africa, diatonic harmonics bor-

The popular music style known in Creole as *cungo* ('let's go') emerged in the 1980s. It is a fusion of brukdown rhythms, guitar riffs influenced by rock, and lyrics reflecting Afrocentric philosophies.

rowed from Europe, and lyrical themes colored with the Belizean creole language and experience. Brukdown became the music of the people, whether rural or urban. The atmosphere that allowed its flourishing resulted from the demand for music at social functions such as children's parties, birthdays, and weddings. Its musical style flourished especially in the late 1800s, after the abolition of slavery, when ex-slaves were allowed more freely to engage in musical activities. Another reason for the evolution and survival of brukdown has been its nature, its flexibility of instrumentation, and its ability to address the issues affecting illiterate people with lyrics often full of double meanings, satire, and humor. The brukdown singer and composer was often a bearer of scandalous news, and his creole words were given credence, since most members of the population believed and still believe that *If Krufi seh da soh, if da no soh, da naily soh* 'If a creole person brings news, the story is almost accurate and valid, even if not totally so'. This role of the brukdown links it clearly with the Jamaican *mento* and the Trinidadian calypso.

As the urbanization and popularization of radios and jukeboxes heightened, brukdown became a music most often heard at Christmastime during parties (*bram, gato*). One of the most prominent personalities and practitioners of brukdown has been Wilfred Peters, Jr. In his mid-sixties in 1997, he carries on the musical family tradition and is considered the grandfather of brukdown music. He has taken brukdown music with his inimitable vocal style to major festivals throughout the Caribbean, the United States, and Mexico. He continues to perform traditional, anonymously composed songs he learned from his grandfather and father. His repertoire also reflects European influence. He does not stop there, however, but has created brukdown songs reflecting his experiences. He has retained the traditional brukdown strophic form: verse (the call) and hook chorus (the response). His songs have ensured the survival of some aspects of Creole.

Popular brukdown

Popular brukdown, like punta-rock, involves synthesized electronic instruments with those of the traditional brukdown ensemble (see Okada 1995: example 1). Electronic instruments include bass, guitar, keyboard, and frequently a drum machine. The content of the lyrics remains similar to that of the traditional form: political commentary, social satire, humor, and often party slang (terms and phrases that become popular in everyday Creole). In reality, the popular Belizean brukdown is most similar to the Trinidadian soca. The most prominent brukdown singer-composer from the 1960s through the 1980s was Lord Rhaburn (Gerald Rhaburn), whose popular band was known as the Lord Rhaburn Combo. Popular brukdown is played by local bands, which also play punta-rock, soca, and reggae.

Cungo

The popular musical style known in Creole as *cungo* 'let's go' emerged in the 1980s.

Its major advocate was Bredda David Obi. A student of Wilfred Peters, he developed a personal style by fusing brukdown rhythms, guitar riffs influenced by rock, and lyrics reflecting Afrocentric philosophies. The name of his band, Bredda David and Tribal Vibes, reflects the synesthesis of musical and philosophical ideals.

FURTHER STUDY

Ethnomusicological research on the Garifuna has been conducted by Emory Whipple (1971), Carol and Travis Jenkins (1982a, 1982b, 1982c), Kenan Foley (1995), and Gina Scott (1996a, 1996b, 1996c). Whipple's master's thesis (1971) describes the musical culture of the Garifuna and discusses percussion instruments, performance, secular song-and-dance forms, and semisacred songs. Carol and Travis Jenkins have made extensive recordings of secular and sacred music and have made cantometric analyses of the music, trying to identify Amerindian and African cultural traits. Foley's master's thesis (1995) contains some musical analyses and transcriptions of interviews with a shaman. Ervin Beck (1980a, 1980b) has extensively studied folk songs in Creole.

Much musical research is yet to be done in Belize. Garifuna research has been substantial, but nothing has been investigated about the music of the mestizos, the largest population in the country.

REFERENCES

Beck, Ervin. 1980a. "Call and Response in Belizean Creole Folk Songs." *Belizean Studies* 8(2):10–20.

———. 1980b. "Folk History in Creole Topical Songs." *Belizean Studies* 8(6):17–20.

Bilby, Kenneth. 1993. *The Spirit Cries: Music from the Rainforests of South America and the Caribbean.* Rykodisc RCD 10250. Compact disc.

Cayetano, E. Roy. 1977. "Garifuna Songs of Mourning." *Belizean Studies* 5(2):17–26.

———, ed. 1993. *The People's Garifuna Dictionary.* Dangriga, Belize: The National Garifuna Council.

Cayetano, Sebastian. 1989. "The Linguistic History of the Garifuna Peoples (Black Caribs) and Surrounding Areas in Central America and the Caribbean from 1220 AD to the Present." Manuscript.

———. N.d. [1990.] "Garifuna History, Language & Culture of Belize, Central America, & the Caribbean." Manuscript.

Gimme Punta-Rock . . . Belizean Music. 1995. Made and distributed by Andy Palacio. Video.

Foley, Kenan. 1995. "Garifuna Music Culture: An Introduction to Garifuna Music Practice with Emphasis on Abaimahani and Arumahani Songs." M.A. thesis, State University of New York at Binghamton.

Foster, Byron. 1982. "Spirit Possession in Southern Belize." *Belizean Studies* 10(2):18–24.

———. 1986. *Heart Drum: Spirit Possession in the Garifuna Communities of Belize.* Belize City: Benque Viejo del Carmen.

Hadel, Richard. 1973. "Carib Dance Music and Dance." *National Studies* 1:4–10.

Healy, Paul. 1988. "Music of the Maya." *Archaeology* 41(1):24–31.

Jenkins, Carol, and Travis Jenkins. 1982a. *Dabuyabarugu: Inside the Temple: Sacred Music of the Garifuna of Belize.* Smithsonian / Folkways FE-4032. LP disk.

———. 1982b. "Garifuna Musical Style and Culture History." *Belizean Studies* 10(3–4):17–24.

———. 1982c. *Traditional Music of the Garifuna (Black Carib) of Belize.* Smithsonian / Folkways FE-4031. LP disk.

Lawrence, Harold G. 1987. "Mandingo Voyages across the Atlantic." In *The African Presence in Early America*, ed. Ivan Van Sertima. New Brunswick, N.J.: Transaction Books.

Mallán, Chicki. 1993. *Belize Handbook.* Chico, Calif.: Moon Publications.

Okada, Yuki. 1995. *Central and South America.* JVC Smithsonian Folkways Video Anthology of Music and Dance of the Americas, 5. Montpelier, Vt.: Multicultural Media VTMV-229. Video.

Palacio, Andy, et al. 1988. *K'ekchi Harp, Florencio Mes & Co. and Top Star.* Sunrise SUN 006. Cassette.

Pillich, G. Simeon. 1992. *Chatuye: Heartbeat in the Music.* Arhoolie Productions CD–383.

Scott, Gina. 1996a. *Berry Wine Days.* Stonetree Records. LP disk.

——— 1996b. *Maya K'ekchi Strings.* Stonetree Records. LP disk.

——— 1996c. *Sewere.* Stonetree Records. LP disk.

Taylor, Douglas. 1951. "The Black Carib of British Honduras." *American Anthropologist* 17:2–167.

Ugundani Dance Company. 1994. Program notes from performance at Bliss Institute, Belize City, Belize.

Wells, Marilyn. 1980. "Circling with the Ancestors: Hugulendii [sic]: Symbolism in Ethnic Group Maintenance." *Belizean Studies* 8(6):1–9.

Whipple, Emory. 1971. "The Music of the Black Caribs of British Honduras." M.A. thesis, University of Texas at Austin.

———. 1976. "Pia Manadi." *Belizean Studies* 4(4):1–18.

Costa Rica
Carlos A. Fernández

The Archaeological Record
Historical and Ethnographic Records of Native Americans
Spanish, Criollo, and Mestizo Music
Education, Mass Media, and Organizations
Further Study

Most inhabitants of the Republic of Costa Rica are descendants of immigrants from Europe (mainly Spain) and from other early Spanish-American colonies. Most of these immigrants settled in the Costa Rican central plateau, which still holds more than half the national population. The Spanish settlers introduced slaves from Africa and frequently relocated native Americans, destroying their social structure and reducing their population. Intermixtures between European, African, and indigenous peoples occurred. Spanish cultural norms predominated during colonial times.

THE ARCHAEOLOGICAL RECORD

Archaeological evidence suggests the existence of two major cultural areas in Costa Rica during later pre-Columbian times. The northwestern Pacific coast was inhabited by the Chorotega, a Mangue-speaking group. To escape Olmec oppression, the Chorotega migrated from Soconusco, Mexico, to the Isthmus of Rivas about A.D. 800. Displaced by intrusions of the Nicarao, a Náhuatl-speaking group, at about A.D. 1200, they moved into the Nicoya Peninsula, where they were first contacted by Gil González Dávila in 1523 (Fowler 1989:35, 68–69).

Globular and tubular duct flutes, whistles, container idiophones (*sonajas*), and various struck idiophones and membranophones (minus their skins) have been found in archaeological sites of the northwestern Pacific coastal area. These instruments exhibit zoomorphic or anthropomorphic shapes. Most are made of clay, but log idiophones similar to Aztecan *teponaztli* and Mayan *tunkul* have also have been found. The globular flutes are of great variety in size, shape, and tuning. Examples with four holes are predominant. Their exterior forms occasionally exhibit abstractly painted or carved designs of Mexican influence—which may point to a dominant Nicarao presence in the area during the Late Polychrome Period (A.D. 1200–ca. 1520).

The rest of the country was inhabited predominantly by peoples of Macro-Chibchan affiliation as the archaeological record and linguistic similarities show (Ferrero 1977). These peoples are distinguished mainly by their patterns of settlement and by the geographic and ecological conditions in which they lived. In the central plateau, they included the Aserrí, the Currirabá, the Guarco, the Huetara, and the Pacaca chiefdoms; in the central Pacific and Tilarán range, they included the

Corobicí and the Garabito; in the northern Atlantic plains, they included the Voto (modern-day Maleku); on the Atlantic coast and in the Talamanca range, they included the Pococí, the Suerre, the Talamanca (modern-day Bribri and Cabécar), the Tariaca, and the Teribe; and in the south Pacific coastal area, they included the Burucac (modern-day Brunka), the Coto, and the Quepo (Guevara and Chacón 1992). The Chánguena and the Guaymí inhabited the region of Bocas del Toro (Panama) and later settled on the south Pacific coast. The names of these peoples often derived from the names of the places where they lived or the caciques that headed them.

Most of the pre-Columbian artifacts mentioned above are housed in the Museo Nacional de Costa Rica, Museo Arqueológico del Instituto Nacional de Seguros, Banco Central de Costa Rica, and private collections (Stone 1966).

HISTORICAL AND ETHNOGRAPHIC RECORDS OF NATIVE AMERICANS

The earliest written accounts of native American music in Costa Rica are from the observations of sixteenth-century travelers. Ferdinand Columbus, Christopher's son, documented such encounters with indigenous peoples along the Caribbean coast of Costa Rica and Panama in 1502, and noted the native use of *cuernos y tambores* 'horns and drums' (Oviedo y Valdés 1851–1855[4]:96–99). According to Columbus, the playing of these instruments accompanied a hostile display toward his expedition. Gonzalo Fernández de Oviedo y Valdés (official chronicler of the Indies from 1532 to 1537) documented Chorotega dances, ritual sacrifices, and festivities that he witnessed during 1529 in the Nicoya Peninsula. Communal song-dances (*mitote*) occurred on various occasions, including rites that involved human sacrifices and rites that celebrated the conclusion of the corn- or cacao-harvest seasons. As part of these events, large groups of people danced to the rhythm of drums while dressed in bird-feather costumes and colorful paint. A ceremony witnessed by Oviedo in the Gran Nicoya region and described in his chronicles appears to be the *volador,* a ceremony well known in Mexico and Guatemala.

Colonial documents prepared by religious and civil authorities reveal important information regarding processes of native American assimilation and resistance to Spanish rule. Beginning in the late sixteenth century, native Americans living in the central plateau were relocated into *reducciones,* settlements of converted populations that provided tribute and labor for Cartago, the colonial capital (Fonseca 1986:110–113). Many of these communities were organized into *cofradías,* sodalities that supported the Church in its activities and celebrations. Indigenous members were required to adorn streets, prepare altars, assist in carrying images of their religious patrons, and perform their own dances and music during processions (*Ordenanza de Creación de la Cofradía de la Inmaculada Concepción de Cartago* 1594). Enforcement of these duties was sometimes contested at the highest authority, as in 1638, when Cartago's parish priest demanded that the governor force all native Americans in the region to attend the Corpus Christi processions (Fernández 1881[1]:278). The governor forced nearby *reducciones*—Aserrí, Currirabá, Tobosi, and others—to attend the processions; however, populations living far from Cartago had governmental permission that exempted them from participating in these festivals.

During the 1600s and 1700s, missionaries converting populations outside the central plateau recorded aspects of musical culture of native populations. In the area of Talamanca, Fray Francisco de San José (1697, quoted in Fernández 1886[5]:369–374) and Manuel de Urcullu (1763, quoted in Fernández Guardia 1975:152–157) observed many native shamanic rituals and described healing practices, including the use of songs. They also reported the indigenous practice of funerary songs and the use of membranophones.

Nineteenth-century native American history and culture were documented by José María Figueroa (1873–1883), whose manuscripts contain descriptions and pictorial renditions of medicine, dance, and music in indigenous communities of the southern Pacific coast and Talamanca. The manuscripts contain the earliest transcriptions of music performed by native Costa Ricans, including that of a *chirimía* (a double-reed aerophone with six holes for fingering) melody "*La sangre de Cristo*" ('Christ's Blood'), performed by the Tobosi of Cartago. The music—diatonic, emphasizing tonic, mediant, and dominant—seems influenced by melodic patterns of Gregorian chant (Salazar 1992:160).

Maleku

The Maleku are a small, indigenous community of about 520 people. They are descendants of the Voto, who inhabited the Atlantic watershed in pre-Columbian times (Stone 1977:79, 161). These peoples moved into the northern savannas of Costa Rica to escape the Spanish *encomienda*, a policy by which the Crown granted Spanish settlers rights to exploit labor or receive tribute from specific indigenous populations. During the 1700s and 1800s, the Maleku resisted colonial and republican expeditions aimed at controlling their territories.

The Maleku inhabit three settlements (*palenques*)—Margarita, El Sol, Tonjibe—in a reservation created in 1976 near San Rafael de Guatuso, Alajuela Province. Despite legislation that assures them access to land and other resources, they are undergoing radical change in their customs, mainly because nonindigenous peoples have seized some of their lands, and they increasingly depend on wages from landowners surrounding the reservation (Guevara and Chacón 1992:99).

Music is an important part of Maleku daily life, religious and secular. In Maleku mythology, Tokú (creator of the earth and the sky) and Maika (receiver of the dead) sing and communicate with each other, deciding the fates of human beings. To call for godly protection against human wrongdoing or evil spirits, specialists sing or recite the prayers *poora* and *jalacomapacuaper* (Acevedo 1986b:52–53). Mythical narratives and religious songs and prayers are commonly transmitted orally from parent to child.

The Maleku practice a traditional burial ceremony (*fiesta de sufrimiento*), which occurs on the third day after an individual's death. Guests extend condolences to the family. As they approach, each plays a funerary melody on a five-holed side-blown cane flute (*karakukua*), specially constructed for the occasion by a family member of the deceased. By playing these flutes, the guests assure the family that the dead person's wrongdoings are being forgiven.

The Maleku call song *napurete*, and songs of love (*curijurijanapuretec*) are common (Acevedo 1986b:53). The text of each song is personal, but the songs usually follow traditional melodic patterns. Singing is often typified by imitative melodic contours and downward glissandi at phrase endings (figure 1). An individual may use the same melody in various contexts, changing the text to suit the situation. The songs are often accompanied by a palm-beaten membranophone (*tali*), which provides a steady accompanying rhythm. Traditionally, the instrument is made of Spanish cedar (*Cedrela alliodora*); however, deforestation has made the wood difficult to find, and it is being increasingly replaced by balsa (Salazar 1992:80–84). The instrument is cylindrical on the outside and shaped like a goblet on the inside. An iguana skin is fitted on one end.

Songs are performed for two Maleku traditional line dances, *napuratengeo* and *nakikonarájari,* in which men and women, usually elders, dance together (Acevedo 1986b:53–55). The music is performed responsorially by a lead singer and the dancers. In addition to *tali*, the Maleku use traditional maracas, a reed flute

FIGURE 1 Melody and percussion of a Maleku song of love (*curijurijanaporetec*), performed by a woman accompanying herself on a *tali* (*Maleku-Guatuso* n.d.:B11). Transcription by Carlos A. Fernández.

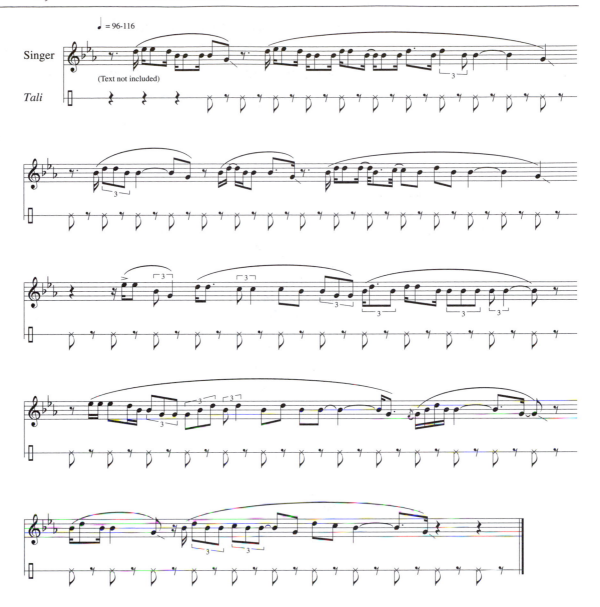

(*naususneusun*), and clay globular flutes and whistles. They also use nonindigenous instruments, including the European guitar and the *güiro*.

Every major event in the community is marked by a fiesta, an occasion for communally sharing foods, drinking corn beer (*chicha*), and performing music and dance. One such occasion occurs at the end of the hunt for turtles (*caza de la tortuga*), held during March, April, and May. An annual event, this hunt involves ritual purification, emphasizing aspects of reciprocity between humans and nature (Bozzoli 1986:19–29).

Through study within the national educational system, travel outside the reservation for work, and exposure to Costa Rican and Nicaraguan radio, many Maleku young people are losing their indigenous heritage. Because of their assimilation of non-Maleku culture and life-styles, they rarely perform their traditional dances, and many ignore the songs. Nevertheless, Maleku young people are adapting indigenous culture and using it in new ways. With traditional songs, instruments, and dances, they present collective dramatizations of Maleku myths and stories in the Malekuan language (Acevedo 1986b:55–56). Exogenous technologies also appear, as Radio Tonjibe, a Maleku-owned station, broadcasts these dramatizations to the community.

During a three-day marathon, the masked *diablos* parade through the village, stopping in homes to perform songs recited with words or vocables, narrating personal experiences.

Brunka and Teribe

The Brunka and Teribe inhabit the savannas of Buenos Aires and the Brunqueña range, both located in southeastern Puntarenas. Their population amounts to more than four thousand in three adjacent indigenous reservations—Boruca (Brunka), Rey Curré (Brunka), Térraba (Teribe)—incorporated by the Costa Rican legislature into the National Indian Reservation system in 1977. These reservations are experiencing some of the problems affecting other indigenous reservations in Costa Rica: displacement of indigenous populations through relocation, reduction of landholdings, invasions of land by nonindigenous farmers, and the use of local fields and forests by national and transnational corporations (Guevara and Chacón 1992:110).

During the early 1600s, Brunka, Coto, and Quepo peoples who inhabited the south Pacific coast were forcibly relocated to Boruca, a *reducción* (Stone 1949:3). Intermixtures occurred, and Brunka cultural patterns predominated. Around 1700, some Teribes were relocated from Talamanca to what would later become Térraba. Since then, the Teribe have assimilated to the cultural patterns of the Brunka. Few of them speak their native languages, despite the efforts of indigenous organizations to incorporate their languages and customs into local educational programs (Bozzoli 1986:60, 66).

Research on the music and dance of the Brunka and the Teribe has focused primarily on the present seasonal festivities, the *fiesta de los negritos* and the *fiesta de los diablitos* (Acevedo 1986b; Salazar 1980; Stone 1949). Both fiestas exhibit the choreological use of hobbymules and hobbybulls, a characteristic shared by other Spanish-derived festivals in Central America and Mexico.

The *fiesta de los negritos* 'fiesta of the little black men', occurring on 8 December, coincides with a celebration in honor of the Virgen de la Purísima Concepción de María Santísima, patron saint of Boruca. Preparations for the event begin on 6 December, when the village council selects the men who will represent the little black men (*negritos*), who formerly wore the skins of forest animals, with their faces painted in mud and soot or coal—a disguise said to accentuate their native identity. The performers still use coal. One dresses as the *sarocla* 'little mule'. The *negritos* go from house to house, dancing around the hobbymule, playing tricks on people, and begging drinks from everyone. They strike the little mule with sticks adorned with multicolored sashes (Salazar 1992:172). According to Brunka respondents, the event celebrates the military supremacy that the Brunka formerly exercised over the Teribe (Acevedo 1986b:73).

The *fiesta de los diablitos* 'fiesta of the little devils', conducted from 30 December to 2 January by little devils (*diablitos*), a society representing the Boruca community, dramatizes the fighting and sacrifice of a bull, said to represent the Spanish conquerors and settlers. Only men participate in its planning and performance, though women are involved in preparing rice tamales and corn beer (Salazar 1985:112). Non-Indians are allowed to participate as spectators. The *diablitos* are organized hier-

FIGURE 2   During the festival of *los diablitos* at Rey Curré Reservation, Puntarenas Province, a Brunka *pitero* (flutist) plays a *kiví* while a *cajero* (drummer) plays a *caja*. Photo by Rodrigo Salazar Salvatierra, 1984. Used with permission.

archically: major devils (*diablos mayores*) are responsible for the event and any problems that may arise; and minor devils (*diablos menores* and *diablas*, female devils, portrayed by men) participate in the event as a bull, herdsmen, sellers, butchers, and musicians (Acevedo 1986b:72–73). A chief major devil organizes the fiesta, coordinates duties, and collects the necessary food and money from the other devils and the rest of the community.

The *diablitos* are traditionally "born" at midnight, 30 December, on Cerro Volcán, residence of Cuasrán, a legendary shaman (*sukia*) who, according to local oral history, never surrendered to Spanish rule (Maroto 1979:77). The fiesta begins with the sounds of cattle horns and conchs. During a three-day marathon, the masked *diablos* parade through the village, stopping in homes to perform *salomas*, songs recited with words or vocables, narrating personal experiences. On the last day, the bull is symbolically sacrificed, cut up, and distributed among the listed buyers (Acevedo 1986b:72–73).

During these and other events, the Brunka and the Teribe play indigenous instruments—maraca, *caja*, *kiví*—and locally crafted nonindigenous instruments, including fiddles and guitars (Salazar 1992:171–175). The maraca, made from a dry calabash (*Crescentia cujete*), is often embossed with scenes depicting regional flora and fauna and abstract designs. Traditionally filled with *platanillo* (*Heliconia* sp.) seeds, the calabash is attached to a wooden handle with a rope. The *caja* is a membranophone made from a cylindrical piece of Spanish cedar, balsa, or *coyol*-palm trunk. Each end is covered with the hide of wild peccary or cattle, fastened with liana rings and laced with maguey cord. The performer strikes the hide with the palms of the hands, or with sticks. The *kiví*, a duct flute, is made of *carrizo* (*Chusquea* sp.), with a beeswax embouchure and five holes for fingering (figure 2). It is reported to have been used in ritual dances of the Brunka. Also known as *pito*, it is being replaced by metal duct flutes and European recorders made of plastic.

Brunka young people also play and dance nonindigenous music, mainly because of their exposure to radio programs and continuous contact with nearby urban centers, such as Buenos Aires de Osa. As early as 1949, the *cumbia*, the *punto chiricano*, and the *vals* were heard in the region. By the late 1970s, ensembles from neighboring towns and local musicians were engaged to play in corn-beer fiestas (*chichadas*), communal meetings (*juntas*), and festivities of *diablitos* and *negritos* in Boruca and Rey Curré. These ensembles performed *cumbias*, *pasodobles*, and other popular musics on nonindigenous instruments, including fiddles, guitars, and concertinas (Salazar 1985:118). By the early 1990s, ensembles were incorporating electric bass guitar and drums and using amplifiers for singers and instruments.

The fiddle was apparently introduced in the Teribe area by Franciscan priests during the colonial period (Salazar 1992:112). In the early 1990s, examples were constructed by local Teribe craftsmen, using wood of *guanacaste* (*Enterolobium cyclocarpum*), a gum extracted from a local palm, and metal guitar strings. The repertoire performed on this instrument is influenced by the community's exposure to national and regional radio programs.

A transcription of a performance of a *pasodoble* by a Teribe fiddler (figure 3) shows melodic contours that outline tonic and dominant triads, with frequent D pedals on an open string.

Guaymí

The Guaymí, originally from Chiriquí, Panama, settled in three main areas of the southeast Pacific coast: Guaymí, Abrojos, and Conte-Burica, all of which are protected as Indian reservations. A highly mobile community of more than twelve hundred,

FIGURE 3 A *pasodoble* performed by a Teribe fiddler has a triadically derived melody (*Guaymí-Térraba* n.d.:B9). Notes in parentheses are barely audible. Transcription by Carlos A. Fernández.

they were recognized as Costa Rican citizens in 1993. They strongly identify with their heritage and struggle to preserve their land, language, and traditions.

Sound is an important aspect of Guaymí medicine and religion. According to local caciques, maracas made of dried cocoa fruits have divinatory powers. Used with other items, these maracas allow healers to expel bad spirits that have taken hold of a patient's body (Salazar 1992:27–28).

The Guaymí practice *mamanchí*, a syncretic religion (also practiced in Panama) that combines Roman Catholicism with indigenous religious and musical elements. In a mixture of Guaymí and Spanish, *mamanchí* priests perform litany-like religious songs and conduct the responses of a women's choir (Bozzoli 1975: 111–112).

Like the Brunka and the Teribe, the Guaymí perform *salomas*. Other secular songs often allude to animals or other elements in the local environment and to aspects of social life and material culture. A transcription of a *canto a la maraca* 'song dedicated to a rattle' (figure 4) shows singing in a canonic manner, one man following the other. Such songs are often accompanied by a *tön*, an embossed, seed-containing calabash rattle having a short, spiked handle.

Two traditional dances still practiced by the Guaymí are a frog dance (*jehio*), usually performed by men, and the *bugutá*, performed by men and women. Both are danced outside at sunset, at night, and during a corn-beer fiesta, a celebration after collective work (Acevedo 1986b:64). In the frog dance, the performers begin in a single file and end in a circle; while crossing one leg behind the other, they march backward. The *bugutá* is danced in a single file, with each dancer holding onto the arms of the one in front. It involves various rapid steps forward, usually initiated by the lead dancer, heading the file. It is executed around a pole, near which the musicians are situated.

These dances are commonly sung and accompanied with *tön* or a *caja*, a short, double-headed, cylindrical membranophone of cedar or balsa, covered with the skin of a wild boar. Each drumhead is attached to the body by two rattan rings. One is tied to the skin. The other holds the head against the body. Both heads are tightened by a W-patterned lacing.

Guaymí dances are sometimes accompanied by *gnelé*, *dru mugata*, and *dru nörá* (Salazar 1992). The *gnelé* is a friction idiophone, a tortoiseshell covered with beeswax, played by softly rubbing the edge of the shell with the palm of the hand; it was formerly used to communicate across mountains. The *dru mugata* is a globular flute made of beeswax; it has two or three holes for fingering and is capable of producing tritonic or tetratonic scales. The *dru nörá* is a double-duct flute made of

FIGURE 4 Excerpt from a *canto a la maraca* 'song dedicated to a rattle', performed by two Guaymí men in a canonic manner, accompanying themselves by shaking calabash rattles (*tön*) (*Guaymí-Térraba* n.d.:A10). Transcription by Carlos A. Fernández.

continues

carrizo, with beeswax forming the instrument's fipples and securing the tubes, tuned a perfect fifth apart.

During the summer, the Guaymí practice *la balsería,* a week-long friendly competition between two communities. The host community provides food, corn beer, and music. Two all-male teams compete against each other, having as their objective the demonstration of strength and agility. One team, armed with balsa logs, tries to hit the other team, which is unarmed; as a strategy of defense, the unarmed team dances out of the way. Hundreds of players have participated.

Afro-Caribbean Music

Little research has been done on the music of people of African descent, the largest ethnic minority in Costa Rica. Nationally, they make up nearly 5 percent of the population. The presence of African peoples in Costa Rica dates back to the 1600s and 1700s, when Spanish settlers imported Bantu-speaking peoples and other Africans to

Amateur musicians performed on locally crafted instruments such as a coconut grater, a double-headed cylindrical wood drum with a tapir-skin membrane, a six-stringed bowed tube zither, a bamboo flute, and a horse-jaw idiophone.

work as slaves (Duncan and Meléndez 1974). These slaves labored in three main areas of colonial economic activity: cacao plantations around Matina, on the Caribbean; small farms in the central plateau, where various crops were harvested; and cattle-raising farms in the Nicoya Peninsula. Except for those who settled in the Matina area during the 1800s, blacks mixed with the European and Amerindian inhabitants and no longer constitute an identifiable ethnic group.

Little documentation about the musical life of these peoples exists; however, many blacks and mulattoes eventually settled in La Puebla de los Angeles, outside the colonial capital of Cartago, where the *cofradía de Nuestra Señora de los Angeles*, a Roman Catholic confraternity founded by mulattoes in 1652, organized annual festivals and religious services to honor its patron (Fernández Guardia 1921:265–287). These festivities involved processions with floats, stagings of comedies, and dances, including the *zarabanda,* a seventeenth-century Spanish dance in triple time. By 1722, criollos were also involved in the *cofradía.*

From the 1870s to the late 1920s, fleeing poverty and economic crises, tens of thousands of African-American English-speaking laborers from Jamaica and other Caribbean islands, Nicaragua, and Panama migrated to Costa Rica. They were attracted by the construction of the railroad between the central plateau and Limón and the United Fruit Company's plantations in the lowlands of Limón. Thousands left the area during the Great Depression of the 1930s, but many blacks remained and went on to become full-time farmers. After the civil war of 1949, many farmers acquired citizenship and were able to register land. From the mid-1950s through the 1960s, with the rise of cacao prices on the world market, these farmers emerged as comfortable landowners (Bourgois 1989:161–164). This period marked the beginning of the economic and cultural integration of the black population into the Costa Rican state.

Religious musical contexts and genres

Pocomía, a syncretic religion incorporating traditional African and Protestant beliefs and practices, existed in Limón around 1900. An important aspect of it was possession by spirits. The celebration of Pocomía included the use of altars and special ceremonial artifacts, drum-accompanied ritual dances in a circle, and the singing of hymns and other sacred songs and the reading of biblical passages (Duncan and Meléndez 1974:103–104).

Since the early 1900s, Protestant (Anglican, Baptist, Methodist) religious services have been important musical occasions among Jamaican immigrants. Hymns composed or arranged by Ira David Sankey (1840–1908) were popular. Concerts of religious music in which soloists, duets, and choirs participated were frequent. Today, Protestant churches attract many people to their services, especially during Holy Week. English hymns, such as those of the *Broadman Hymnal* (1940), continue to be sung by older people. Services include religious songs in Spanish.

Through the 1920s, the people of Limón and other communities on the Caribbean coast organized religious programs that included singing and reciting, in processions and in local churches and halls. Special activities on Easter Monday included games of darts, cricket, and baseball, plus the Maypole dance, which some churches of Limón are reviving. On those occasions, amateur musicians performed on locally crafted instruments such as a coconut grater, a double-headed cylindrical wood drum with a tapir-skin membrane, a six-stringed bowed tube zither, a bamboo flute, and a horse-jaw idiophone (Palmer 1986:56–58, 103). With special foods and dances, the people of Limón commemorated Slavery Day (1 August 1833, when the British government abolished slavery). In December, Harvest was a time to give thanks for a good harvest season and included praying and the singing of hymns. Christmas services were followed by caroling and parties in people's homes. Slavery Day is no longer celebrated, but some Baptist churches still observe Harvest.

Though local economic depression from the 1930s to the 1950s stifled the celebration of these events, local churches, parent-education boards, teachers, and the local offices of the Universal Negro Improvement Association (UNIA), founded in Jamaica by Marcus Garvey in 1919, played a vital role in sustaining the cultural life of the African-derived population. From the 1920s to the late 1940s, they organized concerts—including sacred concerts, rag concerts, and Pleasant Sunday Afternoons—to raise funds for hiring English teachers from abroad and supporting other scholastic and communal activities (Palmer 1986:202–204). Usually held on Saturdays and Sundays, these events were somewhat religious and included the performance of hymns and biblical plays, plus competitions in music. Children performed as soloists and in duets and choirs, and prizes went to the best singer and the best instrumentalist. Women played major roles organizing these events, giving lessons, playing the pedal organ, and directing plays. Today, privately funded English schools and teachers still promote English-speaking creole culture in Limón. Students learn nursery rhymes, rounds and other game-playing songs, hymns, and popular songs from the West Indies, Britain, and the United States. The local UNIA office sponsors bilingual education and the work of various art troops and youth groups.

Wakes continue to be social occasions in which adults and children recite prayers, sing hymns, play traditional Jamaican game-playing songs, and share foods, including *bami* (a baked bread prepared with grated cassava, oil, and salt) and *aid* (a lemonade prepared with brown sugar and ginger). One of the best known game-playing songs is "Go Down Emmanuel Road" (figure 5). People sit next to each other on the floor, forming a circle, each holding a large stone in the right hand. After singing the first two lines of the song, each participant places the stone in front of the person sitting to his or her right, releases the stone, picks up the stone released by the player to the left, then places it in front of the player to the right, and so on. These actions are coordinated with the rhythm of the song, which slowly increases in tempo until one of the players is unable to keep up with the rest.

Another traditional game played during wakes is *balimbo,* which usually involves boys and girls. In a yard outside, players stand in a circle with the leader—an adult called *balimbo*—in the center. The suitor waits outside the ring and then approaches it. The song consists of calls from the leader to the suitor and a joint response by the other participants:

Leader	*Other participants*
Boy, you come, you come.	Yes, *balimbo.*
What you come about?	Yes, *balimbo.*
You come to court a girl?	Yes, *balimbo.*
You have your cocoa farm?	Yes, *balimbo.*

FIGURE 5 Excerpt from "Go Down Emmanuel Road," a song traditionally performed during wakes in Limón, Limón Province. Performed by Ruby Nicholson and John Edwards, 1995. Transcription by Carlos A. Fernández.

You have your house and land?   Yes, *balimbo.*
Walk and view the ring.   Yes, *balimbo.*
Pick the girl you choose.   Yes, *balimbo.*
Girl, you love the boy?   Yes, *balimbo.*
Kiss and make me see.   Yes, *balimbo.*

The suitor is directed to enter the ring and choose a partner; however, the leader decides on the appropriateness of the suitor's choice. Many calls are standard and known to most respondents, but the leader has a great deal of latitude to improvise lines according to the personal traits of the suitor and his selected partner.

Secular musical contexts and genres

Afro-Caribbean immigrants brought to Costa Rica the square dance (*cuadrille*), a traditional dance of rural English origin practiced mainly by the Jamaican middle and upper classes. *Cuadrille* troupes commonly competed during the 1920s and 1930s, and the dance remained popular well into the 1950s. It is still performed in Limón, especially by folk-revival youth groups, with at least four couples and an ensemble usually containing a clarinet, a banjo, a guitar, and a trumpet (Salazar 1984:32–38). The repertoire includes more than fifty dances, each having up to five or six figures or movements, including *vals*, Colombian *pasillo*, Prince Albert, Caledonia, Lancers, and Basquet Cotillion.

During the 1930s, regional musicians became acquainted with country, swing, blues, and other music transmitted by U.S. radio stations. Phonograph records brought to Limón by American, British, and Dutch ships were played on Victrolas at local clubs. From travelers or by mail, self-taught musicians acquired musical scores and books on constructing and playing instruments (Palmer 1986:221–223). Dance-

FIGURE 6 Excerpt from "Monilia," a calypso by Walter "Mr. Gavitt" Ferguson (n.d.:A5), showing a guitar introduction, the vocal melody used in the refrain and the first stanza, and the characteristic guitar-strumming pattern and harmonies. Transcription by Carlos A. Fernández.

(continued)

oriented parties celebrated in Limón and Cahuita began to present local pop orches-tras that often included female musicians, though most members were men. Instrumentation included trumpet, saxophone, guitar, *bajo de caja* (a one-stringed chordophone, resembling a washtub bass), *tumbas* (congas), drums, and a vocalist; the repertoire included square dances, waltzes, swing, blues, fox-trots, and boleros.

Beginning in the 1950s and through the 1960s, calypsonians from Panama and Trinidad, including Lord Cobra, Mighty Sparrow, and Lord Kitchener, became pop-ular. Local clubs and radio stations sponsored competitions among aspiring calypso-nians, who accompanied themselves with guitar or tenor banjo, or with a vocal or percussion ensemble. Prizes were given to those demonstrating the greatest skill at textual and musical improvisation, a skill calypsonians call rhyming. Two well-known Costa Rican calypsonians are Edgar "Pitún" Hutchinson and Walter "Mr. Gavitt"

pasillo   Colombian and Ecuadorian folk music genre that is an adaptation of the Austrian waltz

bolero   Cuban-derived song genre for listening and dancing

guaracha   Cuban genre belonging to the *son* family

rumba   Cuban-derived couple dance

son   Cuban song tradition

FIGURE 6 (*continued*) Excerpt from "Monilia," a calypso by Walter "Mr. Gavitt" Ferguson (n.d.:A5), showing a guitar introduction, the vocal melody used in the refrain and the first stanza, and the characteristic guitar-strumming pattern and harmonies. Transcription by Carlos A. Fernández.

Ferguson (n.d.). As seen in figure 6, calypso provides a vehicle for allusions to an immigrant's history and daily life. This calypso relates the devastation that *Monilia roreri*, an airborne fungus, wreaked on the region's cacao plantations in the 1970s and 1980s. It provides a religious interpretation to the events and cautions audiences to seek repentance:

> I know a woman she name Irene.
> She had a mighty family.
> Monilia plague the gal until she walkin' lean.
> She had to sell out all she property.
>
> Ladies and gents come listen to me;
> I want you all to understand.
> Monilia is a power from a high degree,
> And then it comes to kill off every man.
>
> Who never read the Bible,
> I say they read it now contentedly.
> Get down on they knees and they start to pray;
> Beg their master for sympathy.

After each of these stanzas, the calypsonian sings a refrain:

> Monilia you've come to stay,
> And all you bring is hungry belly.
> You say you no going away,
> Till you bring me down to poverty.

Until the 1970s, local musical ensembles provided live music for boleros, *guarachas, pasillos,* rumbas, and swing. Some musicians played ready-made instruments, including guitar, trumpet, and clarinet. Others made their own, improvising materials for *tumbas* and *bajos de caja.* In the late twentieth century, many clubs began playing recorded music—a practice that decreased wage-earning opportunities for traditional ensembles. Surviving ensembles often included a lead singer, a banjo, a guitar, a *bajo de caja,* a *güiro,* maracas, a bongo, and occasionally a *tres* (six-stringed guitar, with double courses), and *tumbas.* Repertoires may include a wide variety of Afro-Caribbean genres such as bolero, calypso, *guaracha,* rumba, and *son.* Other ensembles, keeping up with younger local, national, and international audiences, have begun to incorporate electronic instruments and broaden their repertoires to include reggae, New York salsa, and North American soul and rock.

Carnaval de Limón is the major annual event of Limón Province. Celebrated during 12–14 October, it commemorates Columbus's landing in America (1492) and is an occasion for thousands of expatriates to return and reestablish social bonds. It was introduced to Limón after World War II by migrant workers who had experienced the Carnaval de Colón in Panama (Salazar 1984:29). Concerts and competitions between local calypsonians are among its outstanding activities. The Carnaval de Limón presents parades in which percussive ensembles and dancers (*comparsas*) compete against each other with elaborate floats, costumes, and the use of clever taunting songs. These ensembles usually include bongos, tom-toms, a bass drum, congas, and *timbaletas,* a pair of single-headed drums tuned a fourth apart and set side by side on a metal stand. The event brings musicians from Panama, Puerto Rico, and the United States and attracts tourists from the entire country and from abroad.

SPANISH, CRIOLLO, AND MESTIZO MUSIC

The first European settlers of Costa Rica were mainly immigrants from Spain (particularly from Andalucía, Extremadura, and New and Old Castile) and other New World Spanish colonies. After initial settlements in Bruselas (near the present-day Pacific port of Puntarenas) and Nicoya (on a peninsula north of Puntarenas), they established in the central plateau in the mid-1500s, founding the village of Garcimuñoz in 1561. In 1564, they moved east to the Guarco Valley, which had better lands and a larger native American population (wanted as labor), and founded Cartago, capital of the colonial province.

During the colonial period (1502–1821), much of the known musical activity of Cartago revolved around Roman Catholic religious services, official visits, and patronal celebrations (Campos 1984:21–42). Corpus Christi, the most important religious festival, often included performances of ethnic music and dance by Spaniards, Africans, and native Americans. The traditional veneration of the Virgen de los Angeles (Virgin of the Angels), practiced since 1635, included the Te Deum or a sung mass, vespers, and processions for which special singers and instrumentalists were engaged. During that era, *saraos,* evening parties with dancing and music, were a common form of entertainment.

By the 1700s, musical events included musical-theatrical representations and popular dances, such as the Andalucían fandango, a lively dance in triple time. European musical instruments—bass viol, bugle, drum, flageolet, guitar, violin—were available to the settlers. In 1785, an inventory of the church of Orosi, a settlement close to Cartago, includes, in addition to the instruments mentioned above, a marimba for use in religious services (Blanco 1974:249–250). By the early 1800s, musicians from Nicaragua and Guatemala were being engaged to perform and teach (Flores 1978:40).

During the 1800s, new institutions and expanded trade brought important changes in musical culture. By the time of national independence (1821), military bands had sprung up in several villages. In 1845, the Dirección Nacional de Bandas, a state agency in charge of providing musical training and securing musical instruments (woodwinds, brass, percussion) for military bands, was created (Flores 1978:71). This agency served as the first public institution for musical instruction in Costa Rica. By the 1880s, military bands performed weekly concerts at town plazas and during Holy Week processions; their repertoire included marches and selections from contemporary European operas.

Throughout the 1800s, woodwind and string instruments were commonly used in social gatherings and other events, such as wakes and processions (Figueroa 1873–1883). With the opening of London markets to coffee exports, local elites imported an increasing number of scores and musical instruments, including pianos and organs. An expanding interest in European art music was stimulated by the creation of the Teatro Nacional (built between 1890 and 1897), which provided a place for visiting European opera companies and artists to perform.

Aspects of musical life during the late 1800s are depicted in José María Figueroa's manuscripts (1873–1883), which include descriptions and drawings of religious services and other social occasions. Among the events Figueroa represents is a child's funeral (*velorio de un angelito*), in which a bass viol, three violins, and two flutes are played. Another drawing illustrates the procession following that funeral, during which musicians also performed.

Musical Instruments

Of the instruments introduced by the Spaniards during the colonial period, the six-stringed acoustic guitar remains the most popular and can be found throughout the country, including among African and indigenous populations. It is used as a solo instrument, to accompany voice, and in *tríos* (three-member ensembles usually performing on voices, guitars, and light percussion), mariachis, and other ensembles. Most manufacturers of guitars are located in the central plateau, mainly in San José, but artisans in rural areas make instruments for local clientele. Native woods commonly utilized are Spanish cedar (*Cedrela alliodora*), mahogany (*Switenia macrophyla*), laurel (*Cordia alliodora*), cristóbal (*Platymiscium pinnatum*), cocobolo or rosewood (*Dalbergia retusa*), and cenízaro (*Pithecelobium saman*); imported woods are also employed (Salazar 1992:128). Some manufacturers produce mandolins, lutes, *requintos* (small guitars, used as lead in *tríos*), and occasionally violins.

The *quijongo* (figure 7) is a musical bow with two gourd resonators. The bow is made of flexible woods, such as laurel and *guácimo ternera* (*Luehea speciosa*). A steel string is attached to either end of the bow; a small piece of wire divides the string into two sections and connects it to a gourd resonator set on the side of the bow opposite the string. Each section of the string produces a fundamental tone, usually tonic and dominant; other tones are produced by striking either section of the string with a wooden or metal rod in one hand while adjusting the opening of the gourd with the other hand. A larger gourd, often replaced by a wooden box or a tin can, is placed on the ground to serve as a resonator for the fundamental tones of the string. The player or an assistant places the lower tip of the bow in contact with the surface of the gourd (Salazar 1992: 119–123). In the hands of a skilled player, these techniques allow for the playing of a melody (harmonics) with a two-layered accompaniment (unresonated or resonated fundamental tones). In colonial Guanacaste, the *quijongo* was popularly used with a guitar or a marimba to accompany dances. Apparently introduced by Africans, it is played mostly by musicians of the Nicoya Peninsula, San Carlos, Matina, and some areas of the central plateau. Known in Honduras as *caramba*, the instrument is also found in El Salvador and Nicaragua with similar traits.

FIGURE 7   A man plays a Costa Rican musical bow (*quijongo*). Matambú, Guanacaste Province. Photo by Rodrigo Salazar Salvatierra, 1976. Used with permission.

The *marimba simple*, diatonic with thirty to forty-two wooden keys, was apparently introduced into Costa Rica from Guatemala by Franciscan missionaries during the late 1700s. During the 1800s, it became popular in the central plateau and Guanacaste, where it accompanied recreational events and dances celebrated in the streets (Pittier and Thiel 1974:306–307). It included gourd resonators with beeswax-attached spiderweb mirlitons; the keyboard's frame was supported by a rattan arc on which the player sat. In 1910, the chromatic marimba was introduced by Guatemalan musicians engaged to perform for communal festivities in Orotina, Puntarenas Province (Salazar 1988:32). Well-known manufacturers of marimbas conduct business in Guanacaste, Puntarenas, and San José. Marimba keys are usually made of *cristóbal* or *hormigón negro* (*Miroxylon balsamum*); resonators are made of *caobilla* (*Guarea* spp.), Spanish cedar, or cypress (*Cupressus lusitanica*). Ensembles with one or two chromatic marimbas, the latter known as *marimba en escuadra*, commonly perform at clubs, restaurants, and hotels.

Two kinds of accordions, known as *concertinas*, are commonly found in the country (Salazar 1992:195–196). One is diatonic and ordinarily of European make; introduced to Costa Rica during the mid-1800s, it is still used by Bribri, Cabécar, Brunka, and Térraba musicians and by people of African heritage in the Atlantic coastal region. The other, introduced during the early 1900s, is chromatic and comes in various sizes; alone or with the accompaniment of other instruments, it is commonly used during wakes, rosary-reciting meetings (*rezos*), baptisms, fairs, and other social events.

Musical genres

Spanish *romances* (ballads), *villancicos* (Christmas carols), *arrullos* (lullabies), and *rondas infantiles* (children's game-playing songs), recited and sung, are important oral traditions in many parts of the country, particularly in the towns and villages of the central plateau, the Nicoya Peninsula, and other areas settled by Spanish settlers and their descendants. The texts of some *romances* are sixteenth-century creations, Christian and Sephardic. Religious ballads include "*Los tres magos del oriente*," "*La calle de la amargura*," and "*Por qué no cantais, la Bella*"; novelistic ballads include "*Bernal Francés*," "*La esposa infiel*," and "*Las señas del marido*" (also known as "*La vuelta del marido*"), well known in the repertoire of Hispanic ballads. The texts often exhibit a great degree of fragmentation, but maintain clear similarities with their Spanish counterparts. Popular *villancicos* include "*Vamos con los magos*," "*Venid, pastorcillos*," and "*Pastores, venid; pastores, llegad*," Children's game-playing songs include "*Qué bonita la panadera*," "*Mañana domingo*," "*Mambrú*" (also known as "*Martín se fue a la guerra*"), "*Estaba una pastora*," and "*Mirón, mirón, mirón*."

Performed with or without guitar accompaniment, ballads are essentially monodic. Melodies are rhythmically simple and regular, and repeat after every four lines of text. They typically lack chromaticism and modulation. Though traditional children's game-playing songs and lullabies exhibit few melodic variations (perhaps a result of having been part of the repertoire of music education since the early 1940s), balladic melodies vary greatly from one version to the next (figure 8).

The genres *retahila* 'string' and *bomba* 'praise', related to the Spanish *copla*, have been popular in the region of Guanacaste but also occur in other areas. The poems of both have eight-syllable verses. The *retahila* (elsewhere known as *ensalada*) involves elaborate consonant or assonant rhymes (*abbccdde, aabbccdd, acbcdfef*) of variable length; it usually links incongruous images and themes to produce humorous effects. Men and women recite examples during parties and other recreational activities. The *bomba*, usually composed of octosyllabic quatrains rhyming *abcb*, is improvised by men, women, and children in various social settings, interjected within songs and

Several Spanish song-dances, among them the *danza*
(also known as *contradanza*) and the *jota,* are still
performed in many areas of Costa Rica.

FIGURE 8   Three
versions of the open-
ing quatrain of "*La
vuelta del marido*"
('The Husband's
Return'), a *romance*
performed in Costa
Rica and collected
by Michèle S. de
Cruz-Sáenz. After
Lathrop 1986:109.

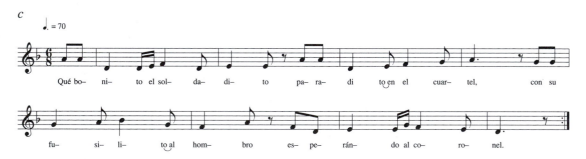

dances or as a part of verbal dueling. As seen in the following examples, collected in
Nicoya, Guancaste, *bombas* often deal with courtship and have humorous texts.

Quién te ve tan galancito,
tan lleno de sonrisas.
Sabe Dios cómo andarán
las faldas de tu camisa.

Las faldas de mi camisa
muy limpiecitas están.
A que vos no me enseñas
los remedos [sic] del fustán.

How deceptively gallant you look,
so full of smiles.
God only knows how
the flaps of your shirt are.

The flaps of my shirt
are extremely clean.
I bet that you don't show me
the patches on your petticoat.

The following *bombas* (after Hernández Viales 1964) are alternated between a man and a woman during the *punto guanacasteco*, a popular couple dance. They occur as the choreographed movements come to a complete halt; each is introduced with the exclamation *¡bomba!*

Morena de ojos quemantes,	Woman of burning eyes,
que al mirarme me adulás,	Who fawns on me with her gaze,
decime, pero cuanto antes,	Tell me, but in a hurry,
¿por qué diablos reculás?	Why the hell do you turn away?
Te quise en el puro invierno;	I loved you in midwinter;
también te quise en verano:	I also loved you in the summer:
sabanero liberiano,	Herdsman from Liberia,
ya soy soga de otro cuerno.	I've now lassoed another horn.
Todas las noches me paso	Every night I pass the time
como los toros, mugiendo;	Like the bulls, mooing;
y hasta me pongo a rascar	And I even scratch myself
pa ver si así te comprendo.	to see if I therefore understand you.

In the late twentieth century, *bombas* have touched on other subjects. "*En los buses de mi pueblo*" describes a bus ride the composer, Hugo Acuña Jiménez (1987), took on his way to work. This excerpt features the exclamation *¡bomba!* followed by a recited quatrain presented as reported speech:

En los buses de mi tierra	In the buses of my land
pasan cosas muy bonitas	Lovely things occur
cuando voy pa' mi trabajo	When I'm heading for work
siempre muy de mañanita.	Early in the morning.
El chofer muy apurado	The driver hastily
va cobrándole a la gente	Charges passengers their fee
mientras toman su café	While they drink their coffee
con arepa bien caliente.	With hot pancakes.
¡Bomba!	*Bomba!*
"¿Diay, qué? ¿Ya no hay caballeros,	"Hey, is it that now there are no gentlemen,
que nadie se va a parar?"	[and] that nobody is going to stand up?"
"Señora, caballeros habemos muchos;	"Lady, we are many gentlemen;
lo que no le quedó fue lugar."	What wasn't left for you was a seat."
¡Bomba!	*Bomba!*
"Y ese señor de sombrero,	"And that man wearing a hat!
que se corra para atrás.	Move on toward the back.
Y usted, por favor, la de vestido rojo,	And you, please, the one in a red dress!
no se me haga del rogar."	Don't make me beg."

Several Spanish song-dances, among them the *danza* (also known as *contradanza*) and the *jota*, are still performed in many areas of Costa Rica. Other regional song-dances, including the Venezuelan *vals criollo*, the Colombian *pasillo* and *bambuco*, and the Mexican *polca*, can also be found. Songs and instrumental pieces are newly composed in these forms, and published collections and recordings exist (Acevedo 1986a; Prado 1962; Rico 1982). Their texts often deal with love, depict local scenery, or make social commentary.

The *son suelto* (also known as *baile suelto*) and *tambito* are popular song-dances. The *son suelto* sometimes exhibits stamping (*zapateado*), a trait common to many traditional Spanish dances. Another song-dance is the *callejera* (or *parrandera*), but there is little agreement about its musical traits. Both names indicate the musical context: the first literally means 'of the street', and the second can be glossed 'reveler'.

Song-dances exhibit binary (AB) or ternary (ABA) formal structures with repeated or double periods. The tonality is often major; tonic, subdominant, and dominant triads (I, IV, V) prevail. When in minor tonalities (as many *danzas* are), these compositions modulate to the relative major from one double period to the other.

Rhythmic and melodic configurations that characterize these song-dances depend on the ensemble performing the music. They may be played by a *quijongo,* a solo singer with guitar, a *trío* (usually a *requinto* [small acoustic lead guitar], a guitar, and a singer, who often plays maracas), an accordion, a variety of marimba ensembles, or a *cimarrona* (a small, traditional ensemble of woodwinds, brass, and percussion).

An excerpt of a *son suelto* (figure 9) shows a texture typical of music for *marimba simple*. One marimbist plays the upper voices (transcribed in treble clef) with a mallet in each hand; the second marimbist plays the middle voices with two mallets in his right hand and one mallet in his left; the third marimbist plays the bass, doubled at the octave. The *son suelto* is performed in a fast compound duple meter with a melodic rhythm of three eighth notes and accompanying rhythms of dotted quarters in middle registers and quarter-note hemiolas in the bass.

The *tambito* is a song-dance whose creation is attributed to the Talolingas, an ensemble from Guanacaste. It has become popular among composers of *música típica* (Ramírez 1986:115), a local term for music of known authorship that utilizes traditional song-dance styles and forms. The guitarists usually provide vocal harmonies. Melodies are often harmonized in parallel thirds or sixths. The guitarists use various techniques of strumming (*rasgueado*): the first and fourth beats are played *apagado* 'stopped'; the second, third, and fifth are left to sound freely (figure 10). The transcribed finger-picking patterns and melodic ornamentation (*requinteo*) are also typical.

Contexts

Ballads and other traditional songs are usually performed at home among family or friends, and on special occasions, including *novenas* (wakes), *veladas escolares* 'public performances at schools', and patronal fiestas. According to Betancourt, Bonamore, and Cohen (1992:12–13), who studied the balladic tradition in Heredia Province, rosary-reciting meetings for Christmas and Holy Week often include the performance of *villancicos* and *romances*, recited or sung, interspersed among devotional prayers and songs of praise (*alabados*).

Birthdays, baptisms, debutante parties (*quinceaños*), weddings, anniversaries, and other small social gatherings are among the occasions when Costa Ricans enjoy singing and listening to music. In urban and rural settings, professional or amateur *tríos* are an important source of music for these occasions. *Serenatas* by *tríos,* considered an essential part of courtship, are often used to amend stressed relationships, to ask parents for their daughter's hand in marriage, and to celebrate a wedding. In urban areas, the music provided by these ensembles may include traditional and popular music, but boleros, particularly those popularized by Trío Los Panchos and Trío Alma de América, are the preferred expressive form. Middle and upper-class *quinceaños* and weddings may feature special parties with dancing to live music or recordings.

Through the 1960s, responsorial singing and the playing of organs remained the

FIGURE 9 Excerpt from "*Mamachilinda*," a *son suelto,* composed and performed by the trio Marimba la Tica (1980:A2), and recorded in San José during the 1978 Somos Como Somos festival. Transcription by Carlos A. Fernández.

continues

primary sources of music for Roman Catholic services. Since the ecumenical council known as Vatican II and amid the growing secularization of Costa Rican society, some urban churches have begun to feature liturgical music played by ensembles that include acoustic (and even electric) guitars and basses, drums, and electronic keyboards. Young people's religious music groups are often encouraged to perform modern religious songs, many of them popular songs (*latino* ballads and rock) with a religious text replacing the original.

Weekly performances by local municipal bands (military bands were eliminated with the 1949 abolition of the Costa Rican army) are common. Such events, known as *retretas* (evening open-air concerts) and *recreos* (Sunday-morning concerts after Mass) usually take place in the municipal plaza or park and include a variety of music, including marches, overtures, and *pasodobles* from Spanish zarzuelas. These

FIGURE 10 Excerpt from "*Homenaje a Guanacaste* ('Homage to Guanacaste'), a *tambito* by Antonio Cedeño Morales, accompanied by a *requinto*, a guitar, and an electric bass (Trío los Juanes 1984:A4). Notice the melodic ornamentation on the *requinto* and the characteristic strumming by the guitarist, who sings the lower vocal part. Transcription by Carlos A. Fernández.

(*continued*)

events provide an opportunity for courtship, other social interaction, and entertainment (Flores 1978:71). Though they are becoming less popular because other forms of recreation are available, municipal bands still perform in parades, religious processions, and official activities.

Fairs and festivals, religious or secular, are important social activities for which entire communities convene. Holding fairs (*turnos*) remains the most effective way to raise money for churches, nursing homes, schools, and other causes. Small-scale weekend events, fairs usually feature live music, raffles and other games, traditional foods, and fireworks.

FIGURE 10 (*continued*) Excerpt from "*Homenaje a Guanacaste* ('Homage to Guanacaste'), a *tambito* by Antonio Cedeño Morales, accompanied by a *requinto*, a guitar, and an electric bass (Trío los Juanes 1984:A4). Notice the melodic ornamentation on the *requinto* and the characteristic strumming by the guitarist, who sings the lower vocal part. Transcription by Carlos A. Fernández.

ción, e- res al- ma de Cos- ta Ri- ca des- de el día de la A-nex- ión. El vein-

ti- cin- co de ju- lio de mil no- ve- cien- tos vein- ti- cua- tro fué la fir- ma más su-

bli- me y en A- mé- ri-ca un im- pac- to.

continues

More than any other activity, annual patronal fiestas, held since early colonial times, evoke communal spirit and devotional fervor. They usually include horse shows and parades in which masqueraders (*payasos*)—men and sometimes adolescents—wear costumes that personify traditional characters, including *el copetón* 'the giant', *la copetona* 'the giantess', *el diablo* 'the devil', and *la muerte* 'death'. Music for these occasions is often provided by a *cimarrona* (figure 11), an ensemble whose instrumentation minimally consists of a trumpet, a tenor saxophone or clarinet, a trombone or baritone saxophone, a bass drum and cymbals (the latter two played by a single musician). Frequently composed of instrumentalists trained in local schools or municipal bands, a *cimarrona* is usually engaged to perform for a fee. The *cimarrona* repertoire usually includes traditional melodies, pop songs, and marches.

FIGURE 11   During the Saint Peter's Day parade at San Pedro de Poás, Alajuela Province, the *cimarrona* La Poaseña and masqueraders (*payasos*) perform. Photo by Eric Carballo, 1992. Used with permission.

Entertainment among the middle and upper classes of the central plateau includes attending seasonal concerts by the National Symphony Orchestra (established in 1926) and the National Symphony Choir, recitals and concerts by chamber ensembles, and performances by local and visiting foreign musicians. These concerts usually present music of the standard international repertoire, but often feature compositions by contemporary Costa Rican composers. In places such as the Teatro Nacional and the Teatro Melico Salazar, opera, symphony, dance, and Latin American music are regularly presented.

EDUCATION, MASS MEDIA, AND ORGANIZATIONS

Institutionalized schooling and mass media have had an important impact on traditional forms of learning and are increasingly shaping the population's musical aesthetic. Musical education is obligatory at the primary- and secondary-school levels; teachers focus on preparing the school band or choir for scholastic activities and official holidays, such as Independence Day (15 September). Educators teach patriotic and traditional songs designed to instill patriotism, moral values, and acceptable attitudes. They have compiled several songbooks for this purpose (Cruz-Sáenz 1986:xxi–xxiii). Their repertoire includes Costa Rican and other Latin American songs. Secondary-school choirs frequently participate in festivals and competitions. They memorize the choral parts and usually perform with instrumental accompaniment.

The Conservatorio Castella, an institution approved by the Ministry of Education, has instituted an eleven-year plan that combines primary- and secondary-school studies with an intensive program in folk and popular music, dance, and drama. Musicians are trained in the Youth Program of the National Symphony Orchestra, founded in 1970 by the administration of José Figueres (Sáenz 1982). Public and private universities offer degrees in musical performance, conducting, composition, musicology, and education. Teachers and students perform in local orchestras, chamber ensembles, choral groups, and popular-music ensembles.

Especially in rural areas and for lower-class people (who have less access to newspapers, books, film, television, or other media), radio is the primary source of information and entertainment. Commercial stations broadcast popular music, soap operas, sports, and news; many specialize in specific genres, including *rancheras* (Mexican *corridos, polcas, valses,* and so on), Caribbean genres, ballads, rock, classical music, and jazz.

Costa Rican television programming relies heavily on imports from Argentina, Mexico, Venezuela, and the United States (Beisanz et al. 1982:166). Local television and cable stations air performances by national and international pop and classical musicians, and feature bands and orchestras on locally produced family-oriented programs. Some transmit videos of pop music from Mexico, Spain, and the United States. The Sistema Nacional de Radio y Televisión Cultural, a national radio-television system, broadcasts folk, popular, and classical music. Throughout the country, it has recorded many folk-based ensembles and popular artists, and it annually sponsors the festival Somos Como Somos.

Music for advertising and consumers is produced by private recording studios, which provide facilities for local musicians to make soundtracks for documentaries, films, "jingles," and records. The studio INDICA (in 1988 acquired by Sony Corporation) produces, records, and publishes music for the Central American market, distributes records and tapes to local radio stations and retailers, and promotes local and visiting label artists.

Despite the effects of mass media on Costa Rican musical culture, many artists have revived popular interest in folk-oriented music and dance through their research and performance. The folklorist Emilia Prieto (1978) has compiled and recorded many traditional songs of the central plateau. Other groups (including Ballet Folclórico Nacional, Cantares, Chubuzú, Curime, and Nacaome) and individual artists (including Guadalupe Urbina and Juan Carlos Ureña) have attained national and international recognition. Much of this success has been achieved through the patronage of state and municipal agencies. Grass-root organizations are promoting traditional arts and music. One of these, the Asociación Aires Costarricenses, furthers research and performance of folk-oriented music and dance of the central plateau. Another, the Asociación de Grupos e Intérpretes de la Cultura Popular, promotes traditional artists and sponsors music events and festivals.

FURTHER STUDY

Of native Americans in Costa Rica, only the music of the Bribri and Cabécar of Talamanca has been studied in detail [see BRIBRI AND CABÉCAR]. Jorge L. Acevedo (1986b) provides a general introduction to many aspects of the musical culture of contemporary indigenous populations. Rodrigo Salazar (1992) contributes a needed organological study with important information regarding musical contexts and instrumental use. Further research is necessary in native musical style and performance, oral composition, musical terminology, aesthetics, and indigenous systems of classifying genres and instruments. Linguistic and oral-poetic analyses of indigenous singing are also lacking.

Quince Duncan and Carlos Meléndez (1974) provide an overview of African history and culture in Costa Rica, including aspects of music and religion. A study by Rodrigo Salazar (1984) discusses the recent history of popular Afro-Caribbean music of Limón. Paula Palmer's study of the coastal communities south of Limón (1986) contributes valuable information about the social and musical life of peoples of the country through the 1970s. More research on Afro–Costa Rican musical composition and poetics, performance, and aesthetics is desirable. Studies of contemporary social contexts of musical performance, particularly life-cycle events, Protestant religious services, and yearly celebrations (such as carnival) are lacking. Research might explore the processes of cultural change in the country since the 1950s, particularly

Despite the effects of mass media on Costa Rican musical culture, many artists have revived popular interest in folk-oriented music and dance through their research and performance.

the effects of non-African settlement and state policies of social and economic integration.

Information about the musical life of Spanish, criollo, and mestizo populations of the colonial and post-independence periods is scattered in historical documents, which rarely deal with the topic specifically. Valuable sources can be found in the works of León Fernández (1881–1907, 1975), Ricardo Fernández Guardia (1921, 1975), and Fernández Guardia and others (1929). Ricardo Blanco (1974) discusses the history of the Roman Catholic Church in Costa Rica and has documented aspects of colonial musical life. A good source for the history of art music, including that of bands and opera, is Bernal Flores (1978). Discussion of cultural policies affecting art and popular music since the 1970s can be found in Guido Sáenz (1982).

Research on Spanish, criollo, and mestizo oral traditions has aimed at publishing textual collections for use in the educational system. Early studies include those by Emma Gamboa (1941), René Aníbal (1944), Julio Fonseca (1950), and Evangelina de Núñez (1956). María Eugenia Monge's *El romancero en Costa Rica* (1946) is the first philological study of traditional Spanish balladry in Costa Rica. Later studies include those by Michèle S. de Cruz-Sáenz (1986), Helia Betancourt (1986) and Betancourt, Alessandra Bonamore, and Henry Cohen (1992), which include textual and musical transcriptions and contextual information. Aspects of Costa Rican religious practice and genres, including prayer and song, can be found in Carlos M. Campos (1984). Acevedo (1986a) provides a general overview of the music of Guanacaste, including aspects of pre-Columbian and colonial culture, instruments, religious sodalities (*cofradías*) and patronal fiestas, and traditional music and dance. Further research is needed on the social history of these traditions, their musical and poetic traits, and their performance. Studies exploring the effects of public education and mass media are also necessary. More work is needed on popular music and the music of other long-standing immigrant communities, such as Jews and Chinese.

REFERENCES

Acevedo, Jorge L. 1986a [1980]. *La música en Guanacaste,* 2nd ed. San José: Editorial Universidad de Costa Rica.

———. 1986b. *La música en las reservas indígenas de Costa Rica.* San José: Editorial Universidad de Costa Rica.

Acuña, Hugo. 1987. *Soy maicero.* Producciones Cabal. Sonimax Colección Emilia Prieto, 1. Audiotape.

Aníbal, René. 1944. *Recados criollos: Folklore costarricense.* San José: Editorial Tecolotl.

Beisanz, Richard, Karen Z. Beisanz, and Mavis H.

Beisanz. 1982. *The Costa Ricans.* Englewood Cliffs, N.J.: Prentice-Hall.

Betancourt, Helia. 1986. *La pájara pinta: Antología de la lírica popular infantil de Costa Rica.* San José: Instituto del Libro.

Betancourt, Helia, Alessandra Bonamore, and Henry Cohen. 1992. *Cancionero y romancero tradicional de Heredia.* San José: Fundación Educativa San Judas Tadeo.

Blanco, Ricardo. 1974. *Historia Eclesiástica de Costa Rica: 1502–1850.* San José: Editorial Costa Rica.

Bourgois, Philippe. 1989. "Blacks in Costa Rica: Upward Mobility and Ethnic Discrimination." In *The Costa Rica Reader,* ed. Marc Edelman and Joanne Kenen, 161–169. New York: Grove Weindenfeld.

Bozzoli, María E. 1975. *Localidades indígenas costarricenses,* 2nd ed. San José: Editorial Universitaria Centroamericana.

———. 1986. *El indígena costarricense y su ambiente natural.* Editorial San José: Editorial Porvenir.

The Broadman Hymnal. 1940. Nashville: Broadman Press.

Campos, Carlos M. 1984. "Devociones populares: Introducción a su estudio en Costa Rica." *Senderos* 21–22:1–236.

Cruz-Sáenz, Michèle S. de. 1986. *Romancero tradicional de Costa Rica.* Hispanic Monographs, series Ediciones Críticas, 3. Newark, N.J.: Juan de la Cuesta.

Duncan, Quince, and Carlos Meléndez. 1974. *El Negro en Costa Rica.* San José: Editorial Costa Rica.

Ferguson, Walter. N.d. *Calypsos of Costa Rica.* Folkways Records FTS 31309. LP disk.

Fernández, León, ed. 1881–1907. *Colección de documentos para la historia de Costa Rica.* 10 vols. Barcelona: Imprenta Viuda de Luís Tasso.

———. 1975. *Historia de Costa Rica durante la dominación española (1502–1821).* San José: Editorial Costa Rica.

Fernández Guardia, Ricardo. 1921. *Crónicas coloniales.* San José: Imprenta Trejos Hermanos.

———. 1975. [1913]. *El Descubrimiento y la Conquista,* 5th ed. San José: Editorial Costa Rica.

Fernández Guardia, Ricardo, et al. 1929. *Costa Rica en el siglo XIX.* San José: Editorial Gutenberg.

Ferrero, Luis. 1977. *Costa Rica precolombina,* 2nd ed. San José: Editorial Costa Rica.

Figueroa, José María. 1873–1883. *Album de Figueroa.* San José: Sala España de la Biblioteca Nacional.

Flores, Bernal. 1978. *La música en Costa Rica.* San José: Editorial Costa Rica.

Fonseca, Elizabeth. 1986. *Costa Rica colonial: La tierra y el hombre.* San José: Editorial Universitaria Centroamericana.

Fonseca, Julio. 1950. "Referencia sobre música costarricense." *Revista de estudios musicales* 1:75–97.

Fowler, William, Jr. 1989. *The Cultural Evolution of Ancient Nahua Civilizations: The Pipil-Nicarao of Central America.* Norman: University of Oklahoma Press.

Gamboa, Emma. 1941. *Canciones populares para niños.* San José: Editorial Antonio Lehmann.

Guaymí-Térraba. N.d. Antología de Música Indígena Costarricense. Asociación Indígena de Costa Rica, Pablo Presbere. Onda Nueva. LP disk.

Guevara, Marcos, and Ruben Chacón. 1992. *Territorios indios en Costa Rica: Orígenes, situación actual y perspectivas.* San José: García Hermanos.

Lathrop, Thomas A., ed. 1986. *Romancero Tradicional de Costa Rica.* Newark, N.J.: Juan de la Cuesta.

Maleku-Guatuso. N.d. Antología de Música Indígena Costarricense. Asociación Indígena de Costa Rica, Pablo Presbere. Onda Nueva. LP disk.

Marimba La Tica. 1980. *Somos Como Somos: Primer Festival Folclórico Costarricense.* San José: Sistema Nacional de Radio y Televisión INDICA PP-458. LP disk.

Maroto, Espíritu Santo, et al. 1979. *Leyendas y tradiciones borucas,* ed. and trans. Adolfo Constenla Umaña. San José: Editorial Universidad de Costa Rica.

Monge, María Eugenia. 1946. *El romancero en Costa Rica.* Licentiate thesis, University of Costa Rica.

Núñez, Evangelina de. 1956. *Costa Rica y su folklore.* San José: Imprenta Nacional.

Ordenanza de Creación de la Cofradía de la Inmaculada Concepción de Cartago. 1594. San José: Curia Metropolitana.

Oviedo y Valdés, Gonzalo Fernández de. 1851–1855. *Historia general y natural de las Indias, islas y tierra-firme del mar océano.* 4 vols. Madrid: Real Academia de Historia.

Palmer, Paula. 1986. *"Wa'apin man": La historia de la Costa Talamanqueña de Costa Rica, según sus protagonistas.* San José: Instituto del Libro.

Pittier, Henri, and Bernardo Thiel. 1974. *Viajeros por Guanacaste.* San José: Ministerio de Cultura, Juventud y Deportes.

Prado, Alcides, ed. 1962. *Costa Rica:Su música típica y sus autores.* San José: Editorial Antonio Lehmann.

Prieto, Emilia. 1978. *Romanzas tico meseteñas.* San José: Ministerio de Cultura, Juventud y Deportes. Serie del Folclor, 2.

Ramírez, José. 1986. *Folclor costarricense.* San José: Jiménez y Tanzi.

Rico, Jaime, ed. 1982. *Las canciones más bellas de Costa Rica.* San José: Academia de Guitarra Latinoamericana.

Sáenz, Guido. 1982. *Para qué tractores sin violines: La revolución musical en Costa Rica.* San José: Editorial Costa Rica.

Salazar, Rodrigo. 1984. *La música popular afro-costarricense.* San José: Organización de Estados Americanos y Ministerio de Cultura, Juventud y Deportes.

———. 1988. *La marimba: Empleo, diseño y construcción.* San José: Editorial Universidad de Costa Rica.

———. 1992. *Los instrumentos de la música folclórica costarricense.* Cartago: Editorial Instituto Technológico de Costa Rica.

Stone, Doris Z. 1949. *The Boruca of Costa Rica.* Cambridge: Peabody Museum, Harvard University. Peabody Museum of American Archaeology and Ethnology, papers, 26 (2).

———. 1966. *Introduction to the Archaeology of Costa Rica.* San José: Museo Nacional.

———. 1977. *Pre-Columbian Man in Costa Rica.* Cambridge, Mass.: Peabody Museum.

Trío los Juanes. 1984. *Mis Campesinos.* Vol. 2. Onda Nueva. LP disk.

El Salvador
Salvador Marroquín

Archaeological Background
Musical Instruments of Spanish and African Inspiration
Musical Contexts and Genres
Music for Entertainment
Social Structure, Musicians, and Behavior
Dynamics of Musical Culture
Further Study

El Salvador, with an area of 21,200 square kilometers featuring mostly rugged topography caused by volcanic and tectonic activity, is the smallest country in the mainland Americas. It has a high population for its size: more than 5 million predominantly rural people. Its largest population density is found in its principal city and capital, San Salvador, located in the Valle de las Hamacas (Valley of the Hammocks), at the foot of the San Salvador volcano. The political and administrative organization of the country includes fourteen departments in four zones: eastern, central, subcentral, and western.

Salvadorans are basically mestizos, though in some places traces of Negroid features are visible. Almost complete racial almagamation between Africans and others occurred during the colonial period, and El Salvador's Amerindian population is totally assimilated (Herring 1968:483).

ARCHAEOLOGICAL BACKGROUND

Archaeological findings from the other countries of Mesoamerica suggest that the first musical instruments in El Salvador were used about twelve thousand years ago. In the Pre-Ceramic Period (from an unknown start to 1200 B.C.), hunter-gatherers are believed to have used stone and bone rasps, turtleshell idiophones, and strings of shells as percussion instruments. Among the aerophones were flutes and a whirled plaque (*palo zumbador* 'bull roarer'). Rasped turtleshells (forerunners of the *güiro*) also appeared. During this period, hunter-gatherers lived within permanent or semipermanent communities that had multiple levels of social status, such as those corresponding to shamanism and other specializations (Castellanos 1970:44).

Throughout Mesoamerica, crops such as corn, squash, and beans had long been raised domestically, and around 1600 B.C. the first agricultural communities appeared. The characteristic feature of this period was that sound-producing materials found in the natural environment were incorporated into ritual and life-cycle practices. The use of naturally hollowed trees from the jungle and humanly hollowed trunks as percussion instruments dates to this period, and the proto-*teponaztli* 'hollowed log idiophone' possibly originated from them. Shamans of this period probably used concussion sticks to scare away evil spirits. The early *tambor simple,* a single-deerskin log drum similar to the Mexican *huéhuetl,* also dates to this period. Among the aerophones of this period were flutes with holes for fingering and the conch trumpet.

The Pre-Classic Period (1200 B.C. to A.D. 250) marked the change to a new means of subsistence; in what is now El Salvador, groups of nomads tended to settle where the surroundings were favorable. The first inhabitants probably settled in the coastal plain because they could enrich their diet with animals and wild fruit from the mountains and marine resources from the coast (Casanova de Párraga 1969:6). The great discovery of this period was the manufacture of ceramic or fired-clay objects—a discovery that led to the experimentation of new sounds from newly created ceramic musical instruments, such as rattles, scrapers, and strings of clay beads. In many cases, these were copies of earlier models of instruments made from other materials. Single-membrane kettledrums in the form of a pot or a vessel with a rounded bottom and later double-membrane drums separated by a partition were made in several sizes. With the use of fired clay, a disproportionate number of aerophones flourished, including ductless edge flutes with U-shaped notched mouthpieces, similar to the Andean *kena;* straight or globular double flutes with a single air channel or two independent ones; globular flutes (ocarinas) with one, two, or three interconnected resonance chambers; single and double whistles; and whistling pots (Castellanos 1970:45).

The characteristic musical feature of the Classic Period (A.D. 250–900) was the organological fusion of aesthetic and empirical concerns, a fusion manifested in an amazing variety and assortment of sound-producing artifacts remade from known materials. These instruments were "improvements" on instruments based on previously known acoustical properties. During this period, one struck idiophone appeared: the *cántaro,* a large jug tuned with water and used musically for low-pitched accompaniment (Contreras Arias 1988:68). Among the aerophones were a great quantity and variety of clay flutes with up to six holes for fingering; straight, piston-type flutes with a rolling ball inside them (their existence suggests that microtones were known in that period); and wooden trumpets about 1.5 meters long. Depictions of these trumpets, which had distal ends shaped like bells, were engraved on an ancient pot that was found in El Salvador and is now in a private collection; on this vessel, performers can be seen resting their trumpets on the ground in about a sixty-degree angle.

Around A.D. 800, just before the beginning of the Post-Classic Period (A.D. 900–1524), the Nahua had learned metallurgy from the peoples who then lived in the areas corresponding to the present-day countries of Peru and Colombia. According to the Spanish chronicler Cieza de León, during this period pre-Columbian bells made of gold were sounded during religious rites, including human sacrifices (Contreras Arias 1988:68–69); they were part of a way of life that had a socially established theocratic structure.

MUSICAL INSTRUMENTS OF SPANISH AND AFRICAN INSPIRATION

Salvadoran culture blends three heritages: the native American (from Mesoamerican ethnic groups whose influences have come down to us through traditional practices), the European (Spanish), and the African (from West African slaves). These broad cultural strands have become syncretically interwoven. The Spanish used musical instruments in military deployments and during times of rest. Many artifacts used in dances by Spanish soldiers—such as clubs, machetes, and swords—functioned as idiophones. Little by little, indigenous peoples incorporated them into their own dances, though the indigenous idiophones of Mesoamerica were so numerous that those contributed by the Spaniards were inconsequential by comparison.

Of the membranophones brought by the soldiers, the *atabales* or *timbales* 'kettle-drums', and *trompetas* 'trumpets', *cornetas* 'bugles' were used along with *sacabuches* 'sackbuts' (forerunners of the trombone) in military maneuvers, battles, and civic and religious ceremonies, where they added splendor. The *timbales* were replaced by two-headed membranophones (*tambores*), still observable in present-day town bands. The European military *tambor* had two rims, between which a W-shaped system of lashing tightened the heads, one with a rustic snare stretched across it. The drum now used in the El Salvador countryside also has two rims, lashings, two skins, a snare, and tuning cords that wrap around the instrument to help twist the lashings into the shape of a W.

Another musical instrument found in the colonial period and today is the pipe and tabor, a one-man ensemble resembling the Basque *txistu*. The flute portion of the ensemble, known as *calambo,* is a two- or three-holed cane duct flute; the tabor, or drum, is small.

Chordophones are the major contribution that El Salvador has received from nonindigenous cultures, principally those of Spain. Since the beginning of the colonial period, strings have played a major role in secular life and religious rites, such as masses, prayers, and weddings. The Spanish aristocracy was interested in bringing over the latest musical innovations from Spain, particularly stringed instruments such as viols, violins, violas, cellos, contrabasses, guitars (*guitarras*), and small guitars (*vihuelas*). In numerous cabinet-making workshops, such stringed instruments were built and repaired. In some workshops today, musical instruments, especially guitars, mandolins, and violins, are made; workshops also exist in penitentiaries located throughout the country. The following European stringed instruments are currently found in El Salvador: guitars with six single courses (six strings) and six double courses (twelve strings); the *guitarrilla* 'little guitar' with four strings (the instrument comes from the medieval flat-backed *guitarilla* of European—mainly Spanish and Italian—origin); the *requinto* 'small guitar'; and the *mandolina* 'mandolin', both the flat-backed European type and the round-backed West Asian type. Because of the local influence of Mexican *ranchera* music, trios, and *mariachi* music, the Mexican *vihuela* (with a rounded back) has joined the Salvadoran inventory of instruments. This kind of *vihuela* does not correspond to the colonial type of instrument, played by plucking; instead, the Mexican *vihuela* in El Salvador, as in Mexico, is strummed and serves as a rhythmic accompanying instrument.

Roman Catholic missionaries during the colonial period installed big bells in high and open places so their ringing could be heard for great distances. Other idiophones included a wooden ratchet (*matraca*) and a wooden rattle (*carraca*), both of Arabic origin and in use during the European Middle Ages. These instruments replaced the bell (*campana*) used in Roman Catholic religious processions. The organ (*órgano*), an aerophone with keyboard, was used in the Roman Catholic liturgy. An example of this is the colonial pipe organ found in the church of Matapán.

Influenced during the 1800s and the beginning of the twentieth century by Italian and French culture, Salvadorans of high social status cultivated the playing of the violin and the piano. On the opposite end of the social continuum were the small village brass bands that developed in the 1840s from the first military bands. With religious music, these bands "were the early manifestations of what would later become Salvadoran national music" (Luna 1971:84).

African slaves added to the instruments of El Salvador by stimulating the development of two types of marimba, the *criolla* 'creole' and the *de arco* 'with bow'—a portable type carried with a strap and whose bow kept the instrument in front of the musician's body while being played. The term *marimba* probably comes from a word of Bantu origin; during the colonial period, the largest number of African slaves came to Mexico from the Guinean coast and the Congo, and from there traveled to El Salvador (Contreras Arias 1988:87).

Other African-derived idiophonic instruments found in El Salvador are the *quijada de burro* 'jawbone of a donkey' (also called *charrasga*), which is struck on its side or scraped along its teeth with a wire, a deer horn, or a piece of wood; claves (concussed wooden sticks); and a scraper (*cacho* 'horn') made from a serrated animal horn and played like a *güiro*. The *cajón* 'big box' is a wooden box struck with the hands; it is a camouflaged version of the ancient *teponaztli* or a substitute for an instrument such as a skin drum, borrowed from Africa. Africa-derived membranophones in El Salvador include the *sacabuche* and the *zambumbia*, friction drums with fixed sticks attached to single heads. Finally, the *caramba*, a musical bow with gourd resonator, is a chordophone that has possibly descended from the African hunting bow.

MUSICAL CONTEXTS AND GENRES

Religious music

Salvadoran music and musical occasions for religious purposes (Roman Catholic or Protestant) can be liturgical, life-cycle related, or festive. Christianity has an extensive ritual structure that usually includes music. There are also rituals for life-cycle events, such as baptism, confirmation, funerals, and marriage, of which only the latter uses song. Parallel to these are popular rituals of a spiritual nature in which singing is sometimes used: the burial of the umbilical cord of a newborn, an ancient ritual connected to notions of the earth as mother; *parabienes* 'congratulatory songs' for brides; *parabienes* sung at wakes for dead children; religious songs or chants for burial; the *bardo*, recited during the first nine days of mourning to help the deceased separate himself or herself from the earthly world; lullabies; children's songs; and birthday songs.

The Roman Catholic Church supports seasonal rituals, some of which reveal syncretism between Amerindian and Spanish sources. The Día de Santa Cruz (Day of the Holy Cross), for example, is a syncretic festival held at the beginning of May. Though priests forced the Cross on the indigenous population, the latter made it out of *palo de jiote* (terebinth, a small tree of the sumac family), which normally peels every year. This wood apparently represents Xipi Totec, the Lord of Spring, and symbolizes the rebirth of nature.

Organizations founded in colonial times by the Roman Catholic Church were called *cofradías* 'confraternities'. Their members took charge of organizing the patron-saint festivals, which priests have never controlled in any way—not even in finances. Patron-saint festivals are syncretic because they mostly involve devotions for animal-accompanied saints; the miraculous element has to do with the animal, not the saint, because it represents the pre-Columbian *nahual*, a spiritual guide or guardian spirit such as an animal that a person has as an inseparable companion. These festivals use religious songs from the church to which the saint and the animal belong, and they all make extensive use of dance and music. Various municipalities in El Salvador hold these festivals for a total of 137 days of the year.

Traditional dances

Traditional Salvadoran dances are syncretic forms of expression, in which traces of dances from past epochs coexist with contemporary traits. Traditional dances are closely related to the celebration of the lives of the saints and the patron-saint festivals. According to the inventory of dances put together by the Cultural Inheritance

In the dance of the mountain hog, one person dresses up like a pig, another like a devil, and two like masked old men. Everyone dances to the sound of a flute and drum.

Agency (Patrimonio Cultural) in 1976, some 116 dances are distributed throughout El Salvador, especially in the west, the center of the country, and in some population centers located in the east. These zones, in which the largest concentration of traditional dances occurs, coincide perfectly with the most densely populated areas, as they did in the prehistoric and colonial eras.

The oldest dances are those of pre-Columbian origin, especially dances connected to Mesoamerican mythology, and in particular, dances named after animals or dedicated to an animal-accompanied saint. To rid them of paganism, the Roman Catholic Church usually adapted them and incorporated them into celebrations and patron-saint festivals. Nevertheless, the dancers' costumes incorporate zoomorphic effigies evoking prehistoric mythological elements.

In the colonial dances, some European subjects survive; in the process of becoming creole, these subjects took on an American flavor. All these dances have original texts or elements that have been passed down from generation to generation.

Salvadoran dances can also be grouped by their contents. There are hunting dances, dances of appeasement, offering dances, dances of courtship, bull-related dances, burlesque or comic dances, festive dances, and war-related dances. This taxonomy is used in the following discussion of major dances.

Hunting dances

The *bailes de cacería* 'hunting dances' are dance-dramas reminiscent of communal hunts that took place thousands of years ago. They concern the sharing of an animal that was part of the fauna of the places where the hunting took place. The dance of the mountain hog and the dance of the jaguar and the deer are examples of such dances. In the dance of the mountain hog, one person dresses up like a pig, another like a devil, and two like masked old men. Everyone dances to the sound of a flute and drum. The devil and the old men hunt the pig, and when the pig has been caught and killed, they symbolically divide up the parts of the animal among everyone in the community, doing so with a humorous dedication.

Tradition has it that because of a miracle that the "Lord of Charity" (Jesus?) granted to them, an elderly couple promised to dance the dance of the jaguar and the deer every year as a form of appeasement. In the dance-drama, the old man, the old woman, and the deer manage to conquer the jaguar after surviving all sorts of dangerous happenings. Once the jaguar is dead, they divide it up in equal shares. The dancers imitate the movements of the animals, and the hunters add comic relief. As the performers symbolically divide up the meat of the jaguar, they sing to their neighbors comments such as the following.

La cabeza para la niña Teresa.	The head for the little girl Teresa.
Lo de adelante para el comandante.	The front part for the commander.
Lo de atrás para e juez de paz.	The back part for the justice of the peace.
El intestino para Don Regino.	The intestine for Don Regino.

This goes on until nothing is left of the jaguar. The whole dance is done to the sound of fife and drum.

Dances of appeasement

The *bailes propiciatorios* 'dances of appeasement' are performed to obtain mercy from saints and other supernatural beings that serve as intermediaries of God. The dance of Saint Benedict and the dance of the big box are good examples of this genre.

For the dance of Saint Benedict, a *charra* (a wide-brimmed women's hat, made of palm fibers) and two little flags (made of China paper, luxurious paper used for printing) are placed atop the altar. After the prayer, two worshipers sing to the saint, asking for permission to dance all night. After the ceremony is over, all the helpers go out to the street, form a circle, and to the accompaniment of chordophones dance the *son* 'song-dance' of Saint Benedict. When the first couple stops dancing, the two dancers pass the hat and the flag to another couple; this procedure is repeated time after time. Everyone who receives the hat and the flag is obligated to dance; if not, he or she will be subject to punishment from the saint. The women's costumes include brightly colored blouses, showy long skirts, hats, and shawls; the men wear shirts of coarse cloth, street pants, and hats. All of them carry small flags in one hand.

The dance of the big box developed during the colonial period, when a wooden statue of the Blessed Virgin Mary was found in a 1.5-meter wooden box in a grotto on La Perla Beach, in the department of La Libertad. People of the area removed the Virgin, took her to the church, and brought the box to the *cofradía* of Saint Ursula. Tradition has it that on some days people find the Virgin with traces of sand on it because she has gone to the beach to bathe. The day of the festival of Saint Ursula includes a vigil that begins at 6:00 P.M. and ends at dawn; cocoa and tamales are served. The dance that ensues is slow, repetitive, and continuously performed around the original box (struck rhythmically with the hands) during the helpers' drinking of alcohol, a ritual act. This dance could be a pre-Columbian ritual that has survived, whereby the Amerindians, to protect themselves from the inquisitive eyes of the Church, camouflaged the *tepunahuaste* by adopting the wooden box of the Virgin as an instrument for dancing.

Offering dances

People perform *bailes de ofrenda* 'offering dances' to thank a supernatural being for some favor that has been obtained. The dance of Saint Tingo is performed by married women, who sing songs and dance to the accompaniment of the *tingo,* a log idiophone, related to the ancient *teponaztli,* personifying Saint Tingo. The participants carry arches adorned with flowers, leaves, and feathers, which sway over the *tingo.* While this could be one of the "replacement" dances that appeared in colonial times, Saint Tingo is not a Roman Catholic saint, though the participants believe that the *tingo* personifies the saint. In prehistoric rituals, the *teponaztli*—then the equivalent of the *tingo*—played an important role.

Dances of courtship

The *bailes de cortejo* 'dances of courtship' are gallant, light, and amiable in character, especially when danced by couples. The dance of the flea and the louse, belonging to the *cofradía* of Santiago Texacuangos, is performed by one group of young men in male clothing and another group of young men in female clothing. Within these groups are pairs of godparents and a bride and groom. The godfather gives away the bride, wearing traditional bridal dress, to the groom, wearing a dark suit. The participants dance to the sound of stringed instruments, talk among themselves, repeat *bombas* (short, witty, improvised verses), and tell jokes among themselves.

Taurine dances

The *bailes taurinos* 'taurine dances' are directly related to bulls or bullfights. One example, the dance of the little spotted bull, parodies bullfighting, a pastime brought from Spain. Eight characters participate: an elder, an old woman, a doctor, a marksman, a mine administrator, a dog, an orangutan, and a little spotted bull. A fife and drum announce the dance, followed by an introduction by the elder:

> Yo soy el viejo mayor. Mi nombre es Don Heracles, esposo de la niña Olimpia, que hemos venido a todos estos lugares en compañía de este torito pinto y este monito orangután, solo por venir a celebrar las fiestas de San Antonio Abad.

> I am the elder. My name is Don Heracles, husband of the young girl Olimpia, and we have come to these parts accompanied by this little spotted bull and this little monkey orangutan, just to celebrate the festivities of Saint Anthony the Abbot.

The participants begin to dance, and Don Heracles avoids the thrusts of the little bull as he follows the rhythm of the fife and drum. Each person introduces herself or himself in a humorous way, and spoken dialogue occurs between fife-and-drum interludes. The little bull gets lost, and the old people speak with the mine administrator to ask for his assistance. With the help of the administrator's dog, Solimán (Mercuric Chloride), the bull is found and returned to its owners. The dance continues, and then the orangutan is lost. The elder and the old woman ask the sharpshooter to go find it and to bring it back. The sharpshooter fires, wounds the orangutan, and returns it to its owners, who run to seek a doctor's assistance. After the orangutan is cured, the sharpshooter asks the two old people to lend it to him so he can ask it questions, wanting to find out if it is intelligent. The questions he asks have double meanings and sexual connotations—implications that make the spectators laugh.

Comic dances

In *bailes burlescos* 'burlesque dances', humor is focused on a sector of the population or some person who has political or economic influence in town. Three dances are representative: *los chapetones* 'the Spaniards', *los tapujeados* 'the masked men', and *la giganta* 'the giantess'.

Los chapetones is a biting satire of colonial Spanish manners. The Spaniards are mocked by how they hold hands and entwine arms while dancing, and by the costumes of the "gentlemen," which consist of white shirts, colored neckties, black vests, black suits with black frock coats, black stovepipe hats, and black umbrellas, sometimes used as canes. The dance-drama itself depicts an agreement occurring between Spain and Turkey about the marriage of Doña Lucrecia of Castille and Don Tomás Raynel. Twelve chancellors—from Argentina, China, Colombia, Eastern Chile, Japan, and elsewhere—are present. During the dance, accompanied by two guitars and a *requinto,* speeches such as the following are made:

> ¿Y qué les parece, señores caballeros? Y dicen que cosa impresiona se pudiera yo casarme con la ya niña Lucrecia de Castilla, ofreciéndole mis caudales, aunque no los tenga aquí, pero mandaré un correo a la ciudad de Uropa, que me traiga mis monedas para poderme casar con ella.

> And what do you think, gentlemen? They say that it would be great if I could already marry the little girl Lucrecia of Castille by offering her my fortune, though I don't have it here, but I will send a message to the city of Uropa [Europe], so my coins will be brought to me so I can marry her.

The other gentlemen answer: *Me parece muy bien, señor caballero* 'It sounds like a good idea, Mr. Gentleman', and tilt their heads in an extreme theatrical exaggeration, which makes the members of the audience laugh.

Los tapujeados is performed by men who disguise themselves with masks and eccentric clothing; their function is to dance jovially through the streets of the town. They accept donations at the end of the dance, usually in the form of alcoholic beverages. The masked men and *los emplumados* 'the feathered men' also participate in the *baile del toro* 'dance of the bull'.

The dance of the giantess is performed by a group of masked people and a doll about 2.5 to 3 meters high, from which the name of the dance derives. The body of the doll has female traits; it is made with wooden framework, its head is made of cloth, and its clothing is made of colorful fabric. A variation of this dance, *baile de la chabelona* 'dance of Big Liz' (from the nickname "Chabela" for Isabel 'Elizabeth'), satirizes the English Queen Elizabeth I (1533–1603).

Festive dances

The *bailes festivos* 'festive dances' are a type of social folklore in which people get together to chat. The *baile de la soguilla* 'dance of the little rope' is a representative example. On 30 November in the town of San Antonio la Cruz, *las capitanas*, the wives of the lead dancers, make a big rope out of pieces of *olote* (the centers of corn cobs), painted in several colors and decorated with cacao seeds; they also decorate a big hat with ribbons and flowers. Popular songs are performed to the accompaniment of stringed instruments. The mayor of the *cofradía* begins the dance by inviting the wife of the sponsor (*mayordomo*) to be his partner. He puts the decorated hat on her head and she puts the rope around his neck. As they dance, they look around to select another couple. In this fashion, everyone ends up going to the center of the patio to participate in the dance. The dance is done in couples, but the dancers do not touch each other.

Christmas dances

Bailes navideños 'Christmas dances' are part of the celebrations dedicated to the birth of the baby Jesus and to the three wise men or to passages from the Old Testament. People of both sexes and all ages participate in these dances; the costumes depend on the portrayed character, whose dialogue and songs are based on religious themes. The dances classified as Christmas dances are *baile de la garza* 'dance of the heron', *baile de los pastores machos* 'dance of the male shepherds', *baile de los herodes* 'dance of Herods', *baile de los pastores o machines* 'dance of the shepherds or white-faced monkeys', *baile del zope* 'dance of the buzzard', *baile de los diablitos* 'dance of the little devils', and *baile de los chiraguaquitos* 'dance of the little Chiragua Indians'.

In the town of Apaneca, Christmas processionals—dramatizations of Mary and Joseph seeking shelter, the Nativity, and the journey of the three wise men—are carried out, and the dance of the heron is performed. The heron character is created from a framework similar to that used for piñatas. Besides a heron, the characters include three policemen, a mayor, a bride, a groom, a rogue, an Indian, an old lady, an old man, and two little monkeys. They all wear everyday clothing but use wooden masks corresponding to the characters they portray. The music is accompanied with strings, and some pieces are ancient Mexican tunes.

The dance of the male shepherds is performed in San Rafael Cedros and the town of Concepción de Ataco on 24 and 25 December. Only men participate. Some dress up like little monkeys, others like old men, and yet others like a little bull, wearing a bull costume made over a wooden framework. The other men wear suits with everyday jackets, put on hats decorated with moss as if from a cold climate, and carry

The dance of the little devils always takes place in the large entrance or entryway of the church or in front of houses where Nativity scenes are erected. The dancers are thirteen people disguised as devils; they wear red, one-piece jumpsuits with long, black tails.

suitcases filled with plates, jugs, and cups, as well as rolled-up sleeping mats on their backs. In their hands, they carry shepherd's crooks. During their journey, they make witty comments and sing verses referring to Jesus's birth.

The dance of the Herods is similar to the dance of the shepherds, except that the sung verses refer to the infanticide ordered by King Herod (Matthew 2:16). The ensemble of chordophones that accompanies it is called *chilamate*. A dance with a similar name, the dance of the shepherds, is done in the city of Nahuizalco from 22 to 27 December to 3 to 7 January. The performers are twelve young men (eight shepherds and four white-faced monkey gods) who are in street dress and wear hats of palm fiber decorated with colored ribbons. Each shepherd uses both hands to hold up his staff (about three meters long), which serves as a support for fifteen balls, strung from the smallest to the largest. Each ball, made of woven vines and newspaper and lined with cloth of many different colors, contains a bell that sounds when shaken, symbolizing happiness for Jesus's birth. The space between balls (the distance of a *jeme,* calculated from the end of the extended thumb to the end of the extended forefinger) is decorated with several garlands of crepe paper that flutter in the wind. The monkey gods have small rattles in their right hands, wear dark cashmere suits, and on their heads have black conical hats (*cucuruchos*) out of whose tips protrude numerous colored ribbons. Dancing in couples, they wittily imitate the movements of monkeys and make reverential gestures among themselves. After this, the shepherds pass before Jesus and describe their offerings:

Aquí te traigo, señora,	Here I bring to you, my Lady,
una ramita de azahar,	A small branch of [orange or lemon] blossom,
para que se la des al niño	So you might give it to the Child
cuando empiece a llorar.	When he begins to cry.

The musical accompaniment for this singing and dancing is provided by a guitar and a *guitarrilla.* This might be a "replacement" dance which fuses an ancient European harvest rite and the tree of life of Mesoamerican mythology. Monkeys, too, are important symbols in Mesoamerican mythology.

The dance of the little devils, performed in Salcoatitán, Sonsonate, always takes place in the large entrance or entryway of the church (but not inside), or in front of houses where Nativity scenes are erected. The dancers are thirteen people disguised as devils; they wear red, one-piece jumpsuits with long, black tails. Within the dance, their hierarchy shows a mixture of Spanish medieval and *cofradía* elements: a guitar leader (*capitán*), a violin leader, a first king of the horn (*cacho*), two vassals who carry snare drums (*zambumbias*), two vassals who carry 'jawbones of donkeys' (*charrasgas*), two vassals with small handheld bells, two vassals using whips, and a main devil. During the performance, dancing—accompanied by violin and the other instruments—alternates with the speeches made by each devil. During the last devil's part, everybody comes together and kneels in front of Jesus, asking him for mercy.

The dance of the little Chiragua Indians is performed in the town of Santo Domingo de Guzmán, Sonsonate. Six young girls and six young boys participate. The girls put on indigenous wrap-around skirts, and the boys wear everyday pants and shirts. All the children carry fruit crates filled with ratchets (*batidorcitos* 'little noisemakers'), tin cans, and little colored flags. Accompanied by accordion and guitar, they sing and dance in the entryway to the church, enter the building to await the birth of Jesus at midnight, and then go to a party in the *cofradía* until dawn the next day.

War-related dances

Bailes guerreros 'war-related dances' portray battles. Performances of these dances were used by the missionaries to destroy Amerindian idols. The conquistadores always triumph, as do their rites and symbols. The *baile de los emplumados* 'dance of the feathered men', the *baile de la partesana* 'dance of the halberd', and the *baile de los moros y cristianos* 'dance of the Moors and Christians' are representative of this genre.

In Cacaopera, department of Morazán, the dance of the feathered men is performed; it is from the area of the Lenca, an indigenous group. It recalls a meeting of eight chiefs that took place before the colonial era. Each had a retinue of warriors (with big spears) and dancers, and each dancer had a retinue of three people. All of them adorned themselves with tufts of feathers of macaw or *torogoz,* a small blue bird, the national bird of El Salvador. Out of this great spectacle, only two dancers remain at the end. The tufts of feathers are still used today for this dance, but are now made of other materials. The musicians who accompany the dance are a drummer, two guitarists, and a violinist.

The dance of the halberd is performed in Santiago Nonualco, in the department of La Paz. A pre-Columbian dance, it features long-poled lances (*falas*) with three metal points on their tips. Jumps executed by the dancer require great agility.

The dance of the Moors and Christians, the dance best known throughout the country, was brought from Europe during the first years of the conquest. Its source of thematic inspiration, its functional relationship with reality, lies in Spanish history during the reconquest from Moorish domination. Pre-Columbian ritual celebrations facilitated the assimilation and diffusion of this dance. Since the 1500s, many versions of it have appeared. The Hispanic structure of the dance never changes; instead, in its several versions, one group of people is replaced with another: the Moors become indigenous people who have not been Christianized, and the Christians become indigenous people who have already been baptized; or the Moors become an indigenous band of warriors commanded by Moctezuma, and the Christians become Hernán Cortés and the conquistadores.

MUSIC FOR ENTERTAINMENT

Music for entertainment is strictly linked to the demands of nocturnal establishments where North American repertoire makes up the largest percentage of the music. Some Salvadorans believe that national music (*música nacional*) has declined in quality by having fallen into the repetitious poverty of foreign music, which, rather than allowing people to think, aims to make them relax, enjoy themselves, and purchase more of it. In the 1990s, however, a high level of musicianship has been displayed in concerts. Excellent directors, guitarists, and pianists from all over the world have participated in these performances. Hotels put on shows designed by the Instituto Salvadoreano de Turismo (Salvadoran Tourism Institute). They are mostly performed by the Ballet Folkórico (Folkloric Ballet), which has represented Salvadorans as much inside the country as abroad. Organizers discover talent by searching for stars via competitions. The major musical figures of El Salvador started their careers by performing in national competitions, and furthered their artistic professions by going abroad.

SOCIAL STRUCTURE, MUSICIANS, AND BEHAVIOR

Salvadoran musicians have always played an important role in rituals, festivities, and entertainment. When musical ensembles or sound systems played popular and fashionable music outdoors, musicians listened to and learned the melodies so they could perform them later in small village pavilions. This is how many pieces that have disappeared from their places of origin have remained in the repertoire.

In El Salvador, Mexican music is mostly heard in the Salvadoran countryside, and North American music is heard in the city. Rural inhabitants have experienced situations similar to those experienced by Mexicans, and since *latino* music has reflected these shared experiences, it is only natural that rural dwellers of other Latin American countries also identify with Mexican music.

The Salvadoran upper class originated in the agricultural system, and the national way of life began in colonial haciendas. The Salvadoran nation was basically rural. Rich people, poor people, foreigners, natives—all had similar dwellings. In colonial times, Spanish music (religious, secular, art, traditional, military, popular), Amerindian music, and African-derived music were performed; these traditions tended to mix. The aristocracy always brought what was new from Europe to America, so there was a constant influx of teachers, musical instruments, and music. Near the end of the 1800s, the phonograph introduced to the Salvadoran countryside additional songs and other music from Europe, the United States, South America (especially Argentina), Cuba, and eventually, above all, music known internationally via the classic movies of the Mexican film industry. The children of landowners studied in Europe, but by the time they did so, they were adolescents or had gone through adolescence and had already incorporated Mexican *ranchera* songs into their heritage. A paradox sometimes arises in El Salvador: though the socioeconomic elite looks down on listening to or singing *rancheras,* this same practice is tolerated if the president of the republic cares to use *ranchera* music for political reasons.

Musical performance in El Salvador has always been a male pursuit; only in a few instances—playing the piano, for example—have women been involved in it. In the 1990s, women have joined bands and orchestras, frequently for decorative purposes; they sometimes sing but are especially seen dancing, often in skimpy attire.

Art music is heard and performed by people who usually have middle- or upper-class backgrounds. They normally prefer music from the European baroque, classical, and romantic periods; contemporary music has a minuscule following. Art music is now broadcast more than before, thanks to Radio Clásica (Classical Radio), a station whose programming has allowed art music to reach a larger part of the population, including people who live in marginal zones. A curious phenomenon in El Salvador is that many mothers who work as maids leave their children alone at home, under lock and key, with Radio Clásica tuned in. Intellectuals, though they have been affected by the backlash of popular music, prefer art music or music with a high degree of social content—music with a message.

North American music, because of the frequency with which the media program it, remains the most popular music in cities. Preadolescents prefer rock because it supposedly suits their rebellious nature. Young people like *rock en español* (rock sung in Spanish), and adults like the music they have grown up with. When the media plan their programming, they do a lot of research to differentiate the sectors of the population.

Salvadoran commercial music basically consists of imitations (covers) of compositions that have already been tried out successfully via public channels. These compositions are limited to translations of North American hits. Original Salvadoran songs are considered worthy of recording only when their composers know the right people and are protected by the owners of the channels of communication; others are excluded, flat out or indirectly, by the costs of recording and manufacturing.

Ideological music is promoted by organized entities. During political campaigns, lyrics of fashionable songs are changed to become vehicles of propaganda. The songs sung by guerrillas during the Salvadoran civil war are another example of this type of music. In El Salvador, bossism (*caciquismo*) fulfills an intermediate role between the countryside and the central government. Monopolies that control channels of social communication reproduce this power structure by becoming intermediaries between the nation and international interest groups. Bills to pass laws that will protect consumers are easily shelved by the Asamblea Legislativa (Legislative Assembly). The Ministry of Education does little about this situation. Because of external pressure in the 1990s, a law favoring copyright protection was passed, but music piracy in El Salvador still occurs.

DYNAMICS OF MUSICAL CULTURE

Salvadoran music is promoted, cultivated, and disseminated institutionally. In the 1880s, the Conservatorio Nacional de Música (National Conservatory of Music) was founded by legislative decree under the direction of Escolástico Andrino. Despite having a small budget, this conservatory used to train the best instrumentalists in the country. It satisfied the demand for trained musicians. As popular music grew in importance, what the conservatory offered could no longer meet the demand for musical training. For this reason, the conservatory was closed in 1969, and the Centro Nacional de Artes (National Center for the Arts) was founded, with the idea of training schoolteachers. The best instrumentalists continue to occupy places in musical groups and commercial orchestras, and the rest devote themselves to teaching in public and private schools.

Traditional methods of teaching

Song was originally the basic means of teaching music, and the traditional method consisted of classes in singing. On the basis of that concept, musicians created mnemonic shortcuts that they later applied to the learning of *zarzuelas* and other year-end presentations. The ideology behind the choice of certain pieces was the instilling of moral and civic values. During the educational reform that began in the 1970s, modern methods of teaching music—those of Dalcroze, Kodály, Martenot, Orff, and Suzuki—were analyzed, and exercises and pieces were chosen and placed in a progressive order, based on how easy they were to sight-read. For the program to continue, it was necessary to produce sufficient didactic materials and to develop a new mentality among the teachers, who had to be retrained so they could judge pedagogical change fairly. Thus, each teacher, by having a new point of view, had to come up with his or her own instructional materials. Besides being clearly planned, this goal appeared easy to accomplish. As it turned out, however, the opposite was true: teachers assimilated the material that they had learned, and they repeated the same exercises for years, finally reaching the saturation point. To discipline and address the children's boredom, teachers, for no pedagogical reason at all, seized on the commercial popular music of the times.

In 1970, several foundations had their cultural projects in place, and a few had permanent musical programs and controlled private concert halls. Little by little, political convulsions ended these initiatives and shows; though they had been programmed, they never reached the public. The Civil War took over all of these spaces,

Popular music in El Salvador has not demonstrated noteworthy originality. The use of electronic equipment has initiated a period of competitive consumption of a product that is valued according to how well it imitates what comes from the United States.

the National Center for the Arts was on the verge of closing its doors, and high-caliber concerts were offered only sporadically.

With the ending of the Salvadoran civil war, a gradual rebirth of cultural activity is being seen. The Teatro Nacional (National Theater), Acto Teatro (Theater of Acts), Teatro Presidente (President's Theater), La Luna (The Moon), and other theaters in the capital and in Suchitoto present artistic events. Activities have been initiated by several foundations, among which the María Escalón de Núñez Foundation has done much work.

The technology of music

Musical technology reached El Salvador toward the end of the 1800s, when the first phonographs arrived. Between 1900 and 1930, a golden age in Salvadoran musical production began, and the Marimba Centroamericana (Central American Marimba Ensemble) recorded for the Victor, Columbia, and Brunswick labels. Their recordings achieved international popularity. From them, municipal bands and marimbists made their own arrangements, which they played during concerts—from kiosks, in local parks, and during social festivities. Composers sent their scores via a local store to New York, where record companies would have orchestras record them, barely acknowledging the composers. This was when Salvadoran popular songs began to be commercialized, a time that coincided with the introduction of electricity and radio to the capital of the country.

In 1926, on the top floor of the National Theater, the government installed the first radio station in El Salvador and Central America. For two hours a day, 6:00 to 8:00 P.M., the station broadcast marimba music and music played by municipal bands. The repertoire of these ensembles included waltzes, foxtrots, Cuban *sones,* tangos, and *rancheras.*

Between 1930 and 1960, several composers, including Felipe Soto, Wesceslao Rodríguez, David Granadino, and José Napoleón Rodríguez, recorded for the Columbia label. Around 1940, the first commercial radio station was installed in the Dirección General de Policía (General Police Headquarters). In 1942, the electric company installed meters in residences, and radio transmission increased to seven hours per day. Other radio stations were created, and programs of entertainment with Salvadoran music ensued. From 1940 to 1950, marimba ensembles, including Cuscatlán, Nima Quiche, Sonora, Nuevo Mundo, Royal, and Atlacatl, popularized swing, mambo, *chachachá,* boleros, and Salvadoran country music. Atlacatl gave concerts in several countries of the Americas and Europe. Beginning in 1945, big dance orchestras sprang up. They stayed in vogue until 1960, when rock began to take over in popularity. In 1960, the first black-and-white televisions arrived in El Salvador, as did youth dance and song competitions that imitated those in the United States and Mexico. From then on, DJs and their programs were oriented toward younger audiences. The one record company in the country was founded during this time, only to disappear in the first half of the 1980s. Computers, Betamax, video games, and video clips all arrived, along with the advances that were made in television.

Improvements in the international and domestic economies have brought positive and negative changes to El Salvador. Since 1990, the importation of technology has produced many musical changes, and the market has generated competition at the regional level. The introduction of electronic instruments and compact recording laboratories has simplified the processes of musical recording and production. Local musicians who, because of the cost, do not participate in this kind of competition remain marginalized in this environment, in which millions of dollars circulate.

Music and identity

Mestizaje, the mixing of cultural elements, and *criollización,* the process of becoming creole, are giving El Salvador a new identity. Latin Americanism is a movement that has strong support and far-reaching ramifications in science and culture. To take on mestizo identity means to cast off one ideological mind-set and to adopt a new one. In this way, the idea of a national culture is being adopted, and direction for the future is being given.

Acculturation is usually a form of penetration and ethnocentric domination that creates inequality in conditions between the center and the periphery. As social strata begin to be defined, social differences also come to be determined. The contribution of Western culture enriched and prepared a world for the Spaniards and other foreigners who came to El Salvador, but the cultural space occupied by the hegemonic class has become so large that most Salvadoran traditions that have not been assimilated into religious practices have disappeared.

Populations are identified by the music they listen to: rock and disco are for preadolescents and urban adolescents; *ranchera* music is for rural and semiurban people; and orchestras have a wide range of followers from adolescents to adults, depending on the repertoire that they perform. Salvadoran society does not approve of adults who have maintained the fashions or genres of yesteryear; if they have not kept up with the musical times, they are directly or indirectly ridiculed.

Popular music in El Salvador has not demonstrated noteworthy originality. The use of electronic equipment—electric guitars, bass guitars, synthesizers, and amplifiers—has initiated a period of competitive consumption of a product that is valued according to how well it imitates what comes from the United States. Rock, in all its forms, is aimed at adolescents, and each generation has its own performers.

FURTHER STUDY

The best source for the general music history of El Salvador, though it is outdated, is by Rafael González Sol (1940). Musical archaeology is more recent, and works by Stanley Boggs (1974) and Salvador Marroquín (1991) are the most valuable. Traditional musical instruments of El Salvador have been studied by Marroquín and Miguel Villegas (1977). In the early 1940s, the Committee of Folkloric Investigation (Comité de Investigaciones Folklóricas) undertook studies of El Salvadoran musical ethnography and folklore, and its transcriptions and other findings were published in 1944. Also in the 1940s, Rafael González Sol (1947) published an informative book about Salvadoran civic and religious festivals and popular exhibitions.

—TRANSLATED BY JANE L. FLORINE

REFERENCES

Boggs, Stanley. 1974. "Notes on Pre-Columbian Wind Instruments from El Salvador." *Baessler-Archiv* 22:23–71.

Casanova de Parraga, Diego A. 1969. *Campanas de Hispanoamerica*. Madrid: Imprenta Aguirre.

Castellanos, Pablo. 1970. *Horizontes de la música precortesiana*. Colección Presencia de México, 14. México, D.F.: Fondo de Cultura Económica.

Comité de Investigaciones Folklóricas y Arte Típico Salvadoreño. 1944. *Recopilaciones de materiales folklóricos salvadoreños*. San Salvador: Ministerio de Instrucción Pública, Imprenta Nacional.

Contreras Arias, Juan Guillermo. 1988. *Colección Atlas Cultural de Mexico, sección Música*. México, D.F.: Secretaria de Educación Pública, Instituto Nacional de Antropología e Historia, Grupo Editorial Planeta.

González Sol, Rafael. 1940. *Datos históricos sobre el arte de la música en El Salvador*. San Salvador: Imprenta Mercurio.

———. 1947. *Fiestas Cívicas, Religiosas y Exhibiciones populares de El Salvador*. 2nd ed. San Salvador: Imprenta Mercurio.

Herring, Hubert. 1968. *A History of Latin America from the Beginnings to the Present*. New York: Alfred A. Knopf.

Luna, David Alejandro. 1971. "Manual de Historia Económica de El Salvador." In *Colección El Tiempo*. San Salvador: Editorial Universitaria de la Universidad de El Salvador.

Marroquín, Salvador. 1991. "Los instrumentos musicales precolombinos y el parentesco cercano con Mexico." In *Chiapas, Serie Memorias: "Encuentro de intelectuales Chiapas-Centroamerica."* Tuxtla-Gutiérrez: Consejo Estatal de Fomento a la Investigación y Difusión de la Cultura, Talleres Gráficos del Estado de Chiapas.

Marroquín, Salvador, and Miguel Villegas. 1977. "Instrumentos musicales tradicionales." *La cofradía* 1(11):1–6.

Museo Nacional David J. Guzmán. 1975. *Exploración etnográfica Departamento de Sonsonate*. San Salvador: Dirección de Publicaciones del Ministerio de Educación.

Guatemala
Linda O'Brien-Rothe

Musical Instruments
Music of the Maya
Music of the Garífuna
Music of Ladinos
European-Derived Art Music
Further Study

Before the Spanish contact in 1524, the territory that is now the Republic of Guatemala was part of the area where Maya civilization developed, flourished, and declined [see MAYA]. By the time Hernán Cortés had sent his envoy Pedro de Alvarado to conquer the territory for Spain, the great Maya temple-cities had long been abandoned, and classic Maya culture lay hidden beneath covers of jungle and time. The Spaniards found the Maya of Guatemala a people divided into more or less mutually hostile, petty kingdoms of the Quiché, Cakchiquel, Ixil, Kekchí, Mam, Pokoman, and Tzutujil clans. Until independence from Spain (1821), Guatemala was part of the political unit known as the Audiencia de Guatemala, which included territory extending from Chiapas, Mexico, to Costa Rica.

From the writings of the ancient Maya (who in the 1500s recorded texts of their myths, clan histories, and dance-dramas using the Western system of writing) we learn about Maya musical life at the time of contact. Principal among the sources are *Los Anales de los Cakchiqueles* (*The Annals of the Cakchiquels*) and the Quiché *Popol Vuh* (*The Book of Counsel*), which contain the history of the people, their myths of creation, and the deeds of their ancestral heroes. Instrumental music, dances, songs, and other arts figure importantly throughout these texts.

These sources show that for the Maya the arts were then, as now, a system of rituals and symbols originated by primordial ancestral heroes. These rituals functioned at the time of Spanish contact, as they do today, to maintain a harmonious relationship between the human world and the world of spirits. In the *Popol Vuh,* the ancestral pair of heroic brothers, Jun Baatz' and Jun Ch'oven (whose names mean 'monkey' and 'artisan'), are proficient in all the arts, since they became flutists, singers, writers, carvers, jewelers, and silversmiths (Edmonson 1971:59). Also demonstrated in these sources is the Maya belief that their ancestors' music has the power to do what it says. When the younger brothers sang and played the spider-monkey hunter's song for the elder brothers on the flute (*zu*) and drum (*k'ojom*), the elder brothers turned into monkeys. The *Popol Vuh* contains the texts of laments that express the sorrow the people felt when they left their homeland in Tula to migrate into highland Guatemala, such as the following (Edmonson 1971:171):

Historical and ethnohistorical records of the music of the Maya in the Audiencia de Guatemala come from journals, letters, and the Spanish colonists' official records and from the accounts of travelers and explorers.

Alas, it is not here that we shall see the dawn,
When the sun is born again
Brightening the face of the earth.

The Annals of the Cakchiquels and *The Title of the Lords of Totonicapán,* sixteenth-century documents relating the origins and myths of the Cakchiquel and the Quiché, mention a bone flute (*zubac*), a conch trumpet (*t'ot'*), a drum (*k'ojom*), and a spiked vessel rattle (*sonaja*). The origin of the latter is related in the following story from the *Popol Vuh* (paraphrase of translation in Edmonson 1971:76):

> The head of the hero, Jun Jun Aj Pu (One One Hunter), was severed by the Lords of the Underworld, and became a living gourd on a calabash tree. The maiden X Kiq (Blood Girl) discovered the head in the branches, and from a drop of spittle the calabash-head let fall on her outstretched hand, conceived the twin heroes Jun Aj Pu (One Hunter) and X Balan Ke (Jaguar Deer).

This story suggests that the magical powers of the spiked vessel rattle stem from its mythical identification with the heroic ancestral twins who conquered the forces of evil, personified as the Lords of the Underworld.

Historical and ethnohistorical records of the music of the Maya in the Audiencia de Guatemala come from journals, letters, and the Spanish colonists' official records and from the accounts of travelers and explorers. References to music and musical instruments in these sources, though scattered and brief, provide a general knowledge of Maya musical instruments and ensembles seen in public performances. An extensive body of manuscripts in Western musical notation of music of European origin or style composed in Spain, Mexico, and Guatemala survives from the 1500s forward. Similarly, after independence, most information collected by ethnographers and anthropologists contains little specifically musical detail, but does include valuable information about the contexts of Maya music.

The present Maya

The Maya in the 1990s constitute more than half of the population of Guatemala, speak a Maya dialect as their primary language, and mostly live in rural areas, engaging in subsistence agriculture, small-scale commerce, and home-based crafts. Their customs and traditions are rooted in ancient Maya religion. Their musical culture tends to retain old and traditional musical styles and instruments and to resist outside influences; nevertheless, the loss of traditional styles is more and more evident. Principal among the agents of this loss are the people's conversion to evangelical Christian religions, whose missionaries identify the music of traditional Maya rituals with the powers of darkness, in which they see a hindrance to salvation; the economic pressure that stems from the fact that, unlike popular styles, the performance of traditional music is not lucrative; and the disruptive effect of the long-term oppression and gradual eradication of the indigenous peoples of Guatemala. As a rule, Maya instruments and styles tend to disappear, rather than be modified.

MUSICAL INSTRUMENTS

The musical instruments and styles typical of Guatemalan music can be conveniently grouped into those commonly used by the indigenous Maya and those more commonly used by the Ladinos (Guatemalans whose primary language is Spanish), though the lines separating Maya and Ladino music are blurred by an overlapping of cultures. Nevertheless, musical instruments and styles are associated mainly with one group rather than the other, though not limited to it. Crossing these lines is international popular music. Radio is accessible virtually everywhere, television and other media are available in cities and larger towns, and recordings of popular artists and styles bring to Guatemala the same music being heard in Mexico, Central America, and Los Angeles.

The Tzutujil classify musical instruments as male or female. Female instruments (*k'ojom*) are those that are struck or plucked; within the Tzutujil cosmos, they represent or are related to the geographic plane or the surface of the earth. The large, double-headed drum is always called *k'ojom* in Tzutujil. Other female instruments may be called simply *k'ojom,* or may be called by Tzutujil names derived from Spanish: *ctar* 'guitar', *arp* 'harp', *mrimp* 'marimba'. Male instruments (*xul*) are those that are blown; they are related to or represent the cosmic tree or central axis that penetrates the geographic plane, communicating with the world of spirits under the earth and above it in the sky. Except for the cane flute (always called *xul* in Tzutujil), male instruments may be called *xul* or by Spanish names: *saxofón* 'saxophone', *chirimía* 'shawm', *trompeta* 'trumpet'. Traditionally, the playing of musical instruments is limited to men.

Because the Tzutujil have delineated their own taxonomy for musical instruments, which is likely accepted by other Maya subgroups who share the same cosmology, musical instruments are presented that way in this essay.

Female instruments

Idiophones

Spiked vessel rattles made of a calabash (Quiché *chin-chin,* Spanish *sonaja,* maraca) are pre-Hispanic ritual instruments used in curing and divination. Today, they are made from various materials including calabash, metal, basketry, and terra-cotta and may contain pebbles, seeds, clay pellets, or (in basket rattles) pellet bells. They are used mainly in dance-dramas (dramatic presentations of part of the Maya world myth, many of them undocumented), but also by ensembles of guitars and *guitarrillas* (small guitars used for local music), and by Maya and Ladino ensembles of popular music. Ceramic replicas are sometimes offered for sale in local markets. Terra-cotta vessel rattles surviving from pre-Columbian times, sometimes in figurine form, are often unearthed during cultivation, and such ancient artifacts—including whistles, nonmusical figurines, and other shards—are especially valued by shamans for use in divination or curing.

Rattles of coins threaded on string or wire across the face of a metal plate are used in some dance-dramas. Rattlesnake rattles are prized for the buzz they add to stringed instruments, flutes, and whistles, when inserted into their cavities or resonators.

A tortoiseshell idiophone (Spanish *tortuga*) struck with a bone, stick, or antler is used by the Ixil of the Department of Quiché in the deer dance (*baile del venado*). It

FIGURE 1   A *c'unc'un* (slit drum) stored under a table with ritual drink, ready to be played during a Mayan ceremony in Santiago Atitlán, Department of Sololá, highland Guatemala. Photo by Linda O'Brien-Rothe, 1971.

commonly accompanies the singing of *posadas,* mainly a Ladino custom during Advent, the pre-Christmas season.

The hollowed log idiophone

The *tun* is an idiophone made from a hollowed-out log of lowland hardwood (*hormigo*), into which an H-shaped slit is cut, creating two tuned tongues (figure 1). When struck with a rubber-tipped mallet, deer antler, or stick, the tongues vibrate and produce two pitches about a fourth apart. A third pitch can be produced by beating the side of the instrument. Other names for the *tun* in Guatemala are Tzutujil *c'unc'un,* and Quiché *tuntun* or *tum;* in Mexico, it is known in Náhuatl as *teponaztli* and in Yucatec-Maya as *teponagua, teponaguastle,* and *tunkul.* Tzutujil men play it daily at sunrise, noon, and sunset, probably as part of the cult of the sun. In the absence of the appointed male ritual official, his wife may fulfill this duty.

The *tun* appears in Maya ritual and dance-dramas, often in differently sized pairs. Probably the most ancient of these is the dance-drama often in colonial documents called *baile del tun* 'dance of the *tun*', in which a *tun* and long wooden trumpets (also called *tun* or *tum,* which may mean 'tube, cylinder') accompany dances and narratives. The log idiophone was used in this presentation with an ensemble of flutes, rattles, skin drums (Spanish *atabales, tambores*), conch trumpets (Spanish *caracoles*), and wooden trumpets. Because the dance represented the sacrifice of a captive taken in battle, the church repeatedly proscribed its performance. It persisted, nevertheless, and survives as the dance-drama *Rabinal Achí* (*Hero of Rabinal*) in Rabinal, Baja Verapaz, and as *Ox Tum* in Ilotenango, Sacatepéquez. Today, it is accompanied by valveless metal trumpets about one meter long with one loop, appearing to be nineteenth-century band instruments, and a log idiophone (Mace 1970).

Other idiophones are small metal clapper bells and pellet bells, rasps of gourd, wood, or bone with transverse grooves, and a wooden ratchet (*matraca*) originating in Spain and used principally during Holy Week, when church bells are customarily silent.

The marimba

The most popular Guatemalan folk-derived instrument is the marimba, a xylophone

FIGURE 2   A *marimba de tecomates* from the
Cakchiquel area of the shores of Lake Atitlán,
Sololá, highland Guatemala. This instrument
was converted from a *marimba de arco* by cutting off the arched branch (its stump visible on
the left) and adding legs. Photo by Linda
O'Brien-Rothe, 1967.

probably introduced from central Africa in the 1500s or 1600s. Evidence for the
African origin of the marimba is chiefly the similarity of the construction of old
gourd-resonator marimbas to that of the xylophones of central Africa, and the
absence of evidence of marimbas in pre-Columbian Mesoamerica. Furthermore, the
word *marimba* resembles *marimba* and *malimba,* African names for the instrument
(O'Brien-Rothe 1982:99–104).

The marimba with gourds (*marimba de tecomates*) is a xylophone of diatonically
tuned wooden slats (the "keyboard") made from lowland hardwood (*hormigo* or
granadillo) suspended above a trapezoidal framework by cord or string which passes
through each slat at its nodal point, and through threading pins between the slats
(figure 2). Tuned gourds for resonation are suspended under the keyboard. Near the
bottom of each gourd is a small hole surrounded by a ring of beeswax, over which a
piece of the membrane from a pig's intestine is stretched as a mirliton. When the slat
is struck, it produces a buzz (*charleo*).

In its oldest form, the marimba was carried by a strap that passed around the
player's neck or shoulders. In this form, called bow marimba (*marimba de arco*), the
instrument had no legs. The keyboard was kept away from the player's body by a
bowed branch (*arco*), which had its ends fixed to the ends of the keyboard. Later
models, called table marimba (*marimba de mesa*), have legs and lack the bow. The
diatonic keyboard (*marimba sencilla* 'simple marimba') has from nineteen to twenty-
six slats that can be tuned by adding a lump of wax, sometimes mixed with bits of
lead, to their undersides; a marimba tuned this way may be called a marimba with
wax (*marimba de ceras*). The slats are struck with mallets (*baquetas*) made of flexible
wooden sticks wrapped with strips of raw rubber: larger and softer mallets are used
for bass slats, smaller and harder ones for the treble range. The marimba with gourds
is played by one, two, or three players, each using two to four mallets.

The marimba was first mentioned in Guatemala in 1680 by the historian
Domingo Juarros (1953), who observed it played by Maya musicians in public festivities. During the 1700s, it became popular and was reported at religious and civil
events. Its growth in popularity among Ladinos in the 1800s led to the extension of
the keyboard to five, six, and seven octaves, and the addition of a fourth player.
During the Guatemalan independence celebration of 1821, it became the national
instrument. Later, the gourd resonators were replaced by harmonic boxes (*cajones*

A small hole, cut into the side of each drum so it can "breathe," is usually ornamented in a style reminiscent of ancient Maya glyphs as a carved six-petaled flower with the hole as its center.

armónicos), wooden boxes fashioned to emulate the shapes of gourds, and the keyboard was expanded to about five diatonic octaves. This form retained the name *marimba sencilla*, referring to its diatonic scale. The *marimba de cinchos* (also called *marimba de hierro* 'marimba with iron' and *marimba de acero* 'marimba with steel') with metal slats also became popular, and even varieties with slats of glass or with bamboo resonators were developed. The marimba with gourds and the diatonic keyboard, the forms most commonly played by the Maya, may be accompanied by a cane flute (*xul*), a shawm, a saxophone, or other band instruments and a drum (Quiché *k'ojom,* Spanish *tambor, tamborón*) or trap set.

The expansion of the marimba keyboard to include the chromatic scale is usually attributed to Sebastián Hurtado in 1894. Its names, *marimba doble* 'double marimba' and *marimba cuache* 'twin marimba', refer to the double row of slats that accommodates the chromatic scale. Unlike the piano keyboard, in which a raised semitone is found above and to the right of its natural, in many Guatemalan marimbas the sharp key is placed directly above its corresponding natural.

The repertoire of the double marimba is more popular and contemporary than that of the diatonic keyboard, though the former is often used to play the traditional *son guatemalteco* or *son chapín,* folkloric dance pieces typically in moderate to rapid 6/8 time that may be sung to four-line verses. Many local variations occur. The *son guatemalteco,* the national dance of Guatemala, is danced with stamping (*zapateado*). Music for the double marimba ranges from these traditional *sones* to light classics and popular music, often elaborately arranged, in which players display a high degree of virtuosity, precise ensemble playing, and expressive effects.

In villages and towns, the double marimba is often combined with saxophones, trumpets, trap set, bass viol with three strings (normally plucked), one or more male singers, and percussion instruments such as maracas, a shaker made of a thermos bottle with pebbles or pellets inside, and percussion sticks, to play music popularized in the media.

In larger towns and cities, double-marimba musicians are more often Ladinos than Maya. The instrument is commonly played in pairs: the *marimba grande* of six and one-half octaves (usually sixty-eight keys) played by four players, and the *marimba cuache* (also *marimba pícolo, marimba requinta, marimba tenor*), which has a range of five octaves (usually fifty keys), played by three musicians.

The traditional repertoire consists mainly of *sones.* When played in the context of Maya culture, these may belong to a body of melodies reserved for calendric rituals of the saints and spirits, which are often danced but seldom sung. *Sones* played by Ladino musicians are drawn from the traditional folk repertoire of the *son guatemalteco* or *son chapín.*

Membranophones

The membranophones most commonly used by the Maya of Guatemala are cylindri-

FIGURE 3 *Chirimía* and *tambor* players accompany the dance of the conquest for the Tzutujil of Santiago Atitlán, Sololá, highland Guatemala. The musicians, Cakchiquel from another town, are hired for the dance in various towns in the area. Photo by Linda O'Brien-Rothe, 1971.

cal, double-headed drums with wooden bodies, made from a single cedar log or bent plywood. They are of two sizes: small (Spanish *tambor,* Quiché *k'ojom*), and large (Spanish *tamborón,* Quiché *nimaj k'ojom*) about 76 centimeters in diameter. Each head, preferably of deerskin or calfskin, is wrapped around a hoop made from a flexible *membrillo* branch, usually held in place by a looped branch or flat wooden frame, around which tensioning cords are laced, or they are simply laced through the head itself. A small hole, cut into the side of each drum so it can "breathe," is usually ornamented in a style reminiscent of ancient Maya glyphs as a carved six-petaled flower with the hole as its center. The *tambor* and the *tamborón* are each played with one or two sticks, sometimes padded or wrapped with crude rubber. In procession, the flutist usually carries the *tambor* or *tamborón* on his back while another musician plays it.

The snare drum (*caja,* also called *tambor de judía* and *pregonero*) has snares made from knotted cords stretched across the head. Most commonly, the *tambor* or the *tamborón* is found in ensemble with the flute or the shawm (*chirimía,* figure 3); a snare drum customarily joins these in the central departments of Sacatepéquez and Chimaltenango.

The *adufe* is a quadrangular double-skin frame drum, roughly 30 centimeters square, sometimes containing a rattle. It is used in some local dances. The *zambomba* (also *zambudia*) is a small friction drum used in the dance of the twenty-four devils (*baile de los veinticuatro diablos*) in Sacatepéquez.

Chordophones

Chordophones in Guatemala stem from stringed instruments introduced from Europe; there is no evidence of them before the Spanish encounter. They include the violin (*violín, rabel*), sometimes crudely constructed, with four holes for tuning pins, but usually only three strings. It is played with a loose horsehair bow, tensioned by the pressure of the thumb. Homemade bows are straight, rather than arched, and are usually gripped partway up the stick. The instrument is held against the chest rather than under the chin. The violin is played as a solo instrument, and it accompanies voices during funerals or calendric rituals. It joins a harp for playing *sones* and other traditional melodies.

A five-stringed guitar (*guitarra*) is documented among the Tzutujil and

FIGURE 4   A harp, two violins, and percussion (a man striking the harp body with drumsticks) play for a family celebration at a Tzutujil home in Santiago Atitlán, Sololá, highland Guatemala. The harpist plays the longest strings with a wooden plectrum. Photo by Linda O'Brien-Rothe, 1972.

Cakchiquel but may be more widespread. It plays alone or accompanies ancestral songs sung by the player. Six- and twelve-stringed guitars tuned in the standard manner are common. In performing *rancheras, corridos,* and popular music, two or three guitarists often play together and sing.

The harp in Guatemala resembles that of the Maya of Chiapas, Mexico. It is about 1.2 meters high, with a straight, carved pillar and a curved neck that may bear elaborately carved decoration. Its back has five panels; the sound board is of a single piece of wood, with three or four sound holes. The tuning pins are of wood, as are the pegs that fasten the strings to the sound board. The harp rests against the player's shoulder and sits on two wooden feet fixed to the base, holding the instrument off the ground. The fingertips of the right hand play the melody on twelve to fifteen diatonically tuned strings of the upper register, and a wooden plectrum held in the left hand is used to play the seven bass strings, tuned to the tonic major triad. There are two or more unstrung pegs between the bass and treble strings. The sound board is sometimes beaten with a padded stick. For playing *sones* and other pieces, the harp often joins a violin, a snare drum, and an accordion (figure 4).

The *guitarrilla* (*tiple*), a now rare five-stringed guitar with a gourd body as resonator, sometimes joins the diatonic harp. Also disappearing is the twelve-stringed *bandurria* (*bandola, bandolín*).

Male instruments

The Maya of Guatemala use various aerophones, but perhaps the most common is the duct flute made of cane, terra-cotta, or metal. Known in various Maya languages as *xul* (pronounced "shool"), *zu, zubac, tzijolaj,* and *cham-cham,* and in Spanish as *pito,* this is a 26-to-36-centimeter-long vertical fipple (duct) flute, open at the distal end, usually with six holes (the *tzijolaj,* being smaller, may have three). It combines with a drum (*tambor* or *tamborón*) to make the most widespread and common ensemble in Guatemala (figure 5). The *xul* is used with the snare drum in the central departments of Sacatepéquez and Chimaltenango. It may be accompanied by the marimba.

A side-blown cane flute (also *xul*) with a rectangular hole for blowing is documented only among the Cakchiquel of San Marcos, Atitlán (Arrivillaga Cortés 1986). It has an inner diameter of about 38 millimeters and is closed at the proximal end by a hollow sphere of black beeswax that has a small perforation over which a

FIGURE 5   In a procession in Sololá, ritual musicians play a cane flute (*xul*) and a drum (*k'ojom*). Photo by Linda O'Brien-Rothe, 1969.

FIGURE 6   Children watch as Cakchiquel musicians in San Marcos La Laguna, Sololá, highland Guatemala, play a *marimba sencilla* and the rare side-blown flute with a mirliton in the proximal end (*xul*). This ensemble plays for the deer dance and other rituals. Photo by Linda O'Brien-Rothe, 1972.

thin membrane, usually from a pig's intestine, is stretched as a mirliton. Rattlesnake rattles are inserted into the cavity of the sphere, where they add to the buzzing of the mirliton. The *xul* commonly has six finger holes. The Cakchiquel of Lake Atitlán play it with a gourd marimba (figure 6) for the deer dance.

The *chirimía* is a small double-reed instrument of the shawm family, with five or six holes for fingering. Unlike its modern European counterpart, the oboe, it has a cylindrical rather than a conical bore, no keys, and a pirouette (mouth disk) like the shawm of Arab countries. Introduced to the Maya in the early years of Spanish colonization, it is widespread in Guatemala. The reed is fashioned from the dried and smoked leaf of a palm or bromeliad. A shawm is commonly played with a *tambor* or snare drum to accompany dance-dramas, but it is also played in processions and other contexts.

The conch trumpet, now rare, is used in some dance-dramas. Valveless metal trumpets (*tun*) about 90 centimeters long with one loop, probably nineteenth-century European band instruments, have replaced the long wooden trumpets described in colonial sources. They are used with *tun* in the *Rabinal Achí* and other dance-dramas.

MUSIC OF THE MAYA

The music of the Maya of Guatemala is a function of the Maya belief system, in which the ancient Maya religion has accommodated a considerable overlay of Christian beliefs, symbols, and practices. Major public musical events are related to a calendar that mixes Maya and Roman Catholic religious observances with the Maya agricultural cycle. Less-public musical events relate to individual life-cycle events (courting, marriage, funerals) and to human needs, such as curing disease, dispelling evil, and protecting or blessing.

Traditional music is understood by the Maya as having been created and handed down from primordial ancestors who established all the customs, including music, that are pleasing to the spirit-lords (Maya gods), as a means of ensuring the continuing harmony of the cosmos. Tzutujil origin stories relate how the spirit-lord Rilaj Mam (Old Grandfather, Spanish Maximón), to begin his service to the people as their guardian, taught them the songs and dances that must be sung and played to invoke his power. Since their ancestral songs translated "Of the Dead" and "Of the Drowned" call into the singer's presence the spirits of the deceased, special precau-

The spirit-lords' prayer has become a tourist attraction in some places, notably in Chichicastenango, where a shaman lights candles and begins to sing on the steps of the church on cue as the daily tourist bus arrives.

tions are taken to protect from fright or harm those singing or listening. Other songs bring rain, contain winds, or control human beings' actions. The faithful performance of the ancestors' music is understood as absolutely essential to the people's well-being. The musical genres and instruments that are part of their tradition (and these often include European introductions, including the dance of the conquest and the playing of the guitar) are believed to be the ancestors' legacy.

In the highland Maya towns of Guatemala, social events are marked by the sound of the marimba. Many of these events follow the Christian calendar of feasts, which often fall on days of solstice, equinox, or other celestial events important in the Maya calendar or are based on Maya customs relating to the agricultural cycle, such as times to pray for rain or sun, good germination, abundant crops, or successful harvest, each accompanied by its own ritual music.

Christian feasts

The manner of celebrating saints' days varies from town to town. Most common are colorful processions of townspeople to or from the church and the house of prayer (*cofradía*), preceded by the *xul* and the *tamborón,* whose music heralds what is coming (see figure 5). The officials of the *cofradía* dedicated to the saint being celebrated might hire an ensemble of harp, violin, accordion, and snare drum to accompany the saint's statue while it is being carried in the procession. Festivities (in the town square or the church patio and in *cofradías*) regularly include the playing of one or more diatonic keyboards, sometimes using a special repertoire of pieces (*sones*) particular to the spirit-lord with whom the saint has been identified. The melodies of these *sones* are commonly believed to have been given or taught directly by the spirit-lord being honored on the occasion. Sometimes the *sones* accompany dancing that takes place later in the *cofradía*; at other times, the festivity includes a dance-drama performed in the town plaza. In all these events, a great many people—adults and children—participate by following the processions, listening, watching, and often dancing. The celebration may include a band (*banda*) consisting of an assortment of brass instruments, snare and bass drums, and sometimes violins; the band plays marches or popular songs. Bands achieved great popularity in the late 1800s and continue to be an important tradition in religious festivals. Most of them play a repertoire of marches that the original members of the band learned several generations ago from the founding teacher, who taught them using musical notation. Now the bandsmen, usually descendants of the original performers, continue the repertoire as an oral tradition and add to it their renditions of popular songs.

Holy Week, from Palm Sunday to the Saturday before Easter, is the occasion for the greatest festivities and the widest variety of musical forms. Characteristic of this time is the clacking of the *matraca* (a large wooden ratchet, swung above the head on a long handle); marimba combos (*conjuntos*) consisting of three-stringed bass viols, saxophones, and other instruments; and the *xul* and the *tamborón.* On Good Friday, bands customarily play slow marches or dirges (reminiscent of Andalucían *saetas*) during the procession that accompanies Jesus' casket. Among the Tzutujil, the rituals of Holy Week include many ancestral songs, played on a five-stringed guitar and often sung. In some places, survivals of European Renaissance genres of sacred music (including motets and settings of the psalms) are still performed.

Great numbers of dance-dramas are performed in highland towns following the yearly calendar of rituals and customs. Four to twenty costumed dancers recite or sing dialogue and dance to instrumental accompaniment. Dancers themselves may play spiked vessel rattles or rasps. Dance-dramas often last several hours and are customarily performed for eight days in succession, beginning on the saint's day or feast being celebrated. Some clearly predate Spanish contact. These include *Rabinal Achí,* which is accompanied by the *tun* (and is therefore sometimes called the dance of the *tun*) and two long trumpets, and the deer dance, which may be accompanied by a gourd marimba and a *xul* or by other instruments. Other dance-dramas are importations from Spain. These include the dance of Moors and Christians (*baile de moros y cristianos*), accompanied by flute and *tambor,* and the dance of the conquest, accompanied by *chirimía* and *tambor.*

Maya ritual contexts

Life-cycle events, particularly rituals of christenings and weddings, may be celebrated with a marimba or by an ensemble that may include strings, marimbas, or guitars, or by a band. For wakes, it is common to engage a violinist or a guitarist to play and possibly sing. Following the casket to the grave, women sing laments. At the burial ceremonies, a local specialist in ritual music (*maestro del coro* 'choirmaster', *maestro cantor* 'song master', *sacristán* 'sacristan, man in charge of ritual') may sing sections of the Roman Catholic burial service, usually in Latin, with violin or other accompaniment.

One of the commonest means of obtaining what is needed from the spirit-lords is to engage a shaman for a ritual that will include the singing of a prayer. Using formalized but flexible texts, praising and petitioning the spirit-lords for what is needed, the shaman sings on a single tone, inflected (at points convenient to the singer and to the significance of the text) by a drop to a lower pitch for a syllable or two before taking a breath to continue. Vocal quality varies greatly—from a stridently marcato style to a relaxed speech-song. This prayer has become a tourist attraction in some places, notably in Chichicastenango, where a shaman lights candles and begins to sing on the steps of the church on cue as the daily tourist bus arrives.

Among the Tzutujil, the yearly rituals for rain and controlling the winds take place in Santiago Atitlán, in a *cofradía* closed and tightly locked to contain the winds the ritual will arouse. A shaman dons a special rainmaking shirt, sings a prayer song, and dances. During these actions, a singer accompanying himself on a five-stringed guitar sings an appropriate ancestral song (*bix rxin nawal*)—apart from the shamanic prayer songs and chants, the only indigenous genre of Maya vocal music documented in Guatemala. Tzutujil ancestral songs are also known as *bix rxin Ruchleu* 'songs of Face-of-the-Earth', the god whose body forms earth, sky, and underworld. Songs of Face-of-the-Earth are identified by titles that describe their functions, such as "Song of San Martín" (the spirit-lord of wind and rain), "Sad Song" (for women's laments), and "Song of the Road" (where a boy courts a girl). They are improvised by the guitarist-singer on a topic associated with the melody, expressed in a generic title such as "song for courting" and "sad song" (figure 7). Thus the same simple melody with many variations, or more accurately, a melodic contour by which it is identified, serves for all courting songs, whether the singer is narrating a famous courting story from the past or improvising a lyrical song of love; and similarly with melodies for

FIGURE 7   A Tzutujil singer of ancestral songs plays his five-stringed guitar at his home in Santiago Atitlán, Sololá, highland Guatemala. Photo by Linda O'Brien-Rothe, 1972.

other titles and themes. This may be sung, hummed, or played on a cane flute or a five-stringed guitar. The simple, diatonic melodic formulas with their accompanying chords on I, IV, and V, in 6/8 time with frequent hemiolas, and the guitar tuning (which places its origin in sixteenth-century Spain) suggest an origin in Spanish music of the colonial period.

That the Tzutujil have a common origin with the Cakchiquel and the Quiché, whose creation and hero stories and clan histories (*The Annals of the Cakchiquels* and *Popol Vuh*) include musical texts, suggests that the ancestral songs of the Tzutujil are part of an old tradition that probably survives in the broader group but has not yet been documented. Tzutujil texts are in Maya couplets (paired lines in parallel syntax, whose second line usually repeats and varies the first). Some are related to the Quiché origin stories of the *Popol Vuh;* the history and customs of the people; prayers of ancestors and gods; songs for mourning, courting, traveling, rain, and so on. The following is an example from "Song to the Sun, Lord of the World":

> Green mountain world,
> Green mountain Face-of-the-Earth,
> You hear us where we stand;
> You hear us where we walk,
> Face-of-the-Earth, God,
> Lamp Samardatina.
> You are in the sky;
> You are in glory.
> Perhaps two hundred,
> Perhaps three hundred steps
> We will take up and down you,
> Oh God, oh World.

The call to be a singer and instruction in singing and playing are received in signs and dreams, and singers belong to the group of ritual specialists who serve the community by maintaining ancestral traditions.

Some traditional Maya music may be heard on commercial recordings, but the most sacred ritual music is rarely issued commercially. In the cities of the United States where Maya refugees from national violence have settled (especially Los Angeles, California, and Indiantown, Florida), traditional Maya music may be heard, usually in a restaurant or at an occasional concert, or at a communitywide social event.

MUSIC OF THE GARÍFUNA

The Caribbean coast of Guatemala, especially the towns of Livingston and Puerto Barrios, is inhabited by the Garífuna, descendants of Arawak and Carib inhabitants of the Caribbean island of St. Vincent and African slaves brought by Spanish colonists (Arrivillaga Cortés 1990:252). The Garífuna came to coastal Central America in the late 1700s and now inhabit the Caribbean coast from Belize south to Islas de la Bahía in Honduras. Large Garífuna communities live in Laguna de las Perlas, Nicaragua, and in New York and Los Angeles.

Garífuna musical ensembles include groups that use at least some traditional instruments and genres. The most traditional combo includes several sizes of *garaón*, *sísira*, and voice. The *garaón primera* (also *garawung*), the lead instrument, is a membranophone fashioned from the trunk of a tree, perhaps 60 centimeters long, of a slightly conical shape. A deerskin head is laced to a branch that has been bent into a hoop. This is fitted to the larger end, tightened by a cord laced around a second hoop fitted above the first, and from there through holes in the body of the drum near the open end. Threaded between the cords are wooden dowels, rotated to regulate tension. Sometimes snares of nylon guitar string or fishing line are strung across the head. The *garaón segunda* is of the same kind, but larger. Two or three of them are used with one *primera*, which plays virtuosically, periodically returning to a basic rhythm between improvisations. The *segunda* often plays an introduction (*llamado*), establishing the rhythm for the other instruments and any dancers; it maintains the basic rhythm throughout. The *garaón primera* is considered male; the *garaón segunda*, female (Arrivillaga Cortés 1990:258). The *sísira*, also called *chíchira*, is a spiked vessel rattle made of a large gourd containing seeds or small stones. Players, often holding two *sísira* in each hand, maintain the basic rhythm. Sometimes a conch trumpet joins the ensemble. These instruments accompany singing led by a soloist and answered by a chorus, gesturing to express the text. The audience participates by singing with the chorus, clapping, commenting, laughing, and sometimes dancing. Afro-Cuban in rhythm and style, the combo's repertoire includes the following genres: *chumba, jungujugu, jungujugu de Chugu (junguledu), parranda, punta, sambay,* and *yankunú* (Arrivillaga Cortés 1990:260–266). Further study is needed to describe these forms and their relation to other Caribbean genres.

Other Garífuna combos include electric guitar, electric bass, electric piano, *batería* (drums and other percussion instruments), congas, sometimes trumpet, trombones or saxophones, and voices. These ensembles play a fusion of traditional rock rhythms in what is called punta rock, plus reggae and other popular styles. Neighborhood combos of boys from the same barrio may be made up of *garaón*, snare and bass drums, cymbals, tortoiseshell idiophones, spiked vessel rattles, claves, and conch trumpets. They play *puntas, parrandas,* calypsos, and other Caribbean genres. Ensembles of guitar and light percussion, such as claves, gourd rasps, and bottle rattles play at parties, in bars, in the street, at home, and at wakes, provided the deceased enjoyed this kind of music. Their repertoire shows Jamaican influence. In the first half of the twentieth century, municipal brass bands played popular rhythms (fox-trot, blues, ragtime) in public parks, at private parties, and for square dances (*seti*). Today, brass bands with *garaón* and *sísiras* play religious or funeral marches for religious festivals and processions.

The *yankunú* is a majestic warriors' dance usually performed by men, dramatizing victory over Europeans. Musically, it is a dialogue between a drummer and masked dancers, who wear shell rattles strung around their calves.

Garífuna songs and dances

Garífuna songs include Christian songs (*lemesidi*) for liturgical use at mass or other services of the Roman Catholic Church; ritual songs for the ancestral cult of the gods Chugu and Yankunú (*Arumajani*), and work-accompanying songs. Most are responsorial between a soloist and a chorus, or antiphonal between a small group and a chorus. The *punta* is the most widely known Garífuna dance-song genre. Topical, erotic, or moral, its texts serve as social regulators. Many are old; some are used at the rituals of Chugu and Yankunu; but new ones are regularly composed. The *punta,* for a dance known as the *culeado,* is usually done by women in the center of the circle formed by musicians and audience; they perform for recreation, on San Isidro's day, and at nine-day wakes (*novenarios*).

The *jungujugu de Chugu* (or *junguledu*) is the most sacred Garífuna genre, used in the ancestor cult of Chugu and Dugu. Drums play a lightly accented rhythm while women and sometimes men dance in a group and may enter trance in which contact is believed to be made with the ancestors. The *jungujugu de fiesta* is played in procession, and its mood is moderate.

The *yankunú* (probably from "John Canoe," a masked dance known as junkanoo in other parts of the Caribbean) is also called *wanaragua* (*enmascarao* in Honduras). This is a majestic warriors' dance usually performed by men, dramatizing victory over Europeans. Musically, it is a dialogue between a drummer and masked dancers, who wear shell rattles (*illacu*) strung around their calves. It is performed on 25 December and 1 and 6 January.

The *parranda* or *zarabanda,* used for celebrating, is usually played while in transit through the streets. Its texts are social regulators of behavior between couples. The *parranda* is done on 12 December for the festival of Our Lady of Guadalupe. The erotic dances *chumba* and *sambay* and the courting song genre *gunyei* have not been studied. There is a growing movement among the Garífuna of Central America, however, to study, rescue, and revitalize traditional Garífuna music and dance. Popular on the commercial media, mainly cassettes, compact discs, television, and radio are the popular Atlantic coastal and Caribbean styles merengue, calypso, soca, and reggae.

Garífuna musical enculturation begins at an early age, usually with children playing the spiked vessel rattle and later with rhythm ensembles of children and youths on the *garaón segunda.* The principal methods of teaching are imitation and example. The development of a clear vocal quality is prized, and singers are usually the composers of their songs. Makers of musical instruments, who often play the instruments, are recognized for their public function during traditional festivals and rituals.

MUSIC OF LADINOS

Ladinos are people who primarily speak Spanish, tend to live in urban areas and engage in nonmanual occupations (such as teaching students, keeping shop, driving a bus), and maintain their own customs and traditions, stemming in part from Spanish traditions. They tend to adopt instruments and styles typical of contemporary Latin American popular music heard on broadcasts, especially those of Mexico and the Caribbean, and more recently, the Andes.

Ladino music flourishes in Guatemala City, in the urban centers of the south coast and eastern lowlands, and among smaller enclaves of Ladinos who live in the predominantly Maya towns of the central cordillera. It does not include Maya ritual music or instruments, but the two cultures share the diatonic keyboard or double marimba, and much of the marimba repertoire of *sones guatemaltecos* and popular music.

In the 1800s, popular music with traditional or local roots—particularly local forms of the *corrido,* the *pasillo,* the *son,* and the *vals*—developed as entertainment in the homes of the elite. Eased by the arrival of printing, songs and dances circulated in elegant salons in Guatemala and other Central American cities, and gradually became differentiated from a pan-Spanish-American style into more or less discrete national styles. Popular music in the early twentieth century included the *corrido,* the fox-trot, the *mazurca* (or *ranchera*), the *pasodoble,* the polka, the *schotís,* and the *vals.* By the 1920s, the influence of African rhythms was notable in the *danza* (or habanera), the merengue, the samba, and other popular styles. The popular music of Guatemala transcends national boundaries, as do the media that transmit it. Nightclubs, restaurants, and hotels support popular styles for urban Ladinos and tourists. Ladinos and urban Maya enjoy latino disco music in clubs. Performances of popular music played by Guatemalan marimba bands can be heard in U.S. cities where numerous Guatemalan immigrants live.

EUROPEAN-DERIVED ART MUSIC

The Spanish Roman Catholic missionaries who accompanied the colonists introduced Spanish religious musical traditions (predominantly of Seville) to the native peoples (Stevenson 1964). Instruction in singing and the playing of wind instruments for the performance of the sacred polyphony of Western Europe began early in the Audiencia de Guatemala. In the 1540s, provision was made for an organist and a cantor at the cathedral of Guatemala (in present-day Antigua, Guatemala), and books of plainchant and polyphony from Seville were acquired. The composer Hernando Franco, the first choir director at the cathedral in Guatemala (1570–1575), had a choir that included paid singers and indigenous instrumentalists. Later, the choir director Gaspar Fernandes copied works of Palestrina, Morales, Victoria, and Pedro Bermudes (chapel master from 1598–1603) for use in the cathedral of Guatemala. In 1645, cathedral musicians were performing polychoral music, and Marcos de Quevedo, choir director in 1698, is credited with the composition of polychoral pieces for their use. An exchange of musical resources among Guatemala, Mexico, and Peru began early and was carried on during the colonial period. Choirbooks containing music by Spanish, Flemish, Italian, and Guatemalan composers for voices and wind instruments circulated in remote villages in the 1500s and 1600s, testifying to a musical life similar to that in the city, developed by churchmen among the Maya in the outlands.

In the early 1700s, the cathedral's collection of music included works by Spaniards Francisco Guerrero, Cristóbal de Morales, and Tomás Luís de Victoria, plus Loyset Compère, Jean Mouton, Claudin de Sermisy, and Philippe Verdelot (Stevenson 1980). The Guatemalan-born composers Manuel José de Quiroz (chapel master from 1738 to 1765) and his nephew Rafael Antonio de Castellanos, who succeeded him, composed *villancicos, jácaras,* and *negros* that have many ethnic and popular stylistic features. In the mid-1700s, the cathedral orchestra maintained fifteen instrumentalists, including string players, an oboist, soprano and tenor bassoonists, and a harpsichordist.

The publishing of music in Guatemala began in 1750 with Fray Antonio Martínez y Coll's *Suma de todas las reglas del canto llano,* which contained music notation. José Domingo Sol was the first published Guatemalan composer, with the publication of his composition for guitar in 1829 in England. Guatemala's first musical press was that of Domingo Toyotti, who in 1897 began to publish so-called national music by Guatemalan composers. Benedicto Sáenz de A., appointed organist at the cathedral in Guatemala City in 1802, composed religious and secular music, including Guatemala's first waltzes and polkas for the piano. He directed the first local orchestral performances of operatic works, and did much to advance musical appreciation.

Guatemala's national anthem, with music composed by Rafael Álvarez to a text written by Ramón P. Molina, was selected in a competition in 1887. Other composers of the late 1800s were Lorenzo Moras (polkas), Rafael Castillo (*valses,* gavottes, mazurkas, *sones,* two-steps), and Fabián Rodríguez (marches).

In the Teatro Oriente in 1853 and 1855, Anselmo Sáenz directed the national premiere of Gioacchino Rossini's *L'Italiana in Algieri, La Cenerentola,* and *La gazza ladra.* The Teatro Carrera was opened in 1859, and thereafter the music season in Guatemala usually consisted of the visit of a traveling Italian opera troupe. The National Conservatory of Music, which opened in 1875, was headed first by Juan Aberle, a violinist and conductor from Naples, and later by Guatemalans, many of whom had been trained in Europe. In 1941, Jesús Castillo (1877–1946) of Ostuncalco, Quezaltenango, composed the first Guatemalan opera, *Quiché Vinak,* which debuted in the Teatro Abril in 1925, and from which selections were played in New York, Washington, and Seville. Other noted composers of the period include Joaquín Orellana (b. 1933 in Guatemala City) whose String Quartet and Trio were premiered at the Inter-American Festivals of 1960 and 1965, and Jorge Álvaro Sarmientos de León, whose Concerto No. 1 for Piano and Orchestra was premiered in 1953.

In the late 1990s, Guatemala has an active symphonic orchestra and folkloric troupe (*baile folklórico*); the latter presents traditional indigenous and early colonial music and dance, stylized for theatrical performance. Public performances in the central park of Guatemala City by one of the national bands or orchestras are seasonal events. Except when dance music is played, audiences participate passively.

FURTHER STUDY

Ethnomusicological research began with Jesús Castillo's investigations among the Mam and the Quiché, published in *La Música Maya-Quiché* in 1927. In the 1940s, Henrietta Yurchenco, working for the Archive of American Folk Song (Library of Congress), documented and recorded Cakchiquel, Ixil, Kekchí, Quiché, Rabinal, and Tzutujil music. In the 1950s, recordings were made by Lise Paret-Limardo de Vela for the Instituto Indigenista de Guatemala. These collections mainly include music for dance-dramas and other public rituals or festivals. Recordings of Maya vocal and ritual music in homes and *cofradías* were made between 1965 and 1975 among the Tzutujil and Cakchiquel of Lake Atitlán by Linda O'Brien-Rothe, resulting in several studies (O'Brien 1975, 1985; O'Brien-Roth 1976). The body of research is significantly expanded by ongoing contributions of the Centro de Estudios Folklóricos of the Universidad de San Carlos de Guatemala, initiated by Manuel Juárez Toledo.

The Guatemalan marimba has been researched by the ethnomusicologist and marimba virtuoso Vida Chenoweth (1964), and by Robert Garfias (1983). These scholars acknowledged a possible African connection for the marimba. O'Brien-

Rothe (1982) wrote an article about Africanisms in Guatemalan marimba music and performance.

The major studies of Garífuna music in Guatemala have been written by Arrivillaga Cortés (1988, 1990), who has focused on drumming ensembles. His anthropological insights and insider status as a Guatemalan scholar make his works particularly useful. Robert M. Stevenson (1964, 1980) has contributed important studies of Guatemalan music in the colonial and preindependence periods. Of particular interest are his analyses of the relationships between the musics of the native people of Guatemala and the Roman Catholic Church.

REFERENCES

Arrivillaga Cortés, Alfonso. 1986. "*Pito, tambor y caja en el área Cakchiquel.*" *Tradiciones de Guatemala* 26:91–102.

———. 1988. "*Apuntes sobre la música del tambor entre la Garífuna de Guatemala.*" *Tradiciones de Guatemala* (Centro de Estudios Folklóricos, Universidad de San Carlos de Guatemala) 29:57–88.

———. 1990. "*La música tradicional Garífuna en Guatemala.*" *Latin American Music Review* 11(2):251–280.

Chenoweth, Vida. 1964. *Marimbas of Guatemala.* Lexington: University of Kentucky Press.

Edmonson, Munro S. 1971. *The Book of Counsel: The Popol Vuh of the Quiché-Maya of Guatemala.* New Orleans: Middle American Research Institute, Tulane University.

Garfias, Robert. 1983. "The Marimba of Mexico and Central America." *Latin American Music Review* 4(2):203–232.

Juarros, Domingo. 1953. *Compendio de la Historia de la Ciudad de Guatemala.* 3rd ed. 2 vols. Guatemala City: Tipografía Nacional.

Mace, Carroll E. 1970. *Two Spanish-Quiché Dance Dramas of Rabinal.* Tulane Studies in Romance Languages and Literature, 3. New Orleans: Tulane University Press.

O'Brien, Linda. 1975. "Songs of the Face of the Earth." Ph.D. dissertation, University of California at Los Angeles.

———. 1985. "Canciones de la Faz de la Tierra," first part. *Tradiciones de Guatemala* (Centro de Estudios Folklóricos, Universidad de San Carlos de Guatemala) 21–22:55–67.

O'Brien-Rothe, Linda. 1976. "Music in a Maya Cosmos." *The World of Music* 18(3):35–42.

———. 1982. "Marimbas of Guatemala: The African Connection." *The World of Music* 25(2):99–104.

Stevenson, Robert M. 1964. "European Music in 16th-Century Guatemala." *Musical Quarterly* 50(3):341–352.

———. 1980. "Guatemala Cathedral to 1803." *Inter-American Music Review* 2:27–71.

Honduras
T. M. Scruggs

Native Americans
Afro-Hondurans
Garífuna
Mestizos
European-Derived Art Music

About two-thirds of the 112,000 square kilometers that make up the Republic of Honduras are mountainous. The remaining one-third consists of valleys, savannas, and low-lying coastal plains. Honduras has a long northern coastline on the Caribbean, a long border with Nicaragua running from the Caribbean southwest to the Atlantic Ocean, a small Atlantic coastline along the Gulf of Fonseca, and shorter borders with El Salvador to the southwest and Guatemala to the west.

The current population, of about four and a half million, is almost 95 percent mestizo, a mixture of indigenous American and European peoples and cultures. During the colonial period, a small number of Africans were brought into what is now Honduras, but this group has mixed so thoroughly with the mestizo population that it no longer exists as a distinct group and is not generally recognized as part of the national makeup. Though the marimba and probably the musical bow (*caramba*) are of African origin, no identifiable retentions of African musical styles currently exist in mestizo music.

NATIVE AMERICANS

The native American population of Honduras represents less than 5 percent of the national total. There are six groups; listed by geographical location from west to east, they are Chorti, Jicaque-Tolupán, Lenca, Paya, Sumu, and Miskitu. These groups are identified as separate from the majority mestizo culture and have retained elements of indigenous culture to varying degrees. All have undergone increased contact with mestizos and national culture in recent years, and this has greatly accelerated acculturation into the majority mestizo population and indigenous language loss.

Chorti

About two thousand Chorti inhabit the department of Copán, on the western edge of the country; more live across the national border in Guatemala. The Chorti are descendants of a Maya group whose state, centered in Copán, disintegrated with the Classic Maya collapse, around A.D. 1000. No research on their music is available.

Jicaque-Tolupán

One group calls itself Tolupán, a name that is gradually replacing the mestizo-given name of Jicaque. In the early 1500s, the Tolupán inhabited a large area possibly extending to the northern coast, but European contact forced survivors to retreat into the interior (Healy 1984:116). There are estimates of five thousand to eight thousand Tolupán located in the department of Yoro (Chávez Borjas 1984; Cruz Sandoval 1988:36). In the mid-1800s, a small group of Tolupán resettled in Montaña de la Flor, in the neighboring department of Francisco Morazán. Despite missionaries' efforts, this group has maintained Tolupán indigenous culture more thoroughly than the major Tolupán population, which has been strongly affected by mestizo culture (Chapman 1984a, 1984b). No systematic research has been done on Tolupán music.

Lenca

The Lenca have moved further along a continuum toward mestizo culture than any other indigenous group in Honduras. The Lenca language was lost earlier in the twentieth century (Campbell 1976), and any ethnic boundary between native American and mestizo is increasingly irrelevant. The most recent figures remain a 1950 estimate of fifty thousand "modified Lenca" and 28,400 Lenca in the process of becoming mestizo (Adams 1959:629). This population is found in the southwestern departments of Santa Bárbara, La Paz, Lempira, and especially Intibucá, and across the border in northern El Salvador. As in the rest of mestizo Honduras, the pipe and tabor (*pito y tambor*) accompany saint's-day dances (Chapman 1984b:550). The long music bow (*caramba,* onomatopoetically named *bumbum*) is played. Doris Stone noted the use of maracas, three- and four-holed bamboo flutes, and drums to accompany dance during annual festivities (1963:214–215). A greater understanding of Lenca music awaits further research.

Paya

About fifteen hundred Paya (calculated from Cruz Sandoval 1984:427) are located in the central eastern part of the country, in the northwestern part of the department of Olancho. Increased encroachment of mestizos into their territory has accelerated the mestizo acculturation of the Paya. Already in the 1920s, Eduard Conzemius had noted that the Paya dressed like mestizos and had adopted the guitar and accordion (1927:283). His descriptions remain the only published documentation of Paya music. He noted the use of a musical bow with a metal string, played with the bow held in the mouth in the same manner as the Miskitu *lungku* [see MISKITU: figure 1]. He listed maracas, flutes from reeds or animal bone, and a frogskin-covered drum made from a hollowed log. These instruments are presumably employed in the *maih-newa* and the *tasnewa,* rituals that mark birth and death, and in the *katik-ka,* large ceremonies held thirty days after death to aid the final voyage of the soul of a deceased person to the afterlife (Conzemius 1927:283, 301).

Sumu

It is estimated that fewer than four hundred Sumu live in Honduras (Cruz Sandoval 1988:36). This population forms several small settlements along the Río Patuca, mostly within the Department of Olancho. Prominent among Sumu instruments are flutes (*bra-tara*). These are a meter long, have four finger holes toward the end, and produce low tones. Early in the twentieth century, Francisco Martínez Landero described long flutes that matched the *bra-tara.* His account of a funerary ritual is undoubtedly that of the *sikro* ceremony (1980:15). *Bra-tara* were seen by Conzemius in the 1920s, though his Sumu encounters possibly occurred in Nicaragua (1932:112–113). No contemporary documentation of the contextual use of the *bra-*

tara survives, but Jesús Muñoz Tábora (1988:127) notes that the music often imitates animal sounds. The Sumu in Honduras (and possibly the Sumu in Nicaragua) play the *liban,* a three-holed globular flute made from a crab's claw and beeswax. The Sumu in Honduras share several instruments with the neighboring Miskitu, instruments that both groups use primarily for hunting. Orange-tree leaves placed between the lips are used to imitate animal sounds while hunting and for recreation. A friction drum (translated in Spanish as *llamador del tigre* 'caller of the jaguar') produces a loud sound of low register, used to flush wildlife during a hunt. It is a large hollow gourd across which goatskin is stretched. The performer produces sound by pulling a horsehair string through a hole in the skin (Muñoz Tábora 1988:127–136) [see NICARAGUA].

Miskitu

About fifty thousand Miskitu live in Honduras (calculated from Ashby 1976:6 and Velásquez 1979:11), located along the coast and major tributaries in the area known as Mosquitia [see MISKITU].

AFRO-HONDURANS

Since the 1890s, West Indians, primarily Jamaicans, came to Honduras as contract laborers on banana plantations along the northern coastal plains. Afro-Hondurans are concentrated in the larger Caribbean ports. No research on their music has been published.

GARÍFUNA

About one hundred thousand Garífuna live in Honduras (calculated from Meléndez 1988:73). Like all Garífuna, they are descendants of the five thousand "Black Caribs" removed by the English from St. Vincent in 1797 and relocated to Roatán Island, in what is now Honduras. Within a generation, the Garífuna had crossed to the Central American mainland and soon spread along the Caribbean coastline. Later migrations established Garífuna communities in Belize, Guatemala, Nicaragua, and more recently, the United States.

Currently, Garífuna live along the northern Honduran coast from Puerto Cortés near the Guatemalan border as far east as Plaplaya, near the mouth of the Paulaya River in the northeastern part of the country. They are concentrated in forty villages along the coast; men often work in nearby ports. For their participation in the struggle for Honduran independence, they were in 1825 granted the status of *morenos libres moradores de los puertos* 'free black residents of the ports'—a condition that helped secure their political and cultural autonomy. Massive conversions to Roman Catholicism in the 1850s blunted the efforts of subsequent Protestant missionaries; currently, the Garífuna in Honduras espouse a mixture of Roman Catholicism and an earlier amalgam of West African and Carib beliefs.

Most significant research on Garífuna music has been conducted with Garífuna in other Central American countries, despite the Garífuna's historical connection with Honduras and the fact that the bulk of the population still resides there [see BELIZE; GUATEMALA; NICARAGUA]. Published research on the Honduran Garífuna is limited. The most thorough treatment is by Crisanto Meléndez (1988), who presents photos, drawings, and summary descriptions of instruments. Ghidinelli and Massajoli confirm the vibrancy of songs and dances found in Garífuna communities in Belize and Guatemala (1984:507–509), and the *iancunú* (dance of masks) are remarked on by Manzanares (1967:128). The only published recordings of traditional Garífuna music in Honduras date from 1953 (Stone) and show a close congruence with similar Garífuna music in other parts of Central America.

The Garífuna in Honduras were the first to organize a folk-oriented troupe of performers: in the mid-1960s, El Ballet Garífuna was founded, and by the 1980s it had achieved national and European success. Though this and other such troupes have stylized traditional music and dance for stage presentation (for example, see *Honduras—Música Folklórica* 1988; *Lita Ariran* 1993), their importance in establishing the presence of the Garífuna within the larger Honduran polity and culture should not be underestimated.

Punta, a genre once part of Garífuna funerary ritual, developed into a new style of popular music in the mid-1980s. Usually sung in Garífuna, it includes at least part of the *garavón* drum ensemble. As it became more popular, it took on non-Garífuna Afro-Caribbean musical influences. In a scenario resembling that of the creole *palo de mayo* in Nicaragua, *punta* became popular with Honduran urban mestizo youth in the late 1980s. The eleven-piece Garífuna group Banda Blanca had tremendous national and international success with their 1990 *punta* hit "*Sopa de Caracol*" ('Snail Soup'), which achieved the highest level of worldwide exposure of any Honduran music (Banda Blanca 1991; Miller 1991).

MESTIZOS

The penetration of Spanish musical culture since European contact has provided the essential foundation for musical expression among the mestizo population. Research on music before independence remains to be done in colonial government and church archives, though the low level of economic enterprise during the colonial period probably limited state and church sponsorship of musical activity. Some ecclesiastical correspondence sketchily documents popular expression during religious festivals. The first mention of festivities that include the dance called *el guancasco* (see below) dates from 1788, when José Ortiz de la Peña wrote of the need to suppress the use of masks and other local expressions (quoted in Ardón Mejía 1987:138).

Beginning in the 1800s, writings by foreign travelers offer another source for information on local musical performances. These data tend to be limited in detail and usually stand as incidental commentary to descriptions of dancing. Nineteenth-century travelers noted an affinity for stringed instruments throughout the country and documented the acceptance and transformation of imported European dances. William Vincent Wells stated that the fandango, danced to solo guitar without the use of castanets, had long been accepted as a national form by 1855, when he witnessed a performance in the eastern area of Olancho (1857:215). Violin, flute, and guitar accompanied singing and dancing atop boards placed on crates—a popular format at the time called *la maroma* 'the acrobatic performance' (Charles 1890:76–79). *La lanza,* a shortening of *la cuadrilla de lanceros* 'the lancers' quadrille' was popular among semiurban middle classes in the early 1880s (Soltera 1884:296–298); it has now entered the local repertoire of peasants' dances.

Traditional mestizo instruments

Idiophones

Several mestizo dances are accompanied with small percussion instruments. The *ayacaste* (*ayakaste*), a wooden handle around 25 to 30 centimeters high, opens into a Y, across which stiff wires lie. Metal spangles, such as metal bottle caps, are strung along these wires, and they vibrate together when the *ayacaste* is shaken. One example of the use of the *ayacaste* is the dance of the little devils (*baile de los diablitos*), annually performed in Comayagua.

Maracas (*sonajas*) are made from a gourd filled with tiny stones or dried seeds, into which a stick is inserted. *Chinchines,* also called *jícaras,* are rattles used in the dance *el guancasco.* Another small idiophone is the *carrasca* (also called *raspador*), a

sonaja (**maraca**)   Spiked vessel rattle made from a gourd or calabash and filled with tiny stones or dried seeds

matraca   Long-handled wooden ratchet of Arabic origin that is swung above the head

marimba   African term for xylophone found in Central America, Mexico, Colombia, and Venezuela

quijongo   Honduran long musical bow

scraper. During Holy Week, the *matraca* rattle is used by dancers and audience during celebrations to produce a high volume of sound.

Marimbas of different sizes are found throughout the western, central, and southern highlands. As in the Central American nations to the south, the large chromatic double marimba (*marimba doble*) was first imported from Guatemala and southern Mexico around the beginning of the twentieth century [see GUATEMALA]. Between then and about 1950, double-marimba ensembles enjoyed substantial popularity in the country's major urban areas. Instrumentation centered on a double marimba whose keys followed the Mexican marimba's piano-keyboard arrangement, not the off-centered Guatemalan one. This marimba was played by four musicians, and a contrabass doubled the bass part. A trap set and a second, smaller marimba doubling the parts of the three musicians with the highest registers on a double marimba were commonly added. This instrumentation was often expanded to include saxophones, trumpets, and/or guitars. The coming of affordable record players and other sound-amplification equipment in mid-century severely contracted the popularity of marimba ensembles. In the late 1990s in the capital, Tegucigalpa, marimba ensembles are reduced to playing in hotels catering to tourists; in the nation's second-largest city, San Pedro Sula, the marimba has disappeared entirely.

Smaller chromatic marimbas, played by one or two musicians, are still common in parts of the highlands, especially in the Comayagua area and the western edge of the country bordering Guatemala. These ensembles can integrate various percussion instruments and continue to provide recreational entertainment and dance in small towns and rural areas. Frequently a guitar and accordion or violin accompanies the marimba—in which case the accordion or violin is usually restricted to doubling the melodic line. These marimba groups accommodate a wide range of repertoire, occasionally even providing music for Roman Catholic and Protestant religious services.

Membranophones

One or more small drums (*tambores*) play with small flutes to accompany several mestizo dances. The *tambor* is always played with sticks, and the head is covered with goatskin, cowskin, or deerskin.

The *sacabuche* or *zambomba* is a friction membranophone constructed from a large gourd, cut and covered with a skin at one end. A stick is inserted through the middle of the skin. Pushing and pulling the stick produces a strong, low tone.

Aerophones

A *pito*, a three- or four-holed end-blown cane duct flute, is used with a small *tambor* to accompany mestizo dances, as in the performance of *el guancasco* in southwestern departments of the country. Peasants use button accordions and piano accordions for song-and-dance music; the button accordion is more popular. The harmonica has found wide acceptance among peasants and is used in various musical contexts.

Chordophones

The impact of Iberian musical culture is evidenced in the prevalence of stringed instruments throughout the mestizo-populated part of the country. By far the most popular instrument in Honduras is the six-stringed Spanish guitar. It is locally manufactured in the more rural parts of the country, where wooden tuning pegs are utilized. Guitar variants include the *requinto,* a smaller, six-stringed instrument found in the central and northwestern parts of the country. Tuned a fourth above the guitar, it primarily serves a melodic function. The *guitarrilla* or *cuatro* is a four-stringed small guitar of local construction. It is featured in the dance *la correa.* The mandolin (*mandolina*), with eight strings in four courses, and the three-stringed *tiple* are used in combination with guitars in various ensembles.

The local violin is most commonly played held at the chest, rather than tucked under the chin. In remoter areas, strings have been made from the mescal fiber, producing unique sonorities.

The *caramba* or *zambumbia* is a monochord more than two meters long. A single string, running from end to end of the long wooden bow, is made from metal in contemporary instruments, but in earlier times a fiber from the *kankulunko* or *caramba* vine was used, hence the instrument's name. The string is stopped close to a midpoint by a tuning noose, another short cord, wrapped around the wooden bow. The nonsymmetrical division of the main string allows for the two principal notes, usually a fifth apart, that sound when the player strikes the string with a small stick in his right hand. The tuning noose holds a small, hollow gourd against the wooden bow. The gourd faces away from the string, toward the player, allowing him to mute the open end of the gourd with the palm of his left hand. Through this muting, he can control the sounding of overtones sufficiently to produce a full range of notes, though always secondarily in volume to the main two pitches created from the string. In addition, the instrument rests upon a *cucurbitácea,* another larger gourd, or open resonator, which amplifies the sound and can be manipulated by one of the player's feet or by an assistant (Manzanares 1967:125–127; Muñoz Tábora 1988:139–140).

The *caramba* has usually been considered of African origin, though Manzanares maintained an American origin for it, and Boilès considered this possibility valid (1966). It is related to the extinct Nicaraguan *quijongo* and the nearly extinct Costa Rican *quijongo.* Its presence is slowly fading, but it is still used in the western area, and in 1970 it was being used in the southern Department of Valle (Manzanares 1972:4). In the far western department of Copán, it accompanies several dances solo; and with an accordion and a guitar, it provides music for the dances *el coyote, la polka,* and *el xique* (Ministerio de Educación Pública 1983).

Musical genres and contexts

Two of the oldest mestizo dances and accompanying music are *el guancasco* and the Moors and Christians (*los moros y cristianos*). Both dances are performed in small communities where a strong component of indigenous culture survives. *El guancasco* is danced in the southwestern part of the country during saint's-day celebrations. The music enjoys a variety of instrumentations. In Yamaranguila, Department of Intibucá, music for the dances is provided by combinations of *sonajas,* small drums, and cane flutes that produce five tones. In nearby Intibucá, two small cane flutes with beveled mouthpieces accompany four pairs of dancers honoring the image of Vara Alta de Moisés, and to the northwest in the city of Gracias, department or Lempira, dancers honoring Saint Lucy (Santa Lucía) are accompanied by violins and guitars (Manzanares 1963:71, 1972:2). *Guancasco* can also refer to festivities held to reaffirm the friendship and social ties between two neighboring communities or villages. Also termed *paisanazgo,* these celebrations often revolve around the physical meeting of images of the patron saints of each community and can include various music, dance, and other expressive cultural forms (Ardon Mejía 1987:129).

The dance *los moros y cristianos* originates from the introduction of the Spanish dance-drama depicting the historical struggle between Moors and Christians but has been transformed over time and frequently integrates other material. The dance-drama, found in several locales, is usually performed during the annual festivities for Saint Sebastian (San Sebastián) on 20 January. The dancers are accompanied by a small *tambor* and a *pito*—never a shawm (*chirimía*), contrary to Ramón y Rivera and Myers (1980:678). A different instrumental piece (*son*) from the *tambor* and *pito* begins each choreographed section of the dance, cues the entrance of main characters, and announces the beginning of important speeches (for discussion and choreography documented in the villages of Ojojona and Lepaterique, Comayagua, located in the central part of the country, see Ardon Mejía 1987:139–149). In the city and environs of Comayagua, the dance is also called the little devils (*los diablitos*) and includes *ayacaste* rhythmic accompaniment (Manzanares 1972:2).

El xique (also spelled *xike* and *sique*) is the most popular and widely dispersed mestizo dance of Honduras. Stone stated that the name was reduced from the word *quisique* (1955:2), but Manzanares maintained that the full name is *xixike,* onomatopoetically derived from the sound of the dancers' sandals sliding on the ground (1965:201–202). The *xique,* in triple meter, is accompanied by varying instrumentations of vocals, accordion, guitar, and other stringed instruments. The music, like that for the overwhelming majority of mestizo dances, has a strongly Iberian musical foundation.

Mestizo dance music is almost uniformly in a major key. Harmonies rarely extend beyond the compass of tonic, subdominant, and dominant chords. Modulation may occur between sections. In the *xique,* the dancing may abruptly halt when a dancer interrupts by crying "¡bomba!" The same dancer then declaims two to four couplets (*coplas,* locally termed *bombas*), octosyllabic quatrains rhyming *abcb.* Traditional *bombas* with humorously romantic themes are used, or the content is improvised to refer directly to other participants [see Costa Rica].

Currently, the bulk of mestizo dance forms and their corresponding musical accompaniment carry the titles of European salon dances that took root throughout the mestizo population during the colonial and early independence period. These dances, found especially in more remote rural areas, often bear only a token similarity to their ostensibly European origins. The most popular include *cuadrilla, contradanza, danza, mazurca, pereke, polka, vals, varsoviana,* and *zapateado* (for more examples, see Manzanares 1972, 1975a, 1975b, 1975c). At least one such dance, the fandango, was probably introduced directly from Spain around three centuries ago. Major tonality, 3/4 or 6/8 meter, and a sectional structure with corresponding changes in meter or tempo are general characteristics of mestizo dances.

Since the city of Omoa once served as an important port of entry from the Caribbean, foreign influences have left their mark on the dances of the area. Notable among these are localized versions of the tango and the rumba, also found to some degree in other northern port cities and their surrounding areas. *Coplas* interjected during a dance are called *valonas* in Omoa but *bombas* in the rest of the country (Manzanares 1972:28, 31).

Prominent among musical forms is the *corrido.* As elsewhere in Spanish-speaking America, the Honduran version is descended from the Spanish romance. The lyrics, structured within the format of the *copla,* usually praise the attributes of local towns or recount the life of major historical figures. "*El Torito Pinto*" ('The Little Painted Bull'), a *corrido* found throughout Central America, conserves lyrics from the Iberian Peninsula and accompanies a dance of the same name. In rural areas, songs with religious content include songs for Christmastime (*canciones navideñas, villancicos*), songs praising the Virgin Mary (*alabados*), motets (*motetes*), and litanies (*letanías*) (Manzanares 1965:200).

EUROPEAN-DERIVED ART MUSIC

Though music of the colonial period in Honduras is a subject that awaits further research, some information, mostly biographical, is available on musical practices in urban areas after independence. José Trinidad Reyes (1797–1855) was a key figure in the early independence period. Besides composing several masses and *villancicos,* he founded the National University and initiated the first school of music in 1834 in the then capital of Comayagua (Valle 1981:192). In the last decades of the 1800s, extending the success of military bands, the central government promoted the development of civil brass bands in major cities across the country. In 1877, the national government contracted the German musician Gustavo Stamm to create an elite concert band, La Banda de los Supremos Poderes (Band of the Supreme Powers) (Adalid y Gamero 1972 [1940]). The fame of this band throughout the Central American region was due in great part to the efforts of Manuel Adalid y Gamero (1872–1947), organist, composer, and director of the band for several years. His output of polkas, *valses,* mazurkas, and marches reflects the musical environment of the Honduran middle class in the first decades of the twentieth century. His major band compositions—"*La suita tropical*" ('Tropical Suite') and "*Los funerales de un conejito*" ('Funeral of a Rabbit')—received international exposure. Ignacio V. Galeano (1885–1954) was noted for an extensive output of religious music, and Rafael Coello Ramos (1877–1967) wrote many children's and patriotic songs that are still used in schools; however, the first large-scale compositions were by Adalid y Gamero's student Francisco Ramón Díaz Zelaya (1896–1977), who wrote four symphonies in romantic style, and Roberto Domínguez Agurcia (1917–1989), recognized for his violin concerto (Cargalv 1983). Leading contemporary composers include Norma Erazo (b. 1947), also an accomplished pianist, and Sergio Suazo (b. 1956), both of whom studied in Quebec and have written in various idioms.

After failed attempts to establish a national conservatory, the current Escuela Nacional de Música in Tegucigalpa was founded in 1953 to offer training for primary and secondary music instructors. There are currently two lower-division conservatories, the Escuela de Artes Musicales Francisco Díaz Zelaya in Tegucigalpa and the Escuela de Música Victoriano López in San Pedro Sula. More advanced study in European classical music is offered in the Facultad de Música in the Universidad Nacional Autónoma de Honduras; however, no course of study on Honduran or other music is available in the country (Ardón Mejía 1990:63). The Dirección General de Cultura and the Departamento de Investigaciones Científicas del Instituto Hondureño de Antropología e Historia have sponsored small research projects into local music since the mid-1970s (Alonso de Quesada 1978:67).

REFERENCES

Adalid y Gamero, Manuel de. 1972 [1940]. "La música en Honduras." *Boletín de la Academia Hondureña de la Lengua* 15(15):97–102.

Adams, Richard N. 1959. *Cultural Surveys of Panama, Nicaragua, Guatemala, El Salvador, Honduras.* Washington, D.C.: Pan American Sanitary Bureau, Scientific Publications, 33.

Alonso de Quesada, Alba. 1978. *Towards a Cultural Policy for Honduras.* Paris: UNESCO.

Ardón Mejía, Mario. 1987. 'Religiosidad Popular: El Paisanazgo entre Ojojona y Lepaterique." *Folklore Americano* 43:127–163.

———. 1990. "Panorama de la cultura popular tradicional de Honduras." *Folklore Americano* 50:61–63.

Banda Blanca. 1991. *Fiesta Tropical.* Sonotone Music POW 6017. Compact disc.

Boilès, Charles L. 1966. "El arco musical, ¿Una

pervivencia? La palabra y el hombre." *Revista de la Universidad Veracruzana,* 2nd series, 39:383–403.

Campbell, Lyle Richard. 1976. "The Last Lenca." *International Journal of American Linguistics* 42(1):73–78.

Cargalv, H. (Héctor C. Gálvez). 1983. *Historia de la música de Honduras y sus símbolos nacionales.* Tegucigalpa: Lithopress Industrial.

Chapman, Anne MacKaye. 1984a. "Los Tolupán de la Montaña de la Flor: ¿Otra cultura que desaparece?" *América Indígena* 44(3):467–484.

——. 1984b. "Los hijos del copal y la candela: Ritos agrarios y tradición oral de los lencas de Honduras." *América Indígena* 44(3):543–552.

Charles, Cecil. 1890. *Honduras: The Land of Great Depths.* Chicago and New York: Rand McNally.

Chávez Borjas, Manuel. 1984. "La cultura jicaque y el proyecto de desarrollo indígena en Yoro." *América Indígena* 44(3):589–612.

Conzemius, Eduard 1927. "Los Indios Payas de Honduras." *Journal de la Société des Américanistes* 19:245–302.

——. 1932. *Ethnographical Survey of the Miskito and Sumu Indians of Honduras and Nicaragua.* Washington D.C.: Smithsonian Institution, Bureau of American Ethnology.

Crisanto Meléndez, Armando. 1988. "Instrumentos musicales pertenecientes a la cultura Garífuna." In *Organología del Folklore Hondureño,* ed. Jesús Muñoz Tábora, 65–124. Tegucigalpa: Secretaría del Turismo y Cultura.

Cruz Sandoval, F. 1984. "Los indios de Honduras y la situación de sus recursos naturales." *América Indígena* 54(3):423–445.

——. 1988. "Honduras—El archipiélago indio." *TRACE* (Travaux et Recherches dans les Amériques du Centre) 13:35–36.

Ghidinelli, Azzo, and Pierleone Massajoli. 1984. "Resumen etnográfico de los caribes negros (garífunas) de Honduras." *América Indígena* 44(3):485–518.

Healy, Paul F. 1984. "The Archaeology of Honduras." In *The Archeology of Lower Central America,* ed. Frederick Lange and Doris Stone, 113–164. Albuquerque: University of New Mexico Press.

Honduras—Música Folklórica. 1988. Tegucigalpa: Secretaría del Turismo y Cultura. LP disk.

Lita Ariran. 1993. *Songs of the Galifuna* [sic]—*Honduras.* JVC VICG- 5337. Compact disc.

Manzanares Aguilar, Rafael. 1963. "La etnomusicología hondureña." *Folklore americano* 11–12:68–73, 91.

——. 1965. "Etnomusicología Hondureña." In *Primera Conferencia Interamericana de Etnomusicología, Feb. 1963, Unión Panamericana,* 199–202. Washington, D.C.: Panamerican Union.

——. 1967. "Instrumentos musicales tradicionales de Honduras." In *Music in the Americas,* ed. George List and Juan Orrego-Salas, 123–128. Bloomington: Indiana University Research Center in Anthropology, Folklore, and Linguistics.

——. 1972. *La danza folklórica hondureña.* Tegucigalpa: Talleres del Partido Nacional.

——. 1975a. *Música y canciones de Honduras.* ELIA 01. LP disk.

——. 1975b. *Música y canciones de Honduras.* ELIA 02. LP disk.

——. 1975c. *Música y canciones de Honduras.* ELIA 03. LP disk.

Martínez Landero, Francisco. 1980. *La lengua y cultura de los sumos de Honduras.* Tegucigalpa: Instituto Hondureño de Antropología e Historia.

Miller, Amy. 1991. "Teaching the World to Punta." *The Beat* 10(4):38–41, 54.

Ministerio de Educación Pública 1983. *Monografía del Departamento de Copán.* Tegucigalpa.

Muñoz Tábora, Jesús. 1988. *Organología del Folklore Hondureño.* Tegucigalpa: Secretaría del Turismo y Cultura.

Ramón y Rivera, Luis Felipe, and Helen Myers. 1980. "Honduras." *The New Grove Dictionary of Music and Musicians,* ed. Stanley Sadie. London: Macmillan.

Soltera, María [Mary Lester]. 1884. *A Lady's Ride across Spanish Honduras.* Edinburgh and London: William Blackwood and Sons.

Stone, Doris. 1953. *The Black Caribs of Honduras.* Folkways FE 4435. LP disk.

——. 1955. *Songs and Dances of Honduras.* Folkways FE 6834. LP disk.

——. 1963. "The Northern Highland Tribes: The Lenca." In *The Circum-Caribbean Tribes.* Handbook of South American Indians, 4. New York: Cooper Square Publishers.

Valle, Rafael Heliodoro. 1981. *Historia de la cultura hondureña.* Tegucigalpa: Editorial Universitaria.

Wells, William Vincent. 1857. *Explorations and Adventures in Honduras.* New York: Harper and Brothers.

Nicaragua
T. M. Scruggs

The largest of the Central American republics at 130,000 square kilometers, Nicaragua is bounded by Honduras to the north, the Caribbean Sea to the east, Costa Rica to the south, and the Pacific Ocean to the south and west. It has two broadly defined cultural regions: the eastern Caribbean coastal region (known as the Atlantic Coast) and the Pacific Coast. This geographic division provides the organizational structure of this essay. Sparsely populated, the Atlantic Coast is the home of native Americans (Miskitu, Rama, Sumu), the Garífuna, and some Creoles and mestizos. The national population is estimated at more than 4 million. Nearly 90 percent of the people live on the Pacific Coast and are overwhelmingly mestizo. Virtually all archaeological and historical documentation of music within Nicaragua has been limited to the Pacific Coast. The following sections are drawn from that material; references available on the music of groups on the Atlantic Coast are included in the sections devoted to those groups.

MUSIC BEFORE 1900

Music before and during the period of initial European contact

Our primary sources for knowledge of the music of the peoples that inhabited the land within the current borders of Nicaragua are archaeological findings and the writings of early Spanish writers (*cronistas* 'chroniclers'). Both sources cover almost nothing but the southern lowlands of the Pacific Coastal region. They account only for musical instruments and make vague references to actual musical practices.

Archaeological evidence suggests that the two principal groups that occupied the lowland region of the Pacific Coast before European contact had different histories. The larger group were the Chorotega, a Mangue-speaking group that may have migrated from Soconusco, Mexico, and established themselves in the Pacific littoral by A.D. 800. The Nicarao, a Náhuatl-speaking group from central Mexico, forced a displacement of the Chorotegans along the Rivas Peninsula beginning about A.D. 1200. Less definite is the place of origin or time of arrival of the Matagalpan people, a smaller group dispersed in the central highland region (Lange et al. 1992; Newson 1987; Stone 1966). Throughout the lowland region, archaeologists have found small

Travelers who crossed Nicaragua beginning in the
1850s with the discovery of gold in California have
left scattered references to folk music.

tubular and globular duct flutes in different sizes and with various numbers of holes
and tunings (d'Harcourt 1941, 1951; Lothrop 1926; Stone 1976).

In 1524, Hernando de Córdoba was the first Spaniard to penetrate the Pacific
coastal plains. Soon afterward, Spanish writers made the first descriptions of indigenous musical performances and interviewed high-ranking members of the
Amerindian societies on musical practices that Spanish authorities had already prohibited or, because of the destruction of native social structures, were no longer being
performed. From these sources, we know that in 1523 the chieftain Diriangén greeted the Spanish conquistador Gil González Dávila with an ensemble of five flutists
before driving him back to Costa Rica (Oviedo 1977:171).

Chorotega and Nahua communities marked the ending of each calendar year
and other occasions with large-scale celebrations that included musical accompaniment for thousands of costumed dancers. In 1540, Giralmo Benzoni witnessed a
large celebration and described the musical instruments as trumpets (*excoletes*), flutes
of reeds and clay, drums, and whistles; he also mentioned *chilchil*, which he termed
small bells, similar to *chischiles,* the current name for small bells sewn onto dancers'
shoes for use in several dances (Brinton 1883: xxvii–xl). Also present in parts of the
Pacific Coast was the *teponaztli*, a log idiophone used by Náhuatl-speaking peoples in
central Mexico, the Nahua homeland.

Colonial and independence periods

During the four centuries of the colonial period, institutionally supported musical
activity in colonial Nicaragua was probably at a low level due to the province's lack of
economic importance and activity. Whatever records might have existed from the
colonial period appear to have been lost during the wars and earthquakes that rav-
aged the cathedrals, the central repositories for written materials from this period.
However, we know that over the centuries, religious musical instruction (primarily
from Spanish hymnals) and continuous contact with secular forms strongly inculcat-
ed European musical structures and aesthetics. Coupled with the weakening and dis-
mantling of Amerindian culture, Spanish musical practices subsumed previous musical expressions and have formed the foundation for all subsequent music making on
Nicaragua's Pacific Coast. Colonial documents record a steady payment to priests for
masses and other religious services that no doubt required musical performance. One
of a handful of musical references to be found in colonial documents indicates that in
the late 1600s the village of El Realejo on the Pacific Coast used its community chest
(*caja de comunidad*) to purchase a *chirimía,* an imported Spanish double-reed instrument, probably for liturgical use. The penetration of Spanish instruments throughout
the Pacific Coast was noted by the traveler Morel de Santa Cruz, who in the early
1750s encountered, deep in the countryside, an instrument he described as a *chirim-
illa* (Romero Vargas 1987 [1977]:98). Nevertheless, some pre-European practices
were retained during this period. In the early 1730s, the English traveler John

Cockburn witnessed a non-Christian ritual that involved singing and dancing around a funeral pyre (Cockburn 1735:183).

Travelers who crossed Nicaragua beginning in the 1850s with the discovery of gold in California have left scattered references to folk music. They documented the widespread use of the guitar and the *marimba de arco* (see below) along the lowland region, from Telica to Rivas. Brass bands were a primary medium for urban musical performance, and interrelated brass and wind orchestras performed for the upper strata of society. European brass and wind instruments gradually became adopted by larger sectors of the population, eventually forming the *bandas de chichero* that are omnipresent in the lowland Pacific Coast. Music schools that promoted the European classical tradition were founded around 1900 in the major cities, and the first documentation of Nicaraguan compositions for wind and brass ensembles dates from this period. The introduction of intensive coffee cultivation helped erode the remaining cultural autonomy of indigenous enclaves on the Pacific Coast. In the 1880s, the United States linguist Daniel Brinton reported that with the death of the previous generation, indigenous languages had disappeared as functioning idioms (1883:xii). Brinton published notations of *sones* that had been performed on pipe and tabor during musical interludes of the play *El Güegüence* (see below)—pieces that show a marked Spanish-derived musical content.

THE ATLANTIC COAST

The estimated current population of 472,000 on the Atlantic Coast contains six distinct ethnic groups. Positioned along a continuum that runs from native American to African, they are mestizos, Sumu, Rama, Miskitu, Garífuna, and Creoles. A large number of mestizos have migrated from the Pacific Coast. This subarticle examines the music of the Atlantic Coast, excepting the mestizos (see Pacific Coast, below) and the Miskitu [see MISKITU]. The Miskitu are evenly divided between the nation-states of Honduras and Nicaragua; their estimated current population within Nicaragua is 120,000.

Historically, the Atlantic Coast's primary cultural and economic relationship with the outside has been with the greater Caribbean basin. Early attempts by the Spanish to control the area effectively were frustrated by resistance from local peoples, competition from the English, and the apparent lack of natural resources that could justify the investment necessary to overcome these obstacles. Beginning in the 1600s, English buccaneers and traders brought African slaves and entered into alliances with the Miskitu. Under the Treaty of Versailles (1787), most of the English population was obliged to depart, but English influence continued, and Spanish authority was never fully exercised. The culture of the various groups on the Atlantic Coast developed with little contact from the Pacific Coast until the end of the 1800s.

Native Americans

Rama

The most recent estimate places the Rama population at fewer than seven hundred (Hale and Gordon 1987:10). Most live on Rama Cay, south of the city of Bluefields, the survivors of a Chibchan-speaking group that once occupied the southern half of the Nicaraguan coast and parts of Costa Rica. European contact and subsequent warfare with Europeans and Miskitu reduced the Rama drastically in numbers, leading to comprehensive deculturation (Loveland 1975). No published studies on their music exist.

Sumu

The term *Sumu* 'uncivilized Indian' is Miskitu. It has been used since the mid-1800s to describe related groups of peoples that currently inhabit tributary headwaters of main rivers on the Atlantic Coast in Nicaragua (part of the northernmost group is also found in Honduras). The Sumu and Miskitu languages are descended from a Macro-Chibcha language, whose speakers once occupied the greater part of the Atlantic Coast (Holm 1978:298; Stone 1966:210). The groups now identified as Sumu shunned contact with the Europeans and Africans who began to arrive in the late 1500s. Their insularity led to the military superiority of the people that because of trade and association with Europeans and Africans became identified as a separate group, known as the Miskitu. Attacks and slaving by the Miskitu over the centuries and repeated incursions in the twentieth century by mestizo and foreign gold prospectors, rubber tappers, and others have driven the groups collectively known as the Sumu upstream.

The current Sumu population in Nicaragua, of about ten thousand, divides into three major communities. From north to south, these are the Twahka, the Panamaka, and the Ulva. Smaller communities include the Bawihka and the Kukra. The Bawihka, located in the central part of the Atlantic Coast, are few and in a process of losing their ethnic identity to that of the Miskitu—a process that has already been completed for the Kukra community, just south of Bluefields (Helms 1971:16–19; Smutko 1985). A small community of Sumu lives upriver in Honduras, along the Río Patusa (Muñoz Tábora 1988:126–136). Despite the divergence of their histories, several elements of Sumu and Miskitu music show marked similarities.

Musical instruments

The Sumu employ rattles made from round or egg-shaped gourds. These are principally played by women during the funerary ritual (*sau*), performed for a deceased woman (see below). In their construction, a stick handle is inserted into the small end of a gourd, or is attached with fiber strings wrapped through perforations made in the gourd. A jaws harp (*yusap*), introduced by Europeans, is popularly used to induce a soothing or tranquil mood in the performer.

Membranophones are played only by men. The most widely used one was introduced by contact with the English, as revealed in its name, *durum*. It is struck with a drumstick (*tiñni*). The indigenous *pantañ* or *panatañ* is an upright hourglass drum, hollowed from a solid block of mahogany or cedar. The ends are of differing diameters, and the smaller end is placed on a pedestal base, bringing the larger end to a height of one meter off the ground. The drumhead can be made of various animal skins, including deer, tapir, toad, and iguana. The skin is secured with a rope and struck with an open palm. The *pantañ* or *panatañ* is used exclusively for the *sikro,* a funerary ceremony for a deceased man (see below).

The *luñku,* a musical bow, is usually played by women. A thin string of silk grass is attached to both ends of a 70-to-90-centimeter length of bamboo or a tough, pliable wooden bough. The player strikes the string with a pick of wood and presses the bow against the mouth, which acts as a resonator.

A single-tone flute made from the femoral bone of a deer, tapir, or other large animal is used in hunting to lure the agouti, for which the instrument is named: *malka kuñin* (Twahka), *malaka kuñini* (Ulva), and *malaka kuñkana* (Panamaka). A similar flute, the *nawa-wakal,* is made from jaguar bone but is used only in the *sikro.* Also used during this ritual are *bara,* two- to four-holed bamboo flutes about 30 to 40 centimeters long with mouthpieces formed from beeswax. A short fife (*una*) is also used in funerary celebrations. The *bra-tara,* a large bamboo flute that can be up to 2 meters long, is played only by the shaman (*sukia*). With one end resting on the ground, he blows through a mouthpiece formed from bird skin and beeswax during curative rituals. A loud, roaring sound issues from a series of holes along the length of the flute. A conch trumpet (*masi*) serves as a signaling device across distances. Exclusive to the *sikro* is a free aerophone instrument consisting of a long pole to which a thin strip of bamboo is attached with horsehair. The instrument is positioned upright with one end in a small hole, and it is then spun so the bamboo strip hums.

Musical genres and contexts

Collective singing plays an important part in the Sumu life cycle and daily activities. Women's collective singing accompanies important rituals, as shown in examples collected by Grossmann (1988:74–75). The following text is an excerpt from a women's song to greet men returning from a hunting expedition:

> Handsome man, strong man,
> Who goes to the jungle and brings meat to the house,
> We thank you, we wish to follow your steps.

A similar text is used for collective singing during the initiation of prospective husbands. After the initiate has passed a test of manhood that includes endurance of a whipping without complaint, the virgin girls of the village greet him with a song that begins:

> Handsome man, strong man,
> Who can endure pain,
> Handsome man, strong man,
> Who knows no fear,
> We want to be under your protection.

The most important Sumu ceremony is the funerary ritual, called *sau* when held for the death of a woman and *sikro* for a man. It is still celebrated by the Twahka and Panamaka Sumu (Conzemius 1932:112–113; Grossmann 1988:78–81). The *sau* and *sikro* (which mean 'ground, world') help guide the departed's spirit to *itwana*, the land of the hereafter. The *sau,* held at the deceased woman's place of residence, involves drinking fermented maize (*puput*) and dancing with the participation of both sexes. The *sikro* is more elaborate, the exclusive domain of men. In the early stages of the ceremony, lasting from two to four days, the village shaman (*sukia*) takes a thin, black thread, spun by the community's women, and unravels it from the grave back to the house of the deceased. The soul of the departed will travel along this thread, which must therefore never touch the ground, and is suspended on tree limbs, and even propped up to cross waterways. The men disguise themselves with black paint, and wear elaborate headdresses, made from bark covered with brightly colored bird feathers, thus preventing the soul of the deceased from forcing them to accompany him to *itwana*. The first night, the shaman sings incantations that invoke the spirit of the deceased. The spirit's arrival along the thread is announced with the sound produced from spinning a pole with an attached bamboo strip (see above). The ritual proceeds to dancing and the inebriation of all the males. No singing takes place, but the dancing is accompanied by reed flutes (*bara*), cedar drums (*pantañ / panatañ*), and short fifes (*una*). After two or three days, a break in the thread is observed, signaling the departure of the soul of the deceased and its entry into *itwana*.

Toward the end of the second day of the ritual, when the sickness has been exorcised, a joyous celebration with secular, recreational dances welcomes the healed person back into the community, and the ensemble is augmented with guitars, a jawbone, a washtub bass, and maracas.

Garífuna

Garífuna, sometimes called Black Caribs, are descendants of a mixed Carib and African people, exiled from St. Vincent to the island of Roatán, Honduras, in 1797. Within forty years most Garífuna had left Roatán and settled along the Caribbean coast. Garífuna migrated to Nicaragua from Honduras and Belize during the economic boom on the Atlantic Coast in the later half of the 1800s (Holm 1978:418–419; Davidson 1980:36–38). With the economic downturn that began in the 1920s, some Garífuna returned north and others mixed with Creoles and Miskitu, leaving reduced communities in the area of Pearl Lagoon (Conzemius 1928:183). The most recent population estimate, two thousand, includes several families in the city of Bluefields (calculated from Hale and Gordon 1987:23). The total Garífuna population in Nicaragua is small in comparison to that in Belize, Guatemala, and Honduras, where more research on their music has been done [see BELIZE; GUATEMALA; HONDURAS].

Salient among the musical practices of the Nicaraguan Garífuna is the curative ritual, *walagallo*. The following description is taken from Suco Campos (1987), the only published study of Nicaraguan Garífuna music. The *walagallo* is held to cleanse a sick member of the community, and lasts from Friday dawn until Sunday morning. It contains the strongest African retentions found in expressive culture in Nicaragua. The music centers on the shaman's singing and a three-drum ensemble (*garavón*). Garífuna shamans are called *sukia*; their having the same name as Miskitu and Sumu shamans demonstrates the closeness of the relationship among these three peoples. The drums and their corresponding dimensions are *libiama garavón* 'first drum, chosen drum' (26 centimeters in diameter and 39 centimeters high), *lingigui garavón* 'main drum, drum of the heart' (30 centimeters in diameter and 45 centimeters high), and *luruvan garavón*, 'third drum, helping drum' (27 centimeters in diameter and 40 centimeters high). The first drum is made from a hollowed trunk of a tree, and the other drums are made from vertical wooden slats held in place by three metal hoops. Deerskin, used for the heads, is rolled at the edges around a circular bent branch and fitted over one end of the drum. Cords laced through holes in the bottom of the drum are wrapped around a second wooden hoop, placed above the first to secure the skin. The performer can adjust the pitch by twisting wooden pins that thread between pairs of these cords. The drums, always played with the hands, produce a range of tones from different positions and placements of the hands on the drumhead. Each drum is assigned a principal rhythmic pattern (figure 1).

As is typical of many African drum ensembles, the lowest-pitched drum, the *lingigui garavón*, plays the leading role. Its player begins the music, and during the series of performances that make up the ritual his improvisations interact with the shaman and/or the dancers. The other two drums, providing accompaniment to the first drum, vary little from their respective patterns.

Toward the end of the second day of the ritual, when the sickness has been exor-

FIGURE 1   Rhythmic patterns of the Garífuna drum ensemble: *a,* first drum (*libiama garavón*); *b,* main drum (*lingigui garavón*); *c,* third drum (*luruvan garavón*). Transcriptions by Idalberto Suco Campos (1987:64, 66–67).

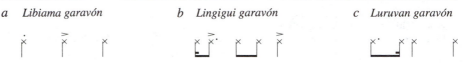

a   Libiama garavón   *b*   Lingigui garavón   *c*   Luruvan garavón

cised, a joyous celebration with secular, recreational dances welcomes the healed person back into the community, and the ensemble is augmented with guitars, a jawbone, a washtub bass, and maracas.

Creoles

The Creole population on the Atlantic Coast totals about forty thousand persons, concentrated primarily in urban areas. Almost half of the Creoles currently reside in the largest city, Bluefields; the remainder live mostly on Corn Island and Pearl Lagoon, and in Puerto Cabezas. A small, growing number reside in Managua (on the Pacific Coast), and many more have migrated to the United States. Unlike the Spanish-speaking, Roman Catholic Pacific Coast population, Creoles are Protestant, and speak a unique Creole English, sometimes termed Misquito Coast Creole (Holm 1978). Most Creoles also speak Spanish and/or standard English.

English traders arrived in the mid-1600s, bringing the first African slaves taken to the Atlantic Coast from the parts of West Africa that today are Benin, Gambia, Ghana, and Togo (Holm 1978:187). In 1787, when the English evacuated the Atlantic Coast, many slaves escaped and stayed behind, joining others of African descent who were already established as "free men of colour." This population was no longer purely African but the result of extensive genetic mixing with Europeans and some of the indigenous population. The economic boom of the late 1800s attracted a new wave of immigrant workers, most of whom came from Jamaica. Only since the 1940s have the more mixed-race Creoles, already established on the coast, fully accepted these arrivals (Gordon 1987:139). The West Indian culture of these more recent immigrants has had a strong impact on creole culture, including music—a connection further strengthened through continual contacts with the islands by Creole sailors and itinerant workers. Beyond occasional reporting on annual festivities in the national press, there are no published studies of creole music.

Folk music

West Indian influence is reflected in the most common musical form, usually called *mento*, which resembles Jamaican *mento*. These songs have duple meter, moderate tempo, major tonality, syncopated rhythmic accompaniment, open vocal style, and a basic structure of alternating verse and chorus. The chorus consists of single lines sung by the lead singer, lines immediately repeated by the chorus in a responsorial fashion. The instrumentation reflects the Creoles' common cultural links with other parts of the English-speaking Caribbean: banjo, ass's jaw, washtub bass, scraper, guitar, and more recently, accordion. Claves, bongos, and congas are also occasionally added. Lyrics typically describe an actual local event, frequently laced with satire. The lyrics to the song "Judith Drowned" (figure 2) can be dated to actual events that took place in the mid-1920s in Bluefields. This section of the song illustrates the structural feature of initiating a song with the chorus section, which will repeat between stanzas. It also shows the pattern of alternating a solo singer and a chorus. The soloist's rising melodic line is answered by the descending melodic line of the chorus—a trait typical of the responsorial sections.

Creoles hold to a number of Protestant faiths, but the Moravian Church has the strongest presence. German Moravian missionaries first arrived in Bluefields in 1849 (Hale 1994:40) and by the end of the 1800s had established several parishes along

FIGURE 2   Vocals from beginning of the Creole *mento* "Judith Drowned" as sung by Samuel "Sabu" Hodgson, with Hubert Perry and Barry Pondler, May 1987. Transcription by T. M. Scruggs.

the coast. Moravian hymnody remains a central musical outlet in the Creole community. Musical performances in Creole Moravian services are close copies of imported European versions and exhibit few African influences.

The maypole is the most widely known traditional dance. Dancers hold on to ribbons attached to the top of a tall pole and twine the ribbons around the pole. In Nicaragua, the dance dates from the 1800s or before, possibly having spread from Pearl Lagoon to other Creole communities. It occurs during festivities that reach their zenith in May, celebrating the earth's fertility. The festivities close with another traditional dance, the *tulu lulu* (or *tulululu*), accompanied by the song of the same name. Dancers pass one at a time under a couple's extended arms while onlookers sing out their names in the song's lyrics.

The chorus of "Mayaya-o" in the traditional *mento* "Mayaya Lost 'im Key" was the basis for the name Mayo-ya (Spanish *mayo ya* 'it's May now') given to the state-sponsored events begun in 1980 to enhance traditional May celebrations. Throughout the 1980s, Mayo-ya became a national event with the additional participation of Pacific Coast music groups and outside tourism. The change of government in 1990 and economic pressures canceled most aspects of Mayo-ya, and current May celebrations more closely resemble those staged before the 1980s.

Popular music

In the 1960s, dance movements from the maypole were transformed into a sensual couple dance that emphasized pelvic movements and close body contact—a development attributed to Bluefields native Harold Hodgson. The sensual aspects of this dance were accentuated in the 1970s when stylistic elements of soca were integrated into the musical accompaniment [see TRINIDAD AND TOBAGO]. The new dance music conserves much of the acoustic, mento-based style, including lyrics, basic melodies, and chordal patterns. However, it transforms the earlier style by increasing tempos and replacing the banjo, the washtub bass, and the accordion with a popular-music instrumentation of trap set, horn sections, and electric instruments, including electric bass, organ, and/or synthesizer. When the song "Judith Drowned" is performed in modern style, the melody and lyrics shown in figure 2 remain intact, though sung at a slightly faster tempo.

Under the Spanish appellation *palo de mayo,* the new dance and music made inroads with mestizo youth on the Pacific Coast. With the success of the Sandinista revolution (1979), *palo de mayo* exploded in popularity nationwide as a symbol of politically and sexually liberated youth—the only time an Atlantic Coast style has gained national acceptance. Mestizos were attracted to it, though the bulk of the repertoire of Creole-led *palo de mayo* groups has always been drawn from a corpus of songs whose lyrics, in Creole English, are unintelligible to the Spanish-speaking Pacific Coast population. The importance of the Pacific Coast's acceptance of this style is reflected in the integration of songs with Spanish lyrics into the repertoire of Creole *palo de mayo* bands. Many bands chose names in Spanish; the earliest group to gain fame in Managua was Los Bárbaros del Ritmo (The Masters of Rhythm) (1976) and the most popular group in the 1980s on both coasts was Dimensión Costeña (Coastal Dimension) (1986, 1989).

Along with African-American popular music from the United States, Jamaican reggae (locally called rasta) has a strong following. The socially committed reggae group Soul Vibrations toured and recorded internationally in 1991—the only Atlantic Coast popular music group to have done so.

Mestizos

The Nicaraguan state's assertion of political control in 1894 and the development of the banana and other industries accelerated the growth of Spanish-speaking mestizo population and influence. About three hundred thousand mestizos currently live on the Atlantic Coast. They are the area's largest group, accounting for 65 percent of the population. Mestizos have established a major presence in the Atlantic littoral urban centers, but 90 percent of them are peasant farmers on the western boundaries of the region (Hale and Gordon 1987:25), mostly migrants from the Pacific Coast's northern area. Uprooted by big economic projects and strong population pressures on the Pacific Coast, they continue to encroach on Miskitu and Sumu territory. During the Sandinista period (1979–90), previously sporadic links between nonmestizo Atlantic Coast communities and the Pacific Coast intensified; these have abated since 1990, in great part because of the nation's economic crisis. The growth of the mestizo population and closer ties to the Pacific Coast have resulted in the increased influence of Hispanic Nicaraguan culture and music.

THE PACIFIC COAST

The subjugation and near-destruction of the Chorotega and Nahua peoples allowed for the subsequent pervasive Spanish acculturation in the Pacific Coast of Nicaragua. Currently, even the isolated pockets of indigenous communities on the Pacific Coast have experienced strong mestizo influences. During the colonial period, Africans were brought to replace the exhausted indigenous population for agriculture and mining (Romero Vargas 1987 [1977]). Over time, this African blood has in some sections of the Pacific Coast so thoroughly blended into the general population that it is not generally recognized as part of the national makeup.

No identifiably African musical stylistic retentions currently exist on the Pacific Coast of Nicaragua, though one prominent local instrument, the marimba, is clearly African in origin. Nicaragua's majority mestizo culture belongs to the general mestizo Pacific Coast culture of Central America—a tradition that runs from southern Guatemala to Costa Rica's *meseta central*. With its neighbors, Nicaragua maintains strong cultural contact with the United States, and especially through the media, with Mexico and the rest of Latin America.

Traditional folk instruments

Idiophones

The *sonaja* is a hand-held semicircular wooden tambourine with metal jingles but

guitarrilla 'Little guitar', guitar with four metal strings placed on the treble side of the Nicaraguan marimba

tambor Spanish term for membranophone; also, double-headed indigenous drum of Nicaragua, still found in Indian enclaves

gigantona Primarily verbal performance, the principal folk expression of León, Nicaragua

atabales Large Nicaraguan and Guatemalan drums the size and shape of standard snare drums but made of wood

quijongo Nicaraguan and Costa Rican monochord of African origin, made from a long wooden bow with a single metal string and one or two gourd resonators

without a membrane. Today, it is unique to the dance-dramas *el toro huaco* and *el gigante* (see below).

The *marimba doble* is a large, chromatic marimba developed in Chiapas (Mexico) and central Guatemala around 1900. *Marimba dobles* were imported and imitated in Nicaragua soon afterward. Sometimes joined with wind and percussion instruments to form dance-accompanying bands, the *marimba doble* has steadily declined since the 1950s and is now rarely heard [see GUATEMALA].

The *marimba de arco* 'hooped marimba', whose epicenter is the region around Masaya and Monimbó, is the only lowland Pacific instrument of African origin. Often touted as Nicaragua's national instrument, it is distinctive from other Latin American marimbas in its construction and national prominence, despite its diminutive size and diatonic limitations relative to other marimbas. The name is derived from a hoop (made from a thick, woody vine and attached to the frame) that makes the instrument easily portable and within which the musician sits to play. The tone of each hardwood slat is reinforced by a resonator, originally made from gourds sized for each slat as in Africa, but later replaced by bamboo and now by hollow cedar cylinders. All Nicaraguan marimbas preserve the mirliton of African marimbas, the buzzing membrane stretched over a hole in each resonator, most commonly derived from dried pig's intestine. The *marimba de arco* is played solo by a single *marimbero* flanked by two stringed instruments positioned to add support to the appropriate register: a *guitarra*, a six-stringed Spanish guitar with metal strings, sometimes modified with extra bass strings, is situated on the bass end of the marimba, and a *guitarrilla*, a four-stringed guitar with metal strings, is placed on the treble side (figure 3).

FIGURE 3   A *marimba de arco* trio of Monimbó, Masaya: *left to right,* Juan Palacios on *guitarrilla,* Manuel Palacios on *marimba de arco,* and Carlos Palacios on guitar. Photo by T. M. Scruggs, 1985.

Membranophones

Several membranophones share a similarity both with Spanish folk instruments and with sixteenth-century descriptions by Spanish chroniclers of indigenous instruments in use in Nicaragua at the time of the Encounter. Two examples of this possibly double origin are the *juco,* a small friction drum once found in the Masaya area (and now extinct), and various sizes of *tambor,* a double-headed drum, still found in Indian enclaves. All Nicaraguan folk drums are double headed and played with two sticks, never by hand.

A medium-size *tambor* (20 to 25 centimeters in diameter) is still used in the indigenous community of Monimbó, played exclusively by the *mayordomo,* the community's elected leader. Until the 1980s, certain rhythms were widely understood to signify specific messages, such as calling the populace to perform particular communal tasks or alerting them to fire or other calamities, but this form of musical communication has fallen into disuse.

Two small drums and one medium-size drum are the traditional accompaniment for *la gigantona,* a primarily verbal performance and the principal folk expression of León, the nation's second-largest city. The drums announce the beginning of the performance and intersperse their sounds with the calling out of *coplas,* four-line rhymed verses shouted by the performer from inside an oversized representation of a female figure, originally derived from the Spanish tradition depicting Queen Isabella.

The largest Nicaraguan drums are the *atabales,* the size and shape of a standard snare drum but made of wood, and the *bombo,* a bass drum. One *bombo* and up to a dozen *atabales* form the type of folk ensemble known as *los atabales,* found exclusively in the city of Granada and performing only in October, during a month-long religious celebration.

Chordophones

By far the most popular and widely distributed instrument throughout Nicaragua (on both coasts) is the six-stringed Spanish guitar (*guitarra*). Throughout the nation, this guitar accompanies solo lyric songs or, especially in the mestizo cultural area, appears in pairs playing parallel thirds and sixths.

The use of the guitar in instrumental settings has been cultivated in Las Segovias and neighboring northern regions of the Pacific Coast more than in other parts of the country. Duo-guitar instrumental pieces are especially associated with the northern region. The most common instrumentation calls for the two guitars to divide the chordal accompaniment and melodic line. The most popular form for these instrumental guitar duos is the mazurka, the triple-meter music and associated dance introduced into the northern coffee-producing regions by Central European immigrants in the latter half of the 1800s. Though found in other departments to the south, it is commonly called *la mazurka segoviana* 'the Segovian mazurka' and remains a vital music-and-dance complex in the northern zone.

Another instrumental music proper to the northern regions of Nicaragua consists of a *violín de talalate* (named for the soft, white *talalate* wood, famed for the ease with which it can be carved into the appropriate shape), accompanied by one guitar or more. Groups featuring a *violín de talalate,* most notably in the Estelí area, perform various musical genres including mazurkas. The musical style of this violin, matching that of the region's vocal aesthetic, avoids vibrato and emphasizes glissandos. The sound of the instrument—thin, sometimes raspy—realizes an aesthetic common to other Latin American violin performances.

The *quijongo,* a monochord of African origin, is made from a wooden bow up to three meters long with a single metal string. To provide rhythmic and melodic accompaniment, a small stick strikes the string [see HONDURAS]. The *quijongo* has been limited to the zone close to the Honduran border and is practically extinct.

Aerophones and combinations of instruments

In the southern coastal zone, a *pito,* a small, straight, wooden fipple flute, is played with one or more *tambores* to accompany traditional dances. Each *tambor* averages 15 centimeters in diameter. Usually considered a Spanish importation, the pipe-and-tabor instrumentation may also have American origins (Boilès 1966). Though references to the local use of the shawm (*chirimía*) survive from the colonial period, this aerophone fell out of use at least a century ago and is no longer found in Nicaragua.

Folk-musical genres and contexts

On the Pacific Coast, one surviving Spanish form is the *romance,* a vocal genre usually sung solo with guitar accompaniment. About twenty *romances* closely retain the original Spanish melodic and lyrical form, though most occur in more than one version. *Romances* in Nicaragua roughly adhere to the standard form of four octosyllabic lines per stanza and range from four to twelve stanzas in length. They can be divided into three categories: secular, religious, and children's songs. Most extant examples are from the first category and recount stories of love, almost invariably with tragic endings.

The Nicaraguan *corrido,* sometimes called the *corrido nacional,* follows the same basic form as the Spanish *romance,* though with greater variation in lyric structure. *Romances* and *corridos* are frequently identified by other names, including *versos, historias, coplas,* and *canciones.* The lyrics of *corridos* can be grouped into four categories: those that treat themes of love; those whose main characters are animals, often as a metaphorical reference to humans; those that propound nationalism and patriotism; and those that give accounts of specific political events that have taken place in the country. Some *corridos* in the last category can be dated to the first half of the 1800s. All *romances* and *corridos* are in a major key throughout, with a narrow melodic range and a descending melodic ending typically leading to the tonic.

Northern areas

Some of the most widely known *corridos* stem from the military and political struggle of Augusto C. Sandino in the northern regions (1928–1933). Denied access to institutional forms of communication and appealing to an illiterate population, these songs popularized the goals and accomplishments of Sandino's movement. *Corridos* about Sandino survived repression by successive régimes of the Somoza family, and a few regained national prominence with the triumph of the Sandinista Revolution.

The most famous *corrido* about Sandino exists in different variations and under several titles, including "*Que se derraman las copas,*" "*A cantarles voy, señores*" (Belausteguigoitia 1934:164) and "*Los dueles de Sandino*" (figure 4), the title of the following text, performed by Los Soñadores de Sarawaska (1980). The lyrics are typical of *corridos* in their use of narrative structure to convey a moral message. This ver-

FIGURE 4   Melody of the beginning of "*Los dueles de Sandino,*" a *corrido nicaragüense* performed by Los Soñadores de Sarawaska (1980:A2). Transcription by T. M. Scruggs.

continues

sion quotes Sandino in a mythical conversation with the then-titular president Sacasa, who advocated accepting the terms of the occupying U.S. Marines. Sandino's apocryphal offer to "sell Americans' heads" refers to the U.S.-trained National Guard's gruesome practice—allegedly introduced by the U.S. Marines—of mutilating and beheading Sandinista troops and civilians.

Pongan cuidado, señores,	Pay attention, gentlemen,
lo que les voy a cantar,	to what I sing to you,
brindándole los sonores	making this musical offering
a un valiente general.	to a valiant general.
Que se derramen las copas;	Let's drain our glasses;
que se aumente más el vino,	Let's have more wine,
y brindemos porque viva	And toast because
Augusto César Sandino.	Augusto César Sandino lives.
"¡Que libere a Nicaragua!"	"Liberate Nicaragua!"
el pueblo de Sandino grita,	Cry Sandino's people,
"y aquel traidor de Moncada	"And rid us of the traitor Moncada,
se vendió hasta la yegüita."	Who's even sold off the mare."
Dijo Sandino una vez,	Sandino once said,
apretándose las manos:	making his hands into fists,
"Yo vendo a diez por centavo	"At ten to the penny
cabezas de americanos."	I sell Americans' heads."
Sacasa dijo a Sandino:	Sacasa said to Sandino,
"Yo me voy a retirar;	"I'm going to give up;
a los Estados Unidos	we can't defeat
no les vamos a ganar."	the United States."
El valiente le contesta,	The courageous one answered,
"Ándate para tu casa;	"Go back to your home.
pues no les tengo miedo:	I don't fear them:
son puritas calabazas."	They're all pumpkinheads."
Que se derramen las copas. . . .	Let's drain our glasses. . . .

Moncada was a general who acquiesced to U.S. intervention after receiving a large payoff.

The impact of the Mexican revolutionary *corrido* is clearly evident in the versification and particularly the music of these songs. Several *corridos* about Sandino utilize the melody of the Mexican *corrido "La Adelita."* The propensity to substitute lyric content using the same music, a trait of the modern Mexican *corrido*, marks other Nicaraguan *corridos*. In the northern regions, a strong commonality with Mexican folk music is noticeable in the thin, nasal vocal quality and the parallel harmony in thirds of melodic lines with descending glissandos at the end of stanzas—traits illustrated in figure 4, and found especially in more remote areas.

Southern areas

The southern zone of the Pacific Coast is rich in musical expressions. Different combinations of the flute (*pito*) and a small *tambor* accompany traditional dances, performed exclusively during a given locality's saint's-day celebrations. For these dances, religious fulfillment is an important part of the context, and the music is considered to have a sacred quality. Though flute-and-drum instrumentation may have originat-

los chinegros 'The blackfaces', Nicaraguan paired dancers, in blackface and dark suits (imitating military uniforms) and armed with wooden swords, who battle one another

cristianos y moros 'Christians and Moors' (also, *moros y cristianos*), dance reenactment of battles between Spaniards and Moors, popular throughout Hispanic America

el güegüence Earliest known Latin American folk drama with text partly in Náhuatl that is still performed in the Diriamba area of Nicaragua

ed in Spanish folk traditions, the musical content is clearly of local origin. In Monimbó and Nindirí (towns known for a high level of indigenous cultural retention), a *pito* and one to three *tambores* provide pieces (*sones*) for *los chinegros,* pairs of dancers—dressed in blackface and dark suit jackets (imitating military uniforms), and armed with wooden swords—who parade and then, on the playing of the appropriate *son,* battle one another (see Okada 1995: example 6). Although the blackface of the dancers might possibly date from the colonial introduction of the Spanish dance depicting *cristianos y moros* (with its blackface representation of Arabs), a more likely explanation is that it reflects the African-Nicaraguan composition of the governmental militia in the provinces of Masaya and Granada in the 1800s. (The African population on the Pacific Coast has since mixed with the general mestizo population to the point that they have disappeared as a recognizable group.) A similar flute and *tambor* accompany the *yegüita,* a dance with music and characters similar to *los chinegros,* found in Granada.

Nearby, in the Diriamba area, musical interludes for the folk dramas *el gigante* and *el güegüence* are provided by a flute and a *tambor,* played by two musicians or with both instruments played by a single musician in pipe-and-tabor fashion. Figure 5 shows the two-musician ensemble. *El güegüence* is famed for being the earliest known Latin American folk drama with partial Náhuatl text that is still performed. Though the text, of mixed Castillian Spanish, Basque, and Náhuatl, dates from the 1700s at the latest, the music cannot be reliably dated to the same era and may be

FIGURE 5 At Diriamba, *sonaja*-playing masked dancers perform the dance-drama *el gigante,* accompanied by *tambor* and *pito.* Photo by T. M. Scruggs, 1988.

FIGURE 6 Excerpt from a *son* played by pipe and tabor for the dance-drama *el toro huaco*. Diriamba, January 1988. Parenthetical notes are indistinct. Transcription by T. M. Scruggs.

(♩) = indistinct note

more recent. In Diriamba proper, a single musician plays a small *tambor* and a two-holed *pito* in pipe-and-tabor fashion to accompany the annual saint's-day performance of *el toro huaco*. Different short *sones* cue the seven complicated series of movements of two dozen masked and elaborately costumed dancers (see Okada 1995: example 7). The triadic implications of the melodic contour reveal a close relationship to European functional harmony (figure 6). Unique to *el toro huaco* is the *sonaja,* a percussion instrument shaken in rhythm by each dancer; its metal jingles complement the shaking of small metal bells (*chischiles*) sewn onto the dancers' shoes.

Dances and ensembles

The pipe-and-tabor instrumentation has also served to accompany folk dances that have begun to disappear. Two important examples are *el baile de moros y cristianos* 'the dance of Moors and Christians' from the area of Boaco and *la vaquita* '[the dance of] the cow' of Managua. *La vaquita* was once performed by a single elderly female dancer in a stylized imitation of a bull's goring onlookers. The only remnants of the tradition are groups of young men dressed in rudiments of the original costume, who carouse through the crowds during the city's annual saint's-day celebrations.

The *marimba de arco* trio accompanies a flirtatious couple dance known under various titles depending on the costuming—*el baile de las inditas* 'the dance of the female Indians', *el baile de las negras* 'the dance of the dark-skinned women' (see Okada 1995: example 8), and so on. These dances, generically called *el baile de la marimba* (the marimba dance), are performed on saint's-day celebrations throughout the Pacific Coast. This dance-music complex remains centered in the greater Masaya area, but its boosters promote it as the national dance—a claim supported by its privileged presentation by national folkloric troupes. The pieces that make up the repertoire for accompanying it are marked by major tonality and ABAB or ABABA structure. The rhythmic feel of the ensemble often clouds the distinction between 6/8 and 3/4 meter. Figure 7, an excerpt from "*El Hombre de Barril*" ('The Barrel-Chested Man'), illustrates how a duple meter is suggested by the bass (which the marimbist plays with the left hand) and a triple meter by the guitar, the *guitarilla,* and the melodic line (which the marimbist plays with the right hand).

TRACK 33

For those outside the tradition's immediate practitioners, and even for many nonmusicians actively involved in *el baile de la marimba*, authorship of the traditional repertoire is considered anonymous, as befits a supposedly genuine folk tradition. Nevertheless, several important pieces were composed in the last two generations (by marimba musicians) or can be traced back a couple of generations to adaptations of popular songs. For expressly secular contexts, *marimba de arco* musicians may aug-

FIGURE 7   Excerpt from *"El Hombre de Barril"* ('The Barrel-Chested Man'), from the *marimba de arco* trio repertoire for accompanying the *baile de la marimba,* as performed by Marco Martínes on *marimba de arco,* Angel Martínes on *guitarrilla,* and Omar Martínes on guitar, 9 March 1989. X-shaped noteheads are stopped. Transcription by T. M. Scruggs.

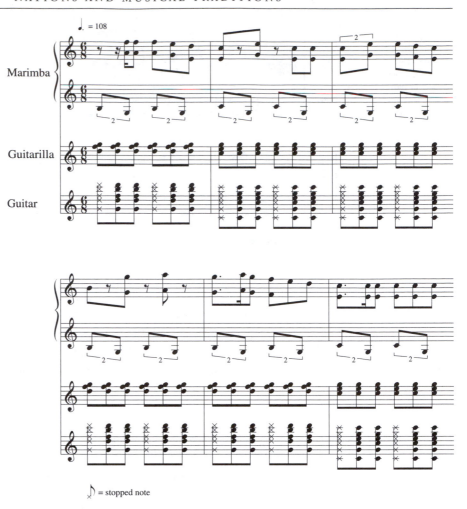

♪ = stopped note

ment the same quasi-religious repertoire with renditions of popular music, especially Mexican-style *cumbias.* In these contexts, the traditional instrumentation is frequently augmented by handheld percussion, most frequently a shaker (*guaya*) and/or a scraper (*güiro*).

Brass and wind bands—called *bandas de chicheros* (from *chicha,* a fermented corn beverage), or more infrequently, *bandas filarmónicas* 'philharmonic bands'—perform important musical functions in rural and urban communities throughout the southern coastal zone. The instrumentation commonly consists of two trumpets, a sousaphone, and a percussion section of snare drum, bass drum, and handheld cymbals; a clarinet, a saxophone, and a trombone may be added. During rodeos and the dance segments of saint's-day festival processions, *chicheros* play *sones de toro* 'bull *sones*' or *sones de cacho* 'bull's-horn *sones*', raucous traditional dance-and-bullfight songs in a quick duple meter. These *sones* may vary from anonymous traditional pieces to military marches to adaptations of popular songs. *Chicheros* provide music for funerary masses and processions, customarily utilizing repertoire written by local composers expressly for brass band. Despite the indispensability of these bands in official church ceremonies and important folk-religious celebrations, the musicians are held in low esteem, as their name indicates.

Sung traditions

The greatest outpouring of religious music on the Pacific Coast takes place in early December with the singing of *purísimas,* songs praising the Virgin Mary (see Okada 1995: example 5). The title refers to the Immaculate Conception (celebrated by the

Roman Catholic Church on 8 December) and possibly dates from as early as the 1700s, when priests distributed images of the Virgin Mary to encourage devotional singing outside of church. Many *purísimas* began as written compositions; the earliest-known publication of one in Nicaragua dates from 1867; however, these songs are now widely regarded as part of an anonymously authored folk-musical repertoire. Their singing is not limited to churches and is dispersed throughout each community. On the night of 7 December (called *la gritería* 'the shouting'), the streets are convulsed with groups of singers, especially children, who approach altars in front of homes, sing one or more *purísimas,* and are rewarded with sweets by the altars' owners.

Less popular are *villancicos navideños*, songs praising the Virgin Mary and the Infant Jesus, sung during the Christmas season. Nicaraguan *villancicos* are exclusively religious and show a remarkable retention of their (originally Spanish) melodic and lyrical form and content. More widely heard during this season are Christmas songs (*sones de pascua*), sometimes called *villancicos*. Most of these compositions are products of local composers, dating back two to four generations, played by brass and other wind ensembles of varying instrumentations.

Popular music

The development of foreign and local popular musical forms corresponds to the growth of a local music industry. Outside musical forms became heavily disseminated in Nicaragua because of two factors: the country's small size limited the extent to which local musical production could compete with the overpowering music industries of more industrialized nations; the Somoza dynasty, which came to power in the mid-1930s, ruled throughout the period when mass media were developing. The elite adopted an outward orientation that gives preference to foreign cultural models, especially those from the United States. As a result of these factors, outside forms had a great impact on Nicaraguan musical culture. The dissemination of Mexican popular music, one of the strongest and most enduring influences, came from radio and records, but movies played a central role. The availability and popularity of Mexican movies that regularly included musical performances began with the 1940s, the Golden Age of Mexican cinema. As a result, throughout the Pacific Coast, the *canción ranchera* (a folk and popular sung genre) and other central and northern Mexican forms have become deeply rooted. The Mexican trio style of guitar- and *requinto*-accompanied singing first popularized in the 1940s is still well accepted. Contemporary trios, including the famous Los Girasoles, integrate local Nicaraguan interpretation and musical sensibilities. Mariachis, in various instrumental combinations, are now found throughout the Pacific Coast. Trios and mariachi musicians available for hire continue to gather nightly in the Bello Horizonte Plaza in Managua.

A series of Afro-Cuban dance musics (rumba, mambo, *cha-cha-chá*) has achieved wide success in urban areas since the 1940s. The Sonora Matancera, an Afro-Cuban group originally popular in the 1950s, still remains a source for programming on radio in Managua. More recently, Mexican and Colombian versions of the *cumbia* have been the most popular styles of dancing. The influence of U.S. popular music has consistently increased over the decades from radio and more recently from television. A host of mostly derivative Nicaraguan rock-playing bands proliferated in the late 1960s and early 1970s. War and economic decline spurred migration to the United States during the 1980s. Ongoing communication with this expatriate population has heightened the profile of North American popular culture in general. In the 1990s, the return of "Miami boys"—children educated in the United States—has had an important cultural impact beyond their actual numbers.

son nica   From *nicaragüense*, 1940s
Nicaraguan song genre deliberately created
by the composer Camilo Zapata as an antidote to Mexican musical influence

volcanto   'Volcano song', Nicaraguan genre of
nueva canción associated with the
Sandinista revolution

The *son nica* (from *nicaragüense*), whose popularity was cemented in the 1940s, was deliberately created as a Nicaraguan antidote to Mexican musical influence. The composer Camilo Zapata (b. 1917) is attributed with inventing it by adapting the *marimba de arco* tradition's major tonalities, melodic phrasing, and 6/8 rhythm. A guitar-accompanied genre, it has achieved recognition as a national idiom, though it is found mostly in the populous lowland region. Important performing composers in this style include Zapata, Victor Manuel Leiva (b. 1925), Jorge Isaac Carvallo (b. 1927), and Otto de la Rocha (b. 1936). Northern musical forms were introduced to the majority population in the lowland area through the immense popularity of recordings by Salvador Cardenal Argüello in the 1950s. The most influential singer-songwriter in the latter half of the century is Carlos Mejía Godoy (b. 1943). His lyrics adroitly draw from peasant culture, and he remains the only composer to set verses to the (traditionally instrumental) northern form of the *mazurka*.

The nation's political upheavals beginning in the mid-1970s paralleled the rise in the local importance of Latin American *nueva canción* 'new song', sometimes dubbed *volcanto* (combining *volcán* 'volcano' and *canto* 'song'). Carvallo's *son nica* "Campesino" ('Peasant') was the first recorded protest song (1964), but Carlos Mejía Godoy established political song as an important genre in the early 1970s. His version of a liberation-theology-inspired Roman Catholic mass set in folk-musical style, the *Misa Campesina* (*Peasant Mass*) (1980), served as a model throughout Latin America in the 1970s and 1980s. The musical style of his younger brother, Luis Enrique Mejía Godoy (b. 1945), typifies that of a younger generation of *volcanto* musicians in his eclectic array of continental musical influences and electric instrumentation. The years just before and after the overthrow of the Somoza government witnessed an explosion of cultural activity that included an outpouring of music with political commentary and social commitment from many short-lived musical ensembles. A milestone was "*Guitarra Armada*" ('Armed Guitar') (1978), a recording of *sones nicas* and other Nicaraguan songs by the Mejía Godoy brothers. The album, recorded in Costa Rica and smuggled into Nicaragua, used humorous lyrics couched in local vernacular to instruct civilian combatants how to use weapons during the final stages of the military struggle. The popularity of *volcanto* ebbed with the fortunes of the Sandinista Revolution—a decline that perhaps was aided by a certain insularity of the new-song movement, which became increasingly based in Managua. Despite the electoral defeat of the Sandinistas in 1990, interest in socially committed song remains high in comparison to the situation in most other Latin American nations. The Mejía Godoy brothers' musical careers have continued, and they remain the nation's most prominent musicians.

EUROPEAN-DERIVED ART MUSIC

On the whole, the classical idiom has remained uncultivated in Nicaragua. The first important secular composers came with the flourishing of the salon tradition in the larger cities around 1900. Waltzes and other dance-related forms typify the works of two most important composers of this period, José de la Cruz Mena (1874–1907) and Alejandro Vega Matus (1875–1937). These and other composers with some classical training devoted much of their efforts toward funeral marches and church-related musical forms, including *sones de pascua,* performed by brass and wind bands in major cities. Many of these works are still performed; however, over time, many have come to be considered part of a folk repertoire of anonymous authorship.

A more fully developed nationalist use of folk materials began with Nicaragua's most widely known composer, Luis A. Delgadillo (1887–1962), the first to write large orchestral works. Educated in Italy at the Milan Conservatory, he lived for many years in the United States, where he had some success in popularizing his works. Though he often claimed the inspiration for his symphonic and shorter works came from indigenous sources (from Nicaragua and other Mesoamerican countries), his output betrays a superficial familiarity with those idioms. More successful in this vein was Juan Manuel Mena Moreno (1917–1989), who arranged dozens of folk melodies for chamber orchestra and especially for the Coro Nacional Nicaragüense (Nicaraguan National Choir) which he directed for many years until his death. His abiding concern with creating a nationally rooted classical repertoire is shown in his last composition, "*Sonnequería No. 2,*" a short concerto scored for the Nicaraguan *marimba de arco* and chamber orchestra. Except for incidental music for film by Pablo Buitrago (b. 1952) in the early 1980s, virtually all Nicaraguan classical music, including the handful of contemporary compositions not already mentioned, is characterized by an essentially romantic style.

INSTITUTIONAL STRUCTURES

Media

Nicaragua's economic infrastructure developed slowly, compared with most of Middle and South America. That and Nicaragua's dependent relationship with the United States were reflected in the creation of media and cultural institutions. The first radio station appeared in 1931, constructed by then-occupying U.S. Marines to meet their own communication needs. By the late 1940s, most of the nation's major urban centers had small radio stations, but the national recording industry was never able to meet the demand for Nicaraguan music for broadcasting. A telling example of the tardiness of the development of the nation's music industry is that the two principal national labels were still producing ten-inch 78-rpm records as late as the early 1960s. Major radio stations were forced to rely heavily on live performances by local musicians for Nicaraguan musical material well into the 1960s—a practice still common in stations in smaller towns.

The 1972 Managua earthquake destroyed much of the nation's recording industry, but the Sandinista Revolution initiated several new institutional structures that had a significant impact on musical production and consumption. The nation's first Ministry of Culture coordinated a new state recording label, ENIGRAC, Empresa Nicaragüense de Grabaciones Artísticas y Culturales (Nicaraguan Company for Artistic and Cultural Recordings). In the first years of the 1980s, ENIGRAC more than doubled the previous output of Nicaragua's private record industry, featuring traditional folk music and *volcanto.* Musics from the Atlantic Coast—Creole *palo de mayo* and Miskitu folk songs—received their greatest degree of exposure at that time. Nevertheless, the new supply of recordings by Nicaraguan musicians did not translate into a qualitative increase in radio programming of Nicaraguan music, even on state-controlled stations with large national audiences—a subject of much debate during the Sandinista period. In the 1990s, severe contraction from the economic crisis has combined with the final exhaustion of Nicaragua's one pressing plant to leave national music production at its lowest level in decades. Despite nationalist rhetoric, national media, especially programming on radio, continue to favor imported popular musics at the expense of national popular music, which has atrophied from lack of exposure.

Other institutions

Founded on the heels of the Revolution, the ASTC, Associación Sandinista de Trabajadores de la Cultura (Sandinista Association of Cultural Workers), offered logistical and limited financial support to politically engaged musicians and other artists located in Managua. Outside the capital, the Ministry of Culture sponsored the creation of a network of CPCs, Centros Populares de Cultura (Centers of Popular Culture). CPCs played a key role in the country's smaller cities and towns, serving as a locus for various cultural activities, including musical instruction and performance.

Folkloric troupes of dancers proliferated during the early 1980s; as many as six were once in regular operation and conducting international tours. As part of the Sandinista project of national integration, folkloric troupes included stylized representations of dance and music from all parts of the country, including the Atlantic Coast. After intensive cultural activity, the ASTC and Ministry of Culture closed in the late 1980s, replaced in part by the Instituto de Cultura (Institute of Culture). In the post-Sandinista period, the CPCs reorganized as autonomous units under the name Casas de Cultura (Houses of Culture) and continue to function on a smaller scale.

The Rubén Darío Theater has served as the nation's central performance venue since the 1960s and was the only significant indoor theater to survive the 1972 earthquake. It was formerly restricted to classical concerts for the nation's richest patrons, but after 1979 it opened its doors to a larger audience and a wider repertoire. Since then, it has offered regular presentations by the nation's folkloric troupes. Large outdoor events are held at La Piñata in Managua, especially annual music festivals and concerts of touring bands. During the 1980s, Managua hosted many continentwide new song (*nueva canción*) festivals. The annual Gastón Festival (named after Rafael Gastón Pérez, a Nicaraguan composer of popular songs) continues to stimulate the performance of romantic popular songs (*canciones románticas*) with a national competition for new material. Most of the nation's clubs that feature local popular musicians, including new song performers, continue to be located in Managua.

The Managua-based Orquesta de Cámara Nicaragüense (Nicaraguan Chamber Orchestra) is virtually the sole organization dedicated to performances of classical music. Some semiclassical works are included in the repertoire of the Coro Nacional Nicaragüense (Nicaraguan National Choir). The Banda Filarmónica de Managua (Managua Philharmonic Band) at times continues the tradition of outdoor concerts, a tradition that dates from the early twentieth century.

Music education

The bulk of musical education takes place on a private basis and is not found within an institutional framework. Music education in primary and secondary schools suffers from a severe shortage of instruments and teachers. The classically oriented Escuela de Música (School of Music) in Managua offers instruction up to university entry level. There is no regular musical instruction at any of the nation's universities. The Orquesta Nacional and the Escuela de Música received regular stipends under the Somoza and Sandinista governments but now face a precarious economic future.

FURTHER STUDY

Beginning in the 1930s, writers and intellectuals involved with the *costumbrista* and *vanguardia* movements turned their attention toward local themes and material for their writings. This inward focus also led to the first attempts at collecting folklore, including traditional music and dance (Cuadra and Pérez Estrada 1978; Delgadillo 1950; Peña Hernández 1968; also see reprints in the *Boletín Nicaragüense de Bibliografía y Documentación* 1982). Ernesto Mejía Sánchez compiled an excellent selection of northern *corridos* and *romances* (1946).

Salvador Cardenal Argüello was the principal investigator of Nicaraguan music. His pioneering accomplishments were many: he made the first field recordings in the 1950s; he contributed writings to the publications of the Granada-based literary circle known as the Taller de San Lucas; he produced records featuring folk music on his own labels; and through broadcasts on his radio station (reaching most of the Pacific Coast) he fostered an urban awareness of more rurally based music. His recordings remain the most comprehensive sources of the nation's folk music and contain a synthesis of his previous writings (Cardenal Argüello 1977, 1992).

Recordings of *marimba doble* ensembles in the 1950s and recordings of *marimba de arco* trios from the 1950s through the 1970s were released by labels based in Managua and Masaya. Luis Felipe Andino released several albums of folk music at this time, primarily *marimba de arco* trios and *bandas de chichero*. These recordings were of variable quality and are now mostly out of print, but more recent recordings of *marimbas de arco* and *chicheros,* and video selections of music and dance traditions are currently available (Scruggs 1988, 1995).

The trio of doctors that performed under the name Los Bisturices Harmónicos (The Harmonizing Scalpels) (1971) stimulated interest in folk music in the 1960s with their collection and popularization of traditional songs. Carlos Mejía Godoy and Wilmor López collected substantial amounts of material in their investigations into folk music in the mid-1970s and early 1980s. Their results have yet to be published, though Mejía Godoy has used the material in his own creative work. Nicaraguan new song has received some scholarly attention (Pring-Mill 1987; Scruggs 1991), and a handful of recordings—Carlos and Luis Enrique Mejía Godoy (1988), Luis Enrique Mejía Godoy and Mancotal (1988), *Nicaragua . . . ¡presente!* (1989)—have been released in the United States.

Nicaragua was neglected by outside academic inquiry before the mid-1970s, but the Sandinista period generated a plethora of publications by foreign authors. Only a few studies offer a comprehensive overview of the nation's history relevant to an understanding of the place of expressive culture in it (Burns 1991; Walker 1991; Woodward 1983). Little attention has been given to music or other forms of expressive culture outside of literature. Marimba traditions and other folk and popular music and dances on the southern Pacific Coast are covered in Scruggs (1988, 1994). Craven (1989) provides good information on governmental agencies that impacted Nicaraguan musical production in his comparison of Cuban and Nicaraguan cultural institutions.

Nicaragua has no central musical archive. Original manuscripts of religious and secular compositions are scattered in uncatalogued private collections. Recording companies have not kept systematic accounts of their past production, and copies of recordings are not available in libraries. After failed initiatives in the first half of the 1980s, contemporary musical investigation has not gone beyond topical reporting in the daily press.

REFERENCES

Los Bárbaros del Ritmo. [1976.] *Palo de Mayo.* Andino 010. LP disk, cassette.

Los Bisturices Harmónicos. [1971.] *¡Son Tus Perfumenes Mujer!* Banco Nicaragüense. LP disk.

Belausteguigoitia, Ramón de. 1934. *Sandino en Nicaragua—La hora de la Paz.* Madrid: Espasa-Calpe.

Boilès, Charles L. 1966. "The Pipe and Tabor in Mesoamerica." *Yearbook for Inter-American Musical Research* 2:43–74.

Boletín Nicaragüense de Bibliografía y Documentación, 48. 1982. Managua: Banco Central.

Brinton, Daniel G. 1883. *The Güegüence: A Comedy-Ballet in the Nahuatl-Spanish Dialect of Nicaragua.* Philadelphia.

Burns, E. Bradford. 1991. *Patriarchs and Folk: The Emergence of Nicaragua, 1798–1858.* Cambridge: Harvard University Press.

Cardenal Argüello, Salvador. 1977. *Nicaragua: Música y canto.* Managua: Banco de América. Liner notes.

Cardenal Argüello, Salvador, compiler. 1992 [1977]. *Nicaragua: Música y canto.* Radio Güegüence. 7 compact discs.

Cockburn, John. 1735. *A Journey over Land from the Gulph of Honduras to the Great South-Sea.* London.

Conzemius, Eduard. 1928. "Ethnographic Notes on the Black Carib (Garif)." *American Anthropologist* 30:183–205.

———. 1932. *Ethnographical Survey of the Miskito and Sumu Indians of Honduras and Nicaragua.* Washington D.C.: Bureau of American Ethnology, Smithsonian Institution.

Craven, David. 1989. *The New Concept of Art and Popular Culture in Nicaragua since the Revolution in 1979: An Analytical Essay and Compendium of Illustrations.* Lewiston, N.Y., and Queenston, Ont.: Edwin Mellen Press.

Cuadra, Pablo Antonio, and Francisco Pérez Estrada. 1978. *Muestrario del folklore nicaragüense.* Managua: Banco de América.

d'Harcourt, Raoul. 1941. "Sifflets et Ocarinas du Nicaragua et du Mexique." *Journal de la Société des Américanistes de Paris* 33:165–174.

———. 1951. "Ocarinas du Nicaragua." *Journal de la Société des Américanistes* 40:241–244.

Davidson, William V. 1980. "The Garífuna of Pearl Lagoon: Ethnohistory of an Afro-American Enclave in Nicaragua." *Ethnohistory* 27(1):31–47.

Delgadillo, Luis A. 1950. "La música indígena y colonial en Nicaragua." *Revista de estudios musicales* 1(3):43–60.

Dimensión Costeña. 1986. *Fiesta de Palo de Mayo.* ENIGRAC CE-6009. LP disk, cassette.

———. 1989. *"Mama let me go."* ENIGRAC CE-6028. Cassette.

Gordon, Edmund T. 1987. "History, Identity, Consciousness, and Revolution: Afro-Nicaraguans and the Nicaraguan Revolution." In *Ethnic Groups and the Nation State: The Case of the Atlantic Coast in Nicaragua,* 135–169. Stockholm: Department of Social Anthropology, University of Stockholm.

Grossmann, Guido. 1988. *La Costa Atlántica de Nicaragua.* Managua: Editorial La Ocarina.

Hale, Charles R. 1994. *Resistance and Contradiction: Miskitu Indians and the Nicaraguan State, 1894–1987.* Stanford: Stanford University Press.

Hale, Charles R., and Edmund T. Gordon. 1987. "Costeño Demography: Historical and Contemporary Demography of Nicaragua's Atlantic Coast." In *Ethnic Groups and the Nation State: The Case of the Atlantic Coast in Nicaragua,* 7–32. Stockholm: Department of Social Anthropology, University of Stockholm.

Helms, Mary W. 1971. *Asang: Adaptations to Culture Contact in a Miskito Community.* Gainesville: University of Florida Press.

Holm, John. 1978. "The Creole English of Nicaragua's Miskitu Coast: Its Sociolinguistic History and a Comparative Study of Its Lexicon and Syntax." Ph.D. dissertation, University College, London.

Lange, Frederick W., et al. 1992. *The Archaeology of Pacific Nicaragua.* Albuquerque: University of New Mexico Press.

Lothrop, Samuel K. 1926. *Pottery of Costa Rica and Nicaragua.* Vol. 1. New York: Museum of the American Indian, Heye Foundation.

Loveland, Franklin. 1975. *Dialectical Aspects of Natural Symbols: Order and Disorder in Rama Indian Cosmology.* Ann Arbor, Mich.: University Microfilms.

McCutcheon, John, compiler. 1989. *¡Nicaragua . . . presente!—Music from Nicaragua Libre.* Rounder Records 4020/4021. 2 LP disks.

Mejía Godoy, Carlos, and Luis Enrique Mejía Godoy. 1988. *Guitarra Armada.* Rounder Records 4022. LP disk. Originally released on INDICA, S.A. (Costa Rica) MC-1147, 1979. Reissued on ENIGRAC MC-015 and MC 1147, 1980.

Mejía Godoy, Carlos, and El Taller de Sonido Popular. [1980.] *La Misa Campesina.* ENIGRAC NCLP–5012. LP disk, cassette.

Mejía Godoy, Luis Enrique, and Mancotal. 1988. *Amando en Tiempo de Guerra / Loving in Times of War.* Redwood Records 8805. LP disk, cassette.

Mejía Sánchez, Ernesto. 1946. *Romances y corridos nicaragüenses.* México, D.F.: Imprenta Universitaria.

Muñoz Tábora, Jesús. 1988. *Organología del Folklore Hondureño.* Tegucigalpa: Secretaría del Turismo y Cultura.

Newson, Linda A. 1987. *Indian Survival in Colonial Nicaragua.* Norman: University of Oklahoma Press.

Okada, Yuki. 1995. *Central and South America.* JVC Smithsonian Folkways Video Anthology of

World Music and Dance of the Americas, 6. Montpelier, Vt.: Multicultural Media VTMV-230. Video.

Oviedo y Valdés, Gonzalo Fernández de. 1977. *Centroamérica en los cronistas de Indias: Oviedo: Introducción y notas de Eduardo Pérez Valle.* Managua: Colección Cultural Banco de América, Banco de América.

Peña Hernández, Enrique. 1968. *Folklore de Nicaragua.* Masaya: Editorial Unión, Cardoza.

Pring-Mill, Robert. 1987. "The Uses of Revolutionary Song: A Nicaraguan Assessment." *Popular Music* 6(2):179–190.

Romero Vargas, Germán José. 1987 [1977]. *Las Estructuras Sociales de Nicaragua en el Siglo XVIII.* Managua: Editorial Vanguardia.

Scruggs, T. M. 1988. *Nicaraguan Folk Music from Masaya.* Chicago: Flying Fish 474. LP disk, cassette.

———. 1991. Review of *Nicaragua . . . presente!— Music from Nicaragua Libre* and *Patria: Music from Honduras and Nicaragua. Latin American Music Review* 12(1):84–96.

———. 1994. "The Nicaraguan *baile de la marimba* and the Empowerment of Identity." Ph.D. dissertation, University of Texas at Austin.

———. 1995. "Nicaragua." In *Central and South America.* Produced by Yuki Okada. JVC Smithsonian Folkways Video Anthology of World Music and Dance of the Americas, 6. Montpelier, Vt.: Multicultural Media VTMV-230. Video. Notes to four video selections.

Smutko, Gregorio. 1985. *La Mosquitia: Historia y cultura de la Costa Atlántica.* Managua: Editorial La Ocarina.

Los Soñadores de Sarawaska. 1980. *Cantos de Tierra Adentro.* Ocarina MC-004. LP disk and cassette.

Soul Vibrations. 1991. *Black History / Black Culture.* Aural Tradition ATRCD 118 (also Redwood Records). Compact disc, LP disk, cassette.

Stone, Doris. 1966. "Synthesis of Lower Central American Ethnohistory." In *Handbook of Middle American Indians,* 4:209–233. Austin: University of Texas Press.

———. 1976. *Arquelogía de la América Central.* Biblioteca Centroamericana de las Ciencias Sociales. Ciudad de Guatemala: Editorial Piedra Santa.

Suco Campos, Idalberto. 1987. *La música en el complejo cultural del Walagallo en Nicaragua.* Havana: Casa de las Américas.

Walker, Thomas W. 1991. *Nicaragua: The Land of Sandino.* 3rd ed. Boulder, Colo.: Westview Press.

Woodward, Ralph Lee, Jr. 1983. *Nicaragua.* Santa Barbara, Calif.: Clio Press.

Panama
Ronald R. Smith

For almost five hundred years, Panama has suffered from a special anonymity, though it has shared its entire history with European, Central American, North American, and South American development. From the 1500s, when Spanish conquistadors landed on its Caribbean shores, to the 1800s and construction of its interoceanic canal, and finally to political independence in the early twentieth century, the isthmus of Panama has served as the so-called Bridge of the Americas. It has been the stage on which millions of people have played out their lives as they crossed the isthmus from the Atlantic Ocean to the Pacific and back.

This land has served as a sociopolitical fulcrum. It has provided the means for building empires in the Americas and Europe; yet rarely has it received attention for its beauty, diversity, and traditions. Few outsiders appreciate the variety of its flora, fauna, peoples, material culture, and music. Few recognize the role that the isthmus of Panama has played in the development of other areas of the world or even in modern history. For people who have spent time in Panama and relished its culinary delights and everyday life, the country presents an exciting and ever-changing social and cultural panorama, a vista through which to enjoy the differences and similarities of the world's musical traditions.

In the form of an S lying on its side, Panama divides into ten provinces. Each province boasts unique traditions, food, music, festivals, and peoples. Customs and genres have been associated with particular towns and provinces, though recent internal migration has fostered a dispersion of traditions across Panamanian territory and a concentration of peoples of different regions in the capital, Panamá (Panama City).

Rodrigo de Bastidas, having received a royal license from Spain to explore in the New World, sailed from Cádiz in October 1501 and late in the year touched the easternmost sector of the isthmus of Panama, near the Atrato River and the Gulf of Urabá, an area now part of Colombia. Columbus sighted the Caribbean coast of Panamá only on his fourth voyage (1502), when he arrived at the western end of the isthmus and the Laguna de Chiriquí. The areas he explored and named—Portobelo and Bastimentos, later called Nombre de Dios (both now in Colón Province)—were to play important roles in the first wave of colonization and the economic boom that drew Europeans to the New World. With economic growth and prosperity, the cultural heritage of Andalucían Spain, especially Seville, was transported to the shores of Panama.

El Camino Real (The Royal Road) was constructed for trans-isthmian travel in the 1500s. Now a collection of cobblestones and streams hidden among luxuriant undergrowth, this road was once the most important highway in Panama, the major route connecting the Caribbean coast (Portobelo) and the Pacific (Panama City). All goods and people who arrived from Spain, the Caribbean islands, and Colombia used the road as a means of communication with Panama City. Traffic, trade goods, and cultural traditions were transported to and from western South America via the Camino Real. Slaves brought from Africa to Portobelo served as muleteers on the roads and oarsmen on the Chagres River, transporting human cargo, gold, silver, wood, manufactured goods, and travelers. Vasco Núñez de Balboa's meeting with native Americans on the isthmus and his sighting the Pacific Ocean encouraged the development of this route, starting the growth of Spanish traditions in this part of the Americas.

The movement and settlement of Spaniards, captive slaves, fugitive slaves, and indigenous populations during the colonial era set the stage for current Panamanian cultural regions and traditions. The strongest manifestations of Afro-Panamanian traditions appear on the Costa Arriba and the Costa Abajo (Colón Province) in the Darién area and on the islands of the Gulf of Panama. The coastal sector of the Caribbean province of Bocas del Toro, site of important banana plantations, is also an area of African descendants. Native American cultures include the Kuna, who reside in the San Blas Islands [see KUNA], the Choco in Darién Province, and the Guaymí and Teribe on the Atlantic side in Veraguas Province. Climatically more temperate, the central provinces—Coclé, Herrera, Los Santos, and Veraguas—became the center of mestizo development and settlement with farmland and cattle ranches. Chiriquí, the westernmost province, has mountains and an extinct volcano with a mean altitude higher than most of the country; suitable for growing vegetables, it is the home of wealthy landowners and mestizo farmers.

The construction of the transisthmian railroad (in the mid-1800s) and the completion of the interoceanic canal (at the end of the nineteenth century) profoundly affected the ethnic mixture and regional identity of Panama. The workforce needed to construct these wonders of engineering was not available in sufficient numbers on the isthmus, so thousands of contract workers from many parts of the world were brought in. Chinese, Greeks, Lebanese, Italians, and others became a new wave of pilgrims to cross the Bridge of the Americas in search of a better life. Communities of their descendants remain in Panama, still practicing ethnic cultural traditions. Among the most numerous contract workers and most visible today are Antilleans, people of African descent from English- and French-speaking Caribbean insular communities, including Antigua, Barbados, Haiti, Jamaica, Martinique, Tobago, and Trinidad.

ETHNIC POPULATIONS AND REGIONAL MUSIC

Self-identification in Panama does not follow regional lines and alliances to rural beginnings. For music, dance, and verbal traditions, associations and personal preferences are often based on ethnic origins and cultural traditions associated with a particular group. Every ethnic group that forms part of the fabric of Panamanian cultural identity has added something of importance to the mixture. Amerindians, Spaniards, and African slaves constituted the principal ethnic groups in colonial Panama; their interaction and exchange in music, dance, and verbal folklore has taken forms that are singular to Panama.

Cultural influences cannot easily be ascribed to the relative numbers within colonial populations. In some regions of Panama, one group or another seems to have predominated in traditional music and dance, though musical instruments illustrate a totally different pattern of dispersion and origin. Officially, Spanish is the national language, spoken by peoples of all groups; nevertheless, Amerindian groups maintain their cultural heritage, and within their own communities speak indigenous languages. Therefore, most verbal forms and vocal music within Panama utilize Spanish as the language of communication. Participants in *congos* (see below) speak a dialect within their communities, though their songs are sung in Spanish (Lipski 1989). People of Antillean descent are essentially bilingual in Caribbean English and Spanish; however, they have had a strong incentive to assimilate, and few examples of Caribbean music and dance survive in their communities.

The Kuna in Panama

Among Amerindian peoples in Panama, the only group for whom any important study and documentation of music and dance exists is the Kuna [see KUNA]. For years, Kuna expressive culture has attracted the interest of European and American researchers. The people have continued to maintain a degree of independence from the center of Panamanian society; a large portion of their population remains in the San Blas Islands, Colón Province. Kuna musical performances and dances are uncommon outside of their own communities. Kuna who reside in urban areas of Panama City or Colón, or in towns within the central provinces, maintain a somewhat separate existence.

The National Museum in Panama City exhibits a small collection of Kuna musical instruments and ceremonial artifacts, as does the Götenberg Museum in Sweden (Izikowitz 1970 [1935]). However, some of these instruments no longer seem to be in use in Kuna society. Folkloric performances at national events, cultural fairs, and regional celebrations (especially in Panama City) often include Kuna traditional music and dance to represent Panama's Amerindian populations. The colorful costumes, especially the women's blouses, multicolored skirts, and golden earrings and nose rings, attract attention.

Spanish heritage

Spanish influence in traditional Panamanian music is strongly represented by the language of lyrics and such instruments as the guitar, the violin, and castanets. Many dances and especially religious celebrations owe their origins to European festivals. Among the most significant folkloric events are carnival, secular holidays that commemorate foundations of towns, and religious commemorations (including Corpus Christi, Holy Week, local patronal feasts, and regional holidays) when music, dance, traditional theater, costume, food, and examples of the plastic arts (traditional masks) all mingle. Though it is often difficult to ascribe a dance or song to one ethnic origin in Panama, dances such as the *punto*, the waltz (*vals*), and the *décima* are important representations of Spanish culture and cultural mixing.

When a Panamanian is asked where to find folklore, often the first response is to refer to the folkloric traditions of the central provinces (Coclé, Herrera, Los Santos, Veraguas). There, the singing of *décimas* is most strongly maintained, the *mejorana* (an instrument and a dance) finds its home, hordes of costumed devils dance, musical parades (*tunas*) move through the streets during festivals, military bands play in the central plaza, and festivals of many varieties fill the calendar. Carnival celebrations in the town of Las Tablas (Los Santos Province) and the roving musical bands that represent its barrios, queens, and entourages are famous throughout the country, attracting thousands of people who have never lived in the region. The central provinces are the birthplace of some particularly Panamanian traditions, including *salomas* and *gritos*.

African heritage

The influence of Africans and the traditions that characterized the cultures from which they came is best portrayed in the *congo* tradition and in such other danced genres as *los diablos de los espejos* of Garachiné (Darién Province), the music and dance of the people of the Pearl Islands, and genres such as *bullerengue, bunde, cuenecué, cumbia,* and *el tamborito,* the national dance. Most performing groups within Panama use African-derived drums, though the ensembles are different and the manner of playing varies for each.

Calypso, a Caribbean genre frequently allied with social commentary and criticism, is usually associated with countries such as Trinidad and Jamaica, but a Panamanian variety is performed in Spanish by Antilleans. Undocumented and virtually unstudied, this Panamanian genre seems to have been popular years ago. It had a resurgence in the 1970s as part of a black awareness and solidarity campaign initiated by bilingual Antillean intellectuals. Though the genre is neither diffused nor performed widely in Panama, it was important in its social context, as it seemed to represent an attempt to build a cultural bridge between English speakers and their Spanish-speaking environment. Calypso is accompanied by guitar, and its text has the same deftness of thought and social commentary that distinguishes calypso in other areas of the Caribbean.

English heritage

Though virtually nonexistent now, except in self-consciously retrospective cultural presentations by clubs or other organizations, English dances, including the quadrille and the contra dance, once flourished among the residents of Antillean towns within the Canal Zone and in the city of Colón. Today, they are but a memory.

Regionalism

The provinces of Colón, Darién, and Panamá, plus the central provinces, have been the focus of important studies of Panamanian music and folklore. Though varied musical customs occur in other areas of Panama, there has been little systematic study. It is common for persons who were born and raised in the interior of the country to preserve a lifelong identification and allegiance to their natal province. Frequently, people now living in the capital return to small towns in the interior to celebrate family occasions, local patronal feasts, national holidays, and regional or local festivals.

MUSICAL INSTRUMENTS, ENSEMBLES, AND CONTEXTS

Archaeologists have dug deep into the soil of Panama to uncover secrets of its pre-Columbian peoples. They have excavated many archaeological sites, though there are no large pyramids or hidden cities to be found as have been in other parts of Middle and South America. Nevertheless, it is clear that for hundreds of years Panama was a major conduit between North and South American Amerindian populations. Researchers have unearthed golden amulets and jewelry; bone, stone, and pottery artifacts; and ceramic tubular and globular flutes. All these objects indicate a flourishing trade and exchange among peoples of different regions over many centuries.

The people of Panama have no traditional system for classifying musical instruments. Native American groups favor idiophones and aerophones, Panamanians of African heritage often employ membranophones, and Panamanians of European

vejiga   Struck, air-filled Panamanian idiophone made from the bladder of an animal, played by the dirty little devils

tamborito   'Little drum', the national couple dance of Panama, featuring drum accompaniment

congo   Afro-Panamanian music, dance, and theater tradition; also, its accompanying African-derived, single-headed drum with wedge-hoop construction

descent and mestizos enjoy Spanish-derived chordophones. The following survey examines the instruments of the African- and European-derived musical traditions.

Idiophones

The idiophones of Panama are associated with particular ensembles, genres, or occasions, adding an important percussiveness to the music and dance. Included within ensembles (*conjuntos*) are maracas and güiros, shaken and scraped idiophones, respectively (figure 1 includes a young musician playing a *güiro*). Dancers such as *los diablicos sucios* 'the dirty little devils' use castanets (*castañuelas*) as personal accompaniments (figure 8), and big devils (*gran diablos*) often have jingle bells attached to their ankles or calves (figures 4 and 9).

Though widely dispersed within Latin American customs, the most unusual among Panamanian percussive instruments is the *vejiga,* an inflated animal bladder worn by devils as part of their costume; when struck with a stick, it functions as a percussion instrument. Because of its material and construction, it is a sort of combination membranophone and idiophone, being made from nonstretched skin. Devils' slippers or shoes (*cutarras*) also function as percussive instruments: the dancers, as they dance, articulate rhythms, with each foot parallel to the ground, accompanied by their castanets.

Membranophones

Drums are the most widespread instruments in traditional Panamanian musical performances. Though the shapes and sizes vary somewhat from town to town and region to region, most are similar in construction and use. Few musical performances could take place if drummers and singers were not available. The excitement created by drummers and their sonic punctuation of dancers' movements are the main source of the dynamism of performances. A drum ensemble may use drums of various kinds and sizes but usually consists of three or four instruments. The *caja* is played with two sticks, on one head and the side. Most often it is placed on the ground and held with one foot while the performer plays (figure 1).

Other drums, played with the hands, may be held between the knees of a seated player or suspended from a cord around his shoulder or neck. Musicians use the latter method to move through streets in parades. All major musical genres and dances are supported by an individual drum with another instrument (such as a guitar or an accordion) or a drum ensemble. The national dance of Panama, *el tamborito,* is the most important drum-accompanied dance within the republic and is danced by couples.

The names of drums vary widely from one town or region to another, but they reveal something important. *Pujador* 'pusher', *repicador* 'chimer', *caja* 'box', *jondo* 'deep', and *seco* 'dry' are names that indicate relationships and timbral affinities within the ensemble, though they do not seem to make much sense in English transla-

FIGURE 1   A typical ensemble (*conjunto típico*) from Panama. *Left to right:* accordion, *güiro*, *caja*, *congo*. Photo by Ronald R. Smith.

tion. Each drum performs a role within the ensemble, and drummers must learn to listen to each other for cues and watch the dancers during a performance. The *caja* often provides a basic rhythmic pattern over which the *pujador* and the *repicador* improvise complicated patterns. The higher-pitched drums often take turns in the role of soloist. The caller (*llamador*) might accompany *los diablicos sucios* of Chitré.

The *congo* ensembles share some of the naming conventions and playing techniques of drummers in other ensembles in Panama (figure 2). Frequently, a *congo* drum will receive a particular name, for example *relámpago* 'lightning', though the practice of baptizing drums [see AFRO-BRAZILIAN TRADITIONS; HAITI] does not occur. Each group has three or four instrumentalists, a chorus of female singers, and a tradition of mimetic dances that recall colonial slavery.

FIGURE 2   A *congo* ensemble from Colón Province performs at the Festival de la Mejorana, Guararé, Los Santos Province, Panama. Photo by Ronald R. Smith.

FIGURE 3 *Congo* drummers from María Chiquita, Colón Province, Panama. Photo by Ronald R. Smith.

Though far less commonly today, *congo* queens, their drum consort, and members of the court travel throughout the Caribbean coastal region in visits (*visitas*) to other so-called kingdoms and palaces (*palacios*). Such visits can be made in cars on the highway, but in earlier days these journeys were quite difficult, as they had to be made in small boats or by walking through the forest. Figure 3 shows one of these visits (ca. 1972), when drummers from the court of Lilia Perea (Colón Province) came to the realm of Tomasa Jaen, Queen of María Chiquita, a small village on the Costa Arriba.

Chordophones

In most instances, chordophones provide melodies within instrumental ensembles. Traditionally, the violin, and in rustic communities the rabel, served in this capacity. The violin is still the instrument of preference for the *punto* because the sweetness and softness of its sound match the elegance and grace of the dance and its participants, but in rural and traditional Panama it has lost much of its importance. More important is the *mejorana*.

The *mejorana* is a small, five-stringed, fretted, guitarlike instrument that in shape and size resembles the Hawaiian ukulele and the Venezuelan *cuatro*. Older instruments used animal material for the strings, but newer ones use synthetics, such as nylon. Its body is made of one piece of fairly soft wood. The front (*tabla* 'table'), with its round sound hole, is carved from another flat piece of wood, affixed to the body. Tuning pegs, carved from a harder wood, are placed in a pegbox at the end of a rather short neck. The *mejorana* is made by hand in rural Panama, though factory-made instruments are now on sale. The preferred instruments are those crafted by masters in the interior.

Panama has a set of commonly named *mejorana* tunings, though there does not appear to be any clear relationship between the names given to tunings and the notes that distinguish their configurations. The most common tunings are known as *por veinticinco* 'by twenty-five' and *por seis* 'by six'. Strings are named in a unique pattern: the two outer strings (1 and 5) are designated firsts (*primeras*), the next two strings on each side (2 and 4) are designated seconds (*segundas*), and the fifth string (3, in the middle) is called third (*tercera*).

The *mejorana* is important within the musical traditions of mestizos from the central provinces and the capital. Performers (*mejoraneros*) accompany singers of *décimas* and the dance that bears the same name. Players learn from their friends, family, and relatives, and by observation within traditional contexts, and they must master a complex set of *torrentes* 'scales' for the accompaniment of *décimas*. The *mejorana* is played with the fingers and can yield single-line melodies, melodic-rhythmic patterns, and chords. Most players do not read staff notation.

Aerophones

Within the mestizo tradition, a flute (*pito*) is sometimes heard playing with drummers and accordionists that travel the streets with the dirty little devils (see below). The *pito* is a small, high-pitched, side-blown flute made from cane. Its tone, being somewhat shrill, easily cuts through the din created by the dancers, other musicians, and the crowd.

The accordion has become an important melodic instrument within many ensembles of traditional Panama; in typical ensembles (*conjuntos típicos*), it carries the major share of musical performance (figure 1). Imported from Germany and Austria during the 1800s, it has taken an honored place among musical instruments, often displacing the violin because of its loudness. The accordion used in Panama has buttons for left-hand chords and buttons or a keyboard for right-hand melodies. Though it functions, in most instances, as a melody instrument, it provides harmonic support. Accordions appear in ensembles that play *cumbias, puntos, tamboritos,* and other popular dances.

MUSIC-DANCE GENRES AND CONTEXTS

Dance

Dance and song are usually linked in Panama: song rarely occurs without dance. Several Panamanian dances require no sung lyrics, but melodies used for those dances may in fact have texts that members of the community know, though these texts may not be sung during the dancing. Each named dance is accompanied by a particular kind of ensemble and is often associated with a specific ethnic group or region.

El tamborito

Among the more popular couple dances, *el tamborito* 'the little drum' is by far the most important. A spectacular drum-accompanied dance, it is considered the Panamanian national dance. Drums play an essential part in the choreography: they communicate with dancers and with each other, and they enter in rhythmic counterpoint with the dancers and their movements. In each region, specific steps (*pasos*) have names that elicit specific patterns from solo drummers. An important part of the performance, after the entrance of each new couple, is the couple's address to the

cumbia Panamanian group circle dance

mejorana Panamanian term denoting a particular song form, dance, scale, and musical instrument

punto Elegant, stately Panamanian couple dance

bunde African-derived dance of Panama and Colombia

bullerengue Afro-Panamanian and Colombian responsorial song and dance genre

drummers. The pair steps toward them, moves backward a few steps, and approaches again. They make this gesture three times. The lead drum (*repicador* 'chimer' or *llamador* 'caller') then "chimes" specific beats (*los tres golpes*), making a high-pitched, bell-like sound on the drum, whereupon each couple makes a fast circular turn and begins the dance. Courtship is the theme, as it is of many dances in the Americas.

Cumbia

Close behind the *tamborito* in popularity is the *cumbia,* a dance featuring grouped couples, popular also among Panama's Colombian neighbors. It is distinguished by the dancers' counterclockwise movement, describing a circle. The group divides into couples, but men or women may dance as two circles moving in tandem, each partner facing the other. A typical ensemble (figure 1) provides music for the *cumbia* in Panama.

Other dances

Other important traditional dances include the *mejorana* and the *punto.* The *mejorana* (which gets its name because it is accompanied by the *mejorana*) features 6/8 or 9/8 rhythms that oscillate between duple and triple pulses. The *punto,* though also in 6/8 duple and triple oscillation, is slower. It is an elegant and graceful couple dance, found mostly in the interior of the country. It affords one of the few occasions where the violin finds a significant role within traditional musical ensembles; in the absence of a violin, an accordion is used. The *bunde* and the *bullerengue,* both of Afro-Panamanian origin, are danced in Garachiné and the towns of the region. The *bunde* is performed at Christmastime in honor of baby Jesus, represented by a doll. Each of these dances is related to the traditions of other Afro-Panamanian groups, especially *congos,* and each is accompanied by drums, a chorus of women, and clapping.

Dance theater

Although most dances in Panama do not have an underlying or background story, there are several important manifestations of dance theater in Panama, namely *congos* and various devils (*diablos*).

Congos

Congos, originally Afro-Panamanian secret societies during colonial days, today perform a kind of dance theater featuring brilliant costumes, drumming (figures 2 and 3), and responsorial singing by people of Afro-Hispanic descent. It is featured during carnival, folkloric festivals, and other celebrations.

Mimetic dance is difficult for the uninitiated to understand on a deep level.

FIGURE 4   Big devils perform in La Chorrera, Panama. Photo by Ronald R. Smith.

Most people see only the dance, experiencing the energy of movements and the drums. Among the *congos,* however, narratives retell oral histories of slave ships, the devil, the Virgin Mary, runaways (*cimarrones*), and everyday activities. The lyrics that accompany the dances do not always coincide with the background narrative; the viewer must know the story and understand what is happening from the dancers' movements and actions.

Devils

The big devils (*gran diablos,* also *diablos de los espejos* 'mirror devils') portray variants of the Christian theme of the battle of good and evil. Figure 4 shows big devils who speak in verse. What they are saying is virtually impossible to understand, as they move through complicated choreographic patterns, and their faces are covered with wooden masks. They act out a drama in which Lucifer, the fallen angel, does battle with the powers of good, personified by the Archangel Michael. Lucifer is vanquished and returned to the grace of God.

Garachiné, a small town on the gulf of San Miguel, is almost inaccessible except by air or water. The people and traditions of this region are related to descendants of runaways who fled to the jungles and the Pearl Islands of Panama. The *diablos de los espejos* tradition is related to the big-devil tradition of Chorrera (Panama Province), but the style of the mask is distinctive, and the theatrical subtext from which they perform their drama is quite different.

Musicians (figures 5 and 6) accompany mirror devils as they enact the defeat of the devil by the Holy Spirit. During the colonial period, such liturgical dramas (here, in spoken verse) were common in Latin America. They instructed the illiterate population in the wonders and mysteries of biblical narratives.

Vocal music

Song and dance are intimately intertwined in the traditional musics of Panama, but song is probably the most important part of the equation. Once, when recording

FIGURE 5   An accordionist performs for mirror devils in Tucutí, Darién Province, Panama. Photo by Ronald R. Smith.

FIGURE 6   A drummer performs for mirror devils in Tucutí, Darién Province, Panama. Photo by Ronald R. Smith.

music in the Pearl Islands, I had to wait until women had gathered to sing. My friends and I were told that if a chorus could not be formed, there would be no dance that night. A typical vocal group consists of a lead singer (*cantalante* among most groups, *revellín* among *congos*) and a chorus of women (*segundas*), who sing and clap on major subdivisions of the pulse. Songs in this configuration are usually responsorial. Most traditions in the country share such a style. Singing loudly in a high register, the soloist often improvises and varies the text at will. A good voice is a powerful voice, which can rise above the chorus, the drums, all other instruments in the ensemble, and ambient noise.

Décima

A solo vocal tradition called *décima* is the province mainly of male singers. It is performed to the accompaniment of the *mejorana*. The singer (*decimero*) must have a powerful voice, but there is an emphasis on the clear and exact enunciation of the text. As one of the singers said, the textual message is the most important part of the *décima*.

The *décima* is a poetic form that encompasses elaborate rhymes and melodic improvisation. The following text is an example of a vocal improvisation by the male singer Santo Díaz. It represents just a section of a longer piece, "*Me duele tu corazón.*"

Me duele tu corazón.	Your heart gives me pain.
Tierra, tú me vas matando.	Land, you are killing me.
Si acaso me oyes cantando,	If by chance you hear me singing,
Yo no grito el mismo son.	I don't shout the same song.
Voy llorando el pasión	I go crying the passion
Que el recuerdo resucita,	That memory revives,
Saber que fuiste mansita	Knowing that you were gentle
Cuando yo te socolaba,	When I rocked you,
Ay, amor, ¡cómo te amaba!	Oh, my love, how I loved you!
Tierra, tierra, ¡qué bonita!	Land, my land, how beautiful!

Saloma

The *saloma*, a vocal melody of undetermined length, appears at the beginning and end of a *décima*. It is a subdued, deeply rhapsodic vocal line, often associated with the *torrente llanto*, used for performances of lyrical themes of sadness and intimacy. It exhibits a striking resemblance to the deep song (*cante jondo*) of Andalucían Spain. It is sung in almost a recitative style, often using vocables and closely following the emphasis of spoken verbal rhythms. Most *salomas* are slow. Their major musical cadences coincide with significant textual phrasal endings. Some singers believe that individuals have characteristic *salomas* or manners of performance. They feel that one must sing a *saloma* at the beginning of a *décima* to release the voice and set the mood.

Shouts

Shouts (*gritos*) ordinarily occur during agricultural activities when it is necessary to communicate in the field. For personal entertainment, men engage in such oral display in homes, on the streets, and in bars. A measure of skill is needed to produce a *grito,* and a degree of stamina is needed to continue it for a concentrated time. It has more musical attributes when men exchange loud, high-pitched yodels. Two or more men sit face to face, or side by side, alternating their *gritos*. Often, after making four or five utterances, they stop for a rest and a drink. When they yodel, each man will often match the alternating pitches and duration of his counterpart in a sort of vocal duel.

Verbal arts

Texts within musical compositions are important in Panama's traditional music. Declamations—dramatic recitations of poems, narratives, and *décima* texts—are often part of public celebrations and family occasions. Little has been collected of the texts of dance-theater presentations, and this is a fertile area for potential research.

FESTIVALS

For many Panamanians, festivals (*fiestas*) are times of release and abandon—occasions to reestablish ties with the supernatural world, families, and regions, and to make public displays of faith. Some festivals, celebrated on a small scale, involve small numbers of people; others involve neighborhoods, towns, or regions. When a festival is shared by the national community, it permits even more possibilities for creative activity and expression. All festival occasions—secular, religious, national—are commemorated with musical ensembles and singing.

Religious festivals

In the interior of Panama on various occasions during the year, especially the Christian holiday of Corpus Christi, dirty little devils roam the streets in brilliant red and black striped costumes and musical ensembles (figure 7). This is such a visually attractive tradition that it has been used to represent Panama—within the republic (figure 8) and outside it. Small companies of devils, accompanied by a guitarist and maybe a *pito* and a drummer (figure 9), move throughout towns, performing for visitors. A special trait of their performance is the use of castanets, *vejigas,* and *cutarras.*

FIGURE 7   During the Festival de la Mejorana in Guararé, Los Santos Province, dirty little devils (carrying *vejigas* and sticks and playing castanets) and a guitarist perform. Photo by Ronald R. Smith.

A marching band's line resembles a large group of dancers. Drummers vigorously lift their drums high in the air, rotating them back and forth so they can strike the heads on opposing sides.

FIGURE 8   During the festival of Corpus Christi in Los Santos Province, Panama, a dirty little devil holds castanets in each hand and carries a *vejiga* and a stick. Photo by Ronald R. Smith.

FIGURE 9   An ensemble of drum and *pito* accompanies dirty little devils during the Corpus Christi festival in Los Santos Province. Photo by Ronald R. Smith.

National festivals

Independence Day, 3 November, occasions great musical activity, especially in the capital. Thousands of citizens crowd the streets in anticipation of parades that feature marching bands and drum-and-bugle corps from the secondary schools of the city and military units of the government. So many people march that the parades last for about five hours. There are two routes, which the musical organizations exchange on the second day, so each has the opportunity of marching and performing for the maximum number of people and showing its prowess on the main street, Avenida Central. The itineraries, organizational names, and pertinent information on each group are published daily in the local papers. Though the bands are composed of instruments common to military bands in most countries, the percussion sections are greatly enlarged, and the rhythms used for the march are more related to *el tamborito* and other drum-accompanied dances of Panama than to those of John Philip Sousa.

A marching band's line resembles a large group of dancers. To discover the more spectacular movements and playing styles, one has only to listen to and watch the bass drum. During each pattern, drummers vigorously lift their drums high in the air, rotating them back and forth so they can alternately strike the heads on opposing sides. Apart from carnival (celebrated in Panama and throughout much of Latin

America), this parade is the most heavily attended musical event regularly presented in Panama.

Folkloric festivals

In the early 1970s, Manuel F. Zárate, Panama's most prominent researcher in folklore, with Dora Pérez de Zárate was instrumental in helping to promote an annual event in his natal province, Los Santos. Each year during the Festival de la Mejorana, performers within the province and from many other cities throughout the country come to Guararé to perform and share their traditions for a week.

ELECTRONIC MEDIA

The impact of radio in Panama has been heavy. For some people who live in isolated areas, radio is the only means of contact with urban areas. Panama has a long history of radio broadcasting. Popular programs still commonly feature traditional singers, musical ensembles, reports of folkloric events, and declamatory presentations. The importance of television and the recording industry is more difficult to ascertain, since they have grown in the recent past, and no studies of these media have been made. There is some indication that recordings of traditional musical performances do reach the public, and it is not difficult to find, on tape and disk, commercial recordings of the more popular *conjuntos típicos.*

FURTHER STUDY

There has been no critical research into musical archaeology and the musical practices of ancient Amerindian groups in Panama. Almost no research has been accomplished in the area of music in colonial Panama. The author has searched in Spanish archives for documents and musical materials that might elucidate this lacuna. It is clear, however, that musical activities were connected to religious brotherhoods (*cofradías*) affiliated with churches: references to musical practices and officers in charge of musical matters appear in their constitutions.

Because the reality of ethnic origins is still strong and provides a basis for a Panamanian worldview, musical terms, musical instruments, and concepts on which people construct interaction, regionalism is an important focus in the study of Panamanian music. Several studies of general interest highlight folkloric traditions in certain regions and among specific ethnic groups, including Amerindian tribes. What is known has been collected by anthropologists and folklorists (Carmona Maya 1989; Densmore 1926; Hayans 1963; McCosker 1974; Sherzer 1983) from such contemporary groups as the Kuna, the Choco, the Guaymí, and the Teribe. These data focus largely on ritual traditions and musical instruments. There are also studies of communities of African descent (Drolet 1980, 1982; Joly 1981; Smith 1976, 1985, 1994), African-derived and mestizo traditions (Cheville 1964, 1977), and mestizo traditions (Garay 1930; D. Zárate 1971; Zárate and Zárate 1968).

Recordings of traditional music from Panama have been collected for many years, but most are not publicly available. Recordings that may be consulted are those deposited at the archive of the National Museum of Panamá, the Archives of Traditional Music at Indiana University (Ronald R. Smith collections), and the INIDEF Archive, created by Drs. Isabel Aretz and Felipe Ramón y Rivera in Caracas, Venezuela. Archival field collections contain a wealth of documentation and musical examples that provide the inquisitive listener with an in-depth view of a range of Panamanian genres (Cheville 1964). Since the 1980s, several commercial recordings of Panamanian traditional musical genres have been released (Blaise 1985; Llerenas and Ramírez de Arellano 1987; Stiffler 1983).

Though linguistic studies in Panamanian folklore are not at the center of musical research, a few studies provide important support for, and insights into, the study of musical traditions of Panama (Joly 1981; Lipski 1989; Sherzer 1983).

The art-music world is probably the most unexplored in the history of the arts in Panama. Though Panamanian artists of international reputation are currently presenting concerts around the world, and though Panama supports a national symphony, many choruses, and a conservatory of music (in the capital), musicology and ethnomusicology do not have an academic home or a cadre of trained Panamanian specialists. The study of folklore, and often folk music, is found within the faculty of history at the University of Panama. There is no university degree program to prepare professionals in this area. Nevertheless, the Panamanian Ministry of Culture has long supported traditional singers, dancers, instrumentalists, and producers of traditional costumes within small schools of performing arts, concentrating their efforts on the teaching of these arts and crafts.

Panamanian musical composition, often the arena in which fine-art music and traditional musical genres and styles interact, has not been studied with serious attention. The lure of Panama—its dances, songs, and festivals—has long been a source of inspiration for Panamanian composers and others in North America.

REFERENCES

Blaise, Michel. 1985. *Street Music of Panama.* 1985. Original Music OML 401. LP disk.

Carmona Maya, Sergio Iván. 1989. *La Música, un fenómeno cosmogónico en la cultura kuna.* Medellín, Colombia: Editorial Universidad de Antioquia. Ediciones Previas.

Cheville, Lila R. 1964. "The Folk Dances of Panama." Ph.D. dissertation, University of Iowa.

———, and Richard A. Cheville. 1977. *Festivals and Dances of Panama.* Panamá: Lila and Richard Cheville.

Densmore, Frances. 1926. *Music of the Tule Indians of Panama.* Smithsonian miscellaneous collections, 77, 11. Washington, D.C.: Smithsonian Institution.

Drolet, Patricia Lund. 1980. "The Congo Ritual of Northeastern Panama: An Afro-American Expressive Structure of Cultural Adaptation." Ph.D. dissertation, University of Illinois at Urbana-Champaign.

———. 1982. *El Asentamiento cultural en la Costa Arriba: Costeños, Chocoes, Cuevas y grupos prehistóricos.* Panamá: Museo del Hombre Panameño, Instituto Nacional de Cultura, Smithsonian Tropical Research Institute.

Garay, Narciso. 1930. *Tradiciones y cantares de Panamá, ensayo folklórico.* Brussels: Presses de l'Expansion belge.

Hayans, Guillermo. 1963. *Dos cantos shamanísticos de los indios cunas.* Translated by Nils M. Holmer and S. Henry Wassén. Göteborg: Etnografiska Museet.

Izikowitz, Karl Gustav. 1970 [1935]. *Musical Instruments of the South American Indians.* East Ardsley, Wakefield, Yorks.: S. R. Publishers.

Joly, Luz Graciela. 1981. *The Ritual "Play of the Congos" of North-Central Panama: Its Sociolinguistic Implications.* Sociolinguistic working papers, 85. Austin, Texas: Southwest Educational Development Laboratory.

Lipski, John M. 1989. *The Speech of the Negros Congos of Panama.* Amsterdam and Philadelphia: J. Benjamins Publishing.

Llerenas, Eduardo, and Enrique Ramírez de Arellano. 1987. *Panamá: Tamboritos y Mejoranas.* Música Tradicional MT10. LP disk.

McCosker, Sandra Smith. 1974. *The Lullabies of the San Blas Cuna Indians of Panama.* Etnologiska stüdier, 33. Göteborg: Etnografiska Museet.

Sherzer, Joel. 1983. *Kuna Ways of Speaking: An Ethnographic Perspective.* Austin: University of Texas Press.

Smith, Ronald R. 1976. "The Society of *Los Congos* of Panama: An Ethnomusicological Study of the Music and Dance-Theater of an Afro-Panamanian group. " Ph.D. dissertation, Indiana University.

———. 1985. "They Sing with the Voice of the Drum: Afro-Panamanian Musical Traditions." In *More Than Drumming: Essays on African and Afro-Latin American Music,* ed. Irene Jackson-Brown, 163–198. Westport, Conn.: Greenwood Press.

———. 1991. Recording review of *Street Music of Panama: Cumbias, Tamboritos, and Mejoranas,"* Latin American Music Review 12(2):216–220.

———. 1994. "Arroz Colorao: Los Congos of

Panama." In *Music and Black Ethnicity in the Caribbean and South America,* ed. Gerard Béhague, 239–266. Miami: North-South Center, University of Miami.

Stiffler, David Blair. 1983. *Music of the Indians of Panama: The Cuna (Tule) and Chocoe (Embera) Tribes.* Folkways Records FE 4326. LP disk.

Zárate, Dora Pérez de. 1971. *Textos del tamborito panameño: Un estudio folklórico-literario de los textos del tamborito en Panamá.* Panamá: Dora Pérez de Zárate.

Zárate, Manuel F., and Dora Pérez de Zárate. 1968. *Tambor y socavón: Un estudio comprensivo de dos temas del folklore panameño, y de sus implicaciones históricas y culturales.* Panamá: Ediciones del Ministerio de Educación, Dirección Nacional de Cultura.

Section 5
Many Islands, Many Sounds

The term *Caribbean* creates many images. It is familiar to all as a tourist haven, the setting for "fun in the sun," the home of "island music," mostly stereotypes created by the tourist industry. In reality, economic, ethnic, meteorological, and political situations have often created many hardships for its people, often reflected in its music. There is much cultural and musical diversity, though certain traits, such as the slave trade to appease the sugar barons' greed, have created superficial similarities in music and dance.

By *Caribbean* we mean the island cultures that lie within the Caribbean Sea and the fringes of the Atlantic and the Gulf of Mexico. This large maritime region is bordered by the United States of America, Mexico, and countries of Central and South America. Though the Caribbean lies within a large area of water, often called the Caribbean Basin, its island polities (some of them departments of France or protectorates of other foreign powers) have had tremendous influence on neighboring mainland countries. Many continental coastal regions share cultural traits with islands in the Caribbean Basin. Sometimes the coasts of those adjacent countries are called Circum-Caribbean regions—a useful term because of cultural and historical similarities.

The photo captures one of the most popular Caribbean musical occasions—carnival in Trinidad. This extremely colorful and elaborate festival several weeks before Easter, like Mardi Gras in New Orleans and Carnaval in Brazil, is a time of merriment, cutting up, and letting loose. It is also a time of great national pride, economic hardship for some, profit for others, and the culmination of months of preparation in the perfecting of musical and dance performances.

An elaborately dressed dancer at carnival in Port of Spain, Trinidad. Photo by Carolyn J. Fulton, 1994.

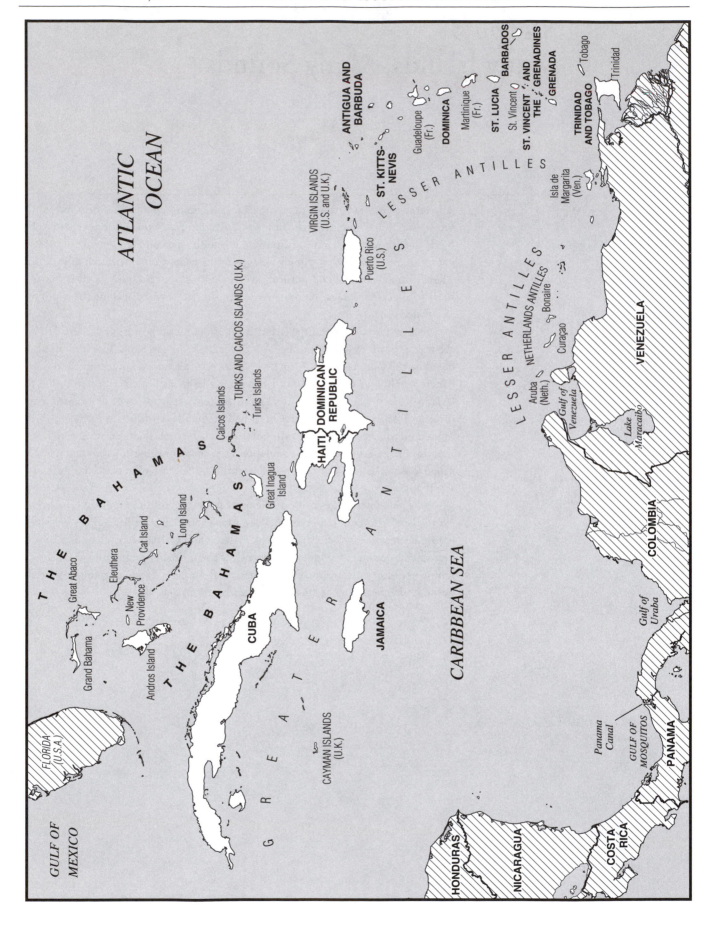

The Music of the Caribbean

Martha Ellen Davis

Economics
Cultural Composition
Musical Culture

(opposite) The Caribbean region

The insular Caribbean region is centered on the islands of the Caribbean Sea, bordered by North, Central, and South America and the Atlantic Ocean, with a total landmass of about 235,700 square kilometers and a current population of about 30 million (map 11). According to some views, the region also includes circum-Caribbean areas, the tropical lowlands bordering the Caribbean Sea. (Those areas are treated separately in this volume.) Because of ecological and sociocultural similarities, especially an African presence, it may even be argued that the circum-Caribbean area reaches down the Atlantic and Pacific coasts of South America and up to southern Florida and the mid-Atlantic island of Bermuda.

The heart of the region is the 3,200-kilometer-long arc-shaped archipelago called the Antilles or the West Indies, stretching between the Yucatán Peninsula and Venezuela. It consists, on the northern side, of the Greater Antilles and the large, mountainous islands of Cuba, Jamaica, Hispaniola, and Puerto Rico (map 12); and, on the eastern side, of the double arc of the Lesser Antilles, comprising the Leeward Islands (northern group) and the Windward Islands (southern group) (map 13). A westward extension of the latter includes Trinidad and Tobago, Aruba and the western Netherlands Antilles (Bonaire and Curaçao), and many small islands off Venezuela. The main islands and groups of the Lesser Antilles, north to south, are the British and American Virgin Islands, St. Martin, Antigua and Barbuda, Montserrat, Guadeloupe, Dominica, Martinique, St. Lucia, St. Vincent, Barbados, and Grenada; many small islands and islets join this chain. Another major group is the Bahamas, north of Cuba.

Unlike those of the Pacific, the Caribbean islands are close together, though some are separated by deep troughs and treacherous currents. The climate is tropical and subtropical (temperate in highlands), with a marked difference between rainy and dry seasons (June–October, November–May). The region is prone to hurricanes and volcanoes. On larger islands, the soils were once rich and supported notable lowland hardwood forests, but the forests have been cut for lumber and the lands cleared for planting sugarcane, depleting the soils.

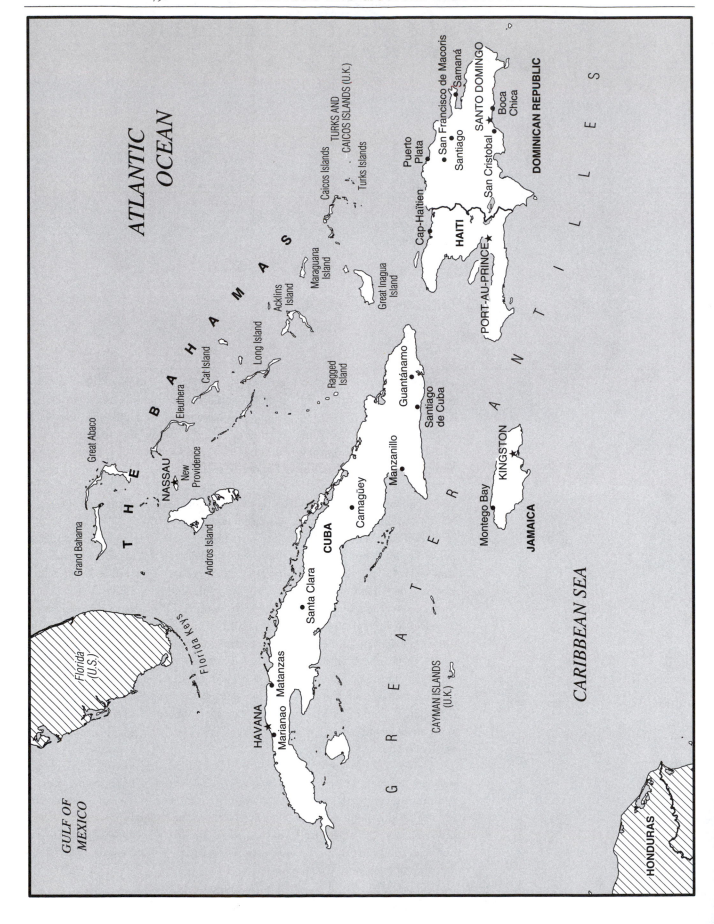

ECONOMICS

The Caribbean was the first region of the New World conquered and settled by Europeans, starting in 1492 with the Spanish colony of Santo Domingo on Hispaniola. By about 1530, the original population of several million Arawak and Carib (for whom the Caribbean was named) had been exterminated by disease, warfare, and suicide. To replace them, African slaves were brought to the Americas in the early 1500s, largely for cultivating sugarcane to produce sugar, molasses, and rum. Sugar became the basis of wealth on these "sugar islands." The raising of cattle became an industry in Cuba and the Dominican Republic. Other tropical cash crops—tobacco (indigenous, starting in the 1500s), cacao (from Central America, starting in the 1500s), coffee (from Arabia, starting in 1714), and copra (dried coconut for oil, of South Pacific origin)—were added later. Vegetables, fruits, and spices are important exports today. Mining, originally of gold on Hispaniola, now includes bauxite (Dominican Republic, Haiti, Jamaica), oil (Curaçao, Trinidad and Tobago), nickel, and other minerals.

Agriculture today remains differentiated into peasant and plantation systems, in highlands and lowlands, respectively, the former entailing diversified subsistence agriculture, and the latter taking the form of "factories in the fields," raising monocrops. The extractive-based economies of the colonial Caribbean differentiated into so-called economic foci (areas of intensive activity), surrounded by economic backwaters. Caribbean plantation economies are also characterized by annual harvest- and off-season boom-and-bust cycles, moderated or exaggerated by trends in world markets. Peasants in the marginal, mainly highland, areas, who may be sharecroppers, sometimes combine their subsistence agriculture with fishing or animal husbandry, cooperatively marketed cash-crop ventures, or seasonal employment on plantations during the harvest season.

Since the mid-twentieth century, tourism and, secondarily, light manufacturing and assembly, first in Puerto Rico and now in free-port zones elsewhere, are becoming the main sources of national and personal revenue. Like agriculture, tourism and industry are economic foci, subject to fluctuating markets. Tourism is also affected by seasonal demand. Caribbean enterprises—mining, cash-crop agriculture, and now tourism and manufacturing—have largely been directed by absentee owners and have often required foreign capital. The allure of cities and urban enterprises, which provide salaried jobs (especially for women), is altering the demographics, socioeconomics, and culture of the region. At the same time, inequities, instability, and psychological insularity have led to large-scale twentieth-century migration to Europe and North America. Émigrés, highly patriotic, send remittances (a substantial source of revenue) and intend to return home with accrued wealth. Post-1959 Cuba provides a variant on this pattern, with its revolutionary expropriations and state ownership of lands and businesses, socioeconomic restructuring for equitability, sugar-price stability (formerly guaranteed by the Soviet market), restrictions on citizens' travel, and regulation of culture, including the arts.

Political structure

It was from Hispaniola that the thrusts of conquest toward the mainlands were launched. The discovery of greater mineral riches in Mexico and the Andes caused Spain to neglect the Caribbean, leading to the loss of much of its territory in the 1600s to France, England, the Netherlands, Denmark, in 1898 to the United States (after the Spanish-American War), and in the 1900s to liberation movements. Many islands have changed hands several times. The consequent ideological pluralism and linguistic fragmentation of the region has continued, with islands grouped politically by governing or former governing powers and culturally by the official colonial lan-

(opposite) The western and northern Caribbean (the Greater Antilles, excluding Puerto Rico) and the Bahamas

Contemporary Caribbean culture is best characterized as creole, a hybrid that has evolved in the New World of Old World influences tempered by New World circumstances.

guages into hispanophone (Spanish-speaking), francophone (French-speaking), and anglophone (English-speaking) islands.

Modern political history started with the Haitian Revolution, which led to the founding in 1804 of the first sovereign republic south of the United States. The Dominican Republic was established in 1844. In contrast, other components of the Insular Caribbean did not gain independence until the twentieth century, mainly mid-century, and some are still governed by, or are actually part of, Europe or the United States. Martinique and Guadeloupe are departments of France, the western and eastern Netherlands Antilles and Aruba are governed by Holland, and Puerto Rico and the U.S. Virgin Islands are respectively a commonwealth and territories of the United States. Former British colonies are members of the British Commonwealth, and some minor island groups are still governed by Britain.

CULTURAL COMPOSITION

Despite political fragmentation, the region is unified by its African heritage. The development of creole languages has provided cultural continuities despite changes in governance. Contemporary Caribbean culture is best characterized as creole, a hybrid that has evolved in the New World of Old World influences tempered by New World circumstances. Simultaneously, certain Old World cultural traits, from Europe and Africa continue, especially in contexts of expressive culture; however, a correlation between race and culture, typical of long-inhabited areas, is increasingly inapplicable in New World societies, which are simultaneously bicultural or multicultural.

The cultural composition of the region is complex and changing. Immigration from Europe has been motivated by a quest for wealth or escape from overpopulation, poverty, and occasionally religious persecution. In addition to emigration from colonial powers and their colonies (as with the Irish to British islands), Sephardic Jewish and Canary Island immigrants have been significant since the early days. The first Africans in the New World, arriving about 1502, were Christians from southern Spain, followed shortly by immigrants directly from Africa. African slaves during the sixteenth through nineteenth centuries were drawn from increasingly southerly points on the West African coast: first Senegambia, later the Bight of Benin, and finally the Congo-Angolan area. However, variations in African sources, the numbers of slaves introduced, the ethnic ratios among them, the ratios of blacks to whites, the continuum between urban and rural locations and opportunities, the kinds of work and crops, and other factors led to the rise of different cultural configurations in different sites. Slavery was abolished throughout the Caribbean during the nineteenth century, last in Cuba in 1886; but the need for cheap labor continued, leading to indentured servitude from colonial powers' other holdings, mainly by Britain from India to Trinidad and Guyana, and by the Netherlands from Java to Surinam. Today's East Indian–derived populations of Trinidad and Guyana are almost 50 percent of the totals. Seasonal workers are currently imported from Haiti to the Dominican

Republic under conditions described as neoslavery, and more than a quarter million Haitians live in Oriente Province, Cuba.

Later musical migrations

Internal migration within the nineteenth- and twentieth-century Caribbean has been caused by flight from political turmoil and persecution and the attraction of economic foci. Pertinent political events have included the Haitian Revolution (1804), Simón Bolívar's liberation of northern South America (1821), the Cuban Revolution (1959), and dictatorships (such as the Dominican Trujillo era, 1930–1961). Important economic events have included the building of the Panama Canal (1904–1914) and booms in the sugar and tourist industries.

Twentieth-century and current immigrants include Spaniards (mainly from Asturias and Galicia) and Portuguese (to Venezuela); Christian Lebanese, Syrians, and Palestinians, collectively called Turks because they emigrated from the Ottoman Empire; Jews fleeing Nazism; Chinese to nineteenth-century Cuba to build the railway, but today from the mainland and Taiwan for business; and secondarily, Japanese as agriculturalists (most importantly in Brazil). These groups have played a tremendous role in twentieth-century commerce and agriculture, but not in musical traditions.

Today's cultural configurations vary by country, island, location (rural or urban), and class. Many of the Lesser Antilles are largely black societies; the black and East Indian societies of Trinidad and Tobago and Guyana are "segmented societies." The hispanophone islands are characterized by substantial white and mulatto populations: the oligarchy (landed elite) and other sectors of the urban upper class, including recent immigrants as merchants, and the subsistence farmers of the mountains, are largely white, though the coastal areas of plantations and former plantations are populated by blacks and mulattos, and urban middle and lower classes are mulatto. Except among endogamous elites, there is a notable trend toward racial and cultural mixture.

MUSICAL CULTURE

The local histories of the Caribbean Islands are embedded in expressive and material culture, including music, dance, ritual, instruments, styles, genres, and texts, all of which serve as cultural artifacts. Collective consciousness of origin and cultural identity is often revealed in music, as with the big-drum dance of Carriacou, a satellite island of Grenada, with its national dances representing various African ethnic groups, followed by its more hybrid and modern creole dances. This pattern—of sacred and European or African components (or both, in that order), followed by secular and hybrid components—is common in the Caribbean, but often the memory of origins is lost, and what exists does not necessarily imply consciousness of what used to exist. Though the flight from the Haitian Revolution may be forgotten, the event is documented in the French rosary in Puerto Rico and the *tumba francesa,* a ballroom dance of Santiago, Cuba.

As an aspect of Caribbean history and reality, music reflects ecology and consequent modes of production. Urban areas provided critical masses to perpetuate culture-specific African religious cults (such as Santería), whereas the mixed ethnic compositions of plantations were more subject to intra-African syncretism or reversion to musical common denominators.

In rural areas, African-derived work-accompanying songs are particular to ecological zones and crops. The entire Caribbean was deforested to the sound of chopping songs. Other work-related songs reinforce the rhythms of labor: digging, pounding, transplanting rice, hauling nets, and so on. They are also sung during

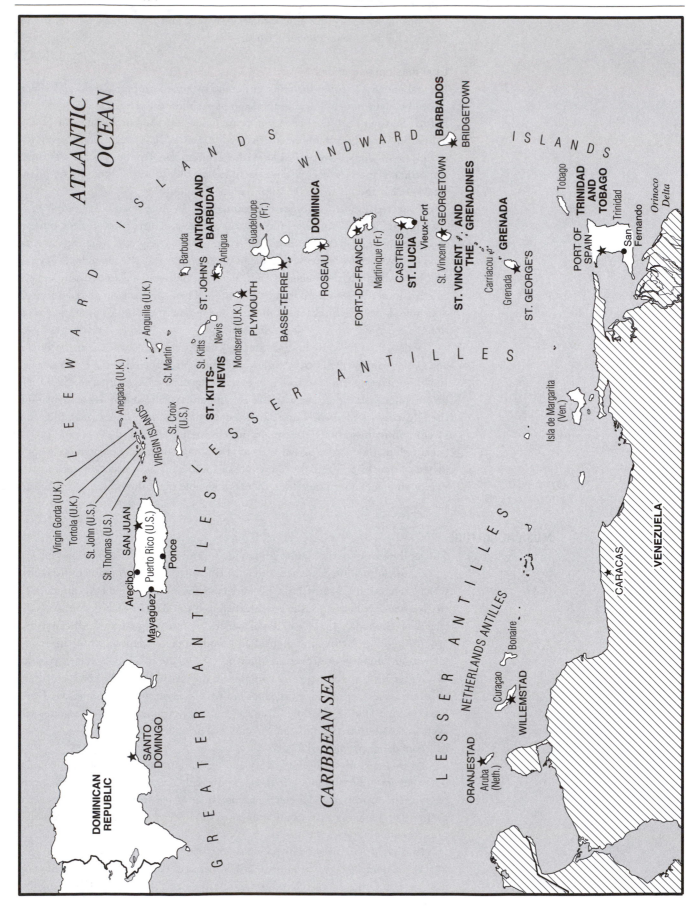

cash-crop harvesting (for example, picking coffee beans) and processing (as when making cigars)—tasks that often involve women. Nonrhythmic tasks may be accompanied by other kinds of music.

Life in particular ecological zones supports special musical cultures: the "cockpit" (sinkhole) country of interior Jamaica is home to Maroons (descendants of runaway slaves) and the birthplace of Rastafarianism; the sugarcane plantations of Haiti and the Dominican Republic are known for their *rará* religious societies; and so forth. The geographic isolation of certain areas leads to the conservation of musical traits, including the sung rosary and other liturgical texts conserved in the Roman Catholicism of areas inaccessible to, and underserved by, priests.

Music and politics

Caribbean musical culture reflects the European political hegemony in civil, military, and religious spheres. To avoid persecution, slave society constructed a Christian façade to camouflage non-Christian beliefs and practices, especially those that honored ancestors and gods. Ritual and musical practices, especially drumming, became the subjects of proscriptive edicts and actions, including a drum-burning campaign in Haiti as late as the 1930s. In seeming contradiction to this policy, masters urged their slaves to participate in African-derived recreational events as an escape valve, an antidote to revolution. These events included patronal and personal saints' festivals, many of which are still celebrated. Certain creole recreational dances—*bamboulá, calenda, juba*—were well-known throughout the Caribbean, albeit with local differences. The Protestant counterparts of religiously proscribed dances are ring games ("plays").

At the same time, European hegemony has been incorporated into local Roman Catholic rituals honoring the saints and the dead with the rosary (such as the Haitian *cantique*) under the guidance of a nonclerical man in a priestly role. In Protestantism, hymns of the literate tradition are juxtaposed with spirituals ("anthems") of the non-literate tradition, and certain hymns—especially "Sankeys," evangelical North American hymns of the late 1800s—are used for lay rituals for the dead and other occasions.

Aspects of African society potentially threatening to European hegemony, including political organizations with royalty and sacred masks, were reinterpreted within playful contexts, including carnival, with its common motifs of a king and a queen, masks and costumes, and the street poetry of mummers. Political structures of colonial or slave society may also be reflected in such organizations as the social structure of the Haitian and Haitian-Dominican *rará* societies of cane communities, whose carnivalesque movements are cued by police whistles and whips.

Slaves' and peasants' emulation of high-class society included eighteenth- and nineteenth-century European-derived ballroom dances: the contredanse, quadrille, mazurka, polka, waltz, and others. Musicians—of lower classes than the members of social clubs—served as conduits of these dances into rural areas, where they have been retained in oral tradition for a century or more after they passed from vogue in urban ballrooms. Musicians also contributed to the development of nineteenth-century creole ballroom dances, including the Puerto Rican *danza*, the Cuban *danzón*, the Haitian *meringue*, the Martinican *biguine*, and others. Bands served, and still serve, as conduits for social mobility and an interface among classes and localities.

Political criticism is rendered more innocuous and political praise more noteworthy if sung, rather than spoken. In this function, the African-influenced man of words has merged in some contexts with the Mediterranean troubadour. The latter's poetic medium is the *décima*, ubiquitous in the hispanophone Caribbean (extending to Venezuela, Veracruz in Mexico, and elsewhere), but with various settings and

(opposite) The eastern and southern Caribbean (the Lesser Antilles and Puerto Rico)

Creole dances of the twentieth century, including the Cuban *son,* the Puerto Rican *plena,* and the Dominican merengue, represent creative hybrids of European textual with African-derived rhythmic structures.

stringed instrumentation. This poetic form and others nourished the development of the Trinidadian calypso, whose seasonal height of creativity is carnival, in which political and social criticism is also expressed through costumes. Songs of commentary can be manipulated by despotic leaders, as when merengue texts were often performed by hired bands and composers in praise of Dominican dictator Rafael Trujillo. In postrevolutionary Cuba, songs of commentary have been cast as songs of protest (*nueva trova,* called *nueva canción* elsewhere, both meaning 'new song').

Musical evolutions

The creole society of the Caribbean is continually changing and evolving. Creole dances of the twentieth century, including the Cuban *son,* the Puerto Rican *plena* (also used for commentary), and the Dominican merengue, represent creative hybrids of European textual with African-derived rhythmic structures. An example of twentieth-century creativity, the steelband, originated in Port-of-Spain, Trinidad, but is now associated with territorially based musical competition in carnival and has become diffused throughout the anglophone Caribbean. It was developed by lower-class young men in the context of social-cultural-sports clubs, using oil drums obtained from Trinidadian oil refineries and tuned to tempered scales. As multi-toned instruments played in ensemble, these are reminiscent of the multi-toned marimbas and marimba orchestras of East Africa, suggesting an African musical retention based on collective memory; but the musical style and repertoire are essentially European.

Other contemporary developments in Caribbean music culture include the newly acquired function of traditional genres as symbols of national and regional identity. In Trinidad, this function is promoted by the annual Best Village competition. The ubiquitous *ballet folklórico,* characterized by inauthentically staged stylization with uniform and flashy costuming, serves as a symbol of national identity. Such genres, with folk-based festivals and other national events, are particularly significant for expatriate communities. A notable example of these activities, the Caribbean Carnival held on Labor Day in New York City, reprises the genuine carnival, held "down home" in the Caribbean five or six months earlier.

Another new development is the increasing commodification of Caribbean expressive culture for export as a new type of extractive industry. Starting in the 1930s or before, Cubans led the way in hispanophone areas, popularizing the *son* even in Africa; based in Miami since the revolution, they still control hispanophone Caribbean popular music. The popular-music enterprise is now larger than the region itself, with recording hubs and performance venues at the site of expatriate communities, not only in Miami, but also in New York and other North American and European cities.

New York is the crucible of encounters between people from countries of the hispanophone Caribbean, divided in the twentieth century by ideology, between the adversaries of Haiti and the Dominican Republic, among language areas of the Caribbean as a whole, and, most important, between any and all of them and U.S. Afro-America, including Afrocentric ideology, jazz, and the world of performance and recorded production. New York, long the site of evolution of Latin jazz, now fosters the development of *plena*-rap, *vodou*-jazz, and other creations born of ethnic fusion.

Antigua and Barbuda
Lorna McDaniel

Popular Music of the 1700s and 1800s
The Twentieth Century

Antigua and Barbuda, with areas of 280 and 161 square kilometers, respectively, are situated in the Leeward Islands. In 1493, Columbus sighted Antigua, which he named after Santa María La Antigua, the cathedral of Seville. Except for a six-month French occupation in 1666, the islands were exclusively under British rule from 1632 to 1981, when they became independent as a united nation.

The present population of about seventy-two thousand (including fifteen hundred persons on Barbuda) is descended mostly from enslaved West Africans. No descendants of aboriginal settlers (Arawaks or Caribs) remain, and except for a few mixed-race descendants of colonizers (Scottish, Irish, English), Antigua and Barbuda remain devoid of the interracial minglings that typify the populations of other Caribbean islands.

Portuguese indentured workers arrived in Antigua in 1860 and soon became shopkeepers. After 1880, when they immigrated to the United States, Lebanese immigrants took their places.

POPULAR MUSIC OF THE 1700S AND 1800S

On Sunday afternoons in the 1780s, as many as a hundred enslaved Africans would participate in open-air dances and exhibit their "fondness of the discordant notes of the banjar and the hollow sound of the toombah" (Luffman 1788). The toombah, a drum with tin jingles and shells, accompanied songs and dances of Africans on Antigua.

A report in 1844 mentions the "tum tum" (toombah) and the "bangoe" (banjar), and the new practice of biweekly subscription balls (Lanigan 1844). At these fancy dress balls, fiddles, a tambourine (employing a "particular way of performing"), and a triangle ("played without any regard to time or melody") reinterpreted the music of European quadrilles.

The musical influence of the colonial churches was overwhelming in its displacement of African music. Acting with similar intensity, postemancipation missionary movements continued adding diverse intonations. Among these were the Salvation Army's brass-ensemble style, and in the late twentieth century, American Baptists' electronic gospel sound. In the 1990s, Jamaican Rastafarians imported Africanesque drumming into Antigua.

Systematic musical research has not yet been undertaken on Antigua, but novels, essays, and editorials allude to the loss of indigenous ethnic forms. Current musical styles appear to have their origins or influence in Europe, Trinidad, Jamaica, and the United States. The highland fling, performed during carnival, survives as a relic of the colonial past, as does the figure-eight quadrille. Young Antiguan choreographers revitalize and Africanize fragments of antique colonial dances by infusing, for instance, the staid dance movements of the maypole (accompanied by a traditional piece, "Country Gardens") with more fluid ones.

Explanations for the loss of African styles may center on peculiar circumstances in Antigua's history:

1. Exclusive British colonial rule (1632–1981), the absence of French culture, and late Roman Catholic presence (1860); islands that underwent periods of French cultural influence show some adherence to African dance, plus ritual syncretisms with Roman Catholic religious forms.
2. The British naval base at Shirley Heights, housing West Indian regiments that guarded against external invasion; the military presence possibly intervened psychologically against internal freedom.
3. The single, dominant sugar proprietorship of the Codrington family.
4. The absence of late-arriving Africans.
5. A unified African ethnicity with little outside cultural competition; on many Caribbean islands with diverse ethnic populations, interracial tension is masked in culturally appropriate ways such as carnival competitions, which work toward the projection of ethnic identity and the revitalization of ancient musical forms.
6. A contemporary climate of an uncertain economy amid charges of governmental corruption.

THE TWENTIETH CENTURY

A Trinidad-inspired carnival, introduced in 1957 to inspire the tourist industry, takes place during the season of celebrations of emancipation. It replaced the Old Time Christmas Festival, some of whose historic themes were adopted by the carnival. To the frustration of older Antiguans, many of the following revered Old Time Christmas masquerade bands are lost to them:

1. Carol trees—lantern-decked poles, carried by carolers, whose singing was accompanied by a concertina;
2. John Bull—participants costumed in banana leaves with animal horns on their heads;
3. Highlander—dancers dressed in Scottish kilts, wearing wire masks, and armed with cowhide whips;
4. Long Ghosts, Moko Jumbie or Jumpa-Ben—robed stilt dancers, accompanied by fife, triangle (cling-a-ching), boompipe (made from a meter-long plumbing joint), and two drums (kettle and bass).

Frank Manning (1977:274) interprets the changing symbolic forms of Antiguan carnival as culturally dissonant with the past in its imitation of North American moral values and consumer ethics introduced by "visitors." The price paid for cultivating the tourist industry is seduction by a culturally imperialistic system that relegates Antiguans to positions as service personnel and "mimic men," robbing the culture of its natural integrity and cultural history.

Calypso

The contemporary Antiguan calypso models its style after the formula set by the Grenadian-Trinidadian calypsonian Mighty Sparrow, but the origin of the early Antiguan calypso is the satiric folk song, the *benna* (or *bennah*). It was sung responsorially by a leader and an audience.

Quarkoo, the legendary traveling singer, is known to have helped generate and popularize the original style of calypso. Performing in the streets, he was the foremost itinerant balladeer and peddler of pencils, matches, and printed songs. He published scandalous texts in a print shop whose owner became a patron of calypso. A satiric *benna,* "Cocoatea," brought about his imprisonment because it broadcast the news that the daughter of a high-placed citizen had become pregnant while living in a convent.

Like the daughter in "Cocotea," Millie was most likely a young woman who, without proper clothing, absented herself, saying she was going to Brazil.

Short Shirt, in his 1977 album *Harambee,* was influential in an attempt to revitalize the *benna.* In the new form, political and racial consciousness comes to the fore. Mighty Swallow, in "Freedom," sang about the oppression in Angola, Rhodesia, and Antigua.

The contemporary political and economic climate has produced a musical reaction—the creation of a direct, humorless type of calypso, the antigovernmental song, as in this example:

> When they have power and authority,
> They don't give a damn about nobody.
> Prostituting this land, to all and sundry,
> They making my people starve.

Jamaica Kincaid (1988:59) accuses the leadership of the small place, Antigua, of "smallness"—corruption, nepotism, oppressive tactics, and trafficking in arms and drugs. Harsh and direct, this chastisement, often sung in calypsos, and less often experienced in print, caused the government little embarrassment. Like Manning, who points to the opposition between carnival economy and cultural continuity, Kincaid reveals the destructive contradiction between the fantasy created for tourists and the reality of local life, the continuing inhibition of culture by greedy politicians, and people's inability to claim power.

REFERENCES

Kincaid, Jamaica. 1988. *A Small Place.* New York: Farrar, Straus and Giroux.

Lanigan, Mrs. 1844. *Antigua and the Antiguans.* 2 vols. London.

Luffman, John. 1788. *A Brief Account of the Island of Antigua.* London.

Manning, Frank E. 1977. "Cup Match and Carnival: Secular Rites of Revitalization in Decolonizing Tourist-Oriented Societies." In *Secular Ritual,* ed. Sally F. Moore and Barbara G. Myerhoff, 265–281. Assen, Netherlands: Van Gorcum.

The Bahamas
Vivian Nina Michelle Wood

Music and Society
Musical Instruments
Religious Music
Secular and Recorded Music
Dance
Festivals
Further Study

The Commonwealth of the Bahamas is an archipelago of some seven hundred islands and more than two thousand cays and rocks, situated in the Atlantic Ocean about 100 kilometers southeast of Florida. The archipelago stretches about 1,224 kilometers toward the northeastern coast of Cuba and the Turks and Caicos Islands. Only thirty of the islands of the Bahamas are inhabited, and more than 50 percent of the country's 255,000 inhabitants live on New Providence, an island 11 kilometers wide and 34 kilometers long, on which Nassau, the country's capital, is located. Except for New Providence and Grand Bahama, the inhabited islands of the Bahamas are known collectively as the Family Islands. Ninety percent of the country's inhabitants are of African descent; the remaining population is primarily of European heritage.

The principal industry of the Bahamas is tourism. More than 3.6 million tourists visit the country each year, primarily from North America. Tourism brings in revenue of about $1.3 billion annually. The tourism industry has had a great effect on local music. Besides sun, sand, and sea, music has always been a form of entertainment made available to visitors at the hotels constructed expressly to accommodate them. In the early years of tourism, these hotels were owned and operated by foreign concerns. Before 1949, most entertainers at these hotels came from the United States. Bahamian musicians performed in nightclubs outside the areas in which the hotels were located. Though the nightclubs catered primarily to the Bahamian population, tourists often found their way to them through the guidance of Bahamian taxi drivers and tour operators. These night spots burgeoned and provided creative outlets for Bahamian musicians. In 1949, a musicians' union was formed. This entity, now known as the Bahamas Musicians and Entertainers Union, protects the interests of Bahamian musicians and establishes employment and salary guidelines.

In 1967, the Bahamas achieved majority rule, and the new government put into place a policy of Bahamianization of jobs and businesses. The government bought many of the large hotels, enabling black musicians to obtain jobs, with the result that each hotel now has a resident group of musicians. Since 1967, the construction of hotels to accommodate increasing numbers of tourists has provided employment for many Bahamian musicians; however, these musicians' moving to the hotels resulted

Bahamian drummers introduced the bomber, a drum made by stretching a goatskin over one end of a washing-machine barrel, and the B-52, made from a 55-gallon oil drum.

in the closing of many nightclubs. Some nightclub acts moved to the hotels in the form of so-called native shows, which eventually became stylized performances of supposedly traditional Bahamian music and dance.

Through the 1980s, the boom in tourism led musicians to perform and record songs familiar to tourists, or covers of songs from other Caribbean countries, limiting the creation of Bahamian music and the development of a local recording industry. It is far more common to hear music from the United States, Jamaica, and Trinidad and Tobago than it is to hear the music of the Bahamas. It is not unusual to hear renditions of country, rock, or rhythm-and-blues songs from the United States, to which Bahamian-like rhythms have been added. Bahamian musicians repeatedly perform for tourists the calypsos made famous in the United States by non-Bahamian performers. Nevertheless, the 1990s have seen a move toward the creation and recording of more original Bahamian music.

MUSIC AND SOCIETY

Musicians in the Bahamas are usually men, and dancers can be men or women. Men, women, and children may make music whenever they wish. There is no caste system in the Bahamas, but a subtle class system permeates Bahamian society. Musicians have traditionally been perceived as belonging to the lower stratum of society, so that persons belonging to the upper and upper-middle classes generally did not choose to become performers of Bahamian music. Many members of the upper classes considered Bahamian music to be unworthy of study or practice. These persons usually opted to learn and play European instruments and European classical music.

A major reason for the disdain of Bahamian music was that it was closer in essence to African than to European musical forms. The similarity to African music was evidenced in the percussiveness of the music, often considered noise. Second, as it was transmitted orally, Bahamian music was not considered "high" art. Furthermore, the development of tourism, the increase in the number of hotels and visitors to the Bahamas, and the subsequent increase in the number of musicians associated with tourism have led to the identification of male musicians as womanizers and drifters.

Despite the stigma locally attached to music, the Bahamas experienced a surge in interest in its traditional music in the 1970s and early 1980s. This interest was due primarily to the country's move toward nationhood, culminating in 1973 with political independence from the United Kingdom and the concomitant nationalism and search for a Bahamian national identity. Since independence, persons from professions such as banking, law, and education have become part-time musicians. Their presence has served to attenuate the stigma formerly attached to musical performers.

MUSICAL INSTRUMENTS

Bahamians create their traditional musical instruments from simple, everyday materials. The dominant musical instrument is the *goombay,* a drum that Bahamian legend says received its name from the sounds made when its head is struck: the *goom* depicts the deep, resonant sound made when the head is struck near the center, and the *bay* (or *bah*) resembles the sound that occurs when the head is struck nearer the edge. However, the term *goumbé* is also found in such West African countries as Senegal and Côte d'Ivoire: in Senegal, *goumbé* is a traditional women's dance associated with the planting season; in Côte d'Ivoire, *goumbé* is a dance popular among young people. Both dances are accompanied by frame drums.

The *goombay* evolved from a frame drum similar to those used in West Africa and in some Caribbean countries. Rarely used in the Bahamas today, the frame drum is made by fashioning a strip of wood into a square or a circle and attaching a skin to one edge. Likewise the *goombay,* which comes in various sizes, is made by stretching the depilated skin of a goat or a sheep over one end of a cylinder. The drum is tuned by heating its skin over or near a fire—an action called bringing the drum up.

Lacking large trees from which to make drums, Bahamians had to be resourceful in finding materials. Before 1971, musicians made drums from wooden kegs that had held imported nails, cheese, or rum. With advances in technology and transportation, foreign manufacturers began shipping their goods in cartons, eliminating the Bahamians' source of materials. Since 1971, Bahamians have used metal barrels to make their drums (Wood 1995:249–250). The use of metal instead of wood has changed the tone of the drum so that it is now slightly less resonant and mellow.

Bahamians have also added new drums, used principally in junkanoo music. In 1985, junkanoo drummers began using the tenor drum from the Western trap set. Lead drummers usually beat this drum, which they call a tom-tom. It does not have to be heated and consequently allows the drummer to perform without interruption. Drummers have also introduced the bomber, a drum made by stretching a goatskin over one end of a washing-machine barrel, and the B-52, made from a 55-gallon oil drum. Though smaller *goombay* are used to play bass rhythms, the bomber and the B-52 provide a more powerful bass.

Other traditional Bahamian instruments include cowbells, a carpenter's saw, a hair comb, a ridged bottle, shak-shaks, and a washtub bass. Before the 1950s, musicians used bronze cowbells imported from Germany. In the 1950s, Bahamian welders began fashioning their own cowbells, making them lighter, longer, and narrower. Cowbells are played in pairs and are shaken in a rhythmic pattern or rung in a sixteenth-note pattern. Cowbell players are known as bellers. In 1993, musicians introduced the concept of multiple cowbells: each bell has two or more heads and two or more clappers, reducing the number of cowbell players needed in an ensemble. Furthermore, since the heads are of varied shapes and sizes, these bells produce various timbres.

The carpenter's saw is a scraped idiophone. The player, holding the handle in one hand and placing its tip against his body, scrapes the serrations with a piece of metal held in the other hand. For tonal variety, he flexes the saw while playing it. The comb and the ridged bottle are scraped with a piece of metal. Sometimes a strip of paper is inserted through the teeth of the comb, over which the player blows to create various tones.

Shak-shaks are dried, seed-filled pods from the poinciana tree, or plastic bottles and tin cans filled with small stones. Both types of shak-shaks are shaken in the same manner as maracas. The washtub bass is a plucked chordophone. It consists of a metal tub, usually turned upside down, to which a staff and a string are attached. Variations in sound are obtained by depressing the string near the upper portion of the staff.

Bahamian musicians also utilize Western instruments including banjos, guitars, accordions, pianos, drum sets, and modern electronic instruments. These are sometimes incorporated into ensembles that include the traditional instruments.

RELIGIOUS MUSIC

The religious music of the Bahamas has its roots in Africa and Europe. African influences are evident in layered voices and polyrhythms, and European influences are in the source of texts, primarily early Wesleyan and Baptist hymns (Bethel 1978:59). The major forms of traditional religious music are the anthem and the rhyming spiritual.

The anthem

The Bahamian anthem is closely related to the spiritual of slaves and other blacks in the southern United States (Hedrick and Stephens 1976:8). This relationship reflects the fact that enslaved Africans came to the Bahamas with whites loyal to Britain in the late 1700s, at the time of the American Revolution.

The Bahamian anthem, performed primarily in the Family Islands, tends to focus on biblical characters and in particular, their relationship to the sea. The anthem is optimistic, creating feelings of joy and celebration by emphasizing life after death. This contrasts with the African-American spiritual of the antebellum South, which was pessimistic and leaned more toward problems being encountered in mortal life.

The most common form of the anthem features a sequence of stanzas containing up to eight lines, held together by a single-line refrain that may be sung after each stanza or after each line in each stanza. It may also comprise four-lined stanzas followed by four-lined choruses sung in multipart harmony. The tenor, which carries the melody, is typically placed between the other parts. Each voice is free to improvise melodically and textually, thus making the anthem highly textured and harmonically varied. The improvisation of the anthem leads to the production of unorthodox chords. Clapping and foot tapping usually provide accompaniment.

The anthem may be performed as a rushin' song. Rushin'—marching or dancing with shuffling steps—is associated with the junkanoo parade, but some congregations rush around their churches on New Year's Eve or during special services. During the rush, the participants sing anthems before performing responsorial chants. The rush recalls the ring shouts performed by slaves in the southern United States.

The rhyming spiritual

The rhyming spiritual, an outgrowth of the anthem, was closely related to the sponging industry, especially on Andros Island. Spongers often sang anthems while performing their tasks. Out of these anthems they created a modified genre of songs that came to be known as rhyming spirituals. Since sponging is locally no longer a viable industry, the art of rhyming—the creation and recounting of sung verse—is gradually disappearing. Rhyming spirituals may sometimes be sung at wakes.

The rhyming spiritual is usually sung unaccompanied by at least two men, but women sometimes participate in the performance. The rhyming spiritual involves singing in parts that may include alto, bass, and more than one tenor. The two most important singers are the lead tenor and the bass. The former, called the rhymer, sings the melody, provides the narrative of the song, and starts and ends each song; the latter, known as the basser, provides an eighth-note ostinato that keeps time and serves as the foundation on which the other parts improvise. The other parts sing above the rhymer so that, as in the anthem, the lead tenor's melody is sandwiched between the other parts.

Though the rhyming spiritual is highly improvised, it is more harmonically restricted than the anthem, and singers tend to adhere to the tonic (I), subdominant (IV), and dominant (V). It consists of stanzas and refrains; each of the singers freely provides rhythmic improvisations in the stanzas, though the refrains are rhythmically uniform. Because of the improvisation in each part and the overlapping of phrases, the rhyming spiritual is performed without evident pauses.

The texts of the rhyming spiritual center on biblical characters and stories, though a rhyming spiritual may recount the story of something that has happened in the community. One of the most famous Bahamian rhymers was the late Joseph Spence. Contemporary performers of the rhyming spiritual include the Dicey Doh Singers.

SECULAR AND RECORDED MUSIC

Before 1970, the secular music of the Bahamas was generically known as *goombay*, a name borrowed from the drum, the primary instrument for this type of music. Today, *goombay* is no longer used to define the entirety of Bahamian music. Instead, the secular music of the Bahamas is divided into several categories, most accompanied by the *goombay* drum. These categories include rake 'n' scrape, goombay, and junkanoo.

Rake 'n' scrape

Rake 'n' scrape historically accompanied quadrilles. The current name, first used publicly in the 1970s by Charles Carter, a radio DJ, derives from the raked and scraped idiophones used to perform this music. A basic rake-'n'-scrape ensemble typically includes a *goombay*, a carpenter's saw, and an accordion to provide melodic interest (figure 1). The Western guitar, banjo, or harmonica may join in if no accordion is present. A washtub bass, a hair comb, a ridged bottle, and shak-shaks may also join in. More modern rake-'n'-scrape ensembles often use electronic instruments;

FIGURE 1   A rake-'n'-scrape band. *Left to right:* carpenter's saw, washtub bass, *goombay,* and accordion. Anonymous photo, 1973. Used with permission of the Department of Archives, the Bahamas.

Junkanoo instruments are all played rhythmically to satisfy the Bahamian aesthetic for a dense mosaic of textures, timbres, and rhythms. Through the use of these instruments, Bahamians continue the African orientation toward intensity in music performance through volume and noise.

FIGURE 2   The rhythm of a carpenter's saw provides the timeline for rake 'n' scrape. Transcription by Vivian Nina Michelle Wood.

the bass drum replaces the *goombay,* the high-hat replaces the carpenter's saw, and the electronic keyboard replaces the accordion.

The definitive trait of rake 'n' scrape is the rhythm usually produced by the carpenter's saw or ridged bottle (figure 2). This rhythm of alternating eighth and sixteenth notes is sustained throughout the performance, providing a timeline. The timeline is provided by the high hat in modern rake-'n'-scrape ensembles. Rake 'n' scrape is performed as dance music, but it is also the foundation for songs whose lyrics address local or foreign events, social problems, and cultural practices.

Goombay

The music now known as *goombay* is that which many non-Bahamians call calypso. It is primarily sung dance music with lyrics that address current affairs or extol male sexual prowess or libido. Unlike in rake 'n' scrape (in which rhythm dominates), melody is important; consequently, melodic instruments such as the Western banjo, electric guitar, and piano are dominant. *Goombay* is the primary form of recorded music in the Bahamas, the music that visitors to the Bahamas are likeliest to hear. Another trait of *goombay* is the continuous strumming of the banjo or the electric guitar to complement the rhythm of the drums.

Famous recording artists and performers of *goombay* included Alphonso "Blind Blake" Higgs, George Symonette (the "King of Goombay"), and Charles Lofthouse. Though these performers are deceased, their tradition continues, thanks to performers including Ronnie Butler, Eric "King Eric" Gibson, and more recently Kirkland "K. B." Bodie and Cyril "Dry Bread" Ferguson.

Junkanoo

Junkanoo is actually traditional *goombay* performed by acoustic instruments within the context of the junkanoo parades at Christmastime. The number of instruments in each junkanoo group may range between ten and five hundred. The traditional instruments used in the parade include the *goombay,* divided into three sections—lead, second, and bass. The lead drums play the more complex rhythm; the second drums match parts of the lead and bass rhythms; and the bass drums carry a steady, metronomic rhythm. The other traditional junkanoo instruments are cowbells, police whistles, foghorns (long black metal horns that emit a sound similar to that of a semi trailer), bicycle horns (which emit a higher-pitched sound) and conchs. A horn blower may often play two or more foghorns together to make a fuller sound and give added reach. Sometimes foghorns and bicycle horns are combined to produce a mixture of textures and a contrast in timbres.

FIGURE 3   Typical rhythms and instrumentation of junkanoo music. Transcription by Vivian Nina Michelle Wood.

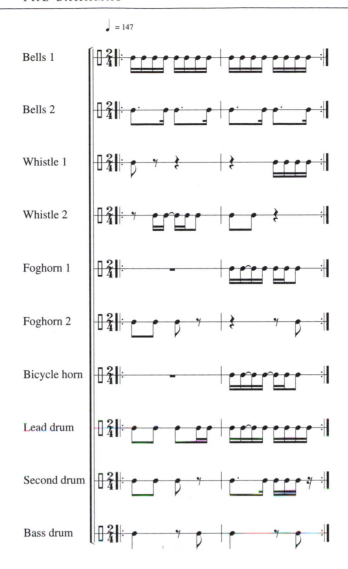

Junkanoo instruments are all played rhythmically to satisfy the Bahamian aesthetic for a dense mosaic of textures, timbres, and rhythms. Through the use of these instruments, Bahamians continue the African orientation toward intensity in music performance through volume and noise.

Since 1976, junkanooers have also used wind instruments, including trumpets, trombones, saxophones, sousaphones, and clarinets. The wind instruments, which play popular melodies, have replaced the traditional practice of singing during the junkanoo parade. A principal reason for the decline of singing was that the junkanoo groups grew to such large numbers that it was impossible to hear human voices over the sounds of the instruments. The use of wind instruments has spawned controversy between those who feel that junkanoo should become a more modern cultural manifestation and those who believe the addition of such instruments removes junkanoo from its tradition and transforms it into an event that too closely resembles carnival in Trinidad and Tobago.

Junkanoo music is multilayered and polyrhythmic (figure 3). Each instrument group has several rhythms, playable with many variations. There are two basic cowbell rhythms—one of repeated sixteenth notes, and the other of alternating dotted eighths and sixteenths. Each beller is free to play variations of these patterns by adding or deleting notes, or by hitting the bells together at some point in the performance. The latter adds another timbre to the layers of music. The same process of variation applies to the foghorns, bicycle horns, and drums. Foghorns and bicycle horns sometimes play together responsorially. Bellers and drummers also blow whistles highly individualized in rhythms that usually contrast with the cowbell and drum rhythms, so that each musician simultaneously plays two rhythms—one on a drum or a cowbell, another on a whistle.

Junkanoo musicians stagger their entries into the overall music performance. In most groups, the leader of the drum section starts the music. Once he has set the tempo, the other drums start to play. After the drummers have settled into a steady rhythm, the leader of the bellers begins to play, followed by the other bellers. Once the drums and cowbells have jelled, the foghorns, bicycle horns, and whistles join in. The brass instruments do not usually begin to play until the entire rhythm section has come together and has established a steady tempo.

Junkanoo music is not limited to the Christmastime parades. It is used in times of celebration or at other important times. Junkanoo bands accompany political rallies and beauty-pageant motorcades. In 1993, they accompanied the Davis Cup match in North Carolina, in which a Bahamian tennis team played against their U.S. counterparts. Junkanoo music broke out each time the Bahamian team scored a point.

Junkanoo and recorded music

The influence of traditional junkanoo on popular recorded music is strongly felt, and the music has evolved from one in which basic rhythms undergirded calypsolike songs to a new form of highly electronic music called junkafunk. Junkanoo's influence on the recorded music of the Bahamas was keenly felt around 1973, when a newly independent nation saw a return to what was perceived as authentic, traditional Bahamian culture. Artists such as Tony "The Obeah Man" McKay and Eddie Minnis and Da Brudders released songs that married, in the case of McKay, traditional junkanoo elements (such as instruments and the imitation of the horns' dominant-tonic melodic intervals) to songs that depicted Bahamian culture. Minnis used an electronic rhythm section to duplicate traditional junkanoo rhythms. The music supported lyrics that addressed contemporary social problems or praised Bahamian traditions. In the early 1980s, a group of musicians led by Tyrone "Dr. Offfff" Fitzgerald and comprising a Western rhythm section, brass players, and traditional junkanoo instruments continued the use of junkanoo in recorded music.

The common denominator in Eddie Minnis' and Dr. Offfff's music was their rhythm section—a six-member group known as High Voltage, which, in 1992, changed its name to "Bahamen." It is responsible for transforming junkanoo music from music of the streets to music of the studio and dance floor. Bahamen has toured the United States, and its recordings have been released around the world. Promoted as junkafunk, their music reproduces traditional junkanoo rhythms on modern electronic instruments. *Goombay* rhythms are reproduced on a Western drum set and bass guitar, whereas whistle and horn patterns are produced by synthesizers. Performances sometimes involve traditional *goombay* drums and cowbells. Despite the use of electronic instruments, junkafunk retains the highly percussive, multilayered character of traditional junkanoo music. Its lyrics sometimes come from traditional *goombay* or rake 'n' scrape songs.

DANCE

The Bahamas has been highly influenced by modern dances from the United States and the Caribbean, but some of its folk dances, such as the quadrille and ring dances, continue to be performed. This is especially true in the Family Islands, which remain somewhat outside the sphere of direct international influence.

FIGURE 4   A fire dance with *goombay* accompaniment. Photo by Stanley Toogood, 1938. Used with permission of the Department of Archives, the Bahamas.

Quadrilles

Bahamian quadrilles derive from an African interpretation of nineteenth-century European set dances. The quadrille, whose format may be a square or two parallel lines, is performed by mixed couples and is accompanied by a traditional rake-'n'-scrape band incorporating a *goombay*, a carpenter's saw, and an accordion or guitar. Drummers and dancers improvise freely, but male dancers tend to be more vigorous than their female counterparts.

A trait of quadrille music is a loud syncopated slap on the *goombay*. The male dancer stamps his foot at the same time as the slap. Foot tapping by each musician also provides rhythmic accompaniment and helps to keep time. Some rake-'n'-scrape bands may add vocal accompaniment.

Ring dances

Ring dances, with roots in Africa, were originally performed in the Bahamas by enslaved Africans. As their name implies, ring dances are done in the center of a ring made by the dancers. Each dancer usually performs alone inside the ring. Traditionally, there would be a fire in the center of the ring, or just outside it; today, a fire is no longer requisite. The *goombay* is the most important instrument used to accompany ring dances.

Three types of ring dances are performed in the Bahamas: the fire dance, the jump-in dance, and the ring-play. The first two are performed by adults; the third, primarily by children.

The fire dance

Originally the fire dance was a form of recreation in which a performer danced in and around a central fire (figure 4). Today, fire dances are performed only on stages in hotel clubs for tourists. Dancers perform around trays engulfed in flames and pass lit torches over their bodies, all to the accompaniment of *goombay* drums.

The jump-in dance

The jump-in dance, also known as the jumping dance, involves solo dancers who use highly individualized and often sensual movements. The sensuality is particularly evi-

Junkanoo and tourism have been closely linked for most of the twentieth century. The costumes and music have been used in television, radio, and print advertisements around the world to attract visitors to the Bahamas.

FIGURE 5   A chant and percussive rhythm used in a jump-in dance. Transcription by Vivian Nina Michelle Wood.

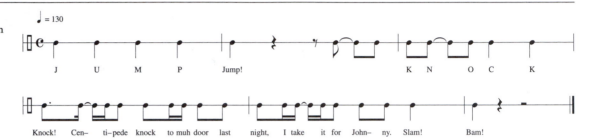

J   U   M   P   Jump!   K   N   O   C   K

Knock! Cen-ti-pede knock to muh door last night, I take it for John-ny. Slam! Bam!

dent at the point in the performance where one dancer approaches another, inviting the latter to take her or his place in the ring. It is often marked by the twisting or shaking of hips and by the suggestive forward thrust of the hips, in tandem with a flourish on the *goombay*. This movement is performed when the dancer is directly in front of and almost touching the replacement. Each person has a turn to perform in the ring, and if possible, chooses a member of the opposite sex as a replacement.

Jump-in dances are usually accompanied by a *goombay,* on-beat claps, and rhythmic chants (figure 5), whose rhythms replicate those of the drum, even if a drum is not present.

The ring-play

Though adults on a few of the islands of the Bahamas such as Cat Island perform ring-plays, these dances are usually performed by children. The ring-play is African derived but heavily influenced by European children's games. As in the jump-in dance, the children form a ring in whose center individuals take turns performing solo. There is no instrumental accompaniment, though adults may use a *goombay*. Adults and children clap on each downbeat.

Ring-plays take the form of a mild jump-in dance, but the songs that accompany them are melodic and longer than those used in jump-in dances (figure 6). They

FIGURE 6   A song and chant used in children's ring-play. Transcription by Vivian Nina Michelle Wood.

Blue Hill wa-ter dry, and there's no-where to wash my clothes. I re-

mem-ber the Sa-tur-day night, boil fish and john-ny cake. Man take one and sa-tis-fied

wo-man take two and she make a moo'!

often contain refrains or responsorial patterns with repetitions of the last line of each call. Sometimes short monotone chants, reminiscent of those used in the jump-in dance, are attached to the ends of the songs in lieu of the refrains. As the chants are being performed, children accelerate their movements, often imitating the sensual hip thrust of their adult counterparts.

FESTIVALS

Junkanoo

Junkanoo is a carnivalesque parade in which costumed participants (called junkanooers) rush to the accompaniment of junkanoo music. The parade originated as a celebration by enslaved Africans, who received two days off for Christmas, and they often spent a portion of this time performing music and dances. After full emancipation (1838), they continued their celebrations. Those on New Providence Island later moved their celebrations to the downtown area of the city of Nassau. The celebrations included the wearing of costumes and the provision of spontaneous music; they were principally the domain of the working class until 1958, when large numbers of middle-class persons began taking part in the parade.

In the 1920s, the government of the Bahamas realized that these celebrations were a possible means of entertaining tourists. They thus sought to organize the celebrations by offering cash prizes for the best costumes to encourage greater participation. As a result, junkanoo and tourism have been closely linked for most of the twentieth century. The costumes and music have been used in television, radio, and print advertisements around the world to attract visitors to the Bahamas. Junkanoo itself has also been exported, with junkanooers taking part in Mardi Gras and the Jazz Festival in New Orleans and at the Orange Bowl parade in Miami. Tourists are encouraged to participate in junkanoo, and it is no longer unusual to see tourists amid the paraders.

With the extensive promotion of junkanoo for the tourist market and the move toward stricter organization, junkanoo has become a spectator event. Bleachers are set up along the sidewalks, and tickets must be purchased for seats. This regimentation has diminished interaction between junkanooers and spectators, but it has allowed more people to view the parade in comfort and safety.

The increased involvement of the government throughout this century and the widespread participation on the part of persons of all colors and classes have made junkanoo the premier cultural manifestation in the Bahamas. Junkanoo parades take place on 26 December and 1 January, between two and eight o'clock in the morning. Junkanoo may be seen on several of the islands, but the most elaborate performance takes place in Nassau. Today, junkanoo is an intensely competitive event involving music, dance, and elaborate costumes made from fringed crepe paper. Several groups of up to a thousand persons each vie for cash prizes and the acknowledgment of being the best performers. The latter acknowledgment is valued far more than the financial reward.

Most junkanooers are men, who were the sole participants until 1946, when women began to participate, primarily as dancers. Women's participation waned after 1958, when the stigma attached to junkanoo began to dissipate. Few women were junkanooers in the 1960s and 1970s, and it was not until 1988 that women began to participate in large numbers, again primarily as dancers. Today, there is only a smattering of female musicians.

Scrap and organized groups

There are two kinds of junkanoo groups: scrap and organized. Organized groups became a part of junkanoo in 1958. Before then, participants were loosely organized, and junkanooers came and went at will during the course of the parade. Today's scrap groups are small. The largest numbers no more than about a hundred members. Their philosophy is closer to that of the traditional junkanooers in that their members take part for pleasure and to release tension and stress. They are not particularly concerned with competing for prizes. Organized groups are extremely competitive. Their performance is more rigid, in that members of the organized groups perform in straight lines and are concerned about presentation and performance. Members of the scrap groups tend to perform in clusters and are more concerned about enjoying themselves and entertaining spectators.

Members of scrap and organized groups perform in costumes. Scrap groups comprise only musicians, but the organized groups also include dancers and large costumed pieces similar to floats but carried by a single performer. About half the members of the organized groups are musicians. All groups receive financial support from business concerns. These funds help defray the expenses of participating in the parade; however, the organized groups receive a higher level of funding, since they are more likely to win the parade and thus provide positive advertising for their sponsors.

FURTHER STUDY

The study of Bahamian music, which has been quite limited, includes an early work by Charles L. Edwards (1895), and articles by Daniel J. Crowley (1958), Zora Neale Hurston (1930), and Elsie Clews Parsons (1928). More recently, in-depth studies have been conducted by Basil C. Hedrick and Jeanette E. Stephens (1976), E. Clement Bethel (1978), and Vivian Nina M. Wood (1995). The works by Hedrick and Stephens, Bethel, and Wood serve as the primary sources for this article. General articles on music in the Bahamas have appeared in local magazines and newspapers, but no official record or archives of Bahamian music exists.

REFERENCES

Bethel, Edward Clement. 1978. "Music in the Bahamas: Its Roots, Development and Personality." Master's thesis, University of California at Los Angeles.

Crowley, Daniel J. 1958a. "Guy Fawkes Day at Fresh Creek, Andros Island, Bahamas." *Man* 58:114–115.

———. 1958b. "L'héritage africain dans les Bahamas." *Présence africaine* 23:41–58.

Edwards, Charles L. 1942 [1895]. *Bahama Songs and Stories.* New York: G. E. Steckert.

Hedrick, Basil C., and Jeanette E. Stephens. 1976. *In the Days of Yesterday and in the Days of Today: An Overview of Bahamian Folk Music.* Museum Studies, 8. Carbondale: Southern Illinois University.

Hurston, Zora Neale. 1930. "Dance Songs and Games from the Bahamas." *Journal of American Folklore* 43:294–312.

Parsons, Elsie Clews. 1928. "Spirituals and Other Folk-Lore from the Bahamas." *Journal of American Folklore* 41:453–524.

Wood, Vivian Nina Michelle. 1995. "Rushin' Hard and Runnin' Hot: Experiencing the Music of the *Junkanoo* Parade in Nassau, Bahamas." Ph.D. dissertation, Indiana University.

Barbados

Janice Millington

Musical Instruments
Musical Contexts and Genres
Social Structure and Change

Sugar plantations and chattel houses perched on coral stones dug from quarries—these are characteristic features of the landscape of Barbados, the most easterly island of the Lesser Antilles chain in the Caribbean. First settled by native Americans (about A.D. 380) who were soon replaced by Island Arawak (about A.D. 1200) and later the Carib, it had a colonial history that included Portuguese settlement before the early 1600s, when England laid claim to it. Barbados has an area of 430 square kilometers and a population of about 260,000 inhabitants, predominantly of African descent but including heritages from Europe (mainly British), China, India, Lebanon, and Syria.

The first Englishmen landed on the island in 1620, when John Powell disembarked from his flagship, *Olive Blossom,* and claimed Barbados for England. In 1627, the ship *William John* brought eighty settlers, including ten African slaves. Sir William Courteen and the Earl of Carlisle were later rivals to the claim of the island, and agreement by law was in favor of the Earl of Carlisle, after whom Carlisle Bay was named. Settlers soon arrived from England, and by 1643 there were thirty-seven thousand whites and about six thousand blacks in residence. Locally grown crops included indigo, cotton, tobacco, and later, sugarcane. More African slaves were brought to work on the plantations, and by 1669 about forty thousand blacks were living on the island. Barbados remained under British rule, producing a rich sugar-export market for England.

Creolization developed a society with Barbadian traits from the 1750s onward. In 1834, Parliament emancipated the slaves, but the plantation system still continued to rule the island's economy and society. Barbadian culture can be detected in the island's cuisine, its architecture, folk music, and language. The blend of African and European elements created a uniquely Barbadian experience. The official language is English, but the popular speech is Bajan, a form of expressive communication combining African grammar and an English lexical base to produce a language commonly used by all Barbadians living in Barbados. *Bajan* is also the term used locally for a person from Barbados.

Because of the lack of archaeological and historical records, the ancient indigenous music of Barbados has not been identified, and the music of immigrants from

The *tuk* band, with its bass drummer, snare drummer, flutist, and triangle, established a sound that, fused with African and British elements, became stamped as a Barbadian expression.

China and India, who came as workers after the abolition of slavery, has not been studied. Music in Barbados is perceived as a syncretization of African and British cultures, juxtaposed with the infusion of other nonindigenous influences (perhaps native American). Classical music performed by local or overseas artists is the accepted form of artistic musical expression for most Barbadians in the capital city, Bridgetown, where orchestral, chamber music, piano, violin, and vocal concerts are performed. The music of the Christian church is influential in urban areas, whereas villagers' expressions are ongoing. Recent interest in national identity and historical bases of study since the 1970s, and interest from radio and television stations in building archives with local performances and data on customs, have encouraged scholars to pursue historical studies of the island and its cultural expressions and influences.

MUSICAL INSTRUMENTS

African slaves were prohibited by laws and circumstances from practicing their traditional customs, including dances, songs, and life-styles of West Africa. Though no record of early African Barbadians and their music survives, there is reference to a group who were roused to battle by lively African music performed on animal horn and conch trumpets and skin drums in a struggle against slavery between 1627 and 1638 (Watson 1979:8–9). In 1675, slave codes banned the playing of any loud instruments and the beating of drums by people of African descent, and by 1688 the use of musical instruments was outlawed among the slaves. This ban, however, did not prohibit the clandestine use of drums for funerals, dances, wakes, and other rituals by the African descendants. Music for them was essential for recreation and dancing and as a part of the life cycle for communication and religious meaning.

Though the British had little expertise in instrumental performance, they encouraged balls and formal parties in the plantation's "great house," using African musicians for entertainment. In 1688, workers emerged at a "crop over" festival, singing in call-and-response fashion to the accompaniment of banjo, bones, struck bottles containing different levels of water, and shak-shaks. The blending of African and British cultural practices created new expressions that were to put their stamp on Barbadian musical development, and today the musical instruments used in performing Barbadian music are varied because of African and British influences. Some instruments are imported from other Caribbean islands.

The most diverse musical instruments in Barbados are idiophones, which include struck instruments such as gongs made from hollow tree trunks, hit with sticks; bottles (with different levels of water inside them to produce differing pitches), tapped with sticks; bones (two bones held between the forefinger and middle finger and struck together); cymbals; triangle; and xylophone. Shaken idiophones include the shak-shak, named after the sound of the mahogany tree pod when shaken with its seeds inside, and *de shot and rattle,* made from a calabash filled with stones and fitted

FIGURE 1   A *tuk* band performs during a festival. *Left to right:* pennywhistle, side drum, triangle, bass drum (congas in background). Note the Landship uniforms as worn by a woman nurse, an older person, and a youth. Photo courtesy of Antonio "Boo" Rudder. Used with permission from the Chief Executive Officer, National Cultural Foundation, Barbados.

with a handle. It is called shak-shak when seeds from a mahogany tree pod are used instead of stones. A scraped idiophone is the rook jaw, which consists of two jagged sticks that are rubbed together.

Membranophones include rural drums called the pump (a hollow tree trunk with goatskin or sheepskin on either end) and the *tum-tum* (a long, hollow tree trunk with skins over each end), played by two men. These instruments are of African inspiration and are made locally.

Also made locally are a double-headed bass drum and a side (snare) drum, the central instruments of the musical ensemble known as the *tuk* band (figure 1). Players and villagers cure the sheepskins and goatskins, and though they used to make the drum bodies from biscuit barrels, today they use plywood. The materials must be light to insure portability. The drums are based on the pattern of the British regimental drums used for military parades on special occasions, such as coronation parades and visits of royalty (as occurred before national independence in 1966). The bass drum is strapped across the musician's shoulder and beaten by a stick stuffed with layers of cloth to form a sturdy beater; in *tuk* bands, it keeps strict time. The side drum is also double headed. Both drums at one time used ropes or other bands to secure their heads, but today the skins are held on with iron rods, bolts, nuts, and spanners (turnbuckles). The *tuk* band, with its bass drummer, snare drummer, flutist, and triangle, established a sound that, fused with African and British elements, became stamped as a Barbadian expression (see Okada 1995: example 1). Other locally used membranophones are the tambourine, the trap set (used for popular music, such as calypso), and the conga and the bongo, imported from the Hispanic Caribbean.

Chordophones include the banjo, the acoustic guitar (often called the box guitar), the electric guitar and bass (used in contemporary performances), the violin (sometimes called the bow-fiddle, often held against the left side of the chest when played in folk music), and the *shukster* (made with guitar string stretched from end to end on the side of a wooden house). The bow-fiddle was used in *tuk* bands but has largely been replaced by the pennywhistle.

Aerophones include instruments made from local materials, though many have been replaced by metal instruments. Once common were the conch trumpet, a bamboo flute with holes for fingering burned into its tube, and a pipe made from the

FIGURE 2   A *tuk* band pennywhistle player during performance at a festival. Photo courtesy of Antonio "Boo" Rudder. Used with permission from the Chief Executive Officer, National Cultural Foundation, Barbados.

vine of a pumpkin. Since the 1980s, a vertical metal fife such as a pennywhistle is used, especially in the *tuk* band (figures 1 and 2). Imported wind instruments include the harmonica, the accordion, alto and tenor saxophones, the trombone, and the trumpet. The last two band instruments are found in calypso and spouge groups, wind bands, and chamber ensembles (see below).

MUSICAL CONTEXTS AND GENRES

Anglican hymns and the practice of the British militia, which provided "security for the free population [while] their regular drills served to intimidate the enslaved group" (Watson 1979:8–9), led to parodies in songs, calypsos, tea meetings, *tuk* bands, and the Barbadian Landship (see below), landmarks for the ratification of Barbadian culture.

Religious forms

With British colonial settlement in Barbados, the Church of England was introduced. In 1641, the island was subdivided into parishes, with a church and a minister for each. This agreement gained acceptance by the locals, and the Bishop of London was named Chief of the Church. Meanwhile, local priests were influenced by the plantocracy, an elite that deemed Christianity unsuitable for slaves. Missionaries, therefore, were sent out by the Church of England to work with the slaves, using religion for building character. All religious routines of African origin were displaced, and slaves were soon converted to Christianity. In 1836, laws were passed to forbid parties on Sundays. The popular Jean and Johnnie dance (a fertility dance, usually performed in the open at plantation festivals and fairs) was forbidden. An energetic dance, it allowed women to show off to admiring men, who often had a chance to do the same. From the late nineteenth and early twentieth centuries, African ideals, religious beliefs, and practices were suppressed, and even missionaries from the Methodist and Moravian churches taught that on Sunday it was incorrect to dance to secular songs with rhythmic beats, saying that such acts suggested worship of the devil. Links, fusion, and tension between African and British cultural expressions are still currently manifested.

Anglican services offer opportunities for performing historical selections of

English and European classical music, evident and accepted in the cultural tradition as anthems, carols, hymns, cantatas, oratorios, and other religious musics, as well as chamber music. The basis of Barbadians' religious experience, however, is the hymn, the sole cultural link where God's work is praised with thanksgiving at the end of the week. For the laboring population, Monday to Saturday are working days; Sunday is reserved for prayer, and all family members dress immaculately, sing together, and praise God for life, seeking strength for the coming week.

Pentecostal music was introduced in the 1920s. Musical performance techniques that became a regular part of church services included tambourines, clapping, and loud, free, spontaneously emotional expression. The Spiritual Baptist religion, whose music and ritual is based on the African-derived Shango cult of Trinidad and Tobago, came from that country in the 1960s. Black American gospel music and work songs have provided new directions and expressive alternatives for Afro-Barbadians. Rastafarianism is currently an alternative to the religious experience for blacks seeking ideas about their ancestral heritage and an aid to redefining themselves in the new global village.

Secular forms

Music as entertainment has been the basis for participation in the artistic and cultural circles of Barbados. Entertainment by Afro-Barbadians was not accepted by the Anglican Church after 1837, and not until World War II was it revived with music for weddings, funerals, tea meetings, plantation fairs, Christmas practices, and Landship parades.

Tea meetings include prolonged solo and group concerts and refreshments; they are held in a school hall or the lodge of a friendly society. Though not popular after the Great War (1914–1918), the tea-meeting concept was revived and is presently popular. Tea meetings begin at 9:00 P.M., when the audience is addressed by the vice-chairman and chairman of the society. At midnight, there is a two-hour break for refreshment. Then songs and speeches resume until daybreak.

The British used music as an enrichment and a reminder of activities at home in the British Isles. Music also provided entertainment at balls, dances, and formal gatherings at the great house. Conversely, African descendants often played drums, sang, and danced. For them, artistic behavior was not separated from life, the universe, or social activity. Many newly created songs were associated with social pastimes and daily workloads. These are now embedded into a rich folk song repertoire, sung individually and during community sings. Dances were held on weekends, at crop over, during Landship festivities, and at major celebrations such as Christmas, Easter, Whitsuntide, and public holidays.

Folk songs

Barbadian folk songs are highly influenced in thought by English practice. Often songs were composed about coronations of the sovereign. Pieces were written about Queen Elizabeth I, King George V, Queen Victoria, and the emancipation of slaves. This tradition dates back to 1650. The stories of "Inckle the English Sailor" and "Yarico the Indian Maid" became topics for English plays. A 1981 collection of narrative, social, and children's songs, *Folk Songs of Barbados* (Marshall, McGeary, and Thompson 1981), belies notions that no indigenous or oral tradition exists in Barbados. The heart of Barbadian song, however, lies with the lower and laboring class of society, which holds onto its social and cultural pasts and traditions. Cultural and dramatic groups now carry on these traditions with performances in concert and tourism settings (figure 3). Archival recordings, however, are rare and exist only in private, inaccessible collections.

Crop over was originally a celebration held to mark the end of the sugarcane harvest. Plantation managers themselves would participate in a drinking competition and a greased-pole climb, singing, dancing, and eating. Slaves participated in song and dance, playing fiddles, guitars, drums, and triangles.

FIGURE 3   A folk group at a crop-over festival sings "Sugar Cane." Dress typifies cane cutters' attire. Photo courtesy of Antonio "Boo" Rudder. Used with permission from the Chief Executive Officer, National Cultural Foundation, Barbados.

Crop over

Crop over was originally a celebration held to mark the end of the sugarcane harvest. At the end of the harvest, which provided lucrative returns for the planters and hard work and daily subsistence for the slaves, a party was permitted in the plantation yard. Plantation managers themselves would participate in a drinking competition and a greased-pole climb, singing, dancing, and eating. Slaves participated in song and dance, playing fiddles, guitars, drums, and triangles. They even climbed the greased pole, ate such delicacies as pudding and souse, cassava pone, and homemade bread; they drank rum punch and enjoyed entertainment, mimicry, and abandon. These practices continue, with newspaper articles telling of choices of venues where dances are organized by a local who is popular and credible in the eyes of the village. Since the 1990s, crop-over singing has been performed during festivals by folk groups wearing sugarcane-cutter costumes (figure 3).

Landship

The Landship Movement, known as the Barbados Landship, was begun in 1837 in Britton's Hall in Seamen's Village by a certain Moses Ward or Moses Wood (oral tradition is not clear about his surname). Its organizational structure, which provided village entertainment from its inception, mirrored the activities, dances, and disciplines of the British navy; its movements and maneuvers depicted the difficulties of a naval ship's passage through rough seas. Landship parades were held, and audiences stood around to encourage meaningful participation by performers from the friendly society.

The Landship Society, advertised as "the only ship that does not sail," patterns its structure on that of the British navy. The Lord High Admiral, the Admiral, Captain, Boatswain, and Blues are representative of ranks and functions within the organization. The "ship" moors to the "dock," which may be a wooden house similar to a chattel house, and meetings of this society are held three times per week at night. All activity begins from the dock. Each unit has a captain, with names like those of seagoing ships—*Director, Vanguard, Iron Duke*—and names of British ships or places in the Commonwealth. Members are governed by the Council of the Barbados Landship Association and are representatives of a ship on the council. Dances during Landship parades and other maneuvers typify European-African fusion: the British military march, jig, hornpipe, and maypole dance of the village green combine with African cross-rhythms and improvisation.

Christmas

During the Christmas season, scrubbers—small bands of strolling musicians singing hymns and hoping for rewards from householders—were often seen in the 1960s going from house to house. This practice was discontinued and has been replaced by concerts at churches or concert halls, where people dress to go and hear caroling. Christmas practices today include community singing of traditional carols and popular North American standards such as "White Christmas" and "Silver Bells." In addition, church choirs sing anthems, oratorios, and works by the English composers William Byrd, Thomas Tallis, Sir Henry Walford Davies, and others. In the 1990s, attempts are being made to use calypso and reggae rhythms and local themes.

Popular music

Calypso

Before the 1930s, *banja,* as calypso was called, was practiced by laborers and confined to village-tenantry areas. Strolling minstrels, including Shilling Agard, Mighty Jerry, and Slammer, were the precursors of calypso; their songs included a combination of free speech, humor, theater, African emotional expression, and lyrics about the feelings of the people. Calypso had its roots in the work of minstrels like them who were not embraced by the community at large but persisted into the 1960s with the commitment to topical song accompanied by guitar or banjo.

In the 1950s, broadcasts on radio introduced Trinidadian and other American musics (samba, merengue, rumba, cha-cha), making calypsonians and their music seem inferior. Efforts by the Mighty Dragon and Lord Silvers to promote shows at the Globe Theatre in 1954 showcased pioneers such as Sir Don Marshall, Mike Wilkinson, Lord Radio and the Bimshire Boys, and Mighty Romeo, who set the style for the development of calypso in the 1960s. Mighty Gabby, Viper, and the Merrymen followed, as did the start of calypso competitions, beginning with five persons in 1960 and expanding to eighteen in 1963 and twenty-one in 1964. The Merrymen established themselves from 1975 to 1985, promoting a Caribbean beat and using folk music and traditional ballads to promote the country as a tourist destination. Their calypso style, known as blue beat, also fused American blues and country with local accents and themes, using harmonicas, guitars, and banjos to identify their particular sound.

The years 1974–1980 gave rise to stage-presented *kaiso* (calypso) and a new concept of crop-over revival in the form of a national festival. Calypsonians increased from twenty-five to two hundred, and with the formation of the National Cultural

Foundation in 1984, the government has had a hand in festival administration. Calypso attracted tourists, and a new kind of calypsonian developed—performers who received greater remuneration by entertaining receptive crowds of foreigners. Support from the Trinidad and Tobago government gave calypso special credence. In the 1990s, analysts, writers, composers, and guardians of calypso culture have surfaced, and many competitions are occurring, giving exposure to new forms of individual vocal and instrumental statements. With governmental support, calypso is received as a meaningful expression of black artistry, and many bajan calypsonians, including the Mighty Gabby and Red Plastic Bag, have become recording artists.

Spouge

British culture (including Welsh, Scottish, and Irish), transmitted through literature and poetry (Shakespeare and Milton), rhymes, folk songs, sea shanties, classical music, hymns, and other songs of praise, has been constantly available, providing entertainment, edification, and general education to all people of Barbados. North American love songs, parlor songs, African-American spirituals and folk hymns, and hillbilly music have also contributed to a cultural mixture in which the love of a song, the expression through movement, and demand for theater continue to be of paramount importance. All of these elements influenced the development of spouge, a Barbadian-styled sound created by the local entertainer Dalton "Manface" Bishop, alias Jackie Opel, who in the 1960s fused the ska beat of Jamaica with calypso rhythms of Trinidad. Spouge employed a special rhythm, played on the cowbell, bass guitar, trap set, and other rhythm and electronic instruments. Added to this were trumpets, a trombone, a saxophone, and vocalists. In the 1960s, there were different types of spouge: the Cassius Clay style (or "dragon spouge") and Draytons Two style (or "raw spouge").

The era from the early 1960s to 1979 saw a sizeable output of spouge recordings by locals, leading to an awareness of a local musical and cultural idiom and the provision for a framework allowing popular bands to grow. Groups such as Lord Radio and the Bimshire Boys, Jiggs Kirton, Antonio "Boo" Rudder, Blue Rhythm Combo, Shirley Stewart, Norman Barrow, Wendy Alleyne and the Dynamics, the Troubadours, and the Draytons Two are all part of the Jackie Opel school. Familiar tunes such as "G-O-Go" and "Play that Spouge Music" (Draytons Two), "Do You Like Sweet Music" (Blue Rhythm Combo), "Are You Sure?" (Troubadours), and "Dance with Me" (Bimshire Boys) all helped advance the work in the popular culture field. In 1989, Calypsonian Commander recorded "Bring Back the Spouge," a song that became a hit.

Other entertainments include performances of North American pop ballads, gospel, and folk songs fused with local practices. Since the early 1980s, the effect of digital technologies on live and studio performances has been important. Major consequences include the proliferation of live bands operating on fairly low budgets, and an unprecedented output from—and growth in numbers of—recording studios, many of which are run by musicians themselves (Michael Alleyne, personal communication). Though little is documented, the contribution of music to the entertainment field in Barbados is significant.

SOCIAL STRUCTURE AND CHANGE

Bajan performers are mainly men, though women participate in calypso music as background vocalists, in folk music, and in classical music (figure 4). No study of the role of women in the development of slave music has been done, but in contemporary folk-musical performances, women are the subjects of derogatory comments in

FIGURE 4 A chamber group at the National Independence Festival of Creative Arts. Photo courtesy of Antonio "Boo" Rudder. Used with permission from the Chief Executive Officer, National Cultural Foundation, Barbados.

calypso texts. Generally, music is perceived as a participatory activity, and its performance encourages dancing and total involvement.

Few schools exist for training the general public, and learning by oral tradition is a common method of transmission. This situation has made the guardians of the cultural heritage within the community especially revered.

With the changing focus of world markets and global awareness, a fusion of local cultural expressions is evolving, yet musicians are profoundly aware of heritage development and identity consciousness. Barbados in its present state of cultural evolution is open to musical changes and the impact of other cultures but remains a strict guardian of its heritage.

REFERENCES

Marshall, Trevor, Peggy McGeary, and Grace Thompson. 1981. *Folk Songs of Barbados*. Bridgetown: Macmarson Associates.

Okada, Yuki. 1995. *The Caribbean*. JVC Smithsonian Folkways Video Anthology of Music and Dance of the Americas, 4. Montpelier, Vt.: Multicultural Media VTMV-228. Video.

Watson, Karl S. 1975. "The Civilised Island, Barbados: A Social History 1750–1816." Ph.D. dissertation, University of Florida.

Cuba
Olavo Alén Rodríguez

Historical Background
Afro-Cuban Music
The Emergence of Cuban Music
Musical Genres
Vocal and Instrumental Ensembles
Musical Education
Administrative Structures and Institutions of Music

About 11 million people inhabit the Republic of Cuba, a nation of more than sixteen hundred keys and islands located in the northwestern Antilles. The main island, Cuba, with a surface area of 105,007 square kilometers, is the largest of the Antilles. Most of the national population is descended from Spaniards (mostly from Andalucía and the Canary Islands) and Africans (mostly Bantu and Yoruba). Small populations derive from Caribbeans of other islands, French, and Chinese. Spanish is the official language, but some Cubans still speak several African-derived languages. Local religions include several derived from African religions, but the largest in membership is Roman Catholicism.

HISTORICAL BACKGROUND

Aboriginal culture

Before Europeans arrived, aboriginal groups occupied the archipelago. Economically and socially, the most developed were an Arawak people, known to later scholars as Taino. According to accounts by early European chroniclers and travelers, the most important cultural activity of the Taino was the feast known as *areito* (also *areyto*), the main social event for the practice of music and dance. We know only a few specifics about Taino music, including the fact that Taino music used jingles, maracas, and the *guamo*, a snail shell opened at its pointed end. But the evidence does not include notated music. Apparently, none of the artistic elements of Taino culture became a part of what centuries later was to be known as Cuban music, though some cultural traits (such as foods and domestic architecture) survived in latter-day Cuban culture.

Beginning at the period of conquest (1492) and during the colonization of the island by Spain, Cuba's autochthonous population died out as a result of exogenous diseases (for which the aborigines had no natural antibodies), the forced labor to which they were subjected (in the quest for nonexistent gold and silver), and mass suicide in response to this labor. About a hundred thousand Amerindians were living in Cuba at the time of its discovery by Spain. Information from fifty to seventy-five years later places the aboriginal population of the island at no more than two thousand.

Early European immigration

The convenience of Cuba's geographical position made it a mandatory way station for Spanish ships traveling to Mexico and South America. Cuba provided facilities for repairing ships and supplies of food and water. The demand for provisions fostered the local development of agriculture, which, since Indian workers were rapidly declining in numbers, necessitated new sources of labor: slaves, brought from Africa. By about 1550, these slaves had replaced indigenous laborers to become the decisive factor in the colony's economic development.

During the colonial era, Spanish settlers and visitors brought music from Spain. The military bands that came over with Spanish troops played an important role in musical life, as did musicians who came to settle. They brought their musical instruments, including the *laúd*, the *bandurria,* and the guitar. A revival of Spanish poetry in meter, such as the *cuarteta* and the *décima*, took place, and even the whole *romancero español* played an important role in the texts of songs.

AFRO-CUBAN MUSIC

The most important African ethnic groups that participated in the amalgamation of the Cuban population were the Yoruba, different groups of Bantu linguistic stock, and some groups from the former area of Calabar (Dahomey). There is little documentation of early African music in Cuba. The music of African people and their descendants in Cuba was played on instruments fashioned after African prototypes. African music found fertile soil for development, particularly as part of the slaves' reorganization of their religions and beliefs. Because all African religions have their own music, the religions brought by African groups to Cuba enriched the art of the entire region. Even now, we often find musical instruments, characteristic ways of playing them, songs, rhythms, dances, and even the use of music for magical functions—all practiced in a way resembling their New World beginnings, much as they must have been when Africans brought them to Cuba, hundreds of years ago.

Yoruba heritage and Santería religion

In Cuba, slaves of Yoruba origin were generally known as Lucumí. Yoruba music has remained, as a rule, more authentically preserved in western Cuba than in eastern Cuba, because most Yoruba slaves (including Egbado, Ijesha, Ketu, Nago, Oyo, and other Yoruba-speakers) were landed on the western coast, mainly in Matanzas, Havana Province, and the city of Havana. The survival of Yoruba music and dance can be partially attributed to the fact that the Yoruba arrived late in the slave trade, between 1820 and 1840 (Marks 1994).

Many African traditions were preserved in Cuba because the Spanish masters allowed slaves to use their traditions of drumming and dance to worship as they had in Africa. The Spanish also allowed the slaves to organize mutual-aid societies so they could better handle their new way of life. These societies often had a king, a queen, and a complex social hierarchy with different levels, conferring prestige on the members of the group who held offices. This relative leniency, combined with compulsory baptism into Roman Catholicism, resulted in the syncretism of West African deities with Christian saints. In this sense, the Yoruba-Cubans went so far as to name their religion Santería, in a frank allusion to the Christian saints. Other Cuban names for this religion are Regla de Ochá (Doctrine of the deity Ochá) and Lucumí (González-Wippler 1973:1).

Many Yoruba and their descendants congregated around temple-homes (*ile-ocha*), headed by a religious godfather (*tata-nganga*) or godmother. These buildings usually had a room (*igbodu*) that held the magical objects devoted to *orishas* 'gods'. It is in these rooms that believers still perform the rhythmic patterns that invoke

FIGURE 1   A famous *babalawo* adjusts the *chaworo* bells on his sacred *batá* drum. Photo courtesy of the Archives of CIDMUC (Center for the Research and Development of Cuban Music), Havana.

orishas. These patterns follow a preestablished order (*oru,* or *oru de Igbadú*). Female priests are known as *iyalochas*; male priests, as *babalochas.* The highest rank, *babalawo,* it is reserved for men, as it was in Africa (figure 1).

Musical instruments

The most important musical instruments used in Santería rituals are two-headed *batá* drums (figure 1), always played in sets of three. These drums have retained the original hourglass shape of their African prototypes, but a clearer differentiation has been established in the diameter of the skins. The drum with the lowest pitch is the *iyá,* the middle drum is the *itótele,* and the smallest one is the *okonkolo* (Cornelius 1990:134). The performer sits and holds a drum horizontally on his lap so he can strike either drumhead at will. The tension of the skin is fixed with tensors, usually made of rawhide. Sometimes bronze jingle bells (*chaworó*) are fastened around the heads of the *iyá.*

Also rebuilt by the Yoruba in Cuba were the *iyesa,* a set of four cylindrical, different-sized double-headed drums. The tension of the skins is maintained with tensors that stretch from one skin to the other. Other Yoruba drums in Cuba are the *bembé,* made in differing sizes from hollowed tree trunks. The skins are nailed on and tightened by heat from a fire. *Bembé* are not used for religious purposes (Ortiz 1954).

Another group of instruments used by the Yoruba in Cuba is a set of shaken idiophones, the *abwe* or *shekere.* These instruments are made from three large gourds covered with bead-studded nets. Each net fits loosely. When the instrument is shaken, the beads (made from seeds) strike the exterior of the gourd. This set of gourds is usually accompanied by a steel hoe blade (*hierro*), struck with an iron bar. In polyrhythmic music, the blade sets and maintains the beat (see Okada 1995: example 2).

Bantu heritage and Congo secret societies

Slaves from the geographical areas of Africa where the Bantu-speaking nations lived contributed heavily to Cuban musical culture. The zone from which most Bantu-speaking slaves were taken is the Congo Basin and both sides of the Congo River. In Cuba, these slaves were generically known as Congos. It would be hard today to identify traits that would distinguish the ethnic groups of this linguistic complex, but the Loango, the Bavili, the Bacongo, the Mayombe, and the Ndongo have provided the greatest contribution to Cuban culture. The Congos also organized mutual-aid societies (*cabildos*) like those of the Yoruba. Like the Yoruba, they congregated around godfathers' temple-homes, creating nuclei of godchildren.

Musical instruments

The Congos brought not only their religion but also the feasts, dances, and music with which they were familiar. They reconstructed many instruments in Cuba. Among these were several wooden idiophonic percussion instruments, of which the *guagua* (or *catá*) is the only survivor. It is a hollowed trunk, struck with two sticks. Membranophonic drums introduced in Cuba by the Congo constituted the *ngoma* ensemble (Ortiz 1954). *Ngoma* drums, made of wooden staves, are single headed and barrel shaped. The drums are usually played alone, but sometimes they are accompanied by the *kinfuiti,* another drum introduced in Cuba by the Congo. The Congo also introduced *makuta* beats and dances, employed in a celebration that is no longer observed. The last record of that festivity is in the early twentieth century, around Sagua la Grande. The Congo instruments that had the greatest cultural impact were *yuka,* drums made from hollowed fruit-tree trunks, with a skin nailed to one end and usually played in a set of three (figure 2). The largest drum is the *caja,* the middle drum is the *mula,* and the smallest is the *cachimbo.* These names seem to have come from the *ngoma* ensemble.

FIGURE 2   An Afro-Cuban ensemble plays *yuka* drums. *Left to right: mula, caja,* and *cachimbo.* Photo courtesy of the Archives of CIDMUC, Havana.

In social and economic spheres and the forms of artistic expression, a distinctively Cuban nationality is thought to have emerged between 1790 and 1868, when there appeared musical genres that, despite having their roots in Spain and Africa, displayed elements of Cuban origin.

Carabalí heritage and Abakuá secret society

The Calabar area of the western coast of Africa, between the Niger and Cross rivers along the Nigeria-Cameroon border, is the place of origin of slaves known as Carabalí. Their *cabildos* were known as Carabalí cabildos, and their mutual-aid societies came to be known in Cuba as Abakuá secret societies or Abakuá powers. These organizations were strong among harbor workers, especially in Havana, Matanzas, and Cárdenas, and they greatly influenced the development of Cuban music. The first of these societies, the Potencia Efik-Buton, consolidated an Apapa Carabalí cabildo founded in the township of Regla in 1836. The members of these societies were called *ñáñigos* in Cuba.

For feasts and ceremonies, the Abakuá followers use two sets of instruments. One set consists of four drums that make a series of isolated sounds having symbolic importance. The other set, the *biankomeko* ensemble, is made up of four drums, each with single heads of goatskin, played only with hands (Courlander 1942:233): *bonkó-enchemiyá, biankomé, obi-apá,* and *kuchí-yeremá.* These drums are accompanied by a cowbell (*ekón*), sticks (*itones*), and two rattles (*erikúndi*).

Ewe and Fon heritages and Arará secret society

From the ancient kingdom of Dahomey (the present-day Republic of Benin) came slaves who founded the Arará *cabildos* in Cuba. They were representatives of several peoples, the most important of which were the Ewe and the Fon. Many Africans enslaved in Dahomey were taken by the French, so French colonies—mainly Haiti and Louisiana—received a large number of Ewe and Fon slaves. The slave rebellion headed by Toussaint L'Ouverture forced many people to flee, and from 1789 to 1804, large numbers of French planters and their faithful slaves emigrated to Cuba. A resulting musical form of this time was the *tumba francesa* 'French drum', referring to Haitian music and dance (Alén Rodrígues 1986). Today, this survives only in performances by national dance troupes (see Okada 1995: example 4).

The most direct transposition from Africa to Cuba, however, was achieved by the Arará, who transferred their festive and religious activities just as they had been performed in Africa. The Arará *cabildos* preserved an ensemble made up of four drums. Their names vary greatly from community to community, but the most frequent names are *hunguedde, huncito, hun,* and *hunga* (see also Courlander 1942:236).

Other West African heritages

The Mina, Manding, and Gange *cabildos* had a much smaller impact on the development of Afro-Cuban music. The Mina *cabildos* took in Ashantis, Fantis, Guaguis, Musinas, and others taken from the former Gold Coast, now the Republic of Ghana. The Manding *cabildos* took in slaves that had come from present-day Sierra Leone and parts of Guinea, representing the Alogasapi, the Bambara, the Lomba, the Sesere, and the Soso. The Gange are of Manding stock, and the Azziero, the Bay, the Gola, the Longoba, the Mani, and the Quisi are among them.

THE EMERGENCE OF CUBAN MUSIC

In social and economic spheres and the forms of artistic expression, a distinctively Cuban nationality is thought to have emerged between 1790 and 1868, when there appeared musical genres that, despite having their roots in Spain and Africa, displayed elements of Cuban origin. There occurred a great surge of music played by Spanish musicians with academic training, who evidenced solid technical foundations in composition and in performance. Musical ensembles were organized around the churches, particularly in Havana and Santiago de Cuba. This period also witnessed the immigration of people of French descent from Haiti, and later from Louisiana.

Another important influence during this period was the introduction of opera and zarzuela companies that came from Italy and Spain. In urban areas, genres such as the Cuban *contradanza* and later the habanera were born. Traditional Cuban song took shape, as did the *orquestas típicas* that played dances. In rural areas, the musical genres that were later to be known as the *punto campesino* (in central and western Cuba) and the *son* (in eastern Cuba) also emerged. In the chapels of Santiago de Cuba and Havana, musicians such as Esteban Salas y Castro (1725–1803) and Juan París (1759–1845) modernized the compositional techniques of Cuban ecclesiastical music.

The period 1868–1898 was marked by rebellions against Spanish rule. The Spanish government abolished slavery gradually in 1880 and definitively in 1886, freeing about a quarter of a million landless blacks, many of whom migrated to urban outskirts and margins. Before 1871, an estimated 150,000 Chinese laborers were brought over, mainly from Canton; though they eventually organized their own Chinatown in Havana and spread throughout the country, their tendency to stick together in closed groups limited their contribution to the common musical culture.

Important Cuban folkloric genres appeared on the urban peripheries during this period. Notable among these were the *rumba* and the *comparsas* (see below).

A vast migration from rural to urban areas, especially to Havana, contributed to the integration of many local traditions that had developed in different areas of the country. The effects of this migration were complemented by the movement of troops resulting from the wars for independence. Concert music changed considerably, particularly piano music in the city of Havana. Outstanding musicians appeared, such as Manuel Saumell (1817–1870), whose *contradanzas* for piano gave rise to Cuba's own concert music.

In 1898, in the last of the three wars for independence, U.S. intervention on behalf of the rebels helped free Cuba from Spanish rule. But U.S. military occupation (1 January 1899 to 20 May 1902) brought North American capital investments in Cuba, and with them came the influence of North American lifeways on Cuban cultural expression.

The republican period, 1902–1959

Under the republic, a national consciousness based on Cuba's position as a politically independent nation began to arise. People became increasingly aware of the need to develop a Cuban musical culture, and simultaneously the music of Cuba began to have influence outside Cuba. The early contacts of Cuban musical genres—particularly the *son*—with American jazz left marked effects on the Cuban genres and jazz, and on the popular music of the United States. In turn, the *rumba* and the *son,* and later the *cha-cha-chá* and the mambo, had impact on Europe during this period.

Cuban musical instruments such as the *tumbadora* and bongos began to be used in diverse instrumental ensembles in cultures outside Cuba.

Concert music, particularly symphonic music, also developed. With the emergence of a strong nationalistic awareness came musicians such as Alejandro García Caturla (1906–1940) and Amadeo Roldán (1900–1939), who used the most up-to-date compositional techniques of the times to create works of a marked national character. The most important contribution to this musical nationalism was through folkloric music.

Professional popular music, with deep roots among the population and intimate links to dance, left its mark too. Professional popular music differed from folk music by the use of technical elements in composition and interpretation that were taken from the music of Europe. This music became easily commercializable because of its ready adaptation to radio and television, the media of mass communication. These media, in turn, affected the development of the Cuban folkloric ensembles of the times. Dance music was by far the most popular, with roots deep in tradition.

Cuban music was nourished by waves of immigrants from the Caribbean, mainly from Haiti and Jamaica. These immigrants were brought to remedy the shortage of manpower in the sugar industry and in the growth of the railroads. The increased importance of radio, the introduction of television (in 1950), the appearance of several small record companies, and the construction of important musical theaters—all fostered a boom in Cuban music, mostly limited to Havana.

By about 1950, the nationalistic movement in musical composition was replaced by a neoclassical trend that centered on the Grupo de Renovación, headed by a composer of Catalonian origin, José Ardévol (1911–1981).

After 1959

The revolution of 1959 began the transition to a socialist society. The government instituted a free educational system whose curriculum included the arts. The National Council of Culture was founded under the Ministry of Education, and in 1976, the council was elevated to the rank of Ministry of Culture. The National Council of Culture aimed to rescue Cuba's folklore. It allocated significant resources to the development of professional music and the Amateur Movement, which eventually produced many professional musicians.

Musicological research was organized, and a cultural policy was designed to find and preserve, in every municipality, the country's musical culture. A national system of music schools was organized, and elementary music schools were opened in practically every important city. A system of enterprises was organized to include all the country's soloists and musical ensembles. These enterprises saw to the contracting and programming of musicians, who were guaranteed steady employment and stable salaries.

The Musical Publications and Recording Studios (EGREM), Cuba's musical publications and recording enterprise, was organized and given the responsibility of producing recordings and publishing scores of Cuban music. One of the spinoffs of EGREM was the National Music Publishing House (Editora Nacional de Música).

A factory was established to mass-produce autochthonous musical instruments that until then had been produced only by individual craftsmen. Consequently, there was an increased availability of bongos, rattles (*chéqueres*), drums of the Abakuá secret society, and other African-Cuban musical instruments. Instruments such as bongos, *tumbadoras,* guitar, and *tres,* which had been produced on a limited scale, were turned out in greater numbers.

The Ministry of Culture fostered the development of institutions that were already doing musicological research. One was the Seminario de Música Popular (Popular Music Seminar). Other, more comprehensive, institutions—the National Museum of Cuban Music and the Center for the Research and Development of Cuban Music (CIDMUC) were also founded.

From its inception, the National Council of Culture and later the Ministry of Culture organized festivals dedicated to music. They included the National Son Festival, the Rumba Festival, the Electro-Acoustic Music Festival in Varadero, the Chamber Music Festival in Camagüey, the National Choral Festival in Santiago de Cuba, and others. Based on the Amateur Movement, a system of *casas de cultura* ('houses of culture') was developed in all the country's municipalities. These institutions not only foster the organization of musical groups of all kinds but also teach music and follow up on amateurs' musical education.

During this period, contemporary music took shape. It accommodated a broad range of aesthetic perspectives, including conventional neoromantic techniques for orchestral work and bold experiments in electroacoustic music. The tendencies that most contributed to the contemporary music of the period were aleatorism and neoserialism.

Professional popular music saw a marked development of the *son,* particularly in connection with *nueva trova,* a nationalistic movement, founded in 1962. The *son,* particularly its urban variants, became practically synonymous with Cuban popular dance music and had a far-reaching impact on the music later known as salsa. The influence of the *son* on the creation of salsa has been so far reaching that many specialists have mistaken one for the other.

Folkloric music became stronger in urban areas. People of central and western Cuba continued singing songs of the *punto guajiro* complex (see below), and the variants of the *son* (including the one called *changüí*) retained their predominance in the rural areas of the eastern provinces. The rumba remains a broadly practiced genre, particularly in Havana and in Matanzas Province. Cuban musicians still compose boleros, *cha-cha-chás, contradanzas, danzones,* and *guarachas,* but none of these is as popular as the *son.*

MUSICAL GENRES

The history of Cuba's musical culture reflects a complex pattern of migrations and cultural confluences, leading to the emergence of widely differing musical traditions in remote areas of the country. These factors contributed to the development of a variegated national musical culture with local musical types. Communication among these areas and among the strata of the population has helped some local traditions gain national popularity and become typical expressions of a Cuban national identity.

The genres of Cuban traditional music divide into five complexes (*son,* rumba, *canción, danzón,* and *punto guajiro*), each comprising related musical genres based on common musical aptitudes and behaviors. These complexes are determined by style, instrumentation, and the makeup of traditional ensembles.

The *son* complex

The combination of plucked strings and African-derived percussion instruments gave birth to a musical genre called *son,* first popular among peasants of eastern Cuba. During the twentieth century, the *son* complex, because of its influence on dance music and its projection into practically all social and functional spheres of musical activity in the country, has been the most important musical genre in Cuba. Its earliest manifestations, perhaps dating as far back as about 1750, were among the first Cuban musical genres or styles about which information survives.

danzón Cuban instrumental dance created by Miguel Failde in 1879

contradanza Cuban genre with French origins that belongs to the *danzón* family

bolero Cuban-derived song genre for listening and dancing, attributed to José "Pepe" Sánchez

son Cuban song tradition forming a complex of genres

FIGURE 3   A *son* ensemble in the mountain area of Oriente. *Left to right: tres, tumbadoras, laúd, contrabajo, tres,* and *tres.* Photo courtesy of the Archives of CIDMUC, Havana.

FIGURE 4   A man plays bongos. Photo courtesy of the Archives of CIDMUC, Havana.

The *son* took shape in rural easternmost Cuba. Its oldest genres include the *son montuno* (from the Sierra Maestra range) and the *changüí* (from the area of Guantánamo). The formal structure of the oldest *sones* is the constant alternation of a soloist with a refrain, typically sung by a small group. When the *son* emerged from rural areas, it acquired another important structural element: the inclusion of an initial closed structure in binary form, followed by a *montuno,* a section in which a soloist alternates with a small choir.

The instrumental ensembles (figure 3) that played *sones* always combined plucked string instruments—guitar, *laúd* (a type of guitar), *tres,* and later the string bass—with percussive instruments such as bongos, *tumbadoras* (congas), claves, maracas, and the *güiro.* The vocal soloist is often the one who plays the claves, and the singers of the refrain are the other instrumentalists in the ensemble.

Within the context of the *son,* musicians exploited two important instruments for Cuban music—the *tres* (a variant of the guitar) and bongos (figure 4). The *tres* is a Cuban plucked stringed instrument that differs from the guitar mainly because of the way the strings are tuned. Three pairs of strings (each with a pitch and its octave) are plucked to build melodies as counterpoints to the main melodies of the singer.

The rumba complex

Another important generic complex in Cuba is the rumba, whose name probably derives from African-Caribbean words (such as *tumba, macumba,* and *tambo*) referring to a collective secular festivity. Originally, in marginal suburbs of Havana and Matanzas, the word meant simply a feast. In time, it took the meaning of a Cuban musical genre and acquired a specific instrumental format for its performance (see Okada 1995: example 3). It even gave rise to its own instruments: *tumbadoras* (often called congas), which have spread throughout the world.

In the beginning, the instruments that played rumbas were different-size wooden boxes. Eventually, they evolved into three barrel-shaped drums, first called *hembra* 'female', *macho* 'male', and *quinto* 'fifth', and later called *salidor* 'starter', *tres-dos* 'three-two', and *quinto*. In African musical cultures, female drums, also called mother drums, are tuned in the lowest registers. Male drums are in the mid-registers, and *quintos* are tuned in the upper registers. The *salidor* is the first drum that plays. *Tres-dos* indicates that the drum will normally be beaten in a combination of three and two beats. These drums were generically called *tumbadoras*. With their appearance, the instrumental format of the rumba was fixed. This ensemble is often complemented by a small *catá,* a hollowed tree trunk, struck with two sticks.

All genres of the rumba have the same structure. The lead singer starts with a section that *rumberos* (rumba players) call the *diana.* The singer then goes into a section of text that introduces the theme, and only after this does the rumba proper begin, with more active instrumental playing and a section alternating between the soloist and the small choir.

Of the genres that make up the rumba complex, the *guaguancó,* the *columbia,* and the *yambú* are the most popular in Cuba. The *guaguancó* has most deeply penetrated into other functional spheres of Cuban music, and is most generally identified with the concept of the rumba. The performance of *guaguancó* may include couple dancing, and the music and the dance have elements that reflect Bantu traits. The ensembles (primarily drums and idiophones) are called *comparsas.*

The *canción* complex

A third generic complex is the *canción* 'song', embodied in Afro-Cuban forms and styles of singing. References to songs written by Cuban composers appear as early as about 1800. These songs, written in the Italian style of the day, had no features that could identify them as Cuban, but they gave rise to Cuban lyrical songs. The earliest appearance of Cuban elements took place in the texts. By about 1850, many songs of this type (such as "*La Bayamesa*" by Carlos M. de Céspedes) were in circulation.

The development of lyrical songs in Cuba led to a new genre, the habanera, which became an important generic prototype after Eduardo Sánchez de Fuentes composed his habanera "*Tu.*" A well-known habanera occurs in Georges Bizet's *Carmen,* premiered in Paris in 1875.

Songs for two voices in parallel thirds and sixths and using the guitar as the instrument of preference have been in frequent use since the 1800s. They laid the foundation for the emergence of another genre of the Cuban song, the *canción trovadoresca,* a genre that takes its name from the name its most important interpreters gave themselves: *trovadores* 'troubadours'. Personalities such as José "Pepe" Sánchez, Sindo Garay, Manuel Corona, and Alberto Villalón decisively shaped the musical genre that has come to be known as the traditional *trova.*

The distinguishing feature of this genre in Cuba is the way the song became closely associated with the singer, who moved around accompanying himself on the guitar, singing about things he knew or whatever struck his fancy. The word *trovador* was probably an attempt by these artists to establish a relation between what they did and the functions they attributed to the troubadours of medieval Europe. This genre developed greatly in Cuba after the 1960s, giving rise to a new movement, *nueva trova,* that developed its own administrative structure and gained throughout the country hundreds of members. Today, the movement has become weak and has given way to boleros and other forms of romantic songs within salsa music.

Before the 1850s, this tradition was intended primarily for listening, not dancing. The situation changed with the rise of the important musical genre known as bolero, born in Cuba from antecedents in the Spanish bolero. Rhythms taken from those played by the Cuban percussive instruments of African origin were added to the traditional forms of the Spanish dance and melody. The creators of the new genre were a group of *trovadores* from Santiago de Cuba who performed the *canción trovadoresca*. They gave the bolero stylistic elements and rhythms from the *son*, then popular only in rural eastern Cuba. José "Pepe" Sánchez is considered the composer of the first Cuban bolero, a genre cultivated by many songwriters and musicians abroad. In some Caribbean countries, it is one of the most important genres of popular music (see PUERTO RICO).

During the 1800s, societies whose only objective was to make music came into being. This is the case with *clave* choirs (*coros de clave*), which originated in Matanzas and Havana. These organizations had repertoires of songs called *claves*, composed by its members. They lost favor and disappeared early in the 1900s, but they contributed to the Cuban musical heritage a genre that preserves the original name.

Another musical genre of the *canción* complex is the *criolla*. It resulted from the continued development of the *clave*. The composer of the first *criolla* was Luis Casas Romero, who wrote his "Carmela" in 1908. *Criollas* are songs written in urban forms and style, with texts referring to rural themes. The tempo is slower than in the *clave*, and the meter is 6/8. The form is binary, and the harmonies are often modal.

With the *clave* appeared another genre, the *guajira*. It is written in 6/8 meter alternating with 3/4, and often includes musical affectations evocative of the rural peoples' plucked stringed instruments. The texts of the *guajira* centered on the beauty of the countryside and pastoral life.

Cuban songs in general, but particularly the bolero and the *canción trovadoresca*, have joined with other Cuban musical genres, such as the *son*, to produce mixed genres that have influenced Cuban dance music.

The *danzón* complex

A large migration of French people and Haitians with French customs arrived in Cuba at the end of the 1700s, when the character of the Cuban nation was taking shape. This migration gave rise to the fourth generic complex, the *danzón,* which had its origins in the early Cuban *contradanzas,* and projects forward in time to the *cha-cha-chá.*

The interpretation in Cuba of French *contredanses*—especially with the violin-piano-flute format—led to the development of a *contradanza* that may be considered Cuban, especially with the later introduction of percussive instruments taken from Afro-Cuban music. The earliest *contradanzas* were played by two different musical ensembles: the *charanga* (a Cuban popular music orchestra consisting of two flutes, piano, *pailas*, claves, *güiro*, two *tumbadoras*, four violins, and eventually a cello) and the *orquesta típica* 'folkloric orchestra'. The development of these orchestras, and the evolution and change experienced by the French and local *contredanses* in Cuba, gave rise to musical genres such as the *danza*, the *danzón*, the *danzonete*, the mambo, and the *cha-cha-chá*.

The *contradanza* acquired its distinctive profile during the 1800s and became the first genre of Cuban music to gain popularity abroad. It had four well-defined routines: *paseo* 'walk', *cadena* 'chain' (taking of hands to make a chain), *sostenido* 'holding of partners', and *cedazo* 'passing through' (as some couples make arches with their arms while others pass under them). Its structure is binary, and each section usually has eight measures. In the mid-1800s, the composer and pianist Manuel Saumell transformed it into a vehicle for concert music; thus, it became the first autochthonous genre included in the concert-hall repertoire.

Danzas cubanas were the result of the evolution of the older *contradanzas*. Played by ensembles known as French *charangas* (*charangas francesas*), they evidenced greater contrast between the first and second parts of the overall binary structure. These pieces gave rise to the most important member of the complex, the *danzón,* of which Miguel Failde composed and premiered the first example, "*Las Alturas de Simpson,*" in Matanzas in 1879.

Like the contradanza, the *danzón* was a square dance, but its figurations were more complex. The transformations brought about in it, particularly through the addition of new parts, gave it the structure of a five-part rondo. This might have been the origin of its name, since the addition of parts enlarged the piece, making it a "big *danza*" (the *-ón* suffix in Spanish is augmentative). The *danzón* is an instrumental genre usually written in 2/4 meter. Once considered the national dance of Cuba, it enjoyed enormous popularity during the late 1800s and early 1900s.

In 1929, another musician from Matanzas, Aniceto Díaz, combined elements from the *son* and the *danzón,* added a vocal part, and created a new style of *danzón* called the *danzonete.* His first composition in this style, "*Rompiendo la rutina* 'Breaking the Routine',*"* established the *danzonete* as a new musical genre. During the 1950s, further transformations of vocal *danzones* and the *danzonetes,* with the addition of new instruments to typical *charangas,* paved the way for Damaso Pérez Prado and Enrique Jorrín to create two new musical genres: the mambo and the *cha-cha-chá.*

The *punto guajiro* complex

The *punto guajiro* and the entire complex of rural musical genres it embraces make up the fifth generic complex of Cuban music. This complex has developed largely within the framework of rural music in central and western Cuba, where country *tonadas, puntos fijos, puntos libres, seguidillas,* and other forms remain common. *Tonadas* are tunes or melodies sung to recite *décimas.* The *punto* can be *fijo* 'fixed' or *libre* 'free': if the accompaniment of the *laúd* and guitar is always present, then the *punto* is *fijo*; if the accompaniment stops to let the singer sing his melody and *décima* alone, the *punto* is *libre.* In the *seguidilla,* the singer uses versification that gives the impression of a never-ending strophe. The *zapateo* or Cuban *zapateo* is the dance used for the *punto. Guateques campesinos* was the name given to the typical parties of the farmers where the *puntos* were sung.

Dances for these genres and the Cuban *zapateo* developed during the 1800s. The *zapateo* is no longer danced. It has been replaced by dance forms borrowed from the *son* and other country dances of the eastern end of the island. The transformation and modernization of the genres of this complex have been slower than in the other complexes of Cuban music, perhaps because it is limited to the rural population. Professional musicians have adopted some of these genres, though usually when combining them with elements of other generic complexes, as in the *son* and the *canción.*

VOCAL AND INSTRUMENTAL ENSEMBLES

The accompanimental requirements of certain musical genres fostered the creation of distinct types of musical ensemble. Plucked stringed instruments, with the guitar and the *tres* as the most central ones, produced the typical sound of most Cuban music. Also important were rhythmic patterns borrowed from the music of the Spanish *bandurria* and played by Cuban rural people on the *laúd.* The *bandurria* and the *laúd* are plucked stringed instruments brought by the Spanish settlers.

Plucked stringed instruments, with the guitar and the *tres* as the most central ones, produced the typical sound of most Cuban music. To the sound of the plucked strings was added that of African-derived percussion instruments.

To the sound of the plucked strings was added that of African-derived percussion instruments. Ensembles took in bongos, *claves*, the *güiro* (and the *guayo*, its metallic counterpart), maracas, and the jawbone rattle (*quijada*), the *botija* (jug), and the *marímbula*. The *marímbula* is made from a large wooden box. Two metal bars are fixed to the side of the box so that metal strips can be inserted and held fast to serve as tongues (*languettes*), which the performer plucks with his fingers. The tuning of the tongues is done by loosening the bars and adjusting the length of the tongues. The performer usually sits on the box with his legs on either side of the *languettes* [see DOMINICAN REPUBLIC]. The acoustic principle of the *marímbula* has antecedents in the idiophone known as *mbira*, which belongs to many Bantu peoples of Africa.

The most important percussive membranophones that developed included the *tumbadoras* (also called congas), *timbales* (big hemispheric drums played with two sticks covered with cloth or leather), and *pailas* (cylindrical metal drums played with two wooden sticks). Many variants of the cowbell (*cencerro*) also developed. In performance, these instruments were often combined with instruments brought from Europe and assimilated into Cuban music in their original organological forms, as happened with the piano, the flute, the violin, the guitar, and other instruments.

This blend of instruments created the instrumental formats that give Cuban music a distinctive character. The most important among them are the *dúo*, the *trío*, the *cuarteto*, the *septeto*, the *conjunto*, the *charanga típica*, the *orquesta típica*, the *piquete típico*, the *órgano oriental*, the *estudiantina*, the *coro de clave*, the *guaguancó* group, the *comparsa*, and the *gran combo* or *gran orquesta*.

The *dúo* consists of two guitars or a guitar and a *tres*. The artists sing two parts or melodic lines, called *primo* and *segundo*. This combination often serves for boleros, *canciones trovadorescas*, *claves*, *criollas*, and *guajiras*. In the eastern provinces, the *dúo* serves frequently for performances of *sones montunos*.

The *trío* retains the two vocal melodic lines. The third performer often sings the *primo* while playing *claves* or maracas. The repertoire of the *trío* resembles that of the *dúo* because both are closely related to the *canción trovadoresca*. When this type of ensemble reached the cities, it took the *son* into its repertoire. Today, *tríos* appear throughout the nation. One of their most outstanding representatives was the Trío Matamoros, famous during the 1940s.

The *cuarteto* format includes two guitars (or guitar and *tres*), *claves*, and maracas. Sometimes, rather than *claves* or maracas, the fourth instrument is a muted trumpet. These groups retain the two melodic lines (*primo* and *segundo*), and base their repertoire on mixed genres such as the *guaracha-son*, the *bolero-son*, and the *guajira-son*. This ensemble was popular during the 1930s.

The instruments of the *septeto de son* are guitar, *tres*, trumpet (usually with mute), maracas, *claves* (played by the vocalist), bongos, and *marímbula* or *botija*. In its most recent version, a string bass replaces the *marímbula*. The *septeto* resulted from adding a muted trumpet to the *sexteto de son*. This combination crystallized in the

1920s, when the *son* was gaining popularity in the cities. One of the most important *septetos* in the history of Cuban music is Ignacio Piñeiro's Septeto Nacional, a paramount example of a traditional Cuban musical ensemble.

The *conjunto,* another type of ensemble, consists of piano, *tres,* guitar, three or four trumpets, bongo, bass, and singers. The singers often play maracas and *claves,* or jawbone and *güiro.* The repertoire of the *conjunto* includes boleros, *guarachas,* and *cha-cha-chás,* and it sometimes plays mixed genres such as *guajira-son* and *bolero-son.* The Cuban *conjunto* enjoyed its greatest popularity in the 1950s, especially after the introduction of television in Cuba. Among the most outstanding representatives are the *conjuntos* of Chappotín, Pacho Alonso, Roberto Faz, and Conjunto Casino.

The *charanga típica* includes a five-key transverse flute, a piano, a string bass, *pailas,* two violins, and a *güiro.* It emerged during the first decade of the twentieth century; after 1940, it doubled the number of violins, and added a *tumbadora* and (later, sometimes) a cello. Some *charangas* have replaced the *pailas* with a complete set of drums and have included electric instruments such as electric bass, electric piano, and synthesizer. The term *orquesta* 'orchestra' has been commonly used since about the 1960s. Foremost in the repertoires of these orchestras was the *danzón,* but now the *son* is the most frequently played genre. During its popularity, these ensembles had no vocalists, but with the creation of the *cha-cha-chá* in the 1950s, they began to feature singers or a small choir. Arcaño y sus Maravillas and the Orquesta Gris are among the most important representatives of the instrumental phase of the *charanga,* and Orquesta Aragón and Enrique Jorrín's orchestra are probably the most important of the phase that included vocalists. One of the most successful *charangas* with electric instruments is Los Van Van.

The *orquesta típica,* a historical ensemble no longer popular, consisted of two clarinets, two violins, a string bass, a cornet or a trumpet, a valve or slide trombone, an ophicleide (*bombardino*), *pailas,* and a *güiro.* The oldest European-derived instrumental ensemble in Cuba, it has fallen into disuse. Its repertoire included *contradanzas,* habaneras, rigadoons (*rigodones*), lancers, *danzas,* and *danzones.* In 1879, Miguel Failde, a musician from Matanzas, composed and played the first *danzón* with one of these orchestras, which he directed.

During the 1800s, wandering musicians organized *piquetes típicos* to play in amusement parks and circuses throughout the country. These ensembles were made up of a cornet or a trumpet, a trombone, a clarinet, an ophicleide, two *pailas,* and a *güiro* (or *guayo*). Their usual repertoire included *danzas, pasodobles, danzones, rumbitas,* and other genres that proved difficult to adapt to other types of ensembles. These groups may have been born of the *orquesta típica* when economic adjustments reduced the number of employed musicians.

The *órgano oriental* is the type of large crank organ imported from Europe to the areas of Manzanillo and Holguín in eastern Cuba beginning around the mid-1800s. Later manufactured in those locations, it served for public dances. The organs were accompanied by *pailas,* a *guayo,* and, at a later stage, *tumbadoras.* Their repertoire included the *danza,* the *danzón,* the polka, and the *son.* The building of such organs became a family tradition in the east of the country. The Borgollas were the most important builders in Manzanillo, and the Ajo de Buenaventura family was the most outstanding in Holguín.

In the late 1700s and early 1800s, the *estudiantina* was made up of two singers who sang *primo* 'first' and *segundo* 'second' while playing maracas and *claves,* plus others performing on a trumpet, two *treses,* a guitar, *pailas,* and a string bass. Some *estudiantinas* also included a *marímbula.* Their repertoire was based mainly on the *son,* but they also played *danzones.* Their tradition centered in Santiago de Cuba.

The *coro de clave* was a choral ensemble with a repertoire based on a musical genre known as *clave*. Each ensemble had a hierarchy in which some members played a featured role. Some were the *clarina,* a powerful-voiced woman who stood out from the choir; the *decimista,* who composed the texts for the songs; the *tonista,* who kept the group in tune and signaled the choir to begin the singing; the *censor,* responsible for the quality of the song texts and the beauty of the melodies; and the director, the most experienced member. These choirs were accompanied by *claves* and a small drum, later replaced by a stringless banjo struck on the resonator box. Some groups included a *botija* and a small diatonic harp. The *coros de clave* disappeared early in the twentieth century.

The *guaguancó* group has a soloist and a small choir, three *tumbadoras, claves,* and occasionally a small *catá.* Its repertoire includes the genres that make up the rumba: *guaguancó, columbia,* and *yambú.* One of the most important groups is Los Muñequitos, in Matanzas (see Okada 1995: example 3).

The instrumentation of *comparsas* has never been stable. They usually require instruments that can be carried and played at the same time. The most frequently used are *tumbadoras,* congas, bass drums, *galletas* 'cookies' (big drums in the shape of a cookie, played with a stick covered with cloth or leather), *bocus* (long, conical drums hung from the player's neck and shoulder and beaten with bare hands), cowbells, plowshares, steel rings, and other improvising instruments. In later phases, *comparsas* have included a trumpet as a solo instrument.

Comparsas accompany dancers who parade through the streets during carnivals. They had their origins in the celebration of Epiphany, 6 January, during the colonial period. (The slaves were treated like children in many ways, and 6 January was Children's Day in the Spanish colonies.) Carrying lanterns and flags, slaves would take to the streets in the typical attire of their homelands. They would dance and parade to the governor's palace, where they would revel in African-derived dramatic presentations, songs, and dances.

Finally, the *gran combo* or *gran orquesta* is another important type of ensemble, influenced by jazz bands in the United States. Particularly after the 1950s, jazz bands began to be organized in Cuba, with repertoires that included *guarachas,* boleros, and *sones montunos.* The instrumentation of these bands consisted of trumpets; trombones; alto, tenor, and baritone saxophones; piano; bass drums; and Cuban percussion. They occasionally included a flute and a clarinet. It was with these bands that the mambo, an important musical genre, was born. One of the most important jazz bands was the Benny Moré Band, which became popular in the 1950s.

MUSICAL EDUCATION

Music was taught in Cuba by settlers who arrived in the 1500s. Historical documents say a musician named Ortiz, living in the town of Trinidad in the 1500s, opened a school to teach dancing and the playing of musical instruments. Manuel Velásquez, the first organist of the cathedral of Santiago de Cuba, taught singing to children who participated in the religious services. Havana's first professor of music was Gonzalo de Silva, who taught singing and organ around 1605.

During the 1700s, the teaching of music was centered in the chapels of the Cathedral of Santiago de Cuba and in the Parroquia Mayor of Havana. Near the end of the 1700s, Esteban Salas y Castro, an important Cuban composer of ecclesiastical music, founded and headed a music chapel at the Cathedral of Havana. *Capilla de música* 'music chapel' was the name given to groups of musicians who performed for Roman Catholic services. They composed church-oriented pieces, including *cantatas, villancicos,* and *pastorelas,* and taught music within the church. Salas y Castro's patience and dedication turned his chapel into Cuba's first real school of music. The wave of French immigrants from Haiti and the Dominican Republic late in the 1700s also had a salutary influence on musical pedagogy.

In a steady flow throughout the 1800s, Spanish musicians came to Havana to play and teach. One of the earliest was José M. Trespuentes, who from the 1830s taught violin, harmony, counterpoint, and composition. The second half of the century saw considerable growth in piano instruction. Piano virtuosos sojourned in Havana and taught talented pupils. Visiting from North America, Louis Moreau Gottschalk (1829–1869) organized spectacular concerts in Havana and Santiago de Cuba and gave piano lessons to Nicolás Ruiz Espadero and others, but eventually left Cuba. Espadero, a great maestro himself, taught the distinguished virtuosos Cecilia Aristi, Gaspar Villate, and Ignacio Cervantes. The last taught the ensuing generation of pianists, represented by his daughter, María Cervantes, and Eduardo Sánchez de Fuentes. In 1885, the Dutch master Hubert de Blanck settled in Cuba and founded the conservatory that bears his name. He designed its curriculum to include the most advanced techniques of the times.

Early in the 1900s, private conservatories were founded in Havana and other important cities. Changes taking place in the teaching of music in the United States spurred changes in Cuba. Eminent musicians such as Amadeo Roldán taught at these conservatories, where many musicians of the period were trained, particularly those who played in the country's chamber-music ensembles and symphony orchestras.

Military bands played an important role in the teaching of music from the late 1800s. Apprentices trained in them later replaced their teachers or joined the bands. This system was particularly important in the larger cities of central Cuba. Remedios, Sancti Spiritus, Cienfuegos, and Caibarién became important musician-training centers.

Under the direction of Guillermo Tomás, the Municipal Conservatory of Music was founded in coordination with the Municipal Band of Havana. This institution has trained several generations of important musicians. It is named after Amadeo Roldán, its director in the middle of the century, who guided the introduction of important changes in the programs and curricula.

Until 1959, the Municipal Conservatory of Havana was the only government-sponsored center for the teaching of music. Since then, provincial schools have been opened in Pinar del Río, Matanzas, Santa Clara, and Camagüey provinces. Two other municipal conservatories were opened in the city of Havana: one in Marianao, named after Alejandro García Caturla, and another in Guanabacoa, named after Guillermo Tomás.

The need for instructors to satisfy the major demand created by the Amateur Movement led to the founding of the School of Arts Instructors in 1961. The National School of Art, with its School of Music, was founded in May 1962; it has trained the most important performers, composers, and musicologists of the late twentieth century. The Higher Institute of Art, founded in 1976, immediately opened its School of Music, Cuba's first university-level school of music. In 1978, to provide facilities for working musicians to take their degree, the National Center for Higher Professional Education was opened. In the 1990s, the progress made in Cuban musical education has led to important results in piano and guitar performance and in musicology.

ADMINISTRATIVE STRUCTURES AND MUSICAL INSTITUTIONS

Between 1959 and 1976, musical activity in Cuba was the responsibility of councils, departments, or divisions of the Ministry of Education. In 1976, the Ministry of Culture was organized and took responsibility for musical activity. In 1989, the Cuban Institute of Music was organized to administer all musical activity within the

The Center for the Research and Development of Cuban Music (CIDMUC) was founded on 26 December 1978 in Havana with the primary objective of fostering knowledge, research, and general information on Cuban music.

Ministry of Culture. All existing government institutions that had to do with music were subordinated to it.

The National Center for Concert Music concerns itself with concert musicians and chamber-music groups. It attends to the programming and promotion of these artists within the country and abroad. The Philharmonic Organization of Havana oversees programming and promotion for the symphony orchestra, other important chamber-music groups, and the country's most important conductors. The National Center for Popular Music, taking responsibility for soloists and ensembles that play popular Cuban music, programs and promotes these artists nationally and internationally.

The Center for the Research and Development of Cuban Music (CIDMUC) was founded on 26 December 1978 in Havana with the primary objective of fostering knowledge, research, and general information on Cuban music. It has two musicological-research departments and an information department. Its Basic Research Department oversees historical and ethnomusicological research, including organological studies and the transcription of Cuban music. Its department of development does research in the fields of the psychology and sociology of music. It also does statistical studies related to professional music activities in Cuba.

The National Museum of Cuban Music, founded in 1971, has a collection that includes valuable musical instruments, old scores of Cuban music, and other documents of historical value. It has hosted research in the field of restoration and has organized lectures, exhibits, concerts, and lecture-recitals based on the documents in its collection.

The Musical Publications and Recording Studios (EGREM) has the responsibility of producing records, cassettes, Cuban musical instruments, and musical scores. It has several recording studios, a record factory, a musical instrument factory, and the National Music Publishing House. In 1986, in cooperation with the last, it founded a quarterly musical magazine, *Clave.*

The Musical Institute for Folk Music Research, founded in 1949 in Havana under the direction of the eminent musicologist Odilio Urfé, was later renamed the Popular Music Seminar, but in 1989 it became the Odilio Urfé Center for Promotion and Information on Cuban Music. It has a huge store of information on the *danzón,* the *teatro bufo,* the *teatro lírico,* and Cuban vaudeville.

The Ignacio Cervantes Professional Music Upgrading Center, a teaching institution for professional musicians who want to complete their academic training, was founded in Havana in 1964. It has branches in every province.

FURTHER STUDY

Major studies of Cuban music before 1960 include those by Alejo Carpentier (1979 [1946]), Emilio Grenet (1939), and Fernando Ortiz (1981 [1951]). Musical instruments have been documented by Harold Courlander (1942), Fernando Ortiz (1954), and others.

Cuban scholars have written many accounts about their own music, especially since the 1970s. One of the most important compendiums about Latin American music is *Ensayos de Música Latinoamericana,* edited by Clara Hernández (1982). It includes eight essays on Cuban music. Studies about socialization and music in Cuba are by Ageliers León (1984) and María Teresa Linares (1974). Odilio Urfé (1984) published a valuable chapter on Cuban music and dance in the book *Africa in Latin America.* Olavo Alén Rodríguez (1986, 1994) has written books on Afro-Cuban music, specifically on *tumba francesa* and *salsa,* respectively. The most widely distributed journal devoted to Cuban music is *Clave,* published in Havana. Its issues contain essays and news about Cuban folk and art music and musicians.

Since the 1980s, North Americans have written numerous studies of Cuban popular music, including salsa and its precursors in Cuba and development in New York City. Vernon W. Boggs (1992b) compiled a book entitled *Salsiology,* which includes chapters by Larry Crook (1992) and Vernon W. Boggs (1992a) about particular aspects of Cuban music. Important studies about Cuban music in the United States are by Steve Cornelius and John Amira (1992), Peter Manuel (1990), James Robbins (1990), and Roberta Singer (1983).

REFERENCES

Alén Rodríguez, Olavo. 1986. *La música de las sociedades de tumba francesa en Cuba.* Havana: Casa de La Américas.

———. 1994. *De los afrocubano a la salsa,* 2nd ed. Havana: Artex S. A. Editions.

Boggs, Vernon W. 1992a. "Founding Fathers and Changes in Cuban Music Called Salsa." In *Salsiology,* ed. Vernon W. Boggs, 97–105. New York: Excelsior Music Publishing Company.

———, ed. 1992b. *Salsiology.* New York: Excelsior Music Publishing Company.

Carpentier, Alejo. 1979 [1946]. *La música en Cuba.* Havana: Editorial Letras Cubanas.

Clave: Revista Cubana de Música. Havana: Dirección de Música, Ministerio de Cultura.

Cornelius, Steven. 1990. "Encapsulating Power: Meaning and Taxonomy of the Musical Instruments of Santería in New York City." In *Selected Reports in Ethnomusicology* 8:125–141.

Cornelius, Steve, and John Amira. 1992. *The Music of Santería: Traditional Rhythms of the Batá Drums.* Crown Point, Ind.: White Cliffs Media.

Courlander, Harold. 1942. "Musical Instruments of Cuba." *Musical Quarterly* 28(2):227–240.

Crook, Larry. 1992. "The Form and Formation of the Rumba in Cuba." In *Salsiology,* ed. Vernon W. Boggs, 31–42. New York: Excelsior Music Publishing Company.

Gonzáez-Wippler, Migene. 1973. *Santería: African Magic in Latin America.* Bronx, N.Y.: Original Products.

Grenet, Emilio. 1939. *Popular Cuban Music.* Havana: Ministerio de Educación, Dirección de Cultura.

Hernández, Clara, ed. 1982. *Ensayos de Música Latinoamericana.* Havana: Casa de las Américas.

León, Ageliers. 1984. *Del canto y el tiempo.* 2nd ed. Havana: Editorial Letras Cubanas.

Linares, María Teresa. 1974. *La música y el pueblo.* Havana: Editorial Pueblo y Educación.

Manuel, Peter. 1990. *Essays on Cuban Music: Cuban and North American Perspectives.* Lanham, Md.: University Press of America.

Marks, Morton. 1994. *Afro-Cuba: A Musical Anthology.* Rounder CD 1088. Compact disc and notes.

Okada, Yuki. *The Caribbean.* JVC Smithsonian Folkways Video Anthology of Music and Dance of the Americas, 4. Montpelier, Vt.: Multicultural Media VTMV-228. Video.

Ortiz, Fernando. 1954. *Los instrumentos de la música afrocubana.* Havana: Cárdenas and Compañía.

———. 1981 [1951]. *Los Bailes y el Teatro de los Negros en el Folklore de Cuba.* Havana: Editorial Letras Cubanas.

Robbins, James. 1990. "The Cuban *Son* as Form, Genre, and Symbol." *Latin American Music Review* 11(2):182–200.

Singer, Roberta L. 1983. "Tradition and Innovation in Contemporary Latin Popular Music in New York City." *Latin American Music Review* 4(2):183–202.

Urfé, Odilio. 1984 [1977]. "Music and Dance in Cuba." In *Africa in Latin America: Essays on History, Culture, and Socialization,* ed. Manuel Moreno Fraginals, 170–188. Translated by Leonor Blum. New York: Holms and Meier.

Dominica
Jocelyne Guilbault

Traits Common to Local Traditions
New Developments

Until the mid-1980s, the ruggedness of Dominica's terrain and coastline made transportation difficult throughout the island. As a result, five distinctive musical cultures—northern, southern, eastern, western, central—evolved almost independently. Though each region has unique cultural traits, they all share one heritage, that of the peoples who settled Dominica: French, West Africans, and English.

A sixth region is the northeast coast (including the villages of Wesley and Marigot), whose inhabitants are direct descendants of settlers who arrived from Antigua and Montserrat during the 1800s. Uninfluenced by the French colonial régime, these people speak English, not Dominica's vernacular, French Creole (Kwéyòl). Although it is the most distinctive region, it has only marginally influenced Dominica's musical traditions.

Caribs, the aboriginal population of Dominica, survive in small numbers on a reserve on the eastern side of the island. They have influenced many local traditions, but have made little or no contribution to the music of the country (Caudeiron 1988:48).

Until the late 1950s, no efforts were made to document, preserve, or promote Dominican culture. As in most other Caribbean islands until then, Dominicans were stigmatized by the colonial régime and the authority of Roman Catholicism, which for more than two centuries had taught them to believe that African-derived traditions were "uncultured," "demonic," and "evil" (Phillip 1986:25). A crusade against these notions was taken up in the 1950s by Mable "Cissie" Caudeiron, who, by organizing productions based on local language, songs, and dances, brought African-derived arts to public recognition (Wason 1987:18).

In 1965, the year England granted to Dominica the political status of associated statehood, Edward Olivier Leblanc, then Chief Minister, inaugurated the National Day Celebrations (later called the National Independence Competitions), which released a new wave of cultural energy and brought governmental recognition to the arts. This day was dedicated to African- and European-derived traditions, both publicly acknowledged as having contributed to Dominica's cultural makeup. For the first time, musicians, dancers, and singers from different regions were introduced to the entire population in an islandwide cultural spectacular, organized as a showcase for local heritages.

In 1978, Dominica's government created a cultural division whose mandate was to plan educational and cultural programs for the public, and to document and promote local culture. This division has organized festivals and set up workshops and cultural exchanges dealing with educationally related cultural studies. Out of these efforts has developed a sense of pride in Dominican musical culture.

TRAITS COMMON TO LOCAL TRADITIONS

All local traditions are passed on orally and learned through observation. Characteristically, instrumentalists are male, but lead singers (*chantwèl*) are mainly female. In 1987, most performers of local traditions were fifty years old and over, or below thirty-five (Phillip 1987:10)—evidence of renewed interest in local arts.

Most local genres include dancing, singing, and playing musical instruments. Lyrics are usually in French Creole, except in the northeast, where they are exclusively in English. All regions emphasize participation through responsorial singing, rhythmic clapping, and the frequent exchange of words between performers and audiences. Improvisation—in lyrics, dancing, and rhythmic accompaniment—is valued and encouraged.

A singer's talent is evaluated by her ability to respond on the spot to any incident and to stimulate the participation of audiences. Players' and dancers' virtuosity is established less by the quantity of new material they introduce than by the impact they achieve. They typically get maximal aesthetic effects by an unexpected breaking away from a steady melodic or rhythmic pattern or dance movement.

Percussion dominates musical ensembles, whether European- or African-influenced, and in both traditions, syncopated rhythmic patterns are prized.

Principal musical genres

Dominican musical genres include song-dances (*bélé*), the quadrille, work songs, storytelling songs, children's musical games, masquerade songs (*chanté mas*), and late-twentieth-century developments such as calypso, chorales, and *cadence-lypso*. Few local musical traditions, however, serve a single purpose.

Song-dances (bélé)

These were usually performed for amusement on full-moon evenings after work but were also performed at wakes (*lavèyé*). Though these traditions have nearly disappeared, *bélé* are still performed on major holidays, such as Christmas, Easter, Independence Day, Jounen Kwéyòl (International Creole Day), and annual parish festivals (held on the anniversary of patron saints). Associated with the lower classes, *bélé* play an important part in Fèt St.-Pierre (fisherman's feast) and the workers' holiday, Fèt St.-Isidore.

Traditionally performed outdoors, these song-dances—including the *bélé soté*, the *bélé djouba*, the *bélé priòrité*, the *bélé rickety*, the *bélé pitjé*, and the *bélé contredanse*—are said to have their roots in rites of mating and fertility (Honychurch 1988:63). All *bélé* are accompanied by a drum of the same name (*tanbou bélé*, a small, single-headed drum barrel about 75 centimeters tall and 30 in diameter, covered at one end by a goatskin stretched by fiber cord and tightened with wooden pegs, and played barehanded by one or occasionally two players), a triangle (*tingting*), and maracas (*chakchak*). The generic term for "drum" in Dominica is *lapo kabwit* 'goatskin'.

The song leader starts, followed by the chorus (*lavwa*). After a few lines, the drummer enters with a steady rhythmic pattern, and the dance begins. The male

dancer (*kavalyé*) demonstrates his physical prowess and skill before being replaced by the female dancer (*danm*), who expresses her approval and in turn tempts him. He tries to seduce her once again, and in the finale, the most intense and heated section of the piece, both dance together. In all *bélé,* the dancers control the drummer's playing, indicating throughout the performance by brakes (stops) and other motions when to stop or speed up.

The quadrille

This is a dance formerly performed by four couples from the same social network—family and friends in private homes, at subscription dances, or at daylong subscription picnics. These practices have been abandoned, replaced by public performances on patron saints' anniversaries and national holidays.

The quadrille usually has four compulsory figures: *pastouwèl, lapoul, lété, and latrinitez.* The last of these, simply called quadrille, comes from Petite Savanne (Phillip 1986), but other regions have variants—sharp, slow, *caristo* (also *aristo*), French, Irish, and Polish. These names differ from community to community, though the versions of the dance may be almost identical. Lancers is another quadrille performed in Dominica, but because its traits are distinctive, it is never confused with the others (Wason 1987:47).

After dancing in a square without joining hands, dancers perform a variable number of closed-couple dances: the merengue (*mereng*), the Viennese waltz (*vals o vyenn*), the *mazouk* (a local form of the mazurka, in many versions), the schottische (*sotis*), the beguine (*bidjin*), and pure polka (*polka pil*).

Musical accompaniment is provided by four instruments (figure 1): an accordion, a tambourine (*tanbou, tambal*), a *gwaj* or *syak* (a combined scraper and rattle, figure 2), and a *boumboum* (a long, hollow wooden tube, serving as a percussion instrument, figure 3)—and by the continuous stamping of the musicians' feet on the floor, sometimes called a jing ping band (see Okada 1995: example 10). Before the late 1940s, when accordions were introduced into the island, a bamboo flute led the ensemble (Cardinal 1989:28). Also used in serenades, the bamboo flute was then in favor. After having been abandoned for a few years, the playing of flutes was revived as part of the National Independence Competitions.

This musical ensemble also accompanies the circle dances called flirtations

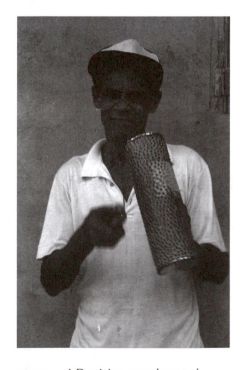

FIGURE 2   A Dominican man plays a *syak.* Photo by Gregory Rabess.

FIGURE 3   A Dominican man plays a *boum-boum*. Photo by Gregory Rabess.

(Wason 1987:60). Whereas *bélé* is traditionally danced in casual attire, a quadrille requires the dancers to dress up in their best clothes—and in formal presentations, to wear the national dress developed by the former slaves shortly after emancipation.

Work songs and other genres

Usually accompanied by the drum *tambou twavay*, work songs were sung by workers to make their task easier, whether maintaining roads, gathering fruit, sawing wood, moving a house, or drawing a fishing boat or fishing net onto the shore. These songs, most of which have disappeared with the use of new technology, were usually short and repetitious, the words and rhythm directly bearing on the work at hand. The *tambou twavay* is a short barrel covered at one end by a goatskin stretched by a circular frame and tightened with cords; a cord with a bead in the middle is attached across the skin to add a buzzing quality to the instrument, which is played with bare hands.

The following is a typical example of a formerly popular wood-sawing song. The leader sings the first line, and the chorus responds with the second (Marie 1977:11).

Papisson ka siyé bwa-la.	Papisson cuts the wood.
Siyé, siyé bwa-la.	Cut, cut the wood.

Storytelling (*kont*) was performed for entertainment on religious feasts and moonlit nights, and during funeral wakes. Today, storytellers are most often heard during National Independence competitions. *Kont* deal with historical facts or local legends and usually conclude with a moralistic message. Most include a short, fixed theme song of no more than one line that recurs throughout the tale, usually in the form of a duet between characters (Caudeiron 1988:52).

Children's musical games, once sung mostly in French Creole, were influenced by French settlers' games. After more than a century of British rule, songs accompanying children's ring games are of English and Scotch-Irish origin, with texts almost entirely in English (see Okada 1995: examples 8 and 9). Nevertheless, they differ from their models in having circle dancing, clapping, and thigh-slapping movements (Stubbs 1972:6).

Masquerade songs (*chanté mas*) consisted of responsorial songs enjoyed by carnival revelers before the calypso era. During two days of masquerading in the streets, each lead singer danced backward in front of her drummer, playing a *tanbou lélé*. The songs sung at masquerades, since they exposed personal shortcomings and commented on events that had taken place during the past year, were loved and feared. Important personages, afraid of scandals, attended rehearsals to pay money to ensure the lead singer's silence. The *tanbou lélé* is a small wooden cylinder drum covered at one end with a goatskin and held by a strap passed around the shoulder; it is played with two sticks.

NEW DEVELOPMENTS

In the early 1960s, calypso was integrated into the Dominican carnival, taking its place alongside masquerade songs. With a fire at carnival in 1963 and the subsequent banning of traditional carnival, calypso and steelband overtook the older genres (Rabess 1989:7). Whereas calypso's rhythmic patterns and instrumentation stood in sharp contrast to the former carnival music, its lyrics continued the social-commentary tradition of masquerade songs. Its success was immediate. The local production of calypsos quickly became, and continues to be, the most important source of musical creativity in the island.

During the same period, chorales—such as Siflé Montan'y, Dominica Folk

Cadence-lypso is a fusion of Trinidadian calypso and Haitian *cadence-rampa*. Its popularity went beyond the confines of the eastern Caribbean—to include Nicaragua, France, French and Portuguese West African countries, and the Cape Verde islands.

Singers, and Lajenn Etwal—came into being. These groups, performing traditional songs and new compositions, began to make recordings in Barbadian studios. In 1972, Ken Robinson set up Dominica's first recording studio, Nature Island Studio.

The following year, Dominica saw the emergence of a new musical form, *cadence-lypso,* created by the group Exile One and developed by other local bands and musicians. *Cadence-lypso* is a fusion of Trinidadian calypso and Haitian *cadence-rampa* (a genre also popular in Guadeloupe). In the 1970s, *cadence-lypso,* sung mainly in French Creole, dominated the annual fêtes, local dances, parish festivals, village feasts, and local airwaves. Its popularity went beyond the confines of the eastern Caribbean—to include Nicaragua, France, French and Portuguese West African countries, and the Cape Verde islands, where a group developed a carbon copy of Exile One and its music.

Though the early 1980s saw a decline of Dominican bands and a loss of popularity for *cadence-lypso,* the genre left its mark on the Dominican people: it gave Dominica a musical identity, as did reggae in Jamaica and calypso in Trinidad (Rabess 1989:9).

Like other small Caribbean islands, contemporary Dominica is striving to counterbalance with local creations the invasion of foreign cultural products via satellite. The governmental radio station, Dominica Broadcasting Station (DBS), has assumed the mandate to encourage local talent by including in its weekly broadcasting a minimum of 20 to 25 percent of local music (out of 60 percent Caribbean music), versus 40 percent North American music.

Educational activities and festivals organized throughout the year— carnival season, the Blue Notes Jazz Festival (launched in 1989), Dominica Art Festival, Traditional Arts Festival, National Independence Competitions, Jounen Kwéyòl— have played important roles in promoting Dominica's national identity and demonstrating its cultural dynamism.

REFERENCES

Cardinal, José. 1989. "La Flûte de Bambou dans Quatre Îles des Antilles (Martinique, Guadeloupe, Dominique et Sainte-Lucie)." Master's thesis, Université de Montréal.

Caudeiron, Mabel "Cissie." 1988. "Music and Songs of Dominica." In *Our Island Culture,* ed. Lennox Honychurch, 48–54. Barbados: Letchworth Press.

Honychurch, Lennox, ed. 1988. *Our Island Culture.* Barbados: Letchworth Press.

Marie, Ophelia Olivacce. 1977. "Dominican Folk Songs." Thesis for a diploma in advanced youth

work, Commonwealth Youth Programme, Caribbean Centre.

Okada, Yuki. 1995. *The Caribbean.* JVC Smithsonian Folkways Video Anthology of Music and Dance of the Americas, 4. Montpelier, Vt.: Multicultural Media VTMV-228. Video.

Phillip, Daryl. 1986. "Twenty Years of Traditional / Folk Dance in Dominica." Thesis for a certificate in dance education, Jamaica School of Dance.

———. 1987. "The Quadrille of Petite Savane."

Thesis for a diploma in dance education, Jamaica School of Dance.

Rabess, Gregory. 1989. "Kwéyòl and Popular Dominican Music." *Kwéyòl Journal* 7–10.

Stubbs, Norris. 1972. *A Survey of the Folk Music of Dominica.* Roseau: Dominica Arts Council.

Wason, Janet. 1987. "Recherches et Études sur les Danses Folkloriques de la Dominique." Report 221/8601–12. Paris: Agence de Coopération Culturelle et Technique.

The Dominican Republic
Martha Ellen Davis

The Dominican Republic shares the island of Hispaniola with Haiti, but the two countries are culturally and musically quite different. When Spain discovered the high cultures and treasures of Mexico (1519) and Peru (1532), it left Hispaniola to languish as a colonial backwater. This policy allowed France to gain a foothold in the island, leading to the 1697 treaty that ceded to France the western third of Hispaniola, called Saint-Domingue as a translation of Santo Domingo, the name of the Spanish colony, which became the Dominican Republic on achieving independence (1844). France commenced to develop Saint-Domingue as the jewel in its colonial crown. By about 1530, with the island's exploitable gold exhausted and the indigenous population drastically reduced, the basis of the accrual of wealth shifted to agriculture, primarily sugarcane cultivation, carried out by African slaves. The millions of Africans brought by the French into Saint-Domingue and their ethnic origins led to the development of a society more densely populated than and culturally different from neighboring Santo Domingo.

THE HISTORICAL BASIS OF NATIONAL CULTURAL POLICY

The racial and cultural contrast between these neighbors lies at the core of Dominican national cultural policy. In 1804, St. Domingue, through slave revolution, became the second free country in the Americas (the first being the United States), taking on the Taino name of *Haïti* and defining itself as a black republic. The Haitian occupation of Santo Domingo (1822–1844) is used by the twentieth-century Dominican elite as justification for the official affirmation of *hispanidad* (Hispanic racial and cultural purity) and the repulsion of all that is black, African, or Haitian. This policy, promoted by dictator Rafael Leonidas Trujillo Molina (1930–1961), has continued under successive governments.

Despite this policy, most members of the intellectual elite would find Spanish and African-derived extremes of Dominican nonliterate music to sound so foreign as to seem "un-Dominican." This is because of the marked gulf in Latin America between rural and urban and between literate and nonliterate cultures. All modern countries, including the Dominican Republic, are culturally heterogeneous with

Like much Taino music, the first music that Europeans brought to Hispaniola was vocal.

regard to region, locale (rural or urban), and social class. "Dominican culture" thus represents different realities to different social sectors.

Since the 1970s, nonelite urban youths have opposed *hispanidad* through their ethnographic search for and artistic expression of an Afro-Dominican identity, at home and in New York (Davis 1994b). At the same time, erudite scholarship, filling a niche in the post-Trujillo era, has documented Afro-Dominican history. Eventually, Dominican scholars, musicians, and the public will probably arrive at a realistic view of Dominican culture as essentially a creole composite, born in the New World of the fusion and evolution of multiple cultural components.

THE TAINO PAST

As elsewhere in the Americas and the world, three principal sources help piece together Dominican musical history: archaeology, the written record, and ethnography (using the living tradition as a key to an unwritten past). The Taino were a sub-group of the Arawak, one of the four huge language families of tropical South America. Seafaring Arawak from the Amazon and the Orinoco populated the Antilles one by one, arriving at Hispaniola (which they called Quisqueya) more than four thousand years ago. When Europeans arrived, the Taino of Borinquen (Puerto Rico) and Quisqueya were being conquered by the bellicose Caribs, another of the four main tropical South American language families.

Taino musical culture is represented by little material evidence, since much of it was vocal. Las Casas (1958) describes the singing of large groups of Taino women when they gathered to grate manioc for toasted cassava cakes (*casabe*). They had neither skin-covered drums nor stringed instruments. Flutes made of clay, bone, and perhaps cane were described, yet few specimens survive. The most important instrument was a hollow log idiophone (*mayohuacán*), struck for the *areito* (also *areyto*), a ritual in which dancers played maracas and may have worn rattles tied to their ankles. The Taino used conch trumpets (*fotutos*) for signaling, as they are still used in some rural areas to announce meat for sale, danger, or death.

The *areito* was the main musical event of Quisqueya, Cuba, and Borinquen. Despite variations based on region and social occasion, it was a large-scale sung dance ritual that could last for hours or days, with a vocal or dance leader and a chorus or dance group of as many as three hundred men or women or both, accompanied by a struck log idiophone. It could be performed for various occasions: to make a petition (as for the fertility of a crop or protection from hurricanes), to render homage (as in Princess Anacaona's *areito* for the governor of Hispaniola, with her three hundred maidservants as dancers), to celebrate an important marriage or a victory in war, to solemnize a funerary memorial, or to foster recreation. The text of the *areito* conserved, reiterated, and commemorated the past and the ancestors and their deeds, sometimes mentioning how each had died. There were also lighthearted, seemingly silly texts. Some celebratory occasions included such prodigious consumption of alcohol that the revels ended in drunkenness.

The vocal chorus and dancers were positioned in a linear, circular, or arch formation, maintaining close contact with one another by holding hands or linking arms. The soloist and chorus moved forward and backward in rhythm with impeccable precision, the dancers playing maracas and perhaps wearing ankle-tied rattles. The leader (*tequina*), a man or a woman (and probably a shaman), sang responsorially with the chorus, who repeated the leader's every line, but at a lower or higher pitch, while the leader kept dancing in silence. A soloist could be replaced but no break would occur until the narrative song was finished; this could take three or four hours, or even from one day to the next. The tune and movements could alter when a new soloist took over, but the narrative had to continue; yet the tune for a new sung story could be the same as the former one.

THE SPANISH HERITAGE

Spain itself was not monolithic at the time of the conquest of the New World; its culture represented the fusion of Sephardic Jewish, Arab, and Celtic-Iberian elements. An impetus toward the New World was the Reconquest, with the final and definitive expulsion of Jews and Arabs from Spain in 1492, only about a month before Columbus began his first voyage. One destination of their flight was the New World. Evidence of Jewish and Arab influence in Hispaniola appears in architecture, dialect, and the oldest musical styles and genres. Other early Spanish immigrants were mainly peasants from Extremadura and Andalucía. In the late 1600s, an important wave of immigrants arrived from the Canary Islands.

Like much Taino music, the first music that Europeans brought to Hispaniola was vocal. On the first voyage, when land was at last sighted, Columbus wrote that his sailors fell to their knees and sang a musical setting of the *Salve Regina*, a Marian antiphon antedating the eleventh century:

Dios te salve, Reina y Madre de Misericordia;
Vida, dulzura y esperanza nuestra, Dios te salve.
A ti llamamos los desterrados hijos de Eva;
A ti suspiramos, gimiendo y llorando en este valle de lágrimas.
Ea, pues, Señora, abogada nuestra; vuelve a nosotros esos tus ojos misericordiosos;
Y después de este destierro, muéstranos a Jesús, Fruto Bendito de tu vientre.
¡Oh clemente! ¡Oh piadosa! ¡Oh dulce Virgen María!
Ruega por nosotros, Santa Madre de Dios,
Para que seamos dignos de alcanzar las promesas de Nuestro Señor Jesucristo. Amen.

Hail, Queen, mother of pity:
Life, sweetness, and our hope, hail.
To you we cry, Eve's exiled children.
To you we sigh, groaning and weeping in this vale of tears.
So ah! our Advocate, turn toward us your pitying eyes.
And after this exile, show us Jesus, blessed fruit of your womb.
O gentle, O devout, O sweet Virgin Mary.
Pray for us, holy Mother of God,
That we may be made worthy of Christ's promises. Amen.

The Dominican *Salve Regina* (Davis 1981b), the sung rosary and other pious prayers, music, iconography, and ritual procedures were introduced by the clergy and then

FIGURE 1   At San Juan de la Maguana, people perform the "*Salve de la Virgen.*" At a saint's festival in the southwest region, men and women may participate in antiphonal performance of the unaccompanied *salve.* The performers often try to outsing each other in the style of the Hispanic *desafío.* Photo by Martha Ellen Davis, 1978.

perpetuated by folk priests (*rezadores*) and other devotees in remote rural areas. The conservation of archaic liturgical practices in folk ritual demonstrates the importance of the oral tradition as a source of historical documentation.

The Dominican *salve* is the musical cornerstone of the saint's festival (*velación, noche de vela, velorio de santo*; *vela* is Spanish for 'candle'), the most frequent and ubiquitous event of Dominican folk Christianity (figure 1). Rural based and individually sponsored, the saint's festival is undertaken initially in payment of a vow for divine healing, but it usually recurs annually as an inherited obligation. Its celebration lasts all night. After each of three rosaries (*tercios*), three sacred "*Salves de la Virgen*" ('Hails of the Virgin') are sung at the altar. In the east, the liturgical *salves* are followed by others in a style representing an African-influenced evolution of the genre (figures 2 and 3); but in the southwest and north, the three sacred *salves* are followed by further *salves* of similar style, sung antiphonally to an infinite number of melodies, until the next of the three rosaries in the event.

FIGURE 2   At the chapel of an Afro-Dominican religious brotherhood, Santa María, San Cristóbal, men and women perform the "*Salve con versos*" with percussive accompaniment by polyrhythmic clapping. Photo by Martha Ellen Davis, 1982.

FIGURE 3 Performance of the "*salve de pan-dero*," an African-influenced extreme of the "*salve con versos*" in the central-south region, entails various small membranophones including the round *pandero* hand drum and the absence of liturgical text. Performed in San Cristóbal at a saint's festival for St. James (pictured on altar, seen under woman's chin on far left). Photo by Martha Ellen Davis, 1976.

Other Dominican traditional musical genres of Hispanic heritage are also vocal, unaccompanied, unmetered, melismatic, and antiphonal. Sung high in male and female registers with tense vocal production, they are often in the minor mode or with a neutral third but are unornamented. The genres include other types of ritual song of folk Christianity for saints' or death ceremonies—the (partially) sung rosary, altar and procession songs other than *salves* (generically called *versos*), songs for children's wakes (*baquiné*), such as the almost extinct *mediatuna* of Cibao, the northern region; *romances* or Spanish ballads (Garrido Boggs 1946); children's songs and games (Garrido Boggs 1980 [1955]); antiphonal, unmetered work songs (*plenas*, not to be confused with Puerto Rican *plenas*); and various improvisatory sung conversations or debates (*desafíos* 'challenges'), performed within the context of agricultural labor (such as the *chuin* of Baní) for social commentary, expression of devotion, or courtship in a festive context, even at the periphery of a wake (such as the *décima*), or as ritual (such as the *tonadas de toros* of the east).

The improvisatory sung conversation or debate (*desafío*), a Mediterranean phenomenon, is a mode of male expression, but in courtship, a woman may use it wittily to evade or metaphorically to accept a man's advances. On the whole, in the Dominican repertoire, improvisatory verbal dexterity in song and the poetic genre of the *décima* are not nearly so important as elsewhere in the Hispanic Caribbean, though their social function is the same. The Dominican *décima* is usually spoken, rather than sung, and when sung is never instrumentally accompanied.

Instrumental music of Spanish influence formerly accompanied largely creole social-dance genres with Spanish-derived stringed instruments: the now extinct treble guitar (*tiple*); the *cuatro* with four double courses of strings (not to be confused with Puerto Rican and Venezuelan *cuatros*); the *tres,* traditionally triangular or guitar-shaped, now only the latter, with six strings in three double courses, tuned E–G–C with the G strings of different thicknesses (Coopersmith 1976 [1949]) (figure 4); and the *guitarra,* the six-stringed Spanish guitar. All these were largely replaced about 1880 by the Höhner button accordion, introduced through trade with Germany, though the *tres*- and guitar-based merengue has been regaining popularity since the 1970s. Brass bands and dance bands (see below) represent another kind of European-derived ensemble; the former play marches, arrangements of art music, and creole dance music, bridging nonliterate and literate musical domains.

Before the 1540s, notable contact occurred between Tainos and Africans in their flight from bondage. In contemporary rural society, Afro-Dominican enclaves are important conservators of Taino material culture.

FIGURE 4   An ensemble of the traditional merengue of the north (Cibao), *merengue típico* or *perico ripiao*, with the *tres* (*left*) as the melodic instrument. The playing of the *tambora* (*right*) in vertical position is atypical for the ensemble (compare figure 6), and depends on the music played. The standing man pays a *güira* or metal scraper, and next to him a man plays a *marimba*. Photo by Dale A. Olsen, 1977.

THE AFRICAN HERITAGE

The native American population of Hispaniola—at least a million persons—was so rapidly reduced by warfare, disease, and suicide that its replacement by an African workforce began as early as 1502. The first Africans (*ladinos*) were Spanish-speaking Christians from Spain, present there in servitude for a century before 1492. They were soon joined in Hispaniola by *bozales*, direct imports from the African continent, starting with Wolof (*golofes*) from the Senegambian region. Later shipments embarked from increasingly southerly points on the West African coast until they were coming from the Congo-Angolan region. In 1822, the Haitian occupation ended the local slave trade. Before the 1540s, notable contact occurred between Tainos and Africans in their flight from bondage. In contemporary rural society, Afro-Dominican enclaves are important conservators of Taino material culture.

The black population of the Dominican Republic was enriched in the nineteenth and twentieth centuries by three immigrations: in 1824–1825, when the whole island was the Republic of Haiti, six thousand Afro-North-American freemen arrived as part of the same initiative that founded Liberia (Davis 1980b, 1980c, 1981a, 1983); in the late 1800s, laborers, stevedores, teachers, and pastors were attracted from the anglophone Lesser Antilles to the booming sugar industry in the Dominican southeast around San Pedro de Macorís (where they are pejoratively called *cocolos*); in the mid-twentieth century, the sugarcane business in many areas required the seasonal importation of thousands of Haitian seasonal workers (*braceros*) under conditions described as neoslavery. Many, estimated up to a million, have stayed and sometimes have intermarried, their children becoming bicultural Dominicans. These components of the population have contributed to the fabric of contemporary national culture, especially nonliterate musical culture.

FIGURE 5 The longdrum dance, *baile de palos,* representing ritual pursuit, a possible descendant of the colonial *calenda.* The women at the left, singing the response, also play single maracas, reflecting influence from the *congo* ensemble of the Villa Mella region, of which Los Morenos is an enclave. Photo by Martha Ellen Davis, 1980.

Genres

Dominican genres of notably African heritage (Davis 1980a) include metered, responsorial work songs (*plenas*), such as wood-chopping songs (*plenas de hacha*); stories about animals, with their characteristic little sung responses (Andrade 1930, 1976); the semi-sacred music of longdrums (*palos, atabales*) associated with Afro-Dominican brotherhoods (Davis 1976) and used in saints' festivals and sometimes *vodú* ceremonies (Davis 1987a) (figure 5); influence on Dominican creole social-dance music (figures 6, 7, 8) and nonliturgical *salves*; also the "*cocolo*" fife-and-drum ensemble (figure 9) and the Haitian-Dominican *gagá* society and ensemble, each associated with a different sugarcane settlement (Rosenberg 1979).

Musical contexts

Musical societies, events, and activities of African influence represent a New World continuity of elements of African political or religious societies, a pan-African polytheism, the attribution of causes and cures of disease and luck to divine forces, the

FIGURE 6 A traditional merengue social-dance ensemble of the northern (Cibao) region, ubiquitous in the Dominican Republic as a folksy musical symbol of national identity. *Left to right:* a *tambora,* an accordion, *güira,* and a *marimba.* Cabral, Barahona. Photo by Martha Ellen Davis, 1980.

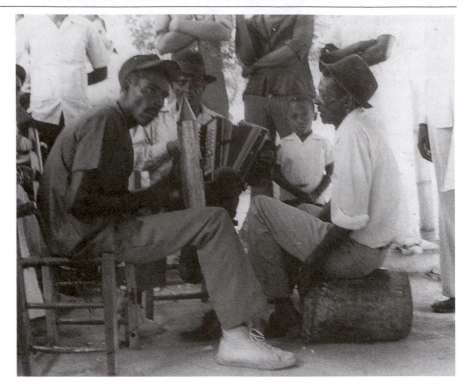

FIGURE 7 The *priprí, a* social dance of the central east and central south. The drum is the *balsié,* known in the colonial Caribbean as the *juba* drum, set on the ground with the player on top, dampening with a heel and beating with the hands on either side of the foot. It is played here for social dancing in the plaza of Villa Mella on Pentecost, the day of the Holy Spirit, patron of the Afro-Dominican brotherhood (*cofradía*) of the Villa Mella region. Photo by Martha Ellen Davis, 1978.

concept of ancestors as elders, systems of collective agricultural labor, and some forms of recreation. Political or religious societies under slavery in the New World were cast in a nonthreatening or Christianized contexts, such as the confraternity or religious brotherhood (*cofradía, hermandad*), or in a playful context, such as carnival (*carnaval*). The elite of colonial slave society is represented in the hierarchy of the Haitian and Haitian-Dominican *gagá* societies [see HAITI].

African polytheism, which syncretized with the polytheism of the Roman Catholic Church, is represented in the configuration of saints served by folk-religious ritual activities, mainly saints' festivals, processions, and pilgrimages. Devotion to

FIGURE 8 In Cabral, Barahona, the southwestern ensemble Belí [Belisario Féliz] y sus Muchachos plays a *priprí,* the rhythmic triptych of *carabiné, mangulina,* and *danza* (and today the merengue) in their own style. *Left to right:* a *güira,* a button accordion, a *balsié* (same name, different instrument from that of the east), and a *pandero* (here, large hand-held drum with laced head). Photo by Martha Ellen Davis,

FIGURE 9   On the patron saint's day of San Pedro de Macorís, carnivalesque mummers of English-island immigrants–the ensemble of Theophilus Chiverton "Primo" (*far left*) and Donald Henderson (*next to drum*)—play, *left to right:* a side-blown flute, a triangle, and a bass drum. Photo by Martha Ellen Davis, 1976.

ancestors is represented in rituals at the deathbed, the wake, the nine-night novena prayer cycle, the final novena (like a second wake), and the anniversary of death (sung rosary for adults, *salves* or the Hispanic *mediatuna* in the north for young children); when the deceased was a member of a religious brotherhood, longdrums are played.

These rituals are related to folk medicine, for they can be undertaken in payment of a vow (*promesa*) after divine healing. If the mortal does not fulfill the vow of undertaking a devotional act promised, the saint may claim his or her due by sending illness or death. Divine healing and counseling may be sought through consultation with a medium (*servidor* or *servidora de misterios*), then publicly celebrated; the initiation of new mediums and patron saints' days of the spiritualist center ("altar") and the medium (its "owner") are also celebrated (with longdrums or nonliturgical *salves*). The *gagá* societies, allied with Haitian Vodoun and protected by its magic, use the *gagá* drum and aerophone ensemble to express death-and-resurrection and celebration-of-life fertility motifs of the Lenten and Easter season (figure 10).

FIGURE 10   The Haitian-Dominican "*gagá*" of the Lenten and Easter season: bamboo tubes of different pitches play in hocket, with *petró* drums, and singing. The dancers twirl staves. Barahona area. Photo by Martha Ellen Davis, 1980.

guayo 'Grater' (also *güira*), Dominican and Cuban metal rasp functioning like the gourd *güiro*, played with a metal scraper

canoíta 'Little canoe', in the Dominican Republic, a pair of wooden idiophones that are struck together, one of which is hollowed out like a little canoe

alcahuete 'Pimp' (also *adulón*), a small, double-headed drum of the Dominican Republic

balsié In the Dominican Republic, the name for two different types of drums: a horizontal drum with tacked head, and a vertical drum with laced head

pandero A Dominican and Puerto Rican round frame drum like a tambourine but without jingles

Instruments and ensembles

Musical instruments and ensembles of the Dominican Republic include various idiophones, membranophones, chordophones, and aerophones.

Idiophones

A metal scraper (*güira* or *guayo* 'grater', figures 4 and 6) is a modern version of the gourd (*güiro*) still played in Puerto Rico. The maraca is a small shaker with a wooden handle, filled with gourd seeds or pebbles and played in pairs or singly in the *congos* ensemble of Villa Mella, which may represent Taino-African syncretism. A stick (*catá*) is beaten on the body of a longdrum in the northeast, including Samaná, where it is called maracas (not to be confused with the shaker of the same name). A pair of wooden idiophones (*canoíta* 'little canoe') resembles Cuban *claves,* but one is much larger and hollowed out like a little canoe and of softer wood; these are played only with the *congos* ensemble.

A recently introduced, definite-pitched, plucked idiophone is the *marimba* (also *marímbola*), a lamellaphone derived from the African *mbira* but much larger and with fewer metal tongues. The player sits on its plywood box. It was probably imported in the 1930s with the popular *sexteto* of the Cuban *son* and was adopted by the folk-merengue ensemble (figures 4 and 6).

Membranophones

Except in central Cibao, large membranophones include longdrums (*palos, atabales*), hand played throughout the country (figure 5). Except in two enclaves, these are made of hollowed-out logs with cowhide heads. All ensembles include responsorial singing by the drummers plus, if for the saints (rather than the dead), a couple dance (*baile de palos*) symbolizing ritual pursuit, perhaps derived from the colonial *calenda.* The master drum (*palo mayor*), the largest and deepest, is the center drum in an ensemble of three; the other drums are generically called *alcahuetes* ('pimps').

Regional variants of longdrum ensembles occur throughout the country except in central Cibao. In the east, two drums have wide, pegged heads and up to three metal scrapers (*güiras*), or one drum plus a pair of maracas in the transitional Monte Plata area, single maracas in the enclave of Los Morenos (figure 5) influenced by the *congos* ensemble of greater Villa Mella, and a stick beaten on the drum body in Samaná. The rhythms are *palos de muerto* 'drums for the dead' for death rituals and *palo corrido* for dancing. A variant in eastern Cibao (Cotuí, San Francisco de Macorís) uses tiny pegs, and the *alcahuete* is called *adulón*. In the central south, there are three drums (with narrow, tacked heads) and no idiophones. The ensemble is called more specifically *canutos* or *cañutos*. The rhythms are for the dead (*palo abajo* and *palo arriba*), joined in sequence everywhere except in Los Morenos, Villa Mella, though they are also danced somberly (figure 5). In the southwest, there are three drums (with wide, pegged heads) and no idiophones. One *alcahuete* is shorter and called the *chivita*. The rhythm is *palo corrido*, the instruments and the rhythm are called *palos del Espíritu Santo* 'palos of the Holy Spirit' because of the mysticism of the region and the instrument's association with the Brotherhood of the Holy Spirit.

Two longdrum special enclaves exist. The Afro-Dominican enclave, the Brotherhood of the Holy Spirit (*Cofradía del Espíritu Santo*) in Villa Mella has two drums (*congos*), one a third the size of the other (with dual goatskin laced heads), one pair of *canoíta* and many single maracas as idiophones. The brotherhood's activities entail mainly death rituals: the ninth and final novena (*rezo* 'prayer') and the anniversary of death (*banco,* probably a Bantu term, meaning unknown). The Afro-Dominican enclave, the Brotherhood of St. John the Baptist from west of Baní (Province of Peravia), now also in town, has three squat drums of dual goatskin-tacked heads; *tambores*, held between the knees for dance accompaniment or under the arm for procession; one *güira*; dance and music generically called *sarandunga*; dance rhythms are *sarandunga* (pieces include *capitana* for the dead and many others), *jacana*, and *bomba-e*. A procession genre is *morano*, in which drums accompany fixed solo and response quatrains. This brotherhood's rituals entail mainly daytime vows sponsored by devotees.

Smaller membranophones include various squat drums, varying in length from some 25 to 75 centimeters and in diameter from some 23 to 38 centimeters, used as the key instruments in social-dance ensembles; the *tambora* of the northern folk merengue, the horizontal, heel-damped tacked head (*balsié*) of the *priprí* ensemble of the east and central south (the Caribbean *juba* drum); the vertical *balsié* (same name, different instrument, with a laced head); and the large, laced frame drum (*pandero*) of the *priprí* (same name, different ensemble) of the southwest. The nonliturgical *salve* ensembles of the central south and east use smaller membranophones: the cylindrical *mongó* or *bongó,* played singly with a polyphonic ensemble of round frame drums; *panderos* (with tacked heads, some 23 to 25 centimeters in diameter and 4 centimeters high), similar to the tambourine but with few and irrelevant jingles, representing syncretism between Spanish (Arab heritage) and African instruments.

Descendants of British immigrants in San Pedro de Macorís favor the ensemble of mummers (*momís, guloyas*), consisting of a fife, a bass drum, and a triangle (figure 9).

Chordophones

A Central African–derived chordophone, the earthbow (*gayumba,* called *tambour maringouin* in Haiti, though it is almost extinct in the island) resembles the American gutbucket, but its resonating chamber is a palm-bark-covered hole in the ground. It plays any kind of music at festive, social occasions.

Aerophones

The conch trumpet (*fotuto*), used for signaling, represents syncretism between a Taino and an African instrument. Aerophones are also used in the following Haitian-Dominican membranophone and aerophone-idiophone ensemble of the *gagá* society: *petró* cult drums and an assortment of single-pitched bamboo trumpets (*vaccines* in Haiti, *bambúes* or *fotutos* in the Dominican Republic), whose players beat little sticks on their bamboo tube as they play; plus other metal aerophones (figure 10).

THE CREOLIZATION OF DOMINICAN MUSIC

Today's Dominican culture is best characterized as creole, the product of a process of adaptation and creative evolution that began in the earliest days of the colony. In recent decades, the evolutionary trend within the creole hybrid has been away from the Spanish heritage and toward greater African influence, marked by the gradual loss of acoustic stringed instruments, nontempered scales, antiphonal structures, and traditional vocal genres, including the *romance* and the *mediatuna*. Some genres, notably dance music and the nonliturgical *Salve*, are the result of creolization; some contexts, genres, styles, and ensembles are New World continuities of Old World cultures. This musical phenomenon is epitomized in the saint's festival.

The saint's festival

In the religious context of the saint's festival, certain musical genres, as part of the ritual, have been slow to change. These genres include the sung rosary, the liturgical *salve,* and sacred drumming. This festival is thus a living museum of the most archaic practices of Spanish and African origin. It shows that "traditional" musical culture and its performers may be bimusical—a common Caribbean occurrence (Davis 1987b, 1994a).

Musical activities in the saint's festival have specific spatial and temporal placement, and they often have gender associations. The rosary and the *salves* are performed at the altar, the sacred European site (erected for the festival against one wall of the folk chapel or of the sponsor's living room), the domain of women's responsibility and authority. Men may participate, but the *salve* is essentially a women's genre. Drumming (*palos*), a male activity, and the drum dance are situated in the center of the room around a center post (the sacred African site), temporally interrupted with *salves* (in the southwest), or outside in a covered patio, with the drums being hauled toward the altar for three sacred pieces after each rosary (in the east). If the festival of the east is a nightlong stop along a pilgrimage route, a separate room with a freestanding table is prepared for sung conversation (*tonadas de toros* 'bull songs') among members of a pilgrimage-associated brotherhood, who take donated alms and bull calves to Higüey, Bayaguana, and three other pilgrimage sites. If, as seldom happens, the sponsor is a *vodú* medium, spirit possession by deities will occur, and while *palos* or *salves* are being played in public, spiritual consultations may take place in an adjacent private room.

Depending on the region of the country, social dance music may be interspersed with drumming, played in a separate site on the festival grounds or played in the morning after the fulfillment of the vow. Rural social-dance genres practiced through the mid-twentieth century included variants of the Spanish *zapateado* called *zapateo* (*sarambo* in Cibao, *guarapo* in El Seybo) or derivatives of the English country dance (the *tumba dominicana*, displaced about 1850 by the merengue: the *carabiné* of the south; and the Haitian-derived *bambulá* in Samaná). In contemporary rural society, social dance includes the merengue from Cibao, the *perico ripiao*; the *merengue redondo* of the east (called *priprí* in the central-south, figure 7); and in the south, the triptych of *carabiné, mangulina,* and *danza* or *vals* (figure 8). The same genres may be danced outside the sacred site and on the occasion of the saint's festival. Secular venues of rural social dancing are bars (*cantinas*) and brothels (*cabarets*). The nickname of the northern merengue, *perico ripiao* 'ripped parrot', is said to have been the name of a brothel in the 1930s in the province of Santiago.

The salve

In today's *salve,* musical elements of different historical origins coexist and have become merged. In the central-south and eastern regions, the *salve* has evolved into two coexisting subgenres: the Hispanic, sacred, liturgical Virgin's *Salve* (*Salve de la Virgen*) and a less sacred *salve* with added text (*salve con versos*). The latter exhibits an appended text and a different, African-influenced musical style: metered and rhythmic, instrumentally accompanied, and responsorial, with a relaxed, mid-register vocal production. Its *versos* entail a secular response inserted between sacred phrases plus added quatrains at the end. It is accompanied by clapping and/or one small, vertical *mongó* (a drum typically played by a man), several small handheld drums (*panderos*, typically played by women), and a *güira* (played by a man). It reaches its most Africanized extreme in the *salve de pandero* of the central-south region, especially around Villa Mella and San Cristóbal, with the addition of many small membranophones played polyrhythmically and the elimination of a sacred text. Within the *salve de pandero*, the variant of the Province of Peravia (Baní) illustrates the coexistence of traditions of two origins within the musical subgenre, with the usual gender associations. Women sing the former positioned in a line in front of the altar, while men, in circular formation at the back of the chapel, accompany them with small membranophones.

The *merengue típico* or *perico ripiao*

Social-dance music, represented today by the folk merengue (*merengue típico* or *perico ripiao*) as a musical symbol of national identity, epitomizes the creolism of Dominican culture. The melodic instrument, formerly strings of the guitar family (figure 4) and now a Höhner accordion (figure 6), is European; the *tambora* has West African influence; the metal *güira* or *guayo* may represent Taino-African syncretism; and the marimba (also *marímbola*, also new since the 1930s) is a Cuban-evolved version of the African *mbira*. The music is based on the quatrain, rendered partially in African responsorial form to African-influenced rhythms in accompaniment of a European-style couple dance with African influence in dance style, such as hip movement. This is the music and dance that Trujillo promoted as the national dance in ballroom adaptations. Though affirming *hispanidad*, he redefined national culture as creole culture, represented by his chosen musical symbol of national identity.

URBAN MUSIC

Since the rise of cities and of literacy, a dialectical relationship of musical exchange bridges rural and urban traditions, as it does literate and nonliterate ones. Cities and towns have literate and nonliterate musical genres, the latter shared among virtually all social classes.

Dominican cities vary in their treatment of literate music. The larger cities and regional capitals have a sizeable educated elite and institutions that support fine-arts education and practice. The most musically active and prolific cities in the country are Santiago and Puerto Plata, and secondarily the capital (Santo Domingo) and San Pedro de Macorís. Smaller and newer towns, especially around sugarcane mills, are largely conglomerations of peasants-turned-proletarians. Since 1965, large numbers of peasants have left the countryside, so the rural-urban dichotomy is now also found in the cities.

Educational institutions

Education, including musical education, is nationally centralized, administered from the capital. The Ministry of Education, Fine Arts, and Religion is housed in a neo-classical complex built in 1956. The Ten-Year Plan for Education, announced in 1992 by presidential degree and in 1996 awarded a loan of $100 million loan from the World Bank and the Inter-American Development Bank, does not mention music education in its four-volume initial document (Congreso Nacional de Educación 1992) but refers to national culture, art, and folklore. Teacher training in music is still poor: only one music-appreciation class occurs in the teacher-training program at the public university. Public-school teachers, especially of elementary classes, have poor and declining skills and are poorly paid; their classrooms lack audiovisual facilities, materials, instruments, and often electricity.

Dominican masking on a national scale emphasizes a bovine motif, perhaps representing a syncretism between horned creatures of two different origins: the Christian devil and the Central African ox.

The National Conservatory of Music was founded in the capital in 1942. Each regional capital has a conservatory that serves elite and middle-class men and women. Young men of the middle and lower classes learn theory and band instruments in public academies of music located in practically every one of the provincial capitals by the 1920s ("Música" 1978:5:77); these academies are in decline because of underfunding. Their purpose is to train musicians for municipal bands. They were supported by Trujillo, whom they honored with military marches on his visits. There are private academies too. Literacy in music provides income and social mobility for musicians of municipal and military bands, as does military service. During the colonial occupation, the military band represented an arm of military conquest and occupation. Since 1844, the municipal and military bands (most notably of Santiago, Puerto Plata, and the capital) have served as training grounds and laboratories for the great conductors and composers of art music and popular song and dance.

Municipal bands also serve public education by providing public access to music. In their regular Thursday and Sunday evening public concerts (*retretas*) in the bandstand (*glorieta*) of the public square (*parque*)—a custom now almost extinct—the band opens the program with the national anthem, then plays musical arrangements, especially of operatic overtures, and then dance music, traditionally ending with a merengue and a reprise of the national anthem.

Contexts for performance

Performances in the capital occur in the theater at the Palace of Fine Arts (built in 1956) and the amphitheater Agua y Luz of the Feria de la Paz government-building complex (1956), the National Theater (1973), neighborhood-club-administered indoor stadiums (including the Mauricio Báez Stadium in the barrio of San Carlos), the national outdoor Quisqueya Stadium (seating about thirty thousand), public basketball courts (including the Sports Palace), the private Casa de Teatro (1974) for counterculture arts, numerous nightclubs, elite social clubs, and public neighborhood cultural-sports clubs. In the southeast near La Romana, the tourist complex Altos de Chavón has a large amphitheater for commercial shows for people mainly from the capital. Venues in Santiago include the Colón Theater, the Centro de la Cultura (about 1982, currently semiprivatized and being expanded into a four-unit Plaza de la Cultura), the Gran Teatro Regional del Cibao (1995, seating eighteen hundred), the Amphitheater of the Pontificia Universidad Católica Madre y Maestra (PUCMM, seating fewer than a thousand), the Cibao Stadium (seating about twenty-five thousand), public basketball courts, and a weekly *peña* (a nocturnal musical gathering in a southern Spanish context, associated with the counterculture in modern Latin America) at the Casa del Arte (in a patio behind the "Alianza Francesa," the French language institute), elite social clubs, and popular neighborhood clubs.

The elite socialize and dance in a town's exclusive social club (*club, casino*). A major event is the *fiesta quinceañera*, the coming-out party for fifteen-year-old girls.

Soirées (*veladas*) may include art-music compositions, choral poetry (*poesía coreada*), and other musical and theatrical genres. Exclusive dance parties are held on public festive events, such as carnival and the patron saint's day.

The neighborhood social-cultural-sports club is a Caribbean urban phenomenon found in cities and towns, and perpetuated in the expatriate community of New York. The club may be the sponsor and organizational site for a carnival group (*comparsa*) or a sports team; it also serves as a site for dances, parties, and men's domino games. Clubs may have a unit of young people dedicated to research on local popular traditions, or a folk-dance ensemble (*ballet folklórico*), often with the same members.

Taverns (*bares*), often open-air and with no restrictions of gender or age, are popular venues for dance parties. Whole families may enjoy a daylong, daytime Sunday event, called a *pasadía*.

Protestants, who do not participate in Roman Catholic festivities, sing hymns (currently from hymnals from Puerto Rico, translations of U.S. hymns) and present entertainment programs in their churches, including dramatizations of biblical events and performances of choral poetry. Traditional English-speaking Protestants of Afro-U.S. and British descent, as in Samaná, end church services with spirituals, called anthems. Seasonal events, such as church anniversaries, include band-accompanied processions; the dead are carried to the cemetery in a cortège with the band.

Public music

Public musical events include biweekly concerts of municipal bands and seasonal events—patronal festivals, carnival (in some towns), and Christmas. Local patron saints may have little to do with actual devotion. Patronal feasts require masses and several days of dances played by bands from other towns. They are traditionally prefaced by the *alborada*, a Spanish-derived predawn procession of a local musical ensemble.

Christmas in rural and urban contexts is characterized by *parrandas*, door-to-door singing for money or liquor. *Parranda*s, not so developed in the Dominican Republic as in Puerto Rico, are more African, with drum-based rather than string-based ensembles. A similar door-to-door circuit is undertaken at Christmas by the *momís* or *guloyas* of the "cocolo" enclave of San Pedro de Macorís, accompanied by a fife, a bass drum, and a triangle, and in cane settlements (*bateyes*) by the Haitian-Dominican *gagá* groups, with musical ensembles and baton-twirling routines of costumed *mayores*.

Throughout Roman Catholic America, carnival is another season for merriment, musical performance, and artistic creativity with masks, costumes, and musical motifs for parade groups. It is celebrated only in Santo Domingo, Santiago, La Vega, Cotuí, Monte Cristi, and Cabral, Barahona. Its date is associated not with the start of Lent, but with the political holidays of 27 February (independence from Haiti) and secondarily 16 August (independence from Spain) except in Cabral, where it is celebrated during the three days after Good Friday. The *gagá* societies also celebrate a carnival these same days in cane communities, at least in those near Barahona. Dominican masking on a national scale emphasizes a bovine motif, perhaps representing a syncretism between horned creatures of two different origins: the Christian devil and the Central African ox.

Musical genres

Urban social dance

Social dances, concert bands, and dance bands are major vehicles of musical exchange between localities, social classes, and traditions. Since 1844 at the latest, dance-band musicians have served as conduits for the introduction of rural genres of dancing into the halls of the urban elite, and conversely, for transmission of urban fashions in social dancing, often of foreign origin, to rural areas. In the late 1700s and early 1800s, the vogue was the *contredanse* and the quadrilles, and in the mid-1800s, the Central European waltz, mazurka, and polka. The *danzón* of Cuba and the *danza* of Puerto Rico—upper-class urban Latin American creole dance genres that became fashionable in the late 1800s—are still enjoyed on radio in the Dominican Republic and are occasionally danced to. By the 1920s, the rage was U.S. dances: one-steps, two-steps, and fox-trots. In the 1920s, the Dominican merengue of Cibao began to be introduced into dance halls (Alberti 1975); it was promoted after 1930 by Trujillo, who had his own dance bands and bandleader-composers. This style of the 1930s to 1950s is still popular as a facet of urban musical patrimony.

At the same time, the orchestrated merengue continues to evolve. Since the 1920s, band instruments have been added to the traditional ensemble, starting with the alto saxophone, the most characteristic instrument of the ballroom merengue band after the *tambora*. During Trujillo's time, the orchestrated merengue was adapted for the ballroom. An initial "stroll" (*paseo*) was added to situate partners on the dance floor. After Trujillo's fall, arrangers added other band instruments to the merengue and made stylistic changes in it, including a marked acceleration. The contemporary merengue bandleader Johnny Ventura (b. about 1940) is credited with compositions and recordings intended for a broader, international audience. Currently, the modern orchestrated merengue is enjoying popularity throughout the Spanish-speaking world as the trendiest Latino dance rhythm (Alberti 1975; Austerlitz 1997), but within Dominican musical culture, the ballroom merengue coexists with its unchanging progenitor, the folkloric *perico ripiao*. The vitality of the merengue is due to its role as a symbol of national identity. The folk merengue represents a rural, traditional identity, and the orchestrated merengue represents an urban, modern one.

Urban song

Merengues were composed for dance bands by composers seeking inspiration in rural, nonliterate genres for the creation of songs and dances of the literate tradition with piano or band accompaniment directed toward urban audiences. Leading composer-conductors of this century included Julio Alberto Hernández (b. 1900) (Hernández 1969) and Alberti (1906–1976). Several songs, including "*Quisqueya*" and danceable merengues such as Alberti's "*Compadre Pedro Juan*," have passed from the literate to the oral urban tradition, and are taken as collective musical symbols of national identity.

Another type of urban music is the sentimental song of *trovadores*, crooners of serenades and parties, who strum acoustic guitars and sing amorous courtship songs in settings where alcohol is consumed. Their songs are transmitted largely orally from person to person, and more recently through recordings and broadcasts. Their medium and function, and certain of their genres (especially the bolero and the *vals*), are shared with their counterparts in other Latin American cities and towns. Other genres are Hispanic Caribbean (such as the Cuban-influenced *son*) or specifically Dominican (such as the *criolla*, a lyrical song in 6/8 time, virtually unknown outside the country). The *son* tradition is maintained in Afro-Dominican sectors in the capital by the old Soneros de Borojols and ensembles of younger musicians in Villa Mella.

Urban folk-based music

Two urban musical genres affirm national identity through the performance of folk-based music: the folk-dance troupe (*ballet folklórico*) and the human-rights-based protest song (*nueva canción*, in Cuba called *nueva trova*). Both are genres unto themselves. The first documented fieldwork-based folk-dance troupe was founded in Miches about 1941 by René Carrasco, a self-made folklorist, and the next was established in the capital by Edna Garrido (b. 1913) at the public university about 1945. Later groups, though essentially derivatives of Carrasco's, lack fieldwork-based authenticity and exhibit the accelerated tempi, the uniform costumery, the synchronized movements, and the entertainment and national-identity agenda typical of this genre throughout Latin America. Starting about 1973, Fradique Lizardo founded a presumably research-based troupe, for which he achieved appointment as National Folk-Dance Troupe (Ballet Folklórico Nacional).

Dominican protest songs share the pan–Latin American style of *nueva canción* or *nueva trova*. They are typically guitar-accompanied and as descendants of the *décima* (the old *trova*) explicitly articulate its ideology. Members of Convite, the group founded about 1975 by Dagoberto Tejeda, were jailed. The lead singer, Luis Días, probably the most authentic and creative of Dominican popular-music composers, was persecuted and now lives in New York. His compositions, based on his rural musical background and later observations, tap Hispanic and Afro-Dominican heritages, fused with the human-rights ideology of *nueva canción*. His compositions have nourished numerous commercial and new-song musicians, including the singer Sonia Silvestre (1994?). Others, mainly of urban origin, have fused Afro-Dominican traditions with new-song verbosity and ideology; they include, in Santo Domingo and New York City, groups led by Toni Vicioso, José Duluc, Edis Sánchez, and William Alemán.

RECORDINGS AND BROADCAST MEDIA

Paralleling the role of yesteryear's bandsmen, the recording and broadcast media serve as conduits between urban and rural areas, and between international and national arenas. The first foreign recordings entered the Dominican Republic in 1913, and the first recordings done there were made by Victor in 1928. The first radio station, HIX, was founded in 1928, and its first live broadcast was by the great baritone Eduardo Brito (Incháustegui 1988). HIN, La Voz del Partido Dominicano (The Voice of the Dominican Party), started broadcasting in 1936. Trujillo's absolute dictatorship stunted the recording and broadcast industries, since he promoted or stymied musicians at will.

During the Trujillo Era, musical broadcasts favored pieces composed in honor of the dictator. Trujillo's fall (1961) allowed a flourishing of broadcast and publishing media. The event virtually coincided with the Cuban Revolution, when Cubans involved in the music industry fled Cuba; some went to the Dominican Republic. At present, there are more than a hundred radio stations in the country, some with local and others with virtually national range. About three, operated by the Roman Catholic Church, transmit educational programs.

The most popular station among the rural and marginal urban sectors is Radio Guarachita, which has almost national coverage and includes a recording enterprise. Its programming focuses largely on folk merengues and the Mexican bolero and *ranchera*, as beloved locally as if they were home-grown genres. Since the 1980s, the station has recorded and promoted a newly commercialized genre, *bachata*, a steel-stringed-guitar-accompanied whiny male lament (Pacini Hernandez 1995). *Bachata*, derived from the *décima* tradition, has probably been in oral traditions for a century, but has only recently been marketed. In the late 1980s and 1990s, Juan Luis Guerra reinterpreted the *perico ripiao* and the *bachata* for marketing to the urban elite. All social sectors enjoy broadcasts of the romantic boleros of *trovadores* and the *gentile*

In the 1980s and 1990s, television, especially live variety shows, has played an important role in disseminating merengue.

nineteenth-century dance music, especially the Puerto Rican *danza* and the Cuban *danzón*; more popular sectors enjoy the Cuban *son* and *guaracha*.

In the 1980s and 1990s, television, especially live variety shows, has played an important role in disseminating merengue. TV has promoted the showy, nightclub bolero (now called *balada*) of pan-Hispanic big business—a far cry from the romantic sincerity and acoustic accompaniment of the *trovador*. Currently, cable television, which brings international broadcasting to the capital, Santiago, and other cities, is a new dimension in broadcast media; it will undoubtedly have some impact on musical taste.

FURTHER STUDY

Further basic ethnographic research is needed on nonliterate rural musical traditions, with the publication of texts and particularly audio and visual recordings, with excellent annotation, preferably in English and Spanish, addressed to Dominicans (many of whom are unfamiliar with the panorama of their national musical culture) and non-Dominicans, and intelligible for the public and specialists.

Folkways published several recordings of various genres by Verna Gillis (1976a, 1976b, 1976c, 1978), but she did not have the ethnographic background to prepare in-depth notes; the one on Haitian *rará* and Dominican *gagá* has been republished with the notes revised by Gage Averill (1991). Republishing needs to be done for the other recordings. Morton Marks published a Folkways recording of a longdrum festival in San Cristóbal Province (1983), and John Storm Roberts published recordings with reliable but short notes (recorded in early 1970s). The field collection of Dominican tales by Manuel J. Andrade (1930, 1976) has been crying for classification; this work should be followed with a restudy with audio recording. Ethnographic work should not merely emphasize the trendy Afro-Dominican traditions; it should include the Hispanic heritage, which represents the oldest folk-European continuities in the New World, including Hispanic or creole dance genres that are virtually extinct. The field collections of Garrido Boggs (about 1947 and following) and J. M. Coopersmith (1944) in the American Folklife Center at the Library of Congress should be annotated, guided by Coopersmith's book and Garrido Boggs's publications, an unpublished manuscript (about 1953), and memory.

There is a need to take down oral histories of song-and-dance composers of the written and oral traditions, bandleaders, and *trovadores,* focusing on the history of popular musical culture through life history. Bernarda Jorge's book (1982) does not do this, missing an important source. The study of brass bands is also needed. This work would entail the collection and conservation of scores of compositions by local bandleaders; this could be the job of the National Archive of Music, but it has no operating budget. Scores and recordings of Dominican art-music compositions also need to be published and recorded.

REFERENCES

Alberti, Luis. 1975. *De música y orquestas bailables dominicanas, 1910–1959*. Santo Domingo: Museo del Hombre Dominicano.

Andrade, Manuel J. 1930. *Folk-Lore from the Dominican Republic*. Memoirs of the American Folklore Society, 23. New York: American Folklore Society.

———. 1976 [1930]. *Folklore de la República Dominicana*. Santo Domingo: Sociedad Dominicana de Bibliófilos.

Austerlitz, Paul. 1997. *Merengue: Dominican Music and Dominican Identity*. Philadelphia: Temple University Press.

Congreso Nacional de Educación. 1992. *Un pacto con la patria y el futuro de la educación dominicana*. Plan Decenal de Educación, A, 1. Santo Domingo: Secretaría de Estado de Educación, Bellas Artes y Cultos.

Coopersmith, J. M. 1976 [1949]. *Music and Musicians of the Dominican Republic / Música y músicos de la República Dominicana*. Edited by Charles Seeger. Pan American Union, Music Series, 15. Santo Domingo: Dirección General de Cultura de la República Dominicana.

Davis, Martha Ellen. 1976. "Afro-Dominican Religious Brotherhoods: Structure, Ritual, and Music." Ph.D. dissertation, University of Illinois at Urbana-Champaign.

———. 1980a. "Aspectos de la influencia africana en la música tradicional dominicana." *Boletín del Museo del Hombre Dominicano* 13:255–292.

———.1980b. "La cultura musical religiosa de los 'americanos' de Samaná." *Boletín del Museo del Hombre Dominicano* 15:127–169.

———. 1980c. "'That Old-Time Religion': Tradición y cambio en el enclave 'americano' de Samaná." *Boletín del Museo del Hombre Dominicano* 14:165–196.

———. 1981a. "Himnos y anthems (coros) de los 'americanos' de Samaná: Contextos y estilos." *Boletín del Museo del Hombre Dominicano* 16:85–107.

———. 1981b. *Voces del Purgatorio: Estudio de la Salve dominicana*. Santo Domingo: Museo del Hombre Dominicano.

———. 1983. "Cantos de esclavos y libertos: Cancionero de anthems (coros) de Samaná." *Boletín del Museo del Hombre Dominicano* 18:197–236.

———. 1987a. *La otra ciencia: El vodú dominicano como religión y medicina populares*. Santo Domingo: Universidad Autónoma de Santo Domingo.

———. 1987b. "Native Bi-Musicality: Case Studies from the Caribbean." *Pacific Review of Ethnomusicology* 4:39–55.

———. 1994a. "'Bi-Musicality' in the Cultural Configurations of the Caribbean." *Black Music Research Journal* 14(2):145–160.

———. 1994b. "Music and Black Ethnicity in the Dominican Republic." In *Music and Black Ethnicity in the Caribbean and South America*, ed. Gerard Béhague, 119–155. Miami: North-South Center, University of Miami.

Garrido Boggs, Edna. 1946. *Versiones dominicanas de romances españoles*. Ciudad Trujillo: Pol Hermanos.

———. 1980 [1955]. *Folklore infantil de Santo Domingo*. Santo Domingo: Sociedad Dominicana de Bibliófilos.

———. 1961. "Panorama del Folklore Dominicano." *Folklore Américas*, 11(1–2):1–23.

Gillis, Verna. 1976a. *The Island of Quisqueya*. Folkways FE 4281. LP disk.

———. 1976b. *The Island of Española*. Folkways FE 4282. LP disk.

———. 1976c. *Cradle of the New World*. Folkways FE 4283. LP disk.

———. 1978. *Songs from the North*. Folkways FE 4284. LP disk.

Gillis, Verna, and Daniel Pérez Martínez. 1978. *Rara in Haiti / Gaga in the Dominican Republic*. Folkways FE 4531. 2 LP disks.

Gillis, Verna, and Gage Averill. 1991. *Caribbean Revels: Haitian Rara and Dominican Gaga*. Smithsonian Folkways CD SF 40402. Compact disc and republished notes.

Hernández, Julio Alberto. 1969. *Música tradicional dominicana*. Santo Domingo: Julio D. Postigo.

Incháustegui, Arístides. 1988. *El disco en la República Dominicana*. Santo Domingo: Amigo del Hogar.

Jorge, Bernarda. 1982. *La música dominicana: Siglos XIX–XX*. Santo Domingo: Universidad Autónoma de Santo Domingo.

Las Casas, Bartolomé de. 1958. *Apologética historia sumaria*. Madrid: Biblioteca de Autores Españoles.

Marks, Morton. 1983. *Afro-Dominican Music from San Cristóbal, Dominican Republic*. Folkways FE 4285. LP disk.

"Música." 1978. *Enciclopedia Dominicana*. 2nd ed. 5:75–88.

Pacini Hernández, Deborah. 1995. *Bachata: A Social History of a Dominican Popular Music*. Philadelphia: Temple University Press.

Roberts, John Storm, compiler. 1972. *Caribbean Island Music: Songs and Dances of Haiti, the Dominican Republic and Jamaica*. Nonesuch H-72047. LP disk.

———. N.d. *Singers of the Cibao*. Tivoli, N.Y.: Original Music OML 403CC. Cassette.

Rosenberg, June. 1979. *El Gagá: Religión y sociedad de un culto dominicano—Un estudio comparativo*. Santo Domingo: Universidad Autónoma de Santo Domingo.

Silvestre, Sonia. 1994? *Quiero andar*. Oi Records, PR 200. LP disk.

Grenada (and Carriacou)
Lorna McDaniel

History of Grenada
Historical Musical Genres of Grenada
Contemporary Grenada
History of Carriacou
Musical Contexts and Genres of Carriacou

Called Camerhogne by Carib settlers and renamed Concepción Island by Columbus on his 1498 voyage, Grenada (named by the British for the ancient Iberian kingdom of Granada) is an independent country with two dependencies, Carriacou and Petit Martinique. Carriacou is the first in the chain of small islands that links Grenada and St. Vincent, called the Grenadines. The southernmost of the Windward Islands, Grenada and its dependencies lie northwest of Trinidad. Its population is about a hundred thousand; its main exports are cocoa, nutmeg, and bananas.

HISTORY OF GRENADA

In 1650, over British objections, Grenada was claimed by France. Caribs, its aboriginal inhabitants, also objected, and armed conflicts arose over a French-Carib agreement. The events of 1652, a dramatic part of Grenada's history, include the French pursuit of Carib warriors to a cliff, where, rather than submitting, they jumped to their deaths. The cliff, Morne des Sauteurs (Leapers' Hill), and a northern village are named after the incident. After this conflict, most local Caribs were expelled or killed, but archaeological sites under excavation document their existence and the extent of their culture of pottery.

France ruled Grenada for more than a century, after which a period of colonial tug of war ensued. After the Seven Years' War (1763), Grenada was awarded to Britain, but in 1779, the island was restored to France. Britain reclaimed Grenada through the Treaty of Versailles (1783) and ruled until 1974, when Grenada became independent. Though France ruled in the distant past, Grenadian culture continues to reflect that past in minor linguistic retentions and other cultural traits.

A few enslaved West Africans were imported from the commencement of France's interest in Grenada, but soon Africans were shipped in great numbers to cultivate indigo and sugar. Beginning at the period of apprenticeship (1834) and after full emancipation (1838), Africans (liberated from slavers' ships), Portuguese, and East Indians served as indentured workers, filling the places of migrating ex-slaves. The system of indenture on Grenada continued to 1885.

A major part of the island's lore centers around historic battles fought over land, alliance, and politics. The modern Marxist struggle, which ended with the ousting of the People's Revolutionary Government by a U.S. invasion in 1983, echoes the revolutions and conflicts of the past. Orally sung histories sustain these tales, inspiring the people to regard the vanquished Caribs, Julien Fedon (who in 1795 led a revolt), and Maurice Bishop (who in 1979 led the New Jewel Movement) as revolutionary heroes.

HISTORICAL MUSICAL GENRES OF GRENADA

Two ancient genres, belair and *kalenda,* were filled with metaphors similar to those above. Further parallels with the old forms are found in the musical structure, and more important, in the function. Like the belair and the *kalenda,* the modern calypso disseminates information, keeps history, bonds people, and molds behavior.

The nineteenth-century *belair* (*bele*) was a dance formed in two lines or in a circle. It was accompanied by two open-bottomed, goatskin-headed drums fashioned from tree trunks or barrels. The first drum, called *tambou* or *ka* (Hearn 1890:143), measured 90 to 120 centimeters tall and 38 to 41 centimeters wide; the second drum (*baboula*), of the same height, was 20 to 23 centimeters wide. The player of the larger drum beats "in time," while the player of the smaller drum beats "as fast as he can and hardly in time" (Bell 1893:32).

Because the colonists considered these dances, especially the *kalenda,* objectionable and related to rebellion, they banned their performance. In teaching more officially acceptable dances (such as the quadrille), they sought to replace the drum with fiddles. The Grenadian quadrille ensemble consists of a fiddle ("scraped with the utmost disregard to tune or time"), a tambourine, and a triangle (whose player used his foot and the floor to drum); dances came to be associated with class, and elegant-dress quadrille parties were hosted by upper-class blacks and "coloureds" (Bell 1893:36).

The belair, the *kalenda,* the quadrille, and African rituals from the era of slavery do not survive on Grenada; however, Yoruba ceremonies from a subsequent era are common. The local existence of Yoruba-Shango rituals is attributed to liberated Africans who entered the colony during the mid-1800s as indentured servants. Likewise, the popularity of other Africanesque religions, such as the Spiritual Baptists, grew out of the presence of African-born immigrants receptive to evangelism.

Rituals and religion

M. G. Smith's transcription (1963) of Norman Paul's autobiography, *The Dark Puritan,* outlines the dynamic between three Grenadian rituals in practice about 1900: the nation dance, Shango, and the Spiritual Baptist religion. After about 1850, the nation dance, the established ceremony of creoles born of enslaved Africans, was overtaken by the newly transplanted Yoruba-based ritual, Shango. At the establishment of the Baptist religion (formerly called Shouters on Grenada), a continuing cycle of syncretic exchange commenced; in it, items and practices were borrowed from and lent to the Shango religion.

A few of the oldest generation, active in Grenada's Shango religion, remember African-born foreparents and preserve a fragmented knowledge of Yoruba learned from them. Grenadian Shango, with specific differences in ritual form and without East Indian ritual contributions, resembles that of Trinidad. According to Pollak-Eltz (1970:823), many Grenadan deities (*orisha*) have Christian counterparts that include Shango (St. John the Baptist), Ogun (St. Michael), Osain (St. Mark), Shakpana or the healer Omolu (Christian counterpart uncertain), Emanya (St. Anne), Oshun (St. Mary), Oshossi (St. Paul), Obatala-Orisanla or Oshala (Jesus Christ, God), Olorun (God), Legbara (Satan), Beji or the Twins (Christian counterpart uncertain), and Egungun (Spirits, or so-called zombies).

Colonial music

Newspaper announcements report the activity and sophistication of musical life of Grenadian colonists. In 1790, an opera in three acts, *The Magnifique,* composed in 1773 by André Ernest Modeste Grétry (1741–1813), was performed by the French and Italian Comedians. It portrayed a "procession of slaves with their redemption and delivery." A comic opera in three acts, *Le Diable a Quatre* 'The Double Metamorphosis', completed the bill. A month later, two operas by "Duny," probably Egidio Romualdo Duni (1709–1775), were staged (*St. George's Chronicle & New Grenada Gazette* 1790).

Advertisements testify to whites' musical activities in Grenada, as in 1827, with an announcement that J. T. Hitchcock—organ builder, piano tuner, music teacher—had become a resident. Shortly after his arrival, invitations for the subscription to a musical society for the purpose of engaging in chamber music (marches, waltzes, quadrilles, strathspeys, reels, overtures, rondos, voluntaries, sonatas, and airs) appeared (*Grenada Free Press and Public Gazette* 1829). This repertoire, especially the dance tunes, influenced all aspects and classes of Grenadian social life.

Carnival

The historic Grenadan carnival (*mas*) included Moko Jumbie 'Stiltdancer', Jab 'Devil' (outfitted with long nails, cattle horns, and a flowing chain), *Shango* (belair dancers), and Donkeyman (accompanied by a drum and a flute). Clowns and *pierrots* continued as carnival favorites for years; the most popular were *Pierrots Grenades* 'Grenadian Clowns', who recited soliloquies and historical narratives in mnemonic contests.

During the 1930s, the string orchestra (guitar, clarinet, triangle), the drum and the flute, or the tamboo-bamboo (bamboo cylinders of varying lengths, struck on the ground and together) were the major instrumental ensembles of carnival. In processions, female songsters marched with special privilege and without harassment (Redhead 1985:107). Each troupe of women, carrying a banner and wearing uniforms, sang a new repertoire, produced expressly for the occasion. The leader, who sang walking backward and facing her ensemble, used maracas (*chac-chac*); when her troupe responded with the chorus, she would turn to march forward. These women were sometimes accompanied by a *cuatro* (a four-stringed Venezuelan guitar).

Apparently, whips rather than weapon-sticks (*bois,* associated with carnival in Trinidad) were the predominant weapon of challenge and symbol of power. One may imagine that whips served as a metaphor of slavery. Social aggression in the guise of physical domination in the prewar carnival was later transmuted to aesthetic supremacy in musical competitions of calypso, pan (steelband), and competitions for king and queen.

CONTEMPORARY GRENADA

Carnival has taken on a new season (early August), a new function (in the interest of tourism), and realistic means of support. Rather than individuals (as was the custom in the earlier form), industries—restaurants, the Grenadian rum distillery, banks—bear the financial burden. Bands dressed as "Arabs," "a restaurant menu," and "sea creatures" march between steelbands mounted on mobile carts of framed steel. The steelbands, pushed by human locomotion, play the winning piece of the pan competition, while engine-powered trucks loaded with high-tech sound equipment disseminate winning calypsos. Participants' costumes are elaborate (figure 1).

In the calypso "Grenada," the Grenadian-Trinidadian Mighty Sparrow, whose style is the prototype of the Caribbean calypso, spoke from an unpopular perspective on the 1983 American invasion of Grenada. Linguistic prowess is essential to the per-

FIGURE 1   A carnival queen in Grenada. Photo by Lorna McDaniel, 1992.

formance of the traditional calypso, and the cleverness of Spanish usage in this excerpt (alluding to Cuba) illustrates that skill:

> *La manera que tengo mi corazón* [From my perspective]
> *¡Viva, viva la revolución!* [Long live, long live the revolution!]
> But if Cuba had arrested Coard and Austin,
> America would not have an excuse to come in.
> *¡Llévame a Grenada, llévame!* [Take me to Grenada, take me!]
> Judas, Lucifer, and Jezebel mustn't get away.

Sparrow describes the characters in the political action, giving them biblical personas: Maurice Bishop, the revolutionary Marxist (painted as a Christ figure), is thought to have been deceived by his closest allies; Bernard Coard, his assistant and Deputy Prime Minister, is cast as Judas, General Hudson Austin as Lucifer, and Coard's wife, Phyllis, as Jezebel.

In 1991, calypso themes seemed strangely apolitical and nonhistorical, probably reflecting intentional decisions. Because of the special weight and influence projected by song, calypsonians rejected the impulse to parody the life-or-death decision of the case in session: for the assassination of Maurice Bishop and members of his cabinet, local courts were trying, and ultimately sentencing to life imprisonment, five persons (including Bernard Coard).

HISTORY OF CARRIACOU

Carriacou lies between Grenada and St. Vincent. It measures 4 kilometers by 12, and its population, mainly West-African-derived people, is about five thousand. Its name (spelled Karyouacou on early maps) is most likely of Carib origin. No Caribs remain, however, and neither East Indians nor liberated Africans were brought to it.

The mixed-race people of Windward Village and neighboring Petit Martinique Island descend from enslaved African women and Scottish shipbuilders or French settlers, who left their genetic print and knowledge of shipbuilding. Carriacou's physical tininess, historical isolation, and absentee proprietorship are among the factors that contributed to the perpetuation of traditional practices among its people.

Carriacou is known for its big-drum tradition, which not only perpetuates the practices of past societies but may have had a role in the formation of the present social structure, beliefs, and behavior.

Excepting the Maroons of Surinam, it has "the most fully articulated system of unilateral descent" of all African-American societies (Mintz and Price 1981:37).

France occupied Carriacou from 1650 to 1763, when Britain was granted ownership. Except for a four-year period (1779–1783) when it reverted to French domination, Britain had control from 1763 until 1974. Late-twentieth-century political struggles include a bloodless Marxist revolution in 1979, led by Maurice Bishop, and the U.S. invasion, after Bishop's murder, in 1983.

MUSICAL CONTEXTS AND GENRES OF CARRIACOU

The current music and dance genres include the historic African-derived dance-ritual, the big drum, the quadrille, the *parang*, the passplay, game songs, music for stringed instruments, ballads, shanties, calypsos, *cantiques*, sankeys, and the vocal styles of the Spiritual Baptist Church. Each musical type is dominated by people of a single age or gender or is owned by a particular district with exclusive domain and function. Colonialism left marks on all musical types, including the big drum. European dances lost in Europe survive in Carriacou.

The big drum, traditionally associated with older people, is controlled principally by women. Middle-aged couples engage in the quadrille, and young men dominate the composition and performance of the *parang*, inspired by Venezuela. The passplay remains a play-song repertoire of children in the southern district of L'Esterre, and string ensemble music, ballads, and shanties are found mainly among mixed-race people in Windward Village. A few *cantiques* remain within the memory of the oldest generation as fragmented remnants of French hymnody, but sankeys, nineteenth-century North American evangelical hymns, form a beloved repertoire, nurtured and reworked by the people for Carriacouan wakes and services. A more recent foreign-church influence is found in the repertoires of the Spiritual Baptists, whose evangelism entered Carriacou via St. Vincent and Trinidad [see TRINIDAD AND TOBAGO].

Contemporary events are documented in Carriacou's modern calypsos, People's Revolutionary Army songs, and *parang*. These songs narrate recent news with the same spirit and intent as big-drum texts once broadcast in patois the great events of the past.

The big drum

Carriacou is known for its big-drum tradition, which not only perpetuates the practices of past societies but may have had a role in the formation of the present social structure, beliefs, and behavior. Established by enslaved African people, this event (also called the nation dance) celebrates ancestral spirits, family reorganization, and changes in social status. It teaches and reinforces knowledge, family lineage, and tradition. It continues to reinforce the current generation's memory of national origin and kinship.

Most likely conceived as a social-religious ceremony, the big drum functions as a family ritual that stimulates the rehearsal of genealogies through song and dance. In this way, the family sponsoring the dance fosters the revival of ancestral memories, not only of their own lineage and nation (African cultural and ethnic tradition), but among neighbors and acquaintances from distant villages.

A two-hundred-item repertoire extant in the 1950s divides into three categories: nation songs, creole songs (*hallecord, bélè kawé, gwa bélè,* juba, old *kalenda,* old bongo), and frivolous songs (*chattam, lora, cariso, chirrup, piké,* man bongo, Trinidad *kalenda, chiffoné*). The nation repertoire, the oldest and most instructive in matters of historical significance, was classified by the people in the nine discrete ethnic groups that represent the origins of the present population: Cromanti, Igbo, Manding, Chamba, Kongo, Arada, Temne, Moko, Banda (Pearse 1956:2).

The Cromanti nation, though principally Akan, was made up of various Gold Coast peoples shipped by the British from the formerly Dutch fort, Cormantine, who received their name from their port of departure. The Igbo, taken from the Bight of Biafra, retained their ethnic title, as did other national groups. The Manding were taken from Senegambia, the Chamba from the Bight of Benin, the Kongo from Kongo, the Arada from Dahomey, the Temne from Sierra Leone, and the Moko from the Bight of Biafra (McDaniel 1986). Because several West African Banda nations exist, there is a problem in pinpointing the origin of the Carriacou Banda. The Banda nation of Carriacou probably came from the Gold Coast interior.

Many nation songs from the era of slavery exhibit themes of supplicating and venerating ancestors. The creole songs, especially the women's *bélè kawé* and *gwa bélè,* project competition and envy between women. The bongo of the creole songs are songs of loneliness and alienation, while the *hallecord* texts most often lament death. The frivolous songs, including satirical songs that speak of social conflict, control, and pleasure, were appropriated from Trinidad and other neighboring islands.

The big drum differs from most other African-based rituals in the New World in persisting as a plural, international type that resists absolute ritual integration. Besides the significance of the classification of the patois songs, data in the African words, places, and ancestral names appear occasionally in the texts that answer historical questions on affiliation, migration, and social structure of the enslaved people. The repertoire is therefore an archive of oral lore.

Donald C. Hill's analysis (1977) of Carriacou migration as a cultural expectation gives meaning to the historic practice of protracted travel for work. Since 1838, sugarcane workers traveled to Trinidad, Grenada, Barbados, Venezuela, Dominica, and Aruba; these names in big-drum texts evidence the people's movements. Hill's thesis—that Trinidad had the longer and greater economic input to Carriacou—is disputed by some but supported by musical evidence. Lyrics mention cities in Trinidad many times, but Aruba (an equally popular magnet since the 1930s) only once. The more recent port of entry for Carriacouans, Aruba is not often coded in the big drum, for which textual composition ended in the 1920s.

The patrilineal code of descent, unusual in the British Caribbean (Smith 1962), is clearly mirrored in the hierarchic musical organization of the big drum, with a musical program that gives preference to agnatic ancestry in the choice of nation songs. The historical matrilineality of the Cromanti is in conflict with the system of patrilineality supported by the big drum, and for this reason Smith contends a non-African origin of the Carriacou system of lineage. For some groups (Cromanti and Kongo), matrilineality probably gave way to patrilineality without losing the essential concepts of Akan inheritance.

For the ritual concert, a standing crowd, including the troupe comprising five to twelve female singers and dancers, surrounds three male drummers. The troupe is

FIGURE 2   Lucian Duncan, chantwell and queen of the big drum, Carriacou, Grenada. Photo by Lorna McDaniel, 1984.

directed by a female lead singer-dancer (*chantwell, chantuelle, chanturelle*), who introduces and controls each song with a maraca (*chac-chac*) (figure 2).

Dancers formerly wore flowing outer skirts (*douiettes*), modeled after nineteenth-century French colonial fashions. Each skirt was split in the front to expose a luxuriant white, starched petticoat made from bleached flourbags, with ribbon woven through an embroidered hem. Dancing barefoot, women integrated an African head-tie and dangling earrings with the colonial gown. Today, women wear a simplified and modified version of this costume. Male dancers do not wear elaborate costumes but use a towel in each hand as extensions of their arms.

Instruments

The full musical ensemble—lead singer, chorus, three drums, maracas, old hoe (a metal idiophone, providing a timeline)—accompanies the ritual libation, which summons ancestors to partake in the festivities. Only in the first of the three Cromanti songs that open the dance is the old hoe played. The names of the drums, *boula* and cutter (*kata*), imply a Congolese origin. Two *boulas* accompany each song with single, specific, reiterative beats that with the style of dancing distinguish the musical category. The cutter drummer, flanked by two *boula* players, improvises multimetric statements that sound above the vocal lead, the chorus, and the rhythm of the *boulas*.

Open-bottomed drums were formerly made from barrels in which rations (salted beef, salted fish) had been imported. Now, using the same techniques, builders take the materials for making drums from empty rum casks. They dismantle the barrel, plane the slats to 1.5 centimeters in depth, and reassemble the slats as a smaller barrel to serve as the body of the drum. A reed hoop wrapped in cloth secures a goatskin head that drummers tighten and tune by tapping the hoop.

The dimensions of drums vary, but the usual height of both types is about 52 centimeters, and the central circumferences are 113 (*kata*) and 104 (*boula*). The *kata* drum is often wider in head diameter than the *boula*. The *boulas* are tuned lower than cutter drums, and their position—heads tilted away from the drummers and the ground—lengthens its body to lower the pitch further. The *kata* drum, sitting squarely on the ground, delivers the higher-pitched part, and the voice of its head, fixed with a snare (straight pins tied to a string), has a bright, distinctive quality. Though the curved-stick technique associated with Yoruba styles of drumming is prevalent in neighboring islands, a stickless, open-palmed style of performing continues on Carriacou to support demographic information offered by the local classification of songs.

The first song performed is appropriate to the family of the host, who leads a procession of his relatives into the dance ring. He pours jack-iron rum (the national drink, high-proof and powerful), his wife sprinkles water, and other participants scatter corn and rice. In the musical exposition of each piece, the lead singer intones the song, the chorus answers on the second statement, and the drummers enter in staggered succession. The *boulas* enter next, and finally the cutter responds. With the entire ensemble playing, the dancer enters the ring. As the performance progresses, the movement is cyclical, the texture is multilinear, and the style is improvisational.

With the loss of knowledgeable drummers, people who sponsor big-drum celebrations express concern over the survival of the nation rhythms and the indifference of the young to the ritual. Because of this concern and with the goal of perpetuating the idiom, a second troupe was formed, made up of young female students and working women. Though traditional performances were mounted in exchange for offerings of food and rum, these ensembles receive token payments from the hosts of the events at which they perform.

Parang

In contrast to the depth of the social organization of the big drum, men and boys sing *parang* (from Spanish *parranda*) without an obvious formal plan. At Christmastime, they form an ensemble of serenaders, visiting porches and yards for impromptu concerts, receiving gifts and rum in return. Their instruments, the *dup* (cardboard barrel used as bass drum), the biscuit tin, and the *baha* (a 1.5-meter-long cardboard tube aerophone), are disposable. With rough pieces of wood and string, boys imitate the guitar and the *cuatro* (a four-stringed small guitar of Venezuela), usually high-quality, handmade instruments, played by leaders. Some boys who follow older musicians become useful to them; others form their own ensemble.

New *parang,* composed during the year, outline the foibles of antisocial persons. At year's end, these satires are presented in open competition, to the delight of the informed public. Probably functioning in similar ways as the big drum, their texts aim at social control through the process of shaming.

Quadrille

The quadrille, a partner dance deriving from square dances of France and England of the eighteenth century, is still practiced by residents of L'Esterre. It has taken on extensive indigenous meaning and stylistic reinterpretation. One of its movements, the *paisade* (or *huit*), imitates, in name and structure, the in-and-out technique of weaving baskets, used in constructing the frame of wattle-and-daub homes. Buildings aptly called mud or African houses have vanished on Carriacou, but these movements keep the memory of the architecture alive.

Each suite has six musical figures. The first two are English tunes, Scottish jigs, or Irish reels. By an accretive process, the others have come to include selections of merengues, French steps (*passe, castian, paseo*), boleros, polkas, mazurkas, waltzes, traditional Caribbean tunes, modern composed tunes ("Whispering Hope"), and a single big-drum tune ("Congo Malabu").

Today, the quadrille is usually held to celebrate the opening of a new shop, as part of an islandwide festival, or as a private anniversary fête. Carriacouans perform the quadrille with violin, bass drum, large tambourine, and triangle (figure 3). All

FIGURE 3   A quadrille band of Carriacou, Grenada plays (*left to right*) tambourine, violin, bass drum, and triangle. Photo by Lorna McDaniel, 1987.

"Dancing the cake" occurs at weddings, when solo dancers balance the bride's and groom's cakes with their hands over their heads.

musicians play seated. The bass drummer strikes the lower head with a hard stick held in his right hand and strikes the upper head with a soft mallet held in his left hand. The triangle player uses his left hand to hold the triangle and damp the sound, altering the pitch and duration of the tones of his pattern. The tambourinist superimposes bold, multimetric, Africanesque rhythmic statements, treating the large instrument like a solo drum, but striking with palm, fist, and elbow.

Other genres

The lancers, an extinct dance, was popular in the central section of the island, where it was performed to an independent repertoire for violin, guitar, banjo and *cuatro*. Formerly, a quadrille and a lancers was a community affair, hosted by a single family. At the end of each event, a bouquet was tossed and caught to designate the next host for the dance.

"Dancing the cake" occurs at weddings, when solo dancers balance the bride's and groom's cakes with their hands over their heads. A white cake symbolizes the bride, and a taller, tiered, pink cake symbolizes the groom. Despite pelvic windings and gyrations, the dancers safeguard the cakes, assuring the ascendancy of the pink cake, which must always—in local notions of husband-wife relationships—dominate the white cake.

"Fighting the flags," a second dance that occurs at weddings, represents conflict between the bride's and groom's families. Two fighters carry flags, with which they duel; the groom's flag must never be allowed to touch the ground, and after the mock-battle, it must wave, symbolic victory of male supremacy. The music that accompanies these dances is played by any combination of violins, guitars, and banjos.

REFERENCES

Bell, Hesketh J. 1893. *Obeah, Witchcraft, in the West Indies.* London: Sampson, Low, Marsten.

Grenada Free Press and Public Gazette. 1829. 19 June.

Hearn, Lafcadio. 1890. *Two Years in the West Indies.* New York: Harper and Brothers.

Hill, Donald C. 1977. *The Impact of Migration on the Metropolitan and Folk Society of Carriacou, Grenada.* Anthropological papers, 54, part 2. New York: American Museum of Natural History.

McDaniel, Lorna. 1986. "Memory Songs: Community, Conflict and Flight in the Big Drum

Ceremony of Carriacou, Grenada." Ph.D. dissertation, University of Maryland.

Mintz, Sidney, and Richard Price. 1981. *An Anthropological Approach to the Afro-American Past: A Caribbean Perspective.* Philadelphia: Institute for the Study of Human Issues.

Pearse, Andrew. 1956. "The Big Drum Dance of Carriacou." Ethnic Folkways Library FE 4011. LP disk and notes.

Pollak-Eltz, Angelina. 1970. "Shango-Kult und Shouter-Kirche auf Trinidad und Grenada." *Anthropos* 65:814–832.

Redhead, Wilfred. 1985. *A City on a Hill.* Barbados: Letchworth Press.

St. George's Chronicle & New Grenada Gazette. 1790. 2 July, 19 August.

Smith, M. G. 1962. *Kinship and Community in Carriacou.* New Haven and London: Yale University Press.

———. 1963. *The Dark Puritan: The Life and Work of Norman Paul.* Kingston, Jamaica: University of the West Indies.

Guadeloupe

Jocelyne Guilbault

Musical Contexts and Genres
Unity in Diversity

Since 1946, Guadeloupe has been a department of France, and its official language is French, though the most commonly spoken language is Creole (Kwéyòl). Today, its population is about 375,000 persons. The colonization of Guadeloupe, which began in the 1600s, brought together African slaves and European planters and administrators. The 1800s saw the arrival of East Indians, who have played an important role in the local economy. Long ignored by the majority, East Indian musical traditions have recently been acknowledged as a constitutive part of the Guadeloupean heritage. They have yet to be documented.

MUSICAL CONTEXTS AND GENRES

Beginning with the period of colonization, musical practices in the island can be divided into two main groups: *bamboulas*, nocturnal sessions of African dancing by slaves, and soirées, in which masters and their friends performed European regional dances (Bertrand 1968:6). The division between these traditions and the social classes sustaining them did not remain static. The sugar-plantation system introduced the possibility of social mobility among slaves, allowing some to develop close cultural contacts with their masters, who tried to maintain racial and social segregation.

The effect of this situation was twofold: whereas segregation provided most slaves with the conditions necessary for a culture of their own, contact between masters and slaves fostered the emergence of a hybrid cultural system. In the context of segregation and a black majority, this system eventually came under the control of the slave population. As a result, European musical traditions were reinterpreted according to African cultural schemes (Lafontaine 1983:2134–2136).

In Guadeloupe, an observer can clearly tell African-derived musical traditions from European-derived traditions but can also locate shared features, easily establishing family resemblances among them. Yet, for generations, questions of what Guadeloupean music is, and what it is not, have been controversial. Since music is part of the power structure (Rosemain 1986:12) and historically served to control slaves, the definition of Guadeloupean music has always had great political significance for the local population. Appropriated by separatist parties and associated with

A successful *léwòz* requires the partcipation of an audience. If someone in the audience feels inspired and wants to sing, he or she will ask to trade places with the main soloist. Spontaneous exchanges also occur between or among the drummers.

their rejection of colonial influences (and thus of any European-derived music), this controversy, articulated most intensively from the late 1970s to the mid-1980s, has incited local musicologists, journalists, and musical activists to hold public debates about their traditions.

The problem remains: by which criteria does one distinguish between traditional and modern music, and between local and imported music? Everyone agrees that drumming is an essential element of Guadeloupean music. But how to evaluate the local quadrille—as a relic of a European tradition? or as a new reality, with a new local meaning? And the beguine—as a variant of European ballroom dances? Instead of engaging in this debate (which would center more on political orientations than on musical practices), I will examine how musical traditions in Guadeloupe show unity in diversity. Since little research has been done in Désirade and Les Saintes, my description concerns mainly Guadeloupe proper and Marie-Galante.

The *léwòz*

The terms *léwòz* and *gwoka* commonly denote the same musical phenomenon: drumming. For practitioners, however, *léwòz* is the name of a genre, and *gwoka* is the general name of the accompanying drums. The term *léwòz* (*la rose*) itself includes two other realities: the evening during which this genre is performed and one of seven basic rhythms characteristic of the genre.

Originally the *léwòz* was performed outdoors on plantations, just after the workers had received their wages. Since the 1970s, however, it has been adopted by Guadeloupean society at large, and *léwòz* soirées (*swaréléwòz*) organically related to the work cycle have become rarities, replaced by informal meetings of musicians (*kout tanbou* 'drum strokes'). The performance of *léwòz* was formerly associated with specific social functions and meanings that had traits in common with another local tradition, the *balakadri*.

The *léwòz* consists of a series of songs and dances accompanied by *gwoka* drums (*boula* and *makyè*): the *boula* produces the lower sounds and steadily plays the basic rhythmic pattern, and the *makyè* produces a higher pitch and engages in a dialogue with a solo dancer by responding in sound to his or her movements. The performance of *léwòz* used to require one *boula* and one *makyè*; later, it required two *boulas* and one *makyè*; today, it allows a variable number of *boulas*, but only one *makyé*. The *léwòz* often includes other percussive instruments, such as a large hollowed calabash (*chacha*) filled with seeds, and two little hardwood sticks (*bwa*) struck against the side of the drum (figure 1).

The lead singer (*chantè, vokal*), usually male, invariably uses a responsorial form, accompanied by a chorus (*répondè*). The leader, by starting a theme, chooses the basic rhythm. The *boula* begins to play this rhythm, which it maintains until the end of the piece. Only after the *boula* has been playing a while does the *makyè* enter.

Like most local traditional music, the songs of *léwòz* are sung in French Creole.

FIGURE I   A *léwòz* performance. Photo
Christian Géber.

According to the Guadeloupean musician and composer Gérard Lockel, they have a
pentatonic scale without semitones (1981).

Improvisation plays an essential role in performance. While singing familiar
tunes, the leader most often composes lyrics on the spot. The *makyè* improvises
because it reproduces the dancer's movements, which, though based on a series of
defined steps, are mostly improvised.

A successful *léwòz* requires the participation of an audience. To this end, a leader
often invites the crowd to mark the beat by clapping (*fwapé lanmen*). After two or
three songs, to rest or dance a little, he may solicit another singer to perform a song
(*ladjé on mòso*). By the same token, if someone in the audience feels inspired and
wants to sing, he or she will ask to trade places with the main soloist. All these dialogues are integrated with the music and enliven the performance. Spontaneous
exchanges also occur between or among the drummers. The dancing is done mostly
by individuals from the audience.

The *léwòz* as a musical genre is acknowledged to comprise seven basic rhythms:
graj, kaladja, léwòz, menndé, padjanbèl, toumblak, and *woulé*. All these rhythms are
binary, except that of the *woulé*, which closely resembles that of the waltz (Lafontaine
1988:75). People in some parts of Guadeloupe believe the *menndé* and the *padjanbèl*
are new rhythms, wrongly included in the *léwòz*. Nevertheless, everyone agrees that
the performance of a *léwòz* ideally includes, in any order, the *graj*, the *léwòz,* and the
woulé before the other rhythms can be added.

Other traditions related to gwoka *music*

Music at wakes (*vèyé boukousou*) is traditionally performed inside and outside the
deceased's house. The music outdoors, which reaches the greatest number of people,
consists of songs accompanied by human instruments: the drum is replaced by throat
sounds (*bouladjèl* 'mouth drum'). Music accompanied by throat sounds, clapping,
and stamping is called *waka* in the region of Basse-Terre, and *sonora* in Grande-Terre
(Gabali n.d.:45). Most melodies at wakes rely on a scale similar to that of *gwoka*
music (Lafontaine 1988:76).

As in the *léwòz,* a male lead singer usually controls performances during wakes.
He begins songs and introduces responses, which the chorus sings in return. In contrast to the *léwòz,* however, the exchange of singers takes the form of a competition,
during which singers challenge and answer each other, frequently begging the audience for support. The element of play is fundamental to outdoor celebrations, which

include storytelling and riddling. It is conceived as a way to support the afflicted family by helping them to forget their grief and loneliness.

The music performed indoors during wakes follows a different set of rules. The singers outdoors have come on their own, but the singers from indoors, most of whom are women, have been invited. They gather around the coffin, singing canticles for the dead (*kantikamò*) throughout the night. Whether sung or psalmodized, the lyrics are traditionally performed responsorially and are also *konmandé,* led by one person in the same way as songs of the *léwòz* tradition (Rey-Hulman 1988:132). Songs performed outdoors support the mourners, but songs performed indoors invoke the spiritual world, dedicated to the dead.

Music at wakes is performed on the evening and night following the death, and during *vénérés,* the eleventh night after the death. This custom is observed only in certain communities in Marie-Galante.

Work songs and other genres

Work songs, especially common in Marie-Galante, include fishermen's songs, which marked the rhythm of paddling in canoes (Bertrand 1968:14), and farmers' songs (*chants-charrue*), sung to keep the draft animals moving (Rey-Hulman 1988:133). Most lyrics dealt with themes related to the land and current events. To perform these songs, at least two *répondè* were required in addition to the leader, who walked in front of the others.

Stylized games of wrestling (*sovéyan, bènaden, mayolè*), each with a unique repertoire and specific rhythms, traditionally involve two *boula* and one *makyè,* a leader, and a chorus (figure 2). Stylized movements— feigned attacks, rapid turns, carefully paced bodily movements—are a big source of entertainment at festivals. These games were sometimes performed at wakes.

Carnival music (*mizik vidé, mizik a mas*) is cheerful, fast, intense. It includes *mizik a mas a Sen Jan, mizik a mas Vyé Fò,* and *mizik a mas a Kongo.* In addition to their respective responsorial songs and typical rhythms, these musical genres have distinctive percussive instruments (the number varying according to the number of players available). The *mizik a mas a Sen Jan* is accompanied by several large, laced, single-headed, barrel-shaped drums (*tanbou bas a yon fas*) and small, high-pitched drums (*tanbou chan*), both played with sticks; the *mizik a mas Vyé Fò,* by double-headed bass drums (*tanbou bas a dé fas*) played with sticks, a large tambourine (*tan-*

FIGURE 2 A *mayolè* performance. Photo Christian Géber.

FIGURE 3   A quadrille ensemble. *Left to right:* large tambourine, accordion, scraper, lead singer, maracas, triangle, concussion sticks. Photo by Christian Géber.

bou dibas), a *chacha,* and bamboo flutes (often replaced by plastic flutes); the *mizik a mas a Kongo,* by two or three single-headed drums played barehanded (*ka,* also called *gwoka*).

Quadrille-music balls (*balakadri*)

This music, deeply influenced by mid-nineteenth-century European traditions, is played by a set orchestra and includes not only the *quadrille au commandement,* which refers to the instructions (*commandements*) that guide the dancers, but also ballroom dances, such as the beguine (*biguine*), the mazurka, the waltz, and the tango.

Like *léwòz* music, quadrille music can be played during an improvised session or a formal ball. *Balakadri* are held throughout the year, except during Lent. Unlike *léwòz,* they are always held indoors and are organized by associations (called societies).

Quadrille orchestras (figure 3) feature a diatonic button accordion (replaced occasionally by a violin), a guitar, a human voice—that of the *konmandè* (who gives instructions)—and various percussive instruments. The latter predominate, and include *tanbou dibas* (also called *boula*), a scraper (*syak*), a pair of maracas (*malakach* or *chacha*), a *bwa* (described above in relation to the *léwòz,* but here struck against one other), and a triangle. In Marie-Galante, the quadrille typically uses fewer instruments.

The dance has four compulsory figures: *pantalon, lété, lapoul,* and *pastourèl,* with *lété* as final repeat (Lafontaine 1988:77). These figures are performed by four couples arranged in a square. Though the performance of the compulsory figures follows a predetermined choreography, it allows room for individual improvisation. After the compulsory figures, the same dancers optionally perform couple dances. These include at least the beguine, to which two or three other dances (such as the waltz, the polka, and the mazurka) can be added.

The meter of the compulsory figures is binary except for the third figure, played in 6/8 time. Highly syncopated, the melodies (played on an accordion or a violin) use the Western tempered scale. New compositions are constantly added to the standard repertoire.

Many believe that, because almost every member of the younger generation stays away from quadrille-music balls, this music is disappearing. In fact, it has always been a music for people over forty. When younger people did attend a ball, they

Because of its reliance on high technology and its primary existence as a recorded music (few live performances occur), *zouk* differs from any other local music previously produced in Guadeloupe.

FIGURE 4   The rhythmic foundation of the beguine. After Benoit 1993:60.

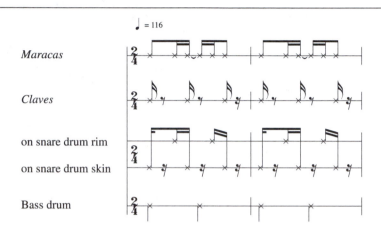

learned, and continued to learn, by observing. A 1988 survey of the number of quadrille societies shows that this tradition is still thriving, especially in rural areas.

Quadrille au commandement is a prime example of the reinterpretation of European traditions, but the beguine stands out as the only ballroom music to have originated in the island. Until the debate brought up by nationalist movements in the late 1970s—which questioned whether the quadrille and the beguine, because of their European influence, should be considered Guadeloupean music at all—the beguine was uncontestedly recognized as the national popular music of Guadeloupe.

Though the origin of the name of the genre (beguine, *biguine, bigin*) remains obscure, the music became internationally famous soon after World War II. The lyrics are sung mostly in French Creole, occasionally in French. The basic rhythm is maintained throughout the piece, whereas the melody, based on a stanza-refrain form, is sometimes sung by the soloist and sometimes played by a saxophone or a trumpet (Benoit 1993:53–67). From the 1940s to the 1980s, ensembles playing beguines varied and included different instruments—in the percussion section, for example, from timbales to bongos to congas, depending on the main influences of the time. In nightclubs, the beguine in the 1960s was typically performed by an orchestra of two trumpets, one alto saxophone, one tenor saxophone, a guitar, a bass, maracas, claves, and a drum set (figure 4). Instrumental improvisation and call-and-response in the accompanimental section are typical. During the 1970s, with the invasion of Haitian popular dance-music (*compas direct*), the beguine lost much of its popularity and has never fully recovered.

UNITY IN DIVERSITY

Balakadri and *léwòz* have similar meanings, social functions, and performative structures. The societies that organize quadrille balls depend on a network of social relations and cooperative support. When participants pay entrance fees for the evening, they write their names in a book so the organizer knows to whom he must return the money when these participants themselves become organizers. The fees hence constitute a loan (*miz*) by which everyone helps the organizer pay expenses and will eventually make a profit.

This system, still operative in quadrille societies, functioned the same way in *léwòz* until the 1980s. But even today, a *kout tanbou* is never solely an entertainment. It follows the same principle: that to receive money, one must spend it. On a structural level, quadrille and *léwòz* are connected: both are based on a series of dances, performed according to a specific order that varies by region.

Through the extensive use of percussive instruments and vocal effects (*bouladjèl* 'syncopation'), all the musical traditions mentioned above feature the preponderance of rhythm over other musical elements. Similarly, improvisation in playing, singing, and dancing is typical.

Zouk

After being invaded by foreign music (Latin and U.S. jazz from the 1940s to the 1960s, and Haitian music for the next twenty years) and while feeling overwhelmed by this invasion, Guadeloupean musicians of the early 1980s succeeded in creating their own music, *zouk* ('party'), which embodies the influences of nationalist movements that in the late 1970s promoted local cultural identity. It is sung in French Creole rather than in French and draws on local rhythms from *mizik vidé* and the beguine, and from Martinican *mizik chouval-bwa* (merry-go-round music), which give the music a distinctive character (Guilbault 1993).

By integrating musical elements from *compas direct,* Trinidadian calypso via Dominican *cadence-lypso* (itself a mixture of *compas direct* and calypso), American funk, and French African *soukous, zouk* reflects influences of the musical genres that have marked local musicians' experience and knowledge. Because of its reliance on high technology and its primary existence as a recorded music (few live performances occur), it differs from any other local music previously produced in Guadeloupe. It has enjoyed a phenomenal success in the Caribbean, Europe, and French Africa.

Its local success must be viewed in relation to important cultural changes that took place locally during the early 1980s. After François Mitterand's election as president of France (1981), the French government decided to reverse thirty-five years of state monopoly and grant licenses for the private operation of radio transmitters. Virtually overnight, twenty-nine stations (*radios libres*) sprang up. Local DJs, eager to boost home-grown products, featured *zouk.*

Recording studios contributed to the rise of the genre. They have had a long history in the island. By the 1960s, Guadeloupe had six studios and a corresponding number of producers, one of whom, Raymond Célini, was the first producer to record traditional music. (From 1966 to 1983, he developed what still constitutes the most important line of commercial recordings of local traditional music.) From the early 1980s, to supply the demand for *zouk,* the studios multiplied their annual production. In parallel, tighter enforcement of copyright laws in the island helped increase the genre's economic success.

For the Guadeloupean music industry, the 1980s were a revolutionary period. With more money at stake and with greater opportunities for success on the transnational market because of *zouk*'s success, the need for greater professionalism and specialization in the music business became an important issue. Youth organizations sponsored workshops on the rights and responsibilities involved in music-related professions. Schools of music grew in number, acquiring a new social meaning in the Antilles.

The development of the Antillean music industry through *zouk* was accompanied by the institutionalization of some artistic practices, and in 1989 the formation of new organizations: Paroliers Musique, the first association of lyricists in Guadeloupe; the Syndicat des Auteurs Compositeurs et des Artistes Musiciens (reorganized); and RCI Productions, the first integrated enterprise for production, distribution, and artist management.

The international success of *zouk* played a major role in the deghettoization of Antillean music on radio. Antillean music is no longer confined to special programs but competes with other international musics on the hit parade. Including women in *zouk* bands helped advertise women's presence in artistic milieus and other marketplaces and hence raised awareness of women's roles in Antillean sociopolitical, cultural, and economic development. All these advancements have played a major role in transforming the status of musician in Guadeloupe into a respected occupation.

REFERENCES

Benoit, Edward. 1993. "Biguine: Popular Music of Guadeloupe (1940–1960)." In *Zouk: World Music in the West Indies,* ed. Jocelyne Guilbault, 53–67. Chicago: University of Chicago Press.

Bertrand, Anca. 1968. "Notes pour une définition du folklore antillais." *Parallèles* 28:5–19.

Clidère, Silvie, ed. 1988. *Les Musiques guadeloupéennes: dans le champ culturel afro-américain, au sein des musiques du monde.* Paris: Éditions Caribéennes.

Gabali, Jocelyn. N.d. *Diadyéé, Gwoka.* Paris: Imprimerie Édit.

Guilbault, Jocelyne, with Gage Averill, Édouard Benoit, and Gregory Rabess. 1993. *Zouk: World Music in the West Indies.* Chicago: University of Chicago Press.

Lafontaine, Céline. 1983. "Le carnaval de l'autre: a propos d'authenticité en matière de musique guadeloupéenne." *Les Temps Modernes* (May): 2126–2173.

———. 1988. "Unité et diversité des musiques traditionelles." In *Les Musiques guadeloupéennes: dans le champ culturel afro-américain, au sein des musiques du monde,* ed. Silvie Clidère, 71–92. Paris: Éditions Caribéennes.

Lockel, Gérard. 1981. *Traité de gro ka modèn: initiation à la musique guadeloupéenne.* Pointe-à-Pitre: Imprimerie Atelier Intégral.

Rey-Hulman, Diana. 1988. "Faiseurs de musique à Marie-Galante." In *Les Musiques guadeloupéennes: dans le champ culturel afro-américain, au sein des musiques du monde,* ed. Silvie Clidère, 115–140. Paris: Éditions Caribéennes.

Rosemain, Jacqueline. 1986. *La musique dans la société antillaise, 1635–1902.* Paris: L'Harmattan.

Haiti

Gage Averill
Lois Wilcken

Neo-African Effects
Traditional Music and Migration
Urban Popular Musics
Musical Style
Musical Education
Music and Public Policy

The earliest known inhabitants of Haiti were the Ciboney, but by 1492, when Columbus arrived, the Arawak had driven them into the southwestern peninsula. Spanish settlers rarely visited the Ciboney, and their fate is unknown. The tools they left say little of their social life and religion, and no musical instruments of their manufacture are known.

Of the Arawak (the first group the Europeans met in Hispaniola), the Taino subgroup was predominant. The Taino used songs to record myths and history, to commemorate the chiefs' marriages and funerals, to tout military victories, and to accompany dancing (Rouse 1948:522–539). Chiefs presided over dances, leading movement and song. Corn beer and snuff fueled Taino *areito* (music and dance events featuring songs that lasted from three to four hours each—or until participants collapsed in exhaustion). Chiefs and their assistants played drums, stone-filled gourd rattles, and castanets made of metal plates, while dancers' kinetic energy generated percussive clattering from strings of snail shells encircling their arms and legs. Songs, drumming, and dances marked an annual procession to the temple to feed the chiefs' sacred stones (*zemi*), and shamans utilized song and sacred rattles in healing.

The Spanish system of exploitation (*repartimiento*) put all male Taino to work in gold mines and on plantations. Many died from overwork and malnutrition, some committed suicide, and others died of smallpox. Fifty years after the Spanish arrived, only a few thousand Taino survived; secure in mountainous retreats, they intermarried with African Maroons (runaway slaves).

Did Taino culture have an impact on that of later Haiti? Linguistic and mythical data may support the argument that some traits of Haitian religion are more readily explained in Arawak than in African terms (Deren 1984:271–286). Early reports of contact between Africans and Taino invite speculation about shared musical concepts and practices. The sacred rattle (*tchatcha,* like a maraca) of the Petro rite of Haitian Vodou probably descended from its Amerindian counterpart. But aside from these traces, Taino culture essentially vanished with its people.

NEO-AFRICAN EFFECTS

As the Taino population waned, the Roman emperor, Charles V, authorized the

Haitians group Vodou songs according to the spirits whom they address, and the songs in a given group may share melodic features, such as scale, contour, and intervallic content.

importation of African slaves. In the late 1600s, with the consolidation of French rule, a period of intense cultivation of sugar ensued, accompanied by a rapid increase in the number of slaves, free blacks, and mulattoes. Neo-African religious groups, particularly in Maroon settlements, raised the political consciousness of the slaves, whose movement led to an uprising in 1791 and independence in 1804. Music and dance were focal points in the religious-political complex.

Despite the role of African belief systems in the Haitian revolution, Roman Catholicism became the state religion. The bourgeoisie's eagerness to appear civilized (à la France), negative international press vis-à-vis Vodou (as the religion came to be called, after a Fon word for "spirit"), and the proselytizing activity of Rome explain the outlawing of neo-African worship in the 1800s. Politico-religious Maroon societies (Sanpwèl, Bizango) trained guerrillas to protect land from seizure by the elite—and, in the 1900s, by U.S. marines.

In the mid-1900s, president-for-life François "Papa Doc" Duvalier (1907–1971) manipulated the ideologies of *négritude* and Vodou to secure power over the masses. In 1986, when his son and successor, Jean-Claude "Baby Doc" Duvalier, fled the country, Vodou priests and priestesses who had openly participated in Duvalierist politics became targets of popular vengeance, and a vitriolic debate between followers of Vodou and Christian leaders ensued. In that climate, the constitution of 1987 became the first to legalize Vodou cults.

The following discussion examines Haiti's neo-African music and dances, with particular attention to Vodou. Because specific African nations (Dahomean, Congolese) became associated with particular geographic niches within colonial Haiti, the regionality of Vodou should be uppermost in the reader's mind. The variety of Vodou discussed below prevails in western Haiti, including Port-au-Prince. Many Haitians maintain that "the real Vodou" is exclusive to rural Haiti, and some believe that Vodou in Port-au-Prince has been commercialized for tourists. The persistence of Vodou in urban Haiti, despite the collapse of the tourist industry in the early 1980s, casts doubt on this claim. In the city, as in the country and in the Haitian diaspora, the structures necessary to Vodou are in place, and Vodou is thus a "vehicle of spiritual, cultural, socioeconomic, and political exchange between urban and rural sectors" (Dauphin 1986:23).

Vodou

Theories and practices of neo-African religion in Haiti (Deren 1984; Métraux 1972) place emphasis on serving the *lwa* (*loa*), a term that comes from a Bantu word for "spirit" (Courlander 1973:19). Devotees acknowledge a supreme being, but only spirits play an active role in human life.

The Vodou *lwa* are organized into nations (*nasyon* in Kwéyòl 'Creole', the dominant language of rural Haiti), corresponding loosely to ethnic groups (of West African and Congolese origin) from which the slaves of colonial Haiti came. Ritual

FIGURE 1 A *manman* drum (the mother drum) used in Rada ceremonies sits in a doorway. Its single cowhide head is fastened into the wooden body with pegs and is struck with a special stick called *agida*. The drum is decorated with the ritual diagram (*vèvè*) for the *lwa* Ezili. Photo by Lois Wilcken.

FIGURE 2 A *baka* drum used in Petro ceremonies leans against the wall of an *ounfò* (inner sanctuary) in Carrefour du Fort, Haiti. Unlike the Rada drum, the Petro goatskin drum has a single head laced to the wooden body and is struck with the hands. The spots painted on this drum serve as protective markings and can also be seen on the wall of the *ounfò*. Photo by Elizabeth McAlister, 1991.

practice evolved in the context of prerevolutionary Haiti, when for the purpose of resistance slaves organized into confederations of nations. The confederative concept is apparent in Vodou rites that salute the national *lwa*. The *lwa* are also associated with natural elements and aspects of human personality: Nagos are known for militancy, Ibos for arrogance, and Kongos for grace and sociability.

The national *lwa* are grouped under two major branches, Rada and Petro. The *lwa* of the Rada branch are cool, beneficent, hierarchical, and formal, and relations between these spirits and their servants are balanced and mutually beneficial (Fleurant 1996). The *lwa* of the Petro branch are hot, aggressive, decentralized, and informal, and they often demand more of their servants than they give.

Music and dance are part of the symbolic web that represents the spirits and calls on them to possess devotees (Wilcken 1992). Dances, songs, percussive patterns, instruments, and performance practices distinguish the nations. Music is most prominent in the evening ceremony (*seremoni* or *dans*), in which a *lwa* may be fed or an individual initiated.

Deren (1984) and Métraux (1972) give details of ritual forms and occasions, personnel, and temples. A priest (*oungan*) or a priestess (*manbo*) officiates over a ceremony, assisted by initiates (*ounsis*) who sing and dance to the accompaniment of a battery of three drums (*manman, segon, boula,* all led by a master drummer) plus a struck iron idiophone (*ogan*). The battery is sometimes embellished by a *bas* or *tanbourin,* a frame drum of low pitch, which keeps a slow pulse. In Rada rites, the priest or priestess keeps time with one type of rattle (*ason*), and then for Petro rites changes to another type (the *tchatcha*). The *poto mitan,* a column in the center of the temple, is a focal point for dancing. The battery is positioned where the master drummer can keep watch over the event.

Vodou percussive instruments intimately interweave to fashion cyclical patterns, in which rhythm and sonority are salient features. A slow pulse, usually defined by the frame drum or the rattle, underlies the patterns, whereas the interrelationships of individual instruments generate a fast pulse. The drums are capable of a range of sonority, colored by the material and construction of the instruments (figures 1 and 2) and controlled by players' techniques. The patterns of *ogan, boula, segon,* and *manman* range from simple to complex, respectively.

Music expresses relationships among the nations, and between the Rada and Petro (Petwo) branches. Figure 3 shows how features of construction, performance, and rhythm are used in accompanying the dances of the major nations. Rada and Nago drums stand out from the others in construction and mode of playing. In Petro dances, the *ogan* plays a 3+3+2 pattern or is embedded in the pattern of the master drum. In a transitional position between Rada and Petro in the ritual order, variously classified by informants, *djouba* (the Vodou dance of the earth *lwa*) shares features of both branches. For playing *djouba,* the drum is laid on the ground and played with hands and feet, because *djouba* spirits live in the earth.

The break (*kase*) of Vodou drumming, a pattern played by the master drummer, cues the dancer to execute a movement also known as a *kase.* Drummers and adepts claim it is an agent of spirit possession. A master drummer is attuned to the kinetics of the ritual. When he sees the onset of possession in an adept, he plays a *kase* to bring the spirit fully to the adept's head. The structure of the master drummer's *kase* is oppositional to the structure of the main pattern. The effect is one of displacement within a continuously cycling pattern.

Haitians group Vodou songs according to the spirits whom they address, and the songs in a given group may share melodic features, such as scale, contour, and intervallic content. A common triadic motif may typify songs for the Rada spirit Ezili Freda (Dauphin 1986:82–83), but more evidence is needed to confirm what the

FIGURE 3 The major nations of the Haitian pantheon, with the types of drumheads, performance techniques, and timeline patterns used for each. Nations are listed from left to right, in ritual order. *Djouba* shares features of Rada and Petro.

Vodou Branches	Rada			Petro			
The major nations	Rada	Nago	Djouba	Petro	Ibo	Kongo	Gede
Drums with cowskin heads	X	X					
Drums with goatskin heads			X	X	X	X	X
Drums played with sticks/hands	X	X					
Drums played with hands only			X	X	X	X	X
Drums have pegged-on heads	X	X					
Drums have laced-on heads			X	X	X	X	X
Drums play 6/12 pulses	X	X	X				
Drums play 8/16 pulses				X	X	X	X
Drums play 3+3+2 patterns				X	X	X	X

experienced listener suspects. The typical scale is anhemitonic pentatonic, but some songs are based on diatonic scales.

Singing is customized to events. To accompany a specific ritual activity, singers exploit the brevity of phrases, the flexibility of responsorial singing, and the possibility of concatenating more than one song. Phrases tend to be two or four *ogan* patterns in length. A priest, a priestess, or a musical specialist (*onjènikon*) sings several phrases, repeated by the chorus of initiates. Before singers change to a new song, they usually alternate the final phrase between soloist and chorus. The number of calls and responses depends on the time necessary to complete whatever ritual action the song accompanies. Many drummers mark with a *kase* the transition from one song to the next.

Vodou and Christianity

Servants of the *lwa* incorporate Christian elements into their practice, not to deceive church authorities but because they believe in the efficacy of these elements (Métraux 1972:358). The Christian constituents of Vodou range from superficial to substantial. Chromoliths of saints (*imaj*), representing *lwa* by virtue of superficial resemblances, synchronize the Christian and the Vodou calendars. The practice of baptism has been incorporated wholesale into Vodou, which baptizes not only servants but all ritual objects as well.

The most striking Christian component of Vodou ceremonies is an opening litany, or *priyè ginen* 'African prayer'. It begins with several Christian songs in French, followed by a long, chanted litany in Creole of saints, and then of Vodou spirits. Steadily intensifying drumrolls accompany it. The officiating priest or priestess leads a prayer and adds a shimmer to the drumrolls by shaking a rattle. The repetition of the chant and the uninterrupted, random percussion keep the congregation in a state of suspense and anticipation, so when the drums break into *yanvalou* (rhythm and dance used in Rada rites) for Legba, the *lwa* who opens the gate to the spirit world, the sense of having arrived is powerful.

TRACK 36

Since the 1930s, Roman Catholic composers have spearheaded a movement to incorporate elements of African-Haitian folklore into their liturgy. In the late 1940s, they began using drums in it, and they worked with Vodou drummers to determine which rhythms were most appropriate to accompany singing in church. In the 1960s, the Second Vatican Council nourished the ideals of their movement. Many folkloric dance companies have been formed under the aegis of local parishes.

Collective labor

Haitians have applied the traditions of collective labor in various contexts, but most notably in agriculture. About 80 percent of the population is rural. Local collective-labor associations have parallels in West Africa (Paul 1962:213–220), and the lack of technological sophistication in the Haitian countryside has fostered the continuity of the associations.

The term *konbit* (possibly deriving from the Spanish *convidar* 'to invite') refers equally to a collective-labor association and to the event it organizes. In some regions, the association is called *sosyete kongo* (Herskovits 1975:70). Most often, the *konbit* meets to till the fields, but it may gather for other activities that benefit from cooperative effort, such as building houses and sorting coffee.

A *konbit* emphasizes music as a propelling force (Courlander 1973:117–118). In the early morning hours, song leaders (*sanba*) and musicians with drums, trumpets, bamboo trumpets (*vaksin*), conch trumpets (*lanbi*), and hoe blades struck with stones signal the *konbit*; they continue to accompany the labor of the day. The leaders and workers sing responsorially. Some songs are old, but newly invented texts use topical material. The rhythms derive from rural dances, including *djouba*. The traditional *konbit* culminates in singing, dancing, and drinking—a party centered on a meal prepared by women. Regional variations of collective-labor parties exist (Paul 1962:205–213).

Secular Songs

Secular songs constitute a major part of Haiti's musical traditions. The composer of the folkloric song is a *sanba* (the same term applied to the song leader of the *konbit*). Haitians classify folkloric songs by social rather than aural criteria. One collector (Dauphin 1981) classifies children's songs by scalar structure, using the Kodály method. Haitian children who grow up with this repertoire identify everyday, calendrical, and occasional songs. A French influence is more pronounced in children's songs than in other categories of folkloric song, possibly because they are diffused by schools in urban and suburban areas (Paul 1962:42).

Songs of social sanction complain of adultery, abuse, duplicity, and so on. Others feature gossip. Many, utilizing Vodou rhythms and melodies, may stem from possession in the Vodou temple (Paul 1962:42–43). This category also incorporates political commentary (Courlander 1973:148–162) typical of *rara* processionals.

Rara

Rara is a seasonal ritual of the countryside (and of lower-class urban neighborhoods). It begins after carnival and builds to its conclusion on Easter weekend (*Caribbean Revels* 1991). Membership in the processional bands (*bann rara*) may be coterminous with membership in a Vodou temple, a secret society, or residence in a particular neighborhood or extended-family compound (*lakou*). The bands demonstrate a widespread African- American predilection for intricate social hierarchies in carnivalesque celebrations that mimic military, governmental, and royal hierarchies. A typical roster might include

1. A *mèt* or *pwezidan*: the "owner" (sometimes a Vodou priest), who made a "promise" to the *lwa* to organize a *rara*.
2. A *kòlonèl*: the director, who carries a whip and a whistle (ritual media, also used by the second in command—the *laplas*—in a Petro ceremony) (figure 4). Both items are rich in symbolic content. Under slavery, the whip was a symbol of power; in *rara*, it has spiritual significance. As in some Petro ceremonies, it dispels malevolent *lwa* and purifies the secular space through which the band will

Rara also has secular features, including an exuberant and sensual celebratory ethos, plus usually topical, bawdy, critical, and allusive musical texts. However, the ritual fulfills an important sacred duty and is connected to issues of life, death, and rebirth.

FIGURE 4   In Léogane, Haiti, *majò jòn* (*center,* a twirler) and *kòlonèl* (*left of center,* the director, with a whip around his neck) lead a *rara* procession. Photo by Elizabeth McAlister, 1991.

pass. The *kolonèl* must disperse spiritual charms (*zanm kongo*) or powders (*poud*), left by other groups to *kraze* 'break, disorganize' the *rara*.

3. *Majò jòn:* twirlers who handle and throw batons, dance, and honor important members of the group and onlookers (figure 4). In the south, they typically wear sequined vests, aprons, short pants with scarves tucked into their belts, sun glasses, baseball caps, and tennis shoes. In the north, the hats tend to be more decorative, and other aspects of the costuming differ. Colors, designs, and banners can represent the group's patron *lwa.* Many groups annually make these outfits and banners anew, only to destroy them after the *rara* season.

4. *Renn:* 'queens' who wear fancy dresses (often red), parade, dance, and collect money for the band.

FIGURE 5   A *vaksin* (single-note bamboo trumpet) player in the *rara* band Modèle d'Haïti in Léogane, Haiti. Photo by Elizabeth McAlister, 1991.

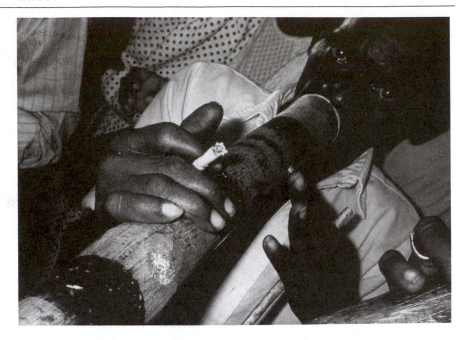

Rara also has secular features, including an exuberant and sensual celebratory ethos, plus usually topical, bawdy, critical, and allusive musical texts. However, the ritual fulfills an important sacred duty and is connected to issues of life, death, and rebirth. *Rara* bands are dedicated to *lwa* such as those from the Petro or the Gede families. Bands "incorporate" during Gede days (around Halloween and All Souls Day) or just after carnival and hold ceremonies to consecrate the band and its instruments. For the *lwa,* they draw maize symbols (*vèvès*) on the ground; they sing and pray for the band's protection. In the *peristil* (an open area for dance in a temple), a band will put to sleep (*kouche*) its musical instruments and batons—a ritual also performed for Vodou drums. Most processional activity occurs at night, with the temple as a point of origin. Because the *rara* traverses public roads and cemeteries, bands invoke *lwa* such as Baron Samdi, Papa Gede (ruler of cemeteries), or Legba (guardian of gateways and crossroads).

🎵 TRACK 37   The musical ensembles that accompany *rara* feature *vaksin* 'bamboo trumpets' (figure 5) and flared *kònè* 'tin horns' (figure 6). Individual pitches on different trumpets interlock in short melodic-rhythmic ostinati. As they are blown, these instruments are struck on their sides with sticks to produce a timeline (*kata*). They are accompanied by *tanbou petro* and *kongo* (single-headed, hand-beaten drums), *kès* (double-headed, stick-beaten drums), frame drums, *graj* (metal scrapers), metal trumpets, *tchatchas,* tin rattles, and other instruments (see Okada 1995: example 11).

Staged folklore

The issue of Haitian cultural identity has been strongly contested since early in the U.S. occupation (1915–1934). During the 1940s, the government institutionalized *négritude* and created the Bureau of Ethnology. New possibilities for the expression of Haitian identity precipitated a folkloric movement. The tourist market also stimulated the development of folkloric companies and their repertoire. In 1949, the intersection of these internal and external forces led to the creation of a government-backed ensemble, La Troupe Folklorique Nationale.

Folkloric companies spotlight dancers, a drum ensemble modeled after the Vodou battery, and a chorus. In choreographies based on carnival and *rara* dances,

FIGURE 6 *Kònè* 'tin horn' players in the *rara* band Vodoule of Port-au-Prince, Haiti, with several *vaksin* in the background. Photo by Gage Averill, 1995.

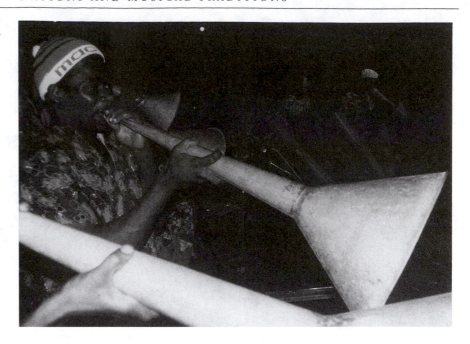

extra players provide the requisite winds and percussion. Folkloric costumes are stylized imitations of peasant clothing. Dances are associated with Vodou, carnival, *rara* festivals, and *konbit*. Dances of European origin (waltz, lancers, polka) are sometimes choreographed as part of an *afranchi* 'freed slave' segment, but staged folklore emphasizes the Africanness of Haiti's past.

The choreography elaborates and varies the basic movements of a given dance and utilizes *vèvè* designs on the floor. Dancers and choreographers continually spin out variations of source material. The master drummer creates accompanying patterns that bind sound and movement. The music on stage is further distinguished from its sources in its use of the *kase*. During a Vodou ritual, the drummer decides when to play a *kase,* and he bases his decision on the psychosocial dynamics in progress. In staged folklore, the points of *kase* are fixed during rehearsal.

Staged folklore replaces the open-ended structures and religious function of Vodou drumming with predetermined forms that function as entertainment. It introduces the notion of *vèvè*; however, it maintains the instrumentation and the songs of its sources. Though the function of the *kase* changes, its form stays intact. Dance, though elaborated, maintains its centrality and—with music and costuming—projects a selected cultural identity.

TRADITIONAL MUSIC AND MIGRATION

Since the Duvaliers came into power, about one million Haitians have emigrated. Haitians in the diaspora tend to cluster in urban neighborhoods, where they seek mutual support. Music and dance can be a means of recreating the familiar and strengthening the support system.

Haitian immigrants include Vodou priests, priestesses, initiates, and drummers. Some have established societies with stable memberships; others fulfill their obligations to the *lwa* as they wait to accumulate the capital to return to Haiti and build temples there. To insure privacy, practitioners often conduct their rituals in basements. Because space is limited, they can only rarely dance around a *potomitan*. In such enclosed spaces, the drumming sometimes overwhelms the singing. Despite these limitations, spirit possession occurs, servants find joy in the rituals, and they pass the repertoire on to their diaspora-born children.

Throughout the 1970s, folk-dance companies appeared regularly in Haitian festivals in New York; but in the 1980s, performances for Haitian audiences declined. Haitian folklore found a more receptive audience among outsiders. Meanwhile, a popular music that incorporated folkloric elements into a commercial framework won Haitian listeners. Both phenomena suggest that the cultural isolation of Haitians in the diaspora was diminishing.

URBAN POPULAR MUSICS

In the early 1800s, peasants fled plantations and established homesteads in inaccessible rural hinterlands, escaping federal oppression and reestablishing neo-African practices of settlement and agriculture. The elite settled in Port-au-Prince and a few small provincial cities, where they managed the country's political system and dominated its economy.

Like *rara,* many ostensibly rural genres made the transition to urban Haiti. Parties (*bambòch*) held in makeshift thatched huts (*tonèls*) in poorer neighborhoods, Vodou ceremonies in family compounds, *rara* bands in carnival, and Christian religious music—all resemble their rural counterparts. As in most of the world (including countries without highly developed industrial sectors), a particularly urban music of syncretic origins depends, for form and coherence, on urban dance contexts, middle- and upper-class patronage, foreign influences, the recording industry, and broadcast media.

Poverty, the gulf between the social classes, and the separation of city and countryside have had important consequences for Haitian urban popular music. Low incomes (in 1997, about U.S. $300 per capita annually) have made development of a highly capitalized music industry impossible. Instead, small businessmen predominate, there is little in the way of development or promotion, and producers focus on short-term gain. For sales, musicians rely on markets in the French Antilles, the American diaspora, and France (Averill 1993). Despite undercapitalization and a depressed market, hundreds of aspiring commercial bands struggle for success. The economics of Haitian music have worked against widespread penetration of foreign-music markets and have kept the technology and standards of recording and performance lagging behind international pop.

Though urban musics are produced in urban areas and disseminated through urban-based media, their impact is felt nationwide. Radio blankets all areas of Haiti, and most Haitians have access to it in some form or another. Because the majority of Haitians are illiterate and more than sixty stations broadcast within the country, radio is critical as a source of news and cultural information. As Haiti urbanizes and children of peasants move to the cities, more and more families have personal connections to the urban environment.

In the early 1900s, urban Haitians gathered at public dances, *douz edmi* ('twelve and a half,' from the men's price of admission in centimes). The standard ensemble for these events was *òkès bastreng,* a French-style string and wind ensemble. After 1945, Port-au-Prince had a lively calendar of *gran bals* for elite classes in hotels, restaurants, and private clubs (such as the Cercle Bellevue and Portauprincienne). Many hotels and restaurants sponsored orchestras such as the Ensemble Riviera, the Ensemble Ibo Lélé, and the Ensemble Aux Calabasses. Nighttime dances (*sware*) took place in *boîtes de nuit* and clubs. At prostitutes' balls (*bal bouzen*) in the brothels of Carrefour, patrons danced with prostitutes to live or recorded music. A type of dance known as *kèmès* grew out of the bazaars and family socials that followed religious ser-

For excitement and impact on commercial music, no single urban event in Haiti can compete with carnival. Since the 1950s, electrified *konpa* bands on floats with massive speakers have dominated the event.

vices in church on Sunday afternoons; eventually, the word *kèmès* came to mean any early afternoon or early evening concert.

For excitement and impact on commercial music, no single urban event in Haiti can compete with carnival. An informal carnival had taken place since colonial times. In addition to commercial and governmental floats, there are always large, popular masques, including *batonyè* 'stick dancers', *trese riban* 'maypole dancers', *chaloska* 'a spoof of military officers' (named after General Charles Oscar), *gwo tèt* 'large heads' (fashioned after famous politicians), *djab* 'devils', *Endyèn Madigra* 'Mardi Gras Indians', and many others.

At carnival, percussion and vocal bands (and many *rara* bands) provided acoustic processional music; but since the 1950s, electrified *konpa* bands on floats with massive speakers have dominated the event. *Mereng koudyay* (or *mereng kanaval*), a genre of fast, marchlike *konpa* similar to the *biguine vidé* of Martinique and the *samba enredo* of Brazil, has developed as the typical carnival rhythm, the basis for the annual competition for best song at carnival.

In 1949, on the waterfront, as part of a bicentennial celebration of the capital, the Théâtre Verdure was built. It was home to weekly concerts of the orchestra Jazz des Jeunes, which accompanied the Troupe Folklorique Nationale. Rebuilt and renamed (Théâtre National), it is used for large concerts. Other concerts take place in movie theaters. In the 1960s, Sunday concerts at movie theaters in Port-au-Prince became a major venue for emerging student *mini-djaz* groups. Gala concerts, featuring a mix of folk-dance troupes, romantic singers, dance bands, and comedians, are held there. In the diaspora, this type of concert (*spèktak*, or *gala*) is popular with well-to-do Haitians.

In the summer, a period of many patronal festivals (*fèt patwonal*), urban bands tour the countryside. The festivals feature ceremonies in church, roving troubadour groups (*twoubadou*), dances under the arbor (*anba tonèl*), and food and drink sold on the street.

Media and the Recording Industry

The first radio station in Haiti, Radio HHK, went on the air in 1927 as a project of the U.S. Marines. In general, however, radio remained a toy of the wealthy until after 1945. A private station, Radio HH3W (later 4VRW, Radio d'Haïti), was launched in 1935; after 1945, it began a series of live *radio-théâtres* from the Ciné Paramount, and eventually from its broadcast-studio auditorium. Radio d'Haïti, owned by Ricardo Widmaier, was the site of the first recordings made in Haiti. In 1937, Widmaier issued a limited-edition recording of Jazz Duvergé, but Joe Anson's label, called Ibo Records, made the first commercial Haitian recordings, beginning with the Ensemble Aux Calabasses in the mid-1950s.

The most active Haitian labels have been a series of four companies based in the diaspora but recording and marketing in Haiti and the diaspora, starting with Ibo

Records. In the mid-1960s, Marc Duverger's Marc Records produced recordings of many *mini-djaz* and larger orchestras. In the 1970s, Fred Paul's Mini Records became the largest producer of Haitian records and sponsored an ensemble, Mini All Stars. Others have produced recordings but mostly as a sideline.

In Haiti, sales of five thousand are considered respectable. Outside the country, especially in the diaspora and in the French Antilles, Haitian artists have done much better. By exploiting the global market through tours and agreements with French labels, some have sold more than fifty thousand albums.

In the 1970s, the pirate-cassette industry dominated the production of music within the country. Record stores marketed copies of legitimate recordings and unauthorized recordings of live concerts. Similar cassettes were sold on the streets. By all estimates, the cheap cassettes (U.S. $2 to $5 typically) vastly outsold the approved ones. In the 1980s, the Haitian music industry typically produced fifty to eighty albums a year.

In 1989, Haitian producers began to market compact discs of current releases and selected previous releases. Few in Haiti itself own CD players, and the Haitian industry is converting only slowly and cautiously to the CD format. Since 1988, many artists with hit records have released videos for Haitian television programs, Creole-language programs in the United States, and programs on French and French-language stations in West Africa and the French Antilles. In the 1990s, musicians such as Emeline Michel and the *mizik rasin* group Boukman Eksperyans have secured international recording contracts.

Many Haitian performers belong to SACEM, the French society of musicians and composers. In 1995 Haiti became a signatory nation of the Berne Convention governing intellectual property.

Commercial genres and ensembles

The Haitian elite traditionally patronized the *mereng-lant* 'slow *méringues*' played by pianists or chamber ensembles (Fouchard 1988). After the popularity of North American jazz in urban Haiti in the 1930s, jazz bands began to arrange *méringues* too. The *méringue* was also performed by troubadour (*twoubadou*) groups—small guitar and percussion bands, patterned after the Cuban *son* trios and quartets (figure 7).

In Port-au-Prince and Cap Haïtien, an influx of tourists after World War II

FIGURE 7 A hotel-style *grenn siwèl* or *twoubadou* ensemble performs *méringues* with *baka* drum, *malinba*, guitars, and maracas. Photo by Steve Winter, 1989.

helped support hotel- and casino-based *méringue* orchestras, such as the Orchestre Casino Internationale. In response to the *négritude* movement and its mandate to develop indigenous forms of popular culture, bands experimented with Vodou rhythms. The most famous of these bands was Jazz des Jeunes, pioneers (after 1943) of the genre *mereng-vodou* or *vodou-jazz*. In this fusion, the instrumentation resembles that of Cuban big bands with the addition of Vodou drums, but the melodic contours, rhythms, and texts come from Vodou and peasant dances. *Négritude* also influenced the composition of art music (*mizik savant*) by Haitian composers, resulting in the production of a corpus of nationalist, Vodou, and merengue-inspired concert pieces, such as Justin Elie's *Fantasie Tropicale* and Werner A. Jaegerhuber's *Complaintes Haïtiennes* (Dumervé 1968; Largey 1991).

In the mid-1950s, the saxophonist Nemours Jean-Baptiste and his ensemble began to restructure the popular Dominican *merengue perico ripiao* or *merengue cibaeño* to produce the *konpa-dirèk* (French *compas direct*), or simply *konpa*. Within a few years, they had established it as Haiti's first commercially successful dance music. The saxophonist and bandleader Wébert Sicot had created a nearly identical dance called *kadans ranpa* (French *cadence remparts*, originally creolized as *rempas*). The contest between these genres and bands enlivened Haitian music for a decade; theirs was the first music to be widely distributed in Haiti on records (78-rpm disks; later, long-playing disks). From their positions on floats, these bands dominated carnival with amplified music.

A younger generation of middle-class boys who played imported rock and roll, locally called *yeye* (from "yeah, yeah, yeah," a refrain by the Beatles), picked up *konpa* and *kadans*. Their *konpa-yeye* hybrid ensembles became known as *mini-djaz*, a term that distinguished them from big bands—and made an analogy with an English term first used in 1965: "miniskirt," the name of a women's fashion style. Instrumentation consisted of two electric guitars, electric bass, conga, bell-and-tom, and tenor saxophone; keyboards and accordions were occasionally added. Groups like Shleu-Shleu, Les Ambassadeurs, Les Fantaisistes de Carrefour, and Les Loups Noirs played in the mid-to-late 1960s at movie theaters for Sunday concerts, student parties, and the like. The most popular bands began to record after 1967. Within a few years, many had emigrated to the United States to perform for Haitian audiences in the diaspora. By 1974, Shleu-Shleu, Tabou Combo, Skah Shah, Volo Volo, Magnum Band (figure 8), and others had become established abroad; they entertained nostalgic émigrés and provided a social context for community gatherings. This was also a period in which Haitian groups became popular in the French Antilles, where they helped spark a *kadans* movement.

In the 1970s, *mini-djaz* borrowed instrumental resources from Caribbean dance bands of Trinidad, Dominica, and Martinique, adding drum sets, extra wind instruments, and finally synthesizers. By the late 1970s, they were no longer so mini: an average band had about twelve or thirteen members.

In the late 1970s and 1980s, more and more Haitian bands and performers—such as Manno Charlemagne, Les Frères Parent, Ti-Manno (Roselin Antoine Jean-Baptiste), and Farah Juste—took part in opposing the Duvalier dictatorship; they produced *mizik angaje* 'politically committed music'. Frustration with a perceived stagnation in popular musics and the search for post-Duvalier cultural forms resulted in new musical directions. A youthful technological-music movement (the *nouvèl jenerasyon* 'new generation') and *mizik rasin,* a neotraditonal music (mixing Vodou, *rara,* and electrified commercial pop), emerged (Averill 1997).

Gender, age, and class in Haitian music

In the production of urban and commercial musics, men are much more in-

FIGURE 8 The *konpa* guitarist Alix "Dadou" Pasquet performs with his Magnum Band at Le Chateau nightclub in the Carrefour District. Photo by Gage Averill, 1989.

volved than women, and the contexts for the urban consumption of music—bars, clubs, even *tonèls*—are frequented more by men than by women. Partly because many Haitians consider unattached women who frequent such establishments disreputable, the number of women who play or sing in commercial bands is negligible. Women have, however, achieved success as patriotic, political, and romantic singers.

Mini-djaz emerged as a phenomenon of youth: an expression of school-age, middle-class boys in Port-au-Prince and a handful of cities in Haiti. The most fervent fans aged with the musicians who invented the genre; by 1995, the bulk of them had reached their forties. The *nouvel jenerasyon* was a reaction to this situation by a younger audience. Musical hits serve as markers of personal and collective history, and older audiences in Haiti and in the diaspora tend to be conservative about the musics that accompanied and helped define their adolescence. A striking change is evident among Haitian teenagers in the diaspora, who readily adopt African-American subcultural norms, disparaging less-acculturated Haitian immigrants as newcomers. Rap and Jamaican-style ragga (dance-hall style of chanting) have become popular among immigrants of this age.

Haitian urban genres carry associations of class, but few genres are exclusive in this way. Most genres appeal to more than one social class, and genres can be subdivided by differences in style that subtly articulate class origins and affiliations. Mediating against a mechanical linkage between style and class is the potential for symbolic upward and downward social mobility through music. Indigenous movements in popular music (*vodou-jazz* and *mizik rasin*) effectively reach downward in class symbolism, aligning musicians and audiences with aspects of peasant or lower-class culture. Music also serves as a means for musicians to socialize with members of elite classes, though this socialization usually occurs within the context of musical employment.

MUSICAL STYLE

Haitian popular music is structured along principles common to many African-Caribbean urban musics. Multiple percussive instruments of different sonorities and pitch levels interact to form a cyclical pattern. In *konpa,* certain melodic instruments play ostinati that articulate changes of chords, and others serve as solo instruments. Harmonic progressions are variable, but most dance sections settle down to a two-chord pattern, often V–I (the tonic is often minor). Most songs begin with an instrumental introduction, progress to a lyrical song section, and end with an ostinato-dominated "groove section," featuring short, responsorial vocals.

Haitians base aesthetic judgments on the singers' vocal quality, the "sweetness" of the overall sound, the subtlety of timing in the rhythm section, but more than any single feature, the degree to which the band moves an audience and creates the proper ambience: *cho* 'hot' for certain occasions, *tèt kole* 'cheek-to-cheek' for others. At large, outdoor events, audiences prefer music that is lively, that gets an audience *anty-outyout* 'carried away' or *anraje* 'worked up'—music with which to *mete de men nan lè* 'put one's hands in the air'. At clubs, the music accompanies close *konpa* dancing, often *kole-kole* 'glued together' or *ploge* 'plugged' together.

Urban commercial music has become nearly ubiquitous in the soundscape of Haitian cities. On cassette and on radio, it provides background music in stores, in restaurants, and on public transportation. On radio and television, it sells commercial products and candidates for public office. Because most Haitians cannot read, urban popular musics serve as part of the technology of advertising, promotion, education, and information.

"Papa Doc" Duvalier's government and his private militia (Tonton Macoutes) commissioned pieces from *konpa* bands and *mini-djaz,* promoted the groups at carnival, and hired them for private parties.

MUSICAL EDUCATION

Formal musical training in Haiti was hard to get. Schooling was reserved for children of the elite, some of whom continued their studies in France or the United States. As part of a French-influenced upbringing, trained musicians provided private lessons for upper-class children. Training was also provided to immediate members of families; and for this reason (until about 1950), parlor, orchestral, and dance-band music was the primarily the province of a limited number of families. Members of other classes could develop musicianship in military brass bands (*fanfa* 'fanfares'), and could parlay their skills into a position with a *meringue* band when they left the armed services. Bandleaders disproportionately came from musical families and brass bands, because it was they who had mastered solfège, a mark of literate musicians. With expansion of religious and public education for the middle classes, musical education became somewhat democratized, though the lack of money, teachers, and instruments marginalized the process. A few *lycées* (equivalent to high schools), such as the Lycée Pétion and the Lycée Saint Louis de Gonzague, have brass bands, and the episcopal school L'Ecole Ste. Trinité has a full orchestra. The main fare for these programs consists of European-American classical music, supplemented by Haitian "autochthonous-school compositions," but some students play jazz or Haitian popular music on their own.

Schools and churches typically have choirs, which serve as another training center for musicians, especially female vocalists. Most women in commercial folk music and popular music received training in religious choirs. Little instruction in anything resembling Haitian traditional music takes place outside of the ethnology program at the Université de l'État (state university).

MUSIC AND PUBLIC POLICY

In 1949, Haiti's first major tourist-oriented extravaganza, the bicentennial of Port-au-Prince, employed folkloric music-and-dance groups. It began a long tradition of government-sponsored performances of these groups, under administrations of varying political ideologies. Many *négritude*-influenced musicians supported "Papa Doc" Duvalier's quest for the presidency and composed folkloric songs in his praise. But the bulk of Duvalier patronage and promotion went to the *konpa* groups, whose popularity was more or less coterminous with his. His government and his private militia (Tonton Macoutes) commissioned pieces from *konpa* bands and *mini-djaz,* promoted the groups at carnival, and hired them for private parties. In addition, local political rallies were considered incomplete without local *konpa* bands or *rara* groups to enliven the occasion and to create an effervescent, *koudyay* 'carnival-like' ambience.

Duvalier's son, "Baby Doc," ardently admired *mini-djaz*; under his rule, as part of an effort to promote a new, more modern, middle-class image of Haiti, these groups received government patronage and commissions. In post-Duvalier Haiti, political instability precluded an active governmental policy toward music, though in 1988 there was a brief appointment of a minister of culture.

The years under de facto military rule (1991–1994) produced a deepening of the gulf between musicians who supported President Jean-Bertrand Aristide (a Roman Catholic priest and proponent of liberation theology, himself a guitarist and songwriter) and those who favored the military and its supporters. Aristide's election (1990) and the restitution of civilian government (1994) inspired some *angaje* 'politically engaged musicians' to participate in the political process as candidates for elected office and advisers to the government—one of whom, Manno Charlemagne, was elected mayor of Port-au-Prince in 1995.

REFERENCES

Averill, Gage. 1993. "'Toujou Sou Konpa': Issues of Change and Interchange in Haitian Popular Dance Music." In *Zouk: World Music in the West Indies,* ed. Jocelyne Guilbault with Gage Averill et al., 68–89. Chicago: University of Chicago Press.

———. 1997. *A Day for the Hunter, a Day for the Prey: Popular Music and Power in Haiti.* Chicago: University of Chicago Press.

Caribbean Revels: Haitian Rara and Dominican Gaga. 1991. Recordings by Verna Gillis. Notes by Gage Averill and Verna Gillis. Smithsonian Folkways SF 40402. LP disk.

Courlander, Harold. 1973. *The Drum and the Hoe: Life and Lore of the Haitian People.* Berkeley: University of California Press.

Dauphin, Claude. 1981. *Brit kolobrit: Introduction Méthodologique Suivie de 30 Chansons Enfantiles Haïtiennes.* Québec: Editions Naaman de Sherbrooke.

———. 1986. *Musique du Vaudou: Fonctions, Structures et Styles.* Sherbrooke: Editions Naaman.

Dumervé, Etienne Constantin Eugene Moise. 1968. *Histoire de la Musique en Haïti.* Port-au-Prince: Imprimerie des Antilles.

Deren, Maya. 1984. *Divine Horsemen: The Living Gods of Haiti.* London and New York: Thames and Hudson. New Paltz, N.Y.: McPherson & Co.

Fleurant, Gerdès. 1996. *Dancing Spirits: Rhythms and Rituals of Haitian Vodun, the Rada Rite.* Westport, Conn.: Greenwood Press.

Fouchard, Jean. 1988. *La Méringue, Danse Nationale d'Haïti.* Port-au-Prince: Editions Henri Deschamps.

Herskovits, Melville. 1975. *Life in a Haitian Valley.* New York: Octagon Books.

Largey, Michael. 1991 "Musical Ethnography in Haiti: A Study of Elite Hegemony and Musical Composition." Ph.D. dissertation, Indiana University.

Métraux, Alfred. 1972. *Voodoo in Haiti.* New York: Schocken Books.

Okada, Yuki. 1995. *The Caribbean.* JVC Smithsonian Folkways Video Anthology of Music and Dance of the Americas, 4. Montpelier, Vt.: Multicultural Media. VTMV-228. Video.

Paul, Emmanuel. 1962. *Panorama du Folklore Haitien: Présence africaine en Haïti.* Port-au-Prince: Imprimerie de l'Etat.

Rouse, Irving. 1948. "The Arawak." In *The Circum-Caribbean Tribes,* ed. Julian H. Steward, 507–546. Handbook of South American Indians, 4. Washington, D.C.: U.S. Government Printing Office.

Wilcken, Lois E., featuring Frizner Augustin. 1992. *The Drums of Vodou.* Tempe, Ariz.: White Cities Media.

Yih, David. 1995. "The Music of Haitian Vodou." Ph.D. dissertation, Wesleyan University.

Jamaica
Olive Lewin

In 1494, when Christopher Columbus on his second voyage to the New World came to Jamaica, he found it inhabited by Arawak Indians. These people did not long survive Spanish colonization. Research has provided us with artifacts and knowledge of their era, but it has not unearthed evidence of their musical culture. As the Arawak work force diminished (mainly from overwork and introduced diseases to which they had little or no resistance), the Spanish began augmenting these laborers by importing slaves from Africa. By the mid-1600s, the Arawak had virtually been eliminated.

In 1655, a British expedition captured Jamaica from the Spanish. Before fleeing the island, the Spanish released their slaves, many of whom took to the mountains and became known as Maroons. During the ensuing years, the British established large sugarcane plantations with the continued use of African slave labor. Some laborers were already in the system; others were imported. All were encouraged to produce children, who automatically inherited their parents' status as slaves.

The Emancipation Act of 1 August 1834 freed all children born after that date and slave children under six years of age. Other slaves became apprentices for varying lengths of time. All were completely free by 1 August 1838. Not all freed Africans—by this time considered Jamaicans—chose to work on plantations, and missing workers had to be replaced. This was done by bringing in indentured laborers, first Central Africans, then (East) Indians, Chinese, and people from Britain. In 1995, according to the governmental census, 76 percent of Jamaicans were of African descent, and 18 percent more of African mixed with European or Asian.

Laborers on plantations could not communicate in their masters' languages, a situation that was to the masters' advantage. Africans had in most cases come from societies in which oral tradition accounted for most learning. Circumstances in Jamaica therefore dictated the development or the continuation of oral traditions in the arts and culture.

MUSICAL INSTRUMENTS

Because of Jamaica's ethnic diversity and dependence on the oral tradition in its cultural development, many musical instruments are found.

Idiophones

Many idiophones are used, with or without voices, in the performance of Jamaican traditional music. Until the 1940s, most of these instruments were handmade or improvised from available materials and items. Maracas, locally called shakkas, were and still are made from dried calabashes with seeds put inside and fitted with wooden handles. The long, dry seed pod of the poinciana tree is sometimes substituted.

The rhumba box, still used in village bands, could be described as a bass *mbira* (similar to the *marímbula* in Cuba and the *marimba* or *marímbola* in the Dominican Republic). Borrowed from the kitchen is the grater, stroked by a large nail or old spoon in syncopated rhythmic patterns or continuously in the manner of a tambourine tremolo. Triangles are made from metal rods bent by heating, or are bought from music shops. Here, too, a large nail serves to beat continuous sounds. If the spirit moves a bystander at a traditional event, he or she is welcome to join in the performance by using a stone, a key, or any such object to tap a striker bell or an empty glass bottle.

In most traditional bands, whether playing for religious or secular purposes, male percussionists predominate. Only occasionally does a woman play a drum, though she may be an expert grater, triangle, tambourine, or maracas player. Clapping, stamping, snapping the fingers, and even thumping the chest sometimes augment percussive sounds with variations of rhythm and pitch. Maroon bands sometimes include a stick, called *aboso,* beaten intermittently against the side of a drum being played; the *kwat,* a length of bamboo, beaten with two sticks; and an *adawo,* a machete, struck with a piece of metal. East Indians in Jamaica make frequent and widespread use of an instrument they call *mangera,* metal cymbals about 10 to 14 centimeters wide.

Membranophones

The drum inherited from Africa is the most significant musical instrument in traditional Jamaican culture. Names and styles of playing vary according to the history of the groups that make and use drums. Dimensions of traditional drums of pre-twentieth-century origin were decided according to the sound produced by various woods in different states of porosity, age, and dryness, rather than by measurements.

The Maroons regard their drums, the *prenting* and the *goombeh,* as having great historic significance for the part they played with the *abeng* (a cow horn) in passing messages and helping to liberate their people from British oppression in 1839.

The *prenting,* a long, cylindrical drum, may be accompanied by a *kwat* and the *adawo.* The *goombeh* is a square goatskin frame drum, tuned with a second wooden frame under the skin. When the correct pitch is achieved, the *goombeh* is seasoned with white rum. *Goombeh* and *prenting* are played with the fingers. *Goombeh* rhythms are quick and sharp. Heavy-pulsed additional patterns are provided by two cylindrical drums, played with unpadded sticks.

Some Maroons also use the *grandy,* similar to the *prenting* and the *goombeh;* the Maroons of Scott's Hall call their cylindrical drums *monkey* and *saliman.* They consider the *goombeh* (or *saliman*) male and the *grandy* (or *monkey*) female.

The Kumina cult includes beliefs and life-styles that are known to have been brought to Jamaica by indentured laborers from the Congo area of Africa in the 1840s. One historian, H. O. Patterson (1973), however, states that it existed in Jamaica as early as 1730. He quotes from *New History of Jamaica* (Leslie 1740), which mentions Dahomean ancestral beliefs and practices of the Kumina cult.

The *goombeh* drum of the Maroons from Accompong Town is normally used only once a year, to celebrate the birthday of Cudjoe (Kojo), their revered warrior.

Otherwise, it is heard on special occasions, such as a leader's funeral. It was Cudjoe who signed on behalf of the Maroons the treaty giving them autonomy over particular areas of Jamaica and formalizing certain conditions. The treaty was also signed by the British Colonel Guthrie in 1739, a full ninety-nine years before African-Jamaican slaves were emancipated. By design, for secrecy, the names of some Jamaican traditional instruments confuse persons from outside the group or location in which they are used.

Drums that appear different to visitors or outsiders may be simply called the drum or the skin. At other times, a similar looking and sounding drum is called by two different names, for example, *grandy* in the hilly eastern interior and *prenting* in similar terrain some 30 kilometers farther east. Each group jealously guards the identity and usage of its drums; for example, in Moore Town the *prenting,* in Accompong the *goombeh,* and in Scotts Hall the *saliman* and the *monkey.*

Kumina cult drums

According to Hazel Carter (1986), a former linguist of the School of African and Oriental Studies in London, rituals and ceremonies of the Kumina cultists in Jamaica maintain cosmological and linguistic links with the Kikongo people of Central Africa.

The cultists use two kinds of drum. The *kbandu,* about 35 to 40 centimeters in diameter and 50 centimeters long, is a single-headed, cylindrical drum. It has a goatskin head stretched over hollow or hollowed-out wood. It invokes the presence of the supreme god of Kumina, King Mzambi, with an ostinato rhythm. The player moves the heel of his foot on and off the stretched skin to alter the pitch.

The *cyas,* a smaller version of the *kbandu,* produces various rhythms chosen to suit the occasion, much as a doctor prescribes medicines. Both drums are played by palms and fingers, with heels changing the pitch. Their combined rhythm controls singers and dancers, invokes spirits, and sometimes induces possession. The players straddle the drums, which face each other at a distance of about one meter. Usually the beating of two sticks (*catta*) on the side of the *kbandu* helps build rhythmic excitement.

Drums used for authentic heritage events, as distinct from those used for festival and stage performances, still are handmade. Some stages of their preparation might even be secret—considered crucial for the successful use of the instrument in healing rituals. Many of these drums are consecrated away from the eyes of the public.

Rastafarian drums

Rastafarianism, a twentieth-century African-Jamaican cult, uses three wooden membranophones, adaptations of traditional *buru,* drums used in Christmas masquerade processions. The drum of lowest pitch, the bass, is played while positioned on its side. About 50 to 75 centimeters in diameter and 50 centimeters long, it is made from barrel staves with goatskin heads at each end, tuned with metal braces and pegs. The player holds it against his body and produces a deep, sonorous tone by striking the center of the drumhead with a heavily padded stick.

The *fundeh,* a Rastafarian drum 23 or more centimeters in diameter, is held between the player's calves, barely touching the ground. Fingers are held together as both hands strike the center of the single goatskin head. The body is made of staves, of strips of wood, or occasionally of a hollowed tree trunk.

The repeater, a short version of the *fundeh,* is held similarly, but it does not touch the ground. Unlike the bass and the *fundeh,* the repeater is played nearer the rim. Fingertips are separated to produce a large variety of rhythms. Rastafarian drums

FIGURE 1   A man plays a bamboo fife, once typical of Jamaican village dance bands. Photo by Olive Lewin, 1971.

are often painted red, green, and gold—the colors of the Ethiopian flag, signifying allegiance to Haile Selassie (1892–1975), emperor of Ethiopia, regarded by the cult as their messiah.

Indian drums

Indian membranophones, all with goatskin heads, include the large, low-toned *dhool,* played with sticks or hands; the higher-pitched, double-headed *dholak,* played mainly with fingers; the small twin, single-headed *tabla* set; and the bowl-shaped *tasa,* played with sticks or fingers. The *tasa* is tuned by being held, skin down, over an open fire. Its bowl is of clay or metal. For playing, the *dhool* is suspended from the shoulder. All the other drums may be played in that position by a drummer sitting cross-legged on the floor or, in some theatrical situations, sitting on a chair or a stool. Indians also use a tambourine called *tambourina.*

Aerophones

A bamboo fife (figure 1), played in florid style, was once typical of village dance bands. Its place has been taken by fifes made from plastic piping or by the orchestral piccolo. These bands now are usually called mento bands, after Jamaica's most long-standing and widespread style of rhythm, song, dance, and music.

Bamboo has also been used for making the Jamaican boompipe, a trumpetlike aerophone or stamping tube. A one-and-a-half- to two-meter length of mature bamboo 10 to 15 centimeters wide, it is buzzed into or pounded against the earth so as to produce a particular note. If two are used in the same band, two different notes are produced.

A bamboo saxophone was once crafted from growing a young, pliable length of bamboo into the shape of the desired instrument. When the right size and maturity were reached, the chosen section of the stalk was cut from the plant, the mouthpiece was fashioned and the other end was sometimes attached to a funnel-shaped length of metal or stiff material. Such instruments are now obsolete. Factory-made saxophones, clarinets, flutes, piccolos, and brass instruments are now sometimes used in village bands and school ensembles. Brass instruments, including bugles and sousaphones, are popular in military and marching bands.

Assisted by the Caribbean Council of Churches, some composers have created a new and growing genre of religious music in Jamaica. The established churches have inspired Jamaicans to embrace their own, long-rejected traditional expressions.

FIGURE 2 A young Maroon blows a rudimentary horn (*abeng*); the disk near the small end is an unusual modern addition. Photo by Dennis Richardson, 1992. By permission of Jampress.

In the 1600s and 1700s, Maroons used the *abeng* (figure 2), a rudimentary horn, mainly for signaling and sending messages during their wars with the British. Some Maroons still play it, imitating the rhythm and the pitch of the drum being used in any situation and in the manner of their ancestors' talking drums (see Okada 1995: example 12).

The only aerophone used by people of Indian heritage is the harmonium, a multiple single-reed portable organ, whose bellows is pumped with one hand while the other hand fingers the keyboard. The harmonium usually accompanies solo or group singing.

Chordophones

A bamboo violin was once an important instrument in traditional Jamaican bands, but the last expert performer died in the 1980s. This instrument has been relegated to museum collections and souvenir shops. A joint of bamboo with about an additional five centimeters at each end was used. A slit about one centimeter wide was cut, and on the opposite side three or four separate fibers were carefully loosened and raised from the main stalk by means of a short bridge, also of bamboo. It took an expert using a 30- to 35-centimeter length of bamboo as a bow, usually moistened with saliva, to produce tunes, some quick and rhythmic, from this instrument. No such experts survive.

Another chordophone that no longer exists in Jamaica is the merrywang. It was occasionally used in one area of the island up to the 1950s but has vanished. A lute made of half a gourd with skin across it, it had six gut or wire strings that were supported by a wooden bridge.

Some Jamaican village or *mento* and quadrille bands have included a fiddle. These were formerly handcrafted from local woods. They produced a pleasing sound, though played by rough-looking bows made of waxed hemp fibers. Only one traditional self-taught fiddler remains in the 1990s. He has a wide repertoire, including tunes, or parts thereof, that have been traced to Scotland. This man's ancestors are said to have arrived three or four generations ago from a ship that ran aground off the south coast near where he and his family live. He now plays a factory-made violin.

The four-stringed banjo has been a popular village instrument. Oral accounts state that field hands used to make and play this instrument in the early 1800s, even before emancipation. These banjo men were often required to play for social gatherings in plantation great houses, the homes of landowners and their associates. Nowadays, few young persons learn to play the banjo, so its music is in the hands of elderly musicians. Each year their number decreases through frailness and death.

The one-stringed bass is now virtually extinct. The bass line in village bands is now played on double bass, rhumba box, and occasionally bass guitar.

Acoustic guitars continue to hold their own, in spite of the prevalence of electronic instruments. They are more suited to accompanying the music of quadrilles, mentos, and folk songs and are indispensable in areas that have no electricity.

The *sitar*, an Indian plucked lute, and the *sarangi*, an Indian bowed lute, are in frequent use, exclusively by Indians, who alone have mastered the techniques for playing them.

MUSICAL CONTEXTS AND GENRES

Religious beliefs and practices

Religious beliefs permeate all levels of Jamaican society. All its ethnic groups participate in religious observances, whether adopted as in the case of Christianity, which embraces people of European, African, and Asian origins, or traditional as in the case of Hindu, Jewish, or Muslim observances.

Christian

The music of Christian ecclesiastical traditions is prominent in Jamaica. Serving the Christian community are denominations including Anglican, Roman Catholic, Baptist, Moravian, Presbyterian, Methodist, Seventh-Day Adventist, and derivatives, plus American-influenced evangelical and Pentecostal churches. Music of the Protestant churches consists of Western traditional hymns and nineteenth-century American "Moody and Sankey" gospel hymns. Organs and pianos are used in most churches having a formal choir to accompany lead singing and occasionally to perform special instrumental pieces. Recitals of sacred music, especially at Easter and Christmas, are normal features of church calendars and often spill over into community activities. A growing trend in the evangelical and Pentecostal churches is the use of bands—drums, guitars, synthesizer or piano, and tambourines—to accompany upbeat singing in American popular gospel styles.

Assisted by the Caribbean Council of Churches, some composers—foremost is the classically trained Jamaican musician Noel Dexter—have created a new and growing genre of religious music in Jamaica. For many Jamaicans, this music satisfies a deep-seated need for spiritual and physical expression in worship. By providing this music, the established churches have inspired Jamaicans to embrace their own, long-rejected traditional expressions, such as Revival and Kumina, in present-day worship.

Though Christianity is the mainstream religious influence, Jamaican cults use religious concepts and practices inherited from African ancestors. These they sometimes mix with Christian beliefs. Judaism, Hinduism, and Islam are also practiced by small sections of the society. Music and sometimes movement are included in most religious services. Even in some churches from the European side of Jamaica's heritage (Roman Catholic and low-church Anglican), religious choruses and hymns are accompanied by bodily movements and clapping.

Cults demonstrate the African-inherited tendency to integrate song, dance, and instrumental accompaniment into the religious experience. Their members believe that ancestral spirits, "the dead," are part of the living world; hence, a god or a spirit can take over or possess the body, the mind, and the character of the living. The leader of the cult mediates between the human and spiritual worlds, using the musical experience as the primary channel of communication to restore lost harmony. These songs, movements, and instrumental accompaniments are sometimes shared by secular and religious activities. The main cults are the Maroon, the Kumina, the Ettu, the Nago, the Tambo, and the Goombeh. Revival and Rastafarianism, also African-based, contain significant European and European-American influences. In all these groups, the membranophonic drum is the significant instrument for musical expression, with the type of drum and the style of drumming dependent on the cult's origins.

FIGURE 3 "Alligator dah walk," a jawbone (used by Maroons for diversion or work), as sung by Mrs. Marie Rennock of Moore Town, Jamaica, 1968. The text means that the alligator is walking and rolling from side to side. Transcription by Olive Lewin.

Maroon

The four main Maroon communities in Jamaica have varying ethnic backgrounds: Africans from the Gold Coast (now Ghana) and the slave coast (Burkina Faso to Benin); creoles, born in Jamaica; and Arawak and Miskito Indians from Central America. These peoples intermingled and created a distinct Maroon culture based on African retentions, a common history of resistance to enslavement, and a sense of the independence for which they fought and which was made real by the signing of the treaty with the British in 1739. This spirit still endures.

Despite the increasing encroachment of mainstream cultures, a distinct Maroon culture exists, particularly in music, dance, and to a lesser extent in linguistic remnants of African languages such as Twi, the language of the Ashanti of Ghana. The strongest survival is in the *kromanti* play or the *kromanti* dance, the main ritual for summoning ancestral spirits to intercede with the supreme being, Nyangkipong. Maroon ceremonies are for healing and cleansing, and the dance involves the spirits through singing, dancing, and drumming to possess a specific person. He or she becomes the channel for diagnosing and treating the malady. The men and women who dance know the properties of herbs for physical and mental cures; each type of medicinal herb has its corresponding type of song and drum rhythm.

Religious dances, which the Maroons call business dances, include songs and music—"Papa" (Ewe), "Mandinga," "Ibo"—named after the particular ethnic groups that brought them (Bilby 1992). These songs and dances have distinctive styles, used to invoke ancestral spirits for instruction and advice and to induce spirit possession. For reasons not shared with outsiders, Maroons call secular *salo* songs jawbone, sale-one, tambu, and ambush. These songs may be sad or happy (figure 3).

The most important Maroon drums, the *prenting* (*oprenting* in Twi) and the *goombeh* (*gumbe*), are used by separate groups on religious and secular occasions. At ceremonies of healing, the *prenting* complements the singing of songs in Cromantin language, used by Cromantee Africans, who came from the Gold Coast in the 1500s (probably Akan; Bilby 1992). For brief periods, a stick called *aboso* is struck against the side of the drum, providing a shifting pulse. The *goombeh* produces quick, sharp rhythms in keeping with the darting, angular dances being accompanied.

Kumina

The Kumina cult is practiced by the descendants mainly of postemancipation indentured laborers from Central Africa. Songs possibly including African-language texts (Kikongo and Kimbundu), complex rhythms, and distinctive dancing are used to honor, appease, and evoke the help of ancestral and other spirits for healing, thanksgiving, memorials for the dead, entombment, and celebrations such as weddings, births, and anniversaries.

Kumina ceremonies use the *kbandu* and *cyas* drums. The *kbandu* rhythm invokes King Nzambi, the supreme god. The complex rhythms produced by the *cyas* drummer invoke other spirits, excite the singers, and induce possession. While the dancers' feet reproduce the *kbandu* rhythm, the *cyas* drummer's improvisatory pat-

FIGURE 4   Excerpt from a Kumina song from Georgia, southeastern Jamaica, as sung in 1971 and said to have been known for at least three generations. The word *chimiah* is said to mean 'see me here'. The song serves to build up excitement, with voices singing in unison and improvising contrapuntally against rhythms from drums and other percussive instruments. Transcription by Olive Lewin.

terns impel the movement of heads, shoulders, arms, and hips. The drummers interact intensely with the singers and the dancers.

The Kumina prayer, responsorially sung and accompanied by drums and other percussive instruments, signals the start of every ritual. Songs in ancestral African languages are used for the more sacred sections of the rituals in which communication with the spirits is sought and achieved. *Baila,* songs using Jamaican Creole, are sung after spirit possession subsides and at recreational events. Singing is in unison or antiphonal unison, usually including high-pitched, loud, forceful tones, improvised contrapuntally (figure 4).

Other cults

Ettu, Nago, Tambo, and Goombeh are small, fading cults found in different parts of the island. They share the African-based belief of ancestral intercession on behalf of the living, and they ceremonially use drumming and dancing to seek assistance for the healing and well-being of individuals and the community.

Ettu and Nago practitioners are descendants of Africans from Abeokuta and the surrounding southwestern area of Nigeria, brought to Jamaica as slaves until about 1700. One of the villages in their part of Jamaica is called Abeokuta. Two musical instruments—the tin (an empty kerosene oil container) and the skin (a double-headed goatskin drum)—are used in Ettu. The tin is also used in Nago events.

Tambo groups describe many of their songs as laments, despite the speed and crispness produced by the *catta.* The drummer communicates with the dancers and singers in phrases of different lengths that build to a climax. Tambo songs are short and repetitive, many lamenting separation from loved ones and from mother Africa. The Goombeh cult uses a *goombeh* similar to that used by Maroons.

Revival

Revival is Jamaica's main African-Christian cult, embracing Revival Pukkumina (also Pukko) and Zion (also Zion Way). Blending Christian and West African concepts, Revival includes singing, dancing, instrumental and percussive accompaniment, healing, divination, and spirit possession. Revival activities may include street meetings to win converts; baptismal baths and fasting for purification; feasts for thanksgiving tables; mourning or memorial rites; and invocations of the spirit world for help.

Revival music that sets the scene for and induces spiritual trance and possession is usually performed with melodic, harmonic, and rhythmic improvisations. Many songs are adaptations of Western-style hymns, but there is also chanting and responsorial singing. Pukko tunes are usually in duple and quadruple time; Zion tunes are sometimes in triple or compound time. The music utilizes syncopation against contrasting rhythmic patterns provided mainly by membranophones and idiophones, and by rhythmic body sounds such as clapping, stamping, moaning, and loud overbreathing (called groaning or trumping). Many Revival songs are based on "Moody

The song "Chi chi bud" appears to be about birds, but really comments on persons such as the overseer, who works for the land master and, like the john crow, as a scavenger, picks at the workers' bones.

and Sankey" hymns. Revivalism continues to be central to the lives of hundreds of Jamaicans, directly or indirectly. Even where the tenets are not accepted, response to the music is fervent and instinctive.

Rastafarianism

Originating among the poor urban class in the 1930s, Rastafarianism is a modern manifestation of the dream of Africa. Its development was influenced by the teachings of Marcus Garvey (1887–1940), who urged black people to look to Africa as their motherland. By the 1970s, the sociocultural influences of Rastafarianism began to be felt among the middle and upper classes, as the tenets (peace, love) and lifestyle (self-expression, self-reliance, dignity) demonstrated by its practitioners attracted a new generation of nationalistic youth. Rastafarianism has affected national life in significant ways, especially the development of the popular music style known as reggae.

A most interesting and significant feature of Rastafarian cult music is *nyabingi* drumming (Bilby 1992). Instrumentalists, playing the three types of wooden membranophones and other percussive instruments (repeater, *fundeh*, and bass), also sing, and with the exception of the drummers, become quite mobile, at times dancing intricate steps (see Okada 1995: example 14). Tunes are sometimes borrowed and adapted from Western hymns, Negro spirituals, or local traditional songs, but the Rasta repertoire is also full of melodies created by devotees, as well as improvised chants.

Indian religions

Indians first came to Jamaica as indentured laborers in 1845 and in these circumstances were able to practice their religions. Since then, links with India have been maintained and strengthened physically by others who have continued to come as farmers, professionals, merchants, and holy men. They have integrated closely into Jamaican society while retaining strong spiritual links with their ancestral land. The Prema Satsangh was formally established as a religious organization in 1994.

Other social contexts and genres

In addition to music associated with religion, there is a repertoire of songs for a variety of social occasions. Lullabies, play songs, love songs, work songs, and funeral songs are common. Clear identification of a certain traditional song with a particular social event, though, is not always possible. Some lullabies are called work songs, since they were identified with work in the plantation's great house, especially caring for the masters' children. Play songs can be work songs also, and some adult games are meant to influence children's development. People have no self-consciousness about using songs for other than their original purposes.

Lullabies can be enhanced by clapping, bouncing the knees, tapping the toes, miming, and any other movement that might amuse and distract an infant from its problem. The same melody, accompanied by gentle rhythms, rocking, and swaying, might then be used to lull the child to sleep.

Many play songs have been adopted from other cultures, mainly African and English, and Jamaicanized by syncopation, improvisation, dramatization, and the use of movements progressing from mime to dancing. The emphasis is on participation and having fun. Songs like "Sally Water," "I Come to See Janie," and "Jane and Louisa" might have been learned through contact with the great house. There are versions of many other well-known English play songs.

Ring games are played by children and adults. The latter might use them at wakes for the dead, or at moonshine *dahlins*—yard entertainment and recreation on moonlit nights. Games with stones evolved out of the task of breaking stones by hand. They allow the players to show off their dexterity and concentration, since any deviation from the rhythm of the song puts one in danger of getting a mashed finger, as in the perennial favorite "Manuel Road."

Jamaica inherited Anansi (also Anancy and Nancy) the spider man from Gold Coast ancestors. Numerous stories are told of his exploits with other animals and human beings. Many Anansi stories incorporate music, mainly songs that comment on the action or are a part of the dialogue. The term *cante-fable* has been applied to some Jamaican traditional stories, but this name is not familiar to Jamaicans, especially storytellers. Like most Anansi stories, cante-fables include singing.

Slavery did not permit the establishment and growth of stable relationships. Traditional love songs, few in number, appear to come from the postemancipation period.

The main occupation of the slaves was work, and the slaves used a significant number of chants and songs to lighten their labor. Work songs vary stylistically, since they had to fit in with many different types of work. They were also used to pass on messages about secret meetings, to laugh at the master's foibles, or to protest against evil treatment without arousing the suspicion that would have earned punishment. The song "Chi chi bud," for example, appears to be about birds, but really comments on persons such as the overseer, who works for the land master and, like the john crow, as a scavenger, picks at the workers' bones (figure 5). The parrot refers to workers who tell tales on their colleagues in an attempt to win favors from the ruling class. Songs also incorporated ways of resting for short periods, such as one out of every four phrases, while singing so as not to arouse the overlord's suspicion and receive punishment. The use of symbols or substitutes in critical commentary on the social system to avoid punishment was widespread. It continues in use by older folk in present-day Jamaica. In modern pop songs, youth are outspoken and direct.

Most songs used for digging, hoeing, and other agricultural labor are responsorial (figure 5). The leader (*bomma*) did not take part in the manual labor. His role was to keep the workers in a buoyant mood, working in concert. He had to be quick witted, able to improvise words and music. The workers responded in a robust chorus

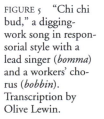

FIGURE 5   "Chi chi bud," a digging-work song in responsorial style with a lead singer (*bomma*) and a workers' chorus (*bobbin*). Transcription by Olive Lewin.

(*bobbin*), frequently improvising harmonies in two to four parts. There are work songs for outdoor and indoor labor. Since many of these songs commented on topicalities, they are invaluable sources of oral history.

The social rituals of death include gathering at the home of the bereaved to assist them through the period of mourning. Wakes, from the setup on the night of death to periods from three to forty nights after, saw people coming together to sing hymns and adaptations of hymns, play ring games, tell stories and riddles, and feast. The most popular wakes are the setup and the nine night, the latter being when the spirit of the dead returns, and if satisfactorily entertained, leaves for the home of the spirits.

Music is an integral part of these wakes, with hymns and solemn tunes being interspersed with lively choruses, Bible readings, and speeches. As the night progresses, secular songs become more prominent, and the mood lightens into ring games and storytelling. Voices and clapping suffice, though a banjo, if available, will be used. Boompipes and small drums are sometimes used.

DANCES AND FESTIVALS

Many forms of music in Jamaica are linked to dance—social dancing and ceremonial dancing for display and entertainment. Most Jamaican music has a movement dimension, expressed spontaneously by Jamaican people of all social strata and ethnic origins. Ritual and deeply traditional music may have characteristics and stylized movements and steps that those outside the particular group find difficult to do. Tapping the toes and clapping the hands often suffice for participation.

The vocal timbres and scalar patterns of some music (like Indian, Maroon, and Kumina) also help maintain their exclusiveness at certain levels. However, this usually applies only to ritual and traditional ceremonial genres. Beyond that, no one cares whether or not the right sounds are being made. Socializing and participation are far more important.

Mento

Mento, Jamaica's indigenous sung, played, and danced style, maintained widespread popularity up to the 1940s. The music is slow and in quadruple time, with a strong accent on the last beat of the bar. *Mento* tunes are usually in major keys, with regular, neatly balanced phrases that lend themselves to harmonization with the primary chords. International pop beats and the popular contemporary dance-hall beat, a close derivative of *mento*, have been influencing the performance of *mento* music and dancing.

In *mento* performance, a great deal of florid ornamentation is improvised, especially when the fife or piccolo is used. Guitar and banjo soloists sometimes embellish the basic tunes to great effect. Nowadays, mento bands play most frequently for maypole dancing. Maypole came to Jamaica via the English great house. Music is provided by a village band playing set pieces that dictate to the dancers which style of ribbon plaiting must be done. Tunes range from Jamaican mento songs to "Rule Britannia" and "The Bluebells of Scotland." These latter are barely recognizable because of the rhythmic Jamaicanization and florid ornamentation on banjo, fiddle, or fife.

The band consists of three types of instruments. Melodies can be played by a clarinet, a fife, a harmonica, a piccolo, a saxophone, a trumpet, or an electronic keyboard; harmonies by a banjo and a guitar (which may also be played melodically), with a rhumba box or a string bass for the bass; and rhythms by drums, maracas, a grater, concussion sticks, and a variety of improvised instruments. The length of an old-time mento ranges from five to twenty minutes, depending on the interplay and excitement generated between dancers and musicians (see Okada 1995:example 16).

Bruckins

Music and dance are central to the annual event known as Bruckins, begun on 1 August 1938 as a celebration of emancipation from slavery. More than just music and dancing, it is a competition in skill and endurance, beginning at nightfall on 31 July and continuing till dawn on 1 August.

The music, played by the side drum (snare drum, often used for marching) using military-sounding beats and accompanying a small group of singers, dictates the sequence of dances. The main characters in the dance are the king, the queen, and courtiers. Each band, one dressed in costumes of red and the other in blue, shows off its skill at playing and dancing. Steps are stylized, and the dance typically has stately dips and glides and exaggerated posturing with swords.

The last practicing traditional group no longer functions, the few remaining members being unable to carry out the demanding dance movements and sustain the necessary energy levels through the night. Young groups now perform the music dance for village festivals and theatrical entertainment.

Jonkunnu

Jonkunnu is the phonetic spelling of what elders called this Christmas masquerade. The British anglicized it as John Canoe, and in more modern times it has been spelled junkanoo in commercial settings.

The slaves celebrated their three- to seven-day Christmas holiday with feasting, music, dancing, and masquerades. A prominent feature was jonkunnu or its variant, horse-head or *buru* processions, the terms used interchangeably by participants. The members of the band were men, costumed to represent a variety of male and female characters.

In the variant *buru* or horse head, the main mask was made from the skull of a horse covered and elaborately decorated. It snapped its jaws at anyone nearby, in the manner of the English midwinter hodening horse and Welsh *mari lwyd* of Christmas to twelfth night. Jonkunnu music was provided by bamboo, and later plastic, home-made fifes and side drums. Styles varied to represent the character whose music was being played. The characters known as Jackna Green and Pitchy Patchy danced differently from Devil or Bride. The fife played short, repetitive snatches of melody in a quick, agitated manner, interspersed with trills accompanied by frequent rolls on the drums (see Okada 1995: example 13).

The variant *buru* or horse head used three drums: bass, *fundeh,* and repeater, playing in quadruple time with a marked accent on the fourth beat of each bar. Melodic lines were provided by mouth organs, paper-covered combs, or singing. The texts were topical, earthy, and often derisive. Jonkunnu bands are now occasionally seen in parades. Those most popular by reputation or judged to be best through national competitions are sponsored for performances in Jamaica's Independence Festival each year on the first Monday in August. Through the tourist industry, jonkunnu bands entertain visitors.

Jamaica quadrille

Jamaica quadrille is a creolization of eighteenth- and nineteenth-century European ballroom dances that the slaves must have learned while serving in the great house. Most of its music is based on European melodic and harmonic styles, with typically Jamaican improvisations, embellishments, and syncopation accenting the upbeat.

The fiddle, merrywang (a now obsolete chordophone), guitar, banjo, maracas, rhumba box, bamboo fife, drums, piccolo, trombone, clarinet, saxophone, harmonica, and mandolin have been used in various combinations. The groupings are flexible and depend on the instruments and the players available at any one place or time.

Limbo is accompanied by music in various styles. This movement was born in slavery, when it was safer to attempt to escape under, rather than over, enclosing fences.

Competent musicians are welcome to join an established group in performance. Set dances such as lancers were a lively part of village life until the 1950s.

The annual August Independence Festival commemorating the 1962 political independence of Jamaica has helped keep maypole, quadrille, and jonkunnu alive in the arena of public performance. Quadrille dancers may be seen performing mazurkas, waltzes, polkas, and schottisches in suites, ending always with a Jamaican mento. There are two styles of dances: ballroom, more formal and favored by adult and sometimes quite elderly performers; and camp style, less stylized and performed by adults and by children as young as eight years of age.

Indian festivals

From arrival, Hindus have held their spring Pagwa or holy festival and autumn Diwali festival of lights. Muslims celebrate Hosay in the summer in commemoration of the victory of good over evil as evidenced in the fatal fight between Hussein and Hassan, grandsons of the prophet Muhammad.

Hosay (Hussein), Pagwa (Pagwah), and Diwali (Divali), though based in ancestral Indian religious observances, include festive features of entertainment. Indian instruments provide music complemented by voices often accompanied by harmonium. Hussein featured stick dancing until discontinued by police because of the possibility of injury to bystanders. Diwali, with its hundreds of lights, whether in private homes or public venues, always includes music and dancing, as does Pagwa, which adds the lighthearted dousing of fellow attendees with colored powders and liquids after the more formal and religious aspects of the occasion.

These festivals are celebrated by all Indians, Hindu and Muslim, plus many Jamaicans of African and other ethnic origins. A deep religious thread runs through all Indian festivals, but they also have value as entertainment. The music of voices and various stringed and percussion instruments, usually accompanied by harmonium, enhances all these occasions. Traditional dances are also featured.

Creole Jamaicans also join in Hosay, the Muslim celebration brought to Jamaica by Indian laborers. Celebrated mainly in the parish of Clarendon, Hosay has seen some Jamaicanization over more than a century of existence on the island. Aspects of its dancing have spilled over into Revival and jonkunnu.

Other dances and theater

Calypso is popular in entertainment circles, as are steelbands, both having been imported from Trinidad and other southern and eastern Caribbean islands. Caribbean students at the University of the West Indies in Jamaica have given life to and improved the quality of these genres. Neither comes naturally to Jamaican musicians but they bring tremendous enjoyment to people of all ages and social strata. Soca, the 1990s combination of soul music and calypso, has become popular but has probably not yet superseded calypso.

Limbo is accompanied by music in various styles, but usually in duple time with vigorous beats. Dancers propel themselves one at a time, knees first, under a pole, sometimes lowered to a height of a third of a meter or less. It is often not realized that this movement was born in slavery, when it was safer to attempt to escape under, rather than over, enclosing fences.

Though Jamaica's modern-dance theater is strongly influenced by the traditional experience, incorporating folkloric music, rituals, gestures, and body movements, contemporary dance uses local and international music. This reflects the mixed influences of Africa and Europe on the culture. The interpretive portrayal of folkloric ceremonies reveals a strong sense of theater, combining music, movement, timing, acting, and in some cases costuming into an integrated experience (see Okada 1995: example 15).

Formal theater has seen a shift from the almost exclusive presentation of foreign companies or plays to more locally written productions. One outstanding example is the annual Christmas pantomime, begun on the British model. Local writers have moved away from that tradition, and the themes, characters, music, and dances are now totally indigenous. Productions of dance and theater draw heavily on local music, traditional and popular.

LEARNING MUSIC

Musical enculturation takes many forms in Jamaica. Among the cults, the secrets of their African retentions, language, styles of drumming, and meaning of rituals are not passed on to young people until or unless they are regarded as ready. An individual may spend years learning to play the rhythms on the special drums. If the teacher, usually an old person, dies before lessons are complete, authenticity can be lost, as only partial learning has occurred.

Aural tradition in learning music is important among Jamaicans, and knowledge of musical notation has not been widely recognized as a requisite to musical participation, even for European-derived musics. A group leader or choirmaster sometimes teaches an hour-long program of choral music, including excerpts from oratorios and cantatas by eighteenth- and nineteenth-century European composers, entirely by rote. A few reading members of vocal ensembles are considered a help but by no means a necessity.

Until the 1950s, schoolteachers and church choirmasters were expected to master Tonic Sol-fa, using syllables, such as *taa ta-te ta-fa-te-fe* for the rhythmic pattern of a quarter note, two eighths, and four sixteenths. However, few Jamaican musicians outside the field of the classics read music. The better pop and jazz musicians master musical notation, but many rely heavily on their ability to memorize and to improvise.

Since few Jamaican pop musicians can read music, most have tended to copy what they have heard. Copyright infringement has not yet been recognized, but the inability to read—and even more, to write—music has led to widespread exploitation of nonliterate Jamaican musicians' musical ideas. Those who work within controlled management situations record their tunes, motifs, and rhythmic patterns for professional transcribers and arrangers to develop. Others are easy prey to pirates.

Formal music education usually ranges from instrumental lessons (often in piano or guitar) given by unaffiliated, individual teachers in their living rooms, to better-organized studios with teachers belonging to the Music Teachers Association, entering students for annual external music examinations leading to diplomas from Trinity College (London) and the Royal Schools of Music (London), to some classroom teaching, usually in secondary schools. A few schools, notably Alpha Boys School (Kingston), have for many years maintained teaching programs that have produced noteworthy players in the genres of brass band and jazz. A more recent introduction is the Jamaica Orchestra for Youth. The effort began by offering lessons in selected schools and special workshops to train first the strings, with the long-term aim of producing a National Youth Orchestra. Schools generally train choirs for festival activities and other special occasions. Marching bands have become a popular feature of youth and community development activities.

Music education is organized at the highest level at the Jamaica School of Music (JSM), a postsecondary institution, one of four schools forming the Cultural Training Centre in Jamaica, now named the Edna Manley Centre for the Visual and Performing Arts, in honor of one of Jamaica's most revered artists and sculptors. The JSM seeks to fill the demand for training for professionals—performers and arrangers of popular music, music teachers in schools, and instrumental specialists who teach privately. Special attention is given to folkloric music, Caribbean and African-American studies, and the use of Caribbean instruments, materials, and indigenous sources of sounds. In addition to a full-time, four-year diploma program, there are part-time courses and individual tuition for children aged seven to seventeen in the junior department. Much learning by individuals occurs outside these systems. Many musicians, especially in popular music, are self-taught. Jamaica's economic problems of the 1990s tended to cause a return of general pre-1960s attitudes to music making. In the intervening years, electronic media and musical instruments seemed to be hustling music making and acoustic instruments off the Jamaican scene. There now appears to be a resurgence of interest, and to a lesser extent activity, in more traditional attitudes to playing. Violins, recorders, guitars, and band instruments lead the way in school, community, and church programs.

Jamaicans expect musicians and students specializing in classical music to read music fluently and write it rudimentarily. By international standards, several Jamaican performers and teachers have excelled. Most seek careers in larger countries or the international music industry.

THE MUSIC INDUSTRY

Traditional music has influenced the development of modern popular music. From ska, to rock-steady, to reggae and dub, contemporary popular beats have recognizable roots in Revival and mento. Rhythms typical of some cults are discernible in the music of enterprising bands such as Third World and Chalice. Jamaica's reggae music gained international recognition mainly through its most popular proponent, Robert (Bob) Nesta Marley (1945–1981), a Rastafarian.

Radio and television

Radio was introduced into Jamaica in 1938, greatly expanding the audience and extending the range of easily accessible musical styles. In 1996, eight full-time stations were operating, and one part time (in the University of the West Indies). For decades, HCJB, a station in Ecuador, has regularly been heard on medium-wave radio sets in Jamaica; Venezuelan stations can be picked up on local shortwave sets. Medium-wave, long-wave, and FM receivers are inexpensive. Cuban stations, North American stations, and a few stations in the Dutch Antilles can be tuned in. A few people use shortwave radios to extend their listening to virtually all areas of the globe.

Increased exposure has influenced not only tastes in listening but also the types of music composed and produced locally. Commercial stations take popularity into account. Methods of production and styles of presentation have been drawn more in line with international standards and, to a large extent, the content of programs also veers in that direction. This trend has had a negative effect on the tapping of Jamaica's rich store of traditional music styles, with the notable exception of reggae.

Jamaica has two television channels, the first of which began transmission in August 1962. Many of its programs are imported, and a wide selection of material originating in North America is available to households, hotels, and businesses via satellite dishes and cable. This medium has intensified the changes in musical presentation and in programming initiated by radio. Local programming is growing and sometimes attains high standards. Unfortunately for the continuity of Jamaican musical traditions, people have tended to imitate even the instrumentation of foreign musical groups—a practice that can be more accurately done from visual models than from radio.

Recordings

Devices for recording sounds were at first in the hands of a small minority of musicians and lovers of music in Jamaica. Reel-to-reel tape recorders were used in Jamaica by media houses, the music industry, scholars, and individuals. By making easy recording, copying, and playback of sounds readily available to a large cross-section of the public, small, battery-operated cassette tape recorders changed this situation.

Analog recordings were in use before the coming of radio. They and the means to play them were expensive and available to a small but growing minority. The cassette tape recorder now enables most Jamaicans to possess and play at will the music of their choice, by means of purchased or copied tapes. It is a much-used tool of researchers. Composers, especially of pop music, most of whom cannot write music, record their works for professional transcription and arranging.

The production of long-playing and 45-rpm records began in Jamaica in 1954. Publicly placed sound systems had earlier dispersed overamplified sounds from imported records, annoying many but creating in others a demand for owning the records. Entrepreneurs such as Clement Dodd, Ken Khouri, Byron Lee, and Duke Reid grasped the opportunity to replace foreign performers with local ones. These performers at first specialized in imported music, but gradually the soundscape changed, and Jamaican composers were encouraged to provide locally inspired material. This led to the development of a Jamaican music industry and the emergence and dissemination of reggae.

In the 1950s and 1960s, the increase in radio ownership and listenership, plus the proliferation of public sound systems, set the stage for the commercialization of music in Jamaica. The program content of radio and sound systems was predominantly imported popular music; however, there was simultaneously a marked and increasing interest in live performances as popular entertainment. The same was true for jazz, which had a smaller but more constant following. The foundations were foreign, but Jamaican musicians, partly responding to audience tastes and demands, introduced deeply ingrained Jamaican modes of musical expression: tunes, rhythmic pulses and patterns, ornamentation, and African-derived responsorial vocal styles. Local music was also influenced by country. This phase of pop music produced brilliant and internationally accepted Jamaican instrumentalists such as Ernie Ranglin (guitar), Monty Alexander (piano, keyboard), and Don Drumond (trombone). These and other talented local musicians formed bands or played as soloists in a thriving music industry.

Other aspects of the Jamaican music industry are related to the trade of imported discs, cassettes, and videotapes, mainly from Britain and North America. By the 1970s, as local entrepreneurs prospered, they set up studios and record-manufacturing plants. Some procured state-of-the-art equipment, run by talented technicians. Consequently, Jamaica has three or four studios of such high quality that they have attracted performers such as the Rolling Stones and Paul Simon.

Also by the 1970s, Jamaica's music industry had become known and recognized

Bob Marley's music astonished listeners, captured imaginations, and won the admiration of fans around the world, including people of diverse political persuasions, religions, ages, and languages.

abroad, mainly in North America and the United Kingdom. It then became easy for Jamaica's music to travel beyond its shores. In the 1960s, ska and rock-steady had followings mainly among Jamaicans who had settled in metropolitan centers overseas or were temporarily working or studying abroad.

Reggae, however, went far beyond these fans. It gained widespread popularity around the world because of the performances of Bunny Wailer, Peter Tosh, Jimmy Cliff, the Third World Band, and others, but it was the music, the message, and the unique communicative skills of Bob Marley (1945–1981) that crowned their efforts. His music astonished listeners, captured imaginations, and won the admiration of fans around the world, including people of diverse political persuasions, religions, ages, and languages. His death left a huge gap, but his musical style and message have been carried on by his children, his widow (Rita Marley), Judy Mowatt, Marcia Griffiths, Bunny Wailer, and others. Jimmy Cliff may not have enjoyed the local chart success that Marley did but continues to be popular internationally. Toots and the Maytals, who emerged from the ska period beginning in 1962, still command a significant following and are prominent in the renewed interest in ska and rock-steady.

Ernie Ranglin, a Jamaican guitarist considered for three to four decades in international circles as one of the finest jazz guitarists in the world, has returned to Jamaica. He now enriches the local scene with his playing, at once virtuosic and expressive. He also has been, and is, a much sought-after arranger, one of the first to take Jamaican folk music into the realms of jazz.

Many other musicians, including Byron Lee, the bandleader, and Peter Ashbourne, the violinist, keyboard player, composer, and arranger, continue to contribute to the local pop scene.

Dance-hall music, with its folk-based rhythms, earthy lyrics, and abandoned movements, which started with youth and people of the lower socioeconomic classes within the 1990s, has become widely popular. Deejays—called rappers in some countries—are the most prolific exponents of dance-hall music. Their messages vary widely, from risqué to humorous, concentrating on local social commentary. Whereas lyrics of traditional mento and work songs, for instance, used veiled references and symbolism in commenting on social situations, modern pop songs are direct in their expression.

FURTHER STUDY

Music, song, and dance have always played a major role in Jamaica's heritage, but there are comparatively few recorded sources of Jamaica's musical history. Researchers have found that human sources of this knowledge often jealously guard their traditions. When bearers of culture have imparted this knowledge, scholars—most of whom have been foreigners, unacquainted with the local language, speechways, and culture—have often misunderstood or misinterpreted it.

Musical records appear in the published works of researchers such as Walter Jekyll (1907), Martha Beckwith (1928), Ivy Baxter (1970), and Olive Lewin (1973). The research procedure was mainly observation involving individuals and groups. Great care was needed to ensure that the meanings of these sources of speech, styles, and symbolism were understood, and that Western notation maintained as much as possible the rhythms and the melodies used.

There are no definitive scholarly studies of Jamaican pop music since the 1980s, but several introductory articles, chapters, and texts can be pointed out. Kenneth Bilby's chapter on Jamaica in Peter Manuel's *Caribbean Currents* (1995) is a good place to begin. For a specific study of reggae, the book by Johnson and Pines (1982) is useful. Studies of more contemporary styles during the mixing and digital age of Jamaican music are by Hebdige (1987) and Jahn and Weber (1992).

REFERENCES

Baxter, Ivy. 1970. *The Arts of an Island: The Development of the Culture and of the Folk and Creative Arts in Jamaica, 1492–1962.* Metuchen, N.J.: Scarecrow Press.

Beckwith, Martha. 1928. *Jamaica Folklore.* New York: American Folklore Society.

Bilby, Kenneth. 1992. *Maroon Music from the Earliest Free Black Communities of Jamaica.* Washington, D.C.: Smithsonian/Folkways CD ST 40412. Notes to compact disc.

———. 1995. "Jamaica." In *Caribbean Currents,* ed. Peter Manuel, 143–182. Philadelphia: Temple University Press.

Carter, Hazel. 1986. "Language and Music of Kumina." *African Caribbean Institute of Jamaica Newsletter* 12:3–12.

Hebdige, Dick. 1987. *Cut 'n' Mix: Culture, Identity and Caribbean Music.* London: Methuen.

Jahn, Brian, and Tom Weber. 1992. *Reggae Island: Jamaican Music in the Digital Age.* Kingston: Kingston Publishers.

Jekyll, Walter. 1907. *Jamaica Song and Story.* London: Folklore Society, London University.

Johnson, Howard, and Jim Pines. 1982. *Reggae: Deep Roots Music.* London: Proteus Books.

Leslie, Charles. 1740. *A New History of Jamaica.* London: Hodges.

Lewin, Olive. 1973. *Forty Folk Songs of Jamaica.* Washington, D. C.: Organization of American States.

Manuel, Peter. 1995. *Caribbean Currents.* Philadelphia: Temple University Press.

Okada, Yuki. 1995. *The Caribbean.* JVC Smithsonian Folkways Video Anthology of Music and Dance in the Americas, 4. Montpelier, Vt.: Multicultural Media VTMV-228. Video.

Patterson, H. O. 1973. *The Sociology of Slavery: An Analysis of the Origins, Development and Structure of Negro Slave Society in Jamaica.* Kingston: Songster's Book Stores.

Martinique
Monique Desroches

Music and the Quest for a Cultural Identity
Contemporary Trends
Cultural Identity

Martinique, an island of the Lesser Antilles, is a young society formed by immigrants from the Caribbean, France, South Asia, and West Africa. Its population is about 320,000, composed largely of the descendants of West African slaves and other cultures that have mixed.

Martinique had been a French colony since the 1600s, but in 1946 it gained the status of an overseas department of France. The island's official language is French, but Creole (Kwéyòl) is used in everyday communication. This type of bilingual society, in which a vernacular tongue remains in active use without an official status, has encouraged the emergence of a parallel culture based on oral tradition. The use of Creole, notably in public contexts, has become a symbol of identification and assertion for the people of Martinique, setting them culturally apart from metropolitan France.

Racial and cultural mixing (*métissage*) has specifically transformed Martinicans' daily life by creating a multiple frame of reference for identity. French, African, Asian, or creole elements might be present during a musical event, depending on where and when it occurs. This phenomenon has caused anthropologists specializing in Creole culture to speak of "cumulative identities" (Fuma and Poirer 1994) and "situational-contextual belongings" (Benoist 1994). Musical practices are also influenced by these processes. The island's traditional and popular music not only contributes to a trend that emphasizes identity, but for many has become a symbol of the quest for a Martinican sense of belonging.

Like other Creole-speaking areas, Martinique is marked by interculturalism, and its musical practices are complex and drawn from multiple sources, old and new:

> The Caribbean serves as a kind of crucible in which the elements of interculturalism can be clearly identified. . . . The extreme healthiness of the culture is the result of the crossbreeding of the diverse elements which have shaped the sensitivity and the reasoning of the people in this region. (René Depestre, quoted in Berrouët-Oriol and Fournier 1994:19)

Despite changes and adjustments, the music of Martinique has maintained expressive elements that distinguish it from other creole traditions. On a more global level, it contributes to the flux of transnational music. How can we then locate identifying traits in a musical practice that shares expressive elements with other musics, especially one that is defined primarily by its capacity of adaptation, even to the point of adopting foreign elements? Could one speak of a stylistic musical continuum?

My aim is to shed light on these questions by surveying musical development in Martinique from 1946 to 1996, and by examining the influence music has on the local identity-seeking process. To understand the links between music and the Martinican quest for identity, one needs to pay special attention to performance contexts and factors that have contributed to the popularity of certain musical genres.

MUSIC AND THE QUEST FOR A CULTURAL IDENTITY

In Martinique, music serves above all to describe the environment, not only in sound, but also in social and cultural aspects. A symbolic universe unto itself, music reflects simultaneously that which binds people together and that which sets them apart. Beyond the rifts that can be traced back to the times of slavery, Martinique has always been a melting pot of ethnic heritages.

Martinican musicians could always choose from five options: conservation of traditional practices, abandonment of traditional practices, adoption of new practices, innovation, and creation (Desroches 1992). However, the choice among these options is not made randomly. While Martinicans have delved deeply into their traditions, they have reinterpreted them in accordance with current contexts and in the light of their quest for cultural identity.

The musical borrowing and reinterpretation characteristic of creole regions is an integral part of the creative process; thus, the term *creolization* was born. The transformation of original elements and the substitution of others, changes in function, attempts to retain ancestral customs, the borrowing of some expressions of modernity and the denunciation of others, the reinterpretation and consequent recreation of certain musical genres—all these traits serve as reminders of how deeply Martinique is anchored in a creole identity. Through Martinicans' style of social expression, oral tradition lives on, from the *krik-krac* tales told at funeral wakes to the *vwa* of the *bélè*-dance singers, and from the parades that occur spontaneously during carnival to Sunday afternoon street music in the capital, Fort-de-France (figure 1).

A comparison of contemporary musical practices with descriptions of early practices reveals that Martinique's musical traditions have followed regional and insular trajectories. This history can be seen as a process through which musical practices have evolved around social, cultural, and economic changes, particularly since 1946.

Beguine, a referential genre

In identifying an authentically Martinican musical genre, discourse on musical tradition singles out the beguine (*biguine, bigin*) because of its early origins and frequent use. The beguine—music and dance—can be distinguished by a binary rhythmic pattern (figure 2*a*). *Mazouk,* another genre associated with popular music in Martinique, is based on a rhythm similar to this, but in triple time (figure 2*b*).

The instrumentation in contemporary musical practice identifies two main types of Martinican beguine: drum beguine (*bigin bélè*) and orchestral beguine. Each of these refers to contexts of a specific origin. The drum beguine comes from a series of *bélè,* dances performed since early colonial times by the slaves who lived in the heart of the great sugar plantations.

Musically, the drum beguine can be distinguished from the orchestral beguine in four ways: its use of a cylindrical single-headed drum (*bélè*) and rhythm sticks (*tibwa*), responsorial singing, soloistic improvisation, and a nasal vocal quality. The beguine figured in fertility rituals practiced in West Africa, the motherland of most

FIGURE 1   In La Savane Park in downtown Fort-de-France, an ensemble plays African-derived musical instruments. *From left:* two *boulè* drums, one *suru* drum, and one *bambú* idiophone; a standing male singer plays a *chacha* rattle. Photo by Dale A. Olsen, 1977.

Martinican slaves (Rosemain 1988), but its ritual significance has disappeared in Martinique. The beguine could be regarded as a continuation of a value system that is in essence African, but with sugar plantations as its social platform. The late singers Ti-Émile, Ti-Raoul, and Eugène Mona remain symbols of the drum *bigin*.

The orchestral beguine has taken a different route. Its ancestry can be traced to Saint Pierre, an urban center that since the 1800s has harbored a notable number of residents of French descent. It keeps the syncopations of the drum *bigin* but takes on an almost Dixieland flavor by virtue of the complexity of its instrumentation (figure 3). The melody, sung in Creole, has a verse-refrain form, bespeaking an unmistakably French influence. The famous "*Mwen désennd Sin Piè*" and many other melodies popularized by Léona Gabriel, the Pierre Rassin Orchestra, Loulou Boislaville, and others, fit into this category.

By highlighting the stylistic elements of both beguines and indicating the place of origin, the table in figure 3 distinguishes their traits. It reveals that in both, the same rhythmic pattern maintained by the rhythm sticks (figure 2a) is present—which suggests that this rhythm characterizes the beguine and is therefore its main identifying trait (see Okada 1995: examples 17 and 18).

Kadans, the birth of a creole identity

For many years, the musical environment with which the population of Martinique identified itself was essentially defined by the two types of beguine (and the *mazouk*

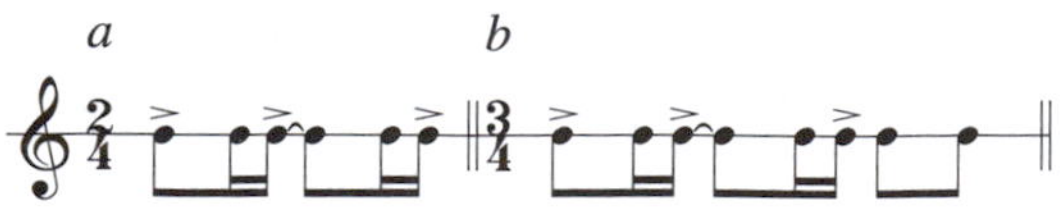

FIGURE 2   The referential Martinican rhythmic pattern: *a*, duple, as in the beguine; *b*, triple, as in the *mazouk*. Transcriptions by Monique Desroches.

FIGURE 3 The distinguishing traits of the drum *bigin* and the orchestrated beguine.

Musical genre	*Bigin bélè*	Orchestrated beguine
Tempo	♩ = 280	♩ = 220
Dance type	circle and quadrille	couple
Formal structure	call and response (soloist improvises)	verse-refrain (8-m. phrases – ABA)
Instrumentation	*bélè* (drum) *ti-bwa* (sticks)	piano, trombone, clarinet, bass, drums, *chacha*
Context	rural (plantation)	urban
Influence	African	European
Basic rhythm	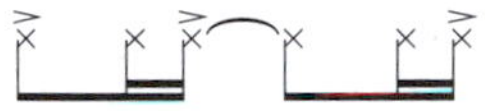	

and the creole waltz), and it was not until the 1970s that this soundscape underwent substantial changes. The causes for this transformation were many, but one is major: the immigration to Martinique of Haitians fleeing their country for political reasons.

To the urban centers of the French West Indies the Haitians brought the *kadans* 'cadence', a musical genre already familiar to some Martinicans via radio. *Kadans* makes a subtle use of musical accents, syncopation, and instrumental color, derived from the mini-jazz orchestras of Haiti (featuring brass, lead and bass guitar, bell, and drums) [see HAITI]. The vocal technique used in *kadans* also contributes to its flavor by the use of onomatopoeia and long, drawn-out tones reminiscent of *bel canto* singing.

This new music upset the relationship that Martinicans had maintained with their music, former ties to island history, and the traditional music of their ancestors; however, the arrival of a popular music from another island served to highlight a sociocultural commonality between the cultures, with their shared history of slavery and a common language. So it was that the island's cultural landmarks were no longer based mostly on Martinican history and society but became something vaster, embracing a larger part of the Caribbean region.

Most music that had previously been produced in Martinique had come from groups formed on the spot at events of an equally spontaneous nature, but *kadans* set a new dynamic into motion with new players, production values, and socioeconomic settings. Here were groups whose status approached the professional, among whom the majority had already recorded commercially and whose success had been transmitted by the media throughout the Creole-speaking Caribbean, setting a standard that local musicians aspired to meet.

Kadans swept the country, and most Martinican musicians turned to its performance and composition, recording on French and West Indian labels, and for the first time the Creole-speaking Caribbean moved to the same music. Singer David Martial and the group La Perfekta are examples of this development.

The result of this upheaval was that the islanders' quest for cultural identity had to be considered creole, not solely Martinican. In the early 1980s, the founding of International Creole Day (Journée Internationale du Créole), held annually on 28

Zouk is a result of the fusion of musical genres from the Caribbean, Africa, and Europe, but it represents Martinicans' desire to put forth an image of the French West Indies that would remain creole while meeting up with modernity.

October, could be seen as the official manifestation of a sense of belonging wherein music played, and still plays, a key cultural role.

Zouk, a musical and social phenomenon

The musical hegemony of *kadans* dominated the musical scene until the mid-1980s, when *zouk* (perhaps glossable as 'dance party') arrived on the scene. Much more than a new concept or a fad, *zouk* reaches beyond the borders of the West Indies to the continents of Africa, Europe, and North America. Its essential expressive elements are drawn from French West Indian traditions, using the *bélè*, the *makè*, or the *boulè* drums to maintain, with the *ti-bwa* and the rattle *chacha*, a rhythm whose basic pulse comes from the drum beguine. Pierre-Edouard Décimus and Jacob Devarieux, the founders of Kassav' (the band that epitomizes the sound of *zouk*), added the festivity and release that mark the spontaneity of the street parade (*vidé*), integrating into the new music and dance some rhythmic elements of the old.

After the fashion of the *balakadri* (from the French *bal à quadrilles*) and the *bal granmoun* (old-time evening balls), a *zouk* then featured the new sound in alternation with dances such as beguines, "slows," and mazurkas to punctuate the evening's ambience. On top of this formula, the creators continued to creolize by slipping in the syncopation of calypso, putting the bass in the foreground (as in reggae), emphasizing guitar solos, and adding staccato brass, all solidly anchored in the ostinato figures of the drums as heard in the contemporary sound of Congo (formerly Zaïre).

The popularity of *zouk* lay in its inventors' ability to engineer and balance its borrowed musical elements so effectively that the resulting atmosphere of joy and release became associated with the genre. *Zouk* gave the region a second wind, perhaps even a new life, and became the common ground, the moment of exchange and synthesis, where all could meet. It could be seen not only as the reinterpretation but as the creation of a music that now expresses Martinican identity.

With *zouk*, Martinican music entered fully into European and American markets, where the recording industry responded to the laws of supply and demand. Unlike *kadans*, in which Martinicans drew their inspiration from foreign musical genres, *zouk* proposed a musical model that united first the entire West Indian community and eventually musicians and fans of African-American music the world over.

In addition, following the example of North American and European rock, Martinican musicians began to take a growing interest in the visual dimensions of performance, in which the stakes had become as important as those of the aural. Into Martinican musical experiences they incorporated theatrical staging: choreography, costumes, lighting. They shifted the appearance of the presentation from that of a dance to that of a spectacle. When one compares the beguine of the 1950s to *zouk* it is clear that a significant transformation took place over thirty years, creating new values and relationships between the people and their music, where the latter is no longer simply intended to be danced to, but also to be watched.

Zouk is a result of the fusion of musical genres from the Caribbean, Africa, and Europe, but it represents Martinicans' desire to put forth an image of the French West Indies that would remain creole while meeting up with modernity—a new identity that followed musical, commercial, and aesthetic trends, and would ultimately characterize a transnational culture.

CONTEMPORARY TRENDS

Tamils came to Martinique from India after the local abolition of slavery (1848), providing labor that had formerly been supplied by slaves. Most came to stay and continued certain of their traditions, including rituals and ceremonial music for rituals (Desroches 1983, 1987, 1992).

Besides the Tamil enclave, three main avenues remain available to today's Martinican musician. The first is the continuation of the trajectory taken by *zouk* in the mid-1980s: the main foundations of the Creole identification process still remain rooted in rhythm, dance, and the employment of Creole, but musicians now cloak themselves in new sounds (such as richer harmonies and orchestral diversity), which I call post-*zouk*. The group Kwak fits into this category.

Return to the source

The second main musical path I call a return to the source. It advocates the return to musical beginnings by favoring music that draws from the past, emphasizing common musical roots. The distinctions formerly made between traditional and popular music are becoming increasingly fine as the latter incorporates more elements from musical practices that are growing progressively rarer because of massive urbanization and migration. These elements include melodic and rhythmic expression, traditional content, and performance context.

This new approach seems to be the chosen avenue of many contemporary musicians, some of whom have revived, at times almost completely, music from ancestral traditions or music from the era preceding Martinique's departmentalization. The group Racines ('roots') is an example of this phenomenon; their 1988 recording *Kali* became a bestseller, hitting the top of the local charts soon after its release.

Other musicians use traditional Martinican rhythms (beguine, mazurka) as a foundation. They sing in Creole but develop and integrate foreign instrumental techniques and harmonies, such as those of jazz and other genres. The success of Mario Canonge's recording *Retour aux sources* (1991) belongs to this category, which could be seen as a continuation of a trend begun as far back as the 1960s by Marius Cultier and the group Fall Fret.

Today, recording companies and distribution and marketing networks alike accept music with an ever-diversifying signature, in which traditional music figures strongly; good examples are the groups Bélè nou and Racines and the singer Max Cilla.

Rap and raggamuffin

The third musical avenue is some people's passion for rap and raggamuffin, adopted part and parcel without having passed through the filter of reinterpretation. Here, identity is linked with black culture, and a variety of concerns are addressed, especially the denunciation of the unequal sharing of power and resources. It will be instructive to follow the progress of these genres in the years to come, to see in which directions the movement will evolve and whether the historical elements of the music are wiped out or forgotten.

CULTURAL IDENTITY

The coexistence of diverse musical aesthetics suggests that Martinican music is at a crossroads in the search for a cultural identity. The choice of performance space, the selection of sonic material, the creation of new musical directions, music that is at once nationalistic and transnational—all these factors indicate a profound preoccupation with the quest for an identity, a search for a musical space that would be simultaneously Martinican, creole, and contemporary.

In Martinique, following the evolution of the dominant musical practices of successive periods amounts to following the island's political, social, and economic history. Haitian immigration has contributed to shaping musical traditions in Martinique, as has emigration to France.

Building up a cultural identity through a musical product is a dynamic, selective process. In Martinique, each genre has defined itself in reaction to the previous one, and musical traditions have been adopted, transformed, abandoned, and revisited. Through this process, Martinicans have gone from an ethnic identity (evidenced in the cleavage between the *bigin bélè*, linked to Africa, and the orchestral beguine, associated with Europe) to a cultural identity, residing in something of an Antillean consciousness. This is what the Martinican writer Edouard Glissant called *antillanité*, a concept that in *zouk* reached out to encompass Caribbean, African, and European features. In reference to earlier Antillanité, the post-*zouk* movement is called *créolité*.

In Martinique, the main debate about identity is found in music. But contrasting with what has happened elsewhere, this debate takes place not only in lyrics (with notable exceptions, such as Mona), but in rhythm, dance, and language. Beyond a product and a process, music must be seen as an issue. In Martinique, cultural identity is deeply rooted in praxis.

FURTHER STUDY

The music of Martinique has been little researched by English-writing scholars. Works in French, however, include two studies by Monica Desroches: *La musique traditionnelle de la Martinique* (1985) and *Les instruments de musique traditionnelle* (1989). Beguine music, which has been studied in neighboring Guadeloupe by Édouard Benoit (1993:53–67), has not been researched in Martinique, even though that French department has produced a number of well-known beguine composers (Benoit 1993:243). Jocelyne Guilbault, in her book *Zouk: World Music in the West Indies* (1993), presents brief but important information about music in Martinique, especially as it relates to music in other French-speaking islands of the Caribbean. She explains that French-produced radio has been influential in introducing African popular music into Martinique (and Guadeloupe): "the musics of Zaire, Congo, and Cameroon were listened to regularly from the late seventies and are still part of the local repertoire" (1993:16). She also explains that certain Caribbean musics such as calypso and reggae were introduced by radio and touring musicians from Trinidad and Jamaica. Likewise, touring groups from Cuba, the Dominican Republic, and Puerto Rico also influenced the development of popular music in Martinique, as did popular musical traditions from Argentina and Brazil (Guilbault 1993:17). All of these, and especially Dominican *cadence-lypso* and Haitian *konpa-dirèk*, were influential in the development of *zouk* in Martinique (and Guadeloupe).

REFERENCES

Benoist, Jean. 1994. "Le métissage: Biologie d'un fait social, sociologie d'un fait biologique." *Métissages* 11:13–21.

Benoit, Édouard. 1993. "*Biguine*: Popular Music of Guadeloupe (1940–1960)." In *Zouk: World Music in the West Indies*, by Jocelyn Guilbault with Gage Averill, Édouard Benoit, and Gregory

Rabess, 53–67. Chicago, University of Chicago Press.

Berrouët-Oriol, Robert, and Robert Fournier. 1994. "Créolophonie et francophonie nord-sud: Transcontinuum." *Canadian Journal of Latin American and Caribbean Studies* 17(34):13–27.

Canonge, Mario, and the ensemble Kann'. 1991. *Retour aux sources.* S.N.A. 150960. Compact disc.

Desroches, Monique. 1981. "Les pratiques musicales: Image de l'histoire, reflet d'un contexte." *Historial Antillais* 1:495–504.

———. 1985. *La musique traditionnelle de la Martinique.* Rapport no. 8. Montréal: Centre de Recherche Caraïbe, Université de Montréal.

———. 1987. "La musique rituelle tamoule à la Martinique: Structure sonore d'un espace sacré." Ph.D. dissertation, University of Montréal.

———. 1989. *Les instruments de musique traditionnels à la Martinique.* Fort-de-France: Bureau du Patrimoine, Conseil régional de la Martinique.

———. 1992. "Créolisation musicale et identité culturelle à la Martinique." *Canadian Journal of Latin American and Caribbean Studies* 17(34):41–53.

Desroches, Monique, and Jean Benoist. 1983. "Tambours de l'Inde à la Martinique, structure sonore d'un espace sacré." *Etudes créoles* 5:39–59.

Fuma, Sudel, and Jean Poirier. 1994. "Métissages, hétéroculture et identité culturelle." *Métissages* 11:49–64.

Guilbault, Jocelyne, with Gage Averill, Édouard Benoit, and Gregory Rabess. 1993. *Zouk: World Music in the West Indies.* Chicago: University of Chicago Press.

Okada, Yuki. 1995. *The Caribbean.* JVC Smithsonian Folkways Video Anthology of Music and Dance in the Americas, 4. Montpelier, Vt.: Multicultural Media VTMV-228. Video.

Racines. 1988. *Kali.* Hibiscus Records HR 88020 CS 750. Compact disc.

Rosemain, Jacqueline. 1988. *La musique dans la société antillaise (1635–1902).* Paris: L'Harmattan.

Montserrat
John Messenger

Social Backgrounds
Musical Contexts and Genres
Jumbie
Carnival, Boxing Day, and Jump-up Day

Montserrat, the southernmost of the Leeward Islands of the West Indies, embraces about 63 square kilometers of mountainous terrain. It had a population of about 12,500 people, of whom one-fifth resided in the capital, Plymouth; the remainder inhabited forty-one villages located mostly along the leeward coast and in the interior. Montserratians were mainly subsistence farmers and migrant laborers in Plymouth. Since the 1960s, many nationals of Canada, England, and the United States had settled in Montserrat, and tourism became a major industry.

Because of the devastating eruptions of the Soufriere Hills Volcano on July 18, 1995, over 8,000 people have left Montserrat, most going to the United Kingdom and Antigua. In 1998 the southern part of the island was almost completely destroyed and is now uninhabited; only about 3,200 people have remained on the northern part of Montserrat. Most of this essay describes the happier days of Montserrat in the 1970s, before the forced out-migration of the late 1990s.

SOCIAL BACKGROUNDS

In prehistoric times, the island was occupied sporadically—first by Arawaks and then by Caribs. The first permanent settlers were Irish, who, because of conflicts between Roman Catholics and Protestants, emigrated from St. Kitts and Virginia in 1632. Though Montserrat has been an English and British colony since that date, it is largely self-governing, with the British connection maintained by local referendum. The first census (in 1678) listed 1,868 Irish, 761 English, and 992 African slaves. By 1805, the slave population had grown to about 9,500, and the white had dwindled to a thousand. A demographic survey conducted in 1946 called 95 percent of Montserratians Negro. Though African phenotypes are dominant in the population, there is much evidence of intermixture, especially among the Black Irish (or "Montserrat Irish"). They are maybe a thousand strong and live in the north, claiming descent from slaves and Irish who married in the 1700s. To maintain Caucasoid phenotypic traits and the Irish heritage, they tend to intermarry.

The culture of Montserrat is an amalgam of African, Irish, and British retentions and reinterpretations, regional borrowings, and internal innovations (Dobbin 1986; Messenger 1968; Philpott 1973). Local culture, largely maintained by the rural underclass and dominated by the African heritage, is most manifested in the local Creole, spoken alongside English, and in religion, folklore, music, song, and dance (Dewer 1977; Dobbin 1986:32–37, 48–59; Messenger 1975:295–299, Philpott 1973:157–163). What remains of the Irish heritage is found in Creole loanwords, the phonology and grammar of local English, religion, and aesthetics. A body of African and Irish cultural imponderables—kinesic habits, values, codes of etiquette, musical styles—though difficult to describe in their subtlety, can be intuited by researchers who have resided in both West Africa and peasant Ireland.

Modernization since the 1970s has dramatically altered the culture. The major modernizing agents have been returning migrant laborers, returning trainees for schools and the civil service, a large real-estate development program (to attract expatriate residents), the enlarging of the airport (built in 1957), governmental plans to emphasize tourism, the establishment of a medical school (serving three hundred fifty students, mostly North Americans), and two local radio stations. Only in the 1960s did traditional patterns of music, song, and dance give way to imported music—steel drums, reggae, and soca. One impetus for this change was provided by a recording studio built in the 1980s. It attracted musical ensembles from all over the world, including the Rolling Stones.

MUSICAL CONTEXTS AND GENRES

African and possibly Irish proverbs and African spider-trickster tales (*anansi*) are common in Montserrat, but folk songs and their texts are far more widespread. Many of these melodies and at least sixty lyrics are usually performed at rituals involving jumbies, ghosts of the dead (good and evil). Islanders love this music and are proud of it as an expression of their cultural identity. Most are experts on the subject, and fights erupt over the proper rendition of tunes and lyrics.

Many tunes, popular with locals and tourists, have been recorded by the Emerald Community Singers (named after an epithet for Montserrat, "Emerald Isle of the Caribbean"), a group formed in 1971. Its first record (1973) featured five traditional songs in highly interpretive performances, somewhat removed from earlier styles. Discussing morality, love, courtship, work, amusing incidents, and magic (*obeah*), the lyrics recount historical events and singular deeds of historical figures on the island.

Two songs of historical significance—"Nincom Riley" and "All de Relief"—are among those often heard. The former heralds emancipation:

> De fus' o' Agus' is cum 'gin.
> Hurrah fo' Nincom Riley!
> If buckra nack, me nack 'ee 'gin.
> Hurrah fo' Nincom Riley!

Here, Nincom Riley reads the proclamation that advocates that freed slaves reply in kind by nacking—kicking—for physical abuse by their former masters. This song combines Irish and African elements: Riley is an Irish surname; Nincom probably derives from the Gaelic *ninc* 'rogue'; *buckra,* a common New World black term for whites, may derive from the Nigerian Ibibio *mbakara* 'he who conquers'. The other song reflects favoritism in the distribution of relief after the hurricane of 1924:

> All de relief dem sen' from town,
> All de relief dem sen' from town,
> Some git some, an' some git none.

Other than those involving jumbies, songs sung in the 1960s were calypsos presented by competitors during carnival and Irish melodies voiced by a few Black Irish elders.

George Allen, who died in 1966, was the last musician to play Irish airs (figure 1). He played a fiddle, held in the crook of his elbow. His daughter, who emigrated soon after his death, could perform Irish step dances, and her English brogue was the most marked on the island. Since the mid-1970s, the local calypsonian Arrow and his soca band have risen to international fame. The demise of traditional music, song, and dance can largely be attributed to his popularity.

JUMBIE

The jumbie dance, probably last performed in 1980, is central to local culture, possibly its focus: "No other single event on the island . . . brings together at one place and one time so much of the culture and historical heritage. . . . No other event . . . contains so much of the traditional lifeways—music, dance, folklore, wisdom, kinship, and friendship values" (Dobbin 1986:153).

Central to this dance is belief in jumbies, who dominate local religion, just as fairies do Irish traditions. Though most Montserratians are members of Christian churches and have been since emancipation, most continue to hold unorthodox beliefs in the supernatural. In addition to jumbies, they recognize a multitude of spirits: the *sukra* and the *jabless,* African spirits, harmful to humans; the Irish mermaid who lives atop a mountain; the animal spirit, resembling the Irish *puca,* who roams the road adjacent to the Roman Catholic church in St. Patrick's Village; and the Jack Lantern, a spirit more menacing than its counterpart in Ireland.

The jumbies of Montserrat are treated much like the fairies of Ireland: when people open a bottle of rum, they spill a few drops in the corner of the room; before they throw water out of a house at night, they direct "Pardon me" to any passing jumbie; on Christmas Eve, people set a table and put out food for ghosts to eat while the family is atttending Mass. At sundown, to prevent evil jumbies from entering, most rural houses close their doors and windows, sometimes marked with white crosses. Ghosts not only leave their graves and voluntarily walk about, but can be called out by *obeahmen,* at whose command they perform good and evil "tricks" (acts); the jumbie dance can summon them, and they can possess dancers.

Some Montserrat-Irish elders hold that the jumbie dance originated before emancipation, when slaves observed and emulated dancing in the "big houses." The jumbie dance differs from the country dance (also called *drum dance* and *goatskin dance*), even though both dances are identical as to musickers (musicians), the instruments played, the songs and dances performed, and the merriment that prevails. The country dance is done for entertainment, "for a spree," and may take place in a home, in a rum shop (a combined provision-and-drinking establishment), even at a hotel as an exhibition. But the jumbie dance is for "dee dead." Danced in a home after a fête, it includes the sponsor's kin and close friends. It is held at times of personal crisis (christenings, weddings, emigrants' departures and returns) and affliction (illness, disputes over property, marital problems). In it, dancers "turn"—become possessed by jumbies, who to those in trance reveal "secrets" that foretell the future, cure sickness, and solve problems.

The musickers, four in number, play a fife or a "pulley" (accordion, concertina, or melodeon), a triangle, and two flat, goatskin-covered drums—one large, called a jumbie drum or a *woowoo* or a French reel, and the other smaller, with or without discs on the edge, called a *babala* or a tambourine. The drums are identical with the Irish *bodhran* in shape and manner of playing—with the back of the hand, the palm, and the fronts of the fingers. When rubbed with the heel of the hands or with a moistened finger, the jumbie drum makes a sound that attracts jumbies—as do (some claim) certain jumbie songs.

Four pairs of men and women dance a series of five quadrilles ("sets") played at

FIGURE 1   George Allen, the last fiddler who played Irish airs. Cudjoe Head, Montserrat. Photo by John Messenger, 1965.

successively faster tempos. After several hours of dancing, with new partners taking over at the end of each five quadrilles, one or more of the dancers will become possessed, aided by the copious consumption of rum, the wildness of the beat, the heat in the house, and the shouts of the crowd. Turning may involve whirling about, apart from the other dancers, or falling to the floor, when the possessed one gasps out a "secret," sometimes in glossolalia. The playing and dancing reveal startling reinterpretations: Western instruments produce Africanesque music, to which dancers perform Irish steps while moving their upper bodies like Africans.

CARNIVAL, BOXING DAY, AND JUMP-UP DAY

Music, song, and dance also abound during carnival (locally called Festival), which occurs between Boxing Day (26 December) and Jump-up Day (1 January). During carnival, and for a fortnight before, masqueraders from various villages parade about the island in colorful costumes, accompanied by musickers (figure 2). Dancers' costumes mimic the uniforms of Grenadier Guards. In a frenzy, the dancers perform sets to music produced by a fife, a triangle, and two deep-barreled, goatskin-covered Africanesque drums ("kettles," "booms"), played in an African manner (figure 3). The dances and the music are African style; the sets, borrowed from the jumbie dance, are almost unrecognizable as such. In 1988, one group survived; in St. John's Village, few attended its performance, preferring to dance to amplified soca music nearby.

On Boxing Day, islanders gather at Sturge Park (adjoining Plymouth) to witness a series of musical events, some of them competitive: music played by steelbands, routines danced by costumed groups from villages and sponsored by local businesses, appearances by ensembles of masqueraders, and the antics of costumed mummers. Between that day and Jump-up Day, organizers produce a beauty pageant, a calypso contest, and nightly dancing in the streets of the capital behind a lorry-drawn platform with a band or the amplified recordings of such. Jump-up Day commemorates emancipation, and its highlight is a parade of brawny weightlifters, carrying chains and dancing to steelband music. From time to time, to symbolize breaking the chains of slavery, they jump high in the air. Masqueraders move about the streets, where thousands of spectators mill about, singing and dancing. During carnival, people do little work; eschewing sleep, they drink heavily.

FIGURE 2   Masqueraders dance to the accompaniment of musickers who play fife and drums. St. John's, Montserrat. Photo by John Messenger, 1972.

During carnival, choral and instrumental groups—
usually small in size and made up of children—visit
homes and hotels, where they performed for food
and money.

FIGURE 3   A band furnishes music for masqueraders to dance. Black Sam Aymers, the conductor, is playing the fife; the other instruments are
a triangle and two drums (only the fife and one
drum are visible). St. John's, Montserrat. Photo
by John Messenger, 1967.

Music, song, and dance also prevail on other important occasions. People meet
in rum shops for gossiping, singing, dancing, and drinking. Musicians often play
accordions, guitars, banjos, and ukuleles (*cuatros*) to entertain the customers and fur-
nish music for dancing. Sometimes on Boxing Day, string bands perform impromptu
in rum shops. During carnival, choral and instrumental groups—usually small in size
and made up of children—visit homes and hotels, where they perform for food and
money. Christmas carols are a staple. A disco in Plymouth, popular with youths,
challenges traditional expressions. Though most calypsos satirically single out political and economic ills, singers sometimes lament the passing of traditional ways, for-
lornly calling for cultural revitalization.

REFERENCES

Dewer, Ann Marie. 1977. "Music in the
Alliouagana (Montserrat) cultural tradition."
Typescript, Montserrat Public Library.

Dobbin, Jay D. 1986. *The Jombee Dance of
Montserrat.* Columbus: Ohio State University
Press.

Emerald Community Singers. 1973. *Emerald Folk
Creations.* Barbados: Trex Records. LP disk.

Messenger, John C., Jr. 1968. "The Irish of
Montserrat." Typescript, Montserrat Public
Library.

———. 1975. "Montserrat: 'The Most
Distinctively Irish Settlement in the New
World.'" *Ethnicity* 2:281–303.

Philpott, Stuart B. 1973. *West Indian Migration:
The Montserrat Case.* London: Athlone Press.

Netherlands Antilles and Aruba
Daniel E. Sheehy

Musical Traditions

Musical Instruments

Musical Contexts and Genres

Popular Music

Art Music

Further Study

Six islands make up the Netherlands Antilles and Aruba, located in the Lesser Antilles chain of the Caribbean Sea: Sint Maarten, Sint Eustatius, and Saba in the northern, windward island group, east of the Virgin Islands; and Aruba, Bonaire, and Curaçao in the southern, leeward group, off the coast of Venezuela. Christopher Columbus sighted the northern islands during his 1493 voyage, and his successors subdued the local Carib population. The Spanish navigator Alonso de Ojeda landed on Curaçao in 1499. In 1527, Spain claimed Aruba, Bonaire, and Curaçao as its own and the Arawak inhabitants as its subjects. After a period of struggle for control among several European colonial powers, all six islands became Dutch possessions in the early 1600s and for the most part remained so thereafter. In 1845, they were officially organized as the Netherlands Antilles, and in 1954, they became an integral part of the Netherlands. In 1986, Aruba separated from the other five islands, attaining equal status as an autonomous part of the Netherlands.

Culturally and geographically, the islands are marked by similarities and regional and local distinctions. Dutch is universally the official language, though the long-standing influence of neighboring islands has made English important in the north and Spanish common in the south. In Aruba, Bonaire, and Curaçao, the most commonly spoken language is Papiamento, a Spanish-dominant creole with borrowings from Dutch and Portuguese. The northern three islands are quite small in area (85 square kilometers total), with diminutive populations: Sint Maarten, twenty-five thousand; Sint Eustatius, fifteen hundred; Saba, one thousand (1989). Sint Maarten shares its island with the French dependency St. Martin.

The southern islands are much larger, and account for most of the Netherlands Caribbean population: Curaçao, 462 square kilometers with 187,500 people (1989); Aruba, 181 square kilometers with sixty-six thousand (1995); and Bonaire, 291 square kilometers with ten thousand (1989). The windward climate is tropical and wet, with lush vegetation; the leeward islands are tropical and arid, with sparse vegetation. The people of the windward group are largely Protestant; the leeward population is predominantly Roman Catholic, with Curaçao being home to the Caribbean's longest-established Jewish community.

People of African ancestry, mostly descendants of slaves imported in the six-

tambú   Also *barí*, a membranophone, the most important African-derived instrument in the Netherlands Antilles

bastel   Also *seoe*, a water drum made from half of a large gourd placed open side down in a water-filled tub and played with the hands

benta   Mouth-resonated bow from Curaçao, made from a local hardwood and strung with coconut fiber

bamba   Stamped tubes of Bonaire that can accompany celebrations of the feasts of St. John and St. Peter

teenth through mid-nineteenth centuries, are prominent throughout the Dutch islands. Their proportion varies from island to island—from only half the population of Saba to 85 percent of the population of Curaçao. In Aruba, an African-Arawak mix predominates; in the other islands, an African-European mix is common. More than forty nationalities have contributed to the cultural makeup of the Netherlands Antilles, including African, European colonial, and more recent immigrant cultures from India, Lebanon, China, and elsewhere.

MUSICAL TRADITIONS

In general, the major currents of musical life in the Netherlands Antilles and Aruba have reflected the islands' historical cultural influences and social divisions. As native populations became extinct or were absorbed into the new colonial cultural majority of Africans and Europeans, so did their musical traditions pass away. Little is known of the music of the local Carib, who long ago disappeared from the northern islands, or of the Arawak inhabitants of the Lesser Antilles, who lost any sense of a separate cultural identity as they intermingled with the African majority. The gourd rasp (*raspu*) may be a descendant of a similar Arawak instrument, though it could as likely have been modeled on rasps imported from elsewhere in the Caribbean. Clearly, African, European, and, more recently, Venezuelan, Colombian, Cuban, other Latin American, and North American musical models have prevailed in the evolution of Dutch Antillean musical practice.

African-derived music

Firmly transplanted in Dutch Caribbean cultural soil, African-derived musical style has profoundly shaped virtually all musical expression in its New World domain. Martinus Joannes Niewindt, the first apostolic vicar of Curaçao (1842–1860), wrote in a letter describing his new see that "the island has become Africa with whites now and then encouraging the wildly drumming and dancing Blacks by passing round the rum bottle" (Walle 1954; quoted in Stevenson 1975:61). Curaçaoan musician and educator Edgar Palm saw the most direct link to his island's African heritage in five stylist traits of the *tambú* music-and-dance complex: the centrality of the *tambú* (from Spanish *tambor* 'drum') to certain rituals and dances, the dance named *tambú*, and the musical group named *tambú*; the separated, individuated style of dancing with the *tambú*; the polyrhythmic relationship between the *tambú*, the singing, and the other instruments; the style of singing, accompanying the dance with improvised, satirical texts; and the highly developed sense of musical rhythm (Palm 1978:19–21).

MUSICAL INSTRUMENTS

There are several important African-derived musical instruments, genres, and performance occasions in the Dutch Leeward Antilles.

Idiophones

Among the idiophones are the *agan*, two metal rods struck together. A water drum (*bastel, seoe*) is half of a large gourd placed open side down in a water-filled tub; a squatting player hits it with his hands (Lekis 1956:224). Other idiophones, though not clearly of African origin, are often used in music of African-derived style. Developed in the Dutch islands from gourd and cow-horn predecessors, the *wiri* rasp is made from an elongated piece of steel, serrated and scraped with a metal rod, producing a louder, sharper sound than its precursors. The *wiri* was originally invented to accompany the *ka'i* (also *kaha di musika, tingilingibox*), an instrument made in Spain and Italy and introduced via Venezuela to Aruba. It spread to Curaçao between 1880 and 1900. The *ka'i* is constructed in the shape of a hand-cranked organ, but instead involves a rotating cylinder with pins that activate hammers, which in turn strike strings. One other instrument distinctive of Dutch Antilles music and that plays in a rhythmic style is the *matrimonial*, a thin plank measuring 60 by 5 centimeters, with four or more sets of copper or tin discs nailed loosely to it. It is held on the knee and beaten, producing a sharp, percussive sound (Lekis 1956:226).

Membranophones

The *tambú* (called *barí* in Bonaire), a membranophone, is the most important African-derived instrument in the Dutch islands of the Leeward Antilles. An earlier, single-headed version made from a hollowed log has been superseded by a double-headed drum made from a herring barrel with sheepskin or goatskin heads struck with both hands.

Chordophones

Resembling African mouth-resonated bows is the *benta*, made on Curaçao from a local hardwood and strung with coconut fiber. Its string is hit with a small wooden stick, and the pitch and timbre are modified by stopping one end of the string with a piece of metal and holding the other end of the string near the oral cavity and changing its shape.

Aerophones

The *cachu*, a cow-horn trumpet, is apparently derived from an antelope-horn Bantu predecessor used for signaling. Pitch may be varied by embouchure tension and/or stopping the open end with the hand, and by interjecting sung pitches. In Curaçao, the *cachu* has been used to call for water to be brought to workers during the sorghum harvest. The *becu* is a transverse double-reed aerophone cut from a sorghum stem and played mainly on the occasion of Simadan (Harvest Festival). In Burkina Faso, a similar instrument has the name *biko* (Gansemans 1982). On Bonaire, stamped tubes (*bamba*) may accompany celebrations of the feasts of St. John and St. Peter.

MUSICAL CONTEXTS AND GENRES

The *tambú* complex of music and dance emerged in the 1800s or earlier. Musically, the *tambú* is generated from a basic repeated rhythmic cycle, with interlocking polyrhythmic patterns providing a framework for an improvising lead drum. The *tambú* dance is traditionally performed by couples, though not touching, except that the man may occasionally put his hand briefly on his partner's shoulder or may briefly hold the ends of her scarf (Lekis 1956:221). When the *tambú* moved to the port of Willemstad, Curaçao's capital, it evolved into an increasingly erotic dance, associated with houses of prostitution and the consumption of alcohol.

Simadan, the sorghum-harvest festival, is another time when the *cachu* might be played, with the *agan* (also used in *tambú* music), beating on pails, and responsorial singing. This music may also have accompanied ceremonial competitive dancing, in which the leaders of two groups of harvest workers would vie for onlookers' favor (Lekis 1956:227), and the *wapa* line dance (see Okada 1995:examples 5, 6, and 7).

European and Latin American marks on Netherlands Antillean musical life are strong, with social dancing, salon music, and the *ka'i* and its music being among the most important influences (Palm 1978:21). European holidays such as Christmas, New Year's, Epiphany, carnival, and patron saints' days are universally important times for music making. In the nineteenth and twentieth centuries, numerous European and Latin American forms of music and dance were laid over the cultural and stylistic base, and some evolved into distinctively local hybrid forms. European dances such as the waltz, the mazurka, the polka, the schottische, and quadrille came into vogue in the 1800s, usually accompanied by European-style string-based ensembles. The waltz in Curaçao maintained its European 3/4 time and harmonic and melodic style, but polyrhythmic additions made for a much more active rhythmic feel. Social dances introduced from Latin American countries included the moderated duple-meter *danza*, derived from the Haitian *contredanse* via nineteenth-century Cuba, and the syncopated duple-meter *tumba*, resembling the Cuban ballroom dance *guaracha* and popular in many parts of the Antilles. The *danza* is danced by two couples with patterns taken from the quadrille; after an introductory polka-time section, the couples curtsy and dance two-step patterns (Lekis 1956:231). Around the mid-twentieth century, the *tumba,* identified with Afro-Caribbean musical tastes since the late 1800s, was the most popular dance and rhythm in all the Netherlands Antilles. It often included socially satirical verses and functioned similarly to Trinidadian calypso in this regard. Proximity to South America brought the *joropo,* the *pasillo,* and other forms from Venezuela, Colombia, and beyond.

With these imported musical genres came several European and Latin American musical instruments that, excepting the *tambú,* have been central to the performance of these forms. Most significant is the *cuatra,* derived from the Venezuelan *cuatro,* a four-stringed guitar strummed rhythmically to accompany a wide range of music. The "standard" six-stringed guitar is also quite common. With the mandolin, string bass, and occasionally other stringed instruments and percussion, these were long the preferred accompaniment to social dance-music, but by the latter decades of the twentieth century, they were more often limited to self-conscious *grupos folklóricos* performing creolized dance-music thought to represent the past more than the present. The *cuatra,* played in the rapid, syncopated triple meter resembling that of the *joropo,* remained central to much social music in traditional contexts, including the annual celebrations for the feasts of Saint John and Saint Peter on Bonaire. In addition, accordions, Cuban *congas* (single-headed barrel drums), the triangle, and other instruments made their way into social dance ensembles.

POPULAR MUSIC

The 1930s and 1940s saw the beginnings of an unending invasion of popular music models from Cuba, the United States, Venezuela, Colombia, and elsewhere in the circum-Caribbean region. Cuban-style orchestras often included Cuban musicians but were composed primarily of Curaçaoans and Arubans dressed in Cuban urban *rumbero* costumes with ruffle-armed shirts. The Cuban instrumentation included trumpet, claves (two wooden rods struck together to mark the basic meter), bongos, *congas, marímbula* (eight metal tongues attached to a deep resonator box and plucked like the African *mbira*), maracas, and guitar. These ensembles played Cuban dance pieces. Other ensembles, called jazz bands, took after North American dance bands with piano, *banzjó* (banjo), saxophone and/or clarinet, trumpet, violin, bass, drums, and lead singer (Martijn 1980:30–31, 49). Through the rest of the twentieth century, imported popular musics from the Americas bombarded the Dutch islands and inspired local imitators. Television stations on Curaçao and St. Maarten, radio, and the commercial music industry have made international popular music a common part of everyday life in the Dutch Antilles.

ART MUSIC

Art music has for more than two centuries maintained a significant niche in Dutch Antillean musical life. Protestant church music has been performed on pipe organs in Curaçao since the late 1700s (Palm 1978:24). Agustín Bethencourt, born in Tenerife in 1826, moved to the island in 1860, organized the first string quartet there, and in 1879 took the lead in founding Harmonie, the first symphonic orchestra on Curaçao (Stevenson 1975:62). Romantic-style art music has been the most influential, particularly that of Spain and Austria, and local composers created a significant repertoire of European salon music. Curaçaoan Jan Gerard Palm (1831–1906), who served as organist for both Fort Amsterdam Church and Mikvé Israel Synagogue, founded a major musical dynasty through his descendants, including Edgar Palm, author of *Muziek en Musici van de Nederlandse Antillen.*

FURTHER STUDY

Art music in the leeward islands has been documented in a small number of publications, including Edgar Palm's book and in Rudolf Frederik Willem Boskaljon's *Honderd jaar muziekleven op Curaçao* (1958) and his article "Het Muziekleven" (1948). Robert M. Stevenson offers a generous gloss of leeward-island music-related references in these and other general publications in his *A Guide to Caribbean Music History* (1975). Although these works offer numerous references and brief descriptions of folk and popular music, and in Palm's book, several chapters devoted to the African and creolized social dance music of the nineteenth and twentieth centuries, description and analysis of Dutch Antilles folk and popular music from an ethnomusicological perspective is severely limited, especially regarding the musical culture of the smaller windward islands. Notable exceptions are "The Origin and Development of Ethnic Caribbean Dance and Music" (1956), an unpublished doctoral dissertation by the dance ethnologist Lisa Lekis, and the annotated recording *Aruba–Bonaire–Curacao: Volksmuziek–musique populaire,* resulting from research and ethnographic recordings made in 1982 by the Belgian Centre Ethnomusicologique Paul Collaer, with notes in Dutch and French credited to Jas Gansemans. This recording was reissued as *Tumba Cuarta & Ka'i* on the Original Music label, with a modified version of the descriptive notes by John Storm Roberts.

REFERENCES

Boskaljon, Rudolf Frederik Willem. 1948. "Het muziekleven." In *Oranje en de zes caraibische parelen Officieel Gedenkboek,* 356–366. Amsterdam: J. H. De Russy.

———. 1958. *Honderd jaar muziekleven op Curaçao* (A hundred years of music on Curaçao). Assen, Netherlands: Van Gorcum.

Gansemans, Jas. 1982. *Aruba-Bonaire-Curaçao: Volksmuziek-musique populaire.* Tervüren, Belgium: Centre Ethnomusicologique Paul Collaer ECPC 01. Notes to LP disk.

———. N.d. *Tumba Cuarta & Ka'i.* Translated and modified by John Storm Roberts. Tivoli, N.Y.: Original Music OMC 202. Notes to LP disk

Lekis, Lisa. 1956. "The Origin and Development of Ethnic Caribbean Dance and Music." Ph.D. dissertation, University of Florida.

Martijn, S. "Yapi." 1980. *Kòrsou Musical, 1e Tomo (Dékada 30, 40 i 50).* Curaçao: Fundashon Promúsiko.

Okada, Yuki. *The Caribbean.* JVC Smithsonian Folkways Video Anthology of Music and Dance of the Americas, 4. Montpelier, Vt.: Multicultural Media VTMV-228. Video.

Palm, Edgar. 1978. *Muziek en Musici van de Nederlandse Antillen.* Curaçao: Druk De Curaçaosche Courant.

Stevenson, Robert M. 1975. *A Guide to Caribbean Music History.* Lima: Ediciones CULTURA.

Walle, J. van de. 1954. *De Nederlandse Antillen.* Baarn, Netherlands: Het Wereldvenster.

Puerto Rico
Héctor Vega Drouet

Musical Instruments
Musical Contexts and Genres
Teaching and Learning
Further Study

Puerto Rico is a small Caribbean island just east of the Dominican Republic and west of the Virgin Islands. Like the U.S. Virgin Islands, Puerto Rico is a colony (commonwealth) of the United States, to which it was ceded by Spain in 1898 following the Spanish-American War. It became the Commonwealth of Puerto Rico in the 1950s. But unlike the people of the Virgin Islands, Puerto Ricans traditionally speak Spanish, though many speak English in urban areas. As a former Spanish colony, Puerto Rico shares much history and culture with Cuba and the Dominican Republic.

Archaeological excavations have yielded evidence that thousands of years ago, native Americans inhabited Puerto Rico. Early inhabitants may have used these and other Caribbean Islands as a bridge in their travels south from North America or north from South America. Later, Arawak Indians from northern South America migrated from Paria Bay into the Caribbean Antilles.

By the time Christopher Columbus came to the Caribbean, the Arawak-speaking Taino were firmly established in the island they called Borinquen, the present Puerto Rico ('Rich Port'). Excavated pottery, domestic items of wood, and stone sculptures of deities confirm their existence. Examination of Arawak middens has revealed evidence of gourd rasps with scrapers (*güiros*); conch trumpets (*guamos*); wooden trumpets; pieces of a hollowed log with an H-shaped slit (similar to the *teponaztli,* an ancient Mexican hollowed log idiophone); shell, clay, wood, and gourd rattles (maracas); clay ocarinas; clay and bone whistles; and a bone flute.

Around 1510, the Spanish colonization of Puerto Rico forced the Taino into hard labor. Many succumbed to European diseases to which they had little or no natural immunity. In official records by the early 1600s, the Taino no longer appeared as a distinct people; however, small bands of them survived by taking refuge in remote and inaccessible hills, areas later called *indieras.*

From the descriptions of Arawak musical activities in the writings of the chroniclers (Cárdenas 1981; Casas 1965; López de Gómara 1965; Pané 1974), it seems that the *areyto* (also *areito*)—a celebration that combined poetry, songs, and dances, with accompanying instruments—was the most important social activity of Taino life. *Areytos* had a historical, religious, ritual, or ceremonial nature. The chroniclers

FIGURE 1   A *güiro* 'gourd scraper' under construction. Photo by Héctor Vega Drouet, 1995.

describe twenty different types. A principal singer or dancer set the order in which poems, songs, and dances were to be performed. Every child was taught the items appropriate for each occasion and how to improvise *areytos* as new situations arose. The *areyto* (*areito*) was the Taino's ideal means of communal socialization and reinforcement of shared beliefs and customs.

Astoundingly, though friars' training in the sixteenth to eighteenth centuries required some knowledge of music, particularly Gregorian chant and polyphonic choral music used in the Roman Catholic Church, chroniclers' reports contain no extensive descriptions, quotations, or analyses of indigenous melodies. We find only three facts pertaining to music: the elderly sang the low voices, while the young sang the upper voices; women sang the soprano, alto, and tenor voices; and indigenous singing was not harsh to European ears.

In Seville, in the Casa de Contracción (Contract Clearinghouse), sixteenth-century inventories detailing items sent to Spanish colonies include jingle bells, *vihuela* strings, clavichord strings, and fifes. Alfonso de Buenaño, boatswain, brought the first *vihuela* to Puerto Rico aboard the ship *Santiago* on 19 September 1512. A Mr. Quintana also brought a *vihuela* to Puerto Rico on 25 December 1512, when he arrived aboard *San Francisco*. Subsequently, other *vihuelas* arrived. Juan Martín, a passenger aboard *San Juan*, brought the first guitar to Puerto Rico on 11 December 1516 (Tanodi 1971).

The 1520s and 1530s were chaotic and disastrous for Puerto Rico, as the discovery of gold in New Spain (Mexico), Peru, and Venezuela lured settlers away. The Spanish population shrank by half. The island became isolated from other colonies; for those who remained, life became austere, and social events were limited. The Roman Catholic Church sponsored the official music activities of the island. Family parties and other informal activities with music were organized by the African slaves and enslaved Indians (*encomendados* 'charges') officially in Spanish hands. In this population—Spaniards, enslaved Africans and Indians, free Arawaks in the *indieras*—lay the foundation for the creolization of Puerto Rico.

By the 1540s, the island was no longer commercially important within the Spanish New World. Most of its merchandise, including musical instruments, was secondhand. For accompaniment to dancing by creole Puerto Ricans, the absence of instruments created a preference for singing, rather than solely instrumental music, and stimulated local craftsmen to build their own instruments.

MUSICAL INSTRUMENTS

Idiophones

Most hard-surface percussive instruments used in Puerto Rico are also found in other Spanish-speaking Caribbean cultures. These instruments include the claves, cowbell, and *güiro* scraper used in salsa and other dance musics, and the maracas used in *jíbaro* music (with the others just listed). Many instruments are machine made, but there are still local makers of the *güiro*, fashioned from a gourd (figure 1).

One distinctly African instrument common in Puerto Rico, as in many parts of the circum-Caribbean area, is the *marímbula*, an idiophone similar to the African *mbira* and *kalimba*, with several tuned metal lamellae mounted over a hole in a wooden box. As is still the practice in Cuba, the player would sit atop the box and pluck the lamellae with his fingers, supplying the bass for a small instrumental ensemble. The *marímbula* and its associated musical tradition arrived with slaves between 1800 and 1880 but quickly dissipated at the beginning of the 1900s. The *marímbula* has not been part of the rural tradition of Puerto Rico since the 1950s,

FIGURE 2   A *marímbula* player. Photo by Héctor Vega Drouet, 1995.

and in the previous five decades there had been but a few isolated builders and players of the instrument (figure 2).

Membranophones

The distinctly Puerto Rican *bomba* drum is a single-headed cylindrical instrument resembling an open-ended straight barrel. The drumhead is about 40 centimeters in diameter and about 75 centimeters long. Originally, the tension of the drumhead was fixed by six pegs. However, after Mr. Aquino, the lone drum builder at Loíza Aldea, discontinued making drums in the 1970s, *bomba* drumheads were fixed by screws, just as on commercial drums. Since 1994, Jesús Cepeda has opened a shop in Loíza Aldea, where he builds pegged *bomba* drums, reestablishing the tradition.

The *bomba* drum is placed between a seated musician's knees and played with the hands only. Two *bomba* drums are usually at the center of an ensemble including rattles, responsorial singers, and often other percussion instruments. One *bomba* plays a relatively fixed pattern, and the other plays a more variable one, improvising in the style of West African drumming.

The *pandereta* is a round frame drum, like a tambourine without jingles. The traditional grouping in Puerto Rico is three *panderetas* of graduated sizes playing three different interlocking parts, with the highest-pitched one having an improvising role. One or more melodic instruments, singers (in a responsorial style with choral refrain), and other percussion instruments are often added.

Many other membranophones are found in Puerto Rico. Most are a part of the *latino* tradition, with origins or parallels in Cuba and/or the Dominican Republic. From Cuban background or influence, for example, are the bongos and congas, and from the Dominican Republic is the *tambora* [see CUBA; DOMINICAN REPUBLIC].

Chordophones

There is no published research on the origins, history, and construction of early European-derived Puerto Rican rural instruments. Notable were four plucked-lute chordophones: *tiple, tres, cuatro,* and *bordonúa* (figure 3). There are no historical data about, nor are informants able to ascertain, the exact date or decade in which these instruments were first made. It appears probable, though, that the musical genre called *seis* (discussed below) was always performed on these instruments, and the *seis* was first used in the early 1600s.

Most of these instruments are hourglass shaped, with occasional regional variations. Respondents mention a three-stringed instrument called *requinto,* with the tuning e_1–a_1–$c\sharp_2$. This instrument is a variant of the common *tres,* similar in size, but with three triple-stringed courses (for a total of nine strings) tuned to A–d–f♯. The *tiple* 'treble' appears to derive from the *timple,* a single-coursed *vihuela* from Andalucía, Spain. It is 56 centimeters long, with a 24-centimeter body, a 16-centimeter neck (*brazo*), and a 14-centimeter pegbox (*pala* or *mano*). The tuning of the five strings is A–e_1–B_1–G–B.

The *cuatro* is the most popular and common of the melodic instruments. Its earlier, four-double-stringed form gave way to its current, five double-stringed courses. The strings of the *cuatro* are tuned in octaves, except for the first two courses (tuned in unison). The present tuning, B_1–E–A–d–g, is the same as that of sixteenth-century *vihuelas* and lutes. The *cuatro* is about 90 centimeters long, with a 50-centimeter body, a 20-centimeter neck, and a 20-centimeter pegbox.

The name of the *bordonúa* comes from the word *bordón* (similar to the French *bourdon*), roughly meaning 'bass'. It resembles late-seventeenth-century Spanish instruments on which low-pitched, double-stringed courses include a thick string tuned an octave lower than its companion. The modern tuning of the *bordonúa* is

FIGURE 3   The Puerto Rican luthier Julio Negrón Rivera in his shop in Morovis. *Left to right: cuatro, tiple,* and *bordonúa.* Photo by Daniel E. Sheehy.

G#–C#–F#–B–e–a, with the first three double-stringed courses tuned in unison and the last three in octaves. It is used primarily to play a bass, rather than a chordal background.

Though craftsmen carve instruments from any native hardwood, they prefer *guaraguao, jagüey,* or *maga.* For the soundboard, they use *yagrumo,* a light softwood. To avoid difficulty attaching the neck to the sound box, native makers carve the entire instrument, except the soundboard, from a single block of wood, and then sand the instrument down to the appropriate dimensions and thickness.

MUSICAL CONTEXTS AND GENRES
Religious forms

The *rosario cantao* 'sung rosary' is an important set of songs, practices, and beliefs that have developed in Puerto Rico around the rosary, a cycle of prayers marked with a circular string of fifty-nine beads. Following Spanish flight from the island around 1530, local versions of Roman Catholic practices began to take shape among the non-Spanish majority population, entirely outside ecclesiastical settings.

There are three types of *rosario cantao*: the *rosario de promesas* 'rosary of promises' (to the Virgin Mary or to a saint), the *rosario a la Santa Cruz* 'rosary to the Holy Cross', and the *rosario para los muertos* 'rosary for the dead'. These sung rosaries are similar to the ecclesiastically sanctioned one, though they are not sung inside a church. Each cycle of fifty-nine prayers (a *tercio del rosario* 'third of a rosary'), corresponds to the two-month lunar cycle of fifty-nine days—a reference to the femininity of the Virgin Mary. The Hail Mary dominates the rosary.

The most common poetic forms found in the sung rosary are couplets (*coplas*), *décimas,* and *decimillas.* The typical *jíbaro* (of the country people) musical ensemble— *tiple* or *cuatro,* guitar, *güiro*—often accompanies all three types. During the *novenario de difuntos,* it performs only between *tercios,* when the singers take a break.

The *rosario de promesas* is the most common category of these rosaries. The organizer of the ritual offers to the Virgin or to a saint a promise in return for the solution to a problem—an exchange between the metaphysical world and the material world.

The devotee keeps an image of the Virgin or saint on an altar at home. Treated as a member of the family, this image receives prayers, petitions, and supplications— and when necessary, scolding and punishment. The devotee may formally present a

The *bomba* dancer begins his improvised dance, which consists mostly of steps, jumps, abrupt body movements, stamping of feet or heels, and/or shoulder movements and whirls. Female dancers favor whirls and arm movements.

petition to the image, with a promise that if the saint intercedes with God and God grants the petition, the devotee will carry out the promise. The promise is specified during the petition, and the quality of the promise will be equal to the importance of the petition. One of the most common promises the *jíbaros* make is to sponsor a complete rosary once a year for so many years.

The rosary of promises begins at vespers the night before the promise is made. It lasts all night. When it ends (usually between six and seven A.M.), the participants say a short daybreak rosary before disassembling the altar. If the organizers have funds left, they will pay the musical group that accompanied the rosary throughout the night or contract a new group to play at a party that will last until noon. Obviously, carrying out a promise can require a lot of effort and money.

The *rosario a la Santa Cruz* follows a similar plan; however, it is performed particularly in May—a remnant of a long-standing Christian tradition of dedicating the month of May to Mary, possibly representing fertility as celebrated in pre-Christian rites of spring (see Davis 1972).

The *rosario para los muertos* is a ritual related to death or dying. It requires thirty-three *tercios*, two novenaries (*novenarios*), and the wake (*velorio*).

This rosary begins with a novenary (nine *tercios*), followed by the wake (thirteen *tercios*). The third section, the novenary for the dead (*novenario de difuntos*), is held for nine consecutive nights after the day of the burial. A *tercio* is said on each of the first eight nights, and three *tercios* are said on the last night. The total of thirty-three *tercios* corresponds to Jesus' supposed age at his death.

Secular forms

Bomba

The first written record of an African musical tradition in Puerto Rico dates from 11 November 1797, when André Pierre Ledrú, a visitor to the island, witnessed an African dance called *bomba* at a party in the farmhouse of a Don Benito in the town of Aibonito (Ledrú 1971:47). Another substantiation is found in a letter dated 9 October 1840 in the Reports of the Spanish Governors of Puerto Rico (entry 23, box 66), whereby Ciriaco Sabat, "King of the Blacks of the Congo Nation," formally requested permission to perform *bomba* dances on the plaza during religious feasts in honor of St. Michael (29 September) and Our Lady of the Rosary (7 October) and reminded the governor that since time immemorial permission to play *bombas* had annually been granted. This suggests that the tradition was then at least a few generations old—which could reasonably date it to the period of 1700–1750. This dating coincides with the belief of the people of Loíza Aldea, who say their tradition of dancing and drumming the *seis de bomba* at the cathedral of San Juan dates to the 1600s as part of the original series of *seises*.

The *bomba* dance was slaves' and free blacks' most important social event and means of expression. They performed it on special dates, at the end of harvesting, and as part of important festivities and private parties—birthdays, christenings, weddings, and the like. It served as an occasion for meetings and as a signal for rebellions. In the eastern, southern, and western part of the island, the traditions of drumming derives from the *musique de maison* 'house music' of Haiti and Martinique, and resemble the *tumba francesa* of Oriente Province, Cuba. This resulted from migrations of French colonizers with their slaves to the southern coast of Puerto Rico during the Haitian Revolution (1780–1805).

Over time, immigration and cultural change led to musical change. African master drummers associated rhythmic patterns with the words they closely paralleled; the patterns served as mnemonic devices for learning and remembering. The loss of African languages meant the demise of this system. From the 1690s to the 1790s, the promise of freedom for African slaves on their arrival in Puerto Rico attracted slaves from around the Caribbean and resulted in musical acculturation. Consequently, *cunyá, leró, yubá, sicá, grasimá, holandés,* and *calindá* are among the types of *bombas* brought to Puerto Rico, thus making *bomba* a generic name.

Each type of *bomba* directly relates to the basic ostinato rhythmic pattern on the second drum (*sonador*). The essence of the *bomba* dance was reduced to a challenge between the improvised beats of the first drum (*repicador*) and the dancer's improvised steps. Since about the 1960s, many drummers have felt the economic necessity of performing in *salsa, merengue,* or *guaguancó* ensembles and have begun to mix rhythms of these musics with those of *bomba*, drastically adulterating the style.

Today in Loíza Aldea in the north and Guayama in the south (Dufrasne-González 1996) the *bomba* is danced by men and women who move separately, within a circle formed by the audience. On one side of the circle are two *bomba* drums. The elders of the community stand to the right of the drums or sit behind the drums. The second drummer begins to play the basic rhythmic pattern, while the first drummer is idle. The singer begins the song, and the dancer approaches the drums from the opposite side of the circle to get the first drummer's attention and challenge him. The dancer now begins his improvised dance, which consists mostly of steps, jumps, abrupt body movements, stamping of feet or heels, and/or shoulder movements and whirls. Male dancers seem to prefer jumps, with exaggerated foot and leg movements. Female dancers favor whirls and arm movements. The central idea is that drummers should be able to synchronize a beat to each dance movement. Naturally, the improvisation is due to the present lack of a drum language. It is not known if a drum language was ever established.

Décima

The *décima* is one of the oldest, commonest, and most popular creole traditions of the rural people (*jíbaros*) of Puerto Rico. Its performance usually combines poetry and music. A poet, according to rural respondents, is a person who can not only compose on a theme according to certain rules of rhetoric, but one who can also improvise. Similarly, a *cantaor* is a person who memorizes *décimas* to sing them. Most esteemed is the *trovador,* who can sing improvised texts on a given topic at the spur of the moment.

The *décima* is the metric combination of ten eight-syllable lines, usually rhyming *abba:accddc.* A pause follows the fourth line (marked by the colon); otherwise, the rhymes of the last five lines mirror those of the first five. This strophe is associated with the Spanish poet Vicente Martínez Espinel (1550–1624), and many people call it the *espinela.*

Another musical-poetic form, the *decimilla* 'little *décima*', has a similar structure, though with only six syllables per line. In Puerto Rico, *decimillas* are almost as popular as *décimas. Decimillas* based on religious topics are called *aguinaldos,* and those based on secular topics are called *seis con décima.*

There are no restrictions on the number of stanzas a poet may join into one text on a single theme. One-stanza *décimas* and *décimas* of dozens of stanzas occur. Most common, though, are four-stanza *décimas* based on a four-line poem called *cuarteta* 'couplet'. The last line of the stanzas are respectively the first, second, third, and fourth lines of the *cuarteta.* The *jíbaros* call this strophe *décima cuarenticuatro* 'forty-four *décima*', but it is known elsewhere in the Hispanic world as *glosa* 'gloss'. In some *décimas* with an indefinite number of stanzas, the tenth line is always the same; this structure is known as *pie forzado* 'forced foot'.

In the verse endings of *décima,* Puerto Rican classical poets prefer consonant rhymes, whereas *jíbaros* seem to be more tolerant of assonantal rhymes. Rural people also show mastery of the inner rhythms of the verses—the syllabic accents at the beginning and middle of the line. Poetic meter is mostly trochaic, dactylic, or mixed. The inner rhythm synchronizes the poetry to the musical form, the *seis.*

Seis

There is no comprehensive or scholarly publication treating the history of the *seis,* the most important creole musical genre. Most published articles are speculations by historians or literary scholars who lack musical training. The *seis* is by far the largest corpus of creole music. The tradition includes names, rhythms, instruments, and possibly styles of singing that manifest the historical amalgamation, probably begun in the 1520s and 1530s, of African, Indian, and Spanish traditions.

The instruments that accompanied the *seis* in earlier times were the *cuatro,* the *bordonúa,* and the Indian gourd rasp now called *güiro.* The *tres* or the *tiple* sometimes replaced the *cuatro;* respondents insist that neither the *tres* nor the *tiple* played simultaneously with it. Eventually, the guitar replaced the *bordonúa.* A second *cuatro* and bongos joined the group, probably in the 1930s (figure 4); for dance-hall settings since about the 1950s, a double bass has given the ensemble a larger sound.

In broad terms, there are two types of *seis:* one, for dancing, is fast and lively; the other, for singing, is slower. Some names of the former type are related to the choreography of the dance: *zapateado* (with fancy footwork, from *zapato* 'shoe'), *amarrao*

FIGURE 4   In a bar in Puerto Rico, a *conjunto jíbaro* performs *música jíbara* 'country music' for their own enjoyment. *Left to right: güiro,* bongos, *cuatro,* and guitar, with another guitar in back. Photo by Daniel E. Sheehy, 1994.

'tied', *valseao* 'waltzed', *del pañuelo* 'with a handkerchief', *del sombrero* 'with a hat', and *juey* 'crab'.

The *seis con décima* is the most common slow *seis* for singing. Some *seises* are known by the names of the towns in which they originate: *orocoveño* (from Orocovis), *bayamonés* (from Bayamón), and *cagüeño* (from Caguas). Others are named after the person who composed or popularized a particular example: *seis fajardeño* (after Mateo Fajardo), *seis de Andino, seis de Pepe Orné, seis Portalatín,* and *seis Villarán. Seises* influenced by Latin American folk music include *seis de milonga, seis gaucho,* and *seis tango* from Argentina; *seis montuno* and *seis habanero* from Cuba; and *seis joropo* and *seis llanero* from Venezuela.

Seises with African influences probably go back to the mid-1500s. The rhythmic pattern of the melody in the *seis mapeyé* (in the minor mode) and the *seis montebello* (in the major mode) resembles the Ghanaian Akan *mpintín,* which comes from the Dagombas of Burkina Faso. The word *bomba* is not of Spanish origin, yet there are a *seis bombeao*—an instrumental example, in which people yell "*bomba!*" and exchange pleasantries in couplets—and a *seis de bomba,* the oldest African dance and drumming tradition in Puerto Rico (discussed below).

The *seis* tradition may have begun in the mid-1500s (López Cruz 1967, Rosa-Nieves 1967). The number of distinct *seises* extant is probably between about ninety and 117. Each *seis* has its own melody, with which its name is most closely identified. The melody is short, usually a phrase or two. The structure of the *seis con décima* is as follows: the instruments play the traditional theme (or melody) twice as an introduction; the singer starts his or her *décima* right after the introduction; the instruments play the theme only once between stanzas and twice to end the performance.

In the modern *seis* ensemble, the first *cuatro* plays the theme and the second *cuatro* plays a duet with it during the introduction and the ending. During other sections of the *seis,* the first *cuatro* improvises, and the second *cuatro* repeats the theme as an ostinato while the *cantaor* sings memorized *décimas* or the *trovador* improvises *décimas* and melodic lines. Proficient *cuatro* players may alternate roles of ostinato and improvisation. The guitar primarily plays a basso continuo, sometimes chordally reinforcing the rhythmic and harmonic framework. The *güiro* player improvises on four basic rhythmic patterns.

Plena

The *plena,* a genre of dance and music, originated in Ponce around 1900. It was first heard in Ponce in the neighborhood Barriada de la Torre, whose population consisted mostly of immigrants from St. Kitts, Tortola, and St. Thomas, who had settled on the island since the late 1800s. At the beginning, sung texts were not associated with the *plena,* which was rendered by guitar, concertina, and tambourine; eventually, in 1907, singing was added.

The first known ongoing *plena* group consisted of Joselito Oppenheimer, tambourine player and leader; Bernabe Aranzamendi, *güiro* player and singer; and Alfredo (last name not known), concertina player. From their base in the neighborhood of Joya del Castillo, the *plena* spread to southern Ponce (San Antón, El Palo de Pan, La Bomba del Agua, los Pámpanos). It became popular in Guayama and Mayagüez about 1906, and reached its peak popularity between 1918 and 1924, when the most famous *plenas* were "*El temporal*" ('The Storm'), "*Submarino alemán*" ('German Submarine'), "*Mamita, llegó el obispo*" ('Mommy, the Bishop Has Come'), "*Tanta vanidad*" ('Such Vanity'), and "*Juana Peña me llora*" ('Juana Peña Cries for Me'). The *plena* became so popular that people throughout the island sang and danced it—especially at planned or impromptu get-togethers on the street and at nightclubs (*casinos*).

The Cuban *danzón* and *contradanza* especially influenced the Puerto Rican *danza*. The Cuban bolero, *son,* and *son montuno* have influenced the music of professional *jíbaro* ensembles.

In the late 1990s, its popularity is still in evidence. New *plenas* appear, in many cases with a new sophistication. Often, they are played by an orchestra with a large percussion section—conga, snare, and bass drum added to or replacing the tambourine. Influential groups, such as El Quinto Olivo and Los Pleneros de la Veintitrés Abajo, increased the number of tambourines and their patterns, and other ensembles have followed suit, including three tambourines in a typical instrumentation.

Popular commercial musics

Other than folk musics, popular commercial music in the 1800s was mostly Spanish dance and march music. Migration to and from Venezuela, Mexico, and Cuba influenced Puerto Rican music. The Cuban *danzón* and *contradanza* especially influenced the Puerto Rican *danza*. The Cuban bolero, *son,* and *son montuno* have influenced the music of professional *jíbaro* ensembles (see Okada 1995: example 19).

The arrival of the U.S. army in 1898 brought American concepts of marching bands, dance bands, and other music, which was locally most obvious in the 1910s. The predominant influences on Puerto Rican music in the twentieth century have been the following, listed chronologically: recruitment of Puerto Ricans by the U.S. army exposed them to dance-band music and big-band music; economic conditions beginning in the 1920s and the Great Depression of the 1930s caused migration to New York, where prominent musicians and composers heard Cuban, Mexican, North American, and other musical traditions; the immigration of Dominicans in the 1950s brought Dominican musical traditions to Puerto Rico; finally, in the 1960s, third- and fourth-generation Puerto Ricans' return to the island brought North American commercial music traditions.

Today, jazz, merengue, rap, rock, and salsa have strong followings. Stadium or beach concerts featuring any of these traditions are common. Nightclubs present artists from all these traditions every night. Most local radio stations program one particular tradition, though many broadcast four or five hours of country (*jíbaro*) music daily.

TEACHING AND LEARNING

The universities of Puerto Rico are teaching institutions. The Fundación de las Humanidades, the local partner of the National Endowment for the Humanities, has a humanist-in-the-community program and a video series on rural traditions; copies of these videos are deposited in libraries and cultural centers in towns throughout the island.

The Casa Paoli Folk Research Center in Ponce sometimes sponsors research. The Institute of Puerto Rican Culture sponsors cultural clubs in every town on the island. Hence, towns or regions can generate festivals and other activities according to their needs and goals.

Supplementing the *seis* tradition in rural areas, the Institute of Puerto Rican Culture sponsors annual town, regional, and national competitions of all the major folk-music traditions.

FURTHER STUDY

An important bibliography for the study of Puerto Rican folk music has been compiled by Donald Thompson (1982), who wrote the only study of the *marímbula* in Puerto Rico and the Caribbean—an instrument he calls "the poor man's bass fiddle" (p. 147). Other studies of African-derived music in Puerto Rico are by Hector Vega Drouet on the *bomba* and *plena* (1969, 1979) and James McCoy (1968) on indigenous and European influences on Puerto Rican music. An important study of a Roman Catholic event, the *rosario* or Fiesta de Cruz in San Juan, was made by the ethnomusicologist Martha E. Davis (1972).

In his annotated bibliography, Thompson (1982) writes: "Recently . . . [ethnomusicological] study has expanded in Puerto Rico to incorporate a growing body of thought concerning urban, as contrasted to rural, folk music" (p. 14). Indeed, since the 1980s, numerous authors have written about Caribbean popular music, including salsa and *plena* in Puerto Rico and New York City. The book *Salsiology* (Boggs 1992) has important chapters by Jorge Duany (1992), Juan Flores (1992), and Quintero Rivera (1992), about salsa, *plena,* and *danza,* respectively.

REFERENCES

Boggs, Vernon W., ed. 1992. *Salsiology.* New York: Excelsior Music Publishing.

Cárdenas Ruíz, Manuel. 1981. *Crónicas Francesas de los Caribes.* San Juan: Editorial Universidad de Puerto Rico.

Casas, Bartolomé de las. 1965. *Historia de las Indias.* Vol. 1. Edited by Agustín Millanes. México, D.F.: Fondo de Cultura Económica.

Davis, Martha E. 1972. "The Social Organization of a Musical Event: The Fiesta de Cruz in San Juan, Puerto Rico." *Ethnomusicology* 16(1):38–62.

Duany, Jorge. 1992. "Popular Music in Puerto Rico: Toward an Anthropology of Salsa." In *Salsiology,* ed. Vernon W. Boggs, 71–89. New York: Excelsior Music Publishing.

Dufrasne-González, J. Emanuelo. 1996. *"Puerto Rico También Tiene . . . ¡Tambó!" Kalinda!* (Spring): 4–5.

Flores, Juan. 1992. "Bumbum and the Beginnings of La Plena." In *Salsiology,* ed. Vernon W. Boggs, 61–67. New York: Excelsior Music Publishing.

Ledrú, André Pierre. 1971. *Viaje a la isla de Puerto Rico.* 5th ed. Edited by Julio L. Vizcarrondo. San Juan: Editorial Coquí.

López Cruz, Francisco. 1967. *La Música Folklórica de Puerto Rico.* Sharon, Conn.: Troutman Press.

López de Gómara, Francisco. 1965. *Historia General de las Indias.* Barcelona: Editorial Iberia.

McCoy, James A. 1968. "The Bomba and Aguinaldo of Puerto Rico as They Have Evolved from Indigenous, African and European Cultures." Ph.D. dissertation, Florida State University.

Okada, Yuki. *The Caribbean.* JVC Smithsonian Folkways Video Anthology of Music and Dance of the Americas, 4. Montpelier, Vt.: Multicultural Media VTMV-228. Video.

Pané, Fray Ramón. 1974. *Relación acerca de las antigüedades de los indios.* Mexico City: Editores Siglo XXI.

Quintero Rivera, Angel G. 1992. "Ponce, the Danza, and the National Question: Notes toward a Sociology of Puerto Rican Music." In *Salsiology,* ed. Vernon W. Boggs, 45–51. New York: Excelsior Music Publishing.

Rosa-Nieves, Cesarro. 1967. *Voz Folklórica de Puerto Rico.* Sharon, Conn.: Troutman Press.

Tanodi, Aurelio, ed. 1971. *Documentos de la Real Hacienda de Puerto Rico: Volume I (1510–1519).* Río Piedras: Centro de Investigación Histórica, Universidad de Puerto Rico.

Thompson, Donald. 1975–1976. "A New World Mbira: The Caribbean Marímbula." *African Music Society Journal* 5(4):140–148.

———. 1982. *Music Research in Puerto Rico.* San Juan: Office of Cultural Affairs, Office of the Governor of Puerto Rico.

Vega Drouet, Hector. 1969. "Some Musical Forms of African Descendants in Puerto Rico: Bomba, Plena and Rosario Francés." M.A. thesis, Hunter College.

———. 1979. "A Historical and Ethnological Survey of the Probable African Origins of the Bomba, including the Festivities of Loíza Aldea." Ph.D. dissertation, Wesleyan University.

St. Lucia
Jocelyne Guilbault

Principal Musical Traditions
Calypso: A Class of Its Own
Late-Twentieth-Century Developments

The political campaigns preceding St. Lucia's independence from Britain in 1979 focused not only on increasing political awareness but also on promoting culture as the symbol of St. Lucian identity. The recognition and celebration of St. Lucian values and cultural practices (advocated in political speeches as a prerequisite for self-determination) reflected the influence of social and ideological forces at the local, regional, and international levels.

These included the black-consciousness movement of the 1960s and early 1970s, which had fueled the civil-rights movement in the United States; the shift of attitude of the Roman Catholic Church (still predominant and influential in St. Lucia) from condemnation of local non-Christian culture to "a radical reappraisal of the theological significance of local culture" after the Second Vatican Council in 1965 (Anthony 1986a:38); and the ensuing inauguration of the Caribbean Ecumenical Consultation for Development in 1971, which called on the forces of the region to foster and disseminate Caribbean cultural values through seminars, exhibits, and cuiltural programs. All these developments helped nurture a sense of pride in local traditions and to instill in key people the notion that culture is an intrinsic part of a country's development.

Many local initiatives have promoted culture since the 1970s, for the most part under the aegis of the Folk Research Centre (FRC, a nongovernmental organization created in 1973), whose goal has been "to promote research into St. Lucian culture" and "to explore and clarify the role of culture in the development of our people." These initiatives have been concerned with promoting the use and appreciation of local arts and of Creole (the vernacular but unofficial national language) "as a weapon for change and integral development" (Anthony 1986a:42).

One of the most effective mobilizations of public support for oral traditions has been the annual observance since 1983 of Jounen Kwéyòl (International Creole Day) on 28 October. This occasion is celebrated by Creole-speaking peoples throughout the world, grouped into Bannzil Kwéyòl, an international organization. Organized by FRC in collaboration with the National Research and Development Foundation and Mouvman Kwéyòl Sent Lisi (St. Lucia Creole Movement), this day of festivities has known such success that it has become a national event (Charles 1986:58).

Besides paying tribute to local skills (such as weaving sisal and building houses), Jounen Kwéyòl celebrates the island's musical traditions. Organized at a different location each year, it honors the master musician, singer, dancer, and other artists from the selected village for their roles in promoting local expression and knowledge.

PRINCIPAL MUSICAL TRADITIONS

Excepting musical genres closely associated with a particular season or occasion (such as carnival and wakes), most local musical traditions described below are performed as part of daily activities.

Activities of leisure (*jwé* 'play')

Jwé are performed mostly in rural areas at beach parties, full-moon gatherings, *débòt* evenings (in which the main dance, *débòt,* accompanied by drumming, is based on two sections, *alé liwon* [introduction] and *débòt* [the dance proper, consisting of a *blòtjé* movement every four beats]), and occasionally at wakes. They provide a source of entertainment, an opportunity to demonstrate verbal and dramatic skills, and a chance to make public commentaries in ways that would otherwise be impossible. Participants laugh at social conventions, criticize laws, and gossip. To minimize the possibility of offending anyone, participants perform all *jwé* with spontaneity and high spirits.

Jwé that use musical elements include storytelling (*listwa*), play-song-dance (*jwé dansé* 'danced play song'), pantomime (*jwé chanté* 'sung *jwé*'), and song-game (*gém*). Sung in Creole, all the songs but *listwa* are responsorial, performed by a leader and a choir. The lyrics, usually improvised, are based on humorous stories or social commentaries. *Listwa* and *jwé chanté* are performed without instrumental accompaniment or dancing, but *jwé dansé* and *gém* involve dancing, typically accompanied by a *ka* (a hollow, barrel-shaped drum, covered at one end with a female goatskin tightly fastened by a cord passed around the edge of the body, and played with bare hands, the drum held between the player's legs in a sitting position) and occasionally by *ti-bwa* (a pair of hardwood sticks, struck against the rim of the drum) (Guilbault 1993).

In most local traditions, men and women may act as lead singers, but instrumentalists are usually men. The success of *jwé* is typically measured by the degree of participation of the audience, who react by clapping hands in rhythm, interjecting comments, and joining in the singing or dancing (figure 1).

Jwé dansé include four play-song-dances: *débòt, yonbòt, jwé pòté,* and *solo.* Except for *solo* (danced by a couple who undulate their hips and sway their pelvises forward and backward), *jwé dansé* are performed in a circle, and include the famous *blòtjé,* a movement consisting of thrusting the pelvis forward and "doing a *touché*" (making contact) with the neighboring dancer.

Jwé chanté, also called *chanté kont,* are usually performed during wakes. In them, the leader uses pantomime to translate visually the meanings of the text. Often the play consists of enacting not the story itself, but the double entendres it may suggest.

In *gém,* all do not play in the same way. The leader plays with language by punning or using ambiguous phrases or metaphors. By adding some personal touch to the choreographed movements while following the rules of the game, other participants demonstrate their agility, imagination, and playfulness.

Not everyone likes to be associated with *jwé.* Many educated people, and those from the higher social class, criticize such activities for their sexual overtones and the singers for singing whatever they please. Most of these critics, though embarrassed to take part, recognize the value of *jwé.* Yet like everyone else in the country, they daily

FIGURE 1   *Ka* drummer from Piaye accompanying a song leader. Photo by Jocelyne Guilbault.

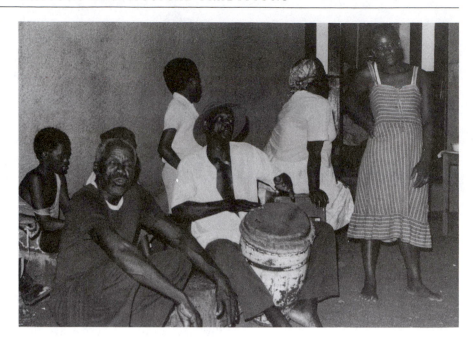

use *jwé* strategies—metaphors, *lang déviwé* (saying the opposite of what is meant), verbal teasing, and other typical text-building techniques of *jwé* lyrics.

Kwadril music

Most *kwadril* evenings, each organized by one person, take place in private houses or rented halls. Invitations specifying the location, date, hour, and fees are sent to prospective guests. The organizer hires and pays essential musicians. Except during Lent, a *kwadril* evening can be organized anytime during the year.

The word *kwadril* is written here in Creole spelling, to differentiate it from the European counterpart from which it originated and to indicate that in St. Lucia the concept of "quadrille" has developed an identity of its own.

A *kwadril* heightens the prestige of every participant. Unlike most other performances (typically based on a few easy steps, allowing room for spontaneity and improvisation), the choreography of *kwadril* has to be learned, memorized, and practiced (see Okada 1995: example 22). These stages of apprenticeship, which do not correspond to the usual norm of learning through doing, are highly valued. They symbolize a particular type of knowledge, believed by many to be of higher quality and more complex than other local traditions. The choreography—which, if performed correctly, is traditionally thought to demonstrate control over behavior, manners, and skills—symbolizes for the executants a set of special values linked with a higher social class.

The *kwadril* tradition is now losing popularity. Especially around the time of independence, European dance styles were seen as out of fashion. The general belief, particularly of youth, was that the traces of colonialism and of colonial values had to be relegated to the past. Only later did some people realize "that certain elements of tradition may play a positive role in the process of change, and should therefore be protected, even promoted and integrated into the development process" (Lutz and El-Shakhs, quoted in Guilbault 1984:179). Since then, in addition to Jounen Kwéyòl, some organizations have actually tried to promote the tradition of *kwadril* by organizing an annual fiddle competition and shows featuring *kwadril* music and dancing.

FIGURE 2   A St. Lucian *kwadril* ensemble from Morne Caillandre. *Left to right: chakchak, skroud* banjo, violin, *cuatro,* guitar. Photo by Jocelyne Guilbault.

A *kwadril* set consists of five compulsory dances: *pwémyé fidji, dézyèm fidji, twazyèm fidji, katwiyèm fidji* (first, second, third, and fourth dance, the fourth also called *avantwa* or *lanmen dwèt*), with a final dance named *gwan won* 'grand round', to which two or three ballroom dances of the musicians' choice are added. These last dances usually include a polka, a schottische, and a *lakonmèt.* Also called *mazouk,* the *lakonmèt* is the only closed couple dance said to have originated in St. Lucia (see Okada 1995: example 21). Whereas the compulsory dances are performed in a square by four couples not joining hands, the other dances are performed freely around the room by the same dancers in a closed-couple position.

The most typical *kwadril* ensemble (figure 2) includes a violin, a banjo (the locally made *skroud* or *bwa pòyé*), a *cuatro* (a locally made four-stringed instrument), a guitar (which plays the bass), and a *chakchak* (rattle). Whenever possible, the ensemble includes a mandolin, and occasionally bones (*zo*). Through syncopation and the *chakchak's* rhythmic effects, the performance strongly emphasizes rhythmic improvisation, especially in the unpredictable sequence of melodic patterns (figure 3).

FIGURE 3
Syncopated rhythms in the St. Lucian *kwadril.*
Transcription by Jocelyne Guilbault.

While the masquerade musicians walked around the village playing their instruments, two costumed male dancers—one playing a woman's role, the other a man's—entertained the crowd by performing contortions.

The La Rose and La Marguerite societies

La Rose (Lawòz) and La Marguerite (Lamargrit), social-support societies that have existed at least since the early 1800s, are competing Roman Catholic organizations found in almost every St. Lucian village (Guilbault 1993). Though they have always declared themselves rivals, they share features. They call themselves societies, as their members enact roles reproducing an elaborate hierarchical system. Following an English model, each society has a king and a queen, a prince and a princess, members of various vocations (such as chief of police and nurses), and lower-class citizens. As members of an idealized society, they share one religion and economic status. They celebrate their respective patron saint annually with a one-day festival.

Except during Lent, both groups meet weekly, La Rose on Saturdays and La Marguerite on Sundays. On these occasions, members of La Marguerite sing together, seated; their lead singer (*chantwèl*) stands. Members of La Rose dance and play musical instruments. La Rose instruments include a tambourine (*tanbouwen*), a *chakchak,* a *baha* (long, hollow tube, blown like a trumpet), sometimes a scraper (*gwaj*), and a guitar. Through these meetings, the members of both organizations enjoy camaraderie and strengthen their will to support each other in case of sickness or death.

The songs of both societies share similar musical genres in stanza-refrain forms, sung by a leader and a chorus. These genres—including *omans* (a type of waltz), *manpa* (a lively dance in duple rhythm), and marches—deal with the same topics: the societies' origin, their patron saint, their flower, and their rival, the other society (see Okada 1995: example 20). The La Rose members perform two other genres, *kwadril* and *lakonmèt,* both rhythmically similar to the dances found in *kwadril* music (figure 4).

No historical document describes the origins of the two organizations or the circumstances that initiated the rivalry between them. One can only observe the profound differences between the two: whereas in performance members of La Marguerite favor reserved behavior, a controlled pace of events, discipline, and order, members of La Rose encourage exuberance, movement, and innovation. The rivalry of these organizations is said to crystallize major tendencies in St. Lucian society. After independence, the government recognized these organizations as symbols of St. Lucian cultural identity by sponsoring every local chapter of La Rose and La Marguerite, and by allowing the societies to meet at central locations on the day of their respective annual celebrations.

Musical traditions for specific occasions

Chanté siay are work songs that accompany sawing wood. Performed by a leader and usually no more than two responders, they are accompanied by a *ka* and the *tibwa,* instruments played in a way that differs from the conventional: instead of holding

FIGURE 4   Rhythmic patterns of La Rose musical styles. Transcription by Jocelyne Guilbault.

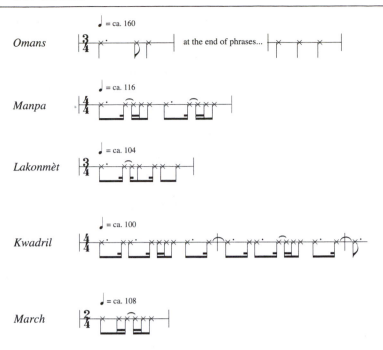

the drum in an upright position, the player lays it on the ground and sits on the barrel, playing on the skin barehanded. The pair of *tibwa* are struck, not against the rim of the drum, but against a bamboo tube or a wooden log resting on a stand. These techniques, associated with the Martinican style of playing these instruments, are encountered mostly in the northeastern part of the island, the region closest to Martinique.

Chanté abwè 'drinking songs' are rarely heard. These were performed mainly during the Christmas season on evenings called *wibòt*. Everyone in a circle of friends took turns receiving the others at home and paying for the food and drinks. The singing of *chanté abwè* was organized as a game in which everyone sitting at a long table in the middle of a room had to sing a new song every time around. Those who could not remember or improvise new songs were sent away. Singers who lasted until the end of the evening won a bottle of rum or other small prizes.

There was no musical accompaniment at a *wibòt*. The entire performance relied on complete participation, since every two lines of text sung by a soloist were repeated by the others. In addition to this form of singing, *chanté abwè* distinguished themselves by their lyrics—French words mixed with Creole expressions. Many lyrics dealt with topics of French origin.

Masquerade and serenade

The masquerade and the serenade (*séwinal*) are nearly extinct. The musical genres played for both activities were the same: merengue, march, and *maynan* (another name for *manpa*).

The masquerade was a celebration organized around holidays such as Christmas, New Year's, and Easter. The orchestra, which included the same instruments used in merry-go-rounds, cockfights, and *séwinal* (a *tanbou tenbal*, a snare drum here called kettledrum, a *chakchak*, and a bamboo flute), left home early in the morning to play, sing, and dance. While the musicians walked around the village playing their instruments, two costumed male dancers—one playing a woman's role (female *mas*), the other a man's (male *mas*)—entertained the crowd by performing contortions. Besides performing for entertainment, the orchestra aimed to earn money through voluntary donations from spectators.

The *séwinal* was usually performed during the four weeks of Advent and, except for Lent, at any other time of the year. Unlike the masquerade, it was performed solely at night or dawn, and no one wore a mask or a costume. It was organized for pleasure, with no expectation of earning money.

Wakes and funeral music

Wakes are performed on the first and eighth nights after a person has died. (Why wakes are celebrated on the eighth instead of the ninth night, as in most other Caribbean islands, remains a mystery.) Depending on the musical tastes and religious affiliations of the deceased, celebrations are accompanied by different kinds of music (drumming or singing hymns), or with no music at all.

When wakes follow the traditional format, however, music is performed inside and outside the deceased's house. In the house, a group of men and women sing hymns and gospel songs (sankeys). Since these songs have been learned at church, all the texts are in English. One person, usually a male singer, lines out the words for the audience. The delivery of the improvised choir is slow, in unison, and without syncopation.

The music performed outside can include *kont,* drumming, or both. Based on local traditions, the lyrics are in Creole. *Kont,* as opposed to *listwa,* are unaccompanied responsorial songs, sung by a leader and a choir. They deal mostly with death, reporting the deceased's last words, or relating various events surrounding the death. Drumming can involve *débòt* and *bélè.* In both instances, song-dances are accompanied by a *ka* and sometimes accompanied by *zo* or *tibwa.* In addition to receiving food and drink, the players, since there are only a few of them and the accompaniment for the whole evening and night depends entirely on them, usually receive money.

In several villages of the southwest (including La Grace, Laborie, and Piaye), a funeral song-dance called *koutoumba* was always performed when a member of the *djiné* died. *Djiné* are people descended from Africans who arrived in the island around the mid-1800s; *koutoumba* also denotes the wake in which the song-dance of the same name is performed. In 1986, with the death of the last drummer who could play this genre, the tradition disappeared. The *koutoumba* differed from all the traditional dances by being performed by only one dancer at a time and by using only two to four lines of text (sung responsorially) to evoke a mood, rather than to recount a story.

TRACK 39   The text of the following *koutoumba* evokes despair (L, leader; C, chorus).

L	Kouman mwen k'alé fè?	What am I going to do?
	Mwen pa ni manman.	I don't have a mother.
C	Kouman nou k'alé fè?	What are we going to do?
L	Manman mwen fini.	My mother is finished [dead].
C	Kouman nou k'alé fè?	What are we going to do?
L	é katapolo.	*é katapolo* [untranslatable].
C	Kouman nou k'alé fè?	What are we going to do?
L	é yangi yanga.	*é yangi yanga* [untranslatable].
C	Kouman nou k'alé fè?	What are we going to do?
L	é nou pa ni papa.	Hey, we do not have a father.
C	Kouman nou k'alé fè?	What are we going to do?
L	An pèyi béké.	In the country of whites' owners.

FIGURE 5 *Kélé* ceremony from the Babonneau region. *Left,* a *tanbou ich; right,* a *tanbou manman.* Photo by Jocelyne Guilbault.

C	Kouman nou k'alé fè?	What are we going to do?
L	é manman nou fini.	My mother is finished [dead].
C	Kouman nou k'alé fè?	What are we going to do?
L	é nou pa nio sésé.	Hey, we do not have a sister.
C	Kouman nou k'alé fè?	What are we going to do?
L	é sésé mwen fini.	My sister is finished [dead].
C	Kouman nou k'alé fè?	What are we going to do?

The term *bèlè* denotes a category of Creole song-dances (including *bèlè atè, bèlè anlè, bèlè matjé,* and *bèlè anlawis*), typically performed by one couple at a time. All four kinds of *bèlè* are sung by a leader and a chorus. Except for the *bèlè anlawis* (which uses a stanza-refrain form), all are responsorial. Their lyrics usually deal with daily preoccupations and miseries in life, such as unhappy relationships and unacceptable behaviors.

Music of the kélé tradition

The *kélé* religious tradition is particular to another group of people from the Babonneau region, who also call themselves *djiné*. Though *kélé* concerns not one deity, but three (Ogun, Shango, Eshu), it is reminiscent of the Ogun festival in Nigeria (Anthony 1986b:114). Rejected by the Roman Catholic Church until the early 1960s, it has been practiced underground since its introduction in the island. It was held "at the New Year or the anniversary of the death of a recent ancestor" (Crowley 1957:8) or to ask African ancestors for protection in all matters of importance, including "good crops, good health, and good fortune" (Simpson 1973:110).

In all of St. Lucia, only one family from Resina, in the Babonneau region, holds *kélés,* claiming "to have authority to perform the ritual and to pass on that authority to their kin" (Anthony 1986b:106). The ritual includes the display of smooth stones (Shango's emblem) and iron and steel tools (in honor of Ogun), the washing of the ram to be offered to Shango, the smashing of a calabash at the end of the ritual (to appease the Yoruba deity Eshu), prayers and incantations (mostly addressed to Ogun), eating, singing, dancing, and the playing of two drums, *tanbou manman* 'mother drum' and *tanbou ich* 'child drum' (figure 5), used only during the ceremony to play four song-dance rhythms—*adan, koudou, kèré, èrè*—each at a prescribed moment.

CALYPSO: A CLASS OF ITS OWN

Calypso has been part of the St. Lucian soundscape since the 1940s. Compared to traditional music, it is now considered at the center of the musical environment because it has kept up to date with new technology and arrangements. It is *the* genre in which St. Lucians express social commentary.

The jump-up, walking steps, and hands in the air—the typical calypso choreography—have become a reflex, performed at the sound of any dynamic, calypsolike music, including soca. All St. Lucian steelbands and nightclub bands compose and perform calypsos, about fifty new ones a year. In the 1980s, a few, usually no more than five, were released on 45-RPM disks. In 1988, an album included songs from several calypsonians, but composite albums remain rare (Charles and Hyppolite 1990:34).

The local business of recording has been hindered by the unavailability of funding and sponsorship, the absence of producers ready to assume the responsibility of recording and marketing, and the few studios available. These conditions are them-

> Calypso has been part of the St. Lucian soundscape since the 1940s. Because it has kept up to date with new technology and arrangements, it is *the* genre in which St. Lucians express social commentary.

selves associated with the widespread dubbing of cassettes, which prevents the local market from developing a significant demand for records.

LATE-TWENTIETH-CENTURY DEVELOPMENTS

Since the 1980s, for the preservation and promotion of the St. Lucian cultural identity, much effort has been made to develop and incorporate educational material on local culture into the school system and mass media. This effort has led to the collection and analysis of traditions, the compilation and publication of information through newspapers and publications sponsored by FRC, the production of a thirty-minute video on *kélé* (1983), several fifteen-minute programs on traditional music for broadcast on radio, photographic exhibits with bilingual texts (English and Creole), and slide presentations in primary schools and colleges.

An audio-visual package of material on St. Lucia's cultural heritage has been prepared under the supervision of FRC, whose five-year cooperative project with the Institut für Völkerkunde of the University of Vienna (1983–1988) and partnership with other institutions since 1988 have laid the groundwork for scientific training in archival and ethnographic work and publications. Since 1987, a *kaiposium* (short for "*kaiso* symposium") has become an annual event. In 1990, to celebrate forty years of local calypso, FRC launched a new journal, *Lucian Kaiso.*

Since 1989, the local radio stations (Radio St. Lucia and Radio Caraïbe International) have aired more presentations in Creole and more short programs on local music. The political campaigns of the late 1970s (which emphasized the need for developing a greater awareness of St. Lucian identities), and the continual efforts by some institutions and individuals to use culture for change and development have helped redefine the meaning and importance of culture in St. Lucian society.

REFERENCES

Anthony, A. B. Patrick. 1986a. "Folk Research and Development: The Institutional Background to the Folk Research Centre, St. Lucia." In *Research in Ethnography and Ethnohistory of St. Lucia,* ed. Manfred Kremser and Karl R. Wernhart, 37–56. Vienna: Ferdinand Berger und Söhne.

———. 1986b. "The Encounter Between Christianity and Culture: The Case of the *Kélé* Ceremony of St. Lucia." In *Research in Ethnography and Ethnohistory of St. Lucia,* ed. Manfred Kremser and Karl R. Wernhart, 103–120. Vienna: Ferdinand Berger und Söhne.

Charles, Embert. 1986. "Oral Traditions in St. Lucia: Mobilisation of Public Support—Jounen Kwéyòl." In *Research in Ethnography and Ethnohistory of St. Lucia,* ed. Manfred Kremser and Karl R. Wernhart, 57–70. Vienna: Ferdinand Berger und Söhne.

Charles, Embert, and Kendel Hyppolite, eds. 1990. *Lucian Kaiso: Tribute to Carro.* Special Series, 1. Castries: Folk Research Centre.

Crowley, Daniel J. 1957. "Song and Dance in St. Lucia." *Ethnomusicology* 1(9):4–14.

Guilbault, Jocelyne. 1984. "Musical Events in the Lives of the People of a Caribbean Island: St. Lucia." Ph.D. dissertation, University of Michigan.

Guilbault, Jocelyne, and Embert Charles. 1993.

Musical Traditions of St. Lucia, West Indies: Dances and Songs from a Caribbean Island. Washington, D.C.: Smithsonian Folkways CD SF 40416. Notes to compact disc.

Kremser, Manfred, and Karl R. Wernhart, eds. 1986. *Research in Ethnography and Ethnohistory of St. Lucia.* Vienna: Ferdinand Berger und Söhne.

Okada, Yuki. *The Caribbean.* JVC Smithsonian Folkways Video Anthology of Music and Dance of the Americas, 4. Montpelier, Vt.: Multicultural Media VTMV-228. Video.

Simpson, G. E. 1973. "The *Kele* (Chango) Cult in St. Lucia: Research Commentaries III." *Caribbean Studies* 13(3):110–116.

Trinidad and Tobago

Lorna McDaniel

Musical Contexts and Genres in History
African Influences
East Indian Influences
National Forms

The Republic of Trinidad and Tobago, a double-island nation of more than one million people, is a culturally diverse society. In 1990, its populations were recorded as about 40 percent East Indian, 40 percent African, 19 percent mixed, and 1 percent white. Its major religions are Roman Catholic, Hindu, Spiritual Baptist, Orisa (Sango), Anglican, and Muslim.

In 1496, when Columbus sailed to the southernmost limits of the Caribbean Sea and passed through the Gulf of Paria, he sighted an island with three mountain peaks, for which he named the island in honor of the Holy Trinity. Until 1688, the Spanish enslaved the original inhabitants, the Arawak, in *encomiendas* (villages benefiting from Amerindian labor) and agricultural enclaves. Though the missions were closed in 1708, Roman Catholic priests continued to rule the local religious system, and the magistrate (*corregidor*) maintained the right to distribute Amerindian labor to Spanish settlers.

Under Spain, Trinidad never evolved into a colonial plantocracy but remained isolated and economically fragile. There was a minor export business in tobacco and cocoa before a crop disaster in 1725. Settlers were devastated by the smallpox epidemic of 1739. The outcomes of slavers' raids, assaults by Caribs, epidemics, and armed confrontations contributed to the decline of the Arawak population. Of an estimated thirty thousand to forty thousand in 1498, only 649 Arawak remained in 1777 (Brereton 1981:5–6). In 1783, under Spanish domination and with a dwindling Amerindian population, Trinidad's local government issued a plan that welcomed white and "free coloured" Roman Catholic colonists.

Before 1793, French Creoles from Dominica, Grenada, Martinique, and St. Vincent embraced the prospect of immigration to Trinidad because their lives had been disrupted by revolution, by the threat of revolution, and by the hostility French subjects experienced on islands ceded to Britain. The influx of Creoles was so rapid that a Francophone culture quickly developed within Trinidad (Wood 1986:32). Gifts of fertile land were offered to the settlers—a practice that continued long after 1797, when British troops invaded and captured Trinidad. Spanish, French, English, and Creole immigrants from the French Antilles and islands formerly owned by France—all continued to expand the local frontier.

Despite a wave of Creole immigrants to Trinidad, overall population growth in the early 1800s was sluggish. In 1807, the slave trade became illegal, and the resultant need for agricultural workers led slave owners to ship enslaved people to Trinidad disguised as planters' servants. The illegal influx, however, could still not meet the demand exacerbated by the emancipation of enslaved Africans in 1838. Soon thereafter, canefield laborers from the Windward Islands were encouraged to immigrate by job offers that included rent-free cottages with small plots of land. Starting in 1845 and ending in 1917, major entries of indentured workers from Africa, China, India, Portugal, and Syria provided the energy to expand the area's economy. Many of these workers became permanent residents, adding further layers of religious practices, languages, and music.

A small, early migration that influenced the musical character of Trinidad was that of about eight hundred African-American enslaved soldiers who had fought on the side of the British in the War of 1812. After their service, they were manumitted and settled as farmers in the Company Villages of southern Trinidad, where they continued Baptist religious rituals and singing developed in North America. Many of their songs have enhanced the musical repertoire of the Spiritual Baptists of Trinidad.

In 1888, the colony of Trinidad merged with the colony of Tobago, an island lying about 30 kilometers northeast of Trinidad. In 1962, the nation of Trinidad and Tobago, now oil rich, received independence within the Commonwealth of Nations; it became a republic in 1974. Despite the union, Tobago's history and culture are distinct. Over a span of two centuries, innumerable Dutch, French, and English colonial contestations were waged over possession of the island, but a predominantly African population remains, preserving untapped reservoirs of musical and linguistic traditions within seaside villages.

MUSICAL CONTEXTS AND GENRES IN HISTORY

In the 1950s, the musics of Trinidad and Tobago, excluding East Indian elements, included the categories *bélè*, bongo, calypso, chanty, congo, *fandang*, pass-play, rada, reel-dance, *parang*, quesh, Sankey, Sango (a later spelling of Shango), steelband, trumpet, work song, *veiquoix, yarraba,* and music for masquerades in carnival (Pearse 1955). The multiculturality of Trinidad is revealed in the names of genres that bear the name of the country of origin and in Spanish genres of Venezuela. The Congo, Rada, Sango, and Yarraba songs had African origins, and the *fandang*, the *parang*, and *veiquoix* had Spanish origins or influence. The *fandang*, which includes the *mazanare*, the *joropo*, and the *gallerón*, are frivolous songs sung at the end of wakes. The *parang* comprises songs such as serenades and *aguinaldos*, accompanied by a *tiple*, a *cuatro*, a *bandol*, a guitar, and a *chac-chac* (maraca) and sung by an ensemble that roves from house to house during the Christmas season. The *veiquoix*, sung at wakes, is accompanied by the same ensemble as the *parang*. Many of these genres are found in Grenada, Carriacou, St. Vincent, Martinique, and Guadeloupe, where they first appeared in the New World. Since the 1950s, they have come to public notice through cultural activities directed by the ministries of cultural affairs.

Under Prime Minister Eric Williams' leadership, the Best Village Competition sponsored the staging of dance, literary, and musical events. Begun in 1963 to enhance cultural awareness, this competition inspired Trinidad and Tobago's music festivals, which grew to include the Annual Classical Indian Singing Competition, the Calypso Competition, the Tassa Competitions, Panorama, the Parang Competition, the Steelband Music Festival, and the Tobago Heritage Festival.

AFRICAN INFLUENCES

Orisa (Sango)

Trinidad's most powerful African-derived religious movement is Orisa, documented as the "Shango cult" (Herskovits 1964 [1947]; Simpson 1965). The communicants worship personal powers (*orisas*), but the religion has been identified with Sango, thunder god and patron of Trinidad and Tobago. An effort to gain acceptance of the name *Orisa* was launched in 1988, during the sesquicentennial celebration of emancipation. An integrated worship service (*ijosin*) was held in honor of the Ooni of Ife, the spiritual head of the traditional religion in Nigeria. The event fostered unity in the organization of the religion and promoted cultural, educational, and economic development, not only by consolidating individual shrines but also in the relationship between Trinidad and Nigeria.

George Simpson (1965) lists the *orisa* and their favorite foods, color codes, and dance implements, describes their personalities, and catalogues their counterparts among Christian saints and mythological figures. Findings of Herskovits' 1939 field studies in Toco, a northern village of Trinidad, bear similarities with Simpson's findings, and with rituals mounted as far south as Oropuche and experienced by me as late as 1989. A contemporary listing of the *orisas* prominent in southern Trinidad's rituals, formulated by practitioners in the Orisa Yin Cultural Organization, is included below. The practitioners' interest in Yoruba orthography and documentation reveals Afrocentric thinking and a commitment to cultural revitalization (Kekera 1988).

Orisa	*Christian and other counterparts, as believed by practitioners*
Ogun	Saint Michael
Oranyan	Saint George
Aganju	Saint Gabriel
Osoosi	Saint Raphael
Soponna	Saint Jerome
Onile	Mother of the Earth (Mama La Terre)
Osanyin	Saint Francis
Ibeji	Saint Peter and Saint Paul (twins)
Dada	Saint Anthony
Erinle Ajaja	Saint Jonah
Sango	Saint John
Orunmila	Saint Joseph
Yemanja	Saint Ann
Osun	Saint Philomena
Oya	Saint Catherine
Oba	Saint Theresa

Several *orisa,* including Elefon, Obalufon, Obatala, and Oduduwa, are related to the highest god, and hence have no named Christian counterparts. They reflect various aspects of the deity.

Among Trinidad's population of Yoruba descent, the system of worship centers on calling and celebrating these gods. Formal ceremonies (the Ebo) include the calling of the *orisa* by drumming; singing; sacrificing fowl, goats, and bulls; and showing the arrival of the deities in possession dances. The ritual feast is a religious duty, a seasonal undertaking by the leader of the temple. It invites worshipers' communities to participate in thanksgiving, the exchange of healing energies, and the welcome and engagement of deities. The musical liturgies of the Orisa religion have not yet been systematically analyzed, nor have the rhythmic emblems of specific deities been notated and published. Three- or four-day feasts by a specific congregation are known to take place yearly or, in the case of the feast for Elefon and Obalufan, every four years; however, for intergroup worship, the congregations constantly visit each other.

The Ebo and the Elefon occur at the shrine compound, a straw-roofed *palais* (a simple, tentlike structure lined with benches), and within the *chapelle* (a small structure housing "tools," the wands used in dancing. Several stools or altars, commemorating various gods, are scattered throughout the compound. Colorful flags, commemorating the deities that commune with members of the congregation, fly on bamboo poles over the stools. Candles burn on the ground near the stools and at the four corners of the room. Before the ritual starts, participants dress the compound in flowing bolts of white cloth, bathe the sacrificial animals in special herbal water, and before the sacrifice, wrap three bulls in white capes.

Music is continuous and essential during the feast, which lasts all night. Three drummers play double-headed drums that rest on their thighs or, in the case of the smallest drum, sit on a stool. In the 1960s, the cylindrical drums with laced double skins, in order from largest to smallest, were named *bemba* (*bembe*), *congo*, and *oumalay* (*omele*) (Simpson 1965:40). With fingers applying pressure to the drumhead, the drummer strikes one head of the *bembe* or *congo* with a curved stick. The smallest drum is beaten with two sticks, in continuous fast and repetitive rhythms. The *bembe* is played with dramatic slams and virtuoso cross-rhythmic statements above the sound of several rattles (chac-chac). This ensemble accompanies the lead singer's call and the participants' monophonic response. The Sango calling song (figure 1) shows the responsoriality of the vocal component, the soloism of the *bembe,* and the repetitiveness of the *omele* and the *congo.*

Melville and Frances Herskovits describe the dance at an Orisa feast and the physical manifestations of possession as the power enters the head and rides the devotee. According to them, the preliminary signs of possession are "the perceptible 'freezing' of the muscles of the face, the sightless stare, the twitching of shoulders and shaking of the knees" (1964:335). Each devotee dances with a wand as a symbol of the *orisa's* power: the dancer represents Sango's appearance with a shepherd's crook; Ogun's with a sword; Soponna's (Sakpata's) with a knife; Yemanja's with a miniature oar; other deities' appearances, with a wooden anchor, a whip, a broom, or a turtle.

Female and male devotees dance beneath a single deity (who enters the head of the dancer) while bearing its symbol and manifesting the personality and dance characteristic of the rider of the *orisa.* Though possession dances are not directed to an audience, observers appreciate the artistry of the exhibition of transcendental postures where the body, with back erect, suddenly becomes supple; or when, with bent torso, the dancer takes long strides or whirls in a stylized movement. The dancer may stop and look forward with wide, sightless eyes, and may then, with extended limbs, advance toward the drum. Expressing intelligence, beauty, defiance, or anger, the devotee's face is transformed, mirroring the *orisa* that has overtaken her or him. At the end of each manifestation, the dancer, under the deity's control, falls unconscious. Water is poured on her or his head as a rite of consecration to the power that governs the devotee. The participants wear simple white dresses or, less often, red dresses (the color associated with Sango) of African fabrics. Sometimes the outfit is a *douiette,* a ruffled skirt open in the front with a white petticoat exposed, recalling nineteenth-century French Creole attire. Every woman in attendance wears a wrap on her head.

Studies of the Trinidadian Orisa religion have noted that most members were

"Lining out" is a practice in which words of a traditional hymn are intoned by a tenor lead singer as a prompt for the congregation, which responds with melodic variations.

FIGURE 1   The beginning of a Sango calling song, "Baba Wa," from an Orisa feast. Oropuche, Trinidad, 1988. Transcription by Lorna McDaniel.

working-class people, and that neither whites nor mixed-race people and only a few Indians participated; however, people of non-African descent adhere to the religion and worship in secret. Not only is involvement often undisclosed, but many participants also worship regularly as Roman Catholics, Anglicans, or Spiritual Baptists (Houk 1992). In the inventory of ritual borrowings, the Yoruba *orisa* Osain and the Muslim saint Hossain are syncretized (Crowley 1957:822). Appropriations from Roman Catholic ritual include prayers, hymns, and such symbols as Bibles, crooks, crosses, and candles, employed during the introductory prayer meeting that precedes the rite (Simpson 1962:1217). La Divina Pastora (Sooparee Mai, the patron saint of Siparia, Trinidad) is often worshipped by Hindu participants, and other bearers of the culture reveal that the powerful Hindu goddess Kali has been accepted by some into the array of *orisa* (Ahye 1978:78). Among these, the deepest syncretism is seen in the reinterpretation of the *orisa* names listed above.

Sometimes there is a total absence of musical syncretism, not only in Orisa feasts but in many repertoires. Despite long cultural contact, extant syncretisms may be imperceptible or appear manipulative, self-conscious, and commercial. The more obvious syncretisms include Indian calypsos and the use of *tassa* drumming in steel-band performances.

Spiritual Baptists

The history of the the Spiritual Baptists ("Shouters") is unclear, and the dates of the sect's inception remain unknown. It traveled to Trinidad and Grenada from St. Vincent, where followers were known as Shakers because of the ecstasy of the religion's worship. This religion endures, though in self-contained and secretive ways, for its practice has resulted in social discrimination and legal suppression. Interdictory laws, particularly against drumming, and the Shouter Prohibition Ordinances (1917) were drawn up against practices seen as related to *obeah* 'magic, witchcraft'. Between 1917 and 1951, police raids of Shouter services were legal.

Cultural amalgamation is obvious in the theology and music of the religion, with its integration of Roman Catholic ritual and many distantly related vocal musical styles including Yoruba songs, Hindu chants, Chinese vocalizations, American spirituals, and Anglican hymns. These styles are superimposed layers of sound during the prayer ritual, the search for trance ("power"), and mental flight. Trance accompanies 'doption singing, which guides participants in mystical journeys to Africa, India, and China. The songs point the direction of travel, and the knowledge of the international repertoire is explained by a supernatural meeting, gained through the practice of mental travel.

Spiritual Baptists are known for their dress, including head ties and monochrome gowns with belts, sashes, and aprons in colors that represent status. Usually led by a male "shepherd," the female majority serves, by rank, as mothers, teachers, pointers, nurses, warriors, healers, and preachers. Status is achieved through initiation ("mourning ground"), which delivers visions, secret gifts of inspiration, and spiritual tests. After each test, an initiate ascends in the hierarchy. Candles, flower-filled gourds, vials of perfumes and oils (altar fluids), a nautical steering wheel laden with candles, a metal Indian plate (*lota*), and a bell are the most distinctive symbols of the movement. These symbols surround the center pole of the room. Spontaneous libations of altar fluids and bell ringing occur there and at the cardinal points or in the corners, punctuating and shaping the progress of the service. The essential symbol, the center pole, "derived from the Ancient African church, represents the timber of Lebanon, which was used for the construction of Solomon's temple" (Thomas 1987:31). The compatibility of the Spiritual Baptist religion with the African Orisa religion made possible the creation of a Sango-Baptist type of worship and other religions that could be placed along a continuum of syncretic styles. The resemblance among the groups is manifest in their vocal styles and borrowed repertoires.

Songs and chants accompany a great portion of the Spiritual Baptist service, and often two songs flowing simultaneously may be joined by a third to form a distinctive polyphonic texture. Traditionally, only claps and stamps occur (see Okada 1995: example 28), though Sango-Baptist services may use drums. The several musical types and practices of the Spiritual Baptist repertoire include lining out, 'doption, trumpets, and spiritual shouts. "Lining out" is a practice in which words of a traditional hymn are intoned by a tenor lead singer as a prompt for the congregation, which responds with melodic variations.

'Doption, a mode of spiritual experience nurtured as part of the initiation practices of the church (Pearse 1953:21), uses vocables to adapt an Anglican tune or a nineteenth-century Sankey hymn into a fast-moving, harmonized, rhythmically

FIGURE 2   A typical trumpet chorus, "Sail Out and Buy." Pearse Archive. Used with permission.

orchestrated song. During the singing of the hymn, syllables (such as *bi mi bim, bam bi-bi bim*) slowly replace the words to imitate drumming; strict eighth-note claps and stamps accompany heterophonic vocal wanderings, grunts, and inhalations, resulting in a jubilant and multirhythmic texture. This practice accompanies the spiritual journey to Africa. Other musical 'doption modes and practices inspire mental travel to China and India. Accompanying the spiritual practice of 'doption, birdlike sounds may be heard interspersed within the language of glossolalia (Williams 1985:49).

Trumpets are rousing choruses, which may be sung in any of the 'doption styles described above. Of a typical trumpet (figure 2), Pearse says: "The movement of this song is "fast rowing," with strong offbeats. It is reiterative, and as it warms up, the accented 'Sail-ee-oh!' cuts in earlier and earlier." Subsequent verses substitute the spiritual gifts, the emblems of church hierarchy: Nurse, Watchman, Captain, Diver, Pumper, Preacher, Teacher (McDaniel 1995:139). Many spiritual shouts and trumpets are songs derived from spirituals brought to Trinidad by American ex-slave soldiers liberated by the British after the War of 1812.

EAST INDIAN INFLUENCES

Many traditional songs and tales in the Bhojpuri language of northern India survive within the East Indian musical cultures of Trinidad. These celebrate marriage, childbirth *(sohar)*, agricultural festivals *(khajri,* after planting rice), and seasonal cycles *(chowtal,* in spring). Others, including songs from the Ramayana, songs from Madras, and the fire-walking ceremony of immigrants from southern India, are no longer performed. Like older classical singing, game songs, and dramatic forms, they once created essential cultural ties for East Indian workers on Trinidad's plantations.

A segment of the Indian population still speaks Bhojpuri, but many sing their traditional songs in Trinidadian Creole or learn Hindi hymns *(bhajan)* taught in schools. A bellows-powered harmonium accompanies these hymns along with a double-headed drum *(dholak)*, an iron rod idiophone *(dandtal)*, clappers with jingles *(kartal)* and small cymbals *(manjira)*. Vedic chant, sung in Sanskrit, is accompanied by a harmonium or a traditional plucked lute, the *tambura* (Myers 1980:149).

East Indian films and recordings have swayed the popular musical taste of Indians in Trinidad more than their schools or oral traditions have. Film scores featuring an American combo accompaniment (electric guitars, organs, bongos, congas, drum set) have diffused East Indian film music to Trinidadian East Indian society. Combos that perform live at traditional weddings and festivals may, depending on the occasion, include various American styles. Because of the depth and ritualized usage, these internationalized styles, instruments, and songs of the combo style are considered by the people to be East Indian.

Besides the Indian Trinidadian combo orchestras and the traditional Hindu and

Muslim religious repertoires is the crossover calypso, a recognizably syncretized form that may insert an Indian topic; integrate an Indian musical theme, vocal style, or instrument; or employ Hindi linguistic elements (Khan 1989:7).

Drumming on a goatskin kettledrum (*tassa*) is done primarily at the yearly Muslim Hosay (Hosein) ritual that celebrates the martyrdom of the grandsons of the Prophet Mohammed. Lavishly ornamented miniature bamboo-framed temple-tombs are carried in procession through the streets of St. James Village to be ritualistically thrown into the river. Traditionally, women followed the procession singing laments (*marseehas*). Vigorous *tassa* drumming and stick fighting (*gatka*), which accompany the procession, symbolize the fierce battle (*jihad*) of Karbalā'. The ensemble, usually made up of three drums (*tassa*), one bass drum, and a cymbal (*jhāñjh*), has historically included Afro-Trinidadians, and the style, though of Indian origin, is considered an indigenous national type, attracting members of the entire population (see Okada 1995: example 23). In 1993, the religious significance of the event was overshadowed by a carnivalesque atmosphere. Apart from Hosay, the main Indian festivals celebrated in Trinidad are the festival of lights Diwālī (locally Divali) and the spring festival Guḍhī Pāḍwā (locally Phagwa).

NATIONAL FORMS

Reel

Tobago, with its separate culture and unified ethnic history, preserves the reel, derived from Scotland, as a vehicle for ancestral contact and veneration. Performed as a prenuptial or healing event, the dances entertain ancestors and ask them to validate a couple's union or remedy a patient's illness. The dances are supported by a violin, a tambourine, and drums, or by any combination of singers, tambourines, triangles, and chac-chacs. Though possession and dance are akin to those of Orisa ceremonies, the Yoruba pantheon of divinities is not a part of this practice.

Bélè

Bélè are dances stemming from the secular French traditions of Guadeloupe, Martinique, and Carriacou. They are sometimes mixed with the calling of ancestors and the pouring of libations. Preserved by festivals and staged productions throughout Trinidad and Tobago, they feature elegant solo and ensemble performances (see Okada 1995: example 24).

Kalenda

Stick fighting, a martial art in Trinidad and Tobago, is often accompanied by singing *kalenda,* dancing, and drumming (figure 3). The *kalenda* is considered one of the most ancient dance styles of African-descended people in the New World. In it, a "stick man" may sing a boastful song before entering the ring; a chorus of male singers responds, all accompanied by drumming. The drums (single-headed and barrel-shaped with heads fastened by hoops), terminology (*cutter, boula*), and style of performance (drums played with open hands) resemble those of the French Antilles rather than that of Orisa ceremonies (see Okada 1995: example 27).

Parang

Throughout Trinidad and Tobago, people perform a musical genre known as *parang* (from *parranda* in Spanish) that has been borrowed from the mainland [see VENEZUELA]. Originally comprising from two to five male singers accompanied by a *cuatro* and maracas (figure 4), a modern *parang* group may have mixed voices with various combinations of guitars, *cuatros*, maracas, woodblock or claves (tock-tock),

> Steelbands, found in much of the Caribbean, achieve their most brilliant applications in Trinidad. An individual instrument, known as a pan, is usually constructed from a 55-gallon metal oil drum.

FIGURE 3 The stick-fighting group Old Time Mas', with one fighter in front and four drummers behind him, Arima, Trinidad. Photo by Carolyn J. Fulton, 1994.

güiro, and a *marímbula,* a bass instrument, also called box bass, resembling a *tonkatonka* or *seprewa* as used by the Akan of Ghana.

In the Venezuelan Christmas *parang* tradition, an ensemble performs *aguinaldos* to serenade families; musicians are received and rewarded with food and drink. In Trinidad, the *parang* serenade has evolved into a national tradition, perpetuated and celebrated in state-sponsored competitions. The late Daisey Voisen, lead singer and founder of the award-winning ensemble La Divina Pastora, stressed in her compositions fine Spanish poetry, traditional musical style, and religious fervor (see Okada 1995:example 29). Sung as entertainment before playful crowds, *parangs* center on the Christmas story and scenes from the life of Jesus.

Steelband

Steelbands, found in much of the Caribbean, achieve their most brilliant applications in Trinidad. An individual instrument, known as a pan, is usually constructed from a 55-gallon metal oil drum. The builder, originally often the player, cuts off the top of the drum, and keeps the length of the side (the skirt) consistent with the range of the instrument: a lead pan has a short skirt, and a bass has a full skirt made from the full length of the barrel. The builder reforms the remaining end by heating and hammering ("sinking") it—an elaborate process that includes depressing the playing head into concavity, chiseling grooves to separate the notes, and hammering in each note. He hammers each bump into the top of the drum from underneath to form a series

FIGURE 4 Marina Gale, age 2, plays maracas while his grandfather plays a *cuatro* in the *parang* band Los Alegres Sin Duda, Port of Spain, Trinidad. Photo by Carolyn J. Fulton, 1992.

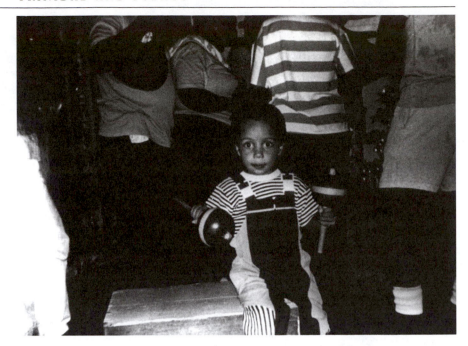

of individual convex impressions (ball-shaped "keys" or bumps), which he then tunes.

Because of the acoustic properties of the hammered metal surface, pitches are not ordered chromatically but are disjunct, creating a distinctive arrangement or pattern unique to each instrument. One of the most important player-builders who has worked toward standardizing the patterns of pitches (into a circle of fifths) is Ellie Mannette, now a teacher of pan at the University of West Virginia. No national standardization has been agreed on, however, because makers prefer to put their personal stamps on instruments they make. Other innovators include Winston "Spree" Simon, Bertie Marshall, and Anthony Williams.

In the late 1940s, names for pans included *tock-tock* (the dominant instrument, today the name for claves in *parang* music), followed by the *belly,* the *base-kettle,* and the *base-bum* (Fermor 1950:171). Because the instruments have continued to develop, there have been wide variations in their construction and use. Today, pans are divided into sections determined by their range and role within the ensemble. Melodic instruments include the tenor pan (formerly called the ping-pong, also known as the lead, the single tenor, the soprano, and the melody pan) and the double tenor (a set of two drums), though other pans will occasionally play the melody. Strumming pans, in imitation of the acoustic guitar, may include the double second, double guitar, quadraphonic, triple guitar, and cello (a set of three drums). The bass, formerly called tuned booms (a set of six to nine drums) and the tenor bass (a set of four drums) play the bass.

Using rubber-tipped mallets, musicians play single notes, double stops (two notes at once), and tremolos (rolls). A traditional parade style, "pan around the neck," gives players mobility, as each instrument is fixed to its player by a harness. For greater mobility in modern parades, the instruments are sometimes placed on car chassis, floats, or trucks. In concerts, the pans are arranged on metal stands or racks (figure 5). Music performed in Trinidad and Tobago is usually learned by rote, but notation is sometimes employed.

Efforts toward the instruments' tonal enhancement, evolution, systematization, and historical documentation continue. National industries sponsor pan orchestras

FIGURE 5   For the finals of Panorama in February 1994, a large pan orchestra on wheeled stands sets up on stage in Queens Park Savannah, Port of Spain, Trinidad. Photo by Carolyn J. Fulton.

and support biennial orchestral, solo, and composition competitions. As Trinidad's national instrument, pan is taught in some schools. As a result, the number of virtuoso panists is growing.

Tales surrounding the discovery of pan abound (Stuempfle 1995). Ownership of its invention is contested throughout the Caribbean and Guyana wherever pan is evident. The earliest record of pan connects it with carnival of the late 1930s, when metallic idiophones joined tamboo-bamboo ensembles (bamboo tubes, struck on the ground and against one another). Because masking at carnival provided the anonymity that encouraged uprisings and membranophonic drumming was associated with revolt, membranophones were outlawed as early as 1797 in Trinidad, especially during carnival. Their twentieth-century replacement, tamboo-bamboo, filled the vacuum and inspired the addition of such tonal resources as bottles, garbage can lids, kettles, oil tins, biscuit pans, and other metal idiophones (see Okada 1995: examples 25 and 26).

No single inventor of the steelband has been ascertained, but the slum environment of Port of Spain, Trinidad, is considered its place of maturation. Its primary nurturers are young African Trinidadian males (Elder 1969:17, 19). By the 1950s, with the support of governmental offices and the sponsorship of Trinidadian industries, pan had begun to be recognized, legitimized, and embraced by all communities and classes. Many pan organizations, once exclusively African descended and male, include East Indian and female participants, though in small numbers.

In state- and industry-sponsored steelband events (most commonly the national competitions Pan is Beautiful and Panorama), classical, new, and popular musical repertoires are performed. Virtuoso interpretations of pieces such as Gershwin's Rhapsody in Blue, Holst's *Planets* (the Mars and Jupiter movements), Rimsky-Korsakov's *Schéhérazade,* Tchaikovsky's *Capriccio Italien* and *Marche Slave,* and Wagner's *Rienzi* overture are created by large orchestras of steel. In formal competitions, besides the Western pieces of choice, each band must play a test piece and a calypso (see Okada 1995: example 31). For carnival, a particular calypso is selected, orchestrated, and used by each steelband as its road march during parades.

Besides a wide choice of fixed and new repertoires, there is experimentation in jazz improvisation, with panist Len "Boogsie" Sharpe as the major contributor. The future direction of Trinidad's composed music for pan is of great concern and incites much discussion in many segments of Trinidad and Tobago society.

Calypso

Calypso is the Caribbean musical genre usually identified with Trinidad. Growing out of the *kalenda* and related to the *bèlè*, it is in constant revision. New compositions, fulfilling cultural expectations and festival needs, appear yearly. The etymology of the word *calypso* is multiple and international. The term was at one time associated with the Hausa word *kaiso* 'serves you right, you deserve no pity', and with its translation in the patois term *sans humanité*. *Kaiso* may have been further confused with the Venezuelan Spanish word *caliso* 'a topical, local song', possibly related to the patois term *wuso* 'to carouse' (French *carrousseaux*) (Hill 1967:364).

The word *kaiso* served as a shout of delight and encouragement after expressive singing; similarly, the response *sans humanité* was offered by crowds at the closure of early patois-text calypsos and in English and macaronic (English and patois) calypsos of the early 1900s. A portion of Lord Executor's "Landing of Columbus," published in 1926, illustrates the use of this tag (after Errol Hill, 1972:63):

> Were you not told what Columbus saw
> When he landed on Iere shore?
> Were you not told what Columbus saw
> When he landed on Iere shore?
> He saw the Caribs so brave and bold,
> The hummingbirds with their wings of gold.
> He was so glad that he called the island Trinidad.
> *Sans humanité.*

Lord Executor's delivery of the same song elicited from the audience an ecstatic unison shout: "Kaiso-o-o!" (Quevedo 1983:37).

Like the *kalenda*, the calypso deploys militant language against political oppression and social infringements; like the *bèlè*, it airs public and individual misdemeanors. Its narrative, while seeking to control social behavior through the dissemination of scandal, informs society, gives lessons in ethnic pride, and parodies and shames exploitative acts. Many texts are fun-loving *picong* (from French *piquant* 'insult'); some belong to the genre known as the war, a battle of words (Warner 1985:13). Others, with sexual double-entendres, employ symbolic metaphors to belittle and insult women. The outrage of maligned religious minorities, like Hindus at the insulting "Om Shanti Om" by Shorti, and the Spiritual Baptists by Blue Boy's "Soca Baptist," invited censorship and rewording of the items.

For forty years, the Mighty Sparrow (Francisco Slinger) has reigned as the most impressive and sophisticated modern practitioner of the art of calypso. His topics exploit international and internal political events, and his musical and linguistic sensibilities have influenced pan-Caribbean calypso styles. His 1956 calypso "Jean and Dinah" ranks as a classic, as does Lord Invader's (Rupert Grant's) "Rum and Coca Cola," a hit during the Second World War.

Inventor (Henry Forbes), Roaring Lion (Hubert de Leon), Atilla the Hun (Raymond Quevedo), Lord Executor (Phillip Garcia), Lord Kitchener (Aldwyn Roberts), Growling Tiger (Neville Marcano), Lord Pretender (Alric Farrell), Lord Beginner (Egbert Moore), King Radio (Norman Span), Lord Caresser, Small Island Pride, and Houdini lead the list of past practitioners (see Warner 1985:15–16). Titles such as "Lord" and "King" are avoided by younger artists, who choose noncolonial-

> Carnival is the major cultural focus and the "national theater" of Trinidad. In its modern form, artists and theatrical professionals assist in a nonstop artistic revelry of parades, dances, concerts, and competitions.

sounding signatures (such as Black Stalin, Watchman, Shortpants, Chalkdust) or retain their own names (as has David Rudder).

In the international climate of the 1980s, a new calypso form *(soca),* with danceable rhythms and pan-African texts, became popular (see Okada 1995: example 30). Though several antiquated calypso forms (Hill 1993:4) and terminologies are revisited by modern calypsonians from time to time, older practitioners fear the complete loss of the fast-moving call-and-response *kalenda* type; the dramatic narrative of the ballad type; the witty, satirical, text-centered, and extemporaneous delivery of the oratorical calypso; and especially the humorous-language duel in duets of an earlier age.

Carnival

Carnival is the major cultural focus and the "national theater" of Trinidad. In its modern form, artists and theatrical professionals assist in a nonstop artistic revelry of parades, dances, concerts, and competitions. Carnival's performances capture the attention of most Trinidadians, children as well as adults (figure 6), and some people dedicate the entire year to its planning. Others simply *play mas'* (join a group organized by similar costume), *jump up* (march or celebrate), and *chip-strut* (strut on the balls of the feet) in the line of march.

The drinking and carousing that sometimes overtake celebrants belie hidden and historically significant aspects of the celebration. This play mirrors society and defines groups while permitting uncloaked behavior. In some way, and among social, cultural, artistic, and even spiritual expectations, Trinidadian carnival still provides the escape valve it did in slave society (Hill 1993: 212)—to relieve anxiety, now caused by current economic problems. The economic impact of the festival is huge.

Preparations for carnival include the cultivation of the national music of Trinidad (pan and calypso) in prescribed ways. Performers introduce newly composed calypsos in tents (urban venues) whose origins were simple thatched structures. Steelbands introduce their repertoires in their pan yards months before the carnival period. In this way, people reach the carnival grounds musically alert and prepared for a season of national artistic involvement.

The carnival parade includes string bands, pan orchestras, and nonmusical troupes of costumed participants, comprising an individual player or groups of hundreds of people whose costumes recreate historical, mythological, or newly created figures (figure 7). People have the choice of joining a same-costumed band and paying a fee for the costume. To an outsider, the cost of participation may seem a major investment, but to many Trinidadians it appears insignificant compared to the privilege and pleasure it provides.

Costumes of the 1800s included the *negre jardin,* a favorite disguise of aristocrats who, well before 1860, adored imitating agricultural servants. This attire was borrowed in the twentieth century by stick-fighting bands, some wearing headbands,

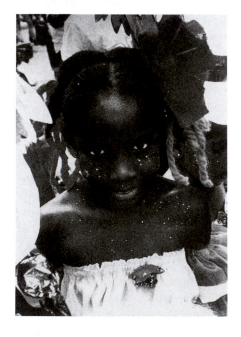

FIGURE 6   A young girl celebrates Children's Mas' during carnival in Port of Spain, Trinidad. Photo by Carolyn J. Fulton, 1994.

FIGURE 7   A male dancer wears a brilliant blue costume resembling a wave during carnival in St. Joseph, Trinidad. Photo by Carolyn J. Fulton, 1994.

trousers turned inside out, or jackets to identify the higher-class patrons of the sport. Early *kalenda* contests were accompanied by tamboo-bamboo orchestras or membranophone drums.

The music that accompanied carnival in the 1800s most likely comprised *kalenda* songs, string music, membranophonic ensembles, and *speech mas'* (a vignette involving poetry or language). In these carnivals, women costumed as bawdy street-walkers (*jamettes*) wore overdressed outfits embellished with flowers and feathers, imitating the high fashion of nineteenth-century France. The word *jamette,* widely used before the turn of the twentieth century, evolved from the French *diamètre,* meaning people below the diameter, the lower half (Pearse 1988:31). They were considered obscene, and their participation was proscribed as was that of the raggedly dressed comic transvestite *pissenlit,* in practice before 1884. The stilt dancer (*moko jumby*) came from Africa, as did *congos* (Sango bands), which parodied the ritual prayers with mock-African language and drumming. Cattle bands, often played by Venezuelans, used cow horns as part of their costumes.

Each "fancy" or "pretty" band of the era before the Great War marched with a king, a queen (figure 8), members of a royal court, and a lead singer (*chantrel*). At carnival from the 1920s to 1947, one lead singer dressed in a silk, velvet, or brocade suit with a cape thrown over his shoulder, a plumed hat, and a sword held in a gloved hand led each band; when he gave the solo call, his masked band, following the line of march, responded by singing (Jones 1947:39). A second fancy band of the same period donned plaid skirts and the complete regalia of caps, sashes, and ornaments; they rode on horseback playing Scottish tunes on bagpipes.

Sailors and "Indian" bands were once the favorite types of organized troops. Originally, "Wild Indians" were probably the so-called Warrahoons of Venezuela, who frequented southern Trinidad until their entry was banned in the 1920s (Crowley 1988:63) [see WARAO]. Colors in names such as "Red Indians," "Blue Indians," and "White Indians" refer to the specific color costuming of the groups. The origin of the "Red Indians" seems to have been Grenada, for that band is the favorite of Grenadians participating in the Trinidad carnival. With unified costuming, language united the "Indian warrior" band fraternities. Phrases taught at rehearsals were incorporated in skits and in the mock stick duels that frequently included utterances of challenges (Crowley 1988:65).

"Black Indians" (played by African Trinidadians), who wear black costumes and use paint to darken their faces, use phrases to imitate African languages. Ritualized language pervaded many old-time portraits and especially that of the old-time clown, the effete Pierrot Grenade. Dressed in an outfit made from burlap bags ornamented with playing cards, old tin cans, and discardable scraps, with erudite, scholarly, and confusing language, he poked fun at Grenadians, at patois, and at English Creole (Carr 1988:197, 204). The pretty-devil band (*jab-jab*) is preferred by East Indians, as is the little donkey (*burroquite*), derived from the Hindu goddess Durga. She is portrayed by her symbol, a horse or donkey whose rider stands behind the head of the animal, surrounded by drapes forming the body. The donkey and the rider dance to a Hindi song. A similar band, called by the same Spanish name, evolved among Venezuelans.

The costumes of fancy bands—created from history, images in comic books, folklore, films, military uniforms, *National Geographic* magazines, mythology, and creative fantasy—were fabulously feathered constructions of papier mâché, fiberglass, and molded wire. Today, brilliant costume extensions are constructed from modern, lightweight materials with unimaginable variety (figure 9).

Cowley (1992) lists the first historical period of carnival (Planter's Carnival, 1797–1833) as being controlled by the upper class, which presented elegant masked

FIGURE 8   A young girl dancer wearing a queen costume celebrates Children's Mas' during carnival in Port of Spain, Trinidad. Photo by Carolyn J. Fulton, 1994.

FIGURE 9 A young girl dancer wearing a butter-fly costume celebrates Children's Mas' during carnival in Port of Spain, Trinidad. The flexible tubing supports her colorful butterfly wings. Photo by Carolyn J. Fulton, 1994.

balls. The second era was during postemancipation (1834–1869); the third, the *jamette* carnival, between 1870 and 1896; and the fourth, the incorporated carnival, from 1897 to 1950. The third era brought about the rise of complaints against obscenity, noise, and workers' drumming, and challenges and riots against police suppression. The riots of 1881 and 1884 were popular uprisings for the right to mount the *cannes brûlées (canboulay,* burning cane), the opening torchlight procession of carnival that recreated the slave-era burning of the canefields. The burning of cane later served as a metaphor denouncing slavery and the establishment (Pearse 1988:18). A famous *kalenda* immortalizes the *cannes brûlées* of 1881, its stick-fighting leader, Joe Talmana, and the notorious captain of police, Captain Baker. This song is among several songs surviving from Trinidad's era of open social conflict (Pearse Archive):

Captain Baker manday pou mois	Captain Baker is asking for me
Ah ya ya, Jo Talmana.	Here I am, Jo Talmana.

It is clear from the costumes—each type with its own mythology, ethnic following, and class organization—that many are representations of the conflicts and struggles in Trinidad's history. In the contemporary carnival, which invites tourists and stresses enjoyment, participants still delight in reversals of class and race. The modern carnival may fulfill a broader, collaborative scheme, even extending into a succeeding year. In the mid-1980s, the grand carnival trilogy "The River," directed by Peter Minshall, enacted the theme of good versus evil in three parts, over three years (Juneja 1988). Larger-than-life carnival theater staged like a religious ritual, it had the people (the culturally diverse "river" of Trinidad) playing themselves in ethnic costumes. Their demise, loss of love (through technology), and search for recovery were elaborately depicted by actors, spectacular bands, and scenes of war between the Princes of Darkness and the Lords of Light. The battle was accompanied by the calypso "Apocalypso," which incorporated the words "I can't see the light."

Modern carnival is charged with new, thought-provoking, universal messages, transmitted with modern effects and high-tech stagecraft. Projecting the future, it reflects the past. Though masks are no longer worn and personal enmities are no longer openly contested, bands must be seen as not only nationalistic and ethnic but also as charged with a spirit of rebellion against ordinary rules of conduct. Mediating racial antipathies and defining social class, carnival bonds its participants in a fierce, competitive nationalization of culture.

REFERENCES

Aho, William R. 1987. "Steel Band Music in Trinidad and Tobago: The Creation of a People's Music." *Latin American Music Review* 8(1):26–58.

Ahye, Molly. 1978. *Golden Heritage: The Dance in Trinidad and Tobago.* Petit Valley: Heritage Cultures Limited.

Ahyoung, Selwyn. 1981. "Soca Fever! Change in the Calypso Music Tradition of Trinidad & Tobago, 1970–1980." M.A. thesis, Indiana University.

———. 1986. "The Music of the Shouter-Baptists of Trinidad, West Indies." *The Hymn* 37(1):19–24.

Brereton, Bridget. 1981. *A History of Modern Trinidad, 1783–1962.* London, Port of Spain: Heinemann Educational Books.

Carr, Andrew T. 1988 [1956]. "Pierrot Grenada." *Trinidad Carnival.* Port of Spain: Paria Printing.

Cowley, John. 1992. "Music and Migration: Aspects of Black Music in the British Caribbean, the United States, and Britain, Before the Independence of Jamaica and Trinidad." Ph.D. dissertation, University of Warwick.

Crowley, Daniel J. 1957. "Plural and Differential Acculturation in Trinidad." *American Anthropologist* 59:817–24.

———. 1988 [1956]. "The Traditional Masques of Carnival." *Trinidad Carnival.* Port of Spain: Paria Publishing.

Elder, Jacob D. 1969. *From Congo Drum to Steel Band.* St. Augustine, Trinidad: University of the West Indies.

Fermor, Patrick. 1950. *The Traveller's Tree: A Journey Through the Caribbean Islands.* New York: Harper and Brothers.

Herskovits, Melville J., and Frances S. Herskovits. 1964 [1947]. *Trinidad Village.* New York: Octagon Books.

Hill, Donald R. 1993. *Calypso Calaloo: Early Carnival Music in Trinidad.* Gainesville: University Press of Florida.

Hill, Errol. 1967. "On the Origin of the Term Calypso." *Ethnomusicology* 11(3):359–367.

——. 1972. *The Trinidad Carnival: Mandate for a National Theater.* Austin: University of Texas Press.

Houk, James T. 1992. "The Orisa Religion in Trinidad: A Study of Culture, Process and Transformation." Ph.D. dissertation, Tulane University.

Juneja, Renu. 1988. "The Trinidad Carnival: Ritual, Performance, Spectacle, and Symbol." *Journal of Popular Culture* 21:87–99.

Jones, Charles. 1947. *Calypso and Carnival of Long Ago and Today.* Port-of-Spain Gazette.

Khan, Aisha. 1989. "Preliminary Survey of Musical Forms Among East Indians in Trinidad." Unpublished paper written for the Smithsonian Institution.

Kekere, Agba. 1988. "Trinidad and Tobago Orisa Yin Cultural Organization, Chaguanas." Unpublished paper.

McDaniel, Lorna. 1995. "Memory Spirituals of the Ex-Slave Soldiers in Trinidad's Company Villages." *Black Music Research Journal* 14(2):119–143.

Myers, Helen. 1980. "Trinidad and Tobago." *The New Grove Dictionary of Music and Musicians,* ed. Stanley Sadie. London: Macmillan.

Okada, Yuki. *The Caribbean.* JVC Smithsonian Folkways Video Anthology of Music and Dance of the Americas, 4. Montpelier, Vt.: Multicultural Media VTMV-228. Video.

Pearse, Andrew. 1953. "My Life: Frank Mayhew." *Caribbean Quarterly* 3(1):13–23.

——. 1955. "Aspects of Change in Caribbean Folk Music." *Journal of the International Folk Music Council* 7:29–36.

——. 1988 [1956]. "Carnival in Nineteenth-Century Trinidad." *Trinidad Carnival.* Port of Spain: Paria Publishing.

Quevedo, Raymond. 1983. *Atilla's Kaiso.* St. Augustine, Trinidad: University of the West Indies.

Ramaya, Narsaloo. 1987. "Towards the Evolution of a National Culture: Indian Music in Trinidad and Tobago." In *Indians in the Caribbean,* ed. I. J. Bahadur Singh, 147–166. New Delhi: Sterling Publishers.

Simpson, George. 1965. *The Shango Cult in Trinidad.* Rio Piedras: Institute of Caribbean Studies, University of Puerto Rico.

——. 1962. "The Shango Cult in Nigeria and in Trinidad." *American Anthropologist* 64:1204–1219.

Stuempfle, Stephen. 1995. *The Steelband Movement: The Forging of a National Art in Trinidad and Tobago.* Philadelphia: University of Pennsylvania Press.

Thomas, Eudora. 1987. *A History of the Shouter Baptists in Trinidad and Tobago.* Trinidad: Calaloux Publications.

Warner, Keith. 1985. *Kaiso! The Trinidad Calypso.* Washington, D.C.: Three Continents Press.

Williams, Mervyn C. R. 1985. "Song from Valley to Mountain: Music and Ritual asmong the Spiritual Baptists ('Shouters') of Trinidad." M.A. thesis, Indiana University.

Winer, Lise. 1986. "Socio-Cultural Change and the Language of Calypso." *Nieuwe West Indische Gids* 60(3–4):113–148.

Wood, Donald. 1986. *Trinidad in Transition.* London: Oxford University Press.

The Virgin Islands
Daniel E. Sheehy

Musical Traditions
Further Study

In 1493, during Columbus's second voyage to the Caribbean, the fleet briefly dropped anchor at the mouth of what is now the Salt River on St. Croix Island. The local inhabitants—Carib Indians, who had long before displaced their Arawak predecessors—discouraged an extended visit, though not enough to keep Columbus from claiming for Spain the island and its neighbors, the westernmost Lesser Antilles. He named these islands Santa Ursula y Las Once Mil Vírgenes (St. Ursula and The Eleven Thousand Virgins), later abbreviated to the Virgin Islands.

By 1600, the Spanish had eliminated or driven out most of the Indians. Over the next five centuries, various of the islands were controlled by as many as six European nations and the United States. Most prominent of these in their impact on modern local culture were the British, the Danish, the Dutch, the French, and the North Americans. Enormously influential in cultural terms were African peoples, brought as enslaved canefield workers as early as 1673, part of the triangle of trade in rum, slaves, and sugarcane. Slavery existed locally until 1848, when it was outlawed in Danish territories.

Today, the Virgin Islands are divided politically into two units: the U.S. Virgin Islands and the British Virgin Islands. The U.S. territory, larger and much more populous, consists of about fifty uninhabited small islets and cays and three principal islands—St. Croix, St. John, and St. Thomas—with a total population of 101,809 (1990). The British crown colony is made up of thirty-two partly inhabited islets and four larger islands—Anegada, Jost Van Dyke, Tortola, and Virgin Gorda—with 16,749 inhabitants (1991). Related to them is the small crown colony of Anguilla, just east of Virgin Gorda. The U.S. portion was a Danish possession for most of the time from the founding of St. Thomas as a colony (in 1671) to its purchase by the United States (in 1917). The other portion was colonized by Britain in 1672. Despite the division between different colonial powers, cultural and economic ties among the islands have long been close. An English-based Creole dominates in both political domains, and the official currency for both is the U.S. dollar.

A shared sense of cultural history and a modern receptivity to English-language popular culture—imported especially from the United States and other English-dominant Caribbean islands—underlie a clear degree of cultural unity, compared with the neighboring islands of Puerto Rico (to the west) and the rest of the Lesser Antilles (to the east and south). Though the American Virgin Islands were under Danish rule until 1917, English had been the dominant language there since the massive nineteenth-century postslavery immigration of workers from the English-speaking Caribbean. Still, Virgin Islands culture has for centuries been marked by a range of cultural backgrounds. Scottish, Irish, Danish, Dutch, French, and other European colonial settlers managed early plantations and maritime trade. Slaves came from the Senegambian, Ghanaian, Nigerian, and Congolese regions of Africa. More recent immigrants—from India, other Caribbean islands (including Antigua, Barbados, Jamaica, and Trinidad), the United States, and Arab countries—have brought a multitude of other cultural traditions. In 1980, fewer than half of U.S. Virgin Islanders were native born (Soule 1993:4).

MUSICAL TRADITIONS

In the mid-twentieth century, Virgin Islands musical traditions were mostly stable, practiced by all generations. Efforts to expand the tourist industry and the diversion of the American tourist trade from Cuba following its 1959 revolution spurred a substantial increase in immigrant labor to fill the service jobs that resulted. At the same time, the growth of television, radio, and the popular music industry brought greater prominence of popular music from the United States and the English Caribbean. These changes served both to dilute local traditions and to divert younger generations from taking them up, favoring the more prestigious and lucrative forms of popular music.

By the 1980s, popular musics such as merengue, reggae, rock, and soca dominated the airwaves, social dances, and record stores. Centers for the performing arts, including the Reichold Center on St. Thomas and the Island Center on St. Croix, offered concerts of jazz, classical music, musical theater, pop stars, and other nonlocal fare. Young people formed Trinidad-style steelbands (pan orchestras), dance bands (with electric guitars, horns, and percussion, playing reggae, rock, and soca), and dance troupes (performing pan-Caribbean genres). Virgin Islanders of Puerto Rican background, accounting for nearly half of St. Croix's 50,139 population (1990), kept an eager ear turned toward Latin Caribbean pop from Puerto Rico and the Dominican Republic, and a few continued to perform music of the Cruz de Mayo and *seis* traditions and domestic music, such as lullabies [see PUERTO RICO].

Musical instruction in schools continues to focus on performance in Western orchestral and concert-band music, with exposure to local traditions through quadrille instruction in several St. Croix schools and a student scratch band (see below) at Charlotte Amalie High School on St. Thomas. The international orthodoxy of Anglican, Methodist, Roman Catholic, and other Christian church music has left little room for distinctively local developments.

Scratch bands

Important exceptions to the near-total eclipse of long-standing Virgin Islands traditions occur. Locally based ensembles, called scratch bands (or *fungi* bands, probably named for *fungi*, a local African-derived stew), have survived by adopting contemporary popular instrumentation and repertoire and identifying with a movement to maintain native cultural traditions. The normal presence in these groups of a squash—the local term for a hollow, open-ended gourd idiophone with notched grooves carved into one side and scratched with a multipronged metal scraper (similar to, but larger than, the Puerto Rican *güiro*)—apparently led the groups to be

FIGURE 1 The scratch band Blinky and the Roadmasters performs at a party on St. Croix. *Left to right:* Lloyd Thomas, conga; Sylvester "Blinky" McIntosh, alto saxophone; Milton Gordon, electric bass; Cyprian King, electric guitar; Norman Edwards, drumset; Anselmo Clarke, squash; and Isidore Griles, steel. Photo by Daniel E. Sheehy, 1991.

called scratch bands, first by continentals (outsiders from the United States) and eventually by local people.

Previously, these ensembles were known as string bands to distinguish them from membrane-based bands, which made more use of drumming. In the more distant past, the precise instrumentation of scratch bands probably varied, but they all included some form of melodic instrument (a violin, a cane flute, or even an accordion) and some form of percussive instrument (a squash, a triangle called "steel," a tambourine, or a locally made double-headed barrel drum, possibly derived from the *tambora* of the Dominican Republic). A six-stringed guitar and a banjo or a ukulele might have supplied rhythmic chords. A car-exhaust tube (known to some as an ass pipe), about 1.2 to 1.5 meters long and played by lip concussion like a tuba, often furnished a bass. These combinations of instruments are not unique to the Virgin Islands and have probably been used in other regions of the anglophone Caribbean.

By the 1980s, the instrumentation had become more standardized (figure 1). The lead melodic instrument was either an alto saxophone or (less frequently) a silver flute. An electric guitar, an electric bass guitar, a squash, a steel (a metal triangle, held and rhythmically dampened with one hand while struck with a metal rod by the other), a dance-band drum set, and a conga were regular components of the ensemble. A banjo or a ukulele, an electric keyboard, and a second saxophone or other melodic instrument were less usual additions.

Scratch bands are most common on St. Croix, where groups such as Blinky and the Roadmasters, Stanley and the Ten Sleepless Knights, and Bully and the Kafooners perform at social dances, festivals, fairs, private parties (such as christenings and wedding receptions), church services of various Christian denominations, "cultural" presentations for tourists, and quadrilles. Their repertoire is eclectic—virtually all dance music. Pieces commonly played range widely: jigs, waltzes, mazurkas, and other European-derived genres generally associated with past generations; boleros, calypsos, merengues, and other English and Latin Caribbean dance music; international American ballads and dance favorites; and locally originated musical genres.

On St. Thomas, the more urban and second most populous island (48,166 in 1990), scratch bands are scarcer than on St. Croix, and their instrumentation and repertoire more closely conform to pan-Caribbean tastes. They also exist in the British Virgin Islands. Elmo and the Sparkplugs, a scratch band from Tortola, performed at the Quelbe [sic] Fest on St. Thomas in 1992, and included a washtub bass (gutbucket) in their instrumentation. More thorough documentation of the British Virgin Islands scratch-band tradition may reveal more general distinctions from their American Virgin Islands counterparts.

Quelbeys and quadrilles

Scratch bands have been central to the continuity of two other musical traditions: quelbeys and quadrilles. Quelbeys are topical songs of local origin. In earlier generations, they were sung most often by individuals in informal gatherings or public celebrations. Their texts "usually contained hidden meaning and sexual innuendo, ridiculed individuals for the words or actions, or immortalized political events such as a boycott or a workers' revolt" (Soule 1993:6). One quelbey, "LaBega Carousel," chastises a carousel owner, Carl LaBega, for having opposed a wage increase for local workers in the early twentieth century (Soule 1993:18):

> I rather walk and drink rum whole night,
> Before me go ride on LaBega Carousel.
> I rather walk, man, and drink rum whole night,
> Before me go ride on LaBega Carousel.
> You no hear what LaBega say,
> "The people no worth more than fifteen cent a day."
> You no hear what LaBega say, man,
> "The people no worth more than half cent a day."

On St. Croix, the quadrille still enjoys a modest following (figure 2). Performances typically take several forms: as social gatherings of aficionados at local public venues such as St. Gerald's Hall in Frederiksted; as educational performances to promote

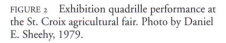

FIGURE 2   Exhibition quadrille performance at the St. Croix agricultural fair. Photo by Daniel E. Sheehy, 1979.

Costumed groups with traditional themes, such as "Wild Indians" or "Mother Hubbard," would play instruments, rhythms, and melodies that signified their special identity as they moved from locale to locale, performing as they went.

local culture in schools or at holiday celebrations; or as spectacles for tourists. The first form of performance is usually open to the public and invites general participation, though skill is required to dance the quadrille. In the traditional fashion, a so-called floor master calls dancers' moves in synchrony with the musical phrases, leading the dancers through the five or six figures (the number being the floor master's choice), each of which is accompanied by a different tune repeated at length (Soule 1993:7). At the latter two performance occasions, an ensemble dressed in color-coordinated traditional garb reminiscent of earlier generations (typified by the St. Croix Heritage Dancers as led by Bradley Christian) might offer a more compact, staged rendition of the principal figures, accompanied by an explanatory narration.

Other traditions

Several other older Virgin Islands musical traditions persist in the memories of older generations or as reconstructed performances by advocates of traditional cultural forms. On St. Croix in the 1990s, a few elderly singers, including Ethel McIntosh and Leona Watson, continued to sing *carisos* dating to the decades just after colony-wide emancipation. Their texts often resembled those of quelbeys in its social censure and commemoration of past events. *Carisos* differ, though, in having a more African-origin melodic style, with more sustained syllables and traditional manner of performance, by women singing in call-and-response fashion. The group sings a fixed refrain, and a male drummer accompanies them.

Cariso continues as a representation of deep Crucian tradition in educational cultural presentations and for special holidays. One famous *cariso* recounts the freedom proclamation of 3 July 1848, ending slavery. The chorus sings a refrain, and a soloist then sings (after Soule 1993:13):

> Clear the road, all you clear the road,
> Clear the road, let the slave them pass,
> We a go for a-we freedom.
>
> Hardship in the morning, suffering at night.
> No one ever help us, it is only Father Ryan.
> They bring we ya from Africa, that we bornin' land;
> Bring we ya in slavery, in the land of Santa Cruz.

The chorus then sings the refrain again.

Many older U.S. Virgin Islanders still remember three traditions of probable origin in the British West Indies: the masquerade jig, the David and Goliath play, and tea meetings. The first two combined theater, oratory, music, and dance to provide an evening's entertainment for those who paid a fee. Each performer would typically intersperse witty monologues with an improvised jig. The biblical plot of David and Goliath served as a point of departure for dramatic and humorous oratory on a wide range of topics. Tea meetings were opportunities for making speeches and singing hymns, nineteenth-century sentimental parlor songs, and the like (Soule 1993:19). These traditions have not retained their former vigor, though they occasionally appear as reconstructed renditions for educational and public display.

Bamboula, an extinct or reconstructed tradition of African-style dance, drumming, and song, is associated with St. Thomas. In the early twentieth century, before it ceased to exist in its traditional form and social context, it apparently consisted of two drummers playing a single drum (one with the hands and heel, the other with two sticks), dance movements (probably of African derivation), and men and women singing songs with collective refrains punctuating often improvised solo texts.

Major holidays, such as festival on St. Croix (Christmas through Three Kings Day, 6 January) and carnival on St. Thomas (after Easter), have for generations provided opportunities for musical performances. Up to the late 1950s, masquerading ("mas'ing") was an important tradition, occurring on several holiday celebrations. Costumed groups with traditional themes, such as "Wild Indians" or "Mother Hubbard," would play instruments, rhythms, and melodies that signified their special identity as they moved from locale to locale, performing as they went. The fife-and-drum ensemble of cane fife, snare drum ("kettledrum"), and double-headed bass drum ("boom-boom," "keg") were often participants. Shortly after the institution of a formal parade and "festival village" (which became the annual focus of such celebration on St. Croix), the older local masquerading traditions there became largely dormant.

Throughout the American Virgin Islands, masquerading of a distinctively local character was gradually replaced at festival and carnival by Trinidadian-style calypso, moko jumbie stilt dancers, pan-Caribbean popular music, and performances by music and dance troupes visiting from other parts of the Lesser Antilles.

FURTHER STUDY

The scholarly documentation of music in the Virgin Islands is not copious. In 1979 and the early 1980s, the sound recordist Mary Jane Soule documented a variety of local traditions and later produced a thoroughly annotated compact disc, *Zoop Zoop Zoop: Traditional Music and Folklore of St. Croix, St. Thomas, and St. John* (1993). The German ethnomusicologist Margot Lieth-Philipp, who collaborated on the descriptive notes for this recording, carried out earlier research that yielded two European publications on Virgin Islands music (1989, 1990). A team of folklorists and other researchers from the Smithsonian Institution's Center for Folklife Programs and Cultural Studies and the Virgin Islands collected musical material in 1989–1990, but except for articles in festival-program booklets (Cadaval 1990; Sprauve 1990), little of it has been published.

REFERENCES

Cadaval, Olivia. 1990. "Folklife of the U.S. Virgin Islands: Persistence and Creativity." In *1990 Festival of American Folklife,* 18–26. Washington, D.C.: Smithsonian Institution.

Lieth-Philipp, Margot. 1989. "*Bamboula:* Historical, Ethnological, and Linguistic Evidence for a Forgotten Caribbean Music." In *Ethnomusicology and the Historical Dimension,* 59–70. Papers Presented at the European Seminar in Ethnomusicology, London, 20–23 May 1986. Ludwigsburg, Germany: Philipp Verlag.

———. 1990. *Die Musikkultur der Jungferninseln:*

Studien zu ihrer Entwicklung und zu Resultaten von Akkulturationsprocessen. Ludwigsburg, Germany: Philipp Verlag.

McIntosh, Sylvester. 1990. *Blinky & the Roadmasters.* Notes by Mary Jane Soule. Rounder Records CD 5047. Compact disc.

Soule, Mary Jane, with Margot Lieth-Philipp. 1993. *Zoop Zoop Zoop: Traditional Music and Folklore of St. Croix, St. Thomas, and St. John.* New York: New World Records. Compact disc and notes.

Sprauve, Gilbert A. 1990. "About Man Betta Man, Fission and Fusion, and Creole, Calypso and Cultural Survival in the Virgin Islands." In *1990 Festival of American Folklife,* 34–36. Washington, D.C.: Smithsonian Institution.

Glossary

Page numbers in *italics* indicate pages on which illustrations appear.

abajeños 'From lower lands', Purépecha instrumental mestizo music for *zapateados* (578–79)

abanderado Chilean conductor of a *baile* or *cofradía* dancing group (365)

abeimahani Unaccompanied Garifuna women's song, a category of *úyanu* (672–73)

abelagudahani 'Bringing-in' song performed at the beginning of the Garifuna *dügü* ritual to escort fishermen to and from the sea (672)

abeng Jamaican cow-horn trumpet (897, 900)

aboio Brazilian *cantoria* cowboy cattle-herding song genre featuring the imitation of cattle (325, 328, 332, 347)

acculturation Changes that occur when members of different cultures come into continuous contact, involving complex relationships of cultural, economic, and political dominance (67, 70–75)

acordeón 'Accordion', in many regions of Spanish-speaking America, a multiple single-reed-concussion aerophone with bellows, either with buttons or keyboard for melody, and buttons for bass notes; *see index under* aerophones

adaha ademi hidi Yekuana garden song festival (179, 181)

adawo Jamaican machete played as an idiophone struck with a piece of metal (897)

ademi Yekuana large group song (181)

adufe Guatemalan quadrangular double-skinned frame drum, with or without rattle inside the body (727)

aerophone 'Air sounder', a musical instrument whose sound is produced by vibrating air, often a column of air (29)

afoxé Contemporary Afro-Brazilian carnival music (308, 338, 351–52)

agachi ngere Suyá day songs in rainy season (145)

agida Lowest-pitched drum of the battery of Maroon ritual drums in Surinam (505)

agogô Brazilian double or triple cone-shaped bell played with metal stick (308–309, 343)

agua 'e nieve Also *agüenieve*, Afro-Peruvian male competition dance (482, 497)

agua larga Colombian *currulao* rhythm (404)

aguinaldo Song genre throughout Hispanic America that is usually sung around Christmas and that involves gifts of coins, candy, food, or drink in exchange for music (531, 538, 615–16)

aires nacionales 'National songs', traditional Mexican and other Latin American melodies arranged for piano (603)

ajköki Bribri songs that tell of birth or death, or are for circumcision rites, first menstrual period, and weddings (634)

akia Suyá individual shout songs (145, 146)

al revés In the Chilean *tonada*, when a quatrain starts with the retrograde of the previous one (368)

alabado Also *albao, alavado*, 'praised', (1) in Colombia and many other Spanish-speaking regions, a folk adaptation of a Catholic hymn (403–404); (2) an announcement played by the *clarinero* in Peru (36)

alabanza 'Praise', (1) unaccompanied religious praise song in Argentina and elsewhere in Spanish-speaking America in two, three, or four voices (258, 457, 571); (2) responsorial Christian hymn in praise of the Eucharist (578)

alabês Afro-Brazilian drummers in Candomblé (343, *345*)

Alacaluf Also Halakwalup, extinct native American culture of Tierra del Fuego (357)

albazo Ecuadorian national folk music genre (417, 424, 427)

alborada Municipal band music for patronal festivals (859)

alcahuete* or *adulón Drums other than *palo mayor* used in the *palos* (854–55)

alcatraz Afro-Peruvian novelty couple dance (482, 496–97)

alé liwon Introduction to the St. Lucian *débòt* dance performed in a circle (943)

aleke A percussive genre of the Maroons of Surinam (439, 509)

alfandoques Ecuadorian tubular rattles (377, 414)

alférez Also *alferéz, alferece*, administrative director, conductor, or main sponsor of a *baile* or *cofradía* dancing group in Chile (291, 362, 365)

altiplano 'High plain', the cold, high central plain of southern Peru and Bolivia (also used for the region around Bogotá, Colombia) (282)

Aluku Maroon people who live on the Maroni

River in French Guiana and Surinam (438–39)

'ama In Tzotzil language, a Guatemalan highland Maya cane flute (654, 722, 723, 726)

ámalihani Complex dance of the Garifuna *dügü* ritual in Belize, characterized by movement in a circular pattern and reversals of direction (672)

amarrao 'Tied', Puerto Rican dance choreography (938–39)

ambush Jamaican *salo* song type (902)

amor fino Afro-Peruvian competitive song form (495)

amto ngere Suyá mouse ceremony (145)

anata Bolivian wooden duct flute, another term for *tarka* (287)

anba tonèl 'Under the arbor', descriptive term for rural, traditional music in Haiti (890)

angara Afro-Peruvian calabash idiophone with one side opened (492–93)

angelitos 'Little angels', songs and instrumental music for deceased infants and children (403–404, 422–24, 462, 571)

angroti ngere Suyá wild pig ceremony (145)

angu'á Paraguayan double-headed membranophone (200–201)

antara Also *andara*, Quechua term for single-unit panpipe in Peru, played by one person (35, 207–208, 467–69)

anthem Bahamian religious song genre closely related to the spiritual of slaves and other blacks from the southern United States (804)

apagado 'Stopped', guitar-strumming technique (698)

apinti Maroon goblet-shaped drum derived from the *apentemma* of the Ashanti in Ghana (505–506)

aras napat Miskitu horse-jawbone idiophone rasped or struck with a deer horn or large nail, like the *quijada* (660, 663)

arca Also *arka*, 'follower' in Aymara, one of the halves (female) of the *siku* (and several other) double-unit panpipe in the central Andes (counterpart of *ira* half, 'leader') (34, 208, 358, 469)

areito Also *areyto*, pre-Columbian music and dance celebratory event of the Taino Indians of the Caribbean (13, 22, 822, 846–47, 888, 932–33)

arisiki Tarahumara bottle gourd rattle (583)

armonías 'Harmonies', brass-band saxhorns (578)

arpa 'Harp', a diatonic harp without pedals, found in many regions of Hispanic America, especially Chile, Ecuador, Mexico, Paraguay, Peru, and Venezuela; *see index under* chordophones

arrasta-pé Dance music genre of northeast Brazil (330, 331, 332)

arrullo (1) Colombian religious folk song (403-404); (2) children's game song and lullaby (408–409, 596, 618, 695)

aruchicos Ecuadorian forceful dances (426)

ason Haitian gourd rattle covered with beads (883)

ass-pipe Car-exhaust tube of the Virgin Islands played like a tuba, often used as a bass instrument (970)

atabales (1) Large Nicaraguan and Guatemalan drums the size and shape of standard snare drums but made of wood (708, 724, 757); (2) longdrum music and instruments associated with saints' festivals (851, 854); (3) single- or double-headed kettledrums (589)

atabaque Brazilian and Uruguayan conical single-headed drum (309, 343, 511, 515)

auto Early religious musical drama and allegorical or religious play throughout the colonial Americas, used by priests for teaching about Christianity (302, 495)

awai Waiãpi ankle shaker (159)

axé Brazilian popular music genre (110, 353–54); (2) Yoruba word for vital spiritual force of Candomblé (353)

ayacachtli Náhuatl name for a gourd or gourd-shaped rattle, made from clay or gold (601)

ayarachi Peruvian panpipe tradition subdivided in three different groups of instruments tuned to the octave (35, 469)

ayotl Náhuatl name for a tortoiseshell idiophone struck with antlers (550, 563, 601)

ayudantes 'Helpers', backup singers for Yuma social dance music (597)

B-52 Drum made from a 55-gallon oil drum (803)

baa wéhai Yaqui idiophone made with a large gourd placed closed side up in a container of water and struck with a stick (550)

babalaô Brazilian 'diviner' of initiation rite (342)

babalorixá Female temple leader in Brazilian Candomblé (342)

baboula Antillean membranophone constructed from a tree trunk or barrel (865)

baguala Argentine song with or without allusive texts (256)

baha (1) Grenadian 1.5-meter-long cardboard tube aerophone (871); (2) St. Lucian tubular trumpet made from wood or plastic (946)

bahanarotu 'Owner of bahana', a Warao shaman in charge of the eastern cosmic realm (189, 193, 195)

baião Brazilian social dance music from Northeast Brazil typically played by trios of

accordion, triangle, and *zabumba* drum (330, 331, 332, 348)

baila Jamaican spirit possession and recreational songs (903)

bailaderos Colombian private-home entertainment businesses (411)

bailados Afro-Brazilian country dramatic dances (347)

bailanta Also *bailable*, Argentine large dance hall (265)

baile 'Dance' in Spanish, referring to dozens of costumed folkloric events in the Hispanic Americas; *see index under* dance and movement

Bajan (1) Form of expressive communication combining African grammar and English (813); (2) the term used locally for a person from Barbados (813)

bajo 'Bass', (1) Bolivian baritone horn (288); (2) *bajo de caja*, one-stringed harp similar to the washtub bass (691, 693); (3) *bajo sexto*, large twelve-stringed Mexican guitar (613)

bajón 'Big bass', (1) Bolivian multiple-tubed trumpet (284, 287); (2) Purépecha bassoon (577); (3) *bajones*, 'big basses', large rafted trumpets of the Moxo (138)

baka aapa 'Cane harp', Yaqui mouth bow (591, 593)

bakánawi Tarahumara curing ceremony (585)

bakohi Warao bamboo and/or cow-horn trumpet used as substitute for conch-shell trumpet (189)

bal granmoun Martinique old-time evening balls (918)

balada Commercially called Latin pop, can be considered the continuation of a long-standing pan-Hispanic tradition of guitar-based romantic song (101, 102–103, 105, 109, 623)

balakadri From the French *bal à quadrilles*, in Martinique, fashion on which *zouk* was based (874, 877–78, 918)

ballet folklórico 'Folkloric ballet', often a Latin American country's professional troupe that performs nationalistic or ideological reinterpretions of rural music and dance practices (796, 859, 861)

balsería Friendly week-long, all-male competition between two Guaymí communities (687)

bamba Stamped tubes of Bonaire that accompany celebrations of the feasts of Saint John and Saint Peter (929)

bambòch Haitian informal party (889)

bamboula An extinct or reconstructed tradition of African-style dance, drumming, and song associated with St. Thomas (973)

bambuco (1) Colombian "national" song and pursuit couple dance genre in compound duple (6/8 + 3/4) meter, musically characterized by syncopation and performed most often on the *tiple* as the main instrument (382–83, 385–89, 404, 409); (2) Mexican romantic, slow, often melancholic vocal genre (613, 620); (3) Ecuadorian pursuit dance, most common of *currulao* genre (428)

bambúes Set of bamboo tubes played in interlocking fashion (855)

bambulá Also *bamboulá*, pan-Caribbean *velación* dance (795, 856)

banbou See vaksin

banda 'Band', usually either a brass band, a large ensemble of mixed European-derived wind instruments, or any ensemble of aerophones and percussion instruments; *see index under* instrumental ensembles

bandola (1) A relative of the mandolin and direct descendant of the Spanish *bandurria* (531); (2) in Colombia, a teardrop-shaped or round lute with sixteen metal strings in four courses of three strings and two courses of two strings (381, 382); (3) four-stringed pear-shaped lute chordophone (540–41); (4) in Chile, an hourglass-shaped lute with four courses of four strings each (358)

bandolim From Italian *mandolino*, small double-course Brazilian chordophone (309, 311)

bandolín Small five-stringed, triple-course plucked lute of Ecuador (417)

bandoneón Argentine button accordion used in tango music, invented in Germany by Heinrich Band in 1854 and brought to Buenos Aires about 1890 (89, 253, 263, 511)

bandurria (1) Guatemalan twelve-stringed lute (728); (2) sixteen- to twenty-stringed chordophone shaped like a mandolin (213)

banja Name for calypso before the 1930s (819)

banjo Fretted, plucked-lute chordophone with circular membranophone resonator (475, 481)

banzjó Banjo of the Netherland Antilles (931)

baquetas Guatemalan marimba mallets (725)

baquiné Also *baquiní*, Ecuadorian, Dominican, and Puerto Rican festive wake, celebrated at the death of an infant or young child (417, 422, 849)

bara (1) Large Miskitu flutes related to the *bra-tara* (662); (2) two- to four-holed Sumu bamboo flutes with mouthpieces formed from beeswax (750, 751)

bardo Recitation during the first nine days of mourning to help the deceased separate himself or herself from the earthly world (709)

barrio Spanish for suburb (420)

bas Also *tanbourin*, Haitian frame drum of low pitch (883)

bastel Also *seoe*, water drum played with hands and made from half of a large gourd placed open side down in a water-filled tub (929)

batidorcitos 'Little noisemakers', ratchets (715)

batucada (1) Brazilian percussion ensemble and percussive dance music (350); (2) drumming session or performance of a samba percussion ensemble (313)

Batuque From Portuguese *bater* 'to hit', (1) Afro-Brazilian religion and dance in Pará, São Paulo, and Rio Grande do Sul states (341, 348); (2) *batuque*, Afro-Brazilian round dance of Angolese or Congolese origin (303, 307, 313, 348); (3) Argentine variant of Afro-Brazilian religion (259–61)

bayamonés Style of *seis* from Bayamón, Puerto Rico (938)

bedug Ritual drum, sounded for the traditional and daily Islamic call to prayer in Guyana (507)

bele, belair (1) Grenadian song-dance (865); (2) Creole precursor of *calypso* (865)

bélè (1) Cylindrical single-headed membranophone of Martinique (915, 918); (2) dance style performed since colonial times in French Caribbean (915); (3) St. Lucian category of song-dances accompanied by drumming (948–49); (4) another name for the *ka* drum (948); (5) Trinidad and Tobago song-dances originating in the French Windwards (953, 959, 963); (6) *bélé*, Dominican song-dances accompanied by drum of the same name (841–42)

beluria In Belize, all-night Garifuna postmortem ritual in commemoration of a recently deceased relative, often concluding with communitywide participation in singing, drumming, and dancing (669, 674–75)

bembe Second drum of the Orisa ensemble (955)

bènaden Stylized Guadeloupe arm wrestling accompanied by drumming and singing (876)

benna Early calypso type of Antigua (800)

benta (1) Mouth-resonated bow from Curaçao, made from a local hardwood and strung with coconut fiber (929); (2) plucked idiophone among Surinam Maroons, similar to the African *mbira* (505)

berimbau (1) Struck musical bow with a calabash resonator common to Bahia, Brazil, and derived from Angola (346); (2) *berimbau de Angola*, another more complete name for the *berimbau* (346); (3) *berimbau de barriga*, 'berimbau of the belly', another name for the Afro-Brazilian musical bow, so called because the calabash resonator is stopped by pressing it against the player's stomach (201, 346)

berusu In Belize, Garifuna musical form for solo voice and guitar for general entertainment, often played at wakes (675)

bhajan Hymns of devotion and praise sung at Hindu religious services in Trinidad (85–86, 444, 958)

bhoom Successful GUYFESTA rhythmic experiment to establish a Guyanese beat (448)

bigin bélè Martinique Creole term for 'drum biguine' type (915, 920)

biguine A social dance music genre in Martinique (795, 915–16)

bikàkla Bribri master of ceremonies (633)

birimbao Also *birimbau*, (1) Argentine criollo jaw's harp (251); (2) Venezuelan jaw's harp (528)

bix rxin nawal Songs of the ancestors in Guatemala (652, 731)

bloco afro Contemporary Afro-Brazilian carnival music (352–54)

blòtjé St. Lucian pelvis-thrusting dance movement (943)

bocina 'Horn', (1) Ecuadorian straight or curved trumpet (416); (2) *bocinas*, colonial Spanish term for 'horns' sounded by the natives in Paraguay prior to an attack (453)

boi 'Bull' in Portuguese, (1) Afro-Brazilian bull character (335, 347); (2) *boi de orquestra*, Afro-Brazilian *aboio* brass-band style (335, 347); (3) *boi de zabumba*, Afro-Brazilian *aboio* style (335, 347)

bolero Cuban-derived song genre for listening and dancing, attributed to José "Pepe" Sánchez (102, 330, 331, 372, 428, 487, 619, 620, 691, 829, 832, 835)

bolero-son Cuban genre that combines elements of the *bolero* and the *son* (834)

bomba (1) Afro-Puerto Rican drum and music/dance genre (936–37); (2) 'praise' interjections by men and women during songs and dances (695–97, 744); (3) Ecuadorian circle dance (often performed around a cross) and its music (415, 425, 427, 430)

bomber Drum made by stretching a goatskin over one end of a washing-machine barrel (803)

bombo (1) European-derived cylindrical double-headed bass drum membranophone, played with sticks (252, 285, 360, 373, 402, 404, 406, 414, 424, 427, 469, 528); (2) for *candombe*, African-derived double-headed conical membranophone (260)

bomma Also singerman, Jamaican leader of agricultural labor call-and-response songs (905)

bongo At a Trinidadian wake, music and dance to placate ancestors (953)

bongos Cuban and Puerto Rican membranophone consisting of two small drums joined by a piece of wood (830, 834)

boompipe Antiguan musical horn made from a plumbing joint (799)

bordón Ostinato bass phrase with slight variation (427)

bordonúa Puerto Rican low-pitched, plucked lute chordophone with six double courses of strings (934–35)

botija Cuban aerophone made from earthen jugs with small hole in the side, through which the performer blows (834)

boula Also *tanbou dibas*, Guadeloupe large tambourine used in *quadrille* (874)

boula (1) Grenadian open-bottomed membranophone of the big drum ceremony (870); (2) small, high-pitched Haitian drum played with two sticks or hands (883)

bouladjèl Guadeloupe rhythmic sounds produced by the throat (875, 879)

boum boum Dominican lip-concussion aerophone used to produce low percussive sounds, similar to the *vaksin* (842)

Bourbon Codex Nahua early colonial codex describing the Aztec world (557)

Boxing Day Day after Christmas, official beginning of carnival in Montserrat (925)

brão Brazilian enigmatic musical genre performed during *mutirões* (301, 307)

bra-tara Large bamboo Sumu flute up to two meters long, played only by the shaman (661, 739, 750)

brazo 'Arm', referring to neck of lute chordophones from Puerto Rico (934)

Bruckins Jamaican annual celebration of emancipation from slavery (907)

brukdown (1) Type of dance and song reflecting usual and unusual events in the life of the common Belizean (677–78); (2) a specific rhythmic organization in Belize (677–78)

bugutá Guaymí dance performed by both men and women (686)

bullérengue Colombian and Afro-Panamanian responsorial song and dance genre (405–406, 773, 778)

bulsique Cabécar dance similar to the Bribri *sörbö* (635)

bumba-meu-boi Dramatic Afro-Brazilian dance that is the last dramatic dance of the *reisado* cycle (335, 347)

bunde (1) African-derived dance of Colombia and Panama (386–87, 778); (2) currently a Colombian funerary song (404)

burro Venezuelan single-headed log drum (528)

burroquite 'Little donkey' of Trinidadian carnival, derived from the Hindu goddess Durga (965)

buru (1) Jamaican masquerade celebration (907); (2) set of drums in Jamaica (898)

business dances Jamaican Maroon religious dances named after particular ethnic groups (902)

buyei Garifuna shaman in Belize (669)

bwa Guadeloupe hardwood sticks that are struck against drum or each other (874, 877)

bwa pòyé St. Lucian banjo (945)

cabildo (1) Secret society in Cuba and other Hispanic-Caribbean areas (825, 826); (2) place for religious conversion by Catholic missionaries in Colombia, Peru, and elsewhere in Spanish-speaking South America (400, 405); (3) Bolivian community authority who may sponsor fiestas (291); (4) Chilean male or female hierarchical organization for patronal festivals (366)

caboclinho Also *terno de caboclos*, Brazilian children's dramatic dance, same as *caiapó* (312, 337)

caboclo Brazilian mestizo of Native American and Portuguese heritages, especially in the northeast (323–33)

cachimbo Northern Chilean dance (365, 373)

cacho (1) Peruvian circular valveless trumpet made of connected bull-horn sections (211, *472*); (2) *cachos*, Venezuelan ductless deerskull flutes played in pairs (533)

cachu Cow-horn trumpet of the Netherland Antilles (929, 930)

cadacada Mapuche shell rasps (234)

cadence-lypso Fusion of Haitian *konpa/kadans* with Trinidadian calypso (841, 844, 879) *cagüeño* Puerto Rican *seis* from Caguas (939)

caiapó Also *terno de caiapós*, Brazilian dramatic dance group that combines Native American, African and Portuguese elements (312)

caj From Spanish *caja* 'box', snare drum among the Quiché Maya (654)

caja 'Box', small membranophone in many Spanish-speaking countries, either single headed or double headed, often with a snare (252, 285, 407, 415, 685, 686, 727, 774–75)

caja chayera Atacameño double-headed, frame snare drum adopted from the Spanish (357, 361)

cajita 'Little box', coastal Afro-Peruvian idiophone made from a small wooden box with a hinged lid, played by shutting the lid in rhythm and striking the box with a stick (492, 494)

cajón 'Big box', (1) Afro-Peruvian and *criollo* idiophone made from a wooden box with a soundhole in the back (475, 493, 709); (2) *cajón de tapeo*, wooden Mixtec box struck with the hands, similar to the *cajón* of Peru (565); (3) *cajones harmónicos*, Guatemalan wooden-box marimba resonators (725–26)

cajuavé Small mouth-resonated bow among the Chaco of Paraguay (455)

calypso (1) Caribbean song form attributed to Trinidad, characterized by humorous language, rhyme, and the improvisational treatment of text and music which are often satirical (86, 95–96, 445–46, 773, 800, 865, 866–67, 908, 953, 963–64); (2) a Trinidadian rhythmical instrumental genre associated with steelbands and carnival (962)

campana 'Bell', (1) used in Roman Catholic religious processions (708); (2) *campanilla*, little Afro-Peruvian handbell, used in the dances of the *hatajo de negritos* (494)

caña (1) Bolivian long cane trumpet (212, 287); (2) Paraguayan 'cane' alcohol in bottles securely balanced on heads of *galoperas* (461, 462); (3) Q'ero vertical, notched, six-note edge aerophone made of reed or plastic pipe (227); (4) long, valveless wooden or cane trumpet (212)

caña de millo Colombian idioglottal transverse clarinet made from cane (39, 402, 406, *407*); *see also* pito

canchis sipas Q'ero panpipes with a double set of seven reed tubes (226)

canción de protesta 'Protest song', any Latin American protest song, often influenced by Cuban revolution (103, 262)

canción ranchera (1) Mexican song type linked to the rise of the popular media and to the popularity of folk-derived ensembles such as the modern mariachi (371, 620–21); (2) folk and popular song genre throughout the Pacific coast of Nicaragua (763)

canción romántica (1) Mexican tradition of the nineteenth-century romantic song (619, 620); (2) romantic popular song tradition sustained at the annual Gastón music festival in Managua, Nicaragua (766)

canción trovadoresca Cuban genre created by singer-composers of Santiago de Cuba (831–32)

canções praieiras Afro-Brazilian fisherman's or beach songs (351)

candombe Afro-Uruguayan dances and dance locales (515–16)

candombe Also *charanda*, *ramba*, Argentine entertainment dance (260–61, 515)

Candomblé (1) Afro-Brazilian religion in Bahia (309, 341); (2) Argentine variant of Afro-Brazilian religion observed in place of Batuque (260); (3) Candomblé de Caboclo, Afro-Brazilian religion in Sergipe (341, 344)

cantalante Lead singer in Panamanian women's chorus (780)

cantaor Also cantador, person who memorizes Puerto Rican *décimas* in order to sing them (937, 939)

cántaro Large jug tuned with water and used for low-pitched accompaniment in El Salvador (707)

cantiques French hymnody surviving on Carriacou (868)

canto 'Song' in Spanish, (1) *canto nuevo*, 'new song', clandestine successor to *nueva canción* ('new song') in Chile after the 1973 coup (103, 373–74); (2) *cantos de ángeles* Chilean 'songs of angels' (366); (3) *cantos de nana*, Mexican coddling songs (618)

canto popular uruguayo 'Popular Uruguayan song' featuring texts that express desire for social and political change (510, 519–20, 521)

cantoria (1) Brazilian secular song traditions of the northeast sung by singer-bards (324–25); (2) Brazilian folk singing usually involving improvised duel, also known as *desafio* (307)

capitán (1) Nahua chief (561); (2) Nahua dancer of Corpus Christi (561); (3) guitar leader of Salvadoran dance of the little devils (714)

capoeira (1) Afro-Brazilian game-fight dance (57, 336, 345–47); (2) *capoeira Angola*, Afro-Brazilian traditional dance of possibly Angolan origin (346); (3) *capoeira regional*, Afro-Brazilian innovative form developed by Mestre Bimba (346)

capoeiristas Afro-Brazilian couples of (usually) male dancer-fighters in *capoeira* (346)

caporal Chilean artistic director of a patronal dance (362)

caquiliztli Náhuatl word for sound or noise (556)

carabiné Dominican Republic imitation dance of nineteenth-century occupying Haitian soldiers (856)

carachacha Also *carraca*, *quijada*, idiophone, scraped or struck, that is made from the lower jawbone of an ass, mule, or a horse (476, 492)

caracol Conch-shell trumpet (724)

caramba Also *zambumbia*, (1) Honduran long music bow (onomatopoetically, *bumbum*) (694, 738, 739, 743); (2) Salvadoran musi-

cal bow with gourd resonator possibly descended from the African hunting bow (709)

carángano Large Afro-Colombian idiochord bamboo tube zither (377, 380–81)

carangueijo Brazilian circular social dance of many variants, especially popular along border areas of Uruguay (307, 516)

cargo During patronal festivals, the musician's role of service to the community to placate the gods and ensure the well-being of the people (291, 657)

caribeño Colombian fusion of *zouk* and *salsa* (410)

CARIFESTA Guyanese festival held since 1972 (447)

carimbó Afro-Brazilian popular dance from Pará (354)

carnaval 'Carnival', (1) secular celebration prior to Lent in Brazil and throughout most of Hispanic America (226, 258–59, 314–15, 335–38, 351–53, 405, 476, 494, 566, 852); (2) Atacameño mestizo agrarian fertility rite in Chile (360–61)

carnival Annual historic, national, theatrical secular celebration prior to Lent in Trinidad and Tobago and elsewhere in English-speaking Caribbean (925–26, 964–66)

carraca Wooden rattle of Arab origin (708)

carrasca Also *raspador*, (1) scraper in Honduras (741–42); (2) scraped idiophone of Colombia (377–78)

carrizo (1) Kogi cane used to make instruments (184); (2) Venezuelan panpipe (533)

cartas anuas Annual reports made by each Jesuit province to the Jesuit general in Rome (200, 453)

casa de baile Dance house of the Aymara region associated with patronal festivals (365)

cascabeles Argentine metal bell jingles (249, 494)

cashua taki Inca line dance (230)

castañuelas 'Castanets', Panamanian struck hardwood idiophones (774)

castillos Ecuadorian fruit-bearing poles along Corpus procession route (421–22)

catá (1) Stick used to hit the body of the long-drum in the Dominican Republic (854); (2) Cuban idiophone made from hollowed-out log and struck with two sticks (831)

cateretê Also *catiretê*, Brazilian social dance genre found in rural areas (301–302, 303, 307, 311)

catta Jamaican sticks beaten on the side of the *kbandu* drum (898, 903)

cavalaria Afro-Brazilian rhythmic pattern (346)

cavaquinho Four-stringed treble guitar used throughout Brazil (305, 309, 311, 329, 330)

caxixí Afro-Brazilian basket rattle, played by the same musician who plays the *berimbau* (346, *347*)

caza de la tortuga 'Turtle hunt' festival among the Maleku, for ritual purification to emphasize aspects of reciprocity between humans and nature (683)

cencerro (1) Cuban metallic idiophone, similiar to a bell with no clapper (834); (2) Bolivian bronze llama bells (285); (3) Ecuadorian cowbells (414)

chacarera Argentine social dance performed during *jineteada* (261)

chac-chac In Grenada and Trinidad and Tobago, gourd-constructed rattle (860, 870, 953)

chacha Guadeloupe large hollowed-out calabash filled with seeds (874, 877, 918)

cha-cha-chá Cuban genre created by Enrique Jorrin during the 1950s (105, 372, 487, 622, 723, 827, 829, 833, 835)

chairígoas Also Yaqui *teneboim*, Guarijio rattles made from the cocoons of the giant silkmoth and wrapped around the dancers' legs from ankle to knee (554)

chakchak (1) Dominican calabash idiophone filled with beads or small pebbles and mounted on stick (841); (2) St. Lucian small calabash idiophone filled with seeds and mounted on a stick (945, 946)

chamamé Argentine polka-derived social dance performed during a *jineteada* (256, 257, 259, 261, 269)

chanántskua Purépecha collective performance game-dance (578)

changüi Cuban genre belonging to the *son* family (829, 830)

chanté 'Sung' in French, (1) *chanté abwè*, St. Lucian 'songs to drink', the songs or their performance during Christmas season (947); (2) *chanté kont*, St. Lucian 'song-drama' often enacted in pantomime and usually performed at wakes (943); (3) *chanté mas*, Dominican masquerade songs based on call and response (841, 843); (4) *chanté siay*, St. Lucian work songs to accompany wood sawing (946–47); (5) *chants-charrue*, songs sung by farmers in Guadeloupe (876)

chantwèl (1) Dominican song leader (841); (2) St. Lucian song leader, typically of the La Rose and La Marguerite societies (946)

chantwell Also *chantrel*, song leader in Caribbean creole cultures (95–96, 870, 965)

chapetones Biting satire dance of colonial Spanish manners (712)

chaqui-capitán Ecuadorian foot-captain (426)

charanga Also *charanga típica*, or *charanga francesa*, (1) Cuban ensemble combining piano, violin, and flute with percussion (832–33, 835); (2) *charanga-vallenato*, Colombian *vallenato* style (410)

charango (1) In the Andes of Argentina, Bolivia, and southern Peru, a small guitar made of wood or an armadillo shell with eight to fifteen metal or nylon strings tuned in five courses (34, 213–14, 251, 284, 288, 289, 469, 473); (2) Bolivian small plucked lute with four or five double courses (293, 295); (3) Ecuadorian small six-stringed plucked lute with double courses (417)

chareos Mixtec dance related to Saint James (566)

charm 1990s Brazilian popular music form (354)

charrango Chilean board zither (360)

charrasca Venezuelan ridged idiophone scraped with a stick (528)

chequeré Cuban idiophone of African origin (828)

chicha (1) Argentine popular alcoholic drink made from *algarrobo* tree (258); (2) corn or maize beer in the Andes (139, 155, 425, 683); (3) distinctly Peruvian variant of *cumbia* that creolized the Colombian *cumbia* rhythms with highland *huayno* melodies (also *cumbia andina*) (101, 102, 293, 484–85)

chicheros 'Chicha drinkers', Nicaraguan musicians who perform in *bandas de chicheros* or *bandas filarmónicas* and provide music for funerary masses and processions (762)

chichodromos Locales for *chicha* events in Peru (485)

chicote Kogi circle dance (185)

chigualo (1) Introductory percussive music of Ecuador (424); (2) Colombian religious wake song (404)

chilamate Ensemble of chordophones that accompanies the Salvadoran dance of the Herods (714)

chilchil (1) Ecuadorian fruit-capsule rattle (414); (2) small Nicaraguan bells (748)

chilena (1) Chilean couple dance, with Afro-Hispanic rhythms and Spanish stanzas, related to the *zamacueca* and the *cueca* of the coast of Peru and Chile (481, 567); (2) Mexican regional style of the Costa Chica, along the Pacific coast of Oaxaca and Guerrero states (610, 611)

chillador 'Screamer' in Spanish, in the Andes (especially northern Chile) a small guitar (like a *charango* but smaller) of five or six courses made of wood or armadillo shell (473)

chimarrita Brazilian folk dance popular along border areas of Uruguay (516)

chimbangueles A set of four to seven Afro-Venezuelan conical drums whose single skins are tightened by hoops and wooden wedges (530–31, 536)

chino 'Humble servant' in Quechua, Chilean dancers who honor the Virgin and who are the oldest type of dancing group comprised of miners in Chilean patronal festivals (27, 258, 359, 362, 364, 365)

chiquit Bolivian special dances at initiation and marriage ceremonies (291)

chiriguano (1) Large panpipes of Huancané, Peru (216); Bolivian tradition of panpipes subdivided into three different groups tuned to the octave (also *chiriwanu*) (285); (3) in the Andes and Paraguay, the name for an Indian culture (also Chiriwano) (469)

chirimía (1) In Bolivia, Guatemala, Mexico (among Purépecha, Maya, and Nahua especially), and parts of Peru, an oboe-type instrument of early Spanish colonial importation played by native Americans or mestizos (33, 36, 283, 384, 396, 402–403, 453, 472, 550, 558, 577–78, 723, 727, 729, 741, 788); (2) a Colombian musical ensemble or band originating in the Chocó region and consisting of brass instruments, *bombo*, *cununo*, and cymbals (406, 407)

chirisuya Type of oboe played in highlands of the Peruvian departments of Lima, Huancavelica, and Ayacucho (33, 36, 472)

chischiles Current name for small bells sewn onto Nicaraguan folk dancers' shoes (748, 761)

chocalho Brazilian idiophone shaker (337)

chonta Ecuadorian palm tree used to make marimba keys (427)

chopí Paraguayan folk couple dance (461)

chordophone 'String sounder', a musical instrument whose sound comes from the vibrations of a stretched string (30)

chorimori Pre-Encounter Atacameño rattle of metal bells without clappers (357)

choro (1) Brazilian dance music ensemble (305, 306); (2) Afro-Brazilian musical genre based on polka-*maxixe* rhythm (350)

chorões 'Weepers', Brazilian strolling street musician-serenaders (305, 306, 313, 350)

chucho Colombian cylindrical rattle (376–77)

chulas Brazilian song texts of *samba de viola* (349)

chumba (1) Guatemalan erotic dance (733, 734); (2) in Belize, old dance performed by a soloist in a highly individualized manner (676)

chunan Mapuche shell rattles (234)

ch'unchu Bolivian caricature dance (286, 362)

chuqila (1) Bolivian ritual vicuña-hunt dance (292); (2) Bolivian vertical end-blown notched flute (286)

churu (1) Conch-shell trumpet in Amazonas (472); (2) Ecuadorian conch-shell trumpet (416, 426)

cifra Argentine traditional *pampa* musical form performed during *jineteada* (261)

cimarrona Small, traditional Costa Rican ensemble of woodwinds, brass, and percussion (698, 700, *701*)

cinco 'Five', (1) Venezuelan small guitar with five strings (531); (2) *cinco de seis cuerdas*, Venezuelan small guitar with six strings (531); (3) *cinco y medio*, Venezuelan small guitar with 'five and a half' strings (531)

ciranda Brazilian children's game-song genre (346)

clarín (1) In Cajamarca, Peru, a long cane side-blown tranverse trumpet in Peru (*118, 212, 471–72*); (2) a long valveless, transverse wooden or cane trumpet in Peru (35–36); (3) in Chile, a pre-Encounter Atacameño two-meter transverse trumpet without resonator made of a cane bound with colored wool (357)

clave 'Key', (1) Cuban rhythm consisting of 3 + 2 or (reverse *clave*) 2 + 3 (832); (2) *claves*, in Cuba and other Latin American regions, two hardwood dowels struck together to mark the *clave* or basic meter (709, 733, 832, 834)

cling-a-ching Antiguan triangle (799)

côco (1) Afro-Brazilian coconut dance (327, 349); (2) *côco-de-décima*, Afro-Brazilian dance based ten-line stanza song structure (349); (3) *côco-de-embolada*, Afro-Brazilian dance based on tongue-twisting song form (327, 349); (4) *côco-de-ganzá*, Afro-Brazilian shaker dance (349)

cofradía 'Confraternity', (1) Roman Catholic religious brotherhood founded for African slaves and their descendants (47, 681, 688, 709); (2) Afro-Peruvian church-sponsored confraternity or sodality devoted to a patron saint (491); (3) Guatemalan Indian prayer house (730, 731)

coliseos Open theaters that were venues of Peruvian music in 1970s in Lima (484)

columbia Cuban music and dance genre belonging to the *rumba* family (831)

combo Cuban name given musical ensembles toward the end of the 1950s (836)

comparsa Cuban characteristic dance in *carnaval* (827, 836)

comuncha Ayacucho guitar tuning pattern (E–B–G–D–B–G) used primarily to play peasant *huaynos* in E minor (473)

concertina Small button accordion in hexagonal shape (695, 799)

conchero Nahua dance accompanied by armadillo-shell guitar, also called by the same name (559, 572, 614)

congo (1) Also *congada*, Brazilian dramatic dance group that combines African and Iberian influences (48, 347); (2) Afro-Panamanian music, dance, and theater tradition (773, 775–76, 778–79); (3) song genre of Sango bands in Trinidadian carnival (953, 965); (4) *congos*, ensemble music of the Brotherhood of the Holy Spirit of Villa Mella (*851*, 854, 855)

conjunto 'Ensemble', (1) throughout Spanish-speaking Americas, a musical ensemble that performs folk music (262, 295, 297, 456, 462, 470, 474, 592, 836); (2) contemporary salsa brass and percussion-based ensembles (101)

contra Chilean alto-register *sikuri* (358, 362)

contradanza (1) Cuban genre with French origins, belonging to the *danzón* family (100, 393, 400, 697, 827, 829, 832–33, 835); (2) Guarijío song-dance in duple meter with a triple subdivision (6/8) (553)

contrapunto Chilean competitive dialogic singing often with improvised quatrains (366, 367)

contrato High voice part of Venezuelan *tonos* ensemble (534)

copla 'Couplet', (1) Spanish-derived narrative musical genre from Chile, Colombia, and other Hispanic-American countries (389–90, 391, 571, 606–607, 744, 757); (2) popular improvised Spanish verse form (389, 400); (3) *copla de carnaval*, Chilean 'carnival couplet', main musical genre of the Atacameño carnival (361, 481); (4) wake song addressed to dead child and its parents (258)

corneta 'Cornet', Andean animal-horn lip-concussion aerophone (287, 453)

corpophone 'Body sounder', the body used as a musical instrument by striking or popping a body part (or parts), such as a hand clap, thigh slap, and so on (31)

corpus See Corpus Christi

Corpus Christi Annual Catholic festival and liturgical holiday in honor of the Eucharist, June 15 (227, 365, 415, 417, 420–22, 468, 494, 537, 578, 681, 693, 772, 781)

corrido (1) Song form descended from the Spanish *romance* with lyrics structured in the format of the *copla* ballad (385, 758–59); (2) narrative song genre of Chile and Mexico (101, 367, 371, 605, 613, 616–17)

cortesía Also *reverencia*, the act of demonstrating respect for the *son* dance (560)

country dance Also drum dance, goatskin dance, five-part Montserrat dance performed by four male-female couples (924)

coyolli Náhuatl name for idiophone rattle made of clay, copper, dried fruit, gold, and nutshells (601)

criolismo "Creolism', (1) a mixing of African and European cultural traits (4); (2) referring to European descendants born in the New World (4)

criolla 'Creole', (1) Cuban urban genre with rural themes belonging to the *canción* family (832); (2) *criollas*, Uruguayan societies whose principal objective is preservation of traditional rural festivals (516)

criollo 'Creole', (1) originally, a black born in the New World, as opposed to an African brought from Africa (4); (2) later applied to anyone born in the colonies (466); (3) more recently applied to a person, a behavior, a music, a style, or some other element that displays or promotes the distinctive traditions, sentiments and customs of the culture of coastal Peru (481); (4) *criollos*, whites, Spanish-Americans (38)

criolloismo Afro-Peruvian philosophy and attitude that reflects nationalistic pride (500)

cronistas 'Chroniclers', early Spanish writers (21)

crop over Originally a celebration held to mark the end of the sugarcane harvest in Barbados (814, 818)

cruz de mayo Venezuelan 'May cross' *velorio* (534)

cuadrilla 'Quadrille', square dance (366, 690)

cuarteada Argentine couple dance named after carried hindquarter of sacrificed animal (257)

cuarteta 'Couplet', four-line Puerto Rican poem (938)

cuarteto (1) Pop music from Córdoba, Argentina (105, 265–66, 273–80); (2) *cuarteto-cuarteto*, musical style based on early *cuarteto* music (274)

cuatra Derived from the Venezuelan *cuatro*, a four-stringed guitar of the Netherlands Antilles (930)

cuatrillo Polyrhythm of four against three (379)

cuatro 'Four', (1) four-stringed small guitar originally from Venezuela and diffused to Colombia, Grenada, Trinidad, and other regions close to Venezuela (301, 387, 524, 531, 849, 866, 945, 953); (2) Puerto Rican ten-stringed guitar with double courses (934); (3) *cuatro y medio*, Venezuelan small guitar with 'four and a half' strings (531)

cueca Also *cueca chilena*, *cueca chilenera*, *cueca porteña*, Chilean folk-urban *criollo* song and couple dance (male pursuit of female) genre that is considered as a national symbol (also found in Bolivia), characterized by composite 6/8 and 3/4 *sesquiáltera*/hemiola meter and song texts that sometimes reveal nationalistic, historical, or social commentary (100, 284, 292, 360, 361, 365, 368–70)

cuíca Single-headed Brazilian friction membranophone used in samba, sounded by rubbing a short stick attached to and protruding from the bottom of the drum skin into the wooden or metal body (309, 378)

cuíca tlamatiliztli Nahua singing (556)

cuicalli Aztec formal schools that included music education (603)

culeado Guatemalan women's *punta* dance (734)

culebrillando Single-file serpentine dance of Ecuador (426)

cumaco Large African-derived drum of Venezuela (528, 530, 536)

cumanana Afro-Peruvian song form, often competitive, accompanied by guitar (495)

cumbia (1) Colombian genre of Caribbean music, existing in both rural and urban forms, the latter popular throughout Latin America's Pacific rim regions from Chile to Central America and Mexico as a salsa genre (39, 101, 102, 265–66, 361, 365, 402–403, 406, 409–10, 484–85, 619, 622); (2) Panamanian group circle dance (773, 778)

cumbiamberos Colombian fusion of *cumbia* and *songo* (410)

cunculcahue Argentine musical bow (253)

cungo 'Let's go', Belizean creole style of popular music that emerged in the 1980s (678–79)

cununo Colombian and Ecuadorian conical single-headed drum from Pacific coast, used in the *currulao* ensemble (402)

curandero 'Curer', a native ritual-healer (652)

curbata In the Venezuelan longdrum ensemble, the short drum that is paired with the *mina* (528)

curijurijanporetec Love songs of the Maleku (682)

currulao Colombian and Ecuadorian couple pursuit dance or marimba dance (404–405, 409, 414, 427–28)

cururu Musical or dance style in Brazil (307)

cuyacas All-female dancing group of Aymara region (362)

cyas Jamaican Kumina ceremonial drum (898, 902–903)

dakoho Warao dance or entertainment song (197)

dalang Person usually of Javanese descent in Surinam who leads the wayang puppet theater (507)

dansaq Scissors dance in Ayacucho, Peru (207, 212, 481)

danza 'Dance', (1) romantic vocal music genre with Afro-Caribbean roots (393); (2) Cuban genre belonging to the *danzón* family, part of the evolution of the *contradanza* (795, 835)

danza Also *danzón*, nineteenth-century Hispanic-Caribbean creole urban dance genre (697)

danzón (1) Cuban instrumental dance genre created by Miguel Failde in 1879; the national dance of Cuba (622, 795, 829, 832–33, 835)

danzonete Cuban genre belonging to the *danzón* family (832–33)

de coleo Chilean *tonada* quatrain starting with the last line of the previous one (368)

de shot and rattle Jamaican calabash spike rattle filled with stones and fitted with a handle (814–15)

dé fas Guadeloupe double-headed, barrel-shaped membranophone (876)

débòt St. Lucian song-dance accompanied by drumming (943, 948)

décima (1) Spanish and Hispanic-American song containing ten-line stanzas, eight syllables per stanza, and a particular rhythm scheme (327, 365, 367–68, 408, 495, 534, 571–72, 607–608, 772, 780, 795–96; (2) sung genre for courtship or expression of religious and social commentary (937–38)

decimilla 'Little *décima*', same as *décima* but with six syllables per line (935, 937–38)

deculturation Loss of culture without the implication of the replacement of it by another (67, 72)

desafío Iberian song duel; *see cantoria*

dholak Guyanese drum for popular music (85, 443, 958)

diablada Also *diabladas*, 'deviled', Bolivian carnival and patronal festival devil dance and dancers (292)

diablicos sucios 'Dirty devils', Panamanian devil dance tradition (775)

diablos 'Devils', costumed dancers in Hispanic-American folkloric events (494, 773)

diana mbajá Dawn trumpet signal to begin patronal feast days in Paraguay (458)

discante Alternative Venezuelan name for *cuatro*, a four-stringed small guitar (531)

distal In organology, the portion of the musical instrument farthest from the mouthpiece (8)

djouba Also *juba*, creole rural dances from colonial times in the French-speaking Caribbean (795, 883)

doble 'Double', (1) Argentine dance (257, 269); (2) combination of a smaller and a larger Chiapan marimba (726)

domingacha Small Peruvian diatonic harp with pear-shaped sound box (473)

'doption Trinidadian song style and possession rite of the Spiritual Baptists (957–58)

douz edmi Early twentieth-century Haitian dance costing twelve and a half centimes (889)

dub Jamaican modern popular music (910)

dueto bambuquero Typical Andean folk music duet in Colombia (377, 382, 387, 390, 393)

dügü Also *adügürühani*, Garifuna feasting the dead, the last of the postmortem rituals (669–72)

dukun Male or female shaman of Javanese descent in Surinam who performs love-controlling magic and curing rituals (507)

ehuru Warao double-headed drum with skins of howler monkeys and a snare on one end, played with one stick (189, 191–92)

el pilón Venezuelan large mortar and pestle used during grain pounding songs (537)

El Güegüence Earliest-known Latin American folk drama with partial Náhuatl text that is still performed in the Diriamba area of Nicaragua (760–61)

electrophone 'Electronic sounder', a musical instrument whose sound is produced by a vibration or action made by electronic means (30–31)

elüwún Mapuche funeral rite (362)

embirekó 'Wife', smaller bow of the Paraguayan *guyrapa* double musical bow (201)

embolada Brazilian 'tongue-twister' song genre performed by dueling singers accompanying themselves on *pandeiro* or *ganzá* (307, 327)

encomienda System by which land and peasants were governed by Spanish landlords (466, 682, 952)

enfloramiento Aymara livestock marking ritual (361)

epena Also *ebena*, *yopo*, Yanomamö hallucinogenic snuff (171, 174–75)

erke (1) Bolivian animal-horn single-reed-concussion aerophone (287); (2) small trumpet made from a single cow or bull horn (211, 253); (3) *erque*, Argentine very long lip-concussion aerophone made from cane (257)

erkencho Also *erquencho*, Argentine single-reed-concussion aerophone without finger holes (253, 256, 415)

escapularios Profane musical performance given by blacks during religious festivities in colonial Mexico (603)

escobillada Afro-Peruvian dance step in which the foot is brushed along the floor or ground (494, 497)

escobillero Acrobatic dancer in Argentine *candombe* (260)

escola de samba Brazilian 'samba school', urban samba group for carnival (61, 309, 313, 315, 350)

espinela Ten-line structure of *décima* (937)

esquinazo Chilean *tonada* performed as a serenade (368)

estilo 'Style', Argentine traditional *pampa* musical form used during a *jineteada* (261)

estudiantina 'Student ensemble', (1) group of musicians playing instrumental music with Spanish-derived instruments, especially common in Colombia and Peru, and in late-nineteenth-century Cuba (*see also lira, rondalla, tuna*) (382, 383, 394, 835); (2) ensemble in Puno that includes guitars, *charangos*, mandolins, and accordion (474–75)

Ettu Jamaican African-based cult (901, 903)

falawatus Also *falawitas*, Andean cane or wooden transverse flute with six finger holes (211)

falsa High voice part of Venezuelan *tonos* ensemble (534)

fandang Trinidadian secular dance used in conjunction with *veiquoix* (953)

fandango (1) Colombian place where festivities occur, or musical dance style (400, 406–407); (2) Venezuelan predecessor of the *joropo* (539); (3) Brazilian generic term for a dance event (309, 334)

fanfa Haitian municipal, school, or military fanfare by wind orchestra (894)

fariseos 'Pharisees', Tarahumara dancers during Lenten celebrations accompanied by pipe-and-tabor musicians (584, 586–87)

favelas Brazilian hillside slums (316, 351, 354)

felu-ko-felu 'Iron-against-iron', two pieces of iron that are hit together by Surinam Maroons (505)

festejo Afro-Peruvian form often interrupted at phrase endings by a sudden pause or long, held pitch (482, 492, 496–97)

festivales de folklore Argentine 'folkloric festivals', annual revivalistic competitions and exhibitions of song and dance (261–62)

fèt patwonal Haitian patron's day festivals (890)

fiesta 'Party', (1) celebration of the feast of a patron saint of the town, according to the Catholic calendar; (2) occasion for communal sharing of foods, drinking, dancing, music making, and merriment; *see index under* festivals

figurines Individual Chilean dancers in a patronal festival (362)

flauta 'Flute', common Spanish term for cane or bamboo transverse flute, usually with six finger holes (283, 286, 379–80)

flautón 'Big flute', Chilean single-tubed *chino* dancer's ductless flute (like a single tube of a panpipe) played in sets (359, 365)

flawta Bolivian duct flute (286)

flor de nube 'Cloud flower', Mixtec song with string accompaniment (566)

Florentine Codex Nahua early colonial codex by Fray Bernardino Sahagún (15, *17*, 557)

flores 'Flowers', Mixtec dance genre accompanied by string music (566)

FM Tango A 1990s Argentine radio station dedicated exclusively to tango (265)

folia Brazilian ensemble that goes from house to house, singing, playing instruments, and collecting donations for popular Catholic festivals, such as the *folia de reis*, 'festival of kings' (Magi) around Christmas (301, 311–12)

forró (1) Brazilian social dance music (319, 324); (2) *caboclo* dance party of Brazil (330–33); (3) accordion-based dance music of northeast Brazil derived from *baião* (332)

fotuto Archaic Colombian gourd, shell, or wooden trumpet (378, 380, 846, 855)

frevo Brass-band carnival march and dance music from Recife, Pernambuco, and electrified version of same in Salvador, Bahia (336-38)

fricote Brazilian carnival dance music (354)

fuga 'Flight', (1) a type of faster coda in Andean music (477); (2) Afro-Peruvian musical appendage used as a lively closing section (477, 481, 496); (3) a Colombian Christmas song (403); (4) a Colombian *currulao* rhythm (404); (5) in Andean music, a contrasting theme in a faster tempo, usually a *huayno* following a *yaraví* (477)

fuká Surinam Maroon *sêkêti* song of hardship (506)

fulia Drum-accompanied Venezuelan responsorial song genre (530, 534)

fundeh Jamaican single-headed membranophone played with hands (898)

furruco Single-headed Venezuelan friction membranophone sounded by rubbing a long stick attached to and protruding from the top of the drum skin (531, 538)

gafieiras Brazilian large dance halls patronized by the urban popular classes (317)

gagá Haitian-derived ensemble in the Dominican Republic (851–52, 859)

gaita Probably from the Arabic *algaita*, a Colombian vertical duct flute (402)

galerón Venezuelan dance music genre (385, 540)

galopa 'Gallop', Paraguayan outdoor fast dance consisting of two contrasting musical sections: a polka and a syncopated section (459, 461)

galoperas Paraguayan women 'dancers' who dance to fulfill religious vows (461)

gamelan Indonesian orchestra consisting mostly of struck idiophones, performed by people of Javanese heritage in Surinam (507)

gamma suid Kuna paired bamboo, single-tubed, end-blown flutes played by puberty chanters (641)

gammu burui Kuna bamboo panpipes played in pairs (641–43)

ganzá Brazilian shaken metal tube filled with beans, seeds, shells or other material (308, 326, 330, 349)

garabato 1940s African-derived musical style in Colombia (405)

garaón Also *garawung*, (1) Garífuna single-headed, conical drum in Guatemala (733); (2) *garaón primera*, the smaller drum of the

set (733); (3) *garaón segunda*, the larger drum of the set (733)

garavón Garífuna single-headed, conical drum in Nicaragua, in a set with distinctions *primera* and *segunda* for smaller and larger, respectively (741, 752)

garawoun Garifuna single-headed, cylindrical drum in Belize, in a set with distinctions *primero* and *segunda* for smaller and larger, respectively (671)

gato 'Cat', (1) Argentine social dance performed during a *jineteada* (261, 422); (2) *gato polceado*, fusion of German polka and Argentine *gato* (89); (3) *gato salvaje* 'wild cat', Yuma song-dance cycle that begins at sunset, with songs about the first stars (597)

gaucho A rural-dwelling nativist, traditionalist, or cowboy of the pampa region of Argentina; also found in Uruguay and in the southern state of Rio Grande do Sul, Brazil (237, 249, 262, 308, 512, 521)

gayumba Central African–derived earth bow in the Dominican Republic (855)

gém St. Lucian games accompanied by singing and drumming (943)

gigante Nicaraguan folk drama (756, 760)

gigantona Primarily verbal performance and the principal folk expression of León, Nicaragua (757)

ginga Brazilian swaying motion (346)

gitanos 'Gypsies', Chilean patronal festival dance group (362, 363, 364)

glorias Argentine unaccompanied religious songs (258)

glosa 'Gloss', Spanish term for four-stanza *décima* (481, 495, 499, 938)

glosador Colombian and Ecuadorian male lead singer (404, 427–28)

gnelé Among the Guaymí of Costa Rica, friction idiophone made of turtleshell covered with beeswax (686)

goke Kuna bamboo panpipes played in sets of three (643)

golpe 'Hit', (1) rhythmic accompaniment performed by hand slaps on a diatonic harp soundbox by an assistant (*golpeador*) in Ecuador (424); (2) Venezuelan dance music genre (540, 541); (3) *golpes*, Brazilian *capoeira* dance figures (346, 347)

golpeador In Ecuador, a person who beats on the box of the harp as a percussion instrument while a harpist plucks the strings (212–13, 418, 425, 428)

goombay (1) Term for calypso in the Bahamas, primarily sung dance music (806); (2) Bahamian onomatopoeic term for a single-headed frame drum (803, 805–806)

Goombeh (1) African-based Jamaican cult (901, 903); (2) *goombeh*, Jamaican square goatskin frame drum played with the fingers, considered male (897–98, 902)

gozos Argentine 'praises' or unaccompanied religious songs (258, 457)

gran diablos 'Great devils', Panamanian devil-dance tradition (774, 779)

grandy Jamaican membranophone similar to the *prenting*, considered female (897–98)

gritería 'Shouting', 7 December Nicaraguan nighttime tradition of singing one or more *purísimas* at different homes for sweets (763)

gritos Shouts of emotional expression during musical and dance performances (401, 773, 780–81)

guabina (1) Humorous, lively, and sometimes melancholy romantic vocal-folk-music genre of Colombia (387, 390–91); (2) *guabina veleña*, an improvised and non-commercialized type of *guabina* from Vélez, Santander, Colombia (391)

guacharaca Colombian stick rasp (39, 378, 401, 407)

guadúa Bamboo resonator or trumpet bell of Ecuador (416, 427)

guaguancó Cuban couple-dance genre belonging to the *rumba* family (831, 836)

guaiá Brazilian rattle (308, 348)

guajira 'Rural peasant', (1) Cuban genre belonging to the *canción cubana* family (831); (2) *guajira-son*, Cuban genre which combines elements of the *guajira* and the *son* (834)

guajolote 'Turkey', Mixtec nuptial dance in which the dancers carry a live turkey and other wedding-banquet foods (567)

gualambau Guaraní term for a musical bow similar to the Brazilian *berimbau* (201, 457)

guamo Conch-shell lip-concussion aerophone used by the pre-Columbian inhabitants of Cuba and Puerto Rico (822, 932)

guaracha Cuban genre belonging to the *son* family (372, 829, 835)

guaránia National song genre tradition of Paraguay, created in 1925 by José Asunción Flores (460, 462)

guarura Venezuelan conch-shell trumpet (533)

guasá Also *guacho*, Colombian and Ecuadorian bamboo or metal rattles played by women (377, 401)

guaya Handheld Nicaraguan shaker (762)

guayo 'Grater', Cuban metal rasp like the gourd *güiro*, played with a metal scraper (834, 854)

guía 'Guide', lead singer of Venezuelan *tonos* ensemble (534)

güiro 'Gourd', perhaps of native or Afro-Cuban or Puerto Rican origin, a scraped gourd idiophone with inscribed grooves or notches, found throughout the Caribbean, Central America, and parts of Mexico (377–78, 774, 834, 854, 932, 939, 960)

guitarra 'Guitar', Spanish term for six-stringed (usually nylon, but also metal in some rural areas of Latin America) plucked or strummed lute chordophone with hour-glass shape (*violão* in Brazil); numerous variants exist with the same name (382, 456, 756, 757, 849); *see index under* chordophones

guitarrilla Also *tiple*, 'little guitar', (1) Guatemalan rare five-stringed guitar with gourd as resonator (723, 727); (2) Bolivian deep-bodied guitar tuned in five courses (288); (3) four-metal-stringed guitar placed on the treble side of the Nicaraguan marimba (756, 761); (4) 'little guitar' of El Salvador with four strings (708, 743); (5) hourglass-shaped chordophone with five double courses of strings and a slightly rounded back (213–14)

guitarrón 'Large guitar', (1) Chilean hourglass-shaped plucked chordophone with twenty-five strings in five courses (360, 367); (2) Mexican bass lute with rounded back, used in mariachi (*546*, 611, *621*, *622*)

guli Kuna bamboo panpipes played in six parts (643)

gumbeh Boom drum, a double-headed membranophone in Belize (677)

gunyei Guatemalan courting songs (734)

GUYFESTA Guyanese British-style music festival (448)

guyrambau Also *lambau*, *mbarimbau*, large mouth bow found among the Mbyá (24, 457)

guyrapa-i Double musical bow in use among various Guaraní groups of Paraguay (201)

guyusa Garifuna predominantly female ritual singers in Belize (672)

gwaj Also *syak*, Dominican and St. Lucian shaken and scraped tin cylinder idiophone pierced with nail holes and filled with pebbles or seeds (842, 946)

gwoka (1) Guadeloupe drum music (874–75); (2) membranophone playing the basic rhythms at *lèwòz* festival in St. Lucia (874–75)

habanera 'From Havana', (1) Cuban genre belonging to the *canción cubana* family (620, 827, 831, 835); (2) Brazilian dance form featuring dotted rhythm (313, 350)

habi-sanuka Small Warao container rattle of calabash with wooden spiked handle (189)

hali' Gourd rattle which is the only traditional musical instrument used by the Guarijio (553)

Hallelujah Guyanese syncretic religion of some native Americans living in the savannah (47, 131, 443)

"Hanacpachap Cussicuinin" Four-part polyphonic piece published in Quechua by the Franciscan Juan Pérez Bocanegra in Lima, 1631 (469)

hanawkwa Yekuana conch-shell trumpet (179)

harawi Also *haraui*, pre-Columbian Incan nostalgic monophonic love song from which the Peruvian *yaraví* is possibly derived (215, 468, 476)

harawiq Group of Andean elder women who sing *harawi* in high-pitched, nasal voices (476)

häwiawan Yanomamö priest-shaman (170)

haylli Call-and-response harvest song in ancient Peru (468, 476)

hebu Warao ancestor spirit which can cause illness (194)

hebu mataro Large Warao container rattle made from a calabash with a wooden spiked handle (189–91)

hekunukabe Warao ductless vertical flute made from plant stalk (189, 192)

hekura Also *híkola*, Yanomamö illness-causing spirit or spirit helper (170–71)

heresemoi Warao conch-shell end-blown lip-concussion aerophone (189, 193)

hermandades Chilean brotherhoods of patronal festivals honoring the Virgin Mary (362)

herranza Marking of animals in the Andes, a context for ritual music making (475, 478)

highland fling Antiguan carnival dance derived from Scottish folk dance (799)

hito Also *wíchu*, *fhidyu*, Yekuana long-tubed vertical duct flute with closed distal end (178)

hoa Warao prayerful song for curing illnesses (188, 196–97)

hoarotu 'Owner of *hoa*', Warao shaman in charge of the western cosmic realm (170, 193–96)

hocket Borrowed European term meaning "interlocking parts," often referring to the alternating manner of playing panpipe halves in the Andes or *vaksin* trumpets in Haiti (161, 207, 236, 285, 359, 365, 887)

hornada 'Batch' or 'ovenful', medley of Venezuelan *revueltas* or *pasajes* (540)

horse head Also *buru*, Jamaican Christmas holiday slave celebration (907)

Hosay Jamaican Muslim celebration brought by indentured workers from India (86, 443, 908)

huada Mapuche calabash rattle (234)

huahua Mixtec danced game (564)

huancar Inca drum (468)

huapango (1) Mexican variety of the *son* (608); (2) *huapango arribeño*, 'highland *huapango*' (571, 573); (3) *huapango huasteco*, played by a string trio at a fast tempo (573)

huapanguera Also *guitarra quinta*, deep-bodied Mexican guitar with eight strings in five single and double courses (608)

huarumu Long, straight tubular trumpet of Ecuador (416)

huaylas Harvest ritual song genre of the central Andes of Peru (476)

huayno Also *wayno*, (1) central Andean dance in fast duple meter with free choreography consisting of two musical phrases in periodic form (*aabb*) (361, 369, 473, 477, 483); (2) native American–derived (Quechua) Peruvian fast duple-meter song and dance form featuring long-short-short rhythmical pattern (477); (3) the most popular highland Peruvian song form, used to transmit narrative texts (59, 101, 133); (4) *huayño*, Bolivian (Aymara) orthography for dance in duple meter (293, 297)

huéhuetl Nahua large, single-headed, cylindrical, hollowed-out log drum, also used by the Maya (550, 556–59, 601–602)

huíbiju Kogi ceramic globular aerophone (184)

huilacapiztli Nahua ceramic globular aerophone (601)

hüngühüngü In Belize, popular Garifuna dance in triple meter with unison singing frequently performed at holidays, processionals, and other festive occasions (676)

huuwai (1) Yekuana shaman (179); (2) malevolent spirit (179)

hwin krã Suyá strung rattle with *piqui* pits or deer or wild pig hooves (144)

ialorixá Brazilian female temple leader in Candomblé 342)

iamuricuma Ceremony in the Xingú region of Brazil (57, 129)

iancunú Garifuna masked dance genre related to Caribbean *junkanoo* (740)

iaren Recitative-like speech form used in Suyá ceremonies (145)

idiophone 'Self-sounder', a musical instrument whose sound is produced by the vibration of the hard qualties of the entire instrument itself (29)

igala Kuna 'language,' 'path', or 'way', characteristic of the systematic nature of instrumental music and chanting traditions (639)

ijexá (1) Afro-Bahian culture associated with Candomblé (351–52); (2) rhythm, style, and dance in Brazilian *afoxé* music (338)

ilê Yoruba 'house' or 'temple' in Cuban Santería (823)

illacu Guatemalan shell rattles strung around calves of dancers (734)

iména 'Husband', the larger half of the Paraguayan *guyrapa* double musical bow (201)

inanka Miskitu laments sung by women at wakes (660, 662–63)

ingá Afro-Peruvian novelty circle dance (482, 496–97)

insuba Also *simbaika*, Miskitu handleless rattle made from a dry gourd filled with small stones or hard seeds (660, 662, 663)

ipála Bolivian special wedding feast song (291)

ira 'Leader' in Aymara, one of the halves (male) of the *siku* (and several other) double-unit panpipe in the central Andes (counterpart of *arca* female half, 'follower') (34, 208, 358, 469)

irak Wayana ceremony that is part of the *marake* initiation ritual (166)

irki Bolivian animal-horn single-reed-concussion aerophone (287)

isimoi Sacred Warao heteroglottal single-reed-concussion aerophone without finger holes (189, 193)

isingni 'Soul', (1) Miskitu deceased (663); (2) manifestation of person's soul in a firefly (663); (3) *isingni ulan*, 'soul mounted', day-long Miskitu curative ritual by shaman to remove dead person's soul from seriously ill patient (662)

iúna Afro-Brazilian rhythmic pattern (346)

jab-jab Trinidadian carnival band characterized by devil costumes (965)

jalajala Colombian bunch rattle (377)

jalacomapacuaper Sung or recited Maleku prayers for protection against human wrongdoing or evil spirits (682)

jantarka Bolivian two-tone pipe played by women during carnival (283)

jarabe Mexican *son* intended especially for dancing (603, 606, 611–12, 619)

jarana (1) Mexican guitar (also *guitarra de golpe*) in a variety of shapes, sizes, courses and strings (565, 608, *609*, 611, *612*); (2) Nahua five-stringed, hourglass-shaped chordophone, often with double courses (559–60); (3) Mexican couple dance resembling the Spanish *jota* in choreography and meter of its music (613); (4) Afro-Peruvian competitive song form (409); (5) early twentieth-century private type of party in lower-class neighborhoods of Peru (500)

jarocho Mestizo culture of Veracruz, Mexico (605–606, 608–609)

jaway Ecuadorian agricultural harvest song (425)

jawbone Jamaican *salo* song type (902)

jebio Guaymí dance which begins in a single file and end in a circle (686)

jhānjh Trinidadian cymbals in the *tassa* ensemble (85, 444, 959)

jíbaros 'Country folk' of Puerto Rico (935)

jíkuri Peyote used by the Tarahumara (585–86)

jineteada Also *jineteada y doma*, Argentine spectacle organized by traditionalist societies, local municipal authorities, or merchants, featuring traditional music and dance (261)

jitarrón Flat-backed *charango*-like instrument played during rainy season in southern Peru and northern Bolivia (283)

jondo Panamanian single-headed drum played with hands (774)

jongo Afro-Brazilian social dance (307, 309, 348)

Jonkunnu Jamaican Christmas holiday slave celebration (907)

Jopará The widespread language mixture of Guaraní and Spanish in Paraguay (452)

Jordanites Members of an African-, Catholic-, and Protestant-derived syncretic religion of Guyana (445)

joropo European-derived "national" couple dance/music genre/event of Venezuela (385, 389, 394, 539–41)

jota Spanish song and dance form using compound duple meter and hemiola or *sesquiáltera* (6/8 + 3/4), from which the *cueca* and other American forms may have developed (422, 481, 613, 657, 697)

Journée internationale du créole 'International Creole Day', annual celebration founded in the 1980s and held on October 28 in Martinique (917–18)

Jovem Guarda (1) Originally a São Paulo television program 1965–1969 (318); *jovem guarda*, a generic term for *iê-iê-iê* (from the Beatles' "Yeah! Yeah! Yeah!"), early Brazilian rock and roll (109, 318)

juco Small friction drum once found in the Masaya area of Nicaragua (757)

juey Puerto Rican 'crab' dance choreography (939)

julajula Large panpipes of La Paz and northern Potosí departments, Bolivia (285, 289, 292)

jumbie (1) Montserrat drum identical to the *babala*, but approximately 76 centimeters in diameter (924); (2) religious dance and music, identical to the country dance (924–25); (3) spirit that can be summoned from the grave by music (923, 924)

jump-in dance (jumping dance) In the Bahamas, a solo dance in which the next dancer who "jumps in" is selected by the current dancer (809–10)

Jump-up Day New Year's Day emancipation celebration in Montserrat (925–26)

junkafunk The Bahamian musical group Bahamen's musical innovation of using junkanoo rhythms on modern electronic instruments (808)

junkanoo In the Bahama Islands, traditional *goombay* music performed by acoustic instruments within the context of the junkanoo parades during the Christmas season (803, 806–808, 811–12)

jwé St. Lucian play activities often accompanied by singing and drumming (943–44)

ka St. Lucian barrel-shaped, single-headed membranophone played with bare hands (946, 948)

kadans Also *kadans-ranpa*, 'cadence', (1) *konpa*-like genre developed in Haiti by Wébert Sicot (892); (2) Haitian-derived musical genre of Martinique (98, 916–19)

kahran kaság ngere Suyá big turtle songs for dry season (145)

kaiso (1) Hausa word suggested as one of the origins of the word *calypso* (819, 963); (2) stage-presented calypso in Trinidad (963)

kalenda Also *calenda*, (1) ancient African song-dance, precursor of calypso (98, 865); (2) Caribbean variations on West African stick fight–dance with musical accompaniment (795, 854); (3) Trinidadian martial sport–dance accompanied by drumming and song (96, 959, 963, 966)

kantikamò Guadeloupe canticles for the dead (876)

kantún Mapuche improvised songs (236)

kantus Double-unit panpipe tradition of Charazani, Bolivia (209, 216)

karakukua Costa Rican five-holed cane flute played by guests at a funeral (682)

karaoke 'Empty orchestra', Japanese recorded pop and folk music minus the singer, a type of "sing-along" to cassette tapes and videos, introduced by Japanese immigrants and popular in South America (41, 85, 87, 89)

kasamintu Bolivian special tuning (291)

kase' 'Break', a radical change in the Haitian master drum's pattern to induce spirit possession (883, 888)

kaseko Also *casser le corps*, 'break the body', (1) creole dance accompanied by drum and song found in French Guiana and Surinam (437); (2) pop genre that merges many Caribbean and African styles, often blending Caribbean calypso, reggae, and *zouk* with West African *soukous* and Surinam Maroon Djuka drumming (508–509)

kashwa Also *cachiua*, cheerful song–circle dance genre of pre-Columbian Andean origins, performed by young, single men and women and usually associated with nocturnal harvest rituals (468, 476, 477)

kaskawilla Chilean bell rattle (358–59)

kata Grenadian open-bottomed, principal membranophone of the big drum ceremony (870)

katikubi Vernacular Mixtec *son* with non-Western structure and improvised texts (567)

ka'um Islamic religious leader of Javanese descent in Surinam (507)

kawadi dejë Yekuana small end-blown deer-tibia ductless flute with internal wax diaphragm (178)

kawina Oldest creole musical form of Surinam (508)

kbandu Jamaican single-headed, cylindrical membranophone played with the hands during Kumina ritual (898, 902)

ke'e Mixtec log idiophone, similar to the Nahua *teponaztli* (563)

keer Also *kitiar*, Ecuadorian bowed-lute chordophone (417)

kélé St. Lucian religious tradition particular to the *djiné* (949)

kèmès Haitian early evening dance (889–90)

kena Spanish orthography *quena*, central Andean end-blown notched flute of Aymara origin with five to eight finger holes (209, 357–58, 416); *see also* quena, qina

kendang Double-headed membranophone of Indonesian origin played in gamelan ensemble in Surinam (507)

kéngi Purépecha elderly native authority of celebrations and responsorial singer (578)

k'epa Inca trumpet (416, 468)

kepu Conch-shell trumpet in Andes (37)

k'illpa Bolivian animal fertility ritual (289)

kin Large, four-stringed Chiapas bass guitar (654–55)

kiringua Purépecha slit-drum idiophone played with two sticks (578)

kitar From English 'guitar', rustically manufactured plucked wooden lute in Guatemala (661)

kitarlawana Also *tiun*, '*kitar* song', Guatemalan songs composed by men, in which the lyric content centers on a woman (663)

klisang Miskitu mirliton made from a piece of cane and a membrane from a bat's wing, a cow's gut, or thin paper and used to sanctify water for curative rituals (660–61, 662) *kodedo* Yekuana turtleshell rubbed or friction idiophone (177)

k'ojom Guatemalan cylindrical, double-headed drum (654, 721, 722, 723, 726, 727)

kokyū Bowed shamisen-type lute played by people of Japanese ancestry in South America (88)

Kolla Suyu Mapuche Southern Kingdom of the Inca empire (232)

konbit Haitian collective labor association that uses music to accompany work (885)

konmandè (1) Guadeloupe call-and-response song leader (876); (2) person who calls quadrille steps (877)

konpa-dirèk Haitian popular dance modeled on the Dominican *merengue* (98, 892, 893)

kont (1) Dominican storytelling with short, fixed, and recurrent song theme (843); (2) St. Lucian unaccompanied songs performed at wakes (948)

korima Tarahumara harvest ceremony (585)

kósi Maroon *sêkêti* song of cursing in Surinam (506)

koten Okinawan classical music, performed by musicians of Okinawan heritage in Argentina, Brazil, and Peru (87)

koto Thirteen-stringed Japanese zither, played by musicians of Japanese heritage in Argentina, Brazil, and Peru (*kutu* in romanized Okinawan orthography) (88)

koudyay Carnival-like Haitian celebration, not necessarily at carnival time (894)

koutoumba St. Lucian wake ceremony or a song-dance performed by the *djiné* (948–49)

krik-krac Martinique oral tradition of tales told at funeral wakes (915)

Krismis From English 'Christmas', Miskitu for 'December', Miskitu calendrical festival dance in a circle (661–62)

krita Miskitu scraper (663)

kromanti (1) Maroon warrior gods, ancestral spirits in Surinam (506); (2) Maroon play or dance in Jamaica (902); (3) Jamaican principal ritual for summoning Maroon ancestral spirits (902)

krywá Cane tube, open on both ends, into which the player hums, played exclusively by women among the Aché-Guayakí of Paraguay (455)

kuísi Also *kuizi*, Kogi vertical cane duct flute with a mouthpiece shaped like a hatchet (made of pitch and ash with a quill for a duct), often played in pairs, one male (*kuísi sigi* or *kuísi macho*) and the other female (*kuísi bunzi* or *kuísi hembra*) (184–85)

kulè 'To speak out or shout', work songs or chants sung by Bribri men (634)

kullkull Mapuche cow-horn lip-concussion aerophone (358)

k'ullu charango Small Bolivian *charango* associated with dry season (213)

kultrún Mapuche single-headed, kettle-shaped membranophone played with one stick by the *machi* shaman (234, 252, 254, 358–59)

Kumina (1) Jamaican religion practiced by the descendants of post-emancipation indentured laborers from Central Africa (901, 902–903); (2) call-and-response song type signaling start of every ritual ceremony (903)

kuminjaré Five-stringed Mbyá shamanic guitar of Paraguay (201–202)

kumú Tukano religious practitioner who cures illnesses caused by the supernatural intrusion of pathogenic agents (stones, splinters, thorns) into the patient's body (153, 154)

kungbi Large Miskitu double-headed cylindrical drum played with the hands (661, 662)

kuraqkuna Bolivian community authority who may sponsor fiestas (291)

kurei Parrot associated with Waiãpi edge aerophones (160)

kuri-kuri Yuma song cycles sung during holidays (597)

kuswa taya Miskitu tortoiseshell idiophone that produces two tones when struck on the free ends of its ventral side with a deer's horn, wooden stick, or large nail (660)

kuwai Wayana shaker attached to legs of dancer or stick, often used by shamans (165)

kwadril 'Quadrille', St. Lucian social dance of European origin (944–45, 946)

kwakwa Maroon squat wooden bench or stool beaten with two sticks in Surinam (505)

kwal taya Miskitu shaman's wake for the deceased (660, 663)

kwat Length of bamboo beaten with two sticks among Jamaican Maroons (897)

la batalla 'The battle', a Venezuelan stick dance (536)

ladainhas 'Litanies', a *capoeira* song repertoire in Brazil (346)

Ladinos (1) Guatemalan urbanites whose primary language is Spanish (651, 655, 723, 734–35); (2) sixteenth-century Spanish-speaking Christians of African descent brought from Spain to the Dominican Republic (850)

lakonmèt Sole closed-couple dance said to have originated in St. Lucia (945, 946)

lambada Brazilian adaptation of *carimbó* popular dance form (94, 354)

lanbi Haitian conch-shell trumpet (885)

lancers English social dance derived from the quadrille (741, 835, 842, 872, 908)

landó Afro-Peruvian song and dance form with a syncopated accompaniment and an underlying (4 + 2)/4 time, said to have come from the Brazilian *lundú* (482, 497–98)

lanigi garawoun 'Heart drum' among the Garifuna in Belize (669–73)

lanza Short for *la cuadrilla de lanceros* 'lancers' quadrille', popular among semiurban middle classes of Honduras in the early 1880s (741)

lapo kabwit 'Goatskin', generic Dominican term for drums (841)

laremuna wadaguman Work-accompanying songs for Garifuna men in Belize (675)

latinos Latin American people, so named because they speak Spanish, a Latin-derived romance language (699)

laúd 'The lute', Cuban Spanish-derived (*la'ud*) twelve-stringed chordophone (833)

laures Venezuelan sticks (also *palos*) beaten on the side of the wooden-bodied *mina* drum (528)

lavwa Dominican chorus that responds to the *chantwèl* (841)

lawatu Bolivian duct flute (286)

lawentuchen 'Small therapies', Mapuche medical ritual (362)

lê Afro-Brazilian smallest *atabaque* drum (343)

lèdèk Female religious dancer of Javanese descent in Surinam (507)

lemesidi Guatemalan Christian songs for liturgical use at Mass or prayer services (734)

leremuna égi Work songs of Garifuna women (675)

levantada (1) Second section of Yuma song characterized by melodic devices and transposition (596); (2) *levantada de muertos*, 'raising of the dead', Mixtec custom in which people in disguises roam around the town accompanied by music (566)

léwòz 'La Rose' in French Creole (Kwéyòl), in Guadeloupe and St. Lucia, a musical genre, the evening of its performance, and its basic rhythm (874–75)

liban Sumu globular flute with three finger holes made from a crab's claw and beeswax (740)

libres Free African-American people of Colombia (401)

lichiwayu Also *lechewayo*, *lichiguayo*, (1) Bolivian notched end-blown flute (209, 286, *287*, 289, 357); (2) *lichiguayo*, thick Chilean *kena* bound with llama tendons (358)

liku Chilean soprano-register *siku* (358, 362)

lingigui garavon 'Main drum' or 'drum of the heart' of the Nicaraguan Garífuna *garavon* drum ensemble (752)

linnet Subgenre of Pame religious song in which two singers, or groups of singers, compete and show off their memory skills (571)

lira In Colombia, a group of musicians playing instrumental music with Spanish-derived instruments (383); *see also estudiantina*, *rondalla*, *tuna*

listwa St. Lucian storytelling, usually including a short song (943)

lóbi Maroon *sêkêti* song of love in Surinam (506)

loncomeo Also *lonkomeo*, (1) Mapuche rhea imitation dance by young boys (254); (2) Mapuche 'moving the head' virtuosic solo dance (236–37)

lopi GUYFESTA rhythmic experiment to establish a Guyanese beat (448)

lué (1) Wayana generic term for aerophones (165); (2) specific flute made from large armadillo's nail (165); (3) *lué kôriró*, Wayana end-blown flute with four finger holes (165)

lumalú Colombian traditional funerary music (404)

lundu Early Brazilian song type derived from Afro-Brazilian folk dance (304, 306, 348, 350)

lunfardo Dialect used by the social classes among which the Argentine tango originated (264)

luñku Also *lungku*, Sumu musical bow that uses the mouth as a resonator, usually played by women (661, 750)

luruvan garavón 'Third drum' or 'helping drum' of the Nicaraguan Garífuna *garavon* or drum ensemble (752)

lwa Also *loa*, Haitian Vodou spirit (882–84, 888)

llakichina 'To make sad', Ecuadorian women's songs to cause to love (430)

llamada Clarín call in northern Peru that tells the workers at a *mita* to begin working (36)

llamado Guatemalan rhythm-establishing introduction (733)

llamador 'Caller', (1) Panamanian single-headed drum (775, 778); (2) *llamador del tigre*, 'caller of the jaguar', friction drum made from a large hollow gourd across which goatskin is stretched, to which a stick is attached and rubbed (740)

llameras All-female dancing group of Aymara region (362)

llanero Adjective referring to the plains (*llanos*) of Colombia and Venezuela (377)

llanto Panamanian *torrente* used to sing sad or love *décimas* (780)

llungur Long valveless, transverse, wooden or cane trumpet in the central Andes (212)

macamaca Afro-Peruvian watermelon harvest festivities (495)

machetero 'Swordsman dance' performed during Moxo festivals (138–40)

machi Mapuche shaman (233, 252, 254, 358–59, 362)

machilwün Mapuche shaman initiation rite (362)

machitún Mapuche shamanic ceremony involving treatment for physical and spiritual illnesses (57, 235)

Macuilxochitl 'Five Flowers', Aztec god of dance and sports (557)

maculelê Afro-Brazilian fighting dance (349–50)

Macumba Afro-Brazilian syncretic religion in Rio de Janeiro (341)

madaka Yekuana shaman's container rattle (177)

mãe de santo Female temple leader in Brazilian Candomblé (342)

maestro del coro Guatemalan *maestro cantor* or sacristan specialist in ritual music (731)

maestros cantores Men who fulfill musical duties of an office established by Franciscan missionaries in colonial times (656)

maipuli (1) Wayana host and participants of

okoma ceremony (166); (2) genre of Wayana dance (166)

majò jon Haitian male baton twirler and dancer in *rara* bands (886)

makawa Chilean double-headed membranophone (358)

makich Ecuadorian fruit-capsule ankle rattle (414)

makyè (1) Guadeloupe drummer who "marks" the choreography of the *lèwòz* dancer (874); (2) membranophone used in *léwòz* dance (874)

malembe 'Softly', 'slowly', or 'take it easy', a Venezuelan rhythm and song (528, 535)

malka kuñin Also *malaka kuñini*, *malaka kuñkana*, single-tone Sumu flute made from the femur of a deer, tapir, or other large animal and used as a hunting lure (750)

Mamanchí Guaymí syncretic religious movement combining Catholicism with indigenous religious and musical elements (686)

mambo Cuban genre of the 1950s belonging to the *danzón* family and created by Orestes López (371, 827, 833)

mampulorios Alternative Venezuelan name for children's wakes (*velorios de angelito*) (535)

mañanitas 'Early morning', nearly synonymous with *serenata*, it includes a range of songs that vary greatly according to local custom in Mexico (613, 618)

manbo Haitian Vodou priestess (883)

manda Musical promise to God, a saint, the Virgin Mary, or some other religious figure throughout Catholic America (549)

mandolina 'Mandolin', either flat-backed Latin type or round-backed West Asian–type plucked chordophone of the lute family, found throughout Spanish-speaking America (531, 572, 708, 743)

mangulina Dance of the southwest Dominican Republic (856)

manman Large drum played by the Haitian master drummer (883)

manpa St. Lucian dance in duple rhythm (946)

mapalé African-derived carnival genre of Colombia (405)

maraca Gourd or calabash container rattle in Cuba, Mexico, Puerto Rico, Venezuela, and many regions of the Americas; usually played in pairs (maracas) (401, 414, 541, 834, 933)

maraka Also *marari*, container rattle played by Waiãpi shamans (159, 161)

marake Wayana cycle of ceremonies that constitute the boys' initiation ritual (166, 437)

mare-hoa Warao prayerful song sung by a man to entice a woman (196)

mareicãe Wayana women's songs sung by men to attract women (166)

maremare 'Happy-happy', a panpipe played by Venezuelan creoles (533)

mariachi The most nationally prominent folk-derived Mexican musical ensemble since the 1930s, usually consisting of guitars, vihuela, *guitarrón*, violins, trumpets, and singers (371, 592, 621–22)

Marian antiphon Antiphonal song in praise of the Virgin Mary (847)

marimba (1) African-derived term for a xylophone found in Central America, Colombia, Mexico, and Venezuela (401, 404, 414–15, 427–28, 655, 667, 693, 708–709, 724–726); (2) African-derived lamellophone in Dominican Republic (*see also marímbola*) (854, 857)

marímbola Also *marímbúla*, African-derived lamellophone consisting of a large wooden box with tuned metal strips or tongues that are plucked, presently from Cuba, Dominican Republic, and Puerto Rico, and rarely in Colombia, Venezuela, and other Caribbean islands (401, 528, 834, 933, 960)

marinera Peruvian dance and song genre in composite 6/8 and 3/4 *sesquiáltera*/hemiola meter, related to the *cueca* (see *zamacueca*) and given its name in honor of seamen who died in the War of the Pacific (1879–1883) (475, 481, 499)

maroma Mixtec acrobatic performance, accompanied by violin, flute, and guitar with singing and dancing atop boards placed on crates (741)

maromeros Mixtec acrobats who do stunts associated with the flier's dance (*baile del volador*) (564)

Maroon 'Runaway', (1) a descendant of African slaves living in the interior of Surinam, French Guiana, Guyana, and Jamaica (164, 438–39, 504–506); (2) Jamaican creole culture and cult of Arawak, Spanish, and predominantly African mix (896, 902)

marujada Dramatic Afro-Brazilian dance (347–48)

mas' In Grenada and Trinidad, short for "masquerade" (866, 964)

mascaritas 'Little masks', Mixtec graceful dances imitating quadrilles of the 1800s (566)

mashramani Celebration after a successful harvest in Guyana featuring steelbands (442, 447)

masi Sumu conch trumpet that serves as a signaling device across distances (751)

masquerade band Costumed Caribbean group in a carnival celebration (446, 799, 964–66)

masquerade jig Paid entertainment of the Virgin Islands that combines theater, oratory, and music (972)

masqueraders Costumed Montserrat dance groups (925)

Mass Games Annual Korean-style mixture of fine arts held during February in Guyana (447)

matachines Also *awieme*, sacred dances in northern Mexico and adjacent areas in the southwestern United States (583, 591)

mataco Tukano double-duct flute (152)

matraca (1) Argentine *criollo* gourd rattle (251); (2) Bolivian cog ratchet (285); (3) Brazilian rattle (347, 348); (4) in El Salvador, Guatemala, and Honduras, a long-handled wooden ratchet of Arab origin that is swung above the head (708, 724, 730, 742)

matrimonial Thin plank with four or more sets of copper or tin discs nailed loosely to it (929)

maxixe Also *maxixi*, Brazilian fast syncopated dance music form from the late nineteenth century until today (94, 305, 350)

mayohuacán Wooden slit drum in ancient Caribbean (13, 846)

mayolè Guadeloupe stylized stick fighting accompanied by drumming and singing (876)

mayordomo Individual steward or sponsor of patronal festivals in the southern Americas (757)

maypole Most widely known traditional dance of Nicaragua (754, 799, 819)

mayura Bolivian minor fiesta sponsor (291)

mazurka Triple-meter music and associated dance introduced into Nicaragua by Central European immigrants in the latter half of the 1800s (757); (2) *mazurka segoviana*, 'Segovian mazurka', music-and-dance complex in northern Nicaragua (757)

mba'e pu ovavá'é Cylindrical drum of the Paraguayan Mbyá used by shamans and to accompany a hunter's propitiatory songs to the animals he has killed (201)

mbaraká (1) Guaraní large spiked shamanic rattle with stones or seeds inside (200, 202, 453, 454, 456); (2) Guaraní name for guitar of standard European design (202)

Mbyá Also Mbïá, native American culture of Misiones Province, Argentina, and parts of Paraguay (Mbïá is Argentine orthography; Mbyá is Paraguayan orthography) (199–201, 254–55)

mborahéi pukú 'Long song', Guaraní song-dance genre (203)

mejorana Panamanian term denoting a particular song form, dance, scale, and musical instrument (772, 776–77, 778)

melanda Wayana genre of love songs performed by adult men (166)

melé Afro-Brazilian friction rattle in southern region (308)

membranophone 'Skin sounder', a musical instrument whose sound comes from the vibrations of a stretched membrane (29)

membrillo Guatemalan branch hoop around which skin is wrapped for drums (727)

mento (1) Jamaican indigenous song/instrumental/dance style and ensemble, popular until 1940s (97, 906); (2) most common folk musical form of Nicaragua with a basic structure of alternating responsorial solo verse and chorus (753–54)

mereng Also *méringue*, (1) Haitian dance/song tradition related to the Dominican *merengue* (98, 798, 842, 891); (2) *mereng koudyay* (also *mereng kanaval*), very fast Haitian carnival composition (890); (3) *mereng-lant*, slow Haitian elite parlour dance (98, 891); (4) *mereng-Vodou*, big-band instrumentation with Vodou temple percussion section (892)

merengue (1) Dominican Republic music and dance genre that has become a symbol of national identity (98, 104–105, 855, 857); (2) *merengue redondo*, 'round merengue', based on circular movements of the dancing couple (856)

merrywang Jamaican fiddle (900)

mesa 'Table', Spanish term in Peru for a shaman's altar on which ritual objects are placed, including musical instruments (229)

mesa de ruidos 'Table of noises' (492); *see tamborete, tormento*

mestisaje **(Port.)**; *mestizaje* **(Span.)** 'Miscegenation', term for the process of mixing of race and culture, usually assumed between native American and Spanish or Portuguese (4, 100, 400, 401, 498, 719)

mestizo Spanish term for an individual of Iberian and native American cultural heritage (4, 249, 359–60, 482–83, 600)

mestre capoeira Brazilian '*capoeira* master' (346)

métissage Martinique intercultural marriages mainly with the French and later with the Tamils (914)

metsaka Tarahumara reference to the Virgin Mary (584)

mihkuhika First change in Nahua dance (561)

mihtutilo Change in Nahua dance (561)

milonga (1) Argentine song (236, 261, 263); (2) Uruguayan musical form used in the *payada* (512)

mimby Generic Guaraní term for flute (201, 452, 455)

mina (1) Venezuelan (Barlovento region) set of two single-headed drums (528–29); (2) the longer drum of the set paired with the shorter *curbata*; the *mina* is the membranophone that plays improvisations (528–29)

mini-djaz Haitian *konpa* ensemble with rock and roll influences (98, 890, 892)

minuete Instrumental genre practiced by the Chichimec and the Pame and unrelated to the European minuet (573, 621)

minyō Japanese folk song, popular among people of Japanese ancestry in South America (87)

mirliton An object or membrane made to sound by the indirect action of the vibration of an instrument to which it is attached; its sound is often described as a buzz (564, 570, 660, 662, 695, 756)

mita Also *minka*, *minga*, communal work effort in the Andes, often accompanied by music (34, 36, 255, 284, 366)

mitote (1) Pre-Hispanic Pame cane flute with four finger holes and one hole near the proximal end covered with matted cobweb that acts as a mirliton (570, 573); (2) Pame dance accompanied by the *mitote* flute; (570, 573); (3) communal song-dances of the pre-Columbian Chorotega used for sacrificial and agricultural harvest rites (681)

mizik angaje Haitian political or socially concerned music (892)

mizik vidé Also *mizik a mas*, Guadeloupe carnival music (876–77, 879)

moçambique Brazilian dramatic dance ensemble similar to the *congada* (309, 312–13)

moda Generic term for a secular song genre both in Brazil and Portugal (307)

moda-de-viola 'Manner of the *viola*', traditional song form of rural south-central Brazil, sung as a duet to the accompaniment of two *violas* (307, 319)

moderno Rock/jazz-based *cuarteto* style in Argentina (274)

modinha Brazilian sentimental song genre, originating in late colonial period (103, 304, 306, 350)

moko jumby (1) Trinidadian carnival stilt dancer of African provenance (965); (2) Moko Jumbie, Caribbean stilt dancer of carnival (799, 866, 973)

Moluche Mapuche warriors and hunters of former times from the pampas (232)

monkey Jamaican cylindrical membranophone of the Maroons (897–98)

montuno Final section of a Cuban *son* (830)

moonshine *dahlins* Jamaican yard entertainment and recreation on moonlit nights (905)

moráo Bolivian ten-tubed panpipe of the lowland Moré (293)

morenada Bolivian black slave carnival dance (292)

morenos Dancing group of mestizo people from the Aymara region of Bolivia (362)

moro Guarijío 'manager' of the *pascola* (554)

moros y cristianos 'Moors and Christians', dance reenactment of Moorish and Spanish battles, popular throughout Hispanic America (494, 561, 566, 731, 743–44, 760, 761)

morrocoyo Kogi rubbed turtleshell idiophone (185)

mpintín Puerto Rican rhythmic pattern derived from the Ghanaian Akan (939)

muakuke Cabécar 'game of the drums' (635)

Muharram Muslim festival that is also celebrated by Hindus in Surinam (86)

muhusemoi Warao deer-bone vertical flute with slightly notched mouthpiece and three finger holes (178, 189, 192)

mukululu Also *mullu*, end-blown notched flute with four finger holes from the department of La Paz, Bolivia (286)

murga (1) Musical/theatrical carnival group in Uruguay (511, 516–19); (2) informal street festival music ensemble in Uruguay (516–19); (3) urban carnival song genre in Argentina (259)

música caipira Brazilian 'country music' (59, 133, 319)

música champeta Colombian pejorative reference to African-derived music (410)

música criolla 'Creole music', (1) in Venezuela, music of Venezuelan peasants of mixed ancestry (526); (2) Catholic-Spanish, Arab-Andalusian, and Chilean foundations of Chilean musical/poetic practice (359); (3) coastal Peruvian music of Afro-Peruvian influence (495)

música cuartetera Also *música de cuarteto*, popular Argentine dance music genre from Córdoba (265–66, 273–80)

música de golpe 'Strike music', a group with violin accompanied by double-headed membranophones such as snare and bass drum (571)

música de proyección folklórica Argentine style based on urbanization of traditional rural repertoires (262)

música nacional 'National music', usually referring to folk music (417, 418, 427)

música regional 'Regional music' (605)

música terapia Colombian feel-good reference to African-derived music (410)

música típica 'Typical music', music of known authors that utilizes traditional song-dance styles and forms in Costa Rica (698)

música tropical 'Tropical music', Afro-Caribbean dance-musics, particularly salsa, cumbia, and merengue, popular throughout the Americas (102, 265–66, 520, 622)

musickers Montserrat musicians (924)

musiñu Also *mohoceño*, Bolivian vertical (small one) and transverse (large one) duct flute (286, *287*)

musiqueada Long Paraguayan *serenata* (462)

mutirães Brazilian voluntary work parties (301)

Nago (1) African-based Jamaican cult (901, 903); (2) a variety of Brazilian Candomblé (341, 342)

nahanamu Warao harvest festival (189, 191, 192, 193)

napurete Maleku name for song (682)

nasis Calabash rattle of the Kuna (640, *641*)

nasyon Lwa Vodou spirit family, usually associated with a West African ethnic group (882)

nawa-wakal Single-tone Sumu flute made from jaguar bone and used in *sikro* funerary ceremony (750)

nawba Early Andalusian musical-poetic tradition developed in colonial times (367)

negre jardin Trinidadian disguise of nineteenth-century aristocrats imitating agricultural servants (964–65)

negritos Also *hatajo de negritos*, (1) Afro-Peruvian young men who perform in front of *nacimiento* dressed as Magi (494, 497); (2) Purépecha dancers wearing masks of black men (579)

neikurrewén Mapuche shamanic initiation rite (362)

netotiliztli Nahua dancing (558)

ngere Suyá word that refers to 'ceremony', 'song-dance', and a specific genre of singing in unison (126, 145–46)

nhimia Generic Waiãpi name for aerophones (159)

nimaj k'ojom Guatemalan large cylindrical, double-headed drum (727)

nine night That part of Jamaican wake when the spirit of the dead person returns to be entertained (906)

Niño Alcalde Argentine 'Child Mayor', theatrical veneration of baby Jesus (258)

nipjiiht Pame end-blown cane flute played during religious rites and processions (570–71)

nolkín Mapuche hollow-stemmed, lip-concussion aerophone played by inhaling (358)

norteño-fronterizo "Near the U.S. border," popular Yuma genre heard on the radio (599)

nouvel jenerasyon Haitian urban technological movement in commercial music of the 1980s (892, 893)

novena Brazilian Catholic religious ritual in honor of a saint or religious figure (*328*, 330, 366)

novenaria Also *última novena*, 'novenary', (1) nine *tercios* or nine-day period of prayer, a Roman Catholic ritual (404); (2) a Colombian and Guatemalan adult wake (404, 734); (3) *novenario de difuntos*, Puerto Rican nine-day period of prayer for the dead (936)

nquillatún Also *ŋillipún*, *nguillatún*, Mapuche annual fertility/harvest rite, a seasonal ritual during which the *trutruka* is played (234, 253, 254, 359, 362)

Nuestra Señora del Rosario 'Our Lady of the Rosary', one of the oldest religious festivals in mestizo Spanish-speaking America (365)

nueva canción 'New song', (1) generic name for pan-Latin American neofolk-protest music that began in Chile in the 1960s and spread throughout the Americas (also *nueva canción chilena*) (32, 60, 81, 90, 103, 298, 373, 764); (2) Dominican Republic counterpart of the Cuban *nueva trova* (861); (3) *nueva canción latinoamericana*, 'new Latin American song', 1970s movement that influenced politically conscious university students (486)

nueva trova 'New song', name given in 1972 to the *canción protesta* 'protest song' created in 1967 and which began in Cuba (103, 486, 796, 829, 831–32)

nung-subaldá Large Kogi calabash trumpet (185)

nurá-mëe 'Horsefly', free-swinging whirled-plaque aerophone ("bullroarer") among the Desana (153)

ñavi maillai Traditional wedding ritual of Ecuador (425)

ñembo'é kaagüy Guaraní fertility-related prayer dance (202, 203)

ñemongaraí Argentine Mbyá annual ceremony related to the ripening of fruits (254–55)

ogan Haitian iron idiophone struck with a stick (883, 884)

okès bastreng Haitian urban, French-influenced string and wind bands (889)

okoma Large Wayana ceremony that is part of the *marake* boys' initiation ritual (166)

öl Mapuche precomposed style of ceremonial song (236)

omans St. Lucian triple-meter dance resembling the waltz (946)

omele Smallest membranophone in the *orisa* drum ensemble in Trinidad (955)

omichicahuaztli Náhuatl name for rasp made from the bone of a deer or deerlike animal (601)

onjènikon Haitian song specialist (884)

ónwehani Among the Garifuna of Belize, the spiritual possession that frequently occurs as female participants dance during the *dügü* ritual (672)

opowe Long cry indicating the end of a vocal or instrumental Waiãpi tune (159)

oratorio Profane musical performance given by blacks during religious festivities in colonial Mexico (603)

orchestral biguine Urban *biguine* of Martinique, with strong French influence and sung in Creole (916)

orisa (1) 'Deity' in Yoruba (Trinidadian spelling), in Trinidadian Orisa (954–56); (2) Orisa, religion that celebrates Yoruba deities in Trinidad (954–57); (3) drum ensemble (955)

orisha 'Deity' in Yoruba (Cuban spelling), in Cuban Santería (823–24)

orixá 'Deity' in Yoruba (Brazilian spelling), in Brazilian Candomblé (341)

orlo Purépecha double-reed, capped, tubular aerophone (similar to the European crumhorn) introduced by colonial missionaries (577)

orocoveño Puerto Rican *seis* from Orocovis (939)

orquesta de toros Ecuadorian ensemble of transverse flute, *caja* and *bombo* (415, 422)

orquesta típica 'Typical orchestra,' (1) Argentine tango ensemble of 1920s (263, 273–74); (2) ensemble in the central Peruvian highlands consisting of saxophones, clarinets, violins, and harp (474); (3) Mexican ensemble in which musicians clad in folkloric garb played regional melodies on a conglomeration of (primarily stringed) instruments (622); (4) instrumental ensemble characteristic of Cuban music (827, 832, 835)

orum The supernatural world in Yoruba cosmovision (352)

oticonte Nahua friction idiophone made from half a calabash covered with a skin onto which a stick is attached and then rubbed (565)

oungan Haitian Vodou priest (883)

ounsi Haitian Vodou initiate (883)

óuu Mixtec single-headed, deep-bodied wooden membranophone resembling the Nahua *huéhuetl* (564)

owirúame Tarahumara curer (585)

Ox Tum Modern-day Guatemalan version of *Baile del Tun* (724)

oyne 'Weeping', long mourning ceremony for Tukano leader or elder (154) *pachallampe* Chilean Aymara potato-sowing ritual (361)

Pachamama 'Mother earth' in the ancient Andes (256, 289)

pagar mandas Also *promesas*, *ofrendas*, throughout the Spanish- and Portuguese-speaking Americas, the fulfilling of religious vows, promises, or offerings for divine intervention (562)

pagode A 1980s variety of Brazilian samba song form with racial and political overtones (351)

pahko Religious fiesta among the Yaqui (590)

pa'i Mbyá religious leader (254–55)

pai de santo Brazilian male temple leader in Candomblé (342)

paichochi Bolivian seed pod rattles worn on the ankles (285)

pailas Cuban paired membranophones with cylindrical metal bodies (834)

paisade Quadrille dance movement that imitates the construction of wattle-and-daub homes in Carriacou (871)

paisanazgo Also *guancasco*, Honduran celebrations with a variety of music and dance that often revolve around the physical meeting of images of the patron saints of each community (743–44)

pajé Term for a shaman in many native South American cultures (161)

Pajelança Brazilian religion in Amazon region (341)

paki Ecuadorian male lead singer (425)

pala Also *mano*, Puerto Rican pegbox (934)

palais Simple tentlike structure in which Orisa feasts are held in Trinidad (955)

Palchasqa Also *Palcha*, Q'ero alpaca fertility ritual in February or March (226–27, 228)

palmetas Colombian wooden spatulas that are struck together (401)

palo 'Stick' or 'log', (1) a long drum and its music, associated with saints' festivals in Dominican Republic (104, 851, 854, 856); (2) *palos*, Venezuelan stick idiophone played on the side of wooden-bodied drums (528)

pampa corneta In Huancavelica, Peru, a vertical wooden trumpet three to four meters long and made of wood (471–72)

pan Single instrument from the steelband tradition of the Caribbean, made from a steel oil drum (96, 953, 960–63)

panalivio Also *penalivio*, Afro-Peruvian sarcastic song of lament about slavery (487, 495)

pandeiro Brazilian frame drum like a tambourine with jingles (309, 326, *328*, 329, 346)

pandero Puerto Rican and Dominican round frame drum, like a tambourine but without jingles (609)

pantañ Also *panatañ*, upright, hourglass Sumu drum, hollowed from a solid block of mahogany or cedar (750–51)

pañuelo 'Handkerchief', Puerto Rican dance choreography that includes swinging a handkerchief (939)

parabién 'Best wishes,' (1) Chilean genre similar to the *tonada*, performed as a marriage greeting and congratulatory song for a bride (368); (2) wake for a dead child (709)

paracá Guarijío harp (553)

parakata uarakua 'Butterfly dance', Purépecha temple priestess dance (576)

paranda From Spanish *parranda*, in Belize, a Garifuna genre resembling a serenade and serving as a vehicle of social criticism, usually composed by men (675)

parang In Grenada and Trinidad and Tobago, a Venezuelan-inspired Christmas caroling tradition accompanied by a *cuatro* guitar; the term is a corruption of *parranda* (538, 868, 871, 953, 959–60)

pareado Chilean two-line stanza of seven and five syllables (369)

pareja In Imbabura, Ecuador, dance music for a child's wake performed on harp with *golpeador*, characterized by a fast 2/4 or 6/8 meter (418, 422–24)

parranda Also *sarabanda*, (1) Christmas caroling tradition in Spanish-speaking America (538, 859); (2) Guatemalan music used for celebrating in the streets (698, 733, 734)

parrilladas Steakhouses that feature Paraguayan folk music (461)

partido-alto Afro-Brazilian folklike dance of primarily black connoisseurs (351)

paruntsi Ecuadorian musical bow (417)

pasacalle Ecuadorian national folk music genre (417, 427)

pasada See *zapateo criollo*

pasaje Venezuelan dance music genre (540)

pasante Bolivian festival ritual sponsor (291)

pascola Guarijío comic dance; ritual host and dancer of the *pahko* (552, 554, 590, 592–93)

pasillo (1) Colombian and Ecuadorian folk music genre that is an adaptation of the Austrian waltz (101, 387, 391–93, 417, 427); (2) *pasillo instrumental*, fast, sectional instrumental genre of Colombia, characterized by alternation of duple and triple meters (382, 383, 391, 392–93); (3) *pasillo lento*, waltzlike vocal folk music genre of Colombia and Ecuador, known for its nostalgic and romantic texts and melancholic melodies (391–92)

pass-play Children's game songs of Carriacou and Trinidad and Tobago (868, 953)

patacoré Rapid, complex *currulao* rhythm of Colombia (404)

Patagon Also *Tehuelche*, extinct native American culture of Tierra del Fuego (357)

patronal festivals Saint's-day celebrations (47, 62; *see index under* festivals)

paya Chilean audience-proposed theme developed as an octosyllabic line (367–70)

payada Uruguayan musical duel or competition (512)

payador (1) Uruguayan singer who improvises poetic texts to a given musical form (512); (2) usually plural, *payadores*, Argentine challenge singers and vocal ensembles (262)

payé Powerful Tukano shaman who cures illnesses, functions as the communicator between Tukano hunters and the supernatural masters of the animals, and presides over life-cycle ceremonies (150–51, 153–54)

pee 'Play', generic term for Aluku ceremonies (439)

peles rojas 'Red skins', Chilean patronal festival dance group that imitates American Indians with dances and costumes derived from North American movies (362, 364)

pelota tatá Activity of the Paraguayan *fiesta de San Juan* in which a tar- and kerosene-soaked ball of rags is set afire and kicked through the crowd (459)

peña (1) Private gathering place or touristic nightclub where folk musicians perform in certain Andean cities where tourism is common (49, 298, 501, 858); (2) in Argentina, a regionally oriented meeting place for dance and food celebrations (262, 263); (3) *peñas folklóricas*, restaurants featuring neofolkloric music (486)

périco ripiao Nickname of small *merengue típico* 'typical merengue' dance music group in Dominican Republic, from the name of a 1930s brothel (856, 857, 860)

peristil Large area of a Haitian temple where dancing takes place (887)

petición de lluvia Mixtec petition for rain on Saint Mark's Day (566)

Petro Creole deities of Vodou in Haiti, possibly with some Taino influence (855, 883, *884*)

pewutún Diagnostic Mapuche medical ritual (362)

peyú vári Also *goo*, 'turtle to scratch', large tortoiseshell idiophone covered with beeswax and rubbed with the musician's hand, producing a low-pitched hum (151)

phalahuita Transverse flute of Peru (471)

phutu wankara Bolivian long double-headed cylindrical drum (285)

pia manadi In Belize, a processional play involving the death and resurrection of one of the characters and displaying traits resembling those of English mumming plays (673–74)

picó Powerful and elaborately decorated mobile sound system in Colombia for playing pop music by disk jockeys (411)

picong Verbal duels or "wars" between calypsonians in Trinidad and Tobago (86, 96, 963)

pie forzado 'Forced foot', style of *décima* in which the tenth line is always the same (938)

Pierrot Grenade Carnival characterization of an effete, shabbily dressed patois-speaker in Grenada and Trinidad and Tobago (866, 965)

piezas sagradas 'Sacred pieces' (573)

pífano Also *pifano*, (1) northeastern Brazilian *caboclo* transverse flute made of cane, plastic, or metal (325, 329); (2) Bolivian cane transverse flute with six finger holes (284, 286, 287); (3) Ecuadorian duct flute with six finger holes (210, 415)

pifülka Also *pifilka*, Mapuche single- and double-tubed ductless flute (panpipe type), usually made from wood but also from cane (233–34, 252–53, 358)

piloilo Chilean two- to five-tubed panpipe made of stone, clay, cane, or wood (358)

pinkui Ecuadorian transverse flute with one blowhole and two finger holes (416)

pinkullu Also *pincollo, pinculu, pincullo, pincullu, pingollo, pinkillo, pinkuyllo, pinquillo,* (1) central Andean end-blown duct flute of Quechua origin with three to eight finger holes (35, 209–10, 250, 280, 286, 289, 468, 470–71); (2) Chilean cane duct flute (*pinquillo*) played alone or accompanied by *bandola* (358); (3) *pingullo,* Ecuadorian end-blown duct flute played in pipe-and-tabor fashion (210, 415); (4) *pinculu,* Q'ero vertical, notched, six-note edge aerophone (226–27)

pinkullwe Mapuche cane vertical flute (358)

pipimemyra End-blown Waiãpi edge aerophone (159, 161)

pirekua (1) Purépecha singing genres influenced by the waltz (578, 579–81); (2) *pirekua-abajeño,* Purépecha song variant of *abajeño* featuring hemiola (579)

pirkansa Ceremonial communal construction music in the Peruvian Andes (478)

pissenlit Trinidadian transvestite band in practice during carnival before 1884 (965)

pisteros Also Spanish *fiesteros,* Tarahumara feast sponsors (587)

pito Also *pitu,* 'pipe', in Spanish, (1) central Andean cane, metal, wooden, or plastic end-blown duct flute of Spanish or indigenous origin with from two to six finger holes, often used with a small tambor to accompany mestizo dances (212, 216, 406, 757); (2) cane or wooden transverse flute with six finger holes in southern Peru and Panama (211, 227, 471, 777, 781, *782*); (3) another name for the Atlantic coastal Colombian *caña de millo,* an idioglottal transverse clarinet of cane or millet with four finger holes, used in the the performance of the traditional *cumbia* (402, 406, *407*); (4) *pito y tambor* 'pipe and tabor', mestizo one-person ensemble of flute and drum to accompany saint's-day dances (406, 739)

pitucahue Mapuche stone panpipes (233)

platillos Colombian cymbals (403)

plena Puerto Rican dance-music genre of the second half of the twentieth century, featuring commentary about work and events (520, 939–40)

Pocomía Syncretic religion incorporating traditional African and Protestant beliefs and practices in Costa Rica (688)

poetas populares Chilean 'popular poets', singer-composers of the *verso* (367)

polca European-derived social dance, from "polka" (89)

Popol Vuh 'Book of Counsel', manuscript from shortly after the Spanish Encounter from the Quiché region of central Guatemala (650, 721, 732)

popygua'i Guaraní idiophone made of two wooden sticks struck together (200)

porfia Brazilian musical duel (307)

pork knockers Guyanese colloquial name for gold diggers (448)

porro Fast rhythmical Atlantic coastal Colombian musical style for ensemble of *gaitas* that developed from the *cumbia* (403, 406)

porteños Argentine 'people of the port' or Buenos Aires residents (264)

posadas (1) Guatemalan pre-Christmas singing, mainly a Ladino custom (653, 724); (2) Mexican musical reenactment of Mary and Joseph's journey to Bethlehem (614–15)

post-zouk Martinique continuation of *zouk* using richer harmonies and orchestral diversity (919)

prato-e-faca Brazilian 'plate-and-knife' idiophone (349)

pre-Columbian Before Columbus, referring to the ancient Americas (555)

precordillera Lower elevations or foothills of the Andes (357)

pregón Peruvian street vendor's call or song (495)

prenting Jamaican long, cylindrical membranophone (897–98, 902)

programas folklóricos 'Folk programs', on several commercial radio stations in Lima, Peru (484)

promeseros Paraguayan festival pilgrims, both children and adults, often dressed as the patron saint (458)

proximal In organology, the portion of the musical instrument closest to the mouthpiece (9)

puel purrún Mapuche 'dance to the east', social dance (236–37)

puerca Gourd-and-membrane friction drum (378)

pujador 'Pusher', Panamanian drum used in *conjuntos* (774–75)

Pukkumina Also Pukko, Jamaican Revival tradition (903)

pulipuli Notched end-blown flute in the central Andes (209)

pulilitu Bolivian animal-horn trumpet (287)

pulley In Montserrat, an accordion, concertina, or melodion (924)

pululu Bolivian gourd trumpet (287)

pump Membranophone made from a hollow tree trunk with goatskin or sheepskin on either end (815)

punta (1) Social-commentary song-and-dance form, the most popular and best-liked Garifuna genre (675, 733, 734, 741); (2) *punta* rock, Guatemalan fusion of traditional *punta* and rock rhythms (675, 676–77, 733)

punteado Spanish term for a picking technique on guitar and other lute-type stringed instruments (288)

punto (1) Elegant, stately Panamanian couple dance (772, 778); (2) Cuban instrumental accompaniment related to the *punto campesino* (833); (3) *punto campesino* (also *punto guajiro*), Cuban song genre associated with the rural population, usually based on the *décima* and its many variants (827, 828, 833)

purahéi asy 'Mournful polka', song on the subject of the Passion (458)

purísimas Referent to the Immaculate Conception, songs of the Nicaraguan Pacific Coast praising the Virgin Mary (762–63)

puro Ecuadorian gourd aerophone (416)

purrum Argentine *nquillatún* song of supplication by women (254)

pututu Small Andean valveless trumpet made from a single cow horn, conch shell, or piece of tin (211, 227, 287, 472)

puwelke Mapuche cane flute (234)

puya Fast, rhythmically complex style in Colombia (406)

qawachan In Peru, contrasting theme in a faster tempo (477)

q'ayma 'Insipid', referring to old Bolivian carnival melodies (294)

qia 'Leader' in the *julajula* Bolivian double-unit panpipe tradition (*285*)

qina, qina-qina Also *kena, quena,* Aymara end-blown notched flute (286, 290)

quadrilha Brazilian social dance or square dance generally associated with festivals in honor of Saint John during the June celebrations in the northeast (309, 331)

quadrille Also set dance, (1) Afro-Caribbean interpretation of nineteenth-century European set dance (773, 798, 799, 802, 809, 842, 865, 871–72, 907–908, 971–72); (2) the five parts of the country and jumbie dances (924–25); (3) *quadrille au commandement,* Guadeloupe quadrille in which the *konmandè* calls the dancers' steps (878)

quebrado 'Broken' or 'turned' motion in Nahua dance (561)

quelbeys Topical songs of local origin in the Virgin Islands (971)

quena Spanish orthography of an Aymara name for a notched, end-blown edge aerophone of the central Andes (467, 469, 470; *see also kena, qina*)

que-que Guyanese action song-dance performed at weddings and wakes (445)

quijada Also *charrasga,* African-derived scraped or struck idiophone made from the defleshed, dried jawbone of an ass, mule, or horse (360, 377, 414, 476, 492, 565, 709, 834)

quijongo Nicaraguan and Costa Rican musical-bow monochord of African origin, made from a long wooden bow with a single metal string and one or two gourd resonators (694, 698, 757–58)

quinceaños 'Fifteen years old', (1) debutante parties in Costa Rica (698); (2) *quinceañera,* girl's fifteenth birthday celebration in Paraguay, a time for music making (461–62) *quinjengue* Afro-Brazilian drum (348)

quinquerche Also *quinquercahue*, Mapuche musical bow (234)

quintillas Five-line *copla* (368, 608)

quinto Smallest and highest pitched of the Cuban *tumbadora* membranophones (831)

quioscos Bandstands set up in town plazas across Mexico in the late 1800s (604)

quipa Also *qquepa*, conch-shell trumpet in Ecuador and Peru (416, 472)

quirquincho Also *charango*, 'armadillo', small guitar made from the shell of an armadillo (473)

quitiplás Venezuelan bamboo stamping tubes (527)

ra'anga Generic Waiãpi category for edge and reed-concussion aerophones (159, 160, 161)

rabeca Brazilian three- or four-stringed bowed lute (309, 311, 329)

rabel Also *violín*, European-derived stringed instrument originating in the Renaissance period, usually with three strings, played with a bow like a violin (255, 360, 727)

Rabinal Achí 'Hero of Rabinal', modern-day version of Guatemalan *Baile del Tun* (653, 724, 729, 731)

Radá White deities of Vodou in Haiti (883, 884)

rada Trinidadian songs of the Arada immigrants from the Dahomean city of Allada (953)

rada-ason See *tchatcha*

Radio Fantástica Argentine FM radio station dedicated exclusively to *música tropical* (266)

Radio Tropical Argentine FM radio station dedicated exclusively to *música tropical* (266)

rajaleña Improvisational street festival *bambuco*-related song genre of Colombia, characterized by African-derived traits such as cross rhythms and responsorial singing, often to insulting, critical, and sexually oriented texts (377, 381, 384, 385–86, 389, 391)

rake 'n' scrape (1) Music historically used to accompany quadrille dances in the Bahamas (805–806); (2) 1990s term derived from the characteristic idiophones used to perform this rhythmic music (carpenter's saw or ridged bottle) (805–806)

rama Advent tradition in Mexico that involves groups of adults and/or children going from home to home asking for gifts (615)

Ramadan Also Pasa, annual monthly celebration which features fasting and other Islamic ritual acts (443, 507)

ramada (1) Rustic dwelling (552); (2) Mapuche song and dance feast (236)

ranchera (1) Mexican song genre (101, 620–21, 703, 716); (2) Argentine social dance performed during a *jineteada* (256, 261); (3) Uruguayan name for the European *mazurca* dance (516); (4) Chilean dance following religious festivals and communal work efforts (366)

rancherías (1) Hamlets of several families, each occupying a one- or two-room house in the Sierra Madre of Mexico (552, 582); (2) slums in Venezuela (542)

rancheros de pastorela Purépecha Christmas shepherds/farmers (579)

rap consciência Afro-Brazilian 'consciousness rap', an alternative to hip-hop (354)

rapá Hunting bow that the Aché-Guayakí use as a musical instrument by placing it over a resonating container (455)

rara (1) Haitian spring processional festival; (2) religious societies of the sugarcane plantations of Haiti and the Dominican republic (795, 885–87)

rasgueado Spanish term for chordal strumming with fingernails on guitar and lute-type stringed instruments (288, 381, 460, 541, 608, 654, 698)

rasguido doble Argentine polka-derived social dance (269)

raspu Gourd rasp of the Netherlands Antilles (928)

Rastafarianism Afro-Jamaican religion based on peace, love, self-expression, self-reliance, and black dignity, musically important for the origins of reggae (97, 898–99, 901, 904)

ravé Mbyá descendant of the *rabel*, a three-stringed bowed chordophone (201)

reaho Yanomamö feast that often celebrates the dead (173)

rêco-rêco Brazilian percussive gourd, metal, or door-spring scraper used in a wide variety of musical traditions (308, 329)

recreos Sunday morning concerts following the church mass in Costa Rica (699)

redoblante (1) Uruguayan snare drum (511); (2) Venezuelan side drum (528)

redondo Venezuelan double-headed drum with internal hourglass shape (527–30, 535)

reducciones 'Reductions', mission towns established by the Jesuits in Paraguay that were important for music teaching and performance by native Americans (453)

reel dance Family ritual of Tobago accompanied by Scottish violin reels (953, 959)

reggae (1) Internationally popular Jamaican music derived from *mento* with Rastafarian influences (97–98, 910, 912); (2) *reggae resistência*, Brazilian 'resistance' synthesis in reggae form (353)

reggaespañol Colombian hip-hop or dance-hall reggae with Spanish lyrics (410)

reisado Brazilian cycle of dramatic dances typically featuring the appearance of a bull (334–35)

repeater Shorter version of the Jamaican *fun-deh* (898)

repicador (1) Panamanian single-headed drum (774–75, 778); (2) Puerto Rican first *bomba* drum (937)

repique Brazilian high-pitched snare drum (309, 352)

répondè Guadeloupe choir that answers the song leader in call-and-response songs (874, 876)

requinteo Melodic ornamentation in Costa Rica (698)

requinto (1) Small acoustic lead-guitar type of El Salvador and Paraguay (457, 708); (2) a four-stringed, narrow-bodied Mexican guitar, plucked with plectrum fashioned from cow horn or a plastic comb (609); (3) small Colombian ten- or twelve-stringed *tiple* (381); (4) small six-stringed guitar, found in the central and northwestern parts of Honduras (743)

resbalosa Amorous Peruvian song and dance with syncopated rhythm, choreography based on *escobillada* (481, 499)

respodadoras Also *respondedoras*, responsorial chorus of women in Colombia and Ecuador (404, 427–28)

responsero Singer of funeral songs in Peru (478)

retirada Final part of *murga* theatrical presentations in Uruguay (517)

retreta Sunday performances by municipal, paramilitary, or military bands in Costa Rica, the Dominican Republic, and Uruguay (516, 699, 858)

Revival Principal Jamaican Afro-Christian cult (901, 903–904)

revuelta Alternate name for Venezuelan *joropo* music (540)

rewe Mapuche altar (236)

reyes (Span.); *reis* (Port.) 'Kings', Christmas music tradition about the Magi or Three Kings throughout Latin America (312)

rezadores Folk priests in the Dominican Republic (848)

rezos 'Prayers' in Spanish; rosary-reciting meetings in Costa Rica (695, 855)

rhyming spiritual Unaccompanied song genre derived from the Bahamian anthem (804–805)

ring dance In Jamaica, African-derived solo dance performed in the center of a ring made by the other dancers (809–11)

ring games Jamaican song-games played by children and adults at wakes and moonshine *dahlins* (905)

ring-play African-derived children's play in Jamaica that is heavily influenced by European children's games and related to the jump-in dance (810–11)

road march Trinidadian music for street dancing (962)

rock en español Rock sung in Spanish (104, 486, 716)

rock steady Short-lived music and dance fad in Jamaica in the late 1960s (910, 912)

rojão Also *baião de viola*, Brazilian syncopated instrumental pattern performed on the *viola* during a *desafio* (327)

romance (1) Spanish colonial narrative song form or ballad, usually sung solo or with guitar accompaniment (57, 389, 616, 695, 758, 849); (2) in Chile, old-style narrative song with an indeterminate number of quatrains recited or sung in one musical sentence (367–68) *roncadora* 'Snorer', a cane or wooden duct flute played in pipe-and-tabor fashion in Ancash Department, Peru (210, 471)

ronda (1) Circular children's game of Mexico (617); (2) Chilean children's game-song derivative of the *romance* (366, 367); (3) *rondas infantiles*, children's game or ring songs (695)

rondador 'One who makes the rounds', a single-unit panpipe from Ecuador with up to thirty tubes, so named because it was once used by night watchmen who made the rounds of Quito, playing their panpipes (208, 416, 426)

rondadorcillos Small eight-tubed single-unit panpipe from Ecuador (210)

rondalla In Colombia, a group of musicians playing instrumental music with Spanish-derived instruments; *see also estudiantina, lira, tuna* (383)

rook jaw In Barbados, scraped idiophone consisting of two jagged sticks that are rubbed together (815)

rosario 'Rosary', (1) *rosario a la Santa Cruz*, Puerto Rican sung rosary to the Holy Cross (936); (2) *rosario cantado* (also *rosario cantao*), sung version of the rosary (795, 935–36); (3) *rosario de promesas*, Puerto Rican sung 'rosary of promises' (935–36); (4) *rosario para los muertos*, Puerto Rican sung rosary ritual for 'good living' or 'dying' (936)

rum Largest Brazilian *atabaque* drum (32, 343)

rum shop Montserrat bar and provision store hosting storytelling, music, song, and dance performers (924, 926)

rumba (1) Nineteenth-century suburban Cuban musical genre at popular secular festivals (827, 832); (2) Cuban-derived couple-dance genre (100, 371, 829, 830–31)

rumpi Middle-sized Brazilian *atabaque* drum (343)

rushin' A form of marching or dancing with shuffling steps in the Bahamas (804)

sacabuche Also *zambomba*, in El Salvador and Honduras, friction membranophone, constructed from a large gourd, cut and covered at one end with a skin into which a stick is inserted and rubbed (709, 742)

saleone Jamaican *salo* song type (902)

saliman Cylindrical membranophone of the Jamaican Maroons (897–98)

salo Jamaican secular song (902)

saloma Panamanian vocal melody or recited chant with words or vocables (685, 686, 773, 780)

salsa Afro-Hispanic Caribbean song and dance form rooted in the Cuban *son* that is today an internationalized form no longer associated with any one country (102, 133, 383, 403, 410, 487, 520, 622, 693, 829)

salsódromos Nightclubs for dancing salsa in Peru (487)

salve (1) Unaccompanied song with religious texts diffused by missionaries since colonial times, sung at *velorios* (258, 366, 533,

536); (2) *salve con versos*, in the Dominican Republic a *salve* with added text in an Africanized musical style (856–57); (3) *Salve Regina*, 'Hail, Holy Queen', Spanish translation of a Marian antiphon (847–48, 850–51)

samba Brazilian generic term designating a wide variety of secular musical and dance styles of African origin (108, 313–17, 348–49, 350–54)

sambay Guatemalan erotic dance (733, 734)

samba caporal Chilean *bailes de salto* of Brazilian-Bolivian origin (362)

sambúda Yekuana cylindrical double-headed drum (177)

San Blás Saint Blaise, patron saint of Paraguay, whose feast is celebrated on 3 February (459)

San Juan Saint John, patron saint throughout the southern Americas, whose feast is celebrated on 24 June (257, 384, 426, 535)

sanba (1) Haitian poet-composer (885); (2) soloist in call-and-response singing of the *konbit* (885)

sangere Suyá invocations to influence the body (145)

Sango African-derived syncretic religion of Trinidad and Tobago (954–57); *see also* Shango

sanha Chilean tenor-register *siku* (358)

sanjuán (1) Popular mestizo dance form in Ecuador (417); (2) in Imbabura, Ecuador, dance music for a child's wake performed on harp with *golpeador*, characterized by its simple duple meter and melodic repetition (418, 423–24, 426–27, 428, 430–31)

sanjuanero Southern Colombian festive *bambuco* (381, 385, 387, 389)

sanjuanito 'Little *sanjuán*', a term used by mestizo and Afro-Ecuadorian musicians to denote an expanded form of *sanjuán*, which in its expanded form may have detailed narrative song texts (426–27)

sankeys St. Lucian gospel hymns named after the evangelist Ira David Sankey (795, 865, 948, 953)

sanshin Three-stringed plucked Okinawan lute, similar to the *shamisen* but covered with snakeskin, played by people of Okinawan heritage in Argentina, Brazil, Paraguay, and Peru (87–88)

Santa Cruz Feast of the Holy Cross (709)

Santa Maria Afro-Brazilian rhythmic pattern (346)

São Bento grande Brazilian *berimbau* rhythmic pattern in *capoeira* (346)

São Bento pequeno Brazilian *berimbau* rhythmic pattern in *capoeira* (346)

sarambo *Velación* genre based on the *zapateo* in the Dominican Republic (856)

sarangi Bowed lute of Indian origin, used as a melodic instrument in Surinam, Guyana, Trinidad, and elsewhere by people of Indian heritage (901)

saraos Evening parties with dancing and music in Costa Rica (693)

sarocla 'Little mule', game-dance in Costa Rica (684)

sau 'Ground', Sumu funerary ritual held for the death of a woman (750–51)

sawaere Wayana body of children's songs learned from the Saramaca Maroons in French Guiana (166)

saya Afro-Bolivian tropical syncretic music style, formerly a praise song (293, 297)

scratch bands Also *fungi* bands, ensembles identified with a movement to maintain native cultural traditions of the Virgin Islands and that perform at social dances, festivals, fairs, and private parties (969–71)

scrubbers Small band of strolling musicians hoping for reward from householders during the Christmas season in Barbados (819)

seco Panamanian single-headed drum (774)

segon Haitian drum of medium size and pitch, that "talks" with the *manman* (883)

seguidilla (1) Cuban genre belonging to the *punto campesino* family (833); (2) Chilean genre with seven-line *cueca* stanzas of five and seven syllables with fourth line repeated (369–70, 607)

segunda 'Second' (supporting) drum of the Garifuna in Belize (671)

seis (1) Puerto Rican lively genre for dancing (934, 938–39); (2) Puerto Rican slow genre for singing (938–39); (3) small Venezuelan guitar with six strings (531)

sekeseke Warao rustic violin played for entertainment (189, 192)

sêkêti Often cryptic Surinam Maroon songs and dances that are a major form of social commentary (506)

Semana Santa Holy Week (419)

semaneros 'Workers by week', Purépecha organized by Friar Juan de San Miguel for study of European organ and choral practice (577)

señalada Mapuche annual animal-branding gathering (237, 256)

senasawim Rattle with a wooden handle and metal discs, like a sistrum, among the Yaqui (590)

senasum Guarijio sistrum (554)

sencilla Chiapas marimba (725–26)

seremoni In Haiti, Vodoun service that includes song, dance, and drumming (883)

serenata 'Serenade', (1) song genre frequently performed at Paraguayan *quinceañeras*; a courting, congratulatory, or devotional serenade (383, 462, 618, 698); (2) *serenatas*, the early hours, when *serenata* performances traditionally occur (698)

sesquiáltera Spanish-derived dual meter consisting of superimposed 3/4 and 6/8, often with alternation or hemiola (369, 395, 409, 415, 428, 460, 481, 540, 929)

set dances European-derived Jamaican dances (908)

seti Guatemalan square dance (733)

set-up Jamaican wake activities on the night of death (906)

sewei Sacred Warao strung rattle (189)

sextilla Six-line *copla* (608)

shabori Also *sablí, sapuli, saboli, shapori, shaboliwa*, Yanomamö shaman (170–71)

shakap Ecuadorian fruit-capsule waist rattle (414)

shakkas Jamaican maracas (897)

shak-shak (1) Onomatopoeic name for idiophone rattle made from mahogany or poinciana tree pod with its seeds inside respectively in the Bahamas and Barbados (803, 814–15); (2) common maracas in Guyana (443)

shakuhachi A Japanese notched vertical bamboo flute with four finger holes and one thumb hole, played by some people of Japanese descent in Brazil (88–89)

shamisen Three-stringed plucked Japanese lute played by people of Japanese heritage in Brazil and Peru (87–88)

Shango (1) Yoruba 'power', music devoted to the *orisa* deity of fire (often spelled Changó in Cuba and Miami; spelled Xangô in Brazil) (865, 953, 955); *see also* Sango

shukster Chordophone made with guitar string stretched from end to end on the side of a wooden house in Barbados (815)

sikro Also *sikru*, 'world', Sumu and Miskitu funerary ritual held for the death of a man (739, 750–51)

siku Also *sico* (pl. *sikuri* in Bolivia), double-unit panpipe consisting of six to eight (or more, seventeen tubes in Bolivia) closed cane tubes per half, requiring two people to play one instrument by interlocking the music (34, 207, 209, 216, 286, 357–58); *see also* arca, ira

sikuri (1) Sets or groups of *siku* or *siku* performers (286, 362, 469); (2) a particular type of music played by particular *siku* groups in Peru (362)

sinebui Garifuna shaman in Belize (670)

sineta Also *adjá*, small bronze bell in Uruguay (515)

sinsiru Bolivian bronze llama bells (285, 291)

sirínus 'Sirens', Andean supernatural beings, often carved into the necks of *charangos* and harps (294)

sísira Container rattle of the main Garifuna shaman in Belize (also *magara*) and Guatemala (also *chíchira*) (670, 733)

siwo Yekuana bark trumpet (179)

ska Jamaican popular dance music that began in the early 1960s (93, 97, 910, 912)

skroud St. Lucian homemade, local banjo (945)

slametan Indonesian ritual that affirms the unity of the Javanese community in Surinam (507)

soca Modern, danceable Trinidadian calypso form, short for *soul calypso* (75, 86, 95, 96, 410, 678, 908, 924, 964)

socabón Also *socavón*, simple Peruvian guitar accompaniment to the *décima* (482, 495)

son Pl. *sones*, diminutive *sonecito*, possibly from *sonar* 'to sound', (1) Mexican genre at the core of most regional musical styles oriented toward accompanying social dance, with vigorous, marked rhythm and fast tempo (550, 560, 603, 605–13); (2) Cuban song

tradition forming a type of *son* complex of genres (101, 827, 829–30)

sonador Second Puerto Rican *bomba* drum (937)

sonaja 'Timbrel' in Spanish, (1) container idiophone of various forms (680); (2) in Honduras and Guatemala, a spiked vessel rattle made from a gourd or calabash and filled with tiny stones or dried seeds (722, 723, 741); (3) Nicaraguan handheld semicircular wooden tambourine with metal jingles but no membrane (755–56, 761)

sonim Also *sones*, melodies among the Yaqui (590)

sontárusi Also Spanish *soldados*, 'soldiers' who take part in Tarahumara feast activities (586–87)

so'o kangwera Small deer-bone edge aerophone among the Waiãpi (159)

soot Ceremonial vessel stick rattle among the Lacandón Maya (657)

sörbö Circle dance to commemorate the creation of the Bribri world and to depict animals of the rain forest (634–35)

soukous Congolese dance music, popular in the Caribbean (93, 508, 879)

sovèyan Guadeloupe stylized hand-to-hand fighting accompanied by drumming and singing (876)

spèktak Also *gala*, Haitian urban music-and-dance concert featuring many performers (890)

spouge A particular rhythm underlying spouge music in Barbados, played on the cowbell, bass guitar, trap set, and other rhythm and electronic instruments (816, 820)

squash Hollow open-ended gourd idiophone of the Virgin Islands with notched grooves carved into one side and scratched with a multi-pronged metal scraper, used in scratch bands (969)

steelband Also pan, Trinidadian ensemble of tuned idiophones formed from metal oil drums, also found in Guyana and elsewhere in the English-speaking Caribbean (86, 96–97, 445–46, 953, 960–63)

stools Trinidadian altars commemorating various gods (958)

strathspey Grenadian slow waltz (866)

string band Late 1980s Montserrat youth band of guitars, banjos, ukuleles, and accordions (926)

stsököl (1) Funerary singer among the Bribri and Cabécar who sings during *sulàr* ceremony (633, 634); (2) *stsököl sini'pa*, assistants of the *stsököl* (634)

suara Kuna single, external duct, bamboo, end-blown edge aerophones played in pairs (641)

suduchu Yekuana five-tubed panpipe (178)

suila jut'as Bolivian heavy metal spurs attached to wooden sandals (285)

sukia (1) Nicaraguan Garífuna shaman (750–51, 752); (2) traditional Miskitu shaman (660)

sulàr 'Music for our people', one of the main funerary ceremonies of the Bribri and Cabécar (634)

supe Kuna single, external-duct, bamboo end-blown edge aerophones played in pairs (640–41)

surdo Brazilian double-headed drum used in many genres of Brazilian music, especially samba and its derivatives (309, 330, 352)

suruídey Sounding device, or vibrating reed, of the Yekuana bamboo clarinet (*tekeyĕ*) (178)

sware Haitian late-night dance (889)

syak Guadeloupe scraper made from a bamboo log ridged with transverse notches and rubbed by thin sticks (877)

tabla charango Bolivian flat-backed *charango* played during rainy season (213)

tablados Uruguayan street stages for carnival musical competitions (516)

taieira Dramatic Afro-Brazilian dance (347)

taita Lead male singer for Moxo *machetero* dance (141)

takipayanaku Bolivian insult songs sung by in-laws at weddings (291)

takuapú Indigenous Paraguayan bamboo stamping tube that may have strings of rattles attached, played by women (200, 454)

talátur Chilean water-praising invocation for irrigation (357, 360–61)

tali Palm-beaten cylindrical wooden membranophone (682)

tambito Local song-dance of Guanacaste, Costa Rica, attributed to the Talolingas ensemble (698)

Tambo Jamaican African-based cult (901, 903)

tamboo-bamboo (1) Grenada bamboo stamping tubes (866); (2) early twentieth-century Trinidadian carnival music played on lengths of bamboo (96, 962)

tambor Generic Spanish masculine term for a membranophone that exists in a variety of forms, either single- or double-headed, the latter often with a snare (*see index under* membranophones)

tambora (1) Generic Spanish feminine term for membranophone (*see index under* membranophones); (2) small, double-headed drum in *merengue* ensembles in Dominican Republic (*851*, 855); (3) long, tubular Afro-Venezuelan membranophone made from a log with two skin heads, played with one stick while held between the knees (528–30)

tamborazos zacatecanos Zacatecas-style Mexican pop bands (622)

tamborero In Peru, a person who beats on the box of the harp as a percussion instrument while a harpist plucks the strings (*see golpeador*) (474)

tambores Ensemble music of the Brotherhood of San Juan Bautista of Baní, Dominican Republic (855)

tamborete Peruvian version of the Chilean *tormento* (492)

tamboril (1) Ecuadorian double-headed drum, varying in size (415); (2) Uruguayan small drum (511, 515–16) *tamborim* Brazilian membranophone consisting of a small metal or plastic frame covered with a tight skin, played with a stick (309)

tamborita Small, double-headed drum of Mexico, played on the head and rim with two drumsticks (611)

tamborito 'Little drum', the national couple dance of Panama, featuring drum accompaniment (773, 774, 777–78)

tambú Also *bari*, (1) music-and-dance complex of Curaçao (928, 929); (2) membranophone, the most important African-derived instrument in the Dutch islands of the Leeward Antilles (929); (3) *tambu*, Brazilian large conical single-headed membranophone (307, 348); (4) *tambu*, Jamaican *salo* song type (902)

tamunangue Venezuelan suite of dances and music (533, 536, 539)

tanbou Membranophone in French or French-influenced locales (841–43, 876–77)

tangará Mbyá ritual dance-song (200, 201, 202)

tango (1) Argentine music and dance of nostalgia and melancholy that originated and is centered around Buenos Aires (90, 263–65, 371, 519); (2) *tango canción*, Argentine sung tango genre (263); (3) *tango característico*, Argentine characteristic sung tango genre (263); (4) *tango romanza*, Argentine instrumental tango genre (263)

tanguería 'Tango place', in Argentina and Uruguay, a recent Argentine name for tango dance club or locale where live tango performers can be heard (263, 520)

tani Kogi calabash container rattle (185)

tanpura Also *tambura*, among East Indian communities in Guyana, Surinam, Trinidad and elsewhere, a plucked lute that provides a drone (85, 950)

tapujeados Dance performed by men who disguise themselves with masks and eccentric clothing in El Salvador (713)

taquirari Bolivian tropical syncretic song style from the lowlands (292, 297, 361)

tara Bolivian broad flute timbre dense with harmonics (296)

tarima Wooden platform for foot-stamping (*zapateado*) dances among the Mixtec (567)

tarka In Bolivia, Chile, and Peru, a square or slightly hexagonal-shaped (cross-section) wooden duct flute with a hoarse sound (210, 287, 289, 295, 358, 471)

tarkeada Music played by a *tarka* ensemble (358, 361, 471)

tarol Brazilian thin snare drum (329)

tarola Spanish term for snare drum (565)

tasnewa Paya ritual that marks both birth and death (739)

tassa Kettle-type drum played with a stick at Muslim festivals and weddings in Guyana and Trinidad and Tobago (85, 444, 957, 959)

tayil Mapuche women's ritual/healing/lineage song (234–35, 236–37, 254)

tchatcha Gourd rattle filled with pellets for use

during Haitian Petro rites, analogous to *rada ason* (881, 883)

teatro callejero Traditional Uruguayan theatrical form (517)

teatro de revistas Type of light comic theater in Montevideo, Uruguay (516, 521)

tecolote 'Owl', whose hoot at dawn signals the end of Yuma social dance (597)

tejón 'Badger', dance among the Mixtec (566)

tekeyë Also *tekeya*, *wanna*, Yekuana ritual bamboo idioglottal clarinet with internal reed (*suruídey*), played in pairs, one male and the other female (34, 178)

temïmbi-púku Argentine vertical flute among the Chiriguano-Chané (253)

temimby ie piasá Transverse flute among the Chriwano of Paraguay (201)

temple 'Tuning', (1) *temple arpa*, Peruvian guitar tuning pattern (E–B–F#–D–A–F#), used to play a *huayno* or *carnaval* in B minor (473); (2) *temple diablo*, Peruvian guitar tuning pattern (E–C–G–D–B♭–G), used to play a *yaraví* in G minor (473)

teneboim Also *chairígoas*, Guarijio leg rattles made of moth cocoons filled with seeds (589, 590)

tenor Also *tenore*, low voice part in Venezuelan *tonos* ensemble (534)

teponahuaste Also *tepunahuaste*, in Mexico, the present-day Nahua *teponaztle* 'log idiophone' used in Christian ceremonies (558); *see also teponaztli, tun, tunkul*

teponaztli Also *teponaztle*, in Mexico, a Nahua hollowed-out log slit drum or gong with H-shaped incision on its top (9, 13, 550, 556–59, 589, 601–602, 680, 711, 724, 748)

tepuzquiquiztli Náhuatl name for a wooden or metal trumpet (601)

tequina Taino responsorial song leader (847)

terno Brazilian generic term for dramatic dance groups that perform during patron saint festivals (312–13)

terokará Board zither with five to seven strings played by the Aché-Guayakí of Paraguay (456)

terreiro 'Temple' in Afro-Brazilian syncretic religious worship in Brazil, Paraguay, and Uruguay (457, 515)

tibwa Martinique rhythm sticks (915, 918, 943, 946–47)

timbalada Afro-Bahian popular genre featuring timbre of the *timbal* (354)

timbales Cuban membranophones constructed from metal semi-spherical closed containers (834)

tina From Spanish 'washtub', Miskitu chordophone consisting of a single string made from vegetable fiber and fixed between the protruding end of a meter-long wooden pole and the bottom of an upturned tin washtub (661)

tingo Salvadoran log idiophone, related to the ancient *tepunahuaste*, personifying Saint Tingo (711)

tingting Dominican triangle (841)

tinka Carnival season celebration in Peru in which a llama is sacrificed and ritual offerings are buried for the deities (477)

tinku 'Encounter', (1) annual community rivalry ritual of Ecuador (426); (2) Bolivian ritual fighting (290)

tiñni Sumu drumstick (750)

tinquy Q'ero intercommunity popular social dance (228)

tinya Small Quechua handheld double-skin frame drum in Peru (206, 211, 469)

tiple 'Treble', (1) a medium-sized twelve-stringed, four-course guitar from Colombia (381, 387–88, 531, 849, 953); (2) three-stringed chordophone in Honduras (743)

tiplero Also *requintador*, 'one who plays treble', player who improvises contrapuntal melodies on *marimba* in Ecuador (427)

tirana Brazilian folk dance popular along border areas of Uruguay (516)

titiru Also *tiroro*, Wayana wooden lip-concussion aerophone used in rituals (165)

tiun 'Song' or 'tune', Miskitu young person's song (660, 663–64)

tiyoo Mixtec tortoiseshell struck with a deer antler, similar to the Nahua *ayotl* (563)

tlapitzalli Náhuatl name for an end-blown clay or bone tubular duct flute with four holes (601)

tlatlazcaliztli Nahua sound of trumpets (556)

toá Bolivian beeswax friction idiophone (285, 289)

toada Brazilian generic term for song, often associated with popular Catholicism (analogous to Spanish *tonada*) (307–309, 312–13, 332)

toá-toré 'Cavity', Tukano log idiophone and the sound it makes (151, *152*)

Todos Santos 'All Saints' or All Souls celebration in Americas (220, 290)

tonada Spanish for 'tune', (1) originally any intoned melody (367); (2) 1990s Chilean song performed by one or two singers in parallel thirds in nasal style (89, 367–68, 370); (3) characteristic Cuban melody in the *punto guajiro* (833); (4) *tonada de toros* 'song of the bulls', improvisatory verbal genre associated with ritualized alms collection in the Dominican Republic (849, 856)

tonadillas escénicas In Mexico, short, simple dramas, replete with new *sones* and other local melodies (603)

tôndáxin Mixtec rattle (563)

tondero Amorous dance and song of northern coastal Peru, related to *marinera* and *zamacueca* (481, 499)

tono 'Tune' or 'tone', (1) European-derived polyphonic song of Venezuela (534); (2) *tono de sikuri*, Chilean pentatonic *sikuri* music for procession (362); (3) *tono y rueda* 'tone and round', principal genre of the Chilean Aymara carnival festival (361)

toombah Eighteenth- to nineteenth-century Antiguan drum fixed with tin jingles and shells (798)

topamiento de comadres Argentine female

funeral dramatization ceremony of carnival (258–59)

toque 'Hit' in Spanish and Portuguese, Brazilian rhythmic pattern played on *berimbau* and other struck instruments in Latin America (346, 347, 352)

toré Among some native South Americans, a single-reed concussion aerophone, or clarinet type (178)

torito 'Little bull', (1) Purépecha musical form for carnival (578); (2) artifact for dance-games (578); (3) *torito kiringua*, slit drum idiophone (578)

tormento 'Storm', a Peruvian and Chilean idiophone made from a sheet of wood on four legs with bottle caps and wood chips placed or partially nailed on top (360, 492)

toro 'Bull', (1) *toro candil*, costume in Paraguay in which one or two men play the part of a fighting bull (459); (2) *toro huaco*, annual saint's day performance in Diriamba, Nicaragua (756, 761); (3) *toro que brinca*, among the Mixtec, '[dance of the] bull that jumps' (566); (4) *toros*, masked youths of Ecuador (415)

torrente Panamanian musical concept similar to scale (777, 780)

tortuga 'Turtle', (1) in Guatemala and elsewhere, a tortoiseshell gong struck on its ventral side with a bone, stick, or antler (653, 723); (2) Mixtec turtle dance (566)

totuma The fruit of a calabash tree used to make rattles, trumpets, and other implements among the Kogi, Warao, and other northern South American cultures (185, 189)

trabajo 'Work', in northern Peru, the working period signified by the music of a *clarín* (36)

tres Cuban six-stringed, double-coursed chordophone of the guitar family (30, 693, 830, 833, 849)

tres-dos Cuban medium-sized *tumbadora* membranophone (831)

trío 'Group of three', (1) in Ibero-American countries, three (usually) male musicians who sing while they accompany themselves on stringed instruments (guitar and guitar types) and possibly percussion (maracas, depending on the country) (694); (2) *trio elétrico*, Brazilian electric guitar trio accompanied by a small percussion group typical of Bahian carnival (337–38); (3) *trío romántico*, a Mexican-derived ensemble of three male musicians who sing sad, nostalgic, and romantic songs while accompanying themselves on guitars (592)

triste Term in Bolivia and Chile for a nostalgic song musically analogous to the Peruvian *yaraví* (477)

trompa (1) Venezuelan jaw's harp (Jew's harp), a plucked lamellophone (528); (2) Uruguayan chronicler's term for a trumpet type (510); (3) *trompe*, Mapuche jaw's harp (359)

trompeta de caracol Spanish term for conch-shell trumpet (533)

tropa 'Troop', Andean group of musicians who play a single type of instrument, such as a *tropa de sikuri* 295)

tropical 'Tropical', (1) Caribbean-based *cuarteto* style (274); (2) *tropicália*, Brazilian avant-garde music movement (318, 351); (3) *tropicalismo*, vanguard popular music movement of the late 1960s in Brazil (109–10)

trote 'Trot', a term used in Chile for the Andean *huayno* (373); *see* wayno, huayño

trova 'Tune', any song of late nineteenth-century to present, performed by Cuban singers called *trovadores* (831, 861)

trutruka Mapuche long end-blast cane trumpet with oblique mouthpiece and attached cow-horn bell (234, 252–53)

tsayantur Ecuadorian musical bow (416–17)

tuburada Solemn ritual of the Guarijío, a subsection of the *túmari* ceremony (552, 553–54)

tuk **band** Barbados ensemble featuring bass drummer, snare drummer, flute player, and triangle featuring a fusion of African and British elements (815–16)

tulé Wayana single-reed aerophone played in ensembles (161, 164)

tulu lulu Also *tulululu*, traditional Nicaraguan song-dance in which dancers pass one at a time under a couple's extended arms while onlookers sing out their names in the song's lyrics (754)

tumank Ecuadorian musical bow that uses the mouth as resonator (416–17)

tumao Cylindrical single-headed log drum of Surinam Maroons (505, 506)

túmari Also *túguri*, *tuwúri*, Guarijío celebration for thanksgiving, benediction, propitiation, fertilization, and/or curing; sometimes related to the agricultural cycle (552–54, 585)

tumba (1) Most popular dance and rhythm of the mid-twentieth century in all the Netherlands Antilles (930); (2) *tumba dominicana*, a *velación* of the northern part of the Dominican Republic (856); (3) *tumba francesa*, former ballroom dance of Santiago de Cuba, now performed only by national troupes (793, 826)

tumbadora Cuban membranophone (basically a conga drum) that originated in the context of the rumba (828, 831, 834)

tumbas Conga drums (691)

tum-tum In Barbados, double-headed log membranophone played by two men (815)

tun (1) In Guatemala, a Quiché Maya hollowed-out log slit drum or gong with H-shaped incision on its top (653, 724, 731) (*see* teponaztli, tunkul); (2) also *tum*, 'cylinder', a long Guatemalan wooden or metal valveless trumpet (729)

tuna (1) A group of musicians playing instrumental music with Spanish-derived instruments, especially common in Colombia and Peru (383) (*see also estudiantina, lira, rondalla*); (2) Panamanian street parade of musicians, singers, and townspeople (772)

tundito Pipe-and-tabor duet among the Otopame, each performer playing both a flute and a drum at the same time (571)

tunga-tunga Accompaniment pattern of Argentine *cuarteto* music (273, *274*)

tunkul In Guatemala, a Yucatec Mayan hollowed-out log slit drum or gong with H-shaped incision on its top (13, 658, 680); *see teponaztli, tun*

tuntui Also *tunduy*, Ecuadorian large slit drum (157, 164)

turas Venezuelan vertical male-female flute pair (533)

ture Also *tule*, *turé*, *tore*, large bamboo single-reed aerophone used throughout the Amazon (160–61, 435)

turélo Guarijío chanter (553)

turning Montserrat possession dance (924, 925)

turno Street fair in Costa Rica (700)

turú Guaraní generic and onomatopoeic name for trumpet (201)

turu-turu Miskitu mirliton made with a bat's wing stretched between two small pieces of reed held together by beeswax (660)

tutuguri The entire Tarahumara pre-Columbian ceremony complex (552, 585)

twoubadou Haitian groups that perform guitar-based music influenced by Cuban *son* groups (890, 891)

tzijolah Among the Guatemalan highland Maya, a three-holed flute that utilizes the harmonic series by a system of overblowing (654)

uaitúge From 'bell', Tukano external strung rattles of dried seeds worn on dancers' ankles and/or upper arms (151)

uaricza araui Pre-Columbian antiphonal dance of men and women sung by the Inca and a choir of young virgins (468)

uatapú Guaraní trumpet used to attract fish (201)

ufisha tayil Mapuche sheep lineage soul chant (235)

ukuku Q'ero costumed representation of a bear during Corpus Christi (229)

ülutún 'Small therapies', Mapuche medical ritual (362)

Umbanda Twentieth-century Afro-Brazilian syncretic religion that borrows from aspects of Candomblé, Macumba, and spiritism (259–61, 341, 344)

umbigada 'Navel', choreographic stomach bump of many Afro-Brazilian circle dances (303, 313–14, 348, 349)

una Short fife used in funerary celebrations among the Sumu (751)

ungá See ingá

upla pruan bara Miskitu wake (663)

urucu Red dye used in body painting and for the Waiãpi shaman (158)

úsêköl High priest among the Bribri (633)

úyanu In Belize, Garifuna unaccompanied, semisacred, usually mournful gesture-accompanying songs in irregular meter (672–73)

vacación In Imbabura, Ecuador, music for a child's wake performed on harp, characterized by its steady tempo and gradually descending melody, meant to drive away the demon from beneath the platform supporting the dead child (418, 424)

vaksin Also *banbou, vaccine*, Haitian single-note lip-concussion aerophone made of bamboo, PVC pipe, or metal and played in groups in interlocking fashion (885, 887)

vallenato (1) Rural musical and dance genre from northern Colombia, featuring accordion, drum, and scraper (39, 407); (2) urban musical and dance genre derived from its rural counterpart of northern Colombia, adding bass, guitar, conga, and cowbell to the rural accordion, drum, and scraper (39, 383, 407–408, 410, 411)

valona Décima-based genre in several parts found in the *tierra caliente* (hotlands), the western part of the state of Michoacán, Mexico (571, 607–608, 611–12)

vals 'Waltz', (1) romantic vocal music genre in triple meter found throughout Spanish-speaking America (387, 393–94, 475, 603–604, 615, 735); (2) Argentine social dance performed during *jineteada* (254, 261, 361); (3) *vals criollo*, 'creole waltz', most popular national music form in coastal Peru with origins in the mid-eighteenth century Viennese waltz (89, 101, 475, 481, 499–500, 697)

valseao Also *valseado*, 'waltzed' choreography (939)

vaquería Colombian cattle song genre, sung by herders to quiet the animals and communicate among themselves (408–409)

vaquita '[Dance of] the cow' in Managua, Nicaragua (761)

veiquoix Trinidadian Spanish-language songs (953)

vejiga Struck air-filled idiophone made from the bladder of an animal in Panama, played by the dirty little devils (380, *381*, 774, 781)

velación (1) Individually sponsored, annually recurring saint's celebration in the Dominican Republic (848); (2) Mixtec wake that lasts all night, accompanied by music (567)

veladas (1) Evening performances among some members of the African-descended population in the Dominican Republic (859); (2) *veladas escolares*, public performances at schools in Costa Rica (698)

velorio (1) Nightlong celebration or night watch to honor a saint or the Holy Cross in many Spanish-speaking countries (530, 534–35); (2) a nightlong wake for a deceased person in many Spanish-speaking countries (406); (3) *velorio de angelito* (also *wawa velorio*), Ecuadorian festive wake for infant or young child, known as *mampulorio* in Venezuela (403–404, 422–24); (4) *velorio de angelito*, Paraguayan wake of a young child (462); (5) *velorio de cruz* 'wake of the Cross' in Venezuela (534)

vénérés Eleventh night after a death in Guadeloupe (876)

veó-páme 'Cane parallel objects', panpipe of the Desana subfamily of Tukano, played antiphonally in male-female pairs (151)

verso 'Verse', (1) sung poetry accompanied by guitar or *guitarrón* in Chile (367);

(2) Dominican Republic ritual song genre for saints in folk Catholicism (849)

vèyé boukousou Guadeloupe wake celebrations (875)

vidé Spontaneous Martinique street parade (438, 918)

viejitos Purépecha dancers who wear old-men masks (579)

vihó Tukano mind-altering snuff inhaled through the nose by the *payé* (153)

vihuela (1) European-derived, five-stringed, hourglass-shaped, plucked chordophone (577); (2) five-stringed Mexican guitar with a convex back (571, 611, *612*, 708); (3) six-course sixteenth-century Spanish guitar (284); (4) *vihuela de mano* 'of the hand', Purépecha six-stringed, hourglass-shaped, plucked and strummed chordophone (577); (5) *vihuela de arco* 'of the bow', Purépecha bowed chordophone introduced by colonial missionaries (577)

villancico 'Rustic song', (1) popular Christmas song genre in Spanish-speaking America (113, 763); (2) Peruvian religious genre sung in Spanish and sometimes in Quechua (494–95); (3) Chilean *tonada* performed as a Christmas carol (367, 368); (4) exclusively religious Nicaraguan songs that show a remarkable retention of their (originally Spanish) melodic and lyrical form and content (763); (5) *villancico navideño*, Nicaraguan song genre praising the Virgin Mary and the Infant Jesus, sung during the Christmas season (763)

viola Brazilian plucked and strummed chordophone of Iberian origin (from *viola de mão*, 'of the hand'), with five double courses of ten or twelve metal strings (309–10, 325, 349)

violão 'Guitar' in Portuguese, the common Iberian six-stringed guitar (*see index under* chordophones)

violín 'Violin' in Spanish, (1) common European violin, introduced by colonial missionaries and disseminated throughout the Americas (*see index under* chordophones); (2) *violín de talalate*, northern Nicaraguan violin named for the soft, white *talalate* wood (751)

virgen 'Virgin', (1) a Roman Catholic icon symbolizing the Virgin Mary, but under different names, the object of devotion in many patronal festivals in the Americas (*62*); (2) Virgen de Guadalupe, religious festivity for all the Mixtec (559, 614); (3) Virgen de La Candelaria, 'Virgin of the Candles', ancient Chilean Catholic festivity (364–65); (4) Virgen de La Tirana, 'Virgin of the Tyrant', largest expression of religious syncretism in northern Chile (363–64); (5) Virgen de Las Peñas, 'Virgin of the Pains', oldest patronal festival among the Chilean Aymara (363); (6) Virgen de Punta Corral, Argentine procession attracting largest number of faithful in province of Jujuy (256)

visitas 'Visiting centers', (1) places where friars introduced European Christian music to Purépecha culture (577–78); (2) small, nearby suburbs of a mission in northwest Mexico (582)

viuda Ecuadorian widow figure of New Year's celebration (426)

Vodou Sometimes Anglicized as *voodoo*, Afro-Haitian religious system and Fon term for 'spirit' in Haiti (882–84)

vodu Also *papagadu*, Maroon ritual to the snake god in Surinam (505)

vodú Dominican Republic ceremony of African heritage characterized by spirit possession (851)

volcanto 'Volcano song', Nicaraguan genre of *nueva canción* associated with the Sandinista Revolution (764, 765)

wada Mapuche gourd rattle (358–59)

waika Also *guaika*, 'to kill a man or animal already dying from wound', an outsider term for some subgroups of the Yanomamö native Americans in southern Venezuela (169)

waka Guadeloupe music accompanied only by throat sounds, hand clapping, and foot stomping (875)

waka pinkillu Bolivian 'bull flute', three-holed duct flute played in pipe-and-tabor fashion (287)

waka tokori Bolivian dance that caricatures a Spanish bullfight (292)

wak'rapuku Also *wakrapuku*, Quechua Peruvian circular or spiral valveless trumpet made of cattle-horn sections or pieces of tin, often played in pairs of *primera* and *segunda* (211, 469, 471–72)

walagallo Curative ritual of the Nicaraguan Garífuna (669, 752–53)

walina Fixed song genre exclusively associated with the ceremonial cleaning of irrigation channels in Peru (476, 478)

waná Tubes used in Yekuana clarinet construction (178)

wanaragua Also John Canoe, old song-and-dance genre, composed and performed solely by men in Belize (673–74)

Wancay Bolivian mythical singer who has the mouth of a toad (283)

wandora Warao *cuatro*, small, four-stringed chordophone (189)

wanka Also *uanca*, Bolivian love song (468, 476)

wankara (1) Bolivian small handheld single-headed cylindrical drum with snare (285); (2) Bolivian large cylindrical double-headed drum (469)

warime Ceremony among the Venezuelan Pairoa (525)

wárini Masked dance that is a prelude to *wanaragua* among the Garifuna of Belize (673–74)

wasaha Yekuana pole or staff rattle (177)

wawallo Ecuadorian festive wake for infant or young child (422)

wayang Javanese puppet theater, performed by people of Javanese descent in Surinam to accompaniment of a gamelan (507)

wayno Also *huayno* in Quechua, *huayño* in Aymara, central Andean fast dance in duple meter, featuring a long-short-short rhythmic pattern (256)

wepasuni Guarijio goat stew served at the end of the *túmari* ceremony (554)

wibòt The evening during which the St. Lucian *chanté abwè* are performed (947)

wiri Rasp made from an elongated piece of steel serrated and scraped with a metal rod (929)

wiriki Also *widiki*, Yekuana quartz pebbles used in container rattles (177)

wisiratu 'Owner of pains', Warao priest-shaman in charge of upper cosmic realm (170, 189–91, 193, 194–95)

witakultruntufe 'Women carrying the drum', Mapuche female healers (235)

woowoo Also French reel, jumbie drum of Montserrat (924)

xácara Brazilian ballad of Iberian origin (307)

xancaa Dance of pre-Hispanic origin among the Otopame (570)

Xangô Portuguese orthography of Shango, a religion in Pernambuco, Brazil (341, 343)

xaxado Men's line dance of northeast Brazil (332)

xayácatl (1) *xayácatl de alastik*, Nahua dance of the flat disguise (561); (2) *xayácatl pasultik*, Nahua dance of the curled disguise (561)

xique Also *xike*, *sique*, most popular and widely dispersed mestizo dance of Honduras (744)

Xocotl Huetzi 'When the fruits fall down', ancient Aztec calendrical month celebration (556)

xote Northeastern Brazilian slow *caboclo* dance genre based on the schottische (332)

xudjiko Also *xudjiku*, Tukano long bark trumpets (155)

xul (1) Guatemalan vertical duct flute, open at the distal end (654, 723, 726, 778); (2)

Maya transverse cane flute with beeswax diaphragm and membrane mirliton (728–29)

yajé *Banisteriopsis caapi*, source of a mind-altering drink used by the Tukano *payé* (153)

yankunu Probably from 'John Canoe', Guatemalan masked warrior dance (734)

yaraví From Quechua *hawari*, in Peru a slow, lyrical and often emotional song section (473, 477)

yarraba African-derived Yoruba songs for secular dances in Trinidad and Tobago (953)

yawera Violin among the Guarijio in northern Mexico (553)

yechumadi Yekuana solo song (181)

yeye Early 1960s Haitian rock music, from the Beatles' "Yeah! Yeah! Yeah!" (892)

yon fas Single-headed, barrel-shaped drum in Guadeloupe (876)

yonbòt St. Lucian song-dance accompanied by the *ka* (943)

yúmari Traditional Tarahumara dance performed in a circle within the larger *tutuguri* ceremony (583, 585)

yuruparí (1) Tukano ceremonial complex (153); (2) huge duct flutes, the most powerful Tukano aerophones, played in male-female pairs (153)

yusap Sumu mouth-resonated jaw's harp or plucked idiophone (750)

zabumba (1) Brazilian large, double-headed bass drum (329–30, 332, 347); (2) name for *banda de pífanos* (329)

zafra Colombian field song sung by farmers for their own entertainment (407, 408–409)

zamacueca Also *zambacueca*, amorous pantomime dance of courtship in nineteenth-century Peru, a predecessor of the *marinera* (481, 498–99)

zambomba Also *zambudia*, (1) Salvadoran friction drum with fixed sticks attached to a single head (709); (2) Guatemalan small friction drum (727); (3) single-headed clay friction drum of Ecuador (378, 414, 415)

zampoña A Spanish term principally used in Chile for the panpipe, especially the double-unit panpipe or *siku* played in northern Chile (207, 286, 357); *see siku*

zampoñero Bolivian large stone statue of panpipe player of c. A.D. 1000 (282)

zapateado See *zapateo*

zapateo From Spanish *zapateado* 'foot stamping', (1) dance technique involving rhythmic striking of heels and toes against the floor or each other (494–95, 561, 567, 578–79, 726, 856, 938); (2) Bolivian energetic stamping dance (290); (3) rural Cuban dance associated with the *punto campesino* (834); (4) *zapateo criollo*, Peruvian dance genre based on foot stamping (469, 497, 499–500)

zarabanda (1) Seventeenth-century Spanish dance in triple meter (688); (2) popular music in highland Guatemala (652, 734)

zarzuela Spanish-derived light opera, especially popular in Argentina and Uruguay (113–14, 517)

zejel Chilean Andalusian musical-poetic tradition, developed in colonial times (367)

Zion Part of Jamaican Revival tradition (903)

zo St. Lucian idiophonic pair of bones or hardwood sticks struck against one another (945, 948)

zouk (1) Martinique dance party (918–19); (2) popular music genre of the French Antilles, developed in the 1980s (93, 98, 879–80)

zubac Guatemalan bone flute (654, 722, 728)

zumbador Mixtec membrane mirliton placed over a hole in the central part of the calabash trumpet (564)

A Guide to Publications

REFERENCE WORKS

Beaudet, Jean-Michel. 1982. "Musiques d'Amérique Tropicale. Discographie analytique et critique des Amérindiens des basses terres." *Journal de la Société des Américanistes* 68:149–203. Paris: Musée de l'Homme.

Béhague, Gérard. 1975. "Latin American Music: An Annotated Bibliography of Recent Publications." *Yearbook for Inter-American Musical Research* 11:190–218.

———. 1993. "Latin America." In *Ethnomusicology: Historical and Regional Studies*, ed. Helen Myers, 472–494. New York: Norton.

Black Music Research Journal. Chicago: Colombia College.

Chase, Gilbert. 1972 [1962]. *A Guide to the Music of Latin America.* 2nd ed. Washington, D.C.: Pan American Union.

Ethnomusicology (Journal of the Society for Ethnomusicology). "Current Bibliography," "Discography," and "Filmography" listed under "Americas." Three issues per year.

Fairley, Jan. 1985. "Annotated Bibliography of Latin-American Popular Music with Particular Reference to Chile and to *Nueva Canción.*" In *Popular Music,* Vol. 5, *"Continuity and Change,"* 305–356. Cambridge: Cambridge University Press.

Figueroa, Rafael, comp. 1992. *Salsa and Related Genres: A Bibliographical Guide.* Westport, Conn.: Greenwood.

Lotis, Howard, comp. 1981. *Latin American Music Materials Available at the University of Pittsburgh and at Carnegie Library of Pittsburgh.* Pittsburgh: Center for Latin American Studies.

Kuss, Malena. 1984. "Current State of Bibliographic Research in Latin American Music." *Fontes Artis Musicae* 31(4):206–228.

Latin American Music Review. Austin: University of Texas Press.

Myers, Helen. 1993. "The West Indies." In *Ethnomusicology: Historical and Regional Studies,* ed. Helen Myers, 461–471. New York: Norton.

Nava, Teresa. 1994. "Dance Research in Mexico." *Dance Research Journal* 26(2): 73–78.

The New Grove Dictionary of Music and Musicians, ed. Stanley Sadie. 20 vols. London: Macmillan.

Rodríguez, David J., et al. 1993. *Puerto Rico Recordings in the Archive of Folk Culture.*

Washington, D.C.: Archive of Folk Culture, American Folklife Center.

Schaeffer, Nancy. 1995. "Directory of Latin American Films and Videos: Music, Dance, Mask, and Ritual." *Latin American Music Review* 16(2): 221–41.

Schechter, John M. 1987a. "A Selected Bibliography on Latin American Urban Popular Music." In *Latin American Masses and Minorities: Their Images and Realities*, Vol. 2, ed. Dan C. Hazen, 679–682. Madison: Seminar on the Acquisition of Latin American Library Materials (SALALM), Memorial Library, University of Wisconsin.

———. 1987b. "Doctoral Dissertations in Latin American Ethnomusicology: 1965–1984." In *Latin American Masses and Minorities: Their Images and Realities*, Vol. 2, ed. Dan C. Hazen, 673–678. Madison: Seminar on the Acquisition of Latin American Library Materials (SALALM), Memorial Library, University of Wisconsin.

———. 1987c. "Selected Bibliographic Sources in Latin American Ethnomusicology." In *Latin American Masses and Minorities: Their Images and Realities*, Vol. 2, ed. Dan C. Hazen, 664–672. Madison: Seminar on the Acquisition of Latin American Library Materials (SALALM), Memorial Library, University of Wisconsin.

Smith, Ronald R. 1972. "Latin American Ethnomusicology: A Discussion of Central America and Northern South America." *Latin American Music Review* 3(1):8–14.

Stevenson, Robert. 1975. *A Guide to Caribbean Music History.* Lima: Ediciones CULTURA.

Steward, Julian H., ed. 1949. *Handbook of South American Indians.* 5 vols. New York: Cooper Square Publishers.

Thomas, Jeffrey Ross. 1992. *Forty Years of Steel: An Annotated Discography of Steel Band and Pan Recordings, 1951–1991.* Westport, Conn.: Greenwood Press.

Thompson, Donald. 1982. *Music Research in Puerto Rico.* San Juan: Office of the Governor of Puerto, La Fortaleza, Office of Cultural Affairs.

Thompson, Donald, and Annie F. Thompson. 1991. *Music and Dance in Puerto Rico from the Age of Columbus to Modern Times: An Annotated Bibliography.* Metuchen, N.J.: Scarecrow Press.

GENERAL

Aretz, Isabel. 1977. *América Latina en su música.* México, D.F.: Siglo XXI.

————. 1991. *Historia de la etnomusicología en América Latina: Desde la época precolombina hasta nuestros días.* Caracas: Ediciones FUNDEF-CONAC-OEA.

Aretz, Isabel, Gérard Béhague, and Robert Stevenson. 1980. "Latin America." In *The New Grove Dictionary of Music and Musicians*, ed. Stanley Sadie. London: Macmillan.

Béhague, Gérard. 1973. "Latin American Folk Music." In *Folk and Traditional Music of the Western Continents*, ed. Bruno Nettl, 2nd ed., 179–206. Englewood Cliffs, N.J. Prentice-Hall.

————. 1979. *Music in Latin America: An Introduction.* Englewood Cliffs, N.J.: Prentice-Hall.

————, ed. 1994. *Music and Black Ethnicity: The Caribbean and South America.* Miami: University of Miami North-South Center.

Béhague, Gérard, and Bruno Nettl. "Afro-American Folk Music in North and Latin America." In *Folk and Traditional Music of the Western Continents*, ed. Bruno Nettl, 2nd ed., 207–234. Englewood Cliffs, N.J.: Prentice-Hall.

Bergman, Billy. 1985. *Hot Sauces: Latin and Caribbean Pop.* New York: Quarto Books.

Boiles, Charles Lafayette. 1978. *Man, Magic and Musical Occasions.* Columbus: Collegiate Publishing, Inc.

Card, Caroline, et al. 1978. *Discourse in Ethnomusicology: Essays in Honor of George List.* Bloomington: Indiana University Archives of Traditional Music (Ethnomusicology Publications Group).

Courlander, Harold. 1976. *A Treasury of Afro-American Folklore.* New York: Crown Publishers.

den Otter, Elisabeth. 1994. *Pre-Colombian Musical Instruments: Silenced Sounds in the Tropenmuseum Collection.* Amsterdam: KIT/Tropenmuseum.

Díaz Roig, Mercedes. 1990. *Romancero tradicional de América.* Serie Estudios de linguística y literatura, 19. México, D. F.: Colegio de México.

Escobar, Luís Antonio. 1985. *La Música Precolombina.* Bogotá: Universidad Central.

Figueroa, Frank M. 1994. *Encyclopedia of Latin American Music in New York.* St. Petersburg, Fla.: Pillar Publications.

Garofalo, Reebee. 1992. *Rockin' the Boat: Mass Music and Mass Movements.* Boston: South End Press.

Greenberg, Joseph. 1987. *Language in the Americas.* Stanford: Stanford University Press.

Hernández, Clara, ed. 1982. *Ensayos de Música Latinoamericana.* Havana: Casa de las Americas.

Heth, Charlotte, ed. 1992. *Native American Dance: Ceremonies and Social Traditions.* Washington, D.C.: National Museum of the American Indian.

Jackson, Irene V., ed. 1985. *More than Drumming: Essays on African and Afro-Latin Music and Musicians.* Prepared under the auspices of the Center for Ethnic Music, Howard University. Contributions in Afro-American and African Studies, 80. Westport, Conn.: Greenwood Press.

List, George, and Juan Orrego-Salas, eds. 1967. *Music in the Americas.* Inter-American Music Monograph Series, Vol. 1. Bloomington: Indiana University Research Center in Anthropology, Folklore, and Linguistics.

Loukotka, Cestmír. 1968. *Classification of South American Indian Languages.* Reference Series, vol. 7. Los Angeles: Latin American Center, University of California, Los Angeles.

Manuel, Peter. 1988. *Popular Musics of the Non-Western World: An Introductory Survey.* New York: Oxford University Press.

Marre, Jeremy, and Hannah Charlton. 1985. *Beats of the Heart: Popular Music of the World.* New York: Pantheon.

Moreno Fraginals, Manuel, ed. 1984 [1977]. *Africa in Latin America: Essays on History, Culture, and Socialization*, trans. by Leonor Blum. New York: Holms and Meier.

Mukuna, Kazadi wa. 1990–1991. "The Study of African Musical Contributions to Latin America and the Caribbean: A Methodological Guideline." *Bulletin of the International Committee on Urgent Anthropological Research* 32–33:47–49.

Murphy, Joseph M. 1994. *Working the Spirit: Ceremonies of the African Diaspora.* Boston: Beacon Press.

Olsen, Dale A., Daniel E. Sheehy, and Charles A. Perrone, eds. 1987. "Music of Latin America: Mexico, Ecuador, Brazil." In *Sounds of the World.* Washington, D.C.: Music Educators National Conference. 3 audio cassettes and study guide.

Olsen, Dale A., and Selwyn Ahyoung. 1995 [1989]. "Latin American and the Caribbean." In *Multicultural Perspectives in Music Education*, ed. William M. Anderson and Patricia Shehan Campbell, 2nd ed., 124–177. Reston, Va.: Music Educators National Conference.

Pineda de Valle, César, comp. 1994. *Antología de la marimba en América.* Guatemala: Librería Artemis-Edinter.

Primera Conferencia Interamericana de Etnomusicología. Unión Panamericana, Washington, D.C., February 1963.

Roberts, John Storm. 1979. *The Latin Tinge: The Impact of Latin American Music on the United States.* New York and Oxford: Oxford University Press.

————. 1998. *Black Music of Two Worlds*, 2nd ed. New York: Schirmer Books.

Robertson, Carol E., ed. 1992. *Musical Repercussions of 1492: Encounters in Text and Performance.* Washington, D.C., and London: Smithsonian Institution Press.

Schechter, John M. 1996. "Latin America/ Ecuador." In *Worlds of Music: An*

Introduction to the Music of the World's Peoples, ed. Jeff Todd Titon, 3d ed., 428–494. New York: Schirmer Books.

Slonimsky, Nicholas. 1945. *Music of Latin America*. New York: Thomas Y. Crowell.

Stevenson, Robert. 1968a. *Music in Aztec and Inca Territory*. Berkeley: University of California Press.

———. 1968b. "The African Legacy to 1800." *Musical Quarterly* 54/4: 475–502.

———. 1991. "Latin American Music Bibliography." In *Libraries History, Diplomacy,*

and the Performing Arts: Essays in Honor of Carleton Sprague Smith, ed. I. J. Katz, 85–99. Stuyvesant, N.Y.: Pendragon Press.

Turino, Thomas. 1992. "Music in Latin America." In *Excursions in World Music*, ed. Bruno Nettl, 232–59. Englewood Cliffs, N.J.: Prentice Hall.

Whitten, Jr., Norman E., and John F. Szwed, eds. 1970. *Afro-American Anthropology: Contemporary Perspectives*. New York: Free Press.

SOUTH AMERICA

Abadía Morales, Guillermo. 1973. *La Música Folklórica Colombiana*. Bogotá: Universidad Nacional de Colombia.

———. 1991. *Instrumentos Musicales: Folklore Colombiano*. Bogotá: Banco Popular.

Alencar, Edigar de. 1965. *O carnaval carioca através da música*. 2 vols. Rio de Janeiro: Livraria Freitas Bastos.

———. 1968. *Nosso Sinhô do samba*. Rio de Janeiro: Civilização Brasileira Editora.

Almeida, Bira (Mestre Acordeon). 1986. *Capoeira—A Brazilian Art Form: History, Philosophy, and Practice*. Berkeley: North Atlantic Books.

Almeida, Raimundo Cesar Alves de. 1993. *Bibliografia crítica da capoeira*. Brasília: DEFER/GDF, Centro de Documentação e Informação Sobre a Capoeira.

Almeida, Renato. 1942. *História da Música Brasileira*, 2nd ed. Rio de Janeiro: F. Briguiet.

Alvarenga, Oneyda. 1982. *Música Popular Brasileira*, 2nd ed. São Paulo: Duas Cidades.

Alves, Henrique L. 1968. *Sua excelência o samba*. Palermo, Brazil: A. Palma.

Andrade, Mário de. 1928. *Ensaio sobre a Música Brasileira*. São Paulo: Martins.

———. 1933. *Compêndio de História da Música*, 2nd ed. São Paulo: Miranda.

———. 1963. *Música, Doce Música*, 2nd ed. São Paulo: Martins.

———. 1975. *Aspectos da Música Brasileira*, 2nd ed. São Paulo: Martins.

———. 1982. *Danças Dramáticas do Brasil*, 2nd ed., 3 vols. Belo Horizonte: Ed. Itatiaia.

———. 1989. *Dicionário Musical Brasileiro*. São Paulo: Editora da Universidade de São Paulo.

Añez, Jorge. 1968. *Canciones y Recuerdos,* rev. ed. Bogotá: Ediciones Mundial.

Appleby, David P. 1983. *The Music of Brazil*. Austin: University of Texas Press.

Araújo, Alceu Maynard. 1964. *Folclore Nacional*. 3 vols. São Paulo: Melhoramentos.

Araújo, Mozart de. 1963. *A Modinha e o Lundu no Século XVIII*. São Paulo: Ricordi Brasileira.

Archivo de Música Tradicional Andina. 1995. *Catálogo del Archivo de Música Tradicional*

Andina. Lima: Pontificia Universidad Católica del Perú, Instituto Riva Agüero.

Aretz, Isabel. 1954. *Costumbres tradicionales argentinas*. Buenos Aires: Huemul.

———. 1967. *Instrumentos musicales de Venezuela*. Cumaná: Editorial Universitaria de Oriente.

———. 1970. *El Tamunangue*. Barquisimeto: Universidad Centro Occidental.

———. 1991. *Música de Los Aborígenes de Venezuela*. Caracas: Fundación de Etnomusicología y Folklore.

Aretz-Thiele, Isabel. 1946. *Música tradicional argentina: Tucumán, historia y folklore*. Buenos Aires: Universidad Nacional de Tucumán.

Arguedas, José María. 1957. *Singing Mountaineers: Songs and Tales of the Quechua People*. Austin: University of Texas Press.

———. 1975. *Formación de una Cultura Nacional Indoamericana*. México: Siglo XXI.

———. 1977. *Nuestra Música Popular y sus Intérpretes*. Lima: Mosca Azul y Horizonte.

———. 1989. *Canto Kechua*, rev. ed. Lima: Horizonte.

Arvelo Ramos, Alberto. 1992. *El cuatro*. Caracas: J. J. Castro Fotografía Infrarroja.

Ayala, María Ignez Novais. 1988. *No Arranco do Grito: Aspectos da Cantoria Nordestina*. São Paulo: Atica.

Ayestarán, Lauro. 1953. *La música en el Uruguay*, vol. 1. Montevideo: Servicio Oficial de Difusión Radioeléctrica.

———. 1967. *El folklore musical uruguayo*. Montevideo: Arca.

———. 1968. *Teoría y práctica del folklore*. Montevideo: Arca.

———. 1994. *Las músicas primitivas en el Uruguay*. Montevideo: Arca.

Aytai, Desiderio. 1985. *O Mundo Sonoro Xavante*. Coleção Museu Paulista, Ethnologia, Vol. 5. São Paulo: Universidade de São Paulo.

Bahiana, Ana Maria. 1980. *Nada Será Como Antes: A MPB dos Anos 70*. São Paulo: Perspectiva.

Barral, P. Basilio María de. 1964. *Los Indios Guaraunos y su Cancionero*. Madrid: Consejo Superior de Investigaciones Científicas, Departamento de Misionología Española.

Basso, Ellen B. 1985. *A Musical View of the Universe.* Philadelphia: University of Pennsylvania Press.

Bastien, Joseph W. 1978. *Mountain of the Condor. Metaphor and Ritual in an Andean Ayllu.* St. Paul: West.

Bastos, Rafael Jose de Menezes. 1978. *A Musicológica Kamayurá.* Brasília: Fundação Nacional do Indio.

Baumann, Max Peter, ed. 1992. *Cosmología y música en los Andes.* Berlin: IITM.

Beaudet, Jean-Michel. 1983. "Les Orchestres de Clarinettes *Tule* des Wayãpi du Haut Oyapock (Guyane Française)." Ph.D. dissertation, Université de Paris X–Nanterre.

Becerra Casanovas, Rogers. 1990. *Reliquias de Moxos.* La Paz: PROINSA.

Béhague, Gerard. 1971. *The Beginnings of Musical Nationalism in Brazil.* Detroit Monographs in Musicology, 1. Detroit: Information Coordinators, Inc.

———. 1979. *Music in Latin America: An Introduction.* Englewood Cliffs, N.J.: Prentice-Hall, Inc.

Bermúdez, Egberto. 1985. *Los Instrumentos Musicales en Colombia.* Bogotá: Universidad Nacional de Colombia.

Biocca, Ettore. 1966. *Viaggi tra gli indi: Alto Rio Negro–Alto Orinoco. Appunti de un Biologo.* 4 vols. Rome: Consiglio Nazionale delle Ricerche.

Blérald-Ndagamo, Monique. 1996. *Musiques et danses Créoles au tambour de la Guyane Française.* Cayenne: Ibis Roque Editions.

Boettner, Juan Max. n.d. (ca. 1956). *Música y músicos del Paraguay.* Asunción: Autores Paraguayos Asociados.

Bolaños, César. 1981. *Música y Danza en el Antiguo Perú.* Lima: Museo Nacional de Antropología y Arqueología, Instituto Nacional de Cultura.

———. 1988. *Las Antaras Nasca.* Lima: Instituto Andino de Estudios Arqueológicos.

———. 1995. *La Música Nacional en los Medios de Comunicación Electrónicos de Lima Metropolitana.* Lima: Universidad de Lima, Facultad de Ciencias de la Comunicación (Cuadernos CICOSUL).

Borges, Bia. 1990. *Música popular do Brasil: Brazilian Popular Music.* São Paulo: B. Borges.

Brandão, Carlos Rodrigues. 1981. *Sacerdotes da Viola.* Petrópolis, Brazil: Vozes.

Browning, Barbara. 1995. *Samba: Resistance in Motion.* Bloomington: Indiana University Press.

Bureau du Patrimoine Ethnologique, ed. 1989. *Musiques en Guyane.* Cayenne: Conseil Régional de la Guyane.

Bustillos Vallejo, Freddy. 1982. *Bibliografía Boliviana de Etnomusicología.* La Paz: Instituto Nacional de Antropología.

———. 1989. *Instrumentos musicales de Tiwanaku.* La Paz: Museo Nacional de Etnografía y Folklore.

Caldas, Waldenyr. 1979. *Acorde na Aurora: Música Sertaneja e Indústria Cultural,* 2nd ed. São Paulo: Nacional.

———. 1985. *Introdução à Música Popular Brasileira.* São Paulo: Atica.

Cameu, Helza. 1977. *Introdução ao Estudo da Música Indígena Brasileira.* Rio de Janeiro: Conselho Federal de Cultura.

Campos, Augusto de. 1974. *Balanço da Bossa e Outras Bossas.* São Paulo: Perspectiva.

Cardozo Ocampo, Mauricio. *Mundo folklorico paraguayo.* 3 vols. Asunción: Editorial Cuadernos Republicanos.

Carpio Muñoz, Juan. 1976. *El Yaraví Arequipeño.* Arequipa: La Colmena.

Carvalho, José Jorge de. 1994. *The Multiplicity of Black Identities in Brazilian Popular Music.* Brasilia: Universidade de Brasilia.

Carvallo-Neto, Pablo de. 1964. *Diccionario del Folklore Ecuatoriano.* Quito: Editorial Casa de la Cultura Ecuatoriana.

———. 1971. *Estudios afros: Brasil, Paraguay, Uruguay, Ecuador.* Serie de Folklore–Instituto de Antropología e Historia, Universidad Central de Venezuela. Caracas: Instituto de Antropología e Historia, Facultad de Humanidades y Educación, Universidad Central de Venezuela.

Cascudo, Luís da Câmara. 1979. *Dicionário do Folclore Brasileiro,* 5th ed. São Paulo: Melhoramentos.

Castro, Donald S. 1991. *The Argentine Tango as Social History, 1880–1955: The Soul of the People.* Lewiston: E. Mellen Press.

Castro, Ruy. 1990. *Chega de saudade: A história e as histórias da Bossa Nova.* São Paulo: Companhia das Letras.

Céspedes, Gilka Wara. 1993. "*Huayno, Saya,* and *Chuntunqui*: Bolivian Identity in the Music of 'Los Kjarkas.'" *Latin American Music Review* 14(1): 52–101.

Claro, Samuel, et al. 1994. *Chilena o cueca tradicional: De acuerdo con las enseñazas de Fernando González Maraboli.* Santiago: Ediciones Universidad Católica de Chile.

Coba Andrade, Carlos Alberto. 1981. *Instrumentos Musicales Populares Registrados en el Ecuador.* Cultura Popular, vol. 1. Otavalo, Ecuador: Instituto Otavaleño de Antropología.

———. 1985. *Danzas y Bailes en el Ecuador.* Quito: Ediciones Abya-yala.

———. 1992. *Instrumentos Musicales Populares Registrados en el Ecuador,* vol. 2. Quito: Ediciones del Banco Central del Ecuador, and Instituto Otavaleño de Antropología.

Collier, Simon. 1990. *The Life, Music, and Times of Carlos Gardel.* Pittsburgh: University of Pittsburgh Press.

Corrêa, Roberto Nunes. 1989. *Viola Caipira.* Brasília: Viola Corrêa.

Costa, Reginaldo de Silveira. 1993. *O caminho do berimbau: Arte, filosofia e crescimento na capoeira.* Brasília: Thesaurus Editora.

Crook, Larry Norman. 1991. "*Zabumba* music from Caruaru, Pernambuco: Musical style, gender and the interpenetration of rural and urban worlds." Ph.D. dissertation, University of Texas.

Dark, Philip. 1970. *Bush Negro Art.* London: Alec Tiranti.

Davidson, Harry C. 1970. *Diccionario Folklórico de Colombia. Música, Instrumentos y Danzas.* 3 vols. Bogotá: Banco de la República.

Delfino, Jean Paul. 1988. *Brasil Bossa Nova.* Aix-en-Provence: Édisud.

den Otter, Elisabeth. 1985. *Music and Dance of Indians and Mestizos in an Andean Valley of Peru.* Delft: Eburon.

Díaz Gainza, José. 1962. *Historia Musical de Bolivia.* Potosí: Universidad Tomás Frias.

Dicks, Ted, ed. 1976. *Victor Jara: His Life and Songs.* London: Elm Tree Books.

Dolabela, Marcelo. 1987. *ABZ do Rock Brasileiro.* São Paulo: Estrela do Sul.

Dolphin, Lynette, comp. 1991. *National Songs of Guyana.* Georgetown, Guyana: Department of Culture.

Domínguez, Luis Arturo. 1992. *Fiestas y danzas folklóricas en Venezuela.* 2nd ed. Caracas: Monte Avila Editores.

Efegê, Jota. 1978/79. *Figuras e coisas da música popular brasileira.* 2 vols. Rio de Janeiro: FUNARTE.

Fernaud, Alvaro. 1984. *El Golpe Larense.* Caracas: Fundación de Etnomusicología y Folklore.

Ferrer, Horacio. 1977. *El libro del tango.* 2 vols. Buenos Aires: Galerna.

Flores, Hilda Agnes Hübner. 1983. *Canção dos Imigrantes.* Porto Alegre: Escola Superior de Teologia São Lourenço de Brindes, Universidade de Caxias do Sul.

Fuks, Victor. 1989. "Demonstration of Multiple Relationships between Music and Culture of the Waiãpi Indians of Brazil." Ph.D. dissertation, Indiana University.

Gallardo, Jorge Emilio. 1986. *Presencia africana en la Cultura de América Latina: Vigencia de los cultos afroamericanos.* Buenos Aires: Fernando García Cambeiro.

Garcilaso de la Vega, El Inca. 1961. *The Royal Commentaries of the Inca,* ed. Alain Gheerbrant. New York: Orion Press/Avon.

Garrido, Pablo. 1943. *Biografía de la Cueca.* Santiago: Ediciones Ercilla.

Godoy Aguirre, Mario. n.d. *Florilegio de la Música Ecuatoriana: La Música Popular en el Ecuador.* Vol. l. No city: Editorial del Pacífico.

Góes, Fred de. 1982. *O país do carnaval elétrico.* São Paulo: Editora Corrupio Comércio Ltda.

Goldfeder, Miriam. 1981. *Por Trás das Ondas da Rádio Nacional.* São Paulo: Paz e Terra.

González, Juan-Pablo. 1991. "Hegemony and Counter-Hegemony of Music in Latin America: The Chilean Pop." *Popular Music and Society* 15(2): 63–78.

González Torres, Dionisio M. 1991. *Folklore del Paraguay.* Asunción: Editora Litocolor.

Gradante, William J. 1991. "'¡Viva el San Pedro en La Plata!': Tradition, Creativity, and Folk Musical Performance in a Southern Colombian Festival." Ph.D. dissertation, University of Texas.

Gruszcynska-Ziólkowska, Anna. 1995. *El poder del sonido: El papel de las crónicas españolas en la etnomusicología andina.* Cayambe, Ecuador: Ediciones Abya-Yala.

Grebe, María Ester. 1980. "Generative Models, Symbolic Structures, and Acculturation in the Panpipe Music of the Aimara of Tarapaca, Chile." Ph.D. dissertation, Queen's University of Belfast.

Guardia Crespo, Marcelo. 1994. *Música popular y comunicación en Bolivia: Las interpretaciones y conflictos.* Cochabamba: U.C.B.

Guillermoprieto, Alma. 1990. *Samba.* New York: Knopf.

Guss, David M. 1989. *To Weave and Sing: Art, Symbol, and Narrative in the South American Rain Forest.* Berkeley: University of California Press.

d'Harcourt, Raoul et M. 1925. *La Musique des Incas et ses Survivances.* Paris: Librairie Orientaliste Paul Geuthner.

———. 1959. *La musique des Aymaras sur les hauts plateaux Boliviens d'après enregistrements sonores de Louis Girault.* Paris: Societé des Americanistes, Musée de l'Homme.

d'Harcourt, Raoul y Marguerite. 1990. *La Música de los Incas y sus Supervivencias.* General translation from the French by Roberto Miro Quesada. Lima: Occidental Petroleum Corporation of Peru.

Harrison, Regina. 1989. *Signs, Songs, and Memory in the Andes: Translating Quichua Language and Culture.* Austin: University of Texas Press.

Herskovits, Melville J., and Frances S. 1969 [1936]. *Suriname Folk-Lore.* Columbia Contributions to Anthropology, Vol. 27, Part III. New York: AMS Press, Inc.

Hickmann, Ellen. 1990. *Musik aus dem Altertum der Neuen Welt: Archäologische Dokumente des Musizierens in präkolumbischen Kulturen Perus, Ekuadors und Kolumbiens.* Frankfurt am Main: Peter Lang.

Hill, Jonathan D. 1993. *Keepers of the Sacred Chants: The Poetics of Ritual Power in an Amazonian Society.* Tucson: University of Arizona Press.

Holzmann, Rodolfo, and José María Arguedas. 1966. *Panorama de la Música Tradicional del Perú.* Lima: Ministerio de Educación Pública, Escuela Nacional de Música y Danzas Folklóricas (Servicio Musicológico), y la Casa Mozart.

Holzmann, Rodolfo. 1986. *Q'ero, pueblo y música.* Lima: Patronata Popular y Porvenir, Pro Música Clásica.

Hurtado Suárez, Wilfredo. 1995. *Chicha Peruana: Música de los Nuevos Migrantes.* Lima: Eco-Grupo de Investigaciones Económicas.

Instituto Nacional de Musicología "Carlos Vega." 1988. *Instrumentos musicales etnográficos y folklóricos de la Argentina: Síntesis de los datos obtenidos en investigación de campo (1931–1988)*. Buenos Aires: Instituto Nacional de Musicología "Carlos Vega."

Izikowitz, Karl Gustav. 1970. *Musical and Other Sound Instruments of the South American Indians: A Comparative Ethnographical Study*, rev. ed. East Ardsley, Wakefield, Yorks.: S.R. Publishers Ltd..

Jara, Joan. 1984. *An Unfinished Song: The Life of Victor Jara*. New York: Ticknor and Fields.

Jijón, Inés. 1971. *Museo de Instrumentos Musicales "Pedro Pablo Traversari."* Quito: Casa de la Cultura Ecuatoriana.

Jiménez Borja, Arturo. 1951. *Instrumentos musicales del Perú*. Lima: Museo de la Cultura.

Koorn, Dirk. 1977. "Folk Music of the Colombian Andes." Ph.D. dissertation, University of Washington.

Labraña, Luis, and Ana Sebastián. 1992. *Tango, una historia*. Buenos Aires: Ediciones Corregidor.

Lange, Francisco Curt. 1966. *A Organização Musical durante o Período Colonial*. Actas do V Coloquio Internacional de Estudos Luso-Brasileiros, Separata do Vol. IV.

Lewis, J. Lowell. 1992. *Ring of Liberation: Deceptive Discourse in Brazilian Capoeira*. Chicago: University of Chicago Press.

Lisboa Júnior, Luiz Américo. 1990. *A presença da Bahia na música popular brasileira*. Brasília: MusiMed.

Liscano, Juan. 1973. *La Fiesta de San Juan El Bautista*. Caracas: Monte Avila Editores.

List, George. 1983. *Music and Poetry in a Colombian Village*. Bloomington: Indiana University Press.

Lopes, Nei. 1992. *O Negro no Rio de Janeiro e sua Tradição Musical: Partido-Alto, Calango, Chula e Outras Cantorias*. Rio de Janeiro: Pallas.

Lloréns, José Antonio. 1983. *Música popular en Lima: Criollos y andinos*. Lima: Instituto de Estudios Peruanos.

Mamani P., Mauricio. 1987. *Los Instrumentos Musicales en los Andes Bolivianos*. La Paz: Museo Nacional de Etnografía y Folklore.

Marcondes, Marcos Antonio, ed. 1977. *Enciclopédia da Música Brasileira: Erudita, Folclórica, Popular*. São Paulo: Editora Arte.

Margullo Osvaldo-Muñz, Pancho. 1986. *El rock en la Argentina*. Buenos Aires: Galerna.

Mariz, Vasco. 1983. *História da Música no Brasil*, 2nd ed. Rio de Janeiro: Civilização Brasileira.

Martín, Miguel Angel. 1991. *Del folclor llanero*, 2nd ed. Sante Fé de Bogotá: ECOE Ediciones.

Martins, Carlos A. 1986. *Música popular uruguaya 1973–1982: Un fenómeno de comunicación alternativa*. Montevideo: Ediciones de la Banda Oriental.

Máximo, Joao, and Carlos Didier. 1990. *Noel Rosa: Una biografia*. Brasília: Editora Universidade de Brasília.

McGowan, Chris, and Ricardo Pessanha. 1991. *The Brazilian Sound: Samba, Bossa Nova, and the Popular Music of Brazil*. New York: Billboard Books.

Mendonça, Belkiss S. Carneiro de. 1981. *A Música em Goiás*, 2nd ed. Goiânia: Editora da Universidade Federal de Goiás.

Menezes Bastos, R. J. de. 1978. *A Musicológica Kamayura: Para Uma Antropologia da Comunicação No Alto Xingu*. Brasília: FUNAI.

Meyer, Augusto. 1958. *Cancioneiro Gaúcho*. Porto Alegre: Globo.

Montoya, Rodrigo, Edwin Montoya, and Luís Montoya. 1987. *La Sangre de los Cerros: Antologia de la poesía quechua que se canta en el Perú*. Lima: CEPES, Mosca Azul Editores y UNMSM.

Moreno Andrade, Segundo Luis. 1923. *La Música en la Provincia de Imbabura*. Quito: Tipografía y Encuadernación Salesianas.

———. 1949. *Música y Danzas Autóctonas del Ecuador* (Indigenous music and dances of Ecuador). Quito: Editorial "Fray Jacobo Ricke."

———. 1972. *Historia de la Música en el Ecuador. Vol. 1: Prehistoria*. Quito: Editorial Casa de la Cultura Ecuatoriana.

Moura, Roberto M. 1986. *Carnaval: Da Redentora a Praça do Apocalipse*. Rio de Janeiro: Jorge Zahar.

Mukuna, Kazadi wa. 1979. *Contribuição bantu na música popular brasileira*. São Paulo: Global Editora.

Núñez Rebaza, Lucy. 1990. *Los Dansaq*. Lima: Instituto Nacional de Cultura, Museo Nacional de la Cultura Peruana.

Nyberg, John L. 1974. "An Examination of Vessel Flutes from Pre-Hispanic Cultures of Ecuador." Ph.D. dissertation, University of Minnesota.

Oliveira, Valdemar de. 1971. *Frevo, capoeira, e "passo."* Recife: Companhia Editora de Pernambuco.

Oliveira Pinto, Tiago de. 1991. *Capoeira, Samba, Candomblé: Afro-Brasilianische Musik im Recôncavo, Bahio*. Berlin: Museum für Völkerkunde Berlin.

Olsen, Dale A. 1980a. "Folk Music of South America—A Musical Mosaic." In *Musics of Many Cultures: An Introduction*, ed. Elizabeth May, 386–425. Berkeley: University of California Press.

———. 1980b. "Symbol and Function in South American Indian Music." In *Musics of Many Cultures: An Introduction*, ed. Elizabeth May, 363–385. Berkeley: University of California Press.

———. 1989. "The Magic Flutes of El Dorado: A Model for Research in Archaeomusicology as Applied to the Sinú of Ancient Colombia." In *Early Music Cultures, Selected Papers from the Third International Meeting of the ICTM Study Group on Music Archaeology*, ed. Ellen Hickman and David Hughes, 305–328. Bonn: N. p.

———. 1996. *Music of the Warao of Venezuela: Song People of the Rain Forest*. Gainesville: University Press of Florida. Book and compact disc.

Ortiz, Alfredo Rolando. 1984 [1979]. *Latin American Harp Music and Techniques for Pedal and Non-Pedal Harpists*, 2nd ed. Corona, Calif.: Alfredo Rolando Ortíz.

Pallavicino, María L. 1987. *Umbanda: Religiosidad afro-brasileña en Montevideo*. Montevideo: Pettirossi Hnos.

Pardo Tovar, Andrés. 1966. *La Cultural Musical en Colombia*. Bogotá: Ediciones Lerner.

———. 1976. *El Archivo Musical de la Catedral de Bogotá*. Bogotá: Publicaciones del Instituto Caro y Cuervo.

Paredes Candia, Antonio. 1980. *Folklore de Potosí*. La Paz: Ediciones ISLA.

Parra, Violeta. 1970. *Décimas: Autobiografía en versos chilenos*. Santiago: Ediciones Nueva Universidad, Universidad Católica de Chile.

———. 1979. *Cantos Folklóricos Chilenos*. Santiago: Editorial Nascimento.

Perdomo Escobar, José Ignacio. 1963. *Historia de la Música en Colombia*, 3rd ed. Bogotá: Editorial ABC.

Pereira-Salas, Eugenio. 1941. *Los orígenes del arte musical en Chile*. Santiago: Publicaciones de la Universidad de Chile.

Pérez Bugallo, Rubén. 1993. *Catálogo ilustrado de instrumentos musicales argentinos*. Biblioteca de cultura popular, 19. Buenos Aires: Ediciones de Sol.

Perrone, Charles A. 1989. *Masters of Contemporary Brazilian Song: MPB 1965–1985*. Austin: University of Texas Press.

Pinnell, Richard. 1993. *The Rioplatense Guitar: The Early Guitar and Its Content in Argentina and Uruguay*. Westport, Conn.: The Bold Strummer.

Pinto, Tiago de Oliveira, ed. 1986. *Welt Musik: Brazilien*. Mainz: Schott.

———. 1991. *Capoeira, Samba, Candomblé. Afro-brasilianische Musik im Recôncavo, Bahia*. Berlin: Staatliche Museen Preussischer Kulturbesitz.

Pinto, Tiago de Oliveira, and Dudu Tucci. 1992. *Samba und Sambistas in Brasilien*. Wihelmshavaen: F. Noetzel.

Plath, Oreste. 1979. *Folklore Chileno*. Santiago: Editorial Nascimento.

Pollak-Eltz, Angelina. 1972. *Cultos Afroamericanos*. Caracas: Universidad Católica "Andres Bello."

Pombo Hernández, Gerardo. 1995. *Kumbia, legado cultural de los indígenas del Caribe colombiano*. Barranquilla: Editorial Antillas.

Preiss, Jorge Hirt. 1988. *A Música nas Missões Jesuíticas nos Séculos XVII e XVIII*. Porto Alegre: Martins Livreiro Editor.

Price, Richard, and Sally Price. 1980. *Afro-American Arts of the Surinam Rain Forest*. Los Angeles: Museum of Cultural History and University of California Press.

———. 1991. *Two Evenings in Saramaka*. Chicago: University of Chicago Press.

Price, Sally. 1984. *Co-wives and Calabashes*. Ann Arbor: University of Michigan Press.

Primera Conferencia Interamericana de Etnomusicología. 1963. Trabajos Presentados, 131–151. Washington, D.C.: Unión Panamericana, Secretaría General de la OEA.

Puerta Zuluaga, David. 1988. *Los Caminos del Tiple*. Bogotá: Damel Publishers.

Ramón y Rivera, Luís Felipe. 1953. *El joropo, baile nacional de Venezuela*. Caracas: Ediciones del Ministerio de Educación.

———. 1967. *Música Indígena, Folklórica y Popular de Venezuela*. Buenos Aires: Ricordi Americana.

———. 1969. *La Música Folklórica de Venezuela*. Caracas: Monte Avila Editores C.A.

———. 1971. *La Música Afrovenezolana*. Caracas: Universidad Central de Venezuela.

———. 1992. La Música de la Décima. Caracas: Fundación de Etnomusicología y Folklore.

Real, Katarina. 1990. *O folclore no carnaval do Recife*. 2nd ed. Recife: Editora Massangana (Fundação Joaquim Nabuco).

Rephann, Richard. l978. *A Catalogue of the Pedro Traversari Collection of Musical Instruments / Catálogo de la Colección de Instrumentos Musicales Pedro Traversari*. Organization of American States and Yale University Collection of Musical Instruments. Quito: Casa de la Cultura Ecuatoriana.

Rodríguez de Ayestarán, Flor de María. 1994. *La danza popular en el Uruguay: Desde sus orígenes a 1900*. Montevideo: Cal y Canto.

Roel Pineda, Josafáto. 1990. *El wayno del Cusco*. Qosqo, Peru: Municipalidad del Qosqo.

Roel Pineda, Josafáto, et al. 1978. *Mapa de los Instrumentos Musicales de Uso Popular en el Perú*. Lima: Instituto Nacional de Cultura, Oficina de Música y Danza.

Romero, Raúl R. 1985. "La Música Tradicional y Popular." In *La Música en el Perú*, 215–283. Lima: Patronato Popular y Porvenir Pro Música Clásica.

———. 1993. *Música, Danzas y Máscaras en los Andes*. Lima: Pontífica Universidad Católica del Perú.

Roth, Walter E. 1924. "An Introductory Study of the Arts, Crafts, and Customs of the Guiana Indians." *Thirty-eighth Annual Report of the Bureau of American Ethnology to the Secretary of the Smithsonian Institution, 1916–1917*. Washington, D.C.: U.S. Government Printing Office.

Salazar, Briseida. 1990. *San Benito: Canta y Baila Con Sus Chimbangueleros*. Caracas: Fundación Bigott.

Sant'anna, Affonso Romano de. 1986. *Música Popular e Moderna Poesia Brasileira*, 3rd ed. Petrópolis: Vozes.

Santa Cruz, César. 1977. *El Waltz y el Vals Criollo*. Lima: Instituto Nacional de Cultura.

Savigliano, Marta E. 1995. *Tango and the Political Economy of Passion*. Boulder, San Francisco, Oxford: Westview Press.

Schechter, John M. 1992. *The Indispensable Harp: Historical Development, Modern Roles, Configurations, and Performance Practices in Ecuador and Latin America*. Kent, Ohio: Kent State University Press.

Schneider, Jens. 1993. "The Nolkin: A Chilean Sucked Trumpet." *Galpin Society Journal* 46:69–82.

Seeger, Anthony 1987. *Why Suyá Sing: A Musical Anthropology of an Amazonian People*. Cambridge: Cambridge University Press. Book and audio cassette.

Setti, Kilza. 1985. *Ubatuba nos Cantos das Praias: Estudo do Caiçara Paulista e de sua Produção Musical*. São Paulo: Atica.

Sherzer, Joel, and Greg Urban, eds. 1986. *Native South American Discourse*. Berlin: Mouton de Gruyter.

Shreiner, Claus. 1993. *Musica Brasileira: A History of Popular Music and the People of Brazil*. New York: M. Boyars.

Sigueira, Batista. 1979. *Modinhas do Passado*, 2nd ed. Rio de Janeiro: Folha Carioca.

Silva Sifuentes, Jorge E. 1978. *Instrumentos Musicales Pre-Colombinos. Serie Investigaciones Nº 2*. Lima: Universidad Nacional Mayor de San Marcos, Gabinete de Arqueología, Colegio Real.

Smith, Robert J. 1975. *The Art of the Festival*. Publications in Anthropology, Number 6. Lawrence: University of Kansas Press.

Sodré, Muniz. 1979. *Samba: O Dono do Corpo*. Rio de Janeiro: Codecri.

Souza, Tárik de, et al. 1988. *Brazil Musical*. Rio de Janeiro: Art Bureau Representações e Edições de Arte.

Stevenson, Robert. 1960. *The Music of Peru: Aboriginal and Viceroyal Epochs*. Washington, D.C.: Organization of American States.

Stobart, Henry. 1987. *Primeros Datos sobre la música campesina del norte de Potosí*. La Paz: Museo Nacional de Etnografia y Folklore.

———. 1994. "Flourishing Horns and Enchanted Tubers: Music and Potatoes in Highland Bolivia." *British Journal of Ethnomusicology* 3: 35–48.

Suzigan, Geraldo. 1990. *Bossa Nova: Música, Política e Educação no Brasil*. São Paulo: Clam-Zimbo.

Tayler, Donald. 1972. *The Music of Some Indian Tribes of Colombia*. London: British Institute of Recorded Sound. Book and 3 LP disks.

Tinhorão, José Ramos. 1974. *Pequena História da Música Popular: Da Modinha a Canção de Protesto*. Petrópolis: Vozes.

———. 1981. *Música Popular—Do Gramofone ao Rádio e TV*. São Paulo: Atica.

———. 1986. *Pequena história da música popularóda modinha ao tropicalismo*, 5th ed. São Paulo: Art Editora.

———. 1988. *Os Sons dos Negros no Brasil*. São Paulo: Arte Editora.

———. 1990. *História Social da Música Popular Brasileira*. Lison: Caminho da Música.

———. 1992. *A música popular no romance brasileiro. Vol. I: Século XVIII–século XIX*. Belo Horizonte: Oficina de Livros.

———. 1994. *Fado, dança do Brasil, cantar de Lisboa: O fim de um mito*. Lisboa: Editorial Caminho.

Traversari Salazar, Pedro Pablo, ed. 1961. *Catálogo General del Museo de Instrumentos Musicales*. Quito: Editorial Casa de la Cultura Ecuatoriana.

Turino, Thomas.1993. *Moving away from Silence: Music of the Peruvian Altiplano and the Experience of Urban Migration*. Chicago: University of Chicago Press.

Ulloa, Alejandro. 1992. *La Salsa en Cali*. Cali, Colombia: Ediciones Universidad del Valle.

Valencia Chacón, Américo. 1983. *El Siku Bipolar Altiplánico*. Lima: Artex Editores.

———. 1989. *El Siku o Zampoña. The Altiplano Bipolar Siku: Study and Projection of Peruvian Panpipe Orchestras*. Lima: Artex Editores.

Vasconcellos, Gilberto. 1977. *Música Popular: De Olho na Festa*. Rio de Janeiro: Graal.

Vasconcelos, Ary. 1991. *Raízes da Música Popular Brasileira*, rev. ed. Rio de Janeiro: Rio Fundo Editora.

Vásquez Rodríguez, Rosa Elena. 1982. *La Práctica Musical de la Población Negra en el Perú: La Danza de Negritos de El Carmen*. Havana: Casa de las Américas/Ediciones Vitral.

Vásquez, Rosa Elena, and Abilio Vergara Figueroa. 1988. *¡Chayraq!: Carnaval Ayacuchano*. Lima: Centro de Desarrollo Agropecuario.

Vega, Carlos. 1944. *Panorama de la música popular argentina, con un ensayo sobre la ciencia del folklore*. Buenos Aires: Losada.

———. 1946. *Los Instrumentos Musicales Aborígenes y Criollos de la Argentina*. Buenos Aires: Ediciones Centurión.

———. 1952. *Las danzas populares argentinas*. 2nd ed. Buenos Aires: Instituto Nacional de Musicología "Carlos Vega."

———. 1953. *La Zamacueca (Cueca, Zamba, Chilena, Marinera)*. Buenos Aires: Ed. Julio Korn.

———. 1956. *El origen de las danzas folklóricas*. Buenos Aires: Ricordi Americana.

———. 1965. *Las canciones folklóricas de la Argentina*. Buenos Aires: Instituto Nacional de Musicología.

Verger, Pierre, ed. *Fiestas y Danzas en el Cuzco y en los Andes*. Buenos Aires: Editorial Sudamericana.

Vianna, Hermanno. 1995. *O mistério do samba*. Rio de Janeiro: Jorge Zahar/ UFRJ.

Vilcapoma I., José Carlos. 1995. *Waylarsh: Amor y violencia de carnaval*. Lima: Pakarina Ediciones.

Whitten, Norman E., Jr. 1965. *Class, Kinship and Power in an Ecuadorian Town: The Negroes of San Lorenzo*. Stanford: Stanford University Press.

———. 1974a. *Black Frontiersman: A South American Case.* Cambridge, Mass.: Shenkman.

———. 1974b. *Black Frontiersmen. Afro-Hispanic Culture of Ecuador and Colombia.* Prospect Heights, Ill.: Waveland Press.

MEXICO AND CENTRAL AMERICA

Acevedo Vargas, Jorge Luís. 1986. *La Música en Guanacaste*, 2nd ed. San José: Editorial Universidad de Costa Rica.

———. 1986. *La Música en las Reservas Indígenas de Costa Rica.* San José: Editorial de la Universidad de Costa Rica.

Andrews V., and E. Wyllys. 1972. *Flautas Precolombinas procedentes de Quelepa, El Salvador.* San Salvador: Ministerio de Educación, Dirección de Cultura, Dirección de Publicaciones.

Anguiano, Marina, and Guido Munch. 1979. *La Danza de Malinche.* Mexico: Culturas Populares, Secretaría de Educación Pública.

Beezley, William H. et al. 1994. *Rituals of Rule, Rituals of Resistance: Public Celebrations and Popular Culture in Mexico.* Wilmington: Scholarly Resources.

Cardenal Argüello, Salvador. 1977. *Nicaragua: Música y canto.* Managua: Banco de América. Liner notes.

Cargalv, H. (Héctor C. Gálvez). 1983. *Historia de la música de Honduras y sus símbolos nacionales.* Tegucigalpa: N. p.

Carmona Maya, Sergio Iván. 1989. *La Música, un fenomeno cosmogónico en la cultura kuna.* Medellin: Editorial Universidad de Antioquia.

Chamorro, Arturo. 1994. *Sones de la Guerra: Rivalidad y emoción en la práctica de la música P'urhépecha.* Zamora: El Colegio de Michoacán.

Chenoweth, Vida. 1964. *Marimbas of Guatemala.* Lexington: University of Kentucky Press.

Cheville, Lila R., and Richard A. Cheville. 1977. *Festivals and Dances of Panama.* Panama: Lila and Richard Cheville.

Crossley-Holland, Peter. 1980. *Musical Artifacts of Pre-Hispanic West Mexico: Towards an Interdisciplinary Approach.* Los Angeles: Program in Ethnomusicology, Department of Music, University of California, Los Angeles.

Cuadra, Pablo Antonio, and Francisco Pérez Estrada. 1978. *Muestrario del folklore nicaragüense.* Managua: Banco de América.

Densmore, Frances. 1926. *Music of the Tule Indians of Panama.* Smithsonian Miscellaneous Collections 77(11): 1–39. Publication No. 2864. Washington, D. C. : Smithsonian Institution.

———. 1932. *Yuman and Yaqui Music.* Bulletin 110. Washington, D.C.: Bureau of American Ethnology.

Drolet, Patricia Lund. 1980. "The Congo Ritual of Northeastern Panama: An Afro-American Expressive Structure of Cultural Adaptation." Ph.D. dissertation, University of Illinois at Urbana-Champaign.

Evers, Laurence J., and Felipe Molina. 1987. *Yaqui Deer Songs/Maso Bwikam: A Native American Poetry.* Tucson: University of Arizona Press.

Flores, Bernal. 1978. *La música en Costa Rica.* San José: Editorial Costa Rica.

Florers y Escalanate, Jesús, and Pablo Dueñas Herrera. 1994. *Cirilo Marmolejo: Historia del mariachi en la Ciudad de México.* México, D.F.: Asociación Mexicana de Estudios Fonográficas.

Franco Arce, Samuel. 1991. *Music of the Maya.* Guatemala: Casa K'ojom.

Garay, Narciso. 1930. *Tradiciones y cantares de Panamá, ensayo folklórico.* Brussels: Presses de l'Expansion belge.

García Flores, Raúl. 1993. *¡Pure mitote!: La música, el canto y la danza entre los chichimecas del Noreste.* Monterrey: Fondo Editorial Nuevo León.

González Sol, Rafael. 1940. *Datos históricos sobre el arte de la música en El Salvador.* San Salvador: Imprenta Mercurio.

Hayans, Guillermo. 1963. *Dos cantos shamanísticos de los índios cunas.* Translated by Nils M. Holmer and S. Henry Wassen. Göteborg: Etnografiska Museet.

Holmer, Nils M., and S. H. Wassén. 1963. *Dos Cantos Shamanísticos de los Indios Cunas.* Etnologiska Studier, No. 27. Göteborgs Etnografiska Museum. Göteborg: Elanders Boktryckeri Aktiebolag.

Jáuregui, Jesús. 1990. *El mariachi: Símbolo musical de México.* Mexico: Banpaís.

Joly, Luz Graciela. 1981. *The Ritual "Play of the Congos" of North-Central Panama: Its Sociolinguistic Implications.* Sociolinguistic working paper no. 85. Austin: Southwest Educational Development Laboratory.

Kaptain, Laurence. 1992. *The Wood That Sings: The Marimba in Chiapas, Mexico.* Everett, Pa.: HoneyRock.

Mace, Carroll E. 1970. *Two Spanish-Quiché Dance Dramas of Rabinal.* Tulane Studies in Romance Languages and Literature, Publication No. 3. New Orleans: Tulane University Press.

Manzanares Aguilar, Rafael. 1960. *Canciones de Honduras/Songs of Honduras.* Washington, D. C.: Secretaría General, Unión Panamericana, Organización de los Estados Americanos.

———. 1972. *La danza folklórica hondureña.* Tegucigalpa: Talleres del Partido Nacional.

Martí, Samuel. 1955. *Instrumentos musicales precortesianos.* México, D. F.: Instituto Nacional de Antropología

———. 1961. *Canto, Danza y Música Precortesianos.* México, D. F.: Fondo de Cultura Económica.

———. 1968. *Instrumentos Musicales Precortesianos.* 1st and 2nd eds. México, D. F.: Instituto Nacional de Antropología e Historia.

Mayer-Serra, Otto. 1941. *Panorama de la música mexicana desde la independencia hasta la actualidad.* México, D. F.: El Colegio de México.

McCosker, Sandra Smith. 1974. *The Lullabies of the San Blas Cuna Indians of Panama.* Etnologiska Studier, No. 33. Göteborgs Etnografiska

Museum. Göteborg: Elanders Boktryckeri Aktiebolag.

Mendoza, Vicente T. 1939. *El romance español y el corrido mexicano: Estudio comparativo*. México, D. F.: Ediciones de la Universidad Nacional Autónoma de México.

———. 1984 [1956]. *Panorama de la Música Tradicional de México*. México, D. F.: Universidad Nacional Autónoma de México, Instituto de Investigaciones Estéticas.

Moreno Rivas, Yolanda. 1989. *Historia de la música popular mexicana*, 2nd ed. México, D. F.: Consejo Nacional para la Cultura y las Artes, Alianza Editorial Mexicana.

Muñoz Tábora, Jesús. 1988. *Organología del Folklore Hondureño*. Tegucigalpa: Ministerio de Educación

Núñez, Evangelina de. 1956. *Costa Rica y su folklore*. San José: Imprenta Nacional.

Peña Hernández, Enrique. 1968. *Folklore de Nicaragua* . Masaya: Editorial Unión, Cardoza y Cia. Ltd.

Pérez Fernández, Rolando Antonio. 1990. *La música afromestiza mexicana*. Xalapa: Biblioteca Universidad Veracruzana.

Pineda del Valle, César. 1990. *Fogarada: Antología de la marimba*. Tuxtla Gutiérrez: Gobierno del Estado de Chiapas, Instituto Chiapaneco de Cultura.

Prado Quesada, Alcides, ed. 1962. *Costa Rica: Su música típica y sus autores*. San José: Editorial Antonio Lehmann.

Reuter, Jas. 1992 [1985]. *La música popular de México: Orígen e historia de la música que canta y toca el pueblo mexicano*. México, D. F.: Panorama Editoria.

Rivera y Rivera, Roberto. 1977. *Los Instrumentos Musicales de los Mayas*. México, D. F.: Instituto Nacional de Antropología e Historia.

Salazar Salvatierra, Rodrigo. 1985. *La música popular afrolimonense*. San José: Organización de los Estados Americanos, Ministerio de Cultura, Juventud y Deportes.

———. 1988. *La marimba: Empleo, diseño y construcción*. San José: Editorial Universidad de Costa Rica.

———. 1992. *Los instrumentos de la música folclórica costarricense*. Cartago: Editorial Instituto Technológico de Costa Rica.

Saldívar, Gabriel. 1934. *Historia de la música en México: Epocas Precortesiana y Colonial*. México, D. F.: Editorial "Cultura."

———. 1937. *El Jarabe, baile popular mexicano*. Mexico: Talleres gráficos de la nación.

Scruggs, T. M. 1998a. "Cultural Capital, Appropriate Transformations and Transfer by Appropriation in Western Nicaragua: *El baile de la marimba*." *Latin American Music Review* 19(1): in press.

———. 1998b. Review essay on publications from Central America. Salvador Cardenal Argüello, comp., *Nicaragua: Música y canto*; *Alcaldía de Managua*; Jesús Muñoz Tábora, *Organología del Folklore Hondureño*; Rodrigo Salazar Salvatierra, *Instrumentos musicales del folclor costarricense*. *Latin American Music Review* 19(1): in press.

———. 1999a. "'Let's Enjoy as Nicaraguans': The Use of Music in the Construction of a Nicaraguan National Consciousness." *Ethnomusicology* 43(2) (forthcoming).

———. 1999b. "Nicaraguan State Cultural Initiative and 'the Unseen Made Manifest'." *Yearbook for Traditional Music* 31 (forthcoming).

Sheehy, Daniel Edward. 1979. "The 'Son Jarocho': The History, Style, and Repertory of a Changing Mexican Musical Tradition." Ph.D. dissertation, University of California at Los Angeles.

Sherzer, Joel. 1983. *Kuna Ways of Speaking: An Ethnographic Perspective*. Texas Linguistics Sseries. Austin: University of Texas Press.

Smith, Ronald R. 1985. "They Sing with the Voice of the Drum: Afro-Panamanian Musical Traditions." In *More Than Drumming: Essays on African and Afro-Latin American Music*, ed. Irene Jackson-Brown, 163–198. Westport, Conn.: Greenwood Press.

Smith, Sandra. 1984. "Panpipes for Power, Panpipes for Play: The Social Management of Cultural Expression in Kuna Society." Ph.D. dissertation, University of California, Berkeley.

Stevenson, Robert. 1952. *Music in Mexico: A Historical Survey*. New York: Thomas Y. Crowell.

———. 1968. *Music in Aztec and Inca Territory*. Berkeley: University of California Press.

Suco Campos, Idalberto. 1987. *La música en el complejo cultural del Walagallo en Nicaragua*. La Habana: Casa de las Américas.

Tello Solís, Eduardo. 1993. *Semblanza de la canción yucateca*. Mérida: Universidad Autónoma de Yucatán.

Varela, Leticia. 1986. *La Música en la Vida de los Yaquis*. Hermosillo: El Gobierno del Estado de Sonora, Secretaría de Fomento Educativo y Cultura.

Zárate, Dora Pérez de. 1971. *Textos del tamborito panameño: Un estudio folklórico-literario de los textos del tamborito en Panamá*. Panamá: Dora Pérez de Zárate.

———. 1996. *Sobre nuestra musica típica*. Panama: Editorial Universitaria.

Zárate, Manuel F., and Dora Pérez de Zárate. 1968. *Tambor y socavón: Un estudio comprensivo de dos temas del folklore panameño, y de sus implicaciones históricas y culturales*. Panamá: Ediciones del Ministerio de Educación, Dirección Nacional de Cultura.

CARIBBEAN

Ahye, Molly. 1978. *Golden Heritage: The Dance in Trinidad and Tobago*. Petit Valley: Heritage Cultures Limited.

Alén Rodríguez, Olavo. 1986. *La música de las sociedades de tumba francesa en Cuba*. Havana: Casa de La Américas.

———. 1994. *De los afrocubano a la salsa.* 2nd ed. Havana: Artex S. A. Editions.

Aparicio, Frances. R. 1998. *Listening to Salsa: Gender, Latin Popular Music, and Puerto Rican Cultures.* Hanover, N.H.: University Press of New England.

Averill, Gage. 1997. *A Day for the Hunter, a Day for the Prey: Popular Music and Power in Haiti.* Chicago: University of Chicago Press.

Benoît, Edouard. 1990. *Musique populaire de la Guadeloupe: De la biguine au zouk, 1940–1980.* Pointe-è-Pitre: Office régional du patrimoine guadeloupéen.

Bigott, Luís Antonio. 1993. *Historia del bolero cubano, 1883–1950.* Caracas: Ediciones Los Heraldos Negros.

Bilby, Kenneth. 1985. *The Caribbean as a Musical Region.* Washington, D.C.: Woodrow Wilson International Center for Scholars.

Boggs, Vernon W., ed. 1992. *Salsiology: Afro-Cuban Music and the Evolution of Salsa in New York City.* New York: Excelsior Music Publishing.

Carpentier, Alejo. 1946. *La música en Cuba.* México, D.F.: Fondo de Cultura Económica.

Constance, Zeno Obi. 1991. *Tassa, Chutney and Soca: The East Indian Contribution to the Calypso.* San Fernando, Trinidad and Tobago: Z. O. Constance.

Coopersmith, J. M. 1949. *Music and Musicians of the Dominican Republic,* ed. Charles Seeger. Music Series No. 15. Washington, D.C.: Pan American Union.

Courlander, Harold. 1973. *The Drum and the Hoe: Life and Lore of the Haitian People.* Berkeley: University of California Press.

Daniel, Yvonne. 1995. *Rumba: Dance and Social Change in Contemporary Cuba.* Bloomington: Indiana University Press.

Dauphin, Claude. 1980. *Guide d'organologie haïtienne.* Montréal: Societé de Recherche et Diffusion de la Musique Haitienne.

———. *Brit kolobrit: Introduction Méthodologique Suivie de 30 Chansons Enfantiles Haïtiennes.* Québec: Editions Naaman de Sherbrooke.

———. 1983. *La chanson haïtienne folklorique et classique.* Montréal: N. p.

———. 1986. *Musique du Vaudou: Fonctions, Structures et Styles.* Sherbrooke: Editions Naaman.

Davis, Martha Ellen. 1976. "Afro-Dominican Religious Brotherhoods: Structure, Ritual, and Music." Ph.D. dissertation, University of Illinois at Urbana-Champaign.

———. 1981. *Voces del Purgatorio: Estudio de la Salve dominicana.* Santo Domingo: Museo del Hombre Dominicano.

Deren, Maya. 1984 [1953]. *Divine Horsemen: The Living Gods of Haiti.* London and New York: Thames and Hudson. New Paltz, N.Y.: McPherson & Co.

Desroches, Monique. 1989. *Les instruments de musique traditionnels à la Martinique.* Fort-de-France: Bureau du Patrimoine, Conseil régional de la Martinique.

———. 1996. *Tambours des dieux: Musique et sacrifice d'origine tamoule en Martinique.* Montréal: L'Harmattan.

Díaz Ayala, Cristóbal. 1994. *Cuba canta y baila: Discografía de la música cubana, Vol. 1, 1898–1925.* San Juan, P.R.: Fundación Musicalia.

Dobbin, Jay D. 1986. *The Jombee Dance of Montserrat.* Columbus: Ohio State University Press.

Dumervé, Etienne Constantin Eugene Moise. 1968. *Histoire de la musique en Haïti.* Port-au-Prince: Imprimerie des Antilles.

Edwards, Charles L. 1942 [1895]. *Bahama Songs and Stories.* New York: G.E. Steckert.

Elder, Jacob D. 1969. *From Congo Drum to Steel Band.* St. Augustine, Trinidad: University of the West Indies.

Fleurant, Gerdès. 1987. "The Ethnomusicology of Yanvalou: A Study of the Rada Rite of Haiti." Ph.D. dissertation, Tufts University.

———. 1996. *Dancing Spirits: Rhythms and Rituals of Haitian Vodun, the Rada Rite.* Westport, Conn.: Greenwood Press.

Fouchard, Jean. 1988. *La méringue, danse nationale d'Haïti.* Port-au-Prince: Editions Henri Deschamps.

Gerard, Charlie, and Marty Sheller. 1989. *Salsa: The Rhythm of Latin Music.* Crown Point, Ind.: White Cliffs Media.

Goddard, George. 1991. *Forty Years in the Steelbands, 1939–1979.* London: Karia Press.

Guilbault, Jocelyne. 1993. *Zouk: World Music in the West Indies.* Chicago: University of Chicago Press.

Hebdige, Dick. 1987. *Cut 'n' Mix: Culture, Identity, and Caribbean Music.* London: Methuen.

Hedrick, Basil C., and Jeanette E. Stephens. 1976. *In the Days of Yesterday and in the Days of Today: An Overview of Bahamian Folk Music.* Southern Illinois University Museum Studies No. 8. Carbondale: Southern Illinois University Press.

Hernández, Julio Alberto. 1969. *Música tradicional dominicana.* Santo Domingo: Julio D. Postigo.

———. 1992. *Música dominicana.* Santo Domingo: Universidad Autónoma de Santo Domingo.

Herskovits, Melville J., and Francis S. Herskovits. 1964 [1947]. *Trinidad Village.* New York: Octagon Books.

Herskovits, Melville. 1975 [1937]. *Life in a Haitian Valley.* New York: Octagon Books.

Hill, Donald R. 1993. *Calypso Calaloo: Early Carnival Music in Trinidad.* Gainesville: The University Press of Florida.

Hill, Errol. 1972. *The Trinidad Carnival: Mandate for a National Theater.* Austin: University of Texas Press.

Incháustegui, Arístides. 1988. *El disco en la República Dominicana.* Santo Domingo: Amigo del Hogar.

Jahn, Brian, and Tom Weber. 1992. *Reggae Island: Jamaican Music in the Digital Age.* Kingston: Kingston Publishers.

Johnson, Howard, and Jim Pines. 1982. *Reggae: Deep Roots Music.* London: Proteus Books.

Laguerre, Michel S. 1980 *Voodoo Heritage.* Sage Library of Social Research, Volume 98. Beverly Hills and London: Sage Publications.

La Motta, Bill, and Joyce La Motta. 1990. *Virgin Island Folk Songs.* St. Thomas: Joyce La Motta's Tsukimaro.

Largey, Michael. 1991. "Musical Ethnography in Haiti: A Study of Elite Hegemony and Musical Composition." Ph.D. dissertation, Indiana University.

Lent, John A., ed. 1990. *Caribbean Popular Culture.* Bowling Green, Ohio: Bowling Green State University Popular Press.

Leon, Algeliers. 1984. *Del canto y el tiempo.* Havana: Letras Cubanas Editorial.

Lewin, Olive. 1973. *Forty Folk Songs of Jamaica.* Washington, D.C.: Organization of American States.

Linares, Maria Teresa. *La música y el pueblo.* Havana: Pueblo y Educación Editorial, 1974.

López Cruz, Francisco. 1991 [1967]. *La Música Folklórica de Puerto Rico.* 9th ed. Sharon, Conn.: Troutman Press.

Malavet Vega, Pedro. 1992. *Historia de la canción popular en Puerto Rico (1493–1898).* Ponce: Pedro Malavet Vega.

Manuel, Peter, ed. 1991. *Essays on Cuban Music—North American and Cuban Perspectives.* Lanham, Md.: University Press of America.

———. 1995. *Caribbean Currents.* Philadelphia: Temple University Press.

McCoy, James A. 1968. "The Bomba and Aguinaldo of Puerto Rico as They Have Evolved from Indigenous, African and European Cultures." Ph.D. dissertation, Florida State University.

Métraux, Alfred. 1972. *Voodoo in Haiti.* New York: Schocken Books.

Moldes, Rhyna. 1975. *Música folklórica cubana.* Miami: Ediciones Universal.

Moore, Robin D. 1997. *Nationalizing Blackness.* Afrocubanismo *and Artistic Revolution in Havana, 1920–1940.* Pittsburgh: University of Pittsburgh Press.

Nolasco, Flérida de. 1939. *La música en Santo Domingo y otros ensayos.* Ciudad Trujillo: Montalvo.

Núñez, María Virtudes, and Ramón Guntín. 1992. *Salsa caribe y otras músicas antillanas.* Madrid: Ediciones Cúbicas.

Ortiz, Fernando. 1954. *Los instrumentos de la música afrocubana.* Havana: Cárdenas y Cia Editorial.

———. 1965. *Africanía de la música en Cuba.* 2nd ed. Havana: N. p.

Ortiz Ramos, Pablo Marcial. 1991. *A tres voces y guitarras: Los tríos en Puerto Rico.* San Juan: N. p.

Paul, Emmanuel. 1962. *Panorama du folklore haitien: Présence africaine en Haiti.* Port-au-Prince: Imprimerie de l'Etat.

Quevedo, Raymond. 1983. *Atilla's Kaiso: A Short History of the Trinidad Calypso.* St. Augustine, Trinidad: University of the West Indies.

Quintero-Rivera, A. G. 1989. *Music, Social Classes, and the National Question of Puerto Rico.* Washington, D.C.: Woodrow Wilson International Center for Scholars.

Rodríguez Demorizi, Emilio. 1971. *Música y baile en Santo Domingo.* Santo Domingo: Librería Hispaniola.

Rohlehr, Gordon. 1990. *Calypso and Society in Pre-Independence Trinidad.* Port of Spain: G. Rohlehr.

Rosa-Nieves, Cesarro. 1991 [1967]. *Voz Folklórica de Puerto Rico.* Sharon, Conn.: Troutman Press.

Rosemain, Jacqueline. 1986. *La Musique dans la Société Antillaise, 1635–1902:* Martinique et Guadeloupe. Paris: Editions L'Harmattan.

Sekou, Lasana M., ed. 1992. *Fête: Celebrating St. Martin's Traditional Festive Music.* Philipsburg, St. Martin: House of Nehesi Publishers.

Simpson, George. 1965. *The Shango Cult in Trinidad.* Río Piedras: Institute of Caribbean Sudies, University of Puerto Rico.

Stuempfle, Stephen. 1995. *The Steelband Movement: The Forging of a National Art in Trinidad and Tobago.* Philadelphia: University of Pennsylvania Press.

Uri, Alex, and Françoise Uri. 1991. *Musiques and musiciens de la Guadeloupe: Le chant de Karukéra.* Paris: Con Brio.

Vega Drouet, Héctor. 1979. "Historical and Ethnological Survey on Probable African Origins of the Puerto Rico Bomba, Including a Description of Santiago Apostol Festivities at Loiza Aldea." Ph.D. dissertation, Wesleyan University.

Verba, Daniel. 1995. *Trinidad: Carnaval, Steelbands, Calypso.* Paris: Editions Alternatives.

Wallis, Roger, and Krister Malm. 1984. *Big Sounds from Small Peoples: The Music Industry in Small Countries.* London: Constable and Co. (New York: Pendragon Press).

Warner, Keith Q. 1985. *Kaiso! The Trinidad Calypso: A Study of the Calypso as Oral Literature.* Washington, D.C.: Three Continents Press.

Waters, Anita M. 1989. *Race, Class, and Political Symbols: Rastafari and Reggae in Jamaican Politics.* New Brunswick: Transaction Publishers.

White, Timothy. 1989. *Catch a Fire: The Life of Bob Marley.* New York: Henry Holt & Co.

Wilcken, Lois. 1992. *The Drums of Vodou.* Tempe, Ariz.: White Cities Media.

Wood, Vivian Nina Michelle. 1995. "Rushin' Hard and Runnin' Hot: Experiencing the Music of the *Junkanoo* Parade in Nassau, Bahamas." Ph.D. dissertation, Indiana University.

A Guide to Recordings

GENERAL

Música de la Tierra: Instrumental and Vocal Music–Vol. II. 1992. Produced by Bob Haddad. Music of the World CDC-207. Compact disc.

Shaman, Jhankri & Néle: Music Healers of Indigenous Cultures. 1997. Written and produced by Pat Moffitt Cook. Roslyn, N.Y.: Ellipsis Arts. CD3550. Compact disc and book.

The Spirit Cries: Music from the Rainforests of South America and the Caribbean. 1993. Produced by Mickey Hart and Alan Jabbour. Notes by Kenneth Bilby. Rykodisc RCD 10250. Compact disc.

SOUTH AMERICA

A bailar la bomba, con los Hermanos Congo. 1985. Quito: FAMOSA-FADISA, 700211. LP disk.

A bailar la bomba. con los Hermanos Congo. 1986. Vol. 2. Guayaquil: Producciones Maldonado-IFE-SA 339-588l. LP disk.

Aboios/Ceará. 1983. Documentário Sonoro do Folclore Brasileiro INF-039. LP disk.

ACONCAGUA. 1995 [1982]. Los Jaivas [Chile]. Colombia CNIA-2-461823. Compact disc.

Afro-Hispanic Music from Western Colombia and Ecuador. 1967. Recorded and edited by Norman E. Whitten. Ethnic Folkways Library FE 4376. LP disk.

Afro-Peruvian Classics: The Soul of Black Peru. 1995. Compiled by David Byrne and Yale Evelev. Luaka Bop 9 45878-2. Compact disc.

Alma del Sur. 1993. Liner essay ("A Celebration of South American Music") by Dale A. Olsen. Narada Collection Series ND-63908. Compact disc.

Amazonia: Cult Music of Northern Brazil. N. d. Produced by Morton Marks. New York: Lyrichord LLST 7300. LP disk.

Amerique du Sud: Musiques Hispaniques. 1993. Auvidis-Ethnic B 6782. Compact disc.

Amerindian Songs from Surinam, the Maroni River Caribs. 1975. Produced by Peter Kloos. Amsterdam: Royal Tropical Institute. LP disk.

Andean Legacy. 1996. Liner essay ("Music of the Central Andes") by Dale A. Olsen. Narada Collection Series ND-63927. Compact disc.

Astor Piazzolla: Octeto Buenos Aires. 1995. Astor Piazzolla [Argentina]. ANS Records ANS 15276-2. Compact disc.

Banda Cabaçal/Ceará. 1978. Documentário Sonoro do Folclore Brasileiro CDFB-023. LP disk.

Bandoneón Pure: Dances of Uruguay. 1993. René

Marino Rivero, bandoneón. Recorded by Tiago de Oliveira Pinto. Notes by Maria Dunkel. Smithson/Folkways CD SF 40431.

Basta. 1995. Quilapayún. Disco Alerce CDAL 0223. Compact disc.

Baú dos oito baixos: Bucho com bucho. 1982. Sebastião Moraes. Som da Gente SDG-011. LP disk.

Bolivia: Calendar Music in the Central Valleys. 1992. Recorded by Bruno Flety and Rosalia Martínez. Notes by Rosalia Martínez. Le Chant du Monde LDX 274938 CM 251. Compact disc.

Bolivia Panpipes/Syrinx de Bolivie. Recorded by Louis Giraullt. Notes by Xavier Bellenger. UNESCO Collection, AUVIDIS D 8009. Compact disc.

Bororo Vive. 1990. Federal University of Mato Grosso and Museu Rondon. Idéia Livre 19 521.404.030. LP disk.

Bossa Nova: Sua história, sua gente. 1991. Notes by Aloyso de Oliveira. Philips/Polygram 848 302-2. 2 compact discs.

Brazil Classics 3: Forró, etc. 1991. Luaka Bop/Warner Bros. 9 26323-2. Compact Disc.

Brazil: The Bororo World of Sound. 1989. Produced by Ricardo Canzio. UNESCO/ AUVDIS D 8201. Compact disc.

Brésil: Amérindiens d'Amazonie—Asurini et Arara/Brazil: American Indians of the Amazon— Asurini and Arara. 1995. Jean-Pierre Estival. Ocora C 560084. Compact disc.

Brésil Central: Chants et danses des Indiens Kaiapo. 1989. Recorded by René Fuerst, George Love, Pascal Rosseels, and Gustaaf Verswijver. Archives Internationales de Musique Populaire. AIMP & VDE-GALLO CD-554/555. 2 compact discs.

Brésil—Musiques du Haut Xingu. 1992. Produced by Pierre Toureille. OCORA Radio

France, Harmonia Mundi, C 580022. Compact disc.

¡Cantando! 1992. Diomedes Díaz and Nicholas "Colacho" Mendoza [Colombia]. GlobeStyle ORB 055. Compact disc.

Cantos Costeõs: Folksongs of the Atlantic Coastal Region of Colombia. 1973. Produced by George List with Delia Zapata Olivella, Manuel Zapata Olivella, and Winston Caballero Salguedo. Ethnosound EST 8003. LP disk.

Capoeira Angola from Salvador, Brazil. 1996. Grupo de Capoeira Angola Pelourinho. Smithsonian/Folkways SF CD 40465. Compact disc.

Capoeira, Samba, Candomblé, Bahia, Brasil. 1990. Recordings and notes by Tiago de Oliveira Pinto. Berlin: Museum Collection. Compact disc.

Chants et rythmes du Chile: Violeta Parra, Los Calhakis, Isabel et Angel Parra. 1991. Arion ARN 64142. Compact disc.

Charango Cuzqueño. 1985. Julio Benavente Díaz, *charango.* Recorded by Xavier Bellenger. Notes by Thomas Turino. GREM G 1504.

Chocolate: Peru's Master Percussionist. 1992. Lyrichord LYRCD 7417.

Colombia 92. 1992. Sony CD80804/Globo Records. Compact disc.

Cuando el indio llora: Los Huayanay. 1989. Quito: FAMOSO LDF-l040. LP disk.

Cumbia/Cumbia 2: La Epoca Dorada de Cumbias Colombias. 1993. Produced by Nick Gold. World Circuit WCD 033. Compact disc.

Dance Music from the Countryside. 1992. Pé de Serra Forró Band, Brazil. Haus der Kulturen der Welt SM 1509-2. LP disk.

Danzas y Cantos Afrovenezolanos. 1978. Caracas: Oswaldo Lares. LP disk.

Danzas y Canciones Para Los Niños. 1981. Caracas: Ediciones Fredy Reyna. LP disk.

Do jeito que a gente gosta. 1984. Elba Ramalho. Barclay 823 030-1. LP disk.

Documental Folklórico de la Provincia de La Pampa. 1973. Produced by Ercilia Moreno Chá. Buenos Aires: Instituto Nacional de Antropología—Dirección de Cultura de La Pampa. Qualiton QF 3015/16. 2 LP disks.

El Charango. 1988. Ernesto Cavour. La Paz: CIMA. LP disk.

Équateur: Le monde sonore des Shuar/Ecuador: The Shuar World of Sound. 1995. Buda 92638-2. Compact disc.

Flutes and Strings of the Andes: Native Musicians from the Altiplano. 1990. Produced by Bob Haddad. Music of the World CDT-106. Compact disc.

Folklore de mi tierra: Conjunto indígena "Peguche." l977. Industria Fonográfica Ecuatoriana S.A. (IFESA). ORION 330-0063. Guayaquil, Ecuador, Dist. by Emporio Musical S.A., Guayaquil and Psje. Amador, Quito. LP disk.

Folklore de Venezuela, Vols. 1–8. 1971. Caracas: Sonido Laffer. 8 LP disks.

Folklore Musical y Música Folklórica Argentina. 1966. Buenos Aires: Fondo Nacional de las Artes. Qualiton QF 3000/5. 6 LP disks.

From Slavery to Freedom: Music of the Saramaka Maroons of Suriname. 1977. Lyrichord LLST 7354. LP disk.

Fuego. 1993. Joe Arroyo y La Verdad. Sony CDZ 81063. Compact disc.

Grandes éxitos, Vol. 2. 1993. Joe Arroyo y La Verdad. Vedisco 1017—2. Compact disc.

Hekura: Yanomamö Shamanism from Southern Venezuela. 1980. Recorded by David Toop and Nestor Figueras. Quartz Publications 004. LP disk.

Huaynos and Huaylas: The Real Music of Peru. 1991. Compiled by Ben Mandelson, notes by Lucy Duran. GlobeStyle Records GDORBD 064. Compact disc.

Indian Music of Brazil. Musique Indienne Brésil. 1972. Recorded with notes by Simone Dreyfus. Ed. Gilbert Rouget. Collection Musée de l'Homme. Vogue VG 403 LDM 30112. LP disk.

Indiens d'Amazonie. N. d. Recorded by Richard Chapelle. Le Chant du Monde LDX 74501. LP disk.

Inti-Illimani 2: La Nueva Canción Chilena. 1991. Monitor MCD 71794.

Jarishimi Kichuapi (La Voz del Hombre en Kichua). 1984. Enrique Males. Teen Internacional LP-4l586. Guayaquil: Fediscos. LP disk.

¡¡Jatari!! 4. 1978. Quito: Fábrica de Discos S.A. (FADISA) 710129. LP disk.

Javanese Music from Suriname. 1977. Lyrichord LLST 7317. LP disk.

La América de Bolívar Canta. N. d. Caracas: Colección INIDEF. V.D. 82-033. LP disk.

La candela vida. 1993. Totó la Momposina y Sus Tambores. Carol/Real World CD 2337-2. Compact disc.

Las canciones folklóricas de la Argentina. Antología. 1984. Buenos Aires: Instituto Nacional de Musicología "Carlos Vega." 3 LP disks.

L.H. Correa de Azevedo: Music of Ceara and Minas Gerais. N. d. Rykodisc-10404. Compact disc.

Lowland Tribes of Ecuador. 1986. Recorded by David Blair Stiffler. Ethnic Folkways Records FE 4375. LP disk.

Lo mejor de la Cumbia Soledeña. 1977. Polydor 2404041. LP disk.

Los Grandes de la Bomba, con Fabián Congo y Milton Tadeo. l989. Ecuador: Novedades, LP323102. LP disk.

Los Masis: El Corazón del Pueblo. 1996. Los Masis. Tumi CD 062. Compact disc.

Marimba Cayapas: Típica Marimba Esmeraldeña. 1979. Guayaquil: ONIX-Fediscos, LP-5003l. LP disk.

Mountain Music of Peru. 1991 [1964]. Produced by John Cohen. Smithsonian Folkways SF 40020 and 40021. 2 compact discs.

Mushuc Huaira Huacamujun. 1979. Conjunto

Indigena "Peguche." Guayaquil: IFESA, RUNA CAUSAY 339-065l. LP disk.

Music from Saramaka. 1977. Produced by Richard Price and Sally Price. Ethnic Folkways Records FE 4225. LP disk.

Music of Colombia. 1961. Recorded by A.H. Whiteford. Folkways Records, FW 6804. LP disk.

Music of the Andes. Illapa, Inti-Illimani, Kollahuara, Quilapayun, and Victor Jara. Hemisphere 7243 8 28190 28. Compact disc.

Music of the Haut Oyopok: Oyampi and Emerillon Indian Tribes, French Guiana, South America. 1981. Recorded with notes by David Blair Stiffler. Ethnic Folkways Records FE 4235.

Music of the Jívaro of Ecuador. 1973. Recorded by Michael J. Harner, Ethnic Folkways FE 4386. LP disk.

The Music of Some Indian Tribes of Colombia. 1972. Produced by Donald Tayler. London: British Institute of Recorded Sound. 3 LP disks.

Music of the Tukano and Cuna Peoples of Colombia. 1987. Recorded by Brian Moser and Donald Tayler. Rogue Records, FMS/NSA 002. LP disk.

The Music of Venezuela. 1990. Memphis: Memphis State University. High Water Recording Company, LP1013. LP disk.

Music of the Venezuelan Yekuana Indians. 1975. Produced by Walter Coppens and Isaías Rodríguez V. Folkways Records Album FE 4104. LP disk.

Music of the Warao. Song People of the Rain Forest. 1996. Recorded and produced by Dale A. Olsen. Gainesville: University Press of Florida. Book and compact disc.

Música Andina de Bolivia. IV festival folklórico "Luz Mila Patiño." 1979. Produced by Max Peter Baumann. Cochabamba: Centro Portales y Lauro y Cía. LP disk.

Música Andina del Perú. 1987. Produced by Raúl Romero. Lima: Archivo de Música Tradicional, Pontífica Universidad Católica del Perú, Instituto Riva Agüero. LP disk.

Música autóctona del Norte de Potosí." VII Festival Folklórico "Luz Mila Patiño." 1991. Produced by Luz Maria Calvo and Walter Sánchez C. Cochabamba: Centro Portales y Lauro y Cia. LP disk.

Música de Venezuela: Cantos y Danzas e La Costa Central. N. d. Caracas: Oswaldo Laress. LP disk.

Música de Venezuela: Indio Figueredo (Homenaje al Indio Figueredo). 1969. Caracas: Oswaldo Lares. LP disk.

Música etnográfica y folklórica del Ecuador. Culturas: Shuar, Chachi, Quichua, Afro, Mestizo. 1990. Recorded by José Peñín, Ronny Velásquez, and Carlos Alberto Coba Andrade. Otavalo: Instituto Otavaleño de Antropología. 2 LP disks.

Música Indígena Guahibo. ca. 1978. Caracas: Fundación La Salle/Instituto Interamericano de Etnomusicología e Folklore. LP disk.

Música Indigena: A Arte Vocal dos Suyá. 1982. Recorded and produced by Anthony Seeger. São Joáo del Rei: Tacape 007. LP disk.

Música Popular Tradicional de Venezuela. 1983. Caracas: Instituto Nacional del Folklore. LP disk.

Música tradicional de Bolivia. VI festival folklórico nacional "Luz Mila Patiño." 1984. Produced by Luz María Calvo and Roberto Guzmán. Cochabamba: Centro Portales y Lauro y Cía. LP disk.

Música Tradicional de Cajamarca. 1988. Produced by Gisela Canepa Koch and Raul R. Romero. Lima: Archivo de Música Tradicional, Pontífica Universidad Católica del Perú, Instituto Riva-Agüero. AMTA-3. LP disk, cassette [1997].

Música Tradicional de Lambayeque. 1992. Edited by Raúl R. Romero. Lima: Archivo de Música Tradicional, Pontífica Universidad Católica del Perú, Instituto Riva-Agüero. AMTA-6. LP disk, cassette [1997].

Música Tradicional de Piura. 1997. Edited by Manuel Ráez Retamozo and Ana Teresa Lecaros. Lima: Archivo de Música Tradicional, Pontífica Universidad Católica del Perú, Instituto Riva-Agüero. AMTA-9. Cassette.

Música Tradional de la Sierra de Lima. 1997. Edited by Manuel Ráez Retamozo and Ana Teresa Lecaros. Lima: Archivo de Música Tradicional, Pontífica Universidad Católica del Perú, Instituto Riva-Agüero. AMTA-8. Cassette.

Música Tradional del Callejón de Huaylas. 1997. Edited by Manuel Ráez Retamozo. Lima: Archivo de Música Tradicional, Pontífica Universidad Católica del Perú, Instituto Riva-Agüero. AMTA-7. Cassette.

Música Tradicional del Cusco. 1992. Edited by Raúl R. Romero. Lima: Archivo de Música Tradicional, Pontífica Universidad Católica del Perú, Instituto Riva-Agüero. AMTA-5. LP disk, cassette [1997].

Música Tradicional del Valle de Colca. 1989. Edited by Manuel Ráez Retamozo and Leonidas Casas Roque. Lima: Archivo de Música Tradicional, Pontífica Universidad Católica del Perú, Instituto Riva-Agüero. AMTA-4. LP disk, cassette [1997].

Música Tradicional del Valle del Mantaro. 1986. Edited by Raúl R. Romero. Lima: Archivo de Música Tradicional, Pontífica Universidad Católica del Perú, Instituto Riva-Agüero. AMTA-1. LP disk, cassette [1997].

Musik im Andenhochland/Bolivien (Music in the Andean highlands/Bolivia.) 1982. Recording and notes by Max Peter Baumann. Edited by Artur Simon. Museum Collection Berlin MC 14. LP disk.

Musique Boni et Wayana de Guyana. 1968. Produced by Jean-Marcel Hurault. Paris: Collection Musee de l'Homme. Disque Vogue LVLX 290. LP disk.

Musique des Indiens Bora et Witoto d'Amazonie colombienne. 1976. Recorded by Mireille Guyot and Jürg Gasche. Paris: Musée de l'Homme. AEM 01. LP disk.

Musique instrumentale des Wayana du Litani (The Wayana of the Litani River). N. d. Buda 92637-2. Compact disc.

The Noble Songbook of Colombia. N. d. Produced by Joaquín Piñeros Corpos. Bogotá: Universidad de los Andes, LP 501–03. LP disks.

Ñanda mañachi 1 (Préstame el camino). 1977. Produced by Jean Chopin Thermes-Ibarra. Guayaquil: LLAQUICLLA—IFESA. LP disk.

Ñanda mañachi 1 and 2 (Préstame el camino). 1977, 1979. Produced by Jean Chopin Thermes-Ibarra. Guayaquil: LLAQUICLLA - IFESA 339-0502. 2 LP disks.

Ñanda mañachi: ¡Churay, Churay! 1983. Guayaquil: LLAQUICLLA. ONIX-Fediscos LP-59003. LP disk.

Ñuca llacta. 1975. Conjunto "Los Tucumbes." Auténtico Conjunto Folklórico interpretando música autóctona de nuestro país. Ritmos indígenas. Quito: Sibelius, S-4256-SIB-12. LP-12501. LP disk.

O bom do carnaval. 1980. Claudionor Germano. RCA/Cadmen 107.0317. LP disk.

O Melhor de Luiz Gonzaga. 1989. Luiz Gonzaga. RCA CDM 10032. LP disk.

Paiter Merewá: Cantam os Suruis de Rondônia. 1984. São Paulo: Discos Memoria 803.146. LP disk.

Pelas ruas do Recife. 1979. Banda de Pau e Corda. RCA 103.0319. LP disk.

Percussions d'Amérique latine (tracks 3, 7, 12, 14, 17). 1986. Arion CD64023. Compact disc.

Percussions d'amérique latine. N. d. Produced by Gérard Krémer. Arion CD64023. LP disk.

Perou: Huayno, Valse Créole et Marinera. 1994. Playasound PS 65133. Compact disc.

Pérou: Taquile, Île du Ciel: Musique Quechua du Lac Titicaca. 1992. Ocora C580 015. Compact disc.

Peru: Ayarachi and Chiriguano. 1983. Xavier Bellenger. UNESCO MTC 1. LP disk.

Perú: Máximo Damián: El Violín de Ishua. 1992. A.S.P.I.C. X55514. Compact disc.

Perú: Música Negra. 1992. A.S.P.I.C. X55515. Compact disc.

Quechua. Margarita Alvear. 1976. Guayaquil: ONIX. Fediscos, LP-50154. LP disk.

Rebellión. 1992. Joe Arroyo y La Verdad. World Circuit WCD 012. Compact disc.

Reisado do Piauí. 1977. Documentário Sonoro do Folclore Brasileiro CDFB-019. LP disk.

Relevamiento etnomusicológico de Salta, Argentina. 1984. Selección de textos: Rubén Pérez Bugallo. Buenos Aires: Instituto Nacional de Musicología "Carlos Vega." 2 LP disks.

Repentes e emboladas. 1986. Manoel Batista and Zé Batista. Phonodisc LP 0-34-405-215. LP disk.

Ritmos e danças: Frevo. N. d. Fundação Nacional de Arte SCDP-PF-01-PE. LP disk.

Ritual Music of the Kayapó-Xikrin, Brazil. 1995. Recorded by Max Peter Baumann. Notes by Lux Boelitz Vidal and Isabelle Vidal Giannini. Smithsonian/Folkways CD SF 40433. Compact disc and booklet.

The Rough Guide to the Music of the Andes. 1996. Produced by Phil Stanton. World Music Network. RGNET 1009. Compact disc.

Selk'nam chants of Tierra del Fuego, Argentina. 1972. Notes and translations of texts by Anne Chapman. Ethnic Folkways FE 4176. 2 LP disks.

Selk'nam chants of Tierra del Fuego, Argentina. 1978. Notes and transcriptions by Anne Chapman. Ethnic Folkways Records FE 4179. 2 LP disks.

Songs of Paraguay: Papi Basaldua and Grupo Cantares. 1994. JVC VICG 5341-2. Compact disc.

Soul Vine Shaman. 1979. Produced by Neelon Crawford and Norman E. Whitten, Jr., with Julian Santi Vargas, María Aguinda Mamallacta, and William Belzner. New York: Neelon Crawford. LP disk.

Surinam: Javanese Music. 1977. Produced by Annemarie de Waal Malefijt and Verna Gillis. Lyrichord LLST 7317. LP disk.

Tango: Zero Hour. 1986. Astor Piazzolla and the New Tango Quintet. Produced by Kip Hanrahan. American Clave. MCA Records. PAND-42138. Compact disc.

Todos os Sons. 1995. Marlui Miranda. São Paulo, Brazil: Associação IHU, Pró Musica e Arte Indigenas. Pau Brasil Som Imagem e Editora, CGC 65.012l.478/0001-87. Compact disc.

Trio elétrico/carnaval de Bahia. 1990. RGE 3 GLO 121. LP disk.

Tropicalísimo. 1989. Peregoyo y Su Combo Vacana [Colombia]. World Circuit WCD 015.

Txai! 1990. Milton Nascimento. Brazil: Discos C.B.S. 177.228/1-464138. Cassette.

Typiquement D.O.M. Compilation 89 Antilles-Guyane. 1989. Produced by Dany Play. Cayenne: TDM production. LP disk.

Vallenato Dynamos! 1990. Meriño Brothers [Colombia]. GlobeStyle ORB 049. Compact disc.

Victor Jara: Canto Libre. 1993. Victor Jara [Chile]. Monitor MCD 71799.

Violas da minha terra. 1978. Moacir Laurentino and Sebastião da Silva. Chantecler: 2-04-405-075. LP disk.

Yanoama: Tecniche Vocali Sciamanismo. 1979. Recorded by Ettore Biocca. Produced by Diego Carpitella. Suoni CETRA SU 5003. LP disc.

Wayãpi Guyane. 1980. Produced by Jean-Michel Beaudet. Paris: Musee de l'Homme, SELAF-ORSTOM CETO 792. LP disk.

Zabumba/SE. 1979. Documentário Sonoro do Folclore Brasileiro CDFB-031(1979). LP disk.

MEXICO AND CENTRAL AMERICA

Amando en Tiempo de Guerra (Loving in Times of War). 1988. Luis Enrique Mejía Godoy and Mancotal. Redwood Records 8805. LP disk.

Antología del Son de México. 1985. Produced by Baruj Lieberman, Eduardo Llerenas, and Enrique Ramírez de Arellano. México, D. F.: Corason. Distributed by Rounder Records Corp., Cambridge, Mass. 3 compact discs.

Berry Wine Days. 1996. Peter's Boom and Chime. Produced by Gina Scott. Stonetree Records. LP disk.

The Black Caribs of Honduras. 1953. Produced by Doris Stone. Folkways FE 4435. LP disk.

Black History/Black Culture. 1991. Soul Vibrations. Aural Tradition ATRCD 118 and Redwood Records. LP disk.

Calypsos of Costa Rica. N. d. Produced by Walter Ferguson. Folkways Records, FTS 31309. LP disk.

Cantos de Tierra Adentro. 1980. Los Soñadores de Sarawaska. Ocarina MC-004. LP disk.

Chatuye: Heartbeat in the Music. 1992. Produced by G. Simeon Pillich. Arhoolie Productions, CD-383. Compact disc.

"Chicken Scratch"—Popular Dance Music of the Indians of Southern Arizona. 1972. Canyon C-6085 and C-6162. 2 LP disks.

Cinco siglos de bandas en México. N. d. Vols. 2–4. México, D. F.: Archivo Etnográfico del Instituto Nacional Indigenista FONAPAS. 3 LP disks.

Dabuyabarugu: Inside the Temple: Sacred Music of the Garífuna of Belize. 1982. Produced by Carol Jenkins and Travis Jenkins. Smithsonian Folkways Records, FE4032. LP disk.

Deer Dancer: Jessita Reyes and Grupo Yaqui. 1991. Talking Taco Records TT 110. Compact disc.

El Conjunto Murrietta Tocando Norteño. 1978. Canyon C–6162. LP disk.

El Mariachi Tepalcatepec de Michoacán: El Michoacano. 1994. Discos Dos Coronas DDC 9401. Compact disc.

El Triunfo: Los Camperos de Valles—Sones de la Huasteca. 1992. Los Camperos de Valles. Produced by Eduardo Llerenas. Música Tradicional MTCD 007. Cassette disc.

En Busca de la Música Maya: Canción de la Selva Lacandona. 1976. Produced by Yuichi Matsumura and Mabuchi Usaburo. Japan: King Records GXH (k) 5001-3. LP disk.

Fiesta de Palo de Mayo. 1986. Dimensión Costeña. ENIGRAC CE-6009. LP disk.

Fiesta Tropical. 1991. Banda Blanca. Sonotone Music POW 6017. LP disk.

Flautas Indígenas de México. 1995. México, D. F.: Departamento de Etnomusicología del Instituto Nacional Indigenista, serie VII: Organología Indígena, vol.1, INI-VII-0. Compact disc.

Guaymi—Térraba. Antología de Música Indígena Costarricense. N. d. Asociación Indígena de Costa Rica, Pablo Presbere. Onda Nueva. LP disk.

Guitarra Armada. 1988. Carlos Mejía Godoy and Luis Enrique Mejía Godoy. Rounder Records 4022. Originally released on INDICA, S.A. (Costa Rica) MC-1147, 1979, re-issued on ENIGRAC MC-015 and MC 1147, 1980. LP disk.

Honduras—Música Folklórica. N. d. [1988]. Tegucigalpa: Secretaría del Turismo y Cultura. LP disk.

Indian Music of Mexico. 1952. Recorded and produced by Henrietta Yurchenko. Folkways FE-4413. LP disk.

Indian Music of Mexico. 1957. Recorded and produced by Laura Boulton. Folkways FW-8851. LP disk.

Indian Music of Northwest Mexico. 1977. Canyon C-8001. LP disk.

Indian Music of Northwest Mexico. 1978. Canyon C-8001. LP disk.

Instrumental Folk Music of Panama. 1994. Danzas Panama. JVC VICG-5338. Compact disc.

Kunda erer ma-ir ranto niuff/Aguilas que no se olvidan. 1996. *Grupo indígena chichimeca de San Luis de la Paz, Guanajuato.* México, D. F.: Departamento de Etnomusicología del Instituto Nacional Indigenista. INI-VI-05. Compact disc.

La Misa Campesina. N. d. [1980]. Carlos Mejía Godoy and El Taller de Sonido Popular. ENIGRAC NCLP—5012. LP disk.

La música en la Mixteca. 1994. México, D. F.: Subdirección de Radio del Instituto Nacional Indigenista and Secretaría de Desarrollo Social, serie "Sonidos del México Profundo," núm.7, INI-RAD-II-7; XETLA. Compact disc.

La música en la Montaña de Guerrero. 1994. México, D. F.: Subdirección de Radio del Instituto Nacional Indigenista and Secretaría de Desarrollo Social; serie "Sonidos del México Profundo," núm.10, INI-RAD-II- 10; XEZV. Compact disc.

La Sierra Gorda que Canta: A lo Divino y a lo Humano. 1995. Recorded and produced by María Isabel Flores Solano et al. Guanajuato: Instituto de la Cultura del Estado de Guanajuato, Dirección General de Culturas Populares y Discos Corazón. Compact disc.

La Voz de la Costa Chica. 1994. Instituto Nacional Indigenista. Subdirección de Radio Difusora XEJAM, "La voz de la Costa Chica," Jamiltepec, Oaxaca, and Secretaría de Desarrollo Social, INI-RAD-I- 3. Compact disc.

La Voz de las Huastecas. 1994. Instituto Nacional Indigenista. México, D. F.: Subdirección de Radio Difusora XEANT, "La voz de las Huastecas," and Secretaría de Desarrollo Social, INI-RAD-I- 2. Compact disc.

La Voz de la Sierra: Segundo Aniversario. 1994. Instituto Nacional Indigenista. México, D. F.: Subdirección de Radio Difusora XEGLO "La voz de la Sierra," and Secretaría de Desarrollo Social, INI-RAD-I- 4. Compact disc.

"Lanlaya"—Canciones de Amor Miskito [Nicaragua]. 1987. Grupo Lanlaya. ENIGRAC CE-021. LP disk.

Maleku—Guatuso. Antología de Música Indígena Costarricense. N. d. Asociación Indígena de Costa Rica, Pablo Presbere. Onda Nueva. LP disk.

"Mama Let Me Go." 1989. Dimensión Costeña. ENIGRAC CE-6028. LP disk.

Mariachi Coculense "Rodríguez" de Cirilo Marmolejo 1926–1936. 1993. Reissue produced by Chris Strachwitz. Arhoolie/Folklyric CD 7011. Compact disc.

MAYAPAX: Música tradicional maya de Tixcacal Guardia, Quintana Roo. 1993. Instituto Nacional Indigenista. México, D. F.: XEPET "La voz de los mayas," INI-RAD I-1 (XEPET). Compact disc.

Sones from Jalisco. 1994. Mariachi Reyes del Aserradero. Produced by Eduardo Llerenas. Corason COCD 108. Distributed by Rounder Records, Cambridge, Mass. Compact disc.

Mariachi Tapatío de José Marmolejo. 1994. Reissue produced by Chris Strachwitz. Arhoolie/Folklyric CD 7012. Compact disc.

Maya K'ekchi Strings. 1996. Produced by Gina Scott. Stonetree Records. LP disk.

Mexico: Fiestas of Chiapas and Oaxaca. 1991. Recorded by David Lewiston. Notes by Walter F. Morris, Jr., and David Lewiston. Elektra/Nonesuch 9 72070-2. Compact disc.

Mexico's Pioneer Mariachis. 1993. Mariachi Coculense de Cirilo Marmolejo and Cuarteto Coculense. Vol. 1. Produced by Chris Strachwitz. El Cerrito, Calif.: Arhoolie-Folklyric CD7011. Compact disc.

Mexico's Pioneer Mariachis, Vol. 3. Produced by Chris Strachwitz. 1992. Mariachi Vargas de Tecalitlán. El Cerrito, Calif.: Arhoolie-Folklyric CD7015. Compact disc.

Mixtecos y triquis en la frontera norte. 1994. México, D. F.: Subdirección de Radio del Instituto Nacional Indigenista and Secretaría de Desarrollo Social, serie "Sonidos del México Profundo," núm. 5, INI-RAD-II-5 (XEQIN). Compact disc.

Modern Maya: The Indian Music of Chiapas, Mexico. 1975. Produced by Richard Anderson. Folkways FE 4377. LP disk.

Música Afroantillana de Mexico: Combo Ninguno, "Traigo este son." N. d. Combo Ninguno. Discos Pentagrama PCD-070. Compact disc.

Música de la Costa Chica de Guerrero y Oaxaca. 1977. Produced by Thomas Stanford. México, D. F.: Instituto Nacional de Antropología e Historia, Serie de Discos INAH 21. LP disk.

Música Indígena de México, Vol. 5—Música Indígena del Noroeste. 1976. Produced by Arturo Warman. México, D. F.: Instituto Nacional de Antropología e Historia. LP disk.

Music of Mexico, Vol.1. 1994. Conjunto Alma Jarocha, "Sones Jarochos" [Veracruz]. Produced by Daniel E. Sheehy and Chris Strachwitz. El Cerrito, Calif.: Arhoolie CD354. Compact disc.

Music of Mexico, Vol. 2. 1994. Ignacio Montes de Oca H. Conjunto Alma de Apatzingán, "Arriba Tierra Caliente" [Michoacán]. El Cerrito, Calif.: Arhoolie CD426. Compact disc.

Music of Mexico, Vol. 3. 1995. La Huasteca; Huapangos y Sones Huastecos; Los Caimanes (1995) and Los Caporales de Pánuco (1978). Produced by Chris Strachwitz. El Cerrito, Calif.: Arhoolie 431. Compact disc.

Music of the Indians of Panama the Cuna (Tule) and Chocoe (Embera) tribes. 1983. Recorded and produced by David Blair Stiffler. Folkways Records, FE 4326. LP disk.

Music of the Miskito Indians of Honduras and Nicaragua. 1981. Recorded and produced by David Blair Stiffler. Smithsonian Folkways Cassette Series 4237. Cassette with liner notes.

Music of the Tarascan Indians of Mexico: Music of Michoacan and nearby mestizo country. 1970. Recorded and produced by Henrietta Yurchenco. New York: Folkways 4217. LP disk.

Music of Veracruz: The Sones Jarochos of Los Pregoneros del Puerto. 1990. Produced by Dan Sheehy and Joe Wilson. Rounder Records CD 5048. Compact disc.

Música Popular Mexicana: Sones Huastecos. 1990. Trío Xoxocapa. Discos Pentagrama PCD 117. Compact disc.

Música Popular Poblana: Homenaje a don Vicente T. Mendoza. 1995. Produced by Garza Marcue and Rosa María. México, D. F.: Fonoteca del Instituto Nacional de Antropología e Historia, INAH 032. LP disk.

Música y canciones de Honduras. 1975. Produced by Rafael Manzanares. ELIA 01—03. 3 LP disks.

Musiques des Communautes indigènes du Mexique. 1969–1970. Produced by Francois Jouffa, Maurice Morea, and Serge Roterdam. Vogue LDM 30103. LP disk.

Nicaragua—música y canto. 1992 (1977). Produced by Salvador Cardenal Argüello. Managua: Radio Güegüence (Banco de América LP). 7 compact discs.

¡Nicaragua...Presente!—Music from Nicaragua Libre. 1989. Produced by John McCutcheon. Rounder Records 4020/4021. LP disk.

Nicaraguan folk music from Masaya: Música Folklórica de Masaya. 1988. Recorded and produced by T. M. Scruggs. Flying Fish FF474. LP disk.

Palo de Mayo. N. d. [1976]. Los Bárbaros del ritmo. Andino 010. LP disk.

Panamá: Tamboritos y mejoranas. 1987. Produced by Eduardo Llerenas and Enrique Ramírez de Arellano. Música Tradicional MT10. LP disk.

Panamanian Folk Music and Dance. 1971 (1968). Produced by Lila Cheville. LP disk.

Qué resuene la tarima. 1990. Grupo Tacoteno. Produced by Modesto López and Juan Meléndez. Discos Pentagrama PCD-146. Compact disc.

Quinto Festival de Música y Danza Indígena. 1994.

México: Departamento de Etnomusicología del Instituto Nacional Indigenista, serie VIII. Archivo sonoro digital de la música indígena INI-ETM-VIII-01. Compact disc.

Saumuk Raya—Semilla Nueva. N. d. [1986, Nicaragua]. ENIGRAC 018. LP disk.

Serie de discos. 1967–1979. Irene Vázquez Valle, general editor. México, D. F.: Instituto Nacional de Antropología. 24 LP disks of Mexican regional and indigenous music with descriptive notes.

Sewere. 1996. Scott, Gina. The Original Turtle Shell Band. Produced by Gina Scott. Stonetree Records. LP disk.

Sistema de Radiodifusoras Culturales Indigenistas. 1995. Testimonio musical del trabajo radiofónico. México, D. F.: Subdirección de Radio del Instituto Nacional Indigenista and Secretaría de Desarrollo Social, INI-RAD-I-5. 2 compact discs.

¡Son Tus Perfumenes Mujer! N. d. [mid-1970s]. Los Bisturices Harmónicos. Banco Nicaraguense. LP disk.

Songs and Dances of Honduras. 1955. Produced by Doris Stone. Folkways 6834. LP disk.

Songs of the Garifuna. 1994. Produced by Lita Ariran. JVC VICG-5337. Compact disc.

Street Music of Panama. 1985. Produced by Michel Blaise. Original Music, OML 401. LP disk.

Tarahumara Matachin Music/Matachines Tarahumaras. 1979. Canyon C-8000.

Tradiciones Populares de Costa Rica. N. d. Grupo Curime. San José: Indica S.A., PP-17-83. LP disk.

Traditional Music of the Garifuna (Black Carib) of Belize. 1982. Produced by Carol Jenkins and Travis Jenkins. Smithsonian Folkways Records, FE4031. LP disk.

The Vanishing Indians: Costa Rica and Panama, Tribes of the Talamanca Division. N. d. Lyrichord Stereo LLST 7378. LP disk.

Yaqui Dances—the Pascola Music of the Yaqui Indians of Sonora, Mexico. 1957. Produced by Samuel Charters. Folkways FW-957. LP disk.

Yaqui Festive and Ritual Music. 1972. Canyon C-6140. LP disk.

Yaqui Fiesta and Religious Music—Historic Recordings from Old Pascua Village. 1980. Produced by Edward H. Spicer. Canyon CR-7999. LP disk.

Yaqui Pascola Music of Arizona. 1980. Canyon CR-7998. LP disk.

Yaqui Ritual and Festive Music. 1976. Produced by Robert Nuss. Canyon C-6140. LP disk.

Yaqui—Music of the Pascola and Deer Dance. 1976. Canyon C-6099. LP disk.

Ye Stsöke: Breve Antología de la Música Indígena de Talamanca. N. d. Indica S.A., PP- 470-A. LP disk.

CARIBBEAN

20 Reggae Classics, Vols. 1–4. Trojan Records. Compact disc.

A Carnival of Cuban Music. 1990. Routes of Rhythm, vol. 1. Produced by Howard Dratch et al. Rounder CD 5049. Compact disc.

Afro-Cuba: A Musical Anthology. 1994. Produced by Morton Marks. Rounder CD 1088. Compact disc.

Afro-Dominican Music from San Cristóbal, Dominican Republic. 1983. Produced by Morton Marks. Folkways FE 4285. LP disk.

Aires Tropicales. Tropical Breeze. 1996–1997. Various artists. Sony CD 82363/2-469889. Compact disc.

Boukman Eksperyans: Vodou Adjae. 1991. Notes and translations by Gage Averill. Mango Records 162-539-899-2. Compact disc.

Calypso Breakaway, 1927–1941. 1990. Rounder Records. Compact disc.

Calypso Calaloo: Early Carnival Music in Trinidad. 1993. Compiled by Donald R. Hill. Gainesville: University Press of Florida. Book and compact disc.

Calypso Pioneers, 1912–1937. 1989. Produced by Dick Spottswood. Rounder Records 1039. Compact disc.

Calypso Season. 1990. Mango Records. Compact disc.

Cantar Maravilloso: Los Muñequitos de Matanzas.

1990. Compiled by Ben Mandelson. Notes by Lucy Duran. GlobeStyle CDORB 053. Compact disc.

Caribbean Carnivals/Carnavals des Caraïbes. 1991. Seeds Records SRC 119. Compact disc.

Caribbean Island Music: Songs and Dances of Haiti, the Dominican Republic and Jamaica. 1972. Produced by John Storm Roberts. Nonesuch H-72047. LP disk.

Caribbean Revels: Haitian Rara and Dominican Gaga. 1991. Recorded by Verna Gillis. Notes by Gage Averill and Verna Gillis. Smithsonian Folkways CD SF 40402. Compact disc.

Carnival Jump Up: Steelbands of Trinidad and Tobago. 1989. Delos DE 4014. Compact disc.

Cien por ciento puertorriqueño. 1997(?). Edwin Colón Zayas y su Taller Campesino [Puerto Rico]. Disco Hit Productions DHCD-8034.

Con un Poco de Songo. 1989. Batacumbelé [Puerto Rico]. Disco Hit Productions DHLP-008-CD.

Cradle of the New World. 1976. Recorded by Verna Gillis. Folkways FE 4283. LP disk.

Cuban Counterpoint: History of the Son Montuno. 1992. Rounder CD 1078. Compact disc.

Cuban Dance Party. 1990. Routes of Rhythm, vol. 2. Produced by Howard Dratch et al. Rounder CD 5050. Compact disc.

Dance! Cadence! N. d. GlobeStyle ORB 002. Compact disc.

Dancehall Stylee: The Best of Reggae Dancehall Music, vols. 1 and 2. 1990. Profile Records PRO-1271 and 1291.

Dansez...chantez. 1992. Ethnikolor. France: Musidisc MU760. Compact disc.

Divine Horsemen: The Voodoo Gods of Haiti. 1980. Recordings by Maya Deren. Produced by Teiji Ito and Cheryl Ito. Lyrichord LLST 7341. LP disk.

Drums of Defiance: Maroon Music from the Earliest Free Black Communities of Jamaica. 1992. Recorded and Compiled by Kenneth Bilby. Smithsonian/Folkways CD SF 40412. Compact Disc.

El Rey y La Reina del Merengue. 1996. Johnny Ventura y Milly [Dominican Republic]. Sony PROD-7060. Compact disc.

En jíbaro y tropical. 1997. Taller Musical Retablo [Puerto Rico]. TMR02CD. Compact disc.

The Golden Age of Calypso: Dances of the Caribbean Islands. 1996. Compiled by Philippe Zani. EPM Musique 995772. Compact disc.

Guadeloupe: Le Gwoka, Soirée Léwòz à Cacao. 1992. Ocora C560 031. Compact disc.

Heart of Steel: Featuring Steelbands of Trinidad and Tobago. 1990. Flying Fish. Compact disc.

Heat in de Place: Soca Music from Trinidad. 1990. Rounder Records.Compact disc.

History of Ska: The Golden Years, 1960–65.

Hurricane Zouk. N. d. Virgin/Earthworks 7 90882-1. Compact disc.

Intensified! Original Ska, 1962–66. N. d. Mongo Records MLPS 9524. Compact disc.

The Island of Española. 1976. Recorded by Verna Gillis. Folkways FE 4282. LP disk.

The Island of Quisqueya. 1976. Recorded by Verna Gillis. Folkways FE 4281. LP disk.

Jazz and Hot Dance in Martinique, 1929–1950. N. d. Harlequin HQ2018. Produced by Bruce Bastin. Notes by Alain Boulanger. Compact disc.

Jazz Jamaica. N. d. Studio One Sol 1140.

Kali. 1988. Racines. France et Switzerland: Hibiscus Records HR 88020 CS 750. Compact disc.

Kassav' Grands succès, vol.1.1987. Productions Georges Debs GDC10501, Sono disc distribution, Martinique and France. Compact disc.

Kassav' Vini Pou. l987. Holland: CBS CB811. Compact disc.

Konbit: Burning Rhythms of Haiti. 1989. Produced by Jonathan Demme, Fred Paul, and Gage Averill. Notes by Gage Averill and Jonathan Demme. A&M Records CD 5281. Compact disc.

Kwak a dé, vlopé!!! l994. Jean-Michel Mauriello, ed. France: Hibiscus Records. Compact disc.

L'Ame Negre en Exil au Bal Antillais: Franco-Creole Biguines from Martinique. 1988. Produced by Chris Strachwitz. Notes by Richard K. Spottswood. Folklyric Records 9050. Compact disc.

La fête antillaise continue . . ., vol 2. 1991.

Ethnikolor. France: Ethnikolor Productions et Carrère Music CA808. Compact disc.

Legend: The Legacy of Bob Marley and the Wailers. N. d. Tuff Gong/Island Records. LP disk.

Los Muñequitos de Matanzas: Vacunao. 1995. Qbadisc QB 9017. Compact disc.

Los Pleneros de la 21 and Conjunto Melodía Tropical: Puerto Rico, Puerto Rico Mi Tierra Natal. 1990. Notes by Howard Weiss, Morton Marks, and Ethel Raim. Shanachie SH 65001. Compact disc.

Mario Canonge (et le groupe Kann') retour aux sources. 1991. S.N.A.150960, Distribution NATAL, France. Compact disc.

Maroon Music from the Earliest Free Black Communities of Jamaica. 1992. Produced by Kenneth Bilby. Washington, D.C.: Smithsonian/Folkways Recordings CD ST 40412. Compact disc.

Music from Oriente de Cuba: The Estudiantina Tradition. 1995. Estudiantina Invasora. Nimbus NI 5448. Compact disc.

Music of Haiti, vols. 1–3: (1) *Folk Music of Haiti*; (2) *Drums of Haiti*; (3) *Songs and Dances of Haiti.* 1952. Recordings and notes by Harold Courlander. Ethnic Folkways FE4403/4407/4432. LP disks.

The Music of Santería: The Oru del Igbodu. 1994. Produced by John Amira. Companion book by John Amira and Steven Cornelius. White Cliffs Media WCM 9346. Compact disc.

Musical Traditions of St. Lucia, West Indies: Dances and Songs from a Caribbean Island. 1993. Compiled by Jocelyne Guilbault and Embert Charles. Smithsonian/Folkways CD SF 40416. Compact disc.

The Original Mambo Kings: An Introduction to Afro-Cubop 1948–1954. 1993. Notes by Max Salazar. Verve 3214-513-876-2. Compact disc.

Orquesta Aragon: The Heart of Havana, vol. 2. 1993. RCA 3488-2-RL. Compact disc.

Pan Champs, vols. 1–2. 1990. Blue Rhythm Records. Compact disc.

Pan Jazz 'n' Calypso: Vat 19 Fonclaire Steel Orchestra—Trinidad. 1991. Delos DE 4016. Compact disc.

Panorama: Steelbands of Trinidad and Tobago. 1991. Delos DE 4015. Compact disc.

Pa' Que Suene el Pandero . . . ¡PLENEALO! [Puerto Rico]. 1997(?). Disco Hit Productions DHCD-8102. Compact disc.

Paracumbé tambó. 1997. Produced by Emanuel Dufrasne González and Nelie Lebón Robles [Puerto Rico]. Distributed by Rounder Records. Ashé CD 2005. Compact disc.

Planet Zouk: The World of Antilles Music. 1991. Compiled by Eric Basset. Rhythm Safari CDL 57165. Compact disc.

Rhythms of Rapture: Sacred Musics of Haitian Vodou. 1995. Produced by Elizabeth McAlister. Smithsonian/Folkways SF CD 49464. Compact disc.

Roots of Haiti: Voodoo, vols. 1–6. 1978, 1979. Directed by Jacques Fortère. Produced by Fred Paul. Mini Records MRS 1063-6, 1071, 1073. LP disks.

Sacred Rhythms of Cuban Santería/Ritmos sagrados de la santería cubana. 1995. Centro de Investigación y Desarollo de la Música Cubana. Smithsonian/Folkways SF CD 40419. Compact disc.

Septetos Cubanos: Sones de Cuba. 1990. Produced by Eduardo Llerenas. Música Tradicional MTCD 113/4. Distributed by Rounder. 2 compact discs.

Sing de Chorus: Calypso from Trinidad and Tobago. 1992. Delos DE 4018. Compact disc.

The Skatalites: Scattered Lights. N. d. Alligator Records AL 8309. Compact disc.

Sones Cubanos: Sextetos Cubanos, vol. 1: Sones 1930. 1991. Produced by Chris Strachwitz and Michael Iván Avalos. Arhoolie CD 7003. Compact disc.

Songs from the North. 1978. Recorded by Verna Gillis. Folkways FE 4284. LP disk.

Spirit Rhythms: Sacred Drumming and Chants from Cuba. N. d. Nueva Generación. Latitudes LT 50603. Compact disc.

This Is Reggae Music, vols. 1–5. N. d. Mango Records. Compact disc.

Voodoo Trance Music: Ritual Drums of Haiti. Recordings and notes by Richard Hill and Morton Marks. 1974. Lyrichord LLST 7279. LP disk.

West Indies: An Island Carnival. 1991. Produced by Krister Malm. Notes by Daniel Sheehy and Krister Malm. Compact disc.

Where Was Butler? A Calypso Documentary from Trinidad. 1987. Produced by Chris Strachwitz. Notes by Richard K. Spottswood. Folklyric 9048. Compact disc.

Zoop Zoop Zoop: Traditional Music and Folklore of St. Croix, St. Thomas, and St. John. 1993. Notes by Mary Jane Soule. New World Records 80427-2. Compact disc.

A Guide to Films and Videos

GENERAL

The Americas II. 1990. Tomoaki Fujii, ed. Produced by Katsumori Ichikawa. JVC Video Anthology of World Music and Dance, vol. 28 (VTMV-58). Videocassette.

Central and South America: Mexico, Nicaragua, Peru, Venezuela. 1995. Yuki Okada, director. JVC/Smithsonian Folkways Video Anthology of World Music and Dance of the Americas, vol. 6 (VTMV-230). Videocassette.

"Teaching the Music of Hispanic Americans." 1991. Organized by Dale A. Olsen, Linda O'Brien-Rothe, and Daniel E. Sheehy for *Teaching Music with a Multicultural Approach*, MENC Preconference Symposium of the Music Educators National Conference Annual Meeting, Washington, D.C., 1990. Reston, Va.: Music Educators National Conference. Videocassette and book.

SOUTH AMERICA

A Festa de Moça (The Girl's Celebration). 1987. Directed by Vincent Carelli. Distributed by Video Data Bank, Chicago, Ill. Videocassette.

Apu Condor (The Condor God). 1992. Directed by Gianfranco Norelli. Distributed by Documentary Educational Resouces, Watertown, Mass. Videocassette.

Bossa Nova: Music and Reminiscences. 1993. Directed by Walter Saslles. Barre, Vt.: Multicultural Media, Videocassette.

Carnival Bahia. 1982. Produced by Carlo Pasini and Peter Fry. Films Incorporated Video, Chicago. Videocassette.

Carnival in Q'eros: Where the Mountains Meet the Jungle. 1990. Written and filmed by John Cohen. Distrubuted by University of California Extension Media Center, Berkeley. Videocassette, 16 mm.

Caxiri or Manioc Beer. 1987. Victor Fuks. Distributed by Indiana University Audio/Visual Center, Bloomington. Videocassette.

Central and South America: Mexico, Nicaragua, Peru, Venezuela. 1995. Yuki Okada, director. JVC/Smithsonian Folkways Video Anthology of World Music and Dance of the Americas, vol. 6 (VTMV-230). Videocassette.

Corpus Christi en Cusco. 1996. Directed by Luis Figueroa. Produced by Juan Ossio [festival in Cusco, Peru]. Archive of Traditional Andean Music, Pontífica Universidad Católica del Perú. VAMTA-7. Videocassette.

Demonstration of Multiple Relationships between Music and Culture of the Waiãpi. 1989. Victor Fuks. Distributed by Indiana University Audio/Visual Center, Bloomington. Videocassette.

El Charanguero: Jaime Torres, the Charango Player. 1996. Produced by Simona and Jeffrey Briggs. Multicultural Media 1007E. Videocassette.

Fiesta de la Virgen del Carmen de Paucartambo. 1994. Directed by Gisela Cánepa Koch [festival in Paucartambo, Peru]. Archive of Traditional Andean Music, Pontífica Universidad Católica del Perú. VAMTA-2. Videocassette.

Gaiteros: The Music of Northern Colombia. N. d. Produced by Egberto Bermúdez. 3/4-inch video-cassette.

Instrumentos y Géneros Musicales de Lamayeque. 1994. Directed by Gisela Cánepa Koch [northern Peru]. Archive of Traditional Andean Music, Pontífica Universidad Católica del Perú. VAMT-3. Videocassette.

José Carlos and His Spirits: The Ritual Initiation of Zelador Dos Orixas in a Brazilian Umbanda Center. 1989. Produced by Sidney M. Greenfield. Department of Anthropology, University of Wisconsin-Milwaukee. Videocassette.

La Fiesta del Agua. 1995. Diected by Gisela Cánepa Koch [festival in Huarochirí, Lima, Peru]. Archive of Traditional Andean Music, Pontífica Universidad Católica del Perú. VAMTA-5. Videocassette.

Las Cruces de Porcón. 1997. Directed by Gisela Cánepa Koch [festival in Cajamarca, Peru]. Archive of Traditional Andean Music, Pontífica Universidad Católica del Perú. VAMTA-6. Videocassette.

Mamita Candelaria. 1996. Directed by Luis Figueroa. Produced by Juan Ossio [festival in Puno, Peru]. Archive of Traditional Andean Music, Pontífica Universidad Católica del Perú. VAMTA-8. Videocassette.

Mountain Music of Peru. 1984. John Cohen. New York: Cinema Guild. Videocassette, 16 mm.

Music, Dance and Festival. 1987. Victor Fuks. Bloomington: Indiana University Audio/Visual Center. Videocassette.

Palenque: Un Canto. 1992. Produced and directed by María Raquel Bozzi [about San Basilio de Palenque, Colombia]. Distributed by María Raquel Bozzi, Los Angeles, CA. Videocasssette.

Peruvian Weaving: A Continuous Warp. 1980. John Cohen. New York: Cinema Guild. Videocassette, 16 mm.

Q'eros, the Shape of Survival. 1979. John Cohen. New York: Cinema Guild. Videocassette, 16 mm.

Shotguns and Accordions: Music of the Marijuana Regions of Colombia. 1983. Beats of the Heart Series. Produced and directed by Jeremy Marre. Shanachie SH-1205. Videocassette.

The Spirit of Samba: Black Music of Brazil. 1983. Beats of the Heart Series. Produced and directed by Jeremy Marre. Shanachie SH-1207. Videocassette.

Survivors of the Rainforest. 1993. Directed by Andy Jillings. Distributed by Channel 4, London. Videocassette.

Tinka de Alpaca. 1994. Directed by Gisela Cánepa Koch [festival in Arequipa, Peru]. Archive of Traditional Andean Music, Pontífica

Universidad Católica del Perú. VAMTA-12. Videocassette.

Toro Pucllay: El Juego del Toro. 1997. Directed by Luis Figueroa. Produced by Juan Ossio [festival in Apurímac, Peru]. Archive of Traditional Andean Music, Pontífica Universidad Católica del Perú. VAMTA-9. Videocassette.

Umbanda: The Problem Solver. Produced by Steven Cross and Peter Fry. Films Incorporated Video, Chicago. Videocassette.

Waiampi Instrumental Music. 1987. Victor Fuks. Distributed by Indiana University Audio/Visual Center, Bloomington. Videocassette.

Waiãpi Instrumental Music. 1988. Victor Fuks. Distributed by Indiana University Audio/Visual Center, Bloomington. Videocassette.

Warao. 1975. Jorge Preloran. University of California, Los Angeles. Videocassette, 16 mm.

Wylancha. 1991. Directed by Gisela Cánepa Koch. Archive of Traditional Andean Music, Pontífica Universidad Católica del Perú. VAMTA-4. Videocassette.Videocassette.

Yanomamö. 1975. Napoleon A. Chagnon and Timothy Asch. Distributed by University of Pennsylvania. Videocassette, 16 mm.

MEXICO AND CENTRAL AMERICA

Central and South America: Mexico, Nicaragua, Peru, Venezuela. 1995. Yuki Okada, director. JVC/Smithsonian Folkways Video Anthology of World Music and Dance of the Americas, vol. 6 (VTMV-230). Videocassette.

The Devil's Dream. 1992. Mary Ellen Davis [about Guatemalan music]. The Cinema Guild, New York. 16 mm.

Enemies of Silence. 1991. Produced by Jeremy Marre [about two mariachi musicians in Mexico]. Harcourt Films, London. Videocassette, 16 mm.

Gimme Punta Rock . . . Belizean Music. 1994. Produced by Peter and Suzanne Coonradt. Available from Partners in Video, 3762 Elizabeth

St., Riverside, Calif. 92506. Videocassette.

Huichol Sacred Pilgrimage to Wirikuta. 1991. Produced by Larain Boyll. University of California Extension Center for Media and Independent Learning, Berkeley. Videocassette.

Maya Fiesta. 1988. Produced by Allan F. Burns and Alan Saperstein [about the San Miguel festival of Guatemalan migrants in Florida]. Indiantown, Fla.: Corn-Maya. Videocassette.

Tex-Mex: Music of the Texas-Mexican Borderlands. Beats of the Heart Series. Produced and directed by Jeremy Marre. Shanachie SH-1206. Videocassette.

CARIBBEAN

Before Reggae Hit the Town. 1992. Produced by Mark Gorney. Berkeley: University of California Extension Center for Media and Independent Learning. Videocassette.

Bob Marley and the Wailers: Time Will Tell. 1991. Commerce, Calif.: Island Visual Arts. Videocassette.

The Bob Marley Story: Caribbean Nights. 1990. Executive Producers: Chris Blackwell and Alan Yentob. Produced by Anthony Walland Nigel Finch. Directed by Jo Mendell and Charles Chabot. Island Records. Videocassette.

Caribbean Crucible. 1984. Directed by Dennis Marks [about African background, Dominican Republic, and Jamaica]. *Repercussions: A Celebration of African-American Music* (series). Videocassette.

Divine Horsemen: The Living Gods of Haiti. 1985. Filmed by Maya Deren. Mystic Fire M101. Videocassette.

En el País de los Orichas. 1993. Conjunto Folklórico Nacional de Cuba. Distributed by Blackmind Book Boutique, Brooklyn, N.Y. Videocassette.

Haiti: Dreams of Democracy. 1987. Produced and directed by Jonathan Demme and Jo Menell. Clinica Estetico. Videocassette.

The King Does Not Lie: The Initiation of a Shango Priest. 1992. Produced by Judith Gleason and Elisa Mereghette. New York: Filmakers Library. Videocassette.

Legacy of the Spirits. 1985. Filmed by Karen Kramer. New York: Erzulie Films. 16 mm.

Los Muñequitos de Matanzas. 1993. Produced by E. Natatcha Estebanez [about Cuban music]. Distributed by WGBH Educational Foundation, Boston. Videocassette.

Mas Fever. 1987. Produced by Glen Micallef and Larry Johnson. Filmsound Video. Videocassette.

Oggun. 1993. Conjunto Folklórico Nacional de Cuba. Distributed by Blackmind Book Boutique, Brooklyn, N.Y. Videocassette.

Pan in A Minor and Steel Bands of Trinidad. N. d. Produced by Daniel Verba and Jean-Jacques Mrejen. Villon Films.

Roots Rock Reggae: Jamaican Music. 1988. Beats of the Heart Series. Produced and Directed by Jeremy Marre. Shanachie SH-1202. Video-cassette.

Routes of Rhythm. ca. 1993. Narrated by Harry Belafonte [Cuban music and dance]. Distributed by Multicultural Media. 3 videocassettes and study guide.

Rumbas y comparsas de Cuba. 1993. Distributed by Blackmind Book Boutique, Brooklyn, N.Y. Videocassette.

Salsa: Latin Pop in the Cities. 1983. Beats of the Heart Series. Produced and directed by Jeremy Marre. Shanachie SH-1201. Videocassette.

Sworn to the Drum: A Tribute to Francisco Aguabella. 1995. Directed by Les Blank. Distributed by Flower Films, El Cerrito, Calif. Videocassette, 16mm.

Voices of the Orishas. 1994. Produced and directed by Alvaro Pérez Betancourt. Berkeley: University of California Extension Center for Media and Independent Learning. Videocassette.

Notes on the Audio Examples

1. Yanomamö male shaman's curing song, excerpt (1:32)

   Performed by the headman Iyäwei, who is chanting to *hekura* under the influence of *ebena*
   Recorded by Pitts (from Coppens Collection, Caracas) on 20 May 1969 in Iyäweiteri, a Yanomamö village, Boca del Ocamo, Amazonas, Venezuela

2. Yekuana male shaman's curing song, excerpt (1:02)

   Performed near a Yekuana village, Amazonas, Venezuela
   Recorded by Walter Coppens

3. Warao male *wisiratu* shaman's curing song, excerpt (1:33)

   Performed by Bernardo Tobal, accompanying himself with his *hebu mataro* rattle
   Recorded by Dale A. Olsen on 25 August 1972 in Yaruara Akoho, Delta Amacura Federal Territory, Venezuela

4. Warao male *hoarotu* shaman's curing song, excerpt (0:49)

   Performed by José Antonio Páez
   Recorded by Dale A. Olsen on 1 August 1972 in Yaruara Akoho, Delta Amacura Federal Territory, Venezuela

5. *Sikuriada* (music for *siku* panpipes) (1:30)

   Performed by musicians from Jachakalla, Charkas, Potosí, Bolivia
   Six *siku* (*zampoña*), including one *sanka* (eight tubes plus seven tubes); two *ch'ilis* (small, one octave higher: eight tubes plus seven tubes); and *bombo* (bass drum)
   Recorded by Henry Stobart in November 1986 in Charkas Province, northern Potosí Department, Bolivia

6. "Kulwa" (*kupla, cobla*) (1:19)

   Approximately forty male musicians from Wapaka community kneel while playing their *julajula* panpipes (five sizes, tuned in octaves)
   Recorded by Henry Stobart in October 1986 in Charka Province, northern Potosí Department, Bolivia

7. *Lichiwayu* notch flutes (1:36)

Notch flutes of two sizes: *jatunta* (big) and *juch'uycito* (small), a fifth apart, and *caja* drum (played with two hard beaters)
Recorded by Henry Stobart in August 1987 in Alonso de Ibañez Province, northern Potosí Department, Bolivia

8. "*Walata Grande*" ('Great Walata') *huayño* (1:21)

Performed by the Tocamarka *tropa* (ensemble) from Walata Grande
Eighteen *musiñu* duct flutes (four sizes playing in parallel fifths, octaves, and dissonant intervals); two *clarinetos* (wooden clarinets); *clarín* (with clarinet mouthpiece); and four *tamboras* (military side drums)
Recorded by Henry Stobart in December 1986 in Lahuachaka, Aroma Province, La Paz Department, Bolivia

9. *Tarkeada* (music for *tarka* flutes) (2:17)

Performed by musicians from Zona Sud
Twenty-six *tarka* duct flutes (two sizes tuned in parallel fifths), three *tamboras* (military side drums), and one *bombo* (bass drum)
Recorded by Henry Stobart in March 1987 in Lahuachaka, Cercado Province, Oruro Department, Bolivia

10. "*Lunesta, martesta*" ('Mondays, Tuesdays') (2:02)

Performers from Ayllu Sikuya, Chayanta Province, Potosí Department, Bolivia
Two female singers accompanied by *charango*
Recorded by Henry Stobart in May 1987 in Chayanta Province, northern Potosí Department, Bolivia

11. *Folia de Reis* (Folia of the Magi) (1:52)

Performed by members of the Folias de Reis Unidos dos Marinheiros, from Itaú, Minas Gerais, Brazil.
Acordeon (accordion), three *pandeiros* (tambourines), *violão* (guitar), *viola* (small guitar), male singer, and chorus
Recorded by Welson A. Tremura on 16 August 1997 in Olimpia, São Paulo, Brazil, during the Thirty-third Folkloric Festival of Olimpia

12. *Moçambique* (1:19)

Performed by members of the Moçambique de Nossa Senhora do Rosário, from Uberlândia, Minas Gerais, Brazil
Five *bumbos* (bass drums), 3 *chocalhos tipo prato* (plate-shaped shakers), *apito* (whistle), *grupo de figurantes* (dancers)
Recorded by Welson A. Tremura on 17 August 1997 in Olimpia, São Paulo, Brazil, during the Thirty-third Folkloric Festival of Olimpia

13. "*É bonito cantar*" ('Singing Is Beautiful'), *cantoria* of the *embolada* genre (1:30)

Performed by Carlito de Arapiraca and Furió on a street corner in Alagoas, Brazil.
Two *pandeiros* played by the singers
Recorded by Larry Crook on 13 July 1984 in Arapiraca, Alagoas, Brazil

14. *Forró do pife* (*forró* for *banda de pífanos*) (1:53)

Performed by the Bandinha Cultural de Caruaru Severino: Pedro da Silva and João Manuel da Silva, *pífanos* (cane fifes); Antônio do Nascimento, *tarol* (thin snare drum); Manuel dos Santos, *zabumba* (bass drum); Maurício Antônio da Silva, *surdo* (tenor drum); and João Alfredo dos Santos, *pratos* (hand cymbals)
Recorded by Larry Crook on 19 April 1987 in Caruaru, Pernambuco, Brazil

15. *Forró de sanfona* (*forró* for accordion) (1:26)

Performed by Toninho de Calderão, keyboard accordion, and unknown musicians playing *zabumba*, *tarol*, *pratos*, and triangle
Recorded by Larry Crook on 19 September 1987 in Caruaru, Pernambuco, Brazil

16. "*Boa noite todo povo*" ('Good Night Everyone'), a *maracatú rural* (rural *maracatú*) (1:46)

Performed by the group Maracatu Leão Brasileiro, featuring a *mestre de toadas* (lead singer) and other anonymous musicians, at a street performance during carnival celebrations
Trumpet, *tarol*, *congué* (iron bell), *onça* (large friction drum), and *ganzá* (metal shaker); one microphone shared by the lead singer and the trumpeter
Recorded by Larry Crook on 27 February 1988 in Recife, Pernambuco, Brazil

17. *Canto a lo pueta* ('song of the poet'), also called *décima* (1:47)

Performed by Santos Rubio, a blind musician who accompanies himself on the *guitarrón*
Recorded by Daniel E. Sheehy in 1973 in Pirque, Puente Alto, Santiago Province, Chile

18. "*Tengo que hacer un barquito*" ('I Have to Make a Little Boat'), *cueca* dance-song (1:43)

Sung by Eufrasia Ugarte, who accompanies herself on button accordion. She is accompanied by Benito Aranda, who strikes carefully loosened slats of a wooden box with his fingers
Recorded by Daniel E. Sheehy in 1973 in San José, Algarrobo, Valparaíso Province, Chile

19. Song by blind *rondador* (panpipe) player (0:59)

Performed by a beggar-musician in the Ibarra market
Recorded by Charles Sigmund in 1975 in Ibarra, Ecuador

20. Song in Quechua about a young man, alone in the world, looking for a wife (2:14)

Performed by Pedro Tasiguano, who accompanies himself on the harp
Recorded by Charles Sigmund in 1975 in Llano Grande, 24 kilometers north of Quito, Ecuador

21. *Huayno* (Andean dance-song) (2:35)

Performed by Narciso Morales Romero on *roncador y caja* (pipe and tabor)
Recorded by Dale A. Olsen on 1 September 1979 in Huaylas, Ancash Department, Peru

22. Festival de la Virgen del Carmen (patronal festival dedicated to the Virgin of Carmen) (1:30)

Performed by local musicians and people from Alto Otuzco, Cajamarca, Peru
Female vocalists, *flauta y caja* (pipe and tabor), two *clarines* (*clarín* trumpets)
Recorded by Dale A. Olsen on 16 July 1979 in Alto Otuzco, Cajamarca, Peru

23. *"No lo cuentes a nadie"* ('Don't Tell Anyone'), *huayno* (2:42)

Performed by the *orquesta típica* Selección del Centro, directed by Julio Rosales Huatuco
Harp, two violins, clarinets, alto and tenor saxophones
Recorded by Dale A. Olsen on Sunday, 24 June 1979 in Acolla, Junín, Peru, during a private party
for the festival of San Juan Bautista (Saint John the Baptist)

24. *"Quien a visto aquél volcán"* ('Whoever Has Seen this Volcano' [El Misti]), *yaraví* from Puquina,
Arequipa (2:44)

Performed by Nicanor Abarca Puma on *charango*
Recorded by Dale A. Olsen on 12 August 1979 in Arequipa, Peru

25. *"Zancudito,"* *hatajo de negritos* (2:02)

Performed by Amador Vallumbrosio, *caporal* (director), and José Lurita, violin
Recorded by William David Tompkins in 1976 in El Carmen, Chincha Province, Peru

26. *"La Catira"* ('The Light-Haired Woman') (2:42)

Performed by José León (Venezuela), *bandola*, and musicians playing *cuatro* (small guitar), *maracas*,
and string bass
Recorded by Dale A. Olsen on 17 March 1982 at the School of Music, Florida State University,
Tallahassee

27. *Festival de San Juan* (patronal festival of Saint John) (1:41)

Private performance during a party on Sunday afternoon
Mina (large drum), *curbata* (small drum), and *laures* (sticks struck on sides of *mina* drum)
Recorded by Dale A. Olsen on 24 June 1974 in Curiepe, Barlovento, Venezuela

28. *"Cuaulleros"* (1:47)

Performed by Nicandro Aquino, harp; José María Isidro and Teódulo Isidro, violins; and Eleazar
Arrollo, *jarana*, with *uaultl* (*palos* or sticks) and *xauanillsll* (*sonajas* or bells)
Recorded by Arturo Chamorro on 1 October 1984 in Pómaro, Michoacán, Mexico

29. *Danza de corpus* (Corpus Christi dance) (1:22)

Recorded by Arturo Chamorro on 2 October 1984, in Pómaro, Michoacán, Mexico

30. "*Siquisirí*," *son jarocho* (3:31)

    Performed by a trio of *jarocho* musicians: Isidoro Gutiérrez, *jarana* and *pregonero* (lead singer); Luis "Huicho" Delfín, *requinto jarocho*; and Gregorio (last name unknown), harp
    Recorded by Danel E. Sheehy on 22 February 1978 in the cantina Las Palomas (The Doves) in Alvarado, Veracruz, Mexico.

31. "*Ámalihaní*," the central rite of ancestor placation in a Garifuna family *dügü* ceremony (2:16)

    Performed in the *dabuyaba* (ancestral temple) in Dangriga, Belize, by the shaman (*buyei*) John Mariano (playing *sísara*), three drummers (playing three *garawoun segunda* drums), a song leader, and singing family members and relatives
    Text: "My grandmother, we are quieting you down. My grandmother, the cock is crowing. It is silent now. I am for you; you are for me. Grandmother, water."
    Recorded by Oliver Greene on 16 July 1996 in Dangriga, Belize

32. "*El Corredizo*" (refers to running, moving) (1:34)

    Music to accompany *chinegros* performance; the second of several *sones* played between the ritual duels of pairs of dancers
    Pito (vertical, wooden flute) and two *tambores* (small, double-headed drums)
    Recorded by T. M. Scruggs in July 1987 in Nindirí, Nicaragua

33. "*Los Novios*" ('The Sweethearts') (2:27).

    This is one of the approximately thirty-six pieces in the Nicaraguan folklore repertoire that accompany the series of dances generically known as *el baile de la marimba* ('the dance of the marimba'). *Marimba de arco* trio: Marco Martínes, *marimba de arco*; Angel Martínes, *guitarrilla*; and Omar "Bigote" Martínes, *guitarra*
    Recorded by T. M. Scruggs on 9 March 1989 outside Masatepe, Nicaragua

34. "*Los Coros de San Miguel*" ('The Choruses of Saint Michael'), *salve* with drums in the style of the southwest Dominican Republic (0:53)

    One *palo mayor* (master drum) and two *alcahuetes* (accompanying drums)
    Recorded by Martha E. Davis in 1979 in Azua, Dominican Republic

35. "*Dice Desidera Arias*" ('According to Desidera Arias'), *merengue* (2:30)

    Performed by a *périco ripiao* (typical merengue ensemble): male vocalist accompanying himself on *tres* (Cuban small guitar), *güira* (metal scraper), *marímbola* (large lamellophone), and *tambor* (drum), and chorus (the other musicians)
    Recorded by Dale A. Olsen on 17 December 1979 in a hotel courtyard in Boca Chica, Dominican Republic

36. Song for Legba, dance for Ogoun (2:02)

    Performed at the *ounfò* (temple) "Kay Nicole"
    Recorded by Lois Wilcken on 31 July 1985 in La Plaine, Haiti

37. *Rara* instrumental music (1:41)

Performed by Rara Sanbout
Recorded by Gage Averill on 19 February 1991 in Les Salines, Port-au-Prince, Haiti

38. Afro-Martinican street music (2:16)

One male singer (*chacha* player), two *boula* drums, one *suru* drum, one *bambú* idiophone, one *chacha* rattle, and male chorus (the other musicians)
Recorded by Dale A. Olsen on 21 December 1977 in La Savane Park, Fort-de-France, Martinique

39. "*Koumen non k'alé fè,*" *koutoumba* music (1:30)

Recorded by Jocelyne Guilbault on 25 June 1981 in St. Lucia

Index

DATE DUE

Cat. No. 23-221

BRODART